good for you

Dana Jacobi

PHOTOGRAPHS
Erin Kunkel

weldon**owen**

start with the plant

The way I like to eat is easy and intuitive. Put simply, it means focusing on plant-based meals that are delicious and creative as well as wholesome. The foundation for the recipes in this book is a Mediterranean-style diet emphasizing fruits and vegetables, whole grains, and legumes. Some recipes add poultry, fish, or meat for heartiness and additional protein. I also believe in using healthy fats, flavorful and low-fat dairy foods, plus herbs and spices to give dishes bold flavors. I love using nuts and seeds to enhance dishes.

The recipes in this book feature short ingredient lists and sensible prep times. In some dishes, a combination may be unexpected or it gives a simple ethnic twist to healthful ingredients, as in Sicilian-Style Shrimp with Cauliflower and Almonds, North African–Style Bulgur and Grilled Vegetable Salad, and Indian Spiced Roasted Beets. Other recipes make healthy versions of favorites such as Three-Berry Cobbler, and Huevos Rancheros.

Sharing good times is also part of well-being, so this is food that brings people together with pleasure. For me, this is as important as eating less meat and using ingredients rich in antioxidants. Good eating also means enjoying variety—a bit of everything in moderation—rather than following strict rules for what you should eat and what to avoid.

What is good for you can also be good for the planet and your community, so I support buying from local farmers and producers, including those who treat livestock humanely. I point out where organic produce may be desirable and share recommendations from the Environmental Defense Fund. All the seafood choices meet sustainability standards used by Monterey Bay Aquarium's Seafood Watch.

I hope that this book ends up a dog-eared kitchen companion, a source of helpful, health-supporting information, and that its dishes become favorites that your family and friends look forward to sharing.

cabbages & crucifers

Brassicas are loaded with vitamins C, A, beta-carotene, and minerals. Sulfur compounds that neutralize carcinogens contribute to their strong taste. Eating just an ounce a day of crucifers can significantly lower cancer risk.

BROCCOLI
Broccoli contains potent substances that help your body neutralize and get rid of cancer-causing toxins. Most of its goodness is in the florets, especially those with a bluish or purple cast. Whirl in some florets while making pesto for a nutrient boost.

BOK CHOY
Loaded with calcium and potassium as well as vitamin A and beta-carotene, this mild-flavored Asian cabbage is good thinly sliced and added raw to salads as well as stir-fried. Separate the creamy, crisp stems to cook first, then add the dark green leaves. Baby bok choy is lower in nutrients.

for more on broccoli/ broccolini see page 146

BRUSSELS SPROUTS

You get 4 grams of protein, along with vitamins A, C, and folate, plus a generous amount of carotenoids in one cup of cooked brussels sprouts. So they cook evenly, select ones that are equal in size. Sauté them, quartered lengthwise or sliced, with garlic in olive oil or broth until tender-crisp.

CABBAGE

Green cabbage gives you lots of folate, fiber, beta-carotene, and vitamin C, while red cabbage provides twice as much vitamin C. Its red color comes from antioxidants that protect against disease-causing free radicals. When cut, cabbage quickly loses nutrients. Cooking it al dente keeps its sweet taste.

NAPA CABBAGE

Napa cabbage, with its light green crinkly leaves, is an excellent source of folate and has nutrients strongly linked to cancer prevention. It is more flexible and less dense than regular green cabbage, so it can be used as a wrapper as you might a tortilla, and is especially good for Asian-style fillings.

CAULIFLOWER

White, green, and purple cauliflower all give you vitamins B5, B6, C, and folate, along with manganese essential for peak brain function and proper sugar metabolism. Serve this versatile crucifer in soups and stews; mashed, puréed, roasted, or steamed; or raw in crudités and salads. Heads should be firm, with no soft or brown spots on the curd.

dark greens

The strong flavor and deep color of these leafy greens means that they offer big health benefits. All are rich in carotenes and carotenoids. Cruciferous greens also contain important sulfur compounds.

MUSTARD GREENS

There are two types of mustard greens. The first has sharp-tasting, big, ruffled leaves, which are second only to collards in calcium content. These are best braised. The second kind, milder-tasting Asian varieties, have smaller leaves, rich in carotenes, that are tender enough to stir-fry.

BROCCOLI RABE

Use the leaves, florets, and all but the toughest part of this leafy green that is rich in beta-carotene. Boiling softens the bitter flavor of this crucifer as does the addition of a touch of lemon juice or vinegar in the dish.

SPINACH

A top source of heart-protective folate, carotenoids, iron, and bone-strengthening vitamin K, spinach is wildly versatile. Spinach can replace lettuce on a sandwich, or be mixed into meatloaf.

for more
on kale
see page 102

CHARD

Cook the shiny leaves and creamy, wide stems of Swiss chard separately to enjoy its earthy, tender, carotene-rich leaves plus mild-tasting fiber-rich crunch. The leaves cook like spinach, and the stems may be braised, or boiled and then sautéed. Ruby and rainbow chard stems may be too tough to eat.

KALE

Among crucifers, kale beats broccoli in beta-carotene and carotenoid content as well as in vitamin A and calcium. There are many types of kale. More tender types can be used for salads and all can be quickly and lightly braised in broth or wine for an easy and healthful side dish.

COLLARD GREENS

This soul food contains as much calcium in a serving as a glass of milk. It is also a powerhouse combination of sulfur compounds. For the sweetest flavor, steam or blanch the shredded leaves, then sauté or braise them with garlic or bacon.

salad greens

The most appealing salads include an assortment of greens. Using a variety makes salads healthier, too. Eating two cups of salad a day is a sure way to get good amounts of folate, vitamins A, C, and K, carotenes, minerals, and an array of the phytonutrients we need to stay healthy.

ROMAINE

Make romaine the heart of a salad—the folate in it will do your heart good. Chromium in its leaves helps to maintain healthy blood sugar levels. Cutting a head of romaine into long wedges and searing them on the grill creates a crisp center and smoky flavor that is wonderful served with a sprinkling of Parmesan shards.

RADICCHIO

The wine-red color and bitter flavor in this leafy chicory come from some of the same antioxidants found in eggplant and red berries. For a classic tri-color salad, combine radicchio with endive and watercress. Pan-Grilled Radicchio with Salsa Verde (page 135) shows how heat softens the bitterness and turns the radicchio leaves a warm brown color.

WATERCRESS

Adding peppery watercress to salads sharpens their flavor. Its zing comes from the same sulfur compounds found in broccoli and other crucifers. In addition, watercress contains calcium, vitamins A and K, and carotenoids. This surprisingly versatile green is also delicious stir-fried with garlic and ginger as a side dish.

ARUGULA

With just five calories in a cup, this zesty green rich in calcium and vitamin C is a smart choice. Arugula's bite tells you that it contains important sulfur-based anticancer phyto-chemicals—even more so in extra-sharp wild arugula. Arrange sliced tomatoes and mozzarella cheese on a bed of feathery arugula for a light meal.

onions & cousins

Eating alliums abundantly—from pungent garlic and onions to milder leeks and green onions—is a prescription for optimum health. The compounds that make their flavors indispensable in cooking also combat heart disease and high blood pressure and help improve blood cholesterol levels.

LEEKS

Leeks contain the same sulfides as other alliums that protect against cancer and thin the blood to help reduce the risk of strokes. They also contain carotenoids and vitamin A good for eye health. Sauté a chopped leek together with onions to give vegetable and bean soups more flavor.

GARLIC

Using garlic raw provides the most nutritional benefits, including anti-inflammatory, antibacterial, and antimicrobial powers. Let chopped garlic stand for 10 minutes to increase its powers and offset the heat of cooking, which diminishes them. Adding garlic later in cooking also helps retain its nutritional benefits.

GREEN ONIONS

Mild in flavor, these immature onions contain a small amount of the sulfur compounds founds in other alliums but they contain useful amounts of vitamin C and folate. These are the easiest kind of onion to eat raw, so add chopped green onions to salads and salsas or sauté them with spinach.

RED ONIONS

Studies have shown that red onions have a higher concentration of health-promoting substances in their outer layers than other types of onions and they are linked to a lower cancer risk. Cutting all onions 5–10 minutes before using releases more of their health-promoting compounds.

YELLOW ONIONS

Antioxidant compounds give onions their color. Onions are also rich in probiotics that nurture the good bacteria in your gut. An easy way to eat more onions is to sear thick slices in a dry heavy skillet or on the grill to serve as a side dish.

SHALLOTS

Blending the flavors of garlic and onion, shallots contain lesser amounts of the beneficial compounds found in both. Use them to add flavor to sauces, soups, stews, and vinaigrettes. Wrap whole shallots in foil and roast at 400°F (200°C) until soft. Serve with fish or veggie burgers, or mixed into egg salad.

roots, tubers & stalks

These roots and tubers, plus asparagus, an above-ground stalk, offer pleasingly assertive or sweet flavors. Most are good both cooked and served raw. Some contain enough sugar to satisfy your sweet tooth naturally. They all contain a useful amount of fiber.

SWEET POTATOES

The amount of vitamins A, C, B6, manganese, potassium, and beta-carotene in sweet potatoes varies, depending on whether their flesh is cream-color, yellow, or deep red-orange—the darker the flesh, the richer they are in phytonutrients. Bake sweet potatoes, then stir their soft flesh with a fork to enjoy the healthiest mashed potatoes.

RADISHES

Actually part of the brassica family, these roots contain known cancer-fighting substances. They are also rich in vitamin C, folic acid, and a host of minerals. Radishes' peppery bite is best preserved by eating them raw, and they can be added to salads or sandwiches or eaten on their own with a sprinkle of sea salt. To tame their taste, steam or sauté sliced radishes.

ASPARAGUS

Whether you prefer fat spears or slim, one cup of asparagus provides as much fiber as a slice of multigrain bread. This fiber includes a particular kind that supports good bacteria in your gut. Asparagus is also an excellent source of vitamins A and K and is rich in anti-inflammatory cancer-fighting compounds.

BEETS

The pigment that colors beets helps detoxify your body. To avoid staining your fingers, insert your hands into plastic sandwich bags while handling beets. The French serve shredded raw beets as a salad. Also try beet tops, which taste like Swiss chard. Steam them and serve drizzled with olive oil and lemon juice.

CARROTS

Cancer-preventive carotenoids and cholesterol-lowering fiber make carrots good for more than just your eyes. They are second only to beets in sugar content. Their fiber helps your body absorb this sweetness gradually. Serve raw, stir-fried, sautéed or roasted.

TOMATO

Tomatoes are rich in vitamins A and C, carotenes, and carotenoids, especially lycopene, a carotenoid believed to protect against heart disease and some types of cancer. As they redden, their carotenoid content increases. Refrigerating retards this, destroys flavor, and turns them mushy, so keep tomatoes on a shady counter. To avoid genetically engineered, ethylene-gassed tomatoes, buying organic is recommended.

SUMMER SQUASH

In summer, watch for crook-neck yellow squash, scallop-edged pattypan, thin-skinned lita, and round avocado and eight-ball squashes. Steaming them in water or broth preserves the modest amounts of vitamins A and C, along with beneficial minerals, in summer squashes.

ZUCCHINI

For the most nutrition, include the skin of zucchini when using it in recipes. And since you are eating the skin, it's always a good idea to choose organic. This summer squash is high in fiber, vitamins A and C, and potassium. Zucchini comes alive when you sauté it with garlic until it is just al dente, then shower on fresh basil.

vegetable fruits

We call all of these ingredients vegetables, but they contain the seeds of a plant, so botanically speaking they all are fruits. Perhaps that is why most of them combine nicely with fruit—try cucumber in mango salsa, green bell peppers and peaches in a green salad, and avocado accompanied by grapefruit sections.

for more
on tomatoes
see page
162

for info
on chiles
see page
72

AVOCADO

Creamy avocado is full of good-for-you fat
and a compound that reduces the risk of blood
clots. The buttery Hass variety—easily identified
by its pebbly skin— contains the highest amount
of these benefits. To enjoy avocado more
often, mash and spread it on toast when
making a sandwich and purée it into smoothies.

BELL PEPPER

Purple, red, orange, and yellow peppers
all are green ones allowed to ripen fully.
Besides sweetening their taste, ripening
also alters their nutrition—green
peppers that are high in vitamin C
become rich in vitamin A and
carotenoids as they turn bright colors.
For an antipasto, serve roasted peppers
drizzled with olive oil and lemon juice.

CUCUMBER

Cucumbers are nutritionally modest but filling. There are just
14 calories in a cup and their juiciness makes them help you feel
full. Select unwaxed cucumbers, preferably organic ones, so you
can enjoy them unpeeled. At the market, squeeze them to check
for freshness—cucumbers should be firm from end to end.

berries & grapes

Berries and grapes are so loaded with antioxidants that eating them daily is a smart practice. Include them in savory or sweet cooking in addition to eating them raw. For example, sauté pork medallions, deglaze the pan with red wine, add halved grapes, swirl in a pat of butter, and enjoy this rosy sauce with the pork.

GRAPES & RAISINS

Red and black grapes are the best choice—their skin contains the same health-supporting compounds found in red wine. Since both grapes and raisins are high in sugar, minimize snacking on them in favor of adding them to cereals, salads, and desserts. Bake focaccia topped with halved grapes and chopped fresh thyme or rosemary for a true Tuscan snack.

BLUEBERRIES

Bluberries are a powerful source of antioxidants that have been linked to improved memory. In addition, they are rich in flavonoids, which protect against cancer and contribute to heart health. Versatile, low in calories, and high in fiber, they are a must-have for a healthy lifestyle.

BLACKBERRIES

These plump berries are loaded with fiber—there is over seven grams in one cup. To use them regularly, top pancakes with blackberries simmered along with a little sugar, and include them with other berries when making a cobbler, crisp, or pie. Choose berries that are entirely black to ensure they are fully sweet—even a touch of purple makes them tart.

RASPBERRIES

Raspberries are amazingly rich in fiber: One cup contains nine grams, which is about one-third of a day's recommended fiber, together with an abundance of antioxidants. Fresh berries are delicate, and best served the day you buy them. If you must store them, spread them on a paper towel-lined baking sheet in one layer before refrigerating.

CRANBERRIES

Cranberries get their puckery taste from tannins, substances also found in red wine and tea. Their deep color tells you they contain other goodness, as well. To eat cranberries year-round while using less sugar, include dried cranberries in salads, trail mix, and alongside fresh or frozen ones in sauces, relish, or other dishes.

STRAWBERRIES

A strawberry's bright red color indicates an abundance of antioxidants helpful in protecting against cancer and giving support to short-term memory. Strawberries also contain lots of vitamin C and a good amount of fiber. Strawberries are often a big hit with kids, so keep them on hand for healthy snacking.

for more on
strawberries
see page 52

for more on
blueberries
see page 212

21

citrus

To perfume a room, simple peel any citrus fruit. The fragrant oils abundant in their skin also provide valuable health benefits. This makes including their juice or zest in recipes a good idea—using organic fruit, if possible. Nearly every kind of citrus contains compounds that are unique so eat a variety of them. Most fruits are at their peak from winter through spring.

CLEMENTINES

This orange-mandarin cross boasts health benefits similar to these fruits. Clementines are smaller than oranges and have deeper color. They are mostly seedless and easy to peel, making them popular with kids. A great snack, clementines are rich in vitamin C, calcium, and potassium.

LIMES

Limes, with similar health benefits to lemons, are an excellent source of vitamin C and a good source of folic acid, vitamin B6, potassium, and phytochemicals. Squeeze limes liberally into drinks and use to flavor and finish Asian and Latin American dishes whenever you can.

KUMQUATS

Kumquats are unique as the only citrus fruit you can eat whole, including the skin, which contains essential oils rich in antioxidants. Fresh kumquats provide high levels of flavonoid compounds, plus vitamins A and C and fiber. Slice them thinly and add them to salads and desserts.

TANGERINES

Tangerines, including petite mandarins, peel so easily that they are called "zipper fruits." Along with other antioxidants, they contain tangeretin, an anti-inflammatory phytochemical that helps thin the blood and protect against cancer. Whole mandarins, thinly sliced, are delicious baked on top of chicken breast or turkey cutlets.

LEMONS

A touch of their juice or zest gives nearly any dish a flavor boost along with cancer protection. Meyer lemons, a cross of lemon and mandarin, are so naturally sweet that you can use them to make unsweetened lemonade.

GRAPEFRUITS

White grapefruits, mainly from Florida, have the sweetest taste and plenty of good nutrition. Pink and red varieties add the benefits of colorful antioxidants. The best-tasting varieties are Star Ruby and Flame or Rio Red.

ORANGES

Along with an abundance of vitamin C and potassium, oranges are particularly rich in flavonoids, active compounds found mostly in citrus fruits. In all, their nutritional riches give oranges too many health benefits to list.

stone fruits

So-called because they contain a large pit, or "stone," in the center, stone fruits come to market in the late spring and summer. The more vibrantly colored they are, the more beneficial substances stone fruits contain—and in higher amounts. So favor golden peaches and nectarines over white, and choose oxheart cherries and the most intensely colored plums when you can.

PLUMS
From yellow and red to blue and green, plums offer a rainbow of colors, each rich in slightly different antioxidants. Sugar-loaded low-acid varieties lack the tart tang of older plum varieties. Roasting is a great way to cook this summer fruit.

PLUOTS
Aprium, plumcots, and pluots—all are slightly different versions of plum-apricot crosses and all boast similar health benefits of the original fruits. Pluots are perhaps the most popular and easy to find, and are good sources of vitamin A, vitamin C, potassium, and fiber. Their sweet-tart flavor is a unique treat, and worth seeking out.

NECTARINES
Nectarines and peaches are so botanically close that nectarines sometimes appear on a peach tree. Provided they show no green tinge, nectarines continue to ripen sitting on the kitchen counter. They are ready when they yield to pressure along the rim that circles them.

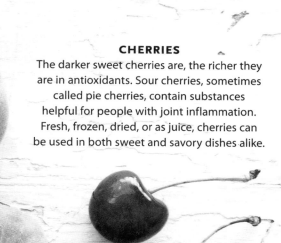

CHERRIES

The darker sweet cherries are, the richer they are in antioxidants. Sour cherries, sometimes called pie cherries, contain substances helpful for people with joint inflammation. Fresh, frozen, dried, or as juice, cherries can be used in both sweet and savory dishes alike.

PEACHES

The best peaches are local, tree-ripened, and eaten out of hand. They're good sources of vitamins A and C and contain valuable antioxidants, to ward off cancer; fiber, to protect the digestive system; and potassium, to help regulate blood pressure. Keep peaches at room temperature until they ripen and them eat them promptly; like tomatoes, peaches turn mushy when refrigerated.

APRICOTS

Eating fresh apricots raw is nutritionally best because when they are cooked or dried a valuable substance in them disappears. Under-ripe fruit gets softer and sweeter when kept at room temperature and its carotenoid content increases. The best tasting dried apricots are Blenheims from California.

tropical fruits

A seductive way to add fiber to your day, eating tropical fruits also provides unique health benefits, including some from enzymes that have important anti-inflammatory activity in your body. To best enjoy the aromatic qualities of tropical fruits, keep them on the counter unless they are already cut.

BANANAS

Bananas are so rich in potassium that eating just one benefits your blood pressure. They contain a probiotic compound that nurtures bacteria necessary for good gut health. Layer sliced banana on a peanut butter sandwich, dip it into melted dark chocolate, and slice and serve over hot breakfast cereal. For creamy and thick dairy-free smoothies, whirl in a banana.

MANGOES

Mangoes are a good source of carotenoids and fiber. A fully ripe one should bathe you in aroma and juice. When shopping for the fruit, go by feel—not color—since some varieties stay green when ripe. Use ripe mango in savory dishes. An unripe one makes good chutney. Use fresh or frozen mango in breakfast smoothies.

COCONUTS

Coconuts and their milk are high in saturated fats, but some experts support them as healthy because they help our immune system to defend against viruses and bacteria. Coconut is a good source of fiber and potassium so use dried coconut in granola and in baking, and sprinkle it on cereal. Use coconut milk in Asian-style dishes.

KIWI

A serving of kiwi contains more vitamin C than an orange, more potassium than a banana, and as much fiber as a bowl of oatmeal. Rock-hard kiwi are unripe and sharply sour. Held at room temperature until they soften slightly, they will taste mildly like wintergreen. Pureed kiwi makes a tangy sauce to serve with grilled halibut or salmon.

PAPAYAS

Squeezing lime juice on a wedge of ripe papaya heightens its tropical flavor. An enzyme in papayas is believed to reduce the risk of rheumatoid arthritis, and lung and color cancer. Papaya seeds look like little black pearls. Sprinkled on a salad they add a peppery flavor.

PINEAPPLES

Pineapples contain an enzyme that is anti-inflammatory and also helps digestion. Pineapples don't get sweeter after picking so look for a ripe one—it will feel heavy and be fragrant. (Forget about pulling a leaf out of the top; it's incorrect.) Use the versatile fruit in salsa for Latin-style fish dishes or whirled into smoothies.

PINTO BEANS

The speckled pattern on the skin of these beige beans disappears during cooking as pinto beans turn an even, rosy pink. The ideal choice when making refried beans or stuffing a burrito, velvety pinto beans are also good puréed, seasoned with cumin, oregano, and roasted garlic, and served as a fiber-rich dip.

LENTILS

Without soaking, protein-rich lentils cook in 20 to 40 minutes. Use flat, green lentils in soups or salads. Red and yellow split lentils are ideal for soups and Indian dal. Black belugas and green Le Puy lentils hold their shape, so think of them for salads.

fresh & dried legumes

In a plant-based diet, dried beans, lentils, and fresh or frozen peas are important protein sources. They are rich in fiber, too. With canned beans, watch their sodium content. Rinsing removes much of the salt, but adding it yourself to bean dishes made using dried beans is better than being stuck with what's in the can.

KIDNEY BEANS

Whether kidney beans are dark red or soft pink, the unique contrast between their firm skin and creamy inside makes them excellent in salads and soups. White kidney or cannellini beans, mashed with herbs and olive oil, make a delicious topping for crostini. The beans are a good source of molybdenum, a mineral that activates enzymes in the body.

ENGLISH PEAS

Fresh English peas, also called garden or green peas, are sugar-sweet when picked. They quickly turn starchy, so unless you can rush them from garden to pot like fresh corn, using frozen peas, always processed at their peak, makes sense. Peas are rich in calcium and a carotenoid that is particularly good for your eyes.

BLACK BEANS

Black beans are exceptionally versatile. Excellent in meatless chili, their firm yet creamy texture is ideal in salads and salsas. The intense, dark color of black beans, also called turtle beans, means they are loaded with important antioxidant phytochemicals.

SNOW PEAS

Besides color and crunch, snow peas add useful protein to a meatless stir-fry. Select pods with fresh-looking leaflets near their stem. They also should snap crisply when broken in half. To avoid overcooking, add snow peas to the pan later. When blanching, give them just a fast plunge in and out of the boiling water.

CHICKPEAS

Also called garbanzo beans, chickpeas are a multi-ethnic bean, delicious in Middle Eastern grain salads and hummus, Italian soups, and Spanish stews. Chickpeas are a good source of calcium, magnesium, potassium, and hard-to-find selenium.

SUGAR SNAP PEAS

A relative newcomer, sugar snap peas were introduced in 1976. Fresh sugar snaps look glossy and make a popping sound when opened. One cup contains 5 grams of fiber, more than a bowl of oatmeal.

whole grains

Studies show that few Americans eat enough fiber. Serving whole grains every day is an important—and delicious—way to change this. Their protein and the full feeling you get from eating them make whole grains fundamental to a plant-based diet. Choosing organically grown grains assures that they are not genetically engineered.

QUINOA
Light-textured and mildly earthy tasting, quinoa cooks in just 20 minutes. Particularly high in protein, this South American grain makes a good hot breakfast cereal, savory pilafs, and satisfying salads. Red quinoa used in place of bulgur makes great gluten-free tabbouleh.

BARLEY
Barley is frequently polished to remove most of the bran. Called pearl barley, it is healthfully high in cholesterol-lowering soluble fiber. Cook barley like oatmeal for breakfast, or make it into risotto for a healthy supper.

FARRO
Nutty, almost sweet tasting farro is an ancient, unhybridized form of wheat. Italians cook it whole—like rice and barley—or use ground farro to make excellent whole-wheat pasta. Eating farro in a salad is a nice introduction to this pleasant grain.

BULGUR
Middle Eastern cooks use bulgur—whole wheat that has been steamed, dried, and cracked—to make tabbouleh. Its pronounced flavor is also good in pilafs served alongside a main course. Bulgur is particularly high in fiber, with over 8 grams in a half-cup serving.

WHOLE-WHEAT FLOUR

Milled including the germ and bran, whole-wheat flour tastes more assertive than white and it can make baked goods weightier. Combining whole-wheat and white flour gives lighter results in baked goods and softens its taste. For dessert baking, try using whole-wheat pastry flour. For pasta, look for whole-wheat semolina.

POLENTA

To be whole-grain, cornmeal and polenta must be stone-ground. Only the ones made from yellow corn include the golden carotenoids that protect your eyes and heart. Made using milk, polenta makes a delicious morning porridge.

BROWN RICE

Brown whole-grain rice is a gluten-free staple in healthy eating. Fluffy brown jasmine and basmati have the same aromatic flavor as white. Nutty-tasting long-grain brown rice has more body. Medium-grain brown rice has a pleasing chewy texture.

OATS

In the morning, serve rolled oats, thick-cut old-fashioned oats, or nubbly steel-cut oats. Use regular or quick-cooking oatmeal—both provide the same amounts of healthful soluble and insoluble fiber. Avoid instant oatmeal, which has minimal fiber or flavor.

cooking grains

To help you incorporate more whole grains into your diet, here are six techniques for cooking versatile grains to use in any meal.

BASIC COOKED QUINOA

Rinse 1 part quinoa with cold water and drain through a fine-mesh sieve. Repeat 3 times, then place in a saucepan. Add 2 parts water and a pinch of salt and bring to a boil. Cover and simmer until the water is absorbed, about 15 minutes. Turn off the heat and let stand at least 5 minutes before using.

BASIC COOKED BARLEY

In a saucepan, bring 4 parts water to a boil. Add 1 part pearl barley and a pinch of salt and simmer until the grains are tender, about 45 minutes. Drain before using.

BASIC COOKED FARRO

In a saucepan, combine 1 part rinsed semi-pearled farro with 2 parts water and a pinch of salt. Bring to a boil, then cover and simmer until the grains are tender and the water is absorbed, about 25 minutes.

BASIC COOKED BULGUR

In a saucepan, combine 1 part medium-grain bulgur and 2 parts water. Bring to a boil, then cover and simmer until the grains are tender, 10–12 minutes.

BASIC SOFT POLENTA

In a saucepan, bring 5 parts broth or water to a boil along with a large pinch of salt. Slowly whisk in 1 part coarse polenta. Simmer, stirring often, until the polenta pulls away from the sides of the pan, 20–45 minutes.

BASIC COOKED BROWN RICE

In a saucepan, combine 1 part rice, 2 parts water, and a pinch of salt. Bring to a boil, then cover and simmer until the rice is tender and the water is absorbed, 45–60 minutes.

lean protein

Protein is essential for maintaining muscle and repairing damaged DNA in your body. So besides eating lean cuts of poultry, beef, or pork, have fish or seafood at least twice a week, particularly ones that contain omega-3s. When grilling any type of protein, marinate it first. This helps to prevent the formation of toxic substances in addition to adding flavor and moisture.

POULTRY

Chicken's white meat is more versatile, but turkey breast has more flavor. Turkey is also slightly leaner and it has less saturated fat than chicken. A sturdier bird, turkey is raised without hormones and using fewer antibiotics, as well. Both chicken and turkey are good sources of tryptophan, the mood-boosting amino acid that also helps sleep.

PORK

Only turkey breast is leaner than pork tenderloin. To help keep this tender cut moist, roast it whole or sauté it in medallions and serve it with a quick pan sauce. In commercially raised pork, antibiotics, stressful living conditions, and the environmental pollution created are concerns. Buying organic or local and humanely raised pork can avoid this.

BEEF

Eating lean beef in moderation provides needed vitamin B-12, zinc, and iron. When it is grass-fed, beef also contains omega-3s and it is leaner than corn-fed, conventionally raised beef. Plus, grass-fed cattle are antibiotic-free and humanely treated. Combine beef with lots of vegetables for a healthy dish.

SALMON

Wild salmon is the food richest in omega-3 fat. Fresh wild salmon is sustainable but it can be costly, so consider canned—most of it is wild Alaska salmon. Try using a can of skinless, boneless salmon to replace the bulgur in tabbouleh, for example. The health benefits from salmon are so important that experts agree that eating farmed is worthwhile if that fits your budget.

SHRIMP

Eating shrimp is another way to get important omega-3s. Although it appears to be fresh, most shrimp is previously frozen and treated with sulfites. To avoid this preservative, ask your fishmonger or read the packaging. Look for shrimp caught wild or farmed in the U.S. Watch, too, for small, sweet, cold-water shrimp from Maine, Canada, or the northern Pacific.

WHITE FISH

Cod, halibut, and black cod— actually sablefish—have at least some omega-3 fat and are rated as Best Choices for sustainability by the Monterey Bay Aquarium's Seafood Watch. Their mild flavor and adaptability in cooking help to make eating fish a couple of times a week appealing. Tiny anchovies are also considered sustainable and boast omega-3 fatty acids and some calcium.

dairy

Eggs, milk, yogurt, and cheese are well-priced sources of complete protein, but choosing dairy products with low amounts of saturated fat is best. Eating dairy foods is also the easiest way to get the calcium you need. Including a small amount of strongly flavored cheese in grain and bean dishes complements their protein and gives a flavor boost.

EGGS

A whole egg provides 6 grams of top-quality protein. The white contains half an egg's protein, while the rest is in the yolk, along with brain-protecting choline. The yolk's color comes from carotenoids, which are important for eye health. Organic eggs are an antibiotic- and hormone-free food. Using eggs laid by pastured hens supports humane treatment.

MILK

A cup of milk delivers nearly one-third of the calcium an adult needs daily for healthy bones, plus vitamins D and K and magnesium that help your body use it. Using reduced-fat (2 percent) and low-fat (1 percent) milk saves calories and significantly reduces saturated fat.

YOGURT

To keep your gut happy and healthy, yogurt must deliver cultures that are both live and active. Always check the label for this. Drink yogurt in a smoothie, combine it with cucumber and mint for a refreshing sauce, or add a dollop of higher-protein, thick Greek-style yogurt to soups and fruit-based desserts.

BUTTERMILK

Buttermilk is made by culturing low fat or skim milk with friendly bacteria. The enzymes these bacteria produce have a tenderizing effect in marinades. Buttermilk lightens pancakes, waffles, and dessert batters and adds a pleasant tang. Use it to make lean, fluffy mashed potatoes and smart, creamy salad dressings.

PARMESAN

Cheesemongers consider authentic Italian Parmigiano-Reggiano the queen of cheeses. Made using partially skimmed milk from grass-fed cows, it is particularly digestible compared to other cheeses. Parmesan from Argentina is a well-priced alternative. Edible Parmigiano rind simmered in a pot of minestrone adds savory umami flavor.

PECORINO

An Italian sheep's milk cheese, the best pecorino comes from near Rome or Sardinia. Its sharp, salty flavor is good with pasta and in lasagna. Mix grated pecorino into meatloaf or chip off chunks and nibble them with a ripe pear. For the most flavor, buy a hunk of pecorino to use as needed.

FETA

Feta is usually sheep's milk cheese pickled in brine, although there are goat and cow's milk versions, too. Feta in chunks should be sold and stored bathed in brine. Crumbled feta may be sold dry. Look for reduced-fat feta in supermarkets. A little crumbled over a salad or blended into turkey burgers adds tangy flavor.

PISTACHIOS

Pistachios get their green color from chlorophyll, which may help to protect against certain cancers and to reduce inflammation. For snacking, a serving—1 ounce of shelled nuts—is a generous 49 pistachios. Look for shelled pistachios at natural food stores.

CASHEWS

Cashews are slightly lower in calories than other nuts. They do contain a fair amount of saturated fat, so serving them as a crunchy element in recipes may a better idea than overindulging by snacking on them. Raw cashews whirled with water, then strained, make a rich, dairy-free milk.

SESAME SEEDS

Rich in calcium, sesame seeds also contain a substance that lowers cholesterol in the liver as well as in the blood. To bring out their flavor, whirl sesame seeds in a dry, heavy skillet until fragrant. Asian toasted sesame oil adds deep, nutty flavor and extra nutrition to Asian-style dishes.

nuts & seeds

The monounsaturated fat in nuts and seeds makes them good for your heart and brain. Eating them also helps you feel satisfied. To keep calories under control, when snacking on nuts, measure out one serving before you start munching.

WALNUTS

Walnuts contain a good amount of omega-3s. Roasted walnut oil drizzled on steamed vegetables gives rich flavor and aroma while adding health benefits. Whirling walnuts in a food processor with walnut oil and a pinch of salt makes delicious nut butter.

PINE NUTS

This protein-rich, rice grain–shaped nut really comes from pine trees. Mediterranean pine nuts have a sweeter taste and softer texture than pine nuts from China. Besides pesto, use pine nuts in green or grain salads to add extra fiber and healthy unsaturated fats.

PUMPKIN SEEDS

Slightly bitter pumpkin seeds blend nicely with other nuts in granola and trail mix. Also use them on top of muffins and tea cakes. A 1-ounce serving, about ¼ cup, contains 8 grams of protein. Pumpkin seeds contain a substance that helps prevent and control an enlarged prostate.

ALMONDS

Compared to other nuts, almonds contain the highest amount of monounsaturated fat and the most fiber. A quarter-cup of almonds contains more protein than an egg. The nutrition in the skin of whole almonds makes them the best choice when you can use them. Almond milk is an excellent choice for dairy-free cooking.

good fats & sweeteners

Yes, fats are high in calories. But some contain anti-inflammatory fatty acids that our body cannot produce and that are essential to our well-being. Using fats in moderation is smart. Sweeteners are a luxury we all deserve on occasion. Used judiciously, these less refined ones include some nutritional goodness or are gentler on blood sugar levels than refined sugar.

GRAPESEED OIL
High in an essential fatty acid the body cannot make, grapeseed oil has a high smoke point, which makes it good for stir-frying, sautéing, and baking. Chefs use this neutral-tasting oil for salad dressings as well as in cooking.

OLIVE OIL
Antioxidants in extra-virgin olive oil help raise good cholesterol and lower bad cholesterol in your blood. The more peppery it tastes, the more of these polyphenols the oil contains. Extra-virgin olive oil is best used in dressings and for drizzling. Heat destroys its antioxidants, so limit its cooking use to quick sautés. Regular olive oil and light olive oil have a high smoke point best for sautéing.

CANOLA OIL
Its neutral taste and favorable omega-3 to omega-6 ratio make canola oil good for salad dressings, sautéing and baking. Using cold-pressed or expeller-pressed canola oil is preferable. Spectrum Naturals High Heat Canola is particularly well suited for cooking.

HONEY

Honey is thirty-five percent sweeter than sugar, so adjust accordingly when using it in baking and cooking. The darker the honey, the stronger it tastes. Wildflower honey's neutral taste is ideal for many dishes. Raw honey is recommended because it contains enzymes and phytonutrients destroyed by pasteurization and filtering.

AGAVE

This liquid sweetener made from a plant related to aloe has a low glycemic index and is twenty-five times sweeter than sugar, so a little goes a long way in recipes. Golden light agave tastes neutrally sweet. Caramel-colored dark agave tastes warm and mellow. Both are good in desserts, drinks, and sauces.

MAPLE SYRUP

Maple syrup contains calcium, potassium, zinc and other minerals. The mild taste of Grade A Fancy syrup goes well with apples, strawberries, and other fruit. Grade B Dark maple syrup has an almost smoky, intense flavor. Use this less expensive grade for hot cereals, in baking, and for glazing sweet potatoes. Dark fudge sauce made with maple syrup is a special treat.

37

working with herbs

In general, only the leaves from fresh herbs are used in cooking. Following is a primer on how to prep them for recipes.

LARGE-LEAFED HERBS

Fresh herbs that boast large or broad leaves, such as basil, sage, and mint, can be either slivered or chopped for recipes. Use your fingers to pull off the leaves one at a time. Stack 5 or 6 leaves on top of one another, then roll the stack lengthwise into a tight cylinder. Using a chef's knife, cut the leaves crosswise into narrow slivers. To chop the herbs, gather the slivers into a pile and rock the blade over them to cut into small pieces.

SMALL-LEAFED HERBS

For herbs such as cilantro, parsley, and tarragon, pull the leaves from the stems one at a time. Heap the leaves together on a cutting board. Rock the blade of a chef's knife back and forth briefly over the leaves to chop coarsely. For finely chopped, continue to re-gather the leaves and rock the knife over them making small, even pieces. For minced, keep chopping until the pieces are as fine as possible.

BRANCHED OR WOODY HERBS

Remove the petal-like leaves from thyme or oregano by gently pulling your thumb and index finger together down the stems. Gather the leaves on a cutting board and follow the instructions for Small-Leafed Herbs (above) to chop or mince.

GENERAL TIPS

- Choose bunches with bright green, fragrant leaves

- Avoid bunches with wilted or discolored leaves, or pluck these from your garden plot

- Rinse herbs just before using and pat dry gently with paper towels

BASIL
Sweet, spicy Genovese basil and pungent Thai basil with its complex citrus, anise, and mint notes are both rich in antimicrobial and anti-inflammatory benefits. Because the aromatic compounds providing these benefits are volatile, add basil late in the cooking process to preserve them and get full flavor.

MINT
Sweet, mild spearmint is soothing, while bitter, sharp peppermint is stimulating. Both help to protect against the bacteria associated with ulcers.

CILANTRO
Widely used in Mexico, the Middle East, and South Asian cooking, cilantro is rich in antioxidants, plus antimicrobials that can protect against salmonella. Sprinkle cilantro on sliced oranges and on buttery carrots. Heat diminishes its flavor so add it later in chili and other cooked dishes.

fresh herbs

The same phytochemical compounds that give herbs their fragrance and flavor also give them proven health benefits. In cooking, use an array of herbs to get the full variety of their powers. Dried herbs quickly lose fragrance, flavor, and health powers, so from a nutritional standpoint, use fresh when possible.

OREGANO

This Mediterranean staple, which gives familiar flavor to Italian red sauce and Greek salad, has the highest antioxidant level of all herbs. When fresh oregano leaves are tough, use dried instead. Keep both pungent Greek oregano and faintly minty Mexican oregano on hand.

PARSLEY

Flat-leaf or Italian parsley tastes better than curly and it contains more phytochemicals. A main ingredient in tabbouleh and Italian salsa verde, you can also use parsley to make gremolata by combining it with garlic, citrus zest, and capers to serve sprinkled on baked fish or lamb shanks.

spices

Fragrant and vibrantly colored, spices have potent health benefits. To maximize their benefits, whenever possible, purchase spices whole and then grind them just before use. Buy spices in the smallest amounts you can, as they lose flavor, fragrance, and nutrients over time.

MUSTARD SEEDS

A brassica related to cabbage and broccoli, mustard seeds contain the same cancer-preventive substances the full-grown plants contain. Their mild heat and nutty flavor enhance vegetable dishes. Brown or black mustard seeds are best in cooking; yellow ones are great for pickling.

CAYENNE

Most cayenne pepper registers 35,000–50,000 on the Scoville (or heat) scale—hot, but not incendiary. If you don't like a lot of heat, you'll still see how a tiny pinch of cayenne pepper simply brightens the flavor in many types of dishes.

CHILE FLAKES

This fiery spice is the seeds and flakes of small dried red chiles. Like fresh chiles, they contain capsaicin, which stimulates endorphins and is beneficial to metabolism. Just a small amount adds bright heat to dishes.

TURMERIC

Golden turmeric contains one of nature's most potent anti-inflammatories. Since it has an unfamiliar, bitter taste, many cooks blend it with other spices or use curry powder containing turmeric. Add a pinch of turmeric to tomato sauce or a pot of lentils, and sprinkle it on cooked carrots.

GINGER

This warming spice has so many health benefits that Indians call it the universal remedy. Asian cooks favor using fresh ginger. Grating it on a rasp helps it blend into dishes nicely. North African and Middle Eastern recipes usually call for dried.

CUMIN

The seed of a member of the parsley family, cumin has a sharp, musky flavor and is used liberally in Indian, North African, and Latin cooking. Studies have shown that cumin may boost immune health and enhance digestion and it is a rich source of iron.

CINNAMON

Most cinnamon today is actually cassia, the bark from a tree growing in Vietnam and China, rather than true cinnamon from Ceylon. Cinnamon's distinctive flavor and fragrance works well in both sweet and savory dishes. Cinnamon helps to control blood sugar levels, so use both kinds liberally.

PAPRIKA

Spanish paprika, called pimentón, is darker and tastes more pungent than the Hungarian kind. Both come in sweet and hot varieties but pimentón has a smoked taste that is great with vegetables.

spice basics

Spices are easy to work with, but require a little care to retain maximum flavor and aroma. To ensure freshness and optimium nutrition, get them from a quality source that has a high turnover.

TOASTING SPICES

To intensify their flavor, put whole spices (such as mustard seeds, cumin seeds, and broken cinnamon sticks) in a dry frying pan over medium heat. Stir constantly until the spices are fragrant and a shade or two darker, 30 seconds to 1 minute. Pour the spices onto a plate to stop the cooking and let cool for about 10 minutes before grinding.

GRINDING SPICES

For grinding small quantities of spices, use a mortar and pestle. For larger amounts, use a small electric coffee grinder reserved only for grinding spices. Grind only the amount you need for a recipe.

COOKING WITH SPICES

Many recipes call for heating ground spices in a small amount of oil prior to incorporating them into a recipe to bring out their flavor. Called "blooming," this also helps spices to blend more readily with other ingredients.

STORING SPICES

Keep spices in tightly closed containers in a cool, dark place that is ideally not beside the stove. If you buy spices in bulk, purchase glass spice jars for storing. Whole spices will last for about 1 year. Ground spices keep for about 6 months.

fruit & vegetable elixirs

Drinking fresh juice helps boost overall heath and well-being, offering vitamins, minerals, and phytochemicals that are easy for the body to absorb. Using a juice extractor or high-speed blender makes raw fruits and vegetables easier to digest. In addition, drinking raw fruit and vegetable juices can help keep you hydrated, providing an energy boost throughout the day. Try these ten favorite combinations, or customize your own.

Pomegranate-Blueberry

Powerful antioxidant tonic that may help reduce cancer risk.

1 cup (6 oz/185 g) pomegranate seeds

2 cups (8 oz/250 g) blueberries

Agave nectar (optional)

In a juice extractor, juice the pomegranate seeds and blueberries. Taste the juice for sweetness and add a little agave if needed.

Makes about 1 cup (8 fl oz/250 ml)

Tomato, Celery, Cucumber & Carrot

Reduces cancer risk and boosts your complexion.

10 tomatoes

2 celery ribs

2 Persian cucumbers

2 carrots

Juice of 1 lemon

Core and quarter the tomatoes. Dice the celery and cucumbers. Chop the carrots. Put the tomatoes, celery, cucumbers, carrots, and lemon juice in a high-speed blender and process until smooth.

Makes about 4 cups (32 fl oz/1 l)

Orange, Celery & Carrot

Reduces cholesterol and helps prevent cancer.

4 navel oranges

4 celery ribs

8 carrots

Peel and quarter the oranges. In a juice extractor, juice the oranges followed by the celery ribs and carrots.

Makes about 2¼ cups (18 fl oz/560 ml)

Pear, Apple & Greens

Builds bones and strengthens the immune system.

1 pear

1 apple

4 oz (125 g) rainbow chard

2 oz (60 g) fresh spinach

½ cup (¾ oz/20 g) chopped flat-leaf parsley

Halve and core the pear and the apple, and chop into chunks. Separate the stems and large veins from the chard leaves and coarsely chop. Put the pear, apple, chard leaves and stems, spinach, and parsley in a high-speed blender and process until smooth. Dilute with water, if desired.

Makes about 4 cups (32 fl oz/1 l)

Beet-Orange

Detoxifies and supports your immune system.

4 navel oranges
3 red beets

Peel and quarter the oranges. Scrub, trim, and quarter the beets. In a juice extractor, juice the oranges and beets.

Makes about 2$\frac{1}{2}$ cups (20 fl oz/625 ml)

Watermelon-Lime

Hydrates and infuses vitamins into your system.

1 seedless watermelon (about 2 lb/1 kg)
2 limes
2 teaspoons honey

Peel and chop the watermelon into small chunks. Peel, quarter, and seed the limes. Put the watermelon chunks, lime quarters, and honey in a blender and process until smooth. Dilute with water, if desired.

Makes about 4 cups (32 fl oz/1 l)

Honeydew-Kiwi

Boosts the immune system and helps balance electrolytes.

$\frac{1}{2}$ honeydew melon
4 kiwis
1 lime
$\frac{1}{2}$ tablespoon agave nectar, plus more if needed

Peel and seed the melon and cut it into chunks. Peel and quarter the kiwis. Peel, quarter, and seed the lime.

Put the melon, kiwis, lime, and agave in a high-speed blender and process until smooth. Dilute with water, if desired. Taste for sweetness and add a little more agave if needed.

Makes 5$\frac{1}{2}$ cups (44 fl oz/1.35)

Mango-Lime

Provides beneficial enzymes that have an anti-inflammatory effect.

3 mangoes
1 lime

Peel the mangoes, cut into large chunks, and discard the pits. Peel, quarter, and seed the lime.

Place the mangoes, lime quarters, and $\frac{1}{2}$ cup (4 fl oz/125 ml) water in a high-speed blender and process until smooth.

Makes 1$\frac{1}{2}$ cups (12 fl oz/375 ml)

Tomato-Pepper-Cucumber

Helps protect against heart disease and boost the immune system.

2 red bell peppers
1 tomato
1 Persian cucumber
$\frac{1}{2}$ jalapeño
Splash of balsamic vinegar

Halve the bell peppers, remove the seeds and ribs, and roughly chop. Quarter and core the tomato. Slice the cucumber. Mince the chile.

Put the peppers, tomato, cucumber, chile, vinegar, and $\frac{1}{2}$ cup (4 fl oz/125 ml) water in a high-speed blender and process until smooth.

Makes about 2 cups (16 fl oz/500 ml)

Wheatgrass-Carrot

Quickly delivers vitamins, minerals, and detoxifying substances.

1 container of wheatgrass
(about 1 cup/1 oz/30 g when trimmed)
4 carrots

Cut off the wheatgrass at the roots. In a juice extractor, juice the wheatgrass and carrots.

Makes about $\frac{3}{4}$ cup (6 fl oz/180 ml)

breakfast

This smoothie couldn't be simpler: just whirl together five superfoods in a blender with ice cubes and you have a balanced breakfast with loads of protein, fiber, and phytochemicals, and you'll have great energy and nutrition before you even leave for work.

Banana-Strawberry-Almond Smoothie

MAKES 2 SERVINGS

1 ripe banana

1 cup (4 oz/125 g) strawberries

1 cup (8 fl oz/250 ml) cranberry juice

1 cup (8 oz/250 g) nonfat plain yogurt

2 tablespoons whole natural almonds

$1/2$ cup (4 oz/125 g) ice cubes

Peel and slice the banana. Hull the strawberries and halve them lengthwise.

In a blender, combine the banana, strawberries, cranberry juice, yogurt, almonds, and ice cubes. Blend until frothy and thoroughly blended.

Divide between 2 tall glasses and serve right away.

Note: Turn to pages 48–49 for more smoothie ideas.

Fresh mango, cranberry juice, and creamy yogurt, blended together with ice cubes, make an unusual and refreshing breakfast drink. Mango is an excellent source of beta-carotene, and both mangoes and cranberries contain vitamin C.

Mango-Yogurt Smoothie

MAKES 2 SERVINGS

1 ripe mango

1 cup (8 fl oz/250 ml) sweetened cranberry juice

1 cup (8 oz/250 g) nonfat plain yogurt

$1/2$ cup (4 oz/125 g) ice cubes

To cut the mango, stand the fruit on one of its narrow sides, with the stem end facing you. Using a sharp knife, and positioning the blade about 1 inch (2.5 cm) from the stem, cut down the length of the fruit, just brushing the large, lengthwise pit. Repeat the cut on the other side of the pit. One at a time, holding each half cut side up, score the flesh in a grid pattern, forming $1/4$-inch (6-mm) cubes and stopping just short of the skin. Push against the skin side to force the cubes outward, then cut across the base of the cubes to free them. Measure out 1 cup (6 oz/185 g) mango cubes; reserve the remainder for another use.

In a blender, combine the 1 cup mango cubes, cranberry juice, yogurt, and ice cubes. Blend until frothy and thoroughly blended.

Divide between 2 tall glasses and serve right away.

The beneficial bacteria in plain yogurt are thought to boost the immune system, increase the absorption of nutrients, and keep the intestinal tract healthy. To ensure optimum benefit, choose unsweetened yogurt that lists live and active cultures on the label.

Carrot-Pineapple Smoothie

MAKES 2 SERVINGS

2 cups (12 oz/375 g) frozen
pineapple chunks

$1/2$ cup (4 fl oz/125 ml) carrot juice

1 cup (8 oz/250 g) nonfat
plain yogurt

$1/2$ cup (4 oz/125 g) ice cubes

In a blender, combine the pineapple and carrot juice. Process until the mixture is smooth, 30–45 seconds. Add the yogurt and ice cubes and process until frothy and thoroughly blended, about 20 seconds longer.

Divide between 2 tall glasses and serve right away.

This crunchy, lightly sweetened nut-and-seed granola is easy to make and lower in fat and sugar than the typical cereal you see in stores. Serve it with yogurt and vitamin-packed blueberries for a great start to the day.

Homemade Granola with Blueberries & Yogurt

MAKES 6 SERVINGS

2 cups (6 oz/185 g) old-fashioned rolled oats

1/2 cup (1 1/2 oz/45 g) raw wheat germ

1/4 cup (1 oz/30 g) coarsely chopped walnuts

1/4 cup (3/4 oz/20 g) sesame seeds

1/4 cup (1 oz/30 g) shredded sweetened coconut

1/4 cup (1 1/4 oz/40 g) raw hulled pumpkin seeds

Pinch of salt

3 tablespoons honey

2 tablespoons grapeseed or canola oil

1 teaspoon ground cinnamon

2 cups (16 oz/500 g) nonfat plain Greek-style yogurt

2 cups (8 oz/250 g) blueberries

Preheat the oven to 400°F (200°C).

In a large bowl, combine the oats, wheat germ, walnuts, sesame seeds, coconut, pumpkin seeds, and salt and stir to mix. Spread the mixture in an even layer on a large rimmed baking sheet. Bake, stirring occasionally, until crisp and golden, about 15 minutes. Transfer to a large plate to cool. (The cooled granola will keep at room temperature in an airtight container for up to 1 week.)

In a small saucepan over low heat, combine the honey, oil, and cinnamon and cook, stirring, just until the mixture is warm and well blended, about 2 minutes. Add half of the honey mixture to the bowl with the granola and toss to combine and coat thoroughly. Add just enough of the remaining honey mixture so that the granola clumps slightly but is not soupy. Reserve any extra for another use.

Divide the yogurt among individual bowls. Top with the granola and blueberries and serve right away.

Strawberries Pack a Punch

Strawberries' bright red color indicates an abundance of antioxidants helpful in protecting against cancer and supporting short-term memory. They also contain lots of vitamin C and a good amount of fiber. Commercial producers of conventionally grown strawberries use toxic chemicals to protect this fragile fruit, so consider using organic, whether you're buying fresh or frozen berries.

Fresh strawberries taste best in early spring through summer, but frozen fruit captures their goodness at other times of the year. Stir a teaspoon of honey or sugar into a bowl of sliced fresh berries and watch them create their own syrup.

Four Ways to Use Fresh Strawberries

Honeyed Strawberries

In a small saucepan over low heat, warm ¼ cup (2 fl oz/60 ml) orange blossom or wildflower honey, stirring, until thinned but not hot, about 1 minute. Remove from the heat. Add 2 tablespoons fresh lemon juice and 1 cup (4 oz/125 g) hulled and sliced strawberries and stir until blended. Cover and let stand at room temperature until ready to serve. Serve with pancakes or waffles. Serves 4.

Strawberry Sauce

In a food processor, combine 2 cups hulled strawberries and 2–3 tablespoons honey (depending on the sweetness of the berries) and pulse just until the berries are puréed. Pour the purée through a fine-mesh sieve set over a bowl, pressing the purée through the sieve with a wooden spoon and leaving the seeds behind. Stir in 1–2 teaspoons fresh lemon juice to brighten the flavor. Cover and refrigerate for up to 5 days. Serve as a topping for hot breakfast cereal or desserts. Makes 2 cups (16 fl oz/500 ml).

Roasted Berries

In a wide, shallow baking dish, combine 2 cups (8 oz/250 g) hulled strawberries, ½ cup (2 oz/60 g) blueberries, ¼ cup maple syrup, and 1 tablespoon fresh orange juice and toss to coat. Spread the berries into an even layer. Roast the berries in a 450°F (230°C) oven until they just begin to soften, 5–7 minutes. Serve warm with crisp, whole-grain cookies or low-fat cake or over low-fat frozen yogurt. Makes about 2½ cups (20 fl oz/750 ml).

Dark Chocolate–Dipped Strawberries

Place 8 oz (250 g) chopped bittersweet chocolate in a heatproof bowl. Place over (not touching) barely simmering water in a saucepan and heat, stirring occasionally, until melted and smooth. Remove from the heat. One at a time, dip 12–16 strawberries about two-thirds of the way into the chocolate and then set on a sheet pan lined with waxed paper. Refrigerate until the chocolate is set, about 15 minutes or up to 2 hours. Makes 12–16 dipped strawberries.

Oatmeal is always a nutritious choice for the morning. Here it is topped with fresh raspberries in fragrant almond syrup for a new twist on an old favorite. Cooking the oats in nonfat milk, rather than water, produces a rich, creamy texture.

Old-Fashioned Oatmeal with Almond-Raspberry Compote

MAKES 4 SERVINGS

$^1/_2$ cup (4 oz/125 g) sugar

2 teaspoons fresh lemon juice

$^1/_4$ teaspoon pure almond extract

$1^1/_2$ cups (6 oz/190 g) raspberries

4 cups (32 fl oz/1 l) nonfat milk

$^1/_4$ teaspoon sea salt

2 cups (6 oz/185 g) old-fashioned rolled oats

In a saucepan over low heat, combine the sugar and $^1/_2$ cup (4 fl oz/125 ml) water and cook, stirring, until the sugar dissolves. Remove from the heat and pour the sugar syrup into a heatproof bowl. Stir in the lemon juice and almond extract. Let the syrup cool to room temperature. Gently stir in the raspberries and set aside.

In a heavy saucepan over medium-high heat, stir together the milk and salt and bring to a boil. Slowly stir in the oats. Reduce the heat to medium and cook at a gentle boil, uncovered, stirring often, until the oatmeal is soft and the milk is absorbed, about 5 minutes. Adjust the heat as needed to keep the oatmeal boiling gently. Remove from the heat, cover, and let stand for 3 minutes.

Spoon the hot oatmeal into individual bowls and top each one with the raspberries, dividing them evenly. Serve right away.

In Italy, breakfast polenta, called "polentina," is a creamier, looser form of polenta than is served at other times of the day. Top the whole-grain cereal with sliced bananas and maple syrup for a novel alternative to traditional oatmeal.

Maple-Banana Breakfast Polenta

MAKES 4 SERVINGS

1²/₃ cups (13 fl oz/410 ml) nonfat milk, or more as needed

1¹/₂ tablespoons sugar

Fine sea salt

³/₄ cup (5 oz/155 g) polenta

2 ripe bananas, peeled and sliced

¹/₂ cup (5¹/₂ fl oz/170 ml) pure Grade B maple syrup, warmed

In a large, heavy saucepan over medium-high heat, combine 1²/₃ cups (13 fl oz/ 410 ml) water and the milk, sugar, and ¹/₄ teaspoon salt and bring to a boil. Reduce the heat to very low and, when the liquid is barely simmering, drizzle in the polenta in a slow, thin stream, whisking constantly in the same direction until all the grains have been absorbed and the mixture is smooth and free of lumps. Switch to a wooden spoon and stir thoroughly every 1–2 minutes until the polenta is loose and creamy, about 15 minutes. (For thicker polenta, cook for up to 30 minutes.) Add a little more water and/or milk if the polenta gets too stiff; this should be a very liquid mixture.

Ladle the polenta into individual bowls. Distribute the bananas over the top. Drizzle with the warm maple syrup and serve right away.

Cinnamon-flavored whole wheat batter produces waffles with a crunchy texture and a nutty taste. They're irresistible topped with vitamin-packed, honey-sweetened berries. Serve these for a weekend breakfast and your family will probably not guess that they're healthy.

Whole-Wheat Waffles with Honeyed Strawberries

MAKES 4 SERVINGS

1 cup (5 oz/155 g) whole-wheat flour

^{1}/$_2$ cup (2^1/$_2$ oz/75 g) unbleached all-purpose flour

2 tablespoons wheat bran

1 tablespoon baking powder

1 teaspoon ground cinnamon

^{1}/$_2$ teaspoon fine sea salt

1^1/$_2$ cups (12 fl oz/375 ml) nonfat milk

2 large eggs

2 tablespoons grapeseed or canola oil, plus more for brushing

2 tablespoons wildflower or orange blossom honey

Honeyed Strawberries (page 53)

In a large bowl, whisk together the flours, bran, baking powder, cinnamon, and salt. In a large glass measuring pitcher, whisk together the milk, eggs, and the 2 tablespoons oil until blended. Add the honey to the milk mixture and whisk until blended. Make a well in the center of the dry ingredients and add the milk mixture. Stir just until blended; do not overmix. The batter will be thick.

Preheat the oven to 200°F (95°C). Preheat a waffle iron for 5 minutes, then brush with oil. Ladle about ½ cup (4 fl oz/125 ml) of the batter into the center of the waffle iron, and spread with a small spatula to fill all the holes. Close the waffle iron and cook until the steam stops escaping from the sides and the top opens easily, 4–5 minutes, or according to the manufacturer's directions.

Transfer the waffle to a warmed platter and keep warm in the oven. Repeat with the remaining batter. Serve the waffles with the honeyed strawberries.

Sweet potatoes are a great source of beta-carotene and are full of fiber. Here, they star along with walnuts in a modern take on traditional pancakes that are dense with nutrition and full of autumn flavors. If you like, serve with Sautéed Apples (page 61).

Sweet Potato Pancakes with Walnuts

MAKES 6 SERVINGS

2 sweet potatoes, scrubbed but not peeled

2 tablespoons unsalted butter

1 1/2 cups (12 fl oz/375 ml) nonfat milk

2 large eggs

2 tablespoons brown sugar

1 1/2 teaspoons pure vanilla extract

1 cup (5 oz/155 g) whole-wheat flour

1/2 cup (2 1/2 oz/75 g) unbleached all-purpose flour

1 tablespoon baking powder

1/2 teaspoon *each* ground cinnamon and freshly grated nutmeg

1/2 teaspoon salt

Canola-oil spray

1/2 cup (2 oz/60 g) walnuts, toasted and coarsely chopped

Warmed pure maple syrup for serving

Preheat the oven to 200°F (95°C). Pierce the sweet potatoes a few times with a fork, and microwave on high until tender, about 8 minutes. Split each sweet potato lengthwise and let cool just until easy to handle, then scoop out and measure 1¼ cups (6 oz/185 g) of the flesh; reserve the remainder for another use.

In a food processor, combine the warm sweet potato flesh and the butter and pulse until incorporated. Add ½ cup (4 fl oz/125 ml) of the milk, the eggs, brown sugar, and vanilla and process until smooth. Transfer to a bowl and whisk in the remaining 1 cup (8 fl oz/250 ml) milk. In a large bowl, combine the flours, baking powder, cinnamon, nutmeg, and salt. Pour the sweet potato mixture into the flour mixture and stir just until combined. Do not overmix.

Place a griddle over medium heat until hot and coat lightly with canola-oil spray. For each pancake, pour about ¼ cup (2 fl oz/60 ml) of the batter onto the griddle and cook until bubbles break on the surface, about 2½ minutes. Flip the pancakes and cook until golden brown on the second sides, about 2 minutes longer. Transfer to a baking sheet and keep warm in the oven. Repeat with the remaining batter.

Serve the pancakes piping hot, sprinkling each serving with the walnuts. Pass the warmed syrup at the table.

An Apple a Day...

Loaded with antioxidants, apples deserve their reputation for leaving doctors idle. Benefits include reducing the risk of lung cancer and cardiovascular problems. A key substance in apples helps people with asthma. An apple's 5 grams of fiber help to lower bad cholesterol and control weight. An apple's skin holds much of its goodness, but it can be contaminated with pesticides, so consider buying organic.

To preserve their heat-sensitive antioxidants, serve apples raw, or cook them lightly, with the peels if possible. You can also mix shredded apple into your oatmeal and layer it on a nut butter sandwich on whole-grain bread.

Four Ways to Use Apples

Apple & Celery Salad

In a small frying pan, toast 1 teaspoon coriander seeds over medium heat, shaking the pan occasionally, until aromatic, 2–3 minutes. Place in a mortar, crush with a pestle, and set aside. Without peeling them, core and cut 4 tart apples into matchsticks and toss in a bowl with the juice of 1 lemon; 1 teaspoon walnut oil; 2 celery ribs, sliced; the toasted crushed coriander; and salt and pepper to taste. Toss to mix well and serve right away. Serves 4.

Belgian Endive with Apples & Walnuts

In a large bowl, whisk together 1 tablespoon grape seed oil, 1 tablespoon lemon juice, 1 teaspoon toasted walnut oil, and 1 teaspoon grated lemon zest. Quarter 2 Braeburn apples, trim away the core, and cut into very thin wedges. Add the apple wedges, coarsely chopped leaves from 2 heads Belgian endive, and 2 teaspoons chopped fresh tarragon to the bowl and toss to mix well. Sprinkle with ¼ cup (1 oz/30 g) coarsely chopped walnuts and serve right away. Serves 2.

Curried Turkey-Apple Salad

In a large bowl, whisk together 6 tablespoons (3 oz/90 g) plain nonfat yogurt, 2 tablespoons fresh lemon juice, 1 teaspoon honey, 1 teaspoon Madras curry powder, and salt to taste. Add 1½ cups (9 oz/280 g) cubed turkey breast; 1 tart apple, cored and diced; ¼ cup (1½ oz/45 g) minced red onion; and 3 tablespoons toasted chopped almonds. Mix well. Serve in romaine lettuce leaves or on slices of whole-grain bread as a sandwich. Serves 2.

Sautéed Apples

In a large saucepan over medium-high heat, melt 2 tablespoons unsalted butter. Add 1 lb (500 g) tart apples, cored and sliced, and sauté until just tender, 5–7 minutes. Drizzle with 2 tablespoons maple syrup, the juice of ½ lemon, and ½ teaspoon ground cinnamon and stir well. Serves 6.

Scrambling eggs with vegetables and greens is a fast and easy way to prepare a nutritious breakfast. Stir in almost any sautéed vegetables that strike your fancy, such as the tomatoes and zucchini used here. Arugula can stand in for the spinach.

Farmers' Market Scramble

MAKES 4 SERVINGS

8 large eggs

2 tablespoons nonfat milk

Sea salt and freshly ground pepper

4 teaspoons olive oil

1 small zucchini, trimmed and diced

1 ripe medium tomato, seeded and diced

1 cup (1 oz/30 g) firmly packed baby spinach leaves

1/4 cup (1 oz/30 g) freshly grated pecorino Romano cheese

In a bowl, whisk together the eggs, milk, and a pinch each of salt and pepper. Continue whisking until the eggs are nice and frothy. Set aside.

Warm the oil in a nonstick frying pan over medium heat. Add the zucchini and another pinch of salt. Cook, stirring, until just tender, about 1 minute. Add the tomato and stir to combine. Reduce the heat to medium-low, add the egg mixture, and let cook, without stirring, until the eggs just begin to set, about 1 minute. Using a heatproof rubber spatula, gently push the eggs around the pan, letting any uncooked egg run onto the bottom of the pan.

When the eggs are about half cooked, 1–2 minutes longer, add the spinach and the cheese. Stir gently to combine and continue cooking until the eggs are completely set but still moist, about another 1 minute.

Transfer the scramble to a warmed platter and serve right away.

Frittatas are another great way to incorporate more vegetables into your diet. They're versatile, easily varied, and can be served warm or at room temperature. To reduce the cholesterol in this recipe, substitute 4 egg whites for 2 of the whole eggs.

Swiss Chard & Onion Frittata

MAKES 4–6 SERVINGS

1 bunch Swiss chard (about 1¹/₄ lb/625 g)

4 tablespoons (2 fl oz/60 ml) olive oil

1 small yellow onion, thinly sliced

Sea salt and freshly ground black pepper

6 large eggs

4 cloves garlic, finely chopped

¹/₄ cup (1 oz/30 g) freshly grated Parmesan cheese

1–2 pinches cayenne pepper

Position a rack in the upper third of the oven and preheat to 350°F (180°C).

Separate the stems from the chard leaves by cutting along both sides of the center vein. Cut the chard stems crosswise into slices ¹/₄ inch (6 mm) thick and coarsely chop the leaves. Set aside separately.

In a large frying pan, heat 2 tablespoons of the olive oil over medium heat. Add the onion and sauté until tender, about 6 minutes. Add the chard stems, season with salt, and sauté until they start to soften, about 4 minutes. Add the chopped chard leaves and sauté until all of the chard is tender, 3–4 minutes longer. Transfer to a plate. Set aside.

In a large bowl, lightly beat the eggs with the garlic and Parmesan. Season with cayenne, salt, and black pepper to taste.

Drain the liquid from the plate holding the chard, squeeze the leaves gently to remove any excess liquid, and stir into the egg mixture. In an 8-inch (20-cm) ovenproof frying pan, heat the remaining 2 tablespoons olive oil over medium-high heat. Add the egg mixture, reduce the heat to medium, and cook without stirring until the eggs are set around the edges, about 5 minutes. Transfer to the oven and bake until completely set, 7–9 minutes longer. Remove from the oven and let cool briefly.

Cut the frittata into wedges and serve straight from the pan, or invert onto a large plate, if desired, cut into wedges, and serve.

Eggs baked in individual ramekins are an easy, cheery breakfast. Just a touch of heavy cream adds silkiness to the dish without too much extra fat. Thick-sliced whole-grain toast is a perfect partner.

Baked Eggs with Spinach

MAKES 4 SERVINGS

Olive-oil cooking spray

1^1/$_3$ cups (3 oz/80 g) coarsely chopped baby spinach

4 extra-large eggs

2 tablespoons heavy cream

Sea salt and freshly ground pepper

Preheat the oven to 375°F (190°C).

Coat the insides of four 6-oz (185-g) ramekins generously with the olive-oil spray. Divide the spinach among the ramekins. Carefully crack an egg into each ramekin over the spinach. Drizzle ½ tablespoon of the cream over each egg and sprinkle with salt and pepper.

Bake until the egg whites are firm and the yolks are cooked to your liking, 10 minutes for soft-set eggs with runny yolks or up to 14 minutes for harder-cooked yolks. Serve right away.

A whole egg baked in a hollowed-out tomato is topped with Parmesan cheese and basil for a novel approach to breakfast. Ripe but firm tomatoes are sturdy enough to hold up to the oven but add lots of sweet juices to the dish.

Eggs Baked in Tomatoes

MAKES 4 SERVINGS

4 medium-size ripe but firm tomatoes

Sea salt and freshly ground pepper

4 large eggs

1/4 cup (1 oz/30 g) freshly grated Parmesan cheese

1 tablespoon extra-virgin olive oil

1/4 cup (1/4 oz/7 g) fresh basil leaves, cut into thin ribbons

Preheat the oven to 450°F (230°C).

Line a rimmed baking sheet with aluminum foil. Using a serrated knife, cut off the top one-fourth of each tomato. Reserve the tomato tops for another use or discard. Using the tip of a spoon, carefully scoop out the insides of the tomatoes, leaving a shell about 1/2 inch (12 mm) thick. Reserve the insides for another use or discard. Place the hollowed-out tomatoes on the prepared baking sheet and sprinkle the insides with a pinch each of salt and pepper.

Carefully crack an egg into each tomato shell and sprinkle 1 tablespoon of the cheese over each egg. Place the baking sheet in the oven and bake until the egg whites are opaque and the yolks have begun to thicken but are still a bit runny, 8–10 minutes.

Remove the egg-filled tomatoes from the oven. Drizzle the tops with olive oil and scatter evenly with the basil. Serve right away.

Pipérade is a Basque-style sauté of sweet onions and colorful peppers. Choose different colors of peppers for the maximum variety of antioxidants, plus a high dose of naturally occurring vitamin C to start your day.

Poached Eggs with Sweet Pepper Pipérade

MAKES 4 SERVINGS

2 tablespoons olive oil

1 small yellow onion, thinly sliced

Sea salt and freshly ground pepper

1 clove garlic, minced

1 *each* red, yellow, and orange bell pepper, seeded and thinly sliced

2 tablespoons white wine vinegar

1 teaspoon sugar

4 large eggs

2 tablespoons chopped fresh flat-leaf parsley

In a frying pan, heat the olive oil over medium heat. Add the onion and a pinch each of salt and pepper. Cook, stirring occasionally, until the onion just begins to soften, 4–5 minutes. Add the garlic and bell peppers and another pinch each of salt and pepper. Cook, stirring occasionally, until the peppers are tender with a bit of a bite and the onion is very soft, 6–8 minutes longer. Stir in 1 tablespoon of the vinegar and the sugar and continue cooking until the vinegar has almost evaporated, 1–2 minutes longer. Cover to keep warm.

Fill a deep sauté pan halfway with cold water. Add 1 teaspoon salt and the remaining 1 tablespoon vinegar and place the pan over medium heat. When the water begins to simmer, break the eggs, one at a time, into a cup and slip each one gently into the water. Cook for 1 minute, then gently slide a spatula under the eggs to prevent sticking. Poach to the desired doneness, 3–5 minutes.

To serve, divide the pepper mixture among individual plates. Using a slotted spoon, scoop the eggs from the simmering water, drain slightly, and place each on top of a serving of peppers. Sprinkle with the parsley and serve right away.

Mexican food can be unhealthy and loaded with fat, although many of its native ingredients, such as beans, tomatoes, and avocados, are considered superfoods. Combined mindfully, as in this dish, they make a healthy south of the border–style breakfast.

Huevos Rancheros

MAKES 4 SERVINGS

4 whole-wheat tortillas

1 tablespoon grapeseed or canola oil, or as needed

4 large eggs

Sea salt and freshly ground pepper

$1^{1}/_{2}$ cups (12 fl oz/375 ml) Roasted Tomato Sauce (page 219), warmed in a wide sauté pan

1 cup (8 oz/250 g) fat-free canned refried black beans, warmed

1 small ripe avocado, halved, pitted, peeled, and sliced

$^{1}/_{3}$ cup ($1^{1}/_{2}$ oz/45 g) crumbled feta or cotija cheese

$^{2}/_{3}$ cup (5 oz/155 g) nonfat plain Greek-style yogurt

1 tablespoon coarsely chopped fresh cilantro

Preheat the oven to 200°F (95°C). Wrap the tortillas in aluminum foil and place in the oven to warm.

In a large frying pan over medium-low heat, warm the oil. Carefully break the eggs into the pan and fry slowly until the whites are set and the yolks have begun to thicken but are not hard, about 3 minutes. Cover the frying pan if you like firm yolks. Season to taste with salt and pepper.

To assemble, remove the tortillas from the oven. Using tongs, dip each tortilla quickly in the warmed tomato sauce and place on warmed individual plates. Spread $^{1}/_{4}$ cup (2 oz/60 g) of the refried beans evenly on each tortilla and top each with a fried egg. Spoon more of the tomato sauce generously over the eggs and tortilla. Top with the avocado, cheese, yogurt, and cilantro. Serve right away.

Eat Spicy to Improve Your Mood

Capsaicin—the substance that makes chiles burn—stimulates feel-good endorphins in the brain, suppresses appetite, and raises metabolism along with helping to prevent ulcers. Green chiles are rich in vitamin C, ripe red ones in vitamin A. Their ribs contain the heat and transfer it to the seeds, so strip out both (wearing gloves) to reduce a pepper's fire. Chiles have complex flavors ranging from floral to smoky or chocolate.

The heat in chiles is measured in Scoville Heat Units (SHU), starting with 500 SHU for Italian-style pickled pepperoncini and up to 7 million SHU for the meanest hot sauce. The dishes below are medium-hot, but you can add additional hot chiles if you like a spicier kick.

Four Ways to Use Chiles

Pan-Grilled Padrón Peppers

Preheat a stove-top grill pan over high heat until smoking. Meanwhile, in a bowl, toss 1 lb (500 g) padrón peppers with 1 tablespoon olive oil until coated. Place the peppers on the hot grill pan and cook, turning occasionally, until the skin has blistered on all sides, 3–4 minutes. Transfer to a plate, season with flaky sea salt, and serve right away. Serves 4 as an appetizer or snack.

Stuffed Poblano Chiles

Slit 2 poblano chiles and remove the seeds and membranes. Stuff with a mashed mixture of goat cheese, nonfat milk, fresh chives, finely chopped shallots, and salt to taste. Roast the chiles at 400°F (200°C) in a lightly oiled baking dish until soft and slightly wrinkled, 30–40 minutes. Serve right away. Serves 2.

Roasted Chiles & Onions

Cut 8 poblano chiles in half lengthwise and remove the ribs, seeds, and stems. Place the chiles cut side down on a baking sheet and broil, turning as needed, until the skin is blackened all over. Transfer to a heatproof bowl, cover with plastic wrap, and let steam for 5 minutes. Using wet fingers, peel off the blackened skin. Cut the chiles into strips and combine with 1 onion, thinly sliced and sautéed in olive oil. Season with salt and pepper. Serve with egg dishes or as a filling for tacos. Serves 4.

Black Bean & Chile Salad

Roast 2 poblano chiles and cut into strips as directed above in Roasted Chiles & Onions. In a bowl, whisk together ¼ cup (2 fl oz/60 ml) extra-virgin olive oil, 2 tablespoons sherry vinegar, 1 tablespoon Dijon mustard, ½ teaspoon ground cumin, and salt and pepper to taste. Add 2 cans (15 oz/470 g) black beans, rinsed and drained; ½ red onion, minced; 1 pint (370 g) cherry tomatoes, halved; and the pepper strips and toss well. Let stand for a few minutes to blend the flavors. Serves 6.

Rich in vitamin A and beta-carotene from the sweet potatoes and antioxidants from the apples, this is an elegant brunch dish that your guests won't guess is healthful. A small amount of nitrite-free ham adds smoky flavor without too much additional fat.

Sweet Potato Hash with Poached Eggs

MAKES 6 SERVINGS

2 medium-size orange-fleshed sweet potatoes (about $^3/_4$ lb/375 g total weight), peeled and cut into slices $^3/_4$ inch (2 cm) thick

4 teaspoons grapeseed or canola oil

1 cup (5 oz/155 g) finely chopped red onion

$^1/_2$ Granny Smith apple, diced

3 oz (90 g) nitrite-free Black Forest ham, diced

2 teaspoons fresh thyme leaves

$^1/_4$ teaspoon sweet paprika

1 tablespoon distilled white vinegar

Sea salt

6 large eggs

In a large saucepan fitted with a steamer basket, bring 1 inch (2.5 cm) water to a boil. Put the sweet potato slices in the basket, spread evenly, cover, and steam until the potatoes are tender but still offer some resistance when pierced gently with a fork, about 8 minutes. Remove the pan from the heat, remove the steamer basket from the pan, and let the potatoes cool to room temperature.

In a nonstick frying pan, heat 2 teaspoons of the oil over medium-high heat. Add the onion and apple and sauté until the onion is lightly browned, about 10 minutes. Cut the sweet potatoes into rough cubes and add them to the pan with the ham, thyme, and paprika. Continue to cook, stirring frequently, until the ingredients are browned and warmed through, 5–10 minutes.

While the hash is cooking, poach the eggs: Fill a deep sauté pan halfway with cold water. Add the vinegar and 1 teaspoon salt and place the pan over medium heat. When the water begins to simmer, break the eggs, one at a time, into a cup and slip each one gently into the water. Cook for 1 minute, then gently slide a spatula under the eggs to prevent them from sticking. Poach to the desired doneness, 3–5 minutes.

Divide the hash among individual plates. Using a slotted spoon, scoop the eggs from the simmering water, drain slightly, and place each on top of a serving of hash. Serve right away.

Quesadillas are popular as a lunch dish, but they also make a versatile breakfast. Start with whole-grain tortillas and stuff them with lean chicken breast, scrambled eggs, spinach, tomato, and avocado. They're easy to vary, so you can also make your own healthy combination.

Chicken, Spinach & Avocado Breakfast Quesadillas

MAKES 4 SERVINGS

Olive oil for greasing, plus 1 tablespoon

1 small boneless, skinless chicken breast half (4–5 oz/125–155 g)

Sea salt and freshly ground pepper

4 large eggs

1 cup (2 oz/60 g) coarsely chopped spinach

1 ripe small tomato, seeded and chopped

Two 10-inch (25-cm) whole-wheat tortillas

1/2 cup (2 oz/60 g) shredded sharp white Cheddar cheese

1/4 cup (2 oz/60 g) nonfat Greek-style yogurt

1 small ripe avocado, pitted, peeled, and sliced

1/4 cup (2 oz/60 g) *pico de gallo* (page 218 or purchased)

Preheat the broiler. Lightly oil a broiler pan and set aside.

Place the chicken between 2 pieces of plastic wrap and lightly pound with a meat pounder to a thickness of about 1/2 inch (12 mm). Brush with oil and season with salt and pepper. Arrange the chicken on the prepared pan and broil, turning once, until lightly browned on both sides and firm when pressed, about 5 minutes total. Transfer to a cutting board and cut into 1/2-inch (12-mm) dice.

In a bowl, whisk together the eggs, 1/4 teaspoon salt, and 1/8 teaspoon pepper. In a frying pan, heat 1 tablespoon olive oil over medium heat. Add the eggs and scramble until starting to set, about 20 seconds. Add the chicken, spinach, and tomato and continue cooking, stirring, until the eggs are just cooked into moist, creamy curds but not dry, about 1 minute. Remove from the heat and set aside.

Warm another frying pan over medium heat. Place 1 tortilla in the hot pan and heat for 1 minute. Flip the tortilla over and sprinkle half of the cheese over the bottom half. Top the cheese with half of the egg-chicken mixture. Fold over the top of the tortilla to cover the filling. Continue cooking until the bottom begins to brown, about 1 minute. Flip and cook until lightly browned on the second side, about 1 minute longer. Transfer to a baking sheet and keep warm in the oven. Repeat to make a second quesadilla.

Cut the quesadillas into wedges. Top each serving with a dollop of yogurt, some avocado slices, and a spoonful of *pico de gallo*. Serve right away.

main dishes

Roasted Tomato & Onion Soup 80

Coconut-Curry Butternut Squash Soup 83

Tuscan-Style Bean & Kale Soup 84

Mushroom & Barley Soup with Fresh Thyme 86

North African–Style Bulgur & Grilled Vegetable Salad 87

Beet & Watercress Salad with Farm Eggs 89

Four Ways to Use Winter Squash 91

Bulgur Salad with Peppers, Chickpeas & Pistachios 93

Quinoa with Tomatoes, Cucumber & Fresh Herbs 94

Whole-Wheat Penne with Spicy Roasted Cauliflower 97

Salmon, Potato & Asparagus Salad 98

Warm Lentil & Kale Salad 101

Four Ways to Use Kale 103

Grilled Salmon with Spicy Melon Salsa 104

Halibut with Roasted Nectarine Chutney 107

Roasted Black Cod with Carrot-Tarragon Purée 108

Sicilian-Style Shrimp with Cauliflower & Almonds 111

Shrimp Tacos with Pineapple Salsa 112

Farro Salad with Turkey, Squash & Dried Cranberries 115

Cashew Chicken Lettuce Tacos 116

Chicken, Broccoli & Mushrooms in Black Bean Sauce 118

Barley Risotto with Chicken, Mushrooms & Greens 119

Four Ways to Use Mushrooms 121

Toasted Quinoa with Chicken & Mango 122

Sautéed Chicken Breasts with Warm Tomato Salad 125

Spicy Ginger Beef & Bok Choy 126

Thai-Style Beef & Herb Salad 129

Steak, Pepper & Onion Salad with Romesco Dressing 130

This simple dish blends three powerful superfoods—tomatoes, garlic, and onions—into a silky soup. The tomatoes are first roasted in a medium-hot oven to concentrate their flavors and enhance their sweetness. Use vegetable broth for a vegetarian version of the soup.

Roasted Tomato & Onion Soup

MAKES 4–6 SERVINGS

3 lb (1.5 kg) ripe tomatoes

2 tablespoons olive oil

2 tablespoons balsamic vinegar

1 clove garlic, minced

2 teaspoons fresh thyme leaves

Sea salt and freshly ground pepper

1 yellow onion, chopped

$1/2$ cup (4 fl oz/125 ml) dry white wine

3 cups (24 fl oz/750 ml) low-sodium chicken broth

2 tablespoons chopped fresh flat-leaf parsley

Preheat the oven to 325°F (165°C).

Cut the tomatoes in half and place, cut side up, on a baking sheet. In a small bowl, whisk together 1 tablespoon of the olive oil, the vinegar, garlic, thyme, $1/4$ teaspoon salt, and $1/4$ teaspoon pepper. Spoon the mixture evenly over the tomatoes. Roast until the tomatoes are soft and wrinkled, about 1 hour.

In a soup pot, heat the remaining 1 tablespoon olive oil over medium-high heat. Add the onion and cook, stirring often and reducing the heat as necessary to prevent scorching, until soft, 5–7 minutes. Add the wine, raise the heat to medium-high, and bring to a boil. Cook until the liquid is evaporated, 2–3 minutes. Stir in the chicken broth and roasted tomatoes, using a wooden spoon to scrape up any browned bits from the bottom of the pan, and return to a boil. Reduce the heat to medium-low, cover, and simmer for 10 minutes to allow the flavors to blend.

In a blender or food processor, working in batches if necessary, process the soup until smooth. Return to the pot and season with salt and pepper. Reheat the soup gently over medium heat just until hot. Ladle into warmed individual bowls, garnish with the parsley, and serve right away.

At once fragrant, sweet, and spicy, this soup is spiked with unexpected Thai flavors. The butternut squash will give the immune system a powerful beta-carotene boost. Garnish it with the leaves and flowers of Thai purple basil leaves, if you like.

Coconut-Curry Butternut Squash Soup

MAKES 4 SERVINGS

1 large butternut squash
(about 4 lb/2 kg)

1 1/2 tablespoons olive oil

4 large shallots, sliced (about 3 oz/90 g)

1 tablespoon peeled and
grated fresh ginger

1 clove garlic, minced

3 cups (24 fl oz/750 ml) low-sodium
chicken or vegetable broth

Sea salt

1 teaspoon Thai red curry paste

3/4 cup (6 fl oz/180 ml) light coconut milk

2 teaspoons fresh lime juice

Using a sharp, heavy knife, trim the stem end from the squash, then cut in half lengthwise. Scoop out the seeds and discard. Cut off the peel, and then cut the flesh into 1-inch (2.5-cm) cubes. (You should have about 9 cups/3 lb/1.5 kg.)

In a soup pot, heat the olive oil over medium heat. Add the shallots and cook until softened, 2–3 minutes. Add the ginger and garlic and cook until fragrant but not browned, about 1 minute. Add the squash, broth, and 1/2 teaspoon salt and bring to a boil over high heat. Reduce the heat to maintain a simmer, cover, and cook until the squash is tender when pierced with a fork, about 20 minutes. Remove from the heat and let cool slightly.

In a small bowl, combine the curry paste and coconut milk and whisk until well blended. In a blender or food processor, working in batches if necessary, process the soup until smooth. Return to the pot and stir in the curry–coconut milk mixture. Reheat the soup gently over medium heat just until hot and season with lime juice and additional salt to taste. Ladle into warmed individual bowls and serve right away.

This humble soup is packed with healthy ingredients. The soup holds well and it tastes even better the next day. If you have leftover soup, for a hearty meal, do as the Tuscans do and add stale whole-grain bread to the pot when reheating it.

Tuscan-Style Bean & Kale Soup

MAKES 8 SERVINGS

1 cup (7 oz/220 g) dried borlotti or cranberry beans, soaked and drained

1 bunch Tuscan kale (about 1/2 lb/250 g)

2 tablespoons olive oil

1 large yellow onion, chopped

1 large carrot, peeled and chopped

1 rib celery, thinly sliced

2 cloves garlic, minced

1 can (28 oz/875 g) whole plum tomatoes

1 bay leaf

Pinch of red pepper flakes

Sea salt and freshly ground black pepper

Pick over the beans for stones or grit. Rinse thoroughly under cold running water and drain. Put the beans in a bowl and add fresh water to cover by 3–4 inches (7.5–10 cm). Let soak for at least 4 hours and up to overnight.

Drain the beans and transfer them to a soup pot. Add water to cover the beans generously. Bring to a boil over high heat, reduce the heat to low, cover partially, and simmer gently until the beans are tender, 1–1½ hours. Drain the beans, pouring their liquid into another pot or a heatproof bowl. Set aside the beans and liquid separately.

Separate the stems from the kale leaves. Stack the leaves, roll them up lengthwise, and cut the leaves crosswise into strips about ½ inch (12 mm) wide. Discard the stems or save them for another use.

In a soup pot, heat the olive oil over medium-high heat. Add the onion, carrot, and celery and sauté until the onion and celery are translucent, 5–7 minutes. Add the kale and stir until wilted, about 5 minutes. Add the garlic and sauté until fragrant, about 1 minute. Pour the tomatoes into a bowl and, using your hands, crush them into small pieces. Add the tomatoes and their juices to the pot and stir to combine.

Measure the bean cooking liquid and add water as needed to total 4 cups (32 fl oz/1 l). Add the beans and the cooking-liquid mixture to the pot along with the bay leaf and red pepper flakes. Bring to a boil over medium-high heat, reduce the heat to medium-low, cover, and simmer just until the beans are heated through, about 10 minutes. Season to taste with salt and black pepper.

Ladle the soup into warmed individual bowls and serve right away.

Dried porcini help to intensify the mushroom flavor in this soup and add an extra savory nuance—umami—to the dish. Simmering barley in a flavorful broth is a pleasing way to get more whole grains in your diet.

Mushroom & Barley Soup with Fresh Thyme

MAKES 4 SERVINGS

$^1/_2$ cup ($^1/_2$ oz/90 g) dried porcini mushrooms

$^1/_2$ cup (4 fl oz/125 ml) dry white wine

1 tablespoon olive oil

2 or 3 large shallots, chopped (about $^1/_2$ cup/2 oz/60 g)

2 cloves garlic, minced

8 oz (250 g) fresh cremini mushrooms, brushed clean and chopped

1 teaspoon minced fresh thyme

Sea salt and freshly ground pepper

3 cups (24 fl oz/750 ml) low-sodium chicken broth

$^3/_4$ cup (5 oz/155 g) pearl barley

1 tablespoon tomato paste

2 teaspoons fresh lemon juice

Rinse the porcini well to remove any dirt or grit. In a small saucepan over medium-high heat, bring the wine to a simmer. Remove from the heat and add the porcini mushrooms. Let stand for 15 minutes. Drain the porcini over a bowl, reserving the liquid, and chop finely.

In a heavy soup pot, heat the olive oil over medium-high heat. Add the shallots and garlic and cook, stirring often, until the shallots are soft, 2–3 minutes. Add the cremini mushrooms, thyme, ¼ teaspoon salt, and ¼ teaspoon pepper and sauté until the cremini release their juices and begin to brown, 4–5 minutes. Add the porcini-soaking liquid to the pot and bring to a boil, using a wooden spoon to scrape up any browned bits from the pan. Cook for 1 minute.

Add the chicken broth, barley, tomato paste, chopped porcini, and 3 cups (24 fl oz/750 ml) water to the pot. Bring to a boil, reduce the heat to medium-low, cover, and simmer gently until the barley is tender, 45–50 minutes.

Transfer about 1 cup (8 fl oz/250 ml) of the soup to a blender or food processor and process until smooth. Return the soup to the pot, reheat gently just until hot, and stir in the lemon juice. Taste and adjust the seasoning.

Ladle the soup into warmed individual bowls and serve right away.

This all-purpose grain salad is easy to vary with your favorite grilled vegetables or seasonings. Chickpeas contribute protein and additional fiber and green onions and mint add freshness. For a heartier dish, add grilled chicken breast or salmon.

North African–Style Bulgur & Grilled Vegetable Salad

MAKES 4 SERVINGS

8–10 spears asparagus, trimmed

2 zucchini, cut on the diagonal into slices about 1/4 inch (6 mm) thick

Boiling water as needed

1 teaspoon olive oil

1 1/2 cups (9 oz/280 g) fine-grind bulgur wheat

3 tablespoons extra-virgin olive oil

2 teaspoons finely grated lemon zest

2 tablespoons fresh lemon juice

2 teaspoons ground cumin

1/2 teaspoon ground turmeric

1/2 teaspoon cardamom seeds, crushed

Sea salt and freshly ground pepper

1 cup (7 oz/220 g) drained cooked or canned chickpeas

2 green onions, white and tender green parts, thinly sliced

30 fresh mint leaves, minced

2 tablespoons minced fresh flat-leaf parsley

Prepare a grill for direct-heat cooking over medium heat and oil the grill rack.

Put the asparagus and zucchini in a heatproof bowl, pour over boiling water to cover, and let stand for 2 minutes to soften slightly. Drain, let cool slightly, and toss with the 1 teaspoon olive oil. When the grill is ready, put the bulgur in a heatproof bowl and add boiling water to cover by 2 inches (5 cm). Let stand for 10 minutes. Meanwhile, grill the asparagus and zucchini until lightly browned on all sides and tender-crisp, 4–5 minutes. Transfer to a cutting board and let cool slightly. Cut the asparagus spears on the diagonal into thirds.

In a nonreactive saucepan, whisk together the extra-virgin olive oil, lemon zest and juice, cumin, turmeric, cardamom, 1 teaspoon salt, and several grindings of pepper to make a vinaigrette. Stir in the chickpeas and warm over medium heat for a couple of minutes, stirring occasionally.

Drain the bulgur. Combine the grilled vegetables, bulgur, green onions, mint, parsley, and chickpeas with the vinaigrette in a large serving bowl and toss to coat evenly. Serve warm or at room temperature.

Assertively peppery watercress is a good foil to the sweet, earthy flavor of the beets. Use two colors of beets if you like, or even striped Chioggia beets, if they are available. For the best flavor and vibrant yolk color, seek out eggs from a local egg farm.

Beet & Watercress Salad with Farm Eggs

MAKES 4 SERVINGS

1¹/₂–1³/₄ lb (750–875 g) baby beets

6–8 large organic eggs

Sea salt and freshly ground pepper

3 tablespoons extra-virgin olive oil

2 tablespoons Champagne vinegar

2 tablespoons fresh orange juice

1 teaspoon finely grated orange zest

4 oz (125 g) watercress, tough stems removed, torn into bite-size pieces

Preheat the oven to 400°F (200°C).

Trim the root and stem ends from the beets and wrap them in heavy-duty aluminum foil, making a separate packet for each color, if using. Bake until the beets are easily pierced with a sharp knife, 45 minutes–1 hour. Unwrap and let cool. Gently peel the beets with your fingers or a paring knife. Cut into quarters and put in a small bowl.

Place the eggs in a saucepan with enough water to cover by 1 inch (2.5 cm). Bring to a boil over medium-high heat. Remove the pan from the heat, cover, and let stand until done to your liking, about 10 minutes for slightly runny yolks and up to 14 minutes for firm yolks. Drain the eggs, then transfer to a bowl of ice water to cool slightly, 2 minutes or so. Peel the eggs and cut them lengthwise into quarters. Sprinkle each quarter lightly with salt and pepper.

In a large bowl, whisk together the oil, vinegar, orange juice and zest, and ¹/₂ teaspoon salt to make a dressing. Pour half of the dressing over the beets and stir to coat. In another large bowl, combine the watercress and remaining dressing and toss to coat.

Mound the watercress on individual plates or on a large serving platter and top with the beets. Arrange the egg quarters around the beets and drizzle with any vinaigrette left behind in the watercress bowl. Sprinkle with a few grindings of pepper and serve right away.

Healthy Cold-Weather Staple

Winter squash comes in an assortment of shapes
and sizes. Inside their colorful, hard shells,
their thick flesh is rich in vitamin A, folate,
carotenes, and carotenoids. Many are also good
sources of fiber. Their flesh may be dense,
fluffy, or wet and stringy, and it may taste
nutty, sweet, or somewhat vegetal.

Winter squash is surprisingly versatile. It can star in a warm salad showered with fresh herbs, as a side dish for Thanksgiving, or as a healthy alternative to mashed potatoes. You can also form it into ribbons for a vegetable-based take on a favorite pasta dish.

Four Ways to Use Winter Squash

Warm Squash Salad

Peel 1 small butternut squash and cut into cubes. Toss with 2 tablespoons olive oil and salt and freshly ground pepper to taste and spread on a baking sheet in a single layer. Roast in a 400°F (200°C) oven until tender, 20–30 minutes. In a bowl, whisk together 2 tablespoons extra-virgin olive oil; 2 tablespoons red wine vinegar; ½ small red onion, diced; 1 small clove garlic, minced; ¼ teaspoon red pepper flakes, and salt to taste. Pour the mixture over the squash and toss to coat. Transfer to a platter, sprinkle with 2 tablespoons torn fresh mint leaves, and serve right away. Serves 4.

Maple-Glazed Acorn Squash

Cut 2 small acorn squashes in half lengthwise and scoop out the seeds. Cut the halves crosswise into ½-inch (12-mm) slices. Season the slices with salt and pepper and arrange in a single layer on an oiled baking sheet. Roast in a 400°F (200°C) oven for 10 minutes. Meanwhile, in a small saucepan, melt 1 tablespoon butter with 2 tablespoons maple syrup, 1 tablespoon chopped fresh thyme, and 2 teaspoons finely grated orange zest. Brush the squash with the syrup mixture and continue to roast until the slices are tender, 10–15 minutes. Serve right away. Serves 4.

Spaghetti Squash Spaghetti

Cut 1 spaghetti squash (about 4 lb/2 kg) in half lengthwise, brush with olive oil, and place, cut side down, on a rimmed baking sheet. Roast in a 400°F (200°C) oven until tender, 40–45 minutes. Let cool slightly, then, using a fork, scrape the flesh to remove it in long, spaghetti-like strands. Top with your favorite tomato sauce, warmed; chopped fresh basil; and freshly grated Parmesan cheese. Enjoy it as you would your favorite pasta. Serves 4.

Winter Squash & Pear Purée with Ginger

Roast 1 small butternut squash as directed above in Warm Squash Salad along with 2 peeled, halved, and cored Anjou or Bosc pears until tender. Purée in a food processor along with 1 tablespoon unsalted butter and ½-inch piece fresh ginger, peeled and chopped. Reheat if needed before serving. Serves 4.

Roasted peppers and dried fruits add bursts of color and sweetness to this vegetarian supper, while toasted pistachios add crunch. Look for pomegranate molasses in a Middle Eastern grocery or specialty food store.

Bulgur Salad with Peppers, Chickpeas & Pistachios

MAKES 6 SERVINGS

1½ cups (9 oz/280 g) medium-grind bulgur wheat

2¼ cups (18 fl oz/560 ml) low-sodium vegetable broth

¼ cup (2 fl oz/60 ml) fresh lemon juice

¼ cup (2 fl oz/60 ml) pomegranate molasses

2 teaspoons sugar

Sea salt and freshly ground pepper

6 tablespoons (3 fl oz/90 ml) extra-virgin olive oil

1 can (15½ oz/485 g) chickpeas, drained and rinsed

2 large red bell peppers

¾ cup (3 oz/90 g) shelled roasted pistachio nuts, toasted

½ cup (¾ oz/20 g) chopped fresh flat-leaf parsley or cilantro

1 cup (4 oz/125 g) dried tart cherries, roughly chopped

Put the bulgur in a large heatproof bowl. Bring the broth to a boil in a saucepan, then pour the boiling broth over the bulgur, cover, and let stand until the liquid has been absorbed, about 30 minutes.

In a small nonreactive bowl, whisk together the lemon juice, pomegranate molasses, sugar, 1½ teaspoons salt, and several grindings of pepper until the sugar dissolves. Slowly whisk in the olive oil to make a dressing. Adjust the seasoning. In a small bowl, stir together the chickpeas and ½ teaspoon salt. Whisk the dressing to recombine, then add it, along with the chickpeas, to the bowl with the bulgur and stir to mix well. Cover and refrigerate for 2 hours.

Preheat the broiler. Place the bell peppers on a small rimmed baking sheet, place under the broiler, and broil, turning occasionally, until the skins are charred on all sides, about 10 minutes. Transfer to a bowl, cover, and let steam for 15 minutes. Remove and discard the skins, stems, and seeds and cut the flesh into small dice.

When ready to serve, in a small bowl, stir together the pistachios and a pinch of salt. Add the pistachios, roasted peppers, parsley, and cherries to the bulgur and toss to mix well. Taste and adjust the seasoning. Divide the salad among individual plates or bowls. Serve right away.

The trio of green onion, parsley, and mint, along with succulent vegetables, brings verdant color and a bold herbal taste to this summery salad. Inspired by traditional Middle Eastern tabbouleh, here protein-rich quinoa stands in for the traditional bulgur.

Quinoa with Tomatoes, Cucumber & Fresh Herbs

MAKES 4 SERVINGS

1¹/₂ cups (12 oz/375 g) quinoa

3 cups (24 fl oz/750 ml) low-sodium chicken or vegetable broth

Sea salt and freshly ground pepper

2 large lemons

2 cloves garlic, minced

1 tablespoon pomegranate molasses

1 teaspoon sugar

¹/₂ cup (4 fl oz/125 ml) extra-virgin olive oil

2 ripe large tomatoes, seeded and diced

¹/₂ large English cucumber, diced

4 green onions, white and tender green parts, thinly sliced

¹/₄ cup (¹/₃ oz/10 g) coarsely chopped fresh flat-leaf parsley

¹/₄ cup (¹/₃ oz/10 g) coarsely chopped fresh mint

Put the quinoa in a fine-mesh strainer. Rinse thoroughly under running cold water and drain. In a saucepan, bring the broth to a boil over high heat. Add the quinoa and ¼ teaspoon salt, stir once, and reduce the heat to low. Cover and cook, without stirring, until all the water has been absorbed and the grains are tender, about 15 minutes. Fluff with a fork and transfer to a large bowl.

Finely grate the zest from 1 of the lemons, then halve both lemons and juice the halves to measure 5 tablespoons (3 fl oz/80 ml). In a small nonreactive bowl, whisk together the lemon juice and zest, garlic, pomegranate molasses, sugar, ½ teaspoon salt, and several grindings of pepper until the sugar dissolves. Slowly whisk in the olive oil to make a dressing. Taste and adjust the seasoning. Add about three-fourths of the dressing to the quinoa and stir to mix well.

In a small bowl, toss the tomatoes with ¼ teaspoon salt and let stand until they release their juice, about 5 minutes, then drain in a sieve set over a second bowl. Place the cucumber in the first bowl along with the green onions and remaining dressing. Toss well, then pour the cucumber mixture over the tomatoes in the sieve to drain. Add the drained tomato-cucumber mixture to the quinoa along with the parsley and mint and stir gently to mix well. Taste, adjust the seasoning, and serve right away.

Roasting cauliflower caramelizes it and brings out its sweetness. Try it in this spicy, Sicilian-style recipe mixed with whole-wheat pasta, capers, and fresh herbs topped with crisp bread crumbs and nutty Parmesan.

Whole-Wheat Penne with Spicy Roasted Cauliflower

MAKES 4–6 SERVINGS

4 slices (each about $1/2$ inch/12 mm thick) country-style whole-grain bread

2 cloves garlic, peeled but left whole

2 heads (about 2 lb/1 kg each) cauliflower

3 tablespoons olive oil

Sea salt

$3/4$ lb (375 g) whole-wheat penne

$1/4$ cup (2 fl oz/60 ml) fresh lemon juice

$1/4$ cup ($1/3$ oz/10 g) chopped fresh flat-leaf parsley

3 tablespoons capers, drained

1 teaspoon red pepper flakes

$1/4$ cup (1 oz/30 g) freshly grated Parmesan cheese

Preheat the oven to 300°F (150°C).

Place the bread slices on a baking sheet and toast until crisp and dry, about 30 minutes. Rub one side of each slice with 1 of the garlic cloves. Let cool, then tear the bread into chunks. Put the chunks in a food processor and process to coarse crumbs. Increase the oven temperature to 400°F (200°C).

Cut each cauliflower into quarters. Discard any leaves and the cores and cut into slices $1/4$–$1/2$ inch (6–12 mm) thick. Mince the remaining garlic clove. Put the cauliflower in a large baking pan, drizzle with the olive oil, sprinkle with the garlic and $1/2$ teaspoon salt, and toss gently to coat evenly. Roast, turning after 10 minutes, until the cauliflower is browned on the edges and tender when pierced with a fork, about 20 minutes.

Meanwhile, bring a large pot three-fourths full of salted water to a boil. Add the pasta to the boiling water and cook until *al dente*, about 12 minutes or according to package directions. Drain, reserving $1/2$ cup (4 fl oz/125 ml) of the cooking water. Return the pasta to the pot and add the cauliflower, lemon juice, parsley, capers, red pepper flakes, and reserved cooking water and toss to combine. Stir in the bread crumbs and cheese and serve right away.

This is one of the most heart-healthy salads you can eat. Perfect for a light supper or a lunch, it can be prepared quickly just before serving, or the salmon, potatoes, and asparagus can be prepared up to 1 day ahead, then dressed just before serving.

Salmon, Potato & Asparagus Salad

MAKES 4 SERVINGS

1 lb (500 g) wild salmon fillet

Sea salt and freshly ground pepper

1 lb (500 g) small red-skinned potatoes, scrubbed

³/₄ lb (375 g) asparagus, trimmed and cut into 1-inch (2.5 cm) lengths

10 oz (315 g) mixed baby salad greens (about 8 cups packed)

Sun-Dried Tomato Vinaigrette (page 218)

3 green onions, white and tender green parts, thinly sliced

Preheat the oven to 400°F (200°C).

Season the salmon fillet generously with salt and pepper. Place the salmon in a baking pan and roast until opaque throughout (use a fork to pull apart a flake of flesh and peek), 10–12 minutes. Transfer the salmon to a plate and let cool.

Meanwhile, put the potatoes in a saucepan and add water to cover. Bring to a boil over high heat, reduce the heat to medium-low, cover, and simmer until the potatoes are tender when pierced with a knife, about 15 minutes. Drain and, when cool enough to handle, peel and cut into slices ½ inch (12 mm) thick.

In a large saucepan fitted with a steamer basket, bring 1 inch (2.5 cm) water to a boil. Add the asparagus to the steamer basket, spread evenly, cover, and steam until tender-crisp, about 3 minutes. Remove the steamer basket from the pan and rinse the asparagus under cold running water until cool. Pat dry.

Cut the salmon into 1-inch (2.5-cm) chunks.

In a large bowl, toss the salad greens with 2 tablespoons of the vinaigrette. Add the asparagus and potatoes along with the remaining vinaigrette and green onions and toss gently. Add the salmon pieces and carefully toss just to gently coat. Serve right away at room temperature.

Here, protein- and fiber-rich brown lentils star alongside roasted carrots, sautéed onions, and earthy kale in a salad that shows off bold tastes, textures, and colors. A small amount of crisped prosciutto lends meaty, savory flavor without much extra fat.

Warm Lentil & Kale Salad

MAKES 6 SERVINGS

1 tablespoon olive oil

4 carrots, peeled and diced

1 large red onion, thinly sliced

Sea salt and freshly ground pepper

Leaves from 1 large bunch Tuscan kale, thinly sliced

1 cup (7 oz/220 g) brown lentils, picked over and rinsed

2 sprigs fresh thyme

4 large cloves garlic

4 cups (32 fl oz/1 l) low-sodium chicken broth

6 thin slices prosciutto

1 teaspoon sherry vinegar

In a large saucepan over medium heat, warm the olive oil. Add the carrots and onion, ¼ teaspoon salt, and several grindings of pepper and sauté until the onion is very soft and lightly caramelized, about 15 minutes. Add the kale leaves to the saucepan, and cook, stirring occasionally, until tender, about 6 minutes. Scrape the contents of the pan into a bowl and set aside. Wipe out the saucepan.

In the same saucepan, combine the lentils, thyme, garlic, chicken broth, ½ teaspoon salt, and ¼ teaspoon pepper and bring to a boil over high heat. Reduce the heat to medium and simmer, uncovered, until the lentils are tender but firm to the bite, 15–20 minutes.

Meanwhile, in a frying pan over medium heat, cook the prosciutto until crisp and browned, about 7 minutes. Let cool, then tear into small pieces.

Drain the lentils in the colander, remove and discard the thyme and garlic, and return the lentils to the saucepan. Stir in the kale mixture, vinegar, and ½ teaspoon salt. Taste and adjust the seasoning. Transfer the lentil mixture to a serving bowl. Top with the prosciutto and serve right away.

One of the Healthiest Foods

Among crucifers, kale beats broccoli in
beta-carotene and carotenoid content as well
as in vitamin A and calcium. Ruffle-edged
curly kale is most familiar. Scallop-edged
Russian kale is more tender and milder tasting.
Tuscan kale, also known as *lacinato* kale,
cavolo nero, and dinosaur kale—so-named because
of the bumpy surface of its long, black-green
leaves—can be meltingly tender and mild.

Ideas abound for using the nutritional powerhouse, kale, such as in a nourishing morning smoothie, as a versatile and simple-to-prepare side dish, stirred into a frittata or pasta sauce, or baked to make crisp, satisfying chips to snack on any time of the day.

Four Ways to Use Kale

Green Smoothie

Using a high-speed blender or masticating vegetable juicer, juice 1 bunch washed kale. Blend the juice into your favorite smoothie, ideally made with fruits, for a healthful elixir to start the day. Or, juice the following in a masticating juicer: 1 pear, 1 apple, 1 bunch kale, and ½ cup (¾ oz/20 g) chopped fresh flat-leaf parsley. Add to a blender along with ½ cup (4 oz/125 g) ice cubes and ½ cup (4 fl oz/125 ml) water; whirl until smooth, and serve. Serves 4.

Wilted Garlicky Greens

Remove the stems and tough ribs from 1 bunch kale. Stack the leaves on a cutting board, roll them up lengthwise, then cut them crosswise into thin strips. Wash the leaves well and drain. In a large frying pan over medium-high heat, warm some olive oil and add 1–2 cloves minced garlic and ¼ teaspoon red pepper flakes. Sauté for about a minute, then add the kale and stir to coat. Add a splash of water to the pan, cover, and cook until the greens are tender, about 5 minutes, adding more water if needed. Serves 2–3 as a side dish.

Frittata or Pasta with Greens

Prepare Wilted Garlicky Greens as directed above, then add to your favorite frittata recipe (1 bunch kale is enough for a 6-egg frittata) or add to pasta sauce to enliven your favorite pasta dish (1 bunch kale is sufficient for 12 oz/275 g of dried pasta.)

Smoky Kale Chips

Tear the leaves from the ribs of 1 bunch washed and dried Tuscan kale into fairly large, chip-size pieces, then toss with about 2 tablespoons olive oil, ½ teaspoon Spanish smoked paprika, and about ½ teaspoon salt. Arrange the leaves in a single layer on 1 or more baking sheets and bake in a 300°F (150°C) oven until dry and crisp. Serves 2 as a snack.

Wild salmon is one of the richest sources of omega-3 fats you can find. A versatile fish, it works well with any fruit-based salsa, such as the mixed melon version here. If you like, swap your favorite tropical fruits such as mango or pineapple for the melon.

Grilled Salmon with Spicy Melon Salsa

MAKES 4 SERVINGS

$1/2$ cup (3 oz/90 g) *each* finely chopped honeydew, cantaloupe, and watermelon

1 serrano chile, seeded and minced

2 tablespoons coarsely chopped fresh cilantro

1 tablespoon honey

2 teaspoons grated lime zest

1 teaspoon fresh lime juice, or to taste

Salt and freshly ground pepper

$1^1/_2$ lb (750 g) wild salmon fillet, skin removed

Canola oil for greasing, plus 1 tablespoon

In a bowl, stir together the melons, chile, cilantro, honey, lime zest and juice, and a generous pinch each of salt and pepper. Mix well and let stand at room temperature for 15–30 minutes to allow the flavors to blend. Taste and adjust the seasoning with lime juice, salt, and pepper. Set aside.

Prepare a grill for direct-heat cooking over medium-high heat and lightly oil the grill rack. (Alternatively, heat a ridged grill pan on the stove top and brush the pan with oil.)

Sprinkle the salmon all over with salt and pepper, then coat with the 1 tablespoon oil. Arrange the salmon on the grill and cook until nicely grill-marked on the first side, 3–4 minutes. Turn and cook until browned on the second side and done to your liking, 3–4 minutes longer.

Transfer the salmon to a platter and serve right away with the melon salsa.

This method is a little unusual, but useful for a busy cook, as everything is cooked in one pan. Here, vitamin C–packed nectarines are baked to become a fragrant chutney and the fish is roasted right on top.

Halibut with Roasted Nectarine Chutney

MAKES 4 SERVINGS

5 ripe yellow nectarines, halved, pitted, and coarsely chopped

1 tablespoon olive oil, plus more for brushing

1/4 cup (1 1/2 oz/45 g) golden raisins

2 tablespoons minced red onion

1 teaspoon fresh lemon juice

1 teaspoon light brown sugar

1 teaspoon peeled and grated fresh ginger

4 halibut fillets, about 5 oz (155 g) each

Sea salt and freshly ground pepper

Chopped fresh flat-leaf parsley for garnish

Preheat oven to 400°F (200°C).

In a baking dish, combine the nectarines, 1 tablespoon olive oil, raisins, onion, lemon juice, brown sugar, and ginger. Stir to coat, then spread evenly in the dish.

Brush the fillets with olive oil, then season on both sides with salt and pepper. Place the fillets on top of the nectarine mixture and roast until the fish is opaque throughout and flakes easily with a fork and the fruit is tender, 15–20 minutes.

To serve, place a fillet on each of 4 warmed individual plates, top each with a spoonful of the chutney, and sprinkle with parsley. Serve, passing the remaining chutney at the table.

Roasted fish is always a healthy choice. Black cod is a silky, moist fish that goes with many accompaniments. The vibrant carrot purée, flavored with anise-like tarragon, is a novel, and nutritious, stand-in for mashed potatoes.

Roasted Black Cod with Carrot-Tarragon Purée

MAKES 4 SERVINGS

4 carrots, peeled and cut into 1-inch (2.5-cm) pieces

Sea salt and freshly ground pepper

2 tablespoons low-sodium chicken broth

2 tablespoons low-fat Greek-style yogurt

3 teaspoons minced fresh tarragon

Olive oil for greasing

4 black cod fillets, each about 6 oz (185 g) and 1 inch (2.5 cm) thick

Preheat the oven to 400°F (200°C).

In a saucepan, combine the carrots with water to cover by 1 inch (2.5 cm) and 1 teaspoon salt and bring to a boil over high heat. Cover, reduce the heat to medium, and simmer briskly until the carrots are very tender, 15–20 minutes. Drain the carrots and transfer to a blender or food processor. Add the chicken broth, yogurt, and 1 teaspoon of the tarragon to the blender and process to a smooth purée. Pour back into the saucepan, then taste and adjust the seasoning.

Lightly oil a baking dish just large enough to hold the fish fillets in a single layer. Brush the fillets with olive oil, then season generously on both sides with salt and pepper. Place in the prepared dish and roast until fish is opaque throughout and flakes easily with a fork, 15–20 minutes.

Gently rewarm the carrot-tarragon purée over medium heat, then divide among warmed individual plates and place a fillet on top. Sprinkle with the remaining 2 teaspoons tarragon and serve right away.

Featuring the typical sweet-sour flavors of Sicilian cuisine, nearly every ingredient in this dish is a superfood. For a heartier dish, serve with steamed brown rice or over your favorite whole-wheat pasta shapes.

Sicilian-Style Shrimp with Cauliflower & Almonds

MAKES 4 SERVINGS

$1/2$ cup (3 oz/90 g) golden raisins

6 cups (6 oz/185 g) cauliflower florets

2 tablespoons olive oil

$1^1/2$ yellow onions, chopped

2 cloves garlic, finely chopped

1 cup (6 oz/185 g) chopped ripe yellow or red tomatoes

$3/4$ lb (375 g) small shrimp, peeled and deveined

4 anchovy fillets, rinsed and patted dry

$1/2$ cup (4 fl oz/125 ml) low-sodium chicken broth

1 teaspoon dried basil

Pinch of red pepper flakes

$1/4$ cup (1 oz/30 g) sliced almonds, toasted

Put the raisins in a small bowl and pour over warm water to cover. Let stand until plumped, about 20 minutes.

In a large saucepan fitted with a steamer basket, bring 1 inch (2.5 cm) water to a boil. Add the cauliflower to the steamer basket, spread evenly, cover, and steam until the cauliflower is tender but still offers some resistance when pierced gently with a fork, about 5 minutes. Remove the pan from the heat, remove the steamer basket from the pan, and set aside. Drain the raisins.

In a sauté pan, heat the olive oil over medium-high heat. Add the onions and sauté until lightly browned, 8–10 minutes. Add the garlic and tomatoes and cook, stirring occasionally, until the tomatoes start to break down, about 5 minutes. Add the shrimp and sauté until bright pink, about 3 minutes. Add the anchovies, mashing them with back of a wooden spoon until creamy. Add the cauliflower, raisins, chicken broth, basil, and red pepper flakes. Reduce the heat to medium and cook until the shrimp are opaque throughout, about 3 minutes longer.

Remove from the heat and stir in the almonds. Transfer to a warmed platter and serve right away.

Any color bell pepper will work in this salsa, but for maximum vitamin C and beta carotene, choose red, orange or yellow. If you can't find fresh pineapple, mango or melon could stand in. This recipe can easily be doubled to serve a crowd.

Shrimp Tacos with Pineapple Salsa

MAKES 4 SERVINGS

1 small pineapple (about 2 lb/1 kg), peeled, cored, and diced

$1/2$ red onion, finely chopped

$1/2$ red bell pepper, seeded and finely chopped

1 small English cucumber, peeled, seeded, and diced

$1/2$ jalapeño chile, seeded and finely chopped

$1/2$ cup ($3/4$ oz/20 g) chopped fresh cilantro

2 tablespoons fresh lime juice

2 tablespoons extra-virgin olive oil

Sea salt and freshly ground pepper

Grapeseed or canola oil for the grill, plus 2 tablespoons

1 lb (500 g) medium shrimp, peeled and deveined

$1/2$ teaspoon chipotle chile powder

1 small clove garlic, minced

8 small (6 inches/15 cm) corn tortillas

In a large bowl, combine the pineapple, onion, bell pepper, cucumber, jalapeño, and cilantro and toss to combine. Add the lime juice and olive oil and season with salt and pepper. Stir to mix well. Cover and refrigerate until ready to serve.

Prepare a grill for direct-heat cooking over medium-high heat. Oil the grill rack. Thread the shrimp onto long metal skewers. In a small bowl, mix together the 2 tablespoons grapeseed oil, chile powder, and garlic. Brush the shrimp with some of the oil mixture.

Using tongs, place the shrimp skewers over the hottest part of the fire and grill until bright pink on the first side, about 2 minutes. Turn and cook until bright pink on the second side, about 2 minutes longer. The shrimp should be firm to the touch at the thickest part. Transfer to a plate.

Lightly brush the tortillas with the remaining oil mixture and place over the hottest part of the grill. Grill until they start to puff up, about 1 minute. Using tongs, turn and grill until puffed on the second side, about 1 minute longer.

Place 1 tortilla on each of 4 warmed individual plates. Arrange the shrimp in the center, dividing them evenly, and top each portion with a large spoonful of the salsa. Serve right away, passing the remaining salsa at the table.

In this grain-based salad, sweet-and-sour dried cranberries contrast with cubes of smoked turkey and earthy butternut squash. Nutty farro serves as a backdrop and adds whole-grain goodness to the meal.

Farro Salad with Turkey, Squash & Dried Cranberries

MAKES 6 SERVINGS

1¹/₃ cups (8 oz/250 g) semipearled farro

4 cups (32 fl oz/1 l) low-sodium chicken broth

Sea salt and freshly ground pepper

1 small butternut squash (about 2 lb/1 kg)

8 tablespoons (4 fl oz/250 ml) extra-virgin olive oil

¹/₄ cup (2 fl oz/60 ml) fresh lemon juice

1 teaspoon honey

1 tablespoon minced fresh flat-leaf parsley

6 oz (185 g) boneless smoked turkey, cut into ¹/₂-inch (12-mm) cubes

²/₃ cup (3 oz/90 g) sweetened dried cranberries

3 green onions, white and tender green parts, thinly sliced

Pick over the farro for stones or grit. Rinse thoroughly under cold running water and drain. In a saucepan, combine the farro, chicken broth and 1 teaspoon salt and bring to a boil over high heat. Reduce the heat to medium-low and simmer gently, uncovered, until all the liquid has been absorbed and the grains are tender, about 30 minutes. Transfer the farro to a large bowl and let cool to room temperature.

Meanwhile, preheat the oven to 400°F (200°C). Using a sharp, heavy knife, trim the stem end from the squash, then cut in half lengthwise. Scoop out the seeds and discard. Cut off the peel and cut the flesh into ½-inch (12-mm) cubes. (You should have about 4½ cups/1½ lb/750 g.) On a rimmed baking sheet, toss the squash cubes with 2 tablespoons of the olive oil, a generous 1 teaspoon salt, and a generous ¼ teaspoon pepper. Spread the squash cubes in an even layer on the baking sheet and roast until tender but still slightly firm to the bite, about 12 minutes. Let cool.

In a small nonreactive bowl, whisk together the lemon juice, honey, parsley, ¼ teaspoon salt, and several grindings of pepper. Slowly whisk in the remaining 6 tablespoons (3 fl oz/90 ml) olive oil to make a dressing. Adjust the seasoning.

Add the dressing, squash, turkey, cranberries, and green onions to the cooled farro and toss to mix well. Serve right away.

This playful spin on tacos starts with a savory Asian-style chicken-and-vegetable stir-fry, then uses crisp, fresh romaine lettuce as a stand-in for tortillas. Chopped cashew nuts add healthy crunch and fresh cilantro adds freshness.

Cashew Chicken Lettuce Tacos

MAKES 4 SERVINGS

2 heads romaine lettuce hearts

¹/₄ cup (2 fl oz/60 ml) low-sodium chicken broth

2 tablespoons hoisin sauce

1 tablespoon low-sodium soy sauce

1 teaspoon rice vinegar

¹/₄ teaspoon Asian sesame oil

1 tablespoon cornstarch

2 tablespoons grapeseed or canola oil

³/₄ lb (375 g) boneless, skinless chicken breasts, cut into ¹/₂-inch (12-mm) cubes

3 cloves garlic, minced

1 medium green bell pepper, seeded and diced

1 large red bell pepper, seeded and diced

4 green onions, white and tender green parts, sliced

1 jalapeño chile, thinly sliced

¹/₂ cup (2 oz/60 g) coarsely chopped raw cashews

Roughly chopped cilantro (optional)

Using your fingers, separate the lettuce leaves from the lettuce heads, tearing out any tough ribs and discarding any blemished or discolored leaves. Place the leaves on a plate, cover with moist paper towels, and refrigerate.

In a small bowl, whisk together the chicken broth, hoisin sauce, soy sauce, vinegar, sesame oil, and cornstarch. Set aside.

In a wok or a large nonstick frying pan, heat the grape seed oil over medium-high heat until almost smoking. Add the chicken and stir-fry until browned, 1–2 minutes. Using a slotted spoon, transfer the chicken to a plate. Add the garlic, bell peppers, green onions, and jalapeño and stir-fry until tender-crisp, about 2 minutes. Return the chicken to the pan and add the cashews. Whisk the soy sauce mixture to recombine, add to the pan, and stir-fry until the chicken is opaque throughout and the sauce is nicely thickened, 2–3 minutes longer.

Scrape the contents of the pan onto a warmed platter. Serve right away with the lettuce leaves. Instruct diners to spoon the chicken-vegetable mixture into the lettuce leaves, add cilantro, if desired, fold them up like tacos, and eat.

Stir-frying calls for cooking foods quickly over high heat in a small amount of fat, which is a healthy choice. Prep all the ingredients for this one—packed with vitamins and lean protein—ahead of time, as the cooking goes quickly.

Chicken, Broccoli & Mushrooms in Black Bean Sauce

MAKES 4 SERVINGS

1 tablespoon fermented black beans

4 tablespoons dry sherry

$^1/_2$ lb (250 g) ground chicken breast

1 teaspoon Asian sesame oil

Sea salt and ground white pepper

2 tablespoons grapeseed or canola oil

6 cloves garlic, chopped

1 tablespoon peeled and grated fresh ginger

2 cups (4 oz/125 g) broccoli florets

2 cups (6 oz/185 g) sliced cremini mushrooms

2 or 3 large shallots, chopped (about $^1/_2$ cup/2 oz/60 g)

2 tablespoons low-sodium chicken broth

Steamed brown rice for serving

$^1/_4$ cup ($^1/_3$ oz/10 g) fresh Thai basil leaves, torn

In a small bowl, soak the black beans in 2 tablespoons of the sherry for 20 minutes. Drain, discarding the sherry.

In a medium bowl, combine the chicken with the sesame oil, ½ teaspoon salt, and ⅛ teaspoon white pepper and stir to coat mix well. Cover with plastic wrap and let stand at room temperature for 20 minutes.

In a wok or a large nonstick frying pan, heat the grapeseed oil over medium-high heat until almost smoking. Add the chicken mixture and stir-fry, breaking up the meat with a spatula until no pink remains, about 2 minutes. Using a slotted spoon, transfer the chicken to a plate. Add the garlic, ginger, and black beans and stir-fry until fragrant, about 30 seconds. Add the broccoli, mushrooms, and shallots and stir-fry until the vegetables begin to soften, about 2 minutes. Add the chicken broth and remaining 2 tablespoons sherry and stir to combine. Return the chicken to pan and stir-fry until the pan is almost dry, 2–3 minutes longer.

To serve, spoon the rice into warmed individual bowls or onto a warmed platter and top with the chicken and vegetables, dividing them evenly. Garnish with the basil and serve right away.

Barley has a pleasantly chewy texture and a sweet, nutty flavor. When simmered in broth over low heat, it cooks into a creamy risotto-style dish. Add meaty mushrooms, shredded chicken, and peppery arugula and you have a delicious fall dinner.

Barley Risotto with Chicken, Mushrooms & Greens

MAKES 6 SERVINGS

6 cups (48 fl oz/1.5 l) low-sodium chicken broth

1¹/₂ tablespoons olive oil

1 yellow onion, chopped

1 clove garlic, minced

2 cups (6 oz/185 g) sliced cremini mushrooms

Sea salt and freshly ground pepper

¹/₂ cup (4 fl oz/125 ml) dry white wine

1 cup (7 oz/220 g) pearl barley

3 cups (4 oz/125 g) firmly packed baby arugula

2 cups (12 oz/375 g) diced or shredded cooked chicken

¹/₂ cup (2 oz/60 g) freshly grated Parmesan cheese

In a saucepan over medium-high heat, bring the chicken broth to a boil. Remove from the heat and cover to keep warm.

In a large saucepan, heat the olive oil over medium-high heat. Add the onion and cook, stirring often, until soft, about 5 minutes. Add the garlic and cook until fragrant, about 1 minute. Add the mushrooms, ¼ teaspoon salt, and a few grindings of pepper. Cook, stirring often, until the mushrooms release their juices and start to brown, 4–5 minutes. Add the wine, bring to a boil, and simmer for 1 minute.

Add 5 cups (40 fl oz/1.25 l) of the hot broth and the barley. Cover and simmer over medium-low heat, stirring occasionally and adding more broth ¼ cup (2 fl oz/60 ml) at a time if barley becomes dry, until the barley is tender, about 45 minutes. Stir in the arugula and more broth to loosen the mixture a little, if needed. Cook, uncovered, until the greens are wilted, about 2 minutes. Stir in the chicken and cook for 1 minute to heat through. Stir in the Parmesan and season to taste with additional salt and pepper. Serve right away.

A Magical Source of Nutrients

The health benefits of mushrooms, particularly shiitakes and wild maitakes, seem almost miraculous. They contain substances unique to mushrooms and so effective that in Asia they are used medicinally to help boost the body's immune system. Even cultivated white button mushrooms, brown cremini, and Portobello mushrooms are rich in anti-cancer selenium and other minerals. They provide good quality protein, as well.

With a pleasing texture and naturally savory flavor, mushrooms make a great snack either on their own topped with pesto, or as a topping for grilled bread. When roasted, they also make a novel side dish or hearty topping for a salad of healthy greens and herbs.

Four Ways to Use Mushrooms

Mushroom Bruschetta

In a small bowl, stir together 3 tablespoons olive oil, 2 tablespoons fresh lemon juice, 1 crushed garlic clove, and salt and pepper to taste. Add 1 lb (500 g) portobello mushroom caps and turn to coat. Brush 8 slices country-style whole-grain bread with olive oil and cook on a medium-hot grill or grill pan until lightly grill-marked, about 1 minute per side. Grill the mushrooms until softened and browned, about 3 minutes per side, then slice and arrange slices on the grilled bread. Sprinkle with chopped fresh basil and shaved Parmesan cheese and serve right away. Serves 4.

Pesto Portobellos

Sprinkle 8 portobello mushrooms caps with lemon juice, salt, and pepper. Cook the mushrooms, gill side down, over a medium-hot grill or grill pan until browned, about 3 minutes. Turn over the mushrooms so they are gill side up, spoon on a little pesto (page 218 or purchased) and cook until the mushrooms are soft and the pesto bubbles, 3–5 minutes. Serve right away. Serves 4.

Garlicky Mushrooms with Pine Nuts

In a bowl, toss 1 lb (500 g) assorted mushrooms with ¼ cup (2 fl oz/60 ml) olive oil, 4 chopped garlic cloves, and salt and pepper to taste. Spread in a roasting pan in a single layer and pour over 2 tablespoons dry white wine or broth. Roast in a 450°F (230°C) oven until they begin to sizzle and brown, about 15 minutes. Add ⅓ cup (2 oz/60 g) pine nuts and continue to roast until tender and browned, about 10 minutes longer. Sprinkle with chopped fresh herbs and serve right away. Serves 4.

Roasted Mushroom Salad

Follow the recipe for Garlicky Mushrooms above, omitting the pine nuts and herbs. Make a dressing from 5 tablespoons (3 fl oz/80 ml) extra-virgin olive oil, ½ teaspoon chopped fresh thyme, ¼ cup (2 fl oz/60 ml) balsamic vinegar, 1 teaspoon fresh lemon juice, a drop of agave nectar, and salt and pepper to taste. In a large bowl, toss together 1 head torn radicchio, 1 small head torn red-leaf lettuce, 1 cup (1½ oz/45 g) fresh flat-leaf parsley, and salt and pepper to taste. Toss with the dressing according to your taste. Divide among plates and top each serving with the warm mushrooms. Serves 6.

This protein-packed dish is simple to make. Its mango-cucumber-yogurt raita features flavors influenced by the cooking of India. You can also serve the raita with grilled or roasted fish or pork.

Toasted Quinoa with Chicken & Mango

MAKES 4 SERVINGS

²/₃ cup (5 oz/155 g) quinoa

3 tablespoons low-fat plain yogurt

1 tablespoon fresh lemon juice

1 teaspoon peeled and grated fresh ginger

1 teaspoon honey

Sea salt and freshly ground pepper

2 cups (10 oz/315 g) diced mango

³/₄ cup (4 oz/125 g) seeded and sliced cucumber

4 boneless, skinless chicken breast halves, about 6 oz (185 g) each

1 tablespoon grapeseed or canola oil

Torn fresh mint for garnish

Put the quinoa in a fine-mesh strainer. Rinse thoroughly under running cold water and drain. Transfer the wet quinoa to a dry nonstick sauté pan and place over medium heat. Toast the quinoa, stirring constantly, with a wooden spatula, until the grains are dry, 2–3 minutes. Raise the heat to medium-high and continue stirring until the grains start popping and the quinoa is lightly browned, about 6 minutes. Remove from the heat and pour in 2 cups (16 fl oz/500 ml) water; be careful, as it will splatter. Return to medium-high heat, cover, and bring to a boil, then reduce the heat to medium-low and simmer gently until tender, about 15 minutes.

Meanwhile, in a bowl, whisk together the yogurt, lemon juice, ginger, honey, and ¼ teaspoon salt. Add the mango and cucumber and stir to coat evenly. Set aside.

One at a time, place the chicken breasts between 2 pieces of plastic wrap and lightly pound with a meat pounder to a thickness of about ½ inch (12 mm). Season the chicken generously on both sides with salt and pepper.

In a large nonstick frying pan, heat the oil over medium-high heat. Working in batches if necessary to avoid crowding the pan, add the chicken and reduce the heat to medium. Cook, turning once, until nicely browned and opaque throughout, 4–5 minutes per side. Transfer each piece to a plate as it is finished and cover with aluminum foil to keep warm.

To serve, fluff the quinoa with a fork and divide among 4 warmed dinner plates. Slice the chicken and place it on top of the quinoa. Top with the mango-yogurt mixture and mint and serve right away.

Cherry tomatoes, which pack a healthful punch, are often seen as a garnish and left behind on the plate. Here, as a sauté atop lean chicken breasts, they make a nutritious, one-dish weeknight supper.

Sautéed Chicken Breasts with Warm Tomato Salad

MAKES 4 SERVINGS

4 boneless, skinless chicken breast halves, about 6 oz (185 g) each

Sea salt and freshly ground pepper

2 tablespoons olive oil

1 or 2 large shallots, minced (about 1/4 cup/1 oz/30 g)

1 clove garlic, minced

1 1/2 cups (9 oz/280 g) cherry and pear tomatoes, preferably a mix of colors and shapes, stemmed and halved

3 tablespoons balsamic vinegar

1/2 cup (1/2 oz/15 g) packed fresh basil leaves, torn

One at a time, place the chicken breasts between 2 pieces of plastic wrap and lightly pound with a meat pounder to a thickness of about 1/2 inch (12 mm). Season the chicken generously on both sides with salt and pepper.

In a large nonstick frying pan, heat the olive oil over medium-high heat. Working in batches if necessary to avoid crowding the pan, add the chicken and reduce the heat to medium. Cook, turning once, until nicely browned and opaque throughout, 4–5 minutes per side. Transfer each piece to a plate as it is finished and cover with aluminum foil to keep warm.

Add the shallots and garlic to the frying pan and cook, stirring often, until softened, 3–4 minutes. Add the tomatoes and vinegar and cook, still stirring often, until the tomatoes begin to soften and split, about 4 minutes. Stir in the basil and season with salt and pepper.

To serve, place a chicken breast on each of 4 warmed individual plates and spoon the warm tomato salad on top. Serve right away.

Lean flank steak is easier to slice if you chill it in the freezer for about 30 minutes. Serve this quick stir-fry with steamed brown rice. If you like, add color and more nutrients to the dish by stir-frying red onions and red bell peppers along with the bok choy.

Spicy Ginger Beef & Bok Choy

MAKES 4 SERVINGS

2 tablespoons dry sherry

1 tablespoon low-sodium soy sauce

1/2 teaspoon Asian red chile paste, plus more if desired

1 lb (500 g) baby bok choy

1 tablespoon grapeseed or canola oil

2 cloves garlic, minced

1 tablespoon peeled and minced fresh ginger

1 lb (500 g) flank steak, thinly sliced across the grain

In a small bowl, stir together the sherry, soy sauce, and chile paste. Set aside.

Trim the stem ends from the baby bok choy and separate into leaves.

In a wok or a large nonstick frying pan, heat 1/2 tablespoon of the oil over high heat. When the oil is hot, add the bok choy and cook, stirring, just until tender-crisp, about 2 minutes. Transfer to a bowl.

Add the remaining 1/2 tablespoon oil to pan. When hot, add the garlic and ginger and cook, stirring often, until fragrant but not browned, about 30 seconds. Add the beef to the pan and cook, tossing and stirring, just until no longer pink, about 2 minutes.

Return the bok choy to the pan along with the sherry mixture and cook for 1 minute until heated through. If you like your food extra spicy, top with additional red chile paste. Serve right away.

This salad contains an abundance of vegetables and fresh herbs that are high in beta-carotene and other protective phytochemicals. Tossed with lean steak and a low-fat vinaigrette featuring Thai flavors, it is reminiscent of salads typical of Southeast Asia.

Thai-Style Beef & Herb Salad

MAKES 4 SERVINGS

3 tablespoons Thai fish sauce

3 tablespoons fresh lime juice

2 teaspoons sugar

1–2 teaspoons minced fresh hot chiles with seeds

Grapeseed or canola oil for greasing, plus 2 teaspoons

1 small flank steak (^{3}/$_4$–1 lb/375–500 g)

Sea salt and freshly ground pepper

1 large head butter or other soft-textured leaf lettuce, torn into bite-sized pieces

1 cup (5 oz/155 g) thinly sliced English cucumber

^{1}/$_2$ cup (1^3/$_4$ oz/50 g) thinly sliced red onion

^{1}/$_2$ cup (2^1/$_2$ oz/75 g) red bell pepper strips

^{1}/$_2$ cup (^{3}/$_4$ oz/20 g) lightly packed torn fresh mint leaves

^{1}/$_2$ cup (^{3}/$_4$ oz/20 g) lightly packed torn fresh cilantro leaves

^{1}/$_4$ cup (^{1}/$_3$ oz/10 g) lightly packed torn fresh basil leaves, preferably Thai

In a large bowl, stir together the fish sauce, lime juice, sugar, and chiles to make a vinaigrette. Set aside.

Prepare a charcoal or gas grill for direct-heat cooking over high heat, or preheat the broiler. Oil the grill rack. Sprinkle the flank steak evenly with salt and pepper and rub them into the meat. Brush lightly on both sides with the 2 teaspoons oil.

Place the flank steak directly over the heat and grill, turning once, until seared on the outside and cooked rare to medium-rare in the center, about 4 minutes per side. (Alternatively, place the flank steak on a broiler pan and slip it under the broiler about 2 inches/5 cm from the heat source. Broil, turning once, until the meat is seared on the outside and cooked rare to medium-rare in the center, about 4 minutes per side.)

Transfer the steak to a cutting board, tent with aluminum foil, and let rest for 20 minutes.

Cut the steak across the grain on the diagonal into very thin slices. Add the slices to the vinaigrette and toss to coat. Add the lettuce, cucumber, onion, bell pepper, mint, cilantro, and basil and toss to coat. Serve right away.

This salad is a riot of garden-fresh color, which also means it is deeply nutritious. Smoked paprika lends intensity and appealing red color to a steak marinade and romesco-style dressing and echoes the charred flavors from the grill.

Steak, Pepper & Onion Salad with Romesco Dressing

MAKES 6 SERVINGS

6 tablespoons (2 fl oz/60 ml) extra-virgin olive oil

$1/3$ cup (3 fl oz/80 ml) sherry vinegar

2 tablespoons fresh orange juice

1 tablespoon Spanish smoked paprika

5 cloves garlic, minced

$1^1/_2$ tablespoons fresh oregano leaves

$1^3/_4$–2 lb (875 g–1 kg) flank steak

2 small red onions, cut into thick slices

3 red, yellow, or orange bell peppers, seeded and cut into wide strips

Sea salt and freshly ground pepper

$1/2$ large head green leaf lettuce, leaves torn into bite-sized pieces

Romesco Dressing (page 218)

2 tablespoons chopped fresh flat-leaf parsley

In a glass dish large enough to hold the steak, whisk together ¼ cup (2 fl oz/ 60 ml) of the olive oil, the vinegar, orange juice, paprika, garlic, and oregano until well blended. Lay the steak in the dish and turn a few times to coat it evenly. Cover and refrigerate for at least 2 hours and preferably overnight, turning once or twice. Let come to room temperature before grilling.

Prepare a grill for direct-heat cooking over medium-high heat. Oil the grill rack.

Brush the onions and peppers with the remaining 2 tablespoons olive oil and season with salt and pepper. Grill, turning once, until softened and lightly charred on both sides, 7–10 minutes for the onions and about 15 minutes for the peppers. Transfer to a plate. Remove the meat from the marinade (discard the marinade) and season both sides with salt and pepper. Grill, turning once, until browned on both sides and cooked to your liking, 10–15 minutes. Transfer to a cutting board and tent with aluminum foil. Cut the peppers into ½-inch (12 mm) strips and separate the onion slices into rings.

In a bowl, toss the lettuce with ⅛ teaspoon salt. Divide the lettuce evenly among individual plates. Cut the steak across the grain on the diagonal into thin slices. Top each mound of lettuce with an equal amount of the steak, onion, and peppers. Spoon the dressing over each salad, dividing evenly, and sprinkle each with a little parsley. Serve right away.

sides & snacks

Grilling bitter radicchio caramelizes and sweetens the leaves. Salsa verde adds piquancy and colorful contrast. Be sure to taste the salsa before seasoning, as its anchovies and capers both have natural saltiness.

Pan-Grilled Radicchio with Salsa Verde

MAKES 4 SERVINGS

4 heads treviso radicchio
(about 1¹/₄ lb/125 g total weight)

Extra-virgin olive oil for drizzling,
plus 8 tablespoons (4 fl oz/125 ml)

Sea salt and freshly ground pepper

1 lemon

2 cloves garlic, smashed

2 tablespoons capers

1 teaspoon prepared horseradish

2 olive oil–packed anchovy fillets,
preferably Italian

Leaves from 1 bunch fresh
flat-leaf parsley

Leaves from ¹/₂ bunch fresh mint

Remove and discard any blemished or discolored leaves from the radicchio heads, then cut each head lengthwise into quarters. Put the quarters on a baking sheet, drizzle them lightly with olive oil, sprinkle lightly with salt and pepper, and toss to coat. Set aside.

Finely grate the zest from the lemon, then halve it and squeeze the juice from one half into a small bowl. Set aside the remaining half.

In a food processor, combine the lemon zest, garlic, capers, horseradish, and anchovies. Process until well chopped. Add the parsley and mint leaves, lemon juice, and 2 tablespoons of the olive oil. Pulse until the mixture forms a coarse purée. With the motor running, slowly pour in the remaining 6 tablespoons (3 fl oz/90 ml) olive oil and process until smooth; the salsa should have the consistency of pesto. Transfer the mixture to a bowl and taste and adjust the seasoning. If desired, add a bit more lemon juice or water to loosen the sauce.

Heat a ridged grill pan on the stove top over medium heat. When the pan is hot, add the radicchio quarters in a single layer and cook until they just begin to wilt and caramelize, 2–3 minutes per side. Transfer to a serving plate and drizzle with the salsa verde. Serve hot or at room temperature.

This trio of chunky vegetables, fresh herbs, and protein-rich quinoa makes a balanced side dish for any meal. It is also a perfect meatless dinner. A small amount of feta cheese adds tanginess and additional protein.

Yellow Squash & Red Quinoa Salad

MAKES 6 SERVINGS

1¹⁄₂ cups (8 oz/250 g) red quinoa

2 tablespoons plus ¹⁄₄ cup (2 fl oz/60 ml) extra-virgin olive oil

1 lb (500 g) yellow crookneck squash, cut into ¹⁄₂-inch (12-mm) chunks

Sea salt

1 clove garlic

¹⁄₄ cup (2 fl oz/60 ml) fresh lemon juice

1 small cucumber, cut into ¹⁄₂-inch (12-mm) chunks

5 green onions, white and tender green parts, cut on the diagonal into ¹⁄₄-inch (6-mm) pieces

¹⁄₄ cup (¹⁄₃ oz/10 g) chopped fresh basil

¹⁄₄ cup (¹⁄₃ oz/10 g) chopped fresh mint

¹⁄₂ cup (2¹⁄₂ oz/75 g) crumbled feta cheese

Put the quinoa in a fine-mesh strainer. Rinse thoroughly under running cold water and drain. In a saucepan, bring 3 cups (24 fl oz/750 ml) water to a boil over high heat. Add the quinoa, stir once, and reduce the heat to low. Cover and cook, without stirring, until all the water has been absorbed and the grains are tender, about 25 minutes. Let it stand for a few minutes, covered, then fluff with a fork and transfer to a large bowl.

Meanwhile, in a large frying pan, heat the 2 tablespoons olive oil over medium-high heat. Add the squash, season with salt, and cook, stirring often, until tender-crisp, 3–4 minutes. Transfer to a plate and let cool.

On a cutting board, using a fork or the flat side of a chef's knife, mash the garlic into a paste with a pinch of salt. In a small bowl, stir together the mashed garlic and lemon juice and let stand for 10 minutes. Whisk in the ¹⁄₄ cup (2 fl oz/ 60 ml) olive oil to make a vinaigrette.

Put the quinoa, squash, cucumber, green onions, basil, mint, and feta in a large bowl. Drizzle with the vinaigrette and toss gently to mix and coat well. Taste and adjust the seasoning. Serve right away.

The deeper green color of leafy greens like broccoli rabe, kale, and chard indicate that they contain higher amounts of vitamins and other nutrients than the lighter greens used in salads. Here is an all-purpose recipe that can be used for any type of dark green.

Spicy Broccoli Rabe with Garlic

MAKES 4–6 SERVINGS

Sea salt

1 lb (500 g) broccoli rabe, trimmed

1 tablespoon olive oil

3 cloves garlic, thinly sliced

$1/4$ teaspoon red pepper flakes

1 tablespoon fresh lemon juice

Bring a large saucepan two-thirds full of salted water to a boil over high heat. Add the broccoli rabe and cook until just tender, about 4 minutes. Drain well.

In a large frying pan, heat the olive oil over medium-high heat. Add the garlic and red pepper flakes and cook, stirring constantly, until the garlic is fragrant but not browned, about 30 seconds. Add the broccoli rabe and $1/2$ teaspoon salt. Stir to coat the broccoli rabe with the seasoned oil and cook just until warmed through, 1–2 minutes. Remove from the heat and stir in the lemon juice.

Transfer to a warmed platter and serve right away.

In this dish, fragrant toasted walnut oil and tart wine vinegar counter the bitterness of the brussels sprouts. Toasted walnuts contribute another layer of warm nuttiness and a crunchy texture.

Sweet & Sour Brussels Sprouts with Walnuts

MAKES 4 SERVINGS

1 lb (500 g) brussels sprouts

1 tablespoon olive oil

Sea salt and freshly ground pepper

1 cup (8 fl oz/250 ml) low-sodium chicken broth

2 tablespoons red wine vinegar

1 tablespoon light brown sugar

2 teaspoons roasted walnut oil

1/4 cup (1 oz/30 g) walnut pieces, toasted

Using a small, sharp knife, trim the bases of the brussels sprouts. Remove and discard any blemished or discolored leaves.

In a large frying pan, heat the olive oil over medium heat. Add the brussels sprouts, spread in a single layer, and sprinkle lightly with salt. Cook, stirring once or twice, until the sprouts are golden brown and caramelized on all sides, about 4 minutes.

Raise the heat to medium-high and add the chicken broth. Bring the broth to a boil and, using a wooden spoon, scrape up any browned bits from the bottom of the pan. Reduce the heat to medium-low, cover partially, and simmer until most of the liquid has evaporated and the sprouts are just tender when pierced with a knife, about 20 minutes.

Add 1/4 cup (2 fl oz/60 ml) water to the pan, stir in the vinegar and brown sugar, and raise the heat to medium-high. Cook, stirring occasionally, until the liquid reduces and thickens to a glaze, 2–3 minutes. Remove the pan from the heat and stir in the walnut oil and walnut pieces. Taste and adjust the seasoning with salt and pepper.

Transfer to a warmed serving bowl and serve right away.

Eating cabbage regularly can significantly lower your risk of cancer and this recipe shows a great way to do it. Green apples bring sweetness and bright flavor, red wine adds depth, and a sprinkle of orange zest contributes freshness to this hearty side dish.

Balsamic-Braised Red Cabbage with Apples

MAKES 4–6 SERVINGS

3 tablespoons olive oil

1 yellow onion, thinly sliced

Sea salt and freshly ground pepper

1 tablespoon honey

1 Granny Smith apple, halved, cored, and thinly sliced

¼ cup (2 fl oz/60 ml) balsamic vinegar

1 cup (8 fl oz/250 ml) dry red wine

1 head red cabbage (about 2 lb/1 kg), cored and cut into thin shreds

Finely grated zest of 1 orange

In a large frying pan, heat the olive oil over medium heat. Add the onion and a pinch of salt and sauté until the onion is soft and translucent, 5–7 minutes. Add the honey and cook for 1 minute longer. Add the apple slices and vinegar, raise the heat to medium-high, and use a wooden spoon to scrape up any browned bits from the bottom of the pan. Bring the liquid to a boil, then add the wine and 1 cup (8 fl oz/250 ml) water. Season with a generous pinch each of salt and pepper and return to a boil. Reduce the heat to medium-low and simmer until the liquid begins to reduce, about 10 minutes.

Add the cabbage. Using tongs, toss to coat well with the liquid in the pan. Cover the pan and cook, stirring occasionally, until the cabbage begins to wilt, 25–30 minutes. Uncover and cook until the cabbage is tender and most of the liquid has evaporated, 25–30 minutes longer.

Taste and adjust the seasoning. Remove the pan from the heat and stir in the orange zest, then transfer the cabbage to a warmed bowl and serve right away.

With its savory blend of mustard, garlic, and smoky bacon, this recipe will turn even the most finicky eater into a brussels sprout fan. The bacon is added sparingly—just a half slice per serving—to give complexity and flavor with just a little fat.

Warm Brussels Sprouts Salad

MAKES 6 SERVINGS

2 tablespoons red wine vinegar

1/2 teaspoon grainy mustard

1 clove garlic, minced

1/4 cup (2 fl oz/60 ml) extra-virgin olive oil

Sea salt and freshly ground pepper

1 1/2 lb (750 g) brussels sprouts

3 slices bacon, cooked until crisp and finely crumbled

In a small bowl, whisk together the vinegar, mustard, and garlic. Whisking constantly, pour in the olive oil in a slow, steady stream to make a vinaigrette. Season with salt and pepper and set aside.

Using a small, sharp knife, trim the bases of the brussels sprouts. Remove and discard any blemished or discolored leaves. Separate the leaves of the sprouts, continuing to use the knife to cut away the cores.

In a large saucepan over medium heat, combine the brussels sprout leaves and 1/2 cup (4 fl oz/125 ml) water. Cover, raise the heat to high, and bring to a boil. Reduce the heat to medium-low and cook until the leaves are bright green and tender, about 7 minutes, adding more water if needed. Drain thoroughly and transfer to a warmed serving bowl.

Drizzle the vinaigrette over the brussels sprouts and toss to coat. Taste and adjust the seasoning. Sprinkle with the bacon and serve right away.

Any color of beet can be used here, but keep in mind that red beets can color your fingers. To avoid stains, wear rubber gloves when peeling them. Chioggia beets, with their concentric red and white rings, bleed only slightly, and golden beets not at all.

Beet, Orange & Fennel Salad

MAKES 4 SERVINGS

4 red or golden beets
(about 1 lb/500 g total weight)

2 teaspoons olive oil

2 oranges

1 fennel bulb

2 tablespoons orange-infused olive oil

1 teaspoon red wine vinegar

1 teaspoon balsamic vinegar

Sea salt and freshly ground pepper

$^1\!/_2$ cup (2 oz/60 g) freshly grated pecorino Romano cheese

$^1\!/_4$ cup (1 oz/30 g) slivered almonds, toasted

Position a rack in the middle of the oven and preheat to 350°F (180°C).

Place the beets in a single layer in a shallow baking dish. Drizzle with the olive oil and rub to coat. Roast, turning occasionally, until the beets are easily pierced with a sharp knife and the skins are slightly wrinkled, about 1¼ hours. Remove from the oven and let cool. When cool enough to handle, cut off the stems and remove the skins with your fingers. Cut each beet into quarters.

Cut a thick slice off the top and bottom of each orange. Working with 1 orange at a time, stand it upright and, following the contour of the fruit, carefully slice downward to remove the peel, pith, and membrane. Holding the orange over a bowl, cut along each section of the membrane, letting each freed section drop into the bowl. Strain the oranges, reserving 2 teaspoons of the juice.

Cut off the stems and feathery leaves from the fennel bulb and set aside. Discard the outer layer of the bulb if it is tough. Quarter the bulb lengthwise and cut off the core and any tough base portions. Cut the fennel lengthwise into slices about ¼ inch (6 mm) thick. Add to the bowl. Add the beets to the bowl with the reserved orange juice, the orange-infused olive oil, the red wine and balsamic vinegars, ½ teaspoon salt, and ¼ teaspoon pepper. Toss gently to coat and mix well.

Divide the salad among individual plates. Chop the fennel fronds. Sprinkle the salad with the cheese, toasted almonds, and fennel fronds and serve right away.

Good for Bone Health

Broccolini is a cross between broccoli and *gai lan*, a Chinese vegetable. Sweeter and milder than broccoli (page 8) it offers as much vitamin C as orange juice. It also provides a substantial amount of folate, vitamin A and potassium, as well as some iron, calcium, vitamin B and fiber.

Broccoli and broccolini make great side dishes when
roasted or steamed and can be seasoned with a wide
variety of flavorings influenced by cuisines around
the globe. Added to pasta, they bring substance
and nutrition to an easy main dish.

Four Ways to Use Broccoli & Broccolini

Roasted Broccoli with Mustard & Pine Nuts

In a large roasting pan, toss 2 lb (1 kg) broccoli florets, with 2 tablespoons olive
oil. Spread in the pan in a single layer, then roast in a 400°F (200°C) oven until
browned and tender, stirring once or twice, 20–30 minutes. In a bowl, whisk
together 2 tablespoons balsamic vinegar, 1 teaspoon grainy mustard, and
1 tablespoon olive oil. Pour over the broccoli and toss well. Sprinkle with
¼ cup (1 oz/30 g) toasted pine nuts and serve right away. Serves 6.

Broccolini with Soy-Sesame Vinaigrette

In a large bowl, whisk together 1 tablespoon toasted sesame oil, 1 tablespoon
low-sodium soy sauce, 2 teaspoons fresh lemon juice, and 1 drop dark agave
nectar. Steam 1½ lb (750 g) broccolini until tender-crisp, 7–10 minutes. Add
the warm broccolini to the soy mixture and toss well to coat. Sprinkle with
2 teaspoons toasted sesame seeds and serve right away. Serves 4.

Broccoli or Broccolini with Orange & Almonds

Toss 1½ lb (750 g) broccoli florets or trimmed broccolini with 1½ tablespoons
olive oil and spread in a roasting pan in a single layer. Roast in a 425°F (220°C)
oven until browned, about 25 minutes. Transfer to a serving dish and drizzle
with 1 tablespoon fresh orange juice, 1 teaspoon grated orange zest, and
2 tablespoons chopped toasted almonds. Serves 4.

Pasta with Broccoli, Garlic & Anchovies

In a large frying pan over medium heat, sauté 6 finely chopped anchovy fillets
and 5 cloves thinly sliced garlic in ¼ cup (2 fl oz/60 ml) olive oil until the garlic
is lightly golden, 1–2 minutes. Add 1 lb (500 g) blanched broccoli florets, a pinch
of red pepper flakes, and salt to taste and sauté for 2–3 minutes to heat through.
Add ¼ cup (2 fl oz/60 ml) dry white wine and cook until nearly evaporated,
1–2 minutes. Toss with 1 lb (500 g) cooked whole-wheat pasta and serve topped
with freshly grated Parmesan cheese. Serves 4–6.

This quick dish pairs tender asparagus with meaty shiitake mushrooms for a satisfying vegetable stir-fry. Sesame seeds are densely nutritious and offer a surprising array of health benefits, including cholesterol-lowering potential.

Stir-fried Asparagus with Shiitakes & Sesame Seeds

MAKES 4–6 SERVINGS

1 lb (500 g) asparagus, tough ends snapped off

3 tablespoons canola or grapeseed oil

1 clove garlic, minced

1 tablespoon peeled and grated fresh ginger

6 oz (185 g) shiitake mushrooms, stems removed, caps brushed clean and thinly sliced

$1/4$ cup (2 fl oz/60 ml) dry white wine or sake

$1/4$ cup (2 fl oz/60 ml) low-sodium chicken broth

$1^1/2$ tablespoons low-sodium soy sauce

2 teaspoons sesame seeds

Cut the asparagus on the diagonal into 2-inch (5-cm) pieces.

In a large frying pan, heat the oil over high heat. Add the garlic and ginger and cook, stirring constantly, until fragrant but not browned, about 30 seconds. Add the mushrooms and cook, stirring often, until they begin to brown, about 2 minutes. Add the asparagus and cook, stirring constantly, until bright green and tender-crisp, about 3 minutes.

Stir in the wine, broth, and soy sauce and cook until the liquid is reduced to a saucelike consistency and all the vegetables are tender, 2–3 minutes longer. Stir in the sesame seeds, transfer to a warmed serving dish, and serve right away.

Of the many types of sweet potatoes, the dark orange-fleshed ones are an especially healthful choice because they are high in fiber and beta-carotene. In this simple recipe, the seasoned potatoes are garnished with antioxidant-rich fresh cilantro.

Roasted Sweet Potatoes with Cumin & Cilantro

MAKES 4 SERVINGS

2 orange-fleshed sweet potatoes (about 1 lb/500 g total weight), peeled

1 tablespoon canola or grapeseed oil

1 teaspoon ground cumin

Sea salt and freshly ground pepper

2 tablespoons finely chopped fresh cilantro

Preheat the oven to 400°F (200°C).

Cut the sweet potatoes crosswise into rounds ½ inch (12 mm) thick. Rinse the slices under cold running water and spread on a clean kitchen towel; blot dry with a second kitchen towel.

Put the sweet potatoes in a bowl. Drizzle with the oil, sprinkle with the cumin, and toss to coat evenly.

Preheat a nonstick baking sheet in the oven for 5 minutes. Remove from the oven and carefully arrange the sweet potatoes in a single layer on the hot baking sheet. Roast the sweet potatoes, turning every 10 minutes, until evenly browned and tender when pierced with a knife, 30–35 minutes.

Transfer the sweet potatoes to a warmed serving dish and sprinkle with ½ teaspoon salt, a grinding or two of pepper, and the cilantro. Toss gently to coat. Serve right away.

Cauliflower is an excellent source of potassium and vitamin C and has cancer-fighting properties. Soaking cauliflower before baking is an important step. Advise each diner to squeeze on a little lemon juice at the table.

Cauliflower with Orange Zest & Green Onion

MAKES 4 SERVINGS

1 head cauliflower (about 1³/₄ lb/875 g), cored and cut into uniform-sized florets

1 tablespoon olive oil

Sea salt and freshly ground pepper

2 tablespoons coarsely chopped green onion

2 tablespoons chopped fresh flat-leaf parsley

2 teaspoons grated orange zest

4 lemon wedges

Put the cauliflower florets in a large bowl and add cold water to cover. Let stand for 20–30 minutes, then drain and pat dry.

Preheat the oven to 400°F (200°C).

Spread the cauliflower in a single layer in a 9-by-13-inch (23-by-33-cm) baking dish. Drizzle with the olive oil, sprinkle with salt and pepper, and toss to coat. Roast, turning every 10 minutes and sprinkling with 1–2 tablespoons cold water each time, until the florets are tender and lightly browned, about 30 minutes.

Pile the green onion, parsley, and orange zest on a cutting board and finely chop them together. Using your fingers, toss the finished mixture on the board to distribute all the ingredients evenly. When the cauliflower is done, remove it from the oven and sprinkle evenly with the green-onion mixture. Spoon the cauliflower into a warmed serving dish and garnish with the lemon wedges. Serve right away.

A trio of spices commonly found in curry blends of India lend an exotic flavor to earthy-sweet roasted beets. If your beets come with tops, cut them off and then save them for sautéeing as you would Swiss chard or kale.

Indian-Spiced Roasted Beets

MAKES 4 SERVINGS

1 teaspoon ground cumin

1 teaspoon ground coriander

1/2 teaspoon ground turmeric

Sea salt and freshly ground pepper

6 red beets (about 1 3/4 lb/875 g total weight)

2 tablespoons canola or grapeseed oil

Fresh cilantro leaves for garnish

Preheat the oven to 350°F (180°C).

In a small bowl, combine the cumin, coriander, turmeric, 1 teaspoon salt, and 1 teaspoon pepper and stir to mix well.

If the beet greens are still attached, cut them off, leaving 1/2 inch (12 mm) of the stems attached. (Save the greens for another use.) Arrange the beets in a shallow baking dish just large enough to hold them in a single layer. Drizzle with the oil and turn to coat, then rub with the spice mixture, coating the beets evenly. Roast, turning occasionally, until the beets are easily pierced with a sharp knife and the skins are slightly wrinkled, about 1 1/4 hours. Remove from the oven and let cool. When cool enough to handle, cut off the stems and remove the skins with your fingers.

Cut each beet lengthwise into wedges, sprinkle with cilantro, and serve warm or at room temperature.

This is an unusual way to prepare broccolini: a half lemon is cut, peel and all, and roasted with the vegetables. The other seasonings are minimal—just garlic, salt, and pepper—for a suprisingly complex flavor from just six ingredients.

Roasted Broccolini with Lemon

MAKES 4 SERVINGS

2 lb (1kg) broccolini, trimmed and coarsely chopped

¹/₂ lemon

1¹/₂ tablespoons olive oil

2 cloves garlic, minced

Sea salt and freshly ground pepper

Preheat the oven to 350°F (180°C).

Trim and coarsely chop the broccolini. Remove the seeds from the lemon and then cut it, peel and all, into ¹/₄-inch (6-mm) dice.

In a frying pan, heat 1 tablespoon of the olive oil over medium-high heat. Add the garlic and cook, stirring constantly, until lightly golden, about 1 minute. Add the broccolini, diced lemon, ¹/₂ teaspoon salt, and a few grindings of pepper. Cook, stirring often, just until color of the broccolini deepens, about 1 minute longer.

Scrape the contents of the frying pan into a baking dish, add the remaining ¹/₂ tablespoon olive oil, and turn to coat. Roast until the broccolini is tender-crisp, 10–12 minutes. Transfer to a platter and serve warm or at room temperature.

Cooking the cauliflower in a smoking-hot pan until well browned brings out its natural sweetness. This dark, caramel-like flavor is enhanced by the spicy glaze and a splash of tart, vitamin C-rich lemon juice.

Sweet & Smoky Caramelized Cauliflower

MAKES 4 SERVINGS

2 tablespoons unsalted butter

3 tablespoons olive oil

1 large head cauliflower (about 3 lb/ 1.5 kg), cored and cut into 1-inch (2.5-cm) florets

Sea salt and freshly ground black pepper

1 shallot, minced

$^1/_2$ teaspoon smoked sweet paprika

$^1/_4$ teaspoon red pepper flakes

2 tablespoons honey

$^1/_2$ lemon

In a large frying pan over medium heat, melt the butter with 2 tablespoons of the olive oil. Add the cauliflower florets, sprinkle with a generous pinch of salt, and toss gently to coat the florets with the seasoned oil. Spread the florets in a single layer in the pan and cook, without stirring, until lightly browned on the bottom, 3–4 minutes. Using tongs, turn each piece and continue cooking, undisturbed, until evenly browned on the second side, 3–4 minutes. Repeat until all sides are evenly browned, 3–5 minutes longer.

Add the remaining 1 tablespoon olive oil, the shallot, paprika, and red pepper flakes to the pan. Cook, stirring occasionally, until the shallot is softened, 1–2 minutes. Add the honey and 2 tablespoons water and sauté until the liquid reduces to a glaze, 2–3 minutes. Squeeze the juice from the lemon half over the cauliflower, stir to combine, and cook just to warm through, about 30 seconds. Remove from the heat. Taste and adjust the seasoning with salt and black pepper.

Transfer the cauliflower to a warmed serving bowl and serve right away.

Traditionally, ratatouille is a dish of summer vegetables that are simmered for a long time in their own juices. In this version, the vegetables are cut into large pieces and roasted briefly, which concentrates and intensifies their flavors.

Roasted Ratatouille

MAKES 6–8 SERVINGS

1 lb (500 g) plum tomatoes, halved lengthwise

4 large cloves garlic, sliced

1 large yellow onion, halved and cut crosswise into slices ¹⁄₄ inch (6 mm) thick

1 small eggplant, trimmed and cut into 1-inch (2.5-cm) chunks

1 small zucchini, trimmed and cut crosswise into slices ¹⁄₂ inch (12 mm) thick

1 small yellow crookneck squash, trimmed and cut crosswise into slices ¹⁄₂ inch (12 mm) thick

1 green bell pepper, seeded and cut into 1¹⁄₂-inch (4-cm) squares

5 tablespoons (3 fl oz/80 ml) olive oil

Sea salt and freshly ground pepper

¹⁄₄ cup (¹⁄₃ oz/10 g) finely shredded fresh basil

2 tablespoons chopped fresh thyme

Preheat the oven to 425°F (220°C).

Combine the tomatoes, garlic, onion, eggplant, zucchini, yellow squash, and bell pepper in a large bowl. Drizzle in the olive oil, sprinkle generously with salt, and toss to coat. Transfer the vegetables to a large rimmed baking sheet and spread in an even single layer.

Roast the vegetables, stirring once or twice, for 20 minutes. Remove from the oven and sprinkle with the basil and thyme. Continue to roast, again stirring once or twice, until the biggest pieces are tender when pierced with a fork, 5–10 minutes longer. Remove the vegetables from the oven and season with salt and pepper.

Transfer the ratatouille to a bowl. Serve hot, warm, or at room temperature.

The Redder the Better

Tomatoes are rich in vitamins A and C, carotenes and carotenoids. As they redden, their carotenoid content increases. Refrigerating retards this, destroys flavor, and turns them mushy, so keep tomatoes on a shady counter. When they are in season, from summer through fall, eat locally grown vine-ripe tomatoes, particularly heirloom varieties in every color available. Since you eat the skins, buying organic is best.

Tomatoes are abundant at the market during summer and early fall. Since they are such nutritional powerhouses, use them often. Cooking tomatoes makes lycopene, a powerful antioxidant, easier for the body to use.

Four Ways to Use Tomatoes

Roasted Tomatoes

Cut 3 lb (1.5 kg) heirloom tomatoes in half and place, cut side up, on a baking sheet. In a small bowl, mix together 1 tablespoon olive oil, 2 tablespoons balsamic vinegar, 1 minced garlic clove, ¼ teaspoon *each* salt and freshly ground pepper, and the leaves from 1 sprig fresh thyme. Spoon the mixture evenly over the tomatoes and bake in a 325°F (165°C) oven until the tomatoes are soft and wrinkled, about 1 hour. Add to pastas, vegetable dishes, sandwiches, and pizzas. Makes about 2 cups (16 oz/500 g).

White Beans with Tomatoes & Basil

In a bowl, mix together 2 cans (15 oz/470 g) each white kidney (cannellini) beans, rinsed and drained; 2 tomatoes, seeded and chopped; ¼ cup finely chopped red onion; 2 tablespoons balsamic vinegar; 1 tablespoon extra-virgin olive oil; 3 tablespoons torn fresh basil leaves, and salt and pepper to taste. Let stand for 30 minutes or refrigerate for up to 4 hours before serving. Serves 4.

Tomato Pesto

Place ½ cup (1½ oz/45 g) dry-packed sun-dried tomatoes in a heatproof bowl, add boiling water to cover, and let stand for 15 minutes to re-hydrate. Drain the tomatoes, then add to a food processor along with 2 plum tomatoes, diced; ½ cup (¾ oz/20 g) packed fresh basil leaves; 1 chopped garlic clove; and ½ teaspoon salt and process until puréed. With the motor running, slowly drizzle in 2 tablespoons extra-virgin olive oil until blended. Use on pizzas, or with pastas or vegetables. Makes about 1 cup (8 oz/250 g).

Heirloom Tomatoes with Sherry Vinaigrette

In a small bowl, whisk together 3 tablespoons extra-virgin olive oil, 1 tablespoon sherry vinegar, 1 minced large shallot, and salt and pepper to taste. Core 1–1½ lb (500–750 g) heirloom tomatoes, preferably in different colors, and cut into thin wedges. Arrange on a platter, drizzle with the vinaigrette, and serve sprinkled with your favorite chopped fresh herbs. Serves 4.

Low-calorie spaghetti squash is a great stand-in for pasta and its long strands take to sauces just as well. This simple side dish is sprinkled with cheese and fresh herbs, but you could also toss the squash with your favorite tomato sauce.

Spaghetti Squash with Garlic, Oregano & Parmesan

MAKES 4 SERVINGS

1 spaghetti squash (about 2 lb/1 kg)

1 tablespoon extra-virgin olive oil

1 small clove garlic, minced

Sea salt and freshly ground pepper

$1/4$ cup (1 oz/30 g) finely grated Parmesan cheese

1 teaspoon minced fresh oregano

Preheat the oven to 350°F (180°C).

Using a sharp, heavy knife or a cleaver, trim the stem end from the squash, then cut it in half lengthwise. Scoop out the seeds and discard. Place the halves, cut side down, in a baking dish and add $1/3$ cup (3 fl oz/80 ml) water. Bake until tender, about 1 hour.

Transfer the squash to a cutting board. When cool enough to handle, use a fork to scrape out flesh in noodlelike strands, scraping all the way to skin. Place the squash in a serving bowl and add the olive oil, garlic, $1/2$ teaspoon salt, and $1/2$ teaspoon pepper. Stir gently to mix well. Sprinkle with the Parmesan and toss to combine. Taste and adjust the seasoning. Sprinkle with the oregano and serve right away.

Yellow tomatoes have a sweeter, less acidic flavor than red tomatoes, but red ones can be substituted for the yellow here, or use equal amounts of each. If using red tomatoes, reduce the amount of red wine vinegar slightly.

Green Bean & Yellow Tomato Salad with Mint

MAKES 4 SERVINGS

1 lb (500 g) long, slender green beans

$^1\!/_2$ cup ($^3\!/_4$ oz/20 g) chopped fresh mint

2 tablespoons extra-virgin olive oil

Sea salt and freshly ground pepper

1 or 2 ripe yellow tomatoes

$^1\!/_2$ cup (2 oz/60 g) thin red onion wedges

2 teaspoons red wine vinegar, or to taste

Bring a large saucepan two-thirds full of water to a boil over high heat. Trim the ends of the beans. Add the beans to the boiling water and cook until tender, 5–7 minutes; the timing will depend on their size. Drain thoroughly and pat dry.

In a large serving bowl, combine the hot green beans, mint, olive oil, and $^1\!/_2$ teaspoon salt and toss to mix. Set aside and let cool to room temperature, about 20 minutes.

Cut the tomatoes into wedges about $^1\!/_2$ inch (12 mm) thick. Just before serving, add the tomatoes, onion, 2 teaspoons vinegar, and a grind of pepper to the bean mixture and toss to mix. Taste and add more vinegar or salt and pepper, as needed. Serve at room temperature.

A small amount of prosciutto or lean bacon used in a dish lends complexity without adding a lot of extra fat. It's a good strategy to use when cooking bland-tasting legumes, such as the lentils here.

Lentils with Shallots & Prosciutto

MAKES 4 SERVINGS

³/₄ cup (5 oz/155 g) brown lentils

1 tablespoon olive oil

³/₄ cup (4 oz/125 g) finely chopped fresh fennel bulb

¹/₄ cup (1 oz/30 g) finely chopped shallots

2 tablespoons sherry vinegar

2 oz (60 g) prosciutto, cut into ribbons

Sea salt and freshly ground pepper

Chopped fresh fennel fronds for garnish

Pick over the lentils for stones or grit. Rinse thoroughly under cold running water and drain. In a saucepan, combine the lentils with water to cover by 2 inches (5 cm) and bring to a boil over medium-high heat. Reduce the heat to medium-low, cover, and simmer gently until the lentils are tender but firm to the bite, about 20 minutes. Scoop out ¼ cup (2 fl oz/ 60 ml) of the cooking liquid and reserve. Drain the lentils thoroughly in a colander, then return to the saucepan.

In a frying pan, heat the olive oil over medium-high heat. Add the fennel and shallots and cook, stirring often, until golden, about 8 minutes. Scrape the contents of the frying pan into the saucepan with the lentils. Add the vinegar and reserved lentil-cooking liquid to the frying pan, bring to a boil, and cook until the liquid is reduced by half, about 3 minutes. Add the hot liquid to the lentils and stir in the prosciutto. Season to taste with salt and pepper.

Transfer the lentils to a serving bowl or platter, sprinkle with the fennel fronds, and serve right away.

A speedy sauté brings out the natural sweetness and enhances the crunch of two kinds of spring peas. Anise-like fresh basil, tart lemon zest, and tangy pecorino cheese are sprinkled on top for a delicious, fresh and fast side dish.

Sautéed Garden Peas with Basil & Pecorino

MAKES 4 SERVINGS

1 tablespoon unsalted butter

1 tablespoon olive oil

$^1/_2$ lb (250 g) sugar snap peas, strings removed

1 lb (500 g) English peas, shelled

Sea salt and freshly ground pepper

1 lemon

Leaves from 4 fresh basil sprigs, torn

About 1 oz (30 g) chunk pecorino Romano cheese

In a large frying pan over medium heat, melt the butter with the olive oil. Add the sugar snap peas and English peas. Pour in ¼ cup (2 fl oz/60 ml) water and add a pinch of salt. Cover and cook for 2 minutes. Uncover and cook, stirring occasionally, until the water has evaporated, about 2 minutes longer. The peas should be tender-crisp and still bright green.

Finely grate 2 teaspoons zest from the lemon, then halve the lemon. Remove the pan from the heat and squeeze the juice from 1 lemon half over the peas (reserve the remaining half for another use). Add the lemon zest, basil, and a pinch each of salt and pepper to the pan. Grate cheese over the top to taste and stir to mix well.

Transfer the peas to a warmed serving dish and serve right away.

Large pieces of winter squash can take a long time to cook, but when sliced thinly, it cooks in about 15 minutes. This means you can take advantage of squash's dense nutrition even on a weeknight, as in this dish that also stars sweet pears and fragrant rosemary.

Butternut Squash & Pears with Rosemary

MAKES 4 SERVINGS

1 Bosc pear

1 tablespoon grapeseed or canola oil

¹/₂ small butternut squash (about ³/₄ lb/ 375 g), peeled, seeded, and thinly sliced

Sea salt

1 tablespoon finely chopped fresh rosemary

Pinch of cayenne pepper

¹/₂ cup (4 fl oz/125 ml) apple juice

Halve and core the pear and cut it lengthwise into thin slices.

In a frying pan, heat the oil over medium-high heat. Add the squash and sprinkle with 1 teaspoon salt. Cook, stirring often, until the squash is browned on the edges and begins to soften, about 5 minutes.

Add the pear, rosemary, cayenne, and apple juice and cook until the liquid evaporates and the squash is tender, 6–8 minutes longer.

Transfer to a serving bowl. Serve hot, warm, or at room temperature.

Medium-grain brown rice has a sticky texture and nutlike aroma and taste. A whole grain with its bran intact, it is far more healthful than white rice. Sesame seeds enhance the rice's nutty flavor and contribute calcium.

Sesame Brown Rice

MAKES 4 SERVINGS

1 cup (7 oz/220 g) medium-grain brown rice

Sea salt

2 teaspoons sesame seeds

1 teaspoon Asian sesame oil

1 tablespoon thinly sliced green onion tops

In a saucepan, bring 2¾ cups (22 fl oz/680 ml) water to a boil over high heat. Add the rice and ½ teaspoon salt, stir once, and reduce the heat to low. Cover and simmer very gently, without stirring, until all the water has been absorbed and the grains are tender, 35–45 minutes.

Meanwhile, in a small, dry frying pan over medium heat, toast the sesame seeds, stirring constantly, until they are fragrant and have darkened slightly, about 2 minutes. Immediately pour the seeds onto a plate to cool. Set aside.

Carefully lift the cover of the saucepan so that no condensation drips into the rice. Drizzle the sesame oil evenly over the top and sprinkle with half of the sesame seeds. Gently fluff the rice with a fork or the handle of a wooden spoon.

Spoon the rice into a warmed serving dish. Sprinkle with the remaining sesame seeds and the green onion. Serve right away.

Whole grain bulgur and easy-to-cook lentils combine
with aromatic vegetables, fragrant spices, and fresh
herbs in a versatile pilaf to accompany any meal.
A topping of toasted almonds lends protein and crunch.

Bulgur & Lentil Pilaf with Almonds

MAKES 4 SERVINGS

³/₄ cup (5 oz/155 g) brown lentils

2 tablespoons olive oil

1 yellow onion, chopped

2 cloves garlic, minced

1 cup (6 oz/185 g) medium-grain
bulgur wheat

1 teaspoon ground coriander

Sea salt and freshly ground pepper

2 cups (16 fl oz/500 ml) low-sodium
vegetable broth or water

¹/₄ cup (1¹/₂ oz/45 g) roasted almonds

¹/₃ cup (¹/₃ oz/10 g) fresh flat-leaf
parsley leaves

1 tablespoon grated lemon zest

2 tablespoons fresh lemon juice

Pick over the lentils for stones or grit. Rinse thoroughly under cold running
water and drain. In a small saucepan, combine the lentils with water to cover
by 2 inches (5 cm) and bring to a boil over medium-high heat. Reduce the heat
to medium-low, cover, and simmer gently until tender but firm to the bite,
about 20 minutes. Drain thoroughly and set aside.

In a large frying pan, heat the olive oil over medium-high heat. Add the onion
and cook, stirring often, until the onion is wilted, 2–3 minutes. Add the garlic,
bulgur, coriander, ¹/₄ teaspoon salt, and ¹/₄ teaspoon pepper and cook, stirring
often, until the garlic is fragrant, about 1 minute. Stir in the lentils and the broth
and bring to a boil. Reduce the heat to low, cover, and simmer for 5 minutes.
Remove from the heat and let stand, covered, for 15 minutes.

Place the almonds, parsley, and lemon zest on a cutting board and coarsely
chop them together. Fluff the pilaf with a fork and stir in the lemon juice. Season
to taste with salt and pepper. Mound the pilaf on a serving platter, sprinkle with
the almond mixture, and serve right away.

When shopping for farro, look for "semipearled," or "semiperlato," which means that it has been partially polished to remove some of its hull. It will cook more quickly, but still retain some whole-grain benefits.

Farro Salad with Artichoke Hearts

MAKES 4–6 SERVINGS

1¼ cups (10 oz/315 g) semipearled farro

Sea salt and freshly ground pepper

½ cup (2½ oz/75 g) pine nuts

¼ cup (1½ oz/45 g) olive oil–packed sun-dried tomatoes

1 jar (14 oz/440 g) artichoke hearts (not marinated)

6 tablespoons (3 fl oz/90 ml) red wine vinegar

3 tablespoons extra-virgin olive oil

½ cup (2½ oz/75 g) finely chopped red onion, rinsed and thoroughly drained

½ cup (¾ oz/20 g) chopped fresh flat-leaf parsley

Pick over the farro for stones or grit. Rinse thoroughly under cold running water and drain. In a saucepan, combine the farro, 2½ cups (20 fl oz/625 ml) water and a generous pinch of salt and bring to a boil over high heat. Reduce the heat to medium-low, cover, and simmer gently until all the water has been absorbed and the grains are tender, 25–30 minutes.

In a small, dry frying pan over medium heat, toast the pine nuts, stirring often, just until fragrant and lightly browned, 2–3 minutes. Be careful not to let them burn. Immediately pour onto a plate to cool. Set aside.

Drain the sun-dried tomatoes, reserving the oil to use in place of some of the olive oil, if you like. Cut the tomatoes into julienne. Drain the artichokes, rinse, and drain again. Cut into quarters.

In a large bowl, whisk together the vinegar and olive oil (or a mixture of the tomato oil and olive oil, if using). Add the farro, tomatoes, artichoke hearts, onion, parsley, and pine nuts and toss gently to mix and coat well. Season generously with salt and pepper. Serve right away.

Give Your Liver a Boost

Eating an artichoke down to its meaty heart takes patience, but it's worth it when you consider it offers good and unique, rarely found, liver-detoxifying compounds. To better preserve their antioxidants and vitamin C, choose steaming over boiling artichokes. An alternative is paring the vegetable while raw and discarding the fuzzy choke to expose its meaty heart and then using it in a variety of dishes.

Serve artichokes Italian-style—thinly sliced raw in a salad. Braising or steaming are other healthy options. So is buying artichoke hearts in a jar or frozen to make Farro Salad with Artichoke Hearts (page 177). (Just make sure they are not sulfite-treated.)

Four Ways to Use Artichokes

Shaved Artichoke Salad

Halve 8 medium artichokes lengthwise and using a small spoon, remove the fuzzy choke. As the artichokes are trimmed, immerse them in lemon water. Slice the artichokes thinly lengthwise, put them in a bowl, and toss with 2 tablespoons extra-virgin olive oil. Add ¼ cup (½ oz/155 g) torn frisée, season with salt and pepper, and squeeze over the juice of 1 lemon half. Toss gently and transfer to a platter. Scatter a small amount of shaved Parmesan cheese on top and serve right away. Serves 4.

Artichokes with Herbed Yogurt Sauce

Arrange 4 trimmed large artichokes, stem end up, in a single layer in a steamer basket and steam over simmering water until the bottoms can be easily pierced with a knife, 30–40 minutes. In a bowl, mix together 1 cup (8 oz/250 g) nonfat plain yogurt, 1 cup (1 oz/30 g) chopped fresh herbs, 1 chopped green onion, 1 small drop agave nectar, and salt and hot pepper sauce to taste. Serve the artichokes with the dipping sauce. Serves 4.

Braised Artichokes with Lemon & Garlic

Trim the fuzzy tips from 6 large artichokes. Halve them lengthwise and, using a melon baller or small spoon, remove the fuzzy choke. Place the artichokes in a saucepan with the juice of ½ lemon. Add 10 halved garlic cloves, 5 fresh thyme sprigs, 2 bay leaves, ½ teaspoon salt, and ¼ cup (2 fl oz/60 ml) olive oil. Add water to cover and bring to a boil over medium-high heat, reduce the heat to medium, and simmer for 5 minutes. Remove from the heat and let cool in the pan, about 1 hour or until tender when pierced with a knife. Sprinkle with chopped fresh parsley and serve right away. Serves 6.

Artichokes Vinaigrette

Trim 1¼ lb (625 g) baby artichokes, arrange in a single layer in a steamer basket, and steam over simmering water until the bottoms can be easily pierced with a knife, 8–10 minutes. Let cool, then arrange in a single layer in a baking dish. Drizzle with 3 tablespoons olive oil and roast in a 400°F (200°C) oven until lightly browned, 10–12 minutes. Pour in 1 tablespoon red wine vinegar, 2 teaspoons minced fresh oregano, ½ clove minced garlic, and salt and pepper to taste. Let stand for a few minutes to blend the flavors. Serves 4.

Toasted spices infuse this crunchy salad of grated root vegetables with their warmth. Harissa, a North African chile-and-spice paste, adds a suggestion of heat to this unique version of crudités.

Moroccan-Style Carrot & Parsnip Salad

MAKES 6 SERVINGS

$^1/_4$ teaspoon ground cinnamon

$^1/_4$ teaspoon ground cumin

$^1/_4$ teaspoon ground coriander

$^1/_8$ teaspoon ground ginger

3 large carrots (about $^3/_4$ lb/375 g total weight)

3 large parsnips (about $^3/_4$ lb/375 g total weight)

$^1/_4$ cup (2 fl oz/60 ml) fresh lemon juice

1 tablespoon honey

$^3/_4$ teaspoon prepared harissa

Sea salt and freshly ground pepper

6 tablespoons (3 fl oz/90 ml) extra-virgin olive oil

$^1/_2$ cup (2 oz/60 g) roasted shelled pistachio nuts, coarsely chopped

$^2/_3$ cup (4 oz/125 g) raisins

$^1/_4$ cup ($^1/_3$ oz/10 g) coarsely chopped fresh cilantro or mint

In a small, heavy frying pan over medium-low heat, combine the cinnamon, cumin, coriander, and ginger and toast, stirring constantly, until fragrant, about 2 minutes. Remove from the heat and let cool to room temperature.

Peel the carrots and parsnips and shred them on the large holes of a box grater-shredder. Set aside.

In a small nonreactive bowl, whisk together the toasted spices, lemon juice, honey, harissa, and a scant $^1/_2$ teaspoon salt. Slowly whisk in the olive oil to make a dressing. Taste and adjust the seasoning.

In a bowl, stir together the pistachios and a pinch of salt. Add the carrots and parsnips, raisins, $^1/_2$ teaspoon salt, several grindings of pepper, and the dressing and toss well. Taste and adjust the seasoning. Transfer to a platter or serving bowl, sprinkle with the cilantro, and serve right away.

Anchovies are loaded with omega-3 fatty acids. They are also wonderful to keep on hand for adding unique, savory flavor to a variety of dishes, including this side of lightly sautéed dark greens, onions, and tomatoes.

Swiss Chard with Tomato, Lemon & Anchovy

MAKES 4 SERVINGS

1 large bunch Swiss chard

3 tablespoons olive oil

$^3/_4$ cup (6 fl oz/180 ml) low-sodium vegetable or chicken broth

2 or 3 anchovy fillets, rinsed and patted dry

2 tablespoons fresh lemon juice

Freshly ground pepper

$^1/_2$ yellow onion, chopped

2 ripe plum tomatoes, seeded and chopped

Separate the stems from the chard leaves by cutting along both sides of the center vein. Stack the leaves, roll them up lengthwise, and cut crosswise into strips about $^3/_4$ inch (2 cm) wide. Trim off the tough bottoms from the stems and cut crosswise into $^1/_2$-inch (12-mm) pieces.

In a frying pan, heat 1 tablespoon of the olive oil over medium-high heat. Add the chard stems and sauté for 5 minutes. Add $^1/_4$ cup (2 fl oz/60 ml) of the broth and cook until the stems are tender and the pan is almost dry, 3–4 minutes. Remove from the heat. Push the chard stems to one side of the pan and add the anchovies to the other. Using the back of a wooden spoon, mash the anchovies until creamy, then stir in the chard stems along with the lemon juice. Season with pepper. Arrange the cooked chard stems on one side of a warmed platter.

In a clean frying pan over medium-high heat, heat the remaining 2 tablespoons olive oil. Add the onion and sauté until golden, 6–7 minutes. Add the chard leaves a few handfuls at a time, stirring each batch until wilted. Add the tomatoes and the remaining $^1/_2$ cup (4 fl oz/125 ml) broth and cook, stirring occasionally, until the chard is tender, about 10 minutes. Spoon the leaves onto the platter with the stems. Serve right away.

Earthy quinoa, pleasantly bitter radicchio, sweet-tart dried cherries, and crunchy pistachios combine in this unexpectedly delicious salad. Be generous with the basil if you like an herbal edge to the dish.

Quinoa & Radicchio Salad with Dried Cherries & Nuts

MAKES 4 SERVINGS

1 cup (8 oz/250 g) quinoa

1/2 head radicchio (about 4 oz/125 g), cored and thinly sliced

1/4 cup (2 fl oz/60 ml) balsamic vinegar

2 tablespoons olive oil

1/4 cup (1 oz/30 g) dried tart cherries

1/4 cup (1 oz/30 g) shelled roasted pistachios, chopped

3 tablespoons chopped fresh flat-leaf parsley

Sea salt and freshly ground pepper

Torn fresh basil for garnish

Put the quinoa in a fine-mesh strainer. Rinse thoroughly under running cold water and drain. In a saucepan, bring 2 cups (16 fl oz/500 ml) water to a boil over high heat. Add the quinoa, stir once, and reduce the heat to low. Cover and cook, without stirring, until all the water has been absorbed and the grains are tender, about 15 minutes. Let stand for 5 minutes, covered, then fluff with a fork and transfer to a large bowl.

Add the radicchio, vinegar, olive oil, cherries, pistachios, and parsley to the warm quinoa and stir gently to mix and coat well. Season with salt and pepper. Sprinkle with basil and serve warm or at room temperature.

desserts

This cobbler shows how to reduce the amount of butter used in the topping by replacing part of it with buttermilk and other lean ingredients. Halving instead of slicing the strawberries keeps them from turning mushy in the filling.

Three-Berry Cobbler

MAKES **6** SERVINGS

Canola-oil spray

2 cups (8 oz/250 g) blueberries

4 cups (1 lb/500 g) raspberries

4 cups (1 lb/500 g) strawberries, hulled and halved lengthwise

1/4 cup (2 1/2 oz/75 g) raspberry jam

1 tablespoon instant tapioca

1/2 cup (2 1/2 oz/75 g) whole-wheat flour

1/2 cup (2 1/2 oz/75 g) unbleached all-purpose flour

2 teaspoons baking powder

1/4 teaspoon baking soda

1/2 teaspoon sea salt

3 tablespoons unsalted butter, at room temperature

1/3 cup (3 oz/90 g) sugar

1/3 cup (3 fl oz/80 ml) nonfat buttermilk

Preheat the oven to 350°F (180°C). Coat an 8-inch (20-cm) square nonreactive metal pan or ceramic baking dish lightly with the canola-oil spray. (Do not use a glass dish for this recipe.)

To make the filling, in a bowl, combine the blueberries, raspberries, strawberries, jam, and tapioca. Using a rubber spatula, stir gently to coat the berries with the jam. Spread the fruit in an even layer in the prepared pan.

To make the topping, in a bowl, whisk together the flours, baking powder, baking soda, and salt. In a bowl, using a handheld mixer, beat together the butter and sugar on high speed until fluffy and pale, about 3 minutes. Reduce the speed to medium and beat in about half of the buttermilk. Add about half of the dry ingredients and beat until almost combined. Beat in the remaining buttermilk. Add the remaining dry ingredients and beat until a thick, sticky batter forms. Do not overmix.

Drop the batter by heaping spoonfuls over the fruit. Spread it as evenly as possible, using the back of the spoon. Some of the fruit will be exposed.

Bake the cobbler until the crust is deep golden brown and the fruit juices bubble up around the edges and through any cracks, about 40 minutes. Transfer to a wire rack and let cool to lukewarm before serving. Scoop the cobbler from the dish onto dessert plates and serve.

Fresh basil is unusual to find in desserts, but in this icy granita, it pairs perfectly with ripe cantaloupe. Be sure to use quality, ripe produce to make the best-tasting granita, especially since the recipe calls for so few ingredients.

Cantaloupe-Basil Granita

MAKES 8 SERVINGS

30 fresh basil leaves
$^1/_4$ cup (2 fl oz/60 ml) fresh lime juice
$^2/_3$ cup (5 oz/155 g) sugar
1 ripe cantaloupe (about 4 lb/2 kg)

Coarsely chop 20 basil leaves; set the remaining 10 leaves aside. In a small nonreactive saucepan, combine the lime juice, sugar, and 2 tablespoons water and bring to a simmer over medium-high heat. Simmer, swirling occasionally, until the sugar is dissolved, about 2 minutes. Remove from the heat, stir in the chopped basil, cover, and let steep for 15 minutes.

Meanwhile, halve the cantaloupe and scoop out and discard the seeds. Cut off the rind and then cut the flesh into 1-inch (2.5-cm) cubes.

Strain the basil mixture through a fine-mesh sieve into a blender. Add half of the melon cubes and pulse a few times, then purée until smooth. Add the remaining melon cubes and pulse a few times, then add the reserved whole basil leaves and purée until the mixture is smooth. Pour the mixture into a 13-by-9-by-2-inch (33-by-23-by-5-cm) glass baking dish. Cover with plastic wrap, place on a rimmed baking sheet, and place in the freezer.

After 1–1½ hours, check the granita. When the mixture starts to freeze around the edges of the dish, stir it with a fork, then return the dish to the freezer. Stir the granita with the fork every 45 minutes or so, until the mixture is completely frozen into icy grains and the texture is fluffy, 2–3 hours longer.

Spoon the granita into bowls and serve right away. (The granita is best when eaten within 2 days. If it becomes very hard and dry in the freezer, let it stand at room temperature for 10–15 minutes before serving.)

Eat for Maximum Hydration

Nearly 90 percent water, melons are also rich in nutrients, including fiber, and low in calories, making them a high-value food that can help you maintain your weight. Watermelons are high in vitamin C and contain the antioxidant lycopene. Cantaloupes boast high amounts of vitamins C and A as well as potassium. Honeydew contains similar nutrients to cantaloupe, but less of them.

Serve melons all day, as they are appropriate for any meal from breakfast to desserts after dinner. Their nutrition-dense and calorie-light qualities also make them terrific for snacks, whether on their own or embellished with spices.

Four Ways to Use Melons

Cantaloupe Agua Fresca

In a blender, combine 4 cups (1½ lb/750 g) seeded and cubed cantaloupe, ⅓ cup (3 fl oz/80 ml) fresh lime juice, ¼ cup (¼ oz/7 g) lightly packed fresh mint leaves, and agave nectar to taste. Blend on high speed until the melon is completely liquefied and the mixture is smooth. Transfer to a pitcher and stir in 4 cups (64 fl oz/1 l) water. Pour over ice to serve. Serves 4–6.

Grilled Prosciutto-Wrapped Honeydew

Wrap wedges of honeydew melon in prosciutto, trimming off the fat from the ham, if you like. Brush lightly with olive oil and grill over medium heat until the fruit is warm and the prosciutto is lightly browned. Serve as a starter or as an accompaniment to an arugula salad. Servings vary.

Watermelon with Chile Salt

In a small bowl, gently stir together 1 teaspoon red pepper flakes, 1 teaspoon grated lime zest, and 1 tablespoon coarse salt. Sprinkle the chile salt on 6 watermelon wedges. Serve right away. Serves 6.

Watermelon-Lime Ice Pops

In a blender or food processor, combine 4 cups (24 oz/750 g) cubed seedless watermelon, 2 teaspoons agave nectar, 2 tablespoons fresh lime juice, and a pinch of salt and blend until very smooth. Divide the purée among ice pop molds and freeze until partially frozen, about 1 hour. If using sticks, insert them and continue to freeze until solid, at least 3 hours or up to 3 days. Makes 6–10, depending on the size of the molds.

In this unusual Spanish version of chocolate mousse, extra-virgin olive oil replaces the usual cream, resulting in a silky texture and a hint of the oil's flavor. Use a mild-tasting oil to let the flavor of the chocolate shine through.

Olive Oil Chocolate Mousse

MAKES 4 SERVINGS

6 oz (185 g) bittersweet chocolate, finely chopped

3 large egg yolks

$1/4$ cup (2 fl oz/60 ml) mild-flavored extra-virgin olive oil

3 tablespoons warm water

$1/4$ teaspoon sea salt

2 large egg whites

$1/8$ teaspoon cream of tartar

$1/4$ cup (2 oz/60 g) sugar

Chocolate shavings
for serving (optional)

In a heatproof bowl set over, but not touching, a pan of barely simmering water, stir the chocolate until melted and smooth. Remove from the heat and whisk in the egg yolks, olive oil, warm water, and salt until well blended.

In a clean bowl, using an electric mixer set on medium-high speed, beat the egg whites with the cream of tartar until frothy. Add the sugar and continue beating until the mixture forms soft peaks. Fold about one-third of the egg-white mixture into the chocolate mixture until no white streaks remain. Gently fold in the remaining egg-white mixture until well incorporated.

Spoon the mousse into 4 custard cups, dividing it evenly, and refrigerate until well chilled, at least 4 hours or up to overnight.

Sprinkle with the chocolate shavings. Serve right away.

Note: This recipe contains raw eggs. If you have health and safety concerns, you may wish to avoid foods made with raw eggs.

Although most kinds of berries can be found year-round, most of them often taste best in the spring and summer. Plump berries with deep color have the most flavor. You can also spoon this over slices of angel food cake.

Warm Berry Compote

MAKES 4 SERVINGS

½ cup (4 oz/125 g) sugar

2 cups (8 oz/250 g) strawberries, hulled and quartered

1 cup (4 oz/125 g) blueberries

1 cup (4 oz/125 g) blackberries

2 teaspoons fresh lemon juice

Pinch of sea salt

2 tablespoons unsalted butter, at room temperature, cut into cubes

Good-quality vanilla frozen yogurt for serving

In a large, nonreactive sauté pan over medium heat, combine the sugar and ¼ cup (2 fl oz/60 ml) water and bring to a boil, stirring to dissolve the sugar. Cook for 2 minutes, then add the strawberries, blueberries, blackberries, lemon juice, and salt. Return to a boil, add the butter, and swirl the mixture in the pan until the butter melts.

Put scoops of frozen yogurt in dessert bowls and spoon the compote over the top, scooping up both berries and sauce. Serve right away.

This is a perfect way to showcase any kind of summer-ripe melon. The ingredients may surprise you, but the cayenne pepper provides a touch of contrasting heat and a pinch of sea salt brings out the sweetness in the fruit.

Sweet & Spicy Melon with Lime

MAKES 4–6 SERVINGS

$^1/_2$ cup (6 fl oz/180 ml) honey

$^1/_4$ cup (2 fl oz/60 ml) fresh lime juice

$^1/_8$ teaspoon cayenne pepper

1 teaspoon grated lime zest

$^1/_2$ small seedless watermelon (about 3 lb/1.5 kg)

1 ripe small cantaloupe (about 3 lb/1.5 kg)

Pinch of sea salt

2–3 tablespoons torn fresh mint

In a small saucepan over medium-high heat, combine the honey, lime juice, and cayenne pepper. Bring to a boil, then reduce the heat to low and simmer for 3 minutes to blend the flavors. Remove from the heat and let cool to lukewarm. Stir in the lime zest. Let cool to room temperature.

Cut the rind from the watermelon and then cut the flesh into bite-sized cubes. Halve the cantaloupe. Scoop out the seeds and discard. Cut off the rind and then cut the flesh into cubes.

Place all of the melon in a wide, shallow serving bowl and drizzle with half of the honey-lime syrup. Toss gently to coat, then drizzle with the remaining syrup. Sprinkle with the salt and mint and serve right away.

This recipe works with any type of stone fruits, but plums go particularly well with the exotic flavors of star anise. You could also make these for a brunch, served over pancakes or with hot cereal, or layered in a parfait with nonfat yogurt and granola.

Roasted Spiced Black Plums

MAKES 4–6 SERVINGS

Canola-oil spray
8 ripe black plums, halved and pitted
1 tablespoon brown sugar
8 star anise pods
Nonfat or low-fat vanilla frozen yogurt
for serving

Preheat the oven to 400°F (200°C). Coat a baking dish just large enough to hold the plum halves in a single layer lightly with the canola-oil spray.

Arrange the plums, cut side up, in the prepared dish. Cut a thin slice off the round side of each half to help them sit flat, if you like. Sprinkle brown sugar over each plum half, dividing evenly, then sprinkle the star anise pods evenly over the top. Roast until the sugar has melted, the plums are warmed through, and the skins are just beginning to wrinkle a bit on the edges, about 15 minutes. Let cool to warm, or use right away.

To serve, put scoops of frozen yogurt in 4 dessert bowls, arrange 2 plum halves on top of each (discard the star anise), and serve right away.

Baked summer fruit is irresistible when topped with a crumbly almond streusel topping. Substitute peaches or plums if you wish. For a delightful contrast in temperature, serve the warm nectarines with dollops of cold nonfat vanilla yogurt.

Baked Nectarines with Cinnamon-Almond Streusel

MAKES 4 SERVINGS

Canola-oil spray

4 ripe but firm nectarines, halved and pitted

6 tablespoons (2 oz/60 g) whole-wheat flour

6 tablespoons (2¹/₂ oz/75 g) firmly packed brown sugar

¹/₂ teaspoon ground cinnamon

¹/₈ teaspoon sea salt

2 tablespoons unsalted butter, cut into pieces

¹/₃ cup (2 oz/60 g) roasted almonds, chopped

Preheat the oven to 400°F (200°C). Coat a 9-by-13-inch (23-by-33-cm) baking dish lightly with the canola-oil spray.

Arrange the nectarines, cut side up, in the prepared dish. Cut a thin slice off the round side of each half to help them sit flat, if you like. Set aside.

In a food processor, combine the flour, brown sugar, cinnamon, and salt and pulse a few times to mix. Add the butter pieces and pulse just until the mixture resembles coarse crumbs. Do not overmix. Stir in the almonds. Squeeze the flour-sugar-butter mixture into small handfuls and distribute it evenly over the nectarine halves, pressing it lightly to adhere.

Bake until the nectarines are tender when pierced with a small knife and the topping is nicely browned, about 20 minutes. Arrange 2 nectarine halves on each of 4 dessert plates and serve warm.

In this recipe, fresh bay leaves lend their intriguing aroma, usually reserved for savory dishes, to a simple dessert of honeyed pears flavored with almond-scented amaretto, toasted nuts, and tart Greek-style yogurt.

Bay-Scented Roasted Pears with Honey & Greek Yogurt

MAKES 6 SERVINGS

$^1/_3$ cup (1$^1/_2$ oz/45 g) slivered almonds

3 ripe but firm Bosc pears

$^1/_3$ cup (4$^1/_2$ fl oz/140 ml) honey

4 fresh bay leaves

3 tablespoons unsalted butter, cut into 6 pieces

2 tablespoons amaretto liqueur

1$^1/_2$ cups (12 oz/375 g) nonfat or low-fat plain Greek-style yogurt

Preheat the oven to 375°F (190°C). Place the almonds on a rimmed baking sheet and toast in the oven, stirring once or twice, until fragrant and lightly browned, 5–6 minutes. Immediately pour onto a plate to cool. Leave the oven on.

Halve the pears lengthwise. Using a melon baller, scoop out the cores.

In a small Dutch oven or heavy ovenproof saucepan, combine the honey and bay leaves and bring to a simmer over medium-high heat. Reduce the heat to medium and continue to simmer, stirring occasionally, until the honey is fragrant and turns a rich amber color, about 3 minutes. Remove from the heat.

Place the butter pieces in the pot with the honey, spacing them evenly. Using tongs, carefully place a pear half, cut side down, on top of each piece of butter. Cover the pot and roast the pears in the oven for 10 minutes. Using the tongs, gently turn the pears over. Switch to a long-handled spoon and baste the pears with the honey mixture. Drizzle the pears with the amaretto and continue to roast, uncovered, until golden brown and a sharp knife slips easily into the centers, 6–8 minutes longer. Remove from the oven and let the pears cool slightly in the honey mixture, about 30 minutes.

In a bowl, whisk the yogurt until smooth. To serve, arrange the pear halves on a platter, drizzle the honey mixture from the pot over the top, and sprinkle with the toasted almonds. Serve right away, passing the yogurt at the table.

Fresh-Picked Nutrients

Pears contain 5 grams of fiber as well as potassium, vitamin C, folic acid, and antioxidants. Their high water content promotes fullness, so pears such as Bartlett and Bosc are great to have on hand as snacks during their prime season in fall and winter. Pears need to be picked green, then ripened off the tree. For fullest flavor, set them on the counter until they yield when gently pressed near the stem.

Adaptable pears go well with a range of different ingredients. Try them raw as a sweet contrast to tart cranberries in a fresh relish, or sliced as part of a salad. Roasted, pears complement sweet vegetables and help offset savory meats and poultry with their bright flavor.

Four Ways to Use Pears

Pear, Orange & Cranberry Relish

In a food processor, process 1 thin-skinned navel orange, halved and cut into thin wedges (including peel); 3 cups cranberries; and 2–3 tablespoons sugar until finely chopped. Transfer to a bowl and stir in 2 firm but ripe pears, peeled, cored, and finely chopped, and ½ teaspoon ground cardamom. Mix well and refrigerate for about 1 hour before serving. Serve with roasted poultry or meat. Makes about 4 cups (32 fl oz/1 l).

Pear & Fennel Salad

In a large bowl, whisk together 1 tablespoon sherry vinegar, 2 tablespoons extra-virgin olive oil, 1 tablespoon coarsely grated pecorino Romano cheese, and salt and pepper to taste. Add 1 bulb fennel, shaved, and toss to coat. Arrange on each plate 1½ cups (1½ oz/45 g) baby arugula leaves and top with some fennel mixture. Top each salad with ½ pear, halved, cored, and thinly sliced. Sprinkle each with 1 tablespoon dried currants. Serves 4.

Pears & Parsnips with Almonds

On a rimmed baking sheet, arrange 1 lb (500 g) parsnips, peeled and quartered, and 3 Bosc or Anjou pears, quartered lengthwise and cored. Sprinkle with 3 tablespoons olive oil and salt to taste, then toss to coat evenly. Spread out in an even layer and roast in a 400°F (200°C) oven until tender when pierced with a small knife and browned, 30–40 minutes. Top with 3 tablespoons toasted almonds and serve right away. Serves 6.

Savory Roasted Pears

Oil a shallow baking dish and drizzle 1 tablespoon maple syrup into the dish. Arrange 4 firm but ripe Bosc, Bartlett, or Anjou pears, halved lengthwise and cored, in the dish, cut-side up. Brush the cut sides with fresh lemon juice and sprinkle with 1 tablespoon chopped fresh sage. Drizzle the pears with 2 tablespoons dry white wine. Roast in a 425°F (220°C) oven until just tender, 22–25 minutes. Drizzle with 2 tablespoons additional wine and ¼ cup (2 fl oz/ 60 ml) water. Continue to roast, basting 1 or 2 times, until the pears are very tender and lightly browned, 12–15 minutes. Serve warm or at room temperature drizzled with the pan juices. Serves 4 as a side dish.

Baked apples stuffed with dried fruits are an alluring dessert. Honey makes a sparkling glaze for the apples. When choosing apricots, avoid the Turkish variety, as they are too sweet. Unsulfered California dried apricots are a good choice.

Baked Apples Filled with Dried Fruits

MAKES 4 SERVINGS

16 dried apricots

4 dried Calimyrna figs

4 soft pitted prunes

2 dried pear halves, each cut into 4 pieces

$^1/_4$ cup (1 oz/30 g) dried cranberries

$^1/_4$ cup ($1^1/_2$ oz/45 g) raisins

$1^1/_3$ cups (11 fl oz/330 ml) unfiltered apple cider

4 baking apples such as Rome Beauty, Fuji, or Jonagold

$^1/_3$ cup ($4^1/_2$ fl oz/140 ml) honey

In a heatproof bowl, combine the apricots, figs, prunes, pears, cranberries, and raisins. In a small saucepan, bring 1 cup (8 fl oz/250 ml) of the cider to a boil. Pour the hot liquid over the fruits. Let stand until the fruits have plumped, 30–60 minutes.

Preheat the oven to 350°F (180°C).

Cut a slice $^1/_2$ inch (12 mm) thick off the stem end of each apple. Using a melon baller, scoop out and discard the core from each apple, being careful not to puncture the base of the fruit. Then, carve out the flesh to leave a shell about $^1/_2$ inch (12 mm) thick. Discard the flesh or reserve for another use. Stand the apples in a baking dish just large enough to hold them upright.

Drain the plumped fruits in a sieve held over the baking dish. Spoon the fruits into the apple cavities, dividing them evenly. Drape squares of aluminum foil over the stuffing in each apple and bake until a knife pierces the bottom of the apples with only slight resistance, 35–40 minutes. Remove from the oven and lift off the foil.

When the apples are cool enough to handle, after about 20 minutes, use a slotted spoon to transfer them to a platter. Spoon any of the fruit stuffing that fell off back in place. Discard the liquid remaining in the dish.

In a saucepan, combine the remaining $^1/_3$ cup (3 fl oz/80 ml) apple cider and the honey. Bring to a boil over medium-high heat, reduce the heat to medium, and simmer until the liquid is syrupy and reduced by about one-third, about 8 minutes. Spoon the hot glaze over the stuffing and apples until it pools in the bottom of the platter. Serve warm or at room temperature.

Naturally sweet and creamy when frozen, bananas are full of potassium. Cover them with dark chocolate and nuts and you have a quick, healthy treat. Choose bright yellow bananas that are not too ripe and freckled but rather still have some firmness.

Dark Chocolate–Banana Pops with Roasted Almonds

MAKES ABOUT 30 POPS; SERVES 8

12 oz (375 g) bittersweet chocolate, chopped

²/₃ cup (4 oz/125 g) roasted almonds or pecans, chopped

2 ripe bananas

In a bowl set over a pan of barely simmering water, melt the chocolate, stirring occasionally, until smooth. Remove the pan from the heat, but leave the bowl of chocolate on top to keep warm.

Put the nuts in a small bowl. Line a baking sheet with waxed paper.

Peel the bananas and cut them into ½-inch (12-mm) rounds. Drop 1 banana slice at a time into the chocolate and turn to coat. Lift out with a fork, tapping the fork gently on the bowl edge to allow excess chocolate to drip back into the bowl. Place the banana slice on the prepared baking sheet and sprinkle with nuts. Repeat to dip and coat the remaining banana slices.

Freeze the coated bananas until the chocolate is set, about 20 minutes, then transfer to an airtight container and store in the freezer for up to 1 week.

A syrup flavored with cardamom offers hints of ginger, allspice, clove, and black pepper, to complement the tropical sweetness of creamy-textured mangoes. Used sparingly, whipped cream adds a touch of indulgence to an otherwise fat-free dessert.

Spiced Mango Pavlovas

MAKES **6** SERVINGS

4 large egg whites, at room temperature

$1/8$ teaspoon cream of tartar

$1^1/_2$ cups (12 oz/375 g) sugar

1 tablespoon cornstarch

5 whole green cardamom pods

3 ripe mangoes, peeled and cut into $1/_2$-inch (12-mm) cubes (see page 48)

Finely grated zest and juice of 1 lime

Sweetened Whipped Cream for serving (page 219)

Preheat the oven to 275°F (135°C). Line a baking sheet with parchment paper.

In a stand mixer, beat the egg whites on high speed until foamy. Add the cream of tartar and continue to beat while gradually adding 1 cup (8 oz/250 g) of the sugar until soft peaks form. Sift the cornstarch over the whites and fold in gently. Spoon 6 dollops of the mixture onto the prepared sheet, dividing it evenly and spacing the mounds about 3 inches (7.5 cm) apart. Using the back of a spoon and working in a circular motion, spread each dollop into a disk about 4 inches (10 cm) in diameter. Finally, make a depression in the center of each. Bake the meringues until they are no longer tacky on the surface and are very lightly golden, about 1 hour. Set the baking sheet on a wire rack and let the meringues cool completely on the pan.

Using the flat side of a chef's knife, lightly crack open the cardamom pods. Add the pods to a saucepan along with the remaining ½ cup (4 oz/125 g) sugar and 2 tablespoons water and bring to a simmer over medium-high heat. Simmer, swirling occasionally, until the sugar is dissolved, about 2 minutes. Let cool to room temperature.

Put the mangoes in a bowl. Squeeze the lime juice over the mangoes, pour the cardamom syrup through a fine-mesh sieve into the bowl, and stir to mix well.

To serve, place each of the meringues on a dessert plate. Spoon a small amount of whipped cream on top of each meringue. Using a slotted spoon, top the whipped cream with some of the mango cubes. Drizzle a little cardamom syrup over the top, sprinkle with lime zest, and serve right away.

Pearl tapioca is a gluten-free starch. While it is not nutritionally dense, it does provide some minerals and fiber. Here it is made into an immunity-boosting pudding with coconut milk and fresh mango and papaya.

Tapioca Pudding with Tropical Fruits

MAKES 4–6 SERVINGS

$^{1}/_{2}$ cup (3 oz/90 g) small pearl tapioca

$^{1}/_{4}$ cup (2 fl oz/60 ml) unsweetened coconut milk

2 tablespoons granulated sugar

1 ripe mango, peeled and diced

$^{1}/_{2}$ ripe medium or large papaya, peeled, seeded, and sliced

Juice of 1 lime

4 teaspoons raw sugar

In a saucepan, bring 4 cups (32 fl oz/1 l) water to a boil over high heat. Reduce the heat to medium, add the tapioca, and simmer gently until translucent, 12–15 minutes. Drain thoroughly through a fine-mesh sieve.

Put the tapioca in a bowl. Add the coconut milk and granulated sugar and stir to mix well and help dissolve the sugar. Cover and refrigerate until well chilled, at least 1 hour and up to 24 hours.

To serve, divide the pudding among dessert bowls and top with the fruit. Drizzle with the lime juice, sprinkle with the raw sugar, and serve right away.

Think Blue for Health

Eating blueberries benefits your heart and helps to stabilize blood pressure. It may boost your memory, as well. Blueberries' power and intense color come from antioxidants called anthocyanins, along with fiber, vitamin C and manganese. Dark, evenly colored blueberries are best. A silver sheen on the berry indicates just-picked freshness—it disappears after a few days.

Blueberries are popular at the breakfast table, often seen in pancakes, muffins, or other baked goods. Their bold color also helps create eye-catching drinks, salads, and vibrant main-course sauces. Layered with nonfat yogurt, honey, and nuts, they also make an easy and healthful dessert.

Four Ways to Use Blueberries

Sparkling Blueberry Lemonade

In a blender, combine the juice of 1 lemon, 1 tablespoon honey, and ¼ cup (1 oz/30 g) blueberries and blend to a smooth purée. Fill a glass with ice, pour in the blueberry purée, and top with a splash of sparkling water. Serves 1.

Blueberry, Almond & Feta Salad

In a large bowl, whisk together 3 tablespoons extra-virgin olive oil, 4 teaspoons raspberry vinegar, and salt and pepper to taste. Add 1 minced shallot, 1½ cups (6 oz/185 g) blueberries, and 2 teaspoons chopped fresh chives. Let stand for 10–15 minutes, then add 1 head butter lettuce, torn, and 3 oz (90 g) crumbled feta cheese and toss well. Serve right away topped with ¼ cup (1½ oz/45 g) toasted almonds. Serves 4.

Wasabi-Spiked Blueberry-Rhubarb Sauce

Heat 1 tablespoon canola oil in a sauté pan over medium-high heat. Add ½ minced red onion and sauté until tender. Add 2–3 thin rhubarb stalks, sliced, and cook, stirring, until the bottom of the pan looks syrupy, 3–4 minutes. Add 1½ cups (6 oz/185 g) blueberries and 2 tablespoons honey. When the berries start to soften, after about 1 minute, reduce the heat to medium. Simmer until the rhubarb is tender and collapsing, about 5 minutes. Remove from the heat and stir in ¼ teaspoon wasabi powder. Serve warm with grilled or roasted salmon, pork, or poultry. Serves 4.

Blueberry-Yogurt Parfaits

For each parfait, spoon ½ cup (4 oz/125 g) plain low-fat or nonfat Greek-style yogurt into a glass. Spoon about ½ cup (2 oz/60 g) blueberries over the yogurt. Sprinkle with 1–2 teaspoons toasted sliced almonds and ½ teaspoon honey. Repeat the layers, ending with the honey. Serves 1 or more.

The lemony-herbal nuances of lemongrass are infused into a sweet syrup and then paired with juicy raspberries in this exotic twist on a classic dessert. It's delicious on its own, but if you feel like splurging, serve with lightly sweetened whipped cream.

Raspberries in Lemongrass Syrup

MAKES 6 SERVINGS

1 stalk fresh lemongrass

1/3 cup (3 oz/90 g) sugar

8 cups (2 lb/1 kg) raspberries

Nonfat plain Greek-style yogurt
for serving

Remove the dry outer leaves of the lemongrass and then trim the stalk to a 3-inch (7.5-cm) piece of the pale green bottom section. Using the back of the blade of a chef's knife, bruise the lemongrass, flattening the stalk and breaking some of the fibers to release its aroma.

In a small saucepan, combine the sugar and ⅓ cup (3 fl oz/80 ml) water and bring to a simmer over medium-high heat. Simmer, swirling occasionally, until the sugar is dissolved, about 2 minutes. Remove from the heat, add the lemongrass, cover, and let steep until cooled completely, about 30 minutes.

Strain the lemongrass syrup through a fine-mesh sieve into a large bowl, pressing on the stalk with the back of a spoon to extract as much syrup as possible; discard the lemongrass.

Add the raspberries to the syrup and stir gently. Divide the raspberries and syrup among 6 dessert bowls. Top with the yogurt and serve right away.

glossary

antibacterial

Helping to destroy or inhibit the growth of bacteria. Ingredients with antibacterial properties include garlic and some fresh herbs, such as peppermint.

anti-inflammatory

Helping to reduce or prevent inflammation in the body tissues. Anti-inflammatory ingredients include deeply pigmented fruits and vegetables, spices such as turmeric, and fresh herbs.

antimicrobial

Helping to destroy or inhibit the growth of microbes, such as salmonella. Ingredients with antimicrobial properties include some alliums and fresh herbs like basil and cilantro.

antioxidants

Antioxidants protect against and repair daily damage to our cells and tissues. They have also been linked to heart health and cancer prevention. Some come in the form of vitamins, such as vitamins C and E. Others are compounds found in plant foods such as phytonutrients like lycopene and beta-carotene, or polyphenols such as ellagic acid. The best sources of antioxidants are colorful fruits, vegetables, nuts, and whole grains.

carbohydrates

There are three main kinds of carbohydrates: starch, sugar, and fiber. Starch and sugar provide our bodies and brains with energy. Although our bodies can't digest fiber, it provides a number of significant benefits. The healthiest sources of carbohydrates are fruits, vegetables, beans, and whole grains such as whole-wheat bread and pasta, brown rice, and quinoa.

capsaicin

The substance in chiles that makes them hot. Capsaicin has a host of health benefits, and is thought to help speed metabolism, relieve pain, fight cancer, and more.

carotenoids

Carotenoids are colored pigments in plants that provide multiple health benefits such as improved vision, enhanced immunity, or protection against cancer. While beta-carotene, the pigment that gives carrots their orange color, is perhaps the most well known carotenoid, others include lycopene from tomatoes and zeaxanthin and lutein from spinach.

cholesterol

Foods from animal sources such as eggs, milk, cheese, and meat contain cholesterol, but the human body makes its own supply as well. While cholesterol in our diets was once thought to be a major contributor to high cholesterol levels, we now know that foods rich in saturated fat raise unhealthy LDL cholesterol in our blood streams more substantially than cholesterol from other food. Plant compounds like phytosterols in wheat germ, peanuts, and almonds and beta-glucan from oats have been shown to lower cholesterol.

fats

Our bodies need fat to absorb certain vitamins, build the membranes that line our cells, and cushion our joints and organs. But fats aren't all created equal. Saturated and hydrogenated fat are linked to chronic ailments such as heart disease, while unsaturated fats can be more healthful.

monounsaturated fats Found in nuts, avocados, olive oil, and canola oil, these fats are less likely to raise levels of unhealthy LDL cholesterol, linked to heart attack and stroke. They also help keep arteries clear by maintaining levels of healthy HDL cholesterol.

polyunsaturated fats These fats can play an important role in helping control cholesterol. While most of us get plenty of the polyunsaturated fat linolenic acid from vegetable, corn, and soybean oil, our diets don't usually contain enough of heart-healthy omega-3 fats. These are found as EPA and DHA in fish or in the form of alpha linolenic acid in flaxseed, canola oil, and walnuts.

saturated fats Found in meats, dairy products, and tropical oils such as coconut oil and palm oil, these fats raise blood levels of unhealthy LDL cholesterol.

trans fats Present in hydrogenated vegetable oils in many processed and fried foods, trans fats may be even more harmful than saturated fats.

fiber

Fiber is the component of plant foods that our bodies can't digest. Insoluble fiber does not dissolve in water and is known for preventing constipation. Soluble fiber softens in water and helps lower blood cholesterol levels. Fiber-rich diets have been linked with improved digestive health and reduced risk for type 2 diabetes and heart disease.

flavonoids

These plant compounds help prevent heart disease and possibly cancer. They include quercetin from onions and apples, anthocyanidins from berries, and isoflavones from soy.

free radicals

These unstable molecules act to damage healthy cells and to cause inflammation in body tissues. Eating antioxidants can help counteract their damage.

glycemic index

A method of measuring the effects of various foods on blood sugar. Foods that quickly raise blood sugar levels rate high on the index, while foods that slowly act on blood sugar rate near the bottom. Foods that produce a slow but sustained release of sugar in the bloodstream are considered best for optimum health.

lycopene

A carotenoid believed to protect against heart disease and some types of cancer. It is found in tomatoes and other red fruits and vegetables.

minerals

Minerals are elements that our bodies need in varying quantities for survival. Major minerals, such as calcium, are required in larger amounts, while trace minerals like iron and zinc are required in smaller amounts.

calcium Vital for bone health, calcium is also important for muscle contraction and blood pressure regulation. Calcium-rich foods include low-fat milk, fish, and vegetables such as broccoli and spinach.

chromium A trace element that is important for metabolism and insulin function in the body.

copper This trace mineral is essential for proper iron processing. It is also involved in healing and metabolism.

folate Folate helps produce and maintain new cell growth and may help fight cancer.

iron This mineral helps the body transport and use oxygen, and also plays a role in immune function, temperature regulation, cognitive development, and energy metabolism.

manganese This trace mineral is needed for proper metabolism of carbohydrates, fats, and proteins. It also keeps bones and teeth healthy.

phosphorus Phosphorus helps build strong bones and teeth, and helps the body get energy from food.

potassium Potassium helps the body maintain water and mineral balance, and regulates heartbeat and blood pressure.

selenium This trace mineral works with vitamin E as an antioxidant to protect cells from damage, and also boosts immune function.

zinc Zinc promotes a healthy immune system and is critical for proper blood clotting, thyroid function, and optimal growth and reproduction.

phytochemicals

Numbering more than 10,000 known to date, these plant-based compounds have a positive effect on the body. Deeply pigmented fruits and vegetables tend to be highest in phytochemicals, but they are also found in tea, chocolate, and nuts. Familiar phytonutrient groups include carotenoids and polyphenols.

phytonutrients

Another word for phytochemicals.

polyphenols

A class of antioxidant chemicals present in deeply pigmented fruits and vegetable as well as tea, which may help protect the heart and fight cancer.

protein

Made of amino acids, protein provides the building blocks our bodies need to synthesize cells, tissues, hormones, and antibodies. It is found in foods of animal and vegetable origin, although animal proteins contain more of the amino acids our bodies need to synthesize protein. Choose lean protein sources like fish, poultry, and legumes.

sulfur compounds

Powerful substances found in cruciferous vegetables that help prevent cancer and contribute to eye health.

vitamins

Our bodies require vitamins in order to function properly. They fall into two categories: fat-soluble vitamins, which require fat for absorption and are stored in our body's fat tissue, and water-soluble vitamins, which cannot be stored and must be replenished often.

vitamin A Found in dairy products, yellow-orange fruits and vegetables, and dark green leafy vegetables, vitamin A promotes healthy skin, hair, bones, and vision. It also works as an antioxidant.

B vitamins This group of water-soluble vitamins can be found in a range of fruits and vegetables, whole grains, and dairy and meat products and includes vitamins B6 and B12, biotin, niacin, pantothenic acid, thiamin, folate, and riboflavin. Each one plays a vital role in bodily functions, including regulating metabolism and energy production, keeping the nerves and muscles healthy, and protecting against birth defects and heart disease. Choline, found in eggs, grains, and other foods, helps with brain and memory development, nutrient transport, and essential cell functions.

vitamin C This water-soluble vitamin helps build body tissues, fights infection, helps keep gums healthy, and helps the body absorb iron. It also works as an antioxidant. It can be found in many fruits and vegetables, especially citrus.

vitamin D Instrumental in building and maintaining healthy bones and teeth, vitamin D can be found in fish such as salmon and sardines, as well as in fortified milk and cereal.

vitamin E Found in nuts and seeds, whole grains, dark green vegetables, and beans, vitamin E helps form red blood cells, prevents oxidation of LDL cholesterol, and improves immunity. It also works in the body as an antioxidant.

vitamin K Necessary for protein synthesis as well as blood clotting, vitamin K can be found in dark green vegetables, asparagus, and cabbage.

basics

These staple recipes include flavorful dressings, sauces, condiments, and seasonings that will enhance a variety of dishes. Use them as part of any healthy meal.

Pico de Gallo

3 tomatoes

½ red onion

2–4 serrano chiles

1 tablespoon finely chopped
fresh cilantro

2 teaspoons fresh lime juice

Sea salt

Finely chop the tomatoes and onion into equal-size pieces. Seed and mince the chiles.

In a large bowl, stir together the tomatoes, onion, chiles, cilantro, lime juice, and 2 teaspoons salt. Let the salsa stand for 1 hour to blend the flavors.

Serve right away, or cover and store in the refrigerator for up to 3 days.

Makes about 1½ cups (12 fl oz/375 ml)

Gremolata

⅔ cup (1 oz/30 g) minced fresh
flat-leaf parsley

Finely grated zest of 1 lemon

2 cloves garlic, minced

In a small bowl, stir together the parsley, lemon zest, and garlic. Serve over cooked fish, chicken, meat, or steamed vegetables.

Makes about ¾ cup (1½ oz/45 g)

Romesco Dressing

2 tablespoons extra-virgin olive oil

1 tablespoon fresh orange juice

2 tablespoons sherry vinegar

¼ teaspoon Spanish sweet smoked paprika

2 cloves garlic, minced

3 jarred piquillo peppers, drained

1½ tablespoons chopped blanched almonds

Sea salt and freshly ground pepper

In a food processor, combine the olive oil, orange juice, vinegar, paprika, garlic, piquillo peppers, almonds,

a scant ½ teaspoon salt, and a few grindings of pepper. Process until a relatively smooth dressing forms, about 15 seconds. Taste and adjust the seasoning.

Makes about ¾ cup (6 fl oz/180 ml)

Sun-Dried Tomato Vinaigrette

4 dry-packed sun-dried tomato halves

Boiling water as needed

¼ cup (2 fl oz/60 ml) extra-virgin olive oil

3 tablespoons fresh lemon juice

1 tablespoon finely chopped fresh
flat-leaf parsley

1 tablespoon finely chopped fresh dill

1 teaspoon grated orange zest

1 small clove garlic, minced

Sea salt and freshly ground pepper

Place the sun-dried tomatoes in a heatproof bowl, pour over boiling water to cover, and let stand for 5 minutes. Drain the tomatoes and finely dice. In a small bowl, whisk together the olive oil, lemon juice, sun-dried tomatoes, parsley, dill, orange zest, garlic, 2 tablespoons water, ½ teaspoon salt, and a grinding or two of pepper until blended.

Makes about ¾ cup (6 fl oz/180 ml)

Pesto

1 tablespoon pine nuts

½ cup (4 fl oz/125 ml) extra-virgin olive oil

2 large cloves garlic

Sea salt and freshly ground pepper

1½ cups (1½ oz/45 g) tightly packed
fresh basil leaves

¼ cup (½ oz/15 g) coarsely chopped
fresh spinach leaves

2 tablespoons freshly grated
Parmesan cheese

In a dry frying pan, toast the nuts until lightly browned and fragrant, about 3 minutes; watch carefully, as they burn easily. Immediately pour onto a plate to stop the cooking and let cool.

In a food processor, combine the olive oil, pine nuts, garlic, and ½ teaspoon salt. Pulse, scraping down the sides as needed, until fairly smooth. Add the basil, spinach, and ¼ teaspoon pepper and process until blended, but still with some texture. Transfer to a glass or ceramic bowl and stir in the cheese.

Makes about 1 cup (8 fl oz/250)

Buttermilk-Herb Sauce

1/3 cup (1/2 oz/15 g) lightly packed,
coarsely chopped fresh flat-leaf parsley

2 tablespoons lightly packed,
coarsely chopped fresh dill

1 tablespoon coarsely chopped fresh mint

1 green onion, including tender green tops,
thinly sliced

1/2 cup (4 fl oz/125 ml) low-fat buttermilk

1/2 cup (4 oz/125 g) nonfat plain yogurt

1 tablespoon extra-virgin olive oil

Sea salt

In a food processor, combine the parsley, dill, mint,
and green onion and process until finely chopped.
Add the buttermilk, yogurt, olive oil, and 1/2 teaspoon
salt and process until the ingredients are blended.

Pour the dressing into a container with a tight-fitting
lid and refrigerate for several hours or overnight before
serving; it will thicken.

Shake or stir well before serving over green salads,
tomatoes, steamed vegetables, chicken, or fish.
It will keep in the refrigerator for up to 3 days.

Makes 1 1/4 cups (10 fl oz/310 ml)

Roasted Tomato Sauce

7 ripe plum tomatoes, cored

2–3 serrano chiles,
seeded and minced

1/2 small onion, chopped

1 large clove garlic, chopped

1 tablespoon canola or grapeseed oil

Sea salt

In a dry frying pan over high heat, roast the tomatoes,
turning them as they char slightly, about 5 minutes.

In a food processor, combine the tomatoes, chiles,
onion, and garlic. Process until blended but still chunky.

In a large frying pan over medium-high heat, warm
the oil. Add the tomato mixture and cook, stirring
constantly, until thickened, about 5 minutes. Taste
and adjust the seasoning.

Makes about 1 1/2 cups (12 fl oz/375 ml)

Sweetened Whipped Cream

1/2 cup (4 fl oz/125 ml) cold heavy cream

2 teaspoons sugar

1/2 teaspoon pure vanilla extract

In a chilled bowl, combine the heavy cream, sugar,
and vanilla. Using a whisk, beat until soft peaks
form. (Alternatively, using an electric mixer, beat
on medium-high speed until soft peaks form.)

Use the cream right away, or cover and refrigerate
until serving time.

Makes about 1 cup (8 fl oz/250 ml)

Fruit Sauce

2 cups (8 oz/250 g) raspberries, strawberries,
blueberries, or mango cubes

2 1/2 tablespoons honey

1 1/2 teaspoons fresh lemon juice

In a food processor, combine the fruit and honey
and pulse just until puréed. Pour the purée through
a fine-mesh sieve set over a bowl, pressing on the
purée with the back of a wooden spoon to remove
any seeds. Stir in the lemon juice. Cover and refrigerate
for up to 5 days. Serve over pancakes, waffles,
angel food cake, fresh fruit, or yogurt.

Makes about 2 cups (16 fl oz/500 ml)

Homemade Yogurt

1 qt (1 l) nonfat milk

1/3 cup instant nonfat dried milk

2 tablespoons plain nonfat yogurt
(make sure it contains live, active cultures
and is made without gelatin or stabilizers)

In a large, heavy saucepan, bring the milk just to a boil,
stirring to prevent a skin from forming. If a skin does
form, skim it off with a spoon. Remove from the heat
and let cool to 112°–115°F (44°–46°C).

Put the dried milk in a clean ceramic or glass bowl.
Gradually whisk in about 1/2 cup of the warm milk
until the mixture is smooth. Whisk in the yogurt until
well blended. Slowly whisk in the remaining warm
milk until blended.

Cover the dish tightly with plastic wrap and set in
a warm place (90°-100°F/35°-38°C) without moving
or disturbing the bowl, until thickened to your liking,
6–8 hours or overnight. (An oven with a gas pilot light
is a good choice; if you have an electric oven, preheat it
to 120°F/49°C, then turn it off. The longer the yogurt
stands, the tarter and thicker it will become.

Use the yogurt right away, or refrigerate it for
up to 4 days.

Makes about 2 cups (16 fl oz/500 ml)

index

weldon**owen**

415 Jackson Street, Suite 200, San Francisco, CA 94111
www.weldonowen.com

GOOD FOR YOU

Conceived and produced by Weldon Owen, Inc.
In collaboration with Williams-Sonoma, Inc.
3250 Van Ness Avenue, San Francisco, CA 94109

A WELDON OWEN PRODUCTION

Copyright © 2013 Weldon Owen, Inc.
and Williams-Sonoma, Inc.
All rights reserved, including the right of reproduction
in whole or in part in any form.

Printed and bound in China

First printed in 2012
10 9 8 7 6 5 4 3

Library of Congress Control Number: 2012949839

ISBN 13: 978-1-61628-494-7
ISBN 10: 1-61628-494-3

Weldon Owen is a division of
BONNIER

WELDON OWEN, INC.

CEO and President Terry Newell
VP, Sales and Marketing Amy Kaneko
Director of Finance Mark Perrigo

VP and Publisher Hannah Rahill
Executive Editor Jennifer Newens

Creative Director Emma Boys
Art Director Ali Zeigler
Designer Rachel Lopez Metzger
Production Director Chris Hemesath
Production Manager Michelle Duggan

Photographer Erin Kunkel
Food Stylist Valerie Aikman-Smith
Prop Stylist Christine Wolheim

ACKNOWLEDGMENTS

Weldon Owen wishes to thank the following people for their generous support
in producing this book: David Bornfriend, Kim Laidlaw, Ashley Lima,
Eve Lynch, Elizabeth Parson, Jason Wheeler

the DICTIONARY of BIBLICAL LITERACY

Compiled by Cecil B. Murphey

OLIVER NELSON

A division of Thomas Nelson Publishers
Nashville

Published in Nashville, Tennessee, by Oliver-Nelson Books, a division of Thomas Nelson, Inc., Publishers, and distributed in Canada by Lawson Falle, Ltd., Cambridge, Ontario.

Much of the information in this book has been adapted from *The Bible Almanac,* Copyright © 1980, and *Nelson's Illustrated Bible Dictionary,* Copyright © 1986, by Thomas Nelson Publishers. Used by permission.

Scripture quotations are from THE NEW KING JAMES VERSION. Copyright © 1979, 1980, 1982, Thomas Nelson, Inc., Publishers. Scripture quotations noted KJV are from The King James Version of the Holy Bible. Scripture quotations noted NIV are taken from the HOLY BIBLE: NEW INTERNATIONAL VERSION. Copyright © 1973, 1978, 1984 by the International Bible Society. Used by permission of Zondervan Bible Publishers. Scripture quotations noted NASB are from the New American Standard Bible, © 1960, 1962, 1963, 1968, 1971, 1972, 1973, 1975, 1977 by The Lockman Foundation. Used by permission. Scripture quotations noted TEV are from the *Good News Bible*—Old Testament: Copyright © American Bible Society 1976: New Testament: Copyright © American Bible Society 1966, 1971, 1976. Used by permission. Scripture quotations noted NEB are from *The New English Bible.* © The Delegates of the Oxford University Press 1961, 1970. Reprinted by permission. Scripture quotations noted RSV are from the Revised Standard Version of the Bible, copyrighted 1946, 1952, © 1971, 1973.

Printed in the United States of America.

Senior Editor: Lila Empson
Senior Copy Editor: Dimples Kellogg
Production Manager: Harold Leach
Design and Typesetting: Bill Parsons of ProtoType Graphics
Copy Editors: Lynne Deming, Christine Benagh, Etta Wilson
Research Consultant: George Knight
Indexer: Steve Nichols
Manuscript Processing: Steve Womack
Photo Coordinators: Carol Martin, Marie Sennett
Proofreaders: Mary Jane Lunn, Beatrice Sussman, Suzanne Olds

ISBN 0-8407-9105-4

1 2 3 4 5 6 — 94 93 92 91 90 89

Contents

Introduction

What should I, as a Christian, know about the Bible? That question prompted the compiling of this information.

About the same time, E. D. Hirsch, Jr., Joseph F. Kett, and James Trefil published *The Dictionary of Cultural Literacy* in which they asked a similar question about the more general knowledge of our culture. The authors pointed out they sought to convey knowledge shared by anyone. They collected the information that, in their opinions, our culture finds useful and worth preserving.

Following that same concept, we have tried to avoid filling the pages of *The Dictionary of Biblical Literacy* with trivia. We also have tried to avoid presenting scholarly debate, to avoid offering information that would be of little interest to most people, and to avoid being so comprehensive that we include everything anybody would ever want to know about the Bible.

We have not attempted to make *The Dictionary of Biblical Literacy* the final word on biblical knowledge. Instead, we have attempted to present material that is
- Basic to an understanding of our shared Christian faith;
- Significant enough to be worth knowing;
- Helpful in its overview of the life, culture, and times covered by the Bible;
- Enjoyable for readers who are interested in the Bible.

As additional features we have surveyed the personalities and movements through the centuries of the church. We have included a couple of who's who lists of names, with brief annotations, that profile the major personalities and forces in the Bible and church history. We also have included overviews of the major denominations and brief explanations of current theological interpretations among conservative Christians.

Ultimately the selections and choices had to be subjective. That means some people can point to specific entries and wonder why they were included; other people can wonder why some items were left out. The only defense I offer is that the material in *The Dictionary of Biblical Literacy* revolves around the kind of information that people want to know.

CECIL MURPHEY

*Abbreviations*_____

The following abbreviations have been used throughout *The Dictionary of Biblical Literacy.*

Testaments

New Testament	NT
Old Testament	OT

Old Testament Books

Alphabetical Order:

Amos	Amos
Chronicles, 1	1 Chron.
Chronicles, 2	2 Chron.
Daniel	Dan.
Deuteronomy	Deut.
Ecclesiastes	Eccles.
Esther	Esther
Exodus	Exod.
Ezekiel	Ezek.
Ezra	Ezra
Genesis	Gen.
Habakkuk	Hab.
Haggai	Hag.
Hosea	Hos.
Isaiah	Isa.
Jeremiah	Jer.
Job	Job
Joel	Joel
Jonah	Jon.
Joshua	Josh.
Judges	Judg.
Kings, 1	1 Kings
Kings, 2	2 Kings
Lamentations	Lam.
Leviticus	Lev.
Malachi	Mal.
Micah	Mic.
Nahum	Nah.
Nehemiah	Neh.
Numbers	Num.
Obadiah	Obad.
Proverbs	Prov.
Psalm, Psalms	Ps., Pss.
Ruth	Ruth
Samuel, 1	1 Sam.
Samuel, 2	2 Sam.
Song of Solomon	Song of Sol.
Zechariah	Zech.
Zephaniah	Zeph.

New Testament Books

Alphabetical order:

Acts	Acts
Colossians	Col.
Corinthians, 1	1 Cor.
Corinthians, 2	2 Cor.
Ephesians	Eph.
Galatians	Gal.
Hebrews	Heb.
James	James
John, 1	1 John
John, 2	2 John
John, 3	3 John
John	John
Jude	Jude

Luke	Luke
Mark	Mark
Matthew	Matt.
Peter, 1	1 Pet.
Peter, 2	2 Pet.
Philemon	Philem.
Philippians	Phil.
Revelation	Rev.
Romans	Rom.
Thessalonians, 1	1 Thess.
Thessalonians, 2	2 Thess.
Timothy, 1	1 Tim.
Timothy, 2	2 Tim.
Titus	Titus

Bible Versions

Alphabetical order:

Jerusalem Bible, The	JB
King James Version	KJV
New American Bible	NAB
New American Standard Bible	NASB
New English Bible	NEB
New International Version	NIV
New King James Version .	NKJV
Revised Standard Version .	RSV
Today's English Version (Good News Bible)	TEV

Animals and
Plants

Animals

The Bible tends to look upon nature more from the perspective of human experience than in terms of scientific interest. Bible writers frequently draw spiritual lessons from their observations, letting us know that God created all things and is concerned for all creation, and that not even a common sparrow falls to the ground without his notice (Matt. 10:29).

The Bible names scores of specific animals, but many of these names are simply the educated guesses of translators. In some cases, the meaning is obvious; in others, the context gives helpful clues. Frequently passages offer no clues as to which specific animals are intended. In those cases, the meaning of animal names has been lost.

This problem is complicated by the fact that animal life in the Middle East has changed over the centuries. One naturalist claimed it was impossible that certain passages of Scripture could really mean *lion* because no lions lived in the Holy Land. But, as is true in many areas of the world, some animals of the biblical world have since become extinct.

Over the centuries the words used to describe certain animals have changed. Scholars who have done much work in the language of the Bible and have studied the evidence from archaeology are not always final in their conclusions. When a single term has as many as ten possible meanings, it is no wonder that different names are given for the same animals in Bible translations.

The Bible classifies animals quite broadly. Sometimes its terms are unfamiliar to modern ears. For instance, Genesis 1:28 divides animal life into fish, fowl, and living things. The words *flesh* and *beast* often imply animal life in general. *Beast* also refers to wildlife, in contrast to *cattle*, which means the domesticated animals (sheep, goats, asses, and pigs, as well as cows and oxen). *Fowl* means all bird life. Since Genesis 1:20 refers to fish, *whales* probably indicates larger sea creatures. *Creeping things* (swarming things) can be used for reptiles, amphibians, insects, and small animals that scamper around, such as mice.

The most basic division of animal life—clean and unclean—was in effect very early in Israel's history. Clean animals, the Jews believed, were acceptable to God for sacrifices and were permitted as food. All others were considered unclean, or unacceptable for sacrificing or eating.

Guidelines for distinguishing between clean and unclean animals are given in detail in Leviticus 11. Of the larger mammals, God said, "Whatever divides the hoof, having cloven hooves and chewing the cud—that you may eat" (Lev. 11:3). Birds were an important source of food, so the few unclean ones were listed. These were mostly scavenger birds that ate flesh. Though neighboring peoples ate lizards, snakes, and turtles, Jews considered all reptiles unclean. Fish with scales and fins were clean; but shellfish, eels, and sharks were unclean. Most insects were unclean, with the exception of locusts, grasshoppers, and some beetles.

Early Christians inherited this historic concern of the Hebrew people with clean and unclean animals. The Christians' concern was whether meat bought in the marketplace might have come from Roman sacrifices. Paul counseled them that nothing was "unclean of itself" (Rom. 14:14).

Since the Fall, people have sacrificed animals to God. The first biblical mention of this practice is Abel's offering of a lamb (Gen. 4:4). Animal sacrifice was an essential part of Jewish worship until the temple in Jerusalem was destroyed in A.D. 70.

Moses spelled out strict rules for animal sacrifice as recorded in the book of Leviticus. Only clean animals were acceptable, and they had to be at least eight days old, with no blemishes or flaws. A bullock, kid, or lamb was the usual offering. In some cases, people could bring doves or pigeons. A poor family, who could not afford even a bird, might offer a measure of flour in its place.

Although they practiced animal sacrifice, the Jewish people believed in humane treatment of their animals. The OT contains warnings against mistreating livestock. The Law provided that animals should receive a day of rest during the week, along with their masters. Unlike their neighbors, the Israelites did not worship animals. Egypt, for instance, considered the bull and cat sacred, and Greece worshiped the serpent. It was common for a nation of the ancient world to be represented by an animal on its coins. The prohibition against making graven images prevented this practice in the nation of Israel.

The following animals are mentioned or implied in the Bible. This list is keyed to the NKJV, with cross-references from five additional popular translations—KJV, NASB, NEB, NIV, and RSV. Animals in this listing include mammals, insects, and reptiles.

Addax. (See *Antelope.*)

Adder. (See *Snake.*)

Ant. Approximately 100 species of ants lived in the Holy Land. Harvester ants are the ones meant in Proverbs 6:6–8 and 30:25. These tiny insects settle near grain fields, carrying seed after seed into their private storehouses. In cold weather they cluster together and hibernate. When winter comes, they have food stored up until the next harvest.

God has provided ants with such amazing instincts that they appear to reason and plan ahead. If stored grain gets wet, they haul it out into the sun to dry. Their hard work was considered a worthy example for human beings by the writer of Proverbs.

Antelope. Antelope are cud-chewing, hollow-horned animals related to goats. Early European Bible translators were unacquainted with antelope, which roamed the grassy plains and forests of Asia and Af-

rica, so they called the antelope *deer* instead. Antelope, or deer, are listed among clean wild game (Deut. 14:5), and among King Solomon's table provisions (1 Kings 4:23).

When threatened, antelope flee in breathtaking leaps. So speedy were they that hunters in Bible times sometimes needed nets to catch them (Isa. 51:20). Sometimes a grazing herd of antelope is joined by other animals that profit from their ability to spot an enemy or smell water at a great distance.

Various Bible translations mention three types of antelope. The *addax* is a large, light-colored antelope with spiral horns. The *oryx* is a large African antelope, whose long horns are nearly straight. Most familiar to Bible writers was the *gazelle*, which stands less than a yard (approximately one meter) high at the shoulders.

The word *gazelle* is Arabic for "affectionate." Young gazelles were taken as pets. Poets made much of their dark, liquid eyes and delicate beauty. King David's soldier, Asahel, gifted with both speed and endurance, was "as fleet of foot as a wild gazelle" (2 Sam. 2:18). The woman of good works whom Peter raised to life was called *Tabitha* (Hebrew for "gazelle"), or *Dorcas* (Acts 9:36). The Dorcas gazelle, once common, almost became extinct. Now protected by the modern nation of Israel, it is an agricultural nuisance.

Ape. King Solomon brought apes from tropical and semitropical regions of the world to Israel. Solomon's zoo probably contained a variety of apes, monkeys, and baboons (1 Kings 10:22; 2 Chron. 9:21). Some commentators suggest that Isaiah's reference to the "satyrs" who "dance" and "cry to [their] fellow[s]" (Isa. 13:21; 34:14, KJV) would fit the dog-faced baboon honored by the Egyptians. (See also *Monkey.*)

Asp. (See *Snake.*)

Ass. (See *Donkey.*)

Baboon. (See *Ape.*)

Badger. Only the skin of badgers is mentioned in the Bible, and even this is questionable. Exodus 26:14 and Numbers 4:6–25 speak of the coverings for the tent of the tabernacle. The Hebrew word *tachash* is translated *badger skins*. However, no one really knows what the Hebrews meant by this word. Other translators render it as *goatskins* (RSV), *porpoise-hides* (NEB), or *hides of sea cows* (NIV).

Possibly this word did mean badgers. Coarse badger hair would certainly be a protective cushion between the fine fabrics in which the articles of worship were wrapped for travel. The KJV translates the word as *badgers' skins* in Ezekiel 16:10, which refers to a foot covering. The RSV translates *leather*.

Bat. Bats are flying mammals. They are included on the list of unclean fowl (Lev. 11:19). About 15 species of bats live in the Holy Land. Most feed on insects or fruit.

Bats hunt their food at night. An amazing built-in sonar system enables them to fly safely in total darkness. They sleep hanging upside down, often with their wings wrapped around them. Some species gather in caves. Isaiah 2:20 pictures discarded idols being cast "to the moles and bats," as if to say that is where such abominations belong.

Bear. In OT times, bears were threats to humans and beasts. They ate honey, fruit, and livestock and harmed both crops and herds. Bears are easily angered, and the Asian black bear is exceptionally fierce. This bear is prone to attack, with or without provocation, as did the two female bears that mauled those who taunted the prophet Elisha (2 Kings 2:24). It was a mark of David's courage that he killed a bear that stole from his flock (1 Sam. 17:34–37).

A bear "robbed of her cubs" (2 Sam. 17:8) was legendary because of her fierceness. Since bears are rather clumsy, they sometimes lie in ambush, waiting for prey to come to them (Lam. 3:10). The era of peace shall arrive when, as Isaiah 11:7 predicts, "the cow and the bear shall graze" side by side.

Bee. Bees are not mentioned often in the Bible, but honey is. Honey was the major sweetening substance for primitive peoples. Beekeeping was practiced in Canaan. Indeed, the Jews spoke of the Promised Land as a region flowing with milk and honey.

Bees remind us of honey, but biblical writers saw angry bees as a symbol of God's wrath (Ps. 118:12). These insects can be ferocious when disturbed or threatened. Wild bees often choose strange hives. They can hide their honeycombs in the crannies of high rocks (Deut. 32:13). One swarm even settled in the carcass of a lion (Judg. 14:8).

Beetle. Beetles fly but they do not leap (Lev. 11:22). Crickets, which are related to locusts, both fly and leap. Some scholars contend that *katydid,* or *locusts,* is more likely the correct translation of this one biblical reference to beetles or crickets.

Behemoth. *Behemoth* could refer to *elephant, crocodile, hippopotamus, water buffalo,* or *mythological monster.* The word appears in Job 40:15 and Job 41:1, where God humbles Job by praising two of his creations, behemoth and Leviathan. *Hippopotamus* is probably the best choice of the possibilities. Hippos submerge themselves in rivers and bask in cool marshes. Yet they can climb up riverbanks and hillsides, devouring vegetation. An angered hippo can bite a person in half or crush a canoe with its enormous jaws.

Bittern. This bird is similar to the heron and was a creature that dwelt in ruined places—a symbol of abandonment (Isa. 14:23, KJV).

Bitterns can be found in marshes all over the world. Their loud cries, hollow and drumlike, boom through the darkness while they hunt their prey. Ancients saw bitterns as omens of desolation and prophecies of evil. Bitterns are large birds, about two feet long, with a gift of camouflage. Because bitterns become statuelike with their long beaks tilted skyward, they can be overlooked among reeds swaying gently in the wind. Bitterns eat frogs, snails, worms, and small fish.

Other translations of the Hebrew word for bittern are *hedgehog* (Isa. 14:23; Zeph. 2:14, RSV) and *porcupine* (Isa. 14:23, NKJV; Isa. 34:11, RSV, NKJV).

Black vulture. (See *Osprey.*)

Boar. (See *Swine.*)

Buck. (See *Deer.*)

Buffalo. (See *Cattle.*)

Bull, Bullock. (See *Cattle.*)

Bustard. (See *Porcupine.*)

Buzzard. (See *Vulture.*)

Calf. (See *Cattle.*)

Camel. Although it is an ugly beast, the camel is prized in desert countries. From the time of Abraham, the Bible mentions camels frequently, mostly in lists of possessions. Large herds of camels were a sign of wealth. For example, Job owned 3,000 camels.

Jeremiah spoke of the "swift dromedary" (Jer. 2:23), a camel raised for riding and racing. Jesus talked of "blind guides, who strain out a gnat and swallow a camel" (Matt. 23:24), and stated, "It is easier for a camel to go through the eye of a needle than for a rich man to enter the kingdom of God" (Matt. 19:24).

In addition to serving as a beast of burden, the camel provided milk and leather for the ancient Hebrew people. PHOTO BY GUSTAV JEENINGA

Camels are bad-tempered, prone to spit and grumble when they take on a load. But they are well suited for harsh desert life. With a heavy coat as insulation, these animals perspire little; and their well-balanced systems do not require much liquid. They can go for weeks without water. When they do drink, they take only enough to replace lost moisture. Each of their three stomachs can hold 23 liters (five gallons) of water. In the hump on their backs, camels store fat for times when food is scarce; the hump shrinks when the body draws on that reserve.

Camels stand 20 meters (six feet) or higher at the shoulder. They are trained to kneel on leathery knees to take on a load. They hold their heads high with what seems to be a haughty air, but they are merely peering out from under bushy eyebrows. Like their tightly closing lips and nostrils, their eyebrows protect against desert sandstorms. Their tough feet are ideal for walking through sharp rocks and hot sands.

The Hebrew people used camels primarily as pack animals. They were indispensable to traveling the desert routes, carrying several hundred pounds on their backs. The Jews also rode camels and milked them, although they considered camels unclean and did not eat them (Lev. 11:4).

The Arabs, however, allowed no part of a camel to go to waste. They ate camel meat and wove the soft hair into warm, durable cloth. John the Baptist was clothed in a garment of camel's hair (Matt. 3:4). The tough hide made good leather for sandals and water bags, and camel-dung chips served as fuel. Even the dried bones of camels were carved like ivory.

Desert tribes rode camels to war (Judg. 7:12), and camels were seized as spoils of war.

Cankerworm. (See *Worm*.)

Cat. Cats were common throughout the ancient world, but they are mentioned only in the Apocrypha (Epistle of Jer. 21). The Hebrews may have avoided cats since the Egyptians worshiped them. The Romans made cats a symbol of liberty. Cats and mongooses were probably used to control rats and mice in places where grain was stored.

Caterpillar. (See *Moth; Worm*.)

Cattle. *Cattle* is usually a general reference to livestock (Gen. 30:32; 31:10, KJV). What we think of as cattle, the Bible calls

oxen. A wild ox—a massive, untamable beast—is also mentioned (Job 39:9–10). The KJV calls it a *unicorn*.

The Bible uses specific terms to refer to cattle: *kine*, for instance, the plural of cow, and *beeves*, the plural of beef. Until she bore a calf, a young female was known as a *heifer*; a young male was a *bullock*.

Some oxen were raised for sacrifice or prime quality meat. Rather than run with the herd, they were fed in a small enclosure. *Fatling, fatted calf, fed beasts, stalled ox, fattened cattle*, and *yearling* described such well-cared-for animals. One translation refers to *buffalo* (2 Sam. 6:13, NEB), when *fatling* seems to be the obvious reference. A similar term, *firstling*, refers to the first offspring of any livestock. All firstborn males belonged to the Lord (Gen. 4:4; Exod. 13:12).

Oxen were hollow-horned, divided-hoof, cud-chewing animals considered clean by the Jews. They needed considerable food and space because of their large size, so a person who kept many of them was rich indeed. The pastures and grain country of Bashan, located east of the Jordan River and south of Damascus, were ideal to raise oxen.

Scripture speaks of oxen as a measure of wealth (Job 42:12), beasts of burden (1 Chron. 12:40), draft animals (Deut. 22:10), meat (Gen. 18:7), and sacrificial offerings (2 Sam. 6:13).

Bulls (as opposed to work oxen) were allowed a large measure of freedom as strong, fearsome beasts. The OT showed concern for the humane treatment of oxen (Deut. 22:4) and provided legal recourse for a person wounded by an ox (Exod. 21:28–36).

While in Egypt, the Hebrews were surrounded by bull worshipers. After the Exodus and while in the wilderness, Aaron melted down their jewelry to make an idol, a golden calf. The people were punished severely for this idolatry, but some of their descendants fell into the same sin (Exod. 32; 1 Kings 12:28).

Chameleon. (See *Lizard*.)

Chamois. The KJV has *chamois* for the goat or antelope of Deuteronomy 14:5. The chamois (goat antelope) of Europe never lived in Canaan. Since the Hebrews were allowed to eat this animal, it must have been familiar in their country. It may have been a wild goat or a type of wild mountain sheep. (See also *Sheep.*)

Chicken. (See *Fowl.*)

Cobra. (See *Snake.*)

Cock. (See *Fowl.*)

Cockatrice. (See *Snake.*)

Colt. (See *Donkey; Horse.*)

Coney. (See *Rock badger.*)

Cormorant. Both the prophets Isaiah and Zephaniah linked the cormorant (KJV, or *pelican,* NKJV) with the bittern to describe the ruin God brings in judgment upon humanity's proud cities (Isa. 34:11; Zeph. 2:14). The cormorant (or *fisher owl,* NKJV) was listed among the few birds the Israelites were not to eat (Lev. 11:17; Deut. 14:17).

Cormorants are large fish-eating birds, related to pelicans, with hooked beaks and webbed feet. They dive into the water to catch fish; they swim well; and they can stay under water for a long time.

The cormorant found in Israel has a black head, yellow-circled eyes, and green highlights in its black plumage. As the prophets suggested (Isa. 34:11; Zeph. 2:14), the cormorant would be an unsettling sight in the swampy pools of a ruined city.

Cow. (See *Cattle.*)

Crane. Cranes are the largest of several migratory birds that fly over the Holy Land in noisy flocks of thousands.

Hezekiah, king of Judah, thinking he was dying, chattered and clamored like a *crane* (Isa. 38:14; *swift,* NIV). With a windpipe coiled like a French horn, cranes produce one of the loudest bird calls in the world.

Cricket. (See *Beetle.*)

Crocodile. The land crocodile appears as an unclean beast in the RSV rendering of Leviticus 11:30. Many scholars assume that the crocodile is the mysterious Leviathan (*whale,* NEB) of Job 41:1–34; it is also mentioned in Psalms 74:14 and 104:26 and in Isaiah 27:1.

Crocodiles used to live in rivers in the Holy Land, including the Jordan, but they have now disappeared. Long, heavy animals, crocodiles have tough hides covered with overlapping scales. Their eyes and nostrils are high on their head, so they can float almost totally submerged. Crocodiles are extremely dangerous, with strong jaws and sharp teeth. They ordinarily eat small animals, birds, and fish, but occasionally will attack larger animals or people.

Crow. (See *Raven.*)

Cuckoo. Cuckoos are insect-eating migratory birds that appear in Israel during the summer. Scholars feel that the Hebrew word was incorrectly rendered *cuckow* in the KJV. There is no obvious reason why the cuckoo would be considered an unclean bird (Lev. 11:16; Deut. 14:15). The NKJV translates *seagull.*

Cuckow. (See *Cuckoo.*)

Deer. From early times, deer were game animals. Isaac's son Esau was "a skillful hunter" (Gen. 25:27). Isaac's craving for deer meat enabled Jacob to steal his dying father's blessing (Gen. 27). Deer were still plentiful in Solomon's day and were served at his table (1 Kings 4:23). Jews could eat deer because this animal chews the cud and divides the hoof.

The Bible contains many references to deer. The animal was admired for its agility and grace, its ability to sense danger quickly, and its swiftness. Biblical writers also noted the doe's gentle care of her young. A young deer is called a *fawn* (Song of Sol. 4:5; 7:3). The psalmist thought of the long journey for water that a deer faces in dry seasons and exclaimed: "As the deer pants for the water brooks, so pants my soul for You, O God" (Ps. 42:1). Isaiah thought of the feelings of joy and elation when he wrote, "The lame shall leap like a deer" (35:6).

Scholars are not sure of the precise species or kind of deer Esau hunted or Solomon served. The terms *stag* or *buck* (male), *hart* (male), and *hind* (female) are used of the red deer common in Europe, which has never lived in Canaan. Likely candidates are the *fallow deer* (Deut. 14:5, KJV), common in Mesopotamia, and the *roe deer*, often called by its male name, *roe buck* (Deut. 14:5, RSV). (See also *Antelope*.)

Dog. In ancient Israel, calling someone a dog was one of the most offensive ways of insulting that person. The Bible mentions dogs frequently, most of them derogatory. Even in NT times, Jews called Gentiles dogs (Matt. 15:26). The term *dog* also referred to a male prostitute (Deut. 23:18). Unbelievers who will be shut out of the New Jerusalem are termed dogs in Revelation 22:15—probably a reference to their sexual immorality. Moslems later applied the insult to Christians.

Although small in size, donkeys were strong enough to carry travelers and transport heavy loads in Bible times.

The dog may have been the first animal in the ancient world to be tamed. Ancient Egyptians raced greyhounds (mentioned in Prov. 30:31, NKJV), and the Greeks raised mastiffs. But dogs were more wild than tame. They often banded together in packs and lived off the refuse and food supplies of a village. Some dogs were useful as watchdogs or guardians of sheep, but even they were not altogether reliable (Isa. 56:10).

Donkey. One of the first animals tamed was the donkey, referred to as the *ass* in the same translations. Wild donkeys (referred to as the *onager* in Job 39:5, NKJV) also roamed the land. "Like a wild donkey" (Hos. 8:9) described a headstrong, untamed nature. But the domesticated donkey was an obedient servant.

Donkeys stand about 1.3 meters (four feet) high. They are gray, reddish-brown, or white. The long-suffering donkey often won the affection of the household and was decorated with beads and bright ribbons. But their true role was to serve as work animals. They trampled seed, turned the millstone to grind grain, and pulled the plow.

Donkey caravans were the freight trains and transport trucks of ancient times. These animals carried great weight in spite of their small size. Since they required only a fraction as much fodder as horses, they were more economical to own. Donkeys were also safe and comfortable to ride, ridden by rich and poor alike. When Jesus entered Jerusalem, he signaled his peaceful intentions by riding a young donkey rather than a prancing war-horse.

The offspring of a male donkey *(jack)* and a female horse *(mare)* is a mule. The mule had the surefootedness and endurance of the donkey, coupled with the greater size and strength of the horse. Crossbreeding like this was outlawed among the Jewish people (Lev. 19:19), but from David's time mules were imported and increasingly used by the Israelites (2 Sam. 18:9; 1 Kings 18:5). Ezra 2:66 records that the Israelites brought 245 mules with them when they returned from captivity in Babylon.

Dove. Doves and pigeons belong to the same family. They are mentioned in the Bible as if they are the same animal. The rock dove is the wild ancestor of our common street pigeon. Turtledoves are migrants. They spend the months of April to October in the Holy Land, filling the air with soft cooing when they arrive each spring (Song of Sol. 2:11–12).

Doves come in several colors, from pure white to the chestnut-colored palm turtledove. Even the plain gray pigeon has a silver sheen. David longed for "wings like a dove" (Ps. 55:6), so he could fly away from his enemies.

Pigeons were probably the first domesticated bird. When people realized doves could travel long distances and always find their way home, they used them to carry messages. Homing pigeons have keen eyes with which they spot landmarks to help them stay on the right route.

Hebrews ate pigeons and, from Abraham's time, used them in sacrifice. Even the poor could provide a pigeon or two for worship, as Joseph and Mary did at Jesus' circumcision (Luke 2:21–24).

Doves appear to express affection, stroking each other, mating for life, and sharing nesting and parenting duties. They are gentle birds that never resist attack or retaliate against their enemies. Even when her young are attacked, a dove will give only a pitiful call of distress.

Because of its innocence and gentle nature, the dove is a common religious symbol. The Holy Spirit took the form of a dove at Jesus' baptism (Matt. 3:16; Mark 1:10; Luke 3:22). The dove also symbolizes peace, love, forgiveness, and the church.

Dragon. Dragons are imaginary beasts with a long history in the folklore of many cultures. Usually the dragon is a crafty creature that represents evil. The word *dragon*, as used in some translations of the Bible, is often confusing. Occasionally this occurs when the intended meaning was probably *jackal* (Lam. 4:3, RSV), *sea ser-pent*, or *serpent* (Ps. 91:13, RSV), or even *crocodile* (Ezek. 29:3–4).

This huge fire-breathing monster with terrifying wings and claws symbolizes Satan (Rev. 12:3–17; 16:13; 20:2). In early Christian history, dragons represented sin. Christian art often depicts a dragon at the feet of Jesus—to show his triumph over sin.

Dromedary. (See *Camel.*)

Eagle. Eagles are included among the unclean birds mentioned in the Bible (Lev. 11:13, NKJV), but they were admired as majestic birds. The golden eagle, which is actually dark brown with sprinkles of gold, has a 26-meter (eight-foot) wingspread. It nests in high places that are inaccessible (Jer. 49:16). There, in a nest made larger each year, the eagle hatches two eggs. Usually only one eaglet survives to adulthood.

Eagles have keen eyesight and can spot their prey while soaring hundreds of feet in the air. Like lightning bolts, they drop to seize it, killing it quickly with their powerful claws. Then they swoop back to their nests to rip the meat apart and share with their young.

Mother eagles carry their eaglets on their back until they master the art of flying. Moses used this familiar picture from nature to describe God's care for the Israelites. God carried his people on his wings (Deut. 32:11–12) as he delivered them from slavery in Egypt.

Eagles can stay aloft for hours, rarely moving their wings and riding wind currents. But many passages in the Bible also speak of the swiftness of the eagles' flight (Deut. 28:49).

The belief that eagles renew their strength and youthful appearance after shedding their feathers gave rise to Psalm 103:5 and Isaiah 40:31. Eagles do have a long life span, living 20 to 30 years in the wild, and longer in captivity.

OT prophets also spoke of eagles as symbols of God's judgment (Jer. 48:40; Ezek. 17:3, 7). In Revelation 12:14, the phrase "two wings of a great eagle" portrays God's intervention to deliver his people from persecution.

Eagle owl. (See *Owl.*)

Elephant. No elephants lived in the Middle East, but they were native to the neighboring continents of Africa and Asia. Wealthy Jews sometimes imported the ivory that came from their great tusks. King Solomon "made a great throne of ivory, and overlaid it with pure gold" (1 Kings 10:18). And King Ahab built an "ivory house" (1 Kings 22:39).

Ewe. (See *Sheep.*)

Falcon. In some translations of the Bible the falcon appears in the lists of unclean birds (Lev. 11:14; Deut. 14:13, NKJV). As a bird of prey, it is often grouped with hawks. But a falcon is not a true hawk. The sport of hunting with trained falcons originated in ancient Persia. Great numbers of falcons are still seen in the Holy Land.

Fallow deer. (See *Deer.*)

Fawn. (See *Deer.*)

Ferret. (See *Lizard.*)

Fish. One authority says 45 species of fish were found in the inland waters and many more lived in the Mediterranean Sea. The Bible gives no details on any specific species of fish.

Fish, like other animals, were divided into clean and unclean. Those with fins and scales were clean and they made a popular meal. Unclean fish included catfish, eels, and probably sharks, lampreys, and shellfish. The Hebrews considered whales and porpoises as fish, since they lived in the sea.

Fishing was a major industry among the Hebrews. Jerusalem had a Fish Gate, and presumably a fish market. Fish were caught with nets (Hab. 1:15), hooks (Isa. 19:8; Matt. 17:27), and harpoons and spears (Job 41:7). The catch was preserved by salting and drying or storing in salt water.

The Bible contains many references to fish and fishing. Habakkuk 1:14–17 compares captive Israel to helpless fish gathered into a dragnet by her enemies. Jesus, on the other hand, called his disciples to become fishers of men (Matt. 4:19; Mark 1:17). From early times, the fish has symbolized Christianity. Believers used the Greek word for fish—*ichthus*—as an acrostic for "Jesus Christ, Son of God, Savior":

I	*Iesous,* "Jesus"
X (CH)	*Xristos,* "Christ"
TH	*Theos,* "God"
U	*Huios,* "Son"
S	*Soter,* "Savior"

Fisher owl. (See *Cormorant.*)

Flea. Fleas flourished in the sand and dust of the Holy Land. Classified as parasites, these tiny insects attach themselves to a body and suck blood from their host. Fleas have no wings, but they do have strong legs and can jump several inches at one leap. The flea that can live on humans is tiny, but it can be very irritating. David described himself as a mere flea being pursued by a king (1 Sam. 24:14; 26:20), meaning that although he seemed insignificant, he irritated King Saul.

Fly. The flies of the Bible included the common housefly and other two-winged insects. Many of these were biting insects. This explains the devouring flies of Psalm 78:45. The plague of flies upon the Egyptians probably included houseflies, stinging sand flies, gnats, and mosquitoes.

The prophet Isaiah's reference to the "fly that is in the farthest part of the rivers of Egypt" (7:18) may have been a symbol of swarms of Egyptian soldiers. Or he could have intended the dreaded tsetse fly of Africa, which spreads sleeping sickness. Still another possibility is the olive fly, which ruined ripe olives.

The "fly in the ointment" (Eccles. 10:1) has become a proverb as well as Jesus' "straining out a gnat"—which referred to the custom of straining wine to take out the impurities before it was served (Matt. 23:24).

Fowl. We assume that hens and roosters (cocks) were common, but the Bible rarely mentions them. Domestic chickens probably descended from the red jungle fowl of Asia. Cocks were bred for the ancient sport of cockfighting before hens were raised for meat and eggs.

The crowing of roosters served as alarm clocks. Cocks crowed about midnight and again about 3:00 A.M. Soldiers often rotated their guard duty at this regular signal. Jesus predicted that Peter would deny him three times before the cock crowed (Matt. 26:34).

Wild or tame, chickens gather in flocks. Jesus must have been familiar with this flocking instinct when he spoke of a mother hen that tucks a whole brood of chicks under her wings for safety (Luke 13:34).

The fatted fowl provided for King Solomon (1 Kings 4:23) may have been geese. Ancient carvings from Megiddo show women carrying fat geese. Geese also appear in Egyptian tomb paintings.

Fox. Foxes were common predators in Bible times. Since they fed on small rodents like rats and mice, they helped to protect the grain crops, but their fondness for grapes caused farmers much grief. Sometimes they tunneled under protective walls to feast on grapevines (Song of Sol. 2:15). Foxes also settled in holes and burrows, often those abandoned by other animals. Jesus used this to say that although foxes have holes, the Son of man had nowhere to lay his head (Matt. 8:20).

Foxes have keen senses of sight, smell, and hearing. They are also clever enough to lie in wait for prey. They may even play dead to attract a bird within striking range. When hunted, they are cunning and devious, misleading their pursuers. Jesus compared Herod, the Roman tetrarch of Galilee and Perea, to a fox because of his crafty, devious nature (Luke 13:32).

The land of Shual mentioned in 1 Samuel 13:17 may have been fox country, for *shual* means *fox* or *jackal*. (See also *Jackal*.)

How Versions of the Bible Sometimes Differ in Translation of Animal Names

This chart shows that five popular translations of the Bible sometimes disagree in their translations of the names of animals in the Bible. These differences exist because scholars disagree on the precise meaning of these words in the original language in which the Bible was written.

Reference	NKJV	KJV	RSV	NIV	NEB
Exod. 8:17	lice	lice	gnats	gnats	maggots
Exod. 36:19	badger skins	badgers' skins	goat-skins	hides of sea cows	porpoise-hides
Lev. 11:18	jackdaw	pelican	pelican	desert owl	horned owl
Num. 23:22	wild ox	unicorn	wild ox	wild ox	wild ox
2 Sam. 6:13	fatted sheep	fatlings	fatling	fattened calf	buffalo
1 Kings 10:22	monkeys	peacocks	peacocks	baboons	monkeys
Ps. 104:18	rock badgers	conies	badgers	coneys	rock-badgers
Isa. 11:8	viper	cockatrice	adder	viper	viper
Isa. 14:23	porcupine	bittern	hedgehog	owl	bustard
Isa. 34:11	pelican	cormorant	hawk	desert owl	horned owl
Jer. 8:7	swallow	swallow	swallow	thrush	wryneck
Lam. 5:18	foxes	foxes	jackals	jackals	jackals
Amos 4:9	locust	palmerworm	locust	locust	locust
Zeph. 2:14	pelican	cormorant	vulture	desert owl	horned owl

Frog. Frogs are mentioned several times in the Bible (Exod. 8:2–13; Ps. 105:30; Rev. 16:13). All but the passage in Revelation refer to the plague of frogs in Egypt. The ancient Egyptians connected frogs with fertility and the life cycle, so they considered frogs sacred. It must have caused great concern when the frogs multiplied uncontrollably, then died, and the Egyptians had to gather these sacred animals into stinking heaps. Revelation 16:13 symbolizes them as unclean spirits.

Gazelle. (See *Antelope.*)

Gecko. (See *Lizard.*)

Gier eagle. (See *Vulture.*)

Glede. (See *Hawk.*)

Gnat. (See *Fly.*)

Goat. Hebrew shepherds treasured the goat because it was such a useful animal. They wove its hair into rough cloth. They drank the goat's milk, which is sweet and more nutritious than cow's and is ideal for making cheese. They used goatskin bottles to transport water and wine. When the hide of these containers wore thin, they leaked and had to be patched (Josh. 9:4; Matt. 9:17).

Goats often grazed with sheep in mixed flocks. Unlike their gentle and helpless cousins, goats were independent, willful, and curious. Bible writers sometimes used goats to symbolize irresponsible leadership (Jer. 50:8). In Jesus' parable of the Final Judgment (Matt. 25:32–33), the goats represent the unrighteous who will not enter his kingdom.

Goats were sacrificed in the worship system of ancient Israel. On the Day of Atonement, the high priest used two goats. He sacrificed one, sprinkling its blood upon the back of the other (the scapegoat). This scapegoat was then sent into the wilderness, symbolically bearing the sins of the people (Lev. 16:10).

Young goats are referred to as *kids* in the Bible (Gen. 27:9, 16; Num. 7:87). The wild goat is known as the *ibex* (Deut. 14:5, RSV, NIV; *mountain goat*, NKJV; *pygarg*, KJV).

Goose. (See *Fowl.*)

Grasshopper. Numerous references to grasshoppers and locusts show what an impact these insects had in the hot, dry lands of the ancient world. Some of these references are literal (Exod. 10:4–19) while others are symbolic (Num. 13:33).

The terms *grasshopper* and *locust* are often used interchangeably. A locust is a kind of grasshopper. Another term used for these insects is *katydid* (Lev. 11:22, NIV), which has a brown-colored body two to three inches long. Airborne, with two sets of wings, the locust was dreaded because of its destructive power as a foliage-eating insect.

The eighth plague that God sent upon the Egyptians was an invasion of locusts. Millions of these insects may be included in one swarm, which usually occurs in the spring. Locusts in such numbers speedily eat every plant in sight, totally destroying the crops. A locust plague is practically unstoppable. Water does not work; for when enough locusts drown, the survivors use their bodies as a bridge. They have also been known to smother fires that had been set to destroy them. Modern farmers still wrestle with this problem, often resorting to poisoning the adults and harrowing fields in the fall to destroy the eggs before they can hatch in the spring.

Revelation 9 presents a nightmarish prospect: locusts with special powers will be unleashed upon the human race for five months.

Locusts do not always appear in swarms. Hot weather normally brings a few solitary grasshoppers and locusts to the Holy Land. Under certain conditions of climate and in times of food scarcity, chemical changes take place in the female locust. These cause more eggs to hatch, sending millions of locusts into the air at the same time in search of food.

Many people, including the Jews, eat locusts (Lev. 11:22). These insects may be boiled, fried, or dried. Locusts were part of the wilderness diet of John the Baptist (Matt. 3:4).

Great lizard. (See *Lizard*.)

Great owl. (See *Owl*.)

Greyhound. (See *Dog*.)

Griffon. (See *Vulture*.)

Grub. (See *Worm*.)

Hare. Hares were plentiful, but they are mentioned in the Bible only as forbidden food (Lev. 11:6; *rabbit*, NIV, NASB). They look like large rabbits with longer ears and legs. The common jackrabbit is actually a hare. Unlike rabbits, hares are born furry and able to see. Hares were mistakenly thought to chew the cud, but they were considered unclean because they did not have divided hooves (Lev. 11:6; Deut. 14:7). Perhaps they were forbidden because they are rodents, but the Hebrews' Arab neighbors did not hesitate to hunt them for food.

Hart. (See *Deer*.)

Hawk. Hawks are fierce little members of the eagle and vulture family. Adult hawks vary from one to two feet in length. They are known for their exceptional eyesight, which is about eight times as keen as a human's. Proverbs 1:17 says, "Surely, in vain the net is spread in the sight of any bird."

Hawks not only detect nets from a distance, but they can see mice, insects, and other birds. They strike with devastating swiftness, their powerful claws crushing their prey, which they eat whole.

Some 18 species of hawks exist in the Holy Land, among them the small sparrow hawk. This hawk, which Egyptians considered sacred, nests in a hollow tree, amid old ruins, or upon a rock. As winter approaches, it migrates to a warmer climate.

Harrier hawks live in the valleys and low-lying plains. They glide near the ground and "harry" other birds by forcing them to land.

Kites (gledes) are a larger breed of hawk, with long narrow wings (Deut. 14:13). Red kites, black kites, and Egyptian kites live throughout the Middle East. Kites in Syria hide their nests by draping them with cloth scraps or animal skins. Just as they abstained from eating other birds of prey, Israelites did not eat hawks (Lev. 11:16; Deut. 14:15).

Hedgehog. (See *Porcupine*.)

Heifer. (See *Cattle*.)

Hen. (See *Fowl*.)

Heron. The Bible mentions herons only in the lists of unclean birds (Lev. 11:19; Deut. 14:18). Several species of herons and egrets made their home in Israel. Egyptian carvings picture herons and their nests among the reeds of marshes and lakes. Tall and graceful, herons fly with their necks curled and their long legs stretched out behind. They eat fish, frogs, and small reptiles, which they spear with their long, sharp beaks.

Hind. (See *Deer*.)

Hippopotamus. (See *Behemoth*.)

Hoopoe. Hoopoes are beautiful birds with a disgusting habit of probing in foul places for insects with their sharp, slender beak. Their wing feathers bear a zebra stripe, and their heads sport lovely crowns of feathers. When frightened, they may flutter their crest or drop to the ground and play dead. The offensive odor picked up from their feeding grounds is enough to drive away most of their enemies.

Called *lapwing* in the KJV, hoopoes are unclean birds (Lev. 11:19).

Horned owl. (See *Owl*.)

Hornet. (See *Wasp*.)

Horse. Horses are mentioned often in the Bible but they were of little importance to the average Hebrew, who found it more practical to keep a donkey to ride or an ox to pull the plow. Horses were traded for food when money failed during a famine in Egypt (Gen. 47:17). Some kings used swift horses rather than camels to carry messages (Esther 8:10, 14). But for the most part, Hebrews thought of horses in terms of war.

Pharaoh's horses and chariots pursued when Moses led the Israelites out of Egypt (Exod. 14:9). Their Canaanite enemies met them with many horses and chariots, but they still fell before the Israelites (Josh. 11:4–9).

Solomon had a sizable cavalry as well as horses to draw war chariots.

Jeremiah used the word *stallion* in speaking of horses (Jer. 8:16; 47:3; 50:11, RSV), warning the nation of Judah that it would fall to a conquering army that would be riding prancing stallions. He also used the symbol of a well-fed, lusty stallion (Jer. 5:8, NKJV) to describe the idolatry and unfaithfulness of God's people.

Revelation 6 predicts four horsemen who will ride out to ravage the earth in the end times. But even more dramatic than this is the entrance of a white horse bearing the King of kings and Lord of lords (Rev. 19:11–16).

Animals in the Bible

Adder (a type of snake)	Prov. 23:32
Ant	Prov. 6:6; 30:25
Antelope (*wild bull* in some translations)	Isa. 51:20
Ape	1 Kings 10:22
Asp (a type of cobra)	Isa. 11:8
Ass	John 12:14
Badger (also translated *coney*)	Exod. 25:5; Lev. 11:5
Bat	Isa. 2:20
Bear	1 Sam. 17:34–37; 2 Kings 2:24; Isa. 11:7; Dan. 7:5; Rev. 13:2
Bee	Judg. 14:8
Beetle	Lev. 11:22
Behemoth	Job 40:15
Camel	Gen. 24:10; Matt. 3:4; 19:24; 23:24
Chameleon	Lev. 11:30
Chamois *(mountain sheep)*	Deut. 14:5
Cock	Matt. 26:34
Cockatrice	Isa. 11:8
Cormorant (large black water bird)	Lev. 11:17
Crane	Isa. 38:14
Cricket (sometimes translated *beetle*)	Lev. 11:22
Crocodile (translated various ways)	Ps. 74:14; Ezek. 29:3; 32:2
Cuckoo (sea gull)	Lev. 11:16
Dog	Judg. 7:5; 1 Kings 21:23–24; Eccles. 9:4; Matt. 15:26–27; Luke 16:21; 2 Pet. 2:22; Rev. 22:15
Dove	Gen. 8:8; 2 Kings 6:25; Matt. 3:16; 10:16; John 2:16
Eagle	Exod. 19:4; Isa. 40:31; Ezek. 1:10; Dan. 7:4; Rev. 4:7; 12:14
Elephant	1 Kings 10:22

Animals in the Bible—*continued*

Falcon (see *Kite*)

Fish	Exod. 7:18; Jon. 1:17; Matt. 14:17; 17:27; Luke 24:42; John 21:9
Flea	1 Sam. 24:14; 26:20
Fly	Exod. 8:16–19; Eccles. 10:1
Fox	Judg. 15:4; Neh. 4:3; Matt. 8:20; Luke 13:32
Frog	Exod. 8:2; Rev. 16:13
Gazelle (often translated *roe* and *roe buck*)	Deut. 12:15

Gecko (see *Lizard*)

Gnat	Matt. 23:24
Goat	Gen. 15:9; 37:31; Lev. 16; Dan. 8:5; Matt. 25:33
Hare (a rodent)	Lev. 11:6
Hart	Deut. 14:5
Hawk	Job 39:26
Heron (stork)	Deut. 14:18
Hoopoe (lapwing)	Lev. 11:19
Hornet	Exod. 23:28; Deut. 7:20; Josh. 24:12
Horse	1 Kings 4:26; 2 Kings 2:11; Rev. 6:2–8; 19:14
Horseleach	Prov. 30:15
Hyena (sometimes translated *beast*)	Eccles. 3:18–19
Jackal	Isa. 34:13
Kite (a bird of prey)	Lev. 11:14
Leopard	Isa. 11:6; Jer. 13:23; Dan. 7:6; Rev. 13:2
Leviathan	Job 41:1
Lion	Judg. 14:8; 1 Kings 13:24; Isa. 65:25; Dan. 6:7; 1 Pet. 5:8; Rev. 4:7; 13:2
Lizard	Lev. 11:30
Locust	Exod. 10:4; Joel 1:4; Matt. 3:4; Rev. 9:3
Louse	Exod. 8:16
Mole (burrowing rat)	Isa. 2:20
Moth	Isa. 50:9; 51:8; Matt. 6:19
Mouse	Isa. 66:17
Mule	2 Sam. 18:9; 1 Kings 1:38
Osprey (fish hawk)	Lev. 11:13
Ossifrage (largest of the vultures)	Lev. 11:13
Ostrich	Lam. 4:3
Owl (sometimes translated *swan*)	Isa. 34:11
Ox (bullock)	1 Sam. 11:7; 15:14; 2 Sam. 6:6; 1 Kings 19:20–21; Isa. 1:3; Dan. 4:25, 32; Luke 14:5, 19
Partridge	1 Sam. 26:20
Peacock	1 Kings 10:22
Pelican	Ps. 102:6
Pygarg (a desert animal)	Deut. 14:5
Quail	Exod. 16:13; Num. 11:31
Raven	Gen. 8:7; 1 Kings 17:4
Rock hyrax	Lev. 11:5
Scorpion	Luke 10:19; Rev. 9:3, 5, 10

Animals in the Bible—*continued*

Serpent	Gen. 3:1; Exod. 4:3; Num. 21:9; Rev. 12:9
Sheep	Gen. 4:2; Exod. 12:5; Luke 15:4; John 10:7
Snail	Ps. 58:8
Sparrow	Matt. 10:31
Spider	Isa. 59:5
Swallow	Isa. 38:14
Swine	Matt. 7:6; 8:32; Luke 15:15–16
Tortoise	Lev. 11:29
Turtledove	Gen. 15:9; Luke 2:24
Unicorn (wild ox)	Num. 23:22
Viper	Isa. 30:6
Weasel	Lev. 11:29
Whale	Gen. 1:21
Wolf	Isa. 11:6; Matt. 7:15
Worm	Job 7:5; 17:14; 21:26; Isa. 14:11; 66:24; Jon. 4:7; Mark 9:43–48

NOTE: *Biblical animals are not always easy to identify, and the names may vary from one translation to another.*

Horseleach. (See *Leech.*)

Hound. (See *Dog.*)

Hyena. Hyenas were plentiful in Bible times. The phrases "doleful creatures" (KJV) and "beasts of the field" (Isa. 13:21; Jer. 12:9) may refer to hyenas. The place named *Zeboim* (1 Sam. 13:18) means "hyena." Members of the dog family, hyenas have square snouts and powerful jaws. They run down prey and may even attack human beings. The Israelites hated hyenas and considered them unclean because they are scavengers. Sometimes they even dug up and devoured dead bodies. Hyenas hunt at night, and their eerie howls sound like demented laughter. A reference by the prophet Isaiah to the hyena is also translated as *jackal* (Isa. 13:22, RSV). (See also *Jackal.*)

Ibex. (See *Goat.*)

Jackal. Isaiah spoke of jackals—wild dogs that make their dens in desolate places (Isa. 34:13). As scavengers, jackals also fed on garbage in towns and villages.

Jackals have an unpleasant smell, and they make yapping, howling noises at night. They are also agricultural pests. Farmers put up shelters for watchmen, who guarded their cucumber fields against jackals. Some heaped up whitewashed stones to frighten the jackals, just as scarecrows are used in other places.

Bible references to jackals are confusing, since *jackal, fox, dragon,* and *wolf* may be used interchangeably, depending on the translation. The foxes to whose tails Samson tied torches were probably jackals, which, unlike foxes, travel in packs (Judg. 15:4). (See also *Fox.*)

Jackdaw. (See *Pelican.*)

Jerboa. (See *Mouse.*)

Katydid. (See *Grasshopper.*)

Kid. (See *Goat.*)

Kine. (See *Cattle.*)

Kite. (See *Hawk.*)

Lamb. (See *Sheep.*)

Lapwing. (See *Hoopoe.*)

Leech. Leeches are worms with suckers at each end of their bodies. One end also contains a mouth. Some species have tiny teeth. Parasitic leeches attach themselves to people or animals and suck blood for nourishment. These leeches secrete chemicals that keep the blood flowing freely.

In primitive times, physicians used leeches to bleed their patients and purge their bodies of what they considered contaminated blood. But untended leeches could cause pain and damage.

Leopard. While leopards were familiar, the Hebrews had good reason to fear them. Smaller and lighter than lions, leopards are better hunters because they are swift, wary, and intelligent, and they can climb trees as easily as domestic cats. Leopards are strong enough to drag their prey to a tree branch, where they can devour it out of reach of lions or hyenas. Although leopards do not usually attack human beings, Jeremiah portrayed one symbolically as an instrument of God's judgment: "A leopard will watch over their cities. Everyone who goes out from there shall be torn in pieces" (Jer. 5:6).

Daniel 7:6 and Revelation 13:2 portray the leopard as a symbol of swift cruelty. Isaiah 11:6, however, speaks of a day of peace when the savage leopard would not harm a young goat.

Leviathan.   (See *Crocodile*.)

Lion.   Lions were the most awesome and dangerous wild beasts. Their tawny hide blended into the golden fields and sandy wastes. Lions hid in forests and sometimes pounced from the thickets near the Jordan River (Jer. 49:19).

Daniel miraculously survived a night in a lions' den (Dan. 6). Samson and David killed lions single-handedly (Judg. 14:5–6; 1 Sam. 17:34–37). Kings hunted lions for sport. According to Ezekiel 19:1–9, lions were also captured with pits and nets.

The lions' majestic appearance and fearsome roar prompted many comparisons. The prophet Joel declared, "The LORD also will roar from Zion" (Joel 3:16). Peter wrote: "Be sober, be vigilant; because your adversary the devil walks about like a roaring lion" (1 Pet. 5:8). (See also Hos. 5:14; *panther*, NEB.)

Largest and grandest of cats, lions are powerful and a swat of their paws can kill. Their massive bodies force them to rely on strength instead of speed for hunting.

Lions look and sound so imposing that they symbolized royalty and courage. The highest compliment biblical writers could give was to indicate that an individual had the face or heart of a lion. *Ari*, the most common term for lion, means "the strong one." Isaiah 29:1 calls Jerusalem *Ariel*, implying that the capital of the Jewish nation was the strong lionlike city of God. In some translations, a young lion is called a *cub* (Gen. 49:9, NIV), while other translations use the word *whelp* (Gen. 49:9, KJV).

The Israelite tribes of Judah, Dan, and Gad—and also the nation of Babylon—adopted the lion as their symbol. Jesus is the "Lion of the tribe of Judah" (Rev. 5:5). Isaiah 9:6–7 and 11:1–9 foretold the Prince of Peace would tame even the fierce heart of the lion.

Little owl.   (See *Owl*.)

Lizard.   Lizards receive little attention in the Bible, although they are commonly found in the Middle East. They appeared on the list of unclean animals (Lev. 11:30) and were thus forbidden as food.

Lizards come in many species. Some of the small lizards often pass for snakes, while larger versions resemble the crocodile. All lizards are cold-blooded reptiles. Since their body temperature depends on their surroundings, they thrive in the tropics and in deserts. When the sun gets too hot for them, they lie in the shade or burrow into the sand. One species is even called a *sand lizard* (Lev. 11:30; *skink*, NIV).

Lizards are ingenious in the different ways they move. Some unfurl skinlike sails and soar from tree to tree. Monitor lizards (probably the *great lizard*, Lev. 11:29, RSV, NIV) swim well. They can also climb trees. Many lizards scamper rapidly across the ground. Others have poorly developed legs or no legs. But the little gecko (*ferret* in KJV, Lev. 11:30) can walk across a plaster ceiling upside down or cling to a pane of glass. Its toes end in a pad made of hundreds of tiny hooks, capped with a hidden claw. This enables it to get a foothold on smooth surfaces.

Most lizards eat insects. Larger species of this reptile also eat small animals or plants. The chameleon's sticky tongue, nearly as long as its body, whips out to catch insects. Chameleons are common. They are so narrow they look as if they have been squashed, and their bulging eyes can see in opposite directions. They have a long tail that can grasp a branch or coil into a spiral when at rest. Chameleons move at a slow, deliberate pace.

Chameleons are known for their ability to change color to match their surroundings. Actually, this is a common protective trait for most species of lizards. Another defensive tactic is the use of tricks or bluffs. Glass snakes, a type of lizard, escape capture by shedding their wiggling tail. Other lizards hiss, puff up, or use their tails as whips.

Locust.   (See *Grasshopper.*)

Louse.   Lice thrive in dry, dusty climates where sanitation is poor. These tiny insects are parasites with flat, colorless bodies. They cling to animals, humans, or plants, sucking blood or sap. The Egyptian nobles and priests shaved their heads and beards so lice could find no hiding place on their bodies. An infestation of lice, the third plague of the Exodus, must have been particularly bothersome (Exod. 8:16–18; *gnats,* RSV, NIV, NASB; *maggots,* NEB).

Maggot.   (See *Louse; Worm.*)

Mare.   (See *Horse.*)

Mole.   The Middle East has no true moles. The few Bible references to moles probably mean burrowing rats that live underground and feed on roots and bulbs to the distress of farmers. Their tiny ears and eyes are nearly hidden in their thick coats of fur. Because mole rats live in darkness, Isaiah referred to them as symbols of the spiritually blind. The NEB cites *dung-beetles* [Isa. 2:20]. (See also *Weasel.*)

Mole rat.   (See *Weasel.*)

Monitor lizard.   (See *Lizard.*)

Monkey.   Monkeys are not natives to the Middle East. King Solomon apparently had them imported from other nations, along with apes and exotic goods such as ivory, silver, and gold. They may have come from India, Africa, or even parts of Lower Egypt. The NKJV has *monkeys* in 1 Kings 10:22 and 2 Chronicles 9:21; other versions use *peacocks.* (See also *Ape.*)

Moth.   Moths are mentioned several times in the Bible to symbolize destructiveness and the perishable nature of earthly goods. In Hosea 5:12, God says, "I will be to Ephraim like a moth." Just as the damage caused by moths takes place slowly and undetectably, so God would quietly, but inevitably, bring judgment upon this backsliding people.

Female moths lay their eggs on garments. When the eggs hatch into caterpillars, they feed on the fibers, eventually leaving the garments full of holes. Jesus warned against placing too much confidence in worldly possessions that could be wiped out easily by moths (Matt. 6:19; Luke 12:33).

Mountain sheep.   (See *Sheep.*)

Mouse.   About 40 kinds of mice live in the Holy Land. These include house and field mice, moles, small rats, jerboas, and even hamsters. Arabs ate hamsters, but the Hebrew people considered all rodents unclean (Lev. 11:29; Isa. 66:17).

In spite of their small size, mice are destructive. Hordes of mice threatened grain crops in ancient times. When the Philistines stole the ark of the covenant, God punished them by sending mice or rats that infected them with a disease (1 Sam. 6:4–5, 11, 18; *rats,* NKJV).

Mule. (See *Donkey*.)

Night creature. (See *Owl*.)

Nighthawk. This is a bird mentioned only on the list of unclean birds (Lev. 11:16; Deut. 14:15). No specific characteristics are given that might help to identify the bird. Nighthawks, also called *nightjars*, live in the Holy Land, but they are not predators. There is no obvious reason why nighthawks would be unclean. Other translations render the Hebrew word for nighthawk as *owl* (NASB) or *screech owl* (NIV). After sunset, nighthawks fly high into the air to hunt for insects. They build nests near the ground in thickets or hedges.

Onager. (See *Donkey*.)

Oryx. (See *Antelope*.)

Osprey. Sometimes called *fish hawks* or *fishing eagles*, ospreys are members of the hawk family. With six-foot wingspans, they are large birds of prey. The osprey appears on the list of unclean birds (Lev. 11:13; Deut. 14:12). Some scholars think the term refers to the black vulture. (See also *Vulture*.)

Ossifrage. (See *Vulture*.)

Ostrich. Several Bible passages that refer to the *owl* in the KJV are rendered *ostrich* in the RSV (Lev. 11:16; Deut. 14:15). This strange bird was a common sight in the deserts of Israel and Sinai in Bible times. Earth's largest living birds, ostriches stand 50 meters (eight feet) tall. While they cannot fly, the unusual animals, with their long steps, which cover 15 feet per stride at top speed, can outrun horses. Sometimes ostriches use their wings as sails to achieve even greater speed. Adult ostriches fear only humans and lions, and may live as long as 70 years.

The popular belief that ostriches hide their heads in the sand is not true. However, when young ostriches sense danger, they will crouch near the ground and stretch out their long neck to lessen the possibility of being seen.

These enormous birds have walnut-sized brains, but God gave them certain helpful instincts along with their physical stamina. Like camels, ostriches are fitted for desert life. They eat coarse food and can go for a long time without water. Their heads, necks, and powerful legs have no feathers, which enables them to keep cool in the hot desert climate. Their huge eyes enable them to spot danger from a great distance, and their long eyelashes protect the eyes from dust and sand. The male ostrich has a cry that is similar to a lion's roar.

Unlike most other birds, ostriches do not build nests to protect their young. Female ostriches deposit their eggs on the desert floor and cover them with sand. These eggs are generally left unattended during the day, since the desert sun serves as a natural incubator. These habits are compared unfavorably with the more traditional nesting instincts of the stork (Job 39:13–18).

Owl. Owls are mentioned several times in the Bible (Lev. 11:16–17; Ps. 102:6; Jer. 50:39; Mic. 1:8). The largest native species are the *great owls*, sometimes called *eagle owls*. Several varieties of smaller owls are also common. Among them are *screech owls*, whose calls and whistles bring an eerie feeling in the night.

Other varieties of owls mentioned by different translations of the Bible include the *short-eared owl* (Lev. 11:16, NKJV, NEB); *long-eared owl* (Lev. 11:16, NEB); *horned owl* (Lev. 11:16, NIV); *little owl* (Lev. 11:17, KJV, NIV, NASB); *tawny owl* (Lev. 11:17, NEB); *fisher owl* (Lev. 11:17, NKJV); *desert owl* (Lev. 11:18, NIV); and *white owl* (Lev. 11:18, NKJV, NIV, NASB).

Owls are no wiser than other birds, but their facial features give them a thoughtful and solemn look. Owls have round faces with a circle of feathers around their heads, framing and highlighting their large eyes. These feathers also serve as a sound collector for the ears. Owls' fluffy feathers make them appear larger than they actually are, and they enable them to fly silently because the edges of their feathers pierce the air with little wind resistance.

Owls stalk their prey at night. Unlike other birds, whose eyes are set on opposite sides of the head, owls look directly ahead. They navigate in the dark mostly by sound. Alerted by noises, they lunge toward their prey with claws spread for the kill.

Owls serve a useful agricultural purpose, since they feed on rats, mice, and other rodents. The Hebrew people considered owls unclean and often associated them with scenes of desolation. The scops owl may be the *satyr* (KJV) of such verses as Isaiah 13:21 and 34:14 (*night creature*, NKJV). It has a horned appearance and does hoplike dances much like a goat.

Ox, Oxen. (See *Cattle*.)

Palmerworm. (See *Worm*.)

Panther. (See *Lion*.)

Partridge. From early times, partridges have been game birds. They were among the birds that could be eaten as clean food by the Jewish people. The meat is tasty, and the bird is clever enough to give the hunter a fine chase. It takes sharp eyes to spot the mottled feathers of the partridge. When alarmed, the bird will hide in a hole, crouch among loose stones, or fly from tree to tree with loudly whirring wings. David compared himself to a partridge when he was fleeing from Saul (1 Sam. 26:20).

Two species, the *sand partridge* (Isa. 34:15, NEB) and the *chukar*, are common. Partridges live in fields, feeding on grain and insects. They usually travel in coveys of 12 to 30.

Jeremiah compared the person who gathered riches by unrighteous means to a partridge that gathers a brood of young birds she has not hatched (Jer. 17:11).

Peacock. According to the KJV, Solomon imported peacocks from other nations for his royal courts in Israel (1 Kings 10:22; 2 Chron. 9:21). A peacock, the male of the species, is about the size of a turkey, with feathers of brilliant blue, green, and purple. He parades in front of the female, spreading his train of gorgeous long plumes behind him like a huge fan. Some versions of the Bible translate this term as *monkeys* or *baboons*.

Pelican. Pelicans are among the largest web-footed birds, often reaching 20 meters (six feet) in length with a 33-meter (10-foot) wingspread. Yet, in spite of their great size, pelicans swim and fly well.

Pelicans live in colonies and are experts at catching fish for food. Their long bills have an elastic pouch on the bottom half. With this pouch pelicans scoop up several quarts of water along with their prey. Pouches serve also as dinner bowls for baby pelicans who dip into them for a partially digested treat.

Beautiful in flight, pelicans are haunting, solitary figures when at rest. Perhaps this was the image in David's mind when he declared, "I am like a pelican of the wilderness" (Ps. 102:6). Other translations render the word as *vulture* (RSV), *desert owl* (NIV), or *jackdaw* (NKJV).

Pig. (See *Swine*.)

Pigeon. (See *Dove*.)

Porcupine. Isaiah and Zephaniah mention a wild creature that lived in desolate ruined places (Isa. 14:23; 34:11; Zeph. 2:14). The KJV calls it a *bittern*, but the RSV refers to the animal as a *hedgehog* or *porcupine* (*bustard*, NEB). The Holy Land does have porcupines, even today. They are small animals with sharp needles all over their backs. When in danger, porcupines roll up into a prickly ball.

Porpoise. (See *Badger*.)

Pygarg. The Hebrew word translated *pygarg* in Deuteronomy 14:5 [KJV] means "leaper." The RSV uses *ibex* and the NKJV has *mountain goat* or *addax* (margin). This animal probably was the white-rumped antelope. (See *Antelope, Goat*.)

Quail. The quail is a migrating species that arrives in droves along the shores of the Mediterranean Sea. With their strong flying muscles, these birds can fly rapidly for a short time. When migrating, however, they stretch their wings and allow the wind to bear them along. Sometimes they reach land so exhausted after their long flight that they can be caught by hand.

Most of the time quail remain on the ground, scratching for food and helping farmers by eating insects. Their brown-speckled bodies are inconspicuous, but they often give away their presence by a shrill whistle.

The Hebrew people probably ate dried, salted quail while enslaved by the Egyptians. When they longed for meat in the Sinai Desert, God promised to provide enough meat for a month. Then he directed thousands of quail to their camp, where the birds dropped in exhaustion (Num. 11:31–34; see also Exod. 16:13; Ps. 105:40).

Rabbit. (See *Hare.*)

Ram. (See *Sheep.*)

Rat. (See *Mouse.*)

Raven. *Raven* is a catchall term for *crows, ravens, rooks, jackdaws, magpies,* and *jays.* All were unclean for the Jewish people (Lev. 11:15). With a wingspread of about 10 meters (three feet), ravens are the largest members of this family.

Ravens are scavengers that will eat almost anything. Their harsh cry has probably contributed to their reputation as birds of ill omen. Since they have keen eyes and strong wings, this may explain why the first bird Noah sent from the ark was a raven (Gen. 8:7). They were also known for their practice of pecking out the eyes of a body—a quick way to determine whether their meal was actually dead (Prov. 30:17).

The Bible indicates that God feeds even young ravens (Job 38:41). Jesus used a similar example to illustrate God's care (Luke 12:24). Because God sent ravens to feed the prophet Elijah, ravens are also associated

with God's protective care (1 Kings 17:4, 6). The expression "black as a raven" comes from the Song of Solomon 5:11.

Rock badger. Rock badgers are rabbit-sized furry animals. With short ears, sharp teeth, and black-button eyes, they resemble overgrown guinea pigs (Lev. 11:5; *coney,* KJV, NIV).

"The rock badgers are a feeble folk, yet they make their homes in the crags," says Proverbs 30:26, holding them up as little things that are "exceedingly wise" (30:24). Feeble, or defenseless they may be, but they find safety in steep, rocky terrain. Their feet have a suctionlike grip that enables them to scamper among rocky outcroppings. Their enemies can easily overlook rock badgers stretched out motionless on sun-warmed rocks.

Rock goat. (See *Sheep.*)

Roe buck. (See *Deer.*)

Sand fly. (See *Fly.*)

Sand lizard. (See *Lizard.*)

Sand partridge. (See *Partridge.*)

Sand viper. (See *Snake.*)

Satyr. (See *Goat; Owl.*)

Scorpion. Scorpions are small crawling animals that look like flat lobsters. Members of the spider family, they have eight legs, two sets of pincers, and tails with poisonous stingers. Scorpions feed on spiders and insects, which they rip apart with their claws. They use their poisonous sting only when threatened or when they attack large prey. Their stings are seldom fatal, but can be painful (Rev. 9:5).

During the day, scorpions escape the desert heat by hiding under rocks. They come out at night to hunt and eat. Inhabitants of Bible lands feared scorpions. These animals were an ever-present danger when Moses led the children of Israel through the hot, rocky wilderness (Deut. 8:15).

Jesus' words in Luke 11:12 about giving a person a scorpion instead of an egg may re-

Several species of the scorpion are found in Palestine. Their bite is poisonous but generally not fatal to human beings (Deut. 8:14–15).

PHOTO BY GUSTAV JEENINGA

fer to a light-colored scorpion, which could be mistaken for an egg when in a coiled position. God told Ezekiel not to be afraid of his enemies, who were referred to symbolically as scorpions (Ezek. 2:6). King Rehoboam's threat did not mean he would use scorpions as whips (1 Kings 12:14), but in those days they called a barbed whip or scourge a scorpion.

Screech owl.   (See *Owl.*)

Sea cow.   (See *Badger.*)

Sea gull.
Sea gulls are birds about the size of pigeons. They have long wings, which they use to swoop and soar gracefully on air currents. Gulls gather in flocks near bodies of water. They are scavengers who eat garbage as well as fish and insects. Sea gulls are mentioned only in some translations of the Bible; in others *cuckoo, sea mew,* or *owl* appears (Lev. 11:16; Deut. 14:15).

Sea mew.   (See *Sea gull.*)

Sea monster.
Several terms are used in the Bible to describe large sea creatures: *sea monsters* or *serpents, dragons, great fish, whales,* and *Leviathan.* All of these do not refer to one animal, but it is impossible to match the terms with specific marine life. For instance, many animals have been mistaken for sea serpents—large eels, sharks, and giant squid. The Mediterranean and Red Seas contain whales and enough other such creatures to provide sufficient material for sea-related scare tales.

Dragons are mythical creatures that appear in many ancient cultures. Ezekiel saw images of dragons on the city gates when he was exiled in Babylon. The book of Revelation refers to Satan as "a great, fiery red dragon" (12:3).

Ezekiel and the writer of Psalm 148 also used the word *dragon* as a synonym for *whale* or *sea creature.* Whales, of course, were real creatures that may have been a common sight in the Mediterranean Sea during Bible times. The NEB refers to them in Psalm 148:7 as *water-spouts,* a possible reference to the sperm whale.

Serpent.   (See *Snake.*)

Sheep.
Sheep are mentioned more frequently than any other animal in the Bible—about 750 times. This is natural since the Hebrew people were known early in their history as a race of wandering herdsmen. Even in the days of the kings, the simple shepherd's life seemed the ideal calling. The Bible makes many comparisons between the ways of sheep and human beings. In the NT the church is often compared to a sheepfold.

Well-suited for Palestine's dry plains, sheep fed on grass, plants, and shrubs. They could get along for long periods without water. Sheep in clusters are easily led, so a single shepherd could watch over a large flock.

The sheep of Bible times were probably brown or a mixture of black and white. Modern farmers clip off the tails of sheep for sanitary reasons, but fat tails were prized on biblical sheep. The Hebrews called this "the whole fat-tail." When they offered this prized part of the sheep as a burnt offering to God, they burned the "entire fat-tail cut off close by the spine" (Lev. 3:9, NEB).

Sheep were also valuable because they provided meat for the Hebrew diet. Mutton was nutritious and could be preserved for winter. Before people learned to spin and weave wool, shepherds wore warm sheepskin jackets.

By nature, sheep are helpless creatures. They depend on shepherds to lead them to water and pasture, to fight off wild beasts, and to rub oil on their faces when a snake nips them from the grass. Sheep are social animals that gather in flocks, but they tend to wander off and fall into crevices or get caught in thorn bushes. Then the shepherd must leave the rest of the flock to search for the stray. Jesus used this familiar picture when he described a shepherd who left 99 sheep in the fold to search for one that had wandered off. God revealed his nurturing nature by speaking of himself as a shepherd in Psalm 23. Jesus also described himself as the Good Shepherd who takes care of his sheep (John 10:1–18).

A unique relationship existed between shepherds and sheep. Shepherds knew them by name, and they recognized their own shepherd's voice. Because he demonstrated purity and trustful obedience to the Father, Jesus was called the Lamb of God (John 1:29, 36).

Wild sheep, high-spirited and independent, lived among the tall mountain peaks. Like their domesticated cousins, they flocked together, but their disposition more nearly resembled goats. They are referred to as *mountain sheep* (Deut. 14:5, NKJV, RSV, NIV, NASB), *chamois* (KJV), and *rock-goat[s]* (NEB).

Wild or domestic, the male sheep is called a *ram;* the female is a *ewe.*

Skink. (See *Lizard.*)

Snail. Snails are small, slow-crawling animals with a soft body protected by coiled shells. They move with wavelike motions of their single foot, secreting a slime as they go, making their travel easier. The psalmist may have had this peculiar motion in mind when he spoke of the snail "which melts away as it goes" (Ps. 58:8).

The snail in Leviticus 11:30 (KJV) is probably a skink, a type of sand lizard.

Snake. A snake is the Bible's first—and final—animal villain (Gen. 3; Rev. 20:2). Several different words for snake or serpent appear some 20 times. Scholars can only make educated guesses as to which of the many species of snakes are meant.

The asp and adder are both common in the Holy Land. The asp is a type of cobra with its familiar hood, although its hood is not as pronounced as the Indian cobra's. There is also a desert cobra, which has no hood. *Adder* and *viper* are two names for the same deadly snake. The *horned viper* and *sawscale,* or *carpet viper,* are native to Israel. Another species mentioned in the Bible is the *sand viper* (Isa. 30:6, NEB).

In the wilderness, the Israelites were

In all periods of biblical history sheep were important because they provided wool, milk, meat, and leather for the Hebrew people.

PHOTO BY GUSTAV JEENINGA

plagued by fiery serpents (Num. 21:6). *Fiery* may indicate the burning fever caused by their bite. Or it may refer to the puff adder, which has yellow flamelike markings. The cockatrice of the KJV was a mythological monster. It had the wings and head of a cock and the tail of a dragon. According to the superstitious legend, its look could kill.

Although most snakes were nonpoisonous, the Jewish people feared and hated all of them. In the Bible the serpent is often referred to as the symbol of evil and wrongdoing (Ps. 140:3; Jer. 8:17).

In spite of this attitude among the Jews, some of Israel's neighbors associated serpents with health, life, and immortality. The kingdom of Lower Egypt took the cobra as its official symbol. Moses once held up a bronze serpent in front of the Israelites at God's command to save the people from the fiery serpents in the wilderness (Num. 21:9). Some Israelites continued to worship the bronze serpent until King Hezekiah destroyed it generations later (2 Kings 18:4).

Snakes are fascinating creatures. Scales on their undersides provide traction. Their forked tongues flick rapidly in and out to collect sensations of touch and smell. Psalm 58:4 correctly speaks of the deaf cobra because snakes have no ears to receive sound waves. They rely on physical vibrations to pick up sounds, proving that cobras are charmed not by music, but by movement.

A snake's spine contains as many as 300 tiny vertebrae, which permit the amazing flexibility to coil and curve. Snakes mouths are hinged to permit them to swallow and eat creatures much larger than themselves. Their eyes are protected by transparent lids that are always open, causing scientists to wonder if snakes ever sleep.

Sow. (See *Swine.*)

Sparrow. *Sparrow* is the name given to several different species of birds in the Bible. They ate grain and insects and gathered in noisy flocks. The psalmist wrote, "I . . . am like a sparrow alone on the housetop" (Ps. 102:7). These tiny birds were such social creatures that a lone sparrow was the symbol of deep loneliness.

Sparrows build their untidy nests in the eaves of houses. Sparrows were not driven away when they built their nests in the temple (Ps. 84:3).

In Jesus' time sparrows sold for a low price—two for a copper coin, five for two copper coins (Matt. 10:29; Luke 12:6). Those who could not afford to sacrifice a sheep or a goat might bring a sparrow. Healed lepers were directed to bring two sparrows for a cleansing ceremony (Lev. 14:1–7).

Sometimes it seems that only God cares for sparrows. Cats, hawks, and naughty boys prey upon them. People complain about how they multiply, considering them pests. Yet, Jesus declared, "Not one of them falls to the ground apart from your Father's will" (Matt. 10:29).

Spider. Hundreds of different species of spiders are found in the Holy Land. Spiders' skill at spinning threads into a web is one of nature's miracles. The fragile web of spiders is used to demonstrate the folly of placing confidence in something other than the stable, dependable God (Job 8:13–14).

Spiders trap their victims in their webs and dissolve them with predigestive juices so they can be eaten. Oil on the spider's body keeps it from being entangled in its own web.

Sponge. Sponges are plantlike animals that live on the ocean floor. They absorb nourishment from water passing through their bodies. When sponges are removed from water, the cells die, leaving skeletons. The skeletons of some sponges are flexible and porous. These have been used for centuries as cleaning and water-absorbing tools. A sponge, dipped in sour wine, was offered to Christ on the cross (Matt. 27:48; Mark 15:36; John 19:29).

Stag. (See *Deer*.)

Stork. These goose-sized birds look ungainly in flight, with their legs dangling and wings slowly flapping. But people were always glad to see the storks on their yearly migration from Europe to Africa. Storks had the reputation of bringing good luck. If they were numerous, people believed crops would be abundant. Farmers welcomed storks because they helped the crops by eating insects.

Both black and white storks were often seen. White storks nest as high as possible—often on chimneys. But since houses in the Holy Land had low, flat roofs, they nested instead in the fir trees (Ps. 104:17). In spite of their commendable features, storks were unclean (Lev. 11:19; Deut. 14:18).

Swallow. Swallows are migratory birds familiar to residents of the Holy Land. Frequently on the move to warmer climates, swallows gather in huge flocks to travel thousands of miles. A chattering flock can make quite a racket (Isa. 38:14). The psalmist makes an interesting distinction between the sparrow, who finds a home, and the swallow, who gets a nest (Ps. 84:3). Only permanent residents need homes. Some translations render the Hebrew word for swallow as *thrush* (Jer. 8:7, NIV, NASB) or *wryneck* (NEB).

Swallows spend much of their time in the air, catching insects on the wing. They are beautiful birds, brightly colored, with forked tails.

Swan. Swans are seen occasionally. As vegetarians, they are related to ducks and geese. Alternate translations of the Hebrew term for swan include *ibis, stork, white owl,* and *water hen.* These are better translations, since there seems to be no reason why swans would have been considered unclean (Lev. 11:18, KJV).

Swift. Swifts were small migratory birds often confused with swallows. Although they are similar, the birds come from different families. Swifts are strong fliers that can travel short distances at over 100 miles per hour and spend much of their time feeding on airborne insects.

Jeremiah wrote of this bird and others that "observe the time of their coming." Unlike them, the rebellious people of the nation of Judah "do not know the judgment of the LORD" (Jer. 8:7).

A flock of storks in the Huleh Nature Reserve in Israel. PHOTO BY WILLEM A. VANGEMEREN

Swine. The Jewish people had nothing to do with pigs, but these animals still received much attention in the Bible. In Psalm 80:13, Israel's enemies were likened to a "boar out of the woods." Vicious wild pigs (boars) ranged throughout the land. Owners of vineyards hated them because they devoured grapes and trampled their vines. Dogs and humans alike feared their razor-sharp tusks. In modern times, boars are the largest game animals in Israel.

Domesticated pigs (swine) were also raised—by Gentiles or unorthodox Jews. Pigs were ceremonially unclean because they did not chew the cud. Symbols of greed and filth, pigs also represented unredeemed human nature (2 Pet. 2:22). Jesus told a story of a son who hit bottom when he had to take care of hogs and eat food intended for them (Luke 15:15–16).

Tawny owl.   (See *Owl.*)

Thrush.   (See *Swallow.*)

Tortoise.   (See *Turtle.*)

Turtle.   Turtles and tortoises and their eggs and meat were eaten. In Numbers 6:10 and Jeremiah 8:7 (KJV), *turtle* is simply an abbreviation of *turtledove.* The context clearly indicates that a bird is meant, not the silent, slow-moving turtle.

Turtledove.   (See *Dove.*)

Unicorn.   Unicorns (KJV) were mythical creatures, similar to horses, with a single spiral horn growing out of their foreheads. In the Middle Ages, the unicorn appeared in paintings as a symbol of purity. Many people believed an animal like this really lived. Most Bible verses that refer to unicorns emphasize their great strength (Num. 23:22; 24:8; Deut. 33:17). Biblical writers may have had the aurochs in mind. The horned wild ox was so large and powerful that no one could control or tame it (Job 39:9–10; Pss. 22:21; 92:10; Isa. 34:7).

Viper.   (See *Snake.*)

Vulture.   Vultures are large, loathsome members of the hawk family. The largest species have a wingspread of about 32 meters (nine to 10 feet). Most vultures have bare heads and necks. However, the *lammergeier* ("bearded vulture") has dirty-white neck feathers and a tassel of dark feathers hanging from its beak. Egyptian vultures also have neck feathers. Griffons' long necks are covered with fine white down.

The lammergeier is also called the *ossifrage* (Lev. 11:13; Deut. 14:12, KJV) or the *gier eagle* (Lev. 11:18; Deut. 14:17, KJV).

Vultures feed on dead bodies. For this reason they were considered unclean animals by the Jewish people (Lev. 11:13; Deut. 14:12–13). Other renderings of this word are *buzzard, falcon,* and *bustard.*

Wasp.   These overgrown relatives of bees are known for their painful sting. Wasps are common throughout the Holy Land. Hornets are a large, savage species of wasp. Egyptian soldiers used hornets as a symbol of their military might. When the people of Israel were marching toward the Promised Land, God said he would send hornets to drive the Canaanites out of the land (Exod. 23:28). Ancient writers claim that entire tribes were sometimes driven out of a country by wasps or hornets.

Weasel.   These animals live in almost every country. They are small and furry, with thin, long bodies and short legs. Weasels eat small animals and have a reputation for stealing eggs. The Bible mentions them only in Leviticus 11:29 (KJV), in the list of unclean animals. Some modern sources believe the *mole* (NASB) or the *mole-rat* (NEB) was meant in this verse.

Whale.   (See *Crocodile; Sea Monster.*)

Wild boar.   (See *Swine.*)

Wild donkey.   (See *Donkey.*)

Wild goat.   (See *Goat.*)

Wild ox.   (See *Cattle; Unicorn.*)

Wolf.   Wolves were a menace to the shepherds, and their first dogs were probably tamed wolf pups. Perhaps this kinship enabled wolves to lurk near sheepfolds and gain their reputation for treachery.

Jacob compared his youngest son to a ravenous wolf (Gen. 49:27). The Hebrew word translated *ravenous* means "to rip and tear." Wolves seem particularly cruel because they seek out the weak, old, and defenseless as victims. The flow of blood incites them to rip and tear even more with their powerful jaws.

In many Bible references, wolves represent ruthless enemies. Jesus warned of false prophets "who come . . . in sheep's clothing, but inwardly . . . are ravenous wolves" (Matt. 7:15).

Worm. Worms have no backbone, legs, or eyes, although their bodies are sensitive to light and temperature. But they do play a useful role. They improve the soil by working decaying vegetation into the earth and aerating it with their tunnels.

The Bible speaks both literally and figuratively of worms. *Worms* also refers to wormlike creatures, such as insect larvae. The palmerworm, cankerworm, and caterpillar of Joel 1:4 (KJV) are all caterpillars, which is the larval stage of various moths. (The NKJV, however, translates these as various kinds of locusts.) *Grub* is another word used for worms in various translations (Isa. 51:8, NEB, NASB). Job 7:5 refers to an infestation of worms, and it probably meant *maggots*, the larvae of flies. Decaying matter often teems with tiny wormlike maggots.

Worms, such as tapeworms and pinworms, are parasites that invade the human body. Herod's death was described as his being eaten by worms (Acts 12:23).

The common earthworm also appears in the Bible. Micah 7:17 refers to worms (*snakes*, NKJV) coming out of their holes. Perhaps it was an earthworm also that God appointed to strike at the root of Jonah's shade (Jon. 4:7). The psalmist lamented: "I am a worm . . . and despised" (Ps. 22:6). Job claimed kinship with the lowly worm (Job 17:14). Isaiah 41:14 uses "you worm Jacob" as a metaphor of weakness. The Jews associated worms and fire with the place reserved for the ungodly dead (Isa. 66:24; Mark 9:44, 48).

Wryneck. (See *Swallow*.)

Plants

The land God promised to Abraham and his descendants was extremely fertile. Because of its diverse climate, the world of the Bible contained many varieties of plants. Botanists have identified 3,500 species of plant life in Israel and Syria. Plants or plant products are mentioned in almost every book of the Bible.

The flora of the Bible have been the subject of much discussion and research, and accurately identifying these plants has taken years of scientific research. The Bible writers were not botanists, and they seldom bothered to describe the plants they mentioned.

In the sixteenth century, Levinus Lemmens wrote the first book on the plants in the Bible. It was not until the middle of the eighteenth century that a botanist traveled to Israel for firsthand knowledge of its vegetation. Since then much valuable information has been learned about these plants.

Many of the biblical writers used general terms to refer to plants. Sometimes a reference is no more specific than *tree, grass,* or *grain.* Even if an individual grain such as *corn* or *wheat* is named, the writer still used a generic term. Some other general terms referring to plant life include *bush, herb, grass, cockle, fruit,* and *verdure.*

Although many types of flowers, such as *irises, roses, anemones, lilies, tulips, hyacinths,* and *narcissus* grow in Israel and other Bible lands, few are mentioned by name.

The Hebrew people were certain that God provided the land for their use, but they were not careful to take good care of it. The land was cultivated continuously for thousands of years without rest until much of the soil was depleted and many areas became devastated wastelands. The great forests of Lebanon and Hermon were eventually destroyed and the soil eroded. The people of that time did not know how to manage their environment intelligently. Eventually the land that once flowed with milk and honey became barren of much of its vegetation. Today many of these barren regions of the Holy Land are being turned again into fertile farm land.

The following specific plants are mentioned in the Bible. This listing is keyed to the NKJV, but variant names from five additional popular translations—KJV, NASB, NEB, NIV, and RSV—are cross-referenced throughout the listing.

Acacia. A large thorny tree with rough gnarled bark. The orange-brown wood was hard-grained, and it repelled insects. It bore long locust-like pods with seeds inside and produced round, fragrant clusters of yellow blossoms. Many species of acacia grew in the desert of Sinai, southern Israel, and Egypt.

Acacia wood was used to build the first tabernacle and the ark of the covenant (Exod. 36:20; 37:1). The acacia is called *shittim* and *shittah* in the KJV (Exod. 25:5, 10; Isa. 41:19).

Algum, Almug. A large leguminous tree native to India and Ceylon. While its identity is uncertain, many consider it to be the red sandalwood. Its blossoms were pealike, and its wood was close grained, dark outside, and red within. It was highly scented, making it resistant to insects. Most authorities believe that algum and almug are two forms of the same wood.

Solomon ordered the almug wood from Ophir and Lebanon (1 Kings 10:11–12; 2 Chron. 9:10–11). The wood was well suited for making musical instruments, cabinets, and pillars for the temple.

Almond. A large tree resembling the peach tree in both size and fruit. The almond was chiefly valued for the nuts it produced, which were used for making oil used in the home and as medicine. The Hebrew word for *almond* means "awakening," an allusion to the almond blossom, which is first to bloom in the spring. The almond's pinkish-white blossoms always appear before its leaves.

The almond played an important role in the history of the Hebrews. Jacob included almond nuts in his gifts to Joseph in Egypt (Gen. 43:11). The decorations on the lampstands in the tabernacle were modeled after the almond blossom (Exod. 25:33), and Aaron's rod was an almond twig (Num. 17:8). The almond also symbolized the dependability of God (Jer. 1:11–12). Many scholars think the *hazel* of Gen. 30:37 (KJV) is the almond tree.

Almug. (See *Algum.*)

Aloes. Two plants, one a tree and the other a flower.

1. The aloes mentioned in Ps. 45:8, Prov. 7:17, and Song of Sol. 4:14 came from a large tree known as *eaglewood*, a plant native to India. The wood of the aloe tree is fragrant and highly valued for perfume and incense. Many authorities believe the *lignaloe* to be the same tree (Num. 24:6, KJV).

2. The aloes brought by Nicodemus to wrap the body of Jesus (John 19:39) were probably the true aloes of the lily family, a beautiful plant with thick, fleshy leaves

An almond tree in full bloom in Palestine. The prophet Jeremiah had a vision of a blossoming almond, symbolizing God's coming judgment against his sinful people (Jer. 1:11–12).
PHOTO BY HOWARD VOS

and red flowers. The aloin derived from the pulp of the aloe leaf was an expensive product used in embalming.

Amaranth. A large family of plants that includes weeds and garden plants. Goodspeed translates the *amaranth,* also called the *rolling thing,* of Isaiah 17:23 as the "tumbleweed." It is sometimes called the *resurrection plant* and the *rose of Jericho.* The Greek word for *amaranth* means "unfading." This describes the bloom's ability to retain its color when dried. This meaning is used symbolically in 1 Pet. 1:4 and 5:4, where the inheritance of the faithful is described as unfading. Thus, the amaranth became a symbol of immortality.

Anise. An annual herb that bears yellow flowers and fragrant seeds. The anise mentioned in the Bible is generally thought to be *dill.* Anise (dill) was used as medicine and for cooking. It grows in Israel today both cultivated and wild.

Jesus used the anise as an illustration when he scolded the Pharisees for keeping part of the law in detail while ignoring the rest (Matt. 23:23).

Apple. A tree that grows about nine meters (30 feet) high and has rough bark and pink blossoms. Many authorities believe this was the *apricot,* a native of Armenia. Other authorities suggest the *quince, peach, citron, orange,* or some other fruit, while some believe it really was the *apple.*

The apple was described as sweet and fragrant (Song of Sol. 7:8; *apricot,* NEB), golden (Prov. 25:11), and suitable for shade (Song of Sol. 2:3). This fruit was used figuratively to show how precious we are to God, and how extremely sensitive God is to our needs (Deut. 32:10; Ps. 17:8; Zech. 2:8).

Apricot. (See *Apple.*)

Ash. (See *Pine.*)

Aspen. (See *Mulberry.*)

Asphodel. (See *Rose.*)

Balm. (See *Balsam.*)

Balsam. A thorny tree growing three to five meters (10 to 15 feet) tall with clusters of green flowers, also known as the *Jericho balsam.* Some think the writers meant the *lentisk* or *mastic tree,* a shrubby evergreen growing one to three meters (3 to 10 feet) tall.

Balsam was highly valued during Bible times. It produced a fragrant, resinous gum called *balm.* This was an article of export (Gen. 37:25) and was given as a gift by Jacob (Gen. 43:11). Balm was used as a symbol in Jer. 8:22 to refer to spiritual healing.

Barley. A grain known since early times. It was well adapted to varied climates, ripening quickly and resistant to heat; it usually was harvested before wheat. Because barley was considered a food for slaves and the very poor, however, it was held in low esteem as a grain.

Barley was first associated with Egypt (Exod. 9:31). It was used as an offering of jealousy (Num. 5:15), for fodder (1 Kings

4:28), as well as food (Judg. 7:13; John 6:5, 13).

Bay tree. The *laurel,* a tree native to Canaan. The laurel grew to heights of 12 to 18 meters (40 to 60 feet) and produced small greenish-white flowers and black berries. Parts of the tree were used in medicine, while its leaves were used as seasoning. The Hebrew word means "a tree in its native soil," a fitting way to describe the natural prosperity of the wicked (Ps. 37:35, KJV; *native green tree,* NKJV).

Beans. A hardy plant about one meter (three feet) tall with pea-shaped fragrant blooms, large pods, and black or brown beans, which were eaten alone or with meat. Beans have always been an important part of the Hebrew diet, especially among the poor, and they have been known since ancient times. When beans were threshed and cleaned, they were often mixed with grains for bread (Ezek. 4:9).

Bitter weed. (See *Wormwood.*)

Black cummin. (See *Cummin, Fitches.*)

Box tree. A tree of hard wood and glossy leaves, which grew to a height of about six meters (20 feet). A native of northern Israel and the Lebanon mountains, the box tree was well suited to beautify the temple (Isa. 60:13). The box tree has been used since Roman times for wood engravings and musical instruments. Isaiah referred to the box tree symbolically to remind the Hebrews of God's perpetual presence (Isa. 41:17–20).

Some scholars have suggested that the box tree might be the *cypress* or *plane.* (See also *Chestnut.*)

Bramble. (See *Thistle* or *Thorns.*)

Brier. (See *Thistle* or *Thorns.*)

Broom. A dense, twiggy bush, almost leafless, which grew to about 3.6 meters (12 feet). It has small white blooms. Common in the desert regions of Israel, Arabia, and Egypt, it was used as charcoal (Ps.

120:4) and provided shade for Elijah (1 Kings 19:4–5). The roots that Job ate were not from the broom, which was not edible, but may have been an edible parasite that infested the bush (Job 30:4). The broom is sometimes referred to as juniper in the NKJV, KJV, and NASB. Many scholars believe this to be the shrub or heath referred to in Jer. 17:6 and 48:6.

Bud. (See *Gourd*.)

Bulrush. (See *Reed* or *Rush*.)

Calamus. A fragrant, reedlike grass growing along streams and riverbanks (Song of Sol. 4:14), also referred to as *sweet cane* (Isa. 43:24; Jer. 6:20). Calamus leaves are fragrant and ginger-flavored when crushed. It is named with other aromatic substances (Ezek. 27:19) and as one ingredient for the anointing oil (Exod. 30:23). (See *Reed* or *Rush*.)

Camel-thorn. (See *Cypress*.)

Camphire. (See *Henna*.)

Cane. (See *Calamus; Reed;* or *Rush*.)

Caperberry. A plant with large white, berry-producing flowers, which grows in clefts of rocks and on walls. Only NEB and NASB refer to the caper. Other versions translate the Hebrew word as *desire* (Eccles. 12:5). (See *Hyssop*.)

Caraway. (See *Cummin*.)

Cassia. A plant with a flavor and aroma similar to cinnamon, but considered inferior. Some believe it could be the Indian perfume, *orris*. Moses included cassia in the anointing oil (Exod. 30:24). It was also an article of trade (Ezek. 27:19).

Cedar. An evergreen tree that sometimes grows more than 30 meters (100 feet) tall with a trunk circumference of 12 to 15 meters (40 to 50 feet). It grows in western Asia, the Himalayas, and Cyprus as well as Lebanon.

The cedar's fragrant wood was rot-resistant and knot-free, making it ideal for building (2 Sam. 5:11; 1 Kings 6:9), shipbuilding (Ezek. 27:5), and crafting idols (Isa. 44:14). The references to cedar in Lev. 14:4 and Num. 19:6 are generally understood to be the *juniper* that grew in the Sinai. (See *Fir, Pine*.)

Cedars of Lebanon on the mountainsides of Lebanon. Reckless cutting of these magnificent trees across the centuries has almost eliminated them from the landscape.
PHOTO BY GUSTAV JEENINGA

Chestnut. A tree of Syria and Lebanon thought to be the plane tree. It grew to a height of about 21 to 27 meters (70 to 90 feet) and had a massive trunk. The word is translated *chestnut* in the NKJV and KJV, but *plane* by the RSV, NIV, NEB, and NASB.

Cinnamon. A member of the laurel family, the cinnamon tree grew to be more than nine meters (30 feet) tall with white flowers and wide-spreading branches. A native of Ceylon, the cinnamon tree produced bark and oil used for the *anointing oil* (Exod. 30:23) and as *perfume* (Prov. 7:17; Rev. 18:13).

Citron. A fragrant wood from the sandarac tree. Citron is sometimes referred to as sweet or scented wood. The sandarac tree never grew to more than nine meters (30 feet) tall. Citron is translated as *thyine* by the KJV (Rev. 18:12).

Coriander. An annual herb, which grew from one-half to one meter (two to three feet) tall and produced grayish seeds used to flavor foods, confections, and in medicine.

Corn. (See *Wheat.*)

Crocus. (See *Rose, Saffron.*)

Cucumber. A climbing vine that produces vegetables. The cucumber was one of the vegetables the Israelites longed for after leaving Egypt (Num. 11:5).

Cummin. An annual seed-producing herb with pinkish-white blooms. Cummin is native to the eastern Mediterranean lands. When harvested, cummin was threshed with sticks (Isa. 28:25, 27), a method still used today. Cummin was used for food flavoring and in medicine.

The NKJV also mentions black cummin, translated *dill* (RSV, NEB, NASB), *caraway* (NIV), and *fitches* (KJV).

Cypress. A tall evergreen tree of hard and durable wood. Cypress wood was suited for building, and was used to fashion idols (Isa. 44:14). The word rendered *gopherwood* by the NKJV, KJV, RSV, and NASB in Gen. 6:14 may be cypress. This was the wood Noah used to build his ark. The word for cypress is also rendered as *camel-thorn* (Isa. 55:13) and *ilex* (Isa. 44:14) by the NEB.

Darnel. (See *Tares.*)

Date palm. (See *Palm.*)

Dill. (See *Anise, Cummin.*)

Dove droppings / Dove dung. A bulbous plant edible after being boiled or roasted. Dove's dung was mentioned as food eaten during the siege of Samaria (2 Kings 6:25). Some believe this was excrement from pigeons and doves, while others interpret it as an edible plant (*seed pods*, NIV; *locust-beans*, NEB).

Dove dung was also referred to as the *Star of Bethlehem*, which Syrians used as food. (See *Locust.*)

Ebony. A large tree that produces edible fruit similar to the *persimmon*. The hard, black wood from the inner portion of the tree is quite valuable and used for fine furniture. Idols were sometimes carved from ebony wood.

Elm. (See *Terebinth.*)

Fig. A fruit-producing plant that could be either a tall tree or a low-spreading shrub. The size of the tree depended on its location and soil. The blooms of the fig tree always appear before the leaves. When Jesus saw leaves on a fig tree, he naturally expected fruit (Mark 11:12–14, 20–21). There were usually two crops of figs a year.

Figs were eaten fresh (2 Kings 18:31), pressed into cakes (1 Sam. 25:18), and used as poultices (Isa. 38:21). Jeremiah used the fig tree as a symbol of desolation (Jer. 8:13). It also signified security and hope for Adam and Eve (Gen. 3:7), the 12 spies (Num. 13:23), and the poets and prophets.

Fir. An evergreen tree of uncertain identity. Although this tree is mentioned several times, authorities question whether this was the true fir or some other evergreen of Israel. Many suggest the *Aleppo pine* would fit this description, while others think it might be the *cypress, juniper,* or *cedar*.

The Israelites valued the timber of the fir tree for building the temple (1 Kings 6:15, KJV), for shipbuilding (Ezek. 27:5), and for making musical instruments (2 Sam. 6:5). The fir is used symbolically to describe the blessings of God for his people (Isa. 41:19, 55:13, KJV).

Fitches. Two different plants mentioned in the KJV:

1. An annual herb one-half meter (one to two feet) tall with finely cut leaves and

blue flowers. It produces black poppy seeds used in curries and sprinkled on breads. It is translated *black cummin* in the NKJV (Isa. 28:25, 27).

2. A plant apparently mislabled by the KJV in Ezek. 4:9. The correct identification is *spelt*. (See *Spelt*.)

Flag. (See *Reed* or *Rush*.)

Flax. A plant growing one meter (three feet) tall with pale blue flowers, used for making cloth. When mature, the entire flax plant was pulled and placed in water to separate the fibers from the stems. It was then laid on housetops to dry (Josh. 2:6), and later woven into linen. Flax was also used as wicks for lamps (Isa. 42:3). (See *Reed* or *Rush*.)

Frankincense. An aromatic gum resin obtained from the Boswellia tree. These trees are large with small, white, star-shaped flowers and leaves resembling the mountain ash. The gum is obtained by cutting into the bark and collecting the resin from the tree. When this substance hardens, it is gathered and used as incense.

Frankincense was part of the sacred anointing oil (Exod. 30:34), used in sacrificial offering (Lev. 2:1), as a fumigant during animal sacrifices (Exod. 30:7), and as perfume (Song of Sol. 3:6). It was also a gift to baby Jesus (Matt. 2:11).

The trees are native to India, Arabia, and Africa. Israel probably obtained this product through foreign trade (Isa. 60:6).

Galbanum. The gum from an herb that grew one to 1.5 meters (three to five feet) high and had greenish-white flowers. Galbanum was the milky substance extracted from the stems, which quickly hardened. It was used in perfume and anointing oil (Exod. 30:34).

Gall. A bitter, poisonous herb. This may have been the *poppy* or other wild poisonous plant. *Gall* is used figuratively to mean "a bitter punishment" (Jer. 8:14; 9:15; 23:15) or any "bitter" experience (Acts 8:23, KJV). Gall and vinegar were offered to Jesus on the cross (Matt. 27:34), but he refused the drink.

Garlic. A strong-flavored herb, resembling the onion. Garlic was eaten with bread and used to flavor food, and is still popular. Garlic was highly esteemed in Egypt and was believed to have been used as wages for workers who built the pyramids. The Hebrews yearned for garlic after leaving Egypt (Num. 11:5).

Gopherwood. (See *Cypress*.)

Gourd. A fast-growing shrub that grew to a height of three to four meters (10 to 12 feet). One of Elisha's servants put the fruit of the gourd into a pot of stew (2 Kings 4:39).

The gourd (Jon. 4:6–10; KJV, NEB) is identified as the plant under which Jonah found shade. Some biblical scholars suggest this may have been *pumpkin, squash,* or *ivy*.

Many types of wild gourds flourished in the Mediterranean region, some of which were poisonous. The decorations used on the temple called ornamental buds (1 Kings 6:18; 7:24) might have been a type of wild gourd.

Grapes. A luscious fruit cultivated on vines. Large clusters of grapes weighing about five kilograms (12 pounds) each (Num. 13:23) have been reported in Israel.

Grapes were used in a variety of ways. They were eaten fresh, dried, and made into wine or vinegar. Dried grapes were called *raisins*. The first suggestion of grapes was in connection with Noah's vineyard (Gen. 9:20).

The soil and climate of Israel were well suited for vineyards, and they were cultivated there long before the Israelites occupied the land (Gen. 14:18). The vineyards of Israel produced immense clusters of grapes (Num. 13:20, 23–24).

Vineyards were hedged or fenced as protection from wild animals (Song of Sol. 2:15). In each vineyard a tower was erected and a guard placed to protect the vines from robbers (Matt. 21:33).

Vinedressers were hired to care for the vines and prune them yearly (Lev. 25:3; Isa. 61:5). The grapes were gathered in baskets in September and October with much festivity (Judg. 9:27; Isa. 16:10). Provision was made for the poor to glean the fields (Lev. 19:10; Deut. 24:21). The choicest grapes were dried or eaten fresh and the rest placed in presses to extract the juice (Isa. 61:5; Hos. 9:2–4), which they drank fresh or fermented.

Jesus alluded to his relationship with the twelve disciples by referring to himself as the vine and to them as the branches (John 15:5). Wine symbolized Jesus' shed blood (Matt. 26:27–29). He also mentioned the vineyard in other parables. (See Matt. 20:1–7; 21:28–32; Luke 13:6–9.)

Hazel. (See *Almond.*)

Heath. (See *Broom.*)

Hemlock. A poisonous plant that grows to about two meters (five feet) tall and has small white flowers. Hemlock is referred to only once in the NKJV (Hos. 10:4). Other translations use the more general term *weeds.* (See *Wormwood.*)

Henna. A plant, used to produce a valuable orange-red dye, that grew two to three meters (seven to 10 feet) tall and bore fragrant white flowers. Solomon compared his beloved to a cluster of *henna* (Song of Sol. 1:14; 4:13; *camphire,* KJV).

Hyssop. A species of marjoram and a member of the mint family. Hyssop was an aromatic shrub under one meter (three feet) tall with clusters of yellow flowers. It grew in rocky crevices and was cultivated on terraced walls (1 Kings 4:33). Bunches of hyssop were used to sprinkle blood on the doorposts on the night of the Exodus from Egypt (Exod. 12:22), and in purification ceremonies (Lev. 14:4–6, 51–52). David mentioned the plant as an instrument of inner cleansing (Ps. 51:7). Hyssop was used at the crucifixion to relieve Jesus' thirst (John 19:29).

The hyssop was very similar to the *caper plant.* It is sometimes rendered *marjoram* by the NEB.

Ilex. (See *Cypress.*)

Juniper. (See *Broom.*)

Laurel. (See *Bay tree.*)

Leek. A bulbous vegetable resembling the onion and growing 15 centimeters (about six inches) high. The stems and bulbs of leeks were eaten raw and used to flavor foods. Named with garlic and onions, the leek was a food the Hebrew people ate in Egypt (Num. 11:5).

Lentil. A small annual plant with white, violet-striped flowers. The seeds of lentils grew in pods similar to the pea. Lentil was threshed like wheat and boiled into a reddish-brown pottage. This was the dish Esau purchased with his birthright (Gen. 25:34). Lentils were used as an ingredient in making bread (Ezek. 4:9).

Lign aloe. (See *Aloe.*)

Lily. A flower with white or rosy-purple blooms measuring up to 30 centimeters (12 inches) across. Many scholars think the lily is sometimes a term applied to flowers in general. Others believe the biblical writers meant specific types such as the *Turks Cap,* the *Madonna,* or the *lotus.*

The lily was used as an ornament for the temple (1 Kings 7:22). The Beloved and the Shulamite used the symbol of lilies to describe their love (Song of Sol. 2:1,16; 2:16; 4:5; 5:13; 6:3).

Locust. An evergreen tree growing about six to nine meters (20 to 30 feet) tall and having small glossy leaves. A native of Syria and Israel, it bears long pods known as *carob* or *locust-beans* (Luke 15:16; *husks,* KJV). These pods may have been used for food in dire circumstances (2 Kings 6:25, NEB).

Lotus. (See *Lily.*)

Mallow. A shrub growing 1.5 to three meters (five to 10 feet) high and having thick, succulent leaves and small purple flowers. The Hebrew word for *mallow* means "salt plant," and it thrived in dry, salty regions especially around the Dead Sea. Although the leaves were sour and had little nutritive value, they were boiled and eaten by the poor during famine.

Mentioned only once in the Bible (Job 30:4), mallow is also translated as *salt herbs* in the NIV and *saltwort* in the NEB.

Mandrake. A fruit-producing plant with dark green leaves and small bluish-purple flowers. The mandrake is a relative of the potato family, which grew abundantly throughout Israel and the Mediterranean region.

The yellow fruit of the mandrake was small, sweet-tasting, and fragrant. It had narcotic qualities and may have been used medicinally. The fruit of the mandrake was also referred to as the *love apple* and was considered an aphrodisiac.

Marjoram. (See *Hyssop*.)

Melon. A type of gourd that bears sweet fruit. Both cantaloupes and watermelons may have grown along the banks of the Nile River in Egypt. Melons were used as food and medicine, and people made an intoxicating drink from their juice.

The Hebrews had become accustomed to eating melons in Egypt and longed for them while in the wilderness (Num. 11:5). This word is translated *watermelon* by the NEB.

Millet. An annual grain-producing grass that was under one meter (three feet) high and produced many seeds. The seeds of millet were smaller than other cereal grains. Millet has been known since ancient times in Israel and Egypt. It was used for bread (Ezek. 4:9) and eaten raw, especially by the poor.

Mint. A sweet-smelling herb that grew to a height of one meter (three feet) and produced spikes of lilac flowers. Mint was used in medicine and to flavor foods.

Mulberry. A tree that grew to a height of about eight to ten meters (25 to 30 feet) and

The lotus, a type of water lily, was the symbol of Upper Egypt.   PHOTO BY HOWARD VOS

produced red berries. A refreshing drink was prepared from the fruit. Jesus used the mulberry tree as an illustration when teaching about faith (Luke 17:6). It is called *sycamine* in the KJV and RSV. The mulberry trees mentioned in 2 Sam. 5:23–24 and 1 Chron. 14:14–15 are believed to be a species of *poplar*.

Mustard. A plant that grew wild along roadsides and in fields, reaching a height of about 4.6 meters (15 feet). The black mustard of Israel seems to be the species to which Jesus referred (Matt. 13:31–32; Mark 4:31–32; Luke 13:19). It was cultivated for its seeds that were used as a condiment and for oil.

The mustard seed was one of the smallest seeds known in Jesus' day (Matt. 13:32). Jesus said that if individuals had faith like a mustard seed, they could move mountains (Matt. 17:20) or transplant mulberry trees in the sea (Luke 17:6).

Myrrh. An extract from a stiff-branched tree with white flowers and plumlike fruit. After being extracted from the wood, myrrh soon hardened and was valued as an article of trade. It was an ingredient used in anointing oil (Exod. 30:23), as perfume (Ps. 45:8; Prov. 7:17; Song of Sol. 3:6), in purification rites for women (Esth. 2:12), as a gift for the infant Jesus (Matt. 2:11), and in embalming (John 19:39). On the cross Jesus was offered wine mingled with myrrh (Mark 15:23). Matthew, however, writes of sour wine mingled with gall (Matt. 27:34).

The reference to myrrh in Gen. 37:25 and 43:11 are likely *labdanum*, sometimes called *onycha*, from a species of rockrose and not the true myrrh. (See *Onycha*.)

Myrtle. An evergreen tree with dark glossy leaves and white flowers. People used the leaves, flowers, and berries for perfume and as seasoning for food. The myrtle tree had a religious significance for the Hebrews (Zech. 1:8–11) and was a symbol of peace and joy. Queen Esther's Hebrew name (Esth. 2:7) meant "myrtle."

Nard. (See *Spikenard*.)

Nettle. Two different plants referred to in the Bible.

1. The nettles mentioned in Isa. 34:13 and Hos. 9:6 are believed to be the true nettle. It is a spiny leaf plant sometimes growing to a height of about two meters (six feet).

2. The nettles referred to in Job 30:7 and Prov. 24:31 are thought to be the *acanthus*, a stinging plant common in Israel.

The nettles of Zeph. 2:9 (KJV) are translated *weeds* by the NKJV.

Oak. A large tree with a massive trunk that grew abundantly in Israel and the surrounding countries. Many Hebrew words refer to the oak. Some scholars think these words could have referred to any large tree such as the *terebinth* or *elm*.

The oak tree was an important historical landmark to the Hebrews. Some specific oak trees are mentioned in the Bible, such as the *oaks of Bashan* (Isa. 2:13; Zech. 11:2); the *oak of Bethel* (Gen. 35:8, KJV; *terebinth tree*, NKJV); and the *oaks of Mamre* (Gen. 13:18, RSV; *terebinth trees*, NKJV).

Oak wood was also used in shipbuilding

(Ezek. 27:6), and for crafting idols (Isa. 44:14). (See *Tamarisk, Terebinth*.)

Oil tree. A tree of uncertain identity. Many oil-producing trees mentioned in the Bible could be identified as the oil tree. Some believe the *oleaster* or *wild olive* is the tree meant. It grew to a height of about 4.5 to six meters (15 to 20 feet) and produced small bitter fruit resembling an olive. The oleaster yielded an inferior oil, which was used medicinally.

The oil tree of Isa. 41:19 is called an olive tree in the RSV, NIV, NEB, and NASB. (See also *Olive*.)

Olive. A fruit-bearing tree about six meters (20 feet) tall with a gnarled, twisted trunk, white flowers, and berries that ripen to a black color. The olive tree grew slowly and continued to bear fruit after reaching a great age. Before it died, new branches sprouted from its roots.

The fruit was harvested by beating the boughs of the olive tree with a stick (Deut. 24:20) or by shaking the tree (Isa. 17:6). People ate the fresh-picked green fruit or made it made into a relish.

The best oil was obtained from the green olive fruit. It was used as fuel for lamps (Exod. 27:20), as anointing oil (Lev. 2:1), as an article of trade (1 Kings 5:11), and for dressing wounds (Luke 10:34).

Olive trees were cultivated in groves or orchards (Exod. 23:11; Josh. 24:13). The most famous olive garden mentioned in the Bible is *Gethsemane*, meaning "oil press" (Matt. 26:36).

Onion. A plant with a large, edible bulb. The onion is mentioned only once in the Bible, as one of the foods the Hebrews longed for in the wilderness (Num. 11:5). The onion was known in Egypt from ancient times. Drawings of the onion have been found on Egyptian tombs.

Onycha. A dark brown gum resin obtained from the stem and leaves of a species of the rockrose, also known as *labdanum*. Onycha was used as an ingredient in the holy anointing oil (Exod. 30:34). It was highly valued for its fragrance and medicinal qualities.

The rockrose was a bush growing to a height of about one meter (three feet) and having large white flowers measuring eight centimeters (three inches) across. Some scholars believe the substance referred to as myrrh in Gen. 37:25 and 43:11 was onycha.

Palm. A tree that grew to a height of about 18 to 30 meters (60 to 100 feet) and had long feathery leaves (branches; Neh. 8:15; John 12:13; Rev. 7:9). These branches were about two to three meters (six to eight feet) long and grew from the top of the trunk. Also called the *date palm,* this tree is believed to live up to 200 years.

Palm branches were considered a symbol of victory (John 12:13; Rev. 7:9). Many places in the Bible were identified by their abundance of palm trees (Exod. 15:27; Deut. 34:3; Judg. 1:16). One of the Hebrew words for palm, *Tamar,* was often used as a woman's name (Gen. 38:6; 2 Sam. 13:1).

Pannag. (See *Millet.*)

Papyrus. (See *Reed* or *Rush.*)

Pine. An evergreen tree of uncertain identity. Scholars believe pine refers to either the *Brutian* or the *Aleppo pine* (Isa. 41:19; 60:13). The Brutian pine grew to a height of about nine to 11 meters (30 to 35 feet). It is smaller and has longer needles than the Aleppo pine, which grew to a height of about 27 meters (90 feet). Both trees grew in Lebanon and in Israel.

Authorities have not agreed on the identity of the many evergreens mentioned in the Bible. Other trees suggested for these references are the *ash, fir, cypress, cedar,* or *juniper.*

Pistachio nut. A product of the pistacia tree, which grows about nine meters (30 feet) tall with wide spreading branches. The pistachio nut is about 2.5 centimeters (one inch) long and has a thin, hard outer shell. The smooth husk or skin that shields the green kernel is red. These nuts

are sweet and considered a luxury. Jacob included them in the gifts sent to Egypt (Gen. 43:11).

Plane. (See *Chestnut.*)

Pomegranate. A round, sweet fruit about 10 centimeters (four inches) across with a hard rind. It is green when young and turns red when ripe. There are numerous edible seeds inside the pomegranate.

The pomegranate tree has been cultivated in Israel and Egypt since ancient times (Num. 13:23; Deut. 8:8). It grew as a bush or small tree, sometimes reaching a height of about nine meters (30 feet) with small, lance-shaped leaves. The blossoms were bright red. The fruit usually ripened in August or September.

Pomegranates were highly esteemed during Bible times. The hem of Aaron's robe was decorated with blue, purple, and red pomegranates (Exod. 28:33–34; 39:24–26). They were listed among the pleasant fruits of Egypt (Num. 20:5). Solomon decorated the temple with the likeness of the

A flowering pomegranate. In biblical times pomegranates were widely cultivated in Palestine (Num. 13:23; Deut. 8:7–8). The juice of the fruit made a pleasant drink (Song of Sol. 8:2).
PHOTO BY GUSTAV JEENINGA

pomegranate (1 Kings 7:18, 20). A spiced wine was made from the juice (Song of Sol. 8:2).

Poplar. A tree that grew to a height of about nine to 18 meters (30 to 60 feet) and had wide spreading branches. The leaves were green with white undersides. Jacob stripped the bark from poplar branches to reveal the white wood. This was supposed to control the color of his cattle (Gen. 30:37).

Hosea refers to the Israelites worshiping idols in the shade of poplar trees. This practice brought God's condemnation for their sin (Hos. 4:13). (See *Willow*.)

Raisin. (See *Grapes*.)

Reed or Rush. Gigantic hollow-stemmed grasses that grew along river banks and in moist areas of Egypt and Israel. Several Hebrew words refer to the marsh plants. They form a large order of plants, such as *flax, flags, bulrush, cane, calamus,* and *papyrus*.

Reeds and rushes grew anywhere from one to six meters (three to 20 feet) high and had long, narrow leaves. A cluster of white flowers formed at the top of each stem.

The reeds were used in various ways, including walking sticks, fishing poles, musical instruments, and pens. People also used them for weaving baskets and mats. The infant Moses' basket was woven from reeds. Papyrus, a particular reed, was used to make paper.

Reeds symbolized weakness. Jesus refers to them as shaking in the wind (Matt. 11:7). A reed was placed in Jesus' hand as the Roman soldiers mocked him (Matt. 27:29).

Rose. The name of two different plants of the Bible:

1. Most authorities think the rose referred to in Song of Sol. 2:1 and Isa. 35:1 is not what we know as the rose, but a low-growing bulbous plant producing two to four yellow flowers on each stalk. This flower is noted for its fragrance. Other scholars have suggested the *mountain tu-lip, anemone, saffron,* or *crocus,* all of which grew wild in Israel. This particular flower is translated *crocus* by the RSV, NIV, and NASB (Isa. 35:1) and *asphodel* by the NEB (Song of Sol. 2:1; Isa. 35:2). The flower we call the *rose of Sharon* is a native of China, and is not the one mentioned in Song of Sol. 2:1.

2. The rose of Sirach 24:14; 39:13 (NEB) is thought to be the *oleander*. This shrub grows to a height of about 3.6 meters (12 feet) and has pink or white flowers.

Rue. A garden herb growing one-half to one meter (two to three feet) high with gray-green foliage and clusters of small yellow flowers. Rue had a strong odor, and was valued for its antiseptic and disinfectant qualities as well as for flavoring foods.

Rye. (See *Spelt*.)

Saffron. The product of many varieties of crocus, a flower that grew from a bulb and produced light-blue flowers.

Crocus blooms were gathered, dried, and pressed into cakes of saffron. Saffron was used as a coloring for curries and stews as well as for a perfume for the floors of theaters and for weddings. Solomon was the only biblical writer to refer to saffron (Song of Sol. 4:14).

Salt herb. (See *Mallow*.)

Saltwort. (See *Mallow*.)

Shittah tree. (See *Acacia*.)

Shittim wood. (See *Acacia*.)

Spelt. An inferior kind of wheat. Although the bread made from this grain was of a poorer quality than that made from wheat, spelt was preferred over barley by many in the ancient world. The KJV translates this word as *rye* in Exod. 9:32 and Isa. 28:25, and as *fitches* in Ezek. 4:9. Spelt was sown later than wheat and thrived in poor soil and under adverse conditions.

Spikenard. A costly oil derived from the dried roots and stems of the *nard,* an herb of Asia. This oil was used as a liquid or made into an ointment. Solomon praised the fragrance of spikenard (Song of Sol. 1:12; 4:13–14).

Spikenard was imported from India in alabaster boxes. These were stored and used only for special occasions. When household guests arrived, they were usually anointed with this oil. We have a record of Jesus being so anointed on two occasions as an honored guest (Mark 14:3; John 12:3).

Many spikes grew from a single nard root that produced clusters of pink flowers. The stems were covered with hair, giving them a woolly appearance. Some translations refer to spikenard as *nard*.

Stacte. A resin believed to be an extract of the stems and branches of the storax tree. Stacte was highly prized as perfume and incense. It was one of the ingredients of anointing oil (Exod. 30:34).

The storax was a small, stiff shrub growing to a height of three to six meters (10 to 20 feet) that flourished in Lebanon and throughout Israel. Its leaves were dark with grayish-white undersides. In spring the storax flowered profusely with highly fragrant white blooms that resembled the orange blossom.

Straw. The dried stalks of various grains such as *spelt, barley, millet,* or many kinds of *wheat*. Straw could also include stalks of wild grasses. Straw was mixed with grain and used as fodder (Gen. 24:25; Judg. 19:19; 1 Kings 4:28). The Egyptians mixed straw with clay for stronger bricks (Exod. 5:7).

Sycamine. (See *Mulberry*.)

Sycamore. An evergreen tree growing to a height of about 12 to 15 meters (40 to 50 feet) with a trunk circumference of over 6.5 meters (20 feet). The trunk forked near the ground, and the branches grew outward.

The leaves of the sycamore, sometimes called the *sycamore fig*, were heart-shaped, resembling the leaves of the mulberry. The fruit was similar to the true fig, but inferior in quality. These yellow figs grew in clusters close to the branches.

Sycamores were trees of the plains (1 Kings 10:27) and could not survive in colder climates (Ps. 78:47). The sycamore was the tree that Zacchaeus climbed to gain a better view of Jesus (Luke 19:4).

Tamarisk. A small tree with thick foliage and spikes of pink blooms. It provided ample shade for desert travelers (1 Sam. 22:6). The word for tamarisk is translated *tree, grove,* or *oak* by the KJV.

Tares. A poisonous grass resembling wheat, but with smaller seeds. The tares were usually left in the fields until harvest time, then separated from the wheat during winnowing. Jesus used tares growing with wheat to illustrate evil in the world (Matt. 13:25–30, 36–40). Tares is translated *weeds* in the RSV and NIV, and *darnel* in the NEB.

Teil. (See *Terebinth*.)

Terebinth. A large spreading tree that grew to a height of six to eight meters (20 to 26 feet) with reddish-green leaves and red berries in clusters. The terebinth is mentioned several times in the Bible and is sometimes translated as *teil* (Isa. 6:13), elm (Hos. 4:13), or oak (Gen. 35:4) by the KJV.

Thistles *or* Thorns. General terms for any spiny plant. Such plants are characteristic of arid and desert regions. Some of these were brambles, briers, thorny bushes, small trees, weeds, and prickly herbs. They grew abundantly in Israel and other Bible lands, especially along roadsides, in fields, and in dry places.

The most noted use of thorns in the Bible was the crown of thorns placed on the head of Jesus on the cross (Matt. 27:29) as a form of mockery.

Some of the thorns and thistles were annuals, scattering their seed in autumn. Industrious farmers would destroy the plants before they seeded (Matt. 13:7). Many of them were used as cooking fuel (Ps. 58:9; Eccles. 7:6; Isa. 33:12).

Thorny shrubs were used as hedges to guard fields and vineyards (Prov. 15:19; Mark 12:1). The prophet Micah declared that even the most upright person is "sharper [more destructive] than a thorn hedge" (Mic. 7:4).

Thyine.   (See *Citron.*)

Vine.   (See *Grapes.*)

Watermelon.   (See *Melon.*)

Wheat.   The most important cereal grass mentioned in the Bible. This was the bearded variety belonging to the genus *Triticum* and was cultivated from early times (Gen. 30:14). Egyptian wheat was the many-eared variety called *mummy wheat*—probably the wheat in Pharaoh's dream (Gen. 41:5–57).

Wheat was sown after barley in November or December. It was usually broadcast and then either plowed or trodden into the soil by oxen or other animals (Isa. 32:20). This grain was used for bread (Exod. 29:32), but was also eaten parched (Lev. 23:14; Ruth 2:14). It was used in ceremonial offerings (Lev. 2:1; 24:5–7) and as an article of trade (Ezek. 27:17; Acts 27:38).

When corn, not known in Bible times, is mentioned, it refers to wheat. Jesus compared his own death to a grain of wheat that must die to produce fruit (John 12:24).

Willow.   A tree that grew to about nine to 12 meters (30 to 40 feet) and had reddish-brown bark; narrow, pointed leaves; and flowers or catkins that hung downward. Willow branches were used to construct the booths for the Feast of Tabernacles (Lev. 23:40). The Israelites hung their harps on willows while in Babylon (Ps. 137:1–2).

Some biblical scholars think the willow mentioned in the Bible was actually the *poplar* or *Euphrates aspen.* The word for willow is consistently translated as *poplar* by the NIV. Isaiah 44:4 is translated *poplar* by the NEB and NASB as well. (See *Poplar.*)

Wormwood.   A woody shrub covered with small green leaves, with greenish-yellow flowers growing in clusters. Wormwood grows in the desert regions of Israel and Syria. This plant is mentioned many times in the Bible. It had a bitter taste and a strong aroma (Jer. 9:15).

Wormwood symbolized any calamity or bitter experience (Deut. 29:18; Prov. 5:4; Amos 5:7; Rev. 8:10–11). An intoxicating drink could also be made from this plant (Lam. 3:15). Wormwood is sometimes translated as *bitter weeds* or *hemlock* (Amos 6:12, KJV).

Archaeology

The word *archaeology* comes from two Greek words meaning "a study of ancient things." But the term usually applies to a study of excavated materials belonging to a former era. Biblical archaeology is the scientific study, by excavation, examination, and publication, of the evidences of cultures and civilizations from the biblical period.

Archaeological findings help us understand the Bible better. They reveal what life was like in biblical times, throw light on obscure passages of Scripture, and help us appreciate the historical context of the Bible.

Archaeology is a complex science, calling on the assistance of other sciences such as chemistry, anthropology, and zoology. Many talented professionals—including engineers, historians, chemists, paleontologists, photographers, artists, and surveyors—are involved in the discovery, interpretation, and publication of archaeological knowledge.

Every object an archaeologist discovers—whether a piece of bone, pottery, metal, stone, or wood—is studied in detail. The archaeologist's work often requires translating ancient writings and studying an ancient city's art and architecture. These detailed studies are carried out in museums and laboratories, but the archaeologist must first recover the material by carefully excavating an ancient city.

For the New Testament period, biblical archaeology has concentrated on a geographical area that parallels the extent of the old Roman Empire. The area is somewhat smaller for Old Testament times, and the focus shifts eastward to include the Mesopotamian Valley and Persia (modern Iran).

The main area for Old Testament research is Palestine or Israel (ancient Canaan), but it fans out to include the great empires in the Nile and Mesopotamian valleys. The culture of Phoenicia (modern Lebanon) was similar to that of Canaan to the south. Syria to the east is also a place of study, because its history often was tied to Israel's. Still farther north, Asia Minor was the homeland of the Hittites and several Greek cultures.

Until the early 1800s, little was known of biblical times and customs, except what we read in the Old Testament. Although the Greek historians preserved considerable background material on New Testament times, they provided little documentation for the Old Testament period. Because Alexander the Great forced the Greek language and customs on all the lands his armies conquered, this policy almost destroyed the languages and culture of Egypt, Persia, Canaan, and Babylon. Before the rise of modern archaeology, we had scarcely any historical evidence available to illustrate or confirm the history and literature of the Old Testament.

Modern Near Eastern archaeology began during the eighteenth century. Before that, some research had been done by collectors of antiquities, usually museums or wealthy individuals. Biblical archaeology probably began with the discovery of the Rosetta Stone during Napoleon's invasion of Egypt in 1799. Discovered by an officer in the expedition, the stone was inscribed in three columns consisting of Greek, Egyptian hieroglyphics, and later-written Egyptian script. With Napoleon's encouragement, the stone was studied and recorded with scientific accuracy, then displayed in the British Museum. This discovery opened the door to the study of the remains of ancient Egypt, a rich resource for biblical researchers.

How Ancient Ruins (Tells) Were Formed

In ancient times, cities were usually built on sites that were easy to defend, and they were located near a source of water and on a good trade route. The homes were constructed primarily of sun-baked bricks, which could be destroyed quite easily by flood, earthquakes, or enemy attack. In rebuilding a town, the inhabitants would usually level the rubble and debris and erect new buildings on the same locations. Cities continued to be destroyed by windstorm, enemy attack, or other catastrophes until gradually a mound of earth containing remnants of buildings, tools, vases, and pottery rose on the site. Eventually, many layers of habitation lay upon one another.

The sites of these mounds in the ancient Near East are called tells, the Arabic word for "mounds." These mounds do not look like natural hills, appearing instead as unnatural rounded humps on the landscape. They often rise from their surroundings by as much as 15 to 23 meters (50 to 75 feet).

If a city was destroyed by famine, disease, earthquake, or some other natural catastrophe, the townspeople might conclude that the gods had cursed their city and that it would be unwise to rebuild on the same site. The area might lie unused for hundreds of years until a new group decided to build again on the strategically located site.

When a site is occupied continuously by the same group of people, one layer or stratum of the mound is very similar to the next. Some slight changes in artifacts and ways of doing things, such as the method of baking pottery or the shape of certain tools, will occur in an orderly fashion from generation to generation. If a long period with no habitation has occurred between layers, the new people who inhabit the mound may have discovered new techniques. Also, peoples with new skills—perhaps the conquerors of the former dwellers—may inhabit the site. A sharp change in the pattern of living or in types of artifacts discovered may indicate a gap in habitation of the site.

As they excavate these ancient sites, archaeologists first find large stationary objects such as houses, monuments, tombs, and fortresses. Also, there are smaller artifacts such as jewelry, tools, weapons, and cooking utensils. Archaeology provides the Bible researcher with the rich remains of material culture over the course of centuries to supplement what is recorded in the Bible, in art, and in literature.

How Archaeologists Do Their Work

In organizing their work (called a dig), archaeologists first divide the site, or area, by a *grid system*, using lines parallel to the longitude and latitude of the area. A *field*, 5.8 meters (19 feet) square, is then divided into four squares or quadrants, leaving room for a catwalk among them to observe the work. Each section has an area supervisor, who in turn works under the supervision of the excavation director. Area supervisors are responsible for directing the actual digging in their areas and recording everything as it comes from the ground. It is better to excavate small areas in detail than to excavate a large area carelessly.

Those who actually work the site are of three categories: *Pickmen* carefully break up the soil, noticing every difference in the hardness of the earth and how it is compacted. It takes skill to distinguish a clay wall from ordinary packed clay or to bring forth a vase or a human bone unharmed. *Hoemen* work over the loosened soil, saving anything of potential interest. *Basketmen* carry off the excavated dirt, perhaps using a sieve to sift the soil—to be sure nothing of value is discarded. Archaeology students often serve as laborers on expeditions.

Everything found in a quadrant of the site is collected in an individual basket and tagged with all pertinent information, including the date and location of discovery. The baskets are photographed and evaluated by experts who record all the data. The materials and information go to laboratories and museums where they are studied in detail. Conclusions are published by the excavation director and circulated to other archaeologists and scholars.

In 1832, while the Danish archaeologist C. J. Thomsen was classifying implements for display in a Copenhagen museum, he wondered about the age of the various tools made of iron, bronze, and stone. Returning to the peat bog where the implements had been found, he discovered that artifacts made of stone were found in the bottom layer. Higher levels contained many tools made of copper and bronze. At the top of the bog were instruments of iron, indicating they were made last. These discoveries are the basis for our designations *Stone Age, Bronze Age,* and *Iron Age.*

Thomsen made a very simple application of the principle of stratigraphy, or keeping track of the layers of soil in which artifacts are found to establish a sequence of events. Archaeologists base many of their conclusions on Thomsen's study and evaluation of the various strata of the mound.

An archaeologist carefully uncovers a skeleton at an excavation near Caesarea Maritima.
PHOTO BY GUSTAV JEENINGA

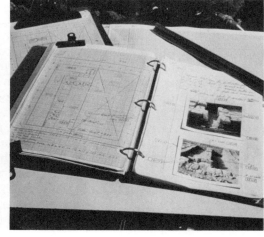

An archaeologist's notebook, containing detailed records of everything uncovered in an excavation.
PHOTO BY GUSTAV JEENINGA

Archaeologists can determine how many times a town has been destroyed and rebuilt, but they will want to know the date of each occupation, how long it lasted, and why it was destroyed. Each level of occupation contains the foundations of walls and buildings and often a layer of debris from the destruction. The levels also contain the articles of everyday living such as weapons, tools, pottery, and ornaments. Sometimes the different strata are separated by thick layers of ash from a great fire. At other times, only a difference in soil color or compactness distinguishes the levels.

Furthermore, during centuries when the mound was not inhabited, erosion and random digging at the site can disrupt a stratum. A new group of settlers may have dug foundations, garbage pits, or trenches deep into an earlier layer, making the job of the archaeologist more difficult.

Pottery. One of the most important keys to dating the strata of a tell. Pottery typology, or the study of various types of pottery, is now refined to an exacting science. Scientists can call on their detailed knowledge of the characteristics of pottery in each period to identify and date their finds, usually within half a century of the exact time when the piece was made. The scientific method of carbon-14 dating is also used to establish the age of some archaeological materials.

Earlier pottery designs were simple and functional; later vessels became more delicate and elaborate, often showing Persian and Greek influences. The method of baking the clay can also indicate the approximate time it was made. Changes in everyday objects such as lamps, tools, weapons, and jewelry help scientists identify broader periods of history. Coin collectors, then as now, might possess old coins, so these are not as reliable a method of identifying a period.

How Archaeology Helps Us Understand the Bible

During the early years of exploring Bible lands, archaeologists hoped to make discoveries that would confirm the main events of Bible history. Today's archaeologists realize that many things about the Bible cannot be proved in a direct way. Instead of providing proof of specific events, archaeology increases our knowledge of the everyday life, the history, and the customs of the people who appear in the Bible's long story—the Egyptians, Phoenicians, Philistines, Moabites, Assyrians, Babylonians, and others, as well as the Hebrews.

For example, discoveries of ancient texts on clay tablets—in many languages—show us what the various peoples of the ancient Near East thought about the gods they worshiped, as well as the types of laws by which they lived. Ancient texts also tell us of alliances, trade agreements, and wars between the great cities and nations of the past.

Archaeological discoveries paint in the background of the Bible, helping to explain many of its events. Thanks to archaeology, we now know that in the time of Abraham (about 2000 B.C.) many thriving cities existed in the ancient Near East. Civilization was already over a thousand years old in Egypt and in the region of the Tigris and Euphrates Rivers. From a city on the Euphrates River, called Ur, Abraham (then called Abram) began a journey that eventually brought him to the land of Canaan (Gen. 11:31). The excavation of Ur early in this century (1922–1934) by Sir Charles Leonard Woolley revealed that Abraham was surrounded by idolatry when God called him to start a new nation of people through whom God could do redemptive work.

The discovery of large bodies of cuneiform literature in Babylon and other places has also proved most revealing. For example, the Amarna Letters from Egypt give an inside glance into conditions in Canaan just before the conquest by Joshua and the Israelites.

In 1890 the famed archaeologist Flinders Petrie began an exploration at Tell el-Hesi in southwestern Palestine. He carefully recorded the pieces and types of broken pottery found at each level of occupation. This exploration helped refine the method known as *ceramic chronology*, which is one of the methods still used to date ancient finds.

Inscriptions and ancient manuscripts have also made an important contribution to biblical study. Today's archaeological work is increasingly concerned with the text of the Bible. Intensive study of more than 3,000 New Testament Greek manuscripts dating from the second century A.D. has shown that the New Testament text has been preserved remarkably well from that time. Not one doctrine has been perverted because of major errors in transmission.

The science of papyrology developed after large quantities of papyri, or ancient writing materials, were discovered in Egypt around the turn of the century. The papyri, written on paper made from the papyrus reeds of Egypt, included a wide variety of topics and were written on in several languages. More than 70 papyri containing portions of the New Testament have been found.

These fragments help confirm the texts of the longer manuscripts dating to the fourth century A.D. and following. Since many of the papyri date to the first three centuries after Christ, the impact of papyrology on biblical studies has been significant. These discoveries make it possible to establish the grammar of the period and, thus, to date the composition of New Testament books to the first century A.D.

The mass of papyri also demonstrated that New Testament Greek was not invented by the New Testament writers. Instead, it was the common language used during the first century of the Christian era. Moreover, the papyri have shown that the New Testament contained good grammar, judged by first-century standards.

The search for buildings and places associated with the ministry of Jesus has been going on for centuries. A synagogue was unearthed in Capernaum, although it is probably not the one in which Jesus taught (Mark 1:21). However, it may well be the successor of the synagogue Jesus knew. Archaeologists think they may have discovered Peter's house at the same site (Matt. 8:14). Graffiti on the plastered wall of this second-century house clearly link it with Peter. Atop Mount Gerizim, excavations have uncovered the foundations of the Samaritan temple. Although tradition has assigned sites for the birth and the crucifixion of Jesus, archaeologists now disagree on the authenticity of some of these locations.

Significant Archaeological Digs and Their Contributions

Many important archaeological discoveries of this century have contributed to Bible knowledge. Following are descriptions of five of these projects, with an analysis of their contributions.

City of Ur. An important city of ancient Babylonia situated on the Euphrates River in lower Mesopotamia (present-day Iraq). The glory of the city was suddenly destroyed about 1960 B.C. Foreigners stormed down from the surrounding hills, captured the reigning king Ibbi-Sin, and reduced the

Even minute particles, such as these microflints and bones, must be carefully sorted and analyzed after they are uncovered by archaeologists.   PHOTO BY GUSTAV JEENINGA

city to ruins. So complete was its destruction that the city lay buried in oblivion until it was excavated in modern times by archaeologists.

Abraham lived in the city of Ur at the height of its splendor. The city was a center of religion and industry. The Babylonians worshiped many gods, but the moon god Sin was supreme. Accordingly, Ur was a theocracy centered in worship of the moon deity. Abraham's father, *Terah*, probably worshiped at the altar of Sin.

God called Abraham out of this polluted atmosphere to begin a new line of people, the Hebrews, who were to be separated from idolatry and who were to become a blessing to all humanity. The archaeological findings of ancient Ur have greatly illuminated the biblical references to the patriarch Abraham and have given a much wider view of the ancient world around 2000 B.C.

Dead Sea Scrolls. The greatest manuscript discovery of modern times began with the uncovering of the Dead Sea scrolls in 1947. A shepherd boy stumbled on a cave south of Jericho containing numerous leather scrolls of Hebrew and Aramaic writing and some 600 fragmentary inscriptions. Excitement quickly spread throughout the archaeological world. In 1952, new caves were found containing fragments of later scrolls in Hebrew, Greek, and Aramaic enclosed in jars. These startling discoveries have been followed by the uncovering of other manuscripts around the Dead Sea area, particularly at Qumran.

After intensive study, scholars date the manuscripts from as early as 250 B.C. to as late as A.D. 68. Although questions have been raised about the age and authenticity of the manuscripts, two lines of evidence establish their integrity. *Radiocarbon count,* a scientific method of dating, places the linen in which the scrolls were wrapped in the general period of 175 B.C. to A.D. 225. Scholars of ancient writing *(paleographers)* date documents by the form of the letters and the method of writing. This line of evidence also places the Dead Sea Scrolls three centuries before A.D. 70.

The scrolls contain ancient texts of parts of the Old Testament, as well as writing that originated between the Old and New Testament periods. The biblical section contains two scrolls of Isaiah, one complete, along with fragments of several Old Testament books. Coins found at the site at Qumran reveal that the settlement was founded about 135 B.C. and abandoned during the Jewish war with the Romans in A.D. 66–73.

The scrolls discovered along the Dead Sea were part of the library of the people at Qumran, possibly the *Essenes,* a religious group mentioned by ancient writers. The sect was even stricter in its interpretation of the religious laws than the Pharisees of the New Testament. Some scholars believe that John the Baptist lived among these

Cave Four at Qumran, where several of the Dead Sea Scrolls were discovered, is visible at upper right. The Dead Sea looms in the background. PHOTO BY GUSTAV JEENINGA

people before beginning his work of announcing the ministry of Jesus.

The Essenes expected the coming of a new age, ushered in by a ruler who would serve as a prophet and priest. Although the finds at Qumran do not relate directly to any events described in the Bible, they shed light on the way certain people thought during the period between the Old and New Testaments.

A full text of the book of Isaiah is the best known of the discoveries at Qumran. The documents make up the oldest existing manuscripts of the Bible in any language. One of the caves yielded 18 scraps of papyri written entirely in Greek, identified as fragments of the earliest New Testament version that has been discovered. One of them, a fragment of Mark's gospel, dates from about 15 years after the events recorded.

Scholars are now studying thousands of clay tablets found at Ebla in northern Syria—a task that will require a generation of careful study and analysis. Dialogue between the biblical text and archaeological finds must continue, because each can help us understand and interpret the Bible.

Lachish letters. In the excavations of Lachish, a city in southwestern Palestine, the most astonishing finds consisted of letters imbedded in a layer of burned charcoal and ashes. Written in Hebrew words but using the ancient Phoenician script, the documents throw additional light on the life and times of Jeremiah. The letters, called *ostraca*, were inscribed on pieces of broken pottery. Most of the letters were written by a citizen named *Hoshayahu*, who was stationed at a military outpost. He sent these letters to Yaosh, evidently a high-ranking officer in the garrison at Lachish.

The Babylonians had attacked and partly burned Lachish ten years earlier during the reign of King Jehoiakim of Judah. These letters were found in the layers of ashes that represent the final destruction of the city. This location dates them from 588–587 B.C., when Nebuchadnezzar of Babylon made his final siege of the Hebrew cities of Jerusalem, Lachish, and Azekah.

One letter lists names, the majority of which are found in the Old Testament; two letters consist largely of greetings; another letter describes movements of troops and makes an interesting reference to an unnamed prophet and his warning. The Lachish letters give an independent view of conditions in Judah during the days before the fall of Jerusalem.

Jeremiah conducted his ministry in these times. His reference to Azekah and Lachish says, "when the king of Babylon's army fought against Jerusalem and all the cities of Judah that were left, against Lachish, and Azekah; for only these fortified cities remained of the cities of Judah" (Jer. 34:7).

Tell ez-Zakariyeh has been identified as the ancient city of Azekah, which had a strong inner fortress buttressed with eight large towers. The Lachish letters concern the time just prior to the fall of the city and

amplify the same conditions of turmoil and confusion revealed in the book of Jeremiah. This information is of immense value in explaining historical backgrounds and illuminating Old Testament Scripture.

Law code of Hammurabi. In 1901 a slab of black marble over seven feet tall and six feet wide, containing over 300 paragraphs of legal inscriptions, was discovered at Susa (Shushan) in ancient Elam. Engraved on the large rock were legal provisions dealing with the social, domestic, and moral life of the ancient Babylonian people of King Hammurabi's time (about 1792–1750 B.C.). The code furnishes important background material for comparison with other ancient bodies of law, such as the law of Moses.

The fact that Hammurabi's code is three centuries older than the laws of Moses has ruined some of the theories of critics and has given rise to others.

This kind of discovery illustrates how archaeology disproves views that place the origin of many of the laws attributed to Moses at a much later time. The discovery of Hammurabi's laws indicates that the law of Moses was not borrowed from, or dependent on, Babylonian laws. Rather, it was divinely given as it claims to be.

The resemblances between the Mosaic laws and the code of Hammurabi are clearly due to the similarity of the general intellectual and cultural heritage of the Hebrews and the Babylonians at that ancient time. The striking differences, however, demonstrate that there is no direct borrowing and that the Mosaic law—although later by three centuries—is in no way dependent upon the Babylonian.

The two law codes are radically different in their origins and morality. The Babylonian laws are alleged to have been received by Hammurabi from the sun god, Shamash. Moses received his laws directly from God. Hammurabi's laws list at least ten varieties of bodily mutilation prescribed for various offenses. For example, if a physician unsuccessfully performed an operation, his hand was to be cut off. By contrast, the Mosaic legislation includes only one instance of mutilation, where a wife's hand is to be severed (Deut. 25:11–12).

In the Hebrew laws, a greater value is placed upon human life. A stricter regard for the honor of womanhood is evident, and masters are ordered to treat their slaves more humanely.

Moabite stone. A black basalt memorial stone discovered in Moab by a German missionary in 1868. Nearly four feet high, it contained 34 lines in an alphabet similar to Hebrew. The stone was probably erected about 850 B.C. by the Moabite King Mesha.

King Mesha's story, as written on the stone, celebrated his overthrow of Israel. This event apparently is recorded in 2 Kings 3:4–27, although the biblical account makes it clear that Israel was victorious in the battle. Mesha honored his god Chemosh in terms similar to the Old Testament reverence for *Yahweh* (the Hebrew name for *God*). The inhabitants of entire cities were apparently slaughtered to appease this deity, recalling the similar practices of the Israelites, especially as described in the book of Joshua. Besides telling of his violent conquests, Mesha boasted on the stone of the building of cities (with Israelite forced labor) and the construction of cisterns, walls, gates, towers, a king's palace, and even a highway.

The Moabite stone has profound biblical relevance. First, from a historical perspective, the stone confirms Old Testament accounts. Second, it sheds light on a theological parallel to Israel's worship of one God. Third, the Moabite stone mentions no less than 15 sites listed in the Old Testament. Fourth, the writing on the stone resembles Hebrew, the language in which most of the Old Testament was originally written.

Ras Shamra tablets. Recovered in another significant excavation were hundreds of clay tablets that had been housed in a library located between two pagan temples in Ugarit, modern Ras Shamra in Syria. These tablets date from about the fifteenth century B.C. and were inscribed in the earliest known alphabet written in wedge-shaped signs. The strange writing was recognized as ancient Canaanite in origin, and it turned out to be religious in nature. The tablets were inscribed in a dialect closely akin to biblical Hebrew and Phoenician.

The famous Moabite Stone, which celebrates the revolt of King Mesha of Moab against the rule of the Israelites. PHOTO BY GUSTAV JEENINGA

So important were the initial discoveries that archaeologist Claude F. Schaeffer continued excavations in the area from 1929 until 1937. Aside from the information they provide about the ancient city of Ugarit, the Ras Shamra texts have great literary importance. The translation of the texts showed the important parallels between the Ugaritic and Hebrew literary style and vocabulary. These texts have been invaluable to scholars studying Hebrew poetry, general style, and vocabulary.

The most important contribution of the religious texts from Ras Shamra is in the background material they provide for careful study of the pagan religions mentioned repeatedly in the Old Testament. As a result of archaeological work, an independent witness to the nature of Canaanite cults is now available. This finding answers the critics who accuse the Old Testament of projecting a bloodthirsty mentality because Joshua ordered the destruction of all Canaanite cities. He gave the order to purge the immoral worship of the Canaanites from the land.

The Bible

Historic Texts and Their Translation

G od's servants wrote the books of the OT many generations before the NT was written. Originally, these were the holy books of the Jewish people. We have received them through channels that were different from the route the NT text has followed. The text of the OT has withstood the rigors of time for centuries more than the NT. Its writers wrote in Hebrew and Aramaic, while all of the NT was written in Greek.

The Old Testament Text

How the Old Testament Was Inspired

Of the OT, Jesus said that "one jot or one tittle will by no means pass from the law till all is fulfilled" (Matt. 5:18). Thus He taught that God had inspired the entire text of the OT, even to the smallest details.

The early church considered the inspiration of the OT basic to its teaching. The NT books were still being written during the first century so when NT writers referred to Scripture, they meant the books that we now know as the OT. However, Paul specifically referred to the books of Moses as the "Old Testament" or "old covenant" in 2 Corinthians 3:14–15. In 1 Timothy 5:18 he was apparently quoting Luke 10:7 as "Scripture."

Peter wrote that "no prophecy of Scripture is of any private interpretation, for the prophecy never came by the will of man, but holy men of God spoke as they were moved by the Holy Spirit" (2 Pet. 1:20–21). Paul told Timothy, "All scripture is given by inspiration of God" (2 Tim. 3:16). And since God inspired these writings, they are "profitable for doctrine, for reproof, for correction, for instruction in righteousness" (2 Tim. 3:16).

Traditionally, the church has taught the plenary inspiration of the Bible. Simply stated, this means:

1. God gave and guaranteed all that the Bible writers had to say on all of the subjects they discussed.
2. God determined for them by inward prompting (plus providential conditioning and control) the manner in which they should express this truth.
3. Scripture was written exactly as God planned, and is as truly his Word as it is human witness. These teachings come from Scripture itself.

OT writers remind us again and again that they are communicating God's Word. The prophets introduce their statements with "thus saith the Lord," "the word of the Lord that came unto me," or something similar. One scholar said that he found nearly 4,000 such declarations in the OT.

Here are two passages that illustrate the point:
- Then the LORD said to Moses, "Write these words, for according to the tenor of these words I have made a covenant with you and with Israel" (Exod. 34:27).
- This word came to Jeremiah from the LORD, saying, "Take a scroll of a book and write on it all the words that I have spoken to you" (Jer. 36:1–2; cf. vv. 21–32).

Each writer explained that he was recording what God had revealed to him, expressing it in the same terms in which he received it from God.

However, God did not dictate the manuscript of the OT to these writers as if they were secretaries. He revealed his truth to them and showed them how they should present it. In so doing, they expressed his Word in terms of their own outlook, interests, literary habits, and peculiarities of style. We can say that while every word in the Bible is the Word of God, it is also the word of a human being.

The writer of Hebrews says that God "at various times and in various ways spoke in time past to the fathers by the prophets" (Heb. 1:1). Instead of binding the OT writers to produce one scripted account of his message, all in the same style, God spoke "in various ways" according to the circumstances and abilities of each writer. This provides a marvelous variety of material from the prophets, poets, historians, wise men, and visionaries through whom God spoke.

The OT writers tell us the methods by which God inspired some phases of their work. At times God revealed the message through visions consisting of sights and sounds. (e.g., Isa. 6:1ff) At other times God spoke directly through them as in 2 Samuel 23:2.

We do not know exactly how God inspired every part of every OT book. It is important that we know the Scriptures are his Word in both their substance and structure.

We can say this only about the original manuscripts and we no longer have them. The technical term for the original manuscripts is *autographs*. How can we be sure that the manuscript copies we have are still the Word of God?

To answer this question, we need to explore the way our ancestors copied the original manuscripts of the OT and passed the copies along to us. Scholars call this process textual transmission.

How We Received the Old Testament Text

When the OT writers finished their scrolls, there were no printing presses to duplicate their writing. They depended on scribes—men who patiently copied the Scriptures by hand when extra copies were needed or when the original scrolls became too worn to use any longer. The scribes attempted to make exact copies of the original scrolls. The scribes who followed them attempted to make exact copies of the copies. Even so, they did not always avoid mechanical slips in copying at some points.

By the time Jesus was born, the most recent OT book (Malachi) had been copied and recopied over a span of 400 years. The books that Moses wrote had been copied this way for more than 1,400 years. Yet during that time the scribes guarded the OT text very well. It has been computed that, on the average, they mistakenly copied one out of every 1,580 letters; and they usually corrected these errors when they made new copies.

The Hebrew language slowly changed, as languages do, across the centuries after the OT was first written. The language of Moses would seem very strange to a modern Israeli, just as the language of Chaucer or even Shakespeare is a long way from our own present-day speech. The meanings of some Hebrew words and some rules of grammar were lost. This has given Bible translators headaches trying to decipher some sections of the OT manuscripts. Yet it's remarkable how much they can understand overall.

Long before the time of the great writing prophets (seventh and eighth centuries B.C.), Hebrew scribes were copying and recopying the Scriptures. Jeremiah is the first to mention the scribes as a professional group: "How can you say, 'We are wise, and the law of the LORD is with us'? Look, the false pen of the scribe (sopherim) works falsehood" (Jer. 8:8). *Sopherim* literally means "the counters." The first scribes earned this title because they counted every letter of every book of Scripture to make sure they didn't leave out anything. To make doubly sure, they checked the letter that appeared in the middle of each book and in the middle of each major section of the book. They took great care to preserve the original wording of the text, even though the changing Hebrew language made it seem archaic.

An important change in the Hebrew language occurred around 500 B.C., when the sopherim began using a square Aramaic script that they learned during their exile in Babylon. (Aramaic had been introduced to Babylon in the Persian royal letters.) From the time of King David, the sopherim had used a rounded Paleo-Hebrew (early Hebrew) script to copy the manuscripts because they could write it on parchment, unlike the wedge-shaped script of the Canaanites.

By 500 B.C. Aramaic had become the common language of commerce and education in the Near East, so the Hebrews adopted its writing system. Papyrus manuscripts from a Jewish colony on Elephantine Island in the Nile Delta prove that the old cursive script was no longer used in 250 B.C. The Dead Sea Scrolls cover this period of transition. Some of them are written in the rounded Paleo-Hebrew script, but most are in the square Aramaic.

But Hebrew scribes did not begin using the Aramaic language. They simply borrowed its script and used it to express their own Hebrew words. They could do this because both Hebrew and Aramaic were Semitic languages. (We call them *Semitic* languages because they were spoken by nations that descended from Noah's son, Shem. See Gen. 10:21–31.) Their scripts stood for the same alphabet, which in turn signified many of the same sounds in both languages.

As a modern parallel, consider English and French. Since they were both shaped by the same classical language, Latin, their alphabets and some of their sounds are the same. Once Hebrew scribes borrowed the Aramaic script, they also started borrowing Aramaic words and phrases to express traditional Hebrew ideas just as we commonly use the French words *coiffure* and *lingerie*. Gradually they inserted Aramaic words into the text to take the place of older Hebrew words they no longer used. Sometimes they added editorial notes in Aramaic to clarify what the text said. Jeremiah 10:11 is such a note.

Paleo-Hebrew had no vowels, and early scribes probably used dots to separate their words as the Phoenicians did. They did not put spaces between words. In the tenth century B.C. the Arameans (now Syrians) had begun putting special letters at the end of each word to indicate final long vowels.

Two centuries later, Moabites of Canaan began doing the same, and they passed the idea on to the Hebrew scribes. Hebrew scribes did not develop a system for showing the vowel sounds until after A.D. 500.

People who read an OT manuscript in the time of Jesus found a continuous string of letters with only simple devices such as dots between words and final long vowels to guide them in identifying, breaking up and pronouncing the words. They had to supply a good deal from memory.

By the time the Hebrew scribes began to insert vowel markings into the text, they had lost the meanings of a few words—most of them ancient or rarely used in the OT. They were able to determine the meaning of most of these words in the light of the surrounding material. We call these later scribes Masoretes, and the manuscripts they produced the Masoretic Text. This term comes from the Hebrew *masora'* (tradition), because the

Masoretic scribes tried to preserve the traditional meaning of the Scriptures. A small Jewish sect in Babylon known as the Qaraites developed an effective system of vowel marks around A.D. 500, which led the Masoretes to deal more seriously with this problem.

A Masoretic family named *ben Asher* produced a better system of vowel markings in the ninth and tenth centuries. Soon afterward, Aaron ben Moshe ben Asher issued a complete text of the OT with the vowel marks. Because the ben Asher system represented the vowels with dots and short dashes, above and below the line of letters, scholars refer to it as vowel pointing. The *ben Naphtali* family of Masoretes developed a different point system and a slightly varied OT text at this same time. Late in the twelfth century A.D., the noted Jewish philosopher Moses Maimonides declared the ben Asher text to be the *textus receptus* (Latin, "received text").

However, the ben Asher text comes to us in several different forms. Our earliest manuscript of the ben Asher text is the Cairo Codex of the Prophets (otherwise known as *Codex C*), which was made in A.D. 950. Moshe ben Asher supplied the vowel markings for this manuscript and presented it to the Qaraite community in Jerusalem.

The crusaders seized it in 1099, but eventually it was returned to the Qaraite community in Cairo. The Leningrad Codex B3 of the Major and Minor Prophets (known as *Codex P*) was written in A.D. 916. The Aleppo manuscript of the ben Asher text *(Codex A)* was probably written before A.D. 940. However, one-fourth of that manuscript was lost during a raid on the Aleppo Monastery in 1948. Finally, the Leningrad Codex B19 A (or *Codex L*) of the OT was finished in A.D. 1008. These manuscripts provide the basic information we have about the ben Asher text.

In 1524, *Jacob ben Hayyim* published a printed text of the Hebrew OT, using manu-

Elephantine Island in the Nile River near Aswan, Egypt. A series of Aramaic papyri and ostraca, written by a colony of Jews stationed here during the Persian era, was found at this site. PHOTO BY GUSTAV JEENINGA

This ostracon from the Dead Sea caves at Qumran contains writing in Hebrew, the language in which most of the Old Testament was originally written. PHOTO BY HOWARD VOS

scripts that had been copied from the ben Asher manuscripts mentioned above. Because this was the first printed edition of the Hebrew OT, it became a standard for printed Bibles. Gerhard Kittel's *Biblia Hebraica*, perhaps the best-known Hebrew OT of the twentieth century, listed the variations of the ben Hayyim text in its footnotes and did not include them in the text.

However, the OT has come down to us in other languages besides Hebrew. Around 300 B.C., Greek versions began to appear. A community of Jewish scholars in Alexandria compiled a Greek version of the OT called the *Septuagint*.

It got this name from the Greek word for seventy. Tradition says that 70 scholars translated the text of the Hebrew Bible into Greek. In print, scholars usually referred to it by *LXX*, 70 in Roman numerals.

After A.D. 200, Jewish scholars began compiling Aramaic paraphrases of the OT. We call these Aramaic versions *targums*. The targums were made from Hebrew manuscripts written in the time of Jesus or later.

The New Testament Text

The writers of the NT completed their manuscripts within about sixty years of Jesus' crucifixion. Being written in an age when literature flourished, and being copied constantly from the start, the NT text has survived the centuries well. We have approximately 15,000 complete manuscripts and quotations of the NT today.

How the New Testament Was Inspired

God moved the writers of the NT faithfully to record his Word as he had the OT writers. Paul and the gospel writers often showed themselves conscious of what the Holy Spirit was doing through them.

Shown at right: *Several stalks of papyrus, reed-like plants used for making a primitive type of paper in Bible times.*

PHOTO BY WILLEM A. VANGEMEREN

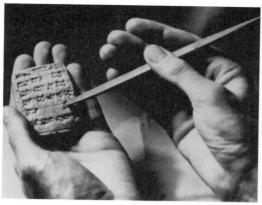

Ancient cuneiform characters were impressed on soft clay tablets with a pointed stylus. These tablets were then baked to form a piece of writing that was virtually indestructible.

PHOTO BY HOWARD VOS

Luke opens his gospel by saying that many others had attempted to write an account of Jesus' life and ministry, but that he himself is doing so because God has given him "perfect understanding of all things from the very first" (Luke 1:3).

We are assured that we can trust John's gospel because the writer was an eyewitness of the events he records (John 21:24). God gave the gospel writers first-hand exposure to the events of Jesus' ministry and perfect understanding of those events which uniquely qualified them for their writing task.

When writing to the churches on practical matters of morals and ethics (1 Cor. 4:14; 5:9), Paul knew he was expressing what the Holy Spirit directed him to write. Of his detailed directions about the conduct of worship in the Corinthian church, he said, "If anyone thinks himself to be a prophet or spiritual, let him acknowledge that the things which I write to you are the commandments of the Lord" (1 Cor. 14:37).

Paul was an apostle, one whom God enabled to declare his revealed wisdom "not in words which man's wisdom teaches but which the Holy Spirit teaches" (1 Cor. 2:13). What Paul laid down was to be received as divine instruction. As Peter said, Paul had written "according to the wisdom given to him" (2 Pet. 3:15).

Again, the apostle John explained that he did not write to the churches to reveal any new instructions from God (1 John 2:7–8). Nor did he write because his readers were ignorant of the truth that Christ had already revealed (1 John 2:21). Rather, he wrote because his readers already knew the truth and his letters would encourage them to obey that truth. This shows that the Holy Spirit inspired the NT writers to work in perfect harmony with the truth that had already been revealed. They knew it was that truth, stemming from Christ himself, that they were expressing and enforcing.

How We Received the New Testament Text

We have many fragments of the NT text that were written in the second century A.D. Some of these are on *ostraka* (scraps of pottery that early writers used as a cheap form of stationery) and talismans (pendants, bracelets, and other objects that early Christians wore to ward off evil spirits). But these objects contain only short quotations from the New Testaments, so they give us little information about the original text.

More important are the papyrus manuscripts of the NT. Written on an early form of paper made from matted papyrus reeds, most of these manuscripts date from the third and fourth centuries after Christ.

The earliest known fragment of a NT papyrus manuscript dates from about A.D. 125 or 140, commonly called the *Rylands Fragment* because it is housed in the John Rylands Library of Manchester, England. A mere 6 centimeters by 9 centimeters (2.5 inches by 3.25 inches), the fragment contains a portion of John 18:32–33, 37–38. Archaeologists recovered the Rylands Fragment from the ruins of a Greek town in ancient Egypt. Despite its early date, the fragment is too small to provide much information about the text of the gospel of John in the second century.

The next oldest papyrus manuscript is one of those called the *Chester Beatty Papyri,* because most of it is owned by the Chester Beatty Museum of Dublin. This manuscript consists of 76 leaves of papyrus (46 at Dublin, 30 at the University of Michigan). Each leaf measures about 16½ centimeters by 28 centimeters (6.5 inches by 11 inches) and contains about 25 lines of writing. Handwriting experts believe that this manuscript was written around A.D. 200. It contains most of Paul's letters.

Another important manuscript is called the *Bodmer Papyrus* (or *Bodmer II*). Also written in about A.D. 200, this manuscript contains chapters 1—14 of John and fragments of the last seven chapters. It is housed in the private library of Martin Bodmer in Cologny, Switzerland.

Jose O'Callagham of Barcelona, a professor of the Pontifical Institute in Rome, believes that some papyrus fragments from Cave 7 of Qumran contain a portion of Mark's gospel. If he is correct, these fragments are the earliest NT finds to date.

It would mean that the gospel was written much earlier than scholars have traditionally supposed. The fragments date from A.D. 50, and it is likely that they are copies of a manuscript written years before that. Therefore, most Bible scholars are doubtful about O'Callaghan's identification of the fragments.

The NT copies made in the third and fourth centuries were written in all capital letters and run together. Scholars call these manuscripts which were written on vellum (parchment) *uncials,* and nearly 275 have been found. Scribes used the uncial style of writing on vellum and papyrus until about the ninth century, when they began copying the manuscripts in a small, cursive Greek script. These later manuscripts are called *minuscules.* We have over 2,700 NT manuscripts written in minuscule style.

Scholars consider *Codex Vaticanus* (or *Vaticanus B*) one of the most important uncial manuscripts. Written shortly after A.D. 300, this manuscript originally contained all of the Septuagint and all the NT. Part of the letter to the Hebrews, the Pastoral Letters, and the book of Revelation have been lost. Some portions of the OT section of this manuscript also have been lost, but what remains is a useful source of information about the text of the OT. It is housed in the Vatican Library.

Another valuable uncial manuscript is called *Codex Sinaiticus,* because Constantine von Tischendorf (1815–1874) found it in a monastery at the foot of traditional Mount Sinai in 1859. Written shortly after Codex Vaticanus, it is the earliest complete manuscript of the NT.

The *Codex Alexandrinus,* an uncial manuscript that dates from just after A.D. 400, originally contained the entire Bible in Greek, along with the apocryphal books of 1 and 2 Clement and the Psalms of Solomon. The Greek Orthodox patriarch of Constantinople gave this manuscript to the British ambassador in 1624, as a gift to England's King James I. It is now housed in the British Museum.

The *Codex Ephraemi Rescriptus,* so called because it contains some of the writings of Ephraem Syrus, was written about the same time as the Codex Alexandrinus. It also contained the entire Greek Bible. Thrifty scribes produced it by erasing the parchment of the earlier manuscript of the Scriptures and jotting the new manuscript of Ephraem's sermons at a right angle to the old one. Scholars call this type of manuscript a *palimpsest* (Grk., "scraped again"). This makes the text difficult to read, but at some points researchers can discern portions of the earlier manuscript as well as the newer one.

Most minuscule manuscripts contain the same type of cursive Greek script. In the nineteenth century, Bible scholars rejected hundreds of these manuscripts as being the poorest examples of the NT text. However, the minuscules have been reconsidered in recent years in an effort to produce what is now called a majority text.

We gain some evidence of the NT text from early *lectionaries* (books containing Scripture lessons to be read on holy days). Also, the early church fathers often quoted NT Scriptures in their writings, however they did not always quote accurately and often paraphrased. Even so, these quotations still serve as an important witness to the original text.

When there came to be many Latin-speaking Christians, the Bible was translated into Latin so those Christians could understand it. It is believed that this was done around A.D. 200, although no Latin manuscripts survive from that time. Christian scribes copied this Old Latin version many times, and eventually their copies picked up some striking differences.

Pope Damasus I commissioned the scholar *Jerome* (A.D. 340–420) to produce a standard text of the Latin Bible which he completed around A.D. 400. His version (called the *Vulgate* because it used the "common language" of early medieval times) was based on the Old Latin versions. Jerome used a good Latin text and compared it with the old Greek manuscripts that were available.

Pope Leo X was the greatest scholar and manuscript collector among the Renaissance popes. He suggested a scholarly edition of the Bible to be edited by Cardinal Ximines of Spain. In 1517, a printer in Alcala, Spain, completed this printed Bible with the Vulgate and the Greek arranged in parallel columns. It became known as the *Complutensian Polyglot* (Latin *Complutum*, "Alcala"; Greek *Polyglot*, "set forth in many languages"). The editors of this edition said they used "very ancient and correct" Greek manuscripts that Pope Leo X provided for their work. But we cannot be sure which manuscripts these were, nor whether they have survived to the present day. They were probably burned in one of the papal wars of Renaissance Italy. The pope did not give permission to release this book until 1522, and by that time another printer named *Joannes Froben* had issued a printed Greek NT.

Froben, a printer in Basel, Switzerland, had persuaded the noted biblical scholar *Erasmus* of Rotterdam to come to Basel to prepare this edition. Using manuscripts from the library of Basel University, Erasmus and Froben produced their Greek text in March 1516. Erasmus' text became the *textus receptus* (Latin, "received text") of the NT and served as a basic guide for the translators of the KJV.

Two hundred years later, scholars began to replace Erasmus' text with printed texts based on earlier Greek manuscripts, which they assumed to be better than the textus receptus. In 1831, *Charles Lachmann* published such a text. Scholars call Lachmann's work the first critical text of the NT. It was called a *critical text* because he set aside the textus receptus and constructed a text from what he considered to be the most ancient witnesses. *Critical* comes from a Greek word meaning "judge."

Later, Constantine von Tischendorf zealously collected ancient manuscripts and issued several editions of the Greek text, with notations of variant readings in the margins. From 1856 to 1879, Samuel Prideaux Tregelles tried to develop an improved text, seeking the best reading at each point where selected manuscripts diverged. Tregelles sought to evaluate the Greek manuscripts by the age of the various readings, not the age of the manuscripts themselves.

Two of the great names in the history of textual studies were *Brooke Foss Westcott* (1825–1901) and *Fenton John Anthony Hort* (1828–1892). After classifying the Greek texts according to the age of the various readings, they concluded that there were four basic text types: *Syrian, Western, Alexandrian,* and *Neutral.* In 1881, after 30 years' work, they published their own Greek text of the NT, entitled *The New Testament in the Original Greek.* It soon replaced Erasmus' text as the textus receptus of the NT. Unfortunately, it began to appear that the classic translations such as the KJV had been made from Erasmus' textus receptus.

Textual study has made some notable advances since the days of Westcott and Hort. Now scholars agree that the early textual history of the Greek NT was more complicated than Westcott and Hort supposed.

The two Anglican scholars assumed that the earliest text would be the purest, with the least difficulties and the simplest readings. Scholars now question that premise. Further, Westcott and Hort knew nothing about papyri or their readings and were unsuccessful in tracing the text back beyond the second century with the approach of text types. Scholars still basically follow the Westcott and Hort principles and conclusions.

Many scholars now believe that internal evidence (i.e., content) should carry more weight than the text types in determining which readings are the most reliable.

Christians can approach their Greek NT today with great confidence. Not one word in a thousand is seriously uncertain, and no established doctrine is called in question by any of the continuing doubts about the correct reading.

English Translations of the Bible

Psalters and Other Early Translations

Bishop Aldhelm of Sherborne (d. A.D. 709) translated the Psalms into Anglo-Saxon, an early form of the English language. Very early, English bards put the Psalms into regular poetic form, making them easy to remember. And so the Psalms became the most popular portion of Scripture in the English tongue. Peasants sang them in the fields and parents taught them to their children. We have manuscripts of the Psalms in Anglo-Saxon dialects dating back to the tenth century.

A tenth-century priest named *Aldred* wrote an English translation of the Gospels between the lines of a Latin text he was copying. This manuscript is our earliest evidence of an English translation of the NT. Around A.D. 1000, Alfric of Bath produced an English translation of the Gospels.

John Wycliffe published the first complete Bible in English in 1382. Wycliffe used primarily the Latin Vulgate, and his translation was weak in some respects. But the common people of England gladly received the book, and Wycliffe organized a group of ministers known as the Lollards, because they used the lollardy (common) speech to travel throughout the country and preach from his translation.

The Roman Catholic Church condemned Wycliffe's work and burned many of the handwritten copies. Nevertheless, about 150 copies of Wycliffe's Version have survived, but only one is complete.

Another Englishman, *William Tyndale,* began printing the next important English translation of the NT at Cologne, Germany, in 1525. Because Tyndale was a close friend of Martin Luther, Roman authorities attempted to halt the project. Yet Tyndale succeeded in finishing the book and smuggled his printed NTs into England. In 1536, after he had completed translations of the Pentateuch and Jonah, British agents captured him in Belgium, strangled him, and burned his body at the stake.

Also in 1535, an Englishman named *Miles Coverdale* published an English translation of the whole Bible in the city of Zurich. This edition had the support of King Henry VIII because Coverdale translated many passages in a way that supported Anglican Catholic doctrine and undermined the use of the Latin Vulgate.

Coverdale then began work on another English Bible that would incorporate the best of Tyndale and other English translators, as well as new insights from the Greek and Hebrew manuscripts. He prepared huge 23 centimeters by 38 centimeters (nine inches by 15 inches) pages for this volume, earning it the name of the Great Bible. He completed it in 1539, and the British government ordered the clergy to display the book prominently in churches throughout the land. This stirred popular interest in the Scriptures.

In 1553, *Mary Tudor* came to the throne of England and enforced strict Catholic policies upon the people. She banned the use of all English Bibles, in favor of the Latin versions. Coverdale and other Bible translators fled to Geneva, Switzerland, where *John Calvin* had established a Protestant stronghold.

William Whittingham of Geneva organized several of these scholars to begin work on a new English Bible, which they published in 1560. It was the first Bible to divide the Scriptures into verses. This was the work of *Robert Estienne,* a Parisian printer of Greek New Testaments. Booksellers called this book the *Geneva Bible* or the *Breeches Bible,* because of the peculiar way it translated Genesis 3:7: "They sewed fig leaves together and made themselves breeches."

Whittingham and his colleagues dedicated this translation to *Queen Elizabeth I,* who had taken the throne of England in 1558. The people of England used the Geneva Bible very widely for the next two generations.

The King James Version

In 1604, James VI of Scotland became *King James I* of England and began a program of peacemaking between the hostile religious factions of Great Britain. That same year he convened a meeting of religious leaders at Hampton Court. *Dr. John Reynolds,* the Puritan spokesman, proposed that a new English translation of the Bible be issued in honor of the king. The KJV was to become an important watershed in the history of English Bible translations.

King James appointed 54 scholars to the task of making a new translation. For the OT, they relied primarily upon ben Hayyim's edition of the ben Asher text. For the NT, they relied upon the Greek text of Erasmus and a bilingual Greek-and-Latin text of the sixth century found by Theodore Beza. The translators followed chapter divisions made by Archbishop Stephen Langton in 1551 and the verse divisions of Robert Estienne.

Because King James had authorized this project, the new Bible became known as the Authorized Version. It was first published in 1611 and revised in 1615, 1629, 1638, and 1762.

An edition of the KJV published by *Bishop William Lloyd* in 1701 was the first Bible to contain marginal notes dating biblical events in relation to the birth of Christ (B.C. and A.D.). Lloyd's edition also contained the chronology laid out by *Archbishop James Ussher* (1581–1656) that dated creation at 4004 B.C. This chronology was first used in an Oxford edition of the KJV published in 1679. Many subsequent editions of the KJV have reprinted this chronology.

The 1762 revision is what most people now know as the KJV.

Revisions of the King James Version

Among the many attempts to revise the KJV, we should not forget the English Revised Version (ERV or RV) and the American Standard Version (ASV). Both of these attempted to maintain the dignity of language that had become a hallmark of the KJV, while drawing upon the new insights provided by recent manuscript discoveries and improved knowledge of Hebrew words and grammar. They also sought to exclude obsolete words and usages left over from the Tudor speech of the King James Version.

English Revised Version

Bishop Harold Browne and *Bishop C. J. Ellicott*—both respected Anglican leaders—headed two committees that attempted to revise the KJV in the 1870s. An American committee joined them in 1872. These groups produced a Revised Version of the NT in 1881, which the public greeted enthusiastically in Great Britain and the United States. The committees issued the Revised Version of the entire Bible in 1885. By that time, the Revised Version had a reputation of being oriented toward British spelling and figures of speech, so the ERV lost popular support in the United States.

American Standard Version

Some members of the American committee for the ERV banded together to produce their own revision of the KJV. Headed by *J. Henry Thayer,* this new committee substituted American expressions for British and reverted to the KJV rendering of many words. The committee also made parallel passages read the same when the Greek text was identical—the KJV had not been consistent in doing this. The ASV committee aimed at a word-for-word translation of the Greek and Hebrew wherever possible. In some cases this made the ASV awkward to read. The complete ASV Bible was published in 1901.

New King James Version

In 1979, Thomas Nelson Publishers issued a new edition of the KJV NT. This edition was based on the 1894 edition of the textus receptus. While it preserved the integrity of the text, it eliminated many archaic expressions that made the KJV difficult to read.

In 1982, Thomas Nelson published the complete NKJV Bible, which quickly gained wide acceptance.

New Translations

Besides revising the KJV, modern scholars have produced several totally new translations of the Bible.

Revised Standard Version. In 1929, the International Council of Religious Education (an agency of the World Council of Churches) began work on a revision of the ASV. After several false starts, the committee resolved on an entirely new translation, based in the NT on the latest scholarly Greek texts. The committee finally settled for an eclectic or reading-by-reading type of text that differed at many points from Westcott and Hort. The NT section of this Revised Standard Version was published in 1946, and the OT in 1952.

The RSV met a mixed response. Many major denominations welcomed it as a more readable translation, and supposedly a more reliable rendering of the ancient texts. It was one of the most consistent translations ever made into English. However, it brought on itself a storm of criticism for two features: (1) It altered the wording of many classic passages. (2) It chose new readings for a number of passages with far-reaching theological implications.

New English Bible. In October 1946, representatives of the major Protestant churches in Great Britain met at Westminster Abbey to commission a new translation that would be better suited to British readers. The NT portion of this New English Bible was released in 1961, exactly 350 years after the publication of the KJV. The complete NEB was released in 1970.

Recent Revisions and Paraphrases.

New American Standard Bible.

In the NASB, evangelical scholars have attempted to update and clarify the ASV.

The NASB translators made it their policy to transliterate (write in English letters) most of the Hebrew and Greek names. They capitalized personal pronouns that referred to deity and used Thou and Thee whenever a biblical speaker addressed God. When a literal translation would confuse the reader, the NASB gave the meaning of the text and put the literal reading in the margin. The marginal notes seem to follow the highly regarded Hebrew text of the Jewish Publication Society, known to scholars as the JPS. The complete NASB appeared in 1971.

New American Bible. A committee of prominent Roman Catholic scholars was gathered in 1944 and worked for many years to produce a new translation. They first established an OT and NT text of their own and then produced an English translation of it. The text chosen for translation varies slightly in character with each section of the Bible. But a textual guide and a complete introduction have been published to inform the reader what judgments were made. The entire NAB was published in 1970 and a complete concordance of it in 1978.

New International Version. This version attempts to give the meaning of the Bible text more effectively than the ASV or the other contemporary versions. It was begun in 1965 by a number of scholars representing a group of evangelical denominations. The group worked for a decade under the direction of the New York Bible Society.

The translation had two basic characteristics: (1) It was to be an ecumenical effort, which would first establish a critical text. The most recent edition of Kittel's *Biblia Hebraica* was used for the OT, but major differences in the Septuagint were noted. The Greek text of the NT was adopted from a number of sources. (2) A principle of translation popularized in the 1960s, known as dynamic equivalence, was used in translating a number of passages. This principle calls for using a word or phrase that makes the impact that the original had on its first readers, rather than using a simple grammatical or lexical equivalent (which in our changed culture might not convey any meaning).

The NT of the NIV was published in 1973 and the OT in 1978. The NIV's English style is quite contemporary and similar to that of the RSV.

The NIV has many helpful features. It seeks to communicate the meaning of the original text in modern English. On the whole, it reads smoothly and is easy for the average reader to understand. The NIV places quotation marks around direct quotes and brackets around words that the translators have supplied to aid the English reader.

Goodspeed's Paraphrase. In 1923, Edgar J. Goodspeed (1871–1962) issued his English-language version of *The New Testament, An American Translation*. To avoid confusing the reader with the structure of Greek sentences, he paraphrased much of the text. This book enjoyed success in the United States, and in 1931 it was combined with a similar translation of the OT by J. M. Powis Smith and others.

J. B. Phillips' Paraphrase. J. B. Phillips' *New Testament in Modern English* appeared in 1957, bringing together a series of paraphrased NT books that Phillips began in 1947 with his *Letters to Young Churches*. Phillips rendered the text freely, often departing entirely from the Greek manuscripts. His paraphrase attracted considerable attention because of its vivid (and sometimes earthy) language.

Today's English Version (*Good News Bible*). This rendering (NT, 1966; OT, 1976) was sponsored by the American Bible Society. The main TEV writer, Robert G. Bratcher (1920–), used a new critical text of the Greek NT which the Bible Society prepared for this project. Bratcher saw his work as one of translation rather than paraphrase, but he used the dynamic equivalence method more liberally than the earlier translations did. This placed the TEV in a class apart. It departs radically from the precise meaning of the Hebrew and Greek at many points.

The Living Bible. Kenneth Taylor (1917–), an editor at a Chicago publishing house, began writing this version, an avowed paraphrase, in an effort to make the Bible more understandable to his children. His colleagues found it helpful, and Taylor founded his own publishing company—Tyndale House—in order to produce a paraphrase of the entire Bible. He published the NT section in 1956 and the OT in 1972.

The Living Bible is marked by great clarity and simplicity, and thousands of readers find that they can understand the TLB more easily than the KJV or other translations. But Bible scholars and religious leaders have criticized the TLB for its free handling of many passages.

English Versions

English readers have had access to many versions of the Bible in the past four centuries. This list gives the date, title, and translator of over 200 English versions of Scripture. It is based upon more extensive lists by John H. Skilton and A. S. Herbert.* Where the translator's name is unknown, or where a group of translators contributed to a particular work, the version is identified by the publisher's name (shown in parentheses):

1526	The New Testament: untitled; William Tyndale.
1530	*The Psalter of David in Englishe;* George Joye. The Pentateuch: untitled; William Tyndale.
1531(?)	*The Prophete Jonas;* William Tyndale.
1534	*Jeremy the Prophete, Translated into Englisshe;* George Joye. *The New Testament;* George Joye.
1535	*Biblia: The Byble;* Miles Coverdale.
1536	*The Newe Testament yet once agayne corrected;* William Tyndale.
1537(?)	The New Testament; Miles Coverdale.
1537	*The Byble;* (Richard Grafton and Edward Whitchurch).
1539	*The Most Sacred Bible* (Taverner's Bible); Richard Taverner. *The Byble in Englyshe* (The Great Bible); (Richard Grafton and Edward Whitchurch). *The newe Testamet of oure Sauyour Jesu Christ;* Miles Coverdale. *The Nevv Testament in Englysshe;* Richard Taverner. *The new Testamet in Englyshe;* (Richard Grafton and Edward Whitchurch).
1540	*The Byble in Englyshe;* Miles Coverdale.
1548(?)	*Certayne Psalmes chose out of the Psalter;* Thomas Starnhold.
1549	*The first tome or volume of the Paraphrase of Erasmus vpon The newe testament;* (Edward Whitchurch).
1557	*Nevve Testament of ovr Lord Iesus Christ;* William Whittingham.
1560	*Bible and Holy Scriptvres conteyned in the Olde and Newe Testament (The Geneva Bible);* William Whittingham.
1562	*The Whole Booke of Psalmes;* Thomas Starnhold and I. Hopkins.
1568	*The holie Bible* (The Bishops' Bible); Matthew Parker.
1582	*The Nevv Testament of Iesvs Christ* (Rheims New Testament); Gregory Martin.
1592	*Apocalypsis;* Thomas Barbar.
1610	*The Holie Bible* (Douay Old Testament); Gregory Martin.
1611	*The Holy Bible* (The King James Version); (Robert Barker).
1612	*The Book of Psalmes;* Henry Ainsworth.
1657	*The Dutch Annotations upon the whole Bible;* Theodore Haak.
1700	*The Psalmes of David;* C. Caryll.
1726	*A new version of all the Books of the New Testament;* (J. Batly and S. Chandler).
1727	*The Books of Job, Psalms, Proverbs, Eccleseastes, and the Song of Solomon;* (J. Walthoe).
1731	*The New Testament . . . Translated out of the Latin Vulgat by John Wiclif . . . about 1378;* John Lewis.
1741	*A new version of St. Matthew's Gospel;* Daniel Scott.
1745	*Mr. Whiston's Primitive New Testament;* William Whiston.
1761	*Divers parts of the holy Scriptures;* Mr. Mortimer.
1764	*All the books of The Old and New Testament;* Anthony Purver. *The New Testament;* Richard Wynne.
1765	*The Psalms of David;* Christopher Smart. *The New Testament;* Philip Doddridge.
1768	*A Liberal Translation of the New Testament;* Edward Harwood.
1770	*The New Testament or New Covenant;* John Worsley.
1771	*The Book of Job;* Thomas Scott.
1773	*The Pentateuch of Moses and the Historical Books of the Old Testament;* Julius Bate.
1779	*Isaiah;* Robert Lowth. *Essay towards a literal English version of the New Testament, in*

English Versions—*continued*

the Epistle of the Apostle Paul directed to the Ephesians; John Callander.

1782 *The Gospel of St. Matthew;* Gilbert Wakefield.

1784 *Jeremiah and Lamentations;* Benjamin Blayney.

1787 *The First (–Fifth) Book of Moses;* David Levi.
The Apostle Paul's First and Second Epistles to the Thessalonians; James MacKnight.

1789 *A new English Translation of the Pentateuch;* Isaac Delgado.
The Four Gospels; George Campbell.

1790 *The Book of Psalms;* Stephen Street.

1791 *The New Testament;* Gilbert Wakefield.

1795 *The New Testament;* Thomas Haweis.

1796 *Jonah;* George Benjoin.
An Attempt toward revising our English translation of the Greek Scriptures; William Newcome.

1797 *The Holy Bible;* Alexander Geddes.

1799 *A Revised Translation and Interpretation of the Sacred Scriptures;* David Macrae.

1805 *The Book of Job;* Joseph Stock.

1807 *The Gothic Gospel of Saint Matthew;* Samuel Henshall.

1808 *The Holy Bible;* Charles Thomson.

1810 *The Book of Job;* Elizabeth Smith.

1811 *Canticles: or Song of Solomon;* John Fry.

1812 *The Book of Job;* John Mason Good.
The New Testament; W. Williams.

1816 *The English Version of the Polyglott Bible;* (Samuel Bagster).

1819 *Lyra Davidis [Psalms];* John Fry.

1822 *The Epistles of Paul the Apostle;* Thomas Belsham.

1825 *The Book of Job;* George Hunt.
The Psalms; J. Parkhurst.

1827 *An Amended Version of the Book of Job;* George R. Noyes.
Liber Ecclesiasticus, the Book of the Church; Luke Howard.

1828 *The Gospel of God's Anointed;* Alexander Greaves.

1831 *The Book of Psalms;* George R. Noyes.

1833 *A literal translation from the Hebrew of the twelve Minor Prophets;* A. Pick.
A New and Corrected Version of the New Testament; Rodolphus Dickinson.

1834 *The Gospel according to Matthew;* William J. Aislabie.

1835 *The Book of the Law from the Holy Bible [The Pentateuch];* Joseph Ablett.

1837 *A New Translation of the Hebrew Prophets;* George R. Noyes.
The Gospel of John; William J. Aislabie.

1843 *The Gospel according to Saint Matthew, and part of the first chapter of the Gospel according to Saint Mark;* Sir John Cheke.
Horae aramaicae: comprising concise notices of the Aramean dialects in general and of the versions of the Holy Scripture extant in them: with a translation of Matthew; J. W. Etheridge.

1846 *The book of Psalms;* John Jebb.
A New Translation of the Proverbs, Ecclesiastes, and the Canticles; George R. Noyes.
The Four Gospels from the Peschito; J. W. Etheridge.

1848 *The New Testament;* Jonathan Morgan.
St. Paul's Epistle to the Romans; Herman Heinfetter.

1849 *The Apostolic Acts and Epistles;* J. W. Etheridge.

1850 *The Bible Revised;* Francis Barham.

1851 *The New Testament;* James Murdock.
The Epistle of Paul to the Romans; Joseph Turnbull.
The Epistles of Paul the Apostle to the Hebrews; Herman Heinfetter.

1854 *The Epistles of Paul the Apostle;* Joseph Turnbull.

1855 *The Book of Genesis;* Henry E. J. Howard.
A Translation of the Gospels; Andrews Norton.

1857 *The Books of Exodus and Leviticus;* Henry E. J. Howard.

English Versions—*continued*

1858　*The New Testament;* Leicester A. Sawyer.

1859　*A Revised Translation of the New Testament;* W. G. Cookesley.

1860　*The Psalms;* Lord Congleton.

1861(?)　*The New Testament . . . As Revised and Corrected by the Spirits;* Leonard Thorn.

1862　*The New Testament;* H. Highton.

1863　*The Holy Bible;* Robert Young.
　　　The Psalms; W. Kay.
　　　The Book of Daniel; John Bellamy.

1864　*The Book of Job;* J. M. Rodwell.
　　　The Emphatic Diaglott; Benjamin Wilson.

1867　*The Minor Prophets;* John Bellamy.

1869　*The Book of Job in metre;* William Meikle.
　　　The Book of Psalms; Charles Carter.

1870　*The New Testament;* John Bowes.

1871　*The Book of Job;* Francis Barham.
　　　The Book of Psalms; Francis Barham and Edward Hare.
　　　St. John's Epistles; Francis Barham.

1871(?)　*The Gospels, Acts, Epistles, and Book of Revelation;* John Darby.

1876　*The Holy Bible;* Julia E. Smith.

1877　*The New Testament;* John Richter.
　　　Revised English Bible; (Eyre and Spottiswoode).

1881　*The New Testament: English Revised Version;* (Kambridgel University Press).

1882(?)　*St. Paul's Epistle to the Romans;* Ferrar Fenton.

1884　*The Psalter . . . and certain Canticles;* Richard Rolle.
　　　The Book of Psalms; T. K. Cheyne.
　　　St. Paul's Epistles in Modern English; Ferrar Fenton.

1885　*The Old Testament Scriptures;* Helen Spurrell.
　　　The Holy Bible: Revised Version; (Oxford University Press).

1894　*A Translation of the Four Gospels from the Syriac of the Sinaitic Palimpsest;* Agnes S. Lewis.

1897　*The New Dispensation: The New Testament;* Robert Weekes.

1898　*The Book of Job;* Ferrar Fenton.
　　　The Twentieth Century New Testa-
ment; (W. and J. Mackay and Co.)
　　　The Four Gospels; Seymour Spencer.

1899　*The Old and New Testaments;* (J. Clarke and Co.).

1900　*St. Paul's Epistle to the Romans;* W. G. Rutherford.

1901　*The Holy Bible: American Standard Version;* (Thomas Nelson and Sons).
　　　The Five Books of Moses; Ferrar Fenton.
　　　The Historical New Testament; James Moffatt.

1902(?)　*The Bible in Modern English;* Ferrar Fenton.

1903　*The Book of Psalms;* Kaufman Kohler.
　　　The New Testament in Modern Speech; Richard Weymouth.
　　　The Revelation; Henry Forster.

1904　*The New Testament;* Adolphus S. Worrell.

1906　*St. John's Gospel, Epistles, and Revelation;* Henry Forster.

1908　*Thessalonians and Corinthians;* W. G. Rutherford.

1912　*The Book of Ruth;* R. H. J. Steuart.

1913　*The New Testament;* James Moffatt.

1914　*The Poem of Job;* Edward G. King.

1916　*The Wisdom of Ben-Sira* (Ecclesiasticus); W. O. E. Oesterley.

1917　*The Holy Scriptures according to the Masoretic text;* (The Jewish Publication Society of America).

1918　*The New Testament* (The Shorter Bible); Charles Foster Kent.

1920(?)　*Amos;* Theodore H. Robinson.

1921　*The Old Testament* (The Shorter Bible); Charles Foster Kent.
　　　Mark's Account of Jesus; T. W. Pym.

1923　*The New Testament. An American Translation;* Edgar J. Goodspeed.
　　　The Riverside New Testament; William G. Ballantine.

1924　*The Old Testament;* James Moffatt.
　　　Centenary Translation of the New Testament; Helen B. Montgomery.

1925　*Hebrews;* F. H. Wales.

1927　*The Old Testament;* J. M. Powis Smith, T. J. Meek, Alexander R. Gordon, Leroy Waterman.

English Versions—*continued*

St. Matthew's Gospel; (T. and T. Clark).

1928 The Psalms Complete; William W. Martin.
The Christian's Bible: New Testament; George LeFevre.

1933 The Four Gospels according to the Eastern Version; George M. Lamsa.
The Four Gospels; Charles C. Torrey.

1936 The Song of Songs; W. O. E. Oesterley.

1937 The Psalms and the Canticles of the Divine Office; George O'Neill.
The New Testament; Johannes Greber.
The New Testament; Charles B. Williams.
St. Paul from the Trenches; Gerald Cornish.

1938 Job; George O'Neill.
The New Testament; Edgar L. Clementson.

1939 Ecclesiasticus; A. D. Power.

1944 The New Testament; Ronald A. Knox.

1945 The Berkeley Version of the New Testament; Gerrit Verkuyl.

1946 The Psalms . . . Also the Canticles of the Roman Breviary; (Benziger Bros.).
The New Testament (Revised Standard Version); (Thomas Nelson and Sons).

1947 The Psalms; Ronald A. Knox.
The New Testament; George Swann.
Letters to Young Churches: Epistles of the New Testament; J. B. Phillips.

1949 The Old Testament; Ronald A. Knox.

1950 The New Testament of Our Messiah and Saviour Yahshua; A. B. Traina.
New World Translation: New Testament; (Watchtower Bible and Tract Society, Inc.).

1951 The New Testament; (Brotherhood Authentic Bible Society).

1952 The Four Gospels; E. V. Rieu.
The Holy Bible: Revised Standard Version; (Thomas Nelson and Sons).

1954 The New Testament; James A.

Kleist and Joseph Lilly.
The Amplified Bible: Gospel of John; The Lockman Foundation.

1955 The Authentic New Testament; Hugh J. Schonfield.

1956 The Inspired Letters in Clearest English; Frank C. Laubach.

1957 The Holy Bible from Ancient Eastern Manuscripts; George M. Lamsa.

1958 The New Testament in Modern English; J. B. Phillips.
The Amplified Bible: New Testament; The Lockman Foundation.

1959 The Holy Bible: The Berkeley Version in Modern English; (Zondervan Publishing Co.).

1960 The Holy Bible (New American Standard); (Thomas Nelson and Sons).
The New World Translation: Old Testament; (Watchtower Bible and Tract Society, Inc.).

1961 The New English Bible: New Testament; (Oxford University Press and Cambridge University Press).

1962 The Children's Version of the Holy Bible; J. P. Green.
Modern King James Version of the Holy Bible; (McGraw-Hill).
Living Letters: The Paraphrased Epistles; Kenneth Taylor.
The Amplified Bible: Old Testament Part II; The Lockman Foundation.

1963 The New Testament in the Language of Today; William Beck.
New American Standard Bible: New Testament; The Lockman Foundation.

1964 The Amplified Bible: Old Testament Part I; The Lockman Foundation.

1966 Good News for Modern Man: The New Testament; (American Bible Society).
The Living Scriptures: A New Translation in the King James Tradition; (American Bible Society).

1968 The Cotton Patch Version of Paul's Epistles; Clarence Jordan.
The New Testament of Our Master and Saviour; (Missionary Dispensary Bible Research).

1969 The New Testament: A New Translation; William Barclay.

English Versions—continued

Modern Language New Testament; (Zondervan Publishing Co.).
The Cotton Patch Version of Luke and Acts; Clarence Jordan.

1970   *New American Bible;* (St. Anthony Guild Press).
New English Bible; (Oxford University Press and Cambridge University Press).
The Cotton Patch Version of Matthew and John; Clarence Jordan.
Letters From Paul; Boyce Blackwelder.
New American Standard Bible; The Lockman Foundation.
King James II Version of the Bible; (Associated Publishers and Authors).
The Living Bible; (Tyndale House).

1973   *The New International Version: New Testament;* (Zondervan Bible Publishers).

The Translator's New Testament; (The British and Foreign Bible Society).
The Cotton Patch Version of Hebrews and the General Epistles; Clarence Jordan.
The Poetic Bible; Veo Gray.

1976   *Good News Bible;* (American Bible Society).

1977   *The Holy Bible in the Language of Today;* William Beck.

1978   *The New International Version;* (Zondervan Bible Publishers).

1979   *The New King James Version: New Testament;* (Thomas Nelson Publishers).

1982   *The Holy Bible, New King James Version;* (Thomas Nelson Publishers).

---

*John Skilton, *The New Testament Student at Work* (Nutley, N.J.: Presbyterian and Reformed, 1975). A. S. Herbert, *Historical Catalogue of Printed Editions of the English Bible,* 1525–1961 (London: British and Foreign Bible Society, 1968).

Authors of the Bible

Author	Book(s) of the Bible	Author	Book(s) of the Bible
Moses	Genesis	Agur	Proverbs 30
	Exodus	Lemuel (another name for Solomon?)	Proverbs 31
	Leviticus		
	Numbers		
	Deuteronomy	Solomon	Ecclesiastes
Joshua	Joshua		Song of Solomon
Job	Job (possible)	Jeremiah	Jeremiah
Samuel	Judges (possible)		Lamentations (probable)
	Ruth (possible)		1 Kings (possible)
	1 Samuel (possible)		2 Kings (possible)
David	Most of the Psalms (see 2 Sam. 23:2)	Ezra	Ezra
			1 Chronicles (possible)
Sons of Korah	Psalms 42, 44—49, 84—85, 87		2 Chronicles (possible)
			2 Samuel (possible)
Asaph	Psalms 50, 73—83	Mordecai	Esther (possible)
Heman	Psalm 88	Prophets whose names they bear	Books of OT prophecy
Ethan	Psalm 89		
Hezekiah	Psalms 120—123, 128—130, 132, 134—136 (see Isa. 38:20)	Luke	Acts
			Luke
Solomon	Psalms 72, 127	John	John
Solomon	Proverbs 1—29		1 John
			2 John

Authors of the Bible—continued

Author	Book(s) of the Bible	Author	Book(s) of the Bible
	3 John		1 Thessalonians
	Revelation		2 Thessalonians
Paul	Romans		1 Timothy
	1 Corinthians		2 Timothy
	2 Corinthians		Titus
	Galatians		Philemon
	Ephesians	Apollos	Hebrews (possible)
	Philippians	Persons whose	Remaining NT epistles
	Colossians	names they bear	and gospels

Languages of
the Bible

Most of the original language of the OT was Hebrew; Greek being the language used in writing most of the NT. Several other ancient languages also had an important bearing on the writing or transmission of the original texts of the Bible.

Aramaic. Spoken from at least about 2000 B.C., Aramaic eventually replaced many of the languages of the ancient world in popularity and usage. Parts of the book of Daniel were written in Aramaic. It was the common language spoken in Israel in the time of Jesus. While the NT was written in Greek, Jesus probably spoke Aramaic. Another name for the Aramaic dialect used in the early churches throughout Asia Minor is Syriac.

Latin. The NT also refers to Latin—the language which sprang from ancient Rome (Luke 23:38; John 19:20). Most people of the Roman Empire also spoke Greek in Jesus' day. But as Roman power spread throughout the ancient world, Latin expanded in use.

Persian. This language was spoken by the people who settled the area east of the Tigris River in what is now western Iran.

Examples of ancient writing in the Hebrew language. The bottom inscription, dating from about 700 B.C., was placed over a tomb near Jerusalem. PHOTO BY GUSTAV JEENINGA

When the Jews were taken as captives to Babylon in 586 B.C., they may have been exposed to this distinctive language form that used a combination of pictorial and phonetic signs in its alphabet. Scholars are uncertain whether Persian was used in the writing of any parts of the OT.

Statistics About the Bible

Old Testament Statistics

39	Books
929	Chapters
23,214	Verses
593,493	Words in the Hebrew text
17	Historical books
5	Poetical books
17	Prophetical books
Psalms	Longest book
Obadiah	Shortest book

New Testament Statistics

27	Books
260	Chapters
7,959	Verses
181,253	Words in the Greek text
4	Gospels
1	Historical book
22	Letters or epistles
Acts	Longest book
3 John	Shortest book

Ten Longest Books in the Bible

Book	Number of Chapters	Number of Verses	Hebrew or Greek Words
1. Psalms	150	2,461	43,743
2. Jeremiah	52	1,364	42,659
3. Ezekiel	48	1,273	39,407
4. Genesis	50	1,533	38,267
5. Isaiah	66	1,291	37,044
6. Numbers	36	1,288	32,902
7. Exodus	40	1,213	32,602
8. Deuteronomy	34	959	28,461
9. 2 Chronicles	36	822	26,074
10. Luke	24	1,151	25,944

Ten Shortest Books in the Bible

Book	Number of Chapters	Number of Verses	Hebrew or Greek Words
1. 3 John	1	14	299
2. 2 John	1	13	303
3. Philemon	1	25	445
4. Jude	1	25	613
5. Obadiah	1	21	670
6. Titus	3	46	921
7. 2 Thessalonians	3	7	1,042
8. Haggai	2	38	1,131
9. Nahum	3	47	1,285
10. Jonah	4	48	1,321

Ten Old Testament Books Most Referred to in the New Testament

Book	Number of Times Referred to	Number of NT Books Where Reference Occurs
1. Isaiah	419	23
2. Psalms	414	23
3. Genesis	260	21
4. Exodus	250	19
5. Deuteronomy	208	21
6. Ezekiel	141	15

Statistics About the Bible—*continued*

Book	Number of Times Referred to	Number of NT Books Where Reference Occurs
7. Daniel	133	17
8. Jeremiah	125	17
9. Leviticus	107	15
10. Numbers	73	4

Ten New Testament Books Containing Material from the Greatest Number of Old Testament Books

NT Book	Number of OT Books Material Taken From	NT Book	Number of OT Books Material Taken From
1. Revelation	32	6. Romans	23
2. Luke	31	7. Hebrews	21
3. John	26	8. 1 Corinthians	18
4. Acts	25	9. James	17
5. Mark	24	10. 1 Peter	15

Most Mentioned Men in the Bible

Name	Number of Times Mentioned	Name	Number of Times Mentioned
David	1,118	Joshua	197
Moses	740	Paul	185
Aaron	339	Peter	166
Saul	338	Joab	137
Abraham	306	Jeremiah	136
Solomon	295	Samuel	135
Jacob	270	Isaac	127
Joseph	208		

NOTE: Jesus is mentioned more than anyone else in the Bible.

Thirty Great Topical Chapters

	Topic	Chapter		Topic	Chapter
1	Ten Commandments	Exodus 20	16	Comfort	John 14
2	Reassurance	Joshua 1	17	Abiding	John 15
3	Faithfulness of God	Joshua 14	18	Justification	Romans 5
4	Shepherd	Psalm 23	19	Sanctification	Romans 6
5	Confession of sin	Psalm 51	20	Glorification	Romans 8
6	Praise of God	Psalm 103	21	Marriage	1 Corinthians 7
7	Word of God	Psalm 119	22	Gifts	1 Corinthians 12
8	Wisdom	Proverbs 8	23	Love	1 Corinthians 13
9	Virtuous woman	Proverbs 31	24	Resurrection	1 Corinthians 15
10	Majesty of God	Isaiah 40	25	Fruit of the Spirit	Galatians 5
11	Great invitation	Isaiah 55	26	Faith	Hebrews 11
12	Beatitudes	Matthew 5	27	Chastisement	Hebrews 12
13	Lord's Prayer	Matthew 6	28	Tongue	James 3
14	Sower and seed	Matthew 13	29	Reason for suffering	1 Peter 4
15	Protection of the sheep	John 10	30	Fellowship	1 John 1

Books of the Bible _____

The Bible: The word means the sacred Book, or collection of books, accepted by the Christian church as uniquely inspired by God, and the guide for faith and behavior.

The Bible contains two major sections known as the Old Testament and the New Testament. The books of the OT were written over a period of about 1,000 years in the Hebrew language, except for a few passages written in Aramaic.

The NT was written over a period of about 100 years. The original language in which it was written was Greek.

Major Divisions and Individual Books of the Old Testament

Books of the Pentateuch, or the Law

Book	Summary
Genesis	Creation and the establishment of the covenant relationship
Exodus	Deliverance of the people of Israel from slavery in Egypt
Leviticus	The ceremonial law
Numbers	Wandering of God's people in the wilderness
Deuteronomy	The second giving of the law by Moses before the people occupy the Promised Land

Books About the History of Israel

Book	Summary
Joshua	The capture and settlement of the Promised Land
Judges	The nation of Israel is rescued by a series of judges, or military leaders
Ruth	A beautiful story of God's love and care
1 & 2 Samuel	The early history of Israel, focusing on the

A Samaritan priest displays a scroll of the five books of Moses, the only Old Testament books which they accept as authoritative.

Major Divisions and Individual Books of the Old Testament—*continued*

Book	Summary
	reigns of kings from the time of Solomon to the captivity of the Jewish people in Babylon
1 & 2 Chronicles	A religious history of Israel, covering the same period of time as 2 Samuel and 1 and 2 Kings
Ezra	The return of the Jewish people from captivity in Babylon
Nehemiah	The rebuilding of the walls of Jerusalem after the exiles returned from Babylon
Esther	God's care for his people under Gentile rule

Books of Wisdom Writings

Book	Summary
Job	An examination of the problems of evil and human suffering
Psalms	The songbook or hymnal of ancient Israel
Proverbs	Wise sayings and observations designed to develop proper attitudes and behavior
Ecclesiastes	A philosophical description of the emptiness of life without God
Song of Solomon	A love song portraying the beauty of a human love relationship as a symbol of divine love

A woven tapestry which portrays the prophet Jeremiah, from the Church of San Vitale in Ravenna, Italy.   PHOTO BY HOWARD VOS

Books of the Major Prophets

Book	Summary
Isaiah	The outstanding prophet of condemnation and messianic consolation
Jeremiah	A message of judgment against Judah's moral and spiritual decay
Lamentations	Jeremiah's five poems of lament over fallen Jerusalem
Ezekiel	A prophecy of judgment during the Babylonian captivity
Daniel	A book of prophecy about the end time

Books of the Minor Prophets

Book	Summary
Hosea	A message of Israel's condemnation followed by God's forgiveness
Joel	A prediction of foreign invasion as a form of judgment by God
Amos	A prophecy consisting of eight pronouncements of judgment against Israel
Obadiah	A book prophesying the total destruction of Edom
Jonah	A reluctant prophet who led Nineveh to repentance
Micah	A prediction of judgment and a promise of messianic restoration
Nahum	A prophecy of the destruction of Nineveh
Habakkuk	A prophet who questioned God and praised his approaching judgment against Judah
Zephaniah	A prediction of destructive judgment followed by tremendous blessing
Haggai	A call to rebuild the temple after the return from Babylon
Zechariah	A messianic prophecy calling for the completion of the temple construction
Malachi	A prophecy of destruction followed by messianic blessing

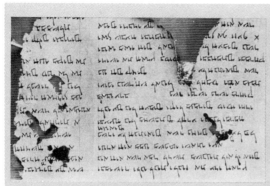

Portions of a commentary on the book of Habakkuk—one of the ancient documents included among the Dead Sea Scrolls.

PHOTO BY HOWARD VOS

Ruins of the civil law court known as the Julian Basilica in ancient Corinth. Some of the charges of the Corinthian Christians against one another (1 Cor. 6:1–11) may have been reviewed on this very site. PHOTO BY HOWARD VOS

Major Divisions and Individual Books of the New Testament

The Gospels

Book	Summary
Matthew	Christ presented as the fulfillment of OT messianic prophecy
Mark	Probably the earliest of the gospels, focusing on Jesus' ministry
Luke	Fullest biography of Jesus, focusing on his perfection and ministry of salvation
John	The most symbolic gospel, which presents Christ as the divine Son of God

History of the Early Church

Book	Summary
Acts	A history of the expansion of the early church

Epistles (Letters) of the Apostle Paul

Book	Summary
Romans	An explanation of the Christian faith for both Jews and Gentiles, addressed to the church at Rome
1 Corinthians	Instructions to the church at Corinth dealing with prob-

Book	Summary
	lems among Christians
2 Corinthians	Paul's defense and explanation of his apostleship
Galatians	An account of the necessity of salvation by divine grace rather than the law
Ephesians	A letter to the church at Ephesus explaining the believer's position in Christ
Colossians	An account of the supremacy of Christ, written to the church of Colossae
1 & 2 Thessalonians	Instructions to the church at Thessalonica about the coming of the Lord
1 & 2 Timothy	Manuals of leadership for the young pastor
Titus	A manual of Christian conduct for church leaders, written to a young pastor
Philemon	An appeal for Christian unity and forgiveness for a runaway slave

Major Divisions and Individual Books of the New Testament—*continued*

General Epistles (Letters)

Book	Summary
Hebrews	A presentation of Jesus Christ as high priest, addressed to Jewish believers
James	Practical instructions for applied Christianity
1 Peter	Encouragement and comfort from Peter to suffering Christians
2 Peter	Peter's warning against false teachers
1 John	John's reminder of the full humanity of Jesus
2 John	John's letter of encouragement and approval
3 John	John's personal note of appreciation to Gaius
Jude	A strong warning against false teachers
Revelation	An encouraging prophecy of the final days and God's ultimate triumph

The Apocrypha ⸺⸺⸺⸺

A*pocrypha* refers to a group of books written during a time of turmoil in the history of the Jewish people, from about 200 B.C. to about A.D. 100 These books fall into two main divisions, OT apocryphal books and NT apocryphal books.

The 15 OT books were written during the period from about 150 B.C. to about A.D. 70, when the Jewish people were in rebellion against the repression of foreign military rulers. These books were excluded from most early versions of the OT. Bibles used by Roman Catholics contain the OT Apocrypha, while these books are seldom included in most Protestant editions of the Bible.

The books known as the NT Apocrypha were written during the second and third centuries A.D., long after the death of the apostles and other eyewitnesses to the life and ministry of Jesus. None of these books were included in the NT because they were judged to be unworthy by officials of the early church and not authoritative.

Old Testament Apocrypha

Events that led to the writing of the OT apocryphal books began in 167 B.C., when the Jews revolted against the king of Syria, Antiochus IV Epiphanes. A pious Jewish priest, Mattathias, and his sons led the rebellion. Mattathias refused to obey Antiochus's command that the Jews worship his gods and offer a pagan sacrifice. Mattathias killed the Syrian official as well as a fellow Jew who was offering the sacrifice and declared: "Follow me, every one of you who is zealous for the law and strives to maintain the covenant" (1 Macc. 2:27–28, NEB).

Guerrilla warfare against the Syrians followed, until the Jews established control of Israel. Early in the revolt one of the sons of Mattathias, Judas Maccabeus (*Maccabeus* means "hammer"), cleansed the temple in Jerusalem from the pollution of the Syrian sacrifices. This day has been celebrated annually by the Jews since that time in the festival known as Chanukah (or Hanukkah), the Feast of Dedication (John 10:22).

These events helped stir the Jewish people to rededicate themselves to the law of Moses. In the fight to establish their independence and uphold their traditions, some Jewish authors wrote to encourage their own people.

From 142 to 63 B.C. the Jews were led in their rebellion against foreign oppression by the family of Mattathias, known as the Hasmoneans. Simon Hasamonaios was the grandfather of Mattathias, and his name was applied to all the members of this great family. In spite of the respect given to the Hasmoneans in the early years of their influence, civil strife again plagued the Jews. The Syrians continued to fight for power over the land of Israel. Judas Maccabeus finally made an agreement with Rome that the Romans would come to the aid of the Jews if they needed assistance in their struggle.

About a century later some of the Jews did appeal to Rome for help. Pompey, a powerful Roman general, brought order to Jerusalem and made Judea part of a Roman province.

In 37 B.C. the land of Israel was placed under the rule of a Roman official, Herod the Great (37–4 B.C.). Herod was actually a Roman vassal and was hated by most of the Jews. In spite of this hostility, Herod managed to launch an ambitious building program in Palestine. He created the magnificent port city of Caesarea on the Mediterranean Sea and improved the temple in Jerusalem. The western wall still stands today in Jerusalem as evidence of Herod's skill as a builder.

After Herod's death (4 B.C.), his sons divided the Holy Land into four regions, ruling the land with varying degrees of success. In A.D. 66 the Jews again grew angry over the foreign domination of their land. Under the encouragement of radical freedom fighters known as Zealots, the Jews started a disastrous war with the Romans. This led to the destruction of Jerusalem and the temple in A.D. 70 and the end of the Jewish nation.

This historical sketch provides the background for the Old Testament apocryphal writings. The Jewish people were continually wondering what God was saying to them through their struggles. Out of their experiences arose the books of the Apocrypha.

> First Esdras
> Second Esdras
> Tobit
> Judith
> The Additions to Esther
> The Wisdom of Solomon
> Ecclesiasticus, or the Wisdom of Jesus,
>   the Son of Sirach
> Baruch
> The Letter of Jeremiah
> The Prayer of Azariah and the Song of
>   the Three Young Men
> Susanna
> Bel and the Dragon
> The Prayer of Manasseh
> First Maccabees
> Second Maccabees

New Testament Apocrypha

The NT Apocrypha contains several writings that were similar to NT books but were not included as a part of the NT. These writings were greatly influenced by the philosophies and religions of the cities or nations out of which they came. Some of the apocryphal gospels were written to replace the Gospels of the NT, but were declared false or inferior writings by officials of the early church.

Often the apocryphal books from the early history of the church present stories and legends meant to fill in information about the apostles and Jesus that is lacking in the NT. For example, some NT apocryphal works claim to give details on the childhood of Jesus (Protevangelium of James, The Gospel of Thomas) or describe how Jesus was raised from the dead (The Gospel of Peter). These writings expand on the accounts found in the NT.

Other apocryphal writings that expand or explain the gospel stories include:

The Gospel of the Egyptians
The Gospel of Truth
The Gospel of the Twelve
The Gospel of Philip
The Gospel of Judas
The Gospel of Bartholomew
The Gospel According to Mary
The Gospel of Nicodemus
The Questions of Bartholomew

These are only a few of the 59 fragments and gospel-related writings in the NT Apocrypha.

The Acts of the Apostles is also paralleled by several apocryphal books. These include stories about the apostles themselves, written in the second and third centuries. Titles of some of these books are

The Acts of John
The Acts of Peter
The Acts of Paul
The Acts of Andrew
The Acts of Thomas

The Acts of John, for example, tells the story of John, his journey from Jerusalem to Rome, and his imprisonment on an island called Patmos off the coast of modern-day Turkey. (See Rev. 1:9.) Other travels of this apostle appear in the book, and he finally dies in Ephesus. Some scholars believe these second-century books may be based on some historical facts. They do give Bible researchers a better understanding of the origin of the early church.

The last group of NT apocryphal writings consists of apocalyptic books. The book of Revelation inspired the early Christians to write their own books that were similar in content and style. Probably the most popular of the apocryphal apocalypses are

Apocalypse of Peter
Apocalypse of Paul
Apocalypse of Thomas

These apocalypses give Bible scholars a clearer picture of the early Christian's view of heaven and hell because they emphasize the state of sinners after death.

While they are interesting and informative, none of these books are considered authoritative like the books of the NT. For various reasons, these books were judged unworthy and were not accepted as authoritative when the NT took its final form in the third century A.D.

New Testament History

Ew Testament writers lived at a time when the art of historical literature was beginning to flower. The historians of Greece and Rome have left us interesting accounts of their cultures. But NT history is more than a cultural report. It is a record of God's interaction with the human race through the life of a man from Nazareth named Jesus.

The Gospels

The Gospels have no parallels in ancient literature.

They are not heroic narratives. The heroic narrative is a single unified story—i.e., one plot. The structure of a gospel is more fragmented. Its elements may be rearranged or even omitted without damaging the movement of the narrative.

In this respect, the Gospels more closely parallel the structure of a chronicle, like the histories of the OT. Yet the OT chronicles focus on the story of the nation whereas the Gospels focus on a main character. The biographies of the OT (e.g., Elijah) bear some similarities to the Gospels but lack the extended discourses and the parabolic devices so prominent in the Gospels.

They are not biography. They lack the detailed reconstruction of the life of the subject. Vast stretches of Jesus' life story are missing—elements that would be indispensable in a biography.

They are not tragedy. Although the main character faces much tragedy and ultimately dies, these accounts do not conform to the structure of tragedy. Jesus is not overcome by uncontrollable fate. He is in complete control of every moment and circumstance. He voluntarily goes to his death—but not as a defeated hero. His death is his victory, crowned by his resurrection three days later. His death is not the result of a tragic moral decision on his part, but it is the climactic step of his consciously chosen way to triumph and glorification. In tragic literature, the hero is admired because he accepts a defeat pressed upon him in spite of his not deserving it.

They are more than theological treatises. Each gospel presents a slightly different portrait of Jesus. But the Gospels lack the systematic discussion of a given theme or themes that typifies the theological treatise.

Like the history of the book of Acts, the Gospels are religious history or religious biography. The distinctive literary quality of Jesus' discourses shows that they originated with a single highly creative personality.

Jesus as a Literary Character

As a literary character, Jesus is unique. In a heroic narrative, the main character is merely exemplary. His behavior is held up as a pattern for all. In the Gospels, however,

Jesus is depicted as more than a human example. He is God incarnate who forgives sin, promises salvation to all who believe, and performs miracles. These are literary themes foreign to heroic narrative.

In mythological narrative tales, the divine or semidivine protagonist (main character) is a literary fiction—not an actual living person. Jesus is clearly a different kind of protagonist. He is an actual historical figure immersed in real life. Since this depiction was published very close to the time of his ministry, it would have been folly for the gospel writers to present fiction as fact. There is no solid reason to think they did so.

As a literary figure, Jesus is an antihero—neither a political king nor a military victor—but a suffering servant and a dying Messiah who overcame death through his resurrection.

Literary Features of the Gospels

A gospel is a collection of stories that are unique in the great amount of action they set forth. The purpose is to publish the facts and meaning of Jesus' life as well as to praise him. There are many forms used in the gospel.

1. Narrative extends in complexity from a simple, bare outline of events to an extended presentation of details surrounding events (e.g., Matt. 27).

2. Dialogue appears with the same wide degree of complexity (e.g., Matt. 13:10–17).

3. Discourses or speeches are frequent (e.g., the Sermon on the Mount in Matt. 5 or the Olivet discourse in Matt. 24).

4. Parable is a story illustrating a single point, in which the details have little meaning (Matt. 13:33), or a story illustrating a major point and other minor points, in which the details are meaningful (e.g., Matt. 13:36–43).

5. Miracle stories as literary devices demand to be taken at face value. The authors fully intend the reader to understand that Jesus performed miracles. To read them otherwise is to ignore the author's intent, and is not responsible literary criticism.

All four Gospels depict Jesus as a literary genius. He is shown to be a master of all the devices of OT poetry: *parallelism* (Matt. 13:13), *metaphor* (Matt. 15:14), *simile* (Matt. 13:47), *paradox* (Matt. 11:30), and *hyperbole* (Matt. 19:24).

His teaching reflects the style and standpoint of both the Prophets and the OT Wisdom Literature. Jesus stands authoritatively in the midst of his disciples, instructing them in the wise ways of living.

Matthew

While each of the Gospels is a unique literary production, it is evident that the first three are related. Most scholars think that Matthew and Luke used some of Mark's material. Matthew wishes to convince his readers that Jesus is the Messiah promised in the OT. He points out that Jesus fulfilled specific OT prophecies. (cf. 1:23; 2:6, 15, 18, 23; 3:3; 4:15–16; 8:17; 12:18–21; 13:35; 21:5; 26:56). Except for 2:6, he prefaces the OT quote with a formula specifying that the Scripture is fulfilled. These quotes appear to be fresh translations of the OT passages, while the other OT citations in the gospel are taken from the Septuagint (the Greek OT).

This gospel has a pronounced OT flavor by emphasizing God's kingdom (chap. 13); Christ the Messiah; the new age (chaps. 24—25); righteousness (chap. 23); and wisdom themes (in the depiction of Jesus' stance among his disciples and in the themes he uses, which is especially true of the contrast between the wise and the foolish in chap. 25).

There are also distinctive features of this gospel:

• Matthew places a unique emphasis on the role of the Gentiles in the new kingdom (e.g., 8:10–12; 10:18).

- Matthew is the only gospel that mentions the church (16:18; 18:17).
- Matthew groups the sayings of Jesus into five blocks of discourses, each ending with the formula, "When Jesus had finished. . . ." (See 5:1—7:29; 10:5—11:1; 13:1–53; 18:1—19:1; 24:4—26:1.)

The book divides the ministry of Jesus into three large sections. First, there is the preparation for his public ministry closed by the phrase "from that time" (4:17). The second division focuses on the opening of his ministry with the closing phrase "from that time" (16:21), followed by emphasis on private instruction of the Twelve and Jesus' death on the cross.

Mark

Mark is distinguished by several aspects of its language:
- Mark uses more Latin words than any other gospel.
- Mark explains a Greek word with a Latin word (12:42; 15:16).
- Mark has a pronounced Aramaic flavor.
- Mark uses rough Greek, marked by broken sentence structure (e.g., 3:30; 7:19) and slang expressions.

Some scholars believe this indicates that Mark wrote down the material as Peter (who was Jewish and knew Aramaic better than Greek) spoke it for a Roman audience.

Mark's gospel moves more rapidly than the other Gospels. Yet Mark is not skimpy with details. In fact, when all three synoptic Gospels (Matthew, Mark, and Luke) report an event, Mark usually gives more details than the others. Mark wrote a book of action, focusing on the deeds of the main character (Jesus) rather than his words. These events pass in rapid succession, emphasized by Mark's use of the word *immediately* more than 30 times.

Mark also depicts Jesus as a teacher and a real human being, emphasizing Jesus' compassion (e.g., 1:41; 6:34), Jesus' indignation (e.g., 3:5), and Jesus' distress and sorrow (e.g., 14:33–34).

This gospel focuses on the training of the Twelve, sometimes painting a poorer picture of them than is found in the other Gospels (e.g., 5:31; 9:10; 10:13–14). Structurally, about 40 percent of the book is given to Christ's passion (i.e., 10:32ff.). Mark pictures Jesus as the Son of God from the beginning (1:1).

Luke

Only the gospel of Luke seeks to bind the stories of Jesus to the secular world. The language of this gospel is literary, somewhat comparable to that of classical Greek. The language of the birth and infancy passages is noticeably different from that of the prologue and the rest of the book. These early narratives have a Semitic flavor. They also relate events otherwise not known.

This writer emphasizes the response of the crowds to Jesus. They were amazed at him (e.g., 5:26; 7:16–17). Yet there is no mention of his compassion for the crowds—only his feelings for individuals. Luke focuses especially on the poor, the rich and their wealth (e.g., 12:13–21), and women. He portrays Jesus as the champion of society's outcasts. Luke also highlights on certain concepts, such as love, joy, praise, and peace.

Some distinguishing aspects of Luke include:
- Luke usually tells us the time and place of the events narrated (e.g., 2:1).
- Luke supplies more details about Jesus' human life than the other Gospels.
- Luke alone gives Jesus the title *Savior* (2:11).
- Luke emphasizes Jesus' mission and traces the parallel between the prophetic pattern and Jesus' ministry.

John

The fourth gospel is written in a simple style with common words, brief statements, picturesque language, and frequent repetition; the effect is profound. The language is distinctive in its diction and its theological concepts (e.g., such key words as "witness," "believe," "life," "love," "abide" or "remain," "truth" or "true," "Jew," "world," "feast," and "light").

The structure of this gospel is artistically balanced between a poetic prologue (1:1–18) and epilogue (chap. 21). Many of Jesus' miracles are especially emphasized and called signs (2:1–12; 4:46–54). However, other miracles are mentioned (2:23; 6:2; 9:1–41; 20:30). John shows that Jesus used the miracles as opportunities to teach spiritual lessons (cf. chap. 9, esp. v. 41).

John has several distinctions:

- John highlights the "I am" sayings of Jesus (e.g., 8:12).
- John places a unique emphasis on the Jewish feasts and festivals that Jesus attended.
- John demonstrates that Jesus was greater than the law (cf. 1:17), the temple (cf. 2:19–21), and the shekinah glory, or visible manifestation of God's presence (cf. 7:37–39).
- Jesus primarily addresses individuals rather than crowds. Some of the main characters associated with Jesus, such as John the Baptist and Judas Iscariot, are pictured more fully in John than elsewhere.
- John puts special emphasis on the deity of Christ.
- John is unique in highlighting his preexistence and in calling him the Word (Greek *logos*). At the same time, John clearly sets forth Jesus' dependence on the Father and his full humanity (Luke 17).

The Book of Acts (The Continuation of Luke's Gospel)

Comparisons of the book of Acts with extrabiblical literature have produced interesting results. Students of classical Greek have concluded that Luke is a church historian in the tradition of Thucydides and Polybius. This is best seen in the speeches recorded in Acts. The Greek historians composed the speeches they reported, but gave careful attention to what the speaker really said.

In writing Acts, Luke probably took shorthand notes of the speeches that he heard, and of others' memories of what they had heard. For example, Paul's address to the Ephesian elders at Miletus (20:18–35) reflects distinctively Pauline concepts. Speeches attributed to Peter (2:14–40; 3:12–26; 4:8–12; 10:34–43) reflect neither Pauline nor Lukan concepts, but the language and concepts of 1 Peter. All the speeches in Acts reflect the same general pattern that probably follows the structure of early Christian preaching.

Like all historians, Luke sets forth an interpretation of history. The overall structure of the book is geared to show how the gospel spread from Jerusalem to "the uttermost parts of the world" (i.e., Rome, the capital of the empire) and how its center shifted from Judaic Christians to gentile Christians. Many things not relevant to this theme are omitted. Especially noticeable in this regard is the way in which the ministry of the apostles is recorded. The only one of the original 12 who is pictured to any degree is Peter, and he is soon eclipsed by the appearance of Paul.

On the other hand, there is clear evidence that this book is a theological creation. Luke's distinctive Greek style marks most of the book. It is the most sophisticated Greek writing in the NT. This is especially true in Luke's "we" passages, where he reports as an eyewitness of the events recounted (cf. Acts 16:10–17; 20:5—21:18; 27:1—28:16). Some of the other sections are couched in the same cultural style.

Commentators disagree about the literary genre to which Acts belongs. It certainly lacks the characteristics of the biography, heroic narrative, or epic because there is no central figure.

Acts has similarities with the OT presentations of the kingdom (1 and 2 Samuel; 1 and 2 Kings; 1 and 2 Chronicles). But these OT chronicles report the history of the kingdom from different theological perspectives, which strongly influence the choice and framing of particular events. Like Acts, they contain summarized speeches. But the speeches of Acts are far more frequent and extended than the speeches of OT histories. Speeches play a significant role in the structure of Acts, such as Peter's sermon at Pentecost (2:14–39), Paul's speech on Mars Hill (17:16–31), and Paul's address to the Ephesian elders (20:18–35).

Luke relates only the relevant details to his central thesis (unlike Greek historians). The end result is high literature. The structure of the work as a whole and of the individual subdivisions presents an excellent balance of simplicity and clarity.

Luke introduces main characters and describes their lives only insofar as they contribute to the main theme. Minor themes are unobtrusively introduced, treated, and set aside. Usually, each unit forms a completed story with a beginning, middle, and end (e.g., chaps. 1—2).

The Epistles

Much of the NT consists of letters that we call epistles—a well-known form of literature among ancient Greeks. We will discuss the book of Hebrews with the epistles, even though it appears to be more of a theological treatise than an epistle.

Paul's Epistles

Paul's epistles (as the rest of the NT letters) are unique literary productions. They differ from all letter styles found in extrabiblical literature.

The extrabiblical letters are structured as follows:

> The author's name and title
> The recipient's name and title
> Sometimes the secretary's or messenger's name
> A standardized greeting
> A discussion of the business in hand
> Closing greetings

In many papyrus letters, the closing greetings are written in a hand different from the rest of the letter. This suggests that the author employed an amanuensis (secretary to write his letter). An amanuensis would listen to what the author wanted to say and then compose the document in his own words. The author would read the amanuensis's work, making sure it said what he intended, and then the author might write closing greetings (cf. Gal. 6:11–12; 2 Thess. 3:17).

Paul's letters follow this general structure. What makes them distinctive is the element of apostolic proclamation and exhortation, which gives them the force of written sermons.

Paul expands the colorless standardized greeting by inserting words such as *grace* and *peace*—characteristic Christian and Hebrew ideas. He replaces his thanksgiving for the recipient's health and happiness in the greeting part of his letters with a blessing (thanksgiving for the blessings received from God).

The main part of Paul's letters opens with a well-known device taken from the rules of Greek and Roman public speaking. Seeking to establish rapport with his readers, Paul makes a request, an appeal, or an injunction. Sometimes he uses a formula of disclosure

("I want you to know" or "I do not want you to be ignorant"). On other occasions, he congratulates his readers on the success of their work (cf. Phil. 1:3–6; 1 Thess. 1:2–10) and their healthy spiritual condition (1 Thess. 1:4–5; 2 Thess. 1:3–4).

Paul's letters sometimes interweave practical and doctrinal concerns (e.g., 1 and 2 Cor.; Phil.; and 1 Thess.), or at other times, he separates these concerns, placing the doctrinal before the practical (e.g., Rom.; Gal.; Eph.). In these cases, the doctrinal sections constitute the basis for the practical application.

Paul closes his epistles with notes of greetings, a doxology, and a benediction.

Characteristic of Paul's letters are the following:
- The tone is not intimate like the typical letter genre.
- He writes not to a single reader (except Timothy, Titus, and Philemon), but to a more general audience.
- He regularly speaks as a public person rather than as a private individual and emphasizes his apostolic ministry.
- Even when he writes to an individual, nearly everything is ultimately a message to the church universal.
- His epistles are thematic extensions of the Gospels—a trait reflected in their literary structure.

Paul proves himself to be a master of rhetoric and eloquent style, using long, suspended sentences that build to a powerful climax. He skillfully uses evocative words such as vivid metaphors, similes, touching allusions to the life and person of Jesus—all devices of effective literary communication. He is especially adept at peroration—attaining a strong climax as seen in Ephesians 6:10–18.

The Epistle to the Hebrews

Considerable debate concerns the literary genre to which Hebrews belongs. It is not really a letter, since it lacks the expected introduction. Yet the opening (1:1–13) serves as an excellent springboard to its argument. The book has several personal allusions (e.g., 2:1). Its argument, however, is much more cohesively developed than in an ordinary epistle, and its style is mostly that of a didactic treatise.

Scholars have differed and concluded that
- Hebrews is an essay. But this literary category fails to include such elements as personal allusions present in Hebrews.
- Hebrews is a written sermon.
- Hebrews is a combination of several sermons.

Hebrews, unique from a literary standpoint, contains elements of the epistle, essay or theological treatise, and sermon all blended together.

Hebrews presents a well-balanced argument. Like Paul's letters to the Romans and Ephesians, it consists of an extended theological or doctrinal presentation (1:1—10:18), followed by a briefer section of practical exhortation (10:19—13:21).

The doctrinal section itself, however, is punctuated by practical admonitions (e.g., 2:1–4; 3:7–19; 5:12–14), exhortations (4:11–13; 6:9–12), and affirmations of the superiority of Christ (4:14–16). These elements are masterfully interwoven.

Hebrews makes frequent reference to the OT and establishes doctrinal points by expounding and applying OT passages. The writer introduces OT passages with formulae showing his respect for them as the utterances of God (e.g., Heb. 4:3; 10:15).

The Epistle of James

This letter was written by James, the brother of Jesus, to the Jewish Christians scattered throughout the Roman Empire.

There is a striking parallel between the sayings of Jesus recorded in Matthew 5—7 and James. Both use many images from nature. Some passages in this letter also remind us of the speech of James in Acts 15.

The epistle exhibits a strong Jewish background, refuting the notion that James structured his letter after the Greek diatribe, common among popular Greek moralists of his day. The diatribe was not geared to speak to a particular historical situation.

The style of this epistle is authoritative, simple, and direct, yet it lacks the cohesiveness of Pauline presentation. Although it is didactic and pastoral in purpose, it is quite different in structure and rhetoric from Paul's writings. The epistle contains many epigrams that demonstrate the influence of the OT poetic style upon James's writing. The same poetic style was prominent in Jesus' teaching, and several passages in this book are obviously dependent upon that teaching. (For example, compare James 1:12 with Matt. 5:11–12.)

Some see James as an example of NT Wisdom Literature. The writer appears as a wise teacher instructing readers in the way of wise living. His short, rather disconnected maxims resemble Proverbs. This feature has led some scholars to suggest that James wrote in the manner in which he taught, which means that the epistle is written as catechetical (instructional) material.

Peter's Epistles

The apostle Peter wrote his first epistle from Rome, addressing it to the predominantly gentile churches of Asia Minor that were enduring severe persecutions at the hands of their unbelieving neighbors.

First Peter is in the form of an epistle:
- It has the expected opening and personal greetings at the beginning.
- It has a benediction at the end.
- It presents the theme of Christian suffering in ever-increasing intensity.
- It has a doxology (4:11) that interrupts the flow of thought only momentarily.

This document has been viewed in a variety of ways:
- As a written baptismal sermon with a general address attached to the end
- As a double letter subsequently combined
- As a letter with an addition for a particular church
- As a general (or circular) epistle used as a vehicle to deliver an exhortation (cf. 5:12)

The style is generally elegant, exhibiting similarities to classical Greek. On the other hand, certain aspects of its style are somewhat rough. This may indicate two writers. The thought and substance are Peter's (the fisherman whose Greek may have been rugged); the composition was mostly, if not wholly, done by the Greek amanuensis Silvanus (1 Pet. 5:12).

A number of passages in 1 Peter are said to be hymnic—reflecting ancient Christian hymns (1:3–12; 2:21–25; 3:18–22). It frequently quotes the OT. The letter uses various figures of speech: simile (2:2), colorful epithets (2:25; 5:4), and metaphor (5:2).

The apostle wrote 2 Peter when he was facing certain death. He addressed the same readers, warning them against false teachers who were spreading dangerous doctrines, and urging his Christian friends to grow in the knowledge of the truth.

The Greek is generally less elegant than that of the first letter. There is a difference in vocabulary. Probably this reflects use of a different amanuensis. Unlike 1 Peter, the second epistle does not refer frequently to the OT. Second Peter 1:5–7 attains an interesting poetic quality by piling phrase upon phrase. The prose is highly descriptive at many points (cf. 2:12–13), employing powerful figures of speech such as the simile in 2:12.

A brother of James and Jesus, Jude picks up the theme of 2 Peter. He condemns the doctrine that taught whatever is done in the body has nothing to do with the soul, or the spiritual part of humanity. Christians who held this position believed that their acts did not affect their salvation, so they committed many sinful acts.

This epistle presents two intriguing literary problems. First, it quotes from 1 Enoch 1:9 and the Assumption of Moses—books written before the time of the NT but not accepted as inspired by the Jewish or Christian communities. Yet Jude used them to make his point. All we can safely say is that he believed what he quoted was true.

Second, a strong similarity exists between Jude and 2 Peter. If they were not penned by the same writer, likely they were written with one another in mind.

Characteristic of Jude are the following points:
• The Greek language is strongly Semitic, possibly due to Jude's intimate knowledge of the Greek OT (Septuagint).
• Jude's style is vivid, vigorous, and at times poetic (vv. 12–13).
• Jude does not use the rugged broken sentence typical of Paul.
• Jude avoids the epigram (short powerful statements) of James.
• Jude's frequent use of a three-point argument and his carefully constructed doxology (vv. 24–25) point to an orderly mind. Only Jude and Paul end their letters with such an elaborate ascription of praise.

John's Letters

The NT contains three epistles from the apostle John to the churches in Asia Minor. They contain notable similarities to his gospel and the book of Revelation. These letters contend against an error that later emerged as the heresy of Gnosticism.

First John is a personal message from the writer. However, it does not have the introduction, writer's greeting, and thanksgiving typical of the epistle genre. Nor does it exhibit the influence of public speaking, typical of the sermon genre. Some scholars have related this epistle to the diatribe genre, but it speaks to a definite historical situation, which diatribes do not.

No unifying theme develops throughout the book. It presents a series of pastoral instructions on topics that appear not to be directly related.

The author is refuting Gnosticism. (*Gnosticism* taught that the body and this world are evil and that salvation is gained by a special kind of knowledge or enlightenment. In particular, Gnostics argued that God could not have become incarnate. They maintained that individuals could do as they wished in this world, as long as they believed the right things—i.e., had the right knowledge.)

This epistle repeats its leading ideas and terms, such as light, truth, and love.

The sentence structure is simple and straightforward, involving parallelism of idea (as in 3:6). The writer tends to present ideas in strong contrast to one another—i.e., in absolute blacks and whites with no theological gray areas. Although these characteristics are similar to OT prophetic writing, 1 John makes only one direct reference to the OT in 3:12.

The epistles of 2 and 3 John are more personal than 1 John. They also speak to specific (but differing) situations and include the opening and personal greetings typical of a letter. Their style, although similar to that of 1 John, is closer to that of the gospel of John.

Apocalyptic Literature

In the broadest sense, *apocalyptic* includes all religious literature that abounds in visions of God or revelations from God concerning the end of the present age. In this sense, apocalyptic includes sections of Joel, Amos, Zechariah, Daniel 7—12, Jesus'

Olivet discourse (Matt. 24—25), 1 Thessalonians 4:13ff., Revelation, and certain extra-biblical literature.

Daniel

Daniel 7—12 is the prototype of apocalyptic literature.

First, Daniel presents a cosmic dualism—two mighty forces (God and evil) locked in a great struggle. Daniel sets forth abundant visions and revelations in highly symbolic language, often alluding to ancient mythological figures and OT prophetic symbolism. Daniel makes symbolic use of numbers, animals, and inanimate objects.

He condemns the evil of the present age, even though the forces of evil apparently triumph. In the higher realm these evil forces are losing the war. Daniel's strong emphasis on divine sovereignty shows that the outcome is never in doubt. His pessimistic outlook on the present political situation is thematically balanced by this optimistic view of divine sovereignty and the outcome of world history. He knows that in the future age God will triumph and bless the faithful.

Another apocalyptic theme of Daniel is the resurrection of the righteous and judgment of the wicked (Dan. 12).

Because it abounds in mysterious figures or symbols, apocalyptic literature such as Daniel's is more difficult to interpret than other OT literature.

Revelation

Revelation, with its unique literary form of letters plus visions of the future, borrows from OT and the apocryphal books, as well as from OT prophetic literature. For example, it highlights the second coming of Jesus Christ, the ultimate glory of the kingdom of God (chap. 21), and the resurrection and final judgment (20:11–15).

Other OT and apocryphal symbols in Revelation include:
- A woman representing a people and a city (cf. 17:18)
- Horns representing authority
- Eyes symbolizing understanding (cf. 5:6)
- Trumpets signifying a superhuman or divine voice (cf. 8:6—11:19)
- White robes referring to the glory of the coming age (cf. 6:11)
- Crowns depicting dominion (cf. 6:2)
- The number seven standing for fullness or perfection (cf. 5:1; 8:6)
- The number 12 symbolizing the ultimately perfect people of God (cf. 7:5–8; 22:2)
- The frequent appearance of angels (cf. 7:1; 10:1)

Apocalyptic writing of this sort was a code, a way of communicating that unbelieving enemies would not understand. Those who wrote such literature could encourage their readers to stand against the pagan state and predict its downfall under divine judgment, without fear of official reprisal. Modern readers often miss this aspect of the apocalyptic genre, just as the ancient pagans did.

An interesting stylistic trait of Revelation is its strong contrasts:
- Conflict *(God against Satan, the saints against the followers of the Beast, the bride of Christ against the harlot Babylon)*
- Imagery *(the Lamb and the dragon, the beautiful but deceptive harlot, the Lamb that is a lion)*
- Actions *(establishment of the New Jerusalem and the destruction of Babylon, Satan being allowed to harm his own human followers but not the followers of the Lamb)*
- Location *(heaven and earth, land and sea)*
- Time *(measurable time as opposed to immeasurable eternity)*

These contrasts vividly convey the sense that vast forces of good and evil are in conflict in this world, and we cannot hope for stability until the day of Christ's triumph.

Figurative Literature in the Bible

Allegory and extended metaphor. The word *allegory* comes from two Greek words (*allos* meaning "other" and *agoreuein* meaning "to speak in an assembly") and refers to a type of literature in which the people, things, and events in the story have a symbolic or hidden meaning. Often allegories are for instructive purposes.

The allegories and extended metaphors of the Bible include:

The Shepherd Psalm	Ps. 23
The grape vine	Ps. 80:8–15
God's vineyard	Isa. 5:1–7
The great eagle	Ezek. 17:1–10
The lioness	Ezek. 19:1–9
The bread of life	John 6:26–51
The sheepfold and shepherd	John 10
The vine	John 15:1–7
The Christian foundation	1 Cor. 3:10–15
The whole armor of God	Eph. 6:10–17
The bondswoman and the free	Gal. 4:21–31

Fable. The Bible, not known for fables, records only two that are genuinely called by that name. *Fables*, by definition, are fictitious, usually about animals or plants that talk and behave like humans. Fables teach a moral.

Here are the two fables, both occurring in the OT:

The fable of the bramble tree related by Jothan to ridicule Abimelech	Judg. 9:7–15
The fable of the thistle bush related by Jehoash, king of Israel, to Amaziah, king of Judah, to ridicule him	2 Kings 14:8–9

Parable. A parable is a short, simple story designed to communicate a spiritual truth, religious principle, or moral lesson. It illustrates a truth by a comparison or example drawn from everyday experiences.

A parable is often no more than an extended metaphor or simile, using figurative language in the form of a story to explain a particular truth. The Greek word for *parable* literally means "laying by the side of" or "a casting alongside," and has come to mean a *comparison* or *likeness*. In a parable something is placed alongside something else so that one can throw light on the other *or* illustrate some less-familiar truth.

Although Jesus was a master of the parabolic form, he was not the first to use parables. Examples of the effective use of parables are found in the OT. Perhaps the best known of these is Nathan's parable of the rich man who took the ewe lamb that belonged to a poor family (2 Sam. 12:1–4). With this illustration, Nathan reproved King David and convicted him of his sin of committing adultery with Bathsheba (2 Sam. 12:5–15). A wise woman of Tekoa also used a parable (2 Sam. 14:5–7) to convince King David to let his son return to Jerusalem.

Jesus' characteristic method of teaching was through parables. His two most famous parables are the parable of the lost son (Luke 15:11–32) and the parable of the good Samaritan (Luke 10:25–37). Both parables illustrate God's love for sinners and God's command that we show compassion to all people.

Actually, the parable of the lost son (sometimes called the prodigal son or the parable of the loving father) is the story of two lost sons: the younger son (typical of tax collectors and prostitutes) who wasted possessions with indulgent living and the older son (typical of the self-righteous scribes and Pharisees) who remained at home but was a stranger to his father's heart.

Some entire chapters in the Gospels are devoted to Jesus' parables, for instance Matthew 13 includes: the parable of the sower (vv. 1–23), the wheat and the tares (vv. 24–30), the mustard seed (vv. 31–32), leaven (v. 33), hidden treasure (v. 44), the pearl of great price (vv. 45–46), and the dragnet (vv. 47–52).

Although parables are often memorable stories, impressing listeners with a clear picture of the truth, even the disciples were sometimes confused as to the meaning of parables. For instance, after Jesus told the parable of the wheat and the tares (Matt. 13:24–30), the disciples needed interpretation to understand its meaning (Matt. 13:36–43).

Jesus sometimes used the parabolic form of teaching to reveal the truth to those who followed him while concealing the truth from those who did not (Matt. 13:10–17; Mark 4:10–12; Luke 8:9–10). The parables fulfilled the prophecy of Isaiah 6:9–10. Like a double-edged sword, they cut two ways—enlightening those who sought the truth and blinding those who were disobedient.

Most of Jesus' parables have one central point. Bible students should not resort to fanciful interpretations that find spiritual truth in every detail of the parable. The central point of the parable of the good Samaritan is that a hated Samaritan proved to be a neighbor to the wounded man. He showed the traveler the mercy and compassion denied to him by the priest and the Levite, representatives of the established religion. The lesson of this parable is that we should extend compassion to others—especially to those who are not of our own nationality, race, or religion (Luke 10:25–37).

In finding the central meaning of a parable, Bible students first need to discover the meaning the parable had in the time of Jesus. They must first relate the parable to Jesus' proclamation of the kingdom of God and to His miracles. This means that parables are not merely simple folk stories but expressions of Jesus' view of God, humanity, salvation, and the new age that dawned in his ministry.

This approach can be demonstrated with the parables dealing with the three "losts" in Luke 15:3–32: the lost sheep, the lost coin, and the lost son.

The historical context is Luke 15:1–2: Jesus had table fellowship with tax collectors and sinners. The Pharisees and scribes, religious leaders of Jesus' day, saw such action as disgusting because, in their view, it transgressed God's holiness. If Jesus truly were a righteous man, they reasoned, he would keep himself pure and separate from sinners.

In response to their murmuring, Jesus told them these parables. God rejoices more, he said, over the repentance of one sinner such as those sitting with him at table than over "ninety-nine just persons who need no repentance" (Luke 15:7)—that is, than over the religious professionals who congratulate themselves over their own self-achieved goodness (cf. the parable of the Pharisee and the tax collector, Luke 18:9–14). Likewise, the prodigal son (Luke 15:11–24) represents the tax collectors and sinners while the older son (Luke 15:25–32) represents the scribes and Pharisees.

A major theme in Jesus' parables is the demand of following him in discipleship. In the parable of the great supper (Luke 14:15–24), Jesus showed that the time for decision is now. In the parables of the unfinished tower and the king going to war

(Luke 14:28–32), Jesus demanded his followers be prepared to give up all. In the parables of the hidden treasure and the pearl of great price (Matt. 13:44–46), Jesus stated that the kingdom of heaven is of such value that all other treasures in life are of secondary worth. Jesus' parables are a call to a radical decision to follow Him, regardless of the cost.

Parables of Jesus that appear only in the gospel of Matthew.

The Wheat and the Tares	Matt. 13:24–30
The Hidden Treasure	Matt. 13:44
The Pearl of Great Price	Matt. 13:45–46
The Dragnet	Matt. 13:47–50
The Unforgiving Servant	Matt. 18:21–35
The Workers in the Vineyard	Matt. 20:1–16
The Two Sons	Matt. 21:28–32
The Wedding Feast	Matt. 22:1–14
The Wise and Foolish Virgins	Matt. 25:1–13
The Talents	Matt. 25:14–30

Parables of Jesus that appear only in the gospel of Mark.

The Growing Seed	Mark 4:26–29
The Watchful Doorkeeper	Mark 13:32–37

Parables of Jesus that appear only in the gospel of Luke.

The Creditor Who Had Two Debtors	Luke 7:40–47
The Good Samaritan	Luke 10:25–37
The Friend Who Came at Midnight	Luke 11:5–8
The Rich Fool	Luke 12:13–21
The Faithful Servant and the Evil Servant	Luke 12:35–48
The Barren Fig Tree	Luke 13:6–9
The Unfinished Tower	Luke 14:28–30
The King Going to War	Luke 14:31–32
The Lost Coin	Luke 15:8–10
The Lost Son	Luke 15:11–32
The Unjust Steward	Luke 16:1–13
The Condescending Master	Luke 17:7–10
The Persistent Widow	Luke 18:1–8

The Pharisee and the Tax Collector	Luke 18:9–14
The Minas	Luke 19:11–27

Parables of Jesus that appear in the gospels of Matthew and Luke.

The Two Builders	Matt. 7:24–27; Luke 6:47–49
The Leaven	Matt. 13:33; Luke 13:20–21
The Lost Sheep	Matt. 18:10–14; Luke 15:1–7

Parables of Jesus that appear in the gospels of Matthew, Mark, and Luke.

The Lamp and the Lampstand	Matt. 5:15–16; Mark 4:21; Luke 8:16
New Cloth on Old Garments	Matt. 9:16; Mark 2:21; Luke 5:36
New Wine in Old Wineskins	Matt. 9:17; Mark 2:22; Luke 5:37–39
A House Divided Against Itself	Matt. 12:25–28; Mark 3:23–26; Luke 11:17–22
The Sower and the Seed	Matt. 13:3–23; Mark 4:1–20; Luke 8:4–15
The Mustard Seed	Matt. 13:31–32; Mark 4:30–32; Luke 13:18–19
The Wicked Vinedressers	Matt. 21:33–41; Mark 12:1–12; Luke 20:9–18
The Fig Tree	Matt. 24:32–35; Mark 13:28–31; Luke 21:29–33

Parables of Jesus that appear only in the gospel of John.

The Bread of Life	John 6:32–58
The Shepherd and the Sheep	John 10:1–18
The Vine and the Branches	John 15:1–8

Paradox. A *paradox* is a statement that seems contradictory but may, in fact, be true. The paradox of the Bible is that of the dual nature of Jesus Christ: He is a total human being, yet he is God.

Following are paradoxical concepts from the Bible:

Of finding one's life, yet eventually losing it	Matt. 10:39; John 12:25
Of losing one's life, yet eventually finding it	Matt. 10:39
Of being unknown, yet being well-known	2 Cor. 6:9
Of dying, yet possessing life	2 Cor. 6:9
Of dying, yet being able to give life	John 12:24
Of being sorrowful, yet always rejoicing	2 Cor. 6:10
Of being poor, yet making many rich	2 Cor. 6:10
Of having nothing, yet possessing all things	2 Cor. 6:10
Of hearing words that cannot be expressed	2 Cor. 12:4
Of being strong when one is weak	2 Cor. 12:10
Of knowing the love of Christ that surpasses knowledge	Eph. 3:19
Of seeing the unseen	2 Cor. 4:18

Paradoxes concerning Christ. The life and ministry of Jesus was itself a divine paradox:

He hungered, yet fed multitudes.	Matt. 4:2; John 6
He thirsted, yet is the Water of life.	John 19:28; 4:14
He grew weary, yet is our rest.	John 4:6; Matt. 11:29–30
He paid tribute, yet is the King of kings.	Matt. 17:27; Rev. 19:16
He prayed, yet hears our prayers.	Mark 14:32–42; John 14:13–14
He wept, yet dries our tears.	John 11:35; Rev. 21:4
He was sold for 30 pieces of silver, yet redeems the world.	Matt. 26:15; 1 Pet. 1:18–19
He was led as a lamb to the slaughter, yet is the Good Shepherd.	Isa. 53:7; John 10:11
He was put to death, yet raises the dead.	John 5:25; 19:33

Paronomasia. *Paronomasia* is a literary term that refers to a type of pun, a rhetori-cal device where similar-sounding words are juxtaposed or opposed in wordplay. Among the ancients it was a common practice to arrange words in a clever fashion and required great skill.

Two kinds of paronomasia predominate in the Bible:

1. A change in the sense of a word by alteration of a letter, as in the Jews' nickname *Epimanes* ("Madman") for Antiochus Epiphanes ("Illustrious").

2. A play upon words that are similar either in sound or sense. Isaiah 5:7 reads:

> He looked for justice *(mispat)*,
> but behold, oppression *(mispah)*;
> For righteousness *(sedaqa)*,
> but behold, a cry for help *(seaqa)*.

Psalms contain paronomasia, and Micah is known for them. Matthew 8:26 reads "a great calm" [*galene megale*] came over the sea.

Paul was especially fond of this device. In Romans 1:29 he spoke of *porneia* ("sexual immorality") and *poneria* ("wickedness"), *phthonou* ("envy") and *phonou* ("murder").

Poetry in the OT. At an early date poetry became part of the written literature of the Hebrew people. Many scholars believe the song of Moses and the song of Miriam (Exod. 15:1–21), celebrating the destruction of Pharaoh's army in the sea, is the oldest existing Hebrew hymn or poetic work, dating perhaps from the twelfth century B.C. Three of the greatest poetic masterpieces of the OT are the song of Deborah (Judg. 5); the song of the bow—David's lament over the death of Saul and Jonathan (2 Sam. 1:17–27), and the burden of Nineveh (Nah. 1:12–3:19).

Approximately one-third of the OT is written in poetry. This includes entire books (except for short prose sections), such as Job, Psalms, Proverbs, the Song of Solomon, and Lamentations. Large portions of Isaiah, Jeremiah, and the Minor Prophets are also poetic in form and content. Many scholars consider Job not only the greatest poem in the OT but also one of the greatest poems in all literature.

The three main divisions of the OT—the Law, the Prophets, and the Writings—contain poetry in successively greater amounts. Only seven OT books—Leviticus, Ruth, Ezra, Nehemiah, Esther, Haggai, and Malachi—appear to have no poetic lines.

Parallelism. Poetic elements such as assonance, alliteration, and rhyme—common to poetry as we know it today—occur rarely in Hebrew poetry. The essential, formal characteristic of Hebrew poetry is parallelism. This is a construction in which the content of one line is *synonymous* (repeated), *antithetic* (contrasted), and *synthetic* (advanced by the content of the next line). Hebrew poetry has a type of sense rhythm characterized by thought arrangement rather than by word arrangement or rhyme. The three main types of parallelism in biblical poetry are synonymous, antithetic, and synthetic.

1. *Synonymous parallelism.* A parallel segment repeats an idea found in the previous segment. With this technique a kind of paraphrase is involved; line two restates the same thought found in line one, by using equivalent expressions. An example of synonymous parallelism is Genesis 4:23: "Adah and Zillah, hear my voice; wives of Lamech, listen to my speech! For I have killed a man for wounding me, even a young man for hurting me."

Another example is Psalm 2:4: "He who sits in the heavens shall laugh; the Lord shall hold them in derision."

2. *Antithetic parallelism.* The thought of the first line is made clearer by contrast—by the opposition expressed in the second line. Examples of antithetic parallelism may be found in Psalm 1:6: "For the Lord knows the way of the righteous, but the way of the ungodly shall perish"; in Psalm 34:10: "The young lions lack and suffer hunger; but those who seek the Lord shall not lack any good thing."

3. *Synthetic parallelism.* This climactic or cumulative parallelism expands the idea in line one with the idea in the following line. Synthetic parallelism has no ascending or descending progression, a building up of thought, with each succeeding line adding to the first.

For example, Psalm 1:3: "He shall be like a tree planted by the rivers of water, that brings forth its fruit in its season, whose leaf also shall not wither; and whatever he does shall prosper."

Alphabetical acrostic. This is another poetic form found in the OT, a form used often in Psalms (e.g., Pss. 9, 10, 25, 34, 37, 111, 112, 119, and 145). In the alphabetical psalms the first line begins with the first letter of the Hebrew alphabet, the next with the second, and so on, until all the letters of the alphabet have been used. Consequently, Psalm 119 consists of 22 groups of eight verses each. The number of groups equals the number of letters in the Hebrew alphabet. The first letter of each verse in a group is (in the original Hebrew text) that letter of the alphabet which corresponds numerically to the group.

Many of the subtleties of Hebrew poetry, such as puns and play-on-word allusions, are untranslatable into English and can be fully appreciated only by an accomplished Hebrew scholar. Fortunately, many good commentaries are available to explain these riches of Hebrew thought.

Poetry in the NT. We find little poetry in the NT, most lines quoted from the OT or hymns included in the worship services of the early church. The beatitudes (Matt. 5:3–10; Luke 6:20–26) have a definite poetic form. The gospel of Luke contains several long poems: Zacharias's prophecy, known as the *Benedictus* (Luke 1:68–79); song of Mary, known as the *Magnificat* (Luke 1:46–55); song of the heavenly host, known as the *Gloria in Excelsis* (Luke 2:14); and blessing of Simeon, known as the *Nunc Dimittis* (Luke 2:29–32).

Examples of parallelism occur in the NT. For instance, synonymous parallelism occurs in Matthew 7:6: "Do not give what is holy to the dogs, nor cast your pearls before swine." Antithetic parallelism occurs in

Matthew 8:20: "Foxes have holes and birds of the air have nests, but the Son of Man has nowhere to lay His head." Synthetic parallelism occurs in John 6:32–33: "Moses did not give you the bread from heaven, but My Father gives you the true bread from heaven. For the bread of God is He who comes down from heaven and gives life to the world."

In the writings of Paul, several poetic passages occur: lyrical celebration of God's everlasting love (Rom. 8:31–39); classic hymn to love (1 Cor. 13); glorious faith in the triumph of the Resurrection (1 Cor. 15:51–58); and thoughts on the humbled and exalted Christ (Phil. 2:5–11).

Who can deny the poetic passion in Paul's words to the Corinthians? "We are hard pressed on every side, yet not crushed; we are perplexed, but not in despair; persecuted, but not forsaken; struck down, but not destroyed" (2 Cor. 4:8–9).

Interpretation of the Bible (Hermeneutics)

Hermeneutics is the science of biblical interpretation. Correct Bible interpretation answers, "How do I understand what this passage means?"

Preparation for Bible Study

Four basic principles are at the heart of preparing us for a sound method of biblical interpretation: pray, use common sense, ask the right questions, and consider the context.

Pray

Because the Bible is a divinely inspired book, and because of our limitation as humans, prayer is an absolute necessity as we study the Bible. Paul teaches that non-Christians and spiritually immature Christians are limited in their ability to know spiritual things (1 Cor. 2:14–3:3). We must pray that God will bridge the gap that separates us from understanding spiritual things, by having the Holy Spirit teach us (John 14:26; 16:13). Without this illumination or insight from God's Spirit, we cannot learn. This need for insight was the concept Paul referred to when he told Timothy to "reflect on what I am saying, for the Lord will give you insight into all this" (2 Tim. 2:7, NIV).

Use Common Sense

The Bible is also a human book and, to a degree, must be interpreted like any other book. This brings us to the principle of common sense. For example, the grammatical-historical method of studying the Bible instructs us to look at the passage carefully to see what it says literally, and to understand a biblical statement in light of its historical background. We understand a historical statement as straightforward and do not change its literal, grammatical sense.

Another example of the common sense principle is illustrated when Jesus says believers can have anything for which they ask (John 15:7). Common sense tells us that there must be some limitation on this statement because we realize that believers do not have whatever they would like. First John 5:14 confirms that the limitation is God's will. Using the common sense principle in this way can be dangerous because it could become an excuse for cutting out any portion of Scripture we do not happen to like. But if our common sense is controlled by God, it is a valid principle of interpreting the Bible.

Ask the Right Questions

We interpret the Bible properly when we learn to ask the right questions of the text. The problem here is that many people do not know what the right questions are, or they are too lazy to learn. Biblical interpretation requires time, energy, and a serious commitment to learn. But when learned, there is much more satisfaction in asking the right questions than in merely guessing.

Consider the Context

The primary rule of biblical interpretation is context. If Bible students would let passages speak for themselves within the context of the paragraph, chapter, or book, the majority of errors in interpretation would be avoided.

The problem is our bias, or our subjectivity. Many times we approach a passage thinking we already understand it. In the process we read our own meaning into the passage. This is called *eisegesis* (*eis* is a Greek preposition meaning "into"). But interpreting the Bible correctly demands that we listen to what the text itself is saying, and then draw the meaning out of the passage. This is called *exegesis* (*ex* is a Greek preposition meaning "out of"). If we let a passage be defined by what it and the surrounding verses say, then we have taken a large step toward interpreting the Bible properly. Only by watching the context carefully and by letting the passage speak for itself do we give Scripture the respect it deserves.

It is impossible to dismiss totally our own bias and subjectivity. Our interpretation will always be colored by our culture and our opinions about the passage, or perhaps by our theological beliefs that are partially based on the passage. But this should not discourage our attempt to let the passage speak for itself, without being weighed down with our personal opinions and views.

Principles of Interpretation

Four words provide the heart of all approaches to finding out what the Bible means: observation, interpretation, evaluation, and application.

Observation

We ask question such as:
- Do I understand all the facts in this passage?
- Do I know the context before and after this passage?
- Do I know the meaning of all the words?
- Do I understand the flow of the discussion?
- Do I understand the cultural background?

For example, in 1 Corinthians 8 the apostle Paul discussed eating meat that had been offered to idols. What is the background? Answer: Meat, received as offerings to idols and not eaten by the priests was sold at the market. Some Corinthian Christians believed it was permissible to eat the meat since idols are nothing but wood and stone. Others said it might appear they were still involved in pagan worship.

Interpretation

What did the author mean in his own historical setting? We must put ourselves in the thinking of the original audience. To answer this question, there are two further questions. First, what does the passage actually say? Many times we forget to look carefully at what a passage says. Some cite Matthew 5:21–22 as proof that to think bad is just as wrong as doing it. Is anger as bad as murder? Of course not. (Common sense tells us that, if nothing else.) But the text does not actually say they are the same. It says the law against murder is not fully obeyed by mere outward obedience, but by maintaining the proper attitude of not being angry, which in turn prohibits the outward act of murder.

Second, does the context help define the meaning of the passage? For example, what does Scripture mean when it says, "There is no God"? (See Ps. 53:1.) Context shows this is a statement made by a fool. What does Paul mean when he says Jesus will return like "a thief in the night"? (See 1 Thess. 5:2.) The context shows it means his coming will be sudden.

Does Jesus' statement, "When you fast, do not be like the hypocrites" (Matt. 6:16) demand that his disciples fast? No, because Matthew 9:14 states that Jesus' disciples did not fast while he was alive. (The beauty of using Scripture to interpret Scripture is that when the Bible answers its own questions, then we know the answer is correct.) The twin matters of what the text actually says and the passage's context help complete the second stage of interpretation.

There are times when even these two questions will not help us understand the meaning of a passage. Sometimes we have to read between the lines and make an educated guess as to what the passage means. But we must remember that we are guessing, and we must keep an open mind to other interpretations.

Integrity is also a necessary element in biblical interpretation.

In interpreting the Bible, we must never forget whose letters we are reading. They have come from God and they demand respect. They demand to speak for themselves. They demand that we be honest and have integrity. We must not put our guesswork on the same level as the words of God.

How do we interpret 1 Corinthians 8? Once we understand the facts and background of the passage, once we have asked what the passage actually is saying and what is its context, then we see that Paul is teaching the principle of voluntarily refraining from a practice which, although not wrong itself, might be harmful to a fellow Christian. We have completed the first step of interpretation. We have seen what the passage meant in the day and age of the author.

Evaluation

We start by asking, what does the passage mean in today's culture? Does this apply to us today? Was it limited to the culture in which it was originally written?

Either the passage applies directly to our culture, or we reapply it because of cultural differences. Much of the NT teaching can be applied directly to our culture. If we love God, regardless of when or where we live, then we must obey his commandments (John 14:15). This teaching is true in any culture for all times.

Yet sometimes a biblical teaching is directed so specifically to the culture of the ancient world that another culture cannot understand it. For example, Western culture today generally does not sacrifice meat to idols, and the meaning of 1 Corinthians 8 may be lost. How then do we evaluate its meaning for us?

We need to distinguish between a cultural expression—a statement that can be understood only within a certain cultural context and an eternal principle—one that God uses to govern the world regardless of culture. "I will never again eat meat, lest I make my brother stumble" (1 Cor. 8:13), is a cultural expression, understandable only within those cultures that offer meat to idols. "God is love" (1 John 4:8) is an eternal principle, understandable in all cultures.

However, every cultural expression in the Bible is the result of an eternal principle. Even though a cultural expression cannot be carried directly to another culture, the eternal principle behind it can.

For example, in Western culture most of us believe in the principle of being polite when we are guests for dinner. In America, this principle could express itself as "Eat all the food on the table; otherwise you insult your host's cooking." But in Uganda, people leave food; otherwise it will appear they are still hungry and that the host hasn't provided sufficiently.

The task of biblical interpreters is to cut through cultural expressions to discover the eternal principles behind them and then to reapply the principles in their own cultures. This is evaluation.

We need to remind ourselves that just as a biblical passage can be set in its culture, so the interpreter is likewise controlled to some extent by his own culture. Many people today do not believe that the biblical accounts of miracles are true. For example, some scholars argue that miracles were a part of first century culture and were believed by the people in Jesus' day. But this is the twentieth century and people do not believe in miracles in this culture. However, these scholars' views on the impossibility of the supernatural are likewise influenced by the materialistic, science-oriented culture in which they live. We must be careful about allowing our own culture to influence our view of Scripture.

Application

It is essential to recognize that the purpose of Bible study is to lead a godly life. Study is not complete until we move beyond the academic and put into our lives what we have learned.

We ask a new question: How can I apply what I have learned to how I live my life? This fuses the academic and the practical. Some people dismiss the academic as boring and trivial. Others reject the application as unnecessary. Both extremes are equally wrong. The faithful Bible interpreter walks the thin line between these approaches.

We have faced the cultural meaning of 1 Corinthians 8 and the question of eating meat previously offered to idols. How do we apply this to our lives? When the Apostle said he would not eat meat again if it offended another Christian, he was not talking about food as a principle. The principle is that of conduct and conscience (my conscience). To apply this verse, I will voluntarily refrain from activities that I might consider harmless or possibly good if they are going to hurt, stumble, or confuse other Christians. This calls for serious self-examination.

We need to go through these four steps because:

1. The Bible was not actually written directly to us, and we need to put ourselves in the mind or thinking of the original audience if we are to understand its message properly.

2. These steps force us to *understand* the meaning of the passage before we *apply* it to ourselves. Surprisingly, this step is often overlooked.

3. The two steps separate us from the text, helping to prevent eisegesis, since it separates what the text says from how it affects us today.

Special Problems in Interpreting the Bible

The Bible, like other books, uses figures of speech and different types of literature that call for special rules for interpretation.

Anthropomorphism

Do rivers have hands to clap? (See Ps. 98:8.) Does God have eyes? (See Ps. 33:18.)

Anthropomorphisms in the Bible describe non-human objects as though they had human characteristics. How do we understand those verses that say God repents? (See Exod. 32:12; Jer. 18:8; *relents, regrets,* NKJV.) Does God change his mind? Answer: These verses describe God from a human point of view.

Apocalyptic Literature

This type of Bible literature is the most often misunderstood because it is no longer used. It has specific rules of interpretation. Its most noticeable characteristic is its use of symbolic figures, such as those in Revelation.

The key to interpreting these figures lies in the book of Revelation itself. The book itself gives us help by telling us the meaning of several of its symbols. For example, in 1:20 the seven stars are interpreted as representing the seven angels, and the seven lampstands signify seven churches. In 17:9–10 the seven-headed beast stands for the seven hills, and in 17:18 the woman is identified as the city that rules the earth.

To understand apocalyptic literature, and Revelation in particular, we must interpret the imagery as figurative and be extremely cautious about accepting anything as literal unless we have good reason for it. The images are describing things and spiritual realities in figurative language.

Hyperbole

An exaggeration used for effect—an overstatement. "I'm so hungry I could eat a horse" obviously is not literally true. It is an exaggeration used to convey the idea of extreme hunger.

In the Bible, for example, John made a statement something like this in his gospel: If everything Jesus ever did were written down, the world could not hold all the books. (See John 21:25.) Wasn't that overstating his point? He used hyperbole to present a graphic picture of how much Jesus did.

Metaphor

A simile makes a comparison by using a word such as *like* or *as:* "Life is like a circus." A metaphor is a similar comparison, except that it omits the word like or as: "All the world is a stage." Metaphors such as "I am the door" (John 10:9) are easily recognized. But what about Jesus' words at the Last Supper? He said, "This is my body." (See Luke 22:19.) Jesus probably intended this statement to be understood metaphorically rather than literally.

Parable

"Once upon a time in a far away land there lived a fairy princess." We do not understand this sentence in a scientific or literal sense. We recognize that it comes from a type of literature that is not historical.

We interpret parables properly by picturing the story in our minds as if we had lived in Jesus' day. We seek for an overall understanding and then for one central point. To understand a parable is to say, "The moral of this story is. . . ."

The difference between allegory and parable is important to understand. An allegory gives a symbolic interpretation to each of the features in the story. The parable of the lost sheep (Luke 15) and the other two in that same chapter have a single truth for the hearers. Each sheep is so important that the shepherd will leave the rest to find a single lost one.

If we allegorized the story, we would have to make each of the sheep have a meaning. The figure 99 would be significant and pregnant with meaning. Leaving the sheep, searching—each fact would have a meaning other than the the literal one.

The famous *Pilgrim's Progress* is probably the best-known type of allegory in Christian literature.

Although a few parables have allegorical elements, most parables teach one point. The parable of the sower (Matt. 13:3–23) is part allegory because the sower, seed, ground, birds, sun, and weeds all stand for something else: Jesus, the Word, Jesus' audience, Satan, persecution, and the cares of the world.

What about the parable of the unjust judge? (See Luke 18:1–14.) If the woman represents the disciple, is God the unjust judge? Is the purpose of the parable of the rich man and Lazarus (see Luke 16:19–31) to teach that we cannot travel between heaven and hell? The procedure for interpreting parables is to find the one main point and to view the details of the story simply as backdrop to make the point, not the direct teaching of the parable.

Poetry

Hebrew poetry does not concentrate on rhythm or rhyme but parallelism. This happens in three ways:

1. Two phrases are joined so that the second repeats the first with different words as in Psalm 95:2.
2. The second states the opposite of the first as Proverbs 15:5.
3. The second line adds a new thought to the first as in Proverbs 15:3.

Prophecy

We need to remember two things when interpreting prophecy. First, what the prophet foresaw as one event may actually be two or more. The OT seers thought of the day of the Lord (see Isa. 2:12) as one event, but the last days actually began at Pentecost (see Acts 2:20) and will conclude at Christ's return (2 Thess. 2:2).

Second, although much OT prophecy is fulfilled in the NT, much was fulfilled in the OT and then again in the NT. For example, Isaiah's prophecy in 7:14 was fulfilled in Isaiah's day, and again by Jesus' birth (Matt. 1:23).

The Church

Religious Groups, Leaders, and Offices ___

Throughout the era covered by the Bible, leaders, groups, offices, factions, sects, and organizations arose. Here are some of those who greatly influenced the world in their time.

Apostles

At the beginning of his ministry, Jesus selected 12 men to travel with him. These men would continue to represent Jesus Christ after he had returned to heaven. Their reputation would continue to influence the church long after they were dead.

"Now it came to pass in those days that He went out to the mountain to pray, and continued all night in prayer to God. And when it was day, He called His disciples to Himself; and from them He chose twelve whom He also named apostles" (Luke 6:12–13).

Most of the apostles came from the area of Capernaum, which was despised by polite Jewish society because it was the center of a part of the Jewish state (only recently added) and was known as "Galilee of the Gentiles." Jesus himself said, "And you, Capernaum, who are exalted to heaven, will be brought down to Hades" (Matt. 11:23).

Jesus molded these 12 men into strong leaders and articulate spokesmen of the Christian faith. Their success bears witness to the transforming power of Jesus' lordship.

None of the gospel writers have left us any physical descriptions of the Twelve. Nevertheless, they give us tiny clues that help us to make educated guesses about how the apostles looked and acted. One very important fact that has traditionally been overlooked in countless artistic representations of the apostles is their youth. If we realize that most lived into the third and fourth quarter of the first century and John into the second century, then they must have been only teenagers when they first took up Christ's call.

Different biblical accounts list the Twelve in pairs. We are not sure whether this indicates family relationships, team functions or some other kind of association between them.

Andrew. The day after John the Baptist saw the Holy Spirit descend upon Jesus, he identified Jesus for two of his disciples and said, "Behold the Lamb of God!" (John 1:36). Intrigued by this announcement, the two men left John and began to follow Jesus. Jesus noticed them and asked what they were seeking.

Immediately they replied, "Rabbi, where are you staying?" Jesus took them to the house where he was staying, and they spent the night with him. One of these men was named Andrew (John 1:38–40).

Andrew soon went to find his brother, Simon Peter and told him, "We have found the Messiah" (John 1:41).

Andrew is our English rendering of the Greek word *Andreas* (literally, manly). Other clues from the Gospels indicate that Andrew was physically strong and a devout, faithful man. He and Peter owned a house together (Mark 1:29). They were sons of a man named Jonah or John, a prosperous fisherman. Both of the young men had followed their father into the fishing business.

Andrew was born at Bethsaida on the northern shores of the Sea of Galilee. Though the gospel of John describes Andrew's first encounter with Jesus, it does not mention him as a disciple until much later (John 6:8). Matthew says that when Jesus was walking along the Sea of Galilee, he hailed Andrew and Peter and invited them to become his disciples (Matt. 4:18–19). This does not contradict John's narrative; it simply adds a new feature. A close reading of John 1:35–42 shows that Jesus did not call Andrew and Peter to follow him the first time they met.

Andrew and another disciple named Philip introduced a group of Greeks to Jesus (John 12:20–22). For this reason, we might say that Andrew and Philip were the first foreign missionaries of the Christian faith.

Tradition says that Andrew spent his last years in Scythia, north of the Black Sea. A small book entitled the *Acts of Andrew* (probably written about A.D. 260) says that he preached primarily in Macedonia and was martyred at Patras.

Roman Catholic tradition says that Andrew was crucified on an X-shaped cross, a religious symbol that is now known as St. Andrew's Cross. They believe he was crucified on November 30, so the Roman Catholic church and Greek Orthodox church observe his festival on that date. Today he is the patron saint of Scotland. The Order of St. Andrew is an association of church ushers who make a special effort to be courteous to strangers.

Bartholomew (Nathanael). We lack information about the identity of the apostle named Bartholomew. He is mentioned only in the lists of apostles. Moreover, while the first three Gospels agree that his name was Bartholomew, John gives it as Nathanael (John 1:45). Some scholars believe that Bartholomew was his surname.

The Aramaic word *bar* means "sons," so *Bartholomew* literally meant "son of Talmai." The Bible does not identify Talmai for us, but he may have been named after King Talmai of Geshur (2 Sam. 3:3). Some scholars believe that Bartholomew was connected with the Ptolemies, the ruling family of Egypt. This theory finds its basis in Jerome's statement that Bartholomew was the only apostle of noble birth.

Jesus called Nathanael "an Israelite . . . in whom is no deceit" (John 1:47).

Tradition says Nathanael served as a missionary in India. The Venerable Bede said that Nathanael was beheaded by King Astriagis. Other traditions say that Nathanael was crucified headdown.

James, son of Alphaeus. The Gospels make only fleeting reference to this James (Matt. 10:3; Mark 3:18; Luke 6:15). Many scholars believe that James was a brother of Matthew, since Scripture says that Matthew's father was also named Alphaeus (Mark 2:14). Others believe that this James was identified with "James the Less"; but we have no proof that these two names refer to the same man (cf. Mark 15:40).

If the son of Alphaeus was the same man as James the Less, he may have been a cousin of Jesus (cf. Matt. 27:56; John 19:25). Some Bible commentators theorize that this disciple bore a close physical resemblance to Jesus, which could explain why Judas Iscariot had to identify Jesus on the night of his betrayal (Mark 14:43–45; Luke 22:47–48).

Legends say that this James preached in Persia and was crucified there, although we have no concrete information about his later ministry and death.

James, son of Zebedee. After Jesus summoned Simon Peter and his brother Andrew, he went a little farther along the shore of Galilee and summoned "James the son of Zebedee, and John his brother, who also were in the boat mending their nets" (Mark 1:19). Like Peter and Andrew, James and his brother responded immediately to Christ's invitation.

James was the first of the Twelve to suffer a martyr's death. King Herod Agrippa I ordered James executed with a sword (Acts 12:2). Tradition says this occurred in A.D. 44, when James would have been quite young. (Although the NT does not describe the martyrdom of any other apostles, tradition tells us that all except John died for their faith.)

The Gospels never mention James alone; they always speak of "James and John." Even in recording his death, Acts refers to him as "James the brother of John" (Acts 12:2). James and John began to follow Jesus on the same day, and both of them were present at the transfiguration of Jesus (Mark 9:2–13). Jesus called both men the "Sons of Thunder" (Mark 3:17).

The persecution that took James's life inspired new fervor among the Christians (cf. Acts 12:5–25). Undoubtedly, Herod Agrippa had hoped to stop the Christian movement by executing leaders such as James, "but the word of God grew and multiplied" (v. 24).

Strangely, John's gospel does not mention James. John was reluctant to mention his own name, and he may have felt the same kind of modesty over reporting the activities of his brother. Once John does refer to himself and James as the "sons of Zebedee" (John 21:2).

Legends say that James was the first Christian missionary to Spain. Roman Catholic authorities believe that his bones are buried in the city of Santiago in northwestern Spain.

John. Fortunately we have a considerable amount of information about the disciple named John. Mark tells us he was the brother of James, son of Zebedee (Mark 1:19). Mark says that James and John worked with the hired servants of their father (Mark 1:20).

Some scholars speculate that John's mother was Salome, who observed the crucifixion of Jesus (Mark 15:40). If Salome was the sister of Jesus' mother, as John suggests (John 19:25), John may have been a cousin of Jesus.

Jesus found John and his brother James mending their nets beside the Sea of Galilee. He ordered them to launch out into the lake and let down their nets to catch fish. They hauled in a tremendous catch—a miracle that convinced them of Jesus' power. "So when they had brought their boats to land, they forsook all, and followed Him" (Luke 5:11). Simon Peter went with them.

John seems to have been impulsive. Soon after he and James entered Jesus' inner circle of disciples, the Master labeled them "Sons of Thunder" (Mark 3:17). The disciples seemed to relegate John to a secondary place in their company. All of the Gospels mentioned John after his brother James; on most occasions, it seems, James was the spokesman for the two brothers. When Paul mentions John among the apostles at Jerusalem, he places John at the end of the list (Gal. 2:9).

John's emotions often erupted in his conversations with Jesus. On one occasion, John became upset because someone else was ministering in Jesus' name. "We forbade him," he told Jesus, "because he does not follow us" (Mark 9:38–40). On another occasion, James and John ambitiously urged that they be allowed to sit on Jesus' right hand in heaven. This idea antagonized the other disciples (Mark 10:35–41).

If John wrote the fourth gospel, the letters of John, and Revelation, he penned more of the NT than any of the other apostles. Conservative scholars advance no sound reason to doubt John's authorship of these books.

Tradition claimed that John was the disciple to whom Jesus committed his mother from the cross (John 19:26–27) and that John cared for Jesus' mother while he was pastor of the congregation in Ephesus and that she died there. Tertullian said that John was taken to Rome and plunged into boiling oil, came out unhurt, and was then exiled to an island. This was probably Patmos, where he wrote Revelation. John likely lived to an old age, and his body was returned to Ephesus for burial.

Judas (not Iscariot).   John refers to one of the disciples as "Judas (not Iscariot)" (John 14:22). It is not easy to determine the identity of this man. Jerome dubbed him Trionius—"the man with three names."

The NT refers to several men by the name of Judas: Judas Iscariot; Judas the brother of Jesus (Matt. 13:55; Mark 6:3); Judas of Galilee (Acts 5:37); and "Judas (not Iscariot)." John wanted to avoid confusion when he referred to this man, especially because the other disciple named Judas had such a poor reputation.

Matthew refers to this man as Lebbaeus, "whose surname was Thaddaeus" (Matt. 10:3). Mark refers to him simply as Thaddeus (Mark 3:18). Luke calls him "Judas the son of James" (Luke 6:16; Acts 1:13). The KJV incorrectly translates Luke as saying that this man was the brother of James.

We are not sure who Thaddaeus's father was. Some think he was James, the brother of Jesus—making Judas a nephew of Jesus. But this is not likely because early church historians report that this James never married. Others think that his father was the apostle James, son of Zebedee. We cannot be certain.

Judas Iscariot.   All of the Gospels place Judas Iscariot at the end of the list of Jesus' disciples. Undoubtedly this reflects Judas's ill repute as the betrayer of Jesus.

Iscariot (Aramaic meaning "man of Kerioth") likely came from Kerioth, a town near Hebron (Josh. 15:25). John tells us that Judas was the son of Simon (John 6:71).

If Judas came from Kerioth, he was the only Judean among Jesus' disciples. Jude-

Traditional tomb of the apostle John in the Church of St. John at Ephesus.

PHOTO BY HOWARD VOS

ans scorned Galileans as crude frontier settlers. This attitude may have alienated Judas Iscariot from the other disciples.

The Gospels do not tell us exactly when Jesus called Judas Iscariot to join his band of followers. Perhaps it was in the early days when Jesus called the others (cf. Matt. 4:18–22).

Judas acted as the treasurer of the disciples. On at least one occasion he manifested a penny-pinching attitude toward their work. When a woman named Mary came to pour a costly oil on the feet of Jesus, Judas complained, "Why was this fragrant oil not sold for 300 denarii, and given to the poor?" (John 12:5). John comments that Judas said this "not that he cared for the poor, but because he was a thief" (John 12:6).

As the disciples shared their last meal with Jesus, the Lord revealed that he was about to be betrayed, and he singled out Judas as the culprit. He told Judas, "What you do, do quickly" (John 13:27). However, the other disciples did not suspect what Judas was about to do. John reports that "some thought, because Judas had the money box, that Jesus had said to him, 'Buy those things that we have need of against the Passover feast'" (John 13:28–29).

Scholars have offered several theories about the reason for Judas's betrayal. Some think that Judas acted out of greed for the money that Jesus' enemies offered him. Luke and John simply say that Satan inspired Judas's actions (Luke 22:3; John 13:27).

Matthew tells us that Judas, in remorse, attempted to return the money to Jesus' captors: "Then he threw down the pieces of silver in the temple and departed, and went and hanged himself" (Matt. 27:5). One legend says that Judas hanged himself on a redbud tree, sometimes called the Judas tree.

In most modern works, Judas is portrayed as a Zealot or extreme patriot who was disappointed at Jesus' failure to lead a mass movement or rebellion against Rome. There is little evidence for this viewpoint.

Matthew. In Jesus' day, the Roman government collected several different taxes from the people. Tolls for transporting goods by land or sea were collected by private tax collectors, who paid a fee to the Roman government for the right to assess these levies. The tax collectors made their profits by charging a higher toll than the law required.

The licensed collectors often hired minor officials called *publicans* to do the actual work of collecting the tolls. The publicans extracted their own wages by charging a fraction more than their employer required. The disciple Matthew was a publican who collected tolls on the road between Damascus and Acco; his booth was located just outside the city of Capernaum.

Normally a publican charged five percent of the purchase price of normal trade items and up to 12.5 percent on luxury items. Matthew also collected taxes from boatmen who brought their goods from cities on the other side of the lake.

The Jews considered a tax collector's money to be unclean, so they would never ask for change. If a Jewish man did not have the exact amount that the collector required, he borrowed from a friend. Jewish people despised the publicans as agents of the hated Roman Empire and the puppet Jewish king. Publicans were not allowed to

testify in court, and they could not tithe their money to the temple. A good Jew would not even associate with publicans in private life (cf. Matt. 9:10–13).

Jews divided the tax collectors in two classes. First were the *gabbai*—they levied general agricultural taxes and census taxes from the people. The second group were the *mokhsa*—officials who collected money from travelers. Most of the mokhsa were Jews, so they were despised as traitors to their own people. Matthew belonged to this class of tax collectors.

The gospel of Matthew tells us that Jesus approached this unlikely disciple as he sat at his tax table. Jesus simply commanded, "Follow Me," and Matthew left his work to follow the Master (Matt. 9:9).

Apparently Matthew was fairly well-to-do because he provided a banquet in his own house: "And there were a great number of tax collectors and others who sat down with them" (Luke 5:29). The simple fact that Matthew owned a house indicates that he was wealthier than the typical publican.

Because of the nature of his work, Matthew likely knew how to read and write. Papyrus tax documents dating from about A.D. 100 indicate that the publicans were quite efficient with figures. (Instead of using the clumsy Roman numerals, they preferred the simpler Greek symbols.)

Matthew may have been related to the disciple James, since each of them is said to have been a "son of Alphaeus" (Matt. 10:3; Mark 2:14). Luke sometimes uses the name *Levi* to refer to Matthew (cf. Luke 5:27–29). Some scholars believe that Matthew's name was Levi before he decided to follow Jesus, and that Jesus gave him the new name, which means "gift of God." Others suggest that Matthew was a member of the priestly tribe of Levi.

Even though a former publican had joined his ranks, Jesus did not soften his condemnation of the tax collectors. He ranked them with the harlots (cf. Matt. 21:31), and Matthew himself classes the publicans with sinners (Matt. 9:10).

We do not know what happened to Matthew after the day of Pentecost. In his *Book of Martyrs*, John Foxe stated that Matthew spent his last years preaching in Parthia and Ethiopia and was martyred in the city of Nadabah in A.D. 60.

Philip.   John's gospel is the only one to give us any detailed information about Philip. Jesus first met Philip at Bethany beyond the Jordan River (John 1:28, RSV) and called him individually while he called most of the other disciples in pairs. Philip introduced Nathanael to Jesus (John 1:45–51), and Jesus also called Nathanael (or Bartholomew) to be his disciple.

When 5,000 people gathered to hear Jesus, Philip asked the Lord how they would feed the crowd. "Two hundred denarii worth of bread is not sufficient for them, that every one of them may have a little," he said (John 6:7).

On another occasion, a group of Greeks came to Philip and asked him to introduce them to Jesus. Philip enlisted the help of Andrew, and together they took them to meet Jesus (John 12:20–22).

While the disciples ate their last meal with Jesus, Philip said, "Lord, show us the Father, and it is sufficient for us" (John 14:8). Jesus responded that they had already seen the Father in him.

These three brief glimpses are all that we see of Philip in the Gospels. The church has preserved many traditions about his later ministry and death. Some say that he preached in France; others, that he preached in southern Russia, Asia Minor, or even India. In A.D. 194, Bishop Polycrates of Antioch wrote that "Philip, one of the twelve apostles, sleeps at Hierapolis." However, we have no firm evidence to support these claims.

Simon Peter.   The disciple named Simon Peter was a man of contrasts. At Caesarea Philippi, Jesus asked, "But who do you say that I am?" Peter immediately replied, "You are the Christ, the Son of the living God" (Matt. 16:15–16). But seven verses later we read, "Then Peter took Him aside, and began to rebuke Him." Rushing from one extreme to another was characteristic of Peter.

When Jesus attempted to wash Peter's feet in the Upper Room, the disciple exclaimed, "You shall never wash my feet!" But when Jesus insisted, Peter said, "Lord, not my feet only, but also my hands and my head!" (John 13:8–9).

On their last night together, Peter told Jesus, "Even if all are made to stumble, yet I will not be" (Mark 14:29). Within hours, however, Peter not only denied Jesus but cursed him (Mark 14:71).

This volatile, unpredictable temperament often got Simon Peter into trouble. Yet the Holy Spirit molded Peter into a stable, dynamic leader of the early church.

The NT writers used four different names in referring to Peter. One was the Hebrew name *Simeon* (Acts 15:14, RSV, KJV), which may mean "hearing." A second name was *Simon*, the Greek form of Simeon. A third name was *Cephas*, Aramaic for "rock." The fourth name was *Peter*, Greek for "rock." The NT writers apply the name Peter to the disciple more often than the other three.

When Jesus first met this man, he said, "You are Simon the son of Jonah: You shall be called Cephas" (John 1:42). *Jonah* was a Greek name meaning "dove" (cf. Matt. 16:17; John 21:15–17). Some modern translations render this name as *John*.

Peter and his brother Andrew were fishermen on the Sea of Galilee (Matt. 4:18; Mark 1:16). He spoke with the accent of a Galilean, and his mannerisms identified him as a native of the Galilean frontier (cf. Mark 14:70). His brother Andrew led him to Jesus (John 1:40–42).

While Jesus hung on the cross, Peter was probably among the group from Galilee that "stood at a distance, watching things" (Luke 23:49). Peter wrote, "I . . . am a fellow elder and a witness of the sufferings of Christ" (1 Pet. 5:1).

Simon Peter heads the list of apostles in each of the gospel accounts, which suggests that the NT writers considered him the most significant of the Twelve. He did not write as much as John or Matthew, but he emerged as the most influential leader of the early church. Although 120 followers of Jesus received the Holy Spirit on the day of Pentecost, the Scripture records the words of Peter (Acts 2:14–40). Peter suggested that the apostles find a replacement for Judas Iscariot (Acts 1:22).

Peter and John were the first disciples to perform a miracle after Pentecost, healing a lame man at the Beautiful Gate of Jerusalem (Acts 3:1–11).

Acts emphasizes the travels of Paul, yet Peter also traveled extensively. He visited Antioch (Gal. 2:11). He may have visited Corinth, since Paul refers to a group in the church at Corinth that followed piety (1 Cor. 1:12). There is also an early tradition that he visited the city of Rome. Eusebius states that Peter was crucified in Rome, probably during the reign of Nero.

Peter felt free to minister to the Gentiles, but is best known as the apostle to the Jews (cf. Acts 10; Gal. 2:8). As Paul took a more active role in the work of the church and as the Jews became more hostile to Christianity, Peter faded into the background of the NT narrative.

The Roman Catholic church traces the authority of the pope back to Peter, for it is alleged that Peter was bishop of the church at Rome when he died. Tradition says that the Basilica of St. Peter in Rome is built over the spot where Peter was buried. Modern excavations under the ancient church demonstrate an ancient Roman cemetery and some graves hastily used for Christian burials.

Simon the Canaanite. Matthew and Mark refer to a disciple named Simon the Canaanite (some translations list him as Canaanaean), while Luke and Acts (KJV) refer to one named Simon Zelotes. These names belong to the same man. *Zelotes* is a Greek word meaning "zealous" and *Canaanite* is an English transliteration of the Aramaic word *kanna'ah*, also meaning "zealous."

The Scripture does not indicate when Simon the Canaanite was invited to join the apostles. Tradition says that Jesus called him at the same time that he called Andrew and Peter, James and John, Judas Iscariot and Thaddaeus (cf. Matt. 4:18–22).

We have several conflicting legends about the later ministry of this man. The Coptic church of Egypt says that he preached in Egypt, Africa, Great Britain, and Persia; other early sources agree that he ministered in the British Isles, but this is doubtful.

Thomas. John gives us a more complete picture of the disciple named Thomas than we receive from the other Gospels or Acts. John tells us he was also called *Didymus* (John 20:24, KJV, Greek for "twin"; the same meaning as the Hebrew word *t'hom*). The Latin Vulgate used Didymus as a proper name and that style was followed by most English versions until the twentieth century. The RSV and other recent translations refer to him as "Thomas, called the Twin."

We do not know who Thomas might have been, nor do we know anything about his family background or how he was invited to join the apostles. However, we know that Thomas joined six other disciples who returned to the fishing boats after Jesus was crucified (John 21:2–3). This suggested that he may have learned the fishing trade.

On one occasion Jesus told his disciples that he intended to return to Judea. The disciples warned Jesus not to go because of the hostility toward him there. Thomas said, "Let us also go, that we may die with Him" (John 11:16).

Most readers forget Thomas's courage and remember only his weakness and doubt. In the Upper Room, Jesus told his disciples, "Where I go you know, and the way you know." But Thomas retorted, "Lord, we do not know where you are going, and how can we know the way?" (John 14:4–5).

After Jesus rose from the dead, Thomas

told his friends, "Unless I see in His hands the print of the nails, and put my finger into the print of the nails, and put my hand into His side, I will not believe" (John 20:25). A few days later Jesus appeared to Thomas and the other disciples to give them physical proof that he was alive. Thomas exclaimed, "My Lord and my God!" (John 20:28).

The early church fathers respected the example of Thomas. Augustine commented, "He doubted that we might not doubt."

Tradition says that Thomas became a missionary in India and was martyred and buried in Mylapore, now a suburb of Madras. His name is carried on by the title of the Mathoma or "Master Thomas" church.

Judas's replacement.

Following the death of Judas Iscariot, Simon Peter said they needed to choose someone to replace the betrayer. Peter's speech outlined qualifications for the new apostle (cf. Acts 1:15–22). The apostle had to know Jesus "from the baptism of John to that day when He was taken up from us." He also had to be "a witness with us of His resurrection" (Acts 1:22).

The apostles found two men who met the qualifications: Joseph surnamed Justus and Matthias (Acts 1:23). They cast lots to decide the matter, and the lot fell to Matthias.

The name *Matthias* is a variant of the Hebrew name *Mattathias,* "gift of God." Unfortunately, Scripture tells us nothing about the ministry of Matthias. Eusebius speculated that Matthias would have been one of the 70 disciples that Jesus sent out on a preaching mission (cf. Luke 10:1–16). Some have identified him with Zacchaeus (cf. Luke 19:2–8). One tradition says he preached to cannibals in Mesopotamia; another says he was stoned to death by the Jews. However, we have no evidence to support any of these traditions.

Some scholars have suggested that Matthias was disqualified and the apostles chose James, the brother of Jesus, to take his place (cf. Gal. 1:19; 2:9). But there appear to have been more than 12 thought of as apostles in the early church, and Scripture gives us no indication that Matthias left the group. (See also *Minister.*)

Apostolic council.

This was the first assembly of church leaders in the NT, consisting of apostles and elders of the church in Jerusalem (see Acts 15). This council debated the question of whether Gentiles had to be circumcised and keep certain laws of the Jewish faith in order to become members of the church. This assembly decided that Gentiles did not first have to become Jews to become Christians.

Assassins.

Known as a fanatical group of Jewish nationalists in the first century A.D., 4,000 assassins followed an Egyptian who promised to lead them in a rebellion against the Romans (Acts 21:38). The Roman commander at Jerusalem wondered if the apostle Paul were a member of this group (Acts 21:38).

Bishop.

The Greek word for bishop, *episkopos,* literally means an "overseer." Although the NT is not clear, scholars think the word covered a broader meaning and included the same title as an elder or a pastor charged with the responsibility of spiritual leadership in a local church in NT times.

Before the church was founded, the Greek word for bishop was used in a general sense to refer to local gods as those who watched over people or countries. The word was later applied to people, including those who held positions as magistrates or other government officers. Eventually the term was extended to refer to officials in religious communities with various functions, including those who supervised the revenues of pagan temples.

In the NT, Jesus is called the "Overseer of your souls" (1 Pet. 2:25). In this passage the word is associated with the term "shepherd."

Bishops were to oversee the flock of God, to shepherd the people, to protect them from enemies, and to teach, exhort, and encourage. They were to accomplish this by being examples to the people, being of a willing and eager spirit, and not by using coercion or pursuing financial gain. To desire a position as bishop, the apostle Paul declared, was to desire a good work (1 Tim. 3:1).

Council. The name given to the Sanhedrin or court of the Jews by NT writers. This council met in the temple area in Jerusalem to interpret and administer the law and to deal with breaches of it. The council was made up of 71 members, including the high priest, former high priests, members of leading priestly families, Pharisees, and scribes. The council came to an end with the destruction of Jerusalem in A.D. 70.

Deacon. The word *deacon* meant a "servant" or "minister"; a deacon is an ordained lay officer in many Christian churches.

The general concept of deacon as a servant of the church is well established in both the Bible and church history. But the exact nature of the office is hard to define, because of changing concepts and varying practices among church bodies through the centuries. Another problem is that the Bible passages associated with deacons are interpreted differently by various church groups.

Deaconess. A deaconess is a female believer serving in the office of deacon in a church.

The only NT reference to deaconess as a church office is Paul's description of Phoebe as a deaconess of the church in Cenchreae (Rom. 16:1, RSV).

Elder. Used throughout the Bible, the term designated different ideas at various times in biblical history. The word may refer to age, experience, and authority, as well as specific leadership roles. In ancient times authority was given to older people with wider experience, who were consid-

ered the most qualified to hold places of leadership.

A governing structure similar to the ruling elders among the Jews was followed in the early church. The title *elder* was continued, but the significance of the office changed. *Elder* as used in the NT refers to the Jewish elders of the synagogue, to the members of the Sanhedrin, and to certain persons who held office in the church. It also implied seniority by reason of age (1 Tim. 5:2; 1 Pet. 5:5).

The presence of elders in the church in the NT indicates that this office was taken over from the synagogue. Elders played an important role in church life through their ministry to the sick (James 5:14–15). They were apparently the teachers also in a local congregation. In addition to ministering to the sick, their duties consisted of explaining the Scriptures and teaching doctrine (1 Tim. 5:17).

Epicureans. These were Greek philosophers who belonged to a school founded by Epicurus about 306 B.C. The Epicureans concerned themselves with the practical results of philosophy in everyday life. Their chief aim in life was pleasure. They believed they could find happiness by seeking that which brought physical and mental pleasure and avoiding that which brought pain.

Only one reference to the Epicureans occurs in Scripture where Paul encountered "certain Epicurean and Stoic philosophers" at Athens (see Acts 17:16–34).

Essenes. Meaning unknown. The Essenes were a religious community that existed in Palestine from about the middle of the second century B.C. until the Jewish war with Rome (A.D. 66–70). The Essenes were noted for their strict discipline and isolation from those who did not observe their way of life.

Although the Bible never mentions the Essenes, they are described by several ancient historians. The Essenes are an important part of the background to the NT, showing the beliefs and practices of one Jewish religious group at the time of John the Baptist and Jesus. People have been especially interested in the Essenes since the discovery of the Dead Sea Scrolls at Qumran. The people who lived at Qumran probably were a group of Essenes.

Evangelist. (See *Minister.*)

Herodians. A political party of Jews who supported Herod Antipas, the ruler of Galilee (4 B.C.–A.D. 39). They joined with the Pharisees in their plot to kill Jesus.

Judges. These were military heroes or deliverers who led the nation of Israel against their enemies during the period between the death of Joshua and the establishment of the kingship. The stories of their exploits are found in the book of Judges.

During the period of the judges, from about 1380 to 1050 B.C., the government of Israel was a loose confederation of tribes gathered about their central shrine, the ark of the covenant. Without a human king to guide them, the people tended to rebel and fall into worship of false gods time and time again. "Everyone did what was right in his own eyes" (Judg. 17:6; 21:25) is how the book of Judges describes these chaotic times. To punish the people, God would send foreign nations or tribes to oppress the Israelites.

The judges or charismatic leaders would rally the people to defeat the enemy. As God's agents for justice and deliverance, they would free the nation from oppression. But the judges themselves were often weak and their work short-lived. The people would enter another stage of rebellion and idolatry, only to see the cycle of oppression and deliverance repeated all over again.

The judges themselves were a diverse lot. Some of them received only a brief mention in the book of Judges. These minor judges were Shamgar (3:31), Tola (10:1–2), Jair (10:3–5), Ibzan (12:8–10), Elon (12:11–12), and Abdon (12:13–15).

The careers of other judges are explored in greater detail in that book:

• Othniel, a nephew of Caleb, was a warrior-deliverer who led the Israelites against the king of Mesopotamia (3:9–11).

• Ehud (3:12–30) was distinguished by left-handedness and his deftness with the dagger.

• Jephthah (11:1—12:7) was a harlot's son whose devotion to God was matched only by his rashness.

• Gideon (6:11—8:35) heeded many encouragements to act upon God's call and finally led 300 Israelites to defeat the entire army of the Midianites.

• Samson's frailties of the flesh led to his capture by the hated Philistines (13:1—16:31).

• Deborah, the most courageous of the judges, prevailed upon Barak to attack the mighty army of the Canaanites (4:4—5:31).

Levite. (See *Priest.*)

Libertines. "Freedmen." Probably Jews who were descended from captives sent to Rome by Pompey and later were liberated. They disputed with Stephen and accused him of blasphemy (Acts 6:9, KJV).

Maccabees. These were members of a Hasmonean family of Jewish leaders and rulers who reigned in Judea from 167 to 37 B.C. The term *Maccabees* especially applies to Judas Maccabeus and his brothers, who defeated the Syrians under Antiochus IV Epiphanes (the Seleucid ruler of Syria about 165 B.C.) and who rededicated the temple in Jerusalem.

Antiochus IV Epiphanes determined to impose the Greek language and culture on all subjects of the empire. (This story is found in the apocryphal book of 1 Maccabees.) He attacked Israel's religious practices and prohibited the observance of the Sabbath and the traditional feasts and festivals. He outlawed the reading of the law of Moses, circumcision, and

Judges of the Old Testament

Othniel	Captured a strong Canaanite city	Judg. 1:12–13; 3:8–11
Ehud	Killed Eglon, king of Moab, and defeated the Moabites in battle	Judg. 3:12–30
Shamgar	Killed 600 Philistines with an ox goad	Judg. 3:31
Deborah	Urged Barak to lead an army that defeated Sisera's troops	Judg. 4—5
Gideon	Defeated 135,000 Midianites with only 300 men	Judg. 6—8
Tola	Delivered Israel from her enemies for 23 years	Judg. 10:1–2
Jair	With his sons delivered 30 Israelite cities from their enemies	Judg. 10:3–5
Jephthah	Defeated the Ammonites after making a vow	Judg. 11:1—12:7
Ibzan	Delivered Israel from her enemies for seven years	Judg. 12:8–10
Elon	Delivered Israel from her enemies for 10 years	Judg. 12:11–12
Abdon	Delivered Israel from her enemies for eight years	Judg. 12:13–15
Samson	Killed 1,000 Philistines with the jawbone of an ass and later tore down the Philistines' temple, killing many more	Judg. 13—16
Samuel	The last of the judges and the first of the prophets	

Kings, Queens, and Rulers

Throughout the Bible, rulers and leaders appear from many nations. Following is a list of the major rulers in the OT and NT.

Amalekite

Agag	Wicked king spared by Saul and put to death by Samuel	1 Sam. 15:8–9 32–33

Ammonite

King of Ammon	Defeated by Jephthah	Judg. 11:12–28
Nahash	First king defeated by Saul	1 Sam. 11:1–11
Hanun	Humiliated David's peace delegation	2 Sam. 10:1–4
Baalis	Hired Ishmael to assassinate Gedaliah	Jer. 40:14

Assyrian

Tiglath-Pileser III (Pul)	Carried off the tribes beyond Jordan	2 Kings 15:29; 16:7, 10
Shalmaneser V	Destroyed Samaria and captured and imprisoned Hoshea	2 Kings 17:1–6; 18:9–11
Sargon II	Finished the sacking of Samaria	Isa. 20
Sennacherib	His armies were destroyed near Jerusalem by the death angel	2 Kings 18—19
Esarhaddon	May have been the ruler to imprison Manasseh	2 Chron. 33
Ashurbanipal (also referred to as Osnapper)	Settled foreigners in Samaria	Ezra 4:10

Kings, Queens, and Rulers—*continued*

Babylonian

Berodach-Baladan	His ambassadors were shown the wealth of Judah by Hezekiah	2 Kings 20:12; *Merodach-Bal adan*, Isa. 39:1
Evil-Merodach	Released the imprisoned Jehoiachin in Babylon	2 Kings 25:27
Nebuchadnezzar	Captured and destroyed Jerusalem and was ruler while Daniel was in Babylon	2 Kings 25; Dan. 1—4
Belshazzar	Saw the divine handwriting on the wall	Dan. 5

Canaanite

Bera	King of Sodom	Gen. 14:2–24
The king of Jericho	Ruler when the walls fell down	Josh. 2:2
Adoni-Zedek	Evil king of Jerusalem who formed a military alliance against Israel	Josh. 10:1–27
Jabin	King of Hazor and the last enemy Joshua defeated	Josh. 11:1–11
Jabin	King of Hazor, whose commander, Sisera, was killed by Jael after his forces were defeated by Barak	Judg. 4:2

Edomite

King of Edom	Refused Israel passage	Num. 20:14–21

Egyptian

Unknown Pharaoh	Pharaoh to whom Abraham lied concerning Sarah	Gen. 12:18–20
Unknown Pharaoh	Made Joseph second ruler in Egypt	Gen. 41:38–45
Thutmose I	Possibly the king who "did not know Joseph"	Exod. 1:8
Thutmose III	Possibly the king who attempted to kill Moses	Exod. 2:15
Amenhotep II	Possibly the king during the 10 plagues and the Exodus	Exod. 5:1
Unknown Pharaoh	Gave Solomon his daughter as a wife	1 Kings 3:1
Shishak	Besieged Jerusalem in the days of Rehoboam	1 Kings 14:25–26
Necho	Killed Josiah in battle and was later defeated by the Babylonians	2 Kings 23:29–30
Hophra	Defeated by the Babylonians in fulfillment of Jeremiah's prophecy	Jer. 44:30

Herodian

Herod the Great	Ruler over Judah at the time of Jesus' birth	Matt. 2:1–20
Herod Archelaus	Oldest son of Herod the Great; king when Joseph, Mary, and Jesus left Egypt	Matt. 2:22
Herod Philip	Another son of Herod the Great and first husband of Herodias, who left him for Antipas, his brother	Matt. 14:3
Herod Antipas	Youngest son of Herod the Great and the king who killed John the Baptist	Matt. 14:1–11
Herod Agrippa I	Grandson of Herod the Great and killer of the apostle James; killed by an angel of the Lord for accepting the people's worship	Acts 12
Herod Agrippa II	Great-grandson of Herod the Great and the king Paul spoke to about becoming a Christian	Acts 25:13—26:32

Kings, Queens, and Rulers—*continued*

Israel (the Northern Kingdom)

Jeroboam I	Perverted the worship of God	1 Kings 11:26—14:20
Nadab	Son of Jeroboam, killed by the rebel Baasha	1 Kings 15:25–28
Baasha	Built a wall to cut off trade with Jerusalem	1 Kings 15:27—16:7
Elah	Son of Baasha, killed by Zimri	1 Kings 16:6–14
Zimri	Committed suicide after ruling for seven days	1 Kings 16:9–20
Omri	Builder of Samaria, the northern capital	1 Kings 16:15–28
Ahab	Son of Omri and wicked husband of Jezebel, condemned by Elijah and killed in battle	1 Kings 16:28—22:40
Ahaziah	Wicked oldest son of Ahab	1 Kings 22:40—2 Kings 1:18
Jehoram	Youngest son of Ahab, who sent Naaman to the prophet Elisha to be healed	2 Kings 3:1—9:25
Jehu	Known for his chariot riding and extermination of Ahab's dynasty	2 Kings 9:1—10:36
Jehoahaz	Jehu's son, who saw his army almost wiped out by the Syrians	2 Kings 13:1–9
Jehoash	Jehoahaz's son, who waged a successful war against Judah and visited Elisha on his deathbed	2 Kings 13:10—14:16
Jeroboam II	Son of Joash, or Jehoash, who reigned during the time of Jonah the prophet	2 Kings 14:23–29
Zechariah	Jeroboam's son and the last of Jehu's dynasty, killed by Shallum	2 Kings 14:29—15:12
Shallum	Reigned for only a month and was killed by Menahem	2 Kings 15:10–15
Menahem	One of the most brutal kings ruling over the 10 tribes	2 Kings 15:14–22
Pekahiah	Son of Menahem, killed by his army commander, Pekah	2 Kings 15:22–26
Pekah	Killed by Hoshea	2 Kings 15:27–31
Hoshea	Dethroned and imprisoned by the Assyrians	2 Kings 15:30—17:6

Judah (the Southern Kingdom)

Rehoboam	Solomon's son, whose stupidity and arrogance sparked the civil war	1 Kings 11:43—12:24; 14:21–31
Abijam (also called Abijah)	Rehoboam's son, helped by God to defeat Jeroboam in battle	2 Chron. 13
Asa	Abijam's son, Judah's first godly king	1 Kings 15:8–24
Jehoshaphat	Asa's son, godly king who built a merchant fleet and made an alliance with Ahab	1 Kings 22:41–50

Kings, Queens, and Rulers—*continued*

Jehoram	Jehoshaphat's son, married to Athaliah, the wicked daughter of Ahab	2 Kings 8:16–24
Ahaziah	Son of Jehoram and Athaliah, killed by Jehu	2 Kings 8:24—9:29
Athaliah	Daughter of Ahab, who assumed the throne on the death of Ahaziah and slaughtered all members of the royal house but one	2 Kings 11:1–20
Joash	Son of Ahaziah, hidden as a boy from Athaliah and ruler after she was executed	2 Kings 11:1—12:21
Amaziah	Son of Joash, defeated by Jehoash (king of the ten tribes) and slain in a conspiracy	2 Kings 14:1–20
Uzziah (Azariah)	Son of Amaziah, struck with leprosy for his sin in the temple	2 Kings 15:1–7
Jotham	Son of Uzziah, who built the temple's upper gate and fortified Jerusalem	2 Kings 15:32–38
Ahaz	Son of Jotham, godless king who sacrificed his son to a pagan god	2 Kings 16:1–20
Hezekiah	Son of Ahaz, reformer, friend of Isaiah, and king when Jerusalem was saved by the death angel	2 Kings 18—20
Manasseh	Son of Hezekiah and Judah's worst king, though later converted	2 Kings 21:1–18
Amon	Son of Manasseh, executed by his own household servants	2 Kings 21:19–26
Josiah	Son of Amon, ruler when the Book of the Law was found in the temple, leader of a national reform, slain in battle against Egypt	2 Kings 22:1—23:30
Jehoahaz	Son of Josiah and ruler after Josiah's death in battle; deposed after only 90 days by Pharaoh Necho and taken to Egypt, where he died	2 Kings 23:31–33
Jehoiakim	Josiah's son who persecuted Jeremiah and burned the prophet's scroll; carried to Babylon by Nebuchadnezzar	2 Kings 23:34—24:5; Jer. 36
Jehoiachin	Jehoiakim's son, who incurred a special judgment from God and was taken to Babylon by Nebuchadnezzar	2 Kings 24:6–16
Zedekiah	Uncle of Jehoiachin, blinded and taken into exile in Babylon while Jerusalem and the temple were destroyed	2 Kings 24:17—25:30

Moabite

Balak	King who hired Balaam to curse Israel	Num. 22—24
Eglon	Obese king assassinated by Ehud	Judg. 3:12–30
Mesha	King who sacrificed his son	2 Kings 3:4–27

Persian and Mede

Cyrus the Great	Issued the return decree for the Jews	2 Chron. 36:22–23; Ezra 1; Isa. 44:28
Darius the Mede	Conqueror of Babylon while Daniel was there	Dan. 6
Darius the Great	Allowed the temple work to continue	Ezra 6:1–12

Kings, Queens, and Rulers—*continued*

Ahasuerus (also known as Xerxes I)	Husband of Esther	Esther 1
Artaxerxes	Befriended both Ezra and Nehemiah	Ezra 7:1; Neh. 2:1
Darius III	His armies were destroyed by Alexander the Great—a fulfillment of Daniel's prophecy	Dan. 8

Philistine

Abimelech	King to whom Abraham lied about Sarah [many scholars believe Abimelech (see Gen. 10) is not a proper name but a general reference to the Philistine king during the times of Abraham and Isaac]	Gen. 20
Abimelech	King to whom Isaac lied about Rebekah	Gen. 26
Achish	King in Gath to whom David fled	1 Sam. 21:10–14; 27—29

Roman

Augustus Caesar	Emperor when Jesus was born	Luke 2:1
Tiberius Caesar	Emperor during Jesus' earthly ministry	Luke 3:1; 20:22–25
Claudius Caesar	Emperor during the ministry of Paul	Acts 11:28; 18:2
Nero Caesar	Emperor Paul appealed to and later the one who probably executed both Peter and Paul [this ruler is not mentioned specifically by name, but he was the ruling emperor during Paul and Peter's time]	Acts 25:10–12

Syrian

Ben-Hadad I	Defeated twice by Ahab	1 Kings 20:1–34
Ben-Hadad II	Sent Naaman to Israel for healing	2 Kings 5:5–6
Hazael	Anointed by Elijah, and later the assassin of Ben-Hadad II	1 Kings 19:15; 2 Kings 8:7–15, 28–29
Rezin	Allied with Pekah in unsuccessful siege against Jerusalem	2 Kings 16:5–9

Tyrian

Hiram	Furnished the wood for the temple	1 Kings 5:1–18
Prince of Tyre	Denounced by Ezekiel	Ezek. 28:1–10

United Kingdom of Israel

Saul	Israel's first king, rejected by God	1 Sam. 9—15
David	Saul's successor, Israel's best-loved king	1 Sam. 16—31; 2 Sam. 1—24
Solomon	David's son, Israel's wisest and richest king	1 Kings 1—11

Queens

Michal	Daughter of Saul and David's first wife	1 Sam. 18:20–28; 2 Sam. 6:20–23
Rizpah	Saul's wife who attempted to protect the bodies of her seven sons until David had them buried	2 Sam. 21:8–14
Bathsheba	Originally the wife of Uriah, then David's wife, and mother of Solomon	2 Sam. 11—12
Queen of Sheba	African or Arabian queen who visited Solomon	1 Kings 10:1–13
Maachah	Idol-worshiping mother of King Asa	1 Kings 15:10; 2 Chron. 15:16
Jezebel	Wicked and idolatrous wife of King Ahab	1 Kings 16:31
Athaliah	Wicked daughter of Ahab and Jezebel	2 Kings 11
Nehushta	Mother of Jehoiachin, who was taken to Babylon	2 Kings 24:8–16
Babylonian queen mother	Advised Belshazzar to call for Daniel	Dan. 5:10–12
Vashti	Disobedient Persian queen deposed by King Ahasuerus	Esther 1
Esther	Jewish maiden who became the wife of Ahasuerus	Esther 2—10
Herodias	Herod Antipas's vicious wife who plotted John the Baptist's death	Matt. 14:1–12
Candace	Ethiopian queen who allowed her servant, the eunuch, to visit Judea	Acts 8:27–28
Bernice	Sister and wife of King Herod Agrippa II	Acts 25:13,23; 26:30

all other religious practices. The penalty for disobedience was death.

Antiochus's ultimate affront to the Jews occurred on the twenty-fifth day of Kislev, 167 B.C., when he dedicated the temple to the pagan Greek god Zeus, set up Zeus's statue in the Holy of Holies, and sacrificed swine on the altar. These actions outraged the people and brought on the revolt of the Maccabees.

The home of Mattathias, a priest at Modein (or Modin), northwest of Jerusalem, became the center of resistance against the Hellenizing policies of Antiochus.

With Mattathias were his five sons. The title *Maccabeus* was first given to Judas, the third son of Mattathias, but it was soon transferred to the entire family. The term probably comes from *makkebeth* (Hebrew) or *makkaba* (Aramaic), meaning "hammer." This alludes to the crushing blows inflicted by Judas and his successors on

their enemies. Judas may have been called the "Hammer" or the "Hammerer" of the enemy (or as some scholars prefer, the "Extinguisher" or the "Quencher").

Antiochus had sent commissioners throughout the entire country of Judea to enforce his decree. Appalled by the sacrilegious acts committed in Judea and Jerusalem and moved by his fervent zeal for the law of Moses, Mattathias killed one of the officers of the king sent to enforce pagan sacrifice. He and his five sons then fled from Modein, taking refuge in the rugged hills nearby. Joined by a growing number of sympathizers who detested the "abomination of desolation" set up on the altar by Antiochus, the Maccabees carried on guerrilla warfare against the Syrians and the Jewish collaborators.

In December 164 B.C. Judas Maccabeus recaptured most of Jerusalem. He forced the loyal priests, those who had not collaborated with Antiochus, to cleanse the holy place and erect a new altar. On the twenty-fifth of Kislev, 164 B.C., precisely three years after Antiochus had defiled it, Judas rededicated the temple.

According to Jewish tradition, only one undefiled cruse of oil could be found. This cruse contained oil for only one day. Miraculously, however, the cruse kept burning for eight days. The Hebrew word *Hanukkah* (literally, dedication) is the name still used for the Jewish Festival of Lights that commemorates this event. Celebrated for eight days from the twenty-fifth day of the month of Kislev to the second day of Adar, Hanukkah occurs near or at the same time as the Christian celebration of Christmas. The Feast of Dedication is mentioned in the NT (John 10:22).

After a short time of peace, war broke out again between the Jews and the Syrians. Leadership of the Maccabees passed from Judas to Jonathan and then to Simon. (The two other brothers had been killed without assuming leadership.) After the death of Simon, the last remaining son of Mattathias, the succession of the Maccabees was maintained by Simon's son John, known later as John Hyrcanus or Hyrcanus I.

Although Judea was nominally still a province of Syria, practical independence was maintained until 63 B.C., when Pompey invaded the country and brought Israel under Roman domination. Mariamne, the wife of Herod the Great, was a descendant of the Maccabees.

The term *Maccabees* has gained wide acceptance and use. The proper name of the family, however, is *Hasmoneans* (or *Asmoneans*), a name probably derived from Chasmon, the great-grandfather of Mattathias.

Minister. To minister is to serve or to be a servant. In the OT this word was used primarily for court servants (1 Kings 10:5; Esther 1:10). During the period between the OT and the NT, it came to be used in connection with ministering to the poor. This use of the word is close to the work of the seven in waiting on tables in the NT (Acts 6:1–7).

In reality, all believers are "ministers." Paul urged the true pastor-teacher to equip the saints so they could minister to one another (Eph. 4:11–12). The model, of course, is Jesus, who "did not come to be served, but to serve" (Mark 10:45). His service is revealed in the fact that he gave "His life a ransom for many" (Matt. 20:28).

Jesus' servanthood radically revised the ethics of Jew and Greek alike because he equated service to God with service to others. When we minister to the needs of the hungry or the lonely, we actually minister to Christ (Matt. 25:31–46). In this light, all who take part in the fellowship of service are ministers.

The concept is strengthened when the use of the Greek word *doulos* is noted. This was the term for a "bondslave," one who was offered his freedom but voluntarily surrendered that freedom in order to remain a servant. This idea typified Jesus' purpose, as described by Paul in Philippians 2:7. This passage alludes to the "Servant of God" passage of Isaiah 52—54.

Following Jesus' example, all believers are bondslaves of God (Rom. 1:1; Gal. 1:10; Col. 4:12). We are to perform good deeds for all with a responsibility especially toward fellow Christians (Gal. 6:10; Heb. 10:24).

Our unselfish service should especially be rendered through our spiritual gifts—given to Christians to minister to one another (1 Pet. 4:10). These gifts are both spiritual and practical (1 Cor. 12:28) and distributed to members of the church so that the union of believers can be expressed in loving service. (See *Spiritual gifts*.)

In Ephesians 4:7–11 the offices of apostles, prophets, pastors, teachers, and evangelists are described as gifts to the church. This is where the officers of the church are linked with the term *minister*. Those who hold these offices minister to the church:

• Apostles through their inspired leadership

• Prophets through their inspired speaking and foretelling
• Evangelists through their traveling missionary work
• Pastor-teachers through their service in local congregations

Yet their primary service was to equip all saints for ministry.

The concepts of *minister* and *ministry* must be broadened today to include all the members of a church. The common concept of pastors as the professional ministers must be discarded, because the biblical pattern is for them to train their congregations for ministry. All the saints are responsible for loving and ministering in various ways to one another, using the spiritual gifts distributed to each by the Holy Spirit. Offices of ministry include apostle, evangelist, pastor, preacher, prophet, prophetess, and teacher.

Apostle. The apostles were special messengers of Jesus Christ, individuals to whom Jesus delegated authority for certain tasks. The word *apostle* is used originally of those 12 disciples Jesus sent out during his ministry in Galilee to preach and heal. On that occasion, evidently, they were first called apostles (cf. Mark 3:14; 6:30).

These same disciples, with the exception of Judas Iscariot, were recommissioned by Jesus after the resurrection to be his witnesses throughout the world (Luke 24:46–49; Acts 1:8). After Jesus' ascension, the apostles brought their number back to 12 by choosing Matthias (Acts 1:23–26).

The word *apostle* is sometimes used in the NT in a general sense of "messenger." For instance, when delegates of Christian communities were charged with conveying those churches' contributions to a charitable fund, they were described by Paul as "messengers [apostles] of the churches" (2 Cor. 8:23). Jesus also used the word this way when he quoted the proverb, "A servant is not greater than his master; nor is he who is sent [literally, an apostle] greater than he who sent him" (John 13:16). Jesus himself is called "the

Apostle . . . of our confession" (Heb. 3:1), a reference to his function as God's special Messenger to the world.

The word *apostle* has a wider meaning in the letters of Paul. It includes people who, like himself, were not included in the original 12, but who saw the risen Christ and were especially commissioned by him. Paul's claim to be an apostle was questioned by others. He based his apostleship on the direct call of the exalted Lord who appeared to him on the Damascus Road and on the Lord's blessing of his ministry in winning converts and establishing churches (1 Cor. 15:10).

Paul also counted James, the Lord's brother, as an apostle (Gal. 1:19). This James was not one of the Twelve; in fact, he was not a believer in Jesus before the Crucifixion (John 7:5). The resurrected Lord "appeared to James" (1 Cor. 15:7), and he presumably commissioned James for his ministry. When Paul says Jesus was seen not only by James but also by "all the apostles" (1 Cor. 15:7), he seems to be describing a wider group than the Twelve.

In 1 Corinthians 12:28 and Ephesians 4:11, apostles are listed along with prophets and other saints as part of the foundation of the household of God. Some scholars have then argued that this means that apostles are confined to the first generation of Christians, but there is no evidence for this.

At an early stage in the church's history it was agreed that apostles to the Jews and

This map of early churches connected with the ministry of Paul and John shows the Seven Churches of Asia Minor. PHOTO BY HOWARD VOS

Gentiles should be divided, with Paul and Barnabas evangelizing the Gentiles. Peter, John, and James (the Lord's brother) were to continue evangelizing Jews (Gal. 2:7–9).

As pioneers in the work of making converts and planting churches, apostles were exposed to special dangers. When persecution erupted, they were the primary targets for attack (1 Cor. 4:9–13). Paul, in particular, welcomed the suffering he endured as an apostle as his way of participating in the suffering of Christ (Rom. 8:17; 2 Cor. 1:5–7).

The authority committed to the apostles by Christ was unique and could not be transmitted to others. The apostles could install elders, teachers and other leaders in the churches.

Evangelist. This word referred to a person authorized to proclaim the gospel of Christ. In a more narrow sense, the word refers to one of the gospel writers: Matthew, Mark, Luke, or John. Literally, however, the word means "one who proclaims good tidings" (Eph. 4:11; 2 Tim. 4:5).

The evangelist was a gift of God to the church (Eph. 4:11). These persons were not attached to any specific local church but traveled over a wide geographical area, preaching to those to whom the Holy Spirit led them.

Pastor. Pastors are the feeders, protectors, and guides (or shepherds) of flocks of God's people in NT times. In speaking of spiritual gifts, Paul wrote that Christ "gave

Ruins of a church at Laodicea, showing engravings of two Latin crosses and the distinctive shape of a Greek cross in the foreground.
PHOTO BY GUSTAV JEENINGA

some to be apostles, some prophets, some evangelists, and some pastors and teachers" (Eph. 4:11). Many believe that pastor-teacher was one office. At any rate, the term *pastor* by this time in church history had not yet become an official title. The term implied the nourishing of and caring for God's people.

The Greek word translated *pastors* (Eph. 4:11) is used elsewhere in the NT for:
• Sheepherders, literally and symbolically (Matt. 25:32)
• Jesus, the Good Shepherd (John 10)
The NKJV used the word *pastor* only in Ephesians 4:11 (cf. Jer. 23:1–2, KJV). (See *Teacher*.)

Preacher. Preachers proclaim God's saving message to the people.

The OT mentions several prominent preachers:
• Noah was a "preacher of righteousness" (2 Pet. 2:5).
• Solomon described himself as a preacher who taught "words of truth" (Eccles. 1:2; 12:9–10).
• Jonah reluctantly preached to the people of Nineveh (cf. Jon. 1—4).
• All the prophets of the OT were regarded as preachers, particularly Isaiah, Jeremiah, Amos, and Micah.

In the NT, the gospel advanced on the wings of preaching. John the Baptist called for repentance in preparation for the Messiah's appearance (Matt. 3:11–12). With a sense of urgency, Jesus and the apostles preached in homes, by the seaside, on the temple steps, and in the synagogues. The zeal generated by Pentecost, coupled with growing persecution of the young church, led the disciples to preach everywhere in the known world (Mark 16:20).

At his home synagogue in Nazareth, Jesus connected his ministry with that of the prophets (Isa. 61:1–2) and identified his mission as one of proclaiming deliverance: "The Lord . . . has anointed Me to preach the gospel to the poor, . . . to proclaim liberty to the captives" (Luke 4:18–19).

Jesus spread the gospel by means of

preaching (Luke 4:43–44). Philip, the preaching deacon, "preached the things concerning the kingdom of God and the name of Jesus Christ" (Acts 8:12). In sending out the Twelve, Jesus commanded them, "As you go, preach, saying, 'The kingdom of heaven is at hand'" (Matt. 10:7). Paul proudly declared his credentials as one whom God "appointed a preacher and an apostle" (1 Tim. 2:7).

NT preaching carries an evangelistic thrust. Paul declared, "It pleased God through the foolishness of the message preached to save those who believe" (1 Cor. 1:21). The redemptive mission of Christ as fulfillment of prophecy—particularly his death and resurrection—was the main theme of apostolic preaching (1 Cor. 1:2–3; 15:14). The preachers' personal testimonies to Christ's power in their own lives were also featured in many sermons (e.g., Acts 4:20).

The distinction between preaching and teaching made in the church today was not evident in the NT. Both Jesus and Paul regarded themselves as preacher-teachers and were so regarded by others. For example, Jesus "taught the people . . . and preached the gospel" (Luke 20:1). Paul testified that he was appointed "a preacher, an apostle, and a teacher of the Gentiles" (2 Tim. 1:11). Paul charged young Timothy to "preach the word! . . . Convince, rebuke, exhort, with all longsuffering and teaching" (2 Tim. 4:2).

Prophet. Prophets spoke for God. In the OT, they communicated God's message to the nation of Israel. In the NT, they became God's "mouthpieces" for the church.

Prophets received their call directly from God. Some, like Jeremiah or John the Baptist, were called before birth (Jer. 1:5; Luke 1:13–16), but this was not a birthright. Their authority came from God whose message they bore (Exod. 7:1–2).

The prophetic call enabled men (and a few women) to be unaffected by human bias and criticism. The call of the prophets required that they not be intimidated or threatened by their audiences (Jer. 1:7–8; Ezek. 2:6).

Prophets sometimes became quite dramatic and acted out their message. For example, Isaiah went naked and barefoot for three years (Isa. 20:2–3); Ezekiel lay on his left side for 390 days and on his right side for 40 more (Ezek. 4:1–8); and Zechariah broke two staffs (Zech. 11:7–14). Making themselves spectacles, prophets not only aroused curiosity but also invited the scorn of their peers (Jer. 11:21).

Except for God's call, prophets had no special qualifications. They appeared from all walks of life and classes of society. They included

• Sheepbreeders and farmers like Amos (Amos 7:14) and Elisha (1 Kings 19:19)
• Princes like Abraham (Gen. 23:6)
• Priests like Ezekiel (Ezek. 1:3)
• Women and children (1 Sam. 3:19–20; 2 Kings 22:14)

In rare circumstances, God used the hesitant or unruly to bear his message. Balaam prophesied the Lord's message (Num. 22:6–24:24) but was actually an enemy of God (2 Pet. 2:15–16; Rev. 2:14).

Some prophets were called for a lifetime, but others spoke only briefly (Num. 11:25–26). In either case, prophets spoke with the authority of the Holy Spirit (Num. 11:29; 24:2–4). One trait characterized them all: a faithful proclamation of God's word and not their own (Jer. 23:16; Ezek. 13:2). Jesus' reference to himself as a prophet in John 12:49–50 rests upon this standard of faithfully repeating God's word to people.

Some scholars deny that prophecy includes the prediction of future events, but fulfillment was, in fact, the test of prophets' genuineness (Deut. 18:20–22). Whether prophets' words were fulfilled within their lifetimes or centuries later, they were fulfilled to the letter (1 Kings 13:3; 2 Kings 23:15–16). But regardless of the time of fulfillment, prophetic messages applied to their generation as well as to ours.

Mainly prophets bore God's word for the purpose of teaching, reproving, correcting,

and training in righteousness (2 Tim. 3:16).
Whether warning of impending danger or
disclosing God's will to the people, they
were similar in function to the modern
preacher in the church.

Prophets were referred to as
• Messengers of the Lord (Isa. 44:26;
Hag. 1:13)
  • Servants of God (Amos 3:7)
  • Shepherds (Jer. 17:16; Zech. 11:4–7)
  • Watchmen (Isa. 62:6)
God has used people in every age to fill
the prophetic role of proclaiming his word.
Here are some examples:
• Noah, a "preacher of righteousness" to
his generation (2 Pet. 2:5)
  • Abraham (Gen. 20:7)
  • Isaac (Ps. 105:9, 14–15)
  • Jacob (Gen. 49).
• Moses, the greatest prophet of all be-
cause of his accomplishments and writings
(Deut. 34:10–12)
• Joshua, commissioned to continue
Moses' work and also assumed the prophetic role (Deut. 34:9; Josh. 1:1, 5)
Following the entrance of the Hebrew
people into the land of Canaan, many
prophets appeared throughout Israel's history to aid and protect the nation. The
prophets mentioned in the Bible probably
represent only a small portion of the total
number of them. Most of the prophets remain obscure because they never wrote
down their message. This indicates their
task required face-to-face confrontations
and a spoken rather than a written message.

Many times the prophets stood alone
and spoke to an unsympathetic or even antagonistic audience. Great courage and independence of spirit were required.

The first prophet mentioned after Joshua
is unnamed (Judg. 6:7–10). Prophets were
to exalt God's word and not seek their own
glory. This unnamed prophet appeared in
the time of Gideon when Israel was falling
back into idolatry. Rather than speak of the
future, he called Israel to remember the
Lord who delivered them from Egypt.

The next prophet was Samuel, whose vo-
cation was apparent to all from his youth
(1 Sam. 3:19–20). Samuel's life was spent
• Serving diligently as a judge (1 Sam.
7:15)
• Leading the army to victory (1 Sam.
7:9–10)
• Establishing the religious and civil life
of the nation (1 Sam. 10:25)
• Appointing (1 Sam. 12:1) and recalling
Saul as the first king of Israel (1 Sam. 15),
then appointing David as Saul's successor
(1 Sam. 16:1–13)
Four prophets appeared in the time of
David, who himself demonstrated the
traits of a prophet (2 Sam. 23:2–3). They
were
  • Gad (1 Sam. 22:5)
  • Nathan (2 Sam. 12:1–15)
  • Zadok (2 Sam. 15:27)
  • Heman (1 Chron. 25:5)
Four prophets also appeared during the
time of Jeroboam I:
  • Ahijah (1 Kings 12:15)
  • "A man of God" (1 Kings 13:1)
  • "An old prophet" (1 Kings 13:25)
  • Iddo the seer (2 Chron. 9:29)
Iddo apparently had visions, but he confined his revelations to writing (2 Chron.
9:29; 12:15; 13:22). A man of God confronted Jeroboam for his intrusion into the
priestly office at the altar and prophesied
the coming of Josiah by name (1 Kings
13:1–9); but his rival, the old prophet in
Bethel, deceived him and brought about
his death (1 Kings 13:11–32). Even though
the old prophet lied, God revealed the
death sentence of the man of God to him
(1 Kings 13:21–23).

The prophet Shemaiah appeared to Solomon's successor, Rehoboam, to stop him
from attempting to reunite the country by
force (2 Chron. 11:2–4). The prophet Iddo
recorded the acts of Abijah (2 Chron. 13:22)
the successor of Rehoboam, who himself
raised a prophetic voice, although he was a
wicked king (1 Kings 15:1–5). The king correctly anticipated victory over Jeroboam's
troops (2 Chron. 13:12).

The next king, Asa, was promised God's
blessing by the prophet Azariah when the

king was returning from his victory over Zerah, the Ethiopian (2 Chron. 15:1–7). But Asa did not remain faithful, seeking help instead from the Syrians when Baasha threatened him. The prophet Hanani was imprisoned for rebuking Asa for not relying upon the Lord alone as in the earlier victory (2 Chron. 16:7–10). The son of Hanani, Jehu, played a more prominent role than his father. He condemned the wickedness of Baasha and declared his dynasty would end (1 Kings 16:1–4).

Jehoshaphat was promised victory over the alliance of Moab, Ammon, and Edom by the prophet Jahaziel (2 Chron. 20:14–17). God alone would supply the victory. Later Jehoshaphat allied with Ahab's son, Ahaziah, in order to build a southern fleet. The prophet Eliezer proclaimed the alliance caused God to destroy the fleet (2 Chron. 20:37).

Five prophets appeared during the reign of Ahab. These included the famous prophets Elijah and Elisha. Elijah was the most unforgettable and dynamic of the Hebrew prophets. He dominated the scene while Ahab was king (1 Kings 17—19; 21), but his ministry continued until the reigns of Ahaziah (2 Kings 1) and Jehoram (2 Kings 2). His impact and eminence were compared with those of Moses, as their joint appearance with Christ in his transfiguration suggests (Matt. 17:1–13). Elijah's spectacular success over the prophets of Baal in the bringing of rain defies comparison. His volatile and dynamic temperament stands in stark contrast to Elisha, who asked for a double portion of Elijah's spirit (2 Kings 2:9).

Although he was called by Elijah in the reign of Ahab, Elisha actually succeeded him in the reign of Jehoram (2 Kings 2—9). Doubly blessed, Elisha performed more miracles than Elijah.

Three prophets confronted kings in person. A man of God told Amaziah of Judah to dismiss his Israelite mercenaries (2 Chron. 25:7–10), while another prophet rebuked Amaziah for saving the idols after defeating Edom (2 Chron. 25:15). Finally,

Oded secured the release of Judeans captured by Israelites during the time of Ahaz (2 Chron. 28:9–15).

These prophets in Joshua, Judges, 1 and 2 Samuel, and 1 and 2 Kings provided those books with the name of *former prophets* in the Hebrew canon. They actually overlapped in time with the *latter* or *writing prophets*, known commonly as the *major* and *minor* prophets. The former prophets dealt more with daily problems and the current state of affairs, while the latter prophets wrote for later generations what would happen in the future.

A few passages in the writing prophets give biographical material about the prophets themselves. Although most of the writing prophets simply present God's message, there are biographical chapters in
- Isaiah (6—7; 20; 37—39)
- Jeremiah (1; 13; 19—21; 24—29; 32; 34—35)
- Daniel (1—6)
- Hosea (1; 3)
- Amos (7:10–17)
- Jonah (1—4)
- Haggai (1—2)
- Zechariah (7—8)

Other parts of Zechariah and Ezekiel tell about the prophets' receiving visions, but these passages have lesser value in portraying the prophets' personalities.

The writing prophets do not appear to be in chronological order, but they provide clues that can be matched with historical facts suggesting their proper sequence. Obadiah spoke against Edom; his ministry may have occurred in the time of Jehoram (853–841 B.C.) when Edom revolted against Judah (2 Kings 8:20–22).

Joel can be dated to the time when Judah's enemies were Tyre and Sidon along with Philistia (Joel 3:4), Egypt, and Edom (Joel 3:19). Since no king is mentioned, the book has been dated to the time of Joash's childhood when Jehoiada, the high priest, was his guardian. The dates of Joash's reign are 835–796 B.C.

In the following century five prophets can be dated to the reigns of various kings.

1. Hosea probably prophesied from about 760 B.C. to past 715 B.C. or from the time of Uzziah and Jeroboam II to Hezekiah.

2. Amos prophesied when Uzziah and Jeroboam II ruled. Their reigns overlapped for at least 15 years (767–753 B.C.) and even longer if Uzziah's coregency with his father, Amaziah, is counted.

3. Jonah was a contemporary of Jeroboam II (793–753 B.C.), but his trip to Nineveh may have been before or after Jeroboam's reign.

4. Isaiah 1:1 says that Isaiah's ministry spanned four kings from the death of Uzziah (Isa. 6:1) through Hezekiah, about whom Isaiah wrote a history (2 Chron. 32:32). That Isaiah ministered after Hezekiah's death in 686 B.C. is evident from his recording of Sennacherib's death in 681 B.C.

5. Micah began his ministry under Uzziah's successor, Jotham, and finished it some time in the reign of Hezekiah (Mic. 1:1). This would suggest his ministry began some time after Uzziah's death in 739 B.C. Since Micah does not mention Sennacherib's invasion of 701 B.C., he likely concluded his ministry before that date.

Four prophets appeared in the next century.

1. Nahum probably wrote his prophecy in the latter half of the seventh century, since Nahum 3:8–10 refers to the destruction of Thebes in 663 B.C. Nahum probably prophesied the 612 B.C. destruction of Nineveh before the ministry of Zephaniah, who also predicted the fall of Nineveh and dates himself to the time of Josiah (640–609 B.C.).

2. Zephaniah's attack on idolatry suggests he wrote his work before the reforms of Josiah in 621 B.C.

3. Habakkuk's prophecy should be dated after 612 B.C., since he made no reference to Assyria. The prophet was concerned about the coming invasion of Babylon, probably the first one of 605 B.C. in the reign of Jehoiakim (609–598 B.C.).

4. Jeremiah began his work in 627 B.C.

(Jer. 1:2–3) and continued ministering in Egypt after the fall of Jerusalem in 586 B.C.

Daniel and Ezekiel ministered during the captivity in Babylon. Daniel was taken to Babylon in 605 B.C. at the time of Nebuchadnezzar's first invasion of Judah. Ezekiel was taken there in 597 B.C. at the time of the second invasion. Daniel ministered until the third year of Cyrus (536 B.C.; Dan. 10:1). Ezekiel was called to begin his ministry in 592 B.C. (Ezek. 1:2) and continued until at least 571 B.C. (Ezek. 29:17).

Haggai, Zechariah, and Malachi ministered after the captivity when the people returned to Judah. Haggai dates his prophecy to 520 B.C. (Hag. 1:1, 15; 2:1, 20). Zechariah began his ministry two months after Haggai (Zech. 1:1).

Probably Malachi was written after 432 B.C. when Nehemiah wrote his book mentioned by Malachi. Problems of the time included priestly carelessness (Mal. 1:6—2:9), intermarriage with foreigners (2:10—3:6), and lack of tithing (3:7—4:3).

Prophetess. A female prophet. God called these women to perform prophetic tasks in Bible times:

• Miriam, the sister of Moses, led the women with her chorus in response to the great song of her brother (Exod. 15:20–21).

• Deborah joined with Barak in song and exulted in their great victory (Judg. 5:2–31).

• Hannah's prayer foretold the founding of David's dynasty (1 Sam. 2:1–10).

• Anna in the temple foretold events (see Luke 2:36–38).

• Elizabeth and Mary prophesied (Luke 1:41–45, 46–55).

First Corinthians 11:5 assumes the female role in prophesying, seen again in Philip's four virgin daughters (Acts 21:9). Other prophetesses such as Noadiah gained a bad reputation (Neh. 6:14).

Teacher. Teachers instruct or impart knowledge and information. As used in the NT, the concept of teaching usually means instruction in the faith. Although some have tried to make a distinction between preaching and teaching, the Bible does not support this position. In the list of spiritual offices in Ephesians 4:11, most scholars now see pastor-teacher as a single office.

Since sound instruction in the faith is essential to the spiritual growth of Christians and to the development of the church, the Bible contains numerous passages that deal with teaching (e.g., Matt. 4:23; Luke 4:15; Acts 13:1–3; Rom. 12:6–8; Gal. 6:6).

Special attention is directed to the danger of false teachings. Christians are warned to test those who pervert the true gospel (2 Tim. 3:1–7; 1 Pet. 2:1–3).

Sound teaching was a concept deeply ingrained in the Jewish mind since OT times. Moses and Aaron were considered teachers of God's commandments (Exod. 18:20). Parents were also directed to teach their children about God and his statutes (Deut. 4:9–10). (See *Pastor*.)

A mosaic of the prophet Joel, who prophesied about the outpouring of God's Spirit in the latter days (Joel 2:28).

Spiritual Gifts

While the gifts such as apostles and evangelists were offices, God gave specific charisms or spiritual gifts to individuals. Those who held these offices exercised some of these gifts.

Essentially spiritual gifts were special talents or abilities bestowed by the Holy Spirit upon Christians for the purpose of building up the church. The list of spiritual gifts in 1 Corinthians 12:8–10 includes wisdom, knowledge, faith, healing, miracles, prophecy, discerning of spirits, speaking in tongues, and interpretation of tongues. Other lists appear in Ephesians 4:7–13, Romans 12:3–8 and 1 Peter 4:10–11.

Paul indicated that these gifts are equally valid but not necessarily equally valuable. Their value is determined by their worth to the church. In dealing with this matter, he used the analogy of the human body. All members of the body have essential functions, Paul declared, but some are more vital to the welfare of the church than others. The service of each Christian should be in proportion to the gifts he possesses (1 Cor. 12—14).

Since these gifts are gifts of grace, their use must be controlled by the principle of love—the greatest of all spiritual gifts (1 Cor. 13).

Of special note among these charisms is the gift of tongues. This is the Spirit-given ability to speak in languages not known to the speaker or in an ecstatic language that could not normally be understood by the speaker or the hearers.

The only reference in the OT to speaking in another tongue or language is possibly Isaiah 28:11: "For with stammering lips and another tongue He will speak to this people." This seems to be a reference to an invasion of the Assyrians. They apparently would speak in another language, one probably unknown to the people of Israel.

Paul later applied this verse to speaking in tongues (1 Cor. 14:21). Peter considered the phenomenon of speaking in tongues that occurred on the day of Pentecost (Acts 2) as the fulfillment of OT prophecy (Joel 2:28–32).

In an appearance to his disciples after the Resurrection, Jesus declared, "And these signs will follow those who believe: In My name they will cast out demons; they will speak with new tongues" (Mark 16:17).

On the day of Pentecost, the followers of Christ "were all filled with the Holy Spirit and began to speak with other tongues, as the Spirit gave them utterance" (Acts 2:4). The people assembled in Jerusalem for this feast came from various Roman provinces representing a variety of languages. They were astonished to hear the disciples speaking of God's works in their own languages. Some have suggested that the miracle was in the hearing rather than in the speaking. This explanation, however, would transfer the miraculous from the believing disciples to the multitude who may not have been believers.

Tongues as a gift of the Spirit is prominent in 1 Corinthians 12 and 14. As one of the several gifts given to believers as manifestation of the Holy Spirit, tongues is intended, with the other gifts, to be exercised for the building up of the church and the mutual profit of its members. Paul puts the gift of tongues in perspective by affirming that though we "speak with the tongues of men and of angels" (1 Cor. 13:1), if we do not have love, the gift of tongues has little value.

In 1 Corinthians 14 Paul deals more specifically with the gift of tongues and its exercise in the church. The tongue was not always an intelligible language, or at least it was not always understood by the listeners. This gift then needed the parallel gift of interpretation.

The gift of tongues was used primarily as a means of worship, thanksgiving, and prayer. While exercising this gift, the individual addressed God, not people. The result was self-edification (1 Cor. 14:2, 4). This gift was intended not for self-exaltation but for the praise and glorification of God. Paul does not prohibit speaking in tongues in a public service (1 Cor. 14:39). But he seems to assign it to a lesser place than the gift of prophecy—unless accompanied by interpretation. When interpreted, it appears to have the same value (1 Cor. 14:5).

The other use of this gift of tongues was to convince unbelievers (1 Cor. 14:22). This was certainly the case on the day of Pentecost when the disciples began to speak in the languages of Jews from all over the known world (see Acts 2:1–13).

Paul claims for himself the gift of tongues-speaking, but apparently he exercised this gift in private or at least in a nondisturbing manner (1 Cor. 14:18–19).

The gift of tongues is to be exercised with restraint and in an orderly way. The regulations for its public use are simple and straightforward. Those who speak in unknown tongues are to pray that they may interpret (1 Cor. 14:13), or someone else is to interpret. Only two or three persons are to speak, with each having an interpretation of what he or she says, and each is to speak in turn. If these criteria are not met, they are to remain silent (1 Cor. 14:27–28). The gifts of speaking in tongues and their interpretation are to be Spirit-inspired.

The phenomenon of speaking in tongues described in the NT is not some psychological arousal of human emotions that results in strange sounds. This is a genuine work of the Holy Spirit.

While not listed in any of the passages that speak of spiritual gifts, unusual manifestations did occur to God's people, either for their own edification or for the upbuilding of others. The following are some of the more unusual spiritual phenemona.

1. A trance is an ecstatic state of mind that gives individuals a sense of detachment from their physical surroundings.

The Greek word for *trance* literally means "standing outside" or "being put outside" normal states of mind. Peter had been in prayer when he "fell into a trance," receiving the vision indicating that the Gentiles were to be included in the church (Acts 10:10). In his defense to the people in Jerusalem, the apostle Paul declared that after his conversion, he fell into a trance and Christ commanded him to leave the city and evangelize the Gentiles (Acts 22:17).

The trances of Peter and Paul involved their seeing and hearing senses. They saw and heard the Lord speaking to them. Both trances took place while they were in prayer, and in both cases the recipients were awake. Neither trance was self-induced; God revealed himself in both.

Paul's vision on the Damascus Road (Acts 9:3–9), the experience recorded in 2 Corinthians 12:2–4, and John's experience of being "in the Spirit" (Rev. 1:10) are other examples of revelatory trances in the Bible.

In the OT the word translated as *blindness* (Gen. 19:11; 2 Kings 6:18) suggests that God caused a trancelike state to fall on the men at Lot's house and on the Syrians. Trances are experiences through which God communicates his will and purpose to the human race.

2. Dreams involve a mental state where images, thoughts, and impressions pass through the mind of those who are sleeping. Dreams have had a prominent place in religious literature of ancient peoples. Dreams—especially those of kings and priests— were believed to convey messages from God (Gen. 31:10–13; Num. 12:6). In the Bible these dreams were sometimes prophetic in nature. Elihu said that God speaks through dreams (Job 33:14–15).

Dreams in the Bible

Jacob received confirmation of the Abrahamic covenant	Gen. 28:12	wisdom and a warning	12; 9:2–9
		Joseph (NT) was assured of Mary's purity	Matt. 1:20
Joseph dreamed of greatness	Gen. 37:5–10	Joseph (NT) was commanded to flee to Egypt	Matt. 2:13
Prisoners dreamed of the future	Gen. 40:5–19	Joseph (NT) was ordered to return to Palestine	Matt. 2:19–22
Pharaoh dreamed of the future	Gen. 41:1–31	The wise men were warned of Herod's evil intentions	Matt. 2:12
Solomon received both	1 Kings 3:5–		

Visions in the Bible

Jacob was instructed to go to Egypt	Gen. 46:2–3	Ananias was ordered to minister to Saul (Paul)	Acts 9:10
David was warned of judgment	1 Chron. 21:16	Cornelius was instructed to send for Peter	Acts 10:3–6
Isaiah saw God's holiness	Isa. 6:1–8	Peter was ordered to minister to Cornelius	Acts 10:10–16
Daniel saw the great Gentile powers	Dan. 7—8	Paul was requested to go to Macedonia	Acts 16:9
Daniel saw the glories of Christ	Dan. 10:5–9	Paul was comforted at Corinth	Acts 18:9
Daniel saw the rise and fall of Alexander the Great	Dan. 8	Paul was comforted at Jerusalem	Acts 23:11
Ezekiel saw the regathering of Israel	Ezek. 37	John the apostle received the book of Revelation	Rev. 1:10

Two special cycles of dreams in which expert interpretation was involved occurred in the OT: first, in the story of Joseph (Gen. 37:5–10ff.); second, in the life of Daniel (Dan. 2:14–15ff.). The dreams in both instances pertained to future events. God granted Joseph and Daniel the ability to interpret those dreams.

In the OT dreams were frequently associated with the prophets (Deut. 13:1–5; Jer. 23:25–32). But dreams, with their proposed prophecies, were not accepted uncritically. Jeremiah, especially, denounced false prophets who spoke with lies.

In the NT, Joseph learned of the forthcoming birth of Jesus in a dream (Matt. 1:20). God also spoke through dreams to protect the infant Jesus (Matt. 2:13–14).

Nazirite. "Separated," "consecrated." An individual who took a vow to separate from certain worldly things and to consecrate himself to God (Num. 6:1–8). Among the Hebrew people any male could take this vow.

Nazirites did not live as hermits; they did follow certain regulations for a specified period of time. While no number of days for the vow is given, Jewish tradition prescribed 30 days or a double period of 60 days or even triple time of 90 to 100 days.

Once a man took this vow, he abstained from wine and other intoxicating drinks. This prohibition was so strict that it included grapes, grape juice, and raisins. He did not cut his hair or shave his beard (see Num. 6:5). The long hair was to serve as a visible sign of the Nazirite's consecration to the Lord (Num. 6:7). A Nazirite also refused to touch or go near a dead body because this would make him ceremonially unclean. A Nazirite could not even help to bury his own relatives.

If a person accidentally broke his Nazirite vow, he had to undergo a ceremony of restoration for cleansing (Num. 6:9–12). He shaved his head and brought two turtle-doves or two pigeons to the priest for offerings, and the priest made atonement for him. In addition, a Nazirite had to present a lamb for a trespass offering.

When the specified period of time was completed, the Nazirite appeared before the priest for the ceremony of release (Num. 6:13–21). After offering a male lamb for a burnt offering, he would then offer a ewe lamb for a sin offering. This was followed by a ram to be used as the peace offering. Next came the usual items for peace offerings (Num. 6:15). The prescribed sacrifices were completed with a meat offering and a drink offering. When the person cut off his hair and burned it on the altar, he was fully released from the vow.

Samson was a Nazirite (Judg. 13:7; 16:17). His parents were told by an angel before his birth that he would "be a Nazirite to God from the womb to the day of his death" (Judg. 13:7).

While Samuel is not specifically called a Nazirite, 1 Samuel 1:11, 28 hints that he probably was. His mother, Hannah, made a vow before his birth, "No razor shall come upon his head" (1 Sam. 1:11). John the Baptist's refusal to drink wine (Matt. 11:18–19) is an indication that he was a Nazirite. His manner of living also indicates this probability (Matt. 3:1–4; Luke 1:15).

The presence of many Nazirites was considered a sign of God's blessings on Israel. There were many Nazirites during the time of the prophet Amos. Amos strongly condemned the people for tempting the Nazirites to break their vows by offering them wine to drink (Amos 2:11–12).

Pharisees. "Separated." Pharisees were a Jewish sect noted for their strict keeping of the written and oral law and their formal show of piety. They were especially hostile to Jesus.

Originally the Pharisees were the spiritual descendants of zealous Jews who observed the law despite the Greek tyranny in the Maccabean wars. They made themselves separate and holy from the unclean pagan world, especially the Gentile influence of Greece and Rome, and dedicated their lives to studying and teaching the law. Pharisees observed the rules of ritual washing, diet, and tithing with scrupulous care and rigidly observed the Sabbath.

Presbyter.   (See *Elder*.)

Presbytery.   In the Bible this word referred to an assembly of elders in one of the early Christian churches (1 Tim. 4:14, KJV). The same Greek noun *(presbuterion)* is also used twice to refer to the Jewish Sanhedrin (Luke 22:66; Acts 22:5).

Priest.   Priests were the official ministers or worship leaders in Israel. They represented the people before God and conducted various rituals to atone for their sins. Before the days of the Law, this function was carried out by the father of a family (Job 1:5) or the head of a tribe. With God's appointment of Aaron as the first high priest, the priesthood was formally established. Aaron's descendants became the priestly line. They carried out the important duties from generation to generation as a special class devoted to God's service.

The Bible often speaks of priests and Levites as if these two offices were the same (e.g., 1 Chron. 23:2; 24:6, 31). They were closely related in that both priests and Levites sprang from a common ancestor—Levi, the son of Jacob. Yet the priests—a specific branch of Levites descended

Priests in the Old Testament

Aaron	Older brother of Moses, and Israel's first high priest	Exod. 28; 39
Nadab and Abihu	Wicked sons of Aaron, who were slain by the Lord for offering profane fire	Lev. 10:1–2
Eleazar and Ithamar	Godly sons of Aaron; Eleazar, Israel's second high priest	Lev. 10:6; Num. 20:26
Phinehas	Son of Eleazar, Israel's third high priest	Num. 25:7
Eli	Descendant of Ithamar, who raised Samuel in the tabernacle	1 Sam. 1—4
Hophni and Phinehas	Godless sons of Eli who were slain by the Lord	1 Sam. 2:12–36; 4:11
Ahimelech	Head of a priestly compound at Nob, later killed by Saul for befriending David	1 Sam. 21—22
Abiathar	One of Ahimelech's sons who escaped the bloodbath at Nob	1 Sam. 22:20–23
Zadok	High priest in the days of David and Solomon	2 Sam. 15; 1 Kings 1
Elishama and Jehoram	Teaching priests in the days of Jehoshaphat	2 Chron. 17:7–9
Amariah	High priest in the days of Jehoshaphat	2 Chron. 19:11
Jahaziel	Priest who assured Jehoshaphat he would be delivered from a terrible enemy threat	2 Chron. 20:14–17
Jehoiada	High priest who saved young Joash from the purge of Queen Athaliah	2 Kings 11—12
Amaziah	Ungodly priest of Bethel who confronted the prophet Amos	Amos 7:10–11
Azariah	High priest who confronted King Uzziah when the ruler foolishly attempted to assume the work of a priest	2 Chron. 26:16–20
Urijah	Compromising priest who built a foreign altar for wicked King Ahaz	2 Kings 16:10–16
Hilkiah	High priest who ministered in the days of King Josiah	2 Kings 22—23
Pashhur	False priest who persecuted the prophet Jeremiah	Jer. 20:1–6

Priests in the Old Testament—*continued*

Joshua	Judah's first high priest after the Babylonian captivity	Hag. 1:1; Zech. 3
Ezra	Great scribe, teacher, and priest during the rebuilding of Jerusalem's walls	Ezra 7:11; Neh. 8
Eliashib	High priest during the days of Nehemiah	Neh. 3:1; 13:4–5
Shelemiah	Priest who was in charge of the administration of storehouses in the time of Nehemiah	Neh. 13:13

Priests in the New Testament

Zacharias	Father of John the Baptist	Luke 1:5–23; 59–64
Annas	The wicked former high priest during the time of Jesus	John 18:13; Acts 4:6
Caiaphas	Son-in-law of Annas and a wicked high priest	Matt. 26:3; Luke 3:2; John 11:47–53; 18:13–14
Ananias	President of the Sanhedrin when Paul was brought before it	Acts 23:2; 24:1
Sceva	False Jewish priest living in Ephesus who unsuccessfully tried to mimic Paul's ministry	Acts 19:14

through Aaron—and Levites—all descendants of Levi in general—performed different duties.

Priests officiated at worship by presenting various offerings on behalf of the nation and in leading the people to confess their sins. The Levites assisted the priests. They took care of the tabernacle (later the temple) and performed menial tasks such as providing music, serving as doorkeepers, and preparing sacrifices for offering by the priests.

As long as the king and the people of Israel remained loyal to God, the priests were highly respected and exercised much influence. The priests eventually sank to immorality and departed from God by worshiping idols along with the rest of the people (Ezek. 22:26).

The prophet Malachi pointed to the neglect and corruption of the priests, saying this was the reason the people neglected the offerings and festivals of the temple—they had lost their respect for the persons who held the office and finally for the office itself (see Mal. 1:6; 2:7–9).

By the NT era, the position of priests had changed considerably. The temple functions were taken over by the "chief priests" while ordinary priests were overshadowed by scribes and Pharisees—two special groups that arose to present the Law and interpret its meaning for the people. In spite of their diminished role, Jesus respected the office and called upon the priests to witness his healing of lepers in keeping with the Law (Mark 1:44; Luke 17:12–14). But the priests themselves were some of the most zealous opponents of Jesus. As leaders of the Sanhedrin (the Jewish high court) they bore much of the responsibility for his crucifixion. They also led the opposition to the apostles and the early church.

Priest, High. This referred to the chief priest of the Hebrew people, especially of the ancient Jewish Levitical priesthood traditionally traced from Aaron. *Head priest, the great one from his brothers,* and *ruler of the house of God*—these are literal translations of references to this officer (Lev. 21:10; 2 Chron. 19:11).

The high priest was the supreme head of his people. Aaron held this position above his sons that was to continue in the first-born of successive holders of the office. The high priest was distinguished from fellow priests by the clothes he wore, the duties he performed, and the particular requirements placed upon him as spiritual head of God's people.

Character and conduct. Although the office of high priest was hereditary, its holder had to be without physical defect as well as holy in conduct (Lev. 21:6–8). He must not show grief for the dead—even his father or mother—by removing his headdress or letting his hair go unkempt.

He must not tear his clothes in grief or go near a dead body. Leaving his duties unperformed because of a death would "profane the sanctuary" (Lev. 21:12). He could marry only a "virgin of his own people" (Lev. 21:14), or a believer in God. She could not be a widow, a divorcee, or an impure woman. He must not, by a bad marriage, spoil his own holiness or endanger the holiness of his son who would succeed him.

Consecration. A high priest was consecrated (installed in office) by an elaborate seven-day service at the tabernacle or temple (see Exod. 29 and Lev. 8). He was cleansed by bathing, then dressed in the garments and symbols he must wear in his ministry, and anointed with special oil. Sacrifices of sin offering, burnt offering, and consecration offering were made for him. He was anointed again with oil and blood from the sacrifice. "Sanctified" (i.e., set apart) to serve as a priest and "consecrated" to offer sacrifice (Exod. 28:41; 29:9), he became "the saint [holy one] of the LORD" (Ps. 106:16).

Clothing. The high priest's special dress represented his function as mediator between God and the people. Over the trousers, coat, girdle, and cap, worn by all priests, the high priest wore an ephod, a two-piece apron reaching to his hips, made of royal colors (blue, purple, and scarlet) and sewed with gold thread. By two onyx stones bearing the names of the 12 tribes of

Israel fastened to the shoulders of the ephod, he brought the whole nation before God in all his priestly acts (Exod. 28:5–14).

The breastplate of judgment, made of the same material, was attached to the front of the ephod (Exod. 28:15–30). On its front were 12 precious stones engraved with the names of the 12 tribes. In its pocket, directly over his heart, were the Urim and Thummim (Exod. 28:30), the medium through which God could communicate his will. The high priest was Israel's advocate before God and God's spokesman to them.

Over the breastplate he wore the blue robe of the ephod (Exod. 28:31). Around its hem were pomegranates, pointing to the divine law as sweet and delicious spiritual food (Deut. 8:3), and bells that would ring as he went "into the holy place before the LORD . . . that he may not die" (Exod. 28:35). The bells announced God's gracious salvation, for he had accepted the people in the person of their advocate, the high priest.

On his forehead the high priest wore the holy crown of gold engraved with the words, "HOLINESS TO THE LORD" (Exod. 28:36–37). He was represented as bearing "the iniquity of the holy things" (Exod. 28:38) that Israel offered to God. He was the crowned mediator, making atonement for the nation so God might accept their gifts and show them favor.

All these garments stood for the "glory and beauty" (Exod. 28:40) that God placed upon his priests, sanctifying them to minister in his name (Exod. 28:3).

Particular services. The high priest held a leadership position in seeing that all responsibilities of the priests were carried out (2 Chron. 19:11). He could participate in all priestly ministry, but certain functions were given only to him. As he alone wore the Urim and the Thummim, Israel came to him to learn the will of God (Deut. 33:8). Joshua went to ask counsel of Eleazar regarding the movements of the army in the conquest of the land of Canaan (Num. 27:21).

The high priest had to offer a sin offering for his own sins and the sins of the whole congregation (Lev. 4:3–21). At the death of the high priest, freedom was granted to all who were confined to the cities of refuge for accidentally causing the death of another person (Num. 35:28).

The most important responsibility of the high priest was to conduct the service on the Day of Atonement, the tenth day of the seventh month each year. On this day he alone entered the Holy Place inside the veil before God. Having made sacrifice for himself and for the people, he brought the blood into the Holy of Holies and sprinkled it on the mercy seat, "God's throne." This he did to make atonement for himself and the people for all their sins committed during the year (Exod. 30:10; Lev. 16). It is with this particular service that the ministry of Jesus as High Priest is compared (Heb. 9:1–28).

Historical development.

Eleazar succeeded Aaron (Num. 20:28) and served at Shiloh where the tabernacle was erected after the conquest of Canaan by the Israelites (Josh. 18:1). He was followed by his son Phinehas (Num. 25:11–12; Josh. 24:33). Eli, a descendant of Ithamar, the younger brother of Eleazar, held the office by the Lord's choice (1 Sam. 2:28) at the end of the period of the judges, the change being unexplained.

Because of the sins of Eli's sons, Samuel appears to have succeeded Eli (1 Sam. 2:12–36; 7:5, 9–10, 17), although he is not called a high priest and did not regularly function at the tabernacle. Ahimelech apparently cared for the tabernacle at Nob after the destruction of Shiloh (1 Sam. 21—22). Abiathar, a descendant of Eli, escaped Saul's slaughter of the priests at Nob (1 Sam. 22:19–21); he took the ephod with him and served with David (1 Sam. 23:9; 30:7).

David appointed Zadok, a descendant of Eleazar, to serve at the tabernacle at Gibeon (1 Chron. 16:39) at the same time that he took the ark to Jerusalem. Zadok crowned Solomon (1 Kings 1:39) and was appointed by him as high priest in the place of Ahimelech when the latter was banished for supporting Adonijah's claim to the throne (1 Kings 2:26–27, 35). This made him the first high priest to minister in the temple. His line of high priests served there until the Babylonian captivity (1 Chron. 6:3–15).

Mutual support and encouragement characterized the Davidic kings and high priests. David organized 24 groups of priests to serve by turn at the temple, supervised by both Zadok and Abiathar (1 Chron. 24:6, 31). Solomon confirmed the appointments of his father (2 Chron. 8:14–15). Jehoshaphat organized priests, Levites, and chief men of Israel under the leadership of the high priest to go through the land teaching the people the Law, encouraging them to faithful, reverent service (see 2 Chron. 19). The high priest Jehoiada protected Joash from Athaliah's murder of the king's sons and organized his coronation and the destruction of Athaliah (2 Chron. 22:10—23:21).

Kings Hezekiah and Josiah assisted the high priests in reform and restoration of the temple and its worship after its desecration by Ahaz and Manasseh (2 Chron. 30—31; 34—35). Ezekiel announced that the sons of Zadok would be priests in the new temple (Ezek. 44:15–16) because they had not rejected God when Israel went astray (1 Kings 12:31; 2 Chron. 11:13–15; 13:9).

After the captivity, Joshua the high priest, of the sons of Zadok (Hag. 1:1), and Zerubbabel of the house of David—the governor appointed by Cyrus—led the rebuilding of the temple. As no further governors were appointed, the high priest became sole political and religious leader. Great care was taken by Ezra and Nehemiah to restore the Mosaic order in purity, but interference by unprincipled civil rulers took a sad toll on the purity and influence of the high priest. The Syrian,

Antiochus IV, removed the Zadokite high priest and replaced him with a man from a nonpriestly family.

In the revolt that followed and the consequent independence, the Hasmoneans, a family of ordinary priests, took political control. In 153 B.C. one of them, Jonathan, assumed the high priest's office and later the royal title. When Herod came to power under Rome in 37 B.C., he arbitrarily deposed and appointed high priests as he pleased, and he did away with anointing them.

During this period until the destruction of the temple in Jerusalem in A.D. 70, five prominent families of high priests held power. Annas was the leader of one of these. His son-in-law Caiaphas, five of his sons, and a grandson held the office. Although Annas had been replaced by Caiaphas before the time of Jesus' ministry, his influence continued (Luke 3:2; John 18:13, 24).

New Testament times. In the NT as in the OT, the "high priest [was] appointed to offer both gifts and sacrifices" (Heb. 8:3), and he was referred to as "God's high priest" and "ruler of [the] people" (Acts 23:4–5). He was the president of the Sanhedrin, the highest ruling body of the Jews (Matt. 26:3). But the office ceased to be hereditary, and it was subject to the whim of the political power, Rome. The high priest's religious influence was weakened by the rising power of the scribes and Pharisees who became known for their materialism and thirst for power.

Above all, the high priest and his fellow priests were threatened by the presence of Jesus because they had changed the temple from a "house of prayer for all nations" (Mark 11:17) to a place of merchandise, a "den of thieves" (Matt. 21:12–13; Luke 19:45–48; John 2:14–16).

The "chief priests" were the holders of the priestly offices of higher rank in the temple and, along with the high priest, were leaders in the Sanhedrin. That they had administrative authority is indicated by their agreement with Judas concerning his betrayal of Jesus (Matt. 27:6; Luke 22:4–6). The chief priests led the opposition to Jesus at his trial (Mark 15:3, 11; Luke 23:23). They were equally prominent in their opposition to the apostles and the church (Acts 4:6; 9:14, 21). Along with the council, the high priest and chief priests condemned Jesus to death (Matt. 26:65–66), mocked him as he was dying (Matt. 27:41), and sealed his grave (cf. Matt. 26—27).

Jesus as High Priest. The NT's most important references to the high priest are found in the book of Hebrews, and they refer to Jesus, who qualified himself to be a merciful and faithful High Priest by becoming a man of the seed of Abraham (2:11–18).

> He is sympathetic with our weaknesses (4:15).
> He did not assume the office of High Priest for glory (5:5), but was called by God to the office.
> He was not of the order of Aaron, but of Melchizedek (5:10).
> He had no need, as the sons of Aaron, to offer sacrifices for his own sins and then for the sins of the people.
> He had no sin (7:26–28).
> He offered his own blood (9:12) once for all (9:26; 10:10, 12).
> He is the eternal High Priest because he lives forever (7:24).
> He performs his ministry in heaven itself (4:14; 9:11), seated at the right hand of God (10:12).
> He has achieved his goal—the sanctification of his people.

We may therefore come directly into the presence of God through the "one Mediator between God and men, the Man Christ Jesus" (1 Tim. 2:5).

Prince. The common elements in the many different words translated as *prince* in the Bible are leadership and authority. The word often denotes royalty, but it just as frequently describes leadership in general. Both Abraham (Gen. 23:6) and Solomon (1 Kings 11:34, KJV) were called princes. Tribal leaders of early Israel were often designated as princes. Jesus was referred to by the prophet Isaiah as the Prince of Peace (Isa. 9:6).

In the NT, Jesus is called the Prince (Author, RSV) of life (Acts 3:15) and a Prince (Leader, RSV) and Savior (Acts 5:31).

Publican.   "Tax gatherers." Outcast Jews who worked for the hated Romans and unjustly demanded more than their due in taxes, in the Bible publicans are mentioned along with sinners and harlots. Jesus befriended publicans and was criticized for visiting and eating with them. Levi (Matthew), a tax collector, became one of Jesus' 12 disciples. Jesus visited the home of Zacchaeus, a chief publican. In one of his parables, Jesus spoke compassionately of the publican (see Luke 18:10–14).

Rabbi.   "Teacher" or "master." Title of respect among Jews. The rabbis taught the meaning of the Law. So far as we know, Jesus was not a trained scholar of the Law, but his teaching was so powerful that many called him by that respectful title.

Ruler of the synagogue.   Jewish elder, leader, or president of a synagogue. As an administrator, he was charged with supervision of all matters pertaining to the synagogue. He was not a dictator over the congregation. He was elected by the board of elders to oversee the worship services

A synagogue at Masada. The synagogue was a place of worship, instruction, teaching of Scripture, and prayer for the Jewish people (Acts 13:13–15).   PHOTO BY GUSTAV JEENINGA

and the upkeep of the building. He chose the men to read the Scriptures, to offer prayer, and to preach or explain the Scripture for each meeting.

If discipline was called for, the ruler of the synagogue could reprimand or excommunicate a member (John 9:22; 16:2), or even order that a scourging or a whipping be carried out (Matt. 10:17; Mark 13:9). Rulers of the synagogue mentioned by name in the NT are Jairus (Mark 5:22; Luke 8:41), Crispus (Acts 18:8), and Sosthenes (Acts 18:17).

Sadducees.   Members of a Jewish faction that opposed Jesus during his ministry. The Sadducees came from the leading families of the nation—the priests, merchants, and aristocrats. The high priests and the most powerful members of the priesthood were mainly Sadducees (Acts 5:17).

Some think the name came from Zadok, high priest in the days of David (2 Sam. 15:24) and Solomon (1 Kings 1:34–35). Many of the wealthy laypeople were also Sadducees—which may be one reason they gave the impression of wanting to preserve things as they were. They enjoyed privileged positions in society and got along well under Roman rule. Any movement that upset order was bound to appear dangerous to them.

They rejected the "tradition of the elders"—the body of oral and written commentary that interpreted the law of Moses. This placed them in direct conflict with another group, the Pharisees, who made the traditions surrounding the Law almost as important as the Law itself. The Sadducees insisted that only the laws written in the law of Moses—the first five books of the OT—were binding.

The Sadducees did not believe in the resurrection of the dead or the immortality of the soul since these doctrines were not mentioned in the law of Moses. They did not believe in rewards or punishments after death. They did not believe in angels or spirits (Acts 23:8). However, they believed in free will—people were responsible for their own prosperity and misfortune. They interpreted the Law literally and tended to support strict justice as opposed to mercy toward the offender.

The NT rarely refers to the Sadducees. They opposed the early church (Acts 4:1–3; 5:17–18) more than the Pharisees did (Acts 5:34–39; 15:5; 23:6–9).

Sanhedrin. "Council" or "assembly." In Roman times, the Sanhedrin was the highest governing Jewish body in the province of Judea. The council, or Sanhedrin, was composed of high priests, elders, and scribes, a total number of 71. The word *Sanhedrin* never appears in the Bible; the writers use the word *council*. This council had the highest authority in legal, governmental, and religious matters. It could exercise these powers as long as they did not infringe on Roman authority. Normally Rome confirmed and carried out death sentences passed by the Sanhedrin.

The Sanhedrin grew out of the council of advisers for the high priest when the Jewish people lived under the dominion of the Persian and Greek empires. Initially, the council was made up of the leading priests and the most distinguished aristocrats among the people. Later, as the influence of the scribes grew, they were also given positions on the Sanhedrin. In this way, the Sanhedrin came to include Sadducees—or "chief priests" and "elders"—and Pharisees and scribes.

The Sadducees and Pharisees were the two main groups within Judaism, and the Sanhedrin usually tried to maintain a balance of power between them. Acts 23:1ff. shows that the Sanhedrin would sometimes divide along party lines. As he stood before them, Paul shrewdly pitted the Pharisees against the Sadducees to his advantage.

After A.D. 6 the official authority of the Sanhedrin extended only to the province of Judea. Still, Jews living elsewhere respected the Sanhedrin highly and would often be guided by its decisions.

Most references in the NT appear in connection with the trial of Jesus (e.g., Matt. 26:59; Mark 14:55). The other references are in connection with the early church (as in Acts 5:21ff.). The Sanhedrin became the focus of Jewish opposition to early Christianity (Acts 4:15; 6:12; 22:30; 23:1; 24:20).

Scribe. Originally scribes were writers attached to the temple and court who kept the official records and copied documents. After the exile, Ezra taught sacred Scriptures to the returning Jews.

In NT times the scribes were sometimes Pharisees and sometimes priests. They constantly opposed Jesus.

Zealots. In some Bible translations this title applied to Simon, the disciple of Jesus (see Luke 6:15). The Zealots were a fanatical nationalistic party in Palestine who wanted to win independence from the Romans by armed rebellion.

Political and Religious Groups in Bible Times

Diaspora	The Jews scattered abroad because of the Assyrian and Babylonian captivities	Acts 2:5, 9–11
Epicureans	Adherents of a hedonistic philosophy developed by Epicurus	Acts 17:18
Galileans	Jewish followers of a rebel named Judas of Galilee	Luke 13:1
Hellenists	Greek-speaking Jews	Acts 6:1
Herodians	A political dynasty from the family Herod, deriving authority from the Roman government	Mark 3:6; 8:15; 12:13–17
Levites	The descendants of Levi, who had charge of the temple	Luke 10:32; John 1:19
Libertines	A group of ex-slaves who apparently had their own synagogue in Jerusalem	Acts 6:9, KJV

Political and Religious Groups in Bible Times—*continued*

Nazirites	Men taking special religious vows	Num. 6; Judg. 13:3–7; Luke 1:15
Pharisees	The separatists, legalists, and guardians of both the written and the oral law	Matt. 12:1–2; 23
Proselytes	Gentile converts to Judaism	Matt. 23:15; Acts 2:10; 13:43
Publicans	The state-appointed, widely disliked tax collectors of Roman revenue	Matt. 9:9; Luke 3:12–13; 19:8
Sadducees	The aristocrats among the Jews who denied belief in angels and the afterlife and believed only in the Torah	Mark 12:18; Luke 20:27
Samaritans	The hated half-Jew, half-gentile people living between the provinces of Judea and Galilee	Matt. 10:5; Luke 10:33; 17:16; John 4:9; 8:48
Sanhedrin	The religious and legal Jewish supreme court	Matt. 26:65–66; 27:1–2
Scribes or Lawyers	The students, interpreters, and teachers of the OT Law	Matt. 16:21; 21:15; 23:2; 26:3
Stoics	A group founded by the philosopher Zeno, who believed life's goal was to rise above all things and to show no emotion in either pain or pleasure	Acts 17:18
Zealots	A group of Jewish patriots, fanatical defenders of theocracy and haters of the Romans	Luke 6:15; Acts 1:13

Forms of Church Government

At first, church organization and government in the NT were flexible to meet changing needs. As the church became better established, it gave attention to the right structures and procedures that would help it accomplish its mission. In the earliest days, the apostles directed the work. Then seven men were chosen to assist with members' needs (Acts 6). Later, evangelists, elders, bishops, and deacons emerged.

No single pattern of government in the early church can be discovered by reading the NT. Numerous forms of church government are in use today to provide order and structure for the work of churches.

Present expressions of church government may be classified into three major forms: congregational, presbyterian, and episcopal.

Congregational

The congregational system of church government recognizes no authority having jurisdiction over more than a single local congregation. This is fairly close to a democratic government in which all members have an equal voice.

Congregational churches include Baptists and those with the word *congregation* in their names. This also includes the Society of Friends (Quakers).

The Quakers reject any type of church ruler or official and almost every form of physical organization. For the Friends, everything depends on the inner light, which any believer has the right and power to receive directly from God. They have no specific rules for receiving members. Decisions are arrived at by mutual agreement among the believers.

Presbyterian

The presbyterian form of church is governed by a board of presbyters (from the Greek word for *elders*). These elders, elected by the congregation, make most of the decisions regarding the operation of the church. They are part of a series of graded courts: *Presbyteries* that rule over local congregations in a geographic area; *Synods* that rule over Presbyteries in a geographic area; and the *General Assembly* that decides on issues affecting the entire church. This is a representative government.

Episcopal

The episcopal form of church government regards bishops as a distinct office (*episcopal* is from a Greek word that means *bishop* or *overseer*) higher than pastors or elders. Each bishop has jurisdiction over a number of congregations and their officers. This form of government is often called a *rule by bishops*.

Aside from the churches with the word *episcopal* in their name, two others fall into this third category: the Roman Catholic church and national church governments.

Roman Catholics view the church as the continuing visible presence of Christ in the world. Christ maintains his life on earth through the church. The clergy form a hierarchy that governs the church with the pope as the highest authority. The pope is the bishop of Rome, and Roman Catholics believe that the papal office has been passed from pope to pope. To Roman Catholics, this authority originated in Christ's declaration of Peter as the first pope. (See Matt. 16:18.)

The Church of England is an episcopal system with the head of state also the head of the church. In other countries, the church itself generally falls under either episcopal or presbyterian forms.

Churches, Denominations, Fellowships, and Conventions

Jesus commanded his disciples to go throughout the entire world and to preach the good news, beginning in Jerusalem. (See Acts 1:8.) Before they left their home base of Jerusalem, differences arose. (See Acts 6.) Greek-speaking widows apparently felt neglected when the Christians met together and distributed food. Peter, the leader from the beginning, asked the followers of Jesus to select seven men of faith and good character to oversee this responsibility. This time they resolved the problem amicably.

As the message of God's love spread, so did the problems. The character of the gospel changed, so that it was no longer the Jewish religion with the added dimension of faith in Jesus as the Messiah. Believers no longer had to go through Jewish rituals and follow specific laws. A council of the leaders in Jerusalem made the decision official (see Acts 15). Preceding the decision and even following, frequent dissension arose between Christians. Paul's writings tell us of the difficulties and differences in the churches he founded.

With an understanding of the lack of full unity at the beginning, we can see how denominations began. Here are two examples.

First, for the first three centuries, sincere Christians argued over the nature of Jesus Christ. Was he just a man with an inspired message? Was he a God who only appeared to be human? Until the first ecumenical council at Nicea in A.D. 325, the churches of Jesus Christ had no official position.

Second, when emperor Constantine moved his capital from Rome to Constantinople (now Istanbul) in 330, he planted the first seeds for the most important split of the church. Until then, the churches of the east and the west had formed one church. In the east, four patriarchs were of equal status with the pope of Rome.

The eastern church was Greek and the west was Latin. After Constantine moved and the Goths invaded Rome, the church of the west appealed to the Franks instead of Constantinople. In gratitude for his aid, the pope of Rome crowned Charles the Great as emperor in 800 and the Roman church became coterminus with the Holy Roman Empire.

Conflict deepened between the heads of the eastern and western church. The split came when the west added the word *filioque* to the Nicene Creed. The eastern church held that the Holy Spirit proceeded directly from the Father; the western church contended that the Holy Spirit proceeded from the Father and the Son—*filioque*. In 1054 the pope excommunicated the eastern patriarch and he, in turn, excommunicated the western pope. This split meant the formation of two distinct churches.

While the western church formed around one pope, the eastern church continued with four patriarchs. No one patriarch is responsible to another, yet all are within the jurisdiction of an ecumenical council of all the churches in communion with the patriarch of Constantinople, who holds the title *Ecumenical Patriarch*.

Today Christendom remains divided into three major sections: Roman Catholic, Eastern Orthodox (often called Greek Orthodox), and Protestant—all groups that do not fit under the first two.

In the United States and Europe our interest has remained primarily with the west—but again, even the western church was never united. All through the centuries individuals arose who differed, cited abuses, or spoke of wrong emphases.

Before Martin Luther's break with the church in 1517, other voices had been protesting for centuries—many of them dying for what they believed. Individuals like John Wycliffe (1320–1384), John Huss (1369–1415), and Savonarola (1452–1498) stand out. The infamous Spanish Inquisition and the Catholic counter-reformation came into being to silence dissenting voices.

At the end of the twentieth century, we sometimes wonder about the plethora of denominations. Yet as long as the church remains on earth and as long as individuals have the right to speak their consciences, we will never have a united church on earth.

Largest U.S. Denominations

The following denominations (or conferences) in the United States each claim a membership exceeding one million. (Membership figures are from 1986.)

African Methodist Episcopal Zion Church	1,202,229	Episcopal Church	2,775,424
American Baptist Churches in the U.S.A.	1,620,653	Greek Orthodox Archdiocese of North and South America	1,950,000
American Lutheran Church	2,339,946	Lutheran Church in America	2,910,281
Assemblies of God	2,036,453	Lutheran Church—Missouri Synod	2,626,133
Baptist Bible Fellowship, International	1,400,900	National Baptist Convention of America	2,668,799
Christian Church (Disciples of Christ)	1,132,510	National Baptist Convention, U.S.A., Inc.	5,500,000
Christian Churches and Churches of Christ	1,043,642	Presbyterian Church (U.S.A.)	3,092,151
Church of God in Christ	3,709,661	Roman Catholic Church	52,286,043
Church of Jesus Christ of Latter-day Saints	3,602,000	Southern Baptist Convention	14,341,821
Churches of Christ	1,600,500	United Church of Christ	1,696,107
		United Methodist Church	9,291,136

Adventist. Adventist Christians believe that the second advent of Jesus Christ is the only hope of the world. Their background stems from the leadership of William Miller (1782–1849) who expected the return of Jesus Christ in 1844. When this event did not take place, most followers left. Those who remained formally organized into smaller bodies. They are conservative and evangelical groups.

Major divisions and their distinctiveness are (1) Advent Christian Church holds to "conditional immortality" and the extinction of the wicked after Christ's return; and (2) Seventh-day Adventists worship on Saturday.

African Methodist Episcopal Zion Church. (See *Methodist*.)

American Baptist Churches in the U.S.A. (See *Baptist*.)

American Lutheran Church. (See *Lutheran*.)

Assemblies of God. (See *Pentecostal*.)

Baptist Churches. In the United States, Baptists constitute twenty-seven groupings and their total membership is approximately 30 million. Baptist churches are completely independent, yet bound together by an amazing common allegiance to principles and doctrines. They claim no founder but Christ, and often claim they have been preaching since the days of John the Baptist.

When the Reformation began in the sixteenth century, scattered Baptist groups in Europe advocated doctrines that eventually united them. As the left wing of the Reformation, they were called *Anabaptists* ("to baptize again") because they immersed those who had been baptized in infancy. They held to a literal application of the Bible, were communal and pacifistic, and opposed capital punishment, taking oaths in court, and the holding of public office. They insisted upon the complete separation of church and state. Undergoing persecution for their then-radical views, they spread all over Europe.

In Holland a group of Mennonites, followers of the former Anabaptist leader Menno Simons, were teaching Anabaptist principles and took in a group of British refugees undergoing persecution under James I. One of their leaders, John Smyth, completely accepted the teaching of the Mennonites. Smyth and his followers were rebaptized, became Anabaptists, and organized the first English Baptist Church in 1609. However, they remained English and refused to take on all the accoutrements of the Mennonites.

As persecution waned, the English Baptists went back across the channel and began a Baptist church in London. Although they spread, they divided again, this time over the theology of the Atonement. The General Baptist churches held that Jesus Christ died for everyone, while others held to the teachings of the Particular Baptist Church—following the teachings of John Calvin—that salvation was only for those predestined by God. The first Particular (British) Baptist Church had its beginning in 1638. A third group, Immersion Baptists, broke away and in 1644 produced a confession of faith that is still in use by many. For the first time, these Christians were popularly known as Baptists.

In 1631 Roger Williams went to America and, although he was not a Baptist, established a Baptist Church at Providence, Rhode Island. In 1814 Baptists organized the General Missionary Convention of the Baptist Denomination in the United States of America for Foreign Missions. This step marked the first real denominational consciousness and united the Baptists. They formed a society for publication as well as for missions and education.

In 1845 came the major split. Southerners seceded from the union and formed their own Southern Baptist Convention to carry on the work of their churches. The others formed the Northern Baptist Convention (later American). They have remained separate.

Baptists generally agree upon the Bible as inspired, the supremacy of Jesus Christ, inherent freedom of individuals to approach God for themselves, salvation by faith through God's grace, two sacraments, or as they prefer to say, ordinances (the Lord's Supper and baptism by immersion), the independence of the local church, the church as a group of regenerated believers, complete separation of church and state, the immortality of the soul, and the ultimate triumph of God's kingdom.

Because Baptists have had freedom of expression in the pulpit and pew, they are quite democratic. This means that liberal and conservative doctrines can be preached freely because each church is autonomous. Local churches license and ordain candidates for the ministry.

The Southern Baptist Convention is the largest, followed by the American Baptist Churches in the U.S.A. Blacks predominate in three large Baptist bodies: the National Baptist Convention of America, the National Baptist Convention U.S.A., Inc., and the Progressive National Baptist Convention, Inc. (500,000 members).

Other groups of Baptists include: Baptist General Conference (approximately 130,000 members); Conservative Baptist Association of America (225,000); General Association of Regular Baptist Churches (300,000); the General Association of General Baptists (75,000); and the North American Baptist General Conference (43,000).

The Baptist World Alliance, a voluntary association of Baptist bodies throughout the world, fosters communication among its members, provides a forum for discussion of doctrine and practice, and organizes the Baptist World Congress meetings (usually held every five years).

American Baptist Churches in the U.S.A.

Originally known as the Northern Baptist Convention, this group changed its name to the American Baptist Convention in 1950 and finally to its present name in 1972.

Most Christians consider this fellowship to be less conservative than the Southern Baptists. American Baptists have open communion (open to all Christians) and have involved themselves in the Protestant trend toward ecumenicity. They are members of the National Council of Churches of Christ in the U.S.A.

Bible Baptist Fellowship, International.

These churches are loosely affiliated with one another in the preaching and teaching of ultraconservative Baptist doctrine. They are biblical literalists, denouncing all modernism and modernistic practices. They recognize only baptism by immersion, and practice closed communion (the Lord's Supper available only to members). They stand adamantly opposed to dancing, drinking, smoking, movies, gambling, and sexual promiscuity.

National Baptist Convention of America.

The year 1773 marks the beginning of the first black Baptist church in America, organized near Augusta, Georgia.

As early as 1700, many slaveholders in the south provided religious instruction and worship. Slaves usually sat in the gallery of the white churches and identified with the faith of their owners. Occasionally a few slaves received their freedom to devote full time to religious work among the slaves.

Following the rebellion led by Nat Turner in 1831, for several years in some sections of the south, slaves could not become Christians or build places to worship.

The first black Baptist association was Providence Baptist Association of Ohio, formed in 1836. An attempt towards a national organization came about in 1880 through the creation of the Foreign Mission Baptist Convention at Montgomery, Alabama. In 1886, blacks formed the American National Baptist Convention in St. Louis. In 1895 in Atlanta, they merged with two other groups and became the National Baptist Convention of America.

Theologically, they hold similar views as most Baptists, although they tend to be a little more Calvinistic.

National Baptist Convention of the U.S.A., Inc.

This group was originally part of the National Baptist Convention of America, until a disruption arose over two major issues: adopting a charter and ownership of a publishing house. Rejecting the charter, the dissidents formed the National Baptist Convention of the U.S.A., Inc. (incorporated under the laws of the District of Columbia). Consequently, members of the two groups often refer to themselves as either unincorporated or incorporated.

Southern Baptist Convention. Southern Baptists tend to hold to a more conservative interpretation of theology than the American Baptists, yet their tenets remain the same. Although they have long moved out of the southern states, their name has not changed.

Brethren. With a heritage from the Pietists of the past two centuries in Europe, they were mostly Lutheran by background. They have taken the name *Brethren* since 1708. Sometimes they are called *Dunkers.* This comes from the German word *tunken* meaning to "dip, immerse." Brethren immerse converts three times.

Brethren Church (Ashland, Ohio). The Brethren Church (Ashland, Ohio) was founded in 1882 by German Baptist Brethren.

Brethren in Christ Church. The Brethren in Christ Church (known as the "River Brethren" because of their original location near the Susquehanna River), was founded in 1778 as an outgrowth of the religious awakening in that part of the country.

Christian and Missionary Alliance. Begun in 1897 (two fellowships that later combined) their purposes were to provide a fellowship of Christians dedicated to experiencing the deeper Christian life and to establish a missionary-sending organization.

Christian Church.

Christian Church (Disciples of Christ). The Christian Church (Disciples of Christ) started on the American frontier at the beginning of the nineteenth century as a movement to unify Christians. Thomas and Alexander Campbell began in Pennsylvania by separating from the Presbyterian Church and calling themselves "Disciples" (detractors often called them Campbellites). Barton Stone started in Kentucky, calling his followers simply "Christians."

In 1932, the two groups merged in Lexington, Kentucky.

The Disciples do not call themselves a denomination but rather a fellowship, because they are independent churches with no formal organization other than in the local congregations. They have no denominational societies, officials, or boards.

They preach a conservative, fundamental theology, stressing the divinity of Christ, the work of the Holy Spirit in conversion, the Bible as the inspired Word of God, future rewards and punishments, and open communion every Sunday.

Churches of Christ. The Churches of Christ, also autonomous congregations, appeal to the Bible alone to determine matters of faith and practice. They also have no central office.

The Churches of Christ shared a common fellowship with the Christian Church (Disciples), but broke away over the introduction of instrumental music in worship and centralization of churchwide activities through a missionary society. In 1906 they formally divided, with the Churches of Christ remaining non-instrumental.

Churches of Christ. (See *Christian Church.*)

Church of God. More than 200 independent religious groupings in the United states claim the name *Church of God.* All of the following are Pentecostal—that is, they practice speaking in tongues: Church of God (Cleveland, Tennessee); Church of God (Huntsville, Alabama); Church of God in Christ; Church of God in Christ (International); Church of God of Prophecy; and the (Original) Church of God, Inc. (See *Pentecostal.*)

Church of God (Anderson, Indiana). (See *Holiness.*)

Church of Jesus Christ of Latter-day Saints. (See *Mormons.*)

Episcopal Church. Known by this name since 1967, the denomination was formerly the Protestant Episcopal Church. This group is the self-governing American branch of the Church of England, and for the first century and a half it bore the name *Church of England.*

The Church of England dates back to 314 when missionaries went there from Gaul. In the days of Henry VIII the church broke away from the supremacy of the pope. Under the reign of Edward VI, the founders published the Book of Common Prayer and the 42 Articles of Religion. They suffered the persecution of Queen Mary until the ascension of Elizabeth I, who united the church and state as Protestant. In 1578, Sir Francis Drake landed in what is now California and claimed the land for the Virgin Queen. Soon other explorations in America followed. By the mid-1600s the Church of England became the established church.

The Revolutionary War almost destroyed the Church of England in America. However, in 1782 William White wrote a pamphlet called "The Case of the Episcopal Churches in the United States Considered" and pleaded for unity and reorganization. The following year delegates met, adopted the name *Protestant Episcopal Church* and the denomination grew instead of dying.

With the outbreak of the Civil War, this is the only one among the major Protestant churches that did not split.

The church is governed nationally by two bodies, the permanent Executive Council and the General Convention, which meets every three years. The principal organizational units are, in descending order of size, provinces, dioceses or missionary districts, local parishes, and local missions.

Bishops, priests, laymen, and laywomen compose the National Council. One bishop is the leader and holds the formal title of presiding bishop. This council is responsible for the missionary, educational, and social work of the denomination.

The General Convention has final authority in matters of policy and doctrine. All acts pass both the House of Bishops and House of Deputies. An equal number of clergy and lay delegates from each diocese make up this latter group.

Several dioceses make up a province, and each has a provincial synod composed of a house of bishops and deputies. Their duty involves coordinating the work of churches in their area. Within a diocese, a bishop is the principal official assisted by the Diocesan Convention (all the clergy in the diocese and lay representatives from each parish). A vestry (pastor and lay members) governs the parish or local church.

The Episcopal Church accepts most of the Articles of the Church of England. Episcopalians believe in the Bible as the word of God and expect their members to be loyal to the doctrine, discipline, and worship of "the one holy catholic and Apostolic Church" in all of the essentials, but allow liberty in nonessentials. They accept two sacraments, baptism (by pouring or immersion for both children and adults) and the Eucharist.

Friends. Better known as *Quakers,* these Christians trace their roots to George Fox (1624–1691) who sought spiritual truth and peace and did not find it in British churches. One day he received the "inner light" (see John 1:9), and from this principle the Quaker movement began. They have no outward forms, ceremonies, rituals or creeds.

Friends General Conference. A fellowship for deepening the spiritual and social testimonies of Friends.

Friends United Meeting. A loose confederation of North American yearly meetings to facilitate a united Quaker witness in missions, peace work, and Christian education.

Religious Society of Friends. The smallest of the three Quaker groups. They emphasize spontaneity, fluidity, variety, and experimentation.

Greek Orthodox. (See *Orthodox.*)

Holiness Churches. Largely an outgrowth of the Methodist movement at the end of the nineteenth century, the holiness groups emphasize sanctification, calling it a second word of grace after regeneration.

The Church of God (Anderson, Indiana). Dating from about 1880, this is not a Pentecostal church but is of the holiness background.

Church of the Nazarene. With 500,000 members, this is one of the larger holiness bodies. It was organized in 1908.

Lutheran   Churches. Lutheran Churches trace their history back to a sixteenth-century priest named Martin Luther whose objections to Roman Catholic practice began the movement known as the *Protestant Reformation.*

Luther held, as his followers still do today, to three basic tenets (1) God—we are justified by faith in God alone; (2) the Bible—the perfect and authoritative guide for humanity; (3) conscience—the individual conscience is responsible only to God.

In 1529 Luther wrote his Longer and Shorter catechisms, which were followed the next year by the Augsburg Confession written by Luther's brilliant helper, Philip Melanchthon.

The Reformation started in Germany, but soon had two distinct branches— Evangelical Lutheranism with Luther and Melanchthon as leaders and the Reformed Church under the leadership of John Calvin, Ulrich Zwingli, and John Knox.

In 1623 the first Lutheran immigrants arrived at Manhattan Island from Holland. By 1649 they had a worshiping congregation, and from there they spread westward. The Civil War brought the first serious break among Lutherans, which was followed by other disruptions. Since 1910, however, Lutherans have been trying to bring about a unification of all Lutheran factions.

Despite their differences, Lutherans share an organizational likeness and hold to the tenets of Luther and Melanchthon.

Twelve Lutheran bodies exist in the United States, six of which account for 95 percent of all Lutherans.

Lutherans recognize two sacraments, baptism (for infants and adults) and the Lord's Supper. They believe that all baptized persons receive the gift of regeneration from the Holy Spirit.

In Lutheran churches the congregation is the basic unit of government, administered by a council headed either by the senior pastor or a lay person elected from the membership of the council. Normally, clergy and elected laypersons compose the council.

Congregations, which are governed by conventions, make up the national church bodies. They are grouped into territorial districts or synods. (The term *synod* is also used in the names of some national bodies.)

American Lutheran Church. With more than two million members, this is the third largest of the Lutheran bodies and theologically is regarded as middle-of-the-road. Through a merger of Lutherans with backgrounds of Danish (United Evangelical Lutheran Church), German (American Lutheran Church), and Norwegian (Evangelical Lutheran Church), they formed the the ALC in 1960. For the first time in this century, major Lutheran groups of different national heritage united.

Lutheran Church in America

The Lutheran Church in America (LCA) is the largest of the three major bodies. It is also less rigid and more liberal in doctrine. This body came into being in 1962 as a result of the merger of four groups with Danish, Finnish, German, and Swedish backgrounds. The LCA traces its roots back to the Dutch Lutheran congregation in New Amsterdam (New York) in the mid-seventeenth century.

Lutheran Church—Missouri Synod. The second largest of the Lutheran bodies, it is the most conservative of the three Lutheran bodies. It began in 1847 in the state of Missouri. In the 1960s a controversy developed within the synod over the question of biblical interpretation. This disagreement resulted in the walkout of most of the faculty members and students from one of their seminaries and the eventual loss of more than 100,000 members.

Lutheran Church in America. (See *Lutheran.*)

Lutheran Church—Missouri Synod. (See *Lutheran.*)

Mennonite. (See *Baptist.*) Menno Simons (1496–1561), a converted priest, organized so many churches in Holland that the movement took on his name. Detractors labeled them Anabaptists or Rebaptizers. Along with rebaptizing those baptized in infancy or by means other than immersion, Mennonites began and have remained pacifists.

The Amish element takes it name from Jacob Amman, who was a strict and conservative Mennonite bishop in Switzerland. He and his followers were such literalists that they divided from other Mennonites.

Beachy Amish Mennonite Churches.
Slightly less conservative in dress, members of this church also worship in church buildings, have Sunday schools, and actively support missionary work.

Church of God in Christ, Mennonite.
The church was organized in 1859 because members felt that the Mennonite church had become apostate.

Hutterian Brethren. Members advocate communal ownership of property.

Mennonite Church. This is the largest group of Mennonites in the United States, with 90,000 members.

Other Mennonites. Other Mennonite churches and conferences include: Conservative Mennonite Conference, Evangelical Mennonite Church, Fellowship of Evangelical Bible Churches, General Conference Mennonite Church, and Mennonite Brethren Church of North America.

Metropolitan Community Churches.
The Universal Fellowship of Metropolitan Community Churches was founded in 1968. This fellowship has a particular but not exclusive outreach to the gay community.

Methodists. The term *Methodist* originated as a nickname for a group of Oxford University students in 1729 because of their methodical application to Bible study and prayer. They also received the sobriquets of Bible Bigots, the Holy Club, and Bible Moths. The three dominant figures of this group were John and Charles Wesley and George Whitefield.

In the beginning the Methodists appealed primarily to the lower classes, mainly through open-air meetings. The first Methodist church society began in London in 1740. Between 1739 and 1744, the organizational elements of Methodism were instituted and a phenomenal growth started. Methodism began as a lay movement, and John Wesley tried to keep it within the Church of England. In 1739 Wesley drew up a set of general rules, which modern Methodists still hold. Wesley died before the Methodists became a recognized church.

The Methodists spread to the new world. By 1773 more than 1600 worshiped in America, but less than half that number existed four years later because the Methodists tended to be pro-British. They seemed doomed to extinction by 1776. Francis Asbury's leadership of the Methodists at this crucial period led them forward, and they prospered. In England Wesley accepted the inevitable changes, ordained ministers for the colonies, and appointed Asbury and Thomas Coke as superintendents. The Methodist Episcopal Church was born in December, 1784 with its first general conference held in 1792.

Circuit riders moved westward with the population and the denomination flourished. They had differences all along, however; some groups split off because of the emphasis upon the Episcopal Church.

Prior to the Civil War the Methodists, like the other denominations, split over the slavery issue. They stayed separate denominations until 1939. The uniting conference of 1939 adopted a new constitution, and this action began the reuniting of Methodists in the United States.

Theologically the Methodists have never been strongly separatist. Many of the churches repeat the Apostles' Creed and the theology is Arminian as interpreted by Wesley.

Methodists believe in the Trinity, the natural sinfulness of humanity, the need for repentance and conversion, freedom of the will, justification by faith, sanctification and holiness, future rewards and punishments, the sufficiency of the Bible for salvation, baptism (infant and adult), the Lord's Supper, the enabling grace of God, and perfection.

United Methodist Church.

The principal Methodist body in the United States is the United Methodist Church, which has member conferences outside the United States. It was formed in 1968 by the merger of the Methodist Church and the Evangelical United Brethren Church.

The government of the United Methodist Church follows a stratified pattern from the General Conference through several intermediate conferences down to the local congregation.

The General Conference, which meets every four years, has final authority in all matters. Its members, half clergy and half lay, are elected by the annual conferences.

Jurisdictional conferences covering major sections of the nation are composed of ministers and lay delegates. Their principal function is to elect bishops. Annual conferences, generally organized along state lines, elect delegates to higher conferences and make official appointments within their areas.

A Methodist bishop presides over a church area—which may embrace one or more annual conferences. Bishops have extensive administrative powers, including the authority to place, transfer, and remove local church pastors—usually done in consultation with district superintendents.

Districts in each conference are responsible for mission work, support of colleges, hospitals and publications, and examination of candidates for the ministry. Members of a congregation form a charge conference and elect officers to a board that assists the pastor.

Methodism in the United States also includes three major black denominations: The African Methodist Episcopal Church, the African Methodist Episcopal Zion Church, and the Christian Methodist Episcopal Church.

United Methodists believe in the Bible as God's Word, the Trinity, the humanity and divinity of Jesus Christ, and they observe two sacraments: baptism (for children and adults), and the Lord's Supper.

African Methodist Episcopal Zion Church.

One of the three largest Methodist groups in the United States, the AME Church began with the withdrawal in 1787 of a number of members of St. George's Methodist Episcopal Church in Philadelphia as a protest against racial discrimination. They formally organized as the AME Church in 1816. From the beginning they provided social, educational, and journalistic services.

The AME church was largely confined to the northern states in the years before the Civil War. Following the war its membership increased in the south, and it is now a a national church.

Moravians.

In 1735 Moravian missionaries of the pre-Reformation faith of John Huss came to America and established the Moravian Church. They are called Moravians because they came from what was then known as Moravia (Czechoslavakia). They are evangelical, liturgical, and consider the episcopacy to be a spiritual office. They insist on the principle of "in essentials unity, in nonessentials liberty, and in all things charity."

Mormons. The Church of Jesus Christ of Latter-day Saints bases its beginning on revelations that Joseph Smith said were brought to him in the 1820s by a heavenly messenger.

After Smith's death in 1844, his followers split into factions, the largest of which is the Church of Jesus Christ of Latter-day Saints. Led west by Brigham Young, these followers founded Salt Lake City in 1847.

The church hierarchy is composed of men known as *general authorities*. Among them, the policy-making body is the First Presidency, made up of a president and two or more counselors. This body has final authority in all spiritual and worldly matters.

The Council of the Twelve Apostles, primarily an advisory body, helps the First Presidency direct church activities. Other general authorities include the church patriarch, a spiritual advisor; a three-member Presiding Bishopric that administers temporal affairs; and the First Quorum of Seventy, in charge of missionary work. Women cannot become general authorities.

The church's basic geographical units are called *stakes* and are governed by a stake presidency, made up of a president and two counselors, and a stake high council. Congregations within a stake are called *wards*. Missions, which oversee members where there are no stakes, are headed by a president and may include one or more congregations known as *branches*.

Mormons believe that Jesus Christ established one church on earth, that it was taken away upon his death, and that it was not restored until Joseph Smith received the divine revelations. After his resurrection, Jesus came to America and visited his people who had migrated to the continent in ancient times.

Among the revelations were directions to gold plates that Smith said he found near Palmyra, New York. He taught that the plates, left by a prophet who lived after the time of Jesus, contained the records of the people Jesus had visited in America.

The Book of Mormon, written by Smith, contains what members believe are his translations of hieroglyphics on the plates. Moroni, the heavenly messenger who led Smith to the plates, later took them away. Smith also wrote the Book of Doctrine and Covenants and Pearl of Great Price. These three books, along with the Bible, are the key church documents, although Mormons believe that revelation continues today through members of the First Presidency.

All faithful male members over the age of 11 are members of the priesthood and can move into leadership positions in the all-lay clergy. They go through a series of ranks from deacon to teacher to priest before becoming elders sometime after their eighteenth birthday.

National Baptist Convention of America. (See *Baptist*.)

National Baptist Convention, U.S.A., Inc. (See *Baptist*.)

Orthodox. The biggest influx of Greeks to America took place between 1890 and 1914, and they naturally brought their faith with them.

Between 1908 and 1922 a period of confusion reigned, with the shifting of jurisdiction of the American churches from the Ecumenical Patriarchate of Constantinople to the Holy Synod of Greece and then back again.

Greek Orthodox Archdiocese of North and South America. The Founding Tome of 1922 established the Greek (Orthodox) Archdiocese of North and South America. It consists of four bishoprics under the auspices of the Archbishop.

Doctrine is based on the Bible, tradition, and the decrees of the seven ecumenical councils. In all liturgies they recite the Nicene Creed, quoted without *filioque*. They reject papal infallibility. They recognize seven sacraments: (1) baptism (adults and infants by threefold immersion), (2) anointing (confirmation or chrismation), (3) communion, (4) penance, (5) holy orders, (6) marriage, and (7) holy unction.

While denying purgatory, they pray for the dead and believe the dead pray for those alive on earth. They insist upon both faith and works as necessary for salvation.

They hold to an episcopal form of government. There are three orders in the ministry: (1) deacons who assist in parish work and in serving the sacrament, (2) priests, and (3) bishops. Candidates for the deaconite and the priesthood may marry before ordination but not afterward. Church services are elaborately ritualistic, with the Eucharist being a reenactment of the gospel account.

Eastern churches.   Other Orthodox-type churches exist. To be truly Orthodox they must be in canonical relationship with the Patriarch of Constantinople and with one another. The following are irregular Eastern churches:

> Albanian Orthodox Archdiocese in America
> American Carpatho-Russian Orthodox Greek Catholic Church
> American Holy Orthodox Catholic Eastern Church
> Antiochian Orthodox Christian Archdiocese of North America
> Bulgarian Eastern Orthodox Church
> Holy Apostolic and Catholic Church of the East (Assyrian)
> Romanian Orthodox Episcopate of America
> Russian Orthodox Church
> Serbian Eastern Orthodox Church in the U.S.A. and Canada
> Syrian Orthodox Church of Antioch (Archdiocese of the U.S.A. and Canada)
> Ukrainian Orthodox Churches

Pentecostal.   *Pentecostal* and sometimes *full gospel* are terms that apply to a large number of revivalistic American denominations and congregations. Many have either a holiness or Baptist background and emphasize the Pentecostal experience (see Acts 2:4).

They believe in original sin, salvation through the atoning blood of Jesus, the virgin birth, the deity of Christ, the inspiration and literal infallibility of the Bible, manifestations of the working of the Holy Spirit (especially the baptism of the Holy Spirit), future rewards and punishments, the Lord's Supper, and believers' baptism by immersion. Many practice divine healing and speaking in tongues. A few (such as the United Pentecostal Church International) deny the Trinity and emphasize the oneness of God, baptizing in the name of Jesus Christ only.

Assemblies of God.   This denomination claims to be the largest and fastest-growing of the Pentecostal groups that stemmed from the revivals at the turn of this century. An evangelical missionary fellowship, it is composed of self-governing churches in 57 districts. Congregations are located in every state of the U.S. and 115 countries of the world. Their founding meeting was in Hot Springs, Arkansas, on April 2–12, 1914.

Church of God in Christ.   The Church of God in Christ, which also claims to be the fastest-growing Pentecostal church, was founded in 1906 in Memphis, Tennessee. Bishop Charles Harrison Mason, a former Baptist minister, led the formal organizing after he had pioneered the holiness teachings for a decade in Mississippi.

The Church of God in Christ organized into four major departments between 1910–1916: (1) Women's Department, (2) Sunday School, (3) Young Peoples Willing Workers, and (4) Home and Foreign Mission.

Doctrinally, the Church of God in Christ believes in the Trinity, the infallibility of the Bible, the necessity of regeneration, and the subsequent baptism of the Holy Spirit. They emphasize holiness as God's standard for Christian conduct. Along with the Lord's Supper and water baptism by immersion, they also practice footwashing as an ordinance. Their church structure is basically episcopal.

Other Pentecostal churches in America include: Calvary Pentecostal Church, Inc., Elim Fellowship, Emmanuel Holiness Church, Independent Assemblies of God, International Church of the Foursquare Gospel, International Pentecostal Church of Christ, International Pentecostal Holiness Church, Pentecostal Assemblies of the World, Inc., Pentecostal Church of God, and Pentecostal Free-Will Baptist Church, Inc.

Presbyterian. Presbyterians take their name from a Greek word that means "elder," which also explains their system of church government—a rule by elders.

They trace their history back to John Calvin (1509–1564), a Frenchman who fled from the Roman Catholics to Geneva and quickly took over the leadership of the Protestants who were Reformed (but not Lutheran). In 1536 Calvin published his first edition of the Institutes of the Christian Religion. While Calvin did not form the Presbyterian Church, he laid the foundation. John Knox of Scotland, a refugee from Bloody Mary, accepted his teachings, and then went back to Scotland. Huguenots from France began to spread Presbyterianism on the continent. Calvin also influenced the Dutch, who established the Dutch Reformed Church.

In Scotland a delegation of ministers, peers, and members of the House of Commons sat in the Westminster Assembly of Divines (1643–1648) and wrote the Westminster Confession of Faith, which all Presbyterians still accept. In the late 1600s multitudes of Presbyterians from the British Isles fled to American shores because of persecution following the reestablishment of the monarchy. However, they trace their first congregation in Virginia back to 1611.

Presbyterians have four levels of authority—local congregations, presbyteries, synods, and a general assembly. Pastors lead congregations. All ministers and an equal number of elders from each congregation in a given geographic district form a Presbytery. Presbyteries unite to form a synod, which normally meets annually. Members of the synod participate by being elected by the presbyteries. Delegates of pastors and elders from each presbytery form the general assembly, which meets yearly with their Presbyterian body to decide on issues of doctrine and discipline.

While relying heavily upon the writings of Calvin and his emphasis upon the sovereignty of God, Presbyterians believe in the Trinity, the Bible as the infallible rule of faith and practice, the humanity and divinity of Jesus Christ, baptism (to children and adults, accepting any form), and the Lord's Supper.

Presbyterian Church (U.S.A.). Presbyterian Church (U.S.A.) is the merger of the northern arm (formerly known as the United Presbyterian Church in the United States of America) with the southern branch (Presbyterian Church in the United States). This 1983 event reunited the two groups, which split at the time of the Civil War when the Presbyterian Church of the Confederate States of America withdrew.

Strongly ecumenical, the PCUSA is the result of at least ten different denominational mergers in the last two and half centuries.

Other Presbyterian bodies include: Associate Reformed Presbyterian Church; Bible Presbyterian Church; Cumberland Presbyterian Church; Orthodox Presbyterian Church; The Presbyterian Church in America; Reformed Presbyterian Church, Evangelical Synod; Reformed Presbyterian Church of North America; and Second Cumberland Presbyterian Church in the United States.

Reformed. (See *Presbyterian*.) This denomination began in Holland during the Reformation and began in 1857 in the United States. It is creedally united in the Belgic Confession of 1561, Heidelberg Catechism of 1563, and the Canons of Dort of 1618. Reformed Churches are Calvinistic in theology and have a modified Presbyterian form of government.

Christian Reformed Church. This denomination has a membership of 224,000.

Hungarian Reformed Church in America.

Reformed Church in America. Established in 1628 by Dutch settlers to New York, it claims to be the oldest Protestant denomination with a continuous ministry in North America. The membership is about 340,000.

Roman Catholic Church. For the first 1500 years after the resurrection of Jesus Christ until the Protestant Reformation, the church in the western world was the Roman Catholic Church—despite the occasional dissension and breakaways of individuals and groups.

By the end of the sixteenth century, Europe (including the British Isles) had divided into Roman Catholic, Lutheran, Anglican, and Reformed (Presbyterian) Churches.

The Roman Catholic Church dates its beginning from the first century when Jesus said, "You are Peter, and on this rock I will build My church" (Matt. 16:18). The RCC contends that its bishops have been established as the legitimate successors of the apostles through generations of ceremonies in which authority was passed down by the laying on of hands.

Responsibility for teaching the faithful and administering the church rests with the bishops. However, the church holds that the pope has final authority over their actions because he is the bishop of Rome, the Vicar of Christ. Although the pope is empowered to speak infallibly on faith and morals, he does so only in formal pronouncements specifically stating that he is speaking from the chair *ex cathedra* of St. Peter. This rarely-used prerogative was most recently invoked in 1950, when Pope Pius XII declared that Mary was assumed bodily into heaven.

The Curia serves as a form of governmental cabinet. Its members, appointed by the pope, handle both administrative and judicial functions. The pope also chooses members of the college of cardinals, who serve as his principal counselors. When they must select a new pope, they meet in a conclave to elect one by majority vote.

In the Latin Rite, used by Catholics in the western world, there are no national churches, although bishops in various nations do organize conferences that develop programs for the church in their nations. The National Conference of Catholic Bishops is the national organization of Roman Catholic bishops in the United States. Its administrative arm is the United States Catholic Conference.

The RCC's principal organizational units are archdioceses, headed by archbishops, and dioceses with bishops, who have final responsibility for activities within their jurisdiction and report directly to Rome.

Below the pope are the cardinal, archbishop, bishop, monsignor, priest and deacon. In religious orders, nonordained men are called "brother."

The RCC is the largest single body of Christians in the nation. They believe in the Trinity, the Incarnation (that the Son became a human being), salvation through Christ, and everlasting heaven and hell. The essential elements of belief are contained in the Bible and in tradition—the body of teachings passed on orally and in writing by the apostles and their successors.

The Mass is central to worship, and Roman Catholics believe Christ is present in the Eucharist.

In addition to the Holy Eucharist, RCCs have six other sacraments: baptism, confirmation, penance (sometimes called the sacrament of reconciliation), marriage, holy orders, and the sacrament of the sick (formerly extreme unction).

Salvation Army. Founded in 1865 by William Booth (1829–1912) in London and introduced to America in 1880. The Salvation Army is an international religious and charitable movement organized and operated on a paramilitary pattern, and is a branch of the Christian Church, with a membership of 420,000.

Southern Baptist Convention. (See *Baptist.*)

United Church of Christ. Although the word *congregational* is still used by some individual congregations, the principal body that used the term dropped it in 1961. At that time, the Evangelical and Reformed Church merged with the Congregational Christian Churches to form the United Church of Christ, which now has a membership of more than 1.6 million people.

Each church is autonomous and responsible for the doctrine, ministry, and ritual of its congregation.

The formation of the United Church of Christ brought together four unique strands from the diverse history of Christian experience.

(1) The Congregational way first achieved prominence among English Protestants during the civil war of the 1640s, groundwork for the Congregational form having been laid by Calvinistic Puritans and Separatists during the preceding half-century. Opposition to state control of their religious worship caused followers of congregationalism to emigrate to America, where they took an active part in colonizing New England.

(2) The Christian Churches originated as a restorationist movement in the United States late in the eighteenth century. Throughout their history, Christians emphasized Christ as the head of the church, the Bible as their only rule of faith, and *Christian* as their only name. United in spirit, they were loosely organized and united. In 1931 the Congregational Churches merged to become the Congregational Christian Churches.

(3) The German Reformed Church represented those who followed Zwingli and Calvin as well as Luther. They wrote the Heidelberg Catechism of 1563 and were united by this confession. They began to emigrate to the New World in the 1700s and settled primarily in the middle Atlantic colonies. They were an independent denomination by 1793.

(4) Early in the nineteenth century in Germany, Enlightenment criticism and Pietism brought about a decrease in the long-standing differences between religious groups. In 1817 this unity resulted in a royal proclamation that merged Lutheran and Reformed people into the United Evangelical Church. Members of this new church migrated to America just as earlier German immigrants moved westward. The Evangelicals settled largely in Missouri and Illinois, continuing their non-controversial emphasis on pietistic devotion and unionism. In 1840 they formed the German Evangelical Church Society in the West. Union with other Evangelical church associations further expanded the movement's membership. In 1877 they changed their name to the German Evangelical Synod of North America.

In 1934, this Synod and the Reformed Church in the U.S. (formerly the German Reformed Church) became the Evangelical and Reformed Church. In both groups the German ethnic traits had lost their influence as the Evangelical and Reformed Church entered the mainstream of American church life. Within their denomination is a blend of the Reformed tradition's desire for unity of the church and the Evangelical's commitment to the liberty of conscience.

United Methodist Church. (See *Methodist.*)

Geography

Geography of the Holy Land

Palestine—the official name of the lands of the Bible until 1948—is the heartland of three major religions of the world. Judaism, Christianity, and Islam trace their beginnings to this small area of land where God revealed himself to the patriarchs and prophets, to Jesus and his apostles.

Studying the geography of the Bible lands is no recent pursuit. Early church fathers such as Jerome felt geography was important for understanding the Bible.

The Holy Land is a magnificent country rich in history, a land of contrasts. Modern and ancient ways of life go on side by side. Barren deserts clash with the lush foliage of oases.

The Great Rift Valley

What can compare with the beauty of the Jordan River valley? Barren slopes of the Judean wilderness loom over the curves of the Jordan River. But since the 1967 cease-fire, this river has marked the boundary between the modern states of Israel and Jordan.

Impressive though it is, the Jordan Valley is only a small part of the Great Rift Valley, which stretches from Syria to Africa. South of the Jordan Valley and the Arabah wilderness, the Red Sea covers over 2,200 kilometers (1,400 miles) of the Great Rift Valley's floor. The Red Sea extends to the Indian Ocean, and its waters lap against east Africa on one side and the Arabian Peninsula on the other.

Thousands of years ago, immense pressures beneath the earth's surface created the Great Rift Valley. As the earth cracked in the upheaval, parts of the earth's crust were pushed up. Thus mountains follow the valley for its full length on both sides.

To the north, the Lebanon and Hermon mountain ranges flank the valley. During certain months of the year these mountains cool the moisture-filled clouds causing heavy rainfall, and in winter they collect snow. Springs and runoff waters create streams that flow into the Sea of Galilee to the south and are eventually channeled out into the Jordan River.

The Jordan meanders southward from the Sea of Galilee through the valley, finally bringing its waters into the Dead Sea. Here the water is trapped, unable to escape except by evaporation, because the ground rises at the south end of the Sea.

The higher ground becomes the Arabah wilderness that reaches from the Dead Sea south to the Gulf of Eilat on the Red Sea. On the east are the sharp mountains of Edom; to the west are the Negev Desert and the Mediterranean Sea.

Biblical authors introduced us to the geographical divisions of the Holy Land. Moses told the people of Israel, "Turn, and take your journey, and go to the mountains of the Amorites, to all the neighboring places, in the plain, in the mountains, and in the lowland, in the South and on the seacoast, to the land of the Canaanites and to Lebanon, as far as the great river, the river Euphrates" (Deut. 1:7). Later we are told that "Joshua conquered all the land: the mountain country and the South and the lowland and the wilderness slopes, and all their kings" (Josh. 10:40).

The subterranean forces that formed the Great Rift Valley are still at work. Even today the land rests uneasily, at the mercy of tremors caused by shifts of the great blocks of land that form the earth's crust. Through the centuries tremors and quakes have shaken the valley.

The Bible mentions some of these earthquakes. Such a forceful quake shook Israel during King Uzziah's reign that Amos dated a message by it: "two years before the earthquake" (Amos 1:1). Zechariah referred to it 270 years later: "you shall flee like as you fled from the earthquake in the days of Uzziah king of Judah" (Zech. 14:5).

Another earthquake took place much later, at the moment Jesus died on the cross: "and the earth quaked, and the rocks were split, and the graves were opened" (Matt. 27:51–52).

Poets and prophets saw earthquakes as instruments of God's judgment: "You will be punished by the LORD of Hosts with thunder and earthquake and great noise, with storm and tempest and the flame of devouring fire" (Isa. 29:6). And "Then the earth shook and trembled; the foundations of the hills also quaked and were shaken, because He was angry" (Ps. 18:7).

Genesis 19:24–28 chronicles the destruction of Sodom and Gomorrah by brimstone and fire. Some believe this was a divinely-ordered earthquake that released an exploding cloud of natural gas. Located in the southern part of the Jordan Valley, the ruins of these cities were gradually covered with the water of the Dead Sea, removing any trace of the wickedness practiced in them.

Ancient sources mention other earthquakes. Archaeologists have unearthed the results of their devastation in Jericho, Qumran, Hazor, and elsewhere.

The Fertile Crescent

God promised the land of Canaan to Abraham and his descendants. It is a fertile country, bounded by deserts to the east and south and shaken by an occasional earthquake.

Canaan is the southern tip of the area known as the Fertile Crescent. Unlike the terrain around it, this narrow semicircle of land in the Near East receives enough moisture to grow crops. The green crescent or horseshoe-shape starts at the Persian Gulf on the eastern end and extends to the southern part of Canaan on the western end. It is bordered by the Mediterranean on the west, mountains to the north, and desert regions to the south and east. From this well-favored strip of land rose the great nations of the OT.

God chose a prominent place for his people to prove themselves to be a "holy nation." The land of Canaan was strategically located between the great civilizations of the Near East. Egypt lay to the southwest, Phoenicia and Aram (Syria) to the north, and Assyria and Babylonia to the east. Unlike Egypt, Canaan could not isolate herself from her neighbors.

In fact, the inhabitants of Canaan were forced to get involved in world politics. In times of war they were never safe, because Canaan was the land-bridge over which Egypt passed on her way to the north. Assyrians, Babylonians, and Greeks trampled Canaan when they headed south in their conquest of the Near East.

Yet there were advantages to being criss-crossed by surrounding cultures. Canaan was enriched by the art and literature of other nations, as well as by their building techniques and scientific accomplishments. In the teeming center of the ancient Near East, God called his people in Canaan to be a challenge to the nations.

"A beautiful heritage of the hosts of nations" (Jer. 3:19) is how Jeremiah described the Promised Land. It is a pleasant land, this southwestern branch of the Fertile Crescent. In contrast to the sea, mountains, and deserts that enclose it, Palestine offers fertile soil, water, and a pleasant climate. These favorable conditions enticed early human beings to settle there. Indeed, whole civilizations rose and fell on the soil of Canaan before Israel claimed it as her own.

By the time Abraham came into the land, Canaan had long been inhabited. The first settlers dwelled in caves in the Mount Carmel region. They lived by hunting wild game and collecting wild grains, vegetables, and fruits. Gradually they moved to small villages and planted fields of wheat, barley, and legumes. Herds and flocks further expanded their diet. As the villagers produced more than they could use, they began trading. The small communities developed road systems for traders to move from village to village with their wares of produce, textiles, pottery, and jewelry.

Jericho is a good example of such developments. This well-watered region is a gorgeous oasis in the desert north of the Dead Sea and several miles west of the Jordan River. Archaeologists have found few signs of the early stages of the city's growth. They surmise that the people lived in flimsy tents and huts. At first the people of Jericho were semi-nomadic, moving from place to place in search of food. But with the development of the flint, sickle, and primitive plow, they could support themselves from a smaller parcel of land. They built houses and the population increased, and gradually the village became a city. To protect against destruction by jealous neighbors or passing enemies, Jericho's early inhabitants erected a wall around the settlement. When Abraham arrived in Canaan, Jericho had already passed through several cycles of building, destruction, and rebuilding.

The Promised Land

Genesis 11:31—12:10 describes the incredible journey Abraham made in search of the land of promise. From the Persian Gulf he traveled the full length of the Fertile Crescent, going as far as Egypt.

In 1866, archaeologists positively identified a site in southern Iraq as Ur, the place of Abraham's birth (see Gen. 11:28). The city was located on the Euphrates River, and in ancient times it was an important commercial center. It prospered for thousands of years, up to the fourth century B.C. Excavations at Ur have unearthed a ziggurat (a three-staged step tower) dedicated to the moon god, Nanna. This discovery might have been the Tower of Babel.

Abraham's father, Terah, led the family's migration from Ur. Abraham, his brother Nahor, and his nephew Lot took their families, servants, and possessions on the long trek. They journeyed over 1,100 kilometers (700 miles) to Haran, another thriving city on one of the trade routes from Assyria to the Mediterranean Sea. Haran was located at the Balikh River, a northern tributary of the Euphrates. Its people worshiped the moon god.

Abraham was 75 years old when God told him, "Get out of your country, from your family, and from your father's house, to a land that I will show you" (Gen. 12:1). He left Haran, taking his wife Sarai and nephew Lot, and their possessions. They followed a road leading through Syria to Damascus.

Beyond that information, we can only speculate on the routes Abraham might have taken to Canaan. From Damascus one road led past the Hermon Mountain range and over the Golan Heights to the Hula Valley. The Hula Lake was a swampy reservoir of water from the melting snow of Mount Hermon, runoff rain water, and springs at the foot of the mountain ranges. South of the lake, the water ran through a narrow canal to the Sea of Galilee. Caravans crossed the narrow canal at a ford. From there the road passed by Hazor and the Sea of Galilee to Megiddo, then through the valley of Dothan to Shechem.

Abraham's caravan might have used the Bashan Road that leads through the Golan Heights (Bashan). At the eastern edge of the Yarmuk gorge, the road turns westward and gradually descends to the Jordan Valley. There the Sea of Galilee, the Jordan River, and the Yarmuk come together. Once in the Jordan Valley, a traveler can quickly go to Beth Shan and from there to Shechem through the valleys of Jezreel and Dothan. This route was not traveled as frequently as the Hula Valley road. The trail from the Golan Heights to the Jordan Valley descended sharply, and part of the way it followed secondary roads less fit for large caravans or troops.

A third route that Abraham may have taken was probably used by Jacob when he deserted Laban in Haran. It led directly south, passing by the cities of Karnaim and Ashtaroth, and between Irbid and Ramoth-Gilead. Ten miles before Rabbath-bene-ammon (the present city of Amman, capital of Jordan), it veered slightly north and due west toward the Jordan Valley. The road descended to the gorge of the Jabbok River, crossed the river at the ford of Mahanaim, then turned southward to Adam, where it could cross the Jordan River. From there to Shechem, the road leading out of the valley followed a rather steep incline by the Wadi Far'a for nearly 32 kilometers (20 miles).

We know Abraham came through Shechem. It was a major intersection, controlling traffic going every direction. Archaeologists believe that Shechem was not a fortified city until the time of Jacob, about 1900 B.C. But it was strategically located at a pass between Mount Ebal on the north and Mount Gerizim on the south. The road from Wadi Far'a came into the Tirzah-Shechem road, which south of Shechem was called "the plain of Meonenim" (Judg. 9:37, KJV), or "the direction of the Diviners' Oak" (RSV). At Shechem a road turned off toward the Mediterranean, connecting Shechem with the major highway of Canaan, the *Via Maris* (meaning "Way of the Sea").

At Shechem, the Lord promised to give the land to Abraham's descendants (Gen. 12:7). As a memorial of the promise, Abraham built an altar on the plain of Moreh (Gen. 12:6). God did not give Abraham exact boundaries, but later assured the patriarch that the land on all four sides would be granted to his descendants (see Gen. 13:14–15).

The promise was confirmed to Isaac (see Gen. 26:3) and to Jacob (cf. Gen. 28:13). God established the relationship between the people and the land.

Land of the Patriarchs

God revealed to the patriarchs the lines of Israel's conquest. Biblical history continued to revolve around the cities, regions, and shrines where the patriarchs lived and worshiped. God commanded Abraham, "Arise, walk in the land through its length and its width; for I give it to you" (Gen. 13:17). Until they could gain control of Canaan, the patriarchs obeyed that command and took the land in faith for their descendants.

The patriarchal family was forced to leave Shechem after Jacob's sons Simeon and Levi killed all the males of the city. Jacob rebuked them: "You have troubled me by making me obnoxious among the inhabitants of the land . . . and since I am few in number, they will gather themselves together against me and kill me; I shall be destroyed, my household and I" (Gen. 34:30).

God sent them to Bethel, where Jacob built another altar. Jacob's household buried all their foreign gods by an oak tree and purified themselves. They went to Bethel where God had revealed himself in Jacob's dream of the ladder twenty years earlier (see Gen. 28). Again at Bethel, God reassured Jacob that his descendants would occupy the land (see Gen. 35:12).

Bethel and Shechem were not the only places where the patriarchs lived and built altars. Their footsteps led to Hebron and as far south as Beersheba in the Negev Desert. They canvassed the area that Joshua would later conquer.

The patriarchs laid the groundwork for both good and ill for their descendants in the land of Canaan. Abraham's and Isaac's involvement with the king of Gerar in the Philistine plain (Gen. 20:1–18; 26:17–22) foreshadowed future conflicts, when the Philistines would press hard against the Israelites in the hill country. But many sacred sites of the Israelites in this period became important cities. Jerusalem, where the priest-king Melchizedek blessed Abraham, became the very center of the Jewish religion after Solomon built the temple there.

Jacob's son Joseph brought the Israelites into Egypt. They entered Egypt as the people or clan of Israel (Jacob) and while there God forged them into a nation. The Egyptians felt threatened by the population explosion of the Israelites. To thwart their growing power, the Egyptians forced the people of Israel to serve as slaves in the land of Goshen.

At the appointed time, God promised them: "And I will bring you into the land, which I swore to give to Abraham, Isaac, and Jacob; and I will give it you as a heritage: I am the LORD" (Exod. 6:8). God sent Moses to lead the people "up out of the affliction of Egypt to . . . a land flowing with milk and honey" (Exod. 3:17).

God planned that his people would enter the Promised Land and become a nation unlike the surrounding nations. They would show their faith in God by grateful obedience. Keeping God's commandments would ensure their success: "Therefore hear, O Israel, and be careful to observe it, that it may be well with you, and that you may multiply greatly" (Deut. 6:3).

God chose the Israelites to be his witnesses in the Promised Land. They could demonstrate the faith of the patriarchs, who had successfully dealt with the nations around them. God's chosen people would grace the chosen land. This was God's third promise to Abraham, that through him and his descendants the nations would be blessed (Gen. 12:3).

Israel's possibilities within the Promised Land—its very future—depended on two things: responsible use of the land and faithful obedience to the terms of the covenant. God looked for the day when Israel's observance of his laws would cause other nations to declare: "Surely this great nation is a wise and understanding people" (Deut. 4:6).

Extent of the Promised Land

We don't know the exact boundaries of Canaan, but God revealed to Abraham that he and his descendants would receive the land. He had originally promised them a much larger area. When Lot's and Abraham's shepherds quarreled over the land, Abraham wisely offered to give his nephew Lot first choice of the territory. Lot decided to settle in the well-watered Jordan Valley in the east. God told Abraham, "Lift up your eyes now, and look from the place where you are, northward, and southward, and eastward, and westward; for all the land which you see will I give to you, and your descendants forever" (Gen. 13:14–15). The boundary lines were not settled, although Abraham's territory obviously ended where Lot's flocks grazed.

God made the land of promise part of his covenant with Abraham because the patriarch "believed in the LORD; and he accounted it to him for righteousness" (Gen. 15:6). In return, God solemnly promised to give to his descendants the land "from the river of Egypt to the great river, the river Euphrates" (Gen. 15:18).

Several hundred years later, when Moses reminded the Israelites of that promise, he described the boundaries of the promised land: the Arabah, the mountainous regions, the Shephelah, and the Negev and the coastal plains by the Mediterranean Sea, from the southern border of Canaan through Lebanon up to the Euphrates (Deut. 1:7).

By this time the Israelites already lived in the Transjordan. God allowed the tribes of Reuben and Gad, as well as part of the tribe of Manasseh, to settle in the newly-occupied land of the Amorites east of the Jordan (Num. 21:21—35:32). This territory extended the borders of the Promised Land even farther. But Moses still did not set a definite eastern boundary.

God ordered Joshua to take all the territory specified by Moses "From the wilderness and this Lebanon as far as the great river, the River Euphrates, all the land of the Hittites, and to the Great Sea toward the going down of the sun, shall be your territory" (Josh. 1:4). However, during the conquest of Canaan the people of Israel failed to take the total area promised them, partly because they were unfaithful to God. God punished the Israelites by holding them back from complete victory. "I swore in My wrath, 'they shall not enter My rest'" (Ps. 95:11). Each tribe lacked part of its inheritance.

Efforts to Expand

During the period of the judges, Israel tried unsuccessfully to enlarge its tribal territories. Even Saul, the first king, was not powerful enough to drive out the other nations.

Yet God allowed Saul's successor, King David, to control the land of promise except for the land of the Hittites. (See Josh. 1:4.) God granted David victory over the Ammonites, Moabites, and Edomites in the east, over the Philistines in the west, and over the marauding nomadic bands in the south. In fact, David's conquests reached almost to the Euphrates River, as far north as Hammath (2 Sam. 8).

Solomon inherited the kingdom at its peak. "For he had dominion over all the region on this side of the River from Tiphsah even to Gaza, namely over all the kings on this side of the River; and he had peace on every side all around him" (1 Kings 4:24). But from the latter part of Solomon's reign, the nation of Israel went steadily downhill. After his death, the kingdom divided into the two nations of Israel and Judah. Wars racked both of these kingdoms until their enemies forced them out of the land.

Fertility of the Land

A tourist from the fertile plains of America might wonder if Moses was in his right mind when he described the Promised Land as "a good land, a land of brooks of water, of fountains and springs that flow out of valleys and hills; a land of wheat and barley, of vines and fig trees and pomegranates, a land of olive oil and honey; a land in which you will eat bread without scarcity, in which you will lack nothing" (Deut. 8:7–9). Moses addressed those words to a people who had just spent 40 years in the desert! The Promised Land held boundless possibilities in contrast to the harsh, dry regions of the Sinai, Negev, and Arabah.

However, the Promised Land was no Garden of Eden. The Israelites may have envisioned endless valleys of crops and hillsides adorned with grasses, herbs, and flowers; but that is not what they found. Thorns and thistles cover the rocky land. During summer months a dull reddish-brown color on the slopes indicates parched vegetation. Nevertheless, the land is highly fertile compared to the surrounding deserts.

The Promised Land offered good opportunities for making a living with its water and tillable soil. However, the Israelites discovered that it was not easy to take advantage of those opportunities. They had to tame the land. The Israelite farmer had to deal with rocks, thorns, and thistles. He feared the sun, which scorched young seedlings that were not rooted deeply enough to draw water from a depth.

Jesus illustrated the farmer's plight with his parable of the sower. The sower spread the seed all over the field, but only the seed that fell on good soil produced a crop. The remaining seed fell on rocks and among thistles and soon died (Matt. 13:3–8).

What the Israelites could accomplish with the soil depended entirely on their relationship with the Lord. He promised to bless them materially for their obedience: "The LORD will open to you his good treasure, the heavens, to give the rain to your land in its season, and to bless all the work of your hand" (Deut. 28:12). Disobedience, however, would bring material judgment: "But . . . if you do not obey the voice of the LORD your God . . . your heavens which are over your head shall be bronze, and the earth which is under you shall be iron. The LORD will change the rain of your land to powder and dust" (Deut. 28:15a, 23–24).

"You shall carry much seed out to the field, but gather little in, for the locust shall consume it. You shall plant vineyards and tend them, but you shall neither drink of the wine nor gather the grapes; for the worms shall eat them" (Deut. 28:38–39). If the Israelites did not heed the Lord, they would lose the land God promised to them: "You shall be plucked from off the land which you go to possess" (Deut. 28:63b). Sadly, that very thing happened.

1. Soil. When the Israelites first occupied the land, they lived in the hill country near the central mountain range of Canaan. The Israelite farmers had to learn how to eke out an existence from the hills, which were largely composed of limestone rock. Though limestone weathers into soil very slowly, it is fertile.

Rains easily wash the rich hillside soil down streams to low-lying valleys. To prevent erosion, farmers planted fruit trees and vines or built terraces.

Terraces abounded in the hill country. Sometimes a layer of rock resisted weathering and formed a natural wall. This held in place the reddish soil that the farmer could plant with wheat, barley, legumes, and vegetables, in addition to fruit trees and vines. When there was no natural wall, the farmer had to clear the area of ever-present stones and use them to build a wall at the lower side of the hill.

Vineyards also abounded in Canaan, and biblical authors often mentioned them symbolically, as Isaiah did: "My Well-beloved has a vineyard on a very fruitful hill. He dug it up, and cleared out its stones, and planted it with the choicest vines" (Isa. 5:1–2). In this passage, God is the owner of the vineyard Israel. The work of preparing the vineyard represents God's love and care for Israel, who nonetheless failed to produce the harvest of righteousness he desired.

Israelite farmers cultivated fruit trees, vines, and grains in the low-lying hills, the Shephelah, and the coastal plains. The soft chalk of the Shephelah weathered easily and mixed with organic materials. Farmers could till this soil at a deeper level, and it was less subject to rain runoff.

2. Precipitation. Farmers counted on the rains of fall, which permitted seeds to germinate and seedlings to develop into strong plants. Equally essential were the latter rains of February and March, which enabled plants to mature in the following months. October to April is considered the winter season and is cold and rainy.

Summer's warm air makes rain unlikely. Rain rarely falls in May and September. Weather varies in the transition months from April to mid-June and during September and October. The onset of cold weather may trigger heavy showers and endanger ripening crops: "As snow in summer and rain in harvest, so honor is not fitting for a fool" (Prov. 26:1).

For the prophets, the rain signaled God's continued blessing and favor upon his children: "Be glad then, you children of Zion, and rejoice in the LORD your God; for he has given you the former rain faithfully, and he will cause the rain to come down for you—the former rain, and the latter rain in the first month" (Joel 2:23).

Hosea likened God's presence to the refreshing spring rain: "He shall come to us like the rain, like the latter and former rain to the earth" (Hos. 6:3b).

Israel's unfaithfulness brought many seasons of drought. Naomi and her family left Bethlehem for the fields of Moab because of drought (Ruth 1:1). Elijah prayed that no rain or dew would fall for three years so that the people of Israel, seeing God's judgment on them, might return to him (1 Kings 17:1; see also Amos 4:7). Of course, drought often led to famine, a condition frequently mentioned in the Bible (for example, Luke 15:14).

The rainfall in Palestine varies widely from place to place. The southern Negev receives 5 centimeters (2 inches) per year, while Mount Hermon may be drenched with 152 centimeters (60 inches) of precipitation.

Israel's rainfall is directly related to the latitude and height of the land. The mountainous regions receive the most—from 61 to 91 centimeters (24 to 36 inches) in northern Galilee and from 51 to 71 centimeters (20 to 28 inches) in Samaria and Judah. South of the line between Gaza and En Gedi a mere 31 centimeters (12 inches) of rain falls; south of Beersheba, only 20 centimeters (eight inches). The rain also decreases from west to east. Perhaps 20 inches falls on the coast at Tel Aviv, or at Jerusalem, but only 10 to 20 centimeters (four to eight inches) falls a few miles to the east at Jericho and the Jordan River.

An estimated 60 to 70 percent of the precipitation is lost through evaporation because of the land's high temperatures and low humidity. Only 10 to 25 percent is absorbed for agricultural purposes.

The dew that falls approximately 250 nights of the year is essential. Some vegetation depends entirely on that source of moisture. We understand why Elijah included dew in his prophecy to Ahab: "there shall not be dew nor rain these years, except at my word" (1 Kings 17:1b).

The Holy Land also gets snow. The majestic snow of Mount Hermon can be seen from a great distance until midsummer. Jeremiah referred to the snowy mountains when he flailed Israel's faithless ways: "Does the snow of Lebanon leave the crags of Sirion? Do the mountain waters run dry, the cold flowing streams? But my people have forgotten me" (Jer. 18:14–15a, RSV).

The hill country of Judah annually averages two days of snow, which melts rapidly when the daytime temperature rises. However, a blizzard hit Palestine in 1950, bringing 69 centimeters (27 inches) of snow to Jerusalem and 53 centimeters (21 inches) to Acre!

3. Winds. Israel's hot climate is eased by cool Mediterranean winds during the day. Chill evenings provide a welcome change from the day's heat in desert and hill country. The moisture-laden seawinds combine with cool air at night to give Palestine its vital dew.

A southeasterly wind marks the change of seasons in Palestine, from spring to summer and from summer to fall. Jeremiah 4:11 mentions "a dry wind of the desolate heights . . . in the wilderness." This dry wind loaded with dust makes the people very uncomfortable.

The Bible's east wind may be what the Arabs call a *khamsin*. The *khamsin* leaves people irritable and they feel like doing nothing because of the oppressive heat. "And it happened, when the sun arose, that God prepared a vehement east wind; and the sun beat on Jonah's head so that he grew faint. Then he wished death for himself, and said, 'It is better for me to die than to live'" (Jon. 4:8).

The land of Israel may be divided into six regions, all related to the Jordan Valley that runs down the center of Palestine:

The Upper Jordan (1) extends from the Lebanon Mountains to the Sea of Galilee. The area that is usually called the Jordan Valley (2) lies between the Sea of Galilee and the Dead Sea.

Galilee (3) is the northernmost area between the Jordan River and the Mediterranean coast. Samaria (4) spreads between these natural boundaries in central Palestine, while Judah (5) does so in the extreme south.

Transjordan (6) is all the land east of the Jordan River, east and south of the Dead Sea. Its eastern border is the Syrian Desert.

The Jordan Valley

The Jordan River courses through the center of Palestine. It has also been the center of Israel's social and economic life, both in ancient times and today.

The Upper Jordan. God first gave the coastal plains to the tribe of Dan for its inheritance. However, as the Philistines grew in power the Danites couldn't hold the land, and they moved to the Upper Jordan Valley, far from the political centers of Jerusalem and Samaria (Judg. 18). They never fully used the 26 square kilometers (11 square miles) of the valley, as it held many streams, swamps, and small lakes. Mountains hedge the valley on three sides: the Naphtali Range to the west, the Hermon Range to the north, and the Golan Heights (Bashan) to the east.

The encircling mountains, drawing abundant rain and snow, give this region the highest precipitation in Israel, seven to 15 centimeters (three to six inches) annually. Runoff water and melting snow flow underground into springs to provide a year-round supply of fresh water.

1. Mount Hermon. The Danites settled in the fruitful valley at the foot of majestic Mount Hermon. They built their towns and planted their crops by the icy waters that flowed to the Sea of Galilee and the Dead Sea via the Jordan River.

Lemon trees at Tel Aviv, Israel, in a modern citrus-farming operation.

PHOTO BY GUSTAV JEENINGA

Traditional tomb of Joseph at Shechem (Ex. 13:19).

PHOTO BY HOWARD VOS

Over 2,700 meters (9,000 feet) high, Mount Hermon juts against the horizon to the northeast. Snow covers its highest peaks until midsummer. The mountain can be seen from a remarkable distance.

The imposing heights, abundant water, and luxurious vegetation struck awe in the hearts of those who settled in the shadows of the Hermon range. Even before the Israelites came, Canaanites linked the region with their fertility god Baal. Part of the range is called Baal Hermon (Judg. 3:3; 1 Chron. 5:23), and there is a city of Baal Gad (Josh. 13:5).

Idolatrous Israelites viewed Mount Hermon as a fertility symbol, just as the pagan Canaanites did. But the Israelites credited fertility and might to the Creator and not to the creation. To them, the power and magnificence of God dwarfed the mighty peaks of the north—Lebanon, Tabor, and Hermon: "The voice of the LORD breaks the cedars, . . . he makes them also skip like a calf, Lebanon and Sirion [Hermon] like a young wild ox" (Ps. 29:5–6). In their eyes, the mountains themselves worshiped Yahweh: "Tabor and Hermon rejoice in your name" (Ps. 89:12).

The many names of Mount Hermon attest its importance. Before the Israelites conquered them, the Amorites called it *Senir* (Deut. 3:9), and the Hebrew of Deuteronomy 4:48 refers to it as *Mount Sion*, although the Syriac version has *Sirian*.

When war threatened Israel's northern border, the Hermon range absorbed the first shock of invading forces. With the Lebanon mountains to the west, it provided a natural barrier to the Aramaean kingdom of the north. But in times of peace the great Mount Hermon still helped the people of Canaan. She quietly gave birth to springs around her base, as melting snows seeped through the porous rocks that make up her foundation.

2. Sources of the Jordan. The Jordan River begins in the Hula Valley. Actually, four rivers—the Senir, Dan, Ayyon, and Hermon—flowed into Hula Lake and their waters emerged at the southern tip of the lake as the Jordan River.

Springs in the northern recesses of Lebanon created the Senir River. These springs are situated 52 kilometers (32 miles) northeast of Metulla, Israel's northernmost settlement, and are fed by runoff water from the western slope of Mount Hermon.

A larger river, the Dan, comes from the ancient springs of Dan. Here the water flows into a crystal pool of ice-cold water and drops quickly into rapids. Smaller springs in the area ooze out of the ground and trickle from the rocks to water the dense foliage of mosses, bushes, and trees.

The tribe of Dan scouted this land and decided it was an ideal spot to settle. So they wiped out the inhabitants of Laish, rebuilt the town, and renamed it Dan. Instead of going to worship at Shiloh, about 128 kilometers (80 miles) away, they set up their own shrine with stolen idols (Judg. 18).

The Ayyon River (which in biblical times drained the Ayyon Valley in Lebanon) contains the Holy Land's most impressive waterfall, the Tannur. At Abel Beth-maacah, a mile south of the waterfall, King David's men besieged Sheba, who drew away Israel's allegiance with his cry: "We have no share in David" (2 Sam. 20:1).

The fourth river feeding into the Jordan River, the Hermon, spills from beneath a high rock wall at what was once the village of Banias. The Banias springs were originally named Paneas, after Pan, the Greek god of forests and meadows. The name *Banias* reflects the Roman term for "bath." There are waterfalls about a mile southwest of this place also.

Herod the Great built a temple at Banias and dedicated the site to Caesar Augustus. Later the tetrarch Philip made his home there and renamed it Caesarea Philippi, after himself.

At Caesarea Philippi, rocks were scattered along the river bank. Idols were nestled in the niches of a high rock wall dedicated to Pan. In Jesus' powerful way he welded the setting to his response: "Blessed art thou, Simon Bar-Jona . . . You are Peter, and on this rock I will build My church, and the gates of Hades shall not prevail against it" (Matt. 16:17–18).

Since they were traveling in the region of Caesarea Philippi, Jesus might have led Peter and James to one of Mount Hermon's ridges to witness his Transfiguration. (Some believe the high mountain of Matthew 17:1 was Mount Tabor, but the preceding passage places the group near Mount Hermon.)

3. Hula Lake. Hula Lake nestles close to the Lebanon and Hermon ranges in the upper Jordan Valley. In Bible times, river waters drained into the shallow water of the Hula swamps, and then into the lake. The swamps north of the lake were filled with semitropical plants. Alligators, hippopotamuses, and water buffalo made their homes there. Since drainage was poor, settlers often contracted malaria, and at certain seasons the area flooded. With so many hazards, the land was not fully used.

A layer of basalt blocked the southern end of Hula Lake. Volcanic activity in the Golan Heights had dumped lava on the mountains north of Galilee. These areas were equally hostile to settlers.

In OT times, river water cut a canal 16 kilometers (10 miles) through the basalt. The canal drops 750 feet in that stretch and deepens as it goes. Consequently, travelers could cross the Jordan at only one point of the canal, just below the lake. Travelers who were willing to wait until the water was low could ford the river there. Caravans loaded with wares from Egypt and Israel regularly crossed the Jordan at that ford on their way north to Damascus or Mesopotamia. In our time, the Bridge of the Daughters of Jacob spans the ancient ford.

Twentieth-century Israelis have made other changes in the region as well. From 1951 to 1958 they drained Hula Lake and reclaimed over 78,000 square kilometers (20,000 acres) of highly fertile land from the lake bed and swamps. They also straightened and deepened the canal to the Sea of Galilee.

The Jordan Valley Proper

The Jordan River valley stretches out in the middle of the Holy Land for 105 kilometers (65 miles). Elevation drops gradually as the Jordan leaves the Sea of Galilee at an altitude of 195 meters (650 feet) below sea level and enters the Dead Sea at 387 meters (1,290 feet) below sea level. Since the river depth varies and the water is full of sandbars, sailors do not try to navigate between the two seas.

About eight kilometers (five miles) south of the Sea of Galilee, the Jordan doubles in size as the Yarmuk River adds roughly 459,000 cubic meters (16.2 million cubic feet) of water to its flow every minute. Other rivers such as the Jabbok swell the Jordan by an additional 94,500 cubic meters (3.3 million cubic feet) per minute.

The watercourse of the Jordan is ever changing. The entire Jordan Valley was once under water. This left debris of loose soil and gravel, especially to the south in a land now called the *qattara* or "badlands." Little rivers feed soil as well as water into the Jordan, and its own currents eat away the riverbed. Earthquakes and tremors have dumped dirt into the river as well, sometimes blocking the Jordan's flow and forcing it to seek a new course.

Desolate mountain ranges flank the river. To the west, Samaria and Bethel reach 450 meters (1,500 feet) in Lower Galilee. East of the Jordan, the humps of the Gilead rise to 600 meters (2,000 feet).

At one point the valley is only three kilometers (two miles) wide. It spreads out to 11 kilometers (seven miles) near Beth Shan and the Jezreel Valley, and by Jericho it widens to a span of 22.5 kilometers (14 miles). A narrow pass in the hill country of Samaria separates the Jordan Valley into the Beth Shan and lower Jordan valleys.

1. A Natural Boundary. The Jordan River served Canaan as a natural boundary, holding back eastern invaders. From the book of Genesis onward, the Scriptures speak of the Jordan River as a boundary or border. Several Scripture texts refer to crossing the Jordan (see Gen. 32:10; Deut. 3:25; 27:4; Josh.1:2).

As the tribes of Israel moved north from the Sinai, they approached the Jordan Valley from the east. At the time, plundering tribes from the desert controlled that land, and the Jordan was a frontier. Three tribes wanted to stay and graze their cattle there, but Moses urged them to go along across the Jordan to help in the conquest of Canaan. They did so with the provision that after the conquest they could return to the eastern shore to settle. The tribes of Reuben and Gad and half the tribe of Manasseh eventually received their inheritance east of the river, as they had requested. Still, the prospect of being separated from the other tribes troubled them: "In time to come your descendants may speak to our descendants, saying, 'What have you to do with the LORD God of Israel? For the Lord has made the Jordan a border between you and us, you children of Reuben and children of God. You have no part in the LORD. So your descendants would make our descendants cease fearing the LORD'" (Josh. 22:24–25).

Many gospel songs have been written about going over the Jordan, and with good reason. It was not an easy river to cross. The Israelites could ford the Jordan only at traditional spots, and even those places were useless when the Jordan flooded its banks.

The Israelites knew the value of the fords and wrested them from their enemies as soon as possible. Ehud's forces "seized the fords of Jordan leading to Moab, and did not allow anyone to cross over" (Judg. 3:28). Gideon recruited men for his army with the cry, "Come down against the Midianites, and seize from them the watering places" (Judg. 7:24).

For the most part, the Jordan Valley was sparsely settled, partly because of the heat and dryness. More people settled in the Beth Shan Valley to the north, where it was at least possible to irrigate crops.

2. The Beth Shan Valley. Tributaries on both sides of the Jordan flood their banks in winter and spring. Though the climate in the Beth Shan Valley resembled a desert, the plentiful amount of water and high temperatures produced dense subtropical brush. The Israelis eventually dug canals to control the flooding and used the Jordan's waters to irrigate crops in the valley.

A modern city of 15,000 people, Beth Shan lies at the foot of Mount Gilboa 24 kilometers (15.5 miles) south of the Sea of Galilee where the Valley of Jezreel meets the Jordan Valley.

The Lower Jordan

The lower Jordan Valley contains three distinct levels. They appear on both sides of the river, and are known as the *zor*, the *qattara*, and the *ghor*.

Closest to the river is the *zor*, a narrow strip of land one or two miles wide that the Bible calls "the thickets of the Jordan" or "the wilderness." Thanks to seasonal floods, the *zor* was a veritable jungle of dense brush, shrubs, and tamarisk trees. Wild beasts hid in its shelter. Jeremiah speaks of "a lion from the flood plain of the Jordan" (Jer. 49:19). The sons of the prophets were cutting down trees in the Jordan thickets when Elisha made an iron ax head float on the river (2 Kings 6:1–7).

John the Baptist prepared the way for the Messiah in the *zor* near Jericho: "John came baptizing in the wilderness and preaching a baptism of repentance for the remission of sins" (Mark 1:4). He also baptized Jesus in the Jordan (Mark 1:9).

Away from the river, beyond the *zor*, are the *qattara* badlands. This territory is covered by ancient deposits of sediment from the lake that once filled the Jordan Valley. Seasonal streams carve deep crevices in the *qattara*. No one grew crops there because the soil was salty. Modern Israeli scientists are reclaiming the soil by washing it with river water.

The *ghor* is a steep but fertile terrace between the *qattara* and the mountains. Farmers irrigate and cultivate these fields.

Galilee

Jesus proclaimed the good news in the lowlands of Galilee. Isaiah had predicted that he would minister in "the land of Zebulun and the land of Naphtali, by the way of the sea, beyond Jordan, Galilee of the Gentiles" (Matt. 4:15).

Volcanoes and earthquakes shaped the landscape of Galilee. The area holds isolated mountains, high plateaus, valleys and gorges, rocky ridges and steep cliffs. Galilee divides naturally into two parts, with obvious differences in altitude, climate, and vegetation.

Upper Galilee

Upper Galilee lies south and west of the Hula Valley. It extends eastward from the Mediterranean Sea to the town of Safed, and south to the Beth Haccerem Valley. In this fertile valley live olive trees that are hundreds of years old.

At one time upper Galilee was probably a single block of mountain, but massive natural forces split it into many pieces. Some parts were thrust up, other sank down, and all were eroded by water.

The tribe of Naphtali settled the mountainous area to the east. From the Naphtali Range (about 600 meters or 2,000 feet above sea level), travelers get a splendid view of the Hula Valley. The scattered peaks of Mount Meiron, Mount Shammai (or Mount Hillel), and Mount Ha-ari, rising between 1,000 and 1,200 meters (3,400 to 3,900 feet), tower above the relatively high mountain ranges of upper Galilee.

Few people settled in upper Galilee. The rugged mountains and sharp cliffs mostly offered protection for fugitives and refugees. King Solomon gave 20 cities in the northwestern territory to King Hiram of Tyre. But the biblical timber baron didn't appreciate the gift: "Then Hiram went out from Tyre to see the cities which Solomon had given him, but they did not please him. So he said, 'What cities are these which you have given me, my brother?' And he called them the land of Cabul, as they are to this day" (1 Kings 9:12–13). Roughly translated, *Cabul* meant "obscurity." Hiram's discourteous remark immediately strained relations with his new subjects in the cities of Galilee.

On upper Galilee's eastern border stands the modern city of Safed, 540 meters (1,800 feet) above sea level. Safed is visible from the northern shore of the Sea of Galilee. The twinkling night lights of such a town might have prompted Jesus' remark: "A city that is set on a hill cannot be hidden" (Matt. 5:14).

Lower Galilee

Lower Galilee is literally lower than upper Galilee, being a plateau about 350 feet above sea level. In lower Galilee we find Jesus' hometown (Matt. 2:23). Nazareth perches atop a steeply tilted hunk of earth. It seems impossible to enter Nazareth from the south, but a tenacious road curves and twists up the narrow ridge into the city. The attempt made on

Jesus' life at Nazareth likely occurred on the cliffs to the south: "And they rose up and put him out of the city, and led him to the brow of the hill on which their city was built, that they might throw him down headlong. But passing through the midst of them he went away" (Luke 4:29–30, RSV).

Looking away from Nazareth people can see Mount Tabor, a cone-shaped volcanic mountain almost 600 meters (2,000 feet) high. In the days of the judges, Deborah sent Barak and his troops to Mount Tabor to attack the Canaanites (Judg. 4:6). Jeremiah evoked the name to pronounce doom on Egypt: "Surely as Tabor is among the mountains and as Carmel by the sea, so he shall come" (Jer. 46:18).

Mount Tabor's beautiful foliage contrasts with the rather barren grassy hills at its base. Some say that Mount Tabor was the site of Jesus' transfiguration.

Another volcanic crater, the Horns of Hittin, can be seen from many parts of Galilee. In A.D. 1187 a decisive battle took place there between the Crusaders and the Arab leader Saladin.

Earthquakes produced two other mountains in Galilee that are actually escarpments with long cliff-like ridges. Mount Arbel rises to only 180 meters (600 feet), yet from it one can see the arena of Jesus' ministry (the valley of Gennosar, the Mount of the Beatitudes, Capernaum, and the blue waters of the Sea of Galilee), and the Golan Heights beyond. Wadi Arbel served as a junction between the road of Galilee (from Hazor and Damascus) and the Horns of Hittim.

The second escarpment overlooks the Jordan Valley, Golan Heights, and the Sea of Galilee. Though Ramat Kokav is the highest mountain in lower Galilee, the Bible does not mention it. The Crusaders built a fortress on its summit. They named the stronghold *Belvoir* ("good lookout point"), because of the excellent view which includes even the snow-capped peaks of Mount Hermon.

The Sea of Galilee

Many people think of this as a large body of water. Actually, the Sea of Galilee is a lake below sea level, and not a large one. Roughly pear-shaped, the water is only 10 kilometers (six miles) wide and 24 kilometers (15 miles) from north to south. It is 39 to 47 meters (120 to 155 feet) deep, and its surface is 206 meters (650 feet) below sea level. Its circumference is about 51 kilometers (32 miles). It is listed as the Lake (or Sea) of Chinnereth on OT maps. Later it was called Lake Gennesaret (Luke 5:1), the Sea of Tiberias (John 6:1), or most frequently, the Sea of Galilee.

The territories of Naphtali, Zebulun, and Issachar bordered Lake Chinnereth in OT times. They constituted the region of Galilee, a subdivision of the northern kingdom. Under Rome's rule, the provinces of Galilee, Judah, and Samaria were part of Herod's kingdom. Herod the Great supposedly rid Galilee of robbers and repopulated the north with Jews. Once known as "Galilee of the nations" (Isa. 9:1, KJV; RSV "Gentiles"), it became a vigorously Jewish region. Still, the people of Judea despised the Jews of Galilee. Yet Jesus conducted most of his ministry in the vicinity of the Sea of Galilee.

Steep hills skirt most of the shoreline. Streams by Bethsaida, Gennesaret, and Sennabris created fertile valleys that the Israelites cultivated. They often built villages on hills and mountaintops. The Arbel cliffs above Magdala offer a panoramic view of the northern region of the lake. The map helps us visualize some familiar NT events.

"And Jesus, walking by the Sea of Galilee saw two brothers, Simon called Peter, and Andrew his brother, casting a net into the sea; for they were fishermen" (Matt. 4:18).

About 3.5 kilometers (2 miles) west of Capernaum stands the Hill of the Beatitudes, where Jesus may have delivered the Sermon on the Mount (Matt. 5—7). On one of these hills he fed the 5,000 with a few loaves and fishes.

When Nazareth rejected Jesus (Luke 4:29–31), he made Capernaum the center of his ministry. Jesus taught in the synagogue, performed many miracles, and then set out on a preaching mission. After the Resurrection, Jesus returned to the shores of Galilee.

Samaria

North of the Dead Sea and west of the Jordan is the hill country of Samaria. A harsh, mountainous land full of fissures and valleys, its boundaries run from the Jordan Valley on the east to the Plain of Sharon on the west. The valleys of Jezreel and Esdraelon border it on the north. The southern boundaries tended to shift, since there is no sharp division between the hill country of Samaria and Judah.

If you were to stand on Mount Nebo and look westward across the Jordan, Samaria might appear to be an impenetrable mountain mass. From the floor of the Jordan Valley, 240 meters (800 feet) below sea level, the Samarian hills climb steeply to 600 meters (2,000 feet) above sea level within 11 kilometers (seven miles). The coastal side drops more gradually, taking 40 kilometers (25 miles) to descend to sea level. Understandably, the west offers easier ways into the hill country of Samaria than the passes of the east.

Mountain passes made Samaria's hills accessible and connected the country with other towns and peoples. Several important routes passed through Samaria. One road passes Beth Shan north of Mount Gilboa to Megiddo, connecting Samaria to the Via Maris, Canaan's major north-south highway. Just west of Mount Gilboa one branch heads south, passing through the Valley of Dothan. Northeast of the Shechem is the pass of Wadi Far'a, by which a traveler can reach the Jordan Valley. The Wadi Far'a descends gradually 300 meters in 16 kilometers (or 1,000 feet in 10 miles), compared to the steep cliffs (750 meters or 2,500 feet) through which it passes.

The Via Maris ran parallel to the main watershed of the Samarian hill country in the Plain of Sharon. From early times, settlers of the hill country maintained connections with the coastal highway for trade and cultural purposes.

Many place-names of Samaria are familiar to Bible readers. At Shechem both Abraham and Jacob built altars (Gen. 12:6–8; 33:18). There the Israelites buried Joseph's bones (Josh. 24:32) and renewed the covenant God had made with Moses.

When the lad Joseph went to look for his brothers, he found them in the Valley of Dothan (Gen. 37:17). Several judges were active in the region: Deborah, Gideon, Tola, and Abdon. The first prophet, Samuel, grew up at the tabernacle of Shiloh. Later he made his birthplace, Ramah, his headquarters and traveled a circuit that included the towns of Bethel, Gilgal, and Mizpah (1 Sam. 1:1—2:11; 7:15–17).

The northern kingdom of Israel made Samaria its capital, and many battles were fought in its open valleys. Such characters as Ahab, Elijah, Jehu, and Elisha appeared in this hilly country to play important parts in the history of Israel.

At the northern tip of Samaria stands Mount Gilboa, a significant place in Israel's military history. Here the Lord instructed Gideon to reduce his forces from 32,000 men to 300 so that it would be obvious that God was responsible for their victory against the Midianites and Amalekites. The "people of the East" had crossed the Jordan and camped in the valley of Jezreel, by the hill of Moreh. Gideon's forces camped near the spring of Harod, at the foot of Mount Gilboa. Gideon obeyed the Lord, and his tiny army routed the enemy (Judg. 7:1–25).

In a later battle, Saul did not fare as well. "Now the Philistines fought against Israel; and the men of Israel fled from before the Philistines, and fell slain on Mount Gilboa" (1 Sam. 31:1). Saul's sons were killed in the battle, and Saul committed suicide. The Philistines hung the bodies of Saul and the royal sons on the wall of Beth Shan in the

Harod Valley (31:10). Upon hearing of their ignoble deaths, David lamented: "O mountains of Gilboa, let there be no dew, nor let there be rain upon you. . . . for the shield of the mighty is cast away there! The shield of Saul, not anointed with oil" (2 Sam. 1:21).

Jesus also visited Samaria and at Jacob's well he met the woman of Samaria. (See John 4:5ff.)

Samaria was one of the three specific places named in the Great Commission Jesus gave before His ascension: "You shall be witnesses to me in Jerusalem, and in all Judea and Samaria, and to the end of the earth" (Acts 1:8). When the early church was scattered by the persecution in Jerusalem, Philip took the gospel to Samaria, where it was well received (Acts 8:1–6, 14).

Judah

No one can state with certainty where the land of Samaria ended and Judah began. Some say the road from Ajalon to Jericho, passing between Bethel and Gibeon, marks the boundary. Others think Samaria ended with the road from Beth-shemesh to Jerusalem. Between the two were the Bethel hills, the shifting border of the northern kingdom of Israel.

Judah encompasses a spine of mountains and the barren desert sands of the wilderness. The hill country of Judah runs parallel to the plateau of Moab, which lies on the other side of the Dead Sea. It goes roughly in a northeast-southwest direction from Bethel to Hebron, with the mountains tapering off in the south, at Beersheba. The mountains are even higher than those of Samaria, rising to 990 meters (3,300 feet).

Bethel Hills

The Bible says little about the Bethel hills, although the tribes of Benjamin and Ephraim settled in this region. Manasseh to the north and Judah to the south are mentioned more frequently in the Scriptures. Yet the Bethel hills contained fertile valleys, such as the plateau between Gibeon and Michmash. Since rainfall was heavy, the region was soon cultivated.

Jerusalem Hills

South of the Bethel hills, in line with the northern tip of the Dead Sea, are the Jerusalem hills and the city of Jerusalem. The city lies 600 meters (about 2,000 feet) above sea level, and the hills that surround it are lower than those of Bethel or Hebron. "As the mountains surround Jerusalem," said the psalmist, "so the LORD surrounds his people" (Ps. 125:2). Even from 13 kilometers (eight miles) away, Jerusalem can be seen from the encircling mountains.

Ravines cut Jerusalem off from all directions but the north, for several valleys converge at this location.

When Jesus came to Jerusalem, the palaces of Herod and the high priest Caiaphas were within the walled city. From their windows they could look down upon the Valley of Hinnom, to the west. King Ahaz had "burned his sons as an offering in the valley of the son of Hinnom, and practiced soothsaying and augury and sorcery, and dealt with mediums and with wizards. He did much evil in the sight of the LORD, provoking him to anger" (2 Chron. 33:6, RSV).

Jesus used the name of the region (Ge-hinnom, in Greek Gehenna) for hell, the ultimate place of God's judgment. Judas, it seems, committed suicide in this valley, where it curves from south to east.

By the Pool of Siloam the Hinnom and Kidron Valleys come together. The Kidron

River runs between the Mount of Olives and the Hill of Jerusalem, also known as Mount Moriah. The events of history mingle in Jerusalem because on Mount Moriah Abraham prepared to sacrifice Isaac (Gen. 22:2). There the Lord appeared to David (2 Chron. 3:1). From the confluence of the Hinnom and Kidron Rivers, rainwater flows through the Judean wilderness to the Dead Sea.

Hebron Hills

Going southward the Hebron range comes next. At over 900 meters (3,000 feet), it is the highest range in Judah. On Hebron's slopes Abraham and Isaac tended their flocks. Near Hebron, Abraham purchased the Cave of Machpelah to bury Sarah, and the patriarchs were also interred there. After Saul's death, David ruled Judah from Hebron for about seven years before he captured Jerusalem.

The Coastal Plains

Alongside the mountain ranges of Judah and Samaria lies the coast of the beautiful Mediterranean Sea. It is a remarkably smooth coastline. Sea currents straightened much of the shoreline by depositing sand picked up from the Nile delta. Northward, the sand deposits decrease until, by the Ladder of Tyre, the coast is rocky.

Because of sand deposits and rocks, it seemed impossible to develop a harbor for international shipping until late in Israel's history. The Phoenicians used the natural harbors at Sidon and Tyre. But on Palestine's stretch of the Mediterranean, only small vessels could dock at Joppa. Solomon's main harbor was Ezion-geber, on the Red Sea's Gulf of Eilat. Other kings of Judah unsuccessfully contested the Edomites for control of that region.

During the rule of Herod the Great, the Romans developed two more ports, Ptolemais (Acre) and Caesarea. Paul docked at Caesarea at the close of his second missionary journey, then visited both Ptolemais and Caesarea after his third journey. Later, Festus sent Paul from Caesarea to Rome as a prisoner (Acts 27:2).

The Palestinian coast has extensive deposits of kurkar, a type of sandstone. Kurkar disintegrates slowly and hardens when it meets water, so it tends to prevent erosion of the shoreline. Little islands of kurkar and a sandstone ridge follow the coastline by Samaria. Until modern times, the Sharon Plain was swampy because that ridge held back water draining from the Samarian hills. Water flooded the plain and rivers slowly carried it to the sea.

The Philistine Coast

The Philistines controlled the coast from the Yarkon River (near Joppa) to Gaza. Dune belts skirt the shore, especially to the south. The dunes are approximately six kilometers (four miles) wide by Gaza, and south of the Philistine coast the sand extends even farther inland. A fertile plain about 16 kilometers (10 miles) wide lies east of the dunes. Sediment and sand create a rich soil, and many types of crops are grown there.

In this region the Philistines lived and worshiped.

Five major cities controlled Philistia and its trade routes. To go from Phoenicia to Egypt, or through Israel's Shephelah into the Judean hills, traders had to pass through Philistia. Gaza, Ashdod, and Ashkelon were near the coast and served as small harbors. Gath and Ekron were further inland, on a road running parallel to the Via Maris. Goliath, the Philistine giant, came from Gath.

The Shephelah

The Shephelah, a strip of land 13 by 64 kilometers (eight by 40 miles) between Philistia's coastal plain and the Judean hills, was a much-disputed territory. Its low-lying hills are mostly of chalk, which easily erodes to form passes and caves. The most important pass into the hills is the Valley of Ajalon, where Joshua said, "Sun, stand still over Gibeon; and, Moon, in the Valley of Aijalon" (Josh. 10:12).

Judah could have been quite isolated, except for the Philistines on the west. International roads crossed through Samaria, but the coastal plains insulated Judah's hills from the Via Maris (Road to the Sea) thoroughfare. Judah could easily check traffic on the road from Shechem to Jerusalem. In times of war with Israel—during the divided kingdom period—Judah simply closed the northern border. The Judean Desert to the east and the Negev Desert on the south helped isolate Judah.

That vulnerable western front remained. The kings of Judah poured much effort and expense into strengthening the fortified cities of the Shephelah. It had been Solomon's idea to flank Jerusalem with defense cities, such as Gezer and Beth-Horon (1 Kings 9:15–17). Rehoboam, Abijah, Asa, and Jehoshaphat reinforced Judah's western frontier (2 Chron. 11:5–12, 23; 13:7; 14:6f.; 17:1ff.).

Modern travelers can still take one of the two roads that led from the domain of the five Philistine kings into the heart of Saul's kingdom in the Shephelah. One road passes through Lachish, one of Judah's military defense centers, then leads northward into the Valley of Elah. The other originates farther north at Ashdod, passes by Gath and reaches the Valley of Elah after a journey of 32 kilometers (20 miles). Merging in the valley, the roads continue northward via Beth-Horon and Gibeon to Michmash, an ancient outpost of the Philistines (1 Sam. 13:5). Saul's son Jonathan boldly routed the Philistine forces at the pass of Michmash, forcing them to retreat to the Valley of Ajalon (1 Sam. 14:1–31).

One famous biblical drama was staged in the Valley of Elah: "Now the Philistines gathered their armies together to battle, and were gathered at Sochoh, which belongs to Judah; they encamped between Sochoh and Azekah, in Ephes-dammim. And Saul and the men of Israel were gathered together, and they encamped in the Valley of Elah, and drew up in battle array against the Philistines. The Philistines stood on a mountain on one side, and Israel stood on a mountain on the other side; with a valley between them. And a champion went out from the camp of the Philistines, named Goliath" (1 Sam. 17:1–4).

The newly anointed but not-yet king, David, heard the challenge as he brought supplies to his brothers. Over the protests of his brothers and despite King Saul's reservations, he met Goliath. David's only assurance was, "The LORD, who delivered me from the paw of the lion and from the paw of the bear, he will deliver me from the hand of this Philistine" (17:37).

The first stone he slung felled the giant, and the Israelites chased the astonished Philistines all the way back to the coastal plains.

The Sharon and Carmel Coast

The Philistine territory ended at the Yarkon River, where the Plain of Sharon begins. Largest of the coastal plains, the Sharon reaches to the Crocodile River in the north.

Although it seemed to be too swampy and shrub-filled to be good for human settlement, the Sharon Valley was quite fertile. The region was best suited for pasturage (Isa. 65:10), and in it the rose of Sharon grew wild (Song of Sol. 2:1). Isaiah spoke of the "excellence of Carmel and Sharon" (Isa. 35:2). Perhaps the Israelites regarded the extensive swamps of the Sharon much as we today value America's wilderness regions.

A few cities dotted the plain: Sochoh (1 Kings 4:10), Gilgal (Josh. 10:7), Aphek, Gathrimmon, Lod, and Ono (1 Chron. 8:12). A small harbor at Dor provided international contacts for the Canaanites.

The Plain of Asher

According to the judge named Deborah, the tribe of Asher "continued at the seashore, and stayed by his inlets" (Judg. 5:17b). This small plain hugs the coast above the Plain of Sharon. For the most part, the Asher Valley is about five miles wide, though it widens south of the port of Accho (modern Acre). At the north end, the mountains of Galilee almost touch the sea, leaving a narrow passage to Phoenicia known as the "Ladder of Tyre."

Because of its strategic location between Phoenicia and Egypt, the plain was important to commerce. In times of peace, the tribe of Asher enjoyed cultural prosperity, but during wars it suffered devastation.

The Dead Sea

The lowest body of water in the world is the Dead Sea, an oblong lake three-fourths as long as the Jordan Valley north of it. Eighty kilometers (50 miles) in length, it does not measure more than 18 kilometers (11 miles) at the widest; across from the Lisan Peninsula it narrows to three kilometers (two miles) or less.

The water surface of the Dead Sea is about 390 meters (1,300 feet) below sea level. Its depth has been estimated at another 1,300 feet.

Tourists enjoy floating on the incredibly buoyant water of the Dead Sea. Because the sea has no outlet and evaporation is high, the concentration of minerals is as much as 30 percent. The water abounds with salt, bromide, magnesium chloride, potassium chloride, and sulfur. Modern Israelis mine the chemical salts of the rich waters for potash, bromine, and other industrial chemicals.

Long ago the Dead Sea was part of a huge inland lake that covered the Jordan Rift from the Hula Valley southward. A salt rock at Mount Sedom (at the southwest corner of the Dead Sea) and the qattara of the Jordan Valley are signs that eroding soil made the ancient lake more salty.

The level of the Dead Sea is dropping. In recent times both Israel and Jordan have diverted huge quantities of water from the Sea of Galilee and the Yarmuk River, so less water flows into it. At one time it was convenient to cross the Dead Sea by the Lisan Peninsula, where the water was about three feet deep. The water level has since dropped so much that only a narrow canal separates the western shore from the widening Lisan.

The third hottest temperature on world record (72 degrees C. or 129 degrees F.) was taken in this area on June 21, 1942. Despite the heat, the precipitation (perhaps five centimeters, or two inches per year), and the bleak scenery, people have settled in the Dead Sea region from ancient times.

This region appeared fertile and desirable to Lot, and he chose it when he and Abraham went their separate ways. Unfortunately, Lot moved into bad company. "But the men of Sodom were exceedingly wicked and sinful against the LORD" (Gen. 13:13). God destroyed Sodom and the nearby city of Gomorrah.

Archaeologists speculate that Sodom and Gomorrah were located in the southern portion of the Dead Sea. When the Lord reduced them to rubble because of their wickedness (Gen. 19), an earthquake probably dropped the land on which they stood and the waters of the Dead Sea inundated the debris.

In the midst of the Judean wasteland bordering the Dead Sea, the oases of En-Gedi and Ein-Faschka provide food and springs of fresh water. Remains of an ancient temple show people settled there as early as 4000 B.C. David and his men hid from Saul at En-Gedi (1 Sam. 24:1). The Song of Solomon speaks of "a cluster of henna blooms in the vineyards of En-Gedi" (1:14).

Near Ein-Faschka is the site of Qumran where the Dead Sea scrolls were found in 1947. During Jesus' time, members of this Essene community believed they were the righteous remnant, sole heirs to God's covenant. They interpreted literally words such as, "The voice of one crying in the wilderness: 'Prepare the way of the LORD; Make straight in the desert a highway for our God'" (Isa. 40:3). Separating themselves from society, they awaited the Lord's coming in the desert. The sweet waters at Ein-Faschka permitted vegetation to grow, supplying the community's physical needs.

The fortress of Masada overlooks the Dead Sea from the rocky Judean wilderness farther south. There the last Jewish forces of a final revolt took their own lives in A.D. 73, rather than submit to Rome's rule.

The Dead Sea region is aptly named. Even fish struggle against being carried into the sea, for its high mineral content brings immediate death. Yet the oases are a vivid reminder of how beautiful the region could be if the lake contained sweet water.

Ezekiel envisioned the restoration of the Dead Sea valley. In his vision, water poured forth from the temple altar and flowed into the Kidron through the Judean wilderness to the Dead Sea (Ezek. 47:8–12).

The Transjordan

Transjordan means "on the other side of the Jordan," and in its widest sense this area includes all the land east of the Jordan River to the Syrian Desert. The area takes in the land east of the upper Jordan Valley as well as that east and southeast of the Dead Sea— and everything in between. Today it includes the nations of Lebanon and Israel, and the Gaza Strip.

From a high vantage point in Palestine, the mountains of Transjordan seem to jump from the valley floor. Higher than Palestine's mountains (though no less bleak), their western rim gently runs down to the plateau of the desert.

Canyon-like riverbeds, running east and west, marked the divisions of tribal territory in the Transjordan.

Bashan is the northern area between the Hermon and Yarmuk Rivers; Gilead lies between the Yarmuk and Jabbok. Next comes the land of the Ammonites (partly shared with the Moabites), whose southern border was the Arnon River. Moab extended from the Arnon to the Zered River. Finally, Edom stretched from the Zered to the Red Sea's Gulf of Eilat and the modern port of Aqaba.

Bashan

Bashan is the biblical name for an area that includes one of the modern world's political problems, the Golan Heights, from which Syria shelled Ein Gev, precipitating Israel's Six-Day War in June of 1967. This highly-coveted district follows the eastern side of the upper Jordan Valley for about 64 kilometers (40 miles), almost to Damascus.

In NT times, Herod the Great made Bashan's wheat lands the granary of the Near East. Even in the OT era, the rich soil of this well-watered tract produced abundant grain. Animal husbandry flourished, and the huge bulls and well-fed cows of Bashan were known far and wide. Exiled in the land of the Chaldeans, Ezekiel spoke of the "fatlings of Bashan" (Ezek. 39:18). Amos railed against the noble women of Samaria, calling them "cows of Bashan, who are in the mountain of Samaria, who oppress the poor, who crush the needy, who say to their husbands, 'Bring, that we may drink!'" (Amos 4:1, RSV). The Psalmist compared his enemies to the powerful beasts: "Many bulls have surrounded me; strong bulls of Bashan have encircled me" (Ps. 22:12).

Mighty oaks grew in Bashan. Isaiah mentioned "all the cedars of Lebanon . . . all the oaks of Bashan" (Isa. 2:13). Although Lebanon's cedars were more highly prized than Bashan's oaks, the Israelites used the timber and even exported it. According to Ezekiel, the oaks of Bashan were used to make oars for Phoenician ships (Ezek. 27:6).

Ten cities in southern Bashan and northern Gilead organized to form the Decapolis. (See Matt. 4:25; Mark 5:20; 7:31.) Each city was a strategic point in the political division of the region. Hippos, for instance, controlled the road to Damascus, on which Paul was traveling in his plan to persecute early Christians. He had the beginning of his conversion experience on that same road (Acts 9:3). Today that road overlooks the modern kibbutz of Ein Gev near the Sea of Galilee.

For the most part, Bashan is unlike the rest of the Transjordan. It is a high country, with mountains rising ever higher to the east. In the north, dense foliage pushes back the desert, compared to a narrow strip of cultivated land south of the Yarmuk River. Most of Bashan gets rain or snow.

The Lower Golan (southern Bashan) starts at the eastern shore of Galilee, below sea level. Not far from the lake, barren hills rise steeply to a plateau about 400 meters (1,600 feet) above the Sea of Galilee. The Lower Golan held a prosperous Jewish community in NT times.

The Upper Golan is breathtaking, with exalted cone-shaped peaks and craters of extinct volcanoes. Erosion of the basalt soil has made a good grazing land. Less rain—3 to 3.5 centimeters (12 to 14 inches)—falls on the plateau to the southeast, which was called *Argob* in the OT. Moses reminded the Israelites that he led them to Bashan: "So the LORD our God also delivered into our hands Og king of Bashan, with all his people, . . . And we took all his cities at that time; there was not a city which we did not take from them; sixty cities, all the region of Argob, the kingdom of Og in Bashan" (Deut. 3:3–4; see also Deut. 3:13; Num. 21:33; 1 Kings 4:13).

Still farther east is the Hauran, which Ezekiel included as part of the northeastern boundary of Israel (Ezek. 47:16, 18). The Hauran is jagged terrain, having once been the center of volcanic activity. Jebel Druz, the mountain of the Arabic-speaking Druze sect, pierces the sky at 1,500 meters (5,000 feet). This rugged country made an ideal hideout for robber bands, and later was a refuge for the persecuted Druze. Yet the area has enough moisture and good soil to grow crops.

Herod the Great took control of Bashan as early as 20 B.C. and left it to his son, Herod Philip, as an inheritance. Philip built up Caesarea Philippi as his capital, naming it in honor of the Caesar as well as himself. The province was given to Agrippa I in A.D. 37.

Gilead

The mountains of Gilead are an eastern counterpart to the hill country of Samaria, and the landscape, vegetation, and climate are somewhat similar. However, the eastern mountains rise higher: 1,000 to 1,200 meters (3,281 to 3,937 feet) as compared with Mount Hebron's 990 meters (3,300 feet). They also receive more rainfall, 75 centimeters (30 inches) per year, instead of the 50 centimeters (20 inches) per annum of the Holy Land.

Those who visit Gilead after being in Palestine are usually surprised at the many springs, villages, and shrub-covered hillsides. From here the famous "balm of Gilead" was exported—probably tiny balls of sap from slashed evergreen trees—to be used for medicinal purposes. Joseph was sold to a caravan from Gilead, on its way to Egypt with "camels, bearing spicery, balm, and myrrh" (Gen. 37:25).

Gilead is an oval dome roughly split in two by the Jabbok River. The half-tribe of Manasseh settled northern Gilead, which was covered with thick brushwood and oaks.

The more mountainous southern Gilead was allocated to Reuben. The high amount of precipitation, plus heavy dew in summer, produced lush growth. Year-round tributaries of the Yarmuka and Jordan rivers drained the excess water.

Two judges of Israel were natives of Gilead:

• Jair ruled Israel for 22 years from Camon, his home in northern Gilead.

• Jephthah was the son of Gilead, but his mother was a harlot, so his stepbrothers refused him a share of the inheritance. He fled to the land of Tob, where he formed a band of raiders. Later his brothers recalled his prowess as a warrior, and promised him the leadership of Gilead if he would lead their army against the Ammonites. Jephthah's forces attacked and defeated the Ammonites (Judg. 11:32).

For the most part, the Ammonites left the Israelites alone until the days of Saul. As Saul was about to assume the reign of Israel, an unsavory character named Nahash besieged the city of Jabesh-Gilead. The inhabitants offered to serve him under a treaty, but he would agree only if they allowed him to gouge out their eyes! And Saul gathered the forces of Judah and Samaria to go to their rescue (1 Sam. 11:1–11). The people of Jabesh-Gilead never forgot this act of kindness: "Now when the inhabitants of Jabesh-Gilead heard what the Philistines had done to Saul, all the valiant men arose and traveled all night, and took the body of Saul and the bodies of his sons from the wall of Beth-Shan; and they came to Jabesh and burned them there. Then they took their bones and buried them under the tamarisk tree at Jabesh, and fasted seven days" (1 Sam. 31:11–13).

Elijah also came from Gilead (1 Kings 17:1). During a three-year famine, he stayed by the brook Cherith in Gilead, where the water refreshed him and ravens brought food (1 Kings 17:36). When his earthly ministry was finished, Elijah again crossed the Jordan into Gilead, where God's chariots snatched him up in a whirlwind (2 Kings 2:8-11).

Perea

A map of the NT era would show the names *Perea* and *Decapolis* on the area of Gilead. Decapolis was roughly equivalent to northern Gilead. Multitudes followed Jesus from this region that extended to both sides of the Jordan River (Matt. 4:25).

"Beyond the Jordan" referred to Perea, a province bordering the Jordan River on the southeast. This was the territory of Herod Antipas, who had John the Baptist beheaded (Mark 6:14–29).

Customarily Jews avoided Samaria, so on his way to Jerusalem, Jesus generally crossed the Jordan to Perea. Opposite Jericho he crossed back over by ford in the Jordan or by taking a ferry, then continued his journey through the Judean wilderness to Jerusalem.

Ammon

Ammon is a vast grassland between the desert on the east and the green mountains of Gilead on the west. The mountains level off into a plateau, and since Ammon has no high mountains, there is little rainfall. At Rabbah, "the city of waters" (2 Sam. 12:27, KJV), springs gush forth to make the beginnings of the Jabbok River. The well-watered areas of Ammon could be cultivated, but it was best suited for pasture. Ezekiel once prophesied that Rabbah would become "a stable for camels and Ammon a resting place for flocks" (Ezek. 25:5).

Moab

Moab was another high pastureland. The 3,000-foot plateau bordering the Dead Sea between the Arnon and Zered rivers was partially planted in wheat and barley. Moab's

King Mesha was a sheep breeder who paid a large tribute to King Ahab of Israel. After years of this, he rebelled against Ahab's successor, Jehoram (2 Kings 3:4–5).

The cities just north of the Arnon River—Dibon (modern Dhiban) and Aroer—were Moab's outposts. But the Moabites wanted the northern tableland of Heshbon and Medeba. Moses told of a time when Sihon, king of Heshbon, had pushed the Moabites back to the Arnon: "For fire went out from Heshbon, a flame from the city of Sihon; it consumed Ar of Moab, the lords of the heights of the Arnon. Woe to you, Moab!" (Num. 21:28–29).

Eventually God gave Sihon's power to Israel. When King Balak of Moab saw what had become of Sihon's Amorites, he panicked at the sight of the Israelites encamped below him in the plains of Moab. He sent for the diviner Balaam to curse the Israelites on his behalf. "I know that he whom you bless is blessed, and he whom you curse is cursed" (Num. 22:6).

God told Balaam, "You shall not curse the people; for they are blessed" (Num. 22:12). Although Balak was furious with Balaam for not doing as he asked, the invasion he feared did not come. Instead the Israelites settled down at Shittim and got into trouble by being overly friendly with the Moabites (Num. 25:1–2).

In the days of the judges, a famine in Judah caused Elimelech and Naomi and their sons to migrate to Moab (Ruth 1:1). The sons married Moabite women. After their husbands died, Naomi and her daughter-in-law, Ruth, returned to Bethlehem, Naomi's former home. Ruth later married Boaz and became the great-grandmother of King David.

Both the Ammonites and the Moabites coveted the fertile Jordan Valley. When the Israelites conquered the kingdoms of Sihon and Og, the Ammonites and Moabites retreated to the safety of their borders. But each time one nation weakened, another would try to expand. Israel, Ammon, and Moab were a constant threat to one another.

The Ammonites and Moabites pressed hard on the Israelites during the period of the judges. Eglon of Moab penetrated beyond the Jordan as far as Jericho (Judg. 3:12–14). Later, when Israel sinned, the Lord "sold them into . . . the hands of the people of Ammon" (Judg. 10:7), who oppressed both the Israelites in Gilead and those west of the Jordan—in Judah, Benjamin, and Ephraim.

King David turned the tables on the Ammonites, forcing them to work for him (2 Sam. 12:29–31). The Ammonites escaped the conquering Babylonians in 586 B.C., and they gloated when Judah was exiled to Babylonia (Ezek. 25:6). Time did not lessen the ancient animosity. When the Jews returned from exile and started to rebuild the walls of Jerusalem, Ammonites showed up to taunt the workmen (Neh. 4:1–9). The Tobiad family ruled the Ammonites from the fifth to the second century B.C., and they never did accept the Jews.

Edom

Edom was another name for Esau, the son of Isaac and brother of Jacob (Gen. 25:30; see also 32:3). Esau went to live in the hills of Seir, southeast of the Dead Sea, and the area came to be known by his name. The people were called *Edomites*.

Edom also means "red," either because of the reddish coloring of Esau or the reddish color of the sandstone mountains in south Edom. In this area is Petra, the fabled red-rose city. In the time of Jesus, the Nabateans built the impenetrable fortress of Sela, carving it from sandstone rocks. They used the natural rocks of Edom for their protection. A narrow passage of steep rocks leads into Petra, and many of the caves they hollowed out and ornately decorated are well preserved to this day.

The stark and imposing mountains of Edom are a radical change from the northern edge of Edom territory, the valley of Zered, as well as from the northern stretch of the King's Highway crossing the tableland of Moab. In Bible times, the northern cities of Tophel and Bozrah had abundant vegetation. Their wood was sent south to make charcoal for the copper smelters at Punon. Even today the village of Tofileh (Tophel) harvests fine olive groves.

The peaks of south Edom exceed 1,500 meters (5,000 feet)—a composite of sandstone, basalt, and crystalline rocks. The 45 to 50 centimeters (16 to 20 inches) of yearly precipitation sometimes includes snow. The resulting vegetation encouraged settlement in biblical times.

Edom and Judah contended fiercely for control of an important highway junction near the port of Ezion Geber. The King's Highway from the northeast met the road to Egypt across the Sinai, and a third highway took caravans farther south to Tema. Edom's economy hinged on access to this junction, but it was also valuable to Israel. Therefore the Israelites fought numerous battles attempting to subjugate Edom, Ammon, and Moab.

David did manage to conquer Edom (2 Sam. 8:13–14). Solomon extracted tribute from the Edomites, and they did not endanger his shipping ventures at Ezion Geber. Soon after Solomon's death they rebelled and shipping became unsafe. Later, King Jehoshaphat of Judah tried to send ships to Ophir for gold, but the ships were wrecked at Ezion Geber (1 Kings 22:48).

In further strife between the two peoples, the Edomites got the upper hand over Judah's King Joram (2 Kings 8:24) and King Ahaz (2 Kings 16:5–18).

Places in the Bible

Bethlehem. Jericho. The Jordan River. These places have long been familiar to readers of the Bible.

The Bible revolves primarily around the land we often still call *Palestine*—the geographical term for the Holy Land from the defeat of the Jews by the Romans in A.D. 135 until 1948 when the region divided into three sections: Israel, Jordan, and the Gaza Strip. Its 100,000 square miles connect three continents at the eastern end of the Mediterranean.

While the Bible concerns itself largely with this land, places such as Egypt, Rome, and parts of Europe also come into view.

The purpose of this chapter is to set down as plainly as possible the essential facts about the important places in the Bible from Abanah to Zion. We have not included the little-known and obscure places.

Abanah. "Stony." The chief river of Damascus. The Abanah flowed through the center of this great city. With the Pharpar, it supplied an abundance of water, making the country around it one of the most beautiful and fertile spots in the world. When Naaman the leper was asked to bathe in the Jordan River seven times, he complained that he would rather bathe in the Abanah or the Pharpar.

Achaia. In Roman times, the name for the whole of Greece, except Thessaly. The Romans gave the region this name when they captured Corinth and destroyed the Achaian League in 146 B.C. Later it comprised several Grecian cities, including Athens.

Achor. "Trouble." A valley near Jericho where Achan was stoned to death during the time of Joshua (Josh. 7:24–26). The prophets used the phrase "the Valley of Achor" (Isa. 65:10) to symbolize the idyllic state of contentment and peace of the messianic age (Hos 2:15).

Acropolis. "Topmost city." An elevated, fortified part of an ancient Greek city, such as Athens, Philippi, and Corinth. The Acropolis of Athens, the most famous of all ancient cities, was located on a hill about 500 feet high. It was adorned with stunning architectural works.

Adriatic. A name for the central part of the Mediterranean Sea south of Italy. It is mentioned in Luke's account of Paul's voyage to Rome (Acts 27:27).

Adullam. "Refuge." A large cave near the city of Adullam (1 Sam. 22:1; 1 Chron. 11:15) where David hid when he was a fugitive from King Saul.

Aenon. "Springs." A place in Palestine near Salim, where John the Baptist was baptizing at the time of Jesus' ministry in Judea (John 3:22–23). Scholars are uncertain of the location of Aenon. Most likely, Aenon was close to the Jordan River, "because there was much water there" (John 3:23).

Ai. "The ruin." A Canaanite city of Palestine (Gen. 12:8; Josh. 10:1), east of Bethel (Gen. 12:8), "beside Beth Aven" (Josh. 7:2), and north of Michmash (Isa. 10:28). Many years before Joshua's time, Abraham pitched his tent at Ai before journeying to Egypt (Gen. 12:8).

Ai figures prominently in the story of Israel's conquest of Palestine. After Joshua conquered Jericho, he sent men from Jericho to spy out Ai and the surrounding countryside. Because Ai was small, the spies assured Joshua that he could take Ai with only a handful of soldiers.

Joshua dispatched 3,000 soldiers to attack Ai. This army was soundly defeated, due to Achan's sin of taking spoils from Jericho, contrary to God's commandment. When God singled out Achan and his family, the people stoned them to death. Joshua then sent 30,000 soldiers against Ai and captured the city by a clever military tactic—an ambush (Josh. 7—8).

Aijalon. "Place of deer." A city in the lowlands west of Jerusalem. It was one of the cities of refuge (Josh. 19:42; 1 Sam. 14:31). It belonged to the tribe of Dan and was assigned to the Kohathite Levites. The area surrounding Aijalon was the scene of the famous battle between Joshua and the five Amorite kings where Joshua made the sun stand still while the Israelites destroyed their enemies (Josh. 10:12–14).

Akeldama. "Field of blood." The name of a field located outside the walls of Jerusalem. This field was purchased by the chief priests with the 30 pieces of silver they paid to Judas for betraying Jesus. Remorseful at having betrayed innocent blood, Judas threw the 30 pieces of silver on the floor of the temple and went out and hanged himself. The priests would not put the coins in the temple treasury, for they were tainted with "the price of blood," so they took the money and bought the potter's field in which to bury strangers (Matt. 27:3–10).

Alexandria. The capital of Egypt during the Greek and Roman periods. Situated on the Mediterranean Sea at the western edge of the Nile Delta, the city was established by Alexander the Great when he conquered Egypt in 331 B.C. After Alexander's death, the capital of Egypt was moved from Memphis to Alexandria; it became one of the most significant cities of the Greek Empire. The population of Alexandria included native Egyptians, learned Greeks, and many Jews. The commercial strength of the city was aided by the famous towering lighthouse that guided ships into port. Paul himself sailed in an Alexandrian ship on his way to Rome (Acts 27:6; 28:11).

The early church father Eusebius recorded the tradition that John Mark was one of the missionaries who first brought the message of Christ to the people of Alexandria. Years earlier, prominent Jews from Alexandria who gathered in Jerusalem strongly opposed Stephen's preaching about Christ (Acts 6:9).

Ammon. The land of Ammon, settled by those who were descended from Ammon (or Ben-Ammi), Lot's son. Ammon was born in a cave near Zoar (Gen. 19:30–38), a city near the southern end of the Dead Sea. The land of the Ammonites generally was located in the area north and east of Moab, a region between the River Arnon and the River Jabbok. Its capital city was Rabbah (Deut. 3:11; 2 Sam. 11:1). Amman, the name of the capital of the modern kingdom of Jordan, continues to use this ancient name.

Amphipolis. "Surrounded city." A city of Macedonia through which the apostle Paul passed on his second missionary journey (Acts 17:1). Amphipolis was situated about 50 kilometers (30 miles) southwest of Philippi. It was almost completely surrounded by a bend in the River Strymon.

Situated on a terraced hill, the city was highly visible from land and sea. A large monument, the Lion of Amphipolis, commemorating a military victory, stands guard today at the ancient site, as it did in Paul's time.

Anathoth. "Answered prayers." A city in the tribe of Benjamin given to the Levites (1 Kings 2:26). Anathoth was the birthplace of the prophet Jeremiah (Jer. 1:1; 29:27). During a time of siege, the Lord instructed Jeremiah to purchase a field in Anathoth. This was to serve as a sign of God's promised redemption of Israel (Jer. 32:7–9). Anathoth was located about five kilometers (three miles) northeast of Jerusalem.

Antioch of Pisidia. A city of southern Asia Minor in Phrygia, situated just north of the territory of Pisidia. Antioch was an important first-century commercial center and significant for the spread of the gospel. Founded by Seleucus Nicator (about 300 B.C.), it became a noted commercial center and was inhabited by many Jews.

The apostle Paul preached in this city's synagogue and founded a church there during his first missionary journey (Acts 13:14–49). Just as Antioch exerted great cultural and political influence over the surrounding area, so also it became a strong base from which to launch the church's evangelistic outreach (Acts 13:42–49). In reaction to Paul's success, the Jews at Antioch caused some influential women to turn against the gospel and had Paul driven out of the city (Acts 13:50).

Antioch of Syria. The capital of the Roman province of Syria, which played an important part in the first-century expansion of the church. Antioch was situated on the east bank of the Orontes River, about 27 kilometers (16.5 miles) from the Mediterranean Sea and 485 kilometers (300 miles) north of Jerusalem. The city was founded about 300 B.C. by Seleucus I Nicator, one of the three successors to Alexander the Great.

The early history of the church is closely connected with Antioch of Syria. One of the first seven deacons, Nicolas, was a proselyte from Antioch (Acts 6:5). After the stoning of Stephen (Acts 7:54–60), great persecution forced the disciples to flee from Jerusalem to Antioch where they preached the gospel to the Jews (Acts 8:1; 11:19). Others arrived later and had success preaching to the Gentiles (Acts 11:20–21).

Aphek. "Fortress."
1. A city on the plain of Sharon. Joshua conquered the king of Aphek while taking the Promised Land (Josh. 12:18).
2. A town mentioned in Joshua 13:4, located at the northern edge of Canaanite territory.
3. A town in the territory allotted to the tribe of Asher (Josh. 19:30; *Aphik*, Judg. 1:31). The Asherites were unable to expel the Canaanites from this city.
4. A town east of the Sea of Galilee where God gave Ahab victory over Ben-Hadad and the Syrian army (1 Kings 20:26–30). Later the prophet Elisha, while on his deathbed, prophesied Israel's victory at Aphek over the Syrian army (2 Kings 13:17).

Appian Way. An ancient Roman road built by Appius Claudius. It ran from Rome to Brundisium on the Adriatic Sea. Paul traveled this road from near the city of Puteoli to Rome, where he was imprisoned (Acts 28:13–16).

Appii Forum. "Marketplace of Appius." A town in Italy located about 64 kilometers (40 miles) southeast of Rome on the Appian Way where the apostle Paul was welcomed by Christians from Rome (Acts 28:15).

Aqueduct. A channel for transporting water from a remote source to a city. Israel's climate provides abundant rainfall in the winter months, but there is seldom any rain from May to October. This, along with the scarcity of good water supplies, made it necessary to build artificial storage areas to catch the winter rains. Elaborate systems of stone and masonry aqueducts and storage pools were sometimes constructed to bring water from the hill country to the cities and larger towns.

The best-known biblical accounts of the building of an aqueduct occur in 2 Kings

20:20 and 2 Chronicles 32:30. King Hezekiah of Judah had a tunnel dug under the city of Jerusalem to bring water from the spring outside the city to the Siloam reservoir inside the city wall. Across part of the course the workmen cut a tunnel through solid rock to complete the aqueduct. Hezekiah's Tunnel is still a major tourist attraction in Jerusalem.

Arabah. "Plain," "desert." A major region of the land of Israel referring usually to the entire valley region between Mount Hermon in the north to the Red Sea in the south (Num. 22:1; Deut. 1:7). The Arabah is more than 390 kilometers (240 miles) long, varying in width from 10 to 40 kilometers (six to 25 miles).

The Arabah includes the Sea of Galilee, the Jordan River Valley, the Dead Sea, and the area between the Dead Sea and the Red Sea. Much of this region lies below sea level, and the Dead Sea, which lies at approximately 394 meters (1,292 feet) below sea level, is the lowest spot on the earth's surface. The NKJV refers several times to the "Sea of the Arabah," meaning the Salt Sea or the Dead Sea (Deut. 3:17; Josh. 3:16; 2 Kings 14:25).

Before their entry into the Promised Land, the people of Israel camped in the Arabah, in an area called "the plains of Moab" (Num. 22:1), just north of the Dead Sea. While the Israelites were camped there, God turned Balaam's curses to blessings (Num. 22:1—24:25), Israel committed idolatrous and immoral acts (Num. 25), Moses renewed the covenant, and Joshua sent out spies to prepare for the invasion of Canaan (Josh. 1:1—3:17).

Arabia. "Wilderness." The large peninsula east of Egypt, between the Red Sea and the Persian Gulf. About 1,300 kilometers (800 miles) wide and 2,300 kilometers (1,400 miles) long, Arabia is nearly one-third the size of the United States. It has almost no rainfall except along the coast, where it measures about 51 centimeters (20 inches) per year. There is only one river and one lake in the entire peninsula. Al-

though a sudden shower may create a short-lived stream, most of the water in Arabia comes from deep wells or desert oases. Consequently, there is little agricultural activity on the peninsula.

The queen of Sheba came from Arabia, bringing gold, spices, and precious stones to Solomon (1 Kings 10:2, 10, 14; 2 Chron. 9:1, 9, 14). Solomon and other kings sent their ships to Ophir in Arabia to bring back gold (1 Kings 9:28; 2 Chron. 9:10). Ophir, Raamah, and Sheba were famous for their gold, silver, and precious stones (Job 22:24; Isa. 13:12; Ezek. 27:22).

The people who lived in Arabia included the children of Joktan (Gen. 10:26–30), Cush (Gen. 10:7), the sons of Abraham and Keturah (Gen. 25:1–6), and Esau (Gen. 36). The "country of the east" (Gen. 25:6) is probably a reference to Arabia. The early history of many of these peoples is unknown. Israel's earliest contacts with the inhabitants of Arabia probably came through their camel caravans. Some of them oppressed the Israelites during the time of the judges, but God delivered Israel from them by raising up the judge Gideon (Judg. 6:11).

David subdued Arabian tribes that were close to Israel (2 Sam. 8:3–14), and Solomon established extensive trade relations with more distant tribes in Arabia to obtain their gold for his building projects (1 Kings 9:28; 10:2, 11). Jehoshaphat, king of Judah, received rams and goats from the Arabians as tribute (2 Chron. 17:10–12), but after his death they revolted and refused to pay tribute to his son Jehoram. Instead, they invaded Jerusalem and carried away Jehoram's wealth, his wives, and all but his youngest son (2 Chron. 21:16–17).

Areopagus. "Hill of Ares." A limestone hill in Athens situated between the Acropolis and the Agora; by association, also the council that often met on the hill. The apostle Paul addressed the Areopagus and attempted to meet the objections of the Epicurean and Stoic philosophers to the gospel (Acts 17:16–34).

Ariel. "Lion of God." The symbolic name of Jerusalem (Isa. 29:1–2, 7), perhaps applied to the city because the lion was the emblem of the tribe of Judah (Gen. 49:9).

Arimathea. "A height." A city in the Judean hills northwest of Jerusalem. It was the home of Joseph, a member of the Jewish Sanhedrin in Jerusalem, who placed the body of Jesus in a new tomb Joseph had prepared for himself (Luke 23:50–53).

Armageddon. "Mountain of Megiddo." The site on which dispensationalists believe a final battle will take place. God will then intervene to destroy the armies of Satan and cast him into the bottomless pit (Rev. 16:16; 20:1–3, 7–10). This place may likely be the valley between Mount Carmel and the city of Jezreel. This valley, known as the Valley of Jezreel and sometimes referred to as the Plain of Esdraelon, was the crossroads of two ancient trade routes and thus was a strategic military site. *Armageddon* is the Greek word for this area, the scene of many ancient battles.

Because of this history, Megiddo became a symbol of the final conflict between God and the forces of evil.

Ashdod. "Fortress." One of the five principal Philistine cities (1 Sam. 6:17), situated five kilometers (three miles) from the Mediterranean coast and 32 kilometers (20 miles) north of Gaza. The city's military and economic significance was enhanced by its location on the main highway between Egypt and Syria.

Ashkelon. "Migration." One of the five major cities of the Philistines (Josh. 13:3). Situated on the seacoast 19 kilometers (12 miles) north of Gaza, Ashkelon and her sister cities (Ashdod, Gath, Gaza, and Ekron) posed a serious threat to the Israelites during the period of the judges. Shortly after Joshua's death, Ashkelon was captured and was briefly controlled by the tribe of Judah (Judg. 1:18). A few years later Samson killed 30 men from this city (Judg. 14:19). During most of the OT era, Ashke-

lon remained politically and militarily independent of Israel.

In the eighth century B.C. Ashkelon was denounced by the prophet Amos (Amos 1:8). Shortly before the Babylonian captivity, Zephaniah prophesied that the Jews would return from Babylon and occupy the ruins of Ashkelon (Zeph. 2:4, 7). Zechariah also prophesied the destruction of Ashkelon (Zech. 9:5). Ashkelon is not mentioned in the NT.

Asia. "Eastern." A Roman province in western Asia Minor that included Mysia, Lydia, Caria, and the coastal islands as well as western Phrygia. The borders of this province were largely those of the earlier kingdom of Pergamos.

Three cities continued to compete for the role of principal city: Ephesus, Smyrna, and Pergamos—the first three cities mentioned in the book of Revelation. (See Rev. 1:11; 2:1–17.) Eventually, Ephesus became the chief commercial center and was known as the most prominent city of the province.

Asia Minor. A peninsula, also called Anatolia, situated in the extreme western part of the continent of Asia. Asia Minor was bounded on the north by the Black Sea, the Sea of Marmara, and the Dardanelles; the Aegean Sea on the west; and Syria and the Mediterranean Sea on the south.

Roughly identical with the modern nation of Turkey, Asia Minor was a high plateau crossed by mountains, especially the Taurus Mountains near the southern coast. In the NT, the term *Asia* is ambiguous, sometimes referring to the peninsula of Asia Minor as a whole (Acts 19:26–27), but more often referring to proconsular Asia, situated in the western part of the peninsula (Acts 2:9; 6:9). The writer of Acts appears to use the term *Asia* to describe the region of the province of Asia Ephesus.

Athens. The capital city of the ancient Greek state of Attica and the modern capital of Greece. Athens was the center of Greek art, architecture, literature, and politics during the golden age of Grecian history (the fifth century B.C.) and was visited by Paul on his second missionary journey (Acts 17:15—18:1).

Babylon, City of. Ancient walled city between the Tigris and Euphrates Rivers and capital of the Babylonian Empire. The leading citizens of the nation of Judah were carried to this city as captives about 586 B.C. after Jerusalem fell to the invading Babylonians. Biblical writers portrayed this ancient capital as the model of paganism and idolatry (e.g., Jer. 51:44; Dan. 4:30).

Babylon was situated along the Euphrates River about 485 kilometers (300 miles) northwest of the Persian Gulf. Its origins are unknown. According to Babylonian tradition, it was built by the god Marduk. We know that around 2300 B.C. the city was destroyed by an invading enemy king. This makes Babylon one of the oldest cities of the ancient world. Genesis 10:10 mentions Babel as part of the empire of Nimrod.

Babylonia. Ancient pagan empire between the Tigris and Euphrates Rivers in southern Mesopotamia. The Babylonians struggled with the neighboring Assyrians for domination of the ancient world during much of their history. At the height of their power, the Babylonians overpowered the nation of Judah, destroyed Jerusalem, and carried the Israelites into captivity about 586 B.C.

The fortunes of the Babylonians rose and fell during the long sweep of OT history—from about 2000 B.C. to about 500 B.C. References to these ancient people—their culture, religion and military power—occur throughout the OT.

Beersheba. "Well of the seven." The chief city of the Negev. Beersheba was situated in the territory of Simeon (Josh. 19:1–2) and was "the limits of the tribe of the children of Judah, toward the border of Edom in the South" (Josh. 15:21). Midway between the Mediterranean Sea and the southern end of the Dead Sea, Beersheba was considered the southern extremity of

The acropolis at Athens, site of the beautiful Parthenon and other buildings of the ancient Greeks. PHOTO BY GUSTAV JEENINGA

the Promised Land, giving rise to the often-used expression, "from Dan [in the north] to Beersheba" (Judg. 20:1) or "from Beersheba to Dan" (1 Chron. 21:2).

Berea. A city of Macedonia about 73 kilometers (45 miles) west of Thessalonica (modern Salonika). On his first missionary journey, the apostle Paul preached at Berea (Acts 17:10) with success. The Bereans were "more fair-minded than those in Thessalonica," because they "searched the Scriptures daily to find out whether these things were so" (Acts 17:11).

Bethany. "House of unripe figs." The home of Mary, Martha, and Lazarus. At Bethany Jesus raised Lazarus from the dead. Mary of Bethany anointed Jesus' feet. Just before his ascension, Jesus blessed his disciples at Bethany.

Bethel. "House of God." A city about 19 kilometers (12 miles) north of Jerusalem. Bethel is first mentioned in the Bible in connection with Abraham (Gen. 12:8; 13:3). The region around Bethel is still suitable for grazing by livestock.

Jacob, Abraham's grandson, had a life-changing experience at this site. He had a vision of a staircase, or ladder, reaching into the heavens with the angels of God ascending and descending on it (Gen. 28:12). Jacob erected a pillar at Bethel to mark the spot of his vision (Gen. 28:22; 31:13). Jacob later built an altar at Bethel, where he worshiped the Lord (Gen. 35:1–16).

Bethesda. "House of grace." A pool in the northeastern part of Jerusalem, near the Sheep Gate. At this pool Jesus healed the man "who had an infirmity thirty-eight years" (John 5:5).

Bethlehem. "House of bread." The birthplace of David and of Jesus. The burial place of Rachel. The home of Ruth and Boaz.

Beth Peor. "House of Peor." Site of Moses' message and his burial place (Deut. 4:44–46; 34:1–6).

Bethphage. "House of figs." Jesus sent two of his disciples to Bethphage to fetch a colt for his ride into Jerusalem.

Bethsaida. "House of fishers." Bethsaida was the home of Peter, Andrew, and Philip. Near there Jesus fed the 5,000.

Beth Shan. "House of security." Where the bodies of King Saul and his son Jonathan were nailed to the wall for public display.

Beth Shemesh. "House of the sun." The birthplace of Samson. At this site a number of men died after looking into the ark of the covenant. (See 1 Sam. 6:19–21.)

Caesarea. Herod the Great built the city in honor of Augustus Caesar. It became the military headquarters of Pontius Pilate when he was governor of Judea. It was also the home of Philip the evangelist. Peter visited Cornelius the centurion at Caesarea. In this same city God struck Herod Agrippa I dead. Paul endured two years of imprisonment at Caesarea before being sent to Rome to stand trial.

Caesarea Philippi. A town near the Jordan River built by Philip the tetrarch and named in honor of Caesar. At Caesarea Philippi Peter confessed that Jesus was the Messiah, the Christ.

Calvary. Latin *calvaria*, Aramaic *Golgotha*, "skull." The place outside the walls of Jerusalem where the soldiers crucified Jesus.

Cana. A village in Galilee where Jesus did two miracles. He turned water into wine at a wedding; he healed the son of a Capernaum official.

Canaan. The OT name of the Promised Land. To this land Moses led the people out of slavery in Egypt. The Bible pictures Canaan as a land flowing with milk and honey, meaning it was fertile.

Canaanites inhabited the land before the Israelites invaded. The land and its people are mentioned throughout the book of Joshua, which tells of the Israelites conquering the land.

Capernaum. A busy and prosperous fishing port with a Roman military station. Jesus visited there with Simon Peter and other fishermen-disciples. Capernaum is the scene of several healings and teachings.

Carmel. A range of hills along the Mediterranean coast of the Holy Land and the place where Elijah contested with the prophets of Baal.

Cenchrea. A seaport town in Greece about 11 kilometers (seven miles) east of Corinth. During his second missionary journey, the apostle Paul sailed from Cenchrea on his return to Syria (Acts 18:18; *Cenchreae*, RSV).

Chebar. A river of Babylon beside which the Jewish exiles settled after the destruction of Jerusalem. It is mentioned in the visions of Ezekiel.

Cilicia *or* Kue. *Kue* appears in the OT. Solomon imported horses from Kue (2 Chron. 1:16, RSV). Tarsus, its major city, was Paul's birthplace. Paul visited the province of Cilicia on his second missionary journey.

Cities of refuge. Places of sanctuary provided by the Mosaic law for people who had unintentionally committed murder and had to flee. They remained unharmed in a city of refuge.

City of David.

1. The stronghold of Zion, the fortified city of the Jebusites, later known as Jerusalem. King David and his men captured it (2 Sam. 5:7, 9).

2. Bethlehem, the birthplace or home of David (Luke 2:4, 11; John 7:42).

Colosse. A city in Phrygia mentioned by Paul at the beginning of his letter to the Colossians. Philemon, Onesimus, Tychicus, and Archippus all came from Colosse.

Corinth. The greatest trading city of ancient Greece. Corinth was not only the marketplace for the goods of the Mediterranean but the source of new ideas. Paul stayed in the city with Aquila and Priscilla, working with them at making tents and arguing in the synagogue every Sabbath.

Crete *or* Caphtor. *Caphtor* appears in the OT. An island in the middle of the Mediterranean Sea. Paul sailed past Crete as a prisoner on his way to Rome.

Cyprus *or* Chittim *or* Kittim. *Chittim* or *Kittim* appears in the OT. An island in the eastern Mediterranean, famous for its copper mines. It was the home of Joseph (or Joses) called Barnabas, Paul's companion. The two men visited Cyprus on their first missionary journey.

Cyrene. The home of Simon who carried Jesus' cross. (See Matt. 27:32.)

Damascus. The capital of Syria and probably the oldest inhabited city in the world. It is situated on the River Abanah, the meeting place of trade routes. Many Jews lived there in NT times. On the road near Damascus Paul of Tarsus was converted.

Dan. The most northerly town in Israel. When the people spoke of "from Dan to Beersheba" they referred to the extreme boundaries. King Jeroboam I of Israel set up a shrine at Dan with a golden image of a calf.

David, City of. (See *City of David*.)

Dead Sea. Often called the Salt Sea or the Eastern Sea in the OT but never mentioned in the NT. It is 53 miles long and 10 miles wide and is the lowest stretch of water in the world. Although the rivers of the Jordan and others run into the Dead Sea, it has no outlet except through evaporation. No fish live there because of the excessive salinity.

Decapolis. "Ten cities." Decapolis was a group of cities built in the Greek style of the first century B.C. Jesus visited the Decapolis and several healings took place.

Derbe. A stopping point on Paul's first missionary journey.

Dothan. Where Joseph's brothers sold the young man into slavery. Elisha asked and God struck the Syrian army with blindness near Dothan. (See 2 Kings 6:18.)

Ebal. "Bare." A mountain north of Shechem and opposite Mount Gerizim (Deut. 11:29). Moses gave instructions to the Israelites about a religious ceremony they should observe after they crossed the Jordan River into the Promised Land. Moses also instructed that stones, whitewashed with lime, be set up on Mount Ebal, and an altar built to the Lord (Deut. 27:4–5).

Joshua and the other leaders of the Israelites did all the things Moses had commanded them and Joshua renewed the covenant by building an altar to God on Mount Ebal and by reading the words of the Law to the assembled multitude (Josh. 8:30 ff.).

When Joshua read the blessings of the Law, the people on Mount Gerizim responded with an "Amen." They said the same word when he read the curses on Mount Ebal which became known as the Mount of Cursing. The tops of the two mountains are about three kilometers (two miles) distant from each other. The modern name of Mount Ebal is Jebel Eslamiyeh.

Eden. The well-watered garden that God created for Adam and Eve. When the couple disobeyed God by eating of the forbidden tree, they were cast out of Eden, never to return.

Edom. "Red." The land belonging to the Edomites, descendants of Esau, Jacob's twin brother. The Edomites constantly fought against Israel.

Egypt. The country in the northeast corner of Africa that extended from the Mediterranean Sea on the north to the first waterfall on the Nile River in the south—a distance of about 880 kilometers (540 miles). The Israelites spent 430 years in this land (Exod. 12:40) between the time of Joseph and Moses. Jesus lived temporarily in Egypt during his infancy (Matt. 2:13–15).

The history of Egypt can be divided into dynasties of three main periods of strength:
- The Old Kingdom (2700–2200 B.C.)
- The Middle Kingdom (2000–1800 B.C.)
- The New Kingdom (1570–1100 B.C.)

These two columns among the ruins of an ancient Egyptian building represented Lower Egypt (left) and Upper Egypt (right).

PHOTO BY HOWARD VOS

Each of these kingdoms was followed by a period of weakness.

After the New Kingdom, Egypt was dominated by Libyan, Ethiopian, Persian, Greek, and finally Roman powers during NT times. The dates for these periods and the length of the reigns of each king are not certain. Egyptologists have been trying to reconstruct a fairly accurate chronology.

Around 3000 B.C., a thousand years before Abraham, all of Egypt was joined under one king at Memphis, and the land was divided into districts called *nomes*. Irrigation and the plow were introduced to increase the nation's agricultural productivity. Shortly afterward, the Old Kingdom period began. During this era, the famous pyramids of Egypt were built.

The New Kingdom period (1570–1100 B.C.) parallels the biblical period just before the birth of Moses until the time of Samuel. The New Kingdom began when the Egyptians managed to drive out the Hyksos and reunite Egypt. This new dynasty was made of kings "who did not know Joseph" (Exod. 1:8). They began to persecute the Hebrews, forcing them to build the cities of Pithom and Raamses (Exod. 1:11). They viewed the Hebrews as foreigners who threatened the security of the nation (Exod. 1:10), so they enslaved them.

The powerful Queen Hathshepsut carried out many building and reconstruction projects and expanded trade relations with several foreign countries. The next king was an aggressive warrior, and he conducted several campaigns into Palestine. Many believe his son, Amenhotep II, was the Pharaoh of the Exodus. Egyptian texts do not mention the 10 plagues, the exodus of the children of Israel from Egypt, or the defeat of Pharaoh and his army in the Red Sea (Exod. 7—15). But this would hardly be expected since the Egyptians seldom recorded any of their defeats.

Many interesting stories come from this period of Egyptian history. "The Tale of Two Brothers" describes how the wife of one brother lied about the sexual advances of the other. This story is similar to the false accusation of Potiphar's wife against Joseph. Tales about the struggles between the gods Horus and Seth and the wisdom "Instructions of Amenemopet," which are in some ways similar to the book of Proverbs, are a few of the important literary compositions from Egypt during these years.

No one knows how the Exodus affected Egypt's religious beliefs. In the middle of the New Kingdom, King Akhenaten rejected the worship of Amon at Thebes and proclaimed that Aten, the solar disk of the sun, was the only god. A beautiful hymn of praise to Aten has been discovered. This shows clearly that Akhenaten was pushing the Egyptians to adopt belief in one god. Religious tension was very high because Akhenaten dismissed the priests at the other temples and moved his capital to El-Amarna.

About 350 letters from Babylon, the Hittites, and many cities in Palestine were found at this capital. These letters reveal that Palestine was undergoing a great deal of political unrest during the time of Joshua and the judges. A few years later the famous King Tut (Tutankhamen), whose burial chambers were found near Thebes, ruled. He brought the nation back to the worship of its traditional gods at Thebes, relieving much of the tension within the nation.

During the final 200 years of the New Kingdom, the capital of Egypt was moved from Thebes to the city of Rameses in the Delta area. Large construction projects at Thebes, Abydos, Abu Simbel, and in the Delta stand as memorials to the greatness and power of these kings. Some believe the Exodus took place during the reign of Rameses (1304–1238 B.C.), but this contradicts the statement of the Bible that the Exodus took place 480 years before Solomon began to build the temple in 955 B.C. (966 plus 480 equals 1446 B.C. for the Exodus). One king, Merneptah, described his defeat of several Canaanite countries and actually mentions his defeat of Israel.

After the New Kingdom, the Late Period

of Egyptian history arrived (1100–330 B.C.). The fragmentation of Egyptian power allowed David and Solomon to establish Israel as a strong nation. The nation was not a strong military power, so more emphasis was placed on trying to form peaceful trade relations with neighboring states.

Model of an Egyptian ship with a double mast discovered in the tomb of Pharaoh Sahure. These ships were used by the Egyptians about 2550 B.C.   PHOTO BY HOWARD VOS

Solomon married the daughter of an Egyptian Pharaoh (1 Kings 3:1), but later in his reign a new king (probably Shishak) provided refuge for two of Solomon's enemies (1 Kings 11:17, 40). A few years after Solomon's death (about 930 B.C.), Shishak, a Libyan who had become Pharaoh, attacked Rehoboam and plundered the gold from the palace and the temple in Jerusalem (1 Kings 14:25–28).

Ethiopian and Saite dynasties controlled Egypt for several hundred years until the destruction of Israel by the Babylonian King Nebuchadnezzar in 587 B.C. These Pharaohs were not particularly powerful because of the political supremacy of the Assyrians and the Babylonians. The Israelite King Hoshea sought the help of Pharaoh around 725 B.C. (2 Kings 17:4) to fight against the Assyrians, but the Egyptians were of little value.

Around 701 B.C. Hezekiah was attacked by the Assyrian King Sennacherib. Tirhakah, the Ethiopian king of Egypt, came to Hezekiah's aid (2 Kings 19:9; Isa. 37:9). The Assyrians themselves marched into Egypt

Entrance to the tomb of Pharaoh Tutankha-men of Egypt in the foreground with the tomb of Ramses VI just behind it.

PHOTO BY HOWARD VOS

in 671 and 664 B.C., destroying the Egyptian forces as far south as Thebes. To strengthen the Egyptian army, the nation hired Greek mercenaries to fight in their army, but this still did not give them any great strength.

Josiah, king of Judah, was killed by the Egyptian Pharaoh Necho in 609 B.C. because Josiah tried to interfere with the Egyptian efforts to help the Assyrians, who were under attack by the Babylonians (2 Kings 23:29). After Josiah's death, Judah came under the control of Egypt; but in 605 B.C. the Egyptians were crushed by the Babylonians.

Many Jews fled to Egypt after the destruction of Jerusalem, although Jeremiah warned them against it (Jer. 39—44). Nebuchadnezzar later defeated Egypt (Jer. 46:13); he was followed by the Persians (525 B.C.) and the Greeks (330 B.C.). After 330 B.C. a group of Ptolemaic kings ruled Egypt, developing the great city of Alexandria as a center of culture and learning.

Many Jews lived in Alexandria during this period. The Greek translation of the OT from Hebrew to Greek was completed so the Greek-speaking Jews would have a Bible in their language. The Romans took control of Egypt around 30 B.C. From the second century A.D. until the Muslim conquest of Egypt in 642, Egypt was primarily a Christian nation.

The religion of Egypt. The Egyptians were polytheists, believing in many gods.

They were often the personification of nature, such as the Nile, the sun, and the earth. Other gods stood for abstract concepts such as wisdom, justice, and order. Some were worshiped on a national level, but most were local deities. Each city had its favorite deity, which was the patron god of that locality (Ptah at Memphis or Amon at Thebes). But the cosmic gods such as Nut (the goddess of the sky), Geb (the god of the earth), and Ra (the sun god), were known throughout the nation.

The beliefs and practices of the Egyptians changed over their 3,000-year history, so any discussion of Egyptian religion must involve generalizations. One of the most confusing aspects of Egyptian religion was its ability to accept the process of syncretism. Through this process one god would take on the characteristics of another and thus eliminate its distinctiveness. Another aspect of Egyptian religion, which is largely hidden, is the extent to which the official beliefs of the priests differed from those of the peasants. Since most information is based on the official records kept in temples and the tombs of the kings, it is likely that these do not represent the beliefs of the poorer people.

The Egyptians believed that the gods were intimately involved with all aspects of life. The gods caused the rain, controlled the growth of crops, determined birth and death, and ultimately were behind everything. They did not give natural explanations for events, because they made no distinction between the secular and the sacred.

Many of these nature deities were represented as animals (bull, crocodile, falcon, ram, jackal) or by a part-human and part-animal statue. These gods were worshiped in temples throughout the land. Huge temples that covered many acres were built for the great cosmic gods and cared for by a large company of priests. The priests were responsible for the regular festivals at the temples and for the daily care of the gods.

Since each god was the king of its own realm of influence, it was treated as a king in its temple. The deity would be awakened, washed, dressed, fed (by an offering), taken for walks, and put to bed.

Pharaoh himself was one of the most important Egyptian gods. While ruling, he was the incarnation of the god Horus and the son of Ra. After his death, he was identified with the god Osiris. The Pharaoh was a mediator between the people and the cosmic gods of the universe and a key factor in determining the fate of the nation.

The worship of Osiris was an important aspect of Egyptian religion. Osiris was the king of the underworld, where people went after death, as well as the god of fertility.

Before the rise of the cult of Osiris, the worship of Ptah at Memphis was dominant. The *Memphite Theology* claimed that Ptah was the supreme god of Egypt who created the world and human beings. The god Amon came to prominence when the kings from Thebes rose to power. Aten received special attention during the reign of Pharaoh Akhenaten. The significance and honor of the Egyptian gods rose and fell according to the religious convictions of the ruling Pharaoh and the political power of the priests at the various temples.

Ekron. "Barren place." The northernmost of the five chief cities of the Philistines. Ekron was apportioned first to the tribe of Judah (Josh. 15:45–46), then given to the tribe of Dan (Josh. 19:40–43). After David killed Goliath, the Israelites pursued the Philistines to the gates of their fortified stronghold (1 Sam. 17:52).

Elath *or* Eloth. A town at the head of the Gulf of Aqabah, near Ezion-Geber. Solomon built a port there for his commercial fleet and established a mining center for smelting and refining copper and iron from the nearby hills. (See 1 Kings 9:26–28.)

Elim. "Large trees." An encampment of the Israelites after they crossed the Red Sea. This encampment was famed for its 12 wells or springs of water and 70 palm trees. The exact location is uncertain.

Emmaus. A village seven miles from Jerusalem toward which two disciples were walking on the day Jesus rose from the dead. They met him on the road and talked with him. When they came to the village, he stayed with them. When they ate a meal together, they finally recognized him.

En Dor. "Fountain of habitation." A town of the tribe of Manasseh where King Saul consulted a medium (1 Sam. 28:7).

En gedi. David hid from King Saul in a cave (1 Sam. 24:1–3).

Ephesus. An important seaport in Asia Minor. The temple of Diana (or Artemis) was one of the seven wonders of the ancient world. Paul stayed in the city for two years, and his preaching harmed silversmiths' business because they sold silver models of the pagan shrines to visitors. As a result, tumult occurred in the city. In Revelation John mentions Ephesus as one of the seven churches.

Eshcol. "Cluster of grapes." A valley north of Hebron, famous for its grapes (Num. 13:23–24). The Hebrew spies cut down a branch with one cluster of grapes from this valley and carried it to Moses to show the fertility of the land.

Ethiopia *or* Abyssinia *or* Cush. Moses married an Ethiopian woman. During King Asa's reign an army of Ethiopians invaded Judah but was defeated. An Ethiopian royal

The Agora, or marketplace, at Ephesus with the remains of shops and government buildings. PHOTO BY GUSTAV JEENINGA

servant named Ebed-Melech rescued Jeremiah from a muddy cistern into which he had been thrown.

In the NT, an important Ethiopian eunuch, the treasurer to Queen Candace, listened to Philip the evangelist preach, believed, and was baptized by him. (See Acts 8:27ff.)

Fair Havens. A small bay on the south side of Crete where the ship on which Paul was a prisoner found shelter in rough weather.

Gadara. One of the towns of the Decapolis ("10 cities") where Jesus healed a man with an unclean spirit. (See Decapolis.)

Galatia. A region in central Asia Minor (modern Turkey). The northern part of the region was settled in the third century B.C. by Celtic tribes that had been driven out of Gaul (France). From these tribes, the region derived its name, Galatia.

Galilee. The hill country in the north of Palestine. At the time of Jesus, Herod Antipas ruled Galilee. All the twelve disciples except Judas came from Galilee.

Galilee, Sea of. *Chinnereth* in the OT. A fresh-water lake in the north of Palestine fed by the Jordan. The New Testament also calls it the Lake of Gennesaret and Sea of Tiberias or "the lake" and "the sea."

Gath. One of the five major Philistine cities on the coast of Palestine. Goliath came from Gath. The Philistines captured the ark of the covenant and kept it at Gath for a time. David conquered this city. Later the Syrians captured Gath, and the Bible never mentions it again.

Gaza. One of the five cities and a trading center of the Philistines. The story of Samson involves the city. Gaza is mentioned only once in the New Testament (Acts 8:26).

Gennesaret. A fertile place on the west side of the Sea of Galilee. The name was also used to refer to the sea itself.

Gilboa. A range of mountains overlooking the pass from the plain of Jezreel to the Jordan valley. Saul and his sons died in battle there with the Philistines.

Gethsemane. The place at the foot of the Mount of Olives, across the Kidron Valley from Jerusalem, where Jesus went with his disciples to pray on the night of his betrayal and arrest.

Gilead. A hilly area to the east of the Jordan River and the home of Elijah the prophet. From resin of the trees the people produced the balm of Gilead used for healing, embalming, and as a cosmetic.

Gilgal. "Circle of stones." The place where Joshua pitched camp after the crossing into Canaan, and set up twelves stones. At Gilgal the people of Israel made Saul their first king, and there Samuel later rejected his leadership.

Gomorrah. "Submersion." One of the five cities of the plain located in the Valley of Siddim (Salt Sea or Dead Sea). The other cities were Sodom, Admah, Zeboim, and Zoar (Gen. 14:2–3). Gomorrah is always closely associated with its twin city, Sodom. Because these cities became the site of intolerable wickedness, they were destroyed by fire.

Goshen. A part of Egypt where the family of Jacob settled with its flocks in the time of Joseph.

Greece. A region or country of city-states in southeastern Europe between Italy and Asia Minor. Greece was bounded on the east by the Aegean Sea, on the south by the Mediterranean Sea, on the west by the Adriatic Sea and Ionian Sea, and on the north by Mount Olympus and adjacent mountains. The OT name for Greece was *Javan* (Gen. 10:2, 4; Isa. 66:19).

In the early years of its history, Greece was a country of self-governing city-states. Politically and militarily, the Greek city-states were weak. Their varied backgrounds led to frictions and rivalries that kept them from becoming one unified nation.

In 338 B.C., Philip II, king of Macedon, conquered the southern peninsula of Greece. Under Philip's son Alexander the Great (356–323 B.C.), the Greek Empire extended from Greece through Asia Minor to Egypt and the borders of India. Alexander's military conquests and his passion to spread Greek culture advanced Greek ideas throughout the ancient world. This adoption of Greek ideas by the rest of the ancient world was known as "Hellenism." So thoroughly did Greek ideas penetrate the other nations that the Greek language became the dominant language of the known world.

Greek learning and culture eventually conquered the ancient Near East and continued as dominant forces throughout the New Testament era. After the rise of the Romans, about 146 B.C., the influence of Greek language, culture, and philosophy remained strong, even influencing the Jewish religion.

Greek religion included many gods. The gods of Egypt, Asia Minor, and Persia were more appealing than the old Greek gods because they promised immortality. However, the Greeks did not abandon their former gods; they simply adopted new gods. A renewed interest in astrology among the Greeks also led to widespread belief that the planets governed the lives and fates of human beings. The Greeks sought to control any turn of fate through worship. They even erected an altar inscribed "to the unknown god" in their capital city of Athens (Acts 17:23).

The peninsula of Greece fell to the Romans in 146 B.C. and later became the senatorial province of Achaia with Corinth as its capital. The apostle Paul visited this area on his second missionary journey, delivering his famous sermon to the Athenian philosophers (Acts 17:22–34). Later he appeared before the proconsul Gallio at Corinth (Acts 18:12–17). On his third mis-

An inscribed altar to unknown gods, perhaps similar to the one Paul saw at Athens (Acts 17:22–24). PHOTO BY HOWARD VOS

sionary journey, he visited Greece for three months (Acts 20:2–3).

Greece is important to Christianity because of its language. In New Testament times Greek was the language spoken by the common people of the ancient world, as far west as Rome and the Rhone Valley in southeastern France. Most of the NT was written originally in Greek. This precise and expressive language provided the most capable vehicle for expressing thought of any language in the ancient world.

Hades. (See *Hell.*)

Haran. A city in northern Mesopotamia associated with Abraham, Isaac, and Jacob. Abraham set out from Haran when God called him to become the father of a great nation. Isaac's wife Rebekah and Jacob's wives Leah and Rachel came from near Haran.

Hebron. Abraham camped at Hebron and built an altar to the Lord. When Sarah died there, Abraham bought a cave in which to bury her. Abraham, Isaac, Rebekah, Jacob, and Leah were later buried at Hebron.

Hebron was one of the cities of refuge. It was also David's first capital and where the men of Judah anointed him king. At Hebron, his birthplace, Absalom began his rebellion against his father David and proclaimed himself king.

Hermon. A range of mountains, more than 9,000 feet above sea level at its highest point and covered with snow the year round. The Psalms make frequent mention of Hermon. This may have been the high mountain that was the scene of Jesus' transfiguration (see Mark 9:2).

Hinnom. Greek *Gehenna.* A valley on the south and west of Jerusalem. The name has evil associations because the people sacrificed children to Molech there in Old Testament times. Jeremiah and others cried out against this pagan custom. Later the valley became a garbage dump, continually on fire. The filth and foul odor suggest the picture of punishment.

Hor, Mount. "Hill, mountain." The mountain on the border of the Edomites where Aaron died and was buried (Num. 20:22–29; Deut. 32:50). Hor is usually regarded as an archaic form of *Har,* the Hebrew word for "mountain." Numbers 20:23 indicates that Mount Hor was situated by the border of the land of Edom. This was the place where the Hebrew people stopped after they left Kadesh (Num. 20:22; 33:37).

Iconium. A city in central Asia Minor visited by Paul on his first and second missionary journeys. Many turned to Jesus Christ but others drove out Paul and Barnabas.

Idumea. "Land of the Edomites." The Greek name for the land of Edom. After the Babylonian captivity, Idumea meant the region south of Judea populated by Edomite refugees fleeing from the invasion of Arabs.

Italy. A long, boot-shaped country that juts into the Mediterranean Sea (Acts 18:2; Heb. 13:24). Its most important city is Rome. During New Testament times, Rome was the capital of the Roman Empire.

Jabbok. One of the main eastern tributaries of the Jordan River (Deut. 2:37). The stream rose in Transjordan, in the hills of Bashan near Rabbah of the Ammonites (modern Amman) and entered the Jordan about 25 kilometers (15 miles) north of the Dead Sea. Near the ford of the Jabbok Jacob wrestled with God and had his name changed to Israel (Gen. 32:22–32).

Jabesh-gilead. "Jabesh of Gilead." A town of Gilead (1 Sam. 31:11; 2 Sam. 2:4), situated about 16 kilometers (10 miles) southeast of Beth Shan and about three kilometers (two miles) east of the Jordan River. It was within the territory assigned to the half-tribe of Manasseh (Num. 32:29, 40).

Jabesh-gilead refused to join in the punishment of the Benjamites (Judg. 21:8–14), an offense for which every man was put to the sword. Four hundred young virgins of Jabesh were given to the Benjamites as wives.

Jacob's well. The well where Jesus talked to the Samaritan woman (John 4:1–26). This is the earliest reference to Jacob's well; it is not mentioned in the OT. The well, known today as *Bir Ya'qub* ("the well of Jacob"), is near Tell Balatah, regarded by some scholars as ancient Shechem.

Jebus. Meaning unknown. An early name for the city of Jerusalem (Judg. 19:10–11). The citadel of Jebus was captured by the army of David, who called it the City of David (2 Sam. 5:7, 9). (See *City of David.*)

Jehoshaphat, Valley of. A valley in which, according to some Christians, God will judge the nations at the end of this age. The Valley of Jehoshaphat was that part of the Kidron Valley between the temple and the Mount of Olives. The name *Jehoshaphat* means "Jehovah is Judge."

Jericho. Meaning unknown. One of the oldest inhabited cities in the world. Situated in the wide plain of the Jordan Valley (Deut. 34:1, 3) at the foot of the ascent to the Judean mountains, Jericho lies about 13 kilometers (eight miles) northwest of the site where the Jordan River flows into the Dead Sea, some eight kilometers (five miles) west of the Jordan.

Since it is approximately 244 meters (800 feet) below sea level, Jericho has a climate that is tropical and at times hot. Only a few inches of rainfall are recorded at Jericho each year; but the city is a wonderful oasis, known as the city of palm trees (Deut. 34:3) or the city of palms (Judg. 3:13). Jericho flourishes with date palms, banana trees, balsams, sycamores, and henna (Luke 19:4).

Three different Jerichos actually existed throughout its long history. Old Testament Jericho is generally identified with the mound of Tell es-Sultan, about two kilometers (a little more than a mile) from the village of er-Riha. This village is modern Jericho, located about 27 kilometers (17 miles) northeast of Jerusalem. New Testament Jericho is identified with the mounds of Tulul Abu el-'Alayiq, about two kilometers (a little more than a mile) west of modern Jericho and south of Old Testament Jericho.

The most imposing site of the three is Old Testament Jericho, a pear-shaped mound which has been the site of numerous archaeological diggings and is a favorite stop for Holy Land tourists.

Jerusalem. The most famous holy city in the world. Jerusalem is first mentioned as a hill stronghold of the Jebusites captured by David, who made it the nation's capital. David placed the ark of the covenant there. Solomon built the temple and a palace in the city.

Nebuchadnezzar of Babylon destroyed the city in 586 B.C. and led royalty and priests away into exile. The Babylonians burned the temple and the gates. Cyrus allowed the Jews to return and to rebuild the temple. In the time of Nehemiah the walls, gates, and towers were rebuilt. The Romans destroyed the city in A.D. 70.

Names for the City of Jerusalem

Ariel, the hearth of God	Isa. 29:1	Holy City	Isa. 48:2; 52:1; Matt. 4:5
City of David	2 Sam. 6:12		
City of God	Ps. 46:4; 48:1; 87:3	Joy of the whole earth	Lam. 2:15
		The Lord is there	Ezek. 48:35
City of the great King	Matt. 5:35		
City of the Lord	Isa. 60:14	Perfection of beauty	Lam. 2:15
City of the Lord of hosts	Psa. 48:8	The Lord our righteousness	Jer. 23:6; 33:16
City of righteousness	Isa. 1:26		
City of Truth	Zech. 8:3	Salem	Gen. 14:18

Important Facts about Jerusalem

It was the place where Abraham fellowshiped with the king-priest Melchizedek.	Gen. 14:18
Joshua later defeated its wicked king Adonizedek during Israel's southern campaign invasion of Canaan.	Josh. 10:1
It was taken temporarily by the tribe of Judah around 1425 B.C.	Judg. 1:8
It was the location of a sexual crime committed by Jebusites who controlled it around 1405 B.C.	Judg. 19:22–30
It was captured by David around 1050 B.C. and made the capital of his kingdom.	2 Sam. 5:6–12; 6:1–19
Temporarily taken by Absalom c. 1020 B.C.	2 Sam. 16:15

Important Facts about Jerusalem—*continued*

Solomon built the temple there, 1005 B.C.	1 Kings 6
Plundered by Shishak of Egypt, during Rehoboam's reign	1 Kings 14:25–28
Plundered by Philistines and Arabians during Jehoram's reign	2 Chron. 21:16–17
Plundered by Syrians during time of Joash	2 Chron. 24:23–24
Plundered by Israel during time of Amaziah	2 Chron. 25:23
Surrounded by Assyrians during reign of Hezekiah	2 Chron. 32
Captured by Pharaoh Necho after Josiah's death	2 Kings 23:28–37
Besieged by Nebuchadnezzar	2 Kings 24:10–16
Nebuchadnezzar destroyed the temple and city.	2 Kings 25
Reconstruction by Cyrus's decree in 536 B.C.	Ezra 1
Walls of city completed under Nehemiah	Neh. 6:15–16
Jerusalem captured by Ptolemy Soter 320 B.C.	
Temple desecrated by Antiochus Epiphanes in 170 B.C.	
Temple cleansed and rededicated by Maccabees in 167 B.C.	
Jerusalem captured by Romans in 63 B.C.	
Antipater rebuilt the walls in 44 B.C.	
In 20 B.C. Herod the Great began to enlarge the temple rebuilt by Zerubbabel.	
It was built of white stone and its facade was plated with gold, so that at a distance it resembled a mountain covered with snow. It cost many millions and took 46 years to complete.	
Jesus was dedicated at the temple.	Luke 2:1–38
Jesus attended the Passover when he was 12.	Luke 2:41–50
Jesus cleansed the temple.	John 2:13–17
He healed an invalid of 38 years.	John 5:8
Jesus forgave an adulterous woman.	John 8:1–11
Jesus healed a man born blind.	John 9:7
Jesus made his triumphal entry.	John 12:12–15
Jesus cursed the fig tree.	Matt. 21:19
Jesus preached on the Mount of Olives.	Matt. 24—25
Jesus wept over the city.	Matt. 23:37–39; Luke 19:41
Jesus met with his disciples in the Upper Room.	John 13—14
Jesus was arrested in Gethsemane.	Matt. 26:47–56
Jesus was condemned to death.	Matt. 27:26
Jesus was crucified.	Matt. 27:27–50
Jesus was buried.	Matt. 27:57–60
Jesus rose from the dead.	Matt. 28:1–10
Jesus visited the Upper Room after his resurrection.	John 20:19–23
Disciples prayed in the Upper Room	Acts 1:12–26
Disciples were filled with the Holy Spirit.	Acts 2
Peter preached his first sermon at Pentecost.	Acts 2:14–41
The lame man was healed by Peter and John.	Acts 3:1–11
Disciples experienced their persecution.	Acts 4:1–3
Ananias and Sapphira killed by God.	Acts 5:1–11
First seven deacons chosen.	Acts 6:1–7
Stephen martyred for the faith	Acts 6:8—7:60

Important Facts about Jerusalem—*continued*

Saul (Paul) returned to Jerusalem after his conversion, and Barnabas vouched for him.	Acts 9:26–28
Jerusalem council meets on issue of law and Gentiles.	Acts 15
Paul arrested	Acts 21:17—23:22
Temple and city of Jerusalem destroyed by Titus the Roman general in A.D. 70	Matt. 24:2

Joppa. A Mediterranean seaport. Although the port for Jerusalem, in Old Testament times, Joppa was a poor and dangerous harbor with heavy surf. The timber for building Solomon's temple went down to the coast from the forests of Lebanon, floated to Joppa, and was dragged through the hills to Jerusalem forty miles away.

In the early days of the church Peter visited Joppa and raised Dorcas from the dead. He stayed at the seaside home of Simon the tanner. On the rooftop he had a vision of a sheet let down from heaven with all kinds of animals and reptiles and birds.

Jordan. The largest and most famous river of Palestine. The Israelites considered the Jordan the boundary of the Promised Land, and it figures into many Bible events. Lot chose its well-watered valley in which to settle. Joshua led the children of Israel across the Jordan on dry ground. King David fled that way during Absalom's rebellion. The Syrian Naaman washed in its waters to be healed. John the Baptist preached along its banks and baptized Jesus in the river.

Judah *or* Judea. The Greek form of the name *Judea* is the form used in the New Testament. Although the name of one of the twelve tribes, it applied not only to the people but also to the part of Canaan they occupied. After the division of the kingdom, Judah and Benjamin formed the southern kingdom in the hill country with its capital at Jerusalem. All rulers were descendants of the house of David.

Kadesh *or* Kadesh-barnea. A desert oasis on the edge of the Negeb where the Israelites spent a year before wandering in the wilderness. Moses' sister Miriam died there. From Kadesh Moses sent out spies to view the hill country of Canaan.

Kidron. A valley between Jerusalem and the Mount of Olives and also a stream that runs through it. Kings of Judah used the valley to burn idols during times of reformation. King David crossed the Kidron when fleeing from his rebellious son Absalom. Jesus went that way on his visit to Gethsemane.

Kirjath Arba. "City of the four." The ancient name of Hebron (Gen. 23:2; *Kiriath-arba*, NIV, RSV). Near this city was the Cave of Machpelah where Jewish tradition says Adam, Abraham, Isaac, and Jacob are buried, and thus, its name, "City of the four." Caleb captured Kirjath Arba from the Anakim, after whose leader, Arba, the city was named (Josh. 14:15). Kirjath Arba was in the hill country district of Judah,

Modern Jaffa on the Mediterranean coast is the successor to the biblical city of Joppa (Acts 10:5–9). Today the city is part of the municipality of Tel–Aviv. PHOTO BY HOWARD VOS

about 32 kilometers (20 miles) southwest of Jerusalem.

Kishon. A small, rushing river in the plain of Jezreel that flowed into the Mediterranean near the modern Haifa. It figures prominently in the story of Deborah and Barak defeating Sisera in the book of Judges. For most of the year Kishon is almost dry, but during the rainy seasons it becomes a raging torrent and floods both banks. The chariots of Sisera's army bogged down in the mud near Kishon and the Israelites easily defeated them.

By the side of Kishon Elijah killed the prophets of Baal after the encounter at Mount Carmel.

Lachish. An important walled fortress city in southern Judah, thirty miles from Jerusalem. Joshua captured the city and Rehoboam fortified it, but it comes to prominence in the days of King Hezekiah when Sennacherib of Assyria made Lachish his military headquarters in his attack on Jerusalem. Hezekiah capitulated and paid tribute to him. A century later when Nebuchadnezzar destroyed Jerusalem, Lachish was one of the two fortified cities that held out for a time.

Lake of Gennesaret. (See *Gennesaret*.)

Laodicea. A city of Asia Minor near Colossae. It was one of the seven churches of Asia that John mentions in Revelation (see Rev. 1:11).

Lebanon. "White mountain." The Lebanon is a chain of mountains a hundred miles long that parallels the coast of the Holy Land and forms the northern boundary of the Promised Land. The peaks rise to 10,000 feet and are always snow-covered. The forests provided mighty cedars in ancient times for building in many empires. Hiram, King of Tyre, supplied David and Solomon with cedar and cypress for the building of the royal palaces and the temple.

Levitical cities. Forty-eight cities assigned to the tribe of Levi. When the land of Canaan was divided among the tribes of Israel, each tribe except Levi received a specific region or territory for its inheritance. The tribe of Levi became the priestly tribe to serve the religious and spiritual needs of the nation. Instead of receiving a territory of their own, the Levites were scattered throughout the land.

Lycaonia. "She-wolf." A Roman province in Asia Minor visited by the apostle Paul (Acts 14:6). In apostolic times part of it (where Paul visited) was a region of the Roman province of Galatia. Because of its remoteness, Lycaonia enjoyed political independence during much of its history, until it fell under Greek control in the period following the conquests of Alexander the Great.

The apostle Paul visited the three main cities of Lycaonia—Iconium, Lystra, and Derbe—on his three journeys to Asia Minor (Acts 13:51—14:6; 2 Tim 3:11). Timothy was from Lycaonia, likely a native of Lystra (Acts 16:1).

Lydda. A town in the plain of Sharon where Peter healed a paralyzed man named Aeneas and where many turned to God.

Lystra. A city of Lycaonia, in modern Turkey, where Paul preached after being driven from Iconium. Lystra was built on a small hill about 46 meters (150 feet) above the plain that stretched northeastward to Iconium and southeastward to Derbe.

Apparently, Lystra was the home of Timothy (Acts 16:1–2). Paul wrote to Timothy mentioning his persecutions and afflictions at Antioch of Pisidia, Iconium, and Lystra (2 Tim. 3:11). At Lystra, when Paul healed a crippled man, the people thought they were gods, calling Barnabas Zeus and Paul Hermes (Mercury). Jews from Antioch and Iconium later came to the city, persuading the multitudes to stone the apostle Paul (Acts 14:19).

Macedonia. Part of northern Greece, which came into prominence under Philip of Macedon and his son Alexander the Great. In the first century it was a Roman province. Paul went to Macedonia after he had a vision at Troas of a Macedonian who begged him to come and help. With Paul's arrival in Philippi, the gospel reached Europe. The apostle visited Thessalonica and other cities of the province where he established churches.

Machpelah. "Double." A field, a cave, and the surrounding land purchased by Abraham as a burial place for his wife Sarah. The cave was to the east of Mamre, or Hebron (Gen. 23:19). At an earlier time, Abraham pitched his tent "by the terebinth trees of Mamre" (Gen. 13:18) and received three visitors who spoke of a child of promise to be born to Sarah.

Abraham purchased the field from Ephron the Hittite. Abraham, Sarah, Isaac, Rebekah, Jacob, and Leah were all buried here (Gen. 49:31; 50:13).

The modern city of el-Khalil (Hebron) is built around the site of Machpelah. The site of the cave was once covered by a Christian church but is now marked by a Moslem mosque. The Moslems have held this site so sacred that for centuries Christians were forbidden to enter the ancient shrine.

Magdala. "Tower." A place on the Sea of Galilee, perhaps on the west shore. Jesus and his disciples withdrew to Magdala after the feeding of the 4,000 (Matt. 15:39; Magadan, NIV, NASB, NEB, RSV). The parallel passage (Mark 8:10) has Dalmanutha. Magdala was either the birthplace or the home of Mary Magdalene.

Mahanaim. "Two armies." An ancient town in Gilead, east of the Jordan River in the vicinity of the River Jabbok. Its exact location is disputed.

On his way home after an absence of 20 years, Jacob was met by angels of God at this site. He named the place *Mahanaim,* meaning "two armies." This was a significant moment for Jacob, who was about to meet his estranged brother Esau.

Following the slaying of King Saul by the Philistines, his son Ishbosheth reigned for

Traditional well of Abraham in the plains of Mamre (Gen. 21:22–32). PHOTO BY HOWARD VOS

two years at Mahanaim (2 Sam. 2:8, 12, 29). Later, Mahanaim became the headquarters for David during the rebellion of his son, Absalom (2 Sam. 17:24). Solomon also made Mahanaim the capital of one of his 12 districts (1 Kings 4:14).

Malta. "Refuge." A small island in the Mediterranean Sea between Sicily and Africa, about 145 kilometers (90 miles) southwest of Syracuse. The apostle Paul was shipwrecked on Malta (Acts 28:1).

With its fine natural harbors, Malta was a convenient haven for ships. Colonized by the Phoenicians, it was captured by the Greeks (736 B.C.), the Carthaginians (528 B.C.), and the Romans (242 B.C.).

Marah. "Bitter." A pool or well of bitter water in the Wilderness of Shur (Num. 33:8–9). Marah was the first place the Israelites stopped after crossing the Red Sea.

Mediterranean Sea. A large sea bordered by many important nations of the ancient world, including the Holy Land. The Hebrews referred to it by several different names. It was called the *Great Sea* (Num. 34:6), the *Western Sea* (Deut. 34:2), the *Sea of the Philistines* (Exod. 23:31, RSV), and simply *the sea* (Josh. 16:8).

Archaeologists believe an open channel once existed that connected the Mediterranean to the Red Sea. This channel was closed off by drifting desert sand and silt from the Nile River, providing a land connection between Asia and Africa.

Many ancient civilizations grew up around this sea and used it for trade. The Hebrews were afraid of the Mediterranean and usually hired others, often Phoenicians (1 Kings 9:27), to conduct their seafaring business for them. The Holy Land itself had few good harbors.

The apostle Paul crossed the Mediterranean Sea during his missionary journeys. He tried to avoid sailing during the winter months, but was shipwrecked on his way to Rome while sailing in late autumn.

Medes. The land of Media lay to the northeast of Mesopotamia between the Black and Caspian Seas. The land is first mentioned when Assyria emerged as a war power. The king of Assyria captured Samaria, carried Israelites to Assyria, and placed them in the cities of the Medes. The Medes joined with the Chaldeans to overthrow Assyria and were themselves eventually overcome by Cyrus and the Persians. The books of Daniel and Esther refer to the laws of the Medes and the Persians.

Megiddo. An ancient fortressed city of strategic importance in northern Palestine. It guarded the pass at the entrance to the plain of Jezreel through which ran the military and trade highways from Mesopotamia to Egypt. All travelers had to go that way. Because of its position Megiddo has been the scene of many critical battles.

Solomon set up a chariot city at Megiddo to stable his horses and chariots. Three hundred years later, King Josiah of Judah fought Pharaoh Neco who was marching north to the aid of Assyria. Josiah died in that battle.

The book of Revelation mentions Armageddon (the hill of Megiddo), and some see it as the actual place where the final battle between good and evil will be fought.

Melita. The island of Malta in the Mediterranean where Paul was shipwrecked on his voyage to Rome.

Memphis. "Haven of good." An ancient royal city during the Old Kingdom period of Egypt's history (about 3000 B.C. to 2200

B.C.). It was situated on the west bank of the Nile River about 21 kilometers (13 miles) south of Cairo. Today little remains to mark the glorious past of the city.

In 670 B.C. Memphis was captured by the Assyrians, and a period of Persian dominance followed. After the Moslem conquest of the city, its ruins were used in the Middle Ages to build Cairo, Egypt's modern capital. The importance of Memphis is demonstrated by the multitude of pyramids and the celebrated Sphinx located near the site of the ancient city.

The word *Memphis* is found only once in the Bible—a translation of the Hebrew word *noph* (Hos. 9:6). In this passage the prophet Hosea condemned the Israelites for their sinfulness and predicted that some of them would be buried by Egyptians from Memphis. In seven other locations the word *noph* refers to Memphis (Isa. 19:13; Jer. 2:16; 44:1; 46:14, 19; Ezek. 30:13, 16). In each passage the NIV has Memphis.

Michmash. "A hidden place." A city of Benjamin about 11 kilometers (seven miles) northeast of Jerusalem. According to 1 Samuel 13:2, Saul gathered an army of 3,000 men in an attempt to meet the Philistine threat. Two thousand of the men were under Saul's personal command at Michmash, and 1,000 were under the command of Jonathan at nearby Gibeah of Benjamin.

When the Philistines moved toward Michmash, Saul fled to Gilgal and many of his soldiers deserted him. Saul offered a sacrifice to the Lord and was severely rebuked by Samuel (1 Sam. 13:5–15). Saul returned to Gibeah while Jonathan and his armorbearer scaled the northern cliff of the gorge of Michmash. By this daring tactical maneuver, they were able to kill the enemy sentries and throw the entire Philistine camp into panic.

Several centuries later, Ezra recorded that 122 men of Michmash returned from the captivity (Ezra 2:27; Michmas, NKJV).

Miletus. An ancient seaport in Asia Minor visited by the apostle Paul (Acts 20:15, 17; 2 Tim. 4:20; Miletum, KJV). Situated on the shore of the Mediterranean Sea, Miletus was about 60 kilometers (37 miles) south of Ephesus and on the south side of the Bay of Latmus. Because of silting, the site is now more than eight kilometers (five miles) from the coast.

Millo. A platform or rampart at the northern end of the City of David, which became part of Jerusalem. Solomon further strengthened this part of the capital and so did Hezekiah.

Mizpah. "Watchtower." One of three names given to a mound of stones erected as a memorial. Jacob set up this memorial in Gilead as a witness of the covenant between him and his father-in-law, Laban (Gen. 31:49). Both Jacob and Laban called this monument "heap of witness." The mound was also called *Mizpah*, meaning "watch (tower)."

Moab. From Mount Nebo in Moab Moses viewed Canaan and there he died. The Israelites had to circumvent Moab on their entry into the Promised Land. Later references to Moab include Ruth, who was a native of that land. David defeated the nation and exacted tribute. In the days of King Jehoram a bloody battle took place in Moab. Nebuchadnezzar conquered the Moabites completely.

Moriah. "Jehovah provides."

1. A land to which God commanded Abraham to take his son Isaac and offer him as a burnt offering on one of the mountains. The mountains of this land were a three-day journey from Beersheba (Gen. 22:2, 4).

2. The hill at Jerusalem where Solomon built the temple. Originally this was the threshing floor of Ornan the Jebusite (2 Chron. 3:1), also called Araunah the Jebusite (2 Sam. 24:16–24), where God appeared to David. David purchased the threshing floor from Ornan (1 Chron. 21:15—22:1) and built an altar on the site.

It was left to Solomon to build the temple.

Jews believe the altar of burnt offering in the temple at Jerusalem was situated on the exact site of the altar on which Abraham intended to sacrifice Isaac. To them the two Mount Moriahs mentioned in the Bible are identical. The Muslim mosque, the Dome of the Rock in Jerusalem, is presently situated on this site.

Mount of the Beatitudes. A slope on the northwest shore of the Sea of Galilee where Jesus is believed to have delivered the Sermon on the Mount (Matt. 5:1–7:29), also known as the Sermon on the Plain (Luke 6:20–49). The level place (Luke 6:17) from which Jesus spoke was not necessarily on the plain, but could have been a plateau on the mountain. A church has been built on the site traditionally recognized as the Mount of Beatitudes, but the actual site cannot be identified with certainty.

Mount of Olives. (See *Olives, Mount of.*)

Nain. A town in Galilee where Jesus restored a widow's son to life.

Nazareth. The home of Mary and Joseph and the town where Jesus was raised. When Jesus taught in the synagogue at Nazareth the people despised him. We have no record that Jesus ever went there again. Nazareth was an obscure, insignificant place. Nathanael asked, "Can anything good come out of Nazareth?" (John 1:46).

Nazarene. An inhabitant or native of Nazareth. The word *Nazarene* is used many times to identify Jesus, both by demons (Mark 1:23–24) and by Jesus himself. When used by his enemies, the term took on a note of contempt. Matthew's gospel stated that Jesus was raised as a boy in Nazareth.

Nebo. A high mountain in Moab. From this mountain peak Moses viewed the Promised Land, and he died there.

Negev. "Dry, parched." A term used in some English translations of the Bible for the southern desert or wilderness area of Judah. Abraham journeyed in the Negev (Gen. 12:9; 13:1, 3; *the South*, NKJV). When the 12 spies explored the land of Canaan, they went up by way of the Negev (Num. 13:17, 22) and saw the Amalekites who lived there (13:29). The Canaanite king of Arad also lived in the Negev (Num. 21:1).

The prophet Isaiah described the Negev as a land of trouble and anguish, hardship and distress, populated by lions and poisonous snakes (Isa. 30:6). Through its arid wastes donkey and camel caravans made their way to and from the land of Egypt.

The Negev contained important copper deposits, and it connected Israel to trade centers in Arabia and Egypt. King Solomon built fortresses in the Negev to guard the trade routes. He also established at Eziongeber, on the Gulf of Aqaba, a port from which he shipped copper to foreign lands. King Uzziah made great efforts to develop the region, building fortresses and expanding agriculture.

The ancient Nilometer, used for measuring the flood stages of the Nile River, was located at Elephantine Island at Aswan, Egypt.

PHOTO BY HOWARD VOS

Nile. The longest river in Africa and the lifeblood of Egypt. Egypt has always depended on the rich soil deposited annually by the flood waters of the Nile, making ancient Egypt the granary of the Mediterranean world. The Nile functioned as a great trade route linking the countries of the Middle East with the wealth of Africa. The OT refers to the Nile as "the River." Goshen, on the fringe of the delta, was the home of the family of Jacob when they left Canaan. Moses was hidden in the reeds of the river when he was a baby. One of the 10 plagues turned the waters of the Nile into blood.

Nineveh. A city on the banks of the Tigris, the mighty capital of the ancient Assyrian empire. Under King Sennacherib the nation reached its height. To the Israelites, Nineveh stood as a symbol of Assyrian oppression. Jonah tried to run away rather than preach to its wicked people. An alliance of the Medes, Babylonians, and Scythians brought the empire to extinction.

Nod. "Wandering." An unidentified land east of the Garden of Eden where Cain fled after he murdered his brother (Gen. 4:16).

Noph. The Hebrew name for *Memphis*, an ancient Egyptian city on the western bank of the Nile and south of modern Cairo.

Obelisk. A stone monument or pillar. These stones are generally associated with Egyptian religion (Jer. 43:13). Stone pillars were raised as monuments to honor Rachel and Absalom (Gen. 35:20; 2 Sam. 18:18).

Oholah. "Her own tent." A symbolic name for Samaria, capital of the northern kingdom, and the ten tribes that made up this nation (Ezek. 23:4–5, 36, 44). The prophet Ezekiel used the allegorical figure of two harlot sisters: Oholah (*Aholah*, KJV) and Oholibah (*Aholibah*, KJV), to represent Jerusalem and the kingdom of Judah. Oholah and Oholibah are pictured as lusting after the Assyrians, Babylonians, and Egyptians.

Olives, Mount of, or Olivet. A line of hills east of Jerusalem across the Kidron Valley. The villages of Bethany and Bethpage flanked its slopes with Gethsemane at the foot of the hill. King David fled from his rebellious son Absalom by way of the Mount of Olives. The Gospels mention the hill a number of times, especially in recounting the night of Jesus' betrayal and arrest.

Ophir. A country on the southwest coast of Arabia, the modern Yemen. Ophir supplied gold to Solomon for his armor, throne, temple, and vessels for his royal table.

Padan Aram. "The plain of Aram." The area of upper Mesopotamia around Iran and the home of Abraham after he moved from Ur of the Chaldeans (Gen. 25:20; *Paddan-aram*, RSV). Abraham later sent his servant to Padan Aram to find a bride for his son Isaac. Much later, Isaac's son Jacob fled to Padan Aram to avoid the wrath of his brother Esau and dwelt there with Laban (Gen. 28:2, 5–7). The region was also referred to as *Padan* (Gen. 48:7; *Paddan*, RSV).

Pamphylia. "A region of every tribe." A Roman province on the southern coast of central Asia Minor (modern Turkey). The province consisted mainly of a plain about 130 kilometers (80 miles) wide. The capital city of Pamphylia, its largest city was Perga (Acts 13:13–14).

Pamphylia is first mentioned in the NT in Acts 2:10. People from Pamphylia were among those present in Jerusalem on the day of Pentecost. In Pamphylia the apostle Paul first entered Asia Minor (Acts 13:13) during his first missionary journey. It was also at Pamphylia that John Mark left Paul and Barnabas (Acts 15:38). On his voyage to Rome, Paul sailed off the coast of Pamphylia (Acts 27:5).

Paran. A wilderness region in the central part of the Sinai Peninsula. Although the boundaries of this desert region are obscure, it probably was bordered by the Arabah and the Gulf of Aqaba on the east.

Paran is frequently mentioned in the OT. Chedorlaomer, one of the four kings who attacked Sodom, conquered as far as "El Paran, which is by the wilderness" (Gen. 14:6). After Hagar was driven from Abraham's household (Gen. 21:21), she fled to this wilderness with her son Ishmael. The Israelites crossed Paran during their exodus from Egypt (Num. 10:12; 12:16), and Moses dispatched spies from Paran to explore the land of Canaan (Num. 13:3).

After the death of Samuel, David fled to Paran (1 Sam. 25:1). After revolting from King Solomon, Hadad went through Paran on his flight to Egypt (1 Kings 11:18).

Patmos. A barren island in the Aegean Sea off the west coast of Asia Minor. John, banished as a political prisoner in the days of Roman persecution, wrote the book of Revelation there.

Penuel or Peniel. "Face of God." A place north of the River Jabbok where Jacob wrestled with God until daybreak and called the place Penuel, "For I have seen God face to face" (Gen. 32:30). A city was built there later, not far to the east of Succoth. When Gideon and his band of 300 men pursued the Midianites, the people of Succoth and Penuel insulted Gideon, refusing to give supplies to his army. Gideon later killed the men of the city (Judg. 8:17). Penuel is about 65 kilometers (40 miles) northeast of Jerusalem.

Perga. Meaning unknown. The capital city of Pamphylia, a province on the southern coast of Asia Minor, twice visited by the apostle Paul. During Paul's first missionary journey, he sailed to Perga from Paphos, on the island of Cyprus (Acts 13:13–14). Later, Paul and Barnabas stopped a second time at Perga (Acts 14:25).

Pergamos. "Citadel." The chief city of Mysia, near the Caicus River in northwest Asia Minor (modern Turkey) and the site of one of the seven churches of Asia (Rev. 1:11; 2:12–17; *Pergamum*, RSV, NIV, NEB, NASB). The city, situated opposite the island of Lesbos, was about 24 kilometers (15 miles) from the Aegean Sea.

Pergamum.   A form of *Pergamos*.

Persia.   An ancient world empire that flourished from 539–331 B.C. The Babylonian Empire fell to the Persians, setting the stage for the return of the Hebrew people to Jerusalem about 538–445 B.C., following their long period of captivity by the Babylonians.

The OT contains many references to the nation of Persia and its representatives. Ezra 9:9 refers to the kings of Persia. Ezra 6:14 cites, "Cyrus, Darius, and Artaxerxes king of Persia." Daniel 8:20 speaks of the kings of Media and Persia. Daniel 10:13 mentions the prince of the kingdom of Persia. The book of Esther refers to the powers of Persia and Media (1:3), the seven princes of Persia and Media (1:14), and the ladies of Persia and Media (1:18). Daniel 5:28 prophesies that Belshazzar's kingdom would be handed over to the Medes and Persians.

The Persians apparently sprang from a people from the hills of Russia known as Indo-Aryans. As early as 2000 B.C., they began to settle in Iran and along the Black Sea coast. Two of these Indo-European tribes settled on the Elamite border and to the east of the Zagros mountain range. The first references to them are made in the inscriptions of Shalmaneser III (858–824 B.C.). They are noted as the *Parsua* (Persians) and *Madai* (Medes).

The first mention of a Persian chieftain refers to his role as an ally aligned against Sennacherib of Assyria. His son was called "King, Great King, King of the City of Anshan." His grandson fathered Cyrus II, who was one of the most celebrated kings of history. He is called by the prophet Isaiah "My shepherd" (Isa. 44:28). In another passage he is referred to as the Lord's anointed (Isa. 45:1), a term used in the OT of the Messiah.

Cyrus II, founder of the mighty Persian Empire, ascended the throne in Anshan in 559 B.C. He conquered the Median King Astyages. He defeated Lydia (about 546 B.C.) and Babylon (about 539 B.C.), finally establishing the Persian Empire. This last conquest is referred to in Daniel 5. Cyrus was the Persian king who issued the decree restoring the Jews to their homeland, following their long period of captivity by the Babylonians (2 Chron. 36:22–23; Ezra 1:1–4).

Cyrus was the founder of the system under which each province, or Persian satrapy, was governed by an official who answered to the great king. However, he allowed a remarkable degree of freedom of religion and customs for the vassal states, including Israel. He developed roads, cities, postal systems, and legal codes, and treated the subject nations kindly and humanely.

Cambyses II (530–522 B.C.), the son of Cyrus, reigned after his father, and Egypt was added to the list of nations conquered by Persia. According to the Greek historian Herodotus, Cambyses accidentally wounded himself with his own sword in 522 B.C. Some believe he committed suicide.

The next Persian king, Darius I (952–486 B.C.), was not a direct descendant of Cyrus but was of royal, Achaemenid blood. He defeated nine kings to claim all 23 Persian satrapies. This conquest was recorded on the famous Behistun Inscription, which was written in the Akkadian, Elamite, and Old Persian languages.

Darius I further unified the Persian Empire by using an efficient gold coinage, state highways, and a more efficient postal system. He was defeated by the Greeks at the Battle of Marathon in 490 B.C. This is the same Darius who, in his second year, ordered the Jewish temple at Jerusalem to be rebuilt after work on it had been discontinued for 14 years (Ezra 4:24; 6:1). He also gave a generous subsidy that made it possible to complete the temple. The extent of the Persian Empire under Darius is reflected in Esther 1:1 and 10:1. The vast territory was nearly 4,900 kilometers (3,000 miles) long and 800 to 2,400 kilometers (500 to 1,500 miles) wide.

Xerxes ruled Persia from 486 to 465 B.C. He was the Ahasuerus of the book of Esther. Esther did not become queen until the seventh year of his reign, about 478 B.C. This was two years after his devastating defeat at Salamis (480 B.C.), which ended Persia's last hope for conquering Greece.

During the reign of Artaxerxes I Longimanus (464–424 B.C.), two of the three returns of the Jewish people from captivity took place. The second return was under Ezra. This was made possible because of the generosity of Artaxerxes. The third return occurred in 445 B.C. (Neh. 1:1). The specific purpose of this return to Jerusalem was to rebuild the city walls.

The religion of the Persians centered on a reformation of the old Iranian religions developed by Zoroaster. He believed in a dualism in which Ahura Mazda (or *Ormazd*) headed the gods of goodness *(Amesha Spentas)* and Angra Mainyu (or *Ahriman*) headed the gods of evil *(daevas)*. Some of this background is revealed in the Jewish apocryphal literature, which developed from the fifth century B.C. to the time of Christ.

Paphos. A town on the west of the island of Cyprus and headquarters of the Roman administrator in the first century. Paul and Barnabas preached to the proconsul Sergius Paulus and he believed in Jesus Christ.

Philippi. A city of Macedonia (Greece) and the first city in Europe to which Paul brought the gospel. Philippi was a Roman colony named after Philip of Macedon, the father of Alexander the Great. In the first century it was an important trade center between Rome and Asia. By the river Paul met a small company of Jewish worshipers, preached Jesus Christ to them, and a wealthy businesswoman, Lydia, believed and became the first baptized Christian in Europe.

Paul and Silas were thrown into prison for healing a slave girl. An earthquake shook the building during the night and the frightened jailer was converted and baptized along with his whole house. To the Christians at Philippi, Paul addressed his letter to the Philippians, thanking them for their gifts and concern.

Petra. "Rock." The capital of Edom and later of Nabatea, situated about 275 kilometers (170 miles) southwest of modern Amman and about 80 kilometers (50 miles) south of the Dead Sea. Petra is not mentioned by name in the Bible, but many scholars believe it was the same place as Sela (Judg. 1:36; 2 Kings 14:7).

Petra is one of the most spectacular archaeological ruins in the Near East and a popular attraction on Holy Land tours. Most of the buildings and tombs of Petra are cut into the rose-red rock cliffs of the area.

Pharpar. Meaning unknown. A river of southern Syria near Damascus (2 Kings 5:12) mentioned by Naaman, the Syrian leper. The Abana probably is the modern Nahr el-Awaj, formed by several streams that descend from Mount Hermon. The river empties into Lake Bahret Hijaneh, east of Damascus.

Philadelphia. "Brotherly love." A city of the province of Lydia in western Asia Minor (modern Turkey) and the site of one of the seven churches of Asia to which John wrote in the book of Revelation (Rev. 1:11).

Philadelphia was situated on the Cogamus River, a tributary of the Hermus (modern Gediz) and was about 45 kilometers (28 miles) southeast of Sardis. It was founded by Attalus II *(Philadelphus)*, who reigned as king of Pergamos from 159 B.C. until 138 B.C. Philadelphia was a center of the wine industry. Its chief deity was Dionysus, in Greek mythology the god of wine (the Roman Bacchus).

Philistia. Meaning unknown. The land of the Philistines, as used in the poetry of the book of Psalms (108:9). This land lay between Joppa and Gaza on the coastal plain of Palestine.

Phoenicia. The land on the eastern shore of the Mediterranean Sea, between the Litani and Arvad Rivers. Phoenicia is a Greek word, a direct translation of the Hurrian word *Canaan*, which means "land of purple." The area was famous in early times for its purple dyes, produced from shellfish.

Phoenicia was a long, narrow country on the seacoast covering much of the territory that today is called Lebanon and southern Latakia (coastal Syria). Like Israel, much of it is mountainous, with only a narrow coastal plain. The low hills and plain are fertile. Phoenicia was famous in biblical times for its lush plant life, which included fruit, flowers, and trees.

The cedars of Phoenicia were cut and shipped as far away as Egypt and eastern Mesopotamia, because most other nations in this part of the world had few trees suitable for timber. Many direct land and sea routes connected Phoenicia to northern Israel. The Phoenicians had many contacts with the Israelites. During their long history, the Hebrew people often fell into paganism and idolatry because of the influence of Phoenician religion.

Phrygia. "Dry, barren." A large province of the mountainous region of Asia Minor (modern Turkey), visited by the apostle Paul (Acts 2:10; 16:6; 18:23). Because of its size, Phrygia was made a part of other provinces. The cities of Colossae, Laodicea, and Hierapolis belonged to Asia, while Iconium and Antioch belonged to Galatia.

The apostle Paul visited Phrygia on three journeys (Acts 13:14—14:5, 21; 16:6; 18:23). He apparently also passed through Phrygia on his third journey (Acts 18:22–24), although his letter to the Colossians suggests he did not found a church there (Col. 2:1). Jews who were at Jerusalem on the day of Pentecost may have been the first Phrygian converts (Acts 2:10). Jews settled in Phrygia during the Seleucid period. Some of them apparently adopted non-Jewish practices. Consequently, strict Jews became hostile to new ideas (Acts 13:44—14:6).

Pisgah. "Cleft." A word that refers to the rugged ridge that crowns a mountain. Pisgah was sometimes identified with Mount Nebo but it more likely refers to the entire ridge of the Abarim Mountains, which extends from the Moabite plateau toward the Dead Sea.

Nebo is the highest peak. From the top of the Pisgah Moses was permitted to survey the Promised Land. The particular peak upon which he stood was on or near Mount Nebo (Num. 21:20; 23:14, Deut. 3:27; 34:1).

Pisidia. Meaning unknown. A mountainous province in central Asia Minor (modern Turkey), twice visited by the apostle Paul (Acts 13:14; 14:24). Pisidia was a wild, mountainous country infested with bandits. When Paul wrote that he had been "in perils of robbers" (2 Cor. 11:26), he may have been referring to his dangerous journey through the mountains of Pisidia. While in Perga Paul intended to travel north through this rugged and dangerous mountain terrain to Antioch of Pisidia. The synagogue in Antioch of Pisidia was the scene of one of Paul's most impressive sermons (Acts 13:16–41).

Pithom. "Temple of Tem." One of the supply cities, or store cities, in Lower Egypt built by the Israelites while they were slaves in Egypt (Exod. 1:11). Pithom was in the general area of Raamses, but the Bible gives no further details about its location. Some archaeologists suggest that the temple, fortress, and storage chambers discovered at Tell el-Maskhutah, in the valley connecting the Nile river and Lake Timsah, are the remains of biblical Pithom. Others believe that Pithom should be identified with Tell er-Ratabah, about 16 kilometers (10 miles) to the west and closer to the land of Goshen.

It is possible that Pithom and Raamses (Exod. 1:11) were built during the reign of Pharaoh Rameses II (who ruled from about 1291–1225 B.C.). Rameses II, however, often made claims to build a city when actually he rebuilt it, or strengthened its fortifications. *Pithom* is supposed by some to be identical with *Succoth* (Exod. 12:37)—*Pithom* being the sacred or religious name and *Succoth* being the secular or civil name.

Pontus. A Roman province in the north of Asia Minor on the shores of the Black Sea. Jews from Pontus came to Jerusalem for the feast of Pentecost (see Acts 2:9). Peter wrote his first epistle to Christians in Pontus and elsewhere in Asia Minor who were undergoing persecution.

Pyramid. An ancient massive structure of Egypt with a rectangular base, outside walls in the form of four triangles that meet in a point at the top, and inner chambers used as tombs for Egyptian royalty. Such monuments were constructed over about 80 royal tombs in ancient Egypt.

The first pyramid was the Step Pyramid of King Djoser (about 2600 B.C.). The structure was made of six ascending steps, each one smaller than the one below. Most of the other pyramids were built during the Old Kingdom (2600–2200 B.C.), before the time of Abraham and well before the Israelite sojourn in Egypt.

The Great Pyramid of Khufu (or Cheops) is the largest. One of the seven wonders of the ancient world, it covered 13 acres and was 768 feet square and 482 feet high. It is situated at Giza, a city of northern Egypt, on the Nile River near Cairo. Some blocks of the Great Pyramid are estimated to weigh more than 54,400 kilograms (60 tons).

As a sacred symbol, the pyramid played an important part in the religious beliefs of the Egyptians. A text inside one pyramid suggests they were considered stairways to heaven for the buried pharaoh, who would be reunited with the sun god Ra.

The pyramids of Egypt are not mentioned in the Bible. Some scholars, however, believe the Tower of Babel (Gen. 11:1–9) was a step pyramid somewhat like those of the Egyptians.

Raamses. (See *Rameses.*)

Rabbah. "Great." The chief city of the Ammonites. Known as "Rabbah of the people of Ammon" (Deut. 3:11; 2 Sam. 12:26), Rabbah is the only Ammonite city mentioned in the Bible. Rabbah was at the headwaters of the Jabbok River, 37 kilometers (23 miles) east of the Jordan.

Rahab-Hem-Shebeth. "Rahab sits idle." A name given by the prophet Isaiah to Egypt (Isa. 30:7), comparing that nation to Rahab the Dragon, a mythological sea monster or primeval dragon of chaos. Israel had sought to establish a political and military alliance with Egypt under the threat of Assyrian aggression. The prophet Isaiah warned that such an alliance was worthless.

Ramah. "Height or hill town." Called Aramathea in the NT. Ramah was the home of the prophet Samuel.

Rameses, Raamses. "House of Ramses." The royal city of the Egyptian kings of the nineteenth and twentieth dynasties (about 1300–1100 B.C.), situated in the northeastern section of the Nile Delta. While the Israelites were slaves in Egypt, they were forced to work on at least two of Pharaoh's vast construction projects— building the supply cities of Pithom and Raamses (Exod. 1:11, KJV, RSV, NASB, NKJV; Rameses, NIV, NEB).

The reference to the land of Rameses (Gen. 47:11) in the story of Joseph, well before Rameses II lived, suggests that the author of Genesis used the name that was common in his day and not the earlier one used during the time of Joseph. This may also be true of the use of Rameses in the account of the Exodus, because the Hebrews apparently left Egypt around 1446 B.C., well before the time of King Ramses.

The land of Rameses (Gen. 47:11) was the best of the fertile district of Egypt. This almost certainly refers to the Land of Goshen, in the northeastern Nile Delta.

Ramoth Gilead. "Heights of Gilead." An important fortified city in the territory of Gad near the border of Israel and Syria. Ramoth Gilead was designated by Moses as one of the cities of refuge (Deut. 4:43; Josh. 20:8). In the time of Solomon, one of the king's 12 district officers was stationed at Ramoth Gilead to secure food for the king's household, since it was a commercial center.

Red Sea. A narrow body of water that stretches in a southeasterly direction from Suez to the Gulf of Aden for about 2,100 kilometers (1,300 miles). It is an important section of a large volcanic split in the earth that goes southward into east Africa and continues north along the Jordan Valley to the Lebanon mountain range.

The Red Sea separates Yemen and Saudi Arabia from Egypt, the Sudan, and Ethiopia. From ancient times the Red Sea has been an impressive sea covering some 169,000 square miles. It measures about 310 kilometers (190 miles) at its widest part and almost 2,900 meters (about 9,500 feet) at its greatest depth. The Red Sea branches at its northern end into two distinct channels, the northeasterly one being the Gulf of Aqaba and the northwesterly one named the Gulf of Suez. The Suez branch is fairly shallow and has broad plains on either side. By contrast, the Gulf of Aqaba is deep and clear with a narrow shoreline.

The Red Sea is usually bright turquoise, but periodically algae grows in the water. When they die, the sea becomes reddish-brown, thus giving it the name, the Red Sea. This body of water has the reputation of being one of the hottest and saltiest on earth because of volcanic slits in the ocean floor that have become filled with salt deposits and other minerals. The sea is heavily traveled because the Suez Canal links it with the Mediterranean. Navigation is difficult at the southern end because of outcroppings of coral reefs that force ships into a narrow channel of water. No large rivers flow into the Red Sea, and there is little rainfall in the area it crosses.

The name Red Sea has found its way into the Bible as a translation of the Hebrew *yam suph*, which means "sea of reeds" and not Red Sea. The term *suph* comes from the Egyptian *twf*, meaning "papyrus." This confusion is unfortunate because papyrus reeds and similar vegetation do not grow in the Red Sea or in the Gulf of Suez. This fact excludes them as the area that witnessed the deliverance of the Hebrew captives at the time of the Exodus.

The best understanding of *yam suph* is that it does not refer to the Red Sea or any of its branches. Instead, it probably refers to a shallow amount of water bordered by papyrus reeds and located somewhere between the southern edge of Lake Menzaleh and the lakes close to the head of the Gulf of Suez that were drained when the Suez Canal was constructed. Such a location for the Exodus would be directly opposite the Wilderness of Shur, which was the first encampment of the Israelites after crossing the *yam suph* (Exod. 15:22).

Rehoboth. "Broad places." A well dug by Isaac in the Valley of Gerar (Gen. 26:22). Rehoboth is probably present-day Wadi Ruheibeh, about 31 kilometers (19 miles) southwest of Beersheba.

Rephidim. "Refreshments." An Israelite encampment in the wilderness (Exod. 17:1–7). The Amalekites attacked the Israelites at Rephidim. During the battle Moses stood on a hill and held the rod of God aloft. Aaron and Hur supported his arms until sundown, and the Israelites won the battle.

Rome. Capital city of the ancient Roman Empire and present capital of modern Italy.

Founded in 753 B.C., Rome was situated 24 kilometers (15 miles) from where the Tiber River flows into the Mediterranean Sea. From its initial settlement on the Palatine Hill near the river, the city gradually grew and embraced the surrounding area. Ultimately, the city was situated on seven hills: Capital, Palatine, Anentine, Caelian, Esquiline, Viminal, and Quirinal.

As capital of the Roman Empire, the city was the seat of Roman government. During its long history, Roman government went through the forms of a monarchy, a republic, and an empire.

The monarchy occurred from 753 to 510

B.C. when Rome was ruled by kings. After Romulus, the first king (ruled 753–714 B.C.), Rome was ruled by six other princes until the decline of the monarchical form of government in 510 B.C.

As a republic, Rome was governed by elected consuls who presided over the senate. Under the republic, Rome expanded its borders and engaged in major internal reforms. The period of the republic lasted until 31 B.C. when Caesar Augustus became the first emperor. He developed Rome into a beautiful and stately city.

During the reign of Augustus as emperor in Rome, Jesus was born in Bethlehem of Judea. At that time and during the entire New Testament period, Judea was under Roman rule. Roman influence penetrated the Jewish community and continued to be felt in the life and mission of the New Testament church. During the reign of Tiberius, successor to Augustus, Jesus' public ministry occurred. The great missionary endeavors of the apostle Paul took place during the reign of Claudius. Under Nero, the city of Rome was burned, Christians were persecuted, and the apostle Paul was martyred.

The book of Acts describes the story of the early church as Christians spread the gospel, beginning at Jerusalem and finally reaching Rome.

The apostle Paul's first known connection with Rome was when he met Aquila and Priscilla at Corinth (Acts 18:2). They had left Rome when Claudius expelled all the Jews from the city. When Paul wrote his letter to the Christians at Rome, his plan was to visit friends in the city on his way to Spain (Rom. 15:24).

Paul went to Rome under different conditions than he had planned. To keep from being killed by hostile Jews in Jerusalem, Paul appealed to Caesar. The binding effect of that appeal ultimately brought him to the capital city as a prisoner where he waited for trial. The book of Acts closes at this point. Tradition says that Paul was martyred by Nero during the emperor's persecution of Christians.

Rosetta. The Rosetta Stone, a black basalt tablet was unearthed in August, 1799, near the village of Rosetta, Egypt, then taken to the British Museum in 1802. The stone was inscribed in three languages: hieroglyphic, Demotic Egyptian, and Koine Greek. This stone was the key that the brilliant young French scholar and Egyptologist, Jean Francois Champollion, needed to decipher Egyptian hieroglyphics. Champollion broke the hieroglyphic code by comparing it with the other two languages, which were translations of the same text. The discovery of this stone made it possible for scholars to translate Egyptian texts and to understand the historical background of Israel's history.

Royal City. A headquarters or capital city, or the center of a king's rule in Bible times. Notable capital cities of the Bible included Jerusalem (Judah), Samaria (Israel), and Damascus (Syria). The term *royal city* is also applied to Rabbah, capital of the Ammonites (2 Sam. 12:26).

Salamis. A thriving port city on the east coast of the island of Cyprus visited by the apostle Paul and Barnabas during Paul's first missionary journey.

Salem. "Peaceful." A city ruled by Melchizedek, the king to whom Abraham gave a tithe (tenth). Salem is usually identified with ancient Jerusalem, or Jebus, the Jebusite city captured by David and turned into the capital city of the nation of Judah (1 Chron. 11:4–9).

Salt Sea. An OT name for the body of water at the southern end of the Jordan Valley (Gen. 14:3). It contains no marine life because of its heavy mineral content. The Salt Sea is also called the *Sea of the Arabah* (Deut. 3:17). Its modern name is the *Dead Sea.*

Salt, Valley of. A barren valley, probably south of the Dead Sea, where the nation of Israel won two important victories over the Edomites. The army of King David killed 18,000 Edomites (2 Sam. 8:13, RSV; *Syri-*

ans, KJV, NKJV; *Arameans*, NASB) in the Valley of Salt. Two centuries later the army of King Amaziah of Judah killed another 10,000 Edomites in this valley (2 Kings 14:7).

Samaria. The capital of the northern kingdom of Israel, fortified in the days of King Omri. The prophet Amos denounced the people of Samaria because they oppressed the poor. The northern kingdom fell to the Assyrians under Sargon in 721 B.C., who deported most of the nationals and filled the land with people from Babylonia and elsewhere. The new inhabitants intermarried with the remaining Israelites and their descendants were called Samaritans. After the exile, Samaria was an area inhabited by these mixed-blood people. The Samaritans tried to stop the rebuilding of the walls of Jerusalem in the time of Nehemiah.

Post-exilic Jews, devoted to purity of race, rejected the Samaritans and an age-long hostility began. The Samaritans erected their own temple on Mount Gerizim in opposition to the temple in Jerusalem. Herod the Great rebuilt the city of Samaria and named it *Sebaste*.

Jesus immortalized the good Samaritan in one of his most memorable parables. Jesus commanded that the disciples take the gospel from Judea to Samaria and to the rest of the world (see Acts 1:8). Soon the disciples preached the gospel in the towns and villages of Samaria (see Acts 8).

Sardis. The capital city of Lydia in the province of Asia, in western Asia Minor (modern Turkey). The church at Sardis was one of the seven churches mentioned by John in the book of Revelation (Rev. 3:1–6).

Sea of Galilee.   (See *Galilee, Sea of*.)

Seir.   "Hairy, rough." The mountainous country stretching from the Dead Sea to the Red Sea, east of the gorge called the *Arabah* (Gen. 14:6). The elevations of Seir range from 183 meters (600 feet) to 1,830 meters (6,000 feet). Two of Seir's outstanding features are Mount Hor, where Aaron

died (Num. 20:27–28), and the ancient city of rock, Petra or Sela (Isa. 16:1). The region was named after a Horite (Hurrian) patriarch whose descendants settled in this area.

God gave this land to Esau and his descendants, who drove out the Horites, or Hurrians (Deut. 2:12). Esau and his descendants, the Edomites, lived in Seir (Deut. 2:29).

Seleucia.   The seaport city of Antioch in Syria. From there Barnabas and Paul sailed to Cyprus on their first missionary journey.

Seven Churches of Asia.   Congregations to which John addressed special messages in the book of Revelation from the Isle of Patmos. These seven churches, found in Revelation 2—3, were Ephesus, the loveless church; Smyrna, the persecuted church; Pergamos, the compromising church; Thyatira, the corrupt church; Sardis, the dead church; and Laodicea, the lukewarm church.

Sharon.   A plain on the Mediterranean coast of Palestine that runs from Joppa to Mount Carmel.

Sheba.   A country on the southwest coast of Arabia, famous for its trade in frankincense, gold, and precious stones. The Queen of Sheba came with a camel caravan to visit Solomon. The names *Seba* and *Sabean* refer to the same place and are always associated with vast wealth.

Shechem.   An ancient fortified city in central Palestine and the first capital of the northern kingdom of Israel. Its name means "shoulder," probably because the city was built mainly on the slope, or shoulder, of Mount Ebal. Situated where main highways and ancient trade routes converged, Shechem was an important city long before the Israelites occupied Canaan. The city has been destroyed and rebuilt several times through the centuries.

Shiloh.   The religious center in the early days of the Israelites' conquest of Canaan.

They placed the ark of the covenant in a shrine at Shiloh and the tribes gathered for religious festivals. Samuel served the Lord at Shiloh when he was a boy. The Philistines captured and destroyed Shiloh and took the ark with them.

Shinar. A name given in the early chapters of Genesis to the land better known as Babylonia.

Shushan. Meaning unknown. The ancient capital of Elam, in southwestern Iran; later a royal residence and capital of the Persian Empire (Neh. 1:1; Susa, NASB, NIV, RSV). The site is present-day Shush, about 240 kilometers (150 miles) north of the Persian Gulf.

Long before the time of Abraham in the OT, Shushan was the center of Elamite civilization. Some scholars believe it was a cult city centering on worship of one of the chief Elamite gods. The city had frequent contacts with Mesopotamia.

The Assyrian King Ashurbanipal (the biblical Osnapper, Ezra 4:10) led a military campaign against Shushan about 642–639 B.C. In about 640 B.C. he sacked the city and carried some of its inhabitants (Susanchites, Ezra 4:9, KJV) into exile in Samaria.

When Cyrus the Great (reigned 550–529 B.C.) established the Persian Empire, he made Shushan its capital. At Shushan Darius the Great (ruled about 521–486 B.C.) built his magnificent royal palace. This palace, when occupied by Artaxerxes II (404–359 B.C.), figured prominently in the story of Esther. In fact, most of the events recorded in the book of Esther took place in Shushan. In Shushan the prophet Daniel had his vision of the ram and the goat (Dan. 8:2), and there Nehemiah lived in exile (Neh. 1:1).

Sidon. Along with Tyre, an important seaport on the northern coast of the Holy Land, in the ancient Phoenician kingdom. Sidonians were sea traders and famous for their woodwork. Their workers helped to build Solomon's temple and palace. After King Ahab married Jezebel, the daughter of the king of Sidon, she introduced Baal worship to Israel.

Sidon rose to prominence again in Roman times and the gospel writers mention the city (see Matt. 11:21; Mark 7:24). Paul visited friends at Sidon on his way to Rome for trial.

Siloam. Also called *Siloah* and sometimes the *King's Pool*. The conduit that carried water from the spring Gihon in the Kidron valley below Jerusalem to a pool inside the city. King Hezekiah brought about this remarkable engineering feet. The name *Siloam* refers to the tunnel and the pool. The gospel of John records the account of Jesus healing a a man born blind and telling him to wash in the pool of Siloam.

Siloam, Tower of. A tower near the Pool of Siloam inside the walls of Jerusalem. The exact site of this tower is unknown. In the time of Christ, a local disaster in which 18 lives were lost by a collapse of this structure was fresh in the minds of the people (Luke 13:4). (See *Siloam*.)

Sinai *or* Mount Horeb. The sacred mountain where Moses saw the burning bush and heard God speak to him. From this mountain Moses gave the law.

Smyrna. "Myrrh." A city in western Asia Minor (modern Turkey) where one of the seven churches in the book of Revelation was situated (Rev. 1:11; 2:8–11). Smyrna's superb natural harbor made the city an important commercial center. In spite of keen competition from the neighboring cities of Ephesus and Pergamum, Smyrna called itself the first city of Asia.

Sodom. "Place of lime." A city at the southern end of the Dead Sea destroyed because of its wickedness (Gen. 19:29; Rom. 9:29). Together with her sister cities—Gomorrah, Admah, Zeboim, and Zoar—Sodom formed the famous pentapolis of the plain or circle of the Jordan (Gen. 10:19; 13:10; 14:2) in the valley that surrounded the Dead Sea.

Although Sodom was a notoriously wicked city, when Lot separated himself and his herdsmen from Abraham, he chose to pitch his tent toward Sodom because the fertile plain that surrounded the city was well watered.

When Sodom was plundered by Chedorlaomer, the goods and captives he carried away had to be rescued by Abraham (Gen. 14:11, 21–24). However, the wickedness of the people of the city continued, and God finally had to destroy Sodom. Fire and brimstone fell from heaven and consumed Sodom and Gomorrah and the other cities of the plain. When Lot's wife looked back at Sodom, she instantly changed into a pillar of salt (Gen. 19:26).

Spain. Meaning unknown. The large peninsula of Europe, now comprising Spain and Portugal, at the western end of the Mediterranean Sea. The Phoenicians had established trading posts here by the time the Israelites conquered Canaan. The Greeks called this peninsula *Iberia* and the Romans referred to it as *Hispania*.

By New Testament times Spain was a part of the Roman Empire. The apostle Paul had a deep desire to visit Spain and preach the gospel (Rom. 15:24, 28). This longing reflects his plan to preach the gospel and establish the church throughout the Roman Empire. But whether he actually visited Spain is uncertain.

Succoth. "Booths."

1. An ancient town in Transjordan where Jacob built booths for his cattle and a dwelling for his family after he and Esau separated (Gen. 33:17). During the period of the judges, this town was severely punished by Gideon for refusing to help him as he chased the Midianites (Judg. 8:5–16).

2. A district or region where the people of Israel pitched their first encampment after leaving Rameses in Egypt (Exod. 12:37). Succoth may be the same place as Thuku, the area around the Egyptian city of Pithom. Some scholars identify Succoth with Tell el-Maskhutah, west of the Bitter

Lakes, in the northeastern part of the Nile delta.

Sychar. Meaning unknown. A city of Samaria mentioned in connection with Jesus' visit to Jacob's Well (John 4:5). Some scholars identify Sychar with ancient Shechem (Gen. 33:18). Jacob's Well, one of the best attested sites in Palestine, is situated on the eastern edge of the valley that separates Mount Gerizim from Mount Ebal.

Syria *or* Aram. Ancient Syria was the nation northwest of Palestine with Damascus as its major city. The northern kingdom of Israel had ill-defined boundaries with the Syrians and suffered continual raids from them. In King Ahab's time the King of Syria laid siege to Samaria and demanded tribute, but the Israelites drove them from the land. Ahab was killed in battle against the Syrians. Shortly after Israel's downfall, Syria fell to the Assyrians. The land came under the domains of Babylon, Persia, and Alexander the Great.

The Romans chose Syria as a province that included the territory from Asia Minor to Egypt, including the Holy Land. Saul (the apostle Paul) was converted on the ancient road to Damascus. Antioch of Syria became the first great missionary center of the Christian church.

Tahpanhes, Tehaphnehes. A city on the eastern frontier of lower Egypt, in the area of the Nile delta (Jer. 2:16; Tahapanes, KJV; Ezek. 30:18, Tehaphnehes). This city was probably named for a powerful general who brought the surrounding area under firm Egyptian control in the 11th century B.C.

Tahpanhes became a place of refuge for Jews who fled their homeland after the assassination of Gedaliah, the Babylonian governor of Judah. Jeremiah warned the Jews against this move, declaring that they would not escape the judgment of God (Jer. 42:16). He dramatically visualized this for them by hiding stones at Tahpanhes for the foundation of the throne of Nebuchadnezzar, the king of Babylon. (See Jer. 43:9–10.)

Tarshish or Tharshish. Location uncertain. It may have been a shipbuilding port in the ancient Mediterranean. Solomon and Jehosaphat had "ships of Tarshish" (see 1 Kings 10:22; 22:48, RSV), meaning they were likely built there. It was Tarshish that Jonah tried to reach when he ran away.

Tarsus. A city in Asia Minor on the banks of the Cydnus River and capital of the Roman province of Cilicia. Tarsus was the birthplace of Paul and the citizens enjoyed the privileges of full Roman citizenship.

Tekoa. The home of the shepherd-turned-prophet Amos. The area is a stony wilderness in the hills that run down to the Dead Sea.

Tel Abib. "Mound of grain." A locality in Babylonia near the River Chebar (a great irrigation canal) where the prophet Ezekiel stayed among the captives for seven days (Ezek. 3:15). These captives had been taken prisoner in Judah and had been deported to Babylon in 597 B.C. The largest city in modern Israel, Tel Aviv, derives its name from *Tel Abib.*

Thessalonica. A wealthy Macedonian city visited by Paul on his second missionary journey. Despite Jews causing an uproar against Paul and Silas, a strong church grew in the city. To the believers Paul wrote two letters of the NT.

Thyatira. A city of the province of Lydia in western Asia Minor (modern Turkey) situated on the road from Pergamos to Sardis. The city was on the southern bank of the Lycus River, a branch of the Hermus River.

Although never a large city, Thyatira was a thriving manufacturing center during New Testament times. Archaeologists have uncovered evidence of many trade guilds and unions. Membership in the trade guilds, necessary for financial and social success, often involved pagan customs and practices.

The book of Revelation refers to a woman known as Jezebel who taught and beguiled the Christians at Thyatira to conform to the paganism and sexual immorality of their surroundings (Rev. 1:11; 2:18–29).

The apostle Paul's first convert in Europe was Lydia, a seller of purple from the city of Thyatira (see Acts 16:14). The modern name of Thyatira is *Akhisar,* which means "white castle."

Tiberias, Sea of. Another name for the *Sea of Galilee,* named after the Roman emperor Tiberius.

Tigris. A major river of southwest Asia. Flowing about 1,850 kilometers (1,150 miles) from the Taurus Mountains of eastern Turkey, the Tigris and Euphrates roughly parallel each other for hundreds of miles in the "land of the two rivers," or Mesopotamia. The Tigris is considered by most scholars to be identical with Hiddekel (Gen. 2:14, KJV, NKJV), one of the four branches of the river that flowed from the Garden of Eden.

Tophet. Meaning unknown. A place southeast of Jerusalem in the Valley of Hinnom, where child sacrifices were offered and the dead bodies were buried or consumed (Isa. 30:33; Jer. 7:31–32). Chemosh, a Moabite god (1 Kings 11:7, 33) and Molech, an Ammonite god (1 Kings 11:7) were worshiped at Tophet through a practice despised by God—infant sacrifice (Jer. 7:31; 19:5).

Transjordan. A large plateau east of the Jordan River, the Dead Sea, and the Arabah. Transjordan is not used in the NKJV, KJV, or RSV, but the general area is called "beyond the Jordan" (Gen. 50:10–11; Deut. 3:20; Judg. 5:17; Isa. 9:1; Matt. 4:15; Mark 3:8).

Tree of Knowledge. One of two special trees in the Garden of Eden. The other was the tree of life (Gen. 2:9). Satan suggested to Adam and Eve that the tree's fruit would make them wise as God (Gen. 3:5). So they disobeyed God. This act of rebellion marked the entrance of sin into the world.

Tree of Life. The tree in the Garden of Eden that bestowed continuing life (Gen. 2:9, 17; 3:1–24). Before Adam and Eve sinned, they had free access to the tree of life; after their act of rebellion, two cherubim guarded the tree. Because of the sin of Adam and Eve, they were subject to death and dying.

Troas. A seaport city of Asia Minor on the Aegean Sea and a Roman colony. In a dream Paul had at Troas, a man from Macedonia begged him to come and help. The apostle left on his first missionary trip to Europe. When Paul preached until midnight, a young man named Eutychus went to sleep and fell from a third-story window. Paul went down and restored him to life.

Tyre. An ancient seaport and trading city of the Phoenicians set on an island off the coast of Palestine. The golden age of Tyre coincided with the reigns of David and Solomon, both of whom made trade alliances with King Hiram. Israel's King Ahab married Jezebel, daughter of the king of Tyre, who brought her pagan worship to Israel. While Tyre survived the attacks of many powerful enemies, the port finally fell to Alexander the Great when he built a causeway from the mainland to the island. Tyre and Sidon are mentioned as places visited by Jesus and Paul.

Ur. Usually known as *Ur of Chaldees.* The place from which Abraham and his father started. Ur was a center of early civilization in Mesopotamia near the mouth of the Euphrates and was the capital city of the Sumerians.

Zarephath. "Place of dyeing." A Phoenician coastal city situated between Tyre and Sidon, where the prophet Elijah lodged with a widow (1 Kings 17:9–10; Obad. 20; Luke 4:26; Sarepta, KJV). The widow of Zarephath showed remarkable faith in feeding Elijah during a time of severe drought and famine. Her faith was re-warded because she never ran out of oil or flour for three years.

Ziklag. Meaning unknown. A city in the Negev or southern Judah (Josh. 15:1, 31), assigned to the tribe of Simeon (Josh. 19:5). When David was pursued by Saul, he and his 600 men fled to the land of the Philistines and found sanctuary with Achish, king of Gath. Achish gave the city of Ziklag to David and his men, and it became David's military base for raids against the nomadic tribes of the Negev (1 Sam. 27:1–12). Many of Saul's followers defected to David and joined David at Ziklag (1 Chron. 12:1–22).

Zin. Meaning unknown. A wilderness through which the Israelites passed on their journey to Canaan (Num. 13:21; 20:1). The Wilderness of Zin stretched along the extreme southern limits of the Promised Land (Num. 13:21).

Zion. The name of the original hilltop fortress captured by David from the Jebusites. It became the oldest part of Jerusalem. Zion came to known as the city of David and eventually the name was applied to the whole of the sacred city. The Psalms frequently referred to Zion as the holy hill. New Testament writers refer to Zion as the idealized city of the living God, the heavenly Jerusalem. (See Heb. 12:22; 1 Pet. 2:6; Rev. 14:1.)

Zoar. "Little." An ancient city apparently situated near the southeast corner of the Dead Sea (Gen. 13:10), and also known as Bela (Gen. 14:2, 8). It was one of five city-states in the area, each with its own king.

Zoar figures prominently in the story of Lot and the destruction of the wicked cities of the plain (Gen. 13:12; 19:29). Warned to flee to the mountains, Lot sought further mercy by asking to go instead to Zoar. His reasoning was that Zoar was only a little city (hence its name). His request was granted and Zoar was spared, while the four other cities (Sodom, Gomorrah, Admah, and Zeboiim) were destroyed (Gen. 19:22–23, 30).

History

Old Testament

From Creation to Abraham

God revealed to Moses that he had created all things, and Moses described creation in Genesis, the first book of the Bible. According to Genesis, God made the world and all that is in it within the space of six days, and he declared it "to be very good." On the seventh day, God rested from creating. Christian scholars disagree about how long these *days* might have been or even if they were periods of time.

By laying our understanding of the meaning of "day" on what the Bible itself has to say, no matter what other questions that remain open, it becomes impossible for conservative scholars to accept the theory that human life evolved over millions of years.

Christians differ on the date of creation. For instance, the Bible's lists of generations might have omitted names, as other genealogies sometimes did. Some feel that we cannot safely add up the ages of the people listed to get the number of years in OT history because the total, just from the record, would be too small. There are other difficulties, too, in figuring the date of creation—difficulties too complex to discuss here.

After God created the man (Hebrew *Adam*), he placed him in a garden called Eden. There, God decreed the first man and woman *(Eve)* to worship him and rule the earth—sometimes called our "cultural mandate." God commanded the couple not to eat fruit from the tree of knowledge of good and evil. If they did, they would know what it meant to participate in evil, and the happy life of Eden would be taken away.

We might think Adam and Eve would have had no trouble obeying this commandment. But someone else entered the picture: Satan, who leads the evil spirits that conspire to defeat God. Satan became a serpent, his lies seduced Eve into eating the forbidden fruit, and Adam joined her. They both sinned against God. Instead of living in harmony with God, they began a life of sin and misery, and they fell from God's favor.

God promised Adam and Eve to send a Redeemer, also called a Savior or a Messiah, who would destroy Satan and restore them to a right relationship with him (Gen. 3:15). The Bible tells how God accomplished this plan of salvation. Of course, since the Bible focuses on that one aspect of world history, we cannot expect it to tell us everything that happened in ancient times.

Several important things happened between the time of Adam and that of Abraham, the "father of all who believe" (Rom. 4:11, NASB). For example, the first murder occurred. Adam and Eve had many sons and daughters (Gen. 5:4), but the Bible names only two because they are important to the history of redemption. Cain jealously killed his brother Abel. God punished Cain by driving him out of the community of people who served God. We know Adam and Eve continued to worship God because their sons offered burnt sacrifices to him (Gen. 4:3–5), and the NT calls Abel a man of true faith

(Heb. 11:4). God saved Cain from the full penalty of his crime by marking Cain so that other people would know God did not want him killed. We are not certain what God's mark was, but it must have been clearly visible to other people.

God gave Adam and Eve a third son, Seth, who replaced Abel. The Redeemer of the world would come from Seth's family.

But what about Cain's family? The Bible shows that Cain's descendant, Lamech, inherited evil ways (Gen. 4:19–24). Lamech boasted that he did not need God's protection, for he could use his sword (Gen. 4:23–24). He rejected God's holy standards of marriage and took more than one wife. He set such a low value on human life that he killed a man for striking him.

Evil spread to all humanity (Gen. 6:1–4). The Bible says human giants or "mighty men" lived during this time, and they did wickedly.

Giants in the Bible

In biblical times, the average man was believed to be about five feet tall. When people appeared that were seven feet or larger, they were referred to as giants. The Bible mentions a number of men labeled as giants.

Anak	Founder of a race of giants that inhabited the Holy Land	Deut. 9:2
Sheshai, Ahiman, and Talmai	Anak's three sons, defeated by Caleb	Josh. 15:14
Sippai	A Philistine giant warrior, slain by the Israelite soldiers	1 Chron. 20:4
Goliath	A Philistine giant, over nine feet tall, killed by David	1 Sam. 17
Lahmi	Brother of Goliath, killed by an Israelite in battle	1 Chron. 20:5
Og	King of Bashan, who slept in a huge iron bed	Deut. 3:11
Ishbi-Benob	Killed by Abishai	2 Sam. 21:16
A Philistine giant	Giant with 12 toes and 12 fingers, killed by David's nephew	1 Chron. 20:6

God sent a great flood to punish sinful humanity, and this was the most important event of the ancient period. However, God preserved the lives of Noah and his family in an ark (a large wooden ship), so that he could eventually keep his promise to redeem the world. God sent the clean animals to the ark seven by seven (Gen. 7:2), and unclean animals two by two (Gen. 7:15).

After the Flood, God set the death penalty for murder and appointed human agents as executioners (Gen. 9:1–7). He also put a rainbow in the sky to remind his people that he would never destroy all human beings by water (Gen. 9:13–17).

Yet right after the flood, Noah's son sinned against God (Gen. 9:20–29). God cursed him because of his disrespect for his father (v. 25).

Then God spoke through Noah to describe the course of subsequent history. He said a descendant of Shem would bring salvation into the world while the descendants of Japheth would share in that salvation. Japheth's family moved north and became progenitors of the Gentiles of NT times (Gen. 10:2).

One more thing happened before Abraham appeared on the scene. Proud city dwellers tried to get to heaven by building a tower in Babel. (See Gen. 11.) God condemned their arrogant ways by breaking them up into different language groups, then scattering them to live in different areas. (See Gen. 10:8–9; cf. 9:1.) This, it seems, is how the large language families of the world began.

These events show us that evil continued to increase from the time of the Flood to Abraham. People during this period worshiped many gods (Josh. 24:2; cf. Gen. 31:29–31), and immorality was rampant. So God, intent upon saving humanity, decided to begin anew in one family through whom all the families would be blessed.

From Abraham to Moses

God chose Abraham as the first in the line that would eventually bring salvation to the rest of humanity. Abraham lived in the city of Ur, capital of the ancient kingdom of Sumer. Sometime around 2000 B.C., God called Abraham to leave his father's home and go to a new land.

The Bible traces Abraham's steps from Ur to Haran, through the land of Canaan, into Egypt, and back into Canaan. God promised to give Abraham a son, whose children would become a great nation. God also promised to make Abraham's descendants a blessing to all nations (Gen. 12:2–3; 17:1–6).

Abraham believed what God said, but as time went on and nothing happened, he apparently had some doubts about how it would happen. He took matters into his own hands. When God didn't give him a son through Sarah as he expected, Abraham took his wife's servant girl Hagar and had a son by her.

Although the ancient world accepted this means of securing an heir, it violated God's law for marriage (Gen. 2:24), and Abraham suffered for his weakness. Thirteen years after Ishmael's birth, God gave Sarah and Abraham a son they named Isaac. Hagar, the mother of his firstborn son Ishmael, turned against Sarah, and Abraham made both Hagar and Ishmael leave.

Abraham came to trust God more completely as the years went by. Finally, God told him to offer Isaac as a burnt sacrifice to prove his love for God. (Cf. Gen. 22.) By this time, Abraham knew that God expected him to obey, and so, trusting God, he laid his son on the altar. (Cf. Heb. 11:17–19.) At the last minute, God ordered him not to kill Isaac and gave him a ram for the sacrifice.

Another time, Abraham asked God to spare the sinful cities where his nephew Lot lived. Lot had failed to be a faithful witness to his community. (Cf. 2 Peter 2:8.) God could not find even 10 righteous individuals there, so he destroyed the cities.

The Bible soon turns its focus to Jacob, Isaac's second son. Jacob lived around 1850 B.C.

Engraved stone tablet from Babylon which describes a great flood. Unlike the Babylonian stories, the biblical account of the Flood emphasizes the sin of humanity and the power and moral judgment of God.

PHOTO BY HOWARD VOS

The rugged Sinai Desert, through which the Israelites passed during the Exodus from Egypt.

PHOTO BY HOWARD VOS

God chose Jacob to inherit the promises he had given to Isaac. He named Jacob's family as the one that would bring the Redeemer to the world.

Jacob tricked his brother Esau and lied to his father so he could steal Esau's birthright. Then he fled to his uncle Laban's home to escape his brother's wrath. God confronted him as he ran away, and yet Jacob held his ground.

So God began a long, slow job of teaching Jacob how to trust him. He gave Jacob a good wife and many possessions. His uncle tricked him into marrying Leah, a girl he did not want, so Jacob pressed on to marry her sister Rachel as well. Jacob grew rich, and his greed led to family trouble. He had to leave Laban's land. He returned to his father's home in Canaan. There he found that God had prepared the way for him, and his brother was no longer angry.

Yet Jacob's troubles were not over. Years later, 10 of Jacob's sons became jealous of their brother, Joseph, because Jacob obviously preferred him. Joseph had dreamed they would bow down to him someday, and he told them the dream. Naturally, the 10 brothers resented this. They trapped Joseph, sold him into slavery, and told their father that a wild animal had killed him.

Slave traders carried Joseph to Egypt where he became one of the Pharaoh's servants. God used Joseph to interpret the Pharaoh's dreams, and the young man rose to become second-in-command under the Pharaoh.

A famine in Canaan drove Joseph's family to Egypt in search of food. His older brothers went first. When they bowed before Joseph, he immediately recognized them but did not tell them who he was. Eventually, Joseph forced them to bring his younger brother Benjamin (by his mother Rachel) to Egypt, too. Then he revealed his identity and forgave them for selling him into slavery. Joseph invited them to bring the entire family. The Pharaoh received them warmly and allowed them to settle in a rich part of Egypt.

From Moses to Saul

The Bible moves its spotlight to Moses (ca. 1526–1406 B.C.), who holds a vital place in the history of salvation.

Jacob's descendants had so many children that the Pharaohs feared they would take charge of the country. So a new Pharaoh put them into slavery and ordered all of the Israelites' boy babies to be killed. Moses' mother put him in a basket and set him afloat in the river, near the place where the Pharaoh's daughter bathed. When the princess found the baby, she took him to the palace to raise as her adopted son. Moses' mother became his nursemaid, and she probably took care of him well beyond the time he was weaned (Exod. 2:7–10).

Moses felt burdened for his people and wanted to bring them out of slavery (Exod. 2:11; Acts 7:24–25). When he was 40, he saw an Egyptian beating an Israelite; he flew into a rage and killed the Egyptian. Afraid the Pharaoh would execute him, Moses fled into the Midian Desert (Exod. 2:14–15). There he married into the family of Jethro (also called Reuel), a pagan priest. Moses agreed to tend Jethro's flock (Exod. 2:16–21).

After 40 years, God spoke to Moses from a bush that burned but was not consumed. He ordered Moses to go back to Egypt and lead the Israelites into Canaan, the land he had promised to Abraham. Moses didn't believe he could do this and made excuses. God sent Moses' brother Aaron along with him, to translate what Moses had to say (Exod. 7:1), and gave Moses power to work miracles that would induce the Israelites to follow him. To Moses, God revealed his holy name *YHWH* (sometimes translated *Jehovah* but scholars now believe should be translated *Yahweh*).

Moses and Aaron persuaded the people of Israel to follow them, but the Pharaoh

Genealogies

A genealogy is a list of ancestors that normally contains the members of each generation in succession. A technical term that means "family history" or "record," the word *genealogy* occurs in several places in the book of Genesis in the phrase, "This is the genealogy of."

This phrase divides the book in such a way as to suggest that the units formed were the actual sources from which the first 37 chapters of Genesis were compiled. These family records sometimes included genealogies (Gen. 10) in much the same way that tablets from ancient Babylonia would occasionally have family trees written on the back. This practice helped to date the tablets since they would obviously belong to the last generation mentioned.

Although these genealogies aid in dating, a more important purpose presents itself—the redemptive purpose of God. For this reason, the Bible follows only the more important links through the successive generations, ultimately leading to Jesus Christ. The genealogy of the human race—reaching through the line of Seth to Noah through Shem to Abraham and then to Isaac, Jacob, Judah, and David to Jesus—is where the providence of God watched and preserved individuals to fulfill his promise to the world.

Although the early chapters of Genesis do the preparation, the important line begins with the promise of the land of Canaan to the offspring of Abraham, Isaac, and Jacob and leads to the separation of the Israelites from the gentile world. The expectation of the Messiah sprang from the tribe of Judah, who was the son of Jacob.

Here are some of the most important genealogies listed in the Bible:

Cain	Gen. 4:16–26	Judah	1 Chron. 2:3–12; 3:1–4
Adam	Gen. 5:1–32	Simeon	1 Chron. 4:24–38
Japheth	Gen. 10:1–5; 1 Chron. 1:5–7	Reuben	1 Chron. 5:1–8
		Levi	1 Chron. 6:1–53
Ham	Gen. 10:6–20; 1 Chron. 1:8–16	Issachar	1 Chron. 7:1–5
		Benjamin	1 Chron. 7:6–12
Shem	Gen. 10:22–31; 11:10–30; 1 Chron. 1:17–27	Naphtali	1 Chron. 7:13
		Asher	1 Chron. 7:30–40
		Jesse	1 Chron. 2:13–17
		Caleb	1 Chron. 2:18–20, 42–55
Abraham	Gen. 25:1–4, 12–18; 1 Chron. 1:28–34	David	1 Chron. 3:1–24
		Ephraim	1 Chron. 7:20–27
Isaac	Gen. 25:19–23	Perez	Ruth 4:18–22
Jacob	Gen. 49:1–27	Jesus (traced through Mary)	Luke 3:23–38
Esau	Gen. 36:1–43; 1 Chron. 1:35–42	Jesus (traced through Joseph)	Matt. 1:1–17

refused to let them leave Egypt. Then God sent 10 devastating plagues on Egypt. The last one killed the firstborn son in every home where the doors had not been marked with blood. Because the people of Israel obeyed God's instructions, the death angel passed over Israel's firstborn. God commanded the Israelites to celebrate this event with a yearly festival, the Passover.

The death plague made the Pharaoh give in; he agreed to let the Israelites go back to their native land. Yet as soon as they left, the Pharaoh changed his mind and sent his army to bring the Israelites back.

God led his people to the Red Sea where he parted the waters and led them through on dry ground. Several scholars estimate that it happened around 1446 B.C.

Moses led the people from the Red Sea to Mount Sinai. On the way, God miraculously gave them food. At Mount Sinai, God revealed through Moses the laws and social plans that would mold the Israelites into a holy nation. These included the Ten Commandments.

From Sinai, God led the Israelites to Kadesh, where they sent spies into Canaan. The spies reported that the land was rich and fertile, yet full of giants. Most of the spies believed that the giants would destroy them if they tried to take the land. Only two—Caleb and Joshua—believed it was worth the fight. The Israelites accepted the skeptical advice of the majority and turned away from Canaan. God condemned them to wander 40 years because they would not trust him.

At the end of their wandering, they camped on the plains of Moab. Moses spoke to them for the last time, and his words were recorded in Deuteronomy. Moses turned his leadership over to Joshua. Moses could not enter the Promised Land because he had rebelled against God at Meribah. (See Num. 20:10ff.) After Moses gave his farewell to the Israelites, God led him to the top of Mount Nebo to see the land they would enter. There he died.

Joshua had proven himself a capable leader of Israel's army in the battle of Amalek (Exod. 17:8–16). Now God used Joshua to lead the people of Israel in conquering and settling the new land. Because they trusted God to give them the land, Joshua and Caleb were the only adults of their generation that God allowed to enter. All the others had died in the wilderness.

Joshua led Israel into Canaan. God rewarded Joshua's faith by helping Israel to take possession of it. First, God divided the overflowing Jordan River so they could cross over on dry land (Josh. 3:14–17). Then the angel of the Lord led the Israelites in their miraculous defeat of Jericho, the first city conquered in Canaan. When the people blew their trumpets as God had ordered, the walls of the city fell down (Josh. 6).

Under Joshua, Israel proceeded to conquer the entire country (Josh. 21:23–45). They suffered defeat only at Ai, when one of their men disobeyed God's battle orders. (See Josh. 7.) Having learned their lesson, the Israelites decided to follow God's orders and try again, and this time they defeated Ai. In all, they conquered 31 kings in the new territory.

Joshua divided the land among the Israelite tribes according to God's directions. Just before he died, Joshua urged his people to keep trusting God and obeying his commands.

After Joshua died, "everyone did what was right in his own eyes" (Judg. 21:25). The leaders of this period acted much like Moses and Joshua; they were military heroes and chief judges in the courts of Israel, and they were called judges. The most noteworthy were

- Othniel
- Deborah (the only woman judge)
- Gideon
- Jephthah
- Samson
- Eli
- Samuel

Samuel, last of the judges and first of the prophets, next dominated the scene.

Samuel's mother had prayed for a son and praised God to see him born (1 Sam. 2:1–10). Samuel's parents gave him to the chief priest Eli so that he could be trained to serve the Lord. While Samuel was still a child, he helped Eli care for the tent of meeting—the place of worship. There he heard God calling him to become the new leader of Israel.

Before Samuel's time, the Israelites called a prophet a *seer*. (See 1 Sam. 9:9; cf. Deut. 13:1–15; 18:15–22.) But Samuel, like other later prophets, was not just a forecaster of the future; he also spoke God's messages to the nation, often rebuking the people for their wicked ways. At God's direction, he anointed Saul as the first human king over Israel (1 Sam. 8:19–22; 10:1), although he later regretted it.

The United Monarchy

In his early reign, Saul appeared as a man of humility and self-control. Over the years, however, his character changed. He became a man of self-will, disobedience, jealousy, and hatred. His anger turned against David, a young warrior who had killed the giant Goliath, and who served as Saul's court musician. He tried to murder David, being jealous of David's popularity (1 Sam. 18:5–9; 19:8–10).

God had secretly chosen David to be the next king, and he promised the kingship to David's family forever. (See 1 Sam. 16:1–13; 2 Sam. 7:12–16.) Yet Saul continued to be king for many years.

After Saul's death, King David brought the ark of the covenant to Jerusalem. (Cf. Deut. 12:1–14; 2 Sam. 6:1–11.) The ark was a wooden box that held the stone tablets on which God wrote for Moses the Ten Commandments; the Israelites had carried it with them through their years of wandering in the wilderness. David brought it to his capital city so that Jerusalem would become the spiritual center of the nation, as well as its political center.

David had the qualities they were looking for—military skill, political savvy, and a keen sense of religious duty. He had made the nation stronger and more secure than it had ever been.

But David was only a man, with weaknesses like everyone else. Among his failings, David

• Had several wives

• Arranged the murder of Uriah, an officer in his army so he could marry the man's wife (Bathsheba) whom he had already impregnated

• Took a census of the men of Israel because he no longer trusted God for military victory and counted upon the strength of his army

God punished David, and because he was the head of the nation, when he sinned against God, all of his people suffered the punishment.

David's son Solomon was Israel's next king. Despite Solomon's legendary wisdom, he did not always live wisely. He carried out David's political plan, strengthening his hold on the territories conquered by his father. He was a shrewd businessman, who made trade agreements that brought vast wealth to Israel (1 Kings 10:14–15). God also used Solomon to build the temple in Jerusalem.

Solomon's lavish style of living increased the burden of taxes upon the common people. He inherited his father's desire for women, and he concluded trade agreements with foreign kings that involved political marriages. He put together a harem of princess-brides from many foreign lands (1 Kings 11:1–8). These pagan wives enticed him to worship pagan gods, and he soon set up their rites and ceremonies in Jerusalem.

The Divided Monarchy

After Solomon, the fortunes of Israel decreased. The nation rebelled against God's laws. God might have destroyed Israel but did not because he still planned to use the house of David to introduce the Messiah who would save the world from sin.

When Solomon died, Israel stumbled into civil war as Solomon's sons and generals fought for the throne. Rehoboam had his father's blessing to be the new king, but his rival Jeroboam wielded more influence among the military chiefs of the land. Rehoboam was left with the southern half of the country and called it Judah. Jeroboam set up his own government in the northern half and retained the name of Israel. Each claimed to be the king God had chosen.

None of Israel's kings served God, and Judah had a poor record. The only kings of Judah who were faithful were

- Asa
- Jehoshaphat
- Joash (Jehoash)
- Amaziah

- Azariah
- Jotham
- Hezekiah
- Josiah

Finally, God allowed the pagan empires of Assyria and Babylonia to destroy both kingdoms and carry the people away into exile.

Two important leaders emerged in the time of the divided monarchy. The first was Elijah the prophet who stands out as a uniquely rugged character. One day he appeared before the wicked King Ahab and declared that God would bring a long drought because the people were so wicked.

After delivering the message, Elijah fled to the wilderness and stopped by the brook Cherith, where God miraculously provided food for him. When the stream dried up, God sent Elijah to help the widow of Zarephath, who was suffering under the drought. She was nearly out of food when Elijah came to her door, but she fed him anyway. Because she did, the prophet stayed at her house, and she was blessed. Her food supplies never ran out while he was there. When her son died, Elijah raised him from the dead.

The prophet returned to King Ahab and told him to summon all the prophets of the pagan god Baal (whom Jezebel, Ahab's wife, worshiped) and meet him on Mount Carmel. There Elijah challenged the prophets to a contest to prove which god was stronger. Elijah asked God to send fire from heaven to light a waterlogged sacrifice, and he did. Elijah killed all the false prophets. (Cf. Deut. 13:5.) Elijah then asked God to end the drought, and God sent a cloudburst of rain.

Jezebel's threats against his life kept Elijah discouraged and frightened, and he asked God to let him die. Instead, God sent angels to minister to Elijah and ordered him to recruit two future kings and his own successor. Elijah obeyed, appointing a farmer named Elisha to be the new prophet.

Elijah confronted Ahab again, condemning him and Jezebel for murdering their neighbor Naboth to get his vineyard. The king sent two companies of soldiers to capture the prophet, but Elijah called fire down from heaven to destroy them. Once more he declared the doom of the king.

Soon after that, Elijah and Elisha went for a walk, discussing the problems their nation faced. When they came to the Jordan River, Elijah divided the water by striking it with his mantle (a cape), and they walked across to the other side. As they stood on the riverbank talking, a chariot of fire swooped down from the sky, picked up Elijah, and carried him away in a whirlwind. His mantle fell on Elisha.

The second great personality of the divided monarchy was Elisha. He was like his teacher in many ways. Both men parted the waters of the Jordan, brought rain in times of drought, increased a widow's supply of food, raised a boy from the dead, performed miracles for Gentiles, pronounced doom upon kings, and destroyed their enemies with supernatural power.

Elisha had an attitude of triumph and confidence. He never seemed to complain or lose courage. The Scriptures show that he performed more miracles than any other prophet of the OT (e.g., 2 Kings 4:38—5:19).

Isaiah, Jeremiah, Amos, Hosea, Micah, Ezekiel, and other prophets warned Israel and Judah that God would punish their wickedness. Isaiah and Ezekiel also had words of consolation for them after they went into exile. God used these men as his holy spokesmen in this crucial epoch of his people's history.

The Kings of Israel

Name	Length of Reign (Years)	Reference
Jeroboam I	22	1 Kings 11:26—14:20
Nadab	2	1 Kings 15:25–28
Baasha	24	1 Kings 15:27—16:7
Elah	2	1 Kings 16:6–14
Zimri	(7 days)	1 Kings 16:9–20
Omri	12	1 Kings 16:16–28
Ahab	22	1 Kings 16:28—22:40
Ahaziah	2	1 Kings 22:40—2 Kings 1:18
Jehoram (Joram)	12	2 Kings 3:1—9:25
Jehu	28	2 Kings 9:1—10:36
Jehoahaz	17	2 Kings 13:1–9
Jehoash (Joash)	16	2 Kings 13:10—14:16
Jeroboam II	41	2 Kings 14:23–29
Zechariah	½	2 Kings 14:29—15:12
Shallum	(1 month)	2 Kings 15:10–15
Menahem	10	2 Kings 15:14–22
Pekahiah	2	2 Kings 15:22–26
Pekah	20	2 Kings 15:27–31
Hoshea	9	2 Kings 15:30—17:6

The Kings of Judah

Name	Length of Reign (Years)	Reference
Rehoboam	17	1 Kings 11:42—14:31
Abijam	3	1 Kings 14:31—15:8
Asa	41	1 Kings 15:8–24
Jehoshaphat	25	1 Kings 22:41–50
Jehoram	8	2 Kings 8:16–24
Ahaziah	1	2 Kings 8:24—9:29
Athaliah	6	2 Kings 11:1–20
Joash (Jehoash)	40	2 Kings 11:1—12:21
Amaziah	29	2 Kings 14:1–20
Azariah (Uzziah)	52	2 Kings 15:1–7
Jotham	16	2 Kings 15:32–38
Ahaz	16	2 Kings 16:1–20
Hezekiah	29	2 Kings 18:1—20:21
Manasseh	55	2 Kings 21:1–18
Amon	2	2 Kings 21:19–26
Josiah	31	2 Kings 22:1—23:30
Jehoahaz	¼	2 Kings 23:31–33
Jehoiakim	11	2 Kings 23:34—24:5
Jehoiachin	¼	2 Kings 24:6–16
Zedekiah	11	2 Kings 24:17—25:30

From the Exile to the Return

The Jewish people were taken into exile more than once. The Assyrians twice conquered the northern kingdom (Israel); the southern kingdom (Judah) was conquered once by Assyria and three times by the Babylonians. Each time, the conquerors carried off many captives. Most often when people refer to the exile, they mean the 70-year Babylonian captivity of Judah.

The Babylonian captivity had three successive phases:

1. Unrealistic hopefulness (cf. Jer. 29; Ezek. 17:11–24)

2. Truer and humbler hopefulness, when God used Ezekiel to comfort the people (Ezek. 36—38)

3. Revived hopefulness in the time of Daniel

The Jews returned from exile in two stages:

1. Led by Sheshbazzar and Zerubbabel (Ezra 1:8—2:70)

2. Led by Ezra and Nehemiah (Ezra 8:1–14)

Just as Isaiah had predicted (Isa. 44:28; 45:1), God raised up a kindhearted pagan king—Cyrus of Persia—who let the Jews return to Canaan. Zechariah and Haggai encouraged the people in their work. Toward the end of this period, Malachi condemned them for slipping back into their sinful ways.

Between the Old and New Testaments

It is not always clear what happened in the 400 years between the writing of Malachi and the time Jesus was born. We call this the intertestamental period because it is the time between the writing of the OT and NT.

We know the restored nation of Israel had serious political upsets. After Alexander the Great conquered the Persian Empire, Greek princes and generals wrestled for the right to govern the Near East. The Seleucid King Antiochus III took Canaan away from Egypt in 198 B.C. and tried to make it a base for building a new empire in the East. Antiochus III was no match for the Roman legions, and they defeated his army in 190 B.C. and made him a puppet ruler in the Roman chain of command.

The Maccabee family (the offspring of the high priest Mattathias) began a civil war against the Seleucid governors and captured Jerusalem in 164 B.C. They weren't able to push the Seleucids completely out of their affairs until 134 B.C. In that year, John Hyrcanus I of the Maccabee family set up his own dynasty, known as the Hasmoneans. They ruled until 37 B.C., when Rome established the Herodian family as the new puppet government.

The books entitled 1 and 2 Maccabees describe the Maccabean revolt and the chaos in Israel up until the time of the Hasmoneans. Roman Catholics include these books and other writings from the intertestamental period in their Bible, but Protestants do not, although translations of them are often included in Protestant versions of the Bible.

New Testament

The Church

The NT brings us to the climax of God's redemptive work, because it introduces us to the Messiah, Jesus Christ, and to the beginning of the church.

The Life of Jesus Christ

The writings of Matthew, Mark, Luke, and John tell us most of what we know about Jesus' ministry. Either these writers were eyewitnesses of Jesus' life, or they wrote down what eyewitnesses told them. However, they do not provide a full biography of Jesus. Everything they recorded happened, but they concentrate on Jesus' ministry and leave gaps elsewhere in the story of his life.

The gospel writers portrayed the person and ministry of Jesus by recording what he did and said. Each writer presents a slightly different viewpoint.

Many people know about the birth and infancy of Jesus Christ with the details, such as the Virgin Mary (the mother of Jesus), Joseph and Mary's trip to Bethlehem, the birth of the baby Jesus in Bethlehem, and the angels who announced his birth to the shepherds.

After Jesus was born, his parents dedicated him at the temple in Jerusalem (Luke 2:22–28). They began training him to live "in favor with God and man" (Luke 2:52).

King Herod wanted to be certain that the people did not rally around the infant king to start a rebellion, so he ordered his soldiers to kill all the boy babies in Bethlehem (Matt. 2:16). Jesus' family fled into Egypt to escape the evil decree. After Herod died, they returned to Israel and settled in the town of Nazareth.

The Bible says nothing more about Jesus until he was 12 or 13 years old. Then, to assume his proper role in the Jewish congregation, Jesus had to make a special visit to Jerusalem and offer a sacrifice at the temple. While he was there, Jesus talked with religious leaders about the Jewish faith. He showed an extraordinary understanding of the true God, and his answers amazed them. Later, his parents started home and discovered that Jesus was missing. They found him at the temple, still talking with the Jewish experts.

The Bible falls silent again until it introduces us to the events that began Jesus' ministry when he was about 30 years old. First, John the Baptist came out of the wilderness and preached in cities along the Jordan River, urging the people to prepare for their Messiah (Luke 3:3–9). John had been born into a godly family, and he grew up to serve God faithfully. Crowds clamored to hear his preaching. He told them to return to God and to obey him. When he saw Jesus, John cried that this was the "Lamb of God who takes away the sin of the world" (John 1:29). John baptized Jesus. As Jesus came up from the water, God sent the Holy Spirit in the form of a dove that settled upon him.

Jesus entered private homes, sat at public feasts, and worshiped with other Jews at their synagogues. He denounced the religious leaders for their hypocrisy. He didn't reject their formal religion but respected the temple and temple worship. (Cf. Matt. 5:17–18.) Most of the Pharisees and other leaders failed to see that Jesus was the Messiah.

Near Galilee, Jesus performed an amazing miracle by taking seven loaves of bread and two fish, blessing them, and breaking them into enough pieces to feed 4,000 people (Matt. 15:32–39). This did not draw more people to faith in Jesus.

Judas Iscariot, one of Jesus' 12 disciples, betrayed him to the hostile leaders of Jerusalem. After a mockery of a trial, the Romans nailed Jesus to a wooden cross to die among common criminals.

Three days later Jesus rose from the grave and appeared to many of his followers, just as he had promised. He also gave final instructions to his closest disciples. As they watched him ascend into heaven, an angel appeared and said they would see him return in the same way—Jesus would come back visibly and in his physical body.

The Ministry of the Apostles

Bible history ends in the book of Acts, which describes the ministry of the early church. In Acts the message of Jesus Christ—the message of redemption—spread from Jerusalem to Rome, the center of the Western world.

Acts shows the expansion of the church in sequential steps: beginning in Jerusalem; from Jerusalem to Judea, Samaria, and the surrounding area; and from Antioch to Rome and the rest of the world

In Jerusalem

The early experiences of Jesus' disciples in Jerusalem reveal a great deal about the early church. Acts shows how earnestly the Christians spread the news about Jesus.

A few days later the disciples replaced Judas, who had killed himself after he betrayed Jesus. They chose Matthias to round out the group of 12.

The risen Christ sent the church his Holy Spirit, who enabled the Christians to fulfill their worldwide task on the day of Pentecost (50 days after the Resurrection).

Peter was the foremost leader of the apostles, and his ministry rallied the enthusiasm of the early church. An apostle (literally, one sent) was a person whom Jesus Christ had chosen for special ministry. (Cf. Gal. 1:12.) Apostles laid the foundation of the church by preaching the gospel of Christ. (Cf. Eph. 2:20; 1 Cor. 3:10–11.) God used Peter to open the door of salvation to the Gentiles.

From Jerusalem to All Judea

The second stage of the church's growth opened with a violent persecution of the church in Jerusalem. All the leaders except the apostles fled from the city (Acts 8:1). Wherever the Christians went they witnessed, and the Holy Spirit used their testimony to win others to Christ. (Cf. Acts 8:3ff.)

At this point the Bible describes the conversion of Saul of Tarsus. Before his conversion, Saul persecuted the church. He obtained letters from the leaders in Jerusalem, authorizing him to proceed to Damascus to make sure that the Christians there were imprisoned and put to death. On his way, Jesus Christ struck him down and challenged him.

Struck blind, Saul was led into Damascus, where God sent a Christian man named Ananias to him. Through Ananias, Saul's sight was restored, and he was filled with the Holy Spirit. Saul underwent a life-changing experience and began his new life in which he used his Roman name, Paul.

From Antioch to Rome

The rest of the book of Acts describes the expansion of the church through the ministry of Paul. Barnabas brought Paul to Antioch (Acts 11:19–26). The Holy Spirit called Barnabas and Paul to be missionaries, and the church ordained them for this task (Acts 13:1–3).

Paul decided to return to the churches he and Barnabas had established on their missionary journey. This time taking Silas, Paul went on his second missionary journey. (See Acts 15:40–41.) Paul received a night vision (i.e., a dream) in which God summoned them to Macedonia (Acts 16:9–10). In Macedonia, they led Gentiles and Jews into the faith.

The next stop was Corinth, where Paul and his friends stayed a year and a half. From there they journeyed back to Antioch via Jerusalem (Acts 18:18–22). All this time, Paul and his companions continued to preach in the synagogues, and they faced opposition from Jews who rejected the gospel (Acts 18:12–17).

The third missionary journey covered many of the same cities Paul had visited on the second journey. He also made a quick visit to the churches in Galatia and Phrygia (Acts 18:23).

In Ephesus he baptized 12 of John the Baptist's disciples who believed in Jesus Christ, and they received the Holy Spirit. (See Acts 19:1–6.) He preached in Ephesus for three years (Acts 20:31).

From Ephesus Paul traveled to Macedonia and back to Philippi. After a brief stay in Philippi he journeyed to Troas, where a young man named Eutychus fell asleep while listening to one of Paul's sermons. He plummeted from a third-story window to his death. God worked through Paul to bring Eutychus back to life (Acts 20:7–12).

In Jerusalem, Paul made a speech in defense of his Christian faith (Acts 22:1–21). Jews charged him with causing trouble, and he was arrested. Eventually, unable to receive justice, Paul appealed to Rome, and the authorities sent him there for trial.

Acts ends with Paul's activities in Rome. We read that he preached to the leading Jews there (Acts 28:17–20). He lived for two years in a rented house, continuing to preach to the people who visited him (Acts 28:30–31).

The Early Church Grows

The Greek word that English versions of the Bible translate as *church* is *ekklesia*, from the Greek *kaleo* (I call or I summon). In secular literature, *ekklesia* referred to any assembly of people—such as a riot, a political rally, an orgy, or a gathering for any other purpose. But the NT uses *ekklesia* only to refer to the gathering of Christian believers to worship Christ. This explains why Bible translators render this word as *church* instead of using a more general term like *assembly* or *gathering*.

The Church Begins

Forty days after his resurrection, Jesus gave final instructions to his disciples and ascended into heaven (Acts 1:1–11). The disciples returned to Jerusalem and secluded themselves for several days of fasting and prayer, waiting for the Holy Spirit, whom Jesus said would come. About 120 of Jesus' followers waited in the group.

Fifty days after the Passover, on the day of Pentecost, a sound like a mighty rushing wind filled the house where the group was meeting. Tongues of fire rested upon each of them, and they began speaking in languages other than their own as the Holy Spirit enabled them. Foreign visitors were surprised to hear the disciples speaking in their own languages. Some of them mocked the group, saying they must be drunk (Acts 2:13).

Peter silenced the crowd and explained they were witnessing the outpouring of the Holy Spirit the OT prophets had predicted (Acts 2:16–21; cf. Joel 2:28–32). Some of the foreign observers asked what they must do to receive the Holy Spirit. Peter said, "Repent, and let every one of you be baptized in the name of Jesus Christ for the remission of sins; and you shall receive the gift of the Holy Spirit" (Acts 2:38). About 3,000 people turned to Jesus Christ (Acts 2:41).

The Jerusalem Community

The first Christians formed a closely knit community in Jerusalem after the day of Pentecost. They expected Christ to return very soon. They shared all of their material goods (Acts 2:44–45). Many sold their property and gave the proceeds to the church, which distributed these resources among the group (Acts 4:34–35).

The church grew so rapidly that the apostles had to appoint seven men to distribute goods to the needy widows. The leader of these men was Stephen, "a man full of faith and of the Holy Spirit" (Acts 6:5). Here we see the beginning of church government. The apostles had to delegate some of their duties to other leaders. As time passed, church offices were arranged in a rather complex structure.

Missionary Efforts

Christ had established his church at the crossroads of the ancient world. Trade routes brought merchants and ambassadors through Israel, where they came into contact with the gospel. In Acts we read of the conversion of officials from Rome (Acts 10:1–8), Ethiopia (Acts 8:26–40), and other lands.

Soon after Stephen's death the church began a systematic effort to carry the gospel to other nations. Peter visited the major cities of Palestine, preaching to both Jews and Gentiles. Others went to Phoenicia, Cyprus, and Antioch of Syria. Hearing that the gospel was well received in these areas, the church in Jerusalem sent Barnabas to encourage the new Christians in Antioch (Acts 11:22–23). Barnabas then went to Tarsus to find the young convert named Saul. Barnabas took Saul back to Antioch, where they taught in the church for over a year (Acts 11:26).

The early Christian missionaries focused their teachings upon the person and work of Jesus Christ. They declared that he was the Sinless Servant and Son of God who had given his life to atone for the sins of people who trusted in him. He was the One God raised from the dead to defeat the powers of sin (Rom. 4:24–25).

Church Government

At first, Jesus' followers saw no need to develop a system of church government. They expected Christ to return soon, so they dealt with internal problems as the need arose—usually in an informal way.

But by the time Paul wrote his letters to the churches, Christians realized their need to organize. The NT does not give us a detailed picture of this early church government. Apparently, one or more elders *presbyters* presided over the affairs of each congregation (cf. Rom. 12:6–8; 1 Thess. 5:12; Heb. 13:7, 17, 24), just as elders did in synagogues. These elders were chosen by the Holy Spirit (Acts 20:28), yet apostles appointed them (Acts 14:23). The Holy Spirit worked through the apostles to ordain leaders for the ministry.

Martyrs

Martyrs have played a significant role in the history of God's people. Here are the biblical martyrs.

Isaiah	Traditionally said to have been sawed asunder by Manasseh	Heb. 11:37
Zechariah	Stoned by his own countrymen for rebuking their sin	2 Chron. 24:20–21
Urijah	Murdered by King Jehoiakim	Jer. 26:20–23
Stephen	The church's first martyr, stoned by the Jews	Acts 7:59
James	The first of the 12 apostles to be martyred	Acts 12:1–2
Paul	Believed to have been beheaded by Emperor Nero	2 Tim. 4:6
Peter	Believed to have been crucified upside down by Nero	John 21:18–19; 2 Pet. 1:14–15
Antipas	Martyred in the city of Pergamos	Rev. 2:13
Two tribulational witnesses	Martyred by the Beast	Rev. 11:3–7
The Sinless Servant and Son of God	Gave his life to atone for the sins of all people who put their trust in him; God raised him from the dead to defeat the power of sin	Rom. 5:8–10; 4:24–25; 1 Cor. 15:17

Some ministers called *evangelists* seem to have traveled from one congregation to another, as the apostles did. Their title means "men who handle the gospel." Some have thought they were all personal deputies of the apostles, as Timothy was of Paul; others suppose that they gained their name through manifesting a special gift of evangelism. The elders assumed the normal pastoral duties between the visits of these evangelists.

In some congregations, the elders appointed *deacons* to distribute food to the needy or care for other material needs (cf. 1 Tim. 3:12). The first deacons were the "men of good reputation" that the elders of Jerusalem appointed to care for widows in the congregation (Acts 6:1–6).

Some NT letters refer to bishops in the early church. This is a bit confusing, since these bishops did not form an upper tier of church leadership as they do in some churches where the title is used today. Paul reminded the elders of Ephesus that they were bishops (Acts 20:28), and he seems to use *elder* and *bishop* interchangeably (Titus 1:5–9). Both bishops and elders were charged with the oversight of a congregation.

Patterns of Worship

As the early Christians worshiped together, they established patterns of worship that were quite different from the synagogue services. We have no clear picture of early Christian worship until A.D. 150, when Justin Martyr described typical worship services in his writings. We do know that the early Christians held their services on Sunday, the first day of the week. They called this "the Lord's Day" because it was the day that Christ rose from the dead.

The first Christians met at the temple in Jerusalem, in synagogues, or in private homes (Acts 2:46; 13:14–16; 20:7–8). Where Christians were persecuted, they had to meet in secret places such as the catacombs (underground tombs) in Rome.

Scholars believe that the first Christians worshiped on Sunday evenings and their service centered on the Lord's Supper. But at some point the Christians began holding two worship services on Sunday as Justin Martyr describes—one in the early morning and one late in the afternoon. The hours were chosen for secrecy and for the sake of working people who could not attend worship services during the day.

The Lord's Supper

The early Christians ate the symbolic meal of the Lord's Supper to commemorate Jesus and his disciples observing the traditional Jewish Passover feast. The themes of the two events were the same. In the Passover, Jews rejoiced that God had delivered them from their enemies, and they looked expectantly to their future as God's children. In the Lord's Supper, Christians celebrated their deliverance from sin by Jesus and expressed their hope for the day when Christ would return (1 Cor. 11:26).

At first, the Lord's Supper was an entire meal that Christians shared in their homes. Each guest brought a dish of food to the common table. The meal began with prayer and the eating of small pieces from a single loaf of bread that represented Christ's broken body. The meal closed with another prayer and the sharing of a cup of wine, which represented Christ's shed blood.

Some people speculated that the Christians were participating in a secret rite when they observed the Lord's Supper, and they fabricated strange stories about these services. The Roman Emperor Trajan outlawed such secret meetings about A.D. 100. At that time Christians began observing the Lord's Supper during the morning worship service, which was open to the public.

Baptism

Baptism was a common event of Christian worship in Paul's time. (Cf. Eph. 4:5.) However, Christians were not the first to use baptism. Jews baptized their gentile converts, some Jewish sects practiced baptism as a symbol of purification, and John the Baptist made baptism an important part of his ministry. The NT does not say whether Jesus regularly baptized his converts, but on at least one occasion before John's imprisonment he did baptize. (It may, however, have been John's baptism that he was administering.) At any rate, the early Christians were baptized in Jesus' name following Jesus' example. (Cf. Mark 1:10; Gal. 3:27.)

It appears that the early Christians interpreted the meaning of baptism in various ways: a symbol of death to sin (Rom. 6:4), cleansing from sin (Acts 22:16; Eph. 5:26), and new life in Christ (Acts 2:41; Rom. 6:3).

Occasionally the entire family of a new convert would be baptized (cf. Acts 10:48; 1 Cor. 1:16), which may have signified their desire to consecrate all they had to Christ.

New Testament Concepts of the Church

Scripture refers to the early Christians as:

- God's family and temple
- Christ's flock and bride
- Salt
- Leaven
- Body of Christ
- The new Israel
- A bulwark sustaining God's truth

There were many other images, too. The church was thought of as a single worldwide fellowship of believers.

Paul described the church as "one body in Christ" (Rom. 12:5) and "His body" (Eph. 1:23) because the church encompasses in a single communion of divine life all who are united to Christ by the Holy Spirit. They are bound together in a community to embody the kingdom of God in the world.

Because they were bound to other Christians, these people understood that what they did with their own bodies and abilities was important (Rom. 12:14; 1 Cor. 6:13–19; 2 Cor. 5:10). They understood that the various races and classes become one in Christ (1 Cor. 12:3; Eph. 2:14–22), and must accept and love each other in a way that shows this to be so.

By describing the church as the body of Christ, the early Christians emphasized Christ as its head (Eph. 5:25). He directed its actions and deserved any praise it received.

The early Christians also identified themselves with Israel, God's chosen people. They believed that Jesus' coming and ministry fulfilled God's promise to the patriarchs (cf. Matt. 2:6; Luke 1:68; Acts 5:31), and they held that God had established a new covenant with Jesus' followers. (Cf. 2 Cor. 3:6; Heb. 7:22; 9:15.)

God, they held, had established the new Israel on the basis of personal salvation rather than family descent. His church was a spiritual nation that transcended cultural and national heritages. Those who placed their faith in God's new covenant by surrendering themselves to Christ became Abraham's spiritual descendants and as such a part of the "new Israel" (Matt. 8:11; Luke 13:28–30; Rom. 4:9–25; 11; Gal. 3—4; Heb. 11—12).

Common Characteristics

Some common qualities emerge from the many images of the church in the NT. They all show that the church exists because God called it into being. Christ has commissioned his followers to carry on his work—the church's reason for existence.

The various NT images of the church stress that the Holy Spirit empowers the church and determines its direction. Members of the church share a common task and common destiny under the Spirit's leading.

The church is an active, living entity. It participates in the affairs of this world, it exhibits the way of life that God intends for all people, and it proclaims God's Word for the present age. The spiritual unity and purity of the church contrast with the enmity and corruption of the world. It is the church's responsibility in all the particular congregations in which it becomes visible to practice unity, love, and care in a way that shows that Christ truly lives in church members.

Trumpets

Moses' two silver trumpets	Num. 10:2	Ezra's trumpets	Ezra 3:10
Joshua's seven rams' trumpets	Josh. 6:4	The trumpet of the return of Jesus	1 Cor. 15:52; 1 Thess. 4:16
Ehud's trumpet	Judg. 3:12–30		
Gideon's 300 trumpets	Judg. 7	The seven judgment trumpets	Rev. 8:2
David's trumpet	2 Sam. 6:15		
Zadok's trumpet	1 Kings 1:39	The regathering of Israel trumpet	Matt. 24:31
Solomon's trumpets	2 Chron. 5:13		

Forms of Hebrew Government

When God created the universe, he brought into being an orderly universe. With the creation of the human race and the multiplication of people throughout the earth, God ordained government for societies and nations. When the people of Israel became a nation, government became a necessity. Various forms of government existed throughout their history.

The Theocracy in the Wilderness

After God delivered his people out of slavery in Egypt, he brought them to Mount Sinai, where they organized into a nation. He constituted them "a kingdom of priests" (Exod. 19:6) with himself as their ruler—a theocracy. (*Theocracy* comes from two Greek words: *theos* meaning "God," and *kratos* meaning "rule," which together mean "rule by God.") From that time on, Israel would always consider itself to be God's kingdom and God to be its ultimate king.

Because Israel's government was given directly by God, it had no true parallel with the city-states of the Canaanites, the great empires of later history, or the Greek republic.

God organized his people into a 12-tribe structure, since he had given Jacob 12 sons. (See Gen. 49.) Other tribes in the Near East organized themselves into units of 12 (cf. Gen. 25:12–16; 36:10–14), but Israel's structure had been mandated by God.

At first, the governmental administration of Israel was simple. Moses was the God-appointed leader to whom was delegated all authority over God's people. But he soon discovered that there were too many people to rule, and he was busy all day (Exod. 18:13).

Jethro, his father-in-law, suggested that Moses appoint judges to rule over groups of thousands, hundreds, fifties, and tens (Exod. 18:25). With God's approval, Moses chose from among the heads of families. He gave them special instructions and commissioned them to judge the people's everyday problems (Deut. 1:12–18). However, Moses continued to decide the most difficult cases (Exod. 18:26).

The system of government, then, was one of a supreme judge and a court system. The courts settled both religious and civil matters. In a theocracy no clear-cut line between religious and civil law could exist; all cases were ultimately brought before God (Exod. 18:19).

Judicial Responsibilities

The court system also included priests and Levites, who were primarily responsible for directly religious cases, such as murder (Deut. 21:1–9) and rituals for leprosy (Lev. 13—14). The judges also had administrative responsibilities, including overseeing of the courts' work (Deut. 19:12; 21; 22:15) and selecting men for warfare (Deut. 20:5–9). Both the judges and the priests were responsible to teach the law to the people (Deut. 17:9; 33:10).

Military Responsibilities

The judges had leadership roles; they were appointed as captains over thousands, hundreds, fifties, and tens. It is estimated that there were 78,000 captains in Israel.

The Theocracy in Canaan

When the people of Israel conquered the land of Canaan and settled in it, certain changes occurred in their government. They were no longer nomads in the desert; they were now living in cities. They had lost the unity they had while wandering in the wilderness. This transition did not change the structure of Israel's government, but it did change the duties of the judges and the manner of their selection.

The judges became responsible for the government of the towns in which they lived. (Cf. Num. 21:25, 32; Judg. 8:6, 14, 16.) The elders of the tribes had exercised general governmental authority since the days of the Egyptian captivity. (Cf. Exod. 3:16–18; 19:7.) When they settled in Canaan, some of these elders were elected as judges in the cities (Judg. 11:5, 11) and sat in the city gates. They judged civil cases at the city gates because that is where most civic business was transacted. (Cf. Ruth 4:1–11.)

In the cities of refuge, the judges tried persons who were accused of murder (Deut. 19:12). They conducted inquests on people who had died (Deut. 21:2) and settled family and marriage problems (Deut. 21:18; 22:15; 25:7). Families generally settled their own problems according to the decision of the patriarch or family leader, but when dissatisfactions still remained, the case could be taken to the judge at the city gates.

During Israel's first settlement of Canaan there was no central authority, king, or ruling body. Each tribe lived in its own area with a minimum of central administration. Since there were few officials, the people had few leaders to whom to give loyalty and obedience.

The United Monarchy

Israel underwent a drastic change when theocracy gave way to monarchy (rule by a king). This period of history is usually divided into two parts, the united kingdom (ca. 1043–930 B.C.) and the divided kingdoms (ca. 930–586 B.C.). Particularly in the first period, the governmental structure grew more complex.

Israel became a monarchy when Saul from the tribe of Benjamin was enthroned. The Israelites had been oppressed by the Philistines for many years and wanted to have "a king to judge us like all the nations" (1 Sam. 8:5). They wanted a permanent military leader who would keep them free of other nations' rule. The phrase "a king to judge" probably emphasizes the military role that the judges played in the preceding centuries rather than the judicial role of settling disputes among the people.

Choosing a King

The king was chosen by God (1 Sam. 9:15–16), as well as by the people (1 Sam. 11:15). But the people's demand for a king was seen as rejection of God's military leadership— they wanted deliverance from their enemies without obedience to God. Had their attitude toward God been different, God would likely have provided a king for his people in due course. This event had been planned for centuries before. (See Deut. 17:14–20.) God agreed to their request but predicted judgment against them. Ultimately the king would oppress the people through heavy taxation and by drafting people to work for him and serve in his army. (See 1 Sam. 8:9–18.)

The Reign of Saul

This prediction began coming true during the reign of Saul. Before he became king, he owned only the usual family property (1 Sam. 9:1–2, 21), but during his reign he distributed fields and vineyards to his officers (1 Sam. 22:7). He must have obtained this property through taxation. At his death he also left considerable property to his heirs (2 Sam. 9:9–10), property he must have gained during his reign.

Government under King Saul continued to be quite simple because he made no known changes from the previous ways. We know of no administrative or bureaucratic developments during his reign. His administrators seemed to have been members of his immediate family. His son Jonathan and his cousin Abner served with him in the army and led the militia (1 Sam. 13:1–2, 16; 14:50–51). We also find that Saul established a permanent army in keeping with the desire of the people (1 Sam. 14:52).

The Reign of David

During the reign of David, many governmental changes occurred. David led the nation into an era of great military power. He subdued Israel's enemies and dominated their lands. He had to consolidate the tribes and centralize the government in order to rule the conquered territories and run the government at home.

Organization of the militia. The army was under the command of a general—Joab—and consisted of three sections. One was the original band of about 600 men under 30 commanders. (Cf. 2 Sam. 23:8–39; 1 Chron. 11:10–47.) The other two were the drafted militia and the hired mercenaries. The militia was organized into 12 sections consisting of 24,000 men each. Each section served on active duty for one month a year, and its tribe was responsible to provide for its needs.

Local government. David either appointed governors over the people whom he conquered (2 Sam. 8:6, 14) or made their kings his vassals (2 Sam. 10:19). These governors and kings were then responsible to carry on the local government for King David. They had to raise the necessary taxes, tributes, levies, and gifts.

David also appointed men over various treasuries, storehouses, and agricultural enterprises (1 Chron. 26:25–31). The lists of his personal holdings show that the shepherd boy who became king gained many possessions and properties during his reign.

Judicial system. As king, David made few changes in the previously existing structure of tribal government. He continued the judicial system established by Moses and allowed cities and tribes to manage their own affairs. The Bible tells us that David used the Levites as civil servants in the court system and as the police force of that period (1 Chron. 26:29–32).

The king's cabinet. The king surrounded himself with able leaders who formed a kind of cabinet, roughly modeled on the form found in Egypt (2 Sam. 8:15–18; 20:23–26; 1 Chron. 18:14–17).

The office of royal scribe or secretary appears frequently throughout the history of the kingdom. This high official seems to have had special assignments from time to time, but his regular duties included writing the royal correspondence and keeping the royal records, the annals of the events during the king's reign (2 Sam. 8:17; 20:25; 1 Chron. 18:16).

The office of recorder seems to have been one of high rank from the reign of King David on. He was called *mazkir* in Hebrew ("one who brings to mind"), and his official duty was to advise the king respecting important events. Jehoshaphat, the son of Ahilud, served as recorder for both David and Solomon (2 Sam. 8:16; 1 Kings 4:3). The recorder represented Hezekiah in public business (2 Kings 18:18, 37).

Minor officials. The Bible mentions a number of minor officials in the king's court during David's reign. One of these was the *saris,* literally translated as "eunuch" or "officer" (1 Chron. 28:1).

The Pharaohs of Egypt had such men, who served as trustees of royal property (Gen. 37:36; 39:1). The neighboring Assyrians had a dignitary called a *sha-reshi,* "he who is at the head," a courtier that may have been a model for the *saris.* The *sha-reshi* was not necessarily a physical eunuch, although he may have been. Scripture indicates that a *saris* in Israel was a trustee much like the Egyptian eunuch or the Assyrian *sha-reshi.* (Cf. 1 Chron. 28:1; 2 Kings 24:15.)

Another official title was *the king's servant* or *the servant of the king.* This seems to have been a general title that applied to the entire group of officials and royal household servants, from the palace guard to the highest office (1 Kings 1:33; 11:26)—to all those who "stood before" the king (1 Sam. 16:21)—the courtiers in the royal palace (1 Kings 12:6). Sometimes it may have been used as a special title, as in the case of Ahithophel (2 Sam. 15:12).

Finally, there was the *superintendent of forced labor.* This office first appears toward the end of David's reign (2 Sam. 20:23). At first, only non-Israelites were subjected to forced labor (Judg. 1:27–33). Under David foreign peoples were used extensively for this work, especially in the king's many building projects. The Hebrew word for forced labor or tribute is *mas* and is of Canaanite origin. Perhaps David borrowed the institution from the Canaanites when the need arose.

The Reign of Solomon

Under Solomon the administrative structure of government increased greatly. His large standing army, his extremely lavish court, and his many building projects required a complex system of government.

David's son built his government on the foundation of existing structures. First, the elder-judge and the priestly-judge institution continued to be the main government of the cities. The elders continued to function as they had under David and for centuries before. Wherever Solomon reorganized the government, he left intact the traditional tribal divisions and loyalties.

The king's cabinet. Solomon kept David's recorder and the office of royal scribe; in fact, Solomon had two secretaries. Some scholars suggest that he did this because of the increased record-keeping responsibilities during his reign.

The son of David's high priest was the high priest during Solomon's reign. Adoram, David's superintendent of forced labor, also kept his job under Solomon. (He is called *Adoniram* in 1 Kings 4:6 and 5:14.) The need for forced labor increased during Solomon's reign because of the building of the temple, as well as the construction of palaces and fortifications.

Solomon's policy was to fortify and hold the territory that David had conquered. He also had extensive personal properties that required maintenance and needed a large work squad. Solomon began using Israelites as well as non-Israelites in forced labor.

During Solomon's reign the superintendent of forced labor held an important office, for he supervised the work of thousands of people. Adoram (or Adoniram) was responsible for 150,000 foreign men in the labor force with 3,600 Israelite supervisors over them. He also had 30,000 Israelites working for him, supervised by 300 officers. The entire structure of nearly 184,000 men must have been well organized and carefully policed, but we have no way of knowing exactly how that was done. We do not know whether the army or a special force was responsible to see that the work was done.

Solomon apparently added two new officials to his cabinet—the chief of the prefects and the officer over the royal household.

The *chief of the prefects* was the cabinet member responsible for all the internal affairs of the kingdom. Under him were the governors or prefects in charge of the 12 districts of the nation created by Solomon. These district governors were responsible for

> Collecting taxes
> Collecting the temple tithe
> Supplying the royal court with food for one month each year
> Lodging soldiers and chariots in the district
> Erecting public buildings in the district
> Constructing and maintaining roads in the district

(See 1 Kings 4:7, 21–28.)

This office was similar to later administrative offices in the Babylonian Empire. Various nations of the Near East organized their government into 12 districts to provide for the court and army throughout the year (one district per month).

The second new official in King Solomon's structure was the *officer over the royal household,* or *vizier* as he was known in other lands. This office continued after Israel split into northern and southern kingdoms.

This official probably was the manager of the king's palace, supervising the maintenance of the grounds, the upkeep of the royal palace, and the assigning of quarters to the court members. He was also responsible for maintaining all royal properties, including Solomon's extensive trade and mining operations.

The revenue of the palace greatly increased during Solomon's reign, and the vizier had to manage all of these finances. The support of the army and the Levites may have been managed by others. But the vizier was responsible for raising all the funds from the royal estates. Archaeological discoveries suggest that these revenues were used to support the palace courtiers, to supply military needs, and perhaps also to provide for the Levites.

The vizier's office can be compared to the Egyptian office of vizier—although under Solomon this official had far less power than his Egyptian counterpart, who was more of a prime minister. He is named toward the bottom of the list of Solomon's court officials (cf. 1 Kings 4:6), and there is no reference to his father.

The queen mother. Solomon was the first of Israel's kings to include a queen mother in his administration—Bathsheba. She received great honor and sat at his right hand (1 Kings 2:19). Her power was not simply that of a mother over her son; she was considered an important adviser.

A similar office existed among the Hittites and among the people of Ugarit. But in these lands the queen mother often became more active in political affairs.

Centralized government. Solomon's changes in the administrative cabinet served to centralize his government. He structured the district governments in a hierarchy of power, stemming from the power of the king.

Solomon's new system eroded the administrative independence of the tribes. He now had a central government with a local administrative staff appointed by the central government. Israel was no longer a kingdom. It had become an empire.

Policy toward the Canaanites. As for the areas where Canaanites still lived, Solomon's policy was to tie them directly to the palace rather than allow the Israelite tribes to have jurisdiction over them. Canaanite leaders were given new positions in Solomon's government. With few exceptions, these leaders were placed over former Canaanite districts. (Cf. Gen. 10:6–20.)

The central province. The tribe of Judah does not appear as one of Solomon's 12 districts. Apparently this territory formed a central province, which itself was divided into 12 sections. The Septuagint mentions a *governor of the land* at the end of the list of Solomon's districts.

In neighboring Assyria, the term *the land* referred to the central province in their civil administration. In the Assyrian form of government, the central province was not considered part of the overall administrative system of government; it was ruled directly from the palace. Perhaps Solomon's structure followed Assyria's.

The Divided Kingdom

The Bible does not tell us much about the administrative structures of the two divided kingdoms, Israel and Judah. We suppose that the structures of Solomon's time were carried over into both kingdoms.

Cabinet officials. We have some evidence that the kings of Israel and Judah continued to use the offices of recorder, scribe, vizier, and others. For example, under King Hezekiah, the recorder Joah went to negotiate with officials of the invading Assyrian king, Sennacherib (2 Kings 18:18, 27; Isa. 36:3, 22). A man named Joah was the son of King Josrah's recorder and was one of the three officials responsible for repairing the temple (2 Chron. 34:8).

When King Jehoash of Judah rebuilt the temple, he entrusted his scribe and high priest with the control of the money (2 Kings 12:10–11). King Hezekiah sent his scribe Shebna with the elders of the priests and his vizier Eliakim to meet Sennacherib's envoy, and later to confer with the prophet Isaiah (2 Kings 19:2). Under King Josiah, Shaphan the scribe joined Joah the son of the recorder and Maaseiah the governor of the city of Jerusalem in restoring the Book of the Law to the temple (2 Chron. 34:8–21).

The office of vizier became more important with the passage of time. In Hezekiah's day, Shebna and his successor Eliakim had great power. Isaiah described the office when he predicted that Eliakim would replace Shebna:

> And I will clothe him with your robe and strengthen him with your belt; I will commit your responsibility into his hand. He shall be a father to the inhabitants of Jerusalem and to the house of Judah. The key of the house of David I will lay on his shoulder; so he shall open, and no one shall shut; and he shall shut, and no one shall open (Isa. 22:21–22).

Adoram, the superintendent of forced labor, continued from David's and Solomon's reigns into the time of Rehoboam. King Rehoboam arrogantly sent Adoram to the northern tribes to assert his rule over them. They showed their contempt for the king of Judah by stoning Adoram (Hadoram) to death (1 Kings 12:18; 2 Chron. 10:18). The office disappeared after the division of the two kingdoms. But in later days King Asa forced some men to fortify Geba and Mizpah (1 Kings 15:22), and Jeremiah denounced King Jehoiakim for forcing his people to build his palace (Jer. 22:13).

During the period of the divided kingdom the capital cities—Jerusalem and Samaria—were under a governor as well as the king. In other Near Eastern countries capital cities were administered by a governor. For example, the governor of the central administrative town of Ugarit had authority over the entire surrounding territory.

Scripture mentions "the governor of the city" of Samaria and Jerusalem (1 Kings 22:26; 2 Kings 23:8; 2 Chron. 18:25).

Early in Israel's history Abimelech appointed a governor over Shechem (Judg. 9:29–30). Much later Ahab ordered Amon, the governor of Samaria, to imprison the prophet Micaiah (1 Kings 22:26–27). In Jehu's day, the governor of Samaria ("he who was in charge of the city"), the vizier ("he who was in charge of the house"), the elders, and "those who reared the children" offered their support and loyalty to him (2 Kings 10:5).

Maaseiah administered Jerusalem under King Josiah (2 Chron. 34:8). In Jezebel's plotting to get Naboth's vineyard, she dealt with the elders and the nobles of the city (1 Kings 21:8–11). We have no evidence of governors in the northern kingdom, except for the capital city of Samaria.

Eunuchs were more prominent in the divided monarchy than at previous times. Jeremiah lists them as men of rank with princes and priests (Jer. 34:19). Earlier, such men took Ahab's message to the prophet Micaiah, summoning him to appear before the king (1 Kings 22:9). These officers or eunuchs restored the Shunammite's goods (2 Kings 8:6). They were also among those who went into the Babylonian captivity under Jehoiachin (2 Kings 24:12; Jer. 29:2), having led the men of Israel in fighting against the Babylonians at the capture of Jerusalem (2 Kings 25:19; Jer. 52:25).

Queen mothers. We find mention of two queen mothers in the divided kingdom. Maachah misused her office and was deposed by King Asa (1 Kings 15:13), and Athaliah later took control of the nation (2 Kings 11:1–16).

Minor officials. In light of the Scripture evidence that cabinet offices continued into this period, we assume that priest administrators, military heads, administrators over local districts, and other minor officials continued in each kingdom.

A new minor official who appears in the divided monarchy is the king's son. He appears to have been some kind of police officer but did not hold high rank in the governmental structure. (Cf. 1 Kings 22:26–27; 2 Chron. 18:25.) Perhaps the title indicates that a king's son originally held this office.

Summary

The government of the nation of Israel began with a theocracy in the wilderness where Israel was a religious community ruled by God with a system of tribal courts. Moses was chief executive over a staff of judges who gave decisions in disputes and apparently served as leaders in battle.

The theocracy in Canaan remained simple, with its civil government centered in the cities where elder-judges settled disputes. Later God raised up another type of judge to deliver the Israelites from their oppressors.

The monarchy in Israel became centralized and more complex. The rule by Kings Saul, David, and Solomon eventually resulted in division of the nation.

Local administration in the divided kingdoms was adjusted from time to time by various reforms and changes of government. But the elders (or judges) still continued as the primary government officials responsible for the judicial processes and local civil needs. This best explains how the returning exiles were able to assume so quickly a form of government that was patterned after the prekingdom administrative structure.

Key Words from
the Bible

When people thoughtfully consider the Christian faith, a number of concepts come to them. Words often flash through their minds, such as *love* and *faith*, or *hope* and *peace*, or *guilt* and *sin*. These are the words we are emphasizing here. Some of the key words have to do with theology, but most of them focus on day-to-day Christian living.

Assurance. Assurance refers to the confidence and conviction of believers that the penalty for their sins has been paid and that they are loved and accepted by God. They inwardly know that they will be with Jesus Christ as their eternal destiny.

Assurance means that Christians possess salvation and they also know that Jesus Christ will continue to work in their lives: "He who has the Son has life" (1 John 5:12).

Church. This word refers to God's people—never a building. God's people—whether in the OT or NT—have certain distinctive marks. They are

• Chosen by God solely on the grounds of his grace (Deut. 7:6–8; 1 Cor. 1:26–29).

• Called covenant people because God enters into a relationship in which he lays down the terms and to which he binds himself (Heb. 8:8–13).

• Redeemed (Exod. 6:6). The Israelites reminded themselves of this at the annual Passover festival while Christians celebrate a greater Passover deliverance (1 Cor. 5:7).

• United and part of one body of believers.

Although repentance and faith in Jesus Christ are the conditions of membership in God's church, it is God who adds people to its number (Acts 2:47) because the church is his.

Coming. God's coming to his people for the final day of reckoning was a constant expectation of OT prophets. Every visitation further assured them of it. Associated with the Day of the Lord—the day when God would make all things right—was a messianic figure, a Davidic King, or a suffering servant.

Some Jews found this so baffling that they finally delineated two separate Messiahs, one a king and the other a priest. Looking backward, Christians grasp that God sent only one Messiah but two comings. Jesus came first as a priest, a servant, a suffering Savior. He will return as a Davidic and triumphant king.

The second coming of Jesus is the hope of all believers through all the ages.

Two Greek words describe this event: *parousia* refers to the "arrival of a ruler," and *apokalypsis* means "unveiling" because it will be the public disclosure of Jesus Christ's glory (1 Pet. 4:13).

Like those of old, we cannot see the end clearly from what God has revealed in the

Bible. We cannot know for certain how and when the details will be filled in, but we know this much:

• The appearing will be sudden and unexpected, like a thief who comes in the night (1 Thess. 5:1–3).

• This momentous event will usher in the final judgment.

• The resurrection of the dead will take place—all will be instantly changed, both the living and those who have already died (1 Cor. 15:51–54).

• For Christians, this means being forever with Christ (1 Thess. 4:17).

Covenant. With the Fall (see Gen. 3:1ff.), sin entered the world, and God prepared the way for human salvation. God's method has been to enter into a covenant with humanity.

Throughout the OT, God made covenants with individuals such as Noah, Abraham, Moses, and David. Each expressed God's grace toward humanity and centered on delivering them from the results of sin. From the promise to all humankind that a flood would not occur again, the divine pledges narrowed down to a specific people with more precise details, culminating in the promises concerning the Messiah through the line of David, which Jesus Christ fulfilled (Luke 1:32–33).

Jesus originated the new covenant, in which all believers—Gentiles and Jews—are incorporated into the people of God (1 Pet. 2:10).

The new covenant achieved what the Mosaic covenant could not; the old covenant (the Law) pointed to a way of life but did not give the power to live it. God's laws are now written upon the hearts of the covenant people who are empowered by the Holy Spirit (2 Cor. 4:6; Heb. 8:10).

Since a covenant involved a sacrifice to seal and bind both parties together (Exod. 24:6–8), the price was the blood of Christ (Mark 14:24). Through giving this covenant, God says, "I will be their God and they shall be my people."

Death. The Bible says, "It is appointed for men to die once" (Heb. 9:27). Yet when it occurs, people have difficulty in accepting the reality of the event.

Paul called death "the last enemy" (1 Cor. 15:26). He also taught that death entered the world as the result of sin (Rom. 5:12), and if there had not been sin, there would have been no death (Rom. 5:17).

Death is more than a natural phenomenon: "The soul who sins shall die" (Ezek. 18:4). When Paul describes death as receiving the "wages of sin," he means much more than its inevitable consequence (Rom. 6:23). Death is God's verdict upon human sinfulness (Rom. 1:32).

Jesus Christ conquered death when he overcame sin and the devil. Spiritually, believers have already passed from death to life (John 5:24), and the broken relationship has been restored.

Believers still face the weakness and pain that accompany dying, but they need not be afraid of death itself. Jesus Christ the victor will finally overcome the last enemy also (1 Cor. 15:26, 54–57).

Faith. The word *faith* (or *trust* or *belief*) occurs frequently in the Bible, expressing the only attitude of God's people toward their loving Creator.

From the Greek word, some scholars see faith as a three-stage movement:

1. Acceptance—of the fact that Jesus Christ died for us (Rom. 10:9)
2. Belief—in the message heard (John 14:21)
3. Commitment—to the message and Jesus Christ (John 3:16)

For Christians, life everlasting is an immediate, present possession (John 5:24) made a reality when they believe. This faith results in active obedience (Rom. 10:16).

Fellowship. Originally the Greek word for fellowship had reference to a business partnership. Early Christians changed the concept and added new meaning. Fellowship binds together, and its primary emphasis is on sharing with others. True fellowship results in wanting to give to others some of what persons enjoy: "If God so loved us, we also ought to love one another" (1 John 4:11). This expression of love is not an emotion but an action—this is true fellowship with others.

Flesh. This word has several meanings. *Flesh* is often a synonym for *people*. True intimacy in marriage makes the two people into one flesh (Gen. 2:24). In the OT, *flesh* often contrasted human weakness with the strength of God's Spirit (Isa. 31:3).

The most significant use of the word is in reference to human nature. This natural part of people is so tainted that Paul says, "I know that in me nothing good dwells (that is, in my flesh)" (Rom. 7:18)—here he obviously refers to human nature.

Flesh, in its most negative sense, means human nature apart from divine influence, making it prone to sin and living in opposition to God. This word includes anything that is weak, low, and tending toward ungodliness. (See Rom. 8:3–6; 2 Cor. 7:5; Gal. 5:16ff.)

Forgiveness. Forgiveness lies at the heart of Christianity. A right relationship with God is the basic human need. Because sin is primarily an offense against God, it is God who forgives.

There is only one sin for which the Father does not promise forgiveness: blasphemy against the Holy Spirit (Matt. 12:32; Mark 3:28–29). The contexts suggest this is the sin of attributing to unclean spirits the work of the Holy Spirit. Some interpreters (including Augustine) have understood it to include a deliberate persistence in doing evil. Some consider this shows itself by an unforgiving spirit. (See Matt. 18:34–35.)

Gospel. The *gospel* is the "good news"— the literal meaning of the Greek word. The good news is a message about Jesus Christ, the Savior. From the start of his ministry, Jesus' preaching rang with a good message

(Mark 1:14–15). Those three years were largely confined to ministry among the Jewish people, but since the Resurrection and Ascension, the gospel has been proclaimed to all nations (Mark 13:10).

Grace. *Grace* means "favor or kindness shown without regard to the worth of those who receive it," and it is offered in spite of what they have done or deserve.

In the OT, the supreme example of grace was God's delivering of the Jews from Egypt and leading them into the Promised Land. (Cf. Deut. 7:1ff.)

Grace is the key word of the Bible. It is the quality repeatedly ascribed to God in dealing with humanity (Exod. 34:6; Acts 20:24). Grace implies the action of a superior to an inferior, and every gracious expression of kindness and mercy is totally undeserved (Lam. 1:18; 3:22).

Guilt. This word and other forms of it *(guilty, guiltiness)* occur about 30 times in the Bible. In the OT, the word translated as *guilty* is usually the Hebrew *asam,* a common word for "trespass offering," and frequently designates the trespass for which the offering was given.

In connection with the sin and trespass offerings, Leviticus 4:13 and 5:2 say that breaking any of God's commands, ceremonial or moral, brings guilt. James 2:10 emphasizes that to offend in one point of the law makes individuals guilty of all.

Hope. The sense of expectation of good and something for which God's people wait in hope. In the Bible, hope stands for the act of hoping (Rom. 4:18; 1 Cor. 9:10) and the thing hoped for (Col. 1:5; 1 Pet. 1:3).

Joy. A positive attitude or pleasant emotion or delight is joy. Many kinds of joy appear in the Bible, making it difficult to give a simple definition. Even the wicked experience joy in their triumph over the godly (1 Cor. 13:6; Rev. 11:10). Many levels of joy are described as gladness, contentment, and cheerfulness.

Joy is distinct from mere happiness because it is possible to have godly joy in the midst of sorrow (1 Cor. 12:26; 2 Cor. 6:10; 7:4).

Knowledge. *To know* sometimes means "to approve" or "to take delight in" (Ps. 1:6; Rom. 8:29), "to cherish" (John 10:27), or "to experience" (Eph. 3:19). It can be used as a euphemism for sexual intercourse (as Gen. 4:1).

Knowledge can be partial (1 Cor. 13:9), and it implies that it is arrived at by discovery or detection. Paul said that through the law comes the knowledge of sin (Rom. 3:20). That is, knowing and understanding the law lead to a discovery of what is right and what is wrong.

Knowledge in the Bible, then, means the truth or facts that people acquire through experience and/or thought. The greatest truth that individuals can possess with the mind or learn through experience is truth about God (Ps. 46:10; John 8:31–32). This knowledge cannot be gained without God's help (Rom. 11:33) and it is acquired only as God shows himself to human beings through nature and conscience (Ps. 19; Rom. 1:19–20), in history or providence (Deut. 6:20–25; Dan. 2:21), and through the Bible (Ps. 119; Rev. 1:1–3).

Life. The physical function of people, animals, and plants is life. Life is also the time between birth and death. Because God is its source, life comes to all humans as a gift from him. He first filled Adam with the breath of life (Gen. 2:7), and he continues to be the source of all life.

Love. Two different Greek words appear in the NT for love: *phileo*, "to have ardent affections and feelings," and *agape*, "to esteem or have high regard."

Love basically means caring. It is an action word and not primarily an emotion. It is a command to do, not to feel. Love for God is to be judged not by intensity of feelings but by obedient action. Jesus said, "If you love Me, keep My commandments" (John 14:15—or it can be translated, "You will keep. . . .")

Obey *or* Obedience. The word translated as *obey* in both Testaments is a contextual rendering of the verb "to hear." Obedience in the Bible signifies an active response to something heard rather than passive listening.

Hearing and obeying are also sometimes attached to believing in both Testaments. Genesis 15:6 states that Abraham believed God, and was accounted righteous. This is defined in Genesis 22:18 as obeying the voice of God. (Cf. Rom. 4:3.)

Overcome. The Christian idea of overcoming has its basis in the declaration of Jesus that he had overcome the world (John 16:33), that is, all that is antagonistic to the will of God. A Stronger One has come and disarmed the antagonistic forces (Luke 11:22) with the result that Christians need fear them no longer.

Peace. The Hebrew word *shalom* means "completeness," "health," "wholeness," "soundness," and "harmony." It involves contentment and prosperity as well as absence of war.

In the NT, peace most often refers to the inner tranquillity of Christians. The peace Jesus Christ promises is a combination of hope, trust, and quietness of heart brought about by a reconciliation with God. Peace and spiritual blessedness are distinct results of faith in Jesus Christ (Rom. 5:1). For the wicked there is no such peace (Isa. 57:21).

Pride. Inordinate and unreasonable self-esteem, attended with insolence and rude treatment of others, defines pride. It is an attempt to appear in a superior light to what we are, with anxiety to gain applause, and it results in distress and rage when slighted.

Theologians have called pride the chief of the capital sins because it prompts and is partially present in all other sins. Pride is the inordinate desire for honor, recognition, and distinction and arises from self-centeredness.

Repentance. The Greek word *metanoia* means "a change of mind." This is the change in individuals who turn from sin to God. Repentance is bound up with faith and is inseparable from it because, without some measure of faith, no one can truly repent. Repentance attains its deepest meaning when sinners realize the grace of God against whom they have sinned.

Some see two stages in repentance: (1) a genuine sorrow or regret because of sin (Ps. 51; 2 Cor. 7:9–10) and (2) an inner repugnance to sin followed by forsaking it (Acts 26:20).

Righteousness. Purity of heart and rectitude to life—the being and doing right—that is righteousness.

The righteousness of the law is obedience to what the law requires (Rom. 3:10, 20; 8:4); righteousness of faith is justification, received by faith (Rom. 3:21–28). The perfect righteousness of Christ is imputed or accounted to believers when they turn to Jesus Christ as their Savior (1 Cor. 1:30; 2 Cor. 5:20–21).

Salvation. The term *salvation* stands for several Hebrew and Greek words, but the central idea is that of safety, deliverance, ease, and soundness.

In the OT, God delivers persons from the snares of the wicked (Ps. 37:40). He grants forgiveness of sins, answers to prayer, joy, and peace (Pss. 79:9; 69:13; 51:12).

In the NT, salvation is shown as triumphing over the power of sin because Jesus Christ is the author of salvation. (Cf. Matt. 1:21; Heb. 2:10.) He freely offers this salvation to all (John 3:16).

Sanctification. When people become Christians, they are sanctified. This term refers to the process of obtaining holiness or being set apart for God. The dominant idea is separation from the secular and sinful and now availability for a sacred purpose. This process is also known as growth.

Sanctification as separation from the world and setting apart for God's service is found all through the Bible.

Believers are sanctified by God the Father (Jude 1), God the Son (Heb. 2:11), and God the Holy Spirit (2 Thess. 2:13; 1 Pet. 1:2). And the purpose of this being set apart is becoming holy or spiritually perfect (Matt. 5:48). That his people should be holy is God's command (1 Thess. 4:7) and purpose.

Sanctification is a process that continues through the entire lives of believers (Heb. 10:14).

Sin. Sin is disobeying a law and a Lawgiver—God. The sinfulness of sin lies in the fact that wrong actions are always against God, even when the wrong is to others or to oneself (Gen. 39:9; Ps. 51:4).

Sin is lawlessness (1 John 3:4) or transgressing God's will either by omitting to do what God requires or by doing what God forbids.

Transgression occurs in thoughts (1 John 3:15), words (Matt. 5:22), and actions (Rom. 1:32).

Walk. Although a familiar word in the NT, it is misunderstood because of having several meanings. It means "to move about," "to accompany someone" or to "travel alone," or "to live" (used figuratively) and refers to conduct or a way of life. This latter meaning is frequently found in Paul's letters. When he says that Enoch and Noah walked with God, he means they maintained a life-style that conformed to God's will.

Wisdom. Although the word has a variety of meanings and four different words in the OT are translated as *wisdom*, there are two dominant meanings.

1. Wisdom is an attribute of God, closely related to knowledge. (See Ps. 104:24; Rom. 11:33; 1 Cor. 1:24.)

2. Human wisdom is not only practical understanding of matters relating to life, but in its highest sense, it is the theoretical and practical acceptance of divine revelation. Wisdom is a divine gift. (See Acts 6:10; 1 Cor. 2:6; 12:8; Eph. 1:17.)

Laws and
Commands

Biblical Laws

Through the giving of the law, God told Moses how the people of Israel should live. Moses recorded these commands in the first five books (the Pentateuch) of the OT. These laws teach us a great deal about OT society. Even today, God still expects believers to honor him in their dealings with one another. As interpreted by Jesus and his apostles, the law forms the foundation of modern Christian ethics.

Uniqueness of Biblical Law

The legal system of the Bible helped to shape the ethics of the West today. We can discern the uniqueness of biblical law when we compare it with other ancient systems of law. Archaeologists have found collections of Near Eastern laws in the ruins of Ur-Nammu, Eshnunna, Sumer, Mari, Ugarit, and other cities.

King Hammurabi of Babylon produced a famous system of law around 1700 B.C. The Hittites of Asia Minor adopted similar ideas when they created their own legal system. The Sumerians, the Babylonians, the Assyrians, and other peoples of Mesopotamia greatly influenced the laws of the world around them. One expert stated that nearly every legal system of the ancient Near East bore the imprint of Mesopotamia.

The law codes of Mesopotamia followed the same general pattern. Instead of providing universal principles, they stated what had been traditionally decided in a series of actual court cases (case law). Scholars call this casuistic law—a term from the Latin word *casus*, meaning "case." The people of the Near East believed their king could apply eternal truth to every new problem. After all, hadn't the gods chosen him to rule them? When the ruler made judgment, all the people were bound by it. Later kings, however, often quoted tradition and did little to codify or modify law to fit current life situations.

Mesopotamian laws told people such things as how to handle their money and property, how to collect damages, and how to get a divorce—but they did not teach moral or religious lessons.

A code of Mesopotamian law usually began by telling how their god or gods gave the king power to rule the land. Then the book listed the rulings on a series of legal cases, arranged by topic. It closed with curses for anyone who disobeyed the laws and blessings for those who kept them. (There are sections of the Pentateuch that list God's rulings according to this pattern.)

Mesopotamian legal codes begin each rule by saying, "Thus you shall do . . ." Often a biblical commandment begins with the words, "Thus says the Lord . . ." There is the basic difference: In the Bible, God gives the command; in Mesopotamian law, the king does.

The content of biblical law often resembles other laws of the Near East. But in many more ways, biblical law is different. Biblical law codes are unique in their form, origin, concept of law, and underlying principles.

The Origin of the Law

Rulers of the Near East were not trying to express universal wisdom through their laws. They were trying to maintain their personal political and economic power and their image as lawgivers. If a previous king had already done this, they borrowed those ideas for their own legal system. A king was supposed to hand down laws that were clear, just, and true, no matter where he got them.

In contrast, God's people received their laws from God. Even laws whose content corresponded to those of other Near Eastern codes are represented as God-given. The Bible says to obey its laws because they are God's commands. Such statements are motive clauses because they bless those who obey God's law and curse those who disobey, or both (e.g., Lev. 26).

Chapters 1—4 of Deuteronomy review Israel's history with a motivating purpose, to remind God's people to obey. The Israelites agreed with their neighbors that the law was eternal and binding, but for a different reason—because God said so.

The Concept of Law

Laws usually deal with a nation's social order; they tell how citizens should act toward one another. The laws of the Bible also tell how to act toward God; they are primarily religious laws.

God introduces the law by saying he chose Israel to be a nation with its own land, not just a clan or a large family (see Gen. 12:2). They heard how to live in harmony with God—the essential message of the Ten Commandments or Decalogue (Greek, "ten words"; see Exod. 20) and the thrust of the civil laws in the legal sections (chaps. 21—23) and the rules of worship (chaps. 24—31). Israel served God by obeying the law; Israel did not make the law.

Hittite law assumed that a god was the *suzerain* ("conquering ruler") of the nation. In the Bible, the relationship between God and Israel is more personal because God calls them "a special treasure" (cf. Exod. 19:3–6).

Biblical law was public law, and this was another important distinction from the pagan laws of the Near East. In many nations, the king carried the laws in his head, as if they were personal possessions. Consequently, individuals could be arrested for breaking laws they had never known. The laws were kept secret, even when people went on trial for breaking them. (There are few instances in which anyone cited the royal codes in a court case.)

In Israel, the leaders of government read the law to the people at regular times of the year (cf. Deut. 31:10–13). All citizens could learn the laws they had to obey. Other peoples of the Near East obeyed laws because they were enforced by the royal establishment and disobedience meant punishment. The Hebrews obeyed the law because they loved God (cf. Deut. 6:5, 20–25).

The claim of the Mosaic law rested on the known character of the Lawgiver. Although the judges and priests interpreted the law, they did not make the law (Deut. 17:8–13). So when people abided by the law, they showed their love for God rather than for the interpreters.

Underlying Principles

The principles behind the laws of the Bible are in marked contrast to those behind other Near Eastern laws. Biblical laws are based upon the revealed character and purpose of

God, point toward a transcendent goal (God's redemption of humanity), show God's protection of each individual's integrity, and reflect that God made human beings the stewards of the earth (cf. Deut. 21:22–23).

Another glaring fundamental difference in the social distinctions embodied in ancient Near Eastern codes is obvious in the *Code of Hammurabi*. This code, for example, preserves three separate social classes and codifies the degradation of the lower class. It is a system designed to protect the position of those at the top of society. Biblical law sees all people as creatures of God, equal to one another.

Other basic themes emerge in biblical law:

1. *All crimes are ultimately against God.* When individuals offended society, they offended God (1 Sam. 12:9–10). Some social offenses were so serious that only God could pardon them.

2. *The law was to bring people to total submission to God.* God's laws showed divine care about every aspect of life. It was not enough to offer formal worship or moral behavior. Since their whole being came from God, they were to serve with their whole being.

God enforced the law when human agents would not (Exod. 22:21–24; Deut. 10:18; Ps. 67:4). God punished his people when they did not apply the law fairly. He was present as Judge at every court trial, no matter what verdict the human judge rendered (cf. Deut. 19:17).

3. *The law was a national responsibility.* God's law was not the private property of the upper class. All Jews knew the law and the penalty for breaking it. At times the whole community punished the lawbreaker because all of the people had to uphold the law (Exod. 21:22–23).

Judges represented God, but they also represented the law-abiding community. Cases of murder required evidence from two or three witnesses, and the verdict was announced publicly at the city gate. If the person was found guilty, the witnesses executed the murderer (Deut. 13:6–10; 17:7); the victim's next of kin did it (Deut. 19:11–12); or the whole community participated (Num. 15:32–36; Deut. 13:6–10).

4. *The law was an individual responsibility.* The Bible stressed personal duty to God as more important than the responsibility to adhere to community policies. If their community was wrong, God still held them individually responsible for their own actions (cf. Exod. 32).

5. *The law respected human life.* Because human beings were created in God's image, the law protected human life. If those from a higher social class injured people of lower social status, they were not excused by the mere payment of a fine. The only equivalent of human life was human life itself. Even before the law, God said, "Whoever sheds man's blood, by man his blood shall be shed; for in the image of God He made man" (Gen. 9:6).

The Book of the Covenant

Technically, the *Book of the Covenant* was everything that Moses read to the Israelites at the foot of Mount Sinai (cf. Exod. 24:3–7), including the Ten Commandments (Exod. 20:2–17). Later Jewish leaders called the book of Deuteronomy "the Book of the Covenant" (2 Kings 23:2). Deuteronomy is generally thought to be "the Book of the Law" discovered during the restoration of the temple under King Josiah of Judah (2 Kings 22:8).

The Israelites accepted the entire law as part of their covenant with God. The Decalogue stated the basic rules of the law, while the other OT laws applied and clarified these principles.

The Holiness Code

God unfolded his laws over a span of many generations. Once given, the Ten Commandments were expanded and explained in Exodus 20:22—23:30. In turn, the laws of Leviticus and Deuteronomy expanded and explained the laws of Exodus. Leviticus explained the first four commandments of the Decalogue—those that had to do with the worship of God—while most of Deuteronomy dealt with the rest of the Decalogue.

The collection of laws in Leviticus 17—26 is called the *holiness code,* and its purpose was to keep Israel holy and pure. Leviticus 20:26 reads, "And you shall be holy to Me, for I the LORD am holy, and have separated you from the peoples, that you should be Mine."

The Deuteronomic Code

Scholars disagree about how much of Deuteronomy makes up the *deuteronomic code.* Some believe that chapters 1—11 continue the discussion of worship from Leviticus and could be included under the holiness code.

The Decalogue (Deut. 5) laid the foundation for Deuteronomy. The laws that governed human relationships would have made no sense without the laws governing human relationship with God. It seems logical to consider Deuteronomy as a complete work and to call the entire book the deuteronomic code. It covers the wide range of ethical and ritual concerns that Moses raised with the Israelites just before they entered the Promised Land.

Exodus divides its case laws from its general legal policies (Exod. 21:1—22:17; 22:18—23:33). The fact that Deuteronomy blends these two forms of law together confirms that it was probably written later.

Further, the laws of Deuteronomy were designed for a more settled way of life. For example, the book adds laws of inheritance (Deut. 21:15–17) and interest on loans (Deut. 23:20) to the Exodus laws. When Deuteronomy was written, the Israelites were no longer wandering in the wilderness but were ready to conquer Canaan and settle down. We find more of these domestic laws in Numbers, such as the laws of a woman's inheritance (Num. 27:1–11; 36:1–12).

Functional Development of Law

The law of Israel developed over several hundred years as God gave each generation the instructions it needed for its way of life. When the laws of the Bible are grouped by topic, we get a picture of how they unfolded through the centuries.

Benevolence laws. Many biblical laws called for humane treatment of the poor and helpless, as well as kindness toward animals.

The law said that every animal was useful, and the Israelites were to feed each animal according to the work it did (Deut. 25:4). God did not allow the cruel beating of animals. They even had to let their animals rest on the Sabbath (Exod. 20:8–11; 23:12).

When Israelites observed beasts carrying loads too heavy for them—even if the animals belonged to neighbors—those observers were expected to take part of the burden themselves (Deut. 22:1–4). Farmers were to leave gleanings in the field for wild animals or the poor. Israelites could not take mother birds and their eggs on the same day, nor cows and their calves, ewes and their lambs (see Lev. 22:28; Deut. 22:6–7).

Scripture directed God's people to take care of the widow, orphan, and foreigner (Exod. 22:22–24). The people did not receive handouts, however; they were to earn their own living (Deut. 24:19–22). The Is-

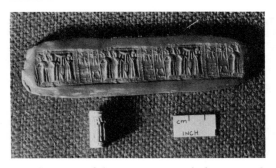

A cylinder seal from ancient Babylonia. Such seals were often used to validate decrees or legalize contracts in Bible times.

PHOTO BY GUSTAV JEENINGA

raelites respected and cared for their elders (Lev. 19:32). They were not allowed to hold grudges (Lev. 19:17–18). They could not inflict excessive punishment on a criminal (Deut. 25:1–3). In every way, God expected his people to show love for their neighbors by their humane treatment.

If an Israelite loaned a coat or some other necessary item, it had to be returned at nightfall. An Israelite could not enter someone's house to collect a bad debt (Deut. 24:10–13). God honored the right of the creditor, but also guarded the right of the debtor.

The Law allowed travelers to enter a field and gather food to eat, but they could not carry off an extra supply (Deut. 23:24–25). Farmers paid wages to hired hands every day, because they needed the money to buy their food (Deut. 24:14–15). They had to lend fellow Israelites money without charging interest (Lev. 25:35–37).

When people could not make a living on their own, they could go into voluntary servitude by signing a contract to become servants. Masters had to treat them kindly, though (Lev. 25:39–43). The freeborn could not be kidnapped and sold into slavery (Exod. 21:16; Deut. 24:7). Israelites had to protect runaway slaves from another country, making sure that their owners did not harm them (Deut. 23:15–16).

Ceremonial laws. The ancient Israelites centered all their activities on the worship of Yahweh. Each person was expected to worship God individually, just as the whole nation was to worship him together. Jesus reinforced this by summing up all the commands of the OT in one—to love God (Matt. 22:37; cf. Deut. 6:5).

The Bible's ceremonial law mentioned several sacred objects that the Israelites kept at the center of their camp as they wandered in the wilderness. The important objects were the ark of the covenant and the central sanctuary.

Ark of the covenant. The ark of the covenant was a wooden box about 122 by 76 by 76 centimeters (4.5 by 2.5 by 2.5 feet), or 2.5 by 1.5 by 1.5 cubits, made of acacia (*shittim,* KJV) wood and covered with gold, inside and out. The Israelites believed this box was God's throne, and they called its solid gold lid the *mercy seat.* Two golden cherubim (angelic statues) stood on opposite ends of the box, facing the mercy seat (Exod. 25:10–22). Inside the box the Israelites kept the stone tablets of the Ten Commandments, a pot of manna, and Aaron's rod that had budded—all reminders of God's love for them.

Central sanctuary. God promised Israel that they would rest in a land of their own (cf. Heb. 4). When that day came, they were supposed to build a central sanctuary where they could worship him.

God chose all of the Israelites to be priests (Exod. 19:6), but because most of them had to earn a living, he ordered that the tribe of Levi represent the whole nation in the sanctuary (Exod. 28:43—29:9). The Levites had to follow special rules to keep themselves pure for this kind of service (e.g., Lev. 10:8–11). From them, God chose one man to be the high priest and gave him even more special rules.

Civil laws. The people of Israel knew themselves called to worship God with their entire lives. This means that their obedience extended to the realm of civil laws as well as religious laws. They consulted God when they selected their leaders, and they looked to God to guide their government. They believed that God had set up the powers of civil government for their own good. These laws dealt with the army, the court system, and the political leaders.

Army. God allowed Israel to raise an army for defense (Num. 2:14–33), but did not want his people to become a warlike nation, greedy for land and power. He would not let them have war horses (Deut. 17:16), nor let them keep anything they captured in war, although they could protect the borders of the land from invaders, and they could crush rebel armies within their country. The generals of Israel could draft soldiers from the men over 20 years of age (cf. Num. 1:20–43), except for the Levites (Num. 1:47–49). God promised to help the army of Israel if the soldiers obeyed his laws (Deut. 23:9–14). Israel must try to make peace with its enemies before going into battle, but often Israel had to destroy its enemies (Deut. 2:34; 3:6). Sometimes God allowed the troops to spare virgins and marry them. If a soldier decided to do this, he could not treat the woman as a slave or captive (Deut. 21:10–14).

Court system. Israel had a dual system of courts. The nation elected judges to hear civil lawsuits while the Levites judged religious matters (cf. Deut. 17:8–13; 2 Chron. 19:8–11). Each court system had layers of lesser courts (cf. Deut. 1:15–16). The judges taught the laws to the people (2 Chron. 17:7–9).

The Law required witnesses to tell the truth or suffer the same penalty as the accused one (Exod. 23:1–3; Deut. 19:15–19). Two or three witnesses had to testify in order to convict anyone of a serious crime. Accused individuals could not be convicted on the basis of only one witness's testimony (Deut. 17:6). Anyone who refused to accept the verdict of the court could be put to death (Deut. 17:12–13).

The courts had room for mercy, though. When individuals committed murder by accident, they could live in a city of refuge (i.e., a city where they could live without being punished; Deut. 19:1–13). But they could enter the city only by convincing the city's judges that the killing was accidental.

Political leaders. God would not allow anyone who had a physical handicap to serve in a position of leadership. He banned from office any male who was sexually maimed or who was born out of wedlock, and anyone who was a Moabite or an Ammonite (mixed races). The Law prevented these individuals from entering the "assembly of the LORD," the chief political body of the nation (Deut. 23:1–3).

God gave Israel specific instructions for choosing a king (Deut. 17:14–20). God required a king who would submit to the laws of the covenant, fully in keeping with the teachings of the rest of the Pentateuch.

Criminal laws. The criminal laws of Israel can be divided into several categories. Of course, all crimes were serious because they were sins against God. But some crimes were more destructive, and they carried a heavier penalty. Crimes against individuals, crimes against morality, crimes against property, crimes against religion, and crimes against society were all covered by legal statutes.

Dedication laws. Israelites learned that the firstborn of every family and animal and the firstfruits of harvests belonged to God. Because God counted Israel his firstborn among the nations, he called the nation to dedicate itself to serving him (Exod. 4:22–23).

God claimed the Israelites as his people while they still lived in Egypt. In response, they followed Moses into the wilderness and entered into a *covenant* (a "treaty" or "agreement") with God at Mount Sinai. They agreed to let the tribe of Levi represent the firstborn of the nation in its worship ceremony (Num. 3:40–41; 8:18). The other Israelites paid a fee to excuse their own firstborn children from this duty (Lev. 27:1–8). Once a year they sacrificed the firstborn of all flocks and herds and produce from the fields to the Lord (Deut. 14:22–27). After the Israelites settled in Canaan, God told them to give these firstfruits to the Levites (Lev. 23:10, 17). This demonstrated that the land and all its yield belonged to God.

The tithe system allowed all of the Israelites to offer their possessions to God. It spread the responsibility for maintaining worship among the rich and the poor, the willing and the unwilling. God ordered the Israelites not to plant their land in the seventh year (Exod. 23:10–11), and did not require a tithe that year. God expected Israel to recognize his lordship, but he demanded only a portion of their property for himself.

In addition to these tithes, every adult male over the age of 20 of the wilderness generation paid a poll tax to raise funds for constructing the tabernacle (Exod. 38:24–31).

Dietary laws. God gave the Israelites a special diet to emphasize that they were a special people (Deut. 12:15). He did not allow them to eat improperly butchered meat (Lev. 7:22–27) or any of the firstfruits from a plant (Exod. 23:19; 34:26).

He gave them many other rules about their diet. Here are some examples. They could not eat

• Blood, because life was in the blood (Deut. 12:23) and because blood was a covering (atonement) for sin (Lev. 17:11).

• Animal fat, because it should be offered to God (Lev. 7:23, 31).

• Animals killed by wild beasts or animals that died of natural causes (Lev. 7:22–27).

• Scavenger animals, such as vultures (Deut. 14:12–19), or organs that remove impurities from an animal's body (Exod. 29:13, 22).

• Water animals with no scales or fins (Deut. 14:9–10).

• Crawling or flying insects, except those of the locust and beetle families (Lev. 11:22–23).

• Anything that had been left open in a room with a dead or dying person (Num. 19:11–22).

• Goat's kid boiled in its mother's milk, because this was a pagan ritual of the Canaanites (Exod. 23:19).

Personal and family rights laws. A survey of the laws of the Bible shows that they guarded the rights of individuals and their families. The Law required children to respect and obey their parents, and parents were to raise their children to serve and obey God (Deut. 6:7). The Bible set strict limits on marriage to make sure that family life would be decent and wholesome.

Slaves kept their dignity as human beings. No Israelite could be forced into slavery. Even when they signed contracts to become servants, God's law canceled the agreement at the end of seven years (Exod. 21:2–6). Slaves could become members of their owner's families. They enjoyed the rights of other family members, except the right of inheritance. If the slaves were foreigners, their owners could circumcise the males and invite them to worship with other Jews (Exod. 12:43–44; Deut. 12:18; 16:10–11).

When owners punished slaves so harshly that they died, the Law branded them as murderers (Exod. 21:20). If the slaves did not die, the Law did nothing—God judged that the owners suffered enough by having disabled slaves (Exod. 21:21). If the owners inflicted a permanent injury—for example, if slaves lost eyes or teeth—the slaves would go free (Exod. 21:26–27).

Even though the Bible allowed slavery, its regulations reminded the Israelites that every person was created in the image of God—including the slave.

The Bible preserved the right to personal property, and a number of laws regulated this. Borrowing was a sacred trust:

• Owners could claim any property that had been lost or stolen.

• Whoever borrowed property had to return it in good condition.

• If borrowers lost the property or if it was stolen, they still had to repay the owner.

• If borrowers schemed to "lose" the property, they had to repay the owner double (Exod. 22:7–15).

God owned the land and set out the rules of inheritance. A firstborn son received a double portion of the property (Deut. 21:15–17; 25:6); however, a wicked son might receive nothing. And if there was no son, a daughter could inherit the property (Num. 27:7–8). In that case, she had to marry a member of her own tribe to keep the property within the family (Num. 36:1–12). Anyone who inherited a piece of property had to use it to care for relatives because he (or she) became the head of the family.

Quarantine laws. God laid down strict rules about death, illness, childbirth, and a woman's menstrual period. The Israelites learned that these things could make them unclean and unfit for acceptable worship (cf. Lev. 12; 14:1–32; 15).

The Israelites knew that God was a God of the living, so they accepted that they must keep death away from their worship. If they touched a corpse, they could not go to a worship service until they had cleansed themselves (Lev. 22:3–7).

God blessed marriage and the raising of a family (Deut. 28:11), but the laws on childbirth reminded the Israelites that they were born in sin. A woman who bore a child had to cleanse herself by rituals, and so did the midwife and anyone else who attended the birth (cf. Lev. 12).

These laws also reminded the Israelites that sexual experiences were not a part of their worship. This set them farther apart from other ancient cultures for whom fertility rites and temple prostitutes formed an important part of worship.

Religious obligation laws. The Law did not simply describe the rights of individuals but also stated their responsibilities to God. All persons owed their lives to Yahweh, and so the community expected them to serve God and remain loyal to God's people.

God bound his people to follow his law and no other. The leaders recorded his law and commanded the people of Israel to study and remember it (Deut. 4:2; Num. 15:37–41; Lev. 18:4–5). God's law demanded their reverence, obedience, and service. And as long as Israel obeyed God's commands, they lived in harmony with him.

Religious symbolism laws. God commanded the Israelites to wear certain symbols to show their dedication. For example, Jewish men wore phylacteries—tiny containers that held key Bible texts. The OT often mentions the phylacteries, but gives no specific command from God concerning them (Exod. 13:9; Deut. 6:8; 11:18). Israelites tied the phylacteries to their foreheads or left hands or to the doorposts of their homes.

God told the Israelites to wear blue fringes (or tassels) on their garments (Num. 15:37–41; Deut. 22:12), which showed their commitment to God's royal law. Jesus wore them (Matt. 9:20), but condemned Jews who made their fringes large to boast of their dedication to God (Matt. 23:5).

Intertestamental Law

The Jewish notion of law changed somewhat between the writing of the OT and the NT. God had given the law of Moses to the people of Israel in the midst of historic events—especially those involving Moses during the Exodus—and the later prophets and priests had interpreted that law for their own day. Their interpretation usually included a hope for national independence and superiority (Isa. 60:1–3; Jer. 31; Joel 3:18f.)—a hope that rested on the Jews' obedience to God's covenant. After centuries of failing to actualize this hope, this theme disappeared from prophecy. In fact, the role of prophecy itself diminished during the intertestamental period.

For the Jews, making the law meaningful for their own day became less important than making it meaningful for that day when God would come to reward them. They began to stress the law's ceremonial prescriptions. Almsgiving, festivals, ritual prayers, and temple rites became significant in the Jewish community.

Jesus and the Law

Jesus' attitude toward the law is a topic of much debate. Some scholars believe he merely interpreted Mosaic law like the Pharisees, without changing it. Others believe that Jesus penetrated past the letter of the law to reveal its great moral and spiritual principles. In more recent years, commentators have noted that some of Jesus' statements seem to be in direct conflict with the Mosaic law. These commentators have made several attempts to resolve these conflicts. At least three of their interpretations have gained some popularity: fulfillment, sovereignty, and inscrutability.

Fulfillment view. Jesus said, "Think not that I have come to abolish the law and the prophets; I have come not to abolish them but to fulfill them" (Matt. 5:17, RSV). Apparent conflicts appear between Jesus' teachings and Mosaic law (e.g., his teachings on divorce). However, the fulfillment view tries to show that, if we look beyond appearances, we can harmonize Jesus' actions with the OT in every case.

Sovereignty view. Commentators of this approach hold that when a disagreement exists between Jesus and Pharisaic law, Jesus' word is authoritative. They base this view upon Jesus' statements such as, "You have heard that it was said, 'You shall love your neighbor, and hate your enemy.' But I say to you . . ." (Matt. 5:43–44, NASB). Exponents of the sovereignty view point out that the OT nowhere says, "You shall hate your enemy." That was a teaching of the Pharisees.

Inscrutability view. Commentators who favor this approach believe that we cannot determine Jesus' attitude toward the law. Even if we could determine his attitude, they doubt if it could be expressed in a clean, neat formula.

Dialogue with the Pharisees

What can we see of the relationship between Jesus' teachings and Moses' law, according to the biblical witness? We rely heavily on the gospel of Matthew, since Matthew and his audience were deeply concerned with Jewish matters.

We find that Jesus said various things concerning the law. For example, in controversies such as that about gathering grain and eating it on the Sabbath (Matt. 12:1–8), Jesus made it clear that he superseded the law. He said, "I tell you, something greater than the temple is here" (v. 6, RSV). The Pharisees were not looking for anything greater than the temple, where God's law was preserved. It amazed them to hear anyone claim that something was greater than the repository of God's Word. Jesus not only refused to submit to their interpretation of the law, but declared himself greater than it: "The Son of Man is also Lord of the Sabbath" (Mark 2:28).

In other instances, though, Jesus preserved the law. For example, in Matthew 23:2ff., Jesus admonished the crowd to do all that the scribes and Pharisees told them, for they "sit in Moses' seat." Then, however, he attacked the Pharisees' hypocrisy. Some have asked if this means that Jesus changed his position in the course of the sermon, or that he was making a distinction between the Pharisees' relaying Moses' law faithfully and embroidering it falsely. Scholars disagree.

Did Jesus bring a new and greater law? Or did he merely challenge the Pharisaic interpretations and hypocrisy? We can see the dialogue between Jesus and the Pharisees in many circumstances, and more than one witness writes about it. Yet several common themes stand out:

• Jesus did not separate himself from Mosaic law (Matt. 5:17).
• Unlike the Pharisees, Jesus emphasized God's love—though he did warn of God's judgment (Matt. 7:21).
• Jesus' behavior fit no mold of this world and he made no attempt to compete as a rabbi among rabbis, nor did he try to fill the traditional role of the Messiah.

Paul and the Law

Paul affirmed and criticized the law. He declared that God had finished with it, but also that he had established it. Many of Paul's teachings on this subject are strongly stated:
• "For Christ is the end of the law for righteousness to everyone who believes" (Rom. 10:4).
• "Do we then make void the law through faith? Certainly not! On the contrary, we establish the law" (Rom. 3:31).
• "For I through the law died to the law that I might live to God" (Gal. 2:19).
How can we integrate these divergent emphases? Here are four things to consider: Paul's world, the Jerusalem council, Paul's theme of faith versus law, and Jesus and Paul.

Paul's World

To make sense of this tension in Paul's teachings, we need to understand the times in which he lived. When Paul wrote, Jerusalem was still intact. The Sadducees and Zealots were powers to be reckoned with, but there was no unified Jewish opposition to Christianity. Paul was part of a fledgling religious community that took its place alongside the other Jewish sects.

As the church spread into gentile territory, a serious question arose: Should Gentiles who are unfamiliar with the law be required to learn and practice it when they become Christians?

The Jerusalem Council

Acts 15 and Galatians 2 describe how the church convened an apostolic council to decide this issue. The congregation at Jerusalem was headed by James, brother of Jesus. James believed that the Jewish Christians should obey Jewish law (although none of them did it fully). Gentile Christians could be permitted a certain amount of freedom from it. A dissenting faction existed in the church, though (Acts 15:5; Gal. 2:4). They believed that all Christians should obey the Jewish law, and they were called Judaizers.

Paul went to Jerusalem to validate his preaching (Gal. 2:1–3), particularly on the relation of the law to the gospel of Christ. The outcome was a brotherly agreement between Paul, James, and Peter.

Unlike Jesus, who wrote nothing that we know of, Paul wrote weighty doctrinal and pastoral letters. Although some of them circulated among several churches (cf. Col. 4:16), Paul often wrote with the local problems of a particular congregation in his mind, such as his letters to the Corinthians.

For this reason, he seems to have different opinions on the law in his letters. At Corinth, for example, Paul's opponents were Hellenistic with little use for the law or its morality. Paul took a conservative stand in responding to them. To the Galatians, on the other hand, he faced the Judaizers and emphasized freedom from law. While there was a definite theological development from the writing of 1 Thessalonians (believed the earliest extant letter) to Romans, Colossians, and Ephesians, we do not want to ignore Paul's specific local themes. It is instructive to compare Paul's letters to congregations where the general disposition is to practice the letter of the law (e.g., the churches of Galatia) and those to congregations where the feeling is opposite (e.g., Corinth).

After Paul left the Jerusalem council, he ministered primarily to Hellenistic Jewish communities. Their people had some notion of Jewish law mixed with gentile ideas. In most congregations, Jewish Christians worshiped beside Gentile Christians. One group was expected to obey the law; the other was released from most of it. It is no wonder that the issue of the law required so much of Paul's attention.

Paul's Theme of Faith Versus Law

Probably the most dominant theme in all of Paul's writings is that the law is subordinate to faith in Christ: "A man is not justified by the works of the law but by faith in Jesus Christ" (Gal. 2:16; cf. Rom. 1—4; Phil. 3).

Paul taught that no law can bring justification. The new covenant is based on the work of the Holy Spirit in the heart, and not on "tablets of stone" (an obvious reference to Mosaic law; 2 Cor. 3:3). Paul knew that God's law could be and was made the basis of a legalistic, self-justifying habit of mind. When it is so abused, the observers are doomed under the law. This legal condemnation is the opposite of being under grace—the grace of Christ's redeeming death (Rom. 6:14). Paul never attacked the righteous content of the law, only the lethal manner in which it operated.

In what way has the law been superseded by faith in Christ? Paul declared that all of us, Jews and Gentiles, have been under the judgment of the law (Rom. 5:12–19), but Christ freed us from this judgment through the cross (Rom. 7:4; 8:1ff.; Gal. 2:21). All of Paul's preaching centered on Christ crucified (1 Cor. 1:17ff.). If we are to understand his attitude toward the law, we must see it in light of Jesus' crucifixion.

Paul understood that Jesus died to open for us a way of salvation (Gal. 2:21)—he died so that we might cease from trying to make ourselves right with God by obeying the law. Jesus substituted himself for us, so that we would not have to bear it (2 Cor. 5:19–21; Gal. 3:13; Col. 2:14).

Jesus and Paul

While Jesus and Paul affirmed the value of Jewish law, they directed early Christians beyond the law. Neither man taught that the Jewish law was evil in itself. They simply pointed out that law cannot justify sinners before God.

The early Christians did not understand the law and gospel as opposites; nor did they simplify their way of relating law and gospel to a formula.

*The Laws of Israel*____

In giving the law to Moses, God gave many laws—all for the welfare of his covenant people. All laws were to help them live in harmony with one another and in right relationship with the God who created them, delivered them from Egypt, and would be with them as their God.

Let's look at these laws and see their practicality.

The Ten Commandments

The Ten Commandments are laws given by God to the Israelites as guidelines for daily living. The first four refer to our relationship with God. Commandments five through 10 pertain to our relationships with one another.

These commandments form the basis of the covenant between God and the nations. These laws are called by several different names: *Ten Words* (Hebrew, Exod. 34:28; Deut. 4:13), *Moral Law, Decalogue* (Greek, "Ten Words"), *Tablets of the Covenant* (Deut. 9:9), *Covenant* (Deut. 4:13), and *Commandments* (Matt. 19:17; Rom. 13:9).

In the OT, two versions appear of the Ten Commandments. The first is Exodus 20, and the other is Deuteronomy 5. They are almost verbally identical except that the reasons given for the observance of the fourth commandment are different. In Exodus, the reason is based on the obligation to God as creator (cf. Gen. 2:3). In Deuteronomy, the reasons are the duty to others and the memory of the bondage in Egypt. Some have concluded that the original law was simply, "Remember the Sabbath day, to keep it holy." It may be that the form in Exodus is the original, and when Moses reviewed the law before leaving the Israelites, he added a fuller reason because of their history.

1. "You shall have no other gods before Me" (Exod. 20:3). Since God's character forms the basis of the covenant with the Hebrew people, he demanded absolute loyalty. When the intent of the heart is to put God first, people's outward actions will reveal it. Others will then see what God's character is like through the actions of his people.

2. "You shall not make for yourself a carved image" (Exod. 20:4). The second commandment is necessary because people do not always keep the first. The Israelites made a golden calf to worship at the very time God was giving the law to Moses. And since Israel had so many contacts with people who did worship images, including replicas of their earthly rulers, God gave them this law. God has never been a tangible, visible Being (Deut. 4:12), but always a Spirit (John 4:24).

3. "You shall not take the name of the LORD your God in vain" (Exod. 20:7). God's name and his character are inseparable. Using his holy name lightly in a frivolous, empty manner is insulting and degrading. Taking God's name in vain happens when individuals perjure themselves in a court of law or when they curse. However, this com-

mandment also applies to hypocritical worship, using God's name in meaningless prayer and praise (Isa. 29:13).

4. "Remember the Sabbath day, to keep it holy" (Exod. 20:8). *Sabbath* means "rest," and God intended for this day to stand for more than an absence of work. It was to be a day of worship as well—a day for setting aside all thoughts of materialistic gain to think about him. God himself set the pattern by ceasing from his labors after creating the world.

5. "Honor your father and your mother, that your days may be long upon the land" (Exod. 20:12). God established parents as authority figures in the family unit. Children get their first impressions about God from their parents. Parents who honestly desire to follow the guidelines of the Scriptures set better examples for their children. And children who want to please God will respect their parents, regardless of pressure from the world and their peers.

6. "You shall not murder" (Exod. 20:13). The breakdown of this guideline has plunged many civilizations into decay. Persons who care about others, beginning with those in the home, do not want to harm them. This law reveals God's attitude toward the human race—created in his image. No one has the right to take that life from another.

7. "You shall not commit adultery" (Exod. 20:14). Technically, this commandment refers to being sexually involved with a married person; but it is traditionally used to prohibit all sexual relationships outside marriage. Again, this commandment involves a right relationship with God and with others. Adultery is possible when people are prepared to hurt others, to enjoy themselves at the expense of other people. A right attitude toward keeping God first and not harming others is tied together in these commandments. People who do not steal will not take others' mates. They do not allow covetous thoughts to grow in their minds because they want God to have their total allegiance.

8. "You shall not steal" (Exod. 20:15). Stealing involves taking something that does not belong to you. This could be another's life, marriage partner, or reputation. This law also emphasizes the importance of getting all you own through lawful channels.

9. "You shall not bear false witness against your neighbor" (Exod. 20:16). A good relationship demands honesty in speaking of another.

10. "You shall not covet" (Exod. 20:17). Jesus elaborated on this commandment by stating, "You shall love your neighbor as yourself" (Matt. 22:39). The negative and the positive work together. You do not harm people you care about.

All of these commandments grow out of loyalty and commitment to God. When people turn their hearts toward God, they will have the right attitude toward others. Consequently, the desires that rise from their inner beings will not cause pain or loss to others. The right motive—pleasing God who is first—will result in obeying the other commandments (not hurting others).

Jesus enlarged on the idea prevalent in the Ten Commandments by emphasizing the heart attitude: "Blessed are the pure in heart, for they shall see God" (Matt. 5:8).

Laws

God commanded the Hebrew people to keep themselves from pagan religious and cultic practices (Exod. 20:3–5; Lev. 19:27). Among these practices were boiling a kid in its mother's milk (Deut. 14:21); shaving one's head in a particular way (Lev. 21:5); worshiping idols (Deut. 7:5, 25; 12:2–3); sacrificing children (Lev. 20:2); participating in homosexuality and temple prostitution (Lev. 19:29); slashing or tattooing one's body (Lev. 19:28); and practicing magic, sorcery, or divination (Lev. 19:26, 31).

God's people were to preserve and study the Lord's law (Deut. 4:2; 6:6–7); revere his name (Deut. 8:6, 11–12); be thankful (Deut. 8:10); and obey, love, and serve their redeemer God (Deut. 6:4–5; 10:14–16; 11:1, 13–14).

Other laws dealt with personal and family rights, property rights, and humane treatment of otherwise defenseless animals and people.

Aliens. Male aliens could convert to Judaism, be circumcised, and become full members of the covenant community (Num. 9:14; 15:12–15). Even if aliens temporarily or permanently living as free people in Israel did not convert, they were to receive full privileges under the civil law (Num. 15:29–30). Unlike Jews, aliens ate foods declared unclean by God. Such foods could be sold or given to them (Deut. 14:21).

Israelites were forbidden to take advantage of poor Hebrews by charging them interest for the loan of food, clothing, money, or anything else (Exod. 22:25; Lev. 25:35–37). However, poor aliens could be charged interest, perhaps because the Israelites considered their status a result of God's judgment (Deut. 23:20).

Animals. Animal laws were also environmental laws. For example, Israel was commanded not to work the land in the seventh year. Whatever grain or fruit grew up was to be left for the animals and the poor. This forced a crop rotation system so the Hebrew people would have some harvest every year (Exod. 23:10–11; Lev. 25:3–7).

They were allowed to eat certain wild beasts and birds but were forbidden to take the mother. Presumably, they could take the young or the eggs, but they were required to let the mother live (Deut. 22:6–7). An ox or any working beast (or human being) was to be fed adequately to give strength for required work (Deut. 25:4). Animals were not to be cruelly beaten or overloaded. They were to rest on the Sabbath (Exod. 20:8–11; 23:12).

Animals, Lost. Straying animals were to be returned to the owners or cared for until claimed (Exod. 23:4–5; Deut. 22:1–4).

Army. An important category of civil law consisted of laws regulating the army.

All Canaan belonged to God. Within its borders his people were commanded to wage war to gain and to maintain the territory. To this end all Israelite males 20 years of age and older formed a militia (Num. 1:20–43), with 50 probably being the exemption age. If only a small-scale war was being fought, a selective service system operated by the casting of lots (Num. 31:3–6). Kings were to maintain only small standing armies.

Certain citizens were exempt from the military: priests and Levites (Num. 1:48–49), men who had not yet dedicated their newly built homes (Deut. 20:5), those who had not gathered the first harvest from a field or vineyard (Deut. 20:6), men who were engaged to be married (Deut. 20:7), and men who had been married within a year of the call to arms (Deut. 24:5).

Within Canaan during wartime every non-Israelite was to be killed and all their possessions and goods offered to God (Deut. 20:16–18). In that way they would purify the territory and guard themselves from Canaanite idolatry. When the Israelites were fighting outside Canaan, a city attacked was to be offered peace before the attack. Refusal triggered the attack. All the citizens and goods of that city then became rightful slaves and booty (Deut. 20:10–15).

Criminals. God defined what a criminal offense was and the proper punishment for each offense. All crimes were sins, or offenses, against God's law. Since there were degrees of punishments, there were degrees of sin under the law. God prohibited the Israelites from punishing criminals excessively (Deut. 25:1–3).

Exclusions. God commanded that several categories of people not be allowed to vote or serve in office. These included the physically handicapped, the sexually maimed, those of illegitimate birth, or persons of a mixed race such as Moabites or Ammonites (Deut. 23:1–3). These laws were another of the repeated attempts by God to teach Israel in a concrete manner that they were to be spiritually clean and perfect before him.

Inheritance laws.   Normally only legitimate sons inherited the family's property. The firstborn son received twice as much as the others (Deut. 21:15–17; 25:6). He was responsible for caring for elderly family members and providing a respectable burial for them. A wicked son could be disinherited. If no sons were born to a family, legitimate daughters were to inherit the property (Num. 27:7–8). Such heiresses had to marry within their own tribe or lose the inheritance (Num. 36:1–12).

Judges.   The judges of the book of Judges functioned as temporary military leaders. They also handled some of the legal functions of modern judges. Israel's kings were different from these judges because they were permanent and maintained a standing army, a governmental network, and a royal court supported by taxation.

Judges were of two classes, priestly and nonpriestly (elders). The priestly judges presided over religious lawsuits, and elders presided over civil lawsuits (Deut. 17:8–13; 2 Chron. 19:8, 11). Judges, also called elders, were to be elected from among heads of households (Exod. 18:13–26).

Judges were charged not to be partial in favor of the rich or against the poor, widows, aliens, or others who might be helpless (Exod. 23:6–9; Deut. 16:18–20; 27:19). Consequently, they were to hear the witnesses carefully, examine the evidence, and make their decisions on the basis of what God had revealed in his written law. They also presided over making or nullifying all contracts.

Land ownership.   Ultimately, the Israelites believed that God owned all the land (Lev. 25:23). He demanded that his tenants rest the land every seventh year by not planting a crop (Lev. 25:1–7). During this seventh year, all travelers and the poor were allowed to eat of the produce of the land without paying for it.

All parcels of land were assigned permanently to certain families; they reverted back to those original owners or their heirs every fiftieth year (Lev. 25:8–24). The land could also be purchased by those owners at its original selling price (Lev. 25:29–31) in the interim. Furthermore, it was a serious matter to move the ancient markers that designated the boundaries of the land. Within walled cities, only Levites owned houses in a permanent sense (Lev. 25:32–34).

Law enforcement.   Refusal to comply with what the court decided (contempt of court) brought a sentence of death (Deut. 17:12–13). The citizens of ancient Israel were the law enforcers and bailiffs (Deut. 16:18). Usually executions were in the hands of the citizens (Deut. 13:9–10). Later, the king's private army enforced his will while Levites also served as officials, or police (2 Chron. 19:11).

Marriage.   God prohibited the Israelites from marrying near relatives and members of their own immediate family (Lev. 18:6–18; Deut. 27:20–23). He also forbade intermarriage with the Canaanites because these pagans would lead their mates into idolatry (Deut. 7:1–4).

If Canaanites converted and became Israelites (members of God's covenantal community), no legal and religious bar prevented marriage with them. A man could marry a woman prisoner of war after she mourned her parents' deaths for a month. This did not necessarily mean her parents were actually dead, but only that this woman now became an Israelite. If her husband divorced her, she had to be set free (Deut. 21:10–14). Her marriage had made her a full citizen under the law—an Israelite.

Special laws also regulated the marriage of priests. A priest could not marry a former harlot, a woman who had been previously married, or a woman who had previously had sexual relations; a priest was to marry a virgin Israelite (Lev. 21:7, 13–15).

Infidelity was punishable by death. Divorce was granted on many grounds other than the breaking of the one-flesh relationship through sexual union with another person or beast and the willful abandonment of the marriage (Deut. 24:1–4). If a man wrongfully accused his wife of infidelity (Deut. 22:17–19), he could not divorce her.

Parents and children. The law assumed that parents would act responsibly and feed and clothe their children even as God fed and clothed them. Parents also were to discipline and teach their children (Deut. 6:6–7). A father was responsible for circumcising his sons (Gen. 17:12–13), redeeming his firstborn from God (Num. 18:15–16), and finding his children proper marriage partners (Gen. 24:4).

Children were commanded to respect and obey their parents (Exod. 20:12). Disrespect in the form of striking or cursing a parent and delinquency (stubbornness and disobedience expressed in gluttony and drunkenness) were punishable by death (Exod. 21:15, 17; Deut. 21:18–21). Minor children were under their parents' authority and could not make binding vows. Unmarried girls were not allowed to make binding vows without their fathers' or their male guardians' agreement (Num. 30:3–5).

Property, Damaged. Property held in trust was protected under the law. Persons caught stealing had to restore to the owners double the value of the goods stolen. If the goods were stolen through carelessness by trustees of the property, trustees had to repay the full amount missing.

Borrowed goods had to be returned. If they were damaged or lost while borrowed, they had to be replaced by the borrowers (Exod. 22:14–15).

Property, Lost. Under Mosaic law, all lost property was to be returned to its owner if the owner was known or if it was to be held until claimed by him (Deut. 22:1–4).

Property, Unsafe. Owners were held responsible for unsafe property. If individuals (or animals) were hurt because of owners' properties, the owners paid a penalty. In the case of a person's death, the property owners lost their own lives (Exod. 21:28–36; Deut. 22:8).

Prophets. God's law strictly prohibited idolatry and provided for the death of those who would lead Israel into idolatry. The test of a true prophet was not his ability to work miracles but his faithfulness to God. The people of Israel were to obey the words of true prophets. If they did not do so, God himself would punish the people.

Refuge cities. Judges controlled the entrance into the refuge cities. These were the cities where those who had committed accidental murder (manslaughter) could flee to safety. When the high priest of the nation died, refugees were free to go home without penalty (Exod. 21:12–14; Deut. 19:1–13). Israel was responsible for keeping the roads to such cities as safe as possible so the fugitive could outrun the avenger—the relative responsible for the fugitive's execution to repay the kinsman's death.

Servants, Hired. God especially protected the poor from the ravages of the rich. One such measure was the law requiring employers to pay their hired help a just and fair wage and to do it at the end of each workday (Lev. 19:13; Deut. 24:14).

Slaves. Slaves were of two classes, indentured and permanent. Hebrews who were unable to pay debts were indentured, or committed to temporary servitude. The indenture lasted only six years or until the year of Jubilee. A male slave might be given a wife while in this state, but the wife and children resulting from the union were bound to the master. Such men could bind themselves permanently to the master either for the master's sake or for that of their family (Exod. 21:2–6).

Israelites indentured because of poverty were not to be thought of or treated as slaves. They were to be treated as hired servants. For example, they were to be paid. 16:12–14). They could be bought out of the situation by relatives or themselves— presumably by savings resulting from their wages while indentured (Lev. 25:39–43, 47–55).

A girl or woman sold to a man as a wife was especially protected. She could be redeemed by her family if the master was not satisfied with her, she could not be sold as a slave to foreign people, and she was to be treated as a daughter and provided for in the same way as other wives. If these laws were disobeyed, her freedom was granted (Exod. 21:7–11).

Permanent slaves could be acquired by purchase or as prisoners of war. They were to be taken only from the nations and peoples outside Canaan (Lev. 25:44–46). Fugitive slaves were not to be returned to their owners or treated as slaves—a provision that forced masters to treat slaves humanely (Deut. 23:15–16).

Slaves were considered permanent members of their masters' households; they were circumcised and admitted to Passover (Exod. 12:43–44) and all the special festivals and sacrifices, except the guilt offering (Deut. 12:17–18; 16:10–11). Slaves could be forced to work; yet if they were beaten severely, they were to be freed (Exod. 21:21, 26–27). If slaves were killed, their masters were punished (Exod. 21:20).

Witnesses. Witnesses were charged by God to tell the truth (Lev. 19:16). If they did not do so, they were judged by him. If their deception was discovered, they were to bear the penalty involved in the case (Exod. 23:1–3; Deut. 19:15–19).

Conviction of serious crimes required two or more witnesses (Num. 35:30). Written documents and other testimony could be used as evidence against the accused.

Crimes

Under God's law, all of life was religious, but some crimes were considered especially directed against the worship system that God had established. Conviction in these cases resulted in death, because such crimes struck pointedly at God and life itself.

Crimes against God included worshiping other gods alongside God (Exod. 22:20; 34:14), turning from God to worship other gods (Deut. 13:1–18), seeking to control other people and future events by magic or sorcery (Exod. 22:18; Deut. 18:9–14), sacrificing children to false gods (Lev. 18:21; 20:2–5), being blasphemous (Lev. 24:16), offering false prophecy (Deut. 18:18–20), and doing work on the Sabbath other than that permitted by God (Exod. 35:2–3; Matt. 21:1–8).

Certain crimes were against society as a whole. Among these were the perversion of justice through bribery, torture of witnesses, and false testimony or perjury (Exod. 23:1–7; Deut. 19:16–21). Judges were commanded to treat all people equally.

Biblical law relating to sexual morality protected and sanctified the family. The sexual union of two persons made them one flesh, and this was the only such union they were to experience.

Crimes of violence against others were serious criminal offenses. Biblical law, unlike other ancient Near Eastern codes, placed a higher value on human life than on possessions. But it also allowed people to have private possessions by protecting them from theft and fraud.

The following crimes are dealt with in the Bible.

Adultery. Under God's law, adultery was a serious crime, perhaps because tearing apart the two who had become one amounted to murder. Those convicted of adultery were to be put to death (Lev. 20:10–12; Deut. 22:22). A betrothed woman (virgin) was protected by the law, but she was also considered to be married in some cases. If she and some man other than her betrothed had sexual union, they were to be put to death (Deut. 22:23–24).

Assault and battery. God's law expected people to live at peace with one another. But realizing that offenses might occur, God provided legislation about assault and battery. If injuring persons caused them to lose time but no further harm was done, the offenders had to pay victims for the time lost. Presumably the courts established the fine in such cases (Exod. 21:18–19). When they maimed their foes in a struggle, they would pay for the lost time and also suffer the same disfigurement at the hands of the court (Lev. 24:19).

God provided for exceptions to this punishment:

• If the victim were a slave, disfigurement resulted in the slave's freedom (a very heavy financial loss to the guilty party).

• If the slave survived and was not disfigured, there was no penalty on the master, except that exacted for loss of time (Exod. 21:20–21, 26–27).

• If a son or daughter attacked either parent, the attacker was to be put to death (Exod. 21:15).

• A woman's hand was to be cut off for attacking a man's genitals, even though she may have been trying to protect her husband (Deut. 25:11–12).

Bestiality. Having sex with a beast (a common feature of Canaanite worship) was an offense punishable by death (Exod. 22:19; Lev. 18:23; Deut. 27:21).

Blackmail and loan fraud. God's law counted these crimes as a kind of theft, mandating heavy fines and possible indentured service as penalties (Exod. 22:1–3; Lev. 6:1–7).

Encroachment. The land was marked into sections by ancient landmarks, according to the allotments made shortly after it was conquered. To move these landmarks resulted in God's curse. This act was considered stealing from neighbors as well as rebellion against God the great landowner (Deut. 19:14; 27:17).

Falsification of weights and measures. Ancient Israel did not use money; transactions were in measured, or weighed, precious metals. God prohibited juggling weights so the goods or metals would be measured to favor thieves. Such thieves had to repay their victims (Lev. 19:35–36; Deut. 25:13–16).

Fornication. In Israel the sexual union was most sacred. A newly married woman charged with premarital sex with a man other than her husband was to be put to death if the charge was proven. If the charge was not proven, her husband had to pay a large fine and keep her as his wife. Also, he could then never divorce her (Deut. 22:13–21).

Homosexuality. Sodomy, or male homosexuality, was pointedly condemned and prohibited. It brought death under God's law (Lev. 20:13). By implication, the same penalty was probably meted out for female homosexuality, or lesbianism.

Incest. Sexual union with one's own offspring or near relative was to result in death (Lev. 20:11–12, 14).

Kidnapping. Capturing individuals to sell or use them as slaves was a capital offense (Deut. 24:7). This prohibition extended to foreigners (unless they were prisoners of war; Exod. 22:21–24), the blind and deaf (Lev. 19:14), and other helpless people (Deut. 27:19).

Miscarriage, Violently induced. Miscarriage or the death of the mother resulting from a blow by someone in a fight brought death upon the attacker. Premature birth caused by this offense required a monetary fine determined by the husband as governed by the courts (Exod. 21:22–23).

Murder. The willful and premeditated taking of a human life was punishable by death. Accidental killing, killing as an act of war, and lawful executions were not considered murder (Exod. 21:12–14; Num. 35:14–34). The sixth commandment said, "You shall not murder." Jesus pointed to the spirit of this commandment when he expanded it to forbid hatred, anger, bitter insults, and cursing (Matt. 5:21–22).

Oppression.   In Israel, the defenseless were to be defended. Those without rights or power to enforce their rights were protected by God. These included the alien passing through the area and the alien who was a temporary or permanent resident. The widow, orphan, deaf, blind, slave, hired hand, and poor were to be given just wages and were to be paid immediately; they were to receive interest-free loans (except aliens) in emergencies, gifts of food at festivals, and the privilege of gleaning (Exod. 22:21–24; Lev. 19:14, 33; Deut. 24:14; 27:18–19).

Prostitution.   Prostitutes of every guise (male or female, cultic or noncultic) were to be put to death (Lev. 19:29; 21:9).

Rape and seduction.   A man who raped a betrothed woman was to be put to death (Deut. 22:25–27). However, if he raped or seduced an unattached woman, he was to pay a large fine and propose marriage. A girl's father could refuse the marriage and keep the money, but if the father approved, the rapist had to marry the girl and could never divorce her (Exod. 22:16–17; Deut. 22:28–29).

If the seduced girl was a betrothed slave, she was considered unattached (for she had not yet been released from slavery). Consequently, the attacker was not put to death. But the man had to bring a guilt offering to God to make restitution for his sin.

Slander.   Slander (making malicious statements about another person) was forbidden and punished if the crime was committed during a trial (Exod. 23:1). This was viewed as a mortal attack on a person (Lev. 19:16).

Stealing.   God prohibited anyone from stealing from another person. Heavy financial penalties were levied upon the thief. For example, if a man stole an ox and could not return it, he had to pay its owner five times the animal's value. If he stole a sheep, he had to pay four times the normal value. (Oxen were worth more because they were beasts of burden.) If the thief was able to return the beast he had stolen, he still had to pay the owner twice its value. If the thief could not afford to pay, he was required to be an indentured servant to pay the debt (Exod. 22:1–5). If the farmer discovered the thief at night and killed him, the judge let the farmer go free.

Life in Bible Times

Agriculture_____

Agriculture refers to the various operations connected with the cultivation of the soil. It includes the sowing and harvesting of vegetables, grains, and fruits or flowers, as well as the raising of animal herds. Hebrew agriculture developed with the growth of the Hebrew nation.

Mosaic law encouraged agricultural development among the landowners (Deut. 26:1–11). When the Hebrews entered the Promised Land, each family received its own allotment of land. The Law did not permit a family to sell its land or to relinquish permanent rights to it; it was to remain the family inheritance (Deut. 19:14).

Conditions Affecting Agriculture

The farmers of Israel found unique challenges in the water and soil of Palestine.

Soil

The country's irregular land surface offered a variety of soil, frequently fertile but shallow and rocky (Isa. 5:2). The soil varied from dark, heavy loam to light, well-aerated sand.

Some areas produced two crops per year because they were so fertile (Amos 7:1). Today, despite much soil erosion, the land still yields rich crops where water is available.

Farmers found a variety of weather patterns in their land. The extreme difference in the rain of the mountains and the drought of the desert, plus the contrast between freezing cold and tropical heat, allowed farmers to grow diverse crops. Snow falls in Jerusalem while open markets only a few kilometers away sell strawberries.

Rainfall Patterns

The pattern of rainfall dictated the way a season would develop. Steady rainfall, coming at critical times, produced better crops than heavy, intermittent rainfall.

Farmers in Palestine had to contend with a five-month rainless period (normally May to October) and if, during the following months, rains were sporadic, the results could be disastrous (Amos 4:7). Three additional months without rain would destroy most crops.

The Bible speaks of early and latter rains (Deut. 11:14). The early rains were the first showers around September or October; the latter rains came in March or April. The early rains prepared the soil for the seed, and the latter rains filled out the crops for harvest. The amount of rain received in different locations varied greatly. For example, today Jericho receives 14 centimeters (5.5 inches) of rainfall per year while areas in upper Galilee have gotten 117 centimeters (47 inches) per year.

However, farmers of Israel could not rely solely upon the rainfall. When the dry season arrived, they depended upon the dews and mist (Gen. 27:28; Deut. 33:28). A heavy dew comes in late August and September. Even today, dew in the hill country and coastal plains will roll off a tent like an early morning rain. This extra moisture provided daily sustenance through the long dry seasons. The absence of dew was considered a sign of God's disfavor (Hag. 1:10).

Control of Water

The Israelites tried to control their supply of water with wells and irrigation. Shepherds and herders generally provided wells for their flocks, often at great expense (2 Chron. 26:10). A well became a natural center for social gatherings (Gen. 24:11), a resting place for weary travelers (John 4:6), and the campsite for hungry armies. It was community property. To stop up a well was considered an act of hostility (Gen. 26:15). Tribes frequently clashed over the right to use a well.

A small stone usually covered the well opening. A low stone wall surrounded the well to protect it from blowing sand and to prevent people and animals from falling in.

The farmers also depended upon cisterns. They dug these reservoirs underground and cemented them tightly to prevent the water from evaporating. Sometimes they carved a cistern out of solid rock, which held the moisture better than a clay-lined cistern. The Nabateans and Romans built dams and reservoirs in the first century B.C. These methods greatly increased the productivity of the land.

The Hebrews practiced irrigation on a smaller scale than the Egyptians. They used artificial trenches to distribute the water. Irrigated water nourished the large city gardens of Israel. Quadrangular plats were subdivided into smaller squares, bordered by walkways and stone-lined troughs that conveyed water to every plant and tree.

Hot Winds

Siroccos (hot winds from the eastern desert) worried farmers from mid-September through October. Siroccos lasted from three days to a week, raising the temperature as much as 20 degrees Fahrenheit above average and the humidity dropped sharply. A prolonged sirocco could spell disaster for farmers (Isa. 27:8; Ezek. 17:10; Hos. 13:15; Luke 12:55).

Insects

Locusts or other insects could destroy a crop. (For a description of insects and the problems they caused, see the chapter on animals.)

Crop Storage

After the harvest, farmers had to dispose of their produce or store it. They stored most of their crops for their own household, although harvests often supplied exports (Ezek. 27:17).

Storage places for grain ranged from clay jars to pits in the ground, as large as 7.6 meters (25 feet) in diameter and nearly as deep. The Hebrews used storage jars to keep their grains, oils, and wines, especially in their homes or shops.

Cisterns and silos stored larger amounts of produce. A circular opening of about 38 centimeters (15 inches) made the top easy to seal. Some farmers built their bins under the women's apartments, the most secluded part of their home.

Jesus described a wealthy man who stored his crops in barns, sometimes called granaries (Luke 12:13–21). The kings of Israel and Judah often built storage cities that were filled with such barns. Solomon built several storage cities to supply his royal court (1 Kings 9:19).

Methods of Cultivation

The farmers of Israel raised a wide variety of crops, and some required special methods of cultivation. (All of the crops mentioned below are discussed more fully in the chapter on plants.)

Grapes

Grapes grew plentifully, and the Hebrews devoted as much time to their vineyards as they did to all other forms of agriculture. The planting, pruning, and cropping of grapevines required hard work, which many people considered menial (2 Kings 25:12). Yet the hill country of Judah offered grapevines a perfect climate. Walled vineyards and watchtowers came to symbolize the land of Judah.

By forbidding farmers to gather grapes for the first three years (Lev. 19:23), Mosaic law guaranteed that the vines would be well-tended in their formative years. The first pruning came in March. After clusters began to form again, the pruners cut off twigs having no fruit. Again the vine grew new clusters, and again the barren branches were pruned.

Wine was squeezed in September, and the Hebrews celebrated this occasion with even more festivity than the harvest (Isa. 16:9–10). It sometimes resulted in wicked mirth (Judg. 9:27).

Grains

Cereal grains were another vital crop. Wheat gave the highest yield. The Plain of Esdraelon (Jezreel) was called the breadbasket of Israel. The area of Galilee produced the best wheat, but every available valley in the rough West Jordan hill country produced grain. The high Transjordan Plateau was also an important grain producer.

Galileans planted fall wheat as the winter rains were beginning, harvesting it between May and June. Farmers in lowland areas like the Jordan Valley harvested their wheat in early May.

The Hebrews harvested abundant barley crops. Since it grew best in the drier climates, they grew much of it in the southeast near the Arabah. Because the climate was too warm to cultivate oats and rye, barley became the Israelites' primary animal feed.

Fitches, spelt, and emmer were inferior grains planted around the border of the fields. They were mixed with wheat or barley to make coarse breads.

Olives

The olive touched nearly every phase of Jewish life: The wood was used in carpentry and as fuel; the fruit was served as food, and the oil was used in a variety of medicines and ointments, as well as being fuel for light.

Olives ripen slowly, and farmers picked them as time permitted. Olives could be eaten after being pickled, but they were valued most for their oil, which was used as a substitute for scarcer animal fats. Farmers extracted the oil in stone presses. They rolled a thick stone wheel over the olives on another flat, circular stone, which was grooved to carry the oil to a basin.

Dates and Figs

Dates flourished, especially in the Jordan Valley north of the Dead Sea. Although the Bible never mentions dates as food, it frequently mentions palm trees, so it is logical to assume that the fruit contributed to the diet of the Hebrews. Ancient writers such as Pliny, Strabo, and Josephus wrote of the syrup made from dates. The Mishna refers to date honey, and the Talmud mentions date wine. Dates also were pressed into cakes.

Figs could be gathered as early as June, but the main crop ripened about August; this main crop was the green fig (Song of Sol. 2:13). Figs came from the tree ready to eat, but could be dried and made into cakes.

Flax

Hebrews made linen cloth and rope from flax (Judg. 15:14; Hos. 2:5, 9), which they harvested in March and April. Farmers used their hoes to chop off the stalks at the ground so that none of the valuable plant would be lost. After the flax was cut, it was laid out to dry in the sun (Josh. 2:6).

Other Crops

Lentils, coarse beans, and chick-peas (garbanzo beans) were also grown in Israel. Cucumbers, onions, leeks, and garlic were other plants on the menu of the Israelites.

Agricultural Tools

Farmers had only primitive tools to help them with their work.

Plows and Harrows

The plow of biblical times was little more than a forked stick with a pointed end. Handles added control. In patriarchal times farmers added a copper point to the plow; later, bronze improved on that. Later still, after the tenth century B.C., the iron plow penetrated the soil to a depth of about 12 centimeters (five inches).

Plows were pulled by oxen, camels, or donkeys, but never by more than a pair of animals. The plow demanded farmers' constant attention to keep it in the ground; only the careless would look away. Jesus used this as an example of one not fit to enter the kingdom of God (cf. Luke 9:62).

Once the early rains came, ground could be broken. Farmers tilled the hard-to-reach places with a mattock, a broad-bladed pickax, or a hoe. Sometimes they would plow their fields twice, crisscrossing directions.

Harrowing broke up the clods after the plowing. Early harrows may have been no more than a wooden plank or log, weighted with stones. Sometimes farmers rode on the harrow.

Sickles

Farmers mowed their fields with hand sickles (cf. Deut. 16:9). The ancient sickle resembled the sickles still used in the Near East; Egyptian monuments show how they looked. Until the early tenth century B.C., the cutting blade of the sickle was made of flint; after that time, it was made of iron.

Workers who reaped grain with a sickle would cut it near the ear, leaving the stubble to be pulled up and used for straw. The grain ears were then carried away in baskets. Sometimes the entire stalk was cut close to the ground, and the stalks were bound into sheaves (Gen. 37:7). Then workers removed the sheaves by cart, stacked them, or stored them.

Winnowing and Threshing Tools

Grain was threshed and then winnowed by throwing it against the wind, which blew away the chaff. Farmers still use this method in much of the Near East.

Ancient threshing places were high, flat summits 15 to 30 meters (50 to 100 feet) in diameter and open to the winds on every side. Each year farmers would level and roll the dirt to keep the threshing floor hard. Often a village had only one threshing floor, and farmers took their turns in a fixed order.

The sheaves were piled in a heap and the grain was beaten out by a machine or by the trampling of oxen's feet. The threshing machine was a square wooden frame holding two or more wooden rollers. On each roller were three or four iron rings, notched like sawteeth. Oxen pulled the machine, and the driver sat on a crosspiece fastened into the frame. As the rollers passed over the grain, it was crushed out on every side, and the straw was shredded for fodder. The threshing machine was a symbol of violence and destruction (cf. Amos 1:3).

Another threshing tool was a wooden plank 90 centimeters (three feet) wide and two to three meters (six to eight feet) long. On the lower side were many holes 2.5 to 5.0 centimeters (one to two inches) in diameter, where farmers fastened pieces of stone, flint, or iron that projected from the board as teeth, tearing the grain loose. Unmuzzled oxen pulled the board behind them across the threshing floor, with the driver standing on the plank.

The grain and chaff gradually formed a big heap at the center of the floor. During the days of threshing, the owner slept nearby to protect the grain from thieves (cf. Ruth 3:2–14).

Farmers winnowed their grain with a fan, which was a semi-oval frame about 90 centimeters (three feet) in diameter with a surface of woven hair or palm leaves. Workers would hold the fan by hand while others poured the mixture of grain and chaff upon it. The winnowers tossed the grain to the winds so the chaff would be blown away and the heavier kernels would fall to the ground (Ps. 1:4). Winnowing was done in the evening, when sea breezes blew the strongest.

Sieves

The first winnowing process did not remove all the unwanted material, so a final step—sifting—was necessary. Amos 9:9 and Isaiah 30:28 describe two kinds of sieves, the *kebarah* in Amos and the *naphah* in Isaiah. We are not sure which type of sieve is meant in either passage. One type of sieve now used in the Near East has a fine mesh that retains the good grain and lets the dust pass through. Another kind, with coarse mesh, allows the desired grain to fall through and retains the larger husks and pods, either to be thrown out or to be rethreshed.

Mills and Presses

Corn and other grains were ground with mortar stones. One or two persons in a household ground grain daily for the family's meals.

Vinedressers cut grapes from the vines with sickles and carried them in baskets to a winepress. This was usually a large stone vat with a small channel that allowed the grape juice to pour out the side into a tub. The grapes were trodden by foot, then pressed by machine. Farmers stored the grape juice in skin bottles, pitchers, and barrels, where it fermented into wine. They also obtained olive oil with presses.

Art

y definition, *art* means the "conscious use of skill and creative imagination, especially in producing beautiful objects."

Except for the descriptions of the tabernacle and the temple in the Bible, art is not discussed. Most of what is known on this subject has been gathered from the work of archaeologists.

Even archaeology has uncovered few samples of the artistic skills of the Israelites. By the time a site is excavated, most writings, paintings, and drawings—even works of art that might have been plastered on walls—have long since disappeared.

Another factor that makes this subject a difficult study is the commandment from the OT Law that directed the Hebrews not to make any graven image (Exod. 20:4). This commandment caused the Israelites to shun certain forms of art, such as painting and sculpture. They expressed their artistic talents and skills through such pursuits as architecture, pottery, metalworking, and bone and ivory carving.

Architecture

The most significant building project for Israel was the temple. Solomon spent seven years and huge sums of money in building God's house in Jerusalem.

Unfortunately, these descriptions, while giving the dimensions and a number of details, do not reveal much about the artistic abilities of the Israelites. Native craftsmen did fashion the furnishings used in the tabernacle. But King Solomon hired thousands of craftsmen to assist in building the temple. He sent to Phoenicia and summoned Hiram of Tyre, a master craftsman who cast the bronze objects and fashioned the latticework that served as furnishings for the temple (1 Kings 7:13–45).

Pottery

Pottery refers to vessels or other objects manufactured from clay and hardened by fire. In modern usage, pottery generally refers only to vessels such as bowls, plates, and jars, but the products of the potter's craft were diverse in Bible times.

The potter's craft is alluded to in numerous biblical passages. This is especially true of the OT, which contains a large ceramic vocabulary, including terms not well understood. Among the references are those to *bowls* of varying sizes (Judg. 5:25; 2 Kings 2:20); *kneading troughs* (Exod. 8:3; 12:34, KJV); *cruses* (1 Kings 17:12, 14; 19:6, KJV); *pots* (Judg. 6:19; 2 Kings 4:38); *jars* and *pitchers* (Gen. 24:14; 2 Kings 4:2; *pot*, KJV); *jugs* (Judg. 4:19; 1 Sam. 26:11); and *lamps* (Exod. 27:20; Prov. 31:18; *candle*, KJV).

The list of ceramic types in the Bible and the actual vessels found in archaeological excavations have provided a clear picture of the pottery of biblical times.

Jeremiah 18:1–6 is the most vivid passage about pottery making in the Bible. It contains a realistic description of the potter's workshop (18:1–4), and it uses figurative language for the potter's craft. The image of God as the Master Potter also appears in Genesis 2:7; Isaiah 29:16; 64:8; Job 10:8–9; and Romans 9:20–24.

The most common forms of Israelite pottery were open bowls, cooking pots of various sizes, jugs for holding liquids, and chalices or goblets for drinking vessels. Some types of pottery were burnished so they had a glossy finish, usually colored red. Some were painted with geometric patterns, while others had pictures of human-headed lions, palm trees, bulls, or fish.

Metalworking

Although the Israelites were experts in the working of metal, few examples of their craft have survived to the present day. Since metal can be easily melted down and recast, this was the probable fate of most metal works of art.

Likely the biggest metalworking project the Israelites undertook was the casting of the bronze Sea for the temple in Jerusalem after it was constructed by Solomon (1 Kings 7:23–26; 2 Chron. 4:2–5). This massive bowl, about 4.5 meters (14 feet) in diameter, rested on the backs of 12 oxen, also cast from bronze. The pillars of Jachin and Boaz, which flanked the entrance to the temple, were also cast from this metal (1 Kings 7:21; 2 Chron. 3:17). Gold leaf was used to cover the doors of the temple and the cherubim and other carved work (1 Kings 6:23–35).

Since iron was a difficult metal to work with, the Israelites used it for objects that required great strength, such as plow points and ax heads. They apparently learned the art of ironworking from the Philistines.

Bone and Ivory Carving

The carving of bone and ivory was an art practiced in Canaan as early as about 4000 B.C. The ivory came from Syria to the north, where elephants were common. The Canaanites and Phoenicians were masters of this craft. A number of ivory pieces were discovered by archaeologists at Samaria, the capital of Israel, from the time of Ahab.

Ivory was sometimes carved into small objects, such as an ointment jar with a hand-shaped stopper found at the ancient city of Lachish. More common was the use of ivory inlays in furniture and wall panels. Amos condemned the excessive wealth and materialism of Israel; he pointed to the beds and houses of ivory as examples (Amos 3:15; 6:4). He was probably referring to the use of such ivory inlays among the wealthy citizens of Samaria, Israel's capital city.

Colors in the Bible

Color as an abstract idea or concept is rarely mentioned in the Bible. The most common Hebrew word translated as *color* actually means: "eye," "appearance," or "aspect" (as Lev. 13:55).

This word expresses color by comparing it with other material. The word describing gems as *colorful* (Isa. 54:11) means "antimony" or "stibium" and probably refers to the dark background that was generally used to set off precious stones. A few objects in the Bible are described as variegated or multicolored (Prov. 7:16; Ezek. 27:24).

Rather than specific hues or tones, a color's brightness or dimness, lightness or darkness, or brilliance or somberness is more often emphasized in the Bible. Shade, rather than hue, seems to be considered more important by the biblical writers.

Natural Colors

Individual colors mentioned in the Bible fall into two major types—natural colors and artificial colors.

Black. Black is one of the more commonly used colors in Scripture. Black describes

- The middle of the night (Prov. 7:9)
- Diseased skin (Job 30:30)
- Healthy hair (Song of Sol. 5:11; Matt. 5:36)
- The color of corpses' faces (Lam. 4:8)
- The sky (Jer. 4:28)
- The darkening of the sun and the moon (Joel 2:10)
- Horses (Zech. 6:2, 6; Rev. 6:5)
- Marble (Esther 1:6)

Blue. Blueness (Prov. 20:30, KJV) may describe the color of a wound, but usually the word refers to the wound itself.

Brown. Brown is a dark color applied only to sheep (Gen. 30:32–33, 35, 40).

Gray. Gray is used only to describe the hair of the elderly (Gen. 42:38).

Green. The words for green normally describe vegetation such as:

- Pastures (Ps. 23:2)
- Herbs (2 Kings 19:26)
- Trees in general (Deut. 12:2; Luke 23:31; Rev. 8:7)
- Grass (Mark 6:39)

A word meaning "greenish" describes plague spots (Lev. 13:49; 14:37).

Red. Several words for red describe such objects as:

- Jacob's stew (Gen. 25:30)
- The sacrificial heifer (Num. 19:2)
- Wine (Prov. 23:31)

- Newborn Esau (Gen. 25:25)
- Judah's eyes (Gen. 49:12, KJV)
- The eyes of drunkards (Prov. 23:29)
- The dragon (Rev. 12:3)

White. The words translated as white describe the color of

- Animals (Gen. 30:35)
- Manna (Exod. 16:31)
- Hair and pustules in leprous sores (Lev. 13:3–39)
- Clothes (Eccles. 9:8; Dan. 7:9)
- Robes of the righteous (Rev. 19:8, KJV)
- Horses (Zech. 1:8; Rev. 6:2; 19:11)
- The shining garments of angels (Rev. 15:6, KJV)
- The transfigured Jesus (Matt. 17:2)
- Hair (Matt. 5:36)
- Gravestones (Matt. 23:27)
- The great throne of judgment (Rev. 20:11)

Yellow. Yellow indicates the cast of gold (Ps. 68:13) and also describes the light-colored hair in a leprous spot (Lev. 13:30, 32).

In addition to black, red, and white horses, certain words suggesting color are used exclusively of horses. The term *sorrel* (Zech. 1:8; *speckled*, KJV *dappled*, NEB) may refer more specifically to a pattern of reddish color mixed with white. *Dappled* (Zech. 6:3; *grizzled*, KJV) probably speaks of a spotted pattern rather than color. The pale horse of Revelation 6:8 (*ashen*, NASB) refers to the color of a corpse.

Artificial Colors

Artificial colors, such as paints and dyes, were used widely in the ancient world. In Babylonia, bricks were made in a variety of colors, some resulting from different kinds of clay, others from special manufacturing processes. Egyptians made dyes from numerous substances. The Israelites had an advanced textile industry. They were skilled not only in weaving but also in dyeing.

Since dyes were made from vegetable sources or from shellfish, quality control was difficult. The completed colors were often impure and inexact. These problems were compounded because many dyes were closely guarded family recipes, which were sometimes lost or changed.

The following dyes or artificial colors are mentioned in the Bible.

Blue. During biblical times, blue was another major dye, also derived from species of shellfish. Fabric dyed this color was used as a part of the pattern for the tabernacle tapestries (Exod. 26:1) and for the hangings in the temple (2 Chron. 2:7). The color was also used for royal trappings (Esther 1:6; 8:15) and clothing for the rich (Jer. 10:9; Ezek. 23:6, KJV).

Purple. The most precious of ancient dyes was purple. In Ugarit, a city of the Canaanites, wool was often dyed this color. Phoenicia derived its name from the source of the dye. The word *Canaan* means "land of the purple." The dye itself was derived from shellfish found in the Mediterranean Sea. A total of 250,000 mollusks was required to make one ounce of the dye, which partly accounts for its great price. It was highly valued within the nation of Israel.

The Lord prescribed the use of purple in several features of the tabernacle, such as the curtains (Exod. 26:1) and the hangings (Exod. 27:16). It was also an essential color of the temple (2 Chron. 2:14).

Purple was the color of
• Royal robes (Judg. 8:26)
• Garments of the wealthy (Prov. 31:22; Luke 16:19)
• Apparel of harlots (Rev. 17:4)
• The robe placed upon Jesus (Mark 15:17, 20).

Robes dyed purple were prescribed for the battle regalia of the Qumran priests, and purple items were highly sought during the Maccabean period. In NT times, purple-dyed textiles were important in trade (Acts 16:14; Rev. 18:12).

Red. Red existed in several shades, and the dye was extracted from the bodies of insects. One of the red colors was *crimson*. Linen of this color was used in the temple trappings (2 Chron. 2:7, 14; 3:14). This artificial color must have been practically indelible or permanent (Jer. 4:30), since crimson is used figuratively of sin (Isa. 1:18).

Another shade of red is *scarlet*. It was the color of
• The cord tied around the wrist of Zerah (Gen. 38:28–30).
• Material used in the tabernacle (Exod. 25:4).
• The cord extended from Rahab's window (Josh. 2:18).
• Prosperity (2 Sam. 1:24; Prov. 31:21).
• The robe placed upon Jesus (Matt. 27:28; since the robe was also described as purple in Mark 15:17, these two colors apparently were not always distinguished during NT times).
• The beast ridden by the harlot (Rev. 17:3).
• Some of the garments of the harlot (Rev. 17:4) and her followers (Rev. 18:16).

Still another shade of red is called *vermilion*, used in decorating the homes of the wealthy (Jer. 22:14) and in the painting of idols (Ezek. 23:14).

Symbolic Significance of Colors in the Bible

Black	Famine and death
Blue	Sometimes describes the sky
Purple	Royalty
Red	Blood; life; the carnage of war
White	Purity, righteousness, and joy; a white horse symbolizes victory

Architecture and Furniture

Modern people admire the architecture of classical Greece and Rome, with its soaring marble pillars and elaborately decorated arches. But Israel produced little architecture that we would call innovative or awe-inspiring. The Israelites designed their buildings and furniture to serve their daily needs, giving little thought to aesthetic features.

Israelite Homes

The Bible tells us that the Israelites built large and costly houses in Judea (see Jer. 22:14; Amos 3:15; Hag. 1:4). But these houses belonged to the wealthy; the common people still lived in tents or crude shelters.

Wealthy people built their houses in the form of a cloister, that is, surrounding an open court. Visitors entered the house by a door that was ordinarily kept locked and tended by someone who acted as a porter (see Acts 12:13). This door opened into a porch, furnished with seats or benches. Visitors then walked through the porch to a short flight of stairs leading to the chambers and the open quadrangular court.

Alliyah. The Jews sometimes built another structure called the *alliyah* over the porch or gateway of the house. It consisted of only one or two rooms and rose one story above the main house. Householders used it as a place to entertain strangers, to store wardrobes, or to rest and meditate.

Jesus probably referred to the *alliyah* when he spoke of going into the "closet" to pray (Matt. 6:6, KJV). Steps led directly from the street to the *alliyah*, but another flight of stairs connected the *alliyah* with the central court of the house. The *alliyah* provided a more private place for worship than the main roof of the house, which might be occupied by the whole family.

Central court. The court was the center of a Jewish house. Probably this is where Jesus sat when a group of men lowered a paralytic man "into the midst" to reach him (Luke 5:19). The court was designed to admit light and air to the rooms around it. Tile or rock paved the floor of the court to shed rain that might come in through the skylight. Sometimes the homeowners built this court around a fountain or well (see 2 Sam. 17:18).

A simple stairway of stone or wood led from the court to the rooms above and the roof. Larger houses might have more than one set of stairs.

Domestic quarters. In ancient Judea, as in Israel today, the people used their ground floor for domestic purposes such as storing food or housing the servants. These ground-floor rooms were small and crudely furnished.

Fireplaces. Ancient houses had no chimneys, even though some versions of the

Bible use this word in Hosea 13:3. Smoke from the hearth escaped through holes in the roof and walls. The hearth itself was not a permanent fixture; it was a small metal stove or brazier (see Jer. 36:22–23). Since the hearth was easy to carry from place to place, kings and generals often used it on military campaigns.

Master's quarters. On the side of the court that faced the entrance was the reception room of the master of the house. It was furnished handsomely with a raised platform and a couch on three sides, which was a bed by night and a seat by day. The guests who entered took off their sandals before stepping upon the raised portion of the room.

The rooms assigned to the wife and daughters were usually upstairs, but sometimes they were on the level of the central court. No one except the master of the house could enter these apartments. Because the owner bestowed the greatest expense upon these rooms, they were sometimes called "citadels" of the house (1 Kings 16:18; 2 Kings 15:25) or "the women's quarters" (Esther 2:3; cf. 1 Kings 7:8–12).

Roof. The roof was an important part of a house in biblical times. Persons could climb to the roof by a flight of stairs along the outside wall. In most cases the roof was flat, although sometimes the builders made domes over the more important rooms. Jewish law required each house to have a balustrade or railing around the roof to keep anyone from falling off (Deut. 22:8). Adjoining houses often shared the same roof, and low walls on the roof marked the borders of each house.

Builders covered roofs with a type of ce-ment that hardened under the sun. If this cracked, householders had to spread a layer of grass on the roof to keep out the rain (see 2 Kings 19:26; Ps. 129:6). Some houses had tiles or flat bricks on the roof.

Upper rooms. When people ascended to the second story by the stairs, they found that the chambers were large and airy, and often furnished with much more elegance than the rooms below. These upper rooms were also higher and larger than the lower rooms, projecting over the lower part of the building so that their windows hung over the street. They were secluded, spacious, and comfortable.

Windows and doors. In ancient houses, the windows were simply rectangular holes in the wall that opened upon the central court or upon the street outside. Sometimes the Israelites built a projecting balcony or porch along the front of the house, carefully enclosed by latticework. They opened the balcony window only for festivals and other special occasions.

The doors of ancient houses were not hung on hinges. The jam (or inner side-piece) of the door projected as a circular shaft at the top and bottom. The upper end of this shaft would fit into a socket in the lintel and the lower end fell into a socket in the threshold. The NKJV loosely uses the word *hinges* in referring to the shaft of the door (1 Kings 7:50; Prov. 26:14).

Often builders equipped the main door of the house with a lock and key. These ancient keys were made of wood or metal; some were so large that they were conspicuous when carried in public (Isa. 22:22). Treasurers or other civic officers carried these huge keys as a symbol of their high office.

Methods of Construction

Although the previous material has described typical houses of the wealthy people, individual houses varied from this floor plan, and some were more elaborate than this. The Israelites used traditional methods of construction in all their homes.

Homes of the Wealthy

The materials for building were abundant in Israel. Well-to-do homeowners could easily obtain stone and brick and the best timber for ornamental work in their houses. They often used hewn stone (Amos 5:11) and highly polished marble (1 Chron. 29:2; Esther 1:6). They also used large quantities of cedar for their wall paneling and ceilings, often with moldings of gold, silver, and ivory (Jer. 22:14; Hag. 1:4). Perhaps their fondness for ivory accounts for the Bible's references to "houses of ivory" and "ivory palaces" (see 1 Kings 22:39; Ps. 45:8; Amos 3:15).

Wealthy landowners also built winter houses and summer houses for their comfort in those seasons (see Amos 3:15). They built the summer houses partly underground and paved them with marble. These houses generally had fountains in the central court and were constructed to bring in currents of fresh air. This made them refreshing in the torrid heats of summer. We know little about the construction of the winter houses.

Homes of the Poor

The houses of the common people were hovels of one room with mud walls. The builders reinforced these walls with reeds and rushes or with stakes plastered with clay. The walls were insecure and often became breeding places for serpents and vermin (cf. Amos 5:19). The family occupied the same room with their animals, although they sometimes slept on a platform above the animals. Their windows were small holes high in the wall, perhaps barred.

Peasants made the doors of their homes low, and individuals had to stoop to enter. This kept out wild beasts and enemies. Some say it was a means of preventing the roving bands of Arabs from riding into the houses.

Furniture

The best-furnished houses (those of the rich) had marble floors covered with beautiful rugs and on the benches were cushions of rich fabric. But the wealthy Israelites did not have a variety of furniture and naturally, the poor had even less.

The rich might have a mat or a skin to recline on during the day, a mattress to sleep on at night, a stool, a low table, and a brazier—this would be the extent of furniture. The rich Shunammite woman furnished the room of Elisha with only a bed (perhaps merely a mattress), a table, a chair, and a lampstand (2 Kings 4:10–13).

Because the floors of more fashionable homes were of tile or plaster, they often needed sweeping or scrubbing (cf. Luke 15:8). At night the residents threw down thick, coarse mattresses to sleep on. The poorer people used skins for the same purpose.

On two or three sides of the rooms of the wealthy were benches, generally 30 centimeters (12 inches) high, covered with stuffed cushions. The masters sat upon these benches in the daytime; but at one end of the room they were more elevated, which was the usual place for sleeping (cf. 2 Kings 1:4). Besides benches, the wealthy had bedsteads made of wood, ivory, or other expensive materials (Deut. 3:11; Amos 6:4). These bedsteads became more common in NT times (cf. Mark 4:21).

Kings and wealthy individuals required a stool for their feet when they sat upon a throne (2 Chron. 9:18), but this piece of furniture was rare in private homes.

On the other hand, lamps were common. They burned olive oil, pitch, naphtha, or wax, and they had wicks of cotton or flax. (A Jewish tradition says that the priests made wicks for the lamps of the temple from their old linen garments.) The poorer Israelites made their lamps of clay, while the wealthy had lamps of bronze and other metals.

The Israelites let their lamps burn all night since light made them feel safer. Many families would rather go without food than let their lamps go out, since that indicated they had deserted their house.

Astrology and Astronomy

Astrology

Astrology refers to the "study of the sun, moon, planet, and stars in the belief that they influence individuals and the course of human events." Astrology attempts to predict the future by analyzing the movements of these heavenly bodies. Although the word *astrology* does not appear in the Bible, the word *astrologers* does. Isaiah taunted the Babylonians by telling them to go to the powerless "astrologers, the stargazers, and the monthly prognosticators" (Isa. 47:13) for their salvation. The word is found eight times in the book of Daniel, in association with magicians, sorcerers, Chaldeans, wise men, and soothsayers (Dan. 1:20; 2:2, 10, 27; 4:7; 5:7, 11, 15).

The idea that one could forecast the future from the stars probably arose naturally in the ancient world. These beliefs would have come from observing that the signs in the heavens and events on earth are sometimes related. For instance, it is evident that the winter season begins when the sun starts to set low in the sky. It takes only one step of logic to conclude that when the sun begins to dip low in the sky, it causes winter to come.

Given the level of scientific thought in the ancient Near East, it required only a further step of logic to conclude that other movements of the sun, moon, and stars affect historical events. An example of this kind of reasoning is found in a letter addressed to the Assyrian King Esarhaddon. "If the planet Jupiter is present during an eclipse," the letter stated, "it is good for the king because an important person in court will die in his stead."

The close association in Babylonian thought between the stars and the gods led ancient sky-watchers to stress their impact on human affairs. This association may be seen clearly in the unique script used to write their language. The sign used to distinguish a god's name was the sign of the star.

The Bible classes astrology with other techniques for predicting the future. Going to the stars for guidance was the same as idolatry to biblical writers. Samuel denounced the two in his condemnation of Saul (1 Sam. 15:23).

The Bible's contempt for astrology is most clearly seen in its prohibition of any technique to aid in predicting the future. Astrology assumes that instead of God's controlling history, history is governed by the affairs of the pagan gods as revealed in the movement of the planets.

Astronomy

On the other hand, *astronomy* is the "scientific study of the solar system and the systematic arrangement of information about the nature, size, and movements of the earth, moon, sun, and stars."

Modern astronomy began with the work of Nicolaus Copernicus (1473–1543), a Polish scientist whose discoveries revolutionized science's view of the universe. Prior to Copernicus, Ptolemy, a Greco-Egyptian astronomer of the second century A.D., had proposed that the earth was stationary at the center of the universe and that the planets moved around it.

Ptolemy's view of our solar system was accepted for over 1,000 years by both scientists and the church until it was overturned by Copernicus's proof that the earth revolves around the sun. This event marked the beginning of astronomy as a modern science.

Early Astronomers

Although the model of the universe accepted by ancient peoples was inaccurate, their attempts to explain how the universe works can be traced back thousands of years. In ancient times, the positions of the planets in relation to one another were thought to have an impact on the course of history. This accounts for astronomy's origins in astrology and similar mystical practices.

The earliest recorded observations of the heavens related to the rising and setting of Venus. These date from around 1650 B.C., and they were probably conducted in an attempt to predict the future. But these observations were also useful in establishing an ancient calendar based on the movement of the sun and stars. Lacking technical devices and a system of mathematics, these ancient astronomers relied solely upon their naked eyes for their observations. This meant that only about 2,000 stars were visible to them.

Importance of Astronomy to Bible Study

The value of astronomy for the study of Scripture lies in its ability to fix absolute dates for some biblical events. Ancient chronologies of major world events were kept carefully. But they usually dated from the year a king was crowned or the year he died; in some cases they date from a great natural disaster. Since those fixed times are no longer precisely known, it is difficult to assign accurate dates for them, although they are well-documented.

The basic orientation of the Bible to astronomy is illustrated in Genesis, which explains why God created the heavenly bodies (chaps. 1—2). The Bible makes only scattered references to them, and none are scientific in the modern sense. Many of these passages refer to the regular movements of the sun and moon to indicate the passage of time. Ancient Israel had a lunar calendar that tied religious events to certain seasons of the year. The times for their annual feasts and festivals depended on the new moon, the full moon, and the position of the sun in both spring and autumn. The planets, by contrast, are referred to by the Bible as objects of idolatry (2 Kings 23:5), probably because the ancient Babylonians were known to practice such forms of idolatry.

Joel may have referred to total eclipses of the sun and moon (Joel 2:31). Falling stars are mentioned in both Testaments (Isa. 34:4; Rev. 6:13). Many scholars believe the star that marked the place where Jesus was born was an astronomical event, perhaps occurring when Saturn and Jupiter lined up along their orbits in the sky. Scientists have documented that such a phenomenon did occur at about the time of Jesus' birth in Bethlehem.

*The Calendar*_____

The calendar of any culture is a system of reckoning time, usually based on a recurrent natural cycle (such as the sun through the seasons or the moon through its phases); it is a table, or tabular register, of days according to a system usually covering one year and referring the days of each month to the days of the week.

Calendar Units

Day

In calendar terms, the day is the smallest and most consistent unit of time. In the ancient world, the term *day* was used in two senses. It described a 24-hour period as well as daylight in contrast to the night (Gen. 1:5). The beginning point of the 24-hour day varied. The Bible contains references to the day beginning in the morning (Gen. 19:34; Acts 23:32) as well as in the evening (Neh. 13:19). In the time of the Roman Empire, the day may have begun at midnight, as indicated by John's gospel (4:6; 19:14). There is also evidence that in OT times the Hebrew people reckoned their day from evening to evening—the period of time between two successive sunsets (Gen. 1:5, 8; Lev. 23:32).

The dawn was the twilight before sunrise (1 Sam. 30:17; Matt. 28:1). The evening was the late afternoon (Deut. 16:6) between the day and the night (Prov. 7:9; Jer. 6:4), or it could mean literally late in the day (Mark 11:19) just before the stars came out (Neh. 4:21). Noon was the end of the morning (1 Kings 18:26), which marked mealtime (Gen. 43:16). Noon was also referred to as midday (Neh. 8:3), broad daylight (Amos 8:9), and heat of the day (2 Sam. 4:5).

The day was divided into three parts: evening, morning, and noon (Ps. 55:17). Midnight was the midpoint of the night (Matt. 25:6; Acts 20:7). In OT times the night was divided into three watches (Exod. 14:24; Judg. 7:19), while it was divided into four watches in NT times (Matt. 14:25; Mark 13:35).

The term *hour* was used to mean "immediately" (Dan. 3:6, 15, KJV), or it could express the idea of one-twelfth of daylight (John 11:9).

Week

The week was a seven-day unit begun at the time of creation (Gen. 1:31—2:2). The word *week* means "seven" (Gen. 29:27; Luke 18:12). In the Bible the days of the week were numbered, beginning with the first day (Gen. 1:8–31; Matt. 28:1), although the seventh day was known as "Sabbath" (Exod. 16:23; Matt. 12:1). The day before the Sabbath was called "the Preparation Day" (Mark 15:42). Christians referred to the first day of the week as "the Lord's Day" (Rev. 1:10).

Month

The month was a unit of time closely tied to the moon's activity. The Hebrew word for *month* also meant "moon" (Deut. 33:14, NIV). The reason for the connection between the month and the moon is that the beginning of a month was marked by a new moon. The moon was carefully observed by the people of Bible times. When it appeared as a thin crescent, it marked the beginning of a new month.

The lunar month was about 29 days long. Therefore, the first crescent of the new moon would appear 29 or 30 days after the previous new moon. At times the crescent was not visible because of clouds. But this was allowed for with a rule that a new moon would never be reckoned as more than 30 days after the last new moon. This prevented too much variation in the calendar.

Year

The Hebrew word for *year* comes from the idea of change or repeated action. Thus the year expresses the concept of a complete cycle of change. Because of the repeated seasons, people set up calendars to account for yearly events and to alert them of the coming seasons. Calendars reckoned the agricultural cycles.

People observed the climatic changes and the length of days in their planting and harvesting. Religious festivals were also established to parallel the agricultural year. No major religious festival, for example, was celebrated during the busy harvest season. They observed that there were four seasons and that the year was about 360 days long. Although the calendars were not always precise, adjustments were made periodically to account for the inaccuracy.

Calendar Systems

Old Testament

The marking of time in OT days primarily revolved around the months, seasonal religious festivals, and the year. The month was marked by the first appearance of the crescent of the new moon at sunset. The first day of each month was considered a holy day marked by special sacrifices (Num. 28:11–15), and it was to be announced with the blowing of trumpets (Num. 10:10; Ps. 81:3).

Originally the months were designated numerically, and the first month of the Hebrew year corresponds to our March-April. In their early history the Israelites adopted Canaanite names for the months connected with agriculture and climate. Only four of these names are mentioned in the OT:

Abib (Exod. 13:4; 23:15) was at the time of the barley harvest. The word *Abib* means "ripening of grain."

Ziv (1 Kings 6:1, 37; *Zif*, KJV) was the second month (April-May). This word means "splendor" and refers to the beauty of flowers blooming at that time.

Ethanim (1 Kings 8:2) was the seventh month (September-October), which occurred during the rainy season.

Bul (1 Kings 6:38) was the eighth month (October-November). Its name may have reference to rain because the eighth month was between the early and the latter rains.

These four names for the months were associated with the most important agricultural times of the year.

In its later history, Israel adopted all 12 months of the Babylonian calendar as the civil calendar. But not all of the 12 months are listed in the Bible. The seven that occur are

- *Nisan,* the first month (Neh. 2:1)
- *Sivan,* the third (Esther 8:9)
- *Elul,* the sixth (Neh. 6:15)
- *Chislev,* the ninth (Zech. 7:1)
- *Tebeth,* the tenth (Esther 2:16)
- *Shebat,* the eleventh (Zech. 1:7)
- *Adar,* the twelfth (Ezra 6:15)

Since Israel was an agricultural society, its calendar worked well for the people and their religious festivals. In the first month the fourteenth day was Passover (Exod. 12:18), the fifteenth day through the twenty-first signaled Unleavened Bread (Lev. 23:6), the sixteenth was Firstfruits (Lev. 23:10–14), dedicating the first-ripe barley sprigs.

The second month marked the celebration of a later Passover for those who had missed the first celebration (Num. 9:10–11).

On the sixth day of the third month, the people celebrated Pentecost, which was also called the Feast of Weeks (Exod. 34:22; Deut. 16:10), in commemoration of the completion of the barley and wheat harvests.

In the seventh month, the first day was the Feast of Trumpets (Lev. 23:23–25; Num. 29:1), celebrating the new year, the tenth day was the Day of Atonement (Lev. 16:29–34; 23:26–32), the fifteenth to the twenty-second days marked the Feast of Tabernacles or Ingathering (Lev. 23:33–43) in commemoration of all the harvests of the year.

Between the Testaments

During the period when the Greeks ruled the ancient world, the Seleucid calendar system was most widely used. Two basic systems were used for reckoning time in the Seleucid era—the Macedonian calendar and the Babylonian calendar. It is difficult to be dogmatic as to which system was used, but the Jewish people seem to have used the Macedonian calendar. This means the Seleucid era in Jewish history began on the first day of their seventh month, Tishri, about 312–311 B.C.

New Testament

The NT contains no references to the Roman or gentile calendar or to the Jewish calendar, except in speaking of the days of the week. There is one reference to the "new moon" (Col. 2:16).

Although the NT makes no references to the Roman or gentile calendar, it does refer to the reigns of rulers. The most specific example is Luke 3:1, "the fifteenth year of the reign of Tiberius Caesar." This refers to the time of the ruler then in office in Judea and the surrounding territories and to the beginning of the ministry of John the Baptist. This must have been in A.D. 28–29, assuming that Luke used either the Julian calendar, which began in January, or the regnal calendar, which began in August. The most general references speak not of the year but of the reigns of

- Caesar Augustus (Luke 2:1)
- Claudius Caesar (Acts 11:28)
- Provincial governor Quirinius (Luke 2:2)
- Provincial governor Gallio (Acts 18:12)
- King Herod (Matt. 2:1; Luke 1:5)
- The ethnarch Aretas (2 Cor. 11:32)

Clothing

The warmth of Israel's climate led the people to prefer loose-fitting clothes, and the drab landscape may have contributed to their preference for bright colors in their garments. Clothing styles remained essentially the same throughout the period covered by the OT and NT.

Every Jewish home had a loom for weaving cloth. Colorful embroidery enlivened the fancier clothes. Purple dye was taken from a Mediterranean shellfish. Red came from insects taken from oak trees. Pomegranate and other plants provided blue dye.

General terms for clothing in the Bible include *attire* and *raiment*. But many specific items of dress are also mentioned. The following list of specific items is keyed to the NKJV. But variant terms from five additional popular English versions—KJV, NASB, NEB, NIV, and RSV—are also cross-referenced to this list.

Apron. (See *Belt* or *Sash*.)

Belt *or* Sash. The belt, made of leather, cloth, or cord, was worn around the waist, much like the belt of today. The Bible mentions belts worn by Elijah (2 Kings 1:8) and John the Baptist (Matt. 3:4). A rich person's leather belt might hold a weapon, such as a sword, dagger, or knife, or an inkhorn for writing. The scribe's reed or pen was also probably carried in the belt (Ezek. 9:2, 11).

The sash was longer than the belt. It consisted of a piece of folded cloth or wool wound two or three times around the waist. When made into a pouch, it might serve as a pocket for carrying money, other valuables (Matt. 10:9; Mark 6:8), or even food. Shepherds might even carry a lamb in their sash.

Other words for belt or sash used by other translations are *girdle* (KJV) and *apron* (NEB).

Cloak. (See *Mantle*.)

Coat. (See *Mantle*; *Tunic*.)

Girdle. (See Belt or *Sash*.)

Mantle. This item of clothing was the distinctive Hebrew outer garment, made of two pieces of thick woolen material sewn together, with slits rather than sleeves for the arms. In OT times the mantle was usually brightly colored. Joseph's "tunic of many colors" (Gen. 37:3) was probably a mantle of woven bright strips.

A handy one-piece garment, the mantle protected them from the weather. Because it fitted loosely, it could also be used to conceal or carry items. The typical Jewish mantle hung below the knees and was decorated with fringe.

Other words for mantle used by various English translations are *cloak, coat, robe,* and *wimple*.

Robe. (See *Mantle*.)

Sandals. The sandals worn by the Hebrew people were of cloth, wood, or dried grass, held on the foot by a thong or strap (Isa. 5:27; Mark 1:7). Sandals were worn by

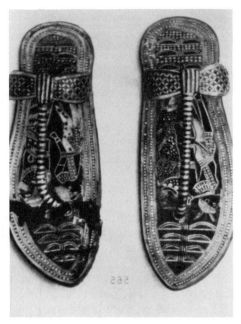

Ornamental sandals, made of papyrus, discovered in the tomb of Pharaoh Tutankhamon (King Tut) of Egypt.   PHOTO BY HOWARD VOS

all classes in Israel, unlike Egypt where some people went barefoot. Women wore

them, too, as noted in the Song of Solomon (7:1). A certain kind of sandal for females had two straps, one between the big toe and the second toe, and another circling the instep and heel.

Another word for sandals used by some English translations of the Bible is *shoes*.

Sash.   (See *Belt* or *Sash*.)

Shirt.   (See *Tunic*.)

Shoes.   (See *Sandals*.)

Tunic.   The tunic was a long piece of cloth folded in half, with holes for the arms and head. Also known as the inner garment, it was worn under the mantle, or outer garment. The tunic was generally made of leather, haircloth, wool, or linen. Jesus' tunic at the Crucifixion was from one piece of cloth and had no seam (John 19:23). Women as well as men wore a tunic, often colored blue. Other words for tunic used by various English translations are *coat* and *shirt*.

Wimple.   (See *Mantle*.)

Clothing for Special Occasions

In addition to the items of everyday dress used by the Hebrews, the Bible also mentions the following clothes used for special occasions.

Mourning or repentance garments. Dark-colored sackcloth of coarse goat's hair was worn by Jacob to lament the loss of his son Joseph (Gen. 37:34). Job wore sackcloth in his time of sorrow (Job 16:15). Eventually "sackcloth and ashes" became a symbol of repentance (Matt. 11:21).

Ornaments.   Ornaments were decorative or religious jewelry items attached to the clothing or body in Bible times. The Bible speaks often of various kinds of ornaments worn by both men and women (Gen. 24:22; Exod. 12:35). These ornaments were worn for dignity (Gen. 41:42), as well as decoration (Song of Sol. 1:10). Rich women were especially adorned in a lavish way

(Isa. 3:16, 18–23), and Jeremiah pointed out that every Jewish maid was attracted to jewelry (Jer. 2:32).

Often amulets or charms were worn as jewelry by pagan people to ward off evil spirits or to please the gods (Gen. 35:4; Judg. 8:24). These might be earrings or pendants around the neck. Some amulets were prayers or curses written on papyrus or parchment, wrapped in linen, and attached to the body.

Jewish men wore phylacteries or frontlets, which consisted of passages of Scripture wrapped in leather and attached to the arm or forehead. These were worn while praying, and the practice countered the idolatrous wearing of amulets.

Phylacteries. These were small square leather boxes or cases containing four strips of parchment inscribed with quotations from the first five books of the OT (e.g., Exod. 13:1–10, 11–16; Deut. 6:4–9; 11:13–21). In Bible times, phylacteries were worn by every male Israelite above age 13 during morning prayer, except on the Sabbath and holy days. Although orthodox Jews still observe this practice, reformed Judaism has discontinued it.

Leather straps were used to fasten them to the left hand and to the forehead during morning worship. The custom of wearing phylacteries traces back to the command, "You shall bind them as a sign upon your hand, and they shall be as frontlets between your eyes" (Deut. 6:8).

The discovery of portions of phylacteries in the Dead Sea caves reveals they were not standardized before the time of Jesus. Certainly not all the people wore them, but the Pharisees possibly wore them consistently.

Robe of honor. Special robes were worn by people of high political positions in the ancient world. Such a robe was given to Joseph by the Pharaoh of Egypt (Gen. 41:42).

Wedding garments. In NT times, the mother of the family often kept her wedding dress for her daughter to use at her wedding. She usually stored it in a box to protect it from moths (as alluded to by Jesus in Matt. 6:19). The wedding dress was usually white silk, perhaps embroidered. The bride also wore a veil and considerable jewelry.

The groom's attire resembled that of a king. He might also wear a garland. Festive robes were worn by the guests at a wedding, as in Jesus' parable where a man was turned away for wearing inappropriate clothes (Matt. 22:11).

Winter clothing. The Hebrews wore fur dresses or animal-skin cloaks in wintertime. The rich wore expensive robes, and the poor made do with common garments of coarse hair (Zech. 13:4).

Priestly Clothing

Priestly dress differed from that of the common Jew. Furthermore, the high priest's clothing differed from that of the common priest.

Priest

Here are the garments worn by priests:

Breeches. Among the Hebrews, breeches were worn only by the priests. In some neighboring countries, both breeches and trousers were worn by common men.

The Jews used fine linen to make this priestly garment. Apparently, it served as an undergarment so that the priest would not be exposed when he climbed the steps of the temple to minister at the altar (Exod. 28:42–43). This undergarment covered the priest's body from the waist to the knees. Rather than being trousers, *breeches* were probably a double apron. (See also Exod. 39:28; Lev. 6:10; 16:4; Ezek. 44:18.)

Cassock *or* Robe. The priests also wore robes of white linen during their temple ministrations. These garments came from the weaver seamless, bound at the waist with a girdle decorated by needlework (Exod. 28:31–34).

Bonnet. A bonnet was worn by the ordinary priest. This bonnet was made of fine linen (Exod. 39:28, KJV; *hat*, NKJV). The Hebrew word *migbaoth* from which *bonnet* was translated means "to be lofty."

Footwear. During their ministrations, the priests were to be barefoot. Before they entered the tabernacle, they were to wash their hands and feet: "He set the laver between the tabernacle of meeting and the altar, and put water there for washing; and Moses, Aaron, and his sons would wash their hands and their feet with water from it" (Exod. 40:30–31).

High Priest

One of the distinctions that separated the high priest from the common priest was the sprinkling of his garments with anointing oil (Exod. 28:41).

Besides that distinction, he wore the following garments.

Breastplate. The high priest's breastplate is described in detail in Exodus 28:15–30. It was a piece of embroidered material about 25.4 centimeters (10 inches) square and doubled over to make a bag or pouch.

This priestly garment was adorned with 12 precious stones, each bearing the name of one of the 12 tribes of Israel (Exod. 28:9–12). The two upper corners were fastened to the ephod, from which it was not to be loosened (Exod. 28:28). The two lower corners were fastened to the girdle. The rings, chains, and other fastenings were of gold or rich lace.

The breastplate and ephod were called a "memorial" (Exod. 28:12, 29) because they reminded the priest of his relationship to the 12 tribes of Israel. It was also called the "breastplate of judgment" (Exod. 28:15), possibly because it was worn by the priest, who was God's spokesman of justice and judgment to the Jewish nation.

Embroidered coat, girdle, and breeches. This particular coat was long-skirted, made of linen, and embroidered with a pattern as if stones were set in it (Exod. 28:4). The common priests also wore this garment.

The girdle of the high priest's garment was wound around the body several times from the breast downward. The ends of the girdle hung down to the ankles (Exod. 29:5). Beneath the priestly garments, the high priest wore the same type of breeches as did the common priest.

Ephod. The high priest's garments were made of plain linen (1 Sam. 2:18; 2 Sam. 6:14), as were the clothes for all priests. But his ephod was made of "gold, blue, purple, and scarlet thread, and fine woven linen" (Exod. 28:6). This indicates that it was a blend of wool and linen, since linen could be dyed only blue. In the same verse, the phrase "artistically worked" signifies some type of embroidery.

There were two parts to the ephod: one covering the back and the other covering the breast of the wearer. The garment was fastened at each shoulder by a large onyx.

The girdle or the band of the ephod was made of blue, purple, scarlet, and gold thread and linen (Exod. 28:8).

Mitre. The mitre, or upper turban, was the official headdress of the high priest (Exod. 28:39). It was made of fine linen, had many folds, and had a total length of about 7.3 meters (eight yards).

This long cloth was wound around the head in turban style. On the front of the mitre was a gold plate bearing the Hebrew words for HOLINESS TO THE LORD (Exod. 28:36; 39:30).

Robe of the ephod. The robe of the ephod was of inferior material to the ephod, dyed blue (Exod. 39:22). It was worn under the ephod and was longer than the ephod. This robe had no sleeves, only slits in the sides for the arms.

The skirt of this garment had a fringe (trimming) of pomegranates in blue, purple, scarlet, with a bell of gold hung between each pomegranate. These bells were attached to the bottom of the high priest's robe so that he would be heard as he came or went from the holy place (Exod. 28:32–35).

Food

God called Canaan the land of "milk and honey" (Exod. 13:5) because food was plentiful, although it required hard work for production. Lack of rainfall or other undesirable weather conditions sometimes caused meager crops.

After conquering and settling Canaan, the Hebrews became farmers. This was different from the nomadic life of their forefathers. Their diet reflected the change, because tillers of the soil eat differently from shepherds and herders. The land that they worked produced foodstuffs in a variety pleasing to the palate and filling to the stomach. Among these were cereal grains, animal protein, vegetables, fruit and nuts, savory spices and herbs, and wine.

Cereal Grains

The cereal grains, often called corn in the KJV, are not to be confused with maize, a product of the Western Hemisphere. The word *corn* in the KJV should be translated as *wheat, barley,* and *millet*. It also included *spelt,* an inferior species of grain related to wheat and called *fitch* in the KJV.

After the grain was harvested, it was ground into flour, mixed and kneaded into dough, and then baked into bread. In Isaiah 3:1 bread is called the "stock and the store."

Grain could be prepared and eaten in ways other than bread. It could be parched, roasted, or cracked and made into a gruel (2 Sam. 17:28).

Animal Protein

Protein, essential to life, was readily available to everyone in the land of Canaan. Although meat was not part of everyday fare, animal products such as milk, butter, and cheese were. A noon meal for workers might consist of two loaves of barley bread—one filled with cheese, the other with olives.

The Hebrews divided animals into two classes—clean and unclean (Lev. 11:1–47; Acts 10:9–15). The law governing this distinction dealt with four-footed animals as well as fish, birds, and insects. Only clean animals could be eaten. These animals chewed the cud and had divided hooves (Lev 11:3). Pigs have divided hooves, but they do not chew the cud, making them ceremonially unclean. Camels chew the cud, but they do not have parted hooves. So they could not be eaten.

Some forbidden foods did serve as health precautions. Pork, for example, must be cooked at high temperatures to kill a dreaded parasite. The people of the land had never heard of trichinosis, but they were protected from it by their food laws.

Fish of some types could be eaten (Lev. 11:9, 12). Oysters and shrimp, which fell within the forbidden list, spoil quickly and become unfit for food in a hot atmosphere with no refrigeration. A total of 20 different species of birds was rejected (Lev. 11:13–19). Insects that had legs and leaped, such as the grasshopper, were fit for food.

Vegetables

While enslaved in Egypt, the Hebrews learned to enjoy vegetables. During their years of wandering in the wilderness, they missed their cucumbers, melons, leeks, onions, and garlic (Num. 11:5). They also longed for their "pots of meat" (Exod. 16:3), which were stew pots filled with simmering meat and vegetables.

Once settled in the land of Canaan, the Hebrews cultivated these favorite vegetables, plus beans, lentils, and squash. The squash they cultivated may have been one of the "melons" they learned to eat in Egypt many years earlier.

Fruit and Nuts

The abundance of food cultivated is indicated by the list of provisions that Abigail furnished David in the desert of Paran (1 Sam. 25:18). Included were bread, wine, mutton, roasted grain, clusters of raisins, and cakes of figs.

Abigail's clusters of raisins were pressed into cakes with the stems still intact. Grapes or raisins might be made into a raisin cake, as she had done, but they could also be eaten fresh or pressed for their juice. In time the fresh-pressed juice could be turned into vinegar or wine.

Along with raisins, Abigail brought figs, dried and pressed into cakes. She may have brought apricots dried and pressed the same way or fresh oranges. The land produced both of them.

Spices and Herbs

Honey was available because the land had both wild and domesticated bees. Honey was made from dates as well. From a small garden Abigail might have brought mint, anise, dill, and cumin. Certainly she could have brought almonds—or pistachios. These trees were common in Canaan. Olives were also plentiful. Olive orchards were scattered throughout the land. The olive was eaten green or ripe or pressed for its oil. Olive oil was used for cooking and seasoning and as fuel for lamps.

Perhaps Abigail brought salt; an abundant supply was available from the nearby Sea of Salt or Dead Sea. But she probably brought no pepper. This seasoning is not mentioned in the Bible.

Wine

Wine is first mentioned in the Bible when Noah became intoxicated after the Flood (Gen. 9:20–21). Because it was a common commodity in Hebrew life, wine is regularly included in summaries of agricultural products (Gen. 27:28; 2 Kings 18:32; Jer. 31:12).

In Canaan, grape harvesting occurred in September and was accompanied by great celebration. The ripe fruit was gathered in baskets and carried to wine presses. The grapes were placed in the upper one of two vats that formed the winepress. Then the grapes were trampled or treaded. The treading was done by one or more individuals, according to the size of the vat. These grape treaders encouraged one another with shouts (Isa. 16:9–10; Jer. 25:30; 48:33).

Sometimes the juice from the grapes was served in an unfermented state, but generally it was stored after fermentation. If the wine was to be kept for some time, a substance was added to give it body (Isa. 25:6). Consequently, the wine was always strained before it was served.

A watchtower, or leaf-covered wooden booth, was often built on a high place overlooking the vineyard (Mark 12:1). This booth was occupied by members of the family during the growing season to protect their crop (Job 27:18) and sometimes by a watchman during the winter. Often a cottage or hut was built in the vineyard. The family lived here during the summer to protect the grapes but abandoned the hut in the winter (Isa. 1:8).

Wine was stored in either clay jars or wineskins, which were made by tying up the holes of skins taken from goats. Old wineskins could not be used a second time because the fermentation process would cause the old skins to burst and the wine would be lost (Matt. 9:17; Mark 2:22; Luke 5:36–38).

Uses of Wine

Wine was a significant trade item in the Near East. Solomon offered Hiram 20,000 baths of wine in exchange for timber (2 Chron. 2:10, 15). Damascus was a market for the "wine of Helbon" (Ezek. 27:18). Fines were sometimes paid with wine (Amos 2:8).

Wine was also used in worship. Libations to false gods were condemned (Deut. 32:37–38; Isa. 57:5–6; 65:11; Jer. 7:18; 19:13), but the drink offering prescribed by the law of Moses was a libation of wine offered to the Lord. The daily offering (Exod. 29:40; Num. 28:7), the offering of the firstfruits (Lev. 23:13), the burnt offering, and the freewill offering (Num. 15:4–5) required one-fourth of a hin of wine. The sacrifice of a ram was accompanied by one-third of a hin of wine (Num. 15:6–7). In the temple organization set up by David, Levites were appointed to supervise these wine offerings (1 Chron. 9:29).

Wine could be drunk with milk (Song of Sol. 5:1). Melchizedek brought wine and bread to Abraham when Abraham returned from battle (Gen. 14:18). Wine was offered by the old man of Gibeah to the traveling Levite (Judg. 19:19). Jesse sent David with bread, a skin of wine, and a young goat as a present when Saul was fighting the Philistines (1 Sam. 16:20). Abigail brought David two skins of wine (1 Sam. 25:18).

Wine was also used as medicine. It was said to revive the faint (2 Sam. 16:2) and was suitable as a sedative for people in distress (Prov. 31:6) or pain. The Samaritan poured oil and wine on the wounds of the injured traveler (Luke 10:34). The apostle Paul charged Timothy, "No longer drink only water, but use a little wine for your stomach's sake" (1 Tim. 5:23).

Misuses of Wine

The dangers of drunkenness are abundantly recognized in the Bible (Prov. 20:1; 23:29–35). Wine often enslaved the heart (Hos. 4:11). The prophets accused Israel of being overcome with wine (Isa. 28:1), of drinking wine by bowlfuls (Amos 6:6), and of wanting prophets who spoke of wine (Mic. 2:11). Some leaders were so interested in drinking that they were not concerned about the ruin of the country (Isa. 5:11–12; 22:13). The list of those drunken with wine in the Bible begins with Noah and includes Lot, Nabal, and Amon (Gen. 9:21; 19:34–35; 1 Sam. 25:36–37; 2 Sam. 13:28).

While the use of wine continued in NT times, Paul admonished his readers to be filled with the Holy Spirit rather than with wine (Eph. 5:18). Wine was a basic commodity in biblical times. But there is no biblical justification for the heavy liquor traffic of modern times.

Music _____

Music played a part of everyday life for the ancient Hebrews. At times music was a form of family merrymaking, such as the homecoming party for the prodigal son (Luke 15:25). Music welcomed heroes and celebrated victories. Miriam and other women sang, danced, and played timbrels when the Israelites miraculously escaped the Egyptians (Exod. 15:20). The Song of Moses (Exod. 15) is the earliest recorded song in the Bible. Jephthah's daughter greeted him with timbrels to celebrate his victory over the Ammonites (Judg. 11:34). David's triumph brought music (1 Sam. 18:6).

The Jews were apparently a musical people. The Assyrian king, Sennacherib, demanded as tribute from King Hezekiah of Judah male and female Judean musicians—a most unusual ransom. The Babylonians demanded "songs of Zion" from the Israelites while they were in captivity (Ps. 137:3). During the period between the Testaments, Strabo, a Greek geographer, called the female singers of Israel the most musical in the world.

Music in the Old Testament

The Bible calls Jubal "the father of all those who play the harp and flute" (Gen. 4:21). But professional musicians do not appear in the Bible before David's time. Even before professional musicians became the norm during David's reign, the concept of court musicians did exist. The young David was called to soothe Saul with music (1 Sam. 16:16–23). In this sense David was a minstrel (2 Kings 3:15, KJV)—a player of stringed instruments.

David introduced music into the sanctuary worship. His son and successor Solomon later retained it after the temple was built (2 Sam. 6:5; 1 Kings 10:12). Music must have been considered an important part of the service, since Hezekiah and Josiah, the two reform kings, saw to it that music was included in the reformation (2 Chron. 29:25; 35:15).

Music in the New Testament

The NT contains little information about music, but it does give some additional hymns, such as the hymns of Mary (Luke 1:46–55, the *Magnificat*) and Zacharias (Luke 1:68–79, the *Benedictus*).

The NT also contains accounts of the early Christians singing hymns for worship and comfort (Acts 16:25; Eph. 5:19; Col. 3:16). Some fragments of early Christian hymns also appear in the NT (Eph. 5:14; 1 Tim. 3:16).

Musical Instruments

Musical instruments used by the Hebrews are of three types:

1. *Stringed* instruments used vibrating strings to make sounds.
2. *Percussion* instruments were struck to produce musical sounds.
3. *Wind* instruments made sounds either by passing air over a vibrating reed or by forcing air through the instrument.

Following is a description of all the musical instruments mentioned in the NKJV. Names of instruments from five other English translations (KJV, NASB, NEB, NIV, and RSV) are cross-referenced to these descriptions from the NKJV.

Bagpipe. (See *Dulcimer*).

Bell. Bells were common in Israel, but they apparently were not used as musical instruments. Tiny bells of pure gold were fastened to the hem of the priest's robe (Exod. 39:25–26). Zechariah also indicated that the people put such tiny bells on the bridles or breast straps of their horses (14:20). (See also *Gong*.)

Bugle. (See *Trumpet*.)

Cornet. (See *Trumpet*.)

Cymbals. Used in priestly functions, cymbals were played only by men and perhaps only by priests. These instruments made a loud, distinctive sound when banged together. They were used to accompany trumpets (Ezra 3:10), the lyre when it was used for worship (1 Chron. 25:1; Neh. 12:27), and "the musical instruments of God" (1 Chron. 16:42). David's chief musician, Asaph, played the cymbals (1 Chron. 16:5).

Dulcimer. This instrument is mentioned only by Daniel. It was one of the Babylonian instruments that signaled the time for Daniel's friends—Shadrach, Meshach, and Abed-Nego—to bow down before a golden image of King Nebuchadnezzar (Dan. 3:5, 7, 10, 15, KJV). Other English versions translate *bagpipe* (NASB, RSV) or *pipes* (NIV).

Fife. (See *Flute*.)

Flute. A flute was a wind instrument that produced a high, shrill sound. Because of its unique sound, the flute was associated with fertility cults and considered appropriate only in a secular setting to show both ecstatic joy and deep sorrow.

The flute is mentioned in connection with the temple only in the Psalms (e.g., Ps. 150:4). However, the Hebrew word *nehiloth* in the title of Psalm 5 means "[with] flutes." Some flutes were made of silver, reeds, wood, or bones. Other words for flute used in various translations of the Bible are *organ* (Gen. 4:21, KJV); *fife* (1 Sam. 10:5, NEB); *pipe* (Job 21:12, RSV); and *reed-pipe* (Jer. 48:36, NEB).

Gong. *Gong* is the word used by some English translations for a type of bell sounded at weddings or other happy occasions (1 Cor. 13:1, RSV, NASB). *Noisy gong* is rendered as *sounding brass* by the KJV and NKJV. The gong may have been similar to a handbell. (See also *Bell*.)

Harp. The musical instrument mentioned more than any other in the Bible is the harp (2 Chron. 29:25; Ps. 147:7; Isa. 23:16). Another word for this instrument used by various translations is *lyre*. Scholars believe these two instruments were similar in function and design, but the harp was probably a larger version.

The harp and the lyre are often spoken of interchangeably in the Bible. Other words used for these two instruments by various translations of the Bible are *psaltery, lute* (1 Kings 10:12, *stringed instrument,* NKJV), and *viol* (Isa. 5:12, KJV). The lute was an even smaller version of the harp or lyre, consisting of only three strings. In the NKJV *stringed instruments* is sometimes used to refer to all these instruments in a collective sense: harp, lute, lyre, psaltery, and viol.

Two specific types of harps or lyres are mentioned in some English translations of the book of Daniel. Daniel's three friends—Shadrach, Meshach, and Abed-Nego—were commanded to bow down and worship an image of the Babylonian king at the sound of various Babylonian musical instruments. These instruments included a *sackbut* (Dan. 3:5, KJV; *trigon*, NASB, RSV; *triangle*, NEB) and a *zither* (Dan. 3:5, NIV). Some scholars believe the sackbut was the seven-stringed lyre used in Babylon, while the zither may have been a 10-stringed lyre or harp that gave its own distinctive sound.

Horn.   (See *Trumpet.*)

Lute.   (See *Harp.*)

Lyre.   (See *Harp.*)

Organ.   (See *Flute.*)

Pipe.   (See *Dulcimer.*)

Psaltery.   (See *Harp.*)

Ram's horn.   (See *Trumpet.*)

Reed-pipe.   (See *Flute.*)

Sackbut.   (See *Harp.*)

Shophar.   (See *Trumpet.*)

Sistrum.   Sistrums were small musical instruments with a U-shaped frame and a handle at the bottom. Strung on bars between the two parts of the U were small pieces of metal or other objects to create a rattling sound. The collection of the Jewish oral law, known as the *Mishnah*, recognized the sistrum, also called a *rattler-sistrum*, as the instrument used by women who mourned the death of a relative or friend.

Tabret.   (See *Timbrel.*)

Tambourine.   (See *Timbrel.*)

Timbrel.   This refers to a percussion instrument carried and beaten by hand. Considered inappropriate for the temple, it was likely played primarily by women (Ps. 68:25). The timbrel may have been excluded from temple instruments because of its great popularity with the Canaanite

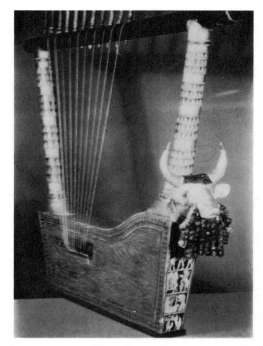

A reconstructed lyre from Mesopotamia. This was a popular musical instrument about 2500 B.C., several centuries before Abraham's time.
PHOTO BY HOWARD VOS

fertility cults. Among the Hebrews, it was associated with merrymaking and processions (Gen. 31:27).

The Hebrew word for timbrel is rendered by other English translations as *tabret* and *tambourine*.

Triangle.   (See *Harp.*)

Trigon.   (See *Harp.*)

Trumpet.   The trumpet is mentioned several times in the Bible. This instrument was used by the priests during services of sacrifice, especially to signal the Day of Atonement (Lev. 25:9). The trumpet was also used to rally troops on the battlefield (Josh. 6:4).

Made of metal or bones, the trumpet featured a sounding air column not quite two feet long. This short length gave this instrument a high, shrill sound. The tone of the trumpet apparently could be regulated (2 Chron. 5:12). Some trumpets were probably made from the horn of animals. *Horn* is used for this instrument in some English translations (1 Chron. 25:5, KJV). Other words used for trumpet include *cornet* (Ps. 98:6, KJV) and *bugle* (1 Cor. 14:8, NASB, RSV).

One distinctive type of trumpet or horn used by the Hebrew people was the ram's horn, also known by its Hebrew name, the *shophar* (Hos. 5:8). The shophar was the greatest of the Jewish ritual instruments. Eventually the horn of a mountain goat was used rather than the horn of a ram. The shophar, or trumpet, was basically a signaling instrument used to assemble the army (Judg. 3:27; 1 Sam. 13:3), sound an attack (Job 39:24–25), or sound an alarm (Jer. 6:1; Amos 3:6). It signaled war and peace, the new moon, the beginning of the Sabbath, approaching danger, or the death of a dignitary.

Some even believed the shophar had power to drive out evil spirits and to heal by magic. The sound of the shophar could be heard from a great distance (Exod. 19:16, 19). It can produce only the first two tones of the musical scale and those not very accurately. The ram's horn is rarely mentioned with other musical instruments. Its main function apparently was to make noise.

Viol. (See *Harp.*)

Zither. (See *Harp.*)

Occupations and Trades

The ancient Near East is often called the cradle of civilization because highly developed cultures flourished in this region of the world long before Abraham (about 2100 B.C.). Many skills that developed into occupations and trades originated here. By Abraham's day civilization was quite complex. Indeed, Abraham himself was a herder of vast flocks of sheep, goats, donkeys, cattle, and perhaps even camels. Many modern scholars think he was also a trader, managing donkey caravans and doing business from Turkey to Egypt.

Throughout their history, the inhabitants of Canaan ranged from primitive to quite advanced peoples. Many skills were required to sustain and promote life in every period of its history.

Canaan was a dry region where water was carefully handled. They dug wells and from about 1200 B.C. constructed cisterns lined with plaster. These processes required a great variety of skills.

The gathering of food was an important aspect of life. Food was secured from the water, forest, and farm. Each of these sources of food demanded a separate set of skills and abilities.

In early history, each wandering family or tribe relied on its members to supply its needs. As society became more complex, however, tribes began to settle into specific areas with larger groups. As this happened, people became more dependent on each other. Skills and occupations became more and more specialized. Farms and other businesses grew in size, demanding servants and hired hands.

As society developed, the skills needed began to change. The early wandering Hebrew herders lived in tents of animal skins, which they could prepare by themselves. When they started to move into houses in towns, they needed a wider variety of skilled laborers such as builders, carpenters, bricklayers, and many other tradesmen.

The more civilized society had a wider variety of needs. It demanded occupations and trades that could fill its clothing needs and provide health care, education, and other needed products and services. Ultimately, society needed skilled rulers and government officials to govern and maintain order.

Young people learned trades through apprenticeships. Older tradespeople would take youngsters in as assistants, teaching them everything they would need to know to be able to continue the trade.

Many necessary occupations and trades existed during Bible times. The following are mentioned or inferred in the Bible.

Ambassador. An official representative of kings and rulers. In ancient times many kings and rulers spoke to other nations through official representatives who offered congratulations (1 Kings 5:1), sought favors (Num. 20:14), made treaties (Josh. 9:4–6), and registered protests (Judg. 11:12). How the other nations treated the ambassador represented how they related to the ruler. If one treated the ambassador rudely, it was an insult to the ruler and could lead to war (2 Sam. 10:4–6).

Apothecary. (See *Perfumer*.)

Mosaic of an archer, discovered at ancient Susa. He may have been a professional soldier in the Persian army. PHOTO BY HOWARD VOS

Archer. Ancient armies had archers who were trained from childhood. Deadly accurate, these warriors were the first to contact the enemy by shooting their bows from a distance. To draw ancient war bows required a pull of 100 pounds. The arrows could pierce almost all armor. The Bible notes how effective archers could be (1 Sam. 31:3; 2 Sam. 11:24; 1 Chron. 10:3).

Armorbearer. A servant who carried additional weapons for commanders. Abimelech (Judg. 9:54), Jonathan (1 Sam. 14:6–17), and Joab (2 Sam. 18:15) had armorbearers. David was once Saul's armorbearer (1 Sam. 16:21).

Armorer. This was the person who manufactured armor. Armorers (smiths skilled in making armor and leather workers skilled in making shields) were primarily Philistines in the days of Saul. While *armorer* is not mentioned directly in the Bible as an occupation, ancient Hebrew soldiers did use shields, helmets, breastplates of scalelike plates, and greaves (leg armor).

Artificer. (See *Metalsmith*.)

Artisan. (See *Metalsmith*.)

Astrologer. These were individuals who sought information from the positions of the sun, moon, and stars in relation to one another and to the zodiac. Astrology and astrologers were widespread in the ancient world, being documented as early as 2000 B.C. in Mesopotamia. From there it spread to Egypt, Greece, China, India, and throughout the ancient world.

The Bible warns against astrologers (Deut. 4:19; 17:2–7; Isa. 47:13–15). Many scholars believe the magi who came to honor Jesus were astrologers. Other names for astrologer used by other translations are *prognosticator, sage,* and *stargazer*.

Attendant. (See *Servant*.)

Baker. Bread was a major food among the ancients, and baking and bakers were common. Home bakers prepared dough from cereal grains and baked it on a rock or in an oven. Towns and villages probably had public bakers who baked bread from dough prepared in their customers' homes. Kings had their own royal bakers (Gen. 40:2).

Banker. Banking and bankers appeared among the Jews during the Babylonian captivity. There is no mention of banking in the OT because lending to other Jews for profit was forbidden (Deut. 23:19–20). Loans were permitted if extended to foreigners. Creditors are mentioned in the Mosaic law (Deut. 15:2). Temples and palaces (citadels and homes of the wealthy) safeguarded much wealth, while others hid their treasures and valuables.

Barber. Tomb pictures of Egyptian barbers at work have been found. The Hebrew word for barbers occurs only in Ezekiel 5:1, where the Lord commanded the prophet to shave his hair and beard. Male Israelites normally let their hair grow long, although they did not let it go uncut as the women did. Barbers most likely served royalty and the rich.

Basketmaker. Women members of the household wove baskets from some kind of natural fiber such as fronds of palms, straw, reeds, rushes, sedges, and grasses. Ancient Near Eastern societies had a need for lightweight containers. Israel used such containers throughout its history.

Baskets came in all sizes and shapes, although the shape resembling earthenware pots was common. Basketmakers made containers large enough to hold a person (Acts 9:25) or a human head (2 Kings 10:7), and small enough to house birds (Jer. 5:27) and carry bread (Exod. 29:3).

Beggar. There are few biblical references to beggars and no term in biblical Hebrew to describe the professional beggar. A person was reduced to begging because of divine judgment or wickedness (1 Sam. 2:7–8; Ps. 109:10; Luke 16:3), a physical handicap (Mark 10:46; Luke 18:35; John 9:8), or laziness (Prov. 20:4).

Blacksmith. (See *Metalsmith*.)

Bleacher. (See *Fuller*.)

Brewer. While brewers are not mentioned in the Bible, scholars know that ancient brewers produced a variety of beer from cereals starting over 8,000 years ago. Beer was known in Egypt and the Mesopotamian valley. Barley was buried in pots to force it to germinate, then it was mixed with water and fermented naturally. Sometime between the tenth and seventh centuries B.C. hops began to be added to the process. Strong drink is mentioned in 21 OT passages, starting from the Exodus period.

Brickmaker. The first OT record of brickmaking occurs in Genesis 11:3. Israel made clay bricks in Egypt, a process depicted on Egyptian wall paintings. Chemicals released by decomposed straw made clay bricks stronger (Exod. 5:6–19).

Brick worker. (See *Brickmaker*.)

Bronze worker. (See *Metalsmith*.)

Builder. Building is an ancient task, beginning with Cain who constructed a walled dwelling to protect himself (Gen. 4:17). Later, the descendants of Noah built a tower to climb into heaven so they might make a name for themselves (Gen. 11:4). In Egypt the Hebrews became a slave corps of builders who built storage cities for Pharaoh (Exod. 1:11). While inhabiting Canaan, the Israelites built walled towns (cities) and unwalled towns (villages), houses, palaces, temples, and many other structures.

Butler. (See *Cupbearer*.)

Camel driver. The existence of camels in Abraham's day is widely questioned. However, the remains of wild camels found in Canaan, Egyptian sculptures of camels from the third and fourth centuries B.C., and similar evidence support the scriptural reports (Gen. 12:16; 24:10).

Carpenter. (See *Builder*; *Woodworker*.)

Carver. The carvers were skilled at whittling, cutting, or chipping wood, stone, ivory, clay, bronze, gold, silver, or glass.

A stone carving from Egypt showing carpenters at work, probably from about 2500 B.C.
PHOTO BY HOWARD VOS

Skilled wood-carvers were rare. Carved panels, windows, and woodwork were signs of great wealth. The tabernacle and temple (1 Kings 6:15–38) were lavishly adorned with such work. Ivory carving—for signet rings and inlays for wooden panels (2 Chron. 9:17), jewelry, furniture, and figurines—was an ancient and highly skilled art.

Caulker. Those skilled in applying tar to hulls of ships to make them watertight were caulkers. Mentioned only in Ezekiel 27:27, caulkers plugged cracks in and between a ship's planks. These caulkers were Phoenicians, the most noted nation in the OT for ships and sea trade. (See *Shipbuilder.*)

Centurion. (See *Soldier.*)

Chamberlain. The chamberlain was responsible for guarding the king's bedroom and harem. These individuals, usually eunuchs to remove all possibility of unfaithfulness, were employed by ancient kings. They were highly trusted and influential officials (Acts 8:27). (See *Eunuch.*)

Chancellor. (See *Government official.*)

Charioteer. (See *Soldier.*)

City clerk. These individuals were important officials of Greek city-states. They were responsible for such things as caring for the city archives, taking minutes at the council meetings, handling official communications (including public readings),

serving on a number of boards, handling many administrative details, and annually distributing money to the poor.

Commander. (See *Soldier.*)

Commissioner. (See *Government official.*)

Comptroller. (See *Government official.*)

Confectioner. (See *Perfumer.*)

Controller. (See *Government official.*)

Cook. The Hebrew word translated *cook* literally means "slaughterer"—one who kills and dresses animals. The king's cooks apparently killed the animals to be prepared for his table. Cooks may have been either women servants (1 Sam. 8:13) or male professionals (Luke 17:8). In the average household, cooking was the women's job (Gen. 18:6; 27:9), although men did the slaughtering and dressing (Gen. 18:7). Gideon was a cook and a baker (Judg. 6:19).

Coppersmith. (See *Metalsmith.*)

Counselor. Ancient kings had trusted officials who served as counselors (1 Chron. 27:32; Ezra 4:5). Not all counselors, however, were professionals (2 Chron. 22:3). Isaiah 9:6 describes the coming Messiah as a Counselor. Joseph of Arimathea is called a counselor (Mark 15:43; Luke 23:50, KJV) and was a member of the Jewish council, the Sanhedrin.

Courtier. (See *Government official.*)

Craftsman. (See *Metalsmith.*)

Creditor. (See *Banker.*)

Cupbearer. This person tasted and served wine to the king. Ancient kings had to be cautious about what they ate and drank. They used trusted servants to taste everything before they consumed it. If the servant lived or did not get sick, the king and queen then ate or drank. The chief butler in the Joseph account (Gen. 40) headed the king's cupbearers. Nehemiah held this highly trusted position under King Artaxerxes (Neh. 1:11), influencing the king politically. King Solomon also used cupbearers (1 Kings 10:5).

Dancer. Professional dancers apparently did not exist among the Hebrews as they did in Egypt, Babylon, and other pagan nations. However, children danced in play (Job 21:11) and adults danced in joy (2 Sam. 6:14). Individuals could dance before God as an act of joy in worship (Exod. 15:20; Pss. 149:3; 150:4). The original Hebrew words reveal that this dancing involved skipping about, whirling, and leaping.

Dealer. (See *Merchant*.)

Designer. Designers are often mentioned with engravers and weavers (Exod. 35:35; 38:23). Artisans during OT times may have been knowledgeable in several crafts.

Disciple. This word means a "follower" or a "pupil." It was common in the ancient world for students or apprentices to attach themselves to a teacher and follow him in learning and discipline (Isa. 8:16). The Pharisees (Mark 2:18), John the Baptist (Matt. 11:2), and Jesus gathered such disciples.

Diviner. This title refers to those who practiced magic, sorcery, and divination. Diviners used the trance, dreams, clairvoyance, and other such means as inspecting the livers of animals to gain information that could not be found by ordinary means. At least once in the OT, it is a proper tool used by the godly (Prov. 16:10).

Doorkeeper. (See *Porter*.)

Drawer of water. (See *Water carrier*.)

Driver. (See *Overseer*.)

Duke. (See *Prince*.)

Dyer. These workers were skilled in permanently coloring cloth. While this is not mentioned as a specific occupation in the Bible, scholars know that dyeing was an ancient craft that often used secret formulas passed on from previous generations.

Embalmer. The Egyptians were well known for this practice. Joseph, a high official in the Egyptian court and an adopted member of the royal family, was embalmed (Gen. 50:26). He had had his father Jacob embalmed (Gen. 50:2–3). This was probably done to preserve the bodies for the trip to the family burial grounds in Canaan (Gen. 50:13–14; Josh. 24:32).

Embroiderer. Ancient embroiderers decorated clothes by using geometrical and stylized designs. The rich and powerful wore clothes beautifully embroidered (Ps. 45:14). Embroiderers participated in decorating tabernacle garments and hangings (Exod. 27:16; 28:4, 15). The embroiderer and the weaver were separate and distinct occupations, but some translations use the terms interchangeably.

Engraver. (See *Metalsmith*.)

Envoy. (See *Ambassador*.)

Eunuch. Frequently, the Hebrew word translated *eunuch* means a man who was castrated to assure he would not become involved sexually with the members of the king's harem (Isa. 56:3). In many passages, however, the word refers simply to an officer. Castrated males were not permitted to approach God's altar (Deut. 23:1).

Executioner. The OT clearly distinguishes between murder (illegally taking another's life, Exod. 20:13) and execution. In God's law many crimes were met with the death penalty (Gen. 9:6; Deut. 13:10; 21:22). It was the executioner's task to exact that penalty. Personal vengeance was prohibited (Deut. 24:16). The NT records several executions that were legal under Roman law but not under divine law (Matt. 14:10).

Fanner. This means those who winnowed or separated grain. The grain was beaten to loosen the kernels. These kernels were then trampled underfoot to loosen the chaff covering the grain. After each stage, the fanner would throw the grain into the air. The wind blew the chaff away and the grain fell to the ground. The fanner used a six-pronged pitchfork in the first stage and a shovel for the second stage (Isa. 30:24).

Farmer. Terms in the Bible that refer to farmer include *plowman* (Isa. 28:24), *husbandman* (2 Chron. 26:10, KJV), *vinedresser* (Isa. 61:5), *gardener* (John 20:15), and *tiller* (Gen. 4:2).

This was one of the major occupations of the ancient Hebrews, along with sheepherding. Farmers of ancient times were responsible for all aspects of farming. All the plowing, planting, tending, and harvesting was done by farmers and their own families. More prosperous farmers were able to hire helpers. In the NT, a farmer is one who owns the land or rents it and raises crops (Matt. 21:33).

Finer.   (See *Metalsmith*.)

Fisherman.   Both amateur and professional fishermen existed in Bible times. They used various kinds of nets, hooks, and lines (Isa. 19:8). Sometimes fishermen used spears (Job 41:7).

Footman.   These were usually runners or messengers. The footmen in Jeremiah 12:5 were couriers. The KJV often uses *footmen* to refer to foot soldiers or infantrymen. (See *Herald*.)

Foreman.   (See *Overseer*.)

Forger.   (See *Metalsmith*.)

Founder.   (See *Metalsmith*.)

Fowler.   Such people hunted and captured birds. The Egyptians were especially known for their taste for bird meat. Ancient fowlers used all kinds of implements and devices such as decoys, traps, nets, bait, bows and arrows, slings, lures, setting dogs, and bird lime smeared on branches to catch their prey.

The Mosaic law forbade taking a mother bird and her young together; only the young were to be taken (Deut. 22:6–7). Wicked, scheming enemies of the righteous are called *fowlers* (Pss. 91:3; 124:7).

Fuller.   This word refers to those who clean, shrink, thicken, and sometimes dye newly cut wool or cloth. The Hebrew word means "to trample" or "to tread," suggesting that action as a major part of the craft.

Fullers removed the oily and gummy substances from material before it could be used by washing it in alkaline such as white clay, putrid urine, or niter, as there was no soap in those days. The alkaline was washed out by treading on the material repeatedly in running or clean water. The material was then dried and bleached by the sun.

The fuller's process created an unpleasant odor. Therefore, it was usually done outside the city gates in an area named Fuller's Field (2 Kings 18:17; Isa. 7:3). God is compared to fullers' soap (Mal. 3:2, KJV).

Gardener.   (See *Farmer*.)

Gatekeeper.   (See *Porter*.)

Glassworker.   Glass was known by 2600 B.C. and so glassworkers date from at least this time. While glassworkers are not mentioned specifically in the Bible, Egyptian glassworkers (about 1400 B.C.) made vessels similar to pottery and small perfume vessels by winding hot glass rods around a sand core and then joining the layers by reheating them.

Gleaner.   (See *Laborer*.)

Goatherd.   (See *Shepherd*.)

Goldsmith.   (See *Metalsmith*.)

Government official.   Many different officials are mentioned in the Bible. Little is known, however, about many of these positions. They may have been government administrators (Gen. 41:34), religious or military overseers (1 Kings 4:5), secretaries or scribes (2 Kings 18:18), commanders (1 Sam. 14:50), or assistants to the king (Esther 1:8)

Government officials referred to in the various translations of the Bible by specific title include *chancellor, commissioner, comptroller, controller, courtier, deputy, magistrate, officer, prefect, president, procurer, recorder, treasurer, trustee,* and *viceroy.*

A quartermaster was an official who made lodging arrangements for the king during his official travels.

Guard.   (See *Soldier.*)

Harvester.   (See *Laborer.*)

Herald.   The heralds were responsible for bearing a message, often in preparation for the appearance of a king or other royal figure. The heralds ran before the king's chariot to announce his coming. Heralds also were responsible for announcing the king's messages (Dan. 3:4). The Aramaic word for *herald* is sometimes translated "to preach" (Matt. 3:1; 4:17) and, consequently, NT preachers are heralds of the King. Heralds are also sometimes referred to as *messengers.* (See *Footman.*)

Hewer.   (See *Woodworker.*)

Hewer of stone.   (See *Stoneworker.*)

Horseman.   (See *Soldier.*)

Hunter.   Hunting for sport was common among ancient kings. It is often depicted on monuments in Egypt and Assyria. In earliest times Nimrod was a noted hunter, adept at using weapons (Gen. 10:9). Later, Esau was a hunter (Gen. 27:3).

Hunters who used traps were called *trappers.*

Husbandman.   (See *Farmer.*)

Innkeeper.   In OT times, most travelers stayed in private dwellings or slept in the open. By NT times some people managed inns (Luke 10:35), which were often not comfortable or safe. Mary and Joseph probably stopped at a larger private dwelling, because it was the custom for such homeowners to rent out dwelling quarters during festival times (Luke 2:7).

Ironsmith.   (See *Metalsmith.*)

Jeweler.   People of the ancient world were fond of jewelry, and jewelry was a sign of wealth and blessing (Isa. 61:10; Ezek. 23:26). It was given to brides as a present (Gen. 24:22, 30, 53) or as part of the dowry.

Judge.   Judges governed and dispensed justice, judgment, and protection. The first judge mentioned is God himself (Gen. 18:25). This divine model is first manifested in human beings in the head of a household (Gen. 21; 22; 27). It was then seen in Moses who judged over all Israel, and in elders appointed to be judges under Moses (Exod. 18:13–27). Israel was ruled by a system of judges described in the book of Judges. The power of judgment was later passed on to the king.

Laborer.   Almost everyone in the Bible worked and worked hard. There were relatively few skilled occupations such as potters, metalsmiths, masons, scribes, dyers, weavers, and jewelry makers. For the most part the life of the average person consisted of long hours of hard work and small incomes (Ps. 90:10). Some laborers worked in the fields at harvest times as harvesters, gleaners, and reapers.

Launderer.   (See *Fuller.*)

Lawyer.   Lawyers are mentioned only in the NT. By Jesus' day the Law, the first five books of the OT, had been expanded by the Jewish leaders. Their intent was to give the people an adequate interpretation and application of divine law to every situation of life. Added to the Law was a vast body of explanation, commentary, and application, which was held to be just as binding as the actual writings of Moses.

The lawyers were experts in this large body of material. They spent their time studying, interpreting, and expounding this law and acting as court judges.

Leatherworker.   (See *Tanner.*)

Lookout.   (See *Watchman.*)

Magistrate.   (See *Government official.*)

Maid *or* Maidservant.   Two Hebrew words are translated *maid* and *maidservant.* Often they refer to a girl or woman whose task was to see to the needs of a wife or daughter of a rich or important man (Gen. 16:1). The Hebrew words may also refer to a female servant (1 Sam. 1:11) or bondservant (Lev. 25:44) whose duties were quite diverse (Exod. 11:5), as well as a female servant who served as a concubine (Judg. 19:9). The NT uses words that mean "young girl" to signify maid. (See *Servant.*)

Mason. (See *Builder; Stoneworker.*)

Merchandiser. (See *Merchant.*)

Merchant. Merchants are referred to by various translations as *traders, dealers,* and *merchandisers.* The OT recognizes a difference between international merchants (Gen. 37:28; Prov. 31:14) and merchants in general (Ezek. 17:4). In Jerusalem in Nehemiah's time, merchants selling similar or the same items were located close to one another (Neh. 3:32; 13:16). Only in the NT was being a merchant as normal an occupation as being a farmer (Matt. 22:5).

Messenger. (See *Footman; Herald.*)

Metalsmith. This occupation included those who dug the ore from the ground, refined the metal, and worked the metal into useful objects. Refining metal was an ancient skill.

The first metalworker mentioned in the Bible was Tubal-Cain, a descendant of Cain (Gen. 4:22). The smiths were often named for the metal they refined, cast, or molded. Goldsmiths worked with gold, silversmiths with silver, coppersmiths with copper, and ironsmiths with iron. Various translations use several different terms to describe metalworkers: *artificer, artisan, blacksmith, bronze worker, craftsman, engraver, finer, forger, founder, refiner,* and *smelter.*

Midwife. Midwives helped women give birth to their children (Gen. 35:17). Midwives were sometimes relatives or friends. Their task involved cutting the umbilical cord, bathing the baby, rubbing it down with salt, and swaddling it (Ezek. 16:4). In swaddling, the baby was wrapped snugly in cloth that bound its arms to its body. These women also marked which twin was the first to come forth or the firstborn (Gen. 38:28). In Egypt, Pharaoh ordered the Hebrew midwives, apparently professionals, to kill all the boy babies at birth, but the women refused to do so (Exod. 1:15–22).

Mourner. Paid professional mourners worked in the ancient world from early times. They are called "mourning women" and "skillful wailing women" (Jer. 9:17), "singing men" and "singing women" (2 Chron. 35:25). These mourners sang or chanted funeral songs or dirges (Amos 5:16), accompanied by musical instruments (Matt. 9:23).

Noble. (See *Prince.*)

Nurse. Such women breast-fed infants or helped raise young children. Pharaoh's daughter hired Moses' mother to suckle him (Exod. 2:7–9), while Naomi helped raise her grandson Obed (Ruth 4:16).

Officer. (See *Government official.*)

Orator. These were teachers of speechmaking or professional writers of speeches. The Jews found an orator's services necessary whenever they appeared before a gentile court. Such courts operated according to given rules of etiquette and oratory (Acts 24:1). Persons could lose their case simply by the crudeness of their speech.

Overseer. These individuals were responsible for controlling and managing a group of people or a task. In the OT, overseers were responsible for getting a job done (2 Chron. 2:8), and they helped to rule the people (Neh. 11:9). A captain in Pharaoh's guard made Joseph the overseer of his house (Gen. 39:4–5).

When overseers were responsible for slaves, they were sometimes called *taskmasters.* The taskmasters over the Israelite slaves in Egypt were particularly cruel (Exod. 1:11–14).

Overseers were also sometimes called

drivers, foremen, and *slavemasters.* In the NT, overseers were church officers whom some scholars equate with the term *elder,* while others see it as a distinct office. Translations do not agree with one another and do not consistently translate the word, which appears in Acts 20:28, Philippians 1:1, 1 Timothy 3:2, and Titus 1:7.

Perfumer. Perfume making is an ancient art. People of the ancient world loved perfumes and used them to cover up unpleasant body odors. The rich, especially royalty, used perfumers (1 Sam. 8:13). Perfumers and cooks are frequently associated in ancient literature, since the skills of both were closely related.

Pilot. (See *Sailor.*)

Plasterer. These workers put plaster on the walls of homes (Lev. 14:42–43) to form a smooth surface. Plastering is an ancient and widespread craft, although homeowners often did their own plastering. Good quality plaster was made by heating broken limestone and gypsum. The lowest quality plaster consisted of clay and straw and was used only in very dry climates. Plaster, also called whitewash (Deut. 27:2–4), was applied to the altar in the tabernacle and engraved while still wet.

Plowman. (See *Farmer.*)

Poet. Poets expressed ideas about things in imagery. Biblical poets used simile, comparing one subject to another (Ps. 125:1); metaphor, referring to a subject in terms of another subject (Ps. 62:2); and other figures of speech. The most famous OT poets are probably Moses (Exod. 15), David (Psalms), and Solomon (Proverbs, Ecclesiastes, Song of Solomon). Several NT writers, including Paul (Rom. 8:31–39) and John (Rev. 18:2–24), wrote poetry.

Porter. These persons guarded the entrance to city and public buildings (John 18:17), temples, homes of the wealthy (Mark 13:34), and sheepfolds (John 10:3). Guards were stationed at any entrance through which someone unwanted might enter, especially at night. This must have been a lowly job because of the contrast implied in Psalm 84:10, where *doorkeeper* is the opposite of the most luxurious and favorable position. Porters were also called *gatekeepers.*

Potter. Pottery is an ancient and developed craft. The pottery wheel appeared about 4000 B.C. In its early history, Israel had professional potters who sat on the edge of small pits, turning pottery wheels with their feet. In treading the clay or kneading it by foot it was important to get the right consistency for a good product. Many potters probably treaded the clay themselves (Isa. 41:25).

Prefect. (See *Government official.*)

President. (See *Government official.*)

Prince *or* Princess. When not royalty, then persons in positions of authority and responsibility. *Prince* is sometimes translated *duke* or *noble* by some English versions.

Procurer. (See *Government official.*)

Prognosticator. (See *Astrologer.*)

Quarryman. (See *Stoneworker.*)

Quartermaster. (See *Government official.*)

Reaper. (See *Laborer.*)

Recorder. (See *Government official.*)

Refiner. (See *Metalsmith.*)

Robber. (See *Criminal.*)

Sage. (See *Astrologer.*)

Sailor. Israel was never a seafaring power. The Phoenicians were the best known and perhaps most skilled sailors who toiled at sea. Jonah traveled on a Phoenician ship (Jon. 1:3). Phoenician sailors were skilled as navigators, pilots, oarsmen, and sailmen who sailed their sturdy ships to distant lands in international trade.

Scribe. (See *Secretary.*)

Sculptor. (See *Stoneworker.*)

Seamster. (See *Weaver.*)

Secretary. Those of this profession did the writing and corresponding for others. In OT society this job was done by a scribe (Jer. 36:26, 32). By NT times scribal duties had increased considerably. The non-Jewish world featured public and private secretaries who wrote, usually in shorthand, from dictation or received the general sense from the author and filled in the rest with appropriate language. Paul may have dictated his letters (Rom. 16:22; Gal. 6:11; 2 Thess. 3:17).

Sentry. (See *Watchman.*)

Sergeant. (See *Soldier.*)

Serpent charmer. This skill in hypnotizing snakes was used by the priests and magicians of Egypt before the Exodus (Ps. 58:5; Eccles. 10:11; Jer. 8:17).

Servant. In Bible times servants could be slaves or persons not free to do their own bidding. Or they could be domestic or hired hands who were paid for their work but free to leave their jobs. They might be neither of these but volunteers choosing to do others' bidding. This idea may be rooted in and governed by the idea of a covenant. Individual believers (Ps. 78:70–72) or God's people as a whole (Isa. 41:8–10) are his servants. Servants are sometimes referred to in the Bible as *attendants*.

Sheepbreeder. (See *Shepherd.*)

Sheepshearer. (See *Shepherd.*)

Shepherd. Abel was the first shepherd mentioned in the Bible. Later Abraham, Isaac, and Jacob became shepherds (Gen. 13:7; 26:20; 30:36). When Israel went into Egypt, the rulers isolated them because they considered shepherds unclean (Gen. 46:34).

In the OT God is often called a shepherd. David used this beautiful metaphor for God (Ps. 23). Isaiah used the same image, comparing God's care of Israel to a shepherd feeding his flock and bearing lambs in his bosom (Isa. 40:11).

Shipbuilder. While they were never a seafaring people, the Hebrews were acquainted with ships, as their historical and poetic literature demonstrates (1 Kings 9:27; Isa. 33:21; Ezek. 27:25). The primary shipbuilders of old were the Phoenicians, who supplied ships for Solomon's trading fleet at Ezion-geber (1 Kings 9:26–27).

In the time between the Testaments, the Greeks and Romans gained prominence as shipbuilders. Smaller fishing boats with a capacity of about 12 men may have been constructed by craftsmen or by the fishermen themselves (Mark 4:1). Shipbuilders were sometimes called *shipwrights*. (See *Caulker.*)

Shipwright. (See *Shipbuilder.*)

Silversmith. (See *Metalsmith.*)

Singer. These were professional vocalists, usually trained. David organized hundreds of Levites as temple musicians (1 Chron. 25). Many of them were probably choir members. Temple singers originally were all men between the ages of 30 and 50. After the captivity, women participated in the choirs (Ezra 2:65).

Slave. In the OT, slaves were both Jewish and gentile. Jews became slaves through their inability to pay their debts or because of poverty and theft. The law protected slaves and granted them certain rights (Exod. 21:2–11; Lev. 25:39–55; Deut. 21:10–14).

Slavemaster. (See *Overseer.*)

Smelter. (See *Metalsmith.*)

Smith. (See *Metalsmith.*)

Soldier. Before Saul, Israel had no professional soldiers, although each tribe specialized in training its adult males in the use of a particular weapon (1 Chron. 12). With a few exceptions (Deut. 20:5–8), all men over the age of 20 were liable to be called to arms in emergencies (Num. 1:3).

These professionals were sometimes referred to in more specific terms. A *guard* was assigned to protect a particular person or thing. A *charioteer* fought from a chariot. As warfare became more developed, chariots were made to hold a driver and one or more fighting soldiers (1 Kings 22:34; 2 Chron. 18:33). A *commander* led other soldiers.

The Romans had an elaborate and detailed army. Specific Roman soldiers are sometimes mentioned in the Bible. A *centurion* was a noncommissioned officer commanding at least 100 men. A *sergeant* was often the local policeman, enforcing the law, with punishment pronounced by the magistrate.

Stargazer. (See *Astrologer.*)

Steward. These workers were entrusted with caring for their superiors' goods. In the OT stewards were over entire households, responsible for managing the material goods (Gen. 43:19). In the NT *stewards* referred to *guardians* or *curators* (Matt. 20:8; Gal. 4:2) in addition to its older meaning as *managers* or *superintendents of households* (Luke 8:2–3; 1 Cor. 4:1–2).

Stonecutter. (See *Stoneworker.*)

Stonemason. (See *Stoneworker.*)

Stoneworker. These workers fashioned stone into usable or ornamental items. Stoneworkers included quarrymen or stonecutters who cut stones or slabs of stone in quarries (1 Kings 5:17; 6:7), stonemasons who shaped the stones and joined them into walls of buildings (2 Kings 22:6; 1 Chron. 22:2; 2 Chron. 24:12), and sculptors. The most skilled stoneworkers in ancient times were from Phoenicia (2 Sam. 5:11; 1 Chron. 14:1). Stoneworkers also hewed out wine vats, cisterns, tombs, and water tunnels.

Tailor. This occupation is implied rather than specifically mentioned in the Bible. In Israel most women made all the family's clothing. This work included preparing the thread or yarn and doing the weaving. Clothing was loose fitting, requiring little design work. The rich, no doubt, had others sew and decorate their clothing for them.

Tanner. These people converted animal skins into leather and made useful or ornamental items from it. Tanning was widespread in the ancient world. Early Israelite families tanned their own hides. But with the growth of cities, leather craftsmen arose. Peter once stayed with a tanner named Simon (Acts 10:6).

Tanning animal skins was an involved process requiring much skill. The hides were soaked until the fat, blood, and hair were removed. After the leather was tanned, it was used for many purposes, including tents (Exod. 26:14), sandals (Ezek. 16:10), hats, skirts, and aprons.

Tapestry maker. (See *Weaver.*)

Taskmaster. (See *Overseer.*)

Tentmaker. An ancient craft, tentmaking consisted of cutting and sewing together cloth, frequently of goat's hair, and attaching ropes and loops. Such crafts were passed from father to son. Paul's native province of Cilicia exported Cilician cloth, a cloth of goat's hair. The only direct reference to tentmakers in the Bible occurs in Acts 18:2–3, where Paul, Aquila, and Priscilla are called tentmakers.

Thief. (See *Criminal.*)

Tiller. (See *Farmer.*)

Townclerk. (See *City clerk.*)

Trader. (See *Merchant.*)

Trapper. (See *Hunter.*)

Treasurer. (See *Government official.*)

Trustee. (See *Government official.*)

Viceroy. (See *Government official.*)

Vinedresser. (See *Farmer.*)

Watchman. These workers guarded or watched over a city or harvest field. Because of the danger of being raided, every city or village had watchmen, especially at night. These watchmen were stationed on the city walls (2 Sam. 18:24), a watchtower (2 Kings 9:17), or a hilltop (Jer. 31:6). Watchmen were responsible for reporting any hostile action or approaching suspicious person. They sometimes patrolled the city, called out the hours of the night, and especially looked forward to dawn (Isa. 21:11–12).

At harvest times watchmen guarded the crops at night. Israel's prophets were responsible for watching for impending divine judgment or blessing (Isa. 21:6; 52:8; Jer. 6:17) and bringing the news to the people. Watchmen are sometimes referred to as *sentries* and *lookouts*.

Water carrier. This lowly job meant going to the well or spring to bring back a household's water. It was assigned to young men (Ruth 2:9) and women (Gen. 24:13; 1 Sam. 9:11) but usually to the lowliest slaves (Josh. 9:21–27). Some translations refer to this occupation as *drawer of water.* Wells and springs were generally situated outside the city gates. Water was carried home in pots and goatskin bags, sometimes borne by a donkey.

Weaver. Weaving was known in the ancient world from about 2000 B.C. Almost every household had a loom, and women spent much time at this task (Prov. 31:13, 19, 22, 24). They sat before their looms and passed the shuttle back and forth through the warp thread while manipulating the loom. They also made their own yarn or thread from animal hair or plant fibers. For instance, flax was made into linen. In other countries, such as Egypt and Assyria, weaving was done mostly by men. Such professional weavers worked in urban areas. Even urban areas in Israel boasted professional weavers.

Well digger. During most of the year there is relatively little rain in the Holy Land, so having wells and cisterns was important. Most scholars believe well diggers were relatively skilled workers, and the wells that they dug were considered valuable. The wells bore specific names (Gen. 26:20–22) and were sometimes fought over by rivals (Gen. 21:25–30).

Starting about the time of the exodus, people of the ancient world also built cisterns that were usually pear-shaped holes lined with plaster and filled with rain water. They were considerably more skilled in digging through rock and earth and in engineering than is often realized. One example of this is Hezekiah's Siloam tunnel in Jerusalem. It was cut through 5,334 meters (1,750 feet) of solid rock, with workers starting at both ends and meeting in the middle.

Woodcutter. (See *Woodworker*.)

Woodworker. Archaeology has demonstrated that ancient Canaan had forests, and yet wood was scarce and expensive. Woodworkers included
• Lumberjacks and woodcutters who felled trees (1 Kings 5:6)
• Hewers who trimmed and readied them for transportation
• Laborers who transported them (1 Kings 5:13–14)
• Carpenters who made them into houses, furniture, tools, and other useful items (2 Kings 22:6)
• Those who carved wood into bas-relief and statue artistry (Isa. 40:20; Jer. 10:3–4).
(See *Builder*.)

Tools and Implements _____

The OT often refers to tools by using the collective Hebrew words *keli* (literally "vessels" or "instruments") and *hereb* ("sword," "knife," or any "sharp cutting instrument"). When Scripture uses one of these general terms, the context helps to determine which tools the writer might have been referring to. Each craft or trade had its own particular tools.

Tools appeared on the scene of history early. The Bible tells us that "Cain was a tiller of the ground" (Gen. 4:2). He must have used some kind of tool to break the ground, though the exact tool is not mentioned. Archaeologists have found flint knives, scrapers, and hoes from the early Neolithic era (ca. 7000 B.C.) in Palestine. Flint was used for rough tools such as reaping hooks even after metal was plentiful (ca. 1000 B.C.). But as metalworkers learned to use copper, bronze, and meteoric iron, they developed various metal tools.

Likely the Israelites were not as skilled in the use of tools as some of their neighbors. This might explain why Solomon employed the craftsmen of Hiram to build the temple (1 Kings 7:13), and why Bezalel and Aholiab were summoned for the building of the tabernacle (Exod. 31:1–11).

Tools of the Egyptians

Archaeologists have learned a great deal about the tools of the ancient world by studying the implements and tools used by the Egyptians. The Egyptian pyramid is a marvel, even in our modern age. But the question of how it was so precisely constructed has puzzled scholars for centuries.

As the Pharaohs' tombs have been excavated, archaeologists have discovered details of Egyptian technology and the tools used in constructing the pyramids. The people of the Nile had a skill for cutting, dressing, transporting, fitting, cementing, and polishing hard and heavy rock.

Having learned to work with metal, Egyptians were able to develop carpentry skills. They designed chisels, hammers, mallets, scrapers, and squares; several specimens of these tools have been found in the ancient tombs.

Tools of the Hebrews

While the Egyptians were skilled in the use of tools, the Hebrews were not. The Bible refers to the use of tools only incidentally, in connection with arts and crafts. The tools of the Egyptians surpassed those of other neighboring cultures as well and enabled Egypt to develop a sophisticated technology that still amazes people today.

Barber's tools. The types of tools used by barbers in Bible times were much the same as those used today. Barber items such as the mirror and razor are certainly familiar to us.

Mirror. Mirrors dating from the Bronze Age have been found in Palestine. These mirrors or looking glasses were made of highly polished metal. Hebrew women may have brought mirrors with them when they came out of Egypt.

The mirrors used by the Egyptians were made of mixed metals, chiefly copper. These could be polished to a high luster, but were liable to rust and tarnish. The Hebrew *gillayon* may refer to mirrors (cf. Isa. 3:23). Isaiah considered them to be extravagant finery.

Razor. The practice of shaving a man's head after he completed a vow indicates that the Israelites had barbers (Num. 6:9; 8:7; Lev. 14:8; Isa. 7:20). In some instances the whole body was shaved (Num. 8:7).

Builder's tools. The Hebrew word *bana* was used to refer to construction workers, both skilled and unskilled. The tools used by master builders as they supervised the construction (1 Cor. 3:10) included the measuring line and the plumb line.

Measuring line. Builders used this tool to survey a building site. Scripture indicates that there may have been more than one type of measuring line. A rope or cord might have been used for this purpose (2 Sam. 8:2; Zech. 2:1); but a string or thread might also have been used. In any case, the measuring line was knotted or marked at one-cubit intervals (cf. 1 Kings 7:15, 23). The cubit (Hebrew *amma*) was an ancient measure of length that equaled about 45 centimeters (17.5 inches). Originally, a cubit was the distance from the tip of the middle finger to the elbow.

In the KJV NT, distance was measured in Roman measures (usually translated by the Elizabethan English term *furlongs*), which were approximately 220 meters (660 feet) long (Luke 24:13; John 6:19; 11:18; Rev. 14:20; 21:16). Sometimes builders took measurements with reeds of a standard length (cf. Rev. 11:1; 21:15).

Plumb line. The Hebrew word *misqelet* is translated as *plummet* in the KJV (2 Kings 21:13). In modern builder's terms, it would be called a *plumb line*.

A plumb line was used to measure and check the vertical line of a structure. This tool was a small lead cone, fastened by cord to a cylindrical piece of wood that was the same diameter as the cone. The wood cylinder was placed against the wall at the top. If the wall was straight, the lead cone at the end of the plumb line should barely touch the wall.

Carpenter's tools. The trade of the carpenter is often mentioned in the Scriptures (cf. Gen. 6:14; Exod. 37). It seems that the carpenter was usually a talented woodcarver (1 Kings 6:18, 29).

Adze. In Bible times the adze was used to shape wood. The blade of this tool was curved and attached to the handle at a right angle.

A typical mirror of Bible times, made of highly polished metal. PHOTO BY GUSTAV JEENINGA

Archaeologists have found the remains of a type of adze used by the Egyptians in about 2000 B.C. This Egyptian adze had a copper blade and was strapped to the wooden handle at a right angle. It is possible that the *planes* mentioned in Isaiah 44:13 was made in the same way.

Awl (aul). Carpenters of Bible times used the awl to poke holes in wood or leather. The awl was a tool with a small pointed blade that stuck straight out the end of the wooden handle. Egyptian monuments picture the awl. The Israelites also used this tool to pierce a hole in the ear of a servant, indicating that he would be a servant forever (cf. Exod. 21:6; Deut. 15:17).

Bow drill. Archaeological discoveries indicate that a type of drill was used in Bible times. The bit, or sharp point, was inserted in the tip of a wooden handle. The string of the bow (shaped like the type used to shoot arrows) was wrapped around the wooden handle of the bit. When the carpenter moved the bow forward and backward, it caused the bow drill to rotate, boring into the wood.

Scripture makes no specific mention of this tool. However, the Bible does mention boring a hole in the lid of a chest (2 Kings 12:9).

Chisel. Archaeological discoveries show that these sharp tools were made of copper. Looking somewhat like a wide screwdriver, the chisel was a thin wedge of metal and had to be continually resharpened. Copper chisels were used by the Egyptians from about 2000 B.C., and it is possible that the same tool was used by the Hebrews.

Compass or Divider. Ancient carpenters used the compass to mark a circle or portions of a circle. No description of the compass is given in the Scriptures, but archaeologists have found the remains of these ancient tools at several sites in Egypt and Palestine.

Marking tool. The *rule* mentioned in Isaiah 44:13 was a measuring line, used much the same as we would use a measuring tape or rule today. After measuring the correct distance on a piece of wood, the carpenter marked it with a stylus or some kind of marking device.

Maul or Hammer. The ancient carpenter's hammer was usually made of heavy stone, drilled with a hole for inserting a handle (cf. 1 Kings 6:7; Isa. 41:7). The maul mentioned in Proverbs 25:18 (KJV) is thought to have been a heavy wooden hammer or mallet that the carpenter may also have used (Judg. 5:26).

Nail. Carpenters used nails to hold pieces of wood together (Jer. 10:4). Iron was used to make these pins or nails (1 Chron. 22:3). Golden or gilded nails were also used (2 Chron. 3:9).

Saw. The ancient Egyptians used saws with teeth pointing toward the handle (instead of away from the handle, like those of modern saws). In most cases, these Egyptian saws had bronze blades, attached to the handle by leather thongs. Some ancient saws in the British Museum have blades inserted into the handle, much as do our modern knives.

Farmer's tools. Although Cain was a tiller of the ground (Gen. 4:2), the Bible does not mention specific farming tools until after the Flood. The tools Cain used were probably made of wood and were very primitive.

Fan. After the threshing machine had done its job, farmers used winnowing fans to throw the stalks and grain into the wind (Isa. 30:24; Jer. 15:7). The breeze separated the grain from the chaff.

The fan is still used in some remote areas of the Middle East. It is a wooden, semi-oval frame, about one meter (one yard) wide.

Isaiah 30:24 mentions that a *shovel* was used in the same manner; but this tool is not described.

File. The file was used to sharpen other types of tools: "Yet they had a file for the mattocks, and for the coulters, and for the forks, and for the axes, and to sharpen the goads" (1 Sam. 13:21, KJV). This is the only scriptural reference, and the exact nature of the tool is not described.

Goad. Hebrew plowmen used a goad for urging on the oxen. The goad was a pole 213 to 240 centimeters (seven to eight feet) long, having a point at one end. The point was sometimes tipped with iron and sharpened (1 Sam. 13:21).

Shamgar used the goad as an effective weapon: "After him was Shamgar the son of Anath, who killed six hundred men of the Philistines with an ox goad" (Judg. 3:31).

Harrow. The harrow was a well-known farming implement (Job 39:10, KJV). Some Scriptures translate this word as "to break the clods," which probably conveys the proper meaning (Isa. 28:24; Hos. 10:11).

The Hebrew noun for harrow *(charitz)* represents an instrument with teeth (cf. 2 Sam. 12:31; 1 Chron. 20:3, KJV). It might have been pulled along by an ox (Job 39:10). It was actually a kind of sled with stone or metal blades mounted on the underside.

Mattock. Israelites used the mattock to break the ground, much as we would use a hoe (Isa. 7:25, KJV). The Hebrew word for mattock *(ma'der)* literally meant "an instrument used to dig in the ground" (Isa. 5:6).

The head of this tool was made of iron, which could be sharpened (1 Sam. 13:20–21) and used as a weapon.

Plow. Deuteronomy 22:10 is the first Scripture reference to the plow. The Law admonished, "You shall not plow with an ox and a donkey together."

This farming tool was made of wood, although the use of iron was known from the time of Tubal-Cain (Gen. 4:22) and the Israelites had iron tools when they entered Canaan (Deut. 27:5).

The primitive Hebrew plow was made of oak. The bent parts were formed by the natural curves in the wood and were held together with iron bands. To this, the farmer fastened a single upright shaft with a short crosspiece to serve as a handle. The single-handed plow was lightweight, allowing farmers to leave one hand free to use the ox goad.

Sickle. Jews used the sickle to harvest grain and other crops (Deut. 16:9). This tool had a short wooden handle, turned toward the point. Ancient Egyptian monuments show the type of sickle that was used in Egypt. Clay and wooden sickles with flint blades have been frequently found in excavations.

Ancient Mesopotamian sickles were made of flint teeth, set in wood. In the tenth century B.C., small curved blades replaced the earlier flint.

Sieve. Israelites used the sieve to separate grain from the grit and dirt after it was threshed and fanned (Isa. 30:28).

Prophets used the sieve as a symbol of God's judgment, which would sift the nations (Isa. 30:28; Amos 9:9). Jesus also used this symbolism (Luke 22:31).

Threshing machine. After the harvest, the grain was spread on the threshing floor—usually a hard-packed patch of ground located at the outskirts of the city. Farmers separated grain from the straw by having oxen trample on it, or by pulling a threshing instrument over it.

There were two types of threshing machines—one made of flat boards and the other that ran on small wheels or rollers (Isa. 28:27–28). The wooden sled-type machine had stones or iron fragments fastened to the underside (Amos 1:3). (See also *Agriculture.*)

Yoke. Israelite farmers seem to have been well acquainted with plowing, since the yoke is often mentioned in Scripture (e.g., Gen. 27:40).

Farmers placed the yoke on the necks of oxen that pulled the plow. It was made of wood and kept the oxen in their places as they pulled. Traces (leather straps) were connected to the yoke and the plow for pulling the plow along.

A pair of oxen were called a "yoke of oxen," as we see in 1 Kings 19:19.

Fisherman's tools. Fish were an abundant food source of Bible times, and we find that fishermen used special tools for catching fish.

Anchor. Ancient fishermen used the anchor much as it is used today. However, early anchors were simply large stones or crooked pieces of wood weighted with stones. These crude tools were not capable of holding a large vessel, and metal anchors with hooks were soon developed.

At first the metal anchor had only one barb to catch the ground; then anchors with as many as four barbs were developed. Acts 27:29 is thought to refer to a four-barbed anchor: "They dropped four anchors from the stern, and prayed for day to come."

Casting line. When Jesus called Simon and Andrew to be his disciples, he found them "casting a net into the sea; for they were fishermen" (Mark 1:16–17; cf. Matt. 4:18). The casting net (Greek *amphiblestron*) had a circular form about 4.5 meters (15 feet) in diameter, with a fine mesh. Fishermen placed lead sinkers around the edge of the net to take the net to the bottom of the lake. They attached a long piece of line to the center of the net. They held this line with the left hand, gathered the net up with the right, and cast it out into the shallow water.

Dragnet or Drawnet. The Greek word *sagene* appears as *dragnet* in Matthew 13:47. Fishermen used this type of net in deeper water (Luke 5:4; Greek *diktuon*). It was a long net—sometimes nearly 100 meters (328 feet) long—and about 2.5 meters (8 feet) wide. The fishermen attached corks to one side to keep it buoyed up, and lead sinkers to the other side to make it sink.

Sometimes the net was stretched between two boats and the boats were rowed in a circle, drawing the net together. The ropes attached to the bottom of the net were drawn in faster than those at the top, which trapped the fish in the net (John 21:6).

Hook. Hooks were also used for fishing. Peter used a fishhook to catch a fish (Matt. 17:27). We know that Assyrian fishermen used the hook and line for fishing, as shown by inscriptions from 700 B.C.

Spear. Hebrew fishermen used the spear, and possibly a type of harpoon, for fishing (Job 41:7). The spear head and the barbs of the harpoons were probably made of iron. Ancient inscriptions prove that such tools were used by the Egyptians.

General tools. Scripture refers to two tools that were used in a variety of trades—the ax and the hammer.

Ax. Seven different Hebrew words are translated as *ax* in English versions. The most commonly used is *garzen,* from a Hebrew root word that means "to be cut" or "sever." This type of ax had a head of iron (Isa. 10:34) fastened to a handle of wood by leather straps. The ax head sometimes slipped off the handle during use (Deut. 19:5; 2 Kings 6:4–7).

Ax blades might be short or long. They were set in the wooden handle, parallel or at a right angle to the handle. Materials for the ax head varied from stone (in the earliest times) to bronze and iron. Modern scholars believe that the Israelites learned ironworking from the Philistines (cf. 1 Sam. 13:20).

Hammer. The ancient hammer looked much like the hammers we use today. More than one Hebrew word was used to denote this tool. The type of hammer used to drive the tent peg into Sisera's head (Judg. 5:26) was called the *halmuth.* But the Hebrew words *makkubhah* and *makkebheth* also referred to the hammer (Judg. 4:21; 1 Kings 6:7; Isa. 44:12; Jer. 10:4).

Householder's tools. Hebrew women used special tools in preparing food for the family. Most of the food preparation was done in a courtyard near their houses.

Knife. The Hebrews used a knife called *ma'akeleth* (literally "eating instrument") for slaughtering animals for food or sacrifice (Gen. 22:6). Another Hebrew word, *hereb*, meant a knife made of flint (Josh. 5:2) or perhaps a knife for shaving (Ezek. 5:1). The flint knife survived well into the Bronze Age for everyday use.

Mill. We first read of the grain mill in Exodus 11:5, which describes the custom of hiring women to turn it: "Even to the first-born of the female servant who is behind the handmill." The wandering Israelites ground manna in mills (Num. 11:8). The mill was such an important item of domestic use that no one was allowed to take it as collateral for a loan (Deut. 24:6).

In Abraham's time, grain was pounded or ground by spreading it on a flat stone and rubbing it with a round stone muller (Gen. 18:6). This type of grinding tool was found in the ruins of Jericho.

The rotary mill came into use during the iron age and consisted of two circular stone slabs 50 centimeters (20 inches) across. A pivot secured the upper slab (Hebrew *rekeb*) to the stone beneath. Women poured grain through the pivot hole in the upper stone, and it was ground as the wheel turned. The flour was forced out between the two stones as more grain was added. Often two women would grind, sitting on either side of the mill. They would turn the mill with a wooden handle attached to the outer surface of the upper stone (cf. Matt. 24:41).

Needle. Hebrew women used needles to make clothing. The first scriptural reference to needlework is Exodus 26:36, which gives specifications for the temple hangings. Needlework was common in Bible times (cf. Exod. 27:16; 28:39; 36:37; 38:18; 39:29; Judg. 5:30; Ps. 45:14).

Oven. Ovens were usually built in the courtyard. These early ovens were hollow

at the top, about 60 centimeters (24 inches) in diameter at the base and about 30 centimeters (12 inches) high. They often were constructed by alternating layers of clay and potsherds (pieces of broken pottery; Job 2:8). The women could bake flat cakes by sticking them to the sides of the oven or placing them over a fire on heated stones (Lev. 2:4; 11:35; 26:26). Archaeologists have found the remains of such ovens in the ruins of Megiddo.

Press. Presses were used to extract the juice of grapes, olives, and other fruit. A full winepress was a sign of prosperity.

Mason's tools. Stone masons used many of the same tools that were used by builders and carpenters of that day, such as the hammer, plumb line, marking tool, measuring line, saw, and chisel.

Masons used saws to cut stone for the temple (1 Kings 7:9). Some Bible passages suggest that they may have used a level and square (Ezek. 41:21), but clear Scripture references to such tools cannot be found. Stones from both Herod's temple and his fortress-palace at Masada show that the stones were cut and fitted before being erected. They often have numbers or mason's marks carved in them.

Metalsmith's tools. In Bible times, the smith was often referred to as he "who blows the coals in the fire" (Isa. 54:16). The metalsmith poured liquid metal from ladles or buckets into clay molds or beat it on an anvil with a forge hammer. The coppersmith and ironworker *(haras barzel)* were also known as hammerers (Isa. 41:7; 44:12), because they flattened and smoothed metal by pounding.

Anvil. The Hebrew for anvil occurs only in Isaiah 41:7: "He who smoothes with the hammer inspired him who strikes the anvil." The earliest anvils were made of bronze. But when Israelites mastered the smelting of iron, they formed it into anvils. The anvil was a metal surface on which the smith would place an object to hammer it

Drawings of several householder's tools excavated at Pompeii and dating to the first century A.D.   PHOTO BY HOWARD VOS

into the desired shape. He might place this metal surface on a large block of wood to deaden the sound of the pounding.

Bellows. The smith used this instrument to force a draft of air through clay pipes to the furnace, producing enough heat to melt metal (Ezek. 22:20). Usually the bellows (Hebrew *mappuach*) was made of sewn goatskin or sheepskin (Jer. 6:29). The skin formed an airtight bag that was fitted in a frame of wood. When the smith compressed this bag, the air was forced out under the pressure.

Furnace. The smith used a furnace that could be heated to high temperatures (Dan. 3:19). But the ancient smiths were never able to get their furnaces hot enough to pour melted iron as they did copper. Iron came from the furnace as a spongy mass of iron, slag, and cinders. The smith hammered it out to remove the slag and air bubbles. Then it was put in the furnace until it

was forged into wrought iron, and finally worked by the skilled blacksmith (1 Sam. 13:18–20). If he needed to sharpen the edges of instruments, such as axes or knives, he might use a whetstone or file (Eccles. 10:10).

Archaeologists have found the remains of smiths' furnaces at Beth Shemesh (Josh. 15:10). There were two different types of furnaces, both made of clay bricks. One had holes in the sides where air could be forced in by a blowpipe. The second type was long and narrow, and open to the air.

Tongs. Often the smith used tongs to lift iron from the furnace or fire (Isa. 44:12). These early tongs were made of bronze; but as iron became available, they were made of that metal.

The smith's tongs had much the same shape as tongs used today. In the archaeological diggings at Tell el-Amarna, Egypt, tongs from 1350 B.C. have been discovered. The grasping ends on the ancient tongs were shaped like human hands.

Potter's tools. Until about 3000 B.C. pottery was hand-molded. After this time, it was made on a potter's wheel. The potter's work is described in Jeremiah 18:3–4.

Furnace. Furnaces were used for baking pottery. The remains of such furnaces or kilns have been discovered at Megiddo.

Paddle and Scraper. From archaeological finds, we know that the potter used various types of paddles and scrapers of wood and stone. But there is no record of these tools in the Scriptures.

Wheel. Examples of the potter's wheel have been discovered in archaeological diggings at Jericho, Megiddo, Gezer, Laish, Hazor, and other cities. These relics show that the potter sat at the edge of a pit in which the wheel stood (Jer. 18:3). The lower stone of the wheel rested in the pit, while the upper stone was on a pivot. A wooden collar encircled the upper stone, and the potter turned this collar with his feet.

Life of
the Family

Birth and Infancy _____

Today, as in biblical times, the birth of a child is a momentous occasion. But today's parents may well be debating questions that the people living in ancient Israel would have found strange and startling. For example, the following questions would not have entered the minds of the Israelites:

Should we have children?

If so, should we limit the number to one or two?

If we do have children, when should we begin?

The ancient Israelites' attitude could be summed up like this: "We want children. We want them now. We will have as many children as we can because children are very important to us. In fact, we would rather be wealthy with children than with money."

The Desire for Children

The first command of God was, "Be fruitful and multiply; fill the earth and subdue it" (Gen. 1:28). The couples in biblical times took this command literally. As one of the Jewish sages declared, "If anyone does not engage in increase, it is as though he were to shed blood or to diminish God's image."

Every Jewish couple wanted children—that was one of the goals of marriage. The couple wanted to be remembered. Only through offspring was this assured. To die without descendants might allow an entire family to be wiped out, forgotten forever.

A Jewish couple hoped that each new child would be a son, but they gladly accepted either a boy or a girl. This was not the case in some of the surrounding cultures. Newborn girls were often left out in the open to die. Some Gentile parents even sold their baby girls into slavery.

The Childless Couple

The story of Rachel and Leah (Jacob's wives) illustrates how important it was for a woman to give her husband sons (Gen. 30:1–24).

Many Israelite couples were unable to bear children. Today we know that couples may be childless because of the husband's or wife's sterility; at that time, however, only the wife was blamed for the problem. (For an exception, see Deut. 7:14.)

Rachel's cry, "Give me children, or else I die!" (Gen. 30:1), expressed the feelings of every bride. And no doubt many a concerned husband agreed with Jacob's response: "Am I in the place of God, who has withheld from you the fruit of the womb?" (Gen. 30:2).

Townspeople ridiculed a barren woman by calling her a reproach (Luke 1:25). Even those who loved her treated her as an object of pity, and placed her in the same category as a widow.

The childless wife was spiritually ruined, socially disgraced, and psychologically depressed. She was married to a husband who wanted a child to assure the continuation of his family line. Her husband might continue to love her, but she felt that was small consolation (cf. 1 Sam. 1:6–8). It was in fact a great mercy, for a resentful husband could have made her life unbearable.

A barren couple spent time examining their past failures to see if any sin had been unconfessed. Through tears the wife repented of all known sin. Then the husband offered a fitting sacrifice to cover any unknown sins (Lev. 4:2).

When sin was ruled out as the cause of the problem, the wife was free to inquire about different kinds of remedies. Her relatives, friends, and neighbors might suggest that she try various love foods or potions that had proved to be helpful to them.

One such food is mentioned in Scripture: Rachel requested *mandrakes* from Leah, her sister (Gen. 30:14–16). Mandrakes were plants believed to produce fertility; they were often used as love charms. Rachel believed that if she ate this food she would conceive. In rabbinic times women sought to overcome their barrenness by changing their diets. Apples and fish were thought to cause a person to become sexually powerful for procreation.

Modern excavations in Israel have produced many clay fertility figures. They were supposed to help a woman get pregnant by sympathetic magic. Each figurine was modeled to look like a pregnant woman. As the barren woman handled it and kept it near her, she hoped to take on the likeness of the pregnant figure.

Women also wore amulets to ensure fertility. Jeremiah noted another common heathen practice: the women of Judah kneaded cakes, gave drink offerings, and burned incense to the "queen of heaven" to assure fertility (Jer. 44:17–19; cf. Jer. 7:18). The queen mentioned in this passage was probably Astarte (Ashtoreth), the Canaanite goddess of sexual love, maternity, and fertility.

If all the remedies were unsuccessful, the woman was considered to be permanently barren. At this point, the husband might take drastic measures. He might marry another wife or, at least in patriarchal times, use a slave to bear children under his name. This is why Sarah gave her servant Hagar to Abraham (Gen. 16:2) and Rachel asked her husband Jacob to impregnate her handmaid, Bilhah (Gen. 30:3).

Adoption was also a method of overcoming the infertility of the wife. The childless couple could adopt an infant or even an adult as their own child. Eliezer of Damascus was a grown man, but Abraham told God that he was to be his heir (Gen. 15:2). The fifteenth-century B.C. tablets discovered at Nuzi show that Abraham was following a common practice for Semitic cultures, although we have few biblical references to it.

Pain in Childbearing

The Pharaoh of Egypt questioned two midwives because they disobeyed his order to kill the Hebrew male infants. They responded, ". . . the Hebrew women are not like the Egyptian women; for they are lively and give birth before the midwives come to them" (Exod. 1:19).

How should we interpret what the midwives said? Were they making up this story because they feared the Lord (Exod. 1:17)? If they were telling the truth, what did they mean? We cannot assume that all Hebrew mothers had painless deliveries; other biblical passages do not back up this theory.

Birth pains were sometimes accompanied by complications. The OT records several occasions where the mother's life was endangered. For example, the child born to Tamar was named Perez, meaning "breach." The midwife noticed that the child had made an unusually large breach or tear in the mother (Gen. 38:28). Jacob's beloved wife Rachel died while giving birth to Benjamin, her second son (Gen. 35:18–20). Also, Phinehas's wife lost her life in childbirth, although the child was saved (1 Sam. 4:20). The birth of a child was painful and often difficult.

The Delivery

In some ancient cultures the mother would lie down to deliver a child; in others, the mother would squat in a crouching position. Although Scripture says little about this phase of birth, there is one reference to a birthstool (Exod. 1:16), which implies that the mother did not lie down. Unfortunately, the birthstool is not described. But such stools are well-known from other cultures of the Middle East.

The mother was usually assisted by a midwife, a woman specially experienced in helping at the time of childbirth. Sometimes these women were mothers themselves; they had learned by experience what kind of assistance was needed. Some midwives were professional people who performed this service as a full-time occupation.

The midwife served several functions. In addition to delivering the baby, she advised and encouraged the woman in labor. On several occasions, Scripture records the words of midwives as they gave assurance and comfort (Gen. 35:17; 1 Sam. 4:20). If twins were born, the midwife had the responsibility of making the distinction between the first- and second-born. As Tamar gave birth to her twins, the midwife took a scarlet thread and tied it on the hand of the firstborn, telling the mother, "This one came out first" (Gen. 38:28).

In biblical times the infant was usually born at home, where the conditions were unsanitary. Probably it would be born on a dirt floor. Farm animals sometimes shared the same living quarters. The water used to cleanse the child was often polluted; the clothing used to wrap the child had been washed in the same impure water. Disease-bearing flies and other insects quickly found the infant. The stable where Jesus was born may have been no worse than some of the homes in Bethlehem.

Immediately following the delivery, several tasks had to be performed. Until recently, a custom prevailed among Arabs that may reflect the procedure in biblical times. First, the umbilical cord was cut and tied. Then the midwife picked up the baby and rubbed salt, water, and oil over its entire body. The infant was wrapped tightly in clothes or clean rags for seven days, then the process was repeated. This continued until the child was 40 days old.

The midwife's duties were finished when she handed the baby to the mother to be nursed. It was considered both a privilege and a duty for the Jewish mother to breast-feed her infant. Infants were actually breast-fed for their first year or more. But sometimes a mother was not physically able to nurse her child. When that happened, a wet nurse was secured. This wet nurse was another nursing mother (usually unrelated to the baby) who fed the baby her own breast milk.

The midwife announced to the mother that the child had been born and was alive and well. If the father was at work in the field or market, she sent word to him. Jeremiah made reference to this practice when he wrote, "Let the man be cursed who brought news to my father, saying, 'A male child has been born to you!' Making him very glad" (Jer. 20:15).

The family's neighbors would ask whether the newborn child was a boy. The birth announcement was simple. It said, "A male child is conceived" (Job 3:3), or "A male child has been born to you!" (Jer. 20:15). This sounds much like the announcement of the Messiah: "For to us a child is born, Unto us a son is given" (Isa. 9:6).

Naming the Children

Names were important in the ancient world. Hebrew names had meanings and they became an important part of the infants' lives. Jewish people believed that they must first know an individual's name before they could know the person. Consider the name of Jacob, which means "heel grabber," to see the importance of a name. To know Jacob's name was to know his basic character! Therefore, the act of choosing a name for an infant was a serious responsibility.

After the exile, the meaning of names was of less importance. Children might be given the name Daniel not because of its meaning, but to honor the famous servant of God. There were exceptions, even during this time. For example, the name Jesus is a Greek form of the Hebrew Joshua, which means, "salvation of Yahweh."

Children's names were chosen by one or both parents. Scripture indicates that the mother usually named the infants. Just as today, other people took it upon themselves to assist in this important task. If Elizabeth's neighbors and kinsfolk had had their way, her son would have been named Zacharias. But Elizabeth protested, insisting the boy would be named John (Luke 1:60–61).

Nowhere does Scripture specifically say when the child was to be named. In some instances, the mother named the child on the day of birth (e.g., 1 Sam. 4:21). By NT times, we know a baby boy was usually named on the eighth day, at the time of his circumcision. (cf. Luke 1:59; 2:21.)

Most of the names in the Bible are theophoric—a divine name was joined with a noun or verb, producing a sentence for a name. For example:
- *Jonathan* means "The Lord has given."
- *Elijah* means "My God [is] the Lord."
- *Matthew* means "A Gift of Yahweh."

This was true of heathen names as well. Many names in the OT contain the word *Baal*. King Saul's grandson was called Merib-baal (1 Chron. 8:34).

Circumstances surrounding the infant's birth sometimes influenced the choice of the child's name. For example, if a woman went to the well for water and had her baby there, she might call the child Beera [born at the well]. A baby born during a winter rainstorm might be called Barak—lightning.

When the Philistines captured the ark of the covenant from Israel, a mother was giving birth to a child. The baby was called Ichabod because, in the words of the mother, "The glory [*chabod*] was departed from Israel!" (1 Sam. 4:21).

Animal names were commonly used for children:
- *Rachel* means "Sheep."
- *Deborah* means "Bee."
- *Caleb* means "Dog."
- *Achbor* means "Mouse."

We can only guess why these animal names were used.

Often the name referred to a personality trait that the parents hoped would describe their children when they reached adulthood. Names like Shobek ("Preeminent") and Azzan ("Strong") can best be understood in this light. In other cases, the name seemed to be the exact opposite of what the parents wanted the child to be. Gareb suggests a "scabby" condition and Nabal makes reference to a "fool."

Some primitive cultures believed that demons want to possess attractive children, so they gave infants names that sounded distasteful. Perhaps names like "Scabby" and "Fool" were therefore given in biblical times to ward off evil spirits.

It is common today to name the firstborn son after the father, but that was not the case in biblical times. One has only to look through the various family trees described in the Scriptures to see this. For example, from Boaz to the last king of Judah, 24 names of kings are listed. And no two of them are alike.

Some names were more popular than others. For example, at least a dozen men mentioned in the OT were called Obadiah ("servant of Yahweh"). In order to distinguish between many children having the same name, the name of the father might be attached. Micaiah's expanded name was "Micaiah ben Imlah," or "Micaiah, the son of Imlah." Peter's name before Jesus changed it was "Simon Bar-Jona," or "Simon, the son of Jona." This custom also served to remind the son of his ancestors.

Another way to distinguish between people with the same name was to identify persons by the names of their hometowns:
- David's father was called "Jesse the Bethlehemite" (1 Sam. 16:1).
- The giant that David killed was "Goliath of Gath" (1 Sam. 17:4).
- One of Jesus' loyal supporters was Mary Magdalene or "Mary of Magdala" (Matt. 28:1).
- Judas Iscariot, the disciple who betrayed Jesus, came from the town of Kerioth.

Sometimes the names of persons were changed after they reached adulthood. The individuals themselves might ask that their names be changed. Ruth's mother-in-law Naomi sought to have her name changed to Mara because, she said, "the Almighty has dealt very bitterly [mara] with me" (Ruth 1:20).

The young Pharisee named Saul had been a Christian for years before he changed his name to Paul, after he converted an important official named Sergius Paulus on the island of Cyprus (Acts 13:1–13).

On other occasions, someone else gave a person a new name. An angel of the Lord gave Jacob his new name, Israel (Gen. 32:28). Jesus changed Simon's name to Peter (Matt. 16:17–18). It is uncertain how often people changed their name in biblical times.

Rituals of Childbirth

Ancient Jewish culture observed certain rituals in connection with childbirth. The Jewish child was born into a deeply religious community. The following rites had special religious meanings in the development of the child.

Circumcising the Males

Many cultures in the world today practice circumcision for hygienic reasons. Some primitive tribes perform the rite on infants and young boys, while others wait until the boys reach the age of puberty or are ready for marriage. These traditions have remained largely unchanged for centuries. Similar practices were common in the Near East in biblical times. Since the Philistines did not practice circumcision, the Jews ridiculed them (1 Sam. 17:26).

The Law of Moses did not stipulate who was to perform the operation on the infant male. It is commonly assumed that an adult male cut off the infant's foreskin. On at least one occasion Scripture records that a woman did this; but the circumstances surrounding that particular event were unusual, for the husband seemed to be dying (Exod. 4:25). The Hebrew word for circumciser and father-in-law is the same. This probably goes back to pre-covenant days when a young man was prepared for marriage by his future father-in-law.

At first, crude instruments such as flint knives were used for this surgery. Even after metal knives were developed, flint knives were used (see Exod. 4:25 and Josh. 5:2). Slowly this tradition was given up, and by NT times flint knives had been replaced by metal ones.

The Jewish boy was to be circumcised on the eighth day. God first delivered this commandment to Abraham (Gen. 17:12) and repeated it to Moses in the wilderness (Lev. 12:3). In earlier periods, the Israelites did not always obey this command. But after the exile, the law was carefully observed. This practice continued through Jesus' time (Luke 2:21) and remains a hallmark of Judaism today. When the eighth day fell on the Sabbath, the circumcision rite was still performed—in spite of many rules and regulations about suspending everyday activities that had been developed to keep the Sabbath holy.

Purifying the Mother

Childbirth was thought to make a woman ceremonially unclean. That meant she was not allowed to participate in any religious observances or touch any sacred objects. Biblical scholars have long speculated about the reason for this. Did it emphasize that the child was born in sin? Did it demonstrate that sexual acts and the birth of a child were somehow sinful? Or was it designed simply as a protection for the mother, to keep her from feeling obligated to journey outside her home soon after the birth of a child? Scripture itself does not give us the reason. However, it is important to remember that anyone—man or woman—was considered ceremonially unclean who had a discharge of blood, semen, or pus. (Cf. Lev. 12; 15.) Other cultures in biblical times had similar taboos.

According to Leviticus 12, the mother was unclean for 40 days after the birth of a son; she was unclean twice as long if a girl was born. Again, no reason is given.

At the end of this period, after the mother had presented a sin offering and a burnt offering at the central place of worship, she was pronounced ceremonially clean. This tradition is unusual, because sacrifices were normally presented by the males. Also, the Law allowed the woman considerable freedom in choosing the type of animal she would sacrifice, depending upon her social status. A wealthy woman was expected to bring a lamb for a burnt offering; but if the family was poor, two turtledoves were allowed. It is interesting that Mary, the mother of Jesus, could afford only the pair of turtledoves at the time of her purification (Luke 2:22–24).

Redeeming the Firstborn

Since all firstborn males were God's possession, it was necessary for the family to redeem, or buy back, that firstborn infant from God. The redemption price was five shekels of silver, given to the priests when the child was one month old (Num. 18:15–16).

Scripture doesn't tell us about the redemption ceremony itself, but by rabbinic times the following procedure had been established. The joyous occasion was celebrated on the thirty-first day of the child's life. (If the thirty-first day happened to fall on the Sabbath, the ceremony was delayed for one day.)

The celebration took place in the infant's home, with a priest and other guests present. The rite began as the father presented the infant to the priest. The priest asked the father, "Do you wish to redeem the child or do you want to leave him with me?"

The father answered that he would redeem the child, and he handed the five silver coins to the priest. As the infant was returned, the father gave thanks to God.

The priest responded by declaring to the father, "Your son is redeemed! Your son is redeemed! Your son is redeemed!" After the priest pronounced a blessing on the child, he joined the invited guests at a banquet table.

If a child was an orphan at birth, the duty of redeeming him fell to one of the child's male relatives.

Childhood _____

Growth Stages

The Hebrews used several words to describe stages of childhood growth: *sucker,* "a nursing infant"; *weaned one*—this change was an important milestone in childhood; *"one who takes quick little steps"* was the next stage.

Another plateau was the reaching of puberty. Young persons at this age were called an *elem* or *almah*, meaning "to be mature sexually."

Five stages of human life are outlined in Leviticus 27:1–8; three of these fit into the age of childhood or adolescence. The first stage was birth until 30 days; the second stage was from one month to five years; the third stage was from five years until the age of 20. The last two stages were adulthood and old age.

Size

The Israelites considered themselves to be smaller than the Canaanites who inhabited the Promised Land before them. When spies returned from scouting out the land, they reported that it was filled with giants. They said, "The people are greater and taller than we; the cities are great and fortified up to heaven; moreover we have seen the sons of the Anakim there" (Deut. 1:28).

The people referred to as "the Anakim" were legendary descendants of a tribe of giants. Archaeologists have found evidence that the Canaanites were of average size and build. It appears that the spies' report was based on fear rather than fact (Deut. 1:28; Num. 13:28).

In every culture there are exceptions to the norm. The Bible says of Saul, "There was not a more handsome person than he among the children of Israel. From his shoulders upward he was taller than any of the people" (1 Sam. 9:2). Goliath was also an exceptionally large man. His height was six cubits and a span (1 Sam. 17:4). A cubit was the distance from the elbow to the tip of the middle finger, or roughly 45 centimeters (18 inches). That would have made Goliath over 270 centimeters (9 feet) tall. At the other end of the scale was Zacchaeus, who had to climb a sycamore tree to see over the heads of the crowd (Luke 19:3–4).

Color of Skin and Hair

The name Esau means "reddish-brown." The descendants of Esau were the reddish-brown people called Edomites. By contrast, the skin of the Israelites was lighter and more yellowish. In our day, Israelis seem to be more dark-skinned people because of their constant exposure to the sun.

Young Israelite girls considered light skin to be beautiful, and they avoided the sun's rays as much as possible. We read in the Song of Solomon that the bride-to-be begged her handmaidens to "look not upon me, because I am dark. Because the sun has looked upon me" (Song of Sol. 1:6). She was embarrassed that her skin was not as light as the skin of the other girls.

The ancient Israelite youths had dark brown or black hair. Song of Solomon 5:11 describes hair as "black as a raven." On several occasions in the Scripture, a youth's hair was likened to a flock of goats moving down a hillside (Song of Sol. 4:1; 6:5); the native goat was black.

Education

The Israelites provided a well-rounded education for their children. It included religious instruction as well as training in practical skills they would need for the workaday world. They were an agricultural people, so only the religious leaders were taught to read and write.

In ancient Israel, education was an informal process. The parent did most or all of the training. There were no classrooms or structured curricula. By the first century, the Jews had adopted a more formal approach to education. They set aside classrooms and qualified teachers to instruct all the children in a village.

Parental Responsibility

The religious education of children was the parents' responsibility (Deut. 11:19; 32:46). No exceptions were made for parents who felt they were too busy to teach.

Even when children came of age and married, the parents' responsibility did not end; they also had an important part in educating the grandchildren (Deut. 4:9). In fact, they often lived in the same house.

Though the Israelite father was ultimately responsible for the education of the children, mothers also played a crucial role, especially until children reached the age of five. During those formative years she was expected to shape the future of her sons and daughters.

When a boy became old enough to work with his father, the father became his principal teacher, even though the mother continued to share in the teaching responsibility (cf. Prov. 1:8-9; 6:20). The mother carried the main responsibility for her daughters, teaching them skills they would need to become in time good wives and mothers.

The Jewish parents' major concern was that their children come to know the living God. In Hebrew, the verb *to know* means "to be intimately involved with a person"; Scripture stated that "The fear [or reverence] of the Lord is the beginning of wisdom: and the knowledge of the Holy One is understanding" (Prov. 9:10). Godly parents helped their children develop this kind of knowledge.

The children learned that the nation of Israel had entered into a covenant with God, and this covenant placed certain restrictions on them. They were not free to seek their own desires. They had a responsibility to God because he had redeemed them. They were diligently taught the guidelines God had given them.

There were probably no formal schools in the early centuries of the nation. Most learning took place amid everyday life. As opportunities arose throughout the day, parents would instruct their children.

The education of a child took a lifetime to complete. The Jewish family took seriously the Lord's instructions, "And these words which I command you today, shall be in your heart. You shall teach them diligently to your children" (Deut. 6:6-7). The phrase "to teach diligently" came from a Hebrew word that usually referred to sharpening a tool or whetting a knife. What the whetstone is to the knife blade, training is to the child. Education prepared children to become useful and productive members of society.

Synagogue Schools

We are not sure when synagogue schools were first established. Some believe the practice dates back to the exile in Babylon. Whenever it began, by the time of Jesus, the synagogue school was a vital part of Jewish life.

Each Sabbath, Jews faithfully gathered at the synagogue to hear their rabbi read the Scriptures and explain the Law. This activity inspired the Muslims to nickname the Jews "the people of the Book." The synagogue sponsored special classes apart from the regular times of worship. During the week, boys came to these classes to study the Scriptures under qualified teachers. The classes supplemented the religious education the boys were receiving from their parents.

Jewish fathers were much more concerned with the character of teachers than with their teaching ability. Naturally, they required teachers to be competent, but they were more concerned that they be examples to the children.

Jewish writings from the first century A.D. give us a partial list of the ideal characteristics of teachers. They must:

Not be lazy	Never discourage children
Have an even temper	Show sin to be repulsive
Never show partiality	Punish all wrong doing
Never become impatient	Fulfill all their promises
Never compromise their dignity by jesting	

Besides learning the Scriptures, Jewish boys also learned etiquette, music, warfare, and practical knowledge. Young David was said to be "skillful in playing [i.e., a musician], a mighty man of valor, a man of war, prudent in speech, and a handsome person, and the Lord is with him" (1 Sam. 16:18). David obviously had a well-rounded education, as did most Jewish boys.

Only the boys received formal training outside the home. They began by meeting in the teacher's house, where they read from scrolls containing small portions from the Scriptures, such as the Shema. This was the elementary school of the day.

When the boys were old enough to learn the sabbatical lessons, they met at the "house of the Book"—the synagogue. Here they entered the room where the Torah scrolls were kept and prepared their lessons under the supervision of the Hazzan, the keeper of the scrolls.

Later they were allowed to discuss questions of the Law with the Pharisaic teachers. These discussions constituted the secondary level of Jewish education.

In NT times, school was in session year-round. During the hot summer months the boys went to school no more than four hours a day. If it were unusually hot, school might be dismissed altogether. The class hours were before 10:00 A.M. and after 3:00 P.M. A five-hour break occurred during the hottest part of the day.

Classes were not organized by age; all the students studied together in the same room. For this reason, their instruction had to be individualized. Teachers copied down a verse for the younger students, and they recited it aloud until they mastered it. Meanwhile the teacher helped the older boys read a passage from Leviticus. The sages believed that if a verse were not repeated aloud, it would soon be forgotten.

Vocational Training

The boys followed their fathers into the fields to work or into the marketplace to buy and sell. They carefully observed their fathers planting, pruning and harvesting. A new world had opened to boys when they were old enough to go with their fathers.

The Israelites believed that undisciplined life would not prepare youth to cope with what faced them. They taught their children the meaning of responsibility early in life, so when the youngsters reached adulthood they were able to meet its demands with confidence.

Since Israel had an agricultural society, much of the practical wisdom handed down from father to son revolved around farming. This included lessons on preparing the soil for planting and the cultivation of various crops, as well as harvesting and storing the bounty. Sons learned these skills by working alongside their fathers throughout their youth. Even when the Jewish people began to seek employment other than farming, they were still "people of the land."

It was also the father's responsibility to teach his sons a trade or craft. If the father was a potter, he taught that skill to his sons. One of the Jewish sages affirmed that "he who does not teach his son a useful trade is bringing him up to be a thief."

While the boys were learning these skills, the girls learned baking, spinning, and weaving under the watchful eyes of their mothers (see Exod. 35:25–26). If there were no sons in the family, daughters might be required to learn the father's work (Gen. 29:6; Exod. 2:16).

Leisure Activities

Young people in biblical times did not have free time, but they still had plenty of time for recreation and leisure.

Toys

Young people had few toys. They could amuse themselves by playing with sticks, bones, or pieces of broken pottery. Terra cotta toys have been found in many excavations.

In Egypt, archaeologists have found simple mechanical toys such as carts and wagons in the royal tombs. Israelite girls played with simple clay dolls clothed with rags.

On one occasion, Isaiah likened God to a person hurling a ball (Isa. 22:18). This is the only biblical reference to such a toy. Unfortunately, the prophet described neither the ball nor the game that was played with it.

Games

The Bible does not describe games the children played, but it does mention their dancing and singing (cf. Job 21:11–12). Jesus said the people of his generation were "like children sitting in the marketplaces and calling to their companions, and saying: 'We played the flute for you, and you did not dance; we mourned to you, and you did not lament'" (Matt. 11:16–17).

Boys of biblical times explored the many caves and crevices that dotted their landscape. Shepherd boys often went off to explore or to trap wild animals. The boys also practiced using a sling or throwing a spear. Even in play, boys were preparing themselves for adulthood.

The Family

Two facts stand out in what the Bible says about the family. First, the roles of family members stayed about the same throughout the biblical period. Changing culture and laws did not significantly affect family customs. Those who lived in the early days of the OT period were seminomadic—often moving from one area to another—so their habits were at some points different from those of settled peoples. The Mosaic law abolished some nomadic practices, such as brothers and sisters marrying each other. But most of the original family life-style persisted into the NT period.

Second, family life in Bible times reflected a culture quite different from our own. We should recognize this difference when we turn to the Scriptures for guidance in raising our own families. We need to search for principles rather than copy directly the specific customs and rituals portrayed. These life-styles were designed for agricultural communities and did not always please God.

The Family Unit

The family was the first social structure. God formed the first family by joining Adam and Eve together as husband and wife. Genesis 2:18 says that God created the woman as a helper for Adam, which indicates that the man and woman were brought together for companionship. She was to help him, and he was to care for her. Together they were to meet the needs of their children.

Husbands

The Hebrew word for "husband" partially means "to dominate, to rule." It can also be translated as "master." As head of the family, the husband was responsible for its well-being. When Abraham and Sarah deceived the pharaoh about their marriage, the ruler challenged Abraham rather than Sarah, who had done the actual lying (Gen. 12:17–20). This does not mean that the Hebrew husband was a tyrant. Rather, he assumed responsibility for the family and sought to serve the needs of those who were under his authority.

The Jewish father assumed spiritual leadership within the family. He functioned as the family priest (cf. Gen. 12:8; Job 1:5). He was expected to lead his family in observing various religious rites, such as the Passover (Exod. 12:3).

Along with the wife, the father was to "Train up a child in the way he should go" (Prov. 22:6). The father also had to convey the written law to his children. He was admonished to "teach them diligently to your children" and to "talk of them when you sit in your house, when you walk by the way, when you lie down, and when you rise up. You shall bind them as a sign on your hand, and they shall be as frontlets between your eyes. You shall write them on the posts of your house and on your gates" (Deut. 6:7–9).

The father had to inflict physical punishment when necessary. This was to be done in such a way as not to "provoke your children to wrath; but bring them up in the training and admonition of the Lord" (Eph. 6:4).

In biblical times, a man who did not provide adequately for his family was guilty of a serious offense, and was shunned and mocked by society (cf. Prov. 6:6–11; 19:7). Paul wrote, "If anyone does not provide for his own . . . he has denied the faith and is worse than an unbeliever" (1 Tim. 5:8).

As husband and father, the man defended his family's rights before the judges when necessary (see Deut. 22:13–19). "The fatherless and the widow" had no man to defend their rights, so they were often denied justice (cf. 10:18).

Wives

In marriage, women took a place of submission to their mates. The wife's responsibility was to be the husband's helper (cf. Gen. 2:18) one who "does him good, and not harm, all the days of her life" (Prov. 31:12). Her main responsibility centered around the home and the children, but it extended to the marketplace and other areas that affected the family's welfare (cf. vv. 16, 25).

A wife's primary goal was to bear children for her husband. Rebekah's family spokesman said to her, "Our sister, may you become the mother of thousands of ten thousands; And your descendants possess the gates of those who hate them" (Gen. 24:60). A Jewish family hoped that the wife would become like a fruitful vine, filling the house with many children (see Ps. 128:3).

As children began to arrive, the mother was tied closer to the home. She nursed each child until the age of two or three, besides clothing and feeding the rest of the family. She spent hours each day preparing meals and making clothes from wool. She often helped her husband in the fields, planting or harvesting the crops.

A mother shared the responsibility for training the children. Children spent their formative years close to their mothers. Eventually, the sons were old enough to go with their fathers into the fields or other places of employment. The mother then turned her attention more fully to her daughters, teaching them how to become successful wives and mothers.

A woman's performance of her tasks determined the failure or success of the family. "An excellent wife is the crown of her husband, but she who causes shame is like rottenness in his bones" (Prov. 12:4). If the wife worked hard at the task laid before her, it greatly benefited her husband. Jews believed that a man could rise to a place among the leaders of Israel only if his wife were wise and talented (cf. 31:23).

Sons

In biblical times, the sons had to support their parents when they became old and then give them a proper burial. For this reason, a couple usually hoped to have many sons. "Like arrows in the hand of a warrior; so are the children of one's youth. Happy is the man who has his quiver full of them; They shall not be ashamed, but shall speak with their enemies in the gate" (Ps. 127:4–5).

The firstborn son held a special place of honor within the family. He was expected to be the next head of the family. All through his life, he was expected to take greater responsibility for his actions and those of his brothers. This explains why Reuben, as the oldest brother, showed greater concern for the life of Joseph when his brothers agreed to kill him (Gen. 37:21, 29).

When the father died, a firstborn son received a double portion of the family inheritance (Deut. 21:17; 2 Chron. 21:2–3).

The fifth commandment admonished, "Honor your father and your mother, that your days may be long upon the land which the Lord your God is giving you" (Exod. 20:12). Both parents were to receive the same amount of respect. However, the rabbis of the Talmud reasoned that if a son ever had to choose, he must give preference to his father. For example, if both parents requested a drink of water simultaneously, the Talmud taught that both the son and the mother should meet the needs of the father.

Daughters

In ancient times, daughters were not prized as highly as sons. Some fathers actually looked upon them as a nuisance. One father wrote, "A daughter keeps him secretly wakeful, and worry over her robs him of sleep; when she is young, lest she do not marry, or if married, lest she be hated, while a virgin, lest she should be defiled or become pregnant in her father's house; or having an husband, lest she prove unfaithful, or, though married, lest she be barren" (Ecclesiasticus 42:9–10, RSV).

However, the Hebrews treated their daughters more humanely than surrounding cultures. The Romans actually exposed newborn girls to the elements, in the hope that they would die. The Hebrews believed that all life—male and female—came from God. For this reason, they would never consider killing one of their babies. When the prophet Nathan described the intimate relationship of a father to a child, he pictured a daughter in her father's arms with her head on his chest (2 Sam. 12:3).

Firstborn daughters held a special place of honor and duty within the family. Lot's firstborn daughter persuaded her younger sister to bear a child for Lot, to preserve the family (Gen. 19:31–38). In the story of Laban and Jacob, the firstborn daughter Leah was given priority over the younger sister (Gen. 29:26).

If a family was without sons, the daughters could inherit their father's possessions (Num. 27:5–8), but they could keep their inheritance only if they married within their own tribe (Num. 36:5–12).

The daughter was under the legal dominion of her father until her marriage. Her father made all important decisions for her, such as whom she should marry. But the daughter was asked to give her consent to the choice of a groom, and sometimes she was even allowed to state a preference (Gen. 24:58; 1 Sam. 18:20). The father had the right to approve all vows the daughter made before they became binding (Num. 30:3–5).

The daughter was expected to help her mother in the home. At a very early age, she began to learn the domestic skills she would need to become a good wife and mother herself. By the age of 12, the daughter had become a homemaker in her own right and was allowed to marry.

Often daughters married at an early age. Although a bride left the dominion of her father, she entered the new domain of her husband and his family. Her mother-in-law stepped in to continue the guidance and training her own mother had given her. The wife and her mother-in-law often developed a deep and lasting bond. This is illustrated in the book of Ruth, when Naomi repeatedly refers to Ruth as "my daughter." Micah described a strife-filled family as one in which "Daughter rises up against her mother, daughter-in-law against her mother-in-law" (Mic. 7:6).

When a young woman went to live with her husband's family, she did not give up all rights in her own family. If her husband died and there were no more brothers-in-law for her to marry, she might return to her father's house. That is exactly what Naomi encouraged her daughters-in-law to do, and Orpah followed her suggestion (Ruth 1:8–15).

The Extended Family

In the most basic sense, a Hebrew family consisted of a husband, a wife, and their children. When the husband had more than one wife, the family then included all the wives and the children in their various relationships (cf. Gen. 30). Sometimes the family included everyone who shared a common dwelling place under the protection of the head of the family. They might be grandparents, servants, and visitors, as well as widowed daughters and their children.

The extended family commonly included sons and their wives and children (Lev. 18:6–18). God counted Abraham's slaves as part of the family group and required Abraham to circumcise them (Gen. 17:12–14, 22–27). In Israel's early history, as many as four generations lived together. This was a normal part of the seminomadic life-style and the later agricultural one.

In OT days, the extended family was ruled by the oldest male in the household, called the father. Often this person was a grandfather or a great-grandfather. For example, when Jacob's family moved to Egypt, Jacob was considered their father—even though his sons had wives and families (cf. Gen. 46:8–27). Jacob continued to rule over his family until his death.

The father of an extended family held the power of life and death over its members. We see this when Abraham nearly sacrificed his son, Isaac (Gen. 22:9–12), and when Judah tried to sentence his daughter-in-law to death because she had committed adultery (Gen. 38:24–26).

Later, the Mosaic law restricted the father's authority. It did not allow him to sacrifice his child on an altar (Lev. 18:21). It allowed him to sell his daughter, but not to a foreigner and not for prostitution (Exod. 21:7; Lev. 19:29). According to the law, a father could not deny the birthright of his firstborn son, even if he had sons by two different women (Deut. 21:15–17).

Some Hebrew fathers violated these laws, as in the case of Jephthah, who vowed to sacrifice whoever came out to greet him upon his victorious return from battle. His daughter was the first. Believing that he had to keep his vow, Jephthah sacrificed her (Judg. 11:31, 34–40). King Manasseh burned his son to appease a heathen god (2 Kings 21:6).

The Clan

The extended family was part of a larger group that we call a clan. The clan might be so large that it registered hundreds of males in its ranks (cf. Gen. 46:8–27; Ezra 8:1–14). Members of a clan shared common ancestry and thus viewed each other as kinsmen. They felt obligated to help and protect one another.

Often the clan designated one male, called a *goel*, to extend help to clan members in need. In English, this person is referred to as the kinsman-redeemer. His help covered many areas of need.

For instance, if a member of the clan had to sell part of his property to pay debts, he gave the kinsman-redeemer the first opportunity to purchase it. The kinsman-redeemer then had to purchase the property if he could to keep it in the clan's possession (Lev. 25:25; cf. Ruth 4:1–6). This situation arose when Jeremiah's cousin came to him saying, "Buy my field which is in Anathoth, for the right of redemption is yours to buy it" (Jer. 32:6–8). Jeremiah purchased the field and used the event to proclaim that the Jews would eventually return to Israel (v. 15).

Occasionally, an army would capture hostages and sell them to the highest bidder. Also, a man might sell himself into slavery to repay a debt. In both cases, the slave's next-of-kin had to find the clan's kinsman-redeemer, who would try to purchase his kinsman's freedom (Lev. 25:47–49).

If a married man died without having had a child, the *goel* had to marry the widow (Deut. 25:5–10). This was called a levirate (brother-in-law) marriage. Any children born through this arrangement were considered the offspring of the deceased brother.

A *goel* also had to avenge a kinsman's murder. In such a case, he was called the avenger of blood (cf. Deut. 19:12). The law of Moses limited this practice by establishing cities of refuge to which killers could flee, but even this did not ensure the killer's safety. If the murder was done out of malice or forethought, the avenger of blood could follow him to the city of refuge and demand his return. In such cases, the murderer would be turned over to the *goel*, who would kill him (cf. Deut. 19:1–13). Joab killed Abner in this manner (2 Sam. 2:26–27).

Erosion of the Family

A family that lives in harmony and in genuine love is a delight to all associated with it. Surely this is what God had in mind when he established the family. Unfortunately, the Bible shows us few families that attained this ideal. Throughout Bible history, families were being eroded by social, economic, and religious pressures. We can identify several of these pressures.

Polygamy

There was continuous domestic strife when two women shared a husband in OT times. The Hebrew word for the second wife literally meant "rival wife" (cf. 1 Sam. 1:6). This term suggests that bitterness and hostility existed between polygamous wives. Nevertheless, polygamy was customary, especially in the time of the patriarchs. If a man was unable to raise the marriage money for a second wife, he considered buying a slave for that purpose or using one he already had in his household.

In a polygamous marriage, the husband invariably favored one wife over another. This caused complications, such as deciding whose child to honor as firstborn son. Sometimes a man wanted to give his inheritance to the son of his favored wife although it was actually owed to the son of the disliked wife (Deut. 21:15–17). Moses declared that the firstborn son had to be rightfully honored, and the husband could not shortchange the firstborn's mother to "diminish her food, her clothing, or her marriage rights" (Exod. 21:10).

After the Exodus, most Hebrew marriages were monogamous. Proverbs never mentions polygamy, even though it touches on many aspects of Hebrew culture. The prophets always used the monogamous marriage to describe the Lord's relationship to Israel. Such a marriage was the ideal of family life.

Death of the Husband

The death of a husband always had far-reaching consequences for his family. After a period of mourning, the widowed wife might follow several courses of action.

If childless, she was expected to continue living with her husband's family, according to the levirate law (Deut. 25:5–10). She was to marry one of her husband's brothers or a near kinsman. If these men were not available, she was free to marry outside the clan (Ruth 1:9).

Widows with children had other options open to them. From the apocryphal book of Tobit we learn that some moved back to the family of their father or brother (1:8). If the widow was elderly, one of her sons might care for her. If she had become financially secure, she might live alone. For example, Judith neither remarried nor moved into the home of a relative, for "her husband Manasseh had left her gold and silver, and men and women slaves, and cattle, and fields; and she maintained this estate" (Judith 8:7).

Occasionally a widow was penniless and had no male relative to depend on. Such women faced drastic hardships (cf. 1 Kings 17:8–15; 2 Kings 4:1–7).

The childless widow of NT times found herself in a more secure position. If she had no customary means of support, she could turn to the church for help. Paul suggested that young widows remarry and that elderly widows be cared for by their children. However, if the widow could turn to no one, the church should care for her (cf. 1 Tim. 5:16).

Rebellious Children

It was a grave sin to dishonor one's father or mother. Moses ordered that a person who struck or cursed his parent should be put to death (cf. Exod. 21:15, 17; Lev. 20:9). We have no record of this punishment being given, but the Bible describes many instances in which children did dishonor their parents. When Ezekiel enumerated the sins of Jerusalem, he wrote, "In you they have made light of father and mother; in your midst they have oppressed the stranger; in you they have mistreated the fatherless and the widow" (Ezek. 22:7). A similar picture is presented in Proverbs 19:26. Jesus condemned many Jews of his day for not honoring their parents (Matt. 15:4–9).

Sibling Rivalry

"A brother offended is harder to win than a strong city; And contentions are like the bars of a castle" (Prov. 18:19). The Bible describes brothers who quarreled for various reasons:
- Jacob stole Esau's blessing (Gen. 27).
- Absalom hated Amnon for raping his sister (2 Sam. 13).
- Solomon destroyed his brother Adonijah when Adonijah tried to get the throne away from him (1 Kings 2:19–25).
- Jehoram ascended the throne and killed all his brothers so that they would never be a threat to him (2 Chron. 21:4).

Adultery

The Hebrews considered adultery a serious threat to the family and punished adulterers swiftly and harshly.

In summary, the family was a unifying thread of the Bible history. When threatened or challenged, the family unit struggled for survival. God used families to convey his message to each new generation.

God has always revealed himself as the Father of his redeemed family (Hos. 11:1–3). He expects honor from his children (Mal. 1:6). Jesus taught his disciples to pray, "Our Father." Even today, children's prayers prepare them to honor God as the perfect Father who is able to meet all their needs.

God ordained the family unit as a vital part of human society. Through the loving experience of a human family, we begin to understand the awesome privilege we have as a part of the family of God.

Marriage

arriage was instituted by God when he declared, "It is not good that man should be alone; I will make him a helper comparable to him" (Gen. 2:18). So God fashioned woman and brought her to man. This passage also emphasizes the truth that "a man shall leave his father and mother and be joined to his wife, and they shall become one flesh" (Gen. 2:24). This suggests that God's ideal is for man to be the husband of one wife and for the marriage to be permanent.

Legislation

God's desire for his people was that they marry within the body of believers. The Mosaic law stated that an Israelite was never to marry a Canaanite. The Israelite would be constantly tempted to embrace the spouse's god as well (Exod. 34:10–17; Deut. 7:3–4). Likewise, Paul commanded the members of the church at Corinth, "Do not be unequally yoked together with unbelievers" (2 Cor. 6:14).

Choosing the Bride

In biblical times, the parents chose the mate for their son. The primary reason for this was that the bride became part of the clan. Although they were married and became "one flesh," the couple remained under the authority of the groom's father. The parents sought to choose someone who would fit into their clan and work harmoniously with her mother-in-law and sisters-in-law.

Sometimes the parents consulted with their children to see if they approved of the choice of mates being made for them. For example, Rebekah was asked if she wanted to marry Isaac (Gen. 24:58). Samson demanded that a certain girl be acquired for him. Although his parents protested, they completed the marriage contract for Samson (Judg. 14:1–4).

People married at a young age, a fact which made the parents' choice a practical matter. By the time of Jesus, the Jewish leaders had decided to establish minimum ages for which a marriage contract could be drawn up. The age was set at 13 for boys and 12 for girls.

An important law involved levirate marriage. This was the marriage prescribed by the law of Moses in which a man was required to marry the widow of a brother who died with no male heir. The term "levirate" means "husband's brother." The purpose of the law was to provide an heir for the dead brother, thereby preserving his name and estate. The law also was designed to provide for the welfare of the widows (Deut. 25:5–10).

Marriage Customs

A number of customs and steps were involved in finalizing a marriage. The first was agreeing on a price to be given to the father of the girl. The payment was compensation for the loss of a worker. The sum was mutually agreed upon (Gen. 34:12; Exod. 22:16–17). It could consist of services instead of money. For example, Jacob agreed to work for seven years for Rachel (Gen. 29: 18–20). The giving and receiving of money was probably accompanied by a written agreement. After this agreement was made, the couple was considered engaged.

In biblical times, a betrothal for marriage was a binding agreement. The agreement was voided only by death or divorce. When Joseph discovered that Mary was pregnant, he did not want to make a public example of her; instead, he decided to divorce her secretly. However, he did not carry out the divorce, because an angel of the Lord convinced him that the baby to be born to Mary was the Son of God (Matt. 1:18–25).

During the engagement period, the groom had certain privileges. For example, if war was declared, he was exempt from military duty (Deut. 20:7). Or if another man raped the groom's betrothed, the act was treated as adultery; and the offender was punished (Deut. 22:23–27). This was considered a more serious crime than the rape of a girl not yet betrothed (Deut. 22:28–29).

The length of engagement varied. Sometimes the couple was married the same day they became engaged. Usually, however, a period of time elapsed between the betrothal and the marriage ceremony. During this time the young man prepared a place in his father's house for his bride, while the bride prepared herself for married life.

On the day of the wedding, the groom and his friends dressed in their finest clothes and went to the home of the bride. Together the couple went back to the groom's house. Their friends sang and danced their way back to his house.

Once at the groom's house, the couple was ushered into a bridal chamber. The marriage was consummated through sexual union while the guests waited outside. Once the fact was announced, the wedding festivities continued, with guests dropping by for the wedding feast. Usually the wedding party lasted for a week.

New Testament Teaching About Marriage

The NT does not contradict the teachings about marriage in the OT. Most marriage teaching comes from Jesus and the apostle Paul.

Jesus performed a miracle in Cana in Galilee when he and his disciples were attending a wedding (John 2:1–11). Our Lord gave his blessing and sanction to the institution of marriage.

On another occasion, when Jesus was asked about marriage and divorce, he quoted two passages from Genesis (1:27 and 2:24): "Have you not read that He who made them at the beginning 'made them male and female,' and said, 'For this reason a man shall leave his father and mother and be joined to his wife, and the two shall become one flesh'? So then, they are no longer two but one flesh. Therefore what God has joined together, let not man separate" (Matt. 19:4–6). He taught that marriage was the joining together of two people so they become "one flesh." Not only did God acknowledge the marriage but he also joined the couple.

In his letter to the Ephesians, Paul showed how a marriage relationship can best function.

First, husband and wife were to submit "to one another in the fear of God" (5:21).

Second, once there was mutual submission, "wives were to submit to their husbands," as to the Lord (v. 5:22). The model for the wife's submission is the church, which is subject to Christ (v. 5:24).

Third, husbands are to love their wives. The role of husband is represented by Jesus Christ, who loved his bride, the church, so much that he died for her (v. 5:25).

Divorce

The divine ideal for marriage is a lifelong bond that unites husband and wife in a one-flesh relationship. The marriage union is a holy condition founded by God and is not to be dissolved at the will of human beings (Matt. 19:5–6).

The law of Moses allowed a man to divorce his wife when she found "no favor in his eyes, because he has found some uncleanness in her" (Deut. 24:1). The primary purpose of this legislation was to prevent him from taking her again after she had married another man—"an abomination before the Lord" (Deut. 24:4).

This law was intended to discourage, rather than encourage, divorce. A public document known as a "certificate of divorce" was granted the woman. This permitted her the right to remarry without civil or religious sanction. Divorce could not be done privately.

The Mosaic law called for severe penalties for certain types of uncleanness. Adultery called for death by stoning for the woman. If a man believed that his wife was not a virgin when he married her, he could have her judged by the elders of the city. If they found her guilty, she could be put to death (Deut. 22:13–21). Although a man was allowed to divorce his wife, the wife was not allowed to divorce her husband for any reason. Legally the wife was bound to her husband as long as they both lived or until he divorced her (1 Cor. 7:39).

The Gospels record four statements by Jesus concerning divorce. In two of these Jesus allowed divorce in the case of adultery. In Matthew 5:32 Jesus commented on the situation of both the woman and her new husband: "Whoever divorces his wife for any reason except sexual immorality causes her to commit adultery; and whoever marries a woman who is divorced commits adultery."

In another statement, Jesus described the position of the man who divorced his wife. "Whoever divorces his wife except for sexual immorality, and marries another, commits adultery; and whoever marries her who is divorced commits adultery" (Matt. 19:9). While these two statements seem to allow divorce because of unfaithfulness, two other statements of Jesus appear to make no provision for divorce (Mark 10:11–12; Luke 16:18).

Paul was essentially in agreement with Jesus' teachings on marriage and divorce. However, the apostle dealt with new situations involving the marital conflict between believers and nonbelievers.

In the case of two Christians, Paul admonished them to follow the Lord's teachings and be reconciled. In any event, neither is to marry another (1 Cor. 7:10–11). Paul further says that a Christian whose mate has abandoned the marriage should be free to formalize the divorce: "If the unbeliever departs, let him depart; a brother or a sister is not under bondage in such cases" (v. 15). Many authorities hold that the phrase "not under bondage" means that a deserted Christian spouse may lawfully go from divorce to remarriage. But other scholars disagree with this interpretation. In any event, Paul encourages believers to keep the marriage together in hope that unbelieving partners might be saved (v. 16).

Women _____

In ancient Israel men were considered more important than women. The father or oldest male in the family made the decisions that affected the whole family, while the women had little to say about them. This patriarchal (father-centered) form of family life set the tone for the way women were treated.

For example, a female was raised to obey her father without question. When she married she was to obey her husband in the same way. If she were divorced or widowed, she often returned to her father's house to live.

Leviticus 27:1–8 suggests that a woman was worth only half as much as a man. A female child was less welcomed into the world than a male. Boys were taught to make decisions and to rule their families while girls were raised to get married and bear children.

Even though most women spent their days as housewives and mothers, there were exceptions. Miriam, Deborah, Huldah, and Esther were more than good wives—they were political and religious leaders who proved they could guide the nation as well as any man could.

The Legal Position of Women

The legal position of a woman in Israel was weaker than that of a man. For example, a husband could divorce his wife if he "found some uncleanness in her," but the wife was not allowed to divorce her husband for any reason (Deut. 24:1–4).

The law stated that a wife who was suspected of having sexual relations with another man must take a jealousy test (Num. 5:11–31). However, there was not test for a man suspected of being unfaithful with another woman. The law also stipulated that a man could make a religious vow and that it was binding on him (Num. 30:1–15), but a vow made by a woman could be cancelled by her father or (if she were married) by her husband. A woman's father could sell her to pay a debt (Exod. 21:7), and she could not be freed after six years, as a man could (Lev. 25:40). In one instance, a man gave his daughter to be used sexually by a mob (Judg. 19:24).

Other laws imply that men and women were to be treated as equals. For example, children were to treat both parents with equal respect and reverence (Exod. 20:12). A son who disobeyed or cursed either parent was to be punished (Deut. 21:18–21). And a man and a woman caught in the act of adultery must both die by stoning (Deut. 22:22). It is interesting to note here that when the Pharisees dragged an adulteress to Jesus and wanted to stone her, they had already broken the law themselves by letting the man get away (see John 8:3–11).

Other Hebrew laws offered protection for women. If a man took a second wife, he was still bound by law to feed and clothe his first wife, and to continue to have sexual relations with her (Exod. 21:10). Even the foreign woman who was taken as a war bride had rights. If her husband tired of her, she was to be set free (Deut. 21:14). Any man found guilty of the crime of rape was to be stoned to death (Deut. 22:23–27).

Usually, only men owned property. When parents had no sons, their daughters could receive the inheritance, but they had to marry within the clan to retain the inheritance (Num. 27:8–11).

Since Israel was a male-dominated society, women's rights were sometimes overlooked. Jesus told a parable about a widow who so pestered the judge who would not listen to her case that he finally agreed to her wishes (Luke 18:1–8). As with many of Jesus' stories, this was something that could really have happened.

Widows were given special privileges. For example, they were allowed to glean the fields after the harvest (Deut. 24:19–22) and share a portion of the third-year tithe with the Levites (Deut. 26:12).

Women at Worship

Women were considered members of the family of faith, and as such, they could enter into most of the areas of worship.

The law directed all men to appear before the Lord three times a year. Apparently the women went with them on some occasions (Deut. 29:10–11; Neh. 8:2; Joel 2:16), but they were not required to go. Perhaps women were excused because of their important duties as wives and mothers.

Hannah went to Shiloh with her husband and asked the Lord for a son (1 Sam. 1:3–5). Later, when the child was born, she told her husband she would not go for the yearly sacrifice "until the child is weaned; then I will take him, that he may appear before the Lord and remain there forever" (vv. 21–22).

As head of the family, the husband or father presented the sacrifices and offerings on behalf of the entire family. But the wife might also be present. Women attended the Feast of Tabernacles (Deut. 16:14), the yearly feast of the Lord (Judg. 21:19–21), and the festival of the New Moon (2 Kings 4:23).

One sacrifice that only a woman gave to the Lord was offered after the birth of a child: "When the days of her purifying are fulfilled, whether for a son or a daughter, she shall bring a lamb of the first year for a burnt offering, and a young pigeon or a turtledove as a sin offering, to the door of the tabernacle of meeting" (Lev. 12:6).

By first century A.D., Jewish women were no longer active in temple or synagogue worship. Although there was a special area at the temple known as the court of women, they were not allowed to go into the inner court. Extrabiblical sources tell us that women were not allowed to read or to speak in the synagogue, but they could sit and listen in the special women's section. The women may have been allowed to enter only the synagogues that were operating on hellenistic principles.

A different picture unfolds in the early Christian church. Luke 8:1–3 indicates that Jesus welcomed certain women as traveling companions. He encouraged Martha and Mary to sit and learn at his feet as disciples (Luke 10:38–42). Jesus' respect for women was something strikingly new.

After Jesus ascended into heaven, several women met with the other disciples in the upper room to pray. Even though Scripture does not say so specifically, these women probably prayed audibly in public. Both men and women gathered at the home of John Mark's mother to pray for the release of Peter (Acts 12:1–17). That both men and women prayed regularly in the church at Corinth is indicated by the apostle Paul's giving instructions to both men and women about how to pray in public (1 Cor. 11:2–16).

Several Bible women were famous for their faith. Included in the list of faithful people in Hebrews 11 are two women, Sarah and Rahab. Hannah was a godly example of the Israelite mother. She prayed, believed that God heard her prayers, and she kept her promise to God (see 1 Sam. 1). Jesus' mother Mary was also a good and godly woman. In fact, Mary must have remembered Hannah's example, for her song of praise to God (Luke 1:46–55) was very similar to Hannah's song (1 Sam. 2:1–10). The apostle Paul reminded Timothy of the goodness of his mother and grandmother (2 Tim. 1:5).

Not all Jewish women in Bible times were loyal to God. According to the book of Jewish writings known as the Talmud, some women were "addicted to witchcraft" (Joma 83b) and the occult. The Talmud also alleged that "the majority of women are inclined to witchcraft" (Sanhedrin 67a). Some rabbis believed this was why God told Moses, "Thou shalt not suffer a witch to live." (Some translations render the Hebrew word for "witch" as "sorceress.")

To be fair, the Scriptures do not indicate that women were any more interested in the occult than the men. Several scriptural references to women who were involved in the occult (e.g., 2 Kings 23:7; Ezek. 8:14; Hos. 4:13–14) imply that men were also involved. And of the four times that sorcery is mentioned in Acts, only once was a woman involved (Acts 8:9–24; 13:6–12; 16:16–18; 19:13–16).

Women in Israel's Culture

In Israelite society a woman's place was in the home. She was expected to find life enjoyable as a wife and mother. Apparently Jewish women accepted that role willingly.

In terms of morality, the law forbade an unmarried woman to have sexual relations. She was to remain a virgin until marriage. If anyone could prove that she was not a virgin when she married, she was brought to the door of her father's house and the men of the city stoned her to death (Deut. 22:20–21).

Sex was an important part of married life. God had ordained the sexual relationship to be enjoyed in the proper place and between the right people—marriage partners. The Jews felt so strongly about this that a newly married man was freed from his military or business duties for a whole year so that he could "bring happiness to his wife whom he has taken" (Deut. 24:5). The only restriction was that the husband and wife were not supposed to have sexual relations during her menstrual period (Lev. 18:19).

Sex was to be enjoyed by the wife as well as the husband. God told Eve, "Your desire shall be for your husband" (Gen. 3:16). In the Song of Solomon, the woman is very aggressive, kissing her husband and leading him into the bed chamber. She expresses her love for him over and over, and she urges him to enjoy their physical relationship (cf. Song of Sol. 1:2; 2:3–6, 8–10; 8:1–4).

By today's standards, we would not consider the daily life of the average Israelite mother very stimulating. It was marked by hard work and long hours. She was up each morning before anyone else, starting a fire in the hearth or oven. The main food in the Jewish diet was bread. In fact, the Hebrew word for food (ohel) was a synonym for bread. One of the jobs of the wife and mother was to grind grain into flour. This involved several steps and many hours.

She used thorns, stubble, or even animal dung to fuel the oven. The children usually had the job of finding the fuel, but if they were not old enough to leave the house, the woman had to find the fuel herself.

Every family needed water. Sometimes they built their own private cistern to store rain water, but more often the water came from a spring or well in the middle of the village. Some OT cities, such as Megiddo and Hazor, were built above underground springs. In Hazor a woman had to walk through the streets to a deep shaft, where she descended two slopes for nine meters (30 feet) and then five flights of stairs to the tunnel, where she followed more stairs to the water level to fill her large jug. She needed considerable strength to climb back out of the watershaft with a heavy jug.

The trips for water gave the women of the village a chance to talk and exchange news. The ladies often made their trips for water in the evening or early morning when it was cool (Gen. 24:11). The woman at the well at Sychar no doubt came in the noon heat because the other women of the town did not want anything to do with her because of her loose living. (John 4:5–30).

The wife was also expected to make her family's clothes. Small children had to be nursed, watched, and kept clean. As the children got older, the mother taught them manners. She also taught the older daughters how to cook, sew, and do the other things a good Israelite wife needed to know.

In addition, the wife was expected to help bring in the harvest (cf. Ruth 2:23). She prepared some crops like olives and grapes for storage.

Women Leaders in Israel

Most Israelite women never became public leaders, but there were some exceptions. Scripture records the names and deeds of several women who became prominent in political, military, or religious affairs.

Military Heroines

The two most famous military heroines in the OT are Deborah and Jael—both had a role in the same victory. God spoke through Deborah to tell the general Barak how to defeat the Canaanites. Barak agreed to the attack, but he wanted Deborah to go with him into the battle. She did so and the Canaanites were duly defeated. However, the Canaanite leader, Sisera, escaped on foot. Jael saw him, went out to greet him and invited him into her tent. After eating he fell asleep, and Jael hammered a tent peg through his head, killing him (see Judg. 4–5).

On another occasion, several woman helped to defend their city of Thebez against attackers. The leader of the attack, Abimelech, moved in close to the tower gate to set it on fire. One of the women saw him at the gate and dropped a millstone on his head. The heavy stone crushed Abimelech's skull. As he lay dying he commanded his armor-bearer, "Draw your sword and kill me, lest men say of me, 'A woman killed him'" (Judg. 9:54). The attack was called off. Later generations gave the unidentified woman credit for the victory (cf. 2 Sam. 11:21).

Queens

Not all the women in the Bible were known for their good deeds. Queen Jezebel is the most notorious woman in the OT. She was a daughter of Ethbaal, king of the Sidonians. She married Ahab, the prince of Israel, and moved to Samaria.

When Jezebel became queen, she enforced her wishes on the people. She wanted the Israelites to bow down to Baal, so she brought hundreds of Sidon's Baal prophets into the country and put them on the government payroll. She also killed as many of the prophets of the Lord as she could find (1 Kings 18:13). Even godly men like Naboth were cut down.

Elijah ran away and hid from Jezebel to save his life. He felt that he was the only true prophet left in the entire country. In fact, in the entire kingdom there were 7,000 people who had refused to worship Baal, but only God knew who they were.

Herodias was another woman who used her power and her beauty to get what she wanted. When John the Baptist spoke out against her marriage to King Herod, she got the king to arrest John and put him into prison. On Herod's birthday, Herodias' daughter danced for the guests. This pleased Herod very much, and he promised to give her anything she asked for. Herodias told her daughter to ask for the head of John the Baptist, thus causing the death of John.

Not all the queens in the Bible were evil. Queen Esther used her power in the Persian Empire to save the Jews.

Queen Mothers

The writers of 1 and 2 Kings and 2 Chronicles tell us much about the queen mothers of Judah. In referring to the 20 different kings who ruled in Judah from the time of Solomon to the time of the Exile, only once do these books fail to mention the queen mother. For example, "In the second year of Joash the son of Jehoahaz, king of Israel, Amaziah the son of Joash, king of Judah, began to reign. He was twenty-five years old when he became king, and he reigned twenty-nine years in Jerusalem. His mother's name was Jehoaddin of Jerusalem. And he did what was right in the eyes of the Lord" (2 Kings 14:1–3).

We assume that the mother of the king must have been an important person in Judah. Unfortunately, nothing is known about her role in the government or the society.

One instance of a queen mother's having decisive influence stands out. Because Adonijah was David's oldest surviving son, he naturally felt he should succeed David. Several high officials agreed with him—including Joab, the general of the army, and Abiathar, the priest. On the other hand, the prophet Nathan and another priest named Zadok believed Solomon, another of David's sons, was God's choice. Bathsheba, Solomon's mother, came to see the king and he reminded her of his promise that Solomon would be king. He immediately took steps to implement his oath (see 1 Kings 1:30–35).

When King Asa brought religious reforms to the country, he removed his grandmother from her position at the court because she had made an image of the goddess Asherah. While King Asa did not kill his mother, he took away her power (1 Kings 15:9–15).

One queen mother who had tremendous power was Athaliah, the mother of Ahaziah. When her son was killed in battle, Athaliah seized the throne and killed all the rightful heirs except for Joash, an infant prince, who was hidden from her. For six years Athaliah ruled Judah cruelly. Then, under the leadership of the high priest, Joash ascended to the throne, and Athaliah was overthrown and killed (2 Kings 11:1–16).

Counselors

Most villages had wise persons whom other people asked for advice. The king's court had wise counselors as well. While there are no Scripture references to women counselors in the king's court, there are several examples of village wise women.

When Joab, the commander-in-chief of David's army, wanted to reconcile David and his son Absalom, he got a wise woman from Tekoa to help him. The woman pretended to be a widow with two sons. She said that one of her sons had killed the other in a fit of anger; now the rest of her family wanted to kill the remaining son. David listened to her story and ruled that she was right to forgive this second son. Then the woman pointed out to the king that he was not practicing what he advocated because he had not forgiven Absalom for a similar crime. David saw that he had been wrong and allowed Absalom to return to Jerusalem (2 Sam. 14:1–20).

Another wise woman saved her town from destruction when Sheba led a revolt against King David. The revolt failed; Sheba ran away and hid in the city of Abel. David's general Joab surrounded the city and was getting ready to attack it when a wise woman from the city appeared at the wall and asked to speak to Joab. She reminded him how important her town had been to Israel. To destroy this city of Abel, she said, would be like killing "a mother in Israel." They agreed to a plan. If Sheba were killed, the city would not be attacked. The wise woman returned and told the townspeople about the plan. They killed the traitor, and Joab and his army rode away (2 Sam. 20:1–22).

Religious Leaders

In Israel, God did not prescribe priestesses, and a woman could not become a priest because that ministry was restricted to the male descendants of Aaron. However, women could perform many other ritual tasks. It is not surprising to find women involved in the public worship of God on various levels.

Women served as prophetesses—spokeswomen—for God. The most famous Hebrew prophetess was Huldah, the wife of Shallum. She was active in this ministry during the days of King Josiah. When the book of the law was found in the temple, the religious leaders came to her to ask what God wanted the nation to do. The whole nation, including King Josiah, carried out her instructions because they were sure God had spoken through her (2 Kings 22:11–23:14).

There were other OT prophetesses, including Miriam (Exod. 15:20), Deborah (Judg. 4:4–16), and Isaiah's wife (Isa. 8:3). The NT mentions that Anna and the daughters of Philip were prophetesses, but we know nothing else about their lives or messages (Luke 2:36–38; Acts 21:9).

Some women used the musical talents God had given them. Miriam and other women sang a song of praise to God after the Israelites had been delivered from the Egyptians (Exod. 15:2). When God helped Deborah and Barak defeat the Canaanites, they wrote a victory song and sang it as a duet (Judg. 5:1–31). Three daughters of Heman were also musicians and performed at the temple (see 1 Chron. 25:5–6).

In the church at Cenchreae (Corinth) was a deaconess named Phoebe, whom Paul described as "a helper of many and of myself also" (Rom. 16:2). In the same letter to the Romans, Paul wrote, "Greet Mary, who labored much for us" (v. 6).

Paul also sent greetings to Andronicus and Junia, "my countrymen." Although this has created arguments, scholarship is now on the side of Junia being a woman, the wife of Andronicus, which is the most natural interpretation of Romans 16:7. This would make her an apostle.

In a letter to Timothy, Paul wrote that wives of deacons "must be reverent, not slanderers, temperate, faithful in all things" (1 Tim. 3:11). But he made it clear that he did not want any woman to teach or to have authority over men (2:12).

Other female leaders of the early church included Priscilla, who helped explain to Apollos "the way of God more perfectly" (cf. Acts 18:24–28)—which is certainly teaching a man, even if in an informal setting.

Euodia and Syntyche were two of the spiritual leaders at Philippi. Paul spoke of them as "women who have labored with me in the gospel, with Clement also, and the rest of my fellow workers" (Phil. 4:3). Thus it appears that they were doing a work similar to his own.

Money, Minerals, and Gems

Money ———————————————————

As soon as ancient people stopped living as wandering hunters and began an agricultural system, a medium of exchange became necessary. A system of barter, or trading of property, preceded the creation of any formal currency that can be called money.

Goods and Services

In OT times, land itself became an immediate asset because it was a possession that could be traded. But produce, and especially livestock, was more convenient because it was so movable. Pharaoh of Egypt supplied Abraham with oxen, sheep, camels, and donkeys (Gen. 12:16). King Mesha of Moab regularly paid a tribute of 100,000 sheep and 100,000 rams to the king of Israel (2 Kings 3:4).

Grain, oil, and wine were also used in bartering. King Solomon traded wheat and olive oil for the cedar and cypress trees needed to build the temple (see 1 Kings 5:11). The Israelites were taxed in the amount of one-tenth of their grain or wine (see 1 Sam. 8:15).

Metals

Gradually, as communities became more organized, traders traveled between settlements. Products circulated from one region to another. Soon metals began to replace goods and services as items of exchange. Copper or bronze was in demand for weapons (2 Sam. 21:16), for farming tools, and for offerings (Exod. 35:5). The early Egyptians, Semites, and Hittites shaped gold and silver into rings, bars, or rounded nodules for easier trading. The children of Jacob used bundles of money (Gen. 42:35), which may have been metal rings tied together with strings.

Silver generally was used in real estate transactions. Omri purchased the village and hill of Samaria for two talents of silver (cf. 1 Kings 16:24).

Gold was sometimes used, along with silver, in the payment of tribute, such as Hezekiah's payment to Sennacherib of Assyria (2 Kings 18:14). Silver was so commonly used as money that the Hebrew word for silver came to mean money.

Gold, the most valuable of metals, was also used for major transactions. King Hiram of Tyre paid 120 talents of gold to Solomon for several cities near his land (1 Kings 9:13–14). Later Hezekiah paid Sennacherib 300 talents of silver and 30 talents of gold to obtain peace (2 Kings 18:14). Bronze (probably an alloy of copper and bronze but rendered as *brass* in KJV) was also used for barter but considered less valuable (e.g., Exod. 35:5; 2 Sam. 21:16; Isa. 60:17). Later these same three metals were used to mint the nation's first coins.

In their early use as money, metals were probably in their raw form or in varying stages of refinement. However, in that form it was difficult to transport them and to determine their true value. The metals were soon refined into the form of a wedge or a bar (Josh. 7:21) or various forms of jewelry.

The Bible frequently refers to "pieces" of silver or gold. The confusing word *shekel* did not denote any one value or weight at first, although it later became the name of a Jewish coin. For instance, there were heavy and light silver shekels (Phoenician), and heavy and light gold shekels (Babylonian). Fifteen heavy Phoenician shekels of silver equaled one heavy Babylonian gold shekel.

Fractions of the shekel are mentioned in the OT as well: the half-shekel, or *bekah* (Exod. 38:26); the third part of a shekel as a covenant obligation (Neh. 10:32); the fourth part of a shekel, or *rebah,* proposed to Saul by the servant as a gift to the prophet Samuel (1 Sam. 9:8); and the twentieth part of a shekel, or a *gerah* (Lev. 27:25), probably a fragment of a gold or silver bar rather than a shaped coin.

The *talent* was the largest unit of silver, shaped in pellets or rings, with approximately the value of one ox.

Before coins with stamped values were introduced, the pieces of precious metal for transactions had to be weighed on a scale. Abraham measured the shekels given to Ephron (Gen. 23:16). Such a system was certainly haphazard. Dishonest practices of weighing were banned (Deut. 25:13) in favor of a "perfect and just weight" (Deut. 25: 15), because "dishonest scales are an abomination to the LORD" (Prov. 11:1).

Stamped Coins

Eventually pieces of metal were standardized, then stamped to designate their weight and value. Coins still had to be weighed, however, since their edges might have been trimmed or filed. Ancient coins often show other marks, indicating they may have been probed to assure their silver content.

The earliest coins were probably struck in Lydia by King Croesus (561–546 B.C.), whose legendary Anatolian mines and stream beds supplied gold and silver. He was conquered by Cyrus the Great, who may have carried the idea of coined money back to Persia. The Persian Darius the Great (522–486 B.C.) minted coins of gold. The coin known as a *daric,* which bore his name, was common with the Israelites during the captivity. It was similar to a U.S. five-dollar gold piece. Ten thousand darics were paid craftsmen for their work on the temple built by Solomon (1 Chron. 29:7).

The Greeks soon adapted the Persian and Babylonian coinage, portraying animals, natural objects, and Greek gods on the coins—which were called *drachmas* (Greek for "handful"). The *tetradrachma* or shekel of Tyre was about the size of an American half-dollar that probably circulated among the Israelites. Archaeologists have uncovered coins of Greek design marked "YHD" (Judah), probably minted by the Persians for use by the Jews. However, these particular coins are not mentioned in the Bible.

Alexander the Great conquered the Persian Empire. In the period between the OT and NT, Greek coins, especially the tetradrachma, poured into Palestine. After Alexander's death, his successors, the Ptolemies, added mints at Gaza, Jaffa, and Tyre for making coins.

The Seleucids seized Palestine about 200 B.C., forcing Greek culture upon the Jews until they rebelled against Antiochus IV around 167 B.C. The right to mint coins was an issue, but the Jewish revolt led by Simon Maccabeus was thwarted. Later Antiochus VII established a mint that struck coins bearing his name. The Seleucids' domination lapsed as the Hasmoneans gained their freedom and began minting their own small bronze coins (one-half, one-third, and one-fourth shekel in weight). These were inscribed to a certain high priest of that time and "the community of Jews." Still the Seleucids issued official gold and silver coins. This brief phase of freedom for the Jews ended when the Romans annexed Palestine in 63 B.C.

Roman coins common in NT times showed a profound Greek influence, including those issued by Herod the Great (36–4 B.C.) and his sons. But because of the second commandment, which prohibited graven images, the coins displayed only traditional, stylized pictures. However, they did include the date of issue.

The basic unit of Roman coinage was the silver *denarius*, probably equal to a laborer's daily wage, as in the parable of the vineyard workers (Matt. 20:9–10, 13). It was also used for paying tribute, or taxes, to the Roman emperor, whose image it carried.

The golden *aureus* was worth about 25 denarii. The "copper coin" (*assarion*, equal to one-sixteenth of a silver denarius) was mentioned by Jesus as being worth no more than two sparrows, in his counsel about God's concern for the smallest creatures as well as the most powerful (Matt. 10:29; Luke 12:6). The *penny* (*quadrans* or *kodrantes*) was equal to one-fourth of the copper assarion. It was also mentioned by Jesus (Matt. 5:26).

Greek coins generally bore religious symbols. They may have been minted at pagan temples, which served as business centers for granting loans and receiving estates. The cult of Astarte may have had a strong influence on the production of coins. Silver for Greek coins was supplied by the rich mines of Laurium. Gold coins were less popular among the Greeks.

The basic Greek coin was the *drachma*, roughly equivalent to a Roman denarius, or one day's wages. Probably the drachma is the lost coin of Jesus' parable (Luke 15:8–10). Paul, when he practiced tentmaking at Corinth, probably exchanged his work for the Corinthian coins that pictured the winged horse Pegasus.

The Greek *didrachmon* (two-drachma piece) was used by the Jews for their half-shekel temple tax (Matt. 17:24). The silver *stater*, or *tetradrachma*, was a four-drachma piece, used to pay the temple tax (Matt. 17:27). The *mina*, equaling 100 drachmas, illustrated Jesus' parable about the wise use of resources (Luke 19:11–27).

The only Jewish coin mentioned in the NT is the "widow's mite" or *lepton*. These were very small copper coins worth only a fraction of a penny by today's standards. Yet, Jesus commended the poor widow who gave two mites to the temple treasury, because "she out of her poverty put in all that she had, her whole livelihood" (Mark 12:44).

Girdles, belts, or waistbands that bound together loose garments and also held money were called "moneybelts." When Jesus sent out the twelve, he told them to take no money in their moneybelts (Matt. 10:9; Mark 6:8; *belts*, RSV, NIV; *purses* KJV, NEB). They were to depend on the generosity of the people in the villages and towns through which they passed.

Bankers who exchanged one nation's currency, or one size of coin, for another were called "moneychangers." These people provided a convenience, charging a fee, often exorbitant, for their services. Moneychangers operated in the temple area called the court of the Gentiles, because all money given to the temple had to be in the Tyrian silver coin. According to Exodus 30:11–16, every Israelite 20 years old or older was required to pay an annual tax of a half-shekel into the temple treasury.

Minerals

Mining is the extraction of minerals or other valuable substances from the earth. Mining operations have been conducted in the biblical world since ancient times. It is not known when people first began to dig into the earth to extract materials. We know it existed in Syria, Israel, the Arabah, Sinai, Egypt, and other Mediterranean lands. Mining was not limited to metallic ores such as gold, copper, silver, iron, lead, and tin. Mining also included other resources such as gems, salt, sand, clays, and many kinds of building stones. A vivid description of mining appears in Job 28.

The first mines were probably placer mines, which involved panning or sifting by hand. Gold, the first metal mentioned in the Bible, was probably mined by this method. Open pit or surface mining was also used in Bible times.

The Hebrews learned mining and metallurgical skills early in their history (Gen. 4:22; Deut. 8:9). The Kenites, who were native to the Arabah, probably introduced the Israelites and the Edomites to the art of mining and metallurgy.

Quarries, which are actually mines, were operated in Israel and Egypt. Masons usually quarried and shaped their own stone (1 Kings 6:7; Isa. 51:1). Deep channels were cut and wedges were driven into the openings and soaked with water. Sometimes these channels were cut along natural breaks by using iron axes.

Salt was also mined from the Dead Sea in "saltpits" (Zeph. 2:9). These were holes or pits dug along the flat coastal area. When the sun evaporated the water, the salt remained.

The Bible mentions six metals known and used by the ancient Hebrews: gold, silver, bronze, iron, tin, and lead (Num. 31:22). Job's reference to metals "taken from the earth" (Job 28:2) seems to indicate a firsthand knowledge of mine operations. The smelting of ores was known apparently in very ancient times with copper the first metal smelted by the Egyptians, about 4500 B.C.

Israel acquired much of its mineral resources through spoils of war (Josh. 22:8) and through trade with foreign countries. This trade reached its greatest height during Solomon's time (1 Kings 10:10–11, 14–15, 22). These minerals proved to be a valuable asset to the physical, material, and spiritual welfare of the people of Bible lands.

The following minerals are mentioned in the Bible. This list is keyed to the NKJV, with cross-references from five additional popular versions: KJV, NASB, NEB, NIV, and RSV.

Alabaster. The most common form of alabaster is a fine-textured variety of massive gypsum (sulfate of lime), soft and excellent for carving. The color is usually white, but it may be gray, yellow, or red.

Large quantities of gypsum were quarried in the Jordan Valley in the days before the Hebrew people occupied this territory. Many articles were fashioned from this stone, including vases, jars, saucers, bowls, lamps, and statues. Mary of Bethany anointed Jesus with costly oil from a flask made of alabaster (Matt. 26:7; Mark 14:3; Luke 7:37).

The ancient variety of alabaster is known as oriental alabaster (carbonate of lime), a form of marble, which is much harder than the gypsum variety but is used for the same purpose. Ancient alabaster was found only in Egypt.

Antimony. A hard mineral, metallic gray in color, usually classed as a metal, antimony was ground into a fine black powder, moistened with oil or water, and used as eye paint to accent the eyelashes and make them appear larger (Jer. 4:30). This was an accepted custom in Egypt and Mesopotamia, but rejected by the Hebrews, although Jezebel and other women of ill repute used the substance (2 Kings 9:30).

Jeremiah and Ezekiel compared Israel to

Bronze head of the Greek god Zeus. In ancient times, bronze was an alloy of copper and tin.
PHOTO BY HOWARD VOS

unfaithful women who adorned themselves with paint for their lovers (Jer. 4:30; Ezek. 23:40). The material David furnished for the temple included antimony. This was mixed with resin and used as a setting for gems (1 Chron. 29:2, RSV).

Ash. (See *Lime.*)

Asphalt. A black mineral substance, a form of bitumen, and derived from crude petroleum (Gen. 11:3; Exod. 2:3), asphalt was found in Mesopotamia and Canaan, especially in the Dead Sea region. Because of the abundance of asphalt around the Dead Sea, the Greeks and Romans referred to it as Lake Asphaltitis (see Gen. 14:10). Other versions translate the word for asphalt as *bitumen, slime, tar,* or *clay.* (See *Bitumen; Clay.*)

Bitumen. Bitumen is a mineral substance consisting chiefly of hydrogen and carbon. Mineral pitch and asphalt are forms of bitumen. It is highly flammable, and its consistency varies from solids to semiliquids (Isa. 34:9). Large deposits of bitumen have existed around the Dead Sea and in Egypt and Mesopotamia since ancient times.

Bitumen was used as caulking to waterproof Noah's ark (Gen. 6:14) and the basket in which Moses was hidden (Exod. 2:3). It was also used as mortar (Gen. 11:3). The pits into which the kings of Sodom and Gomorrah fell were bitumen pits (Gen. 14:10, RSV). Various English versions of the Bible translate the word for bitumen as *asphalt, slime, tar,* or *pitch.* (See *Asphalt.*)

Brass. True brass is an alloy of copper and zinc. However, when brass is mentioned in the Bible, it generally refers to either copper or bronze (1 Cor. 13:1; Rev. 1:15; 2:18; 9:20). The three words, *brass, bronze,* and *copper,* are often used interchangeably in various English translations of the Bible.

Many articles in the ancient world were made from bronze, or brass. These included cooking utensils, shovels, spoons, musical instruments, weapons, and tools. Solomon used copper and bronze in many of the items in the temple (1 Kings 7:14). (See *Copper.*)

Brimstone. A bright yellow mineral usually found near active volcanoes, brimstone is found in large deposits in the Dead Sea region. Highly combustible, it burns with a disagreeable odor.

The Hebrew and Greek words for brimstone denote divine fire (Gen. 19:24; Ezek. 38:22; Luke 17:29). Brimstone (burning stone) is often associated with fire (Rev. 9:17–18; 20:10; 21:8) and barrenness and devastation (Deut. 29:23; Job 18:15). Brimstone was considered an agent of God's judgment (Gen. 19:24). In the NT it symbolically represents God's wrath and future punishment of the wicked (Rev. 9:17–18; 14:10; 20:10). Another word for brimstone used in various translations of the Bible is *sulphur,* or *sulfur.*

Bronze. (See *Brass; Tin.*)

Chalkstone. A variety of fine-grained limestone rock, chalkstone (or chalk) is a soft porous material consisting largely of calcite. It is usually white, but it can be yellow or gray. Limestone is the dominant stone in Bible lands. The Hebrews burned limestone in kilns to make lime (Isa. 33:12). (See *Lime.*)

Chrysolite marble. (See *Marble.*)

Clay. In soil that consists of extremely fine particles of sand, flint, or quartz, some clays were formed of soft limestone with moist grit and flint; others included quartz that formed a harder clay.

Clay was used widely in the ancient world. Archaeologists have found many clay objects dating from about 5000 B.C. at Jericho. Among its many uses, clay was an important building material. The Tower of Babel was constructed of clay bricks (Gen. 11:3). The poorest quality clay was used in making bricks. Both sun-baked and kiln-fired bricks were known (2 Sam. 12:31). Mortar was also usually made of clay. The Hebrew word for clay is translated by some English versions as *asphalt.*

A brick from ancient Babylon impressed with the name of King Nebuchadnezzer.

PHOTO BY GUSTAV JEENINGA

Impressions were made into wet clay with signet rings or cylinder seals to prove ownership (Job 38:14; Dan. 6:17). Clay seals were placed on houses, vessels of various kinds, and perhaps on Christ's tomb (Matt. 27:66).

Clay tablets were used in Mesopotamia for cuneiform writing. Letters were pressed into soft clay with a stylus. The tablet was then sun-baked or kiln-fired to increase its strength. Various kinds of pottery were made of clay. These included lamps, cooking utensils, pots, vases, jars, dishes, and idols. (See *Asphalt.*)

Coal. Coal is a black porous form of carbon (Lam. 4:8, KJV) or live embers of any kind (2 Sam. 22:9, 13). The Hebrews learned to form charcoal by burning wood that had been covered by earth and leaves. The lack of air caused the wood to char. According to Isaiah, cedars, cypress, and oak were some of the trees used for fuel (Isa. 44:14–16). Broom or juniper bushes were also used for charcoal (Ps. 120:4).

The intense heat of charcoal made it a valuable form of fuel in smelting furnaces. The wealthy used charcoal to heat their homes (Jer. 36:22). It was also used for cooking (1 Kings 19:6). Blacksmiths relied on it (Isa. 44:12).

Copper. A reddish brown metal derived from many kinds of ores, copper was the first to be used for making tools. Pure copper was used until it was alloyed with zinc to form brass and with tin to form bronze sometime between 4500 and 3000 B.C.

Ancient copper refineries were located in Sinai, Egypt, Syria, Persia, the Phoenician coast, and Israel. During Solomon's reign (about 971–931 B.C.), an elaborate mining operation existed at Ezion-geber in the Arabah, south of the Dead Sea (1 Kings 9:26). Copper became Solomon's chief article of export.

Many useful articles were made from copper and its alloys, including tools of all kinds, utensils (Lev. 6:28), weapons (2 Sam. 21:16; 22:35; 2 Chron. 12:10), idols, musical instruments, and many furnishings for the temple (2 Kings 25:13). (See *Brass; Tin.*)

Crystal. (See *Quartz.*)

Flint. A hard variety of quartz, dark gray or brown, flint is usually found in chalk or limestone rock. A form of silica, it sparks

An iron stove from the first century A.D. *excavated at Pompeii.*   PHOTO BY HOWARD VOS

when struck by steel or another flint (2 Macc. 10:3).

Archaeologists have found many flint objects, especially knives. These were dated from the Neolithic or Late Stone Age (about 7000–4500 B.C.). Zipporah used a "sharp stone" to circumcise her child (Exod. 4:25; see also Josh. 5:2). The Bible refers to "flinty rock" (Deut. 8:15; 32:13).

Flint is also spoken of in a figurative manner in the Bible, denoting strength and determination (Isa. 5:28; 50:7; Ezek. 3:9). This mineral is still abundant in the limestone rock of Syria, Palestine, and Egypt.

Glass. (See *Quartz.*)

Gold. We find gold mentioned over 500 times in the Bible, more than any other metal. Rich deposits of gold were in Havilah (Gen. 2:11), Ophir (1 Kings 22:48; 2 Chron. 8:18), Sheba (1 Kings 10:1–2), Egypt, Armenia, Asia Minor, and Persia. Gold was at first hammered into desired shapes and sizes. In later periods it was refined and cast. Some scholars believe gold was not refined in Palestine until about 1000 B.C.

Many objects were made of gold, including threads in the high priest's vest (Exod. 28:5), crowns (Ps. 21:3), neck chains (Gen. 41:42), rods (Song of Sol. 5:14; *rings*, KJV), and coins (1 Chron. 21:25; Acts 3:6). Hiram brought gold to Israel for Solomon's palace (1 Kings 10:16–21) and for furnishings for the temple (1 Kings 6:20; 10:11). Gold was also taken as plunder in war (2 Kings 24:13).

Hyacinth. (See *Jacinth.*)

Iron. This mineral is actually a metal obtained from certain rocks or ores. Iron occurs in a variety of minerals. Much of the color of other minerals is due to the presence of iron, which has a steel gray color with a metallic luster.

Meteoric iron is one of the oldest metals known to the human race and it existed in Egypt before 3100 B.C. The presence of nickel in meteoric iron distinguishes it from common iron ore. The ancient Egyptian word for this material meant "metal from heaven." Before the knowledge of smelting ores was available, ancient man fashioned small objects from this ore (Gen. 4:22; Deut. 8:9).

The Hittites in Asia Minor were the first to develop skills in the smelting of iron (about 1400 B.C.). Charcoal-fired furnaces were used for this purpose. Since higher temperatures were required to cast iron, only wrought iron could be made at this time.

When the Philistines overthrew the Hittites (about 1200 B.C.), iron became widely used throughout the ancient world. Iron was definitely in use during the Israelite conquest of the land of Canaan (Josh. 6:24; Judg. 1:19; 4:3). The Philistines became skilled ironsmiths, eventually controlling most of Canaan and later conquering Israel, prohibiting their use of iron (1 Sam. 13:19, 22). After the Israelites' victory over the Philistines, iron became widespread in Palestine.

Iron ore was plentiful in Canaan, Syria, Cyprus, and Asia Minor. Extensive mining operations existed, especially at Eziongeber, south of the Dead Sea. Iron gradually replaced copper and bronze for farming implements, weapons, armor, and tools.

The reference to steel in Psalm 18:34 (KJV) means *copper* or *bronze*, because steel was not known at that time.

Jacinth. An orange or reddish gemstone and a variety of zircon, this mineral is widely distributed in crystal form in volcanic rocks and in fine granules in sand. Jacinth was the first stone in the third row of Aaron's breastplate (Exod. 28:19; *ligure,* KJV; *turquoise,* NEB). Jacinth was used to describe one of the colors in the breastplates of the riders in John's vision (Rev. 9:17; *sapphire,* RSV; *sulfur,* NIV; *hyacinth,* NKJV). Jacinth is also the eleventh foundation stone in the New Jerusalem (Rev. 21:20).

Jasper. (See *Quartz.*)

Lead. A soft, bluish gray metal that, next to gold, is the heaviest of the common metals. Lead is easily worked, but it tarnishes quickly. The ancient Roman name for lead was *plumbum.* The English word *plumber* (worker in lead) comes from this Latin word.

Lead is found in limestone and dolomite rock, usually deposited with other metals, and is sometimes mentioned in the Bible along with other metals (Num. 31:22; Ezek. 22:18, 20). Lead was never used extensively in Canaan, but it was mined in Egypt and the Sinai Peninsula. This metal was also imported from Tarshish (Ezek. 27:12).

Lead was used to purify silver (Jer. 6:29–30; Ezek. 22:18–20), as sinkers for fishing nets (Exod. 15:10), and as weights (Zech. 5:7–8). Job refers to his words being preserved permanently in lead (Job 19:24). Plumb lines may also have been made of lead (Amos 7:7–8).

Ligure. (See *Jacinth.*)

Lime. A calcium oxide derived from limestone rock or chalk, limestone was burned in limekilns and reduced to powder. Then it was used mainly for plastering floors and walls. The earliest mention of lime in the Bible is when God instructed Moses to whitewash stones with lime for a memorial of his covenant with Israel (Deut. 27:2, 4; *plaster,* KJV, NEB, NIV, RSV).

The Hebrew word for lime is also translated by various English versions as *plaster, whitewash,* or *ash* (Deut. 27:2, 4; Isa. 27:9; 33:12; Dan. 5:5; Amos 2:1). Lime was used by the Israelites for mortar and as plaster for walls (Dan. 5:5). The walls of cisterns were also waterproofed with plaster.

Lime may have been used in dyeing to give colors a permanent set in the fabric. Archaeologists have found stone jars containing lime and potash next to dyeing vats. (See *Chalkstone.*)

Lye. Lye is an alkaline material used as a cleansing agent. Both Egypt and Palestine produced some form of soap for washing the body as well as clothes. This may have been natron (niter), a sodium carbonate (soda) available in its natural state in southern Egypt. This substance could have been imported into Israel.

The Hebrew word for lye is *nether*, referring to a mineral alkaline substance. Palestine produced potassium carbonate, an alkaline material made from the ashes of many scrubby plants and mixed with oil to form a soft soap. These plants grew in the Dead Sea region.

Jeremiah declared that the people of Judah were so full of iniquity that it could not be removed, "though you wash yourself with lye" (Jer. 2:22; *nitre*, KJV; *soda*, NIV).

Malachite. (See *Marble.*)

Marble. A crystallized form of limestone, marble is extremely hard and capable of a high polish. Usually white, it is sometimes red or yellow.

The Hebrew and Greek words translated as marble mean "brightness" or "glistening." Marble was obtained from most Bible lands in some form, but the choicest variety came from Arabia.

David supplied an abundance of marble for the temple (1 Chron. 29:2). Solomon alluded poetically to the strength and beauty of marble (Song of Sol. 5:15; *alabaster*, NASB, RSV; Song of Sol. 5:14; chrysolite marble, NIV). It was used in the palace of Shushan, or Susa (Esther 1:6).

In the Greek and Roman periods many public buildings and homes of the wealthy contained marble. Archaeologists have found many marble heads and statues. Marble is included in the merchandise of symbolic Babylon that will be destroyed (Rev. 18:12). Egyptian alabaster was also a form of marble. (See *Alabaster.*)

One distinct type of marble mentioned by several English translations is porphyry (Esther 1:6, NASB, RSV; *malachite*, NEB). This was a purple rock with imbedded crystals of various sizes, used in the pavement of King Ahasuerus's palace at Shushan.

Mercury. A silvery white liquid metal, popularly called quicksilver, mercury

comes from the ores of cinnabar. The Greek word for mercury means "water silver." It is used to extract gold and silver from their ores. This process, called amalgamation, was probably used in the ancient world. Pliny (A.D. 23–79) refers to mercury in this manner.

Mercury is not mentioned in the Bible by name, but it may be implied (Prov. 26:23; Isa. 1:22; Ezek. 22:18–20) by the phrase "silver dross." (See *Vermilion.*)

Mortar. Mortar was a mixture of clay, sand, lime, and water used for building material. Mortar was sometimes made of clay alone or with chopped straw, sand, or crushed stone added for strength. The Hebrews in Egypt may have tempered their bricks and mortar with straw (Exod. 1:14; 5:7).

Lime mixed with sand or small stones was used for mortar. This was used especially for more expensive houses. Mortar was spread on the walls, floors, and roofs of houses for more durability. Nahum suggested the usual method of mixing mortar was treading it (Nah. 3:14).

Nitre. (See *Lye.*)

Oil. In the Bible, oil usually refers to olive oil, although oil from myrrh, spikenard, and other varieties of trees was often used. Olive oil was one of the most important products in the economy and in the daily life of the people. It became a symbol of peace and prosperity (Jer. 31:12), and was looked upon as a blessing from God.

Olives were harvested from September through the middle of November. Olives were gathered by shaking the trees (Isa. 17:6) or by beating the trees with long sticks (Deut. 24:20). The oil was stored in vats for later use. In homes it was stored in jars or flasks for domestic purposes (1 Kings 17:12).

Every household was dependent upon a good supply of oil for the lamps (Exod. 25:6; Matt. 25:3–4, 8) and as an ingredient for bread (1 Kings 17:12). Olive oil was also used as a medicine to treat wounds (Isa. 1:6, NEB).

Ceremonial anointing was a common practice, especially for consecrating the high priest (Exod. 40:13) and anointing the king (1 Sam. 10:1). Oil was also used for personal cleanliness (Ruth 3:3; 2 Sam. 12:20). The early church practiced anointing with oil for healing (Mark 6:13; James 5:14). Oil was an article of trade especially during Solomon's time. Hiram, king of Tyre, received oil each year (1 Kings 5:11), and it was also traded to Egypt.

Probably the most significant use of oil was in religious ceremonies. The best grade of oil was used for cereal offerings (Exod. 29:2; Deut. 12:17), sacrificial offerings (Exod. 29:40), and the sanctuary lamp (Lev. 24:2).

Pearl. (See *Quartz*.)

Pitch. (See *Asphalt*; *Bitumen*.)

Plaster. Plaster was a mixture of clay, lime, and water used to coat various surfaces. The Hebrew word means "to coat" or "overlay." At first plaster was probably made from clay and used to coat floors, walls, and roofs of houses (Lev. 14:42, 45; Dan. 5:5). In later periods lime was mixed with clay or sand to waterproof cisterns and basins.

Porphyry. (See *Marble*.)

Quartz. A hard, glasslike mineral composed of oxygen and silicon, quartz is found in pure crystalline form in such other minerals as agate, flint, sand, and sandstone. It is a common mineral. Job indicated that wisdom was superior to all the precious gems and minerals of the earth, including quartz (Job 28:18; *pearls*, KJV; *glass*, NASB; *alabaster*, NEB; *jasper*, NIV; *crystal*, RSV).

Salt. Salt is sodium chloride, a white crystalline substance used mainly as a seasoning and a preservative (Job 6:6). Salt is not only one of the most important substances mentioned in the Bible, but a necessity for life. The Hebrew people were well aware of the importance of salt to health (Job 6:6).

High concentrations of salt exist in the Dead Sea, a body of water that is nine times saltier than the ocean. The ancient cities of Sodom and Gomorrah may have been located near the south end of the Dead Sea. Here is where the Bible says Lot's wife was turned into a pillar of salt (Gen. 19:26).

An ancient method of extracting salt from seawater was to collect saltwater in saltpits—holes dug in the sand. The water evaporated, leaving the salt behind (Zeph. 2:9). Saltpans were later used for this purpose.

Salt had a significant place in Hebrew worship. It was included in the grain offering (Lev. 2:13), the burnt offering (Ezek. 43:24), and the incense (Exod. 30:35). Part of the temple offering included salt (Ezra 6:9). It was also used to ratify covenants (Num. 18:19; 2 Chron. 13:5). Newborn babies were rubbed with salt in the belief that this promoted good health (Ezek. 16:4).

During times of war, the enemies' lands were sown with salt to render them barren (Judg. 9:45). In Roman times salt was an important item of trade and was even used for money. Roman soldiers received part of their salary in salt.

Jesus described his disciples as the salt of the earth, urging them to imitate the usefulness of salt (Matt. 5:13; Col. 4:6).

Sand. Sand is made up of fine grains of rock that are worn away by wind and rain. Numerous minerals such as quartz, calcite, and mica are found in sand.

Sand was plentiful on the Mediterranean shores, along riverbanks, and in desert regions. It is usually mentioned in the Bible in a figurative manner to symbolize a multitude (Gen. 22:17; Isa. 10:22; Rev. 20:8), weight (Job 6:3), and weakness (Matt. 7:26). Sand was also used in mortar and in the manufacture of glass, which began in ancient Egypt or Phoenicia.

Sapphire. (See *Jacinth*.)

Silver. This mineral is actually a silvery white metal capable of a high polish. In ancient times it was valued next to gold. Silver was harder than gold, but not as hard as copper. It was usually extracted from lead ore, although it was also found in its native state. Silver never tarnishes when exposed to air unless sulfur is present.

The main sources of silver were Asia Minor, Arabia, Mesopotamia, Armenia, and Persia. Israel imported most of its silver from these countries, especially during Solomon's time (about 971–931 B.C.), when "the king made silver as common in Jerusalem as stones" (1 Kings 10:27; 2 Chron. 9:27). Silver was refined and then cast into molds (Judg. 17:4; Ps. 12:6) by silversmiths (Jer. 10:9; Acts 19:24).

Abraham's wealth included silver (Gen. 13:2), which he used as a medium of exchange (Gen. 23:15). Other uses for silver were Joseph's cup (Gen. 44:2), idols (Ps. 115:4; Isa. 40:19; Acts 19:24), various kinds of jewelry (Gen. 24:53; Exod. 3:22), and containers (Num. 7:13; 1 Chron. 28:17; Ezra 1:9–10). Many articles for the tabernacle were made of silver, including trumpets (Num. 10:2), lampstands (1 Chron. 28:15), and sockets (Exod. 26:19).

Slime. (See *Asphalt; Bitumen.*)

Soda. (See *Lye.*)

Steel. Steel was not known during Bible times until the first century A.D. The Hebrew word for copper and brass, or bronze, is incorrectly translated as steel in the KJV (2 Sam. 22:35; Job 20:24; Ps. 18:34; Jer. 15:12).

Sulfur *or* Sulphur. (See *Brimstone.*)

Tar. (See *Asphalt; Bitumen.*)

Tin. A soft bluish white metal smelted from cassiterite, its principal ore, tin was used chiefly as an alloy with copper to produce bronze, a much harder material than either copper or tin. The Hebrew word for tin means a "substitute" or "alloy."

Phoenicia supplied the ancient Mediterranean world with tin obtained from Spain, its chief colony. Some scholars believe the Phoenicians sailed the Atlantic to Cornwall, England, the principal supplier of tin. Tyre received tin from Tarshish (Ezek. 27:12). Some think Persia and Armenia exported tin also.

Tin was among the spoils the Israelites took from the Midianites (Num. 31:22). Ezekiel pictured Jerusalem as being smelted as tin cast in a furnace (Ezek. 22:18–20).

Turquoise. (See *Jacinth.*)

Vermilion. A red pigment obtained from cinnabar, the same mineral ore from which mercury or quicksilver is derived, pure vermilion is a brilliant red, but it is brownish red when impurities such as clay, iron oxides, and bitumen are mixed. This ore is usually distributed in areas of volcanic rocks.

Jeremiah pronounced judgment on Shallum (Jehoahaz) for beautifying his own house with vermilion—decorating it in red (Jer. 22:14, NASB, NIV)—while neglecting the poor and needy. Ezekiel saw the images of the Chaldeans painted in vermilion on the walls (Ezek. 23:14). (See *Mercury.*)

Whitewash. (See *Lime.*)

Gems

S ince the beginning of human history, people have adorned themselves with various kinds of jewelry. To be elaborately decorated with jewelry in the ancient world was a symbol of wealth and status (2 Sam. 1:10; Dan. 5:7, 16, 29). The materials commonly used for jewelry were stones, metals, gems, ivory, shells, and carved horns.

The art of jewelry making probably developed early in Egypt and was known throughout the biblical world. The Hebrews learned this skill from foreign influences, probably from Egypt (Exod. 32:2–3), and obtained much of their jewelry from spoils of war.

The people of the ancient world placed much value on personal ornaments for political and religious purposes. The priestly garments of Aaron, the high priest, were elaborately decorated with jewels. The breastplate contained 12 engraved gems (Exod. 28:17–21). The shoulder pieces of the ephod were engraved onyx stones (Exod. 28:9–12). During Bible times, crowns were also set with gems (Zech. 9:16). Many ornaments were donated to build the tabernacle (Exod. 35:22) and to decorate the temple (1 Kings 7:17).

Bracelets, worn by both men and women, were made of bronze, silver, iron, and gold. Sometimes they wore many bracelets on each arm, covering the entire lower arm. Rebekah's gifts from Abraham included gold bracelets (Gen. 24:22). King Saul wore a bracelet or armlet (2 Sam. 1:10).

Women often wore ornaments for the ankles, made from the same material as the bracelets. Sometimes anklets were fashioned to make a tinkling sound when walking, bringing more attention to the wearer. They attached ankle chains to their feet to encourage smaller steps. Isaiah disapproved of this practice among the women of Jerusalem (Isa. 3:16–18).

Both men and women wore necklaces (cf. Judg. 8:25–26), made of various metals, often inlaid with precious stones. Necklaces of beads made from stone or jewels were strung with cord. Sometimes they attached crescents or pendants to the necklaces (Isa. 3:18–19). Gold chains were given to Joseph (Gen. 41:42) and Daniel (Dan. 5:29), indicating their high positions in government.

Earrings were worn by men, women, and children in the ancient world (Exod. 32:2–3; Num. 31:50; Judg. 8:25–26). They were loops worn alone or with pendants attached. Earrings were made from various metals and stones and were sometimes inlaid with gems. Nose rings were worn mostly by women (Gen. 24:47) and were sometimes decorated with jewels (Isa. 3:21).

Most men wore signet rings for business purposes. These rings were engraved with the owner's name or symbol to show authority or ownership (Gen. 38:18; Exod. 28:11; Esther 8:8; Dan. 6:17). The signet rings were worn on the finger or strung around the neck. They were usually made of gold and set with an engraved gem. Signet rings were given as gifts for the tabernacle (Exod. 35:22).

In NT times jewels were worn much the same way as in OT times. The Greeks emphasized fine, delicately worked jewelry, while the Roman jewelry was much heavier and more elaborate. In the early church the wearing of jewelry was not considered a Christian virtue by Paul, who exhorted women to dress modestly (see 1 Tim. 2:9). James apparently also had a dim view of jewelry (James 2:2).

Gems held a significant place in the life of the Hebrew people and the surrounding nations. In the ancient world the use of precious stones dates back thousands of years before Christ. Myths and superstitions about their use existed. Some say that early humans attributed magical powers to certain gems and even worshiped some of them. This practice, however, is not evident in the OT because the Jewish people valued gems for their beauty, usefulness, and hardness.

No gem deposits existed in the land of Canaan. The Israelites secured their jewels from surrounding nations, which resulted in the art of cutting and engraving gems. Precious stones are mentioned 13 times in the OT, and over 20 specific gems are named in the entire Bible. Since the Hebrews described gems by color or hardness, their precise identification is often difficult.

The majority of gems mentioned in the OT are represented in Aaron's breastplate (Exod. 28:17–20; 39:10–13). Nine of them are mentioned in Ezekiel 28:13, the jacinth, agate, and amethyst being omitted. Jerome (fifth century A.D.) and others have attempted to establish a relationship between the 12 stones in Aaron's breastplate, the 12 months of the year, and the 12 signs in the zodiac; no correlation of this appears in Scripture.

The Bible mentions gems used as personal adornment (as in Exod. 11:2; Isa. 61:10) and as gifts (1 Kings 10:2; Ezek. 16:11, 39). David's crown was set with gems (2 Sam. 12:30). Precious stones were also used to illustrate spiritual truths (Prov. 11:22; 20:15; Matt. 13:45–46). Amber, coral, and pearls are not actually gemstones, but were as highly prized among the ancients as precious stones.

The following gems and precious stones are mentioned in the Bible. This list is keyed to the NKJV, but cross-references are included from five additional popular versions: KJV, NASB, NEB, NIV, and RSV.

Adamant. The exact identity of this substance is unknown; but it is believed to be corundum, the hardest of all minerals next to the diamond. Corundum is not mentioned in the Bible. Pure corundum is colorless and is the source of gems such as rubies and sapphires.

Because of its hardness, Ezekiel used adamant as a symbol of stubborn will of the rebellious Israelites. God strengthened the prophet with a forehead "like adamant stone, harder than flint" to preach to the Israelites (Ezek. 3:9; *emery,* NASB). Other English translations of the Bible render the Hebrew word for adamant as *diamond* (Jer. 17:1; KJV, NASB, RSV) or *flint* (Jer. 17:1, NIV). (See *Diamond.*)

Agate. One of many fibrous varieties of quartz, agate is a form of chalcedony with bands or patterns of various colors. The word comes from a Greek term for the river in Sicily where this stone was abundant. It was also found in Egypt, Arabia, and India. The agate was the middle stone in the third row of Aaron's breastplate (Exod. 28:19; 39:12). The agate was also useful for ornaments (beads) and was considered to possess magical powers. (See *Chalcedony.*)

Amber. Amber is fossilized resin formed from the sap of various trees. Ancient Greeks and Romans regarded amber as a gem and used it for beads and other ornaments. Yellowish orange, it can be polished to a high gloss. Apparently abundant in northern Europe, it reached other countries through trade.

Ezekiel mentioned amber three times. Each time he described it as a brilliant substance (Ezek. 1:4, 27; 8:2). Other English translations use the words *gleaming bronze* (RSV), *brass* (NEB), or *metal* (NASB, NIV) rather than *amber*. Whatever the nature of this substance, Ezekiel compared its brilliance to the awe-inspiring glory of God.

Amethyst. A variety of the mineral corundum, amethyst was used for jewelry, and its color varied from light to deep violet. It was known in Egypt, India, and Ceylon. Amethyst was the third stone in the third row of Aaron's breastplate (Exod. 28:19; 39:12; *jasper*, NEB). It was also included in the foundation of the New Jerusalem (Rev. 21:20).

Bdellium. Found in Havilah in Arabia, a land noted for its precious stones and aromatic gum, bdellium was considered to be a gum resin. In Numbers 11:7, the word for bdellium is rendered as *gum resin* (NEB) and *resin* (NIV). But in Genesis 2:12, bdellium was associated with gold, and therefore it was considered a precious stone. Some scholars suggest that bdellium jewels were pearls from the Persian Gulf. The exact identification of this substance is not certain.

Beryl. A rare silver-white metal similar to aluminum, beryl ranged in color from bluish green to yellow, white, pink, and deep green. It was the first stone in the fourth row of Aaron's breastplate (Exod. 28:20; 39:13). Other English translations render the word for beryl as *chrysolite* (NIV) and *topaz* (NEB). The wheels in Ezekiel's visions were described as resembling beryl (Ezek. 1:16; 10:9; *Tarshish stone*, NASB). The beryl was also the eighth foundation stone in the New Jerusalem (Rev. 21:20).

Carbuncle. (See *Emerald; Turquoise*.)

Carnelian. (See *Sardius*.)

Chalcedony. A translucent variety of quartz occurring in a variety of colors, chalcedony received its name from Chalcedon, a city in Asia Minor. Agate, bloodstone, carnelian, chrysoprase, flint, jasper, and onyx are all varieties of chalcedony. The chalcedony was the third stone in the foundation of the New Jerusalem (Rev. 21:19; *agate*, RSV). (See *Agate; Chrysoprase*.)

Chrysolite. A yellow stone that could have been the same as topaz or some other yellow gem such as beryl, zircon, or a yellow quartz. Its name comes from a Greek word that means "gold stone." Chrysolite was the seventh stone in the foundation of the New Jerusalem (Rev. 21:20). The chrysolite known today is the peridot, an olive green silicate of magnesium and iron. This is not believed to be the same gem as that referred to by Revelation.

Chrysoprase. A variety of chalcedony, chrysoprase was light green, and jewelry made from this precious stone has been found in ancient Egyptian graves. It was the tenth foundation stone of the New Jerusalem (Rev. 21:20; *chrysoprasus*, KJV). (See *Chalcedony*.)

Chrysoprasus. (See *Chrysoprase*.)

Coral. A limestone formation produced by certain kinds of marine life, coral is not a mineral, but it does contain the mineral calcite because of its long exposure to seawater.

When the term *coral* was applied to jewelry, it referred to precious coral—a substance with a polished surface highly prized in the ancient world for various kinds of jewelry (Job 28:18; Ezek. 27:16). Ancients believed it possessed magical powers.

Precious coral was formed in the shape of branches or small bushes, and was found in the warm waters of the Mediterranean

Sea and the Red Sea. The colors included many shades of red.

Cornelian. (See *Onyx.*)

Crystal. A colorless transparent quartz or rock (Job 28:17; Rev. 4:6), this stone was used as jewelry or ornaments. In Roman times it was carved into various household utensils.

There are several different words for crystal in the original languages of the Bible. These words suggest that pearl and glass (Job 28:17–18, RSV) may have been called crystal, too.

Diamond. Pure crystallized carbon, the diamond is the hardest mineral known. The Hebrew word rendered *diamond* in Exodus 28:18; 39:11; and Ezekiel 28:13 by the KJV and NKJV must have been some other hard stone. The diamond was not identified in the Mediterranean lands until the first century. Other English translations render the word as *emerald* (NIV), *jade* (NEB), and *jasper* (RSV).

Emerald. A deep green variety of beryl, the emerald was found in Egypt, Cyprus, and Ethiopia. It was the third jewel in the first row of Aaron's breastplate (Exod. 28:17; 39:10). Emeralds were also articles of trade between Tyre and Syria (Ezek. 27:16). The emerald was the fourth foundation stone of the New Jerusalem (Rev. 21:19), and was used to describe the rainbow around the throne (Rev. 4:3). Various other English translations render the word for emerald as *carbuncle* (KJV, RSV), *beryl* (NIV), *green felspar* (NEB), *turquoise* (NIV), and *purple garnet* (NEB).

Emery. (See *Adamant.*)

Flint. (See *Adamant.*)

Gems. Many precious gems were known in Bible times. Special value was attached to each because of its beauty, rarity, and durability. Although the modern method of cutting gems was not known during Bible times, ancient gem-cutters rounded and polished each stone, engraving some for

seals or signet rings (1 Kings 21:8; Esther 3:10). They were also used for various kinds of jewelry (Exod. 11:2) and as gifts (Gen. 24:22). Precious stones in general are often referred to as gems in the Bible.

Glass. (See *Crystal.*)

Green felspar. (See *Emerald.*)

Gum resin. (See *Bdellium.*)

Jacinth. A yellow-orange variety of the mineral zircon, the jacinth was the first stone in the third row of Aaron's breastplate (Exod. 28:19; 39:12; *ligure*, KJV). In the NT the jacinth was the eleventh foundation stone in the New Jerusalem (Rev. 21:20; *turquoise*, NEB).

Jade. (See *Diamond.*)

Jasper. An opaque variety of chalcedony, or quartz. Jasper is usually red because of the presence of iron, but it can be brown, yellow, or green. It was the third stone in the fourth row of Aaron's breastplate (Exod. 28:20; 39:13; *green jasper*, NEB). Revelation 4:3 describes the one on the throne as "like a jasper." The brilliance of the New Jerusalem was "like a jasper stone, clear as crystal" (Rev. 21:11).

Lapis lazuli. (See *Sapphire.*)

Ligure. (See *Jacinth.*)

Onyx. A form of chalcedony with contrasting layers of colors arranged in parallel lines; the colors are usually black and white or brown and white.

The onyx was used for engraving seals and for various ornaments. It was included in the treasures from Havilah, in Arabia (Gen. 2:12). The shoulder stones of Aaron's ephod were onyx with the names of six tribes of Israel engraved on each stone (Exod. 28:9–10). It was also the second stone in the fourth row of Aaron's breastplate (Exod. 28:20; 39:6). David included the onyx in the material he gathered for the temple (1 Chron. 29:2). Job considered the wisdom from God a greater possession than even the precious onyx (Job 28:16).

The NEB renders the word for onyx in all these passages as *cornelian*.

Pearl. A white translucent jewel created within certain species of mollusks, a pearl is not a mineral, but it is composed of mineral substances. Pearls always have held an important place among the gemstones of the ancient world. Pearls were produced in the Persian Gulf, the Red Sea, and the Indian Ocean.

Pearls were considered valuable jewels and were used for various ornaments. Jesus referred to pearls in a figurative manner to speak of wise thoughts (Matt. 7:6). The apostle Paul admonished women not to adorn themselves with pearls (1 Tim. 2:9). In John's vision of the New Jerusalem, "the twelve gates were twelve pearls: each individual gate was of one pearl" (Rev. 21:21). Jesus taught that we can possess the world's greatest treasure, the "pearl of great price" (Matt. 13:46)—the spiritual wealth of the kingdom of heaven.

Purple garnet. (See *Emerald; Turquoise.*)

Red jasper. (See *Ruby.*)

Ruby. A variety of corundum, the hardest of all minerals next to the diamond, the ruby is deep red because of traces of chromium. Rubies may not have been known in the ancient world until the third century B.C. The Hebrew word translated *rubies* in the NKJV and KJV was probably pink pearl or red coral (see e.g., Job 28:18; Prov. 3:15; 8:11; 20:15; 31:10; Lam. 4:7). Other words for ruby used by other English translations are *agate* (Isa. 54:12, KJV, RSV); *red jasper* (Isa. 54:12, NEB); and *coral* (Lam. 4:7, NASB, NEB, RSV).

Sapphire. The modern sapphire, a blue variety of corundum, was probably not used until the third century B.C. The Hebrew word for sapphire refers to lapis lazuli—a silicate of alumina, calcium, and sodium. It was highly regarded as an ornamental stone (Song of Sol. 5:14; Lam. 4:7; Ezek. 28:13). Rich beds of sapphire were

A ram in a thicket discovered at Ur. This artistic work is made of gold and lapis lazuli (sapphire). It dates from about 2500 B.C.

PHOTO BY HOWARD VOS

found in the mountainous regions of ancient Persia deposited in limestone rock.

Sapphire was the second jewel in the second row of Aaron's breastplate (Exod. 28:18; 39:11). It was also the second stone in the foundation of the New Jerusalem (Rev. 21:19).

Sardin. (See *Sardius.*)

Sardius. A red stone, considered by many to be carnelian (a reddish brown variety of chalcedony), the sardius was used for jewelry and for royal seals. Archaeologists have found many items of jewelry made from sardius in tombs and cities of Egypt and Israel. It was the first stone in the first row of Aaron's breastplate (Exod. 28:17; 39:10) and was included as the covering of the king of Tyre (Ezek. 28:12–13). Sardius was also the sixth foundation stone of the New Jerusalem (Rev. 21:20).

Other words for sardius used by various

English translations of the Bible are *ruby,* *sardin,* and *carnelian.*

Sardonyx.   A red-and-white variety of chalcedony, sardonyx is mentioned only once in the Bible as the fifth foundation stone of the New Jerusalem (Rev. 21:20; *onyx,* RSV). Sardonyx was obtained in Arabia and India and used by the Romans for cameos and signet rings. Some scholars believe the Hebrew word usually translated as *onyx* may refer to sardonyx. (See *Onyx.*)

Tarshish stone.   (See *Beryl.*)

Topaz.   A yellowish green form of chrysolite, the topaz was the second gem in the first row of Aaron's breastplate (Exod. 28:17; 39:10; *chrysolite,* NEB). The "topaz of Ethiopia" (Job 28:19) was famous for its quality. The topaz was also the ninth foundation stone of the New Jerusalem (Rev. 21:20).

Turquoise.   A deep green stone similar to the emerald. A reference to turquoise in the NKJV occurs in Ezekiel's description of the covering of the king of Tyre (Ezek. 28:13; *emerald,* KJV; *carbuncle,* RSV; *purple garnet,* NEB). Many scholars believe this stone is essentially the same as the emerald. (See *Emerald.*)

Numbers, Weights, and Measures

Numbers

Threlated The people of the Bible used numbers in a practical way rather than as part of a mathematical theory. They applied numbers to common problems of everyday life.

Conventional Use of Numbers

Little is known of the arithmetic of the Hebrews, but they seem to have had at least a practical awareness of the science. The Bible itself contains examples of addition (Num. 1:26–27), subtraction (Lev. 27:18), multiplication (Lev. 27:25), and division (Num. 31:27).

A remarkable degree of accuracy in the use of fractions was achieved (Gen. 47:24; Lev. 5:16; Ezek. 4:11; 45:13). Scholars have noted that the proportions of the measurements of Ezekiel's temple would have required considerable skill in mathematics on the part of the prophet as he interpreted this message from God.

Most of the numbers in the Bible indicate specific quantities. But in some cases writers of Scripture did not include exact, official, detailed enumerations or sums. They gave an estimate of the total, which was rounded off. The most frequent numerical data given are enumerations of census, age, or other statistics. These figures provide some difficult textual problems for Bible students.

Ages of people mentioned in the Bible are close to the life span of people today, except in the cases of the people before the Flood and the patriarchs. All of the pre-Flood ages are either a multiple of five or a multiple five plus seven. Scholars are not sure why this phenomenon exists, and they do not know what it means.

Another difficulty with numbers concerns the high census figures for the Hebrews given in some books of the Bible. These high numbers have caused some scholars to question whether the translation of the word *thousand* is accurate. They suggest that its primary meaning in these contexts is something other than the literal number itself.

Rhetorical Use of Numbers

Numbers are often used for poetic or rhetorical impact. This usage is neither literal nor symbolic. Used in this way, these numbers may indicate such concepts as few or many, or they may be used to intensify a point. In Amos 1:9, the phrase "For three transgressions of Tyre, and for four" provides not a catalog but an emphatic statement of Tyre's sins. A similar usage is found in Proverbs 30:18. These are examples of a climactic formula, which builds stylistic progression and anticipation. The quantity itself, in such cases, is indefinite.

The number seven is used almost 600 times in the Bible. Often it expresses the idea of completeness or perfection. To identify any other number as a symbol leaves interpreters on shaky ground. The number 12 may be a primary number on which numbers or decimals were built, and the number 40 may have some significance as a round number.

The only definite mystical use of a number in the Bible occurs in Revelation 13:18. Attempts to identify the meaning of 666 (a few manuscripts have 616) have generally been more clever than convincing. Like every other feature in God's Word, numbers should be studied with considerable care.

Possible Meaning of Numbers

Following is a list of numbers and their occurrences that have led some to make conclusions about their use in the Bible. There is by no means an agreement by scholars about the interpretation of these numbers.

1	The primary number	Absolute singleness (Deut. 6:4; Eph. 4:4–6)
2	The number of witness and support	Two great lights of creation (Gen. 1:16)
		Two angels at Sodom (Gen. 19:1)
		Two cherubim on the ark of the covenant (Exod. 25:22)
		The Ten Commandments written on two stones (Exod. 31:18)
		Two witnesses to establish a truth (Deut. 17:6; Matt. 26:60)
		The good report of the two spies at Kadesh (Num. 14:6)
		Two spies at Jericho (Josh. 2:1)
		Two better than one (Eccles. 4:9)
		Jesus sent disciples out two by two (Luke 10:1)
		Two angels attendant at the Resurrection (Luke 24:4)
		Two angels present at the Ascension (Acts 1:10)
		God's two immutable things (Heb. 6:18)
		The two tribulational witnesses (Rev. 11:3)
3	The number of unity, of accomplishment, and of the universe	The unity of the human race traced to Noah's three sons (Gen. 6:10)
		Three days involved in the crossing of the Jordan (Josh. 1:11)
		Israel's three yearly feasts (Exod. 23:14–17)
		Gideon's mighty victory accomplished through three bands of soldiers (Judg. 7:22)
		Three days of preparation for a revival in Ezra's time (Ezra 10:9)
		Three days involved in the decision to build the walls of Jerusalem in Nehemiah's time (Neh. 2:11)
		Esther's heart prepared for three days before meeting with the king (Esther 4:16)
		Jonah in the fish's belly for three days (Jon. 1:17)
		Jesus in the heart of the earth for three days (John 2:19)
		Jesus' earthly ministry of three years (Luke 13:7)
		Three parts in the tabernacle and the temple—outer court, inner court, Holy of Holies
		Three offices of Jesus Christ—prophet, priest, king
4	An earth-related number	Four directions—north, south, east, west
		Four seasons—summer, winter, fall, spring
		Four great earthly kingdoms (Dan. 7:3)
		Four kinds of spiritual soil (Matt. 13)
		Four horsemen of the Tribulation (Rev. 6)
		Fourfold earthly ministry of Jesus—as told in Matthew (king), Mark (servant), Luke (perfect man), John (mighty God)
5	The number of grace	Five Levitical offerings (Lev. 1—5)
		Five Israelites to chase 100 enemies (Lev. 26:8)
		Five wise virgins (Matt. 25:2)
		Five barley loaves Jesus used to feed the 5,000 (Matt. 14:17)

Possible Meaning of Numbers—*continued*

6	The number of humanity	Creation in six days (Gen. 1:31) Six cities of refuge (Num. 35:6) The number of the Antichrist, 666 (Rev. 13:18)
7	The number of God, or divine perfection	God rested on the seventh day (Gen. 2:2) God's word is as silver purified by fire seven times (Ps. 12:6) Jesus taught Peter to forgive 70 times seven (Matt. 18:22) Seven miracles in the gospel of John Seven sayings on the cross John wrote to seven churches (Rev. 1:4) John saw seven golden candlesticks (Rev. 1:12) Seven stars in Christ's hand (Rev. 1:16) The Father holds a seven-sealed book (Rev. 5:1) Seven angels pronounce judgment (Rev. 8:2)
8	The new beginning number	Eight were saved from the Flood (Gen. 7:13–23) Circumcision performed on eighth day (Gen. 17:12) Thomas saw Jesus eight days after the Resurrection (John 20:26)
9	The fullness of blessing number (9 or its multiples)	Ninefold fruit of the Spirit (Gal. 5:22–23) Sarah was 90 at Isaac's birth (Gen. 17:17)
10	The human government number	The revived Roman Empire will consist of 10 nations. (Dan. 7:24; Rev. 17:12) The northern kingdom had 10 tribes (1 Kings 11:31–35) Local government of 10 men decided the fate of Ruth (Ruth 4:2)
12	The divine government number	Twelve tribes of Israel (Rev. 7) Twelve apostles (Matt. 10) Twelve gates and foundations in the New Jerusalem (Rev. 21)
30	Associated with sorrow and mourning	Israel mourned after Aaron's death for 30 days (Num. 20:29) Israel mourned for Moses 30 days (Deut. 34:8)
40	The number of testing and trial	It rained 40 days during the Flood (Gen. 7:4) Israel spied out the land 40 days (Num. 13:25) Moses spent 40 days on Mount Sinai (Exod. 24:18) Israel wandered 40 years in the desert (Num. 14:33) Goliath taunted Israel for 40 days (1 Sam. 17:16) Jonah preached repentance to Nineveh for 40 days (Jon. 3:4) Jesus spent 40 days in the wilderness before being tempted (Matt. 4:2) There were 40 days between the Resurrection and the Ascension (Acts 1:3)
50	Associated with celebration and ceremony	The Feast of Weeks was 50 days after the Passover (Lev. 23:15–16) The fiftieth year was to be a Jubilee to Israel (Lev. 25:10) Absalom appointed 50 men to run before him (2 Sam. 15:1) Pentecost occurred 50 days after the Resurrection (Acts 2)
70	Associated with human committees and judgment	Moses appointed 70 elders (Num. 11:16) Tyre was to be judged for 70 years (Isa. 23:15) Israel spent 70 years in Babylon (Jer. 29:10) God would accomplish his total plan upon Israel in 70 weeks of seven years each, or a total of 490 years (Dan. 9:24–27) Jesus appointed 70 workers. (Luke 10:1) The Sanhedrin was made up of 70 men.

Weights and Measures

Early in the development of society, people learned to measure, weigh, and exchange commodities. At first this trade was simple barter, exchanging one type of goods for another. As society became more complex, the need for standardized trade values became apparent. Initially each city set up its own standards of weights and measures, creating great confusion in trade between different peoples and cultures.

Weights

The balance was an early method of determining weight. The balance consisted of a beam of wood supported in the middle with a pan suspended by cords on each end. A known quantity of weight would be placed in the pan on one side of the balance and the object to be weighed on the other side. By adding or removing known weights until each side was equal, the weight of the object could be determined.

Both the Canaanites and the Israelites used the Mesopotamian weight system. Each level of weight had four separate standards: common, heavy (twice the common weight), common royal (five percent heavier than the common weight), and heavy royal (five percent heavier than the heavy weight).

Several of these weights are mentioned in the Bible.

Bekah. One-half shekel, the bekah was the weight in silver paid by each Israelite as a religious tax (Exod. 30:13; 38:26). The bekah, spelled *beka* in some translations, is named only once in English translations (Exod. 38:26), but is referred to more often (Gen. 24:22; Exod. 30:13, 15).

Gerah. It is the smallest of the Israelite weights. Exodus 30:13 defines a gerah as one-twentieth of a shekel (cf. Lev. 27:25).

Kesitah. The second heaviest weight in the Hebrew system was the kesitah (Gen. 33:19, *piece of money*; Josh. 24:32, *piece of silver*) and weighed about 125 shekels. Since the root meaning of the word is *lamb*, this particular weight may have been shaped like a lamb. Jacob paid Hamor

of Shechem 100 kesitah for a parcel of land (Gen. 33:19; *sheep*, NEB). At the end of Job's encounter with God, his friends brought him a kesitah and a ring of gold (Job 42:11).

Mina. A weight that was equal to about 50 common shekels, similar to the Canaanite system (1 Kings 10:17; Ezra 2:69; *pound*, KJV). Ezekiel 45:12 seeks to redefine the weight (*maneh*, KJV, NASB), to equal 60 shekels, as in the Mesopotamian system. In Daniel 5:25 the words *Mene, Mene, Tekel, Upharsin* may be interpreted as a play on monetary values of that day ("Mina, mina, shekel, and a half shekel"). The phrase, then, would refer to the Babylonian rulers Nabopolassar, Nebuchad-

Ancient weights were frequently cast in the shapes of animals such as turtles, ducks, and lions to make them easily recognizable and easy to handle. PHOTO BY GUSTAV JEENINGA

nezzar, Nabonidus, and Belshazzar, implying that they were decreasing in importance.

Pim. A weight of about two-thirds of a shekel was the pim. First Samuel 1:21 is difficult to translate, but it probably should read, "And the charge . . . was a pim for the plowshares." This charge is not mentioned in the KJV.

Pound. A Roman weight of about 340 grams, or 12 ounces, is the pound. This term is used in the NKJV to designate the pound of precious ointments used to anoint Christ (John 12:3). The same word is also used to describe the amount of myrrh and aloes used to anoint the body of Jesus in John 19:39.

Shekel. The most common weight in the Hebrew system (Josh. 7:21; Ezek. 4:10) was the shekel, and it weighed about 11.4 grams, or less than an ounce. Its use was so common that in Genesis 20:16, the Hebrew text states "a thousand pieces of silver" without bothering to specify shekel.

The shekel of the sanctuary (Exod. 30:13; Ezek. 45:12) was said to weigh 20 gerahs, the same weight as the common shekel. Possibly the standard for the common shekel was kept at the sanctuary and became known as the sanctuary shekel. There is no clear reference to the use of the heavy shekel in Israel, but the shekel of the king's standard (the royal shekel) is referred to in 2 Samuel 14:26.

Talent. The heaviest unit of weight in the Hebrew system, the talent was used to weigh gold (2 Sam. 12:30), silver (1 Kings 20:39), and many other commodities. The common talent weighed about 3,000 shekels or the full weight that a man could carry (2 Kings 5:23).

Measures

Measurements recorded in the Bible are of three types: measures of *volume*, the amount of dry commodity items such as flour or liquid such as oil that could be contained in a vessel; measures of *length*, for height, width, and depth of an object or person; and measures of *total area*, such as the size of a building, field, or city.

Measures of Volume

Measurements of volume were originally made by estimated handfuls. Eventually containers (jars, baskets, etc.) that held an agreed upon number of handfuls were used as the standard measure. The terms used for such measures were frequently taken from the name of the containers.

Dry volume. The Israelites adapted the Mesopotamian system of measure of volume from the Canaanites. Their system contained several major designations for measuring dry volume.

Ephah. The ephah was equal to one-tenth of a homer (Exod. 29:40; *deal*, KJV; Isa. 5:10).

Homer. The standard unit for dry measure (Ezek. 45:11–14; Hos. 3:2), the homer contained about 220 liters (6.25 bushels). It was a large measure weighing the equivalent of the normal load a donkey could carry. In Leviticus 27:16, a homer of barley seed is worth 50 shekels of silver.

Kab. The kab contained about 1.2 liters or 1.11 quarts and is mentioned only once in the Bible (2 Kings 6:25). During the Syrian siege of Samaria, prices were inflated so badly that one-fourth of a kab of dove's dung was sold for five pieces of silver.

Kor. The same size as the homer (Ezek. 45:14; *cor* KJV), the kor measured flour (1 Kings 4:22), wheat, and barley (2 Chron. 2:10; 27:5).

Omer. An omer is equal to one-tenth of an ephah (Exod. 16:36). Another Hebrew word, *issaron,* is translated as one-tenth of an ephah (Exod. 29:40; Lev. 14:10; Num. 15:4), a dry measure of similar size to the omer.

Seah. A unit of uncertain capacity, but one-third of an ephah is probably correct for a seah (1 Sam. 25:18; 2 Kings 7:1, *measure,* KJV, RSV, NEB, NASB).

Dry capacity. The NT contains four major designations for measuring dry capacity. These Greek words are not mentioned in the English translations.

Choinx. The choinx contained about 1.1 liters or one quart. (See Rev. 6:6; *quart,* NKJV; *measure,* KJV.)

Koros. The koros was a measure of wheat equal to about 453 liters (13 bushels). (See Luke 16:7; *measure,* NKJV, KJV, RSV, NASB; *bushel,* NEB, NIV.)

Modios. The modios contained about nine liters (one-fourth bushel). (See Matt. 5:15; Mark 4:21; Luke 11:33; *basket,* NKJV; *bushel,* KJV, RSV.)

Saton. The saton contained about 13 liters (three-eighths bushel). (See Matt. 13:33; Luke 13:21; *measure,* NKJV, KJV, RSV; *hundredweight,* NEB; *peck,* NASB; *large amount,* NIV.)

Liquid measure, OT. The OT contains five major designations for liquid measure.

Bath. The bath was the equivalent in liquid measure to the ephah in dry measure (Ezek. 45:11, 14). It was the standard liquid measure, equaling about 22 liters (5.83 gallons) and used to measure water (1 Kings 7:26), wine (Isa. 5:10), and oil (2 Chron. 2:10).

Hin. Equal to one-sixth of a bath, a hin was used to measure water (Ezek. 4:11), oil (Exod. 29:40), and wine (Lev. 23:13). One-sixth of a hin was considered the daily ration of water (Ezek. 4:11).

Homer. Containing 10 baths, a homer was the largest liquid measure (Ezek. 45:11–14).

Kor. It was the same size as the homer (Ezek. 45:14).

Log. Found only in Leviticus 14:10–24, a log was a measure of oil in the ceremony for the purification of a leper. The log was equal to one-twelfth of a hin.

Liquid measure, NT. The NT contains three major terms for liquid measure. These words appear in Greek manuscripts but are translated by different words in English versions of the Bible.

Batos. This unit was the next smaller measure. (Luke 16:6; *measures,* NKJV, KJV; *gallon,* NEB, NIV.)

Kestes. A kestes (Mark 7:4, 8; *pitcher,* NKJV; *pot,* KJV; *copper pot,* NASB; *copper bowl,* NEB; *kettles,* NIV; *vessels of bronze,* RSV) was the smallest unit of liquid measure.

Metretes. The largest of these measures (John 2:6; *gallon,* NKJV; *firkin,* KJV; *water-jar,* NEB).

Measures of Length

Linear measure, as with other units of measure, was originally based on parts of the body, such as the hand, arm, or foot. Sometimes the unit was named for the part of the body it represented, such as the palm or finger. Early linear distances were also based upon common but difficult-to-define objects, such as the step, a bowshot, or a day's journey.

Cubit. The distance from the elbow to the fingertip—about 45 centimeters (18 inches)—was a cubit, the standard unit of length. It was the common designation of the height of a person (1 Sam. 17:4) or an object (Ezek. 40:5). There was more than one size of cubit, for the bed of Og, king of Bashan, is described "according to the standard cubit" (Deut. 3:11), while Ezekiel's measuring rod extended "six cubits long, each being a cubit and a handbreadth" (Ezek. 40:5). The long cubit was probably 51.8 centimeters (20.4 inches). The cubit is mentioned several times in the NT (Luke 12:25; Rev. 21:17). In each case it probably refers to the common cubit.

Finger. Smallest subdivision of the cubit, equal to one-fourth of a handbreadth (Jer. 52:21), the finger was also called the cubit.

Fathom. A Greek unit equal to the length of the outstretched arms, about 1.8 meters (six feet), the fathom was about four cubits (Acts 27:28).

Furlong. The furlong measured a distance equal to about 200 meters, or one-eighth of a mile (Rev. 14:20; *stadia*, RSV).

Handbreadth. The width of the hand at the base of the four fingers (1 Kings 7:26; 2 Chron. 4:5), the handbreadth was considered to be one-sixth of a cubit.

Mile. The mile was a Roman measurement of 1,000 paces (five Roman feet to the pace), equaling about 1,477.5 meters, or 1,616 yards (Matt. 5:41).

Rod *or* Reed. These were units of measure equal to six cubits. The rod (Ezek. 40:5) and the reed (Ezek. 29:6) appear to be interchangeable. (Ezek. 40:5 specifies that this measure is according to the long cubit.)

Sabbath day's journey. The *Sabbath day's journey* (Acts 1:12) was the product of rabbinical exegesis of Exodus 16:29 and Numbers 35:5. The rabbis fixed the legal distance for travel on the Sabbath at 2,000 cubits.

Span. The distance between the extended thumb and the little finger (1 Sam. 17:4), the span was equivalent to one-half cubit.

Various distances. Several less definite distances are expressed in the Bible. Before the Babylonian captivity, distance was expressed variously as a *bowshot* (Gen. 21:16), the area plowed by a yoke of oxen in a day (1 Sam. 14:14, NKJV footnote), a *day's journey* (Num. 11:31; 1 Kings 19:4), *three days' journey* (Gen. 30:36; Exod. 3:18; 8:27; Num. 10:33), *seven days' journey* (Gen. 31:23), and *eleven days' journey* (Deut. 1:2).

While no one knows for sure the amount of these distances, a day's journey has been estimated to be approximately 32 to 40 kilometers (20 to 25 miles).

Many modern English translations of the Bible often use modern measurements of length, such as *feet* and *inches* (Gen. 6:15–16, NIV) and *yards* (John 21:8, NASB, NEB, NIV, RSV).

Measures of Area

Measures of area are not well defined in the Bible. Sometimes an area was determined by the amount of land a pair of oxen could plow in a day. Another method of designating area was to estimate the space by the amount of seed required to sow it (Lev. 27:16).

Outline of
the Bible

The Old Testament

O ur word *Bible* comes from the Greek word *biblia* and means "books."
One English text of Jewish Scriptures has 24 books, but these 24 books contain the same material as the Christian 39. The distinction is caused by two different traditions, Jewish and Latin.

Jewish scholars organized the OT into three major sections: the law, or the five books of Moses *(Torah)*, the prophets *(Nebi'im)*, and the writings *(Kethubim)*. The books were arranged according to the official position or status of the writers—Moses, the prophets, and the other writers—though this sequence did not indicate degrees of inspiration. Most modern Jews believe that all the books of their Bible are equally inspired and equally authoritative.

The order of the books in the Hebrew (Masoretic Text) Bible is as follows:

THE LAW. Genesis, Exodus, Leviticus, Numbers, Deuteronomy.

THE PROPHETS. The former prophets: Joshua, Judges, 1 and 2 Samuel, 1 (3) and 2 (4) Kings; the latter prophets: Isaiah, Jeremiah, Ezekiel, and the Twelve (Hosea, Joel, Obadiah, Jonah, Micah, Nahum, Habbakuk, Zephaniah, Hagai, Zechariah, Malachi).

THE WRITINGS. Psalms, Proverbs, Job, Song of Solomon, Ruth, Lamentations, Ecclesiastes, Esther, Daniel, Ezra, Nehemiah, 1 and 2 Chronicles.

Protestants and Catholics follow the order given in the Septuagint, which Jerome changed slightly when he issued the Latin Vulgate in the fourth century A.D. The Septuagint had the Minor Prophets first among the Latter Prophets, while the Vulgate placed Isaiah, Jeremiah, and Ezekiel first. The Vulgate's order—based on topics rather than the importance of the original writers—is the one we know. Most Protestants exclude the books of the Deuterocanon (or Apocrypha) from Scripture, though they are found in the Septuagint and modern Catholic Bibles.

The order of the books in the Christian OT is as follows (deuterocanonical/apocryphal books are shown in italics):

THE PENTATEUCH. Genesis, Exodus, Leviticus, Numbers, Deuteronomy.

HISTORICAL BOOKS. Joshua, Judges, Ruth, 1 and 2 Samuel, 1 (3) and 2 (4) Kings, 1 and 2 Chronicles, Ezra, Nehemiah, *Tobit, Judith,* Esther *including 10:4—16:24.*

WISDOM BOOKS. Job, Psalms, Proverbs, Ecclesiastes, Song of Solomon, *Wisdom of Solomon, Sirach.*

MAJOR PROPHETS. Isaiah, Jeremiah, with Lamentations and *Baruch,* Ezekiel, Daniel, *including after 3:23 the Prayer of Azariah and the Song of the Three Young Men, chapter 13 Susanna, chapter 14 Bel and the Dragon.*

MINOR PROPHETS. Hosea, Joel, Amos, Obadiah, Jonah, Micah, Nahum, Habbakuk, Zephaniah, Haggai, Zechariah, Malachi.

HISTORICAL APPENDIX. *1 and 2 Maccabees.*

ADDITIONAL BOOKS. *1 and 2 Esdras, The Prayer of Manasseh.*

The Pentateuch

We view the books of Genesis, Exodus, Leviticus, Numbers, and Deuteronomy together because they were all written by Moses. Rabbis recognized the close connection of these five, and called them "the five-fifths of the Law."

The first 11 chapters of Genesis constitute a history of creation and of the early generations of the world. Chapters 12–50 focus on Abraham and his descendants. The remainder of Genesis brings us to the death of Joseph. The rest of the Pentateuch gives the history of the Israelites from the death of Joseph to the entrance into Canaan, together with the elaborate code of moral laws and civil government that God revealed to Moses.

The Historical Books

The next section, the historical books, includes 12 books from Joshua to Esther. Jews call the six of them (Joshua, Judges, 1 and 2 Samuel, 1 and 2 Kings) the "former prophets" because prophetic individuals wrote them. The historical books give us the history of Israel from the death of Moses to the reconstruction of the temple under Nehemiah.

The Poetic Books

There are six poetic books: Job, Psalms, Proverbs, Ecclesiastes, Song of Solomon, and Lamentations. We give the name of poetry to compositions that possess imaginative thought, figurative language, and an arrangement in lines of regulated lengths and accents. Hebrew poetry has all of this, yet it uses techniques that are quite different from what we find in English-language poems.

The Prophetic Books

Strictly speaking, prophets are not simply individuals who foretell the future: They also speak for God (or, as one scholar says, "They are mouthpieces for God"); they interpret God's will to his people; and they often predict future events, but not as their primary duty.

The prophetic books contain predictions of the future, but they also contain inspired sermons about conditions in Israel at the time the prophets were writing.

Order of the Old Testament Books

			Song of	Hosea	Habakkuk
Genesis	Ruth	Ezra	Song of	Hosea	Habakkuk
Exodus	1 Samuel	Nehemiah	Solomon	Joel	Zephaniah
Leviticus	2 Samuel	Esther	Isaiah	Amos	Haggai
Numbers	1 Kings	Job	Jeremiah	Obadiah	Zechariah
Deuteronomy	2 Kings	Psalms	Lamentations	Jonah	Malachi
Joshua	1 Chronicles	Proverbs	Ezekiel	Micah	
Judges	2 Chronicles	Ecclesiastes	Daniel	Nahum	

Following are all the books in the OT, arranged in alphabetical order.

Amos. Amos must have written this book soon after the events he describes. He prophesied under King Uzziah of Judah and Jeroboam II of Israel. Although Amos was a native of Judah, he prophesied in Israel.

Authorship. This book tells us that Amos lived in Tekoa, about 19 kilometers (12 miles) south of Jerusalem. He earned his living as a shepherd and a tender of sycamore trees (a fruit tree quite different from the sycamores of North America).

Contents. Israel neglected the worship of God and indulged in extravagant luxury. Rich merchants oppressed the poor and worshiped the pagan idols that Jeroboam I had introduced to the nation.

Chronicles, First.

First and Second Chronicles comprised one book in the Hebrew Bible, called *Divere Hayyanim* ("The words of the days"). The Septuagint translators divided this material into the two books we have today; they called them the *Paraleipomena* (Things omitted"). Jerome's Latin Vulgate gave them the title that we now use: Chronicles. They form a religious history of the monarchy from David on, complementing the more political narrative of the books of Samuel and Kings, which they often summarize.

Authorship. Hebrew tradition says that Ezra wrote Chronicles as well as Ezra. The books do have the same style of language and type of contents: their frequent genealogies, their similar stress upon ritual, and their common devotion to the law of Moses.

Contents. First Chronicles starts by setting forth the genealogies of Jewish priests and laymen. These records were the only proof of individual rights to priestly office and claims to the property of ancestors.

The rest of the book tells the story of David's reign, with special emphasis on the details of Israelite worship during that period.

Chronicles, Second.

This book describes the reign of Solomon, the division of the kingdom, and the subsequent history of the southern kingdom of Judah.

Authorship. Jewish tradition says that Ezra wrote this book, along with the narrative of 1 Chronicles.

Contents. This book describes the history of some of the kings in more detail than the books of Kings. For example, it devotes thirty verses to the religious reforms and military exploits of King Asa, while Kings gives us less than half of that material (1 Kings 15:9–24).

Daniel.

Daniel comes from the Babylonian captivity and recounts several miraculous divine interventions in the lives of certain of the exiles.

Authorship. Daniel spent his adult life in the royal court of the Babylonian and Persian empires. Though he lived after the Jews returned, he probably did not go with them.

The book itself names Daniel as the author and the NT confirms it, even in the words of Jesus, who speaks of "Daniel the prophet" (Matt. 24:15).

Contents. The book of Daniel consists of two parts. The first, including the first six chapters, contains an account of the life of Daniel at the Babylonian court and of various occurrences of the reigns of Nebuchadnezzar, Belshazzar, and Darius.

The second part is prophetic. A wide variety of interpretations have been offered. The traditional view states that it predicts various political changes, the coming of the Messiah, the rebuilding of Jerusalem and the temple, a subsequent second destruction of Jerusalem, and the Messiah's return to judgment.

Deuteronomy.

Our English title comes from the Greek words *deuteronomion touto* ("this second law giving"). The Hebrew manuscripts call it *Elleh Haddevarim* ("These are the words") or *Mishmeh Hattorah* ("Repetition of the law"). This name comes from a phrase in 17:18.

Authorship. Scholars have argued that some later author or authors wrote Deuteronomy. But Christians and Jews have traditionally held that Moses wrote this book, apart from the few verses describing his death (34:5–12). The book itself says that Moses wrote it (31:9, 24).

Contents. Jesus quoted Deuteronomy more often than any other OT book, and the NT refers to it more than eighty times. Deuteronomy tells how God renewed his covenant with the Israelites on the Plains of Moab, just before they entered the Promised Land.

Ecclesiastes. The Hebrew name of this book is *Qoheleth*, which means "Preacher" or "One Who Assembles." The Septuagint translators gave the book its current Greek name, meaning "Member of the Assembly." The book scorns the sinful ways of humanity and condemns the futility of most endeavors.

Authorship. Tradition says that King Solomon wrote this book in his later years after he had repented of his sinful ways. But modern scholars reject this view, saying it was probably written after the exile.

Contents. Ecclesiastes blasts the emptiness of greed and materialism and exhorts the reader to "remember now your Creator" (Eccles. 12:1).

Esther. The Hebrew name of this book is *Megillah Esther* ("The Volume of Esther"). Esther is a name that the Persian royal court gave to Hadassah, the daughter of Abihail; it comes from the Persian word *stara*, meaning "star."

Authorship. We do not know who wrote the book of Esther, although the Jewish historian Josephus says it was Mordecai.

Contents. Jews have valued this book highly as a patriotic rallying point. They like its story of Esther's revenge against the wicked court official Haman, who tried to exterminate the Jews.

The book of Esther does not mention the name of God. This troubled Jewish scholars for centuries, but the book has earned its place in the canon by tradition, and is a telling portrayal of God's hidden hand in providence.

Exodus. Our title for this book comes from the Greek word that means "departure" or "going out." The Hebrew name is the first phrase, "These are the names," or *We'alleh Shemoth.*

Authorship. Moses is the personality of this book, as well as being its author. However, scholars debate his dating of some events.

Contents. Exodus takes up where Genesis leaves off. The period between Joseph and Moses is covered by two verses, 1:6–7.

The favored guests of Pharaoh had become a nation of slaves, as the new ruler sought to control the Hebrews. God prepared Moses, then used him to deliver the Hebrews.

The Exodus influenced the religion and life of Israel more than we can imagine. The Exodus is the central event in the OT, just as the cross is in the NT.

Ezekiel. This prophet's name means "God strengthens." He came from a family of priests and served as a priest in the temple until he was carried away into captivity by Nebuchadnezzar.

Authorship. Ezekiel wrote this book. It reflects the times in which Ezekiel lived, and it carries the burden of his message to the Jews in captivity.

Contents. When Nebuchadnezzar captured the temple in Jerusalem, he stunned the Israelites. They believed God would never allow their enemies to violate the holy sanctuary. But Jeremiah had predicted this would happen, and Ezekiel reminds his fellow exiles that God had brought it to

Ramses II of Egypt bows before his gods with a offering. Many scholars believe this Ramses was the ruling Pharaoh at the time of the Exodus. PHOTO BY HOWARD VOS

pass. His later chapters look forward to restoration from exile and spiritual renewal.

Ezra. This book continues Chronicles. Ezra, a priest and a scribe, was well suited for writing this historical narrative. It begins with Cyrus's decree permitting Zerubbabel to lead the Jews back to Jerusalem and rebuild the temple. It ends with Ezra's moral reform among the Jewish people.

Authorship. Scholars think the priest Ezra wrote part of this book and compiled the rest. They believe Ezra wrote chapters 7—10 from his own experiences and gathered the rest of the material from earlier histories.

Contents. Ezra describes how the Jews returned from exile and restored their worship rituals in Jerusalem.

Genesis. The title comes from a Greek word meaning "origin" or "generation" and occurs frequently in the Septuagint version of this book. The Hebrew title is *Bereshith,* which we translate as "In the beginning."

Authorship. The OT names Moses as the author of the Pentateuch (Josh. 8:31; 23:6; 2 Kings 14:6; 2 Chron. 25:4; 35:12; Ezra 6:18; Neh. 8:1; 13:1). Moses' education in the court of Pharaoh brought him in contact with the literature of the ancient world (Acts 7:22). Moses may well have used these documents of great antiquity in writing his account of creation.

Contents. Genesis sets the stage for all of the rest of the Bible. It surveys God's work of creation and his establishment of a covenant with Abraham's family.

Habakkuk. This prophet lived just before Nebuchadnezzar took the city of Jerusalem. His book denounces the sins of the Jews and predicts that the Babylonians will conquer them as a result.

Authorship. We know nothing about the prophet himself. His name seems to come from a Hebrew word that means "to embrace," and Jerome believed Habakkuk meant "the embracer."

Contents. Most of this book is a stern warning for the people of Judah. However, it closes with a beautiful hymn of petition and praise that the Jews might have sung in their temple services.

Haggai. We know little about the life of Haggai, whose name means "festive." He was the first prophet to address the Jews who returned from exile in Babylon, beginning his work in the second year of King Darius (1:1).

Authorship. The prophet Haggai probably wrote this brief book. It expresses a very natural concern of the time—to renew Israel's cultic covenant with God.

Contents. The Jews had begun rebuilding the temple when they first returned to Jerusalem. But their neighbors harassed and discouraged them and they had suspended work on the project. God sent Haggai to prod them to finish the task.

Hosea. This prophet was a native of Israel and he addressed his prophecies to the people of the northern kingdom. Like the other prophets of this period (such as Isaiah), Hosea seems to have exhorted his people in vain.

Authorship. It seems certain that the prophet Hosea actually wrote this book. God instructed him to marry a prostitute as an object lesson of God's persistent love for Israel. This makes Hosea's prophetic message intensely personal.

Contents. The book consists of threats and denunciations against the wickedness of the Israelites, mingled with predictions of the final restoration of God's people.

Isaiah. The name of this prophet means "Salvation of Yahweh." Though Isaiah lived and wrote later than some of the other prophets, our modern Bibles place his book before the rest because his predictions were so important for the future of Israel and all mankind.

Authorship. Isaiah undoubtedly compiled this book, though he may have been assisted by a scribe or secretary. Some modern critics claim that Isaiah did not write chapters 40—66, but they build their argument on the supposition that God did not reveal the future to his prophets.

Contents. Isaiah proclaimed God's word under a succession of kings, warning them that God would destroy Judah because of their evil ways. They did not heed him, and Jewish tradition says that King Manasseh executed Isaiah by having him sawn in two.

Jeremiah. This name means "the appointed one of the Lord." Jeremiah lived and prophesied about two centuries after Isaiah. He was a priest from the city of Anathoth, and he ministered in Judah for more than forty years. Tradition says that the Jewish refugees stoned him to death in Egypt because he criticized their life during the exile.

Authorship. This book contains the prophecies of Jeremiah as they were recorded by his scribe, Baruch.

Contents. The book of Jeremiah describes the prophet's attempt to call his people back to God just before the Babylonians seized the nation of Judah. Occasionally, the writer used a secret script called *atbash* to conceal the names of nations or cities God has doomed, in case the scroll fell into the hands of enemies.

Job. Some scholars believe this book was written before any other book of the OT—even before the Pentateuch. But most conservative Bible experts think it was written during the reign of King Solomon. Job lived in the land of Uz, somewhere east of Canaan, perhaps in the area of Idumaea.

Authorship. Tradition says that Job himself wrote the book. However, more recent scholars dispute that claim. Across the years, Bible students have supposed that it was written by Moses, Elihu, Solomon, Isaiah, or someone else. We have no proof for any of these theories, and the book does not name its author.

Contents. This book describes Job's questioning of God in the aftermath of several tragedies that befell the "upright man"

of Uz. It addresses the age-old question, "Why do the righteous suffer?"

Joel. In Hebrew, this prophet's name means "Yahweh is God." While scholars disagree about the time of this prophet's ministry, most believe that he lived around 400 B.C.—when the Jews were still under the power of the Persian Empire.

Authorship. Some critics of the nineteenth century supposed that several authors wrote this book. More recent researchers believe it was all penned by Joel, though some later scribes may have changed a few verses.

Contents. The book of Joel takes the opportunity from a plague of locusts to appeal to the Jews to repent, threatens them with destruction otherwise, and predicts the final glory of the Jewish nation.

Jonah. This is the story of an eighth-century prophet who ignored God's call to preach against Nineveh. The book narrates that God prepared a great fish to swallow Jonah, then Jonah had a change of heart.

Authorship. Tradition says that Jonah himself wrote this book, but the book does not name him as its author.

Contents. This book teaches that God will forgive the wicked if they repent. Perhaps God intended the mission of Jonah to have a reforming effect upon the Israelites themselves after his return.

Joshua. The book bears the name of its principal character and continues the historical narrative of the Pentateuch, describing the conquest of Canaan in detail.

Authorship. Although no clear proof exists, many Jews and Christians believe Joshua himself wrote the book. As in the case of Moses, it is believed that the account of his death was added by a later writer.

Contents. The book of Joshua stresses the uniqueness and holiness of the Israelites as they conquered Canaan. By the time of Joshua, Canaanite religious observances had degenerated to licentiousness and brutality, as shown in the Ugaritic tablets and other relics unearthed at Beth Shean and Megiddo.

Judges. The title is a direct English translation of the Hebrew title, *shoffim*. The Septuagint and the Latin Vulgate picked up this title and it has remained in our modern versions.

Authorship. Different scholars have attributed this book to Phinehas, Hezekiah, Jeremiah, Ezekiel, Ezra or to an unknown prophet who drew the materials from public records. Jewish tradition said that Samuel wrote it. We do not know.

Contents. Judges continues the narrative of Joshua. However, it reflects the general social and political chaos at the end of the Amarna Age (ca. 1200 B.C.).

Kings, First. The two books of Kings were originally one in the Hebrew Bible. The translators of the Septuagint divided them, followed by the Vulgate and English versions. The earliest English Bibles called these books 3 and 4 Kings.

Authorship. The book does not identify an author but the Talmud claims that Jeremiah wrote it (because Jeremiah 52 and 2 Kings 24–25 are nearly identical).

Contents. The books of Kings does not present a detailed history of all the kings of Judah and Israel. They give only passing reference to powerful kings like Omri and Jeroboam II, but emphasize the prophets Elijah and Elisha.

The writer evaluates each king by certain standards, such as the king's role in giving support to the temple and its worship. While such support was impossible for the kings of the northern kingdom, the writer believed that was part of God's judgment upon them because they had separated themselves from the temple.

Kings, Second. This book continues the history of Israel and Judah as begun by 1 Kings and carries it up to the Babylonian captivity.

Authorship. Like 1 Kings, this book does not name its author. Probably it was written by the same person who compiled the narrative of 1 Kings.

Contents. Second Kings describes the fall of Israel and the last throes of Judah. Like 1 Kings, it shows that God tried to warn the nations through his prophets, but the corrupt kings ignored him. Here we see the climax of the ministries of Elijah and Elisha.

Lamentations. The Jewish name of this book literally means "Ah, how!"—from the first words of the text. Our present name of the book is the English translation of *Threnoi*, the title the Septuagint translators gave it.

Authorship. Jewish tradition says that Jeremiah wrote this book, and the Septuagint even added a verse of introduction that named Jeremiah as the author.

Contents. The book consists of five separate elegies or lamentations, corresponding to the five chapters of the English version. It is poetical throughout—more elaborately poetical than any other portion of the Bible. Each of the five elegies or chapters is arranged in 22 portions, corresponding with the 22 letters of the Hebrew alphabet.

Leviticus. Leviticus comes from the Greek *Levitikon* ("of the Levites"), part of the book's title in the Septuagint version. The Hebrew title is *Wayyiqra* ("And he called").

Authorship. "They assigned the priests to their divisions and the Levites to their divisions, over the service of God in Jerusalem; as it is written in the Book of Moses" (Ezra 6:18).

Ezra the scribe refers to Leviticus in describing the proper procedure for dedicating the rebuilt temple.

Contents. Leviticus continues the narrative of Exodus without a break. It describes the priestly practices and the rituals of worship in ancient Israel.

Malachi. This name is probably a short form of the Hebrew *Malachiah*, which means "the messenger of the Lord." Malachi was the last prophet to preach to the Jews after they returned from the exile and the last prophet of the OT era.

Authorship. Malachi indicates that the Jews had rebuilt the temple, restored their worship, and then fallen away from God again. This means that Malachi probably wrote late in the fifth century B.C.

Contents. If Malachi prophesied in the time of Nehemiah, the immediate purpose of his prophecy would have been to uphold and perfect the reforms introduced by Nehemiah when he returned from his visit to the Persian court.

Micah. The name of this prophet is a shortened form of *Mikayahu,* which means "Who is like Yahweh?"

Authorship. Some critics doubt that Micah wrote the entire book, because the prophecies seem too sketchy and disjointed. But this argument is weak. It is more reasonable to accept the book's own witness that Micah wrote it (see 1:1).

Contents. Micah declares God's anger against both Israel and Judah. He delivered his prophecies at different times, and it is difficult to follow the historical sequence of the book.

Nahum. *Nahum* means "Consoler." He brought God's message of comfort to Judah just before the Babylonians invaded.

Authorship. Nahum was born at Elkosh, a village of Galilee. He tells the people of Judah that God will destroy the city of Nineveh because its people had opposed the Jews for so long.

Contents. Nahum is a single poem of great eloquence and its theme is "The burden of Nineveh"—that is, the coming punishment of that city and empire in retribution for the Assyrians' cruel treatment of the Jews.

Nehemiah. This book tells the story of the third great leader of the Jews' return from exile. King Artaxerxes sent Nehemiah, a Jew, to serve as governor of the restored city of Jerusalem. The book of Nehemiah recounts this man's struggle to reestablish Israel as a nation.

Authorship. Scholars believe Nehemiah wrote much of the book himself, though later scribes added more material to detail the history of this period.

Contents. Although Nehemiah was not a priest, he proved to be as pious as Ezra, the great religious leader of the period—and a more practical statesman.

Numbers. The title is our English translation of *Arithmoi,* the title of this book in the Greek Septuagint. Various Hebrew manuscripts entitled this book *Wayed habber* ("And he spoke") or *Bemidhbar* ("In the wilderness")—both come from the first words of Numbers.

Authorship. Like the rest of the Pentateuch, this book was written by Moses. Numbers names Moses as its author more than eighty times.

Contents. In Numbers, God teaches his people how to function as a community. He sets their religious, civil, and military economies in order, in preparation for their journeying as a nation.

Laws and instructions are interspersed throughout the book.

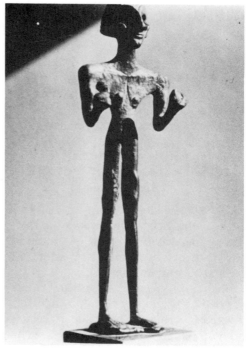

A statue of Baal, a prominent pagan god of the ancient Canaanites. PHOTO BY GUSTAV JEENINGA

Obadiah. This short book of prophecy tells us nothing specific about Obadiah's native land or the time in which he lived. It denounces the Edomites for taking advantage of the Jews when Judah was under attack. Obadiah predicts that God will restore the glory of his people.

Authorship. The first nine verses of this book resemble Jeremiah 49, and so both prophets may have used some statements from earlier prophetic documents.

Contents. Obadiah directs his attention to the Edomites. He condemns them for joining the other enemies of Judah to plunder and burn the city of Jerusalem. He warns that God will judge the Edomites for their actions.

Proverbs. In this case, the Hebrew and English names of the book have the same meaning, since the first words of the book in both languages name its contents—"The Proverbs of Solomon." No doubt this collection of pithy religious and oral sayings was mainly composed by the wise king whose name it bears.

Authorship. Even though Solomon wrote most of Proverbs, the book was not compiled until the time of King Hezekiah, whose scribes "copied" the sayings of Solomon (Prov. 25:1). We do not know the identity of "Agur the son of Jakeh" or the mother of "King Lemuel," who wrote latter portions of the book (Prov. 30—31).

Contents. Proverbs is a collection of ethical precepts about practical living. Like the Psalms, it arranges its material in balanced pairs of thoughts by the method of contrasting parallelism.

Psalms. The Hebrew name for this book means "Praises." The present name is Greek, and was first given in the Septuagint translation; it means "poems with musical accompaniment."

Authorship. Besides 73 psalms that are ascribed to David, we have 30 that are attributed to other authors and 50 that are anonymous. Solomon is supposed to have written Psalms 72 and 127, and he may also have written some of the anonymous psalms. Many are ascribed to Asaph (the head of the temple musicians in David's time) and "the sons of Korah" (probably Levite writers who descended from Korah).

Contents. Psalms is the songbook of the ancient Hebrews. It contains hymns that the priests sang during temple worship and ballads that express the feelings of the Hebrew people at different stages in their history.

Ruth. This book is named after its heroine, a Moabite woman who moved to Bethlehem with her mother-in-law after the death of Ruth's husband. We remember Ruth because she was a foreign ancestor of King David and of Jesus.

Authorship. This pastoral narrative is written by an unknown person, although it has been credited to Samuel, Hezekiah, and Ezra.

Contents. In telling the experiences of Ruth, this book gives us a detailed account of Israelite village life in the time of the judges. The book also demonstrates the ancient law of levirate marriage, by which a male relative would marry a dead man's widow to provide offspring to carry the family name.

Samuel, First. This book receives its name from the key person in its narrative.

Authorship. Most commentators believe Samuel wrote only the sections that deal with the history of Israel prior to his retirement from public office. Some scholars suggest that Abiathar wrote much of 1 and 2 Samuel, especially the parts that describe the court life of David.

Contents. First Samuel continues the history of Israel from the period of the judges down to the establishment of the monarchy under Saul.

The books of Samuel emphasize that God rules in the lives of humans and nations. In judgment and blessing, God works to prepare his people for the coming of the Messiah.

Samuel, Second. Early English Bibles called this book 2 Kings because it is the second book about the kings of Israel. Those same versions called 1 and 2 Kings 3 Kings and 4 Kings. But later publishers attached Samuel's name to this book because he played an important role in setting up the monarchy in Israel.

Authorship. This book does not mention its author (see 1 Samuel above).

Contents. Second Samuel begins by telling of David's men wiping out Saul's family and opening the way for David to rule the nation. The book describes David's reign objectively, showing both his strengths and weaknesses.

Song of Solomon. The Hebrew Bible calls this book "The Song of Songs"—that is, the most beautiful of all songs.

Authorship. Tradition says that Solomon wrote this book, probably while he was a young man. However, it seems more to be about him than by him, and it does not portray him in a favorable light.

Contents. Probably no book of the Bible has been interpreted in as many different ways as the Song of Solomon.

These interpretations fall into two categories—literal and allegorical. The Jewish Talmud teaches that the book is an allegory of God's love for Israel. Many Christian writers feel that it is an allegory of God's love for the church. Some Roman Catholic commentators conclude that it is an allegory of God's love for the Virgin Mary.

On the literal side, Theodore of Mopsuestia (fourth century A.D.) believed the book was a straightforward poem that Solomon wrote in honor of his marriage. Johann David Michaelis believed the book

simply expressed God's approval of marriage, while Johann F. W. Bousset supposed that it was a poetic marriage drama used in ancient times. The modern scholar Calvin Seerveld sees it as an ancient love story with a strong religious and spiritual message.

Despite these differing opinions, the book is one of the most beautiful examples of Hebrew poetry found in the OT.

Zechariah. This prophet lived during the time of Haggai and began work in the second year of Darius's reign (1:1). Like Haggai, Zechariah encouraged his people to rebuild the temple and restore their nation under God.

Authorship. Zechariah delivered his prophecies in Jerusalem after the Jews returned from captivity in 539 B.C. Besides that, we know very little about him.

Contents. Zechariah not only exhorted the people to rebuild God's temple, he also gave them hope for the restored nation.

Zephaniah. The name of this prophet means "the Lord hides."

Authorship. Some Bible students suppose that Zephaniah's father, "Hezekiah" (1:1), was actually King Hezekiah of Judah. But we have no proof of this. Zephaniah prophesied during King Josiah's reign.

Contents. Zephaniah lashes out at the people's hypocrisy and idolatrous worship. Even though King Josiah tried to reform them, they continued to wallow in their sins. Zephaniah foretold that this behavior would lead them to destruction, although there would be a restoration afterwards.

The Deuterocanon, or Apocrypha

Tobit, Judith, Esther (the Greek text), Wisdom of Solomon, Sirach, Baruch, Letter of Jeremiah, Song of the Three Young Men, Susanna, Bel and the Dragon, 1 Maccabees, and 2 Maccabees, formed part of the Septuagint Greek text and were interspersed among other books of the OT.

This Greek text was not only widely used by Jews but was known as well by numerous "God-fearing" Gentiles who were attracted to the high moral teachings of the OT, even though they had not themselves become converts to Judaism. One can thus readily understand how and why early Christianity, as it spread among Greek-speaking Jews and Gentiles, employed this Greek text. In fact, the majority of OT quotations in the NT are based on this translation.

Precisely when Jewish leadership officially adopted the traditional 39 books of the so-called "Hebrew canon" is not known; nor is there agreement as to exactly what criteria were used in determining the canon. According to tradition the determination of the books of the Hebrew canon was made about A.D. 90, but there is evidence to believe that official and widespread agreement on this issue came somewhat later.

Among Christians it was apparently only in the fourth century that the issue of the canonicity of these books arose, a situation which is reflected in Jerome's placing these books in a separated section in his Vulgate translation of the OT.

In 1546 at the Council of Trent the Roman Catholic Church officially declared these books to be sacred and canonical and to be accepted "with equal devotion and reference."

At the time of the Reformation, Martin Luther did not regard these books as Scripture but as "useful and good for reading." In his German translation of the Bible he followed the practice of Jerome in placing them at the end of the OT with the superscription "Apocrypha."

Among Christians who do not accept these books as Scripture there is, however, widespread agreement as to their importance in providing much valuable information in Jewish history, life, thought, worship, and religious practice during the centuries immediately prior to the time of Christ. Accordingly, they make possible a clearer understanding of the historical and cultural situation in which Jesus lived and taught.

Catholics speak of these books as "deuterocanonical" to indicate that their canonical status as Scripture was settled later than that of the protocanonical books. Protestants usually refer to these books as Apocrypha.

Following are all the books in the Deuterocanon, or Apocrypha, arranged in alphabetical order.

Baruch. Many scholars are of the opinion that the various parts of Baruch were written sometime during the early second century B.C. and the middle of the first century B.C., and that the book was edited to appear in its present format about 50 B.C.

Authorship. The traditional author of the book was Baruch, the secretary and confidant of the prophet Jeremiah (1:1). Modern scholarship, based on external and internal evidence, would deny that Baruch is the author. It is generally held that the book is a composite by unknown authors (usually three are mentioned), united by a redactor, and ascribed to Baruch.

Contents. Drawing from various religious traditions, the book of Baruch is addressed to exilic Jews in Babylon.

The books, consisting of prose (1:1—3:8) and poetry (3:9—5:9), is extant today only in Greek, although a Hebrew original was probable for the entire book. The book is not found in the Hebrew Bible or in the Protestant Canon.

Bel and the Dragon. The stories of Bel and the Dragon, along with the Prayer of Azariah and the Song of the Three Young Men, are Greek additions to the Aramaic and Hebrew Masoretic Text.

The story of the priests of Bel. The god Bel is depicted as receiving rich offerings of food from his priests. The king is deceived into thinking that Bel is really alive (v. 6), and that he himself consumes the sacrifices. Actually, the priests remove the food,

presumably for their own use. Daniel cleverly exposes the fraud, proving once again the superiority of the God of the Jews over all the gods of the nations.

The story of the Dragon. This story's plot is similar to the story of Bel: Another Babylonian god, a dragon, is exposed as a false god when Daniel poisons him with food.

Ecclesiasticus. (See *Sirach.*)

Esdras, First. The book of 1 Esdras is united by content, language, interest, and outlook with the canonical books of 2 Chronicles, Ezra, and Nehemiah. The book is quoted by Tertullian, Clement of Alexandria, and Athanasius, among others.

Authorship. Nothing definitive can be said of the author or his purpose in writing this book. "Esdras" is the Greek and Latin translation of the Hebrew *Ezra.* The author of 1 Esdras is probably not the famous scribe, Ezra.

Today, some scholars think that the author of 1 Esdras was a compiler of relevant portions from the Septuagint version of 2 Chronicles, Ezra, and Nehemiah. Others think the author translated into Greek the relevant portions of 1 Chronicles, Ezra, and Nehemiah from an original Hebrew text.

Contents. The story contained in the book of 1 Esdras begins in the middle of Josiah's reign (640–609 B.C.).

The book of 1 Esdras tells the biblical story of Judah from Josiah's Passover (2 Chron. 35) to the reading of the Law by Ezra (Neh. 8). It was known to Josephus, who used it for his account of King Josiah, generally following the order of events found in 1 Esdras.

Esdras, Second. The book of 2 Esdras belongs to the pseudopigraphal writings. It was given the name *Esdras* (the Greek and Latin form of the Hebrew *Ezra*) because Ezra the scribe was revered and honored in Jewish and Christian circles. Ezra's name would attach great authority to the book.

Authorship. Theories abound on the question of the 2 Esdras. According to some scholars, the author is an editor or redactor who used previously existing sources.

Other scholars, while recognizing the secondary character of chapters 1 and 2, as well as 15 and 16, theorize that chapters 3 through 14 are not a compilation from previously existing sources. They assume that one author may have drawn upon memories and observations but did not use major sources.

Contents. The book of 2 Esdras generally contains material of two types. The first is material dealing with apocalyptic and eschatological mysteries. The second is material dealing with religious problems and speculations.

Esther (Greek version).

The book of Esther, as it comes down to us, is a combination of original Hebrew elements with embellishments originally written in Greek.

The book's Greek translation and final additions were made in the Greek period sometime before 114 B.C.

Author. The author is unknown to us since the work is essentially anonymous. At the end of the final Greek section, in the postscript, mention is made of a certain Lysimachus who may have been responsible for the actual Greek translation as well as the addition of the Greek sections.

Contents. The story line of the Greek version of Esther is essentially identical with that of the Esther accepted by non-Catholics. It describes the providence of God for his people living in Persia in the reign of King Xerxes.

Judith.

The setting of the book of Judith is historically so confused that almost all scholars recognize it as a moral tale told in a way that only sounds historical.

Author. The work is anonymous and the author's identity is not known. Extant only in Greek, the book of Judith is probably a Greek translation of an earlier Hebrew form. Its wide-ranging review of Israel's

troubled past suggests that it may have been written after a similar time of crisis.

Contents. The book of Judith has been called a historical romance, written to inspire the Jewish people to continued trust in God, their historic Savior. As such, it falls within the Hebrew *haggadah* literature, largely fictional material in the Jewish Talmud, whose purpose was to make a moral point. The very name *Judith* is Hebrew for "Jewish woman," and thus represents Israel in her faith and courage in times of great crisis.

Letter of Jeremiah.

This work is purported to be written by Jeremiah to his fellow countrymen as they were about to be deported to Babylon by Nebuchadnezzar. Many scholars assign the work to the late fourth century B.C., or early third century B.C. Others prefer a second-century B.C. date.

Authorship. The superscription (v. 1) states that Jeremiah wrote this letter to his fellow countrymen as they were about to be led into exile. This letter was probably attributed to Jeremiah because of its resemblance to an earlier letter that the prophet had sent the exiles in 597 B.C. (Jer. 29:1–23). Modern scholarship holds that the work is a homily, not a letter, and that Jeremiah is not the author.

Contents. The Letter of Jeremiah may be divided as follows: the introduction (vv. 1–7) and the 10-part homily (vv. 8–73).

Maccabees, First.

The book of 1 Maccabees is the first of four books listed in Greek manuscripts under the title "Books of the Maccabees."

The name "Maccabees" comes from the first book. The author introduces the five sons of Mattathias (1 Macc. 2:2–5). To each he gave a second name. He introduces the third son as "Judas (also called Maccabeus)" (1 Macc. 2:4). Although three of the five sons figure prominently in the revolt, described in the first book, Judas is the real hero.

Authorship. The book of 1 Maccabees

does not give us any direct information about the identity of the author.

Several critics think the author was a Sadducee because of his sympathetic attitude toward the priesthood and his tolerance in the question of the Sabbath. But the author actually does not appear to be a man of any particular sect or party.

Contents. The book of 1 Maccabees is a historical book that narrates the exploits of Mattathias and three of his sons in their revolt against the repressive measures of Antiochus IV of Syria and his successors.

Maccabees, Second.

The book of 2 Maccabees tells in further detail the first part of the history covered in 1 Maccabees.

Like 1 Maccabees, 2 Maccabees is basically a historical work. Different from the first book, it is in a Greek style that authors call "pathetic history"—a history narrated with much emotion, moving the reader to share the emotions of the actors.

Authorship. The book of 2 Maccabees gives us no direct teaching about the person of the author.

His competence in the Greek language and the flowery character of his style reveal an Alexandrian Jew, or at least one formed in the schools of the rhetoricians.

Contents. Each of the five tableaus is written to move and persuade. With Onias the High Priest, the reader tastes the peace enjoyed in the regular service of the Temple. Then the reader shares his agony when the Holy Place is threatened, in order to experience the joy of triumph when Heliodorus, chastised, recognizes the holiness of God who dwells there. In the second tableau, the irreverence of humans and the wrath of God are highlighted, from the time of Jason to the time of Menelaus, from the pillage of the Temple to its profanation. In contrast the death of the martyrs, which calms the wrath of God, leaves the reader with an impression of hope. In the last three tableaus Judas is elevated, while his adversaries Antiochus IV (also called Epiphanes), Lysias, Antiochus V (Eupator), and finally Nicanor perish pro-

claiming the glory of the Almighty who reveals himself in his temple.

Prayer of Azariah.

(See *Song of the Three Young Men.*)

Prayer of Manasseh.

Among the apocryphal literature of the intertestamental period is included this beautiful prayer of King Manasseh on the occasion of his personal repentance.

Authorship. Manasseh, son of Hezekiah and father to Amon, ruled Judah from about 687 to 642 B.C. During his long reign in the southern kingdom, the people follow the king's wickedness in idolatry and injustice. The text as it now stands in the apocryphal literature is evidently the product of an unknown Jewish author using the first person form in behalf of King Manasseh, and dates from the period of one hundred years before or after the coming of Christ.

Contents. The text is rooted in the events of 2 Chronicles 33:10–13, which mentions the prayer of repentance by Manasseh after his many offenses against true worship of the Lord.

Sirach.

The book of Sirach, so-called because of the surname of its author, is also known by the designation *Liber Ecclesiasticus*, meaning "Church Book."

Scholars generally agree that Sirach was written sometime between 195 and 168 B.C., probably about 180 B.C.

Authorship. Scholars agree that the author of the book of Sirach is "Jesus (*Joshua* in Hebrew), son of Sirach Eleazar" (50:27). Born and reared in the city, he was probably a scribe, as well as a sage.

Contents. The book of Sirach, a compilation of maxims grouped by affinity, gives the appearance of being a collection of small essays.

Among the various topics dealt with are the following: the rearing of children, pride and humility, patience, respect and obedience of parents, friendship, wealth, relationships with women, table etiquette, control of the tongue, retribution, care of the needy, and above all the quest for wisdom.

Song of the Three Young Men.
The Prayer of Azariah and the Song of the Three Young Men, the story of Susanna, and the stories of Bel and the Dragon, are Greek additions to the Aramaic and Hebrew Masoretic Text. According to Catholic practice, which accepts these additions as Scripture, they are inserted with the book of Daniel and are read as Daniel 3:24–90; 13:1–64; and 14:1–42, respectively.

The Prayer of Azariah. A later author expanded the text of Daniel to include a prayer uttered by Azariah and one of the three young men thrown into the fiery furnace in Daniel 3:23.

The prayer is important theologically, since it interprets the disaster of the fall of Jerusalem as the just punishment of God for the refusal of the Jews to obey the laws of the covenant he had made with them.

The Song of the Three Young Men. This addition follows the Prayer of Azariah and is very similar to the hymn of praise in Psalm 148. It consists of two litanies, the first in verses 52–56, which is a pure hymn of praise.

The second and longer litany invites all of creation to worship the Lord, the God whose "mercy lasts forever" (vv. 67–68, TEV).

Susanna.
Another addition to the Hebrew-Aramaic book of Daniel (along with the Prayer of Azariah and the Song of the Three Young Men and the stories of Bel and the Dragon), the episode of Susanna gives yet another indication of the wisdom of Daniel and of God's providence for his faithful people. The Lord's prophet is led to vindicate Susanna, "a Jewish woman" (v. 57), from the false accusation of adultery made against her by some false elders of the people.

The innocent Susanna has also been interpreted as a symbol of the faithful people of God. Early Christian art used the figure of Susanna to represent the innocent but persecuted church, ultimately freed from injustice.

Tobit.
In the oldest Greek manuscripts, the book of Tobit is placed with Judith and the Greek version of Esther, sometimes after the historical books, and sometimes after the sapiential books.

Authorship. Tradition tells us practically nothing about the author of the book. In the text itself two pieces of data have led several scholars to argue that the book was written by Tobit and his son, Tobias.

Contents. The purpose of the author is to give, not history, but an "edifying story." The book illustrates, in an effective way, many truths concerning the blessing derived from the practice of virtue, particularly from doing acts of charity.

Wisdom.
(See *Wisdom of Solomon.*)

Wisdom of Solomon.
The book of Wisdom, or as it is known in the Septuagint, the Wisdom of Solomon, is not a part of the Hebrew canon of Scripture, yet has long-standing support as one of the deuterocanonical works of the Christian OT.

Its late date makes the Wisdom of Solomon the last book of the Christian canon of the OT.

Authorship. Scholars generally acknowledge today that this book's claim to the person of Solomon as its author is a literary device to lend authority to its message.

Some scholars argue for more than a single author and attempt to divide the book into several sections based on stylistic differences and textual study. There is more support at present for a unity of authorship for the whole book.

Contents. The Wisdom of Solomon was written to offer edification to a Jewish community during times of oppression and political suffering, and to reassure faithful members of that community that God indeed rewards those who remain steadfast in the faith.

The work combines traditional Jewish material with ideas borrowed from Greek philosophy of the age, and has within its text some passages (notably 3:1–8) frequently used in Christian liturgy.

*The New Testament*___

Christians have regarded their collection of Scriptures as being "the Book" since the Council of Carthage drew up the final list of NT books in A.D. 397.

The order of the books in the NT is based on subject categories: the historical books (the Gospels and Acts); the epistles (beginning with the Pauline collection); and the Apocalypse or Revelation.

Early church tradition has the Gospels in the order they are today, with the synoptic Gospels (Matthew, Mark, and Luke) coming first, then the Gospel of John. The early church fathers also arranged the Pauline epistles in two categories—the epistles to the churches and personal letters. They generally arranged the epistles to the churches according to size or length, and the personal letters seemed to follow the same structure, as did the general epistles (non-Pauline writings)—Hebrews was first, followed by the writings of James, Peter, John, and Jude.

This order has been constant since about the fourth century A.D., but many lists circulating during the first three centuries did not include all of the books.

The Historical Books

The historical books of the NT comprise the four Gospels and the book of Acts. The word *gospel* comes from the Anglo-Saxon words *god* ("good") and *spel* ("word" or "tidings"). Gospel is a literal translation of the Greek *euangelion,* which was evidently the title the authors gave to these books.

Bible students often refer to the first three Gospels together as the "Synoptics" [Greek *synoptikos*—"yielding a single view"] because they give a consecutive account of Jesus' life and actions, whereas John concentrates on his character and office.

The book of Acts advances the story about thirty years beyond the crucifixion. Except for what Acts tells us, and incidental statements in the Epistles, we have to depend upon later church and secular history for knowledge of the progress of Christianity.

The Epistles

A collection of letters on theology and practical religion forms the second great division of the NT. These 21 letters were written by five of the apostles—Paul, James, Peter, John, and Jude. Fourteen were written by Paul. The apostles wrote these epistles to congregations of Christian converts or to individuals on different occasions.

The Epistles do not stand in the order in which they were written, but in the order of the importance of the audiences addressed. Romans comes first because Rome was the capital of the empire. Corinthians comes next because Corinth was the next most important city.

Paul's letters to individuals follow those to collective audiences, and our Bible also place them in an order of dignity: first the letter to Timothy, the favorite disciple, then Titus, and finally to Philemon. Hebrews appears last, because there is good reason to doubt whether it was written by Paul.

After Paul's epistles come the seven Catholic, or General, epistles—so called because they were addressed to Christians generally. They appear roughly in the order of their length.

The Apocalypse, or Revelation

This last book of the NT is a prophetic vision of the future. Bible scholars have interpreted it in many different ways, and it remains the most controversial book of the Bible.

Following are the books of the New Testament in alphabetical order.

Acts of the Apostles. This book takes up the history of Christianity and continues it for a period of about thirty years, to the arrival of Paul in Rome.

Authorship. This book does not identify its author, although tradition says it was Luke. The opening verses link it with Luke's Gospel.

Contents. Acts does two crucial things: It describes the Holy Spirit's work in the lives of the apostles, and it shows how God brought the Gentiles into the church.

Acts shows that Jesus fulfilled his promise to send the Holy Spirit to his followers, and silenced the arguments of Jewish Christians who opposed the admission of Gentiles to the church.

Colossians. Paul wrote this epistle at about the same time as Ephesians and probably sent it to the church at Colossae by the same messengers, Tychicus and Onesimus.

Authorship. A few scholars doubt that Paul wrote this letter, but their arguments are not very convincing. The letter is true to Paul's teachings, and its description of the church of Colossae fits what Paul would have known about the congregation.

Contents. Some leaders of the Colossian church said that Gentiles had to adopt Jewish rituals and learn to worship angels when they became Christians. At the same time, these leaders were dabbling in Gnostic philosophy. Paul attempted to correct these trends with this letter.

Corinthians, First. Paul established the church at Corinth on his second missionary journey when he stayed a year and a half in that city. While this church was zealous and prosperous, it was also prone to great troubles.

Authorship. The book identifies Paul as its author, and the early church fathers such as Clement of Rome confirm this fact. The content of the letter also proves Paul's authorship of First Corinthians.

Contents. When most people reflect on this letter, they think of Paul's great rhapsody on Christian love in the thirteenth chapter. But the entire book contains a wealth of practical advice on Christian conduct, designed to help the Corinthians deal with the problems in their congregation.

Corinthians, Second. Paul wrote his second letter to the Corinthian church

---

Order of the New Testament Books

Matthew	Ephesians	Hebrews
Mark	Philippians	James
Luke	Colossians	1 Peter
John	1 Thessalonians	2 Peter
Acts	2 Thessalonians	1 John
Romans	1 Timothy	2 John
1 Corinthians	2 Timothy	3 John
2 Corinthians	Titus	Jude
Galatians	Philemon	Revelation

within a year after the first one. Having dispatched the first epistle, Paul went to Troas, where he expected to meet Titus and learn the effect of his admonitions upon the church at Corinth. Titus was not there, so Paul went on into Macedonia. There he found Titus and received the information he desired. The news was partly good and partly bad. Many of the Corinthian Christians had corrected their beliefs and conduct according to Paul's instructions in the first epistle. But some of them still opposed the Apostle's authority and teaching. So this second letter defends Paul's motives, authority, and labors.

Authorship. Some modern biblical scholars have debated whether Paul wrote this entire letter at one time. They think that 2 Corinthians 6:14–7:1 might have been inserted later, since it seems to break the letter's train of thought.

Ephesians. After Paul arrived in Rome, he wrote the Epistle to the Ephesians in about A.D. 61. So it is one of the last letters he wrote.

Authorship. Virtually no scholars deny that Paul wrote this letter. There are reasons for thinking it was a circular to several churches, of which the church at Ephesus was one. The letter clearly identifies Paul as the author, and its content fits the general pattern of Paul's work.

Contents. In this letter, Paul emphasizes that Christ is the head of the church. He exhorts his fellow Christians to live lives worthy of their high calling as Jesus' disciples.

Galatians. On this third missionary journey, Paul went into Galatia and Phrygia, where he made an inspection tour of the churches, exhorting and advising as he thought necessary. He then proceeded to Ephesus. While there, he heard from the Galatian churches that they were being troubled by persons who were teaching doctrines of a Jewish sort, insisting on circumcision for salvation. They were also attacking the authority of Paul.

Authorship. This letter identifies Paul as the author and its contents support that statement. The letter's contents agrees with Paul's teachings in other epistles.

Contents. This letter refutes the teachings of the Judaizers, who wanted the new Christians to be circumcised and to adopt other Jewish rituals.

Hebrews. Some traditions say that Paul wrote this letter to the converted Jewish congregations in Jerusalem. Others suggest Apollos was the author.

Authorship. This letter does not name its author, but its dissimilarity to Paul's letters in style, language, and method of arguing rules out the idea that Paul composed it.

Contents. This letter displays Jesus as God, human, and high priestly mediator and the fulfillment of Jewish hopes.

Ruins of the library of Celsus at Ephesus from the second century A.D.   PHOTO BY HOWARD VOS

James. This letter is addressed to Hebrew converts and is intended to strengthen them in the Christian life by correcting various tendencies to sin and by instructing them in the truth that faith must show itself alive by the way it works.

Authorship. The man who wrote this epistle was probably the brother of Jesus. Tradition says he was the leader of the Christian church at Jerusalem for many years and was martyred there by a mob. The date of composition was sometime between A.D. 45 and 62.

Contents. This letter challenges Christians to exercise their faith in their daily lives. It calls for vibrant living that glorifies Christ.

John.   A remarkable contrast exists between the Gospel of John and the Synoptics.

Authorship. Some scholars doubt that John wrote this book; however, Irenaeus and other early writers affirm that John was the author.

Contents. The material in the Gospel suggests that, while preparing a history of Jesus' life that would supplement the three previous ones, John wanted to present the teachings of Jesus Christ in a way that would refute heretical doctrines that were then prevailing among Christians.

John, First.   The apostle John probably wrote the three letters that bear his name while in the city of Ephesus, where he spent the later years of his life.

Authorship. Scholars have long debated whether the apostle John or another Christian leader named John wrote these letters.

Contents. This letter dwells on the nature of Jesus Christ, his mission, and the principal doctrines of the Christian life. It also shows the distinction between true and false believers.

John, Second.   Scholars disagree about the identity of the elect lady to whom John addressed this letter. Some think he refers to the whole church, the bride of Christ. Others say this was an individual whose name we do not know.

Authorship. (See the section on 1 John.)

Contents. In this brief epistle, John warns against the heresy of denying the Incarnation and reminds his Christian friends to obey God's commandment of love.

John, Third.   John wrote this epistle to a man named Gaius, who was well known for his hospitality. The epistle simply commends Gaius for his Christian virtues, cautions him against Diotrephes (a schemer and false teacher), and recommends a man named Demetrius.

Authorship. (See the section on 1 John.)

Contents. Obviously John wrote this letter to a real individual, rather than using the name *Gaius* for a group of people. The letter gives Gaius personal praise and advice.

Jude.   We do not know where this epistle was written, and we have no knowledge of the life or labors of Jude.

Authorship. Matthew 13:55 and Mark 6:3 state that a man named Judas was a brother of Jesus. The writer identifies himself as "a brother of James."

Contents. Jude warns his Christian friends to avoid the heresy of Gnosticism, which taught that matter is evil and only spirit is good.

Luke.   This Gospel gives the fullest account we have of Jesus' birth, youth, and ministry. Luke was the first of two volumes, the second being the book of Acts.

Authorship. The early church fathers tell us that Luke, a companion of Paul, wrote this Gospel. Paul called Luke "the beloved physician" (Col. 4:14).

Contents. Luke focuses on Jesus' ministry as the Savior, showing that Jesus lifted lost men and women out of their sins and brought them to God. He describes some events that the other Gospels do not—no doubt distilling this information from the apostles' preaching or from his conversations with other eyewitnesses.

Mark.   This Gospel was recorded sometime before Matthew was written. An ancient tradition says that Mark was only the scribe for this book, and Peter dictated it to him while they were both in Rome.

Authorship. The early church fathers agreed that John Mark, Peter's assistant, wrote down this account of Jesus' life.

Contents. This Gospel was written for Gentile Christians. We can tell by the careful way Mark explains religious terms that would have been familiar to the Jews.

Matthew.   At least part of the Gospel of Matthew was probably first written in the

Syriac, Syro-Chaldaic, Aramaic, or popular Hebrew language.

Authorship. Christian tradition says that the apostle Matthew wrote this book, and we have no reason to doubt his authorship. Matthew's apparent use of Mark's Gospel as a source is no problem; although himself an eyewitness of Jesus, he would naturally have welcomed Mark's pioneer work of putting the story of Jesus' ministry into shape, and availed himself of it.

Contents. Matthew wrote this account of Jesus' life to convince the Jews that Jesus was their Messiah. However, we also see a strong appeal to new Christians in the book because he stresses Jesus' exhortations to his followers.

Peter, First. Peter probably wrote this letter at Rome as early as A.D. 64. He addresses it to "the strangers" in Asia Minor—people converted from Judaism during his several visits to that area.

Authorship. At several points, the letter identifies Peter as its author and most conservative scholars accept this. The different Greek styles of Peter's two letters have raised some doubts about their authorship. Some scholars argue that those who actually wrote down the words put the information in their own writing style. In 1 Peter 5:12 the name of the writer is said to be Silvanus.

Contents. The epistle contains miscellaneous exhortations and instructions to help new Christians persevere in the faith. Also, it shows how to apply the doctrines of Christianity in the duties of daily life.

Peter, Second. We suppose that Peter wrote this letter from Rome to the Christians of Asia Minor. He probably penned it a couple of years after his first letter, since we now see him addressing a new problem on the scene—false teachers.

Authorship. (See the section on 1 Peter.)

Contents. This letter is Peter's last testament of faith. It contains his final instructions and exhortations to his beloved Christian friends. He calls on them to press on in faith, holiness, and hope, and to grow in grace.

Philemon. Paul wrote this brief epistle at the same time he wrote to the Colossians and Ephesians. He sent the letter by Tychicus and Onesimus, along with the other letters. In it he recommends Onesimus to his Christian brother, Philemon. Onesimus had been Philemon's slave and had become a Christian through Paul since running away.

Authorship. Paul wrote this letter to an individual, yet the early church valued it for its pertinent words on Christian fellowship. Congregations shared the letter from an early date, receiving it as an inspired letter from Paul.

Contents. Although the letter to Philemon was supposed to be a personal communication on behalf of Onesimus, Paul's counsel on Christian fellowship makes it useful for all Christian readers.

Philippians. Paul established the first European congregation of the church in the Greek city of Philippi. He wrote this letter from prison to encourage his friends in the Philippian church.

Authorship. This letter names Paul as its author, and the early church fathers testify that this is true. The letter certainly reflects Paul's love for the Philippian church.

Contents. Paul expresses his thanks to the Philippians for a gift they had sent him in prison. In the process, he warns them to correct some problems arising in the church.

Revelation. *Authorship.* The early church fathers reported that the apostle John wrote this book, and we have no sufficient reason to doubt their word.

Contents. We cannot be certain precisely what is meant by all the mysterious pictures in this book, and we have to be cautious in our guesses as to what events John's symbols have in view. The book's powerful prophecy of the final happiness of the good and misery of the wicked makes it an unfailing source of warning and encouragement to Christians.

Romans. Paul wanted to contact the church at Rome for various reasons. Relatives and friends of his were connected with the church. It was an important church, because Rome was the capital of the empire.

Authorship. Paul wrote this letter on his third missionary journey, probably while he was staying in Corinth.

Contents. In this letter, Paul addresses himself to Jewish and Gentile converts. He sets forth a body of Christian doctrine so broadly conceived, so fully stated, that it would accomplish all that Paul could do if he were able to preach in Rome.

Thessalonians, First. Of Paul's many epistles that we now have, this one was probably written first.

Authorship. We have no doubt that Paul wrote both First and Second Thessalonians. In Acts, Luke tells us about the events during the time Paul wrote these letters (see Acts 18).

Contents. In this first letter, Paul reminisces about his earlier work in Thessalonica and encourages the Thessalonians to live holy lives. He also explains the destiny of the dead, giving us one of the most detailed discussions of the Christian hope in the NT.

Thessalonians, Second. Paul wrote his second epistle to the Thessalonians not long after the first.

Authorship. (See the section on 1 Thessalonians above.)

Contents. Paul explains that troublesome times will come before Christ returns to save his people. He urges Christians to guard against laziness or vain confidence, and instructs them in ways they can make the best use of the time that remains.

Timothy, First. We call the two letters to Timothy and the letter to Titus the Pastoral Epistles, because they are letters of advice for exercising the pastoral office. While the dates of all three letters are somewhat uncertain, they were probably written toward the close of Paul's life.

Authorship. The letter identifies Paul as its author, and despite the doubts of some, conservative scholarship holds to Pauline authorship.

Contents. Paul emphasizes the importance of the trust that God has placed in Timothy's hands. He advises the young pastor about the proper function of various classes of people in the Christian congregation.

Timothy, Second. Paul wrote this letter primarily to call Timothy back to Rome. But the letter also contains a kind of spiritual bequest in case Paul died before Timothy arrived. This bequest consists of general instructions for ministerial duty.

Authorship. (See the section on 1 Timothy.)

Contents. This letter follows much the same pattern as the first. But here Paul emphasizes the need to pass the gospel on to faithful Christians who would proclaim the good news to succeeding generations.

Titus. Paul wrote this letter to Titus, another young minister whom he had left as his deputy in Crete, and whom he wanted to instruct in pastoral work.

Authorship. Some scholars doubt that Paul wrote this letter because its language and style differ from his other letters. Also, the letter indicates that the churches had developed a fairly complex system of administration, and some scholars suppose that Paul died before that. But these arguments do not change the fact that the letter identifies Paul as its author.

Contents. Paul explains that sound doctrine should produce a godly life. So a minister like Titus needs to do more than teach the gospel; he must make sure that he and his congregation are putting it into practice.

People

Who's Who in the Bible

The Bible is people. Just the mentioning of their names fills our minds with their stories. When we say Shadrach and Meshach, most of us immediately add Abed-Nego, and we're already recalling the story of the three young men and the fiery furnace. What image does Noah bring? Mary Magdalene? Peter? Ruth?

Biblical literacy revolves around people—and here are the significant people whose names appear within the pages of the Holy Book.

Aaron. Meaning unknown. Brother of Moses and first high priest of the Hebrew nation. Very little is known about Aaron's early life, other than his marriage to Elisheba, daughter of Amminadab (Exod. 6:23).

Abed-Nego. "Servant of Nego." The Chaldean name given to Azariah in King Nebuchadnezzar's court when he was chosen as one of the king's servants (Dan. 1:7; 2:49). With Shadrach and Meshach, Abed-Nego was thrown into the fiery furnace for refusing to bow down and worship a golden image.

Abel. "Breath," "vapor." The second son of Adam and Eve (Gen. 4:2). His brother Cain, who was a farmer, brought an offering to God, and God "respected Abel and his offering, but He did not respect Cain and his offering" (Gen. 4:5). Envious of Abel, Cain killed his brother and was cursed by God.

Abigail. "Father of joy." Wife of Nabal the Carmelite and, after Nabal's death, of David (1 Sam. 25:3, 14–42; 2 Sam. 2:2; 1 Chron. 3:1).

Abihu. "He is my father." Second son of Aaron and Elisheba (Exod. 6:23). Abihu was destroyed, along with his brother Nadab, in the wilderness of Sinai for offering "profane fire" (Lev. 10:1) before the Lord.

Abimelech. "My father is king."
1. The king of Gerar in the time of Abraham (Gen. 20:1–18; 21:22–34).
2. The king of Gerar in the time of Isaac (Gen. 26:1–31).
3. The ruler of the city of Shechem during the period of the judges (Judg. 8:30—10:1; 2 Sam. 11:21).

Abimelech was killed in a battle at Thebez, a city northeast of Shechem, which he surrounded with his army. When Abimelech ventured too close to the city's walls, a woman dropped a millstone on his head, crushing his skull. Abimelech commanded his armorbearer to kill him so it could not be said that he died at the hands of a woman (Judg. 9:50–54; 2 Sam. 11:21).
4. A priest in the time of David (1 Chron. 18:16).
5. A Philistine king whom David met while fleeing from King Saul (Ps. 34, title).

Abishag. A young woman from Shunem employed by David's physicians to care for him in his old age (1 Kings 1:1–4, 15).

Abishai. The oldest son of Zeruiah, David's half sister, and brother of Joab and

Asahel (2 Sam. 2:18). He was one of David's mighty men (2 Sam. 23:18; 1 Chron. 11:20).

Abner. The commander in chief of the army of Saul, first king of Israel (1 Sam. 14:50–51; 17:55).

Abraham. "Father of a multitude"; originally *Abram*, "exalted father." The first great patriarch of ancient Israel and a primary model of faithfulness for Christianity. The accounts about Abraham occur in Genesis 11:26—25:11.

Absalom. The son of David who tried to take the kingship from his father by force.

He was David's third son, and his mother was Maacah, daughter of the king of Geshur. He was a potential heir to the throne.

Because his half brother Amnon raped his (Absalom's) sister Tamar, Absalom killed Amnon and fled.

Upon his return after three years, he schemed against his father and finally proclaimed himself king. David escaped, but Absalom was anointed king (2 Sam. 19:10). Later, Absalom's forces fought those of David, and Absalom was killed.

Achan. "Trouble." Son of Carmi of the tribe of Judah who unintentionally brought about the Israelites defeat at Ai (Josh. 7:1, 18–24).

During the destruction of Jericho, Achan took some goods—although before the battle God had forbidden it—and hid the things. Because of his sin Israel was cursed and defeated in the next battle.

Adam. The first man, created by God on the sixth day of creation and placed in the Garden of Eden. God said "Be fruitful and multiply" (Gen. 1:26–28). He and his wife disobeyed by eating from a forbidden tree and were cast out of the garden.

Adoni-Bezek. A king of Bezek, which was located in the territory allotted to Judah. After he was captured by the Hebrew army, his thumbs and big toes were cut off (Judg. 1:5–6). Adoni-Bezek reaped what he

had sown—he himself had previously cut off the thumbs and big toes of 70 kings (Judg. 1:7).

Adonijah. "Jehovah is my Lord." The fourth of the six sons born to David while he was at Hebron (2 Sam. 3:4). Adonijah's mother was Haggith. With the exception of Absalom, David apparently favored Adonijah over his other five sons. When David was old, Adonijah attempted to seize the throne, although he probably knew that his father intended Solomon to succeed him (1 Kings 1:13).

Adonijah foolishly made another attempt to become king—this time after David's death. He asked that the beautiful Abishag, who had cared for David in his old age, be given to him in marriage. According to the custom of the day, claiming a king's wife or concubine amounted to the same thing as claiming his throne. This time Solomon ordered that Adonijah be killed (1 Kings 2:13–25).

Adoni-Zedek. "My lord is justice." One of the five kings of the Amorites who fought against Joshua at Gibeon (Josh. 10:1–27). When Adoni-Zedek and his four allies took refuge in a cave near Makkedah, Joshua had them sealed inside while he pursued their armies. Later, the Israelites returned to the cave, removed the five kings, and put their "feet on their necks" (Josh. 10:24) as a sign of triumph. After they were killed, their bodies were hung on five trees for public display. Then they were taken down and cast into the cave, which was sealed with stones.

Agabus. "Desire." A Christian prophet of Jerusalem who went to Antioch of Syria while Paul and Barnabas were there, and "showed by the Spirit that there was going to be a great famine throughout all the world" (Acts 11:28). Later, when Paul and his companions were at Caesarea, Agabus the prophet gave a symbolic demonstration of Paul's impending arrest (Acts 21:10–11).

Agag. Meaning unknown. The name of two kings in the OT. The better known of the two was a king of the Amalekites whose army was defeated by the forces of Saul. Instead of slaying Agag as God told him to do, Saul spared his life. Because of his disobedience, Saul was rebuked by the prophet Samuel and rejected by the Lord. David was then anointed king in Saul's place (1 Sam. 15:1–33).

Agrippa I. Roman ruler of Galilee and eventual ruler of the territory previously governed by his grandfather, Herod the Great. Agrippa persecuted the Christians in Jerusalem (Acts 12:1–23) during his reign in Judea from A.D. 41 until his death in A.D. 44.

Agrippa II. Son of Herod Agrippa I and great-grandson of Herod the Great. He was appointed by the Roman Emperor Claudius as ruler of Abilene, part of Galilee, Iturea, and Trachonitis. Shortly before the apostle Paul was taken prisoner to Rome, he appeared before Herod Agrippa II (Acts 25:13—26:32).

Ahab. "Father is brother." The son of Omri, and an early king of Israel (1 Kings 16:30). Under the influence of Jezebel, his wife, Ahab gave Baal equal place with God. Ahab also built a temple to Baal in which he erected a "wooden image" of the Canaanite goddess Asherah (1 Kings 16:33). At Jezebel's urging, Ahab opposed the worship of Jehovah, destroyed his altars, and killed his prophets. He reigned over Israel in Samaria for 22 years [873–853 B.C.] (1 Kings 16:29).

Ahasuerus. "Mighty man." The name of two kings in the OT:

1. A king of Persia and the husband of the Jewess Esther. Scholars generally agree that Ahasuerus is the same person as Xerxes I (485–464 B.C.).

2. A king of the Medes and the father of Darius (Dan. 9:1).

Ahaz. "He has grasped." A son of Jotham and the eleventh king of Judah (2 Kings 15:38; 16:1–20). He was an ungodly king who promoted the worship of Molech, with its pagan rites of human sacrifice (2 Chron. 28:1–4).

Ahaziah. "Jehovah sustains." The name of two kings in the OT:

1. The son and successor of Ahab as king of Israel (1 Kings 22:40, 49, 51). Ahaziah reigned from 853 to 852 B.C. The son of Jezebel, Ahaziah followed policies that showed evidence of his mother's pagan influence.

2. The son and successor of Joram, and the nephew of Ahaziah No. 1 (2 Kings 8:24–26). Ahaziah is also called Jehoahaz (2 Chron. 21:17; 25:23) and Azariah (2 Chron. 22:6). He is the sixth king of Judah.

Ahimaaz. "Powerful brother." A son of Zadok the high priest. Ahimaaz kept David informed of Absalom's revolt after the king was forced to flee Jerusalem (2 Sam. 15:27).

Ahimelech. "My brother is king." The name of two men in the OT:

1. A high priest at Nob who helped David when he fled from King Saul (1 Sam. 22:11–18).

2. A Hittite who befriended David when he hid in the wilderness from King Saul (1 Sam. 26:6).

Ahithophel. "Brother of folly." One of David's counselors who assisted Absalom in his revolt.

Alexander. "Defender of men."

1. A son of Simon, a Cyrenian who carried the cross for Jesus (Mark 15:21), and a brother of Rufus.

2. A Jew who lived at Ephesus during the riot started by Demetrius and the silversmiths who opposed Paul's preaching (Acts 19:21–41).

Alphaeus. "Leader" or "chief." The name of two men in the NT:

1. The father of James the Less, the apostle and writer of the epistle that bears his name (Matt. 10:3; Acts 1:13).

2. The father of Levi (or Matthew), the apostle and writer of the first gospel (Mark 2:14).

Amalekites. An ancient wandering tribe descended from Esau's grandson Amalek (Gen. 36:12, 16; 1 Chron. 1:36). Throughout the OT the Amalekites were bitter foes of the Israelites.

Amasa. "Burden-bearer." David's nephew, the son of Jether and Abigail (1 Chron. 2:17). Amasa was also the cousin of Joab, a captain in David's army (2 Sam. 17:25). When Absalom rebelled against his father David, he appointed Amasa commander of the rebel army. After Absalom was defeated and killed by Joab (2 Sam. 18:14), David forgave Amasa and appointed him commander of the royal army in place of Joab (2 Sam. 19:13).

Amaziah. "Jehovah is mighty." The son of King Joash (2 Kings 14:1–20; 2 Chron. 25:1). Amaziah was 25 years old when he began his reign as the ninth king of Judah. He followed in the steps of his father, doing "what was right in the sight of the LORD" (2 Kings 14:3). However, he permitted the high places of false worship to stand (2 Kings 14:4).

Following a stunning victory over the Edomites, Amaziah embraced the gods of Edom (2 Chron. 25:14). The folly of his action was exposed by the ironic question of a godly priest, "Why have you sought the gods of the people, which could not rescue their own people from your hand?" (2 Chron. 25:15). Amaziah challenged the king of Israel, Joash, or Jehoash, to war and suffered defeat at Beth Shemesh (2 Chron. 25:20–24). Amaziah outlived Joash by 15 years. Learning of a conspiracy against him in Jerusalem, he fled to Lachish. However, his enemies followed and assassinated him there, ending a reign of 29 years (2 Chron. 25:25–28).

Ammon. "Kinsman" or "people." The son of Lot by his younger daughter. He is the same person as Ben-Ammi and is described as "the father [ancestor] of the people of Ammon" (Gen. 19:38).

Ammonites. A nomadic race descended from Ammon, Lot's son, who became enemies of the people of Israel during their later history. During the days of the Exodus, God instructed the Israelites not to associate with the Ammonites (Deut. 23:3).

In the days of the judges, Eglon, king of Moab, enlisted the aid of the Ammonites in taking Jericho from the Hebrew people (Judg. 3:13). The prophets of the OT often pronounced God's judgment against the Ammonites (Jer. 9:26; Amos 1:13–15).

Amnon. "Faithful." The oldest son of David, born at Hebron while that city was still capital of the nation of Israel (2 Sam. 3:2; 1 Chron. 3:1). Amnon raped Tamar, his half sister, incurring the wrath of Absalom, Tamar's full brother. After two years, Absalom had Amnon murdered.

Amon. "Faithful." A son of Manasseh and a king of Judah (2 Kings 21:18–26; 2 Chron. 33:20–25). Amon became king at the age of 22 and reigned for only two years. His reign was characterized by idolatry, and he turned his back on the God of Israel.

Amorites. "Westerners." The inhabitants of the land west of the Euphrates River, which included Palestine, Lebanon, and Syria. The Amorites were one of the major tribes, or national groups, living in Canaan. The OT frequently uses *Amorites* as a synonym for Canaanites in general. The book of Genesis cites Canaan as the ancestor of the Amorites (10:15–16).

Amos. "Burden-bearer." The famous OT shepherd-prophet who denounced the people of the northern kingdom of Israel for their idol worship, graft and corruption, and oppression of the poor. His prophecies and the few facts known about his life are found in the book of Amos.

Amram. "Exalted people." A son of Kohath and the father of Moses, Aaron, and Miriam by Jochebed, Kohath's sister (Exod.

6:18, 20). Amram was the father of the Amramites, the Levitical family that served in the wilderness tabernacle and perhaps in the temple in Jerusalem (Num. 3:27; 1 Chron. 26:23).

Anakim. "Giants." A race of fierce giants (Deut. 1:28; 2:10–11; Josh. 14:12, 15) descended from Anak. So gigantic were they that the spies sent out by Moses considered themselves as mere grasshoppers compared to them (Num. 13:33).

Ananias. "God is glorious."

1. A Christian in the early church at Jerusalem (Acts 5:1–11). With the knowledge of his wife, Sapphira, Ananias sold a piece of property and brought only a portion of the proceeds from its sale to Peter, claiming this represented the total amount of the sale. When Peter rebuked him for lying, Ananias fell down and died. Sapphira later repeated the same falsehood, and she also died.

2. A Christian disciple living in Damascus at the time of Paul's conversion (Acts 9:10–18; 22:12–16). In a vision the Lord told Ananias of Paul's conversion and directed him to go to Paul and welcome him into the church. Ananias went to Paul and laid his hands upon him, the blinded man's sight was restored, and he received the Holy Spirit.

3. The Jewish high priest before whom Paul appeared after his arrest in Jerusalem following his third missionary journey, about A.D. 58 (Acts 23:2).

Andrew. "Manly." Brother of Simon Peter and one of Jesus' first disciples. Both Andrew and Peter were fishermen (Matt. 4:18; Mark 1:16–18) from Bethsaida (John 1:44), on the northwest coast of the Sea of Galilee. They also had a house at Capernaum.

All lists of the disciples name Andrew among the first four (Matt. 10:2–4; Mark 3:16–19; Luke 6:14–16; Acts 1:13). According to tradition, Andrew was martyred at Patrae in Achaia by crucifixion on an X-shaped cross. According to Eusebius, An-

drew's field of labor was Scythia, the region north of the Black Sea. For this reason he became the patron saint of Scotland.

Anna. "Favor." A widow who was at the temple in Jerusalem when Mary and Joseph brought Jesus to be dedicated (Luke 2:27). Anna recognized Jesus as the long-awaited Messiah (Luke 2:37–38).

Annas. "Grace of Yahweh." One of the high priests at Jerusalem, along with Caiaphas, when John the Baptist began his ministry, about A.D. 26 (Luke 3:2). Quirinius, governor of Syria, appointed Annas as high priest about 6 or 7. Although Annas was deposed by Valerius Gratus, the procurator of Judea, about 15, he was still the most influential of the priests and continued to carry the title of high priest (Luke 3:2; Acts 4:6).

Antediluvians. Nonbiblical term for people who lived before the Flood. They possessed some skills that compare with modern technology. For example, Cain built cities (Gen. 4:17), Jubal was a musician (Gen. 4:21), and Tubal-Cain was an "instructor of every craftsman in bronze and iron" (Gen. 4:22). Such crafts imply the skills to mine, smelt, and purify brass and iron. That Noah could construct his huge ark is witness to the engineering skills and tools that were available. The antediluvians also lived long lives. Adam lived 930 years; Seth, 912 years; Mahalalel, 895 years; Jared, 962 years; Methuselah, 969 years; Lamech, 777 years (Gen. 5:5–31).

Antiochus. "Withstander." The name of 13 members of the Seleucid dynasty of Syria. The Seleucids governed Palestine from 280 B.C., following the division of Alexander the Great's empire, until the Roman commander Pompey made Syria a Roman province in 63 B.C.

Apollos. "Destroyer." A learned and eloquent Jew from Alexandria, Egypt, and an influential leader in the early church. Well-versed in the OT, Apollos was a disciple of John the Baptist. When Aquila and Priscilla, two other leaders in the early church, arrived in Ephesus, they instructed Apollos "more accurately" in the way of God (Acts 18:26).

Aquila. "Eagle." A Jewish Christian living in Corinth with his wife Priscilla at the time of Paul's arrival from Athens (Acts 18:2). Aquila was born in Pontus (located in Asia Minor) but lived in Rome until Emperor Claudius commanded that all Jews leave the city. He and Priscilla moved to Corinth, where Aquila took up his trade of tentmaking.

Arameans. An ancient desert people who flourished along with the Israelites during much of their history, sometimes as enemies and sometimes as friends.

The region of the Arameans, the land of Aram, extended from the Lebanon Mountains on the west eastward to the Euphrates River and from the Taurus Mountains on the north southward to Damascus.

Archelaus. "People's chief." The elder son of King Herod the Great by Malthace (Matt. 2:22).

Areopagite. A member of the court, or council, of the Areopagus (Acts 17:34).

Aristarchus. "The best ruler." A Macedonian of Thessalonica who traveled with Paul on his third missionary journey through Asia Minor (Acts 19:29; 20:4; 27:2).

Artaxerxes. "Possessor of an exalted kingdom." A king of Persia, Artaxerxes I Longimanus, at whose court Ezra and Nehemiah were officials (Ezra 7:1, 7, 11–12; Neh. 2:1; 5:14).

Asa. "Healer." The third king of Judah and an ancestor of Christ (1 Kings 15:8—16:29; Matt. 1:7–8).

Asahel. "God is doer." A son of Zeruiah, David's half sister, and the brother of Joab and Abishai. Asahel was "as fleet of foot as a wild gazelle" (2 Sam. 2:18), but his ability to run swiftly was his downfall. When Asa-hel pursued Abner in battle, Abner killed him with his spear (2 Sam. 2:23).

Asher. "Happy." The eighth son of Jacob, the second by Leah's maidservant, Zilpah (Gen. 30:12–13). On his deathbed Jacob blessed Asher: "Bread from Asher shall be rich, and he shall yield royal dainties" (Gen. 49:20).

Athaliah, "Jehovah is strong." The queen of Judah for six years (2 Kings 11:1–3). Athaliah was the daughter of King Ahab of Israel. Presumably, Jezebel was her mother.

Augustus. "Consecrated," "holy," "sacred." A title of honor bestowed on Octavian, the first Roman emperor. Luke refers to him as *Caesar Augustus* (Luke 2:1).

Avenger of blood. A relative responsible for avenging an injury to a member of his family or clan—especially murder (Deut. 19:6, 12; 2 Sam. 14:11).

Baasha. "Boldness." The third king of the northern kingdom of Israel, Baasha succeeded Nadab, the son of Jeroboam I by assassinating him. He was a wicked king (1 Kings 15:16—16:33).

Balaam. A magician or soothsayer (Josh. 13:22) who was summoned by the Moabite King Balak to curse the Israelites. Instead God put words of blessing in his mouth (Num. 22—24).

Barabbas. "Son of Abbas." A man chosen by the mob in Jerusalem to be released instead of Jesus. Barabbas had been imprisoned for insurrection and murder (Luke 23:19, 25; Mark 15:7).

Barak. "Lightning." Summoned by Deborah, a prophetess who judged Israel at that time, Barak and the women raised a militia of 10,000 men to fight Jabin, king of Canaan, who had oppressed Israel for 20 years.

Bar-Jesus. "Son of Jesus." A false prophet who opposed Barnabas and Paul at Paphos, a town on the island of Cyprus (Acts 13:4–12). He is also called *Elymas*, which means a "magician" or "sorcerer."

Bar-Jonah. "Son of Jonah." Family name of the apostle Peter (Matt. 16:17; John 1:42; 21:15–17).

Barnabas. "Son of encouragement." An apostle in the early church (Acts 4:36–37; 11:19–26) and Paul's companion on his first missionary journey (Acts 13:1—15:41). Barnabas was a Levite from the island of Cyprus, and his given name was Joseph, or Joses (Acts 4:36). When he became a Christian, he sold his land and gave the money to the church in Jerusalem.

Barsabas. "Son of the sabbath."

1. Joseph, surnamed Justus, one of the two disciples nominated to replace Judas Iscariot as an apostle (Acts 1:23; *Barsabbas*, NASB, NEB).

2. A disciple who, along with Silas, was sent as a delegate to accompany Paul and Barnabas to Antioch of Syria (Acts 15:22, 27).

Bartholomew. "Son of Tolmai." One of Jesus' 12 disciples (Matt. 10:3; Mark 3:18). He is probably the same as Nathanael.

Baruch. "Blessed." A scribe or secretary of Jeremiah the prophet (Jer. 32:12–16; 36:1–32).

Barzillai. A man who befriended David when he fled from Absalom (2 Sam. 17:27–29).

Bathsheba. Meaning unknown. Wife of Uriah the Hittite and later of King David (2 Sam. 11; 12:24). Bathsheba was the mother of Solomon.

Beloved disciple. A term used for one of the 12 disciples of Jesus (John 13:23; 19:26; 20:2; 21:7, 20). Many believe it refers to the apostle John.

Belshazzar. "Bel, protect the king." The last king of the Neo-Babylonian Empire (Dan. 5:1–30; 7:1; 8:1).

Belteshazzar. "May Bel protect his life." Hebrew form of the Babylonian name given to Daniel by the chief of Nebuchadnezzar's eunuchs (Dan. 1:7; 5:12).

Ben-Hadad. "Son of [the god] Hadad." The name (or possibly a title meaning "ruler") of two or three kings of Damascus in Syria during the ninth and eighth centuries B.C. Because more than one king was known as "the son of Hadad," it is not always possible to be certain which king is meant.

Benjamin. "Son of the right hand." Jacob's youngest son, born to his favored wife, Rachel (Gen. 35:18, 24). After giving birth to Benjamin, the dying Rachel named him Ben-Oni (Gen. 35:18), which means "son of my pain." But Jacob renamed him Benjamin.

Bernice. "Victorious." Oldest daughter of Herod Agrippa I, who ruled Palestine A.D. 41–44 (Acts 25:13).

Bildad. Meaning unknown. One of the friends or comforters of Job. In his three speeches to Job (Job 8:1–22; 18:1–21; 25:1–6), Bildad expressed the belief that all suffering is the direct result of one's sin. He had little patience with Job's questionings and searchings.

Boanerges. "Sons of thunder." The name Jesus gave the sons of Zebedee—James and John (Mark 3:17)—referring to their fervent spirit and boldness (Matt. 20:20–24; Mark 9:38; Luke 9:54).

Boaz. "Swiftness." A wealthy farmer of Bethlehem who befriended Ruth, a Moabite widow of one of his kinsmen. The story ends with Ruth becoming his wife. The child born to them was the grandfather of David and an ancestor of Jesus.

Caesar. The name taken by successors of Julius Caesar. Caesars mentioned in the NT are Augustus (Luke 2:1), Tiberius (Luke 3:1), Claudius (Acts 11:28), and Nero (the "Augustus Caesar" of Acts 25:24–25).

Caiaphas. Joseph Caiaphas was high priest at the trial of Jesus. Annas, whom he succeeded, was his father-in-law.

Cain. The first born son of Adam and Eve in the Genesis story. Cain killed his brother Abel, was cursed by God, and became a wanderer.

Caleb. "Dog." One of the 12 spies sent by Moses to investigate the land of Canaan (Num. 13:6, 30; 14:6, 24, 30, 38).

Canaan. "Low." A son of Ham and grandson of Noah (Gen. 10:6–19; 1 Chron. 1:8, 13). Possibly a reference to the inhabitants of Canaan.

Cephas. The Aramaic form of the name *Peter*, meaning "rock" or "stone." It was the name Jesus gave to Simon, his first disciple (John 1:42).

Candace. A dynastic title of Ethiopian queens (Acts 8:27).

Chaldeans. Ancient people who formed the dominant population in Babylonia, especially after the empire of Nebuchadnezzar II (king of Babylon from 605 to 562 B.C.).

Chedorlaomer. A king of Elam who warred against Sodom and Gomorrah (Gen. 14:1–24).

Claudius Caesar. Roman emperor who banished Jews from Rome (Acts 18:2).

Claudius Lysias. A Roman officer, chief captain in Jerusalem, who arrested Paul (Acts 23:26ff.).

Cleopas. One of the two disciples who met the risen Jesus on the road to Emmaus on the first day of the week after the Crucifixion.

Cornelius. A Roman centurion of the Italian Cohort stationed at Caesarea on the coast of Palestine. Cornelius was sympathetic to the Jewish faith. After having a vision, he sent for Peter who explained to him about faith in Jesus Christ. He believed and was baptized along with his household (Acts 10).

Crispus. A ruler of the synagogue at Corinth who was converted to Jesus Christ (Acts 18:7–8; 1 Cor. 1:14).

Cush. Eldest son of Ham (Gen. 10:6–8; 1 Chron. 1:8–10).

Cyrus. Cyrus the Great founded and ruled the Persian Empire (558–529 B.C.). He conquered Babylon in 539 B.C. and proclaimed that the exiled Jews could return to Jerusalem to rebuild their temple. Isaiah speaks of Cyrus as God's shepherd and as the Lord's anointed servant (Isa. 44:28; 45:1).

Dan. One of the sons of Jacob and father of one of the 12 tribes of Israel.

Daniel. "God is my judge." A prophet during the period of the captivity of the Jews in Babylon and Persia (Dan. 1:6—12:9; Ezek. 14:14; Matt. 24:15). Daniel also wrote the OT book that bears his name.

Daniel was probably still a teenager when he was taken from Jerusalem into captivity by the Babylonians in 605 B.C. That would make him over 80 when he received the vision of the prophecy of the 70 weeks (Dan. 9).

Darius. The sub-king of Cyrus who received the kingdom of Belshazzar (Dan. 5:30—6:28). He is also known as Darius the Mede.

Dathan. A chief of the tribe of Reuben who tried to overthrow Moses and Aaron (Num. 16; 26:9; Deut. 11:6).

David. Only one David appears in the Bible—and that name more than 1,000 times. The son of Jesse of Bethlehem, he is the ideal king of Hebrew history. Samuel anointed him to succeed Saul, Israel's first king. David was a shepherd, a skillful musician, and a valiant man of war. David killed the Philistine giant Goliath with a stone from his sling; he became Saul's armor bearer and captain over the men of war; he became the intimate friend of Saul's son Jonathan and married Saul's daughter Michal. Because of the jealousy of King Saul, David had to flee the court, and he became an outlaw leader. Following the deaths of Saul and Jonathan while battling the Philistines, the men of Judah made David their king.

Later all the tribes of Israel acknowledged him. David reigned for 33 years over all Israel. He broke the power of the Philistines, united the nation, brought the ark of the covenant to Jerusalem, and made that city the religious center of the nation.

Deborah. An Israelite prophetess and influential judge mentioned in the book of Judges. She summoned Barak to gather the tribes to attack Sisera by the Kishon River. After their overwhelming victory, Deborah sang a triumph song of praise to God (Judg. 4—5).

Delilah. A Philistine woman who enticed Samson to reveal the secret of his great strength and then betrayed him to the Philistine rulers (Judg. 16).

Demas. A fellow worker with Paul who eventually proved unreliable and left the apostle (2 Tim. 4:10).

Didymus. "Twin." A name given in John's gospel to Thomas, one of Jesus' 12 disciples (John 11:16; 20:24; 21:2).

Dinah. "One who judges." Jacob's daughter by Leah (Gen. 30:21; 34:1). When she was raped by Shechem, the son of Hamor the Hivite, her brothers were enraged. Later, when Shechem wanted Dinah for his wife, he asked his father to make arrangements for him to marry her. Dinah's brothers consented on the condition that all the Hivites be circumcised.

The Hivites agreed; after they had been circumcised, Simeon and Levi, two of Dinah's brothers, suddenly attacked the males while they were still in pain (Gen. 34:25) and killed all of them.

Dionysius. A member of the supreme court at Athens converted by Paul (Acts 17:34).

Doeg. "Anxious," "cared for." A servant of King Saul who executed the priests of Nob on Saul's orders (1 Sam. 21:7; 22:9–19).

Dorcas or Tabitha. Aramaic, "gazelle." A Christian widely known for her good works of charity, particularly for making clothes for widows. When she died the Christians called Peter, who prayed and raised her to life (Acts 9:36–42).

Drusilla. A Jewess, the daughter of Herod Agrippa I and wife of Felix. She and Felix heard a powerful message by Paul (Acts 24:24–25).

Ebed-Melech. The Ethiopian eunuch of the king's house in Jerusalem who rescued the prophet Jeremiah from the deep cistern where his enemies had thrown him. He sent down old rags and worn-out clothes for the prophet to put under his armpits before he drew Jeremiah up with ropes. The prophet promised Ebed-Melech that he would be saved when the city fell (Jer. 38—39).

Edom. "Red." The name given to Esau, the elder son of Isaac and twin of Jacob, because of his red skin (Gen. 25:30).

Eglon. "Young bull." A Moabite king who reigned during the period of the judges (Judg. 3:12–25). Allied with the Ammonites and the Amalekites, Eglon invaded the land of Israel. His army captured Jericho, and he exacted tribute from the Israelites.

Having endured 18 years of Eglon's rule, Ehud the Benjamite, a left-handed man, stabbed Eglon in the belly with a dagger. Because Eglon was so overweight, "even the hilt went in after the blade, and the fat closed over the blade, for he did not draw the dagger out of his belly" (Judg. 3:22).

Ehud. "Strong." A judge of Israel (Judg. 3:15—4:1). This left-handed man of the tribe of Benjamin assassinated Eglon, king of Moab, who was Israel's oppressor.

Eleazer.

1. Third son of Aaron and successor to the high priest's office (Exod. 6:23; Num. 3:32; 20:28).

2. A man set apart to keep the ark of the covenant (1 Sam. 7:1).

3. A priest who accompanied Ezra when he returned to Jerusalem (Ezra 8:33).

4. A priest who assisted at the dedication of the walls of Jerusalem (Neh. 12:42). Possibly the same as Eleazar No. 3.

Eli. A priest at Shiloh where the Israelites kept the ark of the covenant before the building of the temple. He was a judge—a weak one. It was to Eli that Hannah brought young Samuel to give him to God's service. When he was elderly and blind, he fell dead at the news that the Philistines had captured the ark.

Elias. The Greek form of Elijah, which is used in Mark 8:28 (KJV).

Eliezer.
1. Abraham's chief servant (Gen. 15:2).
2. The second son of Moses and Zipporah (Exod. 18:4).
3. A priest who assisted with bringing the ark of the covenant to the temple (1 Chron. 15:24).
4. A prince of Reuben in the time of David (1 Chron. 27:16).

Elihu. "He is my God." The youngest of Job's friends, Elihu spoke to Job after the three friends—Eliphaz, Bildad, and Zophar—failed to give convincing answers to Job's questions. Like Job's other friends, Elihu was probably from the Transjordan area southeast of Israel.

Elijah. The stormy prophet of Israel in the ninth century B.C. who rebuked King Ahab and his Phoenician wife, Jezebel. He challenged the people of the northern kingdom to reject Baal worship and return to the God of their fathers. Elijah appeared wearing clothes of haircloth with a girdle of leather around his waist, and he lived in caves.

Elijah's fame springs from his being God's spokesman at a time of national apostasy. Elijah never died but was taken out of this world in a whirlwind from heaven after he had chosen his disciple Elisha as his successor.

Malachi declared that Elijah would come again as God's messenger to announce the "great and dreadful day of the LORD" (4:5). Jesus said that John the Baptist fulfilled that prophecy. Moses and Elijah are the two men who appeared with Jesus at the Mount of Transfiguration (Mark 9:1ff.).

Elimelech. The husband of Naomi and father-in-law of Ruth. He died in Moab (Ruth 1:2–3; 2:1).

Eliphaz. The leader of Job's three friends who confronted him and accused him of secret sins (Job 2:11; 4:1; 15:1).

Elizabeth. "Oath of God." The wife of Zacharias and the mother of John the Baptist (Luke 1:5–57).

Elisha. The disciple of Elijah the prophet and his anointed successor in ninth-century B.C. Israel. Elisha took up the prophet's mantle and the work of Elijah when his master disappeared in a heavenly whirlwind.

The books of 1 and 2 Kings record eight miracles done by Elijah and 16 by Elisha, who received a double portion of the Spirit. He held his position for 55 years (1 Kings 19:6–17, 19–21; 2 Kings 2—6; 13).

Elymas. A false prophet who opposed Saul (Paul) and Barnabas at Paphos (Acts 13:8). He was also called *Bar-Jesus* (v. 6).

Enoch *or* Henoch.
1. The eldest son of Cain (Gen. 4:17–18).
2. Son of Jared and an ancestor of Jesus (Gen. 5:18–19, 21; Luke 3:37; Heb. 11:5).

Epaphras. A Christian worker with Paul who served as missionary to Colosse (Col. 1:7; 4:12; Philem. 23).

Ephraim. The second son of Joseph by Asenath. Although Ephraim was the younger son, he received the firstborn's blessing. He was an ancestor of one of the 12 tribes of Israel (Gen. 41:52; 46:20; 50:23).

Esarhaddon. The son of Sennacherib and a powerful king of Assyria (2 Kings 19:37; Ezra 4:2; Isa. 37:38).

Esau. "Hairy." Elder son of Isaac and the twin brother of Jacob. He is the progenitor of the tribe of Edom (Gen. 25:25). He sold his birthright to Jacob (Gen. 25:26–34; 27:36).

Eshcol. The brother of Mamre and Aner who helped Abraham defeat Chedorlaomer (Gen. 14:13–24).

Esther. "Star." The Persian name of Hadassah, who was chosen by Ahasuerus to be his queen. The book of Esther tells her story.

Eutychus. A young man at Troas whom Paul restored to life (Acts 20:6–12).

Eve. "Life," "life-giving." The first woman and Adam's wife (Gen. 3:20; 4:1).

Evil-Merodach. The king of Babylon who released Jehoiachin from imprisonment. He succeeded his father, Nebuchadnezzar (2 Kings 25:27–30; Jer. 52:31).

Ezekiel. "God strengthens." A prophet of a priestly family carried captive to Babylon in 597 B.C. when he was about 25 years old. His call to the prophetic ministry came five years later. Ezekiel prophesied to the captives who dwelt by the River Chebar at Tel Abib. He is the author of the book of Ezekiel.

Ezra. A priest and a scribe in exile in Babylonia during the reign of Artaxerxes, king of Persia. He returned to Jerusalem with a company of priests, Levites, singers, and temple servants, bringing offerings of silver and gold from the Persian king and the exiled Jews. This return took place when Nehemiah was governor in Jerusalem. The people gathered in front of the Water Gate to hear Ezra read from the book of the Law from early morning until midday. Ezra ordered the Jews who had foreign wives to put them and their children away from them. He also reinstituted the Feast of Booths.

Felix. The governor of Judea appointed by Emperor Claudius. Following a riot in Jerusalem, Paul was taken to Caesarea where he appeared for a trial before Felix. The governor listened to Paul's defense, eventually adjourned the hearing, and ordered Paul to be kept under open arrest. He allowed the apostle's friends to visit. When Felix was recalled two years later by Nero, Paul was still a prisoner (Acts 24).

Festus. Porcius Festus succeeded Felix as the governor of Judea appointed by Nero. He heard Paul's defense and wanted to send him to stand trial at Jerusalem. But Paul, fearing for his life if he was returned there, appealed to Caesar, and Festus sent him to Rome (Acts 25—26).

Gabriel. The name of an archangel who acts as the messenger of God. Gabriel appeared to Daniel (Dan. 8:16), Zacharias (Luke 1:19), and the Virgin Mary (Luke 1:26–38).

Gad.
1. Seventh son of Jacob and the father of one of the 12 tribes of Israel. He was the firstborn of Zilpah, Leah's maid. Moses praised Gad for his bravery and faithfulness to duty (Deut. 33:20–21).
2. A prophet described as David's "seer" (1 Chron. 21:9). Gad commanded David to buy the threshing floor of Ornan (or Araunah) the Jebusite that became the site of the temple. Gad also helped arrange the tabernacle music (2 Chron. 29:25).

Gaius. The name of four men in the Bible, and we know little of any of them:
1. A native of Macedonia and Paul's companion (Acts 19:29).
2. A man of Derbe who accompanied Paul to Asia (Acts 20:3).
3. A Corinthian baptized under Paul's ministry (1 Cor. 1:14).
4. A man to whom John addressed his third letter, and John commended his generosity (3 John 1, 5).

Galilean. A native or inhabitant of Galilee. After the captivity, Galilee was only sparsely resettled by Jews. It came to be known as "Galilee of the Gentiles." Jesus (Luke 23:6) and all of his disciples except Judas came from Galilee. The name *Galilean* was sometimes used as a term of contempt when applied to the disciples of Jesus (Luke 22:59).

Gallio. The Roman proconsul of Achaia before whom Paul appeared during his first visit to Corinth (Acts 18:12–17).

Gamaliel. A famous member of the Jewish Sanhedrin and a teacher of the Law. He taught Paul (Acts 22:3) and advised the Sanhedrin to treat the apostles with moderation.

Gedaliah. A person of high birth appointed governor of Judah by Nebuchadnezzar (2 Kings 25:22–25). Gedaliah governed Judah from Mizpah, where after only a very brief rule he was assassinated by Jewish nationalists.

Gehazi. A servant of Elisha (2 Kings 4:8–37). His true character came out in the story of Naaman the Syrian, whom Elisha cured of leprosy. Elisha refused any reward, but Gehazi ran after Naaman to claim something for himself, telling the man that Elisha wanted a talent of silver and two changes of clothing for the needy. Because of Gehazi's greed, lying, and misuse of the prophetic office, Elisha cursed him with the same disease from which Naaman had been cured (2 Kings 5).

Gentiles. A term used by Jewish people to refer to foreigners or any persons who were not Jewish.

Gershon. The oldest of the three sons of Levi; his brothers were Kohath and Merari (Gen. 46:11). He was also called *Gershom.* He was the founder of the Gershonites, one of the three main divisions of the Levitical priesthood.

Gibeonites. The Canaanite inhabitants of the city of Gibeon (2 Sam. 21:1–9). When the Gibeonites heard of Joshua's victories at Jericho and Ai, they pretended to be ambassadors from a far country to make a peace treaty with the invading Israelites (Josh. 9:4–5). When the deception was discovered, the Israelites permitted the Gibeonites to live; however, they were made slaves (Josh. 9:21).

Gideon. A military hero and spiritual leader who delivered Israel from the oppression of the Midianites. As the conquering warrior, Gideon was invited to become king (Judg. 8:22), but he declined.

Gog. "High," "mountain."
1. A descendant of Reuben (1 Chron. 5:4).
2. A prince of Rosh, Meshech, and Tubal (Ezek. 38:2; 39:1).
In Revelation 20:8 Gog appears to have become a nation as is Magog, indicating the name is to be understood symbolically.

Goliath. A Philistine giant whom David killed with a stone from his sling (1 Sam. 17:4–51). Goliath, who lived in Gath, was probably a descendant of a tribe of giants known as the *Anakim,* or descendants of Anak (Num. 13:33). Scholars figure that Goliath was about nine feet tall.

Gomer. A harlot who became the wife of Hosea the prophet (Hos. 1:1–11).

Habakkuk. "Embraced [by God]." A courageous prophet and author of the book of Habakkuk. The Scriptures say nothing of his ancestry or place of birth. A man of deep emotional strength, Habakkuk was both a poet and a prophet.

Hadassah. "Myrtle." Hebrew for *Esther* (Esther 2:7). Some scholars consider *hadassah* a title given to her—a title also used for the Babylonian fertility goddess Ishtar—when she became queen. *Esther* would then be the Hebrew form of Ishtar.

Hagar. The Egyptian maidservant of Sarah and wife-concubine of Abraham. Hagar bore Ishmael to Abraham when Sarah was childless. When Sarah's own son, Isaac, was born, Abraham cast out Hagar and Ishmael to wander in the desert. Muslims claim Ishmael as the ancestor of Arabs and Abraham as their father.

Haggai. "Festive." An OT prophet and author of the book of Haggai. He encouraged the captives who had returned to Jerusalem to complete the reconstruction of the temple.

Ham. "Hot." Youngest of Noah's three sons (Gen. 5:32). Ham, along with the rest of Noah's household, was saved from the great Flood by entering the ark (Gen. 7:7). After the waters went down and Noah's household left the ark, Ham found his father naked, drunk, and asleep in his tent. Ham told his brothers, Shem and Japheth, who covered their father without looking on his nakedness. Noah was furious because Ham had seen him naked, and he placed a curse on Ham and his descendants, saying that the offspring of Ham would serve the descendants of Shem and Japheth.

Haman. Meaning unknown. The evil, scheming prime minister of Ahasuerus (Xerxes I), king of Persia (485–464 B.C.). When Mordecai refused to bow to Haman, Haman plotted to destroy Mordecai and all of the Jews in the Persian Empire. Queen Esther intervened and saved her people. Haman was hanged on the very gallows he had constructed for Mordecai (Esther 3:1—9:25).

Hannah. The mother of Samuel. The childless woman prayed in deep distress and promised that if God would give her a son she would give him back to the Lord. She bore a son (and others). While Samuel was still a child, Hannah kept her promise and took him to the high priest (1 Sam. 1). Samuel served God faithfully all his life.

Hebrew people. An ethnic term designating the lineage of the Jewish people, the nation of Israel. The origin of the term *Hebrew* is a mystery to scholars.

Abraham, or Abram, was the first person in the Bible to be called a Hebrew (Gen. 14:13). Thereafter, his descendants through Isaac and Jacob were known as Hebrews (Gen. 40:15; 43:32).

Herod. Several Roman rulers in the Palestine region during Jesus' earthly min-

istry and the periods shortly before his birth and after his resurrection.

1. Herod the Great (37–4 B.C.). The title refers not so much to Herod's greatness as to the fact that he was the eldest son of Antipater. He did show some unusual abilities. He was a ruthless fighter, a cunning negotiator, and a subtle diplomat.

After Herod became governor of Galilee, he established himself in the entire region. For 33 years he remained a loyal friend and ally of Rome. Later, he was appointed as king of Judea where he was in direct control of the Jewish people.

Jesus was born in Bethlehem during the reign of Herod the Great.

2. Herod Archelaus (4 B.C.–A.D. 6). He inherited his father Herod's vices without his abilities. He was responsible for much bloodshed in Judea and Samaria. Jewish revolts, particularly those led by the Zealots, were brutally crushed. Antipas and Philip did not approve of Archelaus's methods, so they complained to Rome.

3. Herod Philip the Tetrarch (exact dates unknown). Philip, who inherited the northern part of his father Herod the Great's kingdom (Luke 3:1), must have been the best of Herod's surviving sons.

4. Herod Antipas (4 B.C.–A.D. 39). Another of Herod the Great's sons, he began as tetrarch over Galilee and Perea. He ruled over Judea during Jesus' life and ministry.

Antipas's contacts with Jesus occurred at the same time as the ministry of John the Baptist. The NT records that the relationship between Jesus and Antipas must have been strained. Jesus' popularity and teachings seem to have threatened Antipas because he wanted to kill Jesus (Luke 13:31).

The next encounter between Antipas and Jesus occurred at the trial of Jesus (Luke 23:6–12). Luke indicated that Herod could not find anything in the charges against Jesus that deserved death, so he sent Jesus back to Pilate for a final decision.

5. Herod Agrippa I (A.D. 41–44). Agrippa took over Antipas's territory after Antipas

fell from favor. Agrippa's power and responsibilities extended far beyond his ability.

Very little about Agrippa I is recorded in the Bible. From the comments in Acts 12:1–23, it appears that Agrippa wanted to win the favor of his Jewish subjects by opposing the Christians.

6. Herod Agrippa II (A.D. 50–100). Agrippa II was judged to be too young to assume leadership over all the territory of his father, Agrippa I. So Emperor Claudius appointed Cuspius Fadus procurator of the land. In A.D. 53, Agrippa II was appointed as the legitimate ruler over part of this territory.

The only reference to Agrippa II in the NT occurs in Acts 25:13—26:32, which deals with Paul's imprisonment in Caesarea.

Herodias. The first wife of Philip, son of Herod the Great, who then became the wife of his brother Herod Antipas. She was herself a granddaughter of Herod the Great so she married her uncles.

Hezekiah. Son of Ahaz and king of Judah 716–687 B.C. The Bible mentions Hezekiah as one who did what was right in God's sight. He destroyed pagan worship and brought about some reform.

Hiram. The name of a line of kings of Tyre, the Phoenician port of Palestine's northern coast. The Hiram at the time of David was an ally of Israel who supplied the nation with carpenters, masons, and raw materials in exchange for wheat and oil. During the reign of Solomon, he sent skilled workers and an architect to build the temple and the palace.

Hittites. Early inhabitants of Canaan whom the Israelites fought in their conquest of the Promised Land.

Hivites. A tribe in Canaan whom the Jewish people conquered in their battle for the Promised Land.

Hobab. The father-in-law or brother-in-law of Moses (Num. 10:29; Judg. 4:11). The phrase "father-in-law" in Judges 4:11 may possibly mean just that or perhaps Jethro was also named Hobab; but the identity is uncertain.

Horites. Inhabitants of Mount Seir before its conquest by the Edomites (Gen. 14:6; Deut. 2:12, 22) and the descendants of Seir the Horite (Gen. 36:20).

Hosea. A prophet in the northern kingdom of Israel in the second half of the eighth century B.C., during the reign of Jeroboam II. We know nothing of Hosea beyond the book that bears his name.

Huldah. A prophetess in the days of King Josiah (2 Kings 22:14; 2 Chron. 34:22).

Ichabod. A son of Phinehas and grandson of Eli, the high priest. Several national and family tragedies prompted the wife of Phinehas to name her child Ichabod, declaring, "The glory has departed from Israel!" (1 Sam. 4:21).

Irijah. A sentry who arrested Jeremiah during the siege of Jerusalem by the Babylonian army (Jer. 37:11–14).

Isaac. "To laugh." The only son of Abraham by his wife Sarah; father of Jacob and Esau. God promised to make Abraham's descendants a great nation that would become God's chosen people. But the promised son was a long time in coming. Isaac was born when Abraham was 100 and Sarah 90 (Gen. 17:17; 21:5). Both Abraham and Sarah laughed when they heard they would have a son in their old age (Gen. 17:17–19; 18:9–15).

Isaiah. Famous OT prophet who predicted the coming of the Messiah. He is the author of the book of Isaiah. He was probably born in Jerusalem of a family related to the royal house of Judah. He spent his early years as an official of King Uzziah of Judah (2 Chron. 26:22). When Uzziah died (740 B.C.) Isaiah received the prophetic call (Isa. 6).

Isaiah's ministry extended from about

Michelangelo's painting of the prophet Isaiah in the Sistine Chapel in Rome.

PHOTO BY HOWARD VOS

740 B.C. until at least 701 B.C. His 40 years of preaching doom and promise did not turn the nation of Judah from their move toward destruction.

According to a popular legend, Isaiah met his death by being sawed in half during the reign of the evil King Manasseh of Judah.

Iscariot. The surname of Judas, one of the 12 disciples of Jesus and the betrayer (John 6:71; 12:4; 13:2, 26).

Ishbosheth. A son of Saul whom Abner proclaimed king after Saul's death (2 Sam. 2:8–10), and 11 tribes followed him. The tribe of Judah proclaimed David their king. For years each side attempted unsuccessfully to gain control of the entire kingdom (2 Sam. 2:21—3:1).

Ishbosheth made a grave mistake in charging Abner with having sexual relations with Saul's concubine, Rizpah. In anger, Abner changed his allegiance to David (2 Sam. 3:6–21). When Joab murdered Abner in Hebron, Ishbosheth became discouraged. Then two captains of the guard assassinated Ishbosheth and carried his severed head to David. David put the assassins to death (2 Sam. 4:5–12).

Ishmael. The first son of Abraham by his wife's Egyptian maidservant, Hagar. Although God had promised Abraham an heir (Gen. 15:4), Abraham's wife, Sarah, had been unable to bear a child. When Abraham was 85, Sarah offered her maid to him to fulfill the promise (Gen. 16:1–2).

After Hagar learned she was pregnant, she began to despise Sarah. Sarah's harsh treatment in retaliation caused Hagar to flee into the wilderness. An angel of God met Hagar there and told her to return. The angel promised Hagar that her son, who would be named *Ishmael* (literally "God hears"), would have uncounted descendants. Hagar then returned and bore her son (Gen. 16:4–15).

After the birth of Isaac, Sarah demanded that Hagar and Ishmael be cast out. Reluctantly, Abraham agreed. Hagar and Ishmael wandered in the wilderness of Beersheba. When the water was gone and they were weary, the angel of God again contacted Hagar and showed her a well that saved their lives. Ishmael grew up in the wilderness of Paran and gained fame as an archer.

Ishmael was the father of the Ishmaelites, a nomadic nation that lived in northern Arabia. Modern-day Arabs claim descent from Ishmael.

Israel. The name given to Jacob after his struggle with God at Peniel (Gen. 32:28; 35:10). The name *Israel* has been variously interpreted as "prince with God" or "let God rule." The name was later applied to the descendants of Jacob. The 12 tribes were called Israelites, children of Israel, and the house of Israel.

Issachar. The ninth son of Jacob, the fifth by his wife Leah (Gen. 30:17–18; 35:23). He is the father of the tribe that bears his name.

Jacob. "Trickster" or "supplanter." Grandson of Abraham. Jacob was the child of Isaac and Rebekah, and the twin of Esau. He was a crafty, skillful, intelligent, and self-reliant man. Because he was his mother's favorite, she helped him to deceive his father, Isaac, and steal the birthright from Esau.

Jael. "Mountain goat." Woman who killed Sisera, Israel's mighty enemy, by driving a tent peg through his temple while he slept (Judg. 4:17–22). Sisera accepted Jael's invitation to seek refuge in her tent. She covered him with a mantle, gave him milk to quench his thirst, promised to stand guard against intruders, and then killed him as he slept.

Jairus. A ruler of a synagogue who begged Jesus to come and heal his only daughter. Jesus brought the child back to life.

Jambres. One of the Egyptian magicians who opposed Moses (Exod. 7:9–13; 2 Tim. 3:8).

James.
1. The Galilean fisherman, son of Zebedee, and brother of John. He was one of the 12 disciples of Jesus. His name always appears with John. Jesus called them *Boanerges* (sons of thunder). James, along with John and Peter, made up Jesus' inner circle.
2. James, the son of Alphaeus, another of Jesus' disciples. We know nothing else about him.
3. Jesus' brother, who is mentioned in the Gospels (Matt. 13:55). He appears in the Acts of the Apostles and in the writings of Paul as an important leader of the early church, possibly the pastor in Jerusalem.

Jannes. "He who seduces." According to Paul, Jannes and Jambres resisted Moses (2 Tim. 3:8). Although Jannes and Jambres are not named in the OT, they are common figures in late Jewish tradition. Legend has it that they were Egyptian magicians who opposed Moses' demand that the Israelites be freed. They sought to duplicate the miracles of Moses in an attempt to discredit him before Pharaoh (Exod. 7:11–12, 22).

Japheth. One of the three sons of Noah and brother of Shem and Ham (Gen. 5:32; 6:10; 1 Chron. 1:4), and presumed to be the youngest. Japheth and his wife were two of the eight people who entered the ark and were saved from the destructive waters of the Flood (Gen. 7:7; 1 Pet. 3:20).

Jebusites. Original inhabitants of Canaan from whom David captured the fortress of Jerusalem, which he made his capital city.

Jehoahaz. "God sustains."
1. The son and successor of Jehu and a king of Israel (2 Kings 10:35). His 17-year reign (815–798 B.C.) was a disaster for the nation of Israel. By not renouncing the idolatry of the golden calves set up by Jeroboam I at Dan and Bethel, Jehoahaz "did evil in the sight of the LORD." Hazael of Syria and his son Ben-Hadad severely punished Israel during Jehoahaz's reign. This drove Jehoahaz to the Lord, who heard his prayer and granted temporary deliverance from Syria (2 Kings 13:2–5). After the danger had passed, Jehoahaz abandoned his faith. Jehoahaz was succeeded by his son Joash (or Jehoash).
2. Son of King Josiah and ruler of Judah for three months (609 B.C.). At the battle of Megiddo, King Josiah was defeated and slain by the powerful Pharaoh Necho of Egypt. Jehoahaz was appointed king in his place at the age of 23, but he was deposed by Pharaoh Necho (2 Kings 23:30–34; 2 Chron. 36:1–4). Jehoahaz was also called *Shallum* (1 Chron. 3:15).
3. The youngest son of Jehoram, king of Judah (2 Chron. 21:17; 25:23). The reign of Jehoahaz lasted only one year (842 or 841 B.C.). Jehoahaz is usually called *Ahaziah* (2 Kings 8:24—14:13; 2 Chron. 22:1–11). An inscription of the Assyrian King Tiglath-Pileser III refers to Ahaz, king of Judah, as Jehoahaz, evidently his full name, but the Bible always used *Ahaz.*

Jehoash.   (See *Joash.*)

Jehoiachin.   The next to the last king of Judah and the son of Jehoiakim. He reigned only three months before being carried into Babylon. He fared well in exile, and he was freed from prison in the thirty-seventh year of his stay. He was then given a position of honor by being allowed to live at court and eat at the royal table the rest of his life.

Jehoiada.   The name of several OT men, the most famous being the chief priest of the temple during the reign of Queen Athaliah of Judah. Jehoiada plotted a conspiracy against the queen and saved the life of the infant Joash, son of Ahaziah. When the boy was seven, Jehoiada brought the child to the temple, proclaimed him king, and had Athaliah slain. He then worked to wipe out pagan Baal worship.

Jehoiakim.   A king of Judah, a son of Josiah, and the puppet king of Pharaoh Necho of Egypt. Jehoiakim levied heavy taxes on his people. He reigned during the time of Jeremiah who warned of attacks from Nebuchadnezzar of Babylon and rebuked Jehoiakim's pagan practices. When Nebuchadnezzar attacked and overthrew Jerusalem, Jehoiakim perished.

Jehoram.
   1. The son and successor of Jehoshaphat to the throne of Judah and an ancestor of Jesus (2 Kings 8:16–24; Matt. 1:8).
   2. A king of Israel, slain by Jehu (2 Kings 1:17; 3:1–6; 9:24).
   (See also *Joram.*)

Jehoshaphat.   One of the good kings of Judah. Jehoshaphat fortified the cities of Judah, gained immense wealth for his kingdom, and made an alliance with Ahab of the northern kingdom of Israel.

Jehu.   An army commander of Israel whom Elisha had anointed as king. He was to destroy the house of Ahab. He successfully routed the enemy, killed King Joram, the son of Ahab, and the Queen Mother Jezebel. Proverbially, people remember Jehu as a fast driver.

Jephthah.   An outstanding warrior in the book of Judges. His tribe called him to lead them against the Ammonites, and he did it successfully. However, Jephthah vowed that he would sacrifice whatever came out of the door of his house when he returned victoriously. Even though the person was his daughter, Jephthah kept his vow.

Jeremiah.   The book bearing this prophet's name gives us our information about him. He lived during the seventh century B.C. and came from Anathoth near Jerusalem. He began to prophesy during the reign of King Josiah.
   Bound up with the fate of Jerusalem, he is often thought of as the weeping prophet. He was beaten, thrown in a hole, and put into stocks. The leaders heard him speak but refused to obey his messages. He predicted the destruction of Judah and also pointed to the return of the people from captivity. When the Babylonians overthrew Jerusalem, Nebuchadnezzar gave special orders to care for the prophet. Tradition says he died in Babylon.

Jeroboam.
   1. Jeroboam I was the son of Nebat and the overseer of forced labor at the time of Solomon. The prophet Ahijah encouraged him to rebel against the king. Solomon tried to have him killed, but the man fled to Egypt, returning when Solomon's son, Rehoboam, ascended to the throne. He pleaded the discontent of the northern tribes, but the new king would not listen. Jeroboam left, taking 10 tribes with him to form the kingdom of Israel with its capital at Samaria. War waged continually between the two kingdoms. Jeroboam was a wicked king who instituted pagan worship.
   2. Jeroboam II was the son of King Jehoash (or Joash) of Israel. We know little of him except that "he did evil in the sight of the LORD" (2 Kings 14:24).

Jerubbaal. "Let Baal plead." A name given to Gideon, one of the judges of Israel, by his father after Gideon destroyed the altar of Baal at Ophrah (Judg. 6:32).

Jesse. The grandson of Ruth and Boaz, and the father of David. He was a farmer near Bethlehem.

Jesus. "God is salvation." The central figure of the NT. We know of his birth, almost nothing of his childhood, and only scattered pieces of information about his adult life, but much about his three years of public ministry.

Because of opposition to Jesus' teaching, Judas betrayed him to the Jewish leaders. After a hurried trial, the Romans crucified him at Calvary. Three days later he rose from the dead, instructed his disciples for fifty days, and then ascended to heaven. He promised to return.

Jews. This name at first referred to a descendant of the tribe of Judah. In the Bible, the word appears only after the fall of the northern kingdom to refer to those who went into Babylonian exile. Later the word came to mean the entire Hebrew race.

Jezebel. A princess of Tyre and wife of King Ahab of Israel. She worshiped Baal, brought in priests from Tyre, and persecuted the prophets of God.

When Jehu came into power, Jezebel was thrown from a high palace window and eaten by dogs (2 Kings 9:30–37).

Joab. Commander of David's army and a man of great influence over the king. He murdered Abner, a relative of King Saul and an honorable man. David rebuked Joab, yet feared his treachery. As David rose to greater power, Joab was at his side. Joab tried to heal the breach between David and Absalom. When the son conspired against his father, Joab sided with the king, eventually killing Absalom in battle. Later Solomon ordered Joab to be killed because of a request made by David before his death.

Joanna. "Yahweh has been gracious." Wife of Chuza, the steward of Herod Antipas. Along with Mary Magdalene, Susanna, and others, she provided for the material needs of Jesus and his disciples from her own funds (Luke 8:3). Joanna was one of the women who witnessed the empty tomb and announced Christ's resurrection to the unbelieving apostles (Luke 24:1–10).

Joash. A king of Judah; the son of Ahaziah. When Joash's grandmother, Queen Athaliah, destroyed the family of her son Ahaziah, the priest Jehoiada hid the boy in the temple. When the boy was seven, Jehoiada proclaimed him king, and the loyal guard killed Athaliah. Joash (under the priest's influence) immediately brought reform to the land. He repaired the temple with freewill offerings and routed out pagan ways. In the end, however, Joash paid tribute to the king of Syria to save Jerusalem from attack. In an uprising, Joash's own men killed him.

Job. A man of faith in the OT noted for his faith in God, in spite of his suffering and moments of frustration and doubt. The book of Job is a long poetic narrative consisting mostly of Job's discussions about God and his ways with his three "comforters"—Eliphaz, Bildad, and Zophar.

Jochebed. "Yahweh is honor." Mother of Aaron, Moses, and Miriam. To protect Moses from Pharaoh's command that every male Hebrew child be killed, she placed him in an ark of bulrushes on the river. After Pharaoh's daughter discovered the baby, Jochebed became his nurse.

Joel. A prophet who wrote a book bearing his name. He was the son of Pethuel, and we know nothing else about him.

John. The son of Zebedee, the brother of James, and a Galilean fisherman, he was one of the first disciples Jesus chose. The two brothers' names nearly always appear together, and Jesus called them *Boanerges* (sons of thunder). John, along with Peter and James, formed Jesus' inner circle among the 12 disciples.

John the Baptist. The son of Elizabeth and Zacharias; also Jesus' cousin. He behaved much like Elijah the prophet, and Jesus compared him to Elijah, calling him the fulfillment of the promise of Elijah to come again. John preached a baptism of repentance for the forgiveness of sin. He baptized Jesus. Later he was beheaded as a favor to the daughter of Herodias.

Jonah. "A dove." The prophet who was swallowed by a great fish before he obeyed God's command to preach repentance to the Assyrian city of Nineveh.

He is likely the same prophet who predicted the remarkable expansion of Israel's territory during the reign of Jeroboam II (ca. 793–753 B.C.; 2 Kings 14:25).

Joram. "Yahweh is exalted."

1. A son of Toi, king of Hamath (2 Sam. 8:9–10). When David defeated the army of Hadadezer, Toi sent Joram—with gifts of gold, silver, and bronze—to greet and bless David.

2. The son and successor of Jehoshaphat, king of Judah (1 Chron. 3:10–11), also called *Jehoram* (1 Kings 22:50). Joram reigned eight years (2 Kings 8:17) while his brother-in-law, also named Joram, reigned in Israel. His marriage to Athaliah, Ahab's daughter, marked the beginning of Joram's downfall. Athaliah influenced Joram to promote Baal worship in Judah.

3. A king of Israel, slain by Jehu (2 Kings 8:16–29; 9:14–29). The son of Ahab and Jezebel, Joram succeeded his brother, Ahaziah, as king. He was also called *Jehoram* (2 Kings 1:17). His 12-year reign was characterized as an evil time, although he did restrain Baal worship (2 Kings 3:1–3).

4. A Levite who worked as a treasury official in the tabernacle in David's time (1 Chron. 26:25).

Joseph.

1. The son of Jacob and Rachel, and his father's favorite. Joseph is the central figure in Genesis 37–50. His jealous brothers sold him into slavery; he was taken to Egypt where he eventually triumphed as Pharaoh's right-hand man. Later he reunited with his family and arranged for all of them to live in Egypt during the years of famine. The book of Genesis ends with the death of Joseph.

2. The husband of Mary who was Jesus' mother. Matthew described him as a son of David. He was a carpenter in Nazareth who went with his wife to Bethlehem for a census count. Jesus was born in Bethlehem during their visit to the city.

3. The brother of Jesus.

4. A wealthy man from Arimathea. He was a member of the Jewish council and a secret disciple of Jesus. After the Crucifixion, he asked Pilate for the body of Jesus, wrapped him in a shroud, and laid him in the new tomb Joseph had arranged for his own burial.

5. Called Barsabas. He had accompanied Jesus during his ministry and witnessed the Resurrection. He and Matthias became candidates to take the place of Judas Iscariot among the Twelve. The lot fell on Matthias.

Josephus, Flavius. A Jewish historian and a general of the Galilean Jewish army in the war against Rome (A.D. 66–70). Josephus does not appear in the Bible, but his historical works provide important background information for the NT and the late intertestamental period. He supplied details about agriculture, geography, politics, religion, social traditions and practices, and insights into outstanding personalities such as Herod, Pilate, and Felix. He also referred to John the Baptist; James, the Lord's brother; and Jesus.

Joshua. "God is Savior" (the Greek form is *Jesus*). The son of Nun, servant and successor to Moses. He led the armies in their fight against the Amalekites. The book bearing his name tells of Joshua's divine commission to lead the people into the Promised Land. Under his leadership the 12 tribes divided the land and conquered their enemies.

Josiah. King of Judah who came to the throne at the age of eight when his father, Amon, was murdered. The OT says he was one who did right in the eyes of the Lord. He instituted religious reforms in the land, calling the people back to the worship of the one true God.

Jotham.

1. The youngest son of Gideon. Jotham stood atop Mount Gerizim and told the men of Shechem the parable of the trees that wanted to anoint a king over them and they chose the bramble (Judg. 9:7–15).

2. A godly king of Judah; the son of Uzziah (Azariah).

Judas.

1. The son or brother of James, and both men were among Jesus' 12 disciples (Luke 6:16; John 14:22).

2. A brother of Jesus (Matt. 13:55).

3. Iscariot who betrayed Jesus. He went to the chief priests and betrayed Jesus for 30 pieces of silver. He led a crowd to Gethsemane, kissed Jesus as a sign, and delivered his master into their hands. After Jesus' condemnation, Judas repented and brought back the money, throwing the silver down in the temple. He hanged himself.

4. A Galilean rebel mentioned by the Pharisee Gamaliel (Acts 5:37).

Jude. The opening words of the letter of Jude in the NT say that he was a brother of James, which would also make him a brother of Jesus. We know nothing else about him (Jude 1).

Kenites. The name of a wandering tribe of desert people who were enemies of the Israelites (Num. 24:21–22).

Keturah. A wife of Abraham (Gen. 25:1–4). She is also called Abraham's concubine (1 Chron. 1:32–33).

Korah. The Levite who, along with Dathan, Abiram, and On of the tribe of Reuben, led a revolt against the leadership of Moses and Aaron (Num. 16:1–49).

Laban. A descendant of Nahor, a wealthy shepherd of Mesopotamia, and the brother of Rebekah (who married Isaac). When Jacob had to flee from the anger of his twin brother Esau, Rebekah sent him to seek refuge with Laban. Jacob married Laban's two daughters, Leah and Rachel.

Lazarus.

1. Brother of Mary and Martha of Bethany. When he died, Jesus raised him back to life after four days (John 11).

2. The name of the beggar in Jesus' parable about a rich man and a poor man (Luke 16:19–31).

Leah. The elder daughter of Laban. Through her father's trickery, she became Jacob's first wife.

Lemuel. "Devoted to God." An unknown king who wrote Proverbs 31. Some of the early Jewish rabbis identified Lemuel with Solomon. Other scholars believe he was Hezekiah, or even an anonymous Arabian prince.

Levi.

1. The third son of Jacob and Leah; the father of the priestly tribe of Levites.

2. The son of Alphaeus, a tax collector whom Jesus called as one of the Twelve. The name *Levi* does not appear in the list of the 12 disciples, but most scholars think this is another name for Matthew (Matt. 9:9; Mark 2:14; Luke 5:27).

Levites. The tribe descended from Levi, the son of Jacob. God set them apart to minister as priests.

Lo-Ammi. "Not my people." Symbolic name given by the prophet Hosea to his second son (Hos. 1:9–10; 2:23) to symbolize God's rejection of the nation of Israel (Rom. 9:25–26).

Lois. "Desirable." Mother of Eunice and grandmother of Timothy. A devout Jewess, Lois instructed her daughter and her grandson in the OT. Paul gave both Lois and Eunice credit for Timothy's spiritual instruction (2 Tim. 3:15).

Lot. Nephew of Abraham. Lot traveled with Abraham from Ur to Haran and then to Canaan. Both men grew rich with their flocks and soon had to split up because the land was insufficient for both of them. Abraham offered Lot his choice, and the younger man chose the well-watered Jordan Valley. He became an inhabitant of Sodom and later had to flee the fire and brimstone that fell on Sodom and Gomorrah.

Luke. Called the beloved physician, he traveled with the apostle Paul. He wrote the third gospel and the Acts of the Apostles. Luke was likely a Gentile. The "we" sections of the Acts indicate that he traveled with the Apostle during his second and third missionary journeys and his trip to Rome.

Lydia. Meaning unknown. Prosperous businesswoman of the city of Thyatira who became a convert to Christianity after hearing the apostle Paul speak (Acts 16:12–15, 40). Thyatira was noted for its beautifully dyed purple cloth. Already a worshiper of God, the usual designation for a proselyte to Judaism, Lydia believed the gospel when Paul preached in Philippi. She became the first convert to Christianity in Europe.

Magdalene. "Of Magdala." Designation given to a woman named Mary, one of Jesus' most prominent Galilean female disciples, to distinguish her from the other Marys.

Mary Magdalene has been described as a woman of bad character and loose morals. We have no evidence that she was the same person as the sinful woman whom Simon the Pharisee treated with contempt (Luke 7:36–50), although such an identification is possible. Mary Magdalene was among the women who followed Jesus from Galilee (Matt. 27:55) and was one of the women at Calvary when Jesus died on the cross (John 19:25). She was at Joseph's tomb when the body of Jesus was wrapped in a fine linen cloth and a large stone was rolled against the door of the tomb (Matt. 27:61; Mark 15:47). She was the first witness of Jesus' resurrection (Matt. 28:1–8; Mark 16:1–10; Luke 24:10; John 20:1ff.).

Magog. "Land of Gog." Descendants of Magog (Ezek. 38:2), possibly a people who lived in northern Asia and Europe. The Jewish historian Josephus identified these people as the Scythians, known for their destructive warfare. *Magog* may be a comprehensive term that means "northern barbarians." The people of Magog were skilled horsemen (Ezek. 38:15) and experts in the use of the bow and arrow (Ezek. 39:3, 9).

Malachi. "My messenger." OT prophet and author of the prophetic book bearing his name. Nothing is known about Malachi's life except the few facts that may be inferred from his prophecies. He apparently prophesied after the captivity when Nehemiah was leading the people to rebuild Jerusalem's wall and recommit themselves to following God's Law.

Malchus. "Ruler." Servant of the high priest who was present at the arrest of Jesus in the Garden of Gethsemane. Simon Peter stuck Malchus with a sword and cut off his ear (John 18:10).

Manasseh.

1. The elder son of Joseph and ancestor of one of the tribes of Israel (Gen. 41:50–51). His mother was Asenath, daughter of an Egyptian priest.

2. Son of King Hezekiah and called the most wicked king of Judah (2 Kings 21). He had a long reign and was the vassal of the Assyrians. He built pagan shrines and encouraged Baal worship.

Manoah. Samson's father, to whose wife an angel of the Lord appeared to tell her she would bear a son to deliver Israel from the Philistines.

Mark, John. Associate of Peter and Paul, and the probable author of the second gospel. Mark's lasting impact on the Christian church comes from his writing rather than his life. He was the first to develop the literary form known as the gospel.

John Mark appears in the NT only in association with more prominent personalities and events. His mother, Mary, was an influential woman of Jerusalem who possessed a large house with servants. The early church gathered in this house during Peter's imprisonment under Herod Agrippa I (Acts 12:12).

Martha. The sister of Mary and Lazarus of Bethany. A close friend of Jesus, Martha welcomed him to their home but complained that Mary would not help to prepare the meal. Jesus rebuked Martha for her fretting. On another occasion, Martha appealed to Jesus for help when her brother Lazarus died, and Jesus raised him from the dead.

Mary.

1. The mother of Jesus. The Gospels contain little information about her. She was a virgin, a kinswoman of Elizabeth, who was the mother of John the Baptist.

2. Mary of Magdala, which was a town on the Sea of Galilee. Known also as Mary Magdalene, she was one of the women who followed Jesus from Galilee; she witnessed the Crucifixion and went to the empty tomb on Sunday morning to anoint Jesus' body. The longer ending of Mark's gospel tells us that the risen Jesus appeared first to Mary Magdalene, out of whom he had cast seven demons.

3. Mary, the mother of James (the younger) and Joses, the disciples of Jesus (Matt. 27:56). She was one of the women who followed Jesus and ministered to him; she was present at the Crucifixion and at the tomb early on the morning of the Resurrection.

4. Mary, the wife of Clopas. We know only that she was among the women at the cross when Jesus died (Matt. 27:61). She may be the same person as Mary number 3.

5. Mary of Bethany, the sister of Martha and Lazarus. She sat at Jesus' feet and listened while her sister fretted. Jesus praised Mary for her devotion to him. Jesus raised her brother Lazarus from the dead. Mary anointed Jesus with ointment and wiped his feet with her hair.

6. Mary, the mother of John Mark, in whose house in Jerusalem Christians met for prayer.

Matthew. "Gift of Yahweh." One of the 12 apostles of Jesus (Matt. 9:9). Matthew's name appears seventh in two lists of apostles (Mark 3:17–18; Luke 6:14–16), and eighth in two others (Matt. 10:3; Acts 1:13).

Before he followed Jesus, Matthew was a tax collector who worked in or around Capernaum under the authority of Herod Antipas.

Matthias. The man chosen by lot to replace Judas Iscariot as an apostle. We know nothing else about him.

Melchizedek. The priest-king of Salem met Abraham and blessed the patriarch. His name came to symbolize the ideal priesthood (Gen. 14:18; Ps. 110:4; Heb. 7:1–21).

Mephibosheth. Meaning unknown. Son of Jonathan and grandson of Saul. Mephibosheth was also called *Merib-Baal* (1 Chron. 8:34; 9:40), probably his original name, meaning a "striver against Baal." His name was changed because the word *Baal* was associated with idol worship.

Merab. "Increase." Older daughter of King Saul (1 Sam. 14:49). When Goliath defied and taunted the Israelites, Saul promised that the man who killed him would be given great riches as well as Merab in marriage (1 Sam. 17:25). When David killed the giant, however, Saul changed his mind and gave his younger daughter, Michal, to David for his wife.

Merodach-Baladan. "The god Marduk has given an heir." King of Babylon (721–710 and 704 B.C.) who sent emissaries to

King Hezekiah of Judah (Isa. 39:1; *Berodach-Baladan,* 2 Kings 20:12).

Meshach. Meaning unknown. Chaldean name given to Mishael, one of Daniel's companions (Dan. 1:7). Along with Shadrach and Abed-Nego, Meshach would not bow down and worship the pagan image of gold set up by Nebuchadnezzar. They were cast into the fiery furnace, but were preserved from harm by the power of God.

Methuselah. "Man of the javelin." Son of Enoch and the grandfather of Noah. At the age of 187, Methuselah became the father of Lamech. After the birth of Lamech, Methuselah lived 782 years; he died at the age of 969. He lived longer than any other human. He was an ancestor of Jesus (Luke 3:37).

Micah. "Who is like Yahweh." OT prophet and author of the book of Micah. A younger contemporary of Isaiah, Micah was from Moresheth Gath (Mic. 1:1, 14), a town in southern Judah. His prophecy reveals his country origins; he uses many images from country life (Mic. 7:1).

Michal. "Who is like God." Younger daughter of King Saul who became David's wife. After David had become a hero by slaying Goliath, Saul offered to give Michal to David as his wife. But instead of a dowry, Saul requested of David 100 foreskins of the Philistines (1 Sam. 18:25), hoping that David would be killed by the Philistines. Instead, David killed 200 Philistines and brought their foreskins to the king. Then Saul presented Michal to David to become his wife (1 Sam. 18:27–28).

After their marriage, the ark of the covenant was brought from the house of Obed-Edom to the city of David. Caught up in an inspired frenzy of religious fervor, David was filled with joy at being able to bring the ark back to Jerusalem: "Then David danced before the LORD with all his might; and David was wearing [only] a linen ephod [loincloth, kilt, or apron]" (2 Sam. 6:14). Whatever garment David was wearing, it

apparently scandalized Michal, who accused him of lewd behavior—"uncovering himself today in the eyes of the maids" (2 Sam. 6:20).

Michal's sarcasm was met by David's response that he was dancing joyfully for God. Michal died barren (2 Sam. 6:21–23)—one of the most terrible fates that could befall a Hebrew woman.

Midianites. Nomadic clan that frequently raided Canaan in the early days of Israelite settlement. When Moses fled from Pharaoh's wrath, he found shelter with a priest of Midian and married the man's daughter. Israel frequently fought against the Midianites.

Mighty men. Brave warriors who risked their lives for David both before and after he became king of Israel. The names of David's mighty men are given in 2 Samuel 23:8–39 and 1 Chronicles 11:10–47. The phrase "mighty men of valor" is also used of the courageous warriors who served under Joshua (Josh. 1:14; 6:2).

Miriam. The sister of Moses and Aaron. She watched over the infant Moses when he was laid in the reed basket, and she summoned a nurse from among the Hebrew women when Pharoah's daughter found him. In the wilderness she led in dance and song among the Hebrews (Exod. 15:20–21).

Mixed multitude. People of different races and nationalities (Exod. 12:38; Num. 11:4; Neh. 13:3; Jer. 25:20, 24). Each of the uses of this term, however, has a slightly different interpretation. In Exodus 12:38, the Hebrew expression means a group of people of different races. In Numbers 11:4, it refers to rabble. These people may not be the same as those in Exodus 12:38. In Nehemiah 13:3, which refers to the situation after the return from captivity, the term refers to the foreigners with whom Israel had made marriages and the children of those marriages (Ezra 9:1–2; Neh. 13:23–24). In Jeremiah 25:20, 24, the reference is to foreign nations that, like Judah, were to be conquered by Nebuchadnezzar, king of Babylon.

Mordecai. "Related to Marduk." Hero of the book of Esther. Mordecai may have been born in Babylonia during the years of the captivity of the Jewish people. He was a resident of Susa (Shushan), the Persian capital during the reign of Ahasuerus (Xerxes I), the king of Persia (485–464 B.C.).

Mordecai took his orphaned cousin, Hadassah (Esther), into his home as her adoptive father (Esther 2:7). When two of the king's eunuchs conspired to assassinate King Ahasuerus, Mordecai discovered the plot, exposed it, and saved the king's life (Esther 2:21–22). Mordecai's good deed was recorded in the royal chronicles of Persia (Esther 2:23).

Mordecai showed his loyalty to God by refusing to bow to Haman, an official second to the king (Esther 3:2, 5). According to the Greek historian Herodotus, when the Persians bowed before their king, they paid homage to him as a god.

Haman was succeeded by Mordecai who used his new position to encourage his people to defend themselves against the massacre planned by Haman. Persian officials also assisted in protecting the Jews, an event celebrated by the annual Feast of Purim (Esther 9:26–32).

Moses. "Drawn out." Hebrew prophet who delivered the Israelites from Egyptian slavery and who was their leader and lawgiver during their years of wandering in the wilderness. He was the son of Amram and Jochebed (Exod. 6:18, 20; Num. 26:58–59) of the tribe of Levi and the brother of Aaron and Miriam.

Moses built a nation from a race of oppressed and weary slaves. In the covenant ceremony at Mount Sinai, where the Ten Commandments were given, he founded the religious community known as Israel. As the interpreter of these covenant laws, he was the organizer of the community's religious and civil traditions. His story is told in the books of Exodus, Leviticus, Numbers, and Deuteronomy.

In the NT, Moses appears at the Mount of Transfiguration along with Jesus and Elijah, the inference being that Jesus was superior to the two great prophets of the OT.

Naaman. A leper and commander of the Syrian army at the time of Elisha. He went to Elisha for healing, and after reluctantly bathing in the Jordan, he was healed.

Nabal. "Empty person." Wealthy sheepmaster and a member of the house of Caleb (1 Sam. 25:2–39). Nabal pastured his sheep near the town of Carmel on the edge of the wilderness. Nabal was "harsh and evil in his doings," and no one could reason with him (1 Sam. 25:3, 10–11).

Naboth. A man of Jezreel who had a fertile vineyard near the palace of King Ahab. Ahab offered to buy the land, and when Naboth refused, Queen Jezebel plotted his death and the Crown confiscated the land.

Nadab. "Liberal" or "willing." Son of Aaron and Elisheba (Exod. 6:23). Nadab is always mentioned in association with Abihu, Aaron's second son. Nadab accompanied Moses, Aaron, Abihu, and 70 elders of Israel when they ascended Mount Sinai to be near the Lord (Exod. 24:1–10). Along with his father and brothers—Abihu, Eleazar, and Ithamar—he was consecrated a priest to minister at the tabernacle (Exod. 28:1).

Later, Nadab and Abihu were guilty of offering "profane fire before the LORD" in the wilderness of Sinai; and both died when "fire went out from the LORD and devoured them" (Lev. 10:1–2).

Nahum. "Compassionate." A prophet and author of the book of Nahum whose prophecy pronounced God's judgment against the mighty nation of Assyria.

Very little is known about Nahum. His hometown, Elkosh (Nah. 1:1), has not been located. He likely lived shortly before 612 B.C., the year when Assyria's capital city, Nineveh, was destroyed by the Babylonians. Nahum announced that God's judgment would soon fall upon this pagan city.

Naomi. The mother-in-law of Ruth. When Naomi was widowed and her two sons died in the land of Moab, she returned to Bethlehem. Ruth, her loving Moabite daughter-in-law, went with her.

Naphtali. Second son of Jacob and Bilhah (Rachel's maid) and the father of the tribe of Naphtali.

Nathan. A prophet in the time of King David. After David sent Uriah the soldier to his certain death in battle so that David could take his widow Bathsheba, the prophet confronted the king with his crime. When David was dying, Nathan conspired with Bathsheba to make sure that the king's choice, Solomon, ascended to the throne.

Nathanael. (See *Bartholomew*.)

Nazarene. A native of Nazareth. The term more often refers to Jesus.

Nazirite. "Separated," "consecrated." Those who took a vow to separate from certain worldly things and to consecrate themselves to God (Num. 6:1–8). Among the Hebrew people any male could take this vow.

Nebuchadnezzar *or* Nebuchadrezzar. Emperor of Babylon and the most famous ruler of his day. He defeated Judah, the southern kingdom, making it a vassal state with a puppet king on the throne. Because of the continued rebellion of the Jews, he attacked Jerusalem three times, looted the treasures, and carried many of the leading people into exile. In 586 B.C. the city fell and Nebuchadnezzar's army broke down the walls, burned the gates, and destroyed everything.

Nebuzaradan. "Nebo has given offspring." Captain of Nebuchadnezzar's bodyguard who played an important part in the destruction of Jerusalem in 586 B.C.

Necho *or* Nechoh. Pharaoh of Egypt who killed King Josiah of Judah at Megiddo. Later Nebuchadnezzar of Babylon defeated Necho.

Nehemiah. Cupbearer to Artaxerxes I, king of Persia. After learning that the walls of Jerusalem were broken down and its gates destroyed, he asked the king for permission to rebuild. Artaxerxes appointed him governor, supplied him with building materials, and sent him to Jerusalem. The book of Nehemiah tells of the organizing and rebuilding and of local opposition to the work.

Nephilim. A word of uncertain meaning (Gen. 6:4; Num. 13:33, NIV, NEB, NASB, RSV), translated as *giants* by the KJV and NKJV. Some scholars believe the Nephilim were descended from famous rulers, outstanding leaders, and mighty warriors who lived before the Flood. These men, so the theory goes, gathered great harems and were guilty of the sin of polygamy. The Nephilim were the product of these marriages.

Nero. Fifth emperor of Rome (A.D. 54–68), known for his persecution of Christians. Nero began his reign with the promise that he would return to the policies of the great Emperor Augustus. For several years he succeeded. Under his reign Rome extended its borders, solidified certain territories of the Roman Empire, and incorporated some good qualities of Greek culture.

Many of Nero's cruelties are linked to the time of the great fire in Rome (A.D. 64). Nero was accused of setting fire to the city in order to divert attention from himself, but this has never been proven with certainty.

Nero became a kind of apocalyptic figure, a person associated with the end times. Rumors persisted that he was alive and would someday return and reign again. Some interpreters of the Bible believe that Nero is the beast from the sea whose "deadly wound was healed" (Rev. 13:3, 12).

Nicodemus. "Conqueror of the people." Pharisee and a member of the Sanhedrin who became a disciple of Jesus (John 3:1, 4, 9; 7:50). He was described by Jesus as "the teacher of Israel" (John 3:10), implying he was well trained in OT law and tradition.

Nicodemus was a wealthy, educated, and powerful man—well respected by his people and a descendant of the patriarch Abraham.

Nimrod. The great-grandson of Noah and a legendary hunter.

Noah. The hero of the Flood story (Gen. 6–9). God told Noah to build an ark of gopherwood to save his family and every kind of animal, bird, and creeping thing. God destroyed everything living on the earth except those in the ark.

Obadiah. "Servant of Yahweh." One of the minor prophets (i.e., he wrote one of the shorter books of the OT), Obadiah's message was directed against Edom.

Omri. Commander of the Israelite army at a time of civil war (ninth century B.C.). He seized power and made himself the king of Israel.

Onesimus. "Useful." Slave of Philemon and an inhabitant of Colosse (Col. 4:9; Philem. 10). When Onesimus fled from his master to Rome, he met the apostle Paul. Paul witnessed to him, and Onesimus became a Christian. In his letter to Philemon, Paul spoke of Onesimus as "my own heart" (Philem. 12), indicating that Onesimus had become like a son to him.

Some scholars believe this Onesimus is Onesimus the bishop, praised in a letter to the second-century church at Ephesus from Ignatius of Antioch.

Othniel. "Powerful one." First judge of Israel (Judg. 1:13; 3:9, 11). Othniel was a son of Kenaz and probably was a nephew of Caleb. When the Israelites forgot the Lord and served the pagan gods of Canaan, the king of Mesopotamia oppressed them for eight years. When the Israelites repented of their evil and cried out to the Lord for deliverance, Othniel was raised up by the Lord to deliver his people.

Pagan. Follower of a false god or a heathen religion. After the return from the captivity, Ezra and Nehemiah carried on a vigorous campaign against the practice of marriage between Israelites and the pagan women of the land (Ezra 10:2, 10–18, 44; Neh. 13:26–27, 30).

Patriarch. Title applied to the forefathers of the Hebrews, especially to Abraham, Isaac, and Jacob and his 12 sons from whom the tribes of Israel descended.

Paul. Most influential interpreter of Christ's message and teaching; an early Christian missionary who wrote letters to several churches.

The relevance of Paul's teaching for human life today may be brought out in a summary of four of his leading themes.

1. True religion is not a matter of rules and regulations. God does not deal with men and women like an accountant, but he accepts them freely when they respond to his love. He implants the Spirit of Christ in their hearts.

2. In Christ men and women have come of age. God liberates his people then to live as responsible sons and daughters.

3. People and human needs matter more than things, principles, and causes. The highest of principles and the best of causes exist for the sake of people. Personal liberty itself is abused when it is exercised against the well-being of others.

4. Discrimination on the ground of race, religion, class, or sex is an offense against God and humanity alike.

Pekah. "God has opened the eyes." Son of Remaliah and a king of Israel (2 Kings 15:25–31; 2 Chron. 28:5–15). Pekah became king after he assassinated King Pekahiah. Pekah continued to lead Israel in the idolatrous ways of Jeroboam (2 Kings 15:28).

Pekahiah. "Yahweh has opened." Son of Menahem and the seventeenth king of Israel (2 Kings 15:22–26). Pekahiah assumed the throne after his father's death. He was an evil king who continued the idolatrous worship first introduced by King Jeroboam. After reigning only two years (about 742–

740 B.C.), Pekahiah was killed by his military captain, Pekah, and 50 Gileadites. Then Pekah became king.

Peter. Greek *petra*, Aramaic *Cephas*, "rock" or "stone." The name Jesus gave to Simon Bar-Jonah, the Galilean fisherman and the first of the 12 disciples. Peter's mother-in-law is mentioned in an early miracle story.

The obvious leader of the Twelve, Peter was also part of Jesus' inner circle that included James and John.

Pharaoh. The title of the king of Egypt. From the time of Abraham onward, the OT mentions one Pharaoh after another. The last Pharaoh mentioned in the OT was Necho who killed King Josiah of Judah (2 Kings 23).

Pharisees. "Separated." The Pharisees were a Jewish sect noted for their strict keeping of the written and oral law and their formal show of piety. They were especially hostile to Jesus.

Philemon. A Christian to whom Paul wrote a personal letter that bears his name. Because there was a church in his house and he owned slaves, we assume he was wealthy.

Philetus. "Beloved." False teacher of the early church. Along with Hymenaeus, Philetus was condemned by the apostle Paul because he claimed the resurrection was already past (2 Tim. 2:17–18).

Philip.

1. One of the 12 apostles.
2. One of the seven men chosen to care for the widows in the church in Jerusalem. When persecution broken out after the death of Stephen, Philip went to Samaria where he preached and saw many healings. He encountered the Ethiopian eunuch and interpreted the writings of Isaiah for him. The man believed. Paul and his companions stayed with Philip at Caesarea on their journey to Jerusalem.

Philistines. A non-Semitic seagoing people who had five walled cities and controlled the trade routes and most of the central highlands of Canaan. Superior to the Israelites because of their weapons and chariots and tools of iron, they remained a constant enemy until David defeated them. After that they never rose to power again.

Phinehas. "The Nubian."

1. A son of Eleazar and grandson of Aaron (Exod. 6:25). During the wilderness wandering, Phinehas killed Zimri, a man of Israel, and Cozbi, a Midianite woman whom Zimri had brought into the camp (Num. 25). This action ended a plague by which God had judged Israel for allowing Midianite women to corrupt Israel with idolatry and harlotry. For such zeal Phinehas and his descendants were promised a permanent priesthood (Num. 25:11–13).

Phinehas became the third high priest of Israel, serving for 19 years. His descendants held the high priesthood until the Romans destroyed the temple in A.D. 70, except for a short period when the house of Eli served as high priests.

2. The younger of the two sons of Eli the priest (1 Sam. 1:3). Phinehas and his brother, Hophni, were priests who disgraced their priestly office by graft, irreverence, and immorality (1 Sam. 2:12–17, 22–25). The Lord told Eli his two sons would die (1 Sam. 2:34). They were killed in a battle with the Philistines. When Phinehas's wife heard the news, she went into premature labor and died in childbirth. The child was named Ichabod, which means "the glory has departed from Israel" (1 Sam. 4:22). Because of the evil actions of Phinehas and Hophni, the high priesthood later passed from Eli's family.

Pilate. Pontius Pilate was a Roman procurator, or governor, of Judea. He lived at Caesarea but came to Jerusalem during the important festivals such as the Passover. Pilate sentenced Jesus to be crucified.

Potiphar. "Dedicated to Ra." Egyptian to whom the Ishmaelites sold Joseph when he was brought to Egypt as a slave. Potiphar was a high officer of Pharaoh and a wealthy man (Gen. 37:36). In time, he put Joseph in charge of his household. Potiphar's wife became attracted to Joseph and attempted to seduce him. When he rejected her advances, she falsely accused him and had him imprisoned (Gen. 39:6–20).

Priscilla *or* Prisca. Wife of Aquila and a leader in the early church. She and her husband were tentmakers. Paul, who followed the same trade, worked with them in Corinth.

Proselyte. A person who converted from one religion to another. In the Bible it means a Gentile who turned to the Jewish faith. The male convert received circumcision and pledged to keep the Mosaic law. In the NT Gentiles came to the Jewish faith, and some Jewish proselytes became Christians.

Ptolemy. General title similar to *Pharaoh* of the 14 Greek kings who ruled Egypt between the conquest of Alexander the Great (323 B.C.) and the Roman conquest of Egypt in 30 B.C.

Publicans. "Tax gatherers." Outcast Jews who worked for the hated Romans and unjustly demanded more than their due in taxes. In the Bible they are mentioned along with sinners and harlots. Jesus befriended publicans and was criticized for visiting and eating with them. Levi (Matthew), a tax collector, became one of Jesus' 12 disciples. Jesus visited the home of Zacchaeus, a chief publican. In one of his parables, Jesus spoke compassionately of the publican (see Luke 18:10–13).

Quirinius. Meaning unknown. Roman governor of Syria at the time of Jesus' birth (Luke 2:1–5; *Cyrenius*, KJV). Quirinius is mentioned in connection with a census taken for tax purposes. The census was not a local affair; the Roman Emperor Augustus (ruled 31 B.C.–A.D. 14) had decreed that all the world (the Roman Empire) should be taxed or counted. For this purpose, Joseph and Mary made their pilgrimage to Bethlehem. While they were there, Jesus was born.

Rabbi. "Teacher" or "master." Title of respect among Jews. The rabbis taught the meaning of the law. So far as we know, Jesus was not a trained scholar of the law, but his teaching was so powerful that many called him by that respectful title.

Rabshakeh. Meaning unknown. Title of an Assyrian military official under Sennacherib, king of Assyria (2 Kings 18:17–37; Isa. 36:2–22). The Rabshakeh accompanied the Rabsaris and the Tartan from Lachish to Jerusalem. They presented Sennacherib's demand that Hezekiah, king of Judah, surrender the city of Jerusalem.

Rachel. The younger daughter of Laban and the wife whom Jacob loved. She became Jacob's wife after he had served Laban seven years for her and another seven for her older sister Leah. Rachel was the mother of Joseph and died after giving birth to Benjamin.

Rahab. A harlot in Jericho who hid two spies sent by Joshua. She secretly let them down by a rope through a window in her house that was built into the city wall. When Jericho fell to the Israelites, they spared only Rahab and those in her house. She later married a man from Judah and became an ancestor of Jesus.

Rebekah. The sister of Laban, wife of Isaac, and mother of the twins Esau and Jacob.

Rechabites. This clan aided Jehu in his revolt against King Ahab and the destruction of the worshipers of Baal. The Rechabites were noted for not drinking wine and not cultivating the land. They lived in tents long after other tribes settled in towns.

Rehoboam. Son and successor of King Solomon. Immediately after Rehoboam's ascension to the throne, a man named Jeroboam led a revolt against the heavy taxation. Ten tribes rallied behind Jeroboam, and they formed the northern kingdom, Israel. Only the tribes of Judah and Benjamin remained loyal. Rehoboam was a bad king who encouraged pagan customs.

Reuben. Oldest son of Jacob and Leah and the head of one of the 12 tribes of Israel.

Rezin. "Dominion." Last king of Syria. Rezin was killed by Tiglath-Pileser III, king of Assyria, in 732 B.C. Rezin allied himself with Pekah, king of Israel, to try to take away Judah's throne from Ahaz and the line of David (2 Kings 15:37; 16:5–9). Together Rezin and Pekah besieged Jerusalem, but they were unable to capture Ahaz's stronghold. The prophet Isaiah counseled Ahaz not to fear Rezin and Pekah (Isa. 7:4).

Rhoda. "Roses." A girl in the Jerusalem house of Mary, mother of John Mark. When Peter miraculously escaped from prison and went to Mary's house, a startled Rhoda answered the door.

Rizpah. "A glowing stone." Daughter of Aiah who became a concubine of King Saul (2 Sam. 3:7; 21:8, 10–11). She bore two sons, Armoni and Mephibosheth. After Saul's death, Abner had sexual relations with Rizpah (2 Sam. 3:7)—an act that amounted to claiming the throne of Israel. Ishbosheth (also called *Esh-Baal*), one of Saul's sons by another woman, accused Abner of immorality and, by implication, of disloyalty to Ishbosheth's authority.

Ruler of the synagogue. Jewish elder who was responsible for the day-to-day administration of the worship and work of the synagogue.

Ruth. "Friendship." Mother of Obed and great-grandmother of David. A woman of the country of Moab, Ruth married Mahlon, one of the two sons of Elimelech and Naomi. With his wife and sons, Elimelech had migrated to Moab to escape a famine in the land of Israel. When Elimelech and both of his sons died, they left three widows: Naomi, Ruth, and Orpah (Ruth's sister-in-law). When Naomi decided to re-turn home to Bethlehem, Ruth chose to accompany her, saying, "Wherever you go, I will go" (Ruth 1:16).

Salome.
1. Tradition says this is the name of the daughter of Herodias who danced for the birthday party of Herod Antipas, although her name does not appear in the Bible. She so pleased the ruler that he promised to give her whatever she wanted. Prompted by her mother, she asked for the head of John the Baptist. Herod had John killed.
2. A woman who witnessed the Crucifixion. She also went to the tomb early on the first day of the week, the day of the Resurrection.

Samson. An Israelite judge noted for his conflicts with the Philistines. He was a man of enormous physical strength but weak moral character. Delilah learned the secret of his strength and told the Philistines. They cut off his hair, gouged out his eyes, and bound him, making him grind at the prison mill. Samson's hair—the secret of his strength—grew again. The Philistines sent for the blind Samson so they could laugh at him. He felt for the pillars on which the house rested, pulled them down, and died with his enemies.

Samuel. The last of the judges and the first of the prophets. He appeared at a critical time for the tribes of Israel, after being dedicated to God for as long as he lived by his mother, Hannah.

His call came when Samuel served as a boy during the time of Eli the high priest. "The word of the LORD was rare in those days; there was no widespread revelation" (1 Sam. 3:1), which meant that God was not speaking through prophets and seers.

Sanballat. "The god sin has given life." Leading opponent of the Jews after their return from the Babylonian captivity. He tried to hinder Nehemiah in his work of rebuilding the walls of Jerusalem (Neh. 2:10, 19–20; 4:1–23; 6:1–19; 13:28).

Sapphira. "Beautiful." A dishonest woman who, along with her husband, Ananias, gave an offering, yet held back part of the money from the early Christian community after saying it was the total amount. Because of their hypocrisy and deceit, both husband and wife were struck dead by God (Acts 5:1–11).

Sarah or Sarai. The wife of Abraham. When old and childless, Sarah bore her promised son, Isaac.

Saul. "Asked."

1. First king of Israel (1 Sam. 9:2—31:12; 1 Chron. 5:10—26:28). Saul lived in turbulent times. For many years, Israel had consisted of a loose organization of tribes without a single leader. In times of crisis, leaders had arisen, but there was no formal government. Samuel was Saul's predecessor as Israel's leader—a religious leader, not a king. Threatened by the warring Philistines, the people of Israel pressured Samuel to anoint a king to lead them in their battles against the enemy. Samuel gave in to their demands and anointed Saul as the first king of the nation of Israel.

2. The original name of Paul, a persecutor of the church, who became an apostle of Christ and a missionary of the early church (Acts 7:58—9:26; 11:25—13:9).

Scribes. Originally writers attached to the temple and court who kept the official records and copied documents. After the exile, a priest and scribe known as Ezra taught sacred Scriptures to the returning Jews.

In NT times the scribes were sometimes Pharisees and sometimes priests. They constantly opposed Jesus.

Scythians. Barbaric race that lived in Scythia, an ancient region of southeastern Europe and southwestern Asia (now the Soviet Union). In biblical times, the Scythians were a tribe of nomadic raiders notorious for their cruelty and barbarism.

Sennacherib. Son of King Sargon II of Assyria. He attacked Judah at the time of King Hezekiah and made the Jews pay tribute. The Bible tells of a plague breaking out

that killed 185,000 Assyrian troops. The Assyrians withdrew. Sennacherib returned home to Nineveh, and his two sons assassinated him.

Seth. "Appoint," "compensate." Third son of Adam and Eve, born after Cain murdered Abel (Gen. 4:25–26; 5:3–8). The father of Enosh (or Enos) and an ancestor of Jesus Christ (Luke 3:38), Seth died at the age of 912.

Seventy, The. In Luke's gospel, a group of 70 disciples sent by Jesus to heal the sick and preach the good news of the kingdom of God (Luke 10:1–17).

Shadrach. "Command of Aku." One of the three faithful Hebrews who refused to worship the golden image that King Nebuchadnezzar of Babylon set up (Dan. 3:1). Along with his two companions, Meshach and Abed-Nego, Shadrach was thrown into the fiery furnace (Dan. 3:11–27), but they were protected by God.

Shalmaneser. "Shulmanu is chief." Shalmaneser V (727–722 B.C.), the son and successor of Tiglath-Pileser III (745–727 B.C.; called *Pul* in 2 Kings 15:19).

Shalmaneser received tribute from Hoshea, king of Israel. Then he imprisoned Hoshea and besieged Samaria for three years (2 Kings 17:3–6; 18:9–10), until it fell in 723/22 B.C. This marked the end of the northern kingdom of Israel.

Shamgar. Meaning unknown. Third judge of Israel (Judg. 3:31) who delivered the nation from the oppression of the Philistines. Using an ox goad as a weapon, Shamgar killed 600 Philistines who terrorized the main travel routes.

Shem. "Renown." Oldest son of Noah and brother of Ham and Japheth. Shem was born when Noah was 500 years old (Gen. 5:32). He was one of eight people who entered Noah's ark and survived the Flood (Gen. 7:7, 13).

Shimei. "Yahweh is fame." A man from the tribe of Benjamin (2 Sam. 16:5–13;

1 Kings 2:8). Shimei grew bitter because David had taken the throne from the family of Saul. He insulted the king who was fleeing from his own son, Absalom. When David regained the throne, Shimei repented. David accepted Shimei's apology and promised to let him live. After David's death, his son and successor, Solomon, would not allow Shimei to go beyond Jerusalem's walls. Shimei obeyed Solomon's command at first, but eventually he left the city and was promptly executed at Solomon's command.

Shishak. Libyan war chieftain who became Pharaoh of Egypt (reigned from about 940 B.C. to about 915 B.C.). Shishak is known for his expedition against the southern kingdom of Judah after the united kingdom split into two nations following Solomon's death about 920 B.C.

Shulamite. Young woman mentioned in Song of Solomon 6:13 (*Shulammite*, RSV, NIV, NEB, NASB). Many scholars interpret Shulamite as Shunammite—a woman from the city of Shunem (1 Sam. 28:4). Others believe this woman was Abishag, the lovely young Shunammite brought to David in his old age (1 Kings 1:1–4, 15) and who later may have become part of Solomon's harem.

Sihon. Meaning unknown. King of the Amorites defeated by the Israelites during their journey toward the land of Canaan. Moses asked Sihon to let the Israelites pass peacefully through his kingdom, located east of the Jordan River. Sihon refused and later attacked the Israelites at Jahaz. In the battle, Sihon and his army were killed (Num. 21:21–32), and his territory was given to the tribes of Gad and Reuben and half of the tribe of Manasseh (Num. 32:33). Sihon's defeat is mentioned often in the OT (Deut. 1:4; Josh. 2:10; Ps. 135:11; Jer. 48:45).

Silas *or* Silvanus. A prophet and companion to Paul. The church leaders sent him with Paul and Barnabas to Antioch to announce the decision of the new relationship between Jew and Gentile believers (Acts 15). Paul later chose Silas to accompany him on his second missionary journey through Syria and Cilicia. He was imprisoned with Paul at Philippi.

Simeon. "God hears."

1. The second son of Jacob and Leah (Gen. 29:33). Simeon's descendants became one of the 12 tribes of Israel. He and his brother Levi tricked the Hivites and massacred all the males because one of them had raped Dinah, their sister (Gen. 34:2, 25, 30). Simeon was the brother whom Joseph kept as security when he allowed his brothers to leave Egypt and return to their father Jacob in the land of Canaan (Gen. 42:24).

2. A devout Jew who blessed the infant Jesus in the temple (Luke 2:25, 34). The Holy Spirit had promised Simeon that he would not die until he had seen the long-awaited Messiah. Simeon recognized the child as the Messiah when Mary and Joseph brought him to the temple to present him to the Lord.

Simon. "God has heard."

1. Simon Peter, the Galilean fisherman who became an apostle of Christ (Matt. 4:18; 10:2). Simon was the son of Jonah (Matt. 16:17; John 21:15) and a brother of the apostle Andrew (John 1:40). (See *Peter*.)

2. Another of the Twelve, called *the Canaanite* to distinguish him from Simon Peter. The name may also indicate that he was a member of a fanatical Jewish sect, the Zealots (Matt. 10:4; Mark 3:18; Luke 6:15; Acts 1:13). Members of this group were opponents of Roman rule in Israel. As a Zealot, Simon would have hated any foreign domination or interference.

3. One of Jesus' brothers (Matt. 13:55).

4. A former leper in whose house Mary, the sister of Lazarus, anointed Jesus' feet with a precious ointment (Matt. 26:6–13; Mark 14:3–9; John 12:1–8). Both Martha and Lazarus were present when this happened, and Martha also took an active part in serving the dinner. This has led to specu-

lation that Simon was a member of the family or was a close friend.

5. A man of Cyrene who was forced to carry Jesus' cross (Matt. 27:32; Mark 15:21; Luke 23:26). Simon was the father of Alexander and Rufus, men who were known to the early Christians in Rome (Rom. 16:13).

6. A Pharisee in whose house Jesus ate (Luke 7:36–50). On that occasion a woman who was a sinner anointed Jesus' feet. Simon felt that Jesus should not have allowed her to come near him. But Jesus explained that sinners like her were the very ones who needed forgiveness.

7. The father of Judas Iscariot (John 13:2). Both father and son are called *Iscariot*. The RSV has "Judas the son of Simon Iscariot" (John 6:71; 13:26).

8. A sorcerer known as Simon Magus, or Simon the magician, who tried to buy spiritual powers from the apostle Peter (Acts 8:9–24).

Simon's feats were so impressive that the people of Samaria declared, "This man is the great power of God" (Acts 8:10), and followed him. But when Philip the evangelist preached, the Samaritans believed and were baptized. Simon also believed and was baptized.

9. A tanner of Joppa and friend of the apostle Peter (Acts 9:43; 10:6, 17, 32).

Sisera. Canaanite commander whose army oppressed the Israelites in the days of the judges. The prophetess Deborah and Barak fought with Sisera's army in the valley of the Kishon River. Rain fell and bogged down Sisera's chariots, and the Israelites won the battle. Sisera escaped on foot and sought refuge in the tent of Jael. She killed him with a tent peg through his head while he lay asleep.

Solomon. "Peaceable." Also called **Jedidiah.** "Beloved of Yahweh." He was the son of David and Bathsheba and a famous king of Israel.

By intermarriage with many foreign women, Solomon courted spiritual declension and gross idolatry. Of the numerous deities to whom his foreign wives turned

his heart, the best known in the ancient world was Ashtoreth, a goddess of fertility (1 Kings 11:5, 33). Solomon died disillusioned, and the breakup of the monarchy soon followed.

Sosthenes. "Of sound strength." Ruler of the synagogue at Corinth during the apostle Paul's first visit (Acts 18:17). When the Roman ruler of the area refused to deal with the angry mob's charges against Paul, they beat Sosthenes. This may be the same Sosthenes greeted by Paul in one of his Corinthian letters (1 Cor. 1:1).

Stephen. "Crown." The first of the seven men chosen by the church to feed the Greek-speaking widows. He was a powerful preacher whom the Jews falsely accused and tried for blasphemy. He then accused them of betraying and murdering their Messiah. The council stoned Stephen. Saul (later known as the apostle Paul) witnessed his death.

Stephen was the first Christian believer to die for his faith. His dying words closely parallel those of Jesus on the cross.

Tamar. "Palm."

1. The widow of Er and Onan, sons of Judah (Gen. 38:6–30; Matt. 1:3). According to the law of levirate marriage, Judah's third son, Shelah, should have married Tamar, and their first child would have been regarded as his brother's and carried on his name. However, Judah withheld his third son from marrying Tamar. Tamar disguised herself as a harlot and offered herself to Judah. Twin sons, Perez and Zerah, were born of their union. Judah and Tamar became ancestors of Jesus through Perez (Matt. 1:3).

2. The lovely daughter of David by Maacah and sister of Absalom (2 Sam. 13:1–22, 32; 1 Chron. 3:9). Tamar was raped by her half brother, Amnon. She fled to her brother Absalom, who plotted revenge. Two years later Absalom got his revenge for Tamar by arranging Amnon's murder.

3. Absalom's only surviving daughter,

possibly named after his sister Tamar (2 Sam. 14:27).

Terah. The father of Abraham.

Teraphim. Primitive idols or household gods.

Tertullus. "Third." Professional orator hired to prosecute the Jews' case against the apostle Paul (Acts 24:1–2). Tertullus accompanied Ananias the high priest and the elders from Jerusalem to Caesarea to accuse Paul before Felix, the Roman governor of Judea.

Thaddeus. One of Jesus' 12 disciples. Other than his being named by Matthew (10:3) and Mark (3:18), we know nothing about him.

Theophilus. Called "most excellent" (Luke 1:3) and the person to whom Luke wrote his gospel and the Acts of the Apostles.

Thomas. One of the Twelve. John calls him the Twin (Greek "didymus"). Thomas refused to believe in Jesus' resurrection until he saw the nail prints in Jesus' hands. Upon Jesus' appearance, he cried out his confession of faith, "My Lord and my God!" (John 20:28).

Tiberius. Roman emperor called Caesar. He ruled at the time of the ministry and crucifixion of Jesus.

Timothy. "Honorer of God." Paul found Timothy in Lystra, Asia Minor, on his second missionary journey. Timothy was already a Christian. His father was Greek and his mother Jewish. Paul circumcised Timothy so that he would be more acceptable to the Jews as he spread the Gospel. Paul's letters referred to him with affection and "as a son with his father" (Phil. 2:22). Paul wrote Timothy two letters that contain fairly strong rebukes.

Tishbite. Name applied to Elijah the prophet (1 Kings 17:1; 21:17; 2 Kings 9:36). Most scholars believe Elijah was from Transjordan, an area east of the Jordan River, specifically in the land of Gilead.

Titus. Greek fellow worker of Paul. Paul wrote him a short letter. One tradition said that Titus was Luke's brother.

Tobiah. An Ammonite who unsuccessfully attempted to prevent Nehemiah from rebuilding the walls of Jerusalem.

Trophimus. "Nourishing." Gentile Christian who lived in Ephesus and who accompanied the apostle Paul to Jerusalem at the end of Paul's third missionary journey (Acts 20:4). When Jews from Asia saw Trophimus the Ephesian with Paul in Jerusalem, they supposed that Paul had brought uncircumcised Gentiles into the inner court and thus defiled the temple (Acts 21:28–29).

The people seized Paul, dragged him out of the temple, and tried to kill him. But Paul was rescued by the commander of the Roman garrison and eventually sent to Rome for trial. Apparently Trophimus accompanied Paul on the trip toward Rome. To Timothy, Paul revealed, "Trophimus I have left in Miletus sick" (2 Tim. 4:20).

Uriah. A Hittite and a soldier in King David's army. David plotted his death in battle so that he could then marry Uriah's wife, Bathsheba, with whom he had committed adultery. Nathan the prophet rebuked David for this sin.

Urijah. "Flame of Yahweh." A priest in Jerusalem who built an altar according to the pattern provided by King Ahaz (2 Kings 16:10–16). When the wicked Ahaz sought help from the Assyrian King Tiglath-Pileser, he embraced pagan worship at an Assyrian altar and instructed Urijah to build a replica for his worship in Jerusalem. The priest made the heathen altar, putting it in the court of the temple in the place of the bronze altar of God. Without protest, he complied with Ahaz's instructions, presenting all sacrifices and offering on the new altar.

Uzzah. One of the drivers of a new cart on which the ark of the covenant was placed when the Israelites brought it from the house of Abinadab. When the oxen stumbled, Uzzah put out his hand to steady the ark. For this sacrilegious act, God struck him dead.

Uzziah *or* Azariah. The son of Amaziah, king of Judah during one of the most prosperous periods of the divided kingdom. Uzziah contracted leprosy as God's punishment and withdrew from public, reigning with his son Jotham as co-regent. It was "in the year that King Uzziah died" that Isaiah heard the prophetic call from God (Isa. 6).

Vashti. "One who is desired." Beautiful queen of King Ahasuerus (Xerxes I) who was banished from court for refusing the king's command to make an appearance during a period of drunken feasting (Esther 1:11). Her departure allowed Esther to become Ahasuerus's new queen and to be used as God's instrument in saving the Jewish people from destruction.

Zacchaeus. "Pure." The chief tax collector in Jericho. When Jesus came to his city, Zacchaeus, being a short man, climbed into a tree to see him. Jesus called the man down and ate with him in his house. Zacchaeus offered to restore everything he had stolen.

Zacharias. The father of John the Baptist and a priest of the temple. The angel Gabriel appeared to him to announce that his elderly wife would bear a son named John. The news made him speechless until the child was born.

Zadok. A loyal priest in the time of David and Solomon. Zadok guarded the ark of the covenant in Jerusalem when David fled during Absalom's revolt. Through his son, Ahimaaz, he was able to warn the king about Absalom's battle plans and helped to bring about the interloper's defeat. When David was dying, Zadok supported the succession of Solomon, whom he anointed as king.

Zealots. In some translations this title applied to Simon, the disciple of Jesus (Luke 6:15). The Zealots were a fanatical nationalistic party in Palestine who wanted to win independence from the Romans by armed rebellion.

Zebedee. The father of James and John, two of Jesus' 12 disciples.

Zebulun. "Dwelling." The tenth of Jacob's 12 sons, sixth and last son of Leah (Gen. 30:19–20; 35:23; 1 Chron. 2:1), and the father of the tribe that bears his name.

Zechariah. "Yahweh remembers." Prophet in the days of Ezra (Ezra 5:1; 6:14; Zech. 1:1, 7; 7:1, 8) and author of the book of Zechariah. A leader in the restoration of the nation of Israel following the Babylonian captivity, Zechariah was a contemporary of the prophet Haggai, the governor Zerubbabel, and the high priest Joshua.

Zedekiah. The last king of Judah. When Nebuchadnezzar overpowered Jerusalem, he made Zedekiah his vassal king. He rebelled and Nebuchadnezzar's army again laid siege to Jerusalem. After three years the Babylonians won. Zedekiah fled but was captured at Jericho. His eyes were put out, and he was led captive to Babylon.

A painting of the prophet Zechariah by Michelangelo, in the Sistine Chapel in Rome.

PHOTO BY HOWARD VOS

Zelotes. "Full of zeal." Nickname of Simon, one of the 12 apostles of Jesus, to distinguish him from Simon Peter. Modern versions translate as the *Zealot*.

Zephaniah. A descendant of King Hezekiah of Judah, he prophesied in Jerusalem in the days of Josiah. He wrote the book that bears his name.

Zerubbabel. He went back to Jerusalem with the first group of Jews liberated by the Persian King Cyrus. Zerubbabel helped to rebuild the temple. The second temple was commonly referred to as Zerubbabel's temple.

Ziba. "Post," "salute." Servant of King Saul (2 Sam. 9:2–4, 9–12; 16:1–4; 19:17, 29). When Saul and Jonathan died following a battle with the Philistines at Mount Gilboa, David wished to remember his promise to Jonathan and asked if any descendants of Saul still lived. Ziba answered that a son of Jonathan, Mephibosheth, lived in the house of Machir in Lo Debar (2 Sam. 9:3–6). David brought Mephibosheth to Jerusalem and decreed that he should eat bread at the king's table (2 Sam. 9:10–11). He also commanded Ziba to work the land for Mephibosheth.

When Absalom revolted against David, Ziba took David some much-needed provisions. David rewarded Ziba by giving him part of Mephibosheth's land (2 Sam. 19:24–30).

Zilpah. Meaning unknown. Mother of Gad and Asher (Gen. 30:9–13; 35:26).

Zilpah was one of the female slaves of Laban, the father of Leah and Rachel. When Leah married Jacob, Laban gave her Zilpah to serve as her maid (Gen. 29:24; 46:18). Later, Leah gave Zilpah to Jacob as a concubine.

Zimri. "My protection." Fifth king of Israel (1 Kings 16:8–20). Before he became king, Zimri was a servant of King Elah and commander of half of his chariots. One day, Zimri killed the drunken Elah and proclaimed himself king. When Omri, the commander of Elah's army, heard about the assassination, he abandoned the siege of Gibbethon and besieged Tirzah, the capital city. When Zimri saw that the city was taken, he "burned the king's house down upon himself" (1 Kings 16:18). Zimri's reign lasted only seven days (1 Kings 16:15).

Zipporah. "Little bird." Daughter of Jethro, priest of Midian, and wife of Moses (Exod. 2:21–22; 4:25; 18:2–4).

Zophar. "Twittering bird." One of Job's friends. He is called a Naamathite (Job 2:11; 11:1; 20:1; 42:9), indicating he was from Naamah, in northern Arabia. Zophar's two discourses are found in Job 11:1–20 and 20:1–29. He accused Job of wickedness and hypocrisy, urged Job to turn from his rebellion, and charged that God was punishing Job far less than his sins deserved (Job 11:6).

Who's Who in Church History

From preachers to writers to lay leaders to singers to theologians to televangelists—these are the people who are the church.

The people listed in this chapter have helped to shape the destiny of the church in its attempt to be faithful to the mandate of Jesus Christ to fulfill the Great Commission:

> Go therefore and make disciples of all the nations, baptizing them in the name of the Father and of the Son and of the Holy Spirit, teaching them to observe all things that I have commanded you; and lo, I am with you always, even to the end of the age (Matt. 28:19–20).

Abelard, Peter. *1079–1142.* French philosopher and theologian. He was a keen thinker, and scholars say he had "the brightest mind in the twelfth century."

Alford, Henry. *1810–1871.* Biblical scholar and critic. His great life work was his edition of the Greek NT in four volumes.

Ambrose. *340–397.* Bishop of Milan. He began his bishopric A.D. 374 and labored for 23 years. Although a firm disciplinarian, he was greatly loved. One significant result of his preaching was the conversion of Augustine.

Anselm. *1033–1109.* Abbot of Bec, Italy, in 1093 archbishop of Canterbury. In this office he stoutly maintained the church's privileges against the arrogance of the king. He wrote a treatise on the incarnation and atonement of our Lord, *Cur Deus Homo.* Some consider him the most original thinker in the church following the days of Augustine.

Apollinaris. *Second century.* Apologist; bishop of Hierapolis in Phrygia, from A.D. 171. One of the most active and esteemed Christian writers of his day, he was acquainted with pagan literature and used this knowledge in refutation of heresy, the chief one being Phrygian Montanism. Perhaps his chief writing was *Apology Addressed to Emperor Marcus Aurelius,* sometime after A.D. 174.

Arius. *256–336.* Heretic. He taught that Jesus, although the Son of God, could not be coeternal with his Father; that he must be regarded as external to the divine essence; that he was only a creature. He gained a strong following and persisted in his views. The Arian controversy raged until 381; the question was officially settled by the church when the Council of Constantinople adopted the Nicene Creed.

Asbury, Francis. *1745–1816.* First Methodist bishop ordained in America. After the Revolutionary War the Methodists were organized into an independent church, as the Methodist Episcopal Church. Thomas Coke and Francis Asbury became joint superintendents at the Christmas Conference in 1784.

Athanasius. *296–372.* Presbyter and bishop of Alexandria, defender of orthodoxy. He was an archdeacon under Bishop Alexander during the rise of the Arian controversy about A.D. 320. At the time of the first ecumenical council at Nicaea (325) he was a young presbyter in the Alexandrian church but came into prominence as a celebrated leader and theologian by being the chief defender of the trinitarian doctrine.

Augustine, Aurelius. *354–430.* Bishop of Hippo and one of the greatest of the church fathers. Augustine was the leading genius of many of the church synods of North Africa, including the Synod of Carthage in 397 when the Holy Scriptures were finally canonized. Augustine exerted a powerful influence as bishop, theologian, defender of the faith, preacher, and writer. His defense of the faith included preaching and writing against the Manichaeans, the Donatists, and the Pelagians. Chief of his writings were *The City of God* and *Confessions*.

Bakker, James Olsen. *B. 1940.* Clergyman, formerly with Assemblies of God. Wife: Tammy Faye LaVelley. Founder and host of TV's "700 Club" in 1965, he established the "PTL Club" and was the host until 1987. Author of several books, Bakker has been involved in scandal over sexual impropriety and misuse of funds.

Barnes, Albert. *1798–1870.* American Presbyterian preacher and Bible expositor. An active advocate of total abstinence, the abolition of slavery, and the Sunday school cause, he wrote *The Scriptural Views of Slavery, The Church and Slavery,* and *Lectures on the Evidences of Christianity.* He is best known for his voluminous *Notes on the New Testament* and *Notes on the Old Testament.*

Barrows, Cliff. *B. 1923.* Song leader. After meeting Billy Graham in 1945 and joining him as song leader, Barrows has been with him since. He is in charge of all music in the Graham Crusades and serves as director of congregational singing and director of the massed choir.

Barth, Karl. *1886–1968.* Swiss theologian. After World War I, Barth was increasingly convinced that liberal theology was bankrupt, and he emphasized the "otherness" of God—that Christianity is a matter of divine revelation—God breaking into our world and coming to us. He was the chief exponent of neoorthodoxy or, as it sometimes called, the theology of crisis. Barth held a view of a transcendent and sovereign God as opposed to the immanent subjective view of God. He stated that we cannot know God by reason or sensation but salvation can come only through the miraculous supernatural piercing of history by God through the person of Jesus Christ.

Basil the Great. *329–379.* The administrator and prelate among the "Three Cappadocians," the three brilliant leaders of Christian orthodoxy in the fourth century—St. Basil, St. Gregory of Nazianzus, and St. Gregory of Nyssa. In 370 St. Basil was elected bishop of Caesarea and archbishop of all Cappadocia. He endeavored to fight Arianism by appointing orthodox bishops in all the churches.

Baxter, Richard. *1615–1691.* English Puritan divine. Baxter was one of the most successful preachers and pastors of the Christian church and a man with a voluminous output of more than 100 books. Chief among them were *The Saints' Rest, The Reformed Pastor,* and *A Call to the Unconverted.*

Bede, the Venerable. *672–735.* English monk, scholar, and church historian. Bede's best-known and most valuable writing is *Ecclesiastical History of the Saxons,* translated from the Latin by King Alfred into Anglo-Saxon.

Beecher, Henry Ward. *1813–1887.* American Congregational clergyman and reformer. He became known as a revivalist of great power and as a preacher of delightful humor and originality. Active and courageous in the cause of antislavery, he deplored revolutionary measures.

Benedict of Nursia. *Ca. 480–ca. 550.* Founder of a monastic order. In 529 he founded the renowned monastery of Monte Cassino, which marked the beginning of organized monasticism. The monastic order bears his name, and he presided over it for 14 years and composed the Benedictine Rule. This rule soon superseded all former and contemporary rules of a similar nature, and became the code to be followed by later monastic orders. He produced a fourfold plan for the monastic life.

The influential Benedictine order was the forerunner of other great religious orders and added much power to the Roman Catholic church.

Bernard of Clairvaux. *1091–1153.* Schoolman, and sometimes called "the father of Western mysticism."

Bliss, Philip Paul. *1838–1876.* Hymnist and gospel singer. His hymns include: "Let the Lower Lights Be Burning"; "Hold the Fort"; "Man of Sorrows! What a Name!"; "The Light of the World Is Jesus"; "Almost Persuaded"; and "Wonderful Words of Life."

Bonar, Andrew Alexander. *1810–1892.* Writer and minister in the Free Church of Scotland. He was identified with evangelical and revival movements.

Bonar, Horatius. *1808–1889.* Scottish Presbyterian poet-preacher. An older brother of Andrew A. Bonar, he was theologically conservative and a premillenarian. His best work was done in hymnody. He wrote "What a Friend We Have in Jesus," "I Heard the Voice of Jesus," and 600 other hymns and poems.

Bonaventura, Giovanni. *1221–1274.* The "Seraphic Doctor." He was a scholastic, mystic, and cardinal in the Franciscan order. The order regarded him as one of its greatest doctors. Apart from his personal influence, his writings were influential in settling the disputes argued by many church councils. Bonaventura marks the transition in scholastic theology.

Bonhoeffer, Dietrich. *1906–1945.* German Lutheran clergyman and theologian. Bonhoeffer, active in the anti-Hitler resistance movement, refused to leave Germany when Hitler came to power. He was imprisoned in 1943 for smuggling Jews into Switzerland and was hanged in 1945. *The Cost of Discipleship* (1937) was his most famous book.

Boniface, *or* **Winfrid** *or* **Wilfrith.** *672–755.* English Benedictine missionary. He was known as the "Apostle to the Germans."

Boniface VIII. *Ca. 1235–1303.* Benedetto Gaetani was Pope Boniface VIII (1294–1303). In 1296 he issued his famous *Clericis Laicos,* a bull directed against Philip IV of France, prohibiting the taxation of church property without the consent of the Holy See. Both France and England objected. When Boniface made further demands upon Philip, the king burned the bull. Then Boniface ventured on the boldest course of his life, the "greatest mistake ever made by a Roman pontiff." In 1302 he issued the *Unum Sanctum,* the high mark of papal claims in which he stated the papacy held absolute authority over civil power. When the king refused to accept it, both excommunication and interdict were exercised against him. Instead of bowing to the pope, the king had Boniface seized and confined to prison in Anagni for three days. Boniface was then rescued and taken to Rome.

Booth, Catherine Mumford (Mrs. William). *1829–1890.* British welfare worker and "Mother of the Salvation Army."

Booth, Evangeline Cory. *1865–1950.* A general of the Salvation Army, daughter of General William Booth. Trained by her father for work in the Salvation Army, she supervised the field operations of the Salvation Army in Great Britain, Canada, and the Klondike. In 1904, she took over the command of the Salvation Army in the United States, during which time the Army made rapid progress and growth. She was elected general of the Salvation Army in 1934, holding that position until she retired in 1939.

Booth, William. *1829–1912.* Founder and leader of the Salvation Army. In 1865 Booth began preaching and doing missionary work among the poor, lower classes in the Whitechapel neighborhood in East London where the Salvation Army had its beginning as the East London Christian Revival Society. By 1878 Booth had formed his society into an organization with military form, name, and discipline and called it the Salvation Army.

Bounds, Edward McKendree. *1835–1913.* Methodist minister and writer of spiritual life books, including *Preacher and Prayer, Purpose in Prayer, Prayer and Praying Men,* and *Power Through Prayer.*

Brainerd, David. *1718–1747.* Missionary to the American Indians.

Bray, Billy. *1794–1868.* English evangelist.

Bright, William Rohl. *B. 1921.* Founder (1951) and President of Campus Crusade for Christ, Bright received the 1973 Special Award from Religious Heritage of America. Since 1961 he has been the editor of *Worldwide Challenge* magazine.

Broadus, John Albert. *1827–1895.* American Baptist scholar, teacher, and preacher. For a time he was the assistant professor of Latin and Greek at the University of Virginia and pastor of the Baptist church at Charlottesville, Virginia.

Brooks, Phillips. *1835–1893.* American Protestant Episcopal minister and author. He was one of the most eloquent, spiritual, successful, and highly esteemed clergymen of his time.

Bryan, William Jennings. *1860–1925.* American political leader, editor, and lecturer.

Bultmann, Rudolf. *1884–1976.* Highly influential German theologian. His *History of the Synoptic Tradition* (1921) concluded that the historical reliability of the Gospels as reports of facts was questionable. By using "form criticism" he was pessimistic about the extent of historical knowledge of Jesus.

He taught that every "form" or type of material in the Gospels reflects a typical situation in ancient Israel or the earliest churches and the "forms" behind them were often preaching or teaching but hardly ever that of historical reporting.

Bunyan, John. *1628–1688.* Puritan preacher and writer. While in prison, he wrote his famous allegory, *The Pilgrim's Progress.* Bunyan also wrote *The Life and Death of Mr. Badman, The Holy War,* and *Grace Abounding.*

Bushnell, Horace. *1802–1876.* Congregational minister. Among his writings was *Christian Nurture,* in which he advocated the leading of children to Christ in the home rather than in revivals.

Calvin, John. *1509–1564.* Genevan Reformer. In 1536 he published the first edition of his *Institutes of the Christian Religion,* which became the guide for all Reformed churches. Calvin became a great leader of the Reformation, making Geneva the "Rome of Protestantism." His churchstate was almost an OT theocracy.

Campbell, Alexander. *1788–1866.* Founder of the Disciples of Christ; the son of Thomas Campbell, a Scots-Irish minister who broke away from the Church of Scotland.

Carey, William. *1761–1834.* The father of modern missions. In 1792, he preached his memorable sermon, "Expect Great Things from God, Attempt Great Things for God." In that same year he helped to organize the English Baptist Missionary Society. The next year he went to India as one of its first missionaries. Carey advocated two important missionary principles: (1) equality of missionaries and nationals and (2) self-sustaining missions.

Carmichael, Amy Wilson. *1867–1951.* Founder of the Dohnavur Fellowship in India. Her work began with rescuing girls who had been dedicated to a life of servitude in Hindu temples. This led to the establishment of a home for children at Dohnavur, Tirunelveli (Tinnevelly) South India. The Dohnavur Fellowship grew out of this ministry. Miss Carmichael was also a prolific writer.

Catherine of Siena. *1347–1380.* Roman Catholic Italian mystic. She became a Dominican nun and later devoted herself to helping the sick and plague-stricken people and worked for the conversion of sinners. The chief cause of her fame was her reputation for visions and prophecies. Catherine claimed that Christ often appeared to her, that her union with him was confirmed by the espousal ring he placed on her finger and by the stigmata of the five wounds in her body.

Celsus. *Second century* A.D. *180.* Eclectic Platonist and polemical writer against Christianity. Although his arguments against Christianity were weak and superficial, Origen felt them important enough to call forth his answer to them 70 years later, in *Against Celsus.*

Chafer, Lewis Sperry. *1871–1952.* American Presbyterian clergyman and educator. In 1924 he helped to found Texas (now Dallas) Theological Seminary, Dallas, Texas. He was its president and also a professor of systematic theology.

Chrysostom, John (John of Antioch). *347–407.* Bishop of Constantinople, known for his speaking eloquence, which won for him the title, *Chrysostom,* (golden-mouthed). He was also known for his practical writings on the priesthood and other church matters.

Clara Sciffi (Scefi). *1194–1253.* Founder of the order of Poor Clares or the Clarisses.

Clark, Glenn. *1882–1956.* College professor and founder of The Camps Farthest Out. He edited *Clear Horizons* magazine and authored several books on prayer and Christian living such as *I Will Lift Up Mine Eyes, How to Find Health Through Prayer,* and *What Would Jesus Do?*

Clarke, Adam. *1762–1832.* English Methodist preacher, commentator, and theologian. His chief literary work was a commentary on the Bible in eight volumes, which took him 45 years. He also published *Biographical Dictionary* in six volumes.

Clarke, George R. *1827–1892.* Cofounder of the Pacific Garden Mission, Chicago.

Clement I (of Rome). *Ca. 30–100.* One of the earliest bishops of Rome. He may possibly have been the Clement mentioned by Paul in Philippians 4:3. His *Epistle to the Corinthians* is the oldest specimen of postapostolic literature.

Coke, Thomas. *1747–1814.* First bishop of the Methodist Episcopal Church in the United States.

Columba *or* **Columcille.** *521–597.* Irish Celtic missionary called the "Apostle of Chalcedonia."

Columban *or* **Columbanus.** *543–615.* Irish missionary.

Constantine the Great. *Ca. 288–337.* Roman emperor. By 324 he was the sole emperor in both the East and the West. Sensing that his future success as emperor depended on uniting his subjects, he built his policies around the Christian church as an aid to the unity and power of the Roman Empire. He used the term *catholic* in his imperial edicts, chose Christian men as advisers, gradually exempted the clergy from military and civil duty, legalized bequests to the churches, enjoined the civic observance of Sunday, contributed liberally to the building of churches, and gave his sons a Christian education. In 325 he called the first ecumenical council at Nicaea to settle disputed doctrines and to unify the church.

Cook, David Caleb. *1850–1927.* American editor and publisher of Sunday school literature. Because of the lack of Sunday school materials and helps, he prepared and published his own. He called his first publication *Our Sunday School Quarterly.*

Cook, Robert Andrew. *B. 1912.* American clergyman. Cook was the president of Youth for Christ International (1948–1957) and has been the president of King's College since 1962. He was president of National Association of Evangelicals, 1962–1964.

Cotton, John. *1585–1652.* Puritan minister of Boston, called the "Patriarch of New England." He earned a wide reputation for piety and learning, and wielded a powerful influence over affairs in New England as the virtual head of Congregationalism in America.

Coverdale, Miles. *1488–1568.* English translator of the Bible. Under the commission of Thomas Cromwell, he superintended the printing of a revised English version for the Anglican church, known as the Great Bible (1538–1539). In 1540 he edited Cranmer's Bible, a revised edition of the Great Bible.

Cowper, William. *1731–1800.* English poet and hymn writer.

Cranmer, Thomas. *1489–1556.* English Reformer, and first Protestant archbishop of Canterbury. Cranmer urged that the question of the divorce of Henry VIII and Catherine be taken out of the hands of the lawyers and referred to the theologians of the universities. His proposal met the immediate favor of Henry and led to rapid political and ecclesiastical advancement for Cranmer, until the king in 1533 appointed him archbishop.

After Henry's death in 1547, Cranmer became more active in the English reformation of the church. He was responsible for the production and acceptance of the Thirty-nine Articles.

When Catholic Queen Mary ascended the throne (1553), he was martyred along with Ridley and Latimer because they refused to recant.

Crosby, Fanny (Mrs. Frances Jane Crosby Van Alstyne). *1820–1915.* American hymn writer. The total number of her hymns and poems likely exceeded 8,000. Her hymns became favorites of Moody and Sankey and increased their popularity in England and America. A few of her hymns are "Safe in the Arms of Jesus," "Pass Me Not, O Gentle Saviour," "Rescue the Perishing," "Blessed Assurance," and "Saviour, More Than Life to Me."

Crowther, Samuel Adjai. *Ca. 1810–1891.* First Negro bishop of the Anglican church.

Cruden, Alexander. *1701–1770.* Scottish bookseller, and Bible concordance compiler. In 1737 he issued his immortal work, *A Complete Concordance of the Holy Scriptures of the Old and New Testaments.*

Cyprian, Thrascius Caecilius. *195 or 200–258.* Bishop of Carthage.

Cyril *or* Cyrillus, *original name* Constantinus. *827–869.* Missionary to the Slavs.

Cyril of Alexandria. *376–444.* Patriarch of Alexandria.

Cyril of Jerusalem. *Ca. 315–386.* Bishop of Jerusalem.

Darby, John Nelson. *1800–1882.* Chief founder and early leader of the Plymouth Brethren.

Donatus the Great. *D. ca. 355.* Bishop of Carthage. In the time of Diocletian when the lapsed Christians were being received back into the church after persecution, a new puritanic, rigoristic movement opposed reinstating them, taking its name from Donatus.

Dwight, Timothy. *1752–1817.* American Congregational clergyman and grandson of Jonathan Edwards. He was president of Yale College. His remarkable ability as a teacher and his evangelical Christian character did much to raise the standard of the college. He published his famous *Theology Explained and Defended.* Dwight also wrote several other works and was the author of the famous hymn, "I Love Thy Kingdom, Lord."

Eckhart, Meister (Johann). *1260–1327.* German mystic and theologian. His burden of preaching was to bring the soul into conscious, mystic union with God. For him good works did not make people righteous, but he said people must first be righteous to do righteous works. His most famous work was *Opus Tripartitum,* of which only a fraction is extant.

Eddy, Mary Morse (Baker). *1821–1910.* Founder of Christian Science.

Edersheim, Alfred. *1825–1889.* Bible scholar and theologian. He made an intensive study of doctrines, practices, and conditions of Judaism as they related to the NT. He wrote many books, among which are *History of the Jewish Nation after the Destruction of Jerusalem by Titus, The Temple and Bible History* (in seven volumes), and *The Life and Times of Jesus the Messiah* (in two volumes), his greatest work.

Edwards, Jonathan. *1703–1758.* American theologian and preacher. The Great Awakening of 1734–1744 broke out in his and other New England churches. His sermons had a powerful effect upon audiences and greatly influenced the theology of George Whitefield, who worked with him during the Great Awakening. Besides being a pastor, he was also a missionary to the Housatonic, Mohawk, Oneida, and Tuscarora Indians. His best-known book, *Freedom of the Will,* is a defense of the doctrines of foreordination, original sin, and eternal punishment. Many consider his the keenest philosophical intellect that colonial America produced.

Eliot, John. *1604–1690.* Apostle to the American Indians.

Erasmus, Desiderius. *1466–1536.* Dutch scholar, prince of the humanists. He stands in the front rank of the humanists and forerunners of the Reformation, and on the dividing line between the Middle Ages and modern times. He prepared the way for the work of the Reformers, but had little creative or organizing power. He was an expert Greek scholar, and his Greek NT, issued in 1516, was a valuable aid to the work of Luther.

Eusebius of Caesarea (Eusebius Pamphili). *Ca. 260–ca. 340.* Bishop of Caesarea in Palestine, and the "father of church history." Eusebius wrote a valuable history of the Christian church from the time of the apostles down to his own time (ca. 325). Many prominent men and facts are known to us today only from the pages of this history.

Euthymius, Zigabenus. *D. ca. 1118.* Byzantine theologian and exegete. At the order of the emperor, Alexius Commenus, he wrote against all heresies in *Panoplia Dogmatica.* The most interesting part of the book is the section on the Bogomiles, which gives us our chief information on this sect.

Falwell, Jerry. *B. 1933.* Clergyman. Falwell founded the Moral Majority, Inc. in 1979 and has since been its president. He has published widely, and in 1979 he received the clergyman of the year award from the Religious Heritage of America. In 1982, *U.S. News and World Report* listed him as one of the 20 most influential people in the United States.

Farel, Guillaume. *1489–1565.* Reformer. Some called this pioneer of Protestantism in western Switzerland "the Elijah of the French Reformation" and "the scourge of the priests."

Fenelon, Francois de Salignac de la Mothe. *1651–1715*. French mystic and quietist.

Fillmore, Charles. *1854–1948*. Cofounder (with his wife) of the Unity School of Christianity.

Finney, Charles Grandison. *1792–1875*. Congregational revivalist, theologian, and college president. As an evangelist, he initiated the "anxious bench" and dwelt upon the importance of hearers coming to immediate decision and of rising in public attestation of the decision to become a Christian. Among his writings are *Lectures on Systematic Theology* and *Lectures on Revivals*.

Fox, George. *1624–1691*. Mystic and founder of the Society of Friends (Quakers). Fox placed great emphasis on the immediate, personal teaching of the Holy Spirit or inner light; every member is a priest of God, rejecting a professional ministry; anyone, man or woman who is called of God, may preach; the sacraments, including baptism and the Eucharist, are inner and spiritual only; oaths are needless and wrong for the Christian; war is unlawful for a Christian; slavery is abhorrent. He said, "The final test of everything in religion is the test of experience."

Francis de Sales. *1567–1622*. Roman Catholic preacher, devotional writer, and mystic.

Francis of Assisi. *1182–1226*. Founder of the Franciscan order.

Frelinghuysen, Theodore Jacob. *1691–1747*. Colonial Dutch Reformed revivalist. In 1737 he initiated the first formal move to organize an assembly for the Dutch Reformed in America.

Gaebelein, Arno Clemens. *1861–1945*. American clergyman, author, and teacher.

Goforth, Jonathan. *1859–1936*. Canadian Presbyterian missionary to China.

Gordon, Adoniram Judson. *1836–1895*. Baptist minister. His church became a center of missionary support and activity in Boston with work among the Jews, the Chinese, and black people, an industrial home, rescue work for fallen women, evangelistic work on the wharves, in hospitals, in streetcar stables, and in weak churches. He also established a school for the training of missionaries and pastors' assistants. Among Gordon's writings are *When Christ Came to Church, The Ministry of the Spirit*, and *The Ministry of Healing*.

Graham, William Franklin, Jr. (Billy). *B. 1918*. Considered the world's most successful Christian mass evangelist in history. He has been holding mass evangelism meetings since 1949. He was the first evangelist of the Youth For Christ movement. In 1950 he formed the Billy Graham Evangelistic Association and initiated a radio program called "Hour of Decision" (later a TV program). He was the president of Northwestern College (1947–1952). Graham has authored a number of best-selling books beginning with *Peace with God* (1952).

Gray, James Martin. *1851–1935*. Clergy, teacher, writer, and Bible school president.

Gregory the Great (Gregory I). *540–604*. "Rome's greatest pope," 590–604. During his reign monasticism began its rising popularity. Although Gregory was considered equal to Augustine, Jerome, and Ambrose as one of the four great doctors of the church, he was not an original theologian, but more of a transmitter.

Gregory VII (Hildebrand). *Ca. 1020–1085*. Pope, 1073–1085. He was one of the greatest popes of the Roman Catholic Church. His great concern was for its reform. His idea of the Catholic church was that of a theocracy based upon the Mosaic model, canon law, and absolute sovereignty of the church in the world with the pope as the vicar of Christ.

Gregory IX. *1145–1241.* Pope, 1227–1241. A disciplinarian and strong churchman, while still a cardinal he supported Francis of Assisi in establishing the Franciscan order.

Gregory XI (Pierre Roger de Beaufort). *1331–1378.* Pope, 1370–1378. His reign involved constant warfare with cities of Italy. Through the persistent entreaties of Catherine of Siena (1347–1380), and in order to quell a revolt on the banks of the Tiber, he returned from Avignon to Rome in 1377, thus ending the "Babylonian Captivity." That year he issued five bulls ordering the arrest of John Wycliffe of England.

Gregory XII (Angelo Corrario). *1327–1417.* Last of the Roman popes in the Papal Schism. He ruled 1406–1415.

Gregory of Nazianzus. *330–390.* Poet and orator of the "Three Cappadocians."

Gregory of Nyssa *Ca. 330–ca. 395.* Philosopher and student. He became one of the strongest defenders of the faith against Arianism.

Groot, Gerhard (Gerrit) de. *1340–1384.* Founder of the Brethren of the Common Life, and a Dutch religious reformer.

Groves, Anthony Norris. *1795–1853.* Joint founder of the Plymouth Brethren movement, and a missionary to Baghdad and India.

Guyon, Jeanne Marie Bouvier de la Motte. *1648–1717.* French quietist writer.

Harnack, Karl Gustav Adolph Von. *1851–1930.* German Lutheran theologian and church historian. Recognized as one of the leaders of the critical school of theology, he also became an authority on ante-Nicene church history.

Havergal, Frances Ridley. *1836–1879.* English hymn and devotional writer. Her first accepted poem was "I Gave My Life for Thee" but her most widely used hymn is "Take My Life and Let It Be."

Helwys, Thomas. *Ca. 1550–ca. 1616.* Founder of the first English Baptist church.

Henry, Carl F. *B. 1913.* Clergyman. *Time* magazine named him evangelicalism's leading theologian in 1978 after the publication of his six-volume *God, Revelation and Authority.*

Henry, Matthew. *1662–1714.* Nonconformist clergyman and Bible commentator. He is best known for his *Exposition of the Old and New Testaments,* now commonly called *Matthew Henry's Commentaries.*

Herman, Nicholas (Brother Lawrence). *Ca. 1605–1691.* Carmelite mystic. He is known for writing *The Practice of the Presence of God.*

Herzog, Johann Jakob. *1805–1882.* German Reformed theologian. *Realencyclopadie fur Protestantische Theologie und Kirche* (22 volumes) was his greatest contribution to the Protestant church. After his death a condensed edition was prepared by Philip Schaff (three volumes) and later revised as *The New Schaff-Herzog Encyclopedia of Religious Knowledge* in 13 volumes.

Hippolytus. *Ca. 170–236.* Apologist, writer, and bishop. A younger contemporary of Cyprian, he belonged to the North African school of thought. He was a voluminous writer of the Roman church in the third century. His writings dealt with the heresies that were plaguing the Christian church.

Hooker, Richardy. *Ca. 1553–1600.* Church of England writer on ecclesiastical polity. His reputation rests upon his great work, *The Laws of Ecclesiastical Polity,* written in defense of the high church polity of Anglicanism, and as an answer to Calvinistic Puritanism.

Hugel, Baron Friedrich von. *1852–1925.* Roman Catholic lay theologian. In 1905 he founded the London Society for the Study of Religion.

Hurlbut, Jesse Lyman. *1843–1930.* American Methodist Episcopal clergyman. He wrote 30 books on Bible study, Bible history, and Sunday school work, including *Bible Atlas: A Manual of Bible Geography and History, Studies in the Old Testament,* and *Story of Jesus.*

Huss, John. *Ca. 1369–1415.* Bohemian reformer. He made the Bible the only rule in matters of religion and faith. In 1415 he was burned at the stake.

Ignatius. *Ca. 35–ca. 107.* Bishop of Antioch. He was a pupil of the apostle John, and was the second or third bishop of the church at Antioch, Syria.

Ignatius of Loyola. *1491 or 1495–1556.* Founder of the Society of Jesus.

Irenaeus. *Ca. 130–202.* Bishop of Lyons. His greatest literary work was *Against Heresies, a defense of the faith against the Gnostics and other heretics.* He was the first of the church fathers to make full use of the NT.

Ironside, Henry Allan. *1876–1951.* American clergyman. Author of more than 60 volumes, many of which were pulpit messages comprising notes, lectures, and expositions of the books of the Bible.

Jackson, Jesse. *B. 1941.* Baptist clergyman, civic leader. Jackson helped found Operation Breadbasket, a project of the Southern Christian Leadership Conference, in 1966, and in 1971 he founded—and has remained executive director of—PUSH (People United to Serve Humanity). He has been a Democratic presidential candidate (1983–1984 and 1987–1988).

James I. *1566–1625.* King of Great Britain (1603–1625); only son of Mary Stuart, Queen of Scots. During his reign a group of learned divines began the translation of the Bible. After its completion in 1611, it became known as the Authorized or King James Version. He reigned as James VI of Scotland (1567–1603).

Jansen, Cornelius Otto. *1585–1638.* Dutch Roman Catholic theologian, bishop of Ypres, and father of Jansenism. He urged a return to an acceptance of the Pauline and Augustinian view of conversion or salvation through irresistible grace.

Jerome (Hieronymus, Sophronius Eusebius). *Ca. 340–420.* Biblical scholar. When the pope wanted a new translation of the Scriptures made from the original Hebrew and Greek, he commissioned Jerome to the task. By the eighth century Jerome's translation of the OT and NT and the Apocrypha, known as the Latin Vulgate, became the officially recognized and authorized version of the Bible for the Catholic church.

John of the Cross (Juan de la Cruz, baptized Juan de Yepes). *1542–1591.* Spanish Carmelite mystic and poet. His major writing is *The Dark Night of the Soul.*

John of Damascus *or* John Damascene. *Ca. 675–ca. 749.* Last of the Greek fathers. Since John's time there has been little change in the doctrinal statement of the Eastern church. John is known for his theological writings on the nature and work of the Holy Spirit.

John XXIII (Angelo Giuseppe Roncallie). *1881–1963.* Pope who convened the Second Vatican Council that encouraged ecumenism. He issued eight encyclicals that updated papal social teaching.

Johnson, Torrey. *B. 1909.* Founding president of Youth for Christ (YFC), 1944. Pastor of Midwest Church in Chicago, 1933–1953; affiliated with Bibletown U.S.A. in Boca Raton, Florida, 1968–1983. Now minister-at-large for YFC International.

Jones, Rufus Matthew. *1863–1948.* American Quaker. The first editor of the *American Friend.* He was largely responsible for the development of the American Friends Service Committee.

Jones, Samuel Porter (Sam). *1847–1906.* American evangelist.

Jowett, John Henry. *1864–1923.* English Congregational clergyman.

Judson, Adoniram. *1788–1850.* American Baptist missionary to Burma. In 1812 the American Board of Commissioners for Foreign Missions was incorporated, and appointed Judson to go to India.

Justin Martyr. *Ca. 100–165.* Philosopher, martyr, apologist. Justin devoted himself to the vindication and spread of the Christian religion with the conviction that Christianity is the oldest, truest, and most divine of philosophies.

Kanamori, Tsurin Paul. *Ca. 1856– ca. 1928.* Japanese evangelist.

Kierkegaard, Soren. *1813–1855.* Danish philosopher. He published *Either-Or* and *Fear and Trembling* among many other works. The word *existential* is closely associated with Kierkegaard. He used the term to contrast existence with mere life. "Existence is reached by the inner decisions of the individual," he said. "Religion is a matter of the individual soul."

King, Martin Luther, Jr. *1929–1968.* Baptist pastor; civil rights leader. Brought up in the black evangelical tradition and influenced by the social gospel movement, he saw Christianity as a force to transform individuals and society. Advocating a nonviolent approach, he gave a philosophy and strategy to the civil rights movement. King received the Nobel Peace Prize in 1964. He was assassinated in 1968.

Knox, John. *Ca. 1513–1572.* Scottish Reformer. By the time of his death the triumph of the Scottish Reformation was complete.

Kuyper, Abraham. *1837–1920.* Dutch theologian and statesman. In 1880 he founded the Free Reformed University at Amsterdam and later the Free Reformed Church. He wrote many valuable theological and devotional books, including, *The Work of the Holy Spirit* and *The Encyclopedia of Theology.*

Latimer, Hugh. *Ca. 1485–1555.* English bishop and reformer. Because he refused to sign the king's Six Articles, which represented a return to the Romanist position, he was burned at the stake along with Ridley.

Law, William. *1686–1761.* English divine and mystic. Best known for his *Serious Call to a Devout and Holy Life,* he also wrote *On Christian Perfection* and other works. To defend the Christian faith against the prevailing deism, he wrote *The Case for Reason.*

Lewis, Clive Staples. *1898–1963.* The most popular defender of orthodox Christianity in the English-speaking world in the mid-twentieth century. Extraordinarily brilliant, he wrote *The Screwtape Letters* (1942) which brought him fame. He has been called the "Apostle to the skeptics."

Lightfoot, Joseph Barber. *1828–1889.* English scholar, textual critic, and bishop of Durham. Lightfoot's works on the NT and the church fathers won him great fame.

Livingstone, David. *1813–1873.* Scottish missionary and explorer. He opened Africa to missions, working with a threefold goal: (1) to make Christ known to Africa; (2) to find the source of the Nile and open Africa to the West; and (3) to eradicate slave traffic.

Lloyd-Jones, D. Martyn. *1899–1981.* British medical doctor and pastor of Westminster Chapel, London. He began as assistant pastor in 1939, became senior pastor in 1943, and remained in that position until his retirement in 1968. Widely hailed for his commentaries on biblical books, he was affectionately called "the Doctor."

Luther, Martin. *1483–1546.* German Reformer. He was deeply influenced by Augustine's writings, Paul's epistles, and German mysticism. In 1517 he established what has come to be known as the three great Reformation principles:

1. Justification is by faith alone.
2. Every believer has direct access to God.
3. The Bible as the sole source of authority for faith and life.

Luther is often called the "father of the Protestant Reformation."

Macartney, Clarence Edward Noble. *1879–1957.* Presbyterian minister, lecturer, and author of 47 works, consisting mainly of sermons and Bible studies.

Maclaren, Alexander. *1826–1910.* English Baptist preacher and evangelical Bible scholar.

McPherson, Aimee Semple. *1890–1944.* Founder of the International Church of the Foursquare Gospel.

Maier, Walter Arthur. *1893–1950.* Missouri Synod Lutheran radio preacher and college professor.

Makemie, Francis. *1658–1708.* American Presbyterian minister and missionary to America.

Marcion. *D. ca. 160.* Founder of an early heretical sect that merged Gnosticism and orthodox Christianity. His church also resembled Manichaeanism, which arose at a later date. Like both the Gnostics and the Manichaeans, he was sharply dualistic and violently antagonistic to Judaism. He considered the NT unduly colored and contaminated by the Jewish faith and he completely rejected the OT. He formed a canon consisting of only 11 books—an expurgated gospel of Luke and ten of the Pauline Epistles.

Marshall, Peter. *1902–1949.* Chaplain of the United States Senate and Presbyterian minister. He is widely known for his two books of prayers and a book of sermons, *Mr. Jones, Meet the Master,* published shortly after his death.

Martyn, Henry. *1781–1812.* Missionary to India and Persia.

Mather, Cotton. *1663–1728.* Colonial clergyman; eldest son of Increase Mather.

Mather, Increase. *1639–1723.* Colonial minister. Occupying the position of leading clergyman in the Puritan theocracy, he wielded great power from the pulpit for 59 years and published nearly 100 books.

Maximilla. *D. 179.* Montanist prophetess and cofounder of Montanism. (See *Montanus.*)

Melanchthon, Philipp (b. Phillipp Schwarzert). *1497–1560.* German humanist and Reformer. He cast his lot with the German Reformation and became Luther's right-hand man. Scholars acknowledge him as the formulating genius of the Reformation.

Melville, Andrew. *1545–1622.* Scottish theologian. Successor of John Knox in the Scottish Reformation and "Father of Scottish Presbyterianism."

Meyer, Frederick Brotherton. *1847–1929.* English Baptist clergyman. He wrote devotional, biographical, and interpretative books that remain popular. For many years Meyer was closely associated with the Keswick Convention, an annual gathering of evangelical Christians for prayer and Bible study.

Miller, William. *1782–1849.* Early advocate of the Adventist movement. Through his study of the Scriptures he arrived at the premillennial position, and concluded that Christ would return to earth in 1843 or 1844. By 1844 he had more than 50,000 adherents, many of whom disposed of their property, settled their accounts, and waited prayerfully for the eventful day.

Moffat, Robert. *1795–1883.* Pioneer missionary to South Africa.

Moffatt, James. *1870–1944.* Scholar. He translated the OT and NT into modern English, and Adolf Harnack's *Expansion of Christianity* from German into English.

Montanus. *Second century.* Heretic; likely a priest of Cybele worship in Phrygia, Asia Minor. After becoming a Christian about the middle of the second century, he appeared in a small town in Phrygia as a prophet and reformer of Christianity. Since coldness, worldliness, and laxity were creeping into the church, he felt it his duty to recall the church to primitive purity and holiness.

Moody, Dwight Lyman. *1837–1899.* Evangelist. He injected new life into the Young Men's Christian Association (YMCA) and in 1865 was made president of the association. Never ordained, Moody was an effective preacher and evangelist. In 1886 he started the first Bible school of its kind in this country, the Chicago Evangelization Society (later called Moody Bible Institute).

Mott, John Raleigh. *1865–1955.* Methodist layman, leader in the Young Men's Christian Association (YMCA), and founder of the Christian Student Movement.

Moule, Handley Carr Glyn. *1841–1920.* Bishop of Durham.

Muhlenberg, Henry Melchior. *1711–1787.* Patriarch of the Lutheran tradition in America.

Muller, George. *1805–1898.* Evangelist and philanthropist in England.

Murray, Andrew. *1818–1917.* Dutch Reformed minister in South Africa. His still-popular books include *The Children for Christ, Like Christ,* and *With Christ in the School of Prayer.* Murray emphasized the deepening of the spiritual life.

Nestorius. *D. ca. 451.* Patriarch of Constantinople (428–431); founder of the Nestorian church.

Newberry, Thomas. *1811–1901.* Editor of *the Englishman's Bible* (often called *the Newberry Bible*).

Niebuhr, Reinhold. *1893–1971.* Pastor. Considered the most important theologian in America in his day, Niebuhr found liberalism and moral idealism inadequate for the pastoral problems he faced in Detroit during the Great Depression years. He was particularly concerned with social and political ethics, and his *Moral Man and Immoral Society* (1932) set forth his ideas. *Nature and Destiny of Man* (1941–1943) stressed that the final answers to human problems lay beyond history and in the love of God and the cross of Christ.

Ninian. *Ca. 360–432.* The first missionary and monastic bishop of northern Britain.

Owen, John. *1616–1683.* Puritan divine. Owen ranks with Richard Baxter and John Howe as the most eminent of the Puritan divines. His prolific writings include *Doctrine of Justification by Faith, On the Holy Spirit, The Divine Origin of the Scriptures,* and *Saint's Perseverance.*

Papias. *Ca. 60–130.* Bishop of Hierapolis. He is thought to have been a disciple of the apostle John, a friend of Polycarp, and the Bishop of Hierapolis in Phrygia, Asia Minor.

Parker, Daniel. *D. after 1837.* Founder of the Two-Seed-in-the-Spirit-Predestinarian-Baptists. He crusaded against all forms of organized church work, including missionary, Bible, and temperance societies, as well as Sunday schools, colleges, theological seminaries, and instrumental music in the churches. He promulgated the idea that two seeds were planted in Eve, one by God and one by the devil. The good seed was elected to salvation, and the bad seed was destined to be damned.

Paul VI (Giovanni Battista Montini). *1897–1978.* Pope and successor to John XXIII. He continued the reforms and spirit of ecumenism begun by John XXIII.

Peale, Norman Vincent. *B. 1898.* Pastor of Marble Collegiate Reformed Church in New York City since 1932. Peale shot into fame with the publication of his *Power of Positive Thinking* and has remained a man of vast influence in both the Christian and the secular worlds. He founded *Guideposts*, a religious magazine. He was president of the Reformed Church of America (1969–1970).

Pelagius. *Early fifth century.* British theologian. He and Celestius developed the Pelagian doctrine, although Celestius was the chief proponent of it.

Pelagianism taught the following precepts:

• Humanity has no original sin inherited from Adam; sin is a matter of will and not of nature.

• Individuals are created with perfect freedom to do good or evil, making a sinless life possible. Salvation can come by good works.

• Infant baptism is unnecessary because there is no original sin.

• While salvation is possible without the law and the gospel or divine grace, these greatly facilitate the attainment of salvation. Christ helps by his good example.

Peter the Hermit (Peter of Amiens). *Ca. 1050–1115.* French monk and preacher of the First Crusade.

Peter the Lombard. *Ca. 1100–1160.* Latin theologian and schoolman. He was considered the greatest teacher and representative of scholastic philosophy in his time. His *Four Books of Sentences* made a tremendous impact on the theology of his century and of the centuries following. The Roman Catholic church calls him the "father of systematic theology."

Pierson, Arthur Tappan. *1837–1911.* American Presbyterian pastor, missionary advocate, editor, and writer.

Pius IX (Giovanni M. Mastai-Ferretti). *1792–1878.* Pope who in 1854 made the Roman Catholic dogma official that the Virgin Mary was "kept free from all stain or original sin" from her conception. This had been an issue of debate for centuries.

Pius XII (Eugenio Pacelli). *1876–1958.* Pope who defined the doctrine of the assumption of the Virgin Mary, stating that she, "having completed her earthly course, was in body and soul assumed into heavenly glory." Pius XII opposed Nazism and was strongly anticommunistic.

Polycarp. *Ca. 69–155.* Church father. He was a disciple of the apostle John, a friend of Ignatius, and a teacher of Pothinus and Irenaeus.

Priscilla *or* Prisca. *Second century.* Montanist prophetess and cofounder of Montanism. (See *Montanus.*)

Quadratus. *Second century.* Early Christian apologist from Asia Minor. According to Eusebius, he claimed to have been a disciple of the apostles.

Raikes, Robert. *1735–1811.* Founder of the modern Sunday school movement.

Ramsey, Arthur. *1904–1988.* One hundredth archbishop of Canterbury and avid ecumenist.

Rauschenbusch, Walter. *1861–1918.* American Baptist minister. His strong interest in Christian socialism made him emphasize the necessity of economic as well as political democracy as a method of realizing the kingdom of God upon earth.

Ridley, Nicholas. *Ca. 1500–1555.* English reformer and martyr.

Ritschl, Albrecht Benjamin. *1822–1889.* German Protestant theologian. Although his Christian views were Bible centered, he interpreted theology and church history from a pragmatic, historical, and higher critical viewpoints.

Roberts, Granville Oral. *B. 1918.* Preacher. Beginning as an evangelist in 1936, he was with Pentecostal Holiness

Movement but became a Methodist in 1968. In 1947 Roberts started the Worldwide Evangelistic Crusade. He is the founder and president (since 1963) of Oral Roberts University. He also founded the City of Faith Medical Research Center, Tulsa, Oklahoma.

Robertson, Archibald Thomas. *1863–1934.* American Baptist theologian. Robertson's greatest contribution to biblical scholarship was in the field of NT Greek with his *Grammar of the Greek New Testament.*

Robertson, Marion Gordon (Pat). *B. 1930.* Religious broadcaster. Robertson is the president of CBN-TV and a frequent host of the "700 Club." He has been chancellor of CBN University since 1980. In 1987–1988, Robertson was an unsuccessful Republican candidate for president.

Russell, Charles Taze. *1852–1916.* Founder of Jehovah's Witnesses. He used the Bible, but deleted the doctrine of hell and rejected the Trinity, the deity of Christ, his physical resurrection and return, and the doctrine of eternal retribution for sin.

Ryle, John Charles. *1816–1900.* Low church Anglican bishop, who published a number of books of sermons and devotional literature.

Sabellius. *D. after 260.* Founder of the Sabellians (or Modalists). He held to a trinity of successive divine revelations and not a simultaneous trinity of essence, stating that the Godhead reveals only one member at a time—God in the OT, Jesus at the incarnation, and the Holy Spirit in inspiration.

Sankey, Ira David. *1840–1908.* Gospel singer and hymn composer. His singing attracted the attention of Dwight L. Moody, and they joined in evangelistic endeavors.

Savonarola, Girolamo (Jerome or Hieronymus). *1452–1498.* Italian reformer. He became the most conspicuous figure in Italy and preached against the evils of the day, especially the sins of the clergy.

Schaff, Philip. *1819–1893.* Theologian and church historian. He wrote *History of the Christian Church* (eight volumes), *The Creeds of Christendom* (three volumes), and *Theological Propaedeutic, A Companion to the Greek Testament and the English Version.*

Schleiermacher, Friedrich Ernst Daniel. *1768–1834.* German theologian and philosopher. He defined religion as feeling, or as the immediate consciousness of absolute dependence upon God. The Christian consciousness alone became the interpreter of religion and the standard for testing the truth and for knowing God. Jesus of Nazareth, his ideal, was merely a superior, sinless man, unique in his God-consciousness. He believed that Christ redeems us from ignorance rather than from sin.

Schuller, Robert. *B. 1926.* Senior pastor and founder, in 1955, of Garden Grove Community Church in California. Schuller is one of the best-known preachers in the world, since 1970, with weekly TV broadcasts called the "Hour of Power" (since 1970) from the Crystal Cathedral.

Scofield, Cyrus Ingerson. *1843–1921.* Bible student and author. The work for which he is best remembered is his Scofield Reference Bible.

Scott, Walter. *1796–1861.* Cofounder of the Disciples of Christ. He is noted for his use of the five-finger exercise in preaching: faith upon proof, repentance motivated by promises, baptism in obedience to command, remission of sins, and the gift of the Holy Spirit.

Servetus, Miguel. *1511–1553.* Spanish physician and heretic. His theological views developed into antiTrinitarianism.

Shea, George Beverly. *B. 1909.* Singer. Beginning as a soloist with the Billy Graham Crusades in 1947, he has remained the featured soloist. He has recorded more than 50 albums and received a Grammy Award in 1966. In 1978, the Gospel Music Hall of Fame inducted Shea into its membership.

Simpson, Albert Benjamin. *1844–1919.* American Presbyterian minister and founder of the Christian and Missionary Alliance. He edited the *Alliance Weekly,* wrote more than 70 books on the Bible, theology, missions, and the spiritual life, as well as many poems and hymns. He organized two missionary societies, the Christian Alliance and the International Missionary Alliance. Later the two combined under the name of the Christian and Missionary Alliance.

Singh, Sadhu Sundar. *1889–1929.* Indian Christian. Born into a high caste Sikh family, after his conversion Singh traveled across India with his Bible. He wore the saffron robe of the holy man, and for the rest of his life he was a Christian sadhu, going barefooted from village to village as a messenger for Christ.

Slessor, Mary. *1848–1915.* Scottish missionary to Africa.

Smith, George Adam. *1856–1942.* Scottish divine and biblical scholar.

Smith, Hannah Whitall. *1832–1911.* American Quaker philanthropist and author, best known for her book *The Christian's Secret of a Happy Life.*

Smith, Joseph. *1805–1844.* Founder of the Mormons.

Smith, Rodney (Gipsy). *1860–1947.* British evangelist.

Spangenberg, August Gottlieb. *1704–1792.* Bishop of the Moravian tradition. Next to Zinzendorf he is its most illustrious leader.

Spener, Philip Jacob. *1635–1705.* Founder of German Pietism. Spener wrote *Pia Desideria* (Heart's Desires), in which he urged six means of spiritual instruction and improvement of the Christian life.

Spurgeon, Charles Haddon. *1834–1892.* English Baptist preacher. He published more than 2,000 of his sermons. Some regard him as the greatest English preacher of the nineteenth century. His 49-volume *Metropolitan Pulpit* was a mammoth work. Other writings include *The Treasury of David* (a homiletic commentary on the Psalms in seven volumes).

Stott, John. *B. 1921.* Senior minister of All Souls Church of Langham Place, London. Immensely popular as a writer and speaker, Stott has been called the one who introduced "scholarly evangelism."

Strong, James. *1822–1894.* Methodist biblical scholar and educator. He is best known for his *Exhaustive Concordance of the Bible.*

Studd, Charles T. *1860–1931.* Missionary pioneer. He dedicated his life and inherited wealth to Christ. He and six others, the "Cambridge Seven," offered themselves to Hudson Taylor for missionary service in the China Inland Mission. They learned the language, donned Chinese garb, and ate with and like the Chinese, trying to substitute Chinese for Western ways to identify themselves with the natives.

Stylites, Simeon. *Ca. 390–459.* The father of the pillar saints.

Sunday, William (Billy) Ashley. *1862–1935.* American evangelist.

Swaggart, Jimmy. *B. 1936.* One of the best-known American televangelists. His popularity declined when he was charged with sexual improprieties.

Swedenborg, Emanuel. *1688–1772.* Mystic, scientist, and founder of the Church of the New Jerusalem.

Talmage, Thomas DeWitt. *1832–1902.* American Presbyterian minister and lecturer. For many years he edited the *Christian Herald*.

Tauler, Johann. *Ca. 1300–1361*. German mystic and preacher.

Taylor, James Hudson. *1832–1905*. Founder of China Inland Mission.

Taylor, Jeremy. *1613–1667*. Anglican divine and devotional writer.

Taylor, Kenneth Nathaniel. *B. 1917*. Publishing company executive. Taylor was director of Inter-Varsity Christian Fellowship, 1965–1969, and chairman of Unilit, 1972–1973. Since 1963 he has been the president of Tyndale House Publishers, which he founded. Taylor began his paraphrase of the Bible with the publication of his *Living Letters* in 1962 and the entire NT by 1967. In 1971, Taylor released the entire paraphrased *Living Bible*.

Ten Boom, Corrie. *1892–1983*. Dutch lay Christian, noted for her stance in Holland during World War II when she and her family sheltered Jews. She was later imprisoned. She traveled widely and authored *The Hiding Place* (1971), *In My Father's House*, and a number of other books.

Teresa (Theresa de Jesus) of Avila. *1515–1582*. Spanish mystic. She claimed to have had a vision of the image of Christ, who came to be present in her in bodily form. Her writings comprise chiefly mystical treatises, such as *The Way of Perfection* and *The Interior Castle*.

Teresa, Mother. *B. 1910*. Albanian nun who went to India to a convent in 1928. In 1946, Mother Teresa left the convent to work among the poor in the streets of Calcutta. In 1979, she received the Nobel Prize for Peace.

Tertullian, Quintus Septimius Florens. *Ca. 160–ca. 220*. Latin church father and apologist. He defended the Christian faith against heathen, Jew, and heretic, and urged pursuing the strictest morality of life.

Tetzel, Johann. *Ca. 1465–1519*. Commissioner of indulgences. Tetzel promised that indulgences would give complete forgiveness for all sin. The unscrupulous and shameful manner in which these indulgences were sold led Martin Luther to post his Ninety-five Theses on the church door at Wittenberg on October 31, 1517.

Theodoret of Cyrrhus. *Ca. 390–ca. 458*. Greek theologian and historian. His *Ecclesiastical History*, in five volumes continues the history of Eusebius from 325 to the year 429.

Thomas à Kempis. *1380–1471*. Compiler of *Imitation of Christ*.

Thomas Aquinas. *Ca. 1227–1274*. Roman Catholic schoolman. His great work *Summa Theologica* bears witness to his industry, logical discernment, depth of thought, and Catholic orthodoxy. His early study of Aristotle left its deep impression upon him, and his work bears the distinct marks of Aristotelianism.

Thomas, William Henry Griffith. *1861–1924*. Minister, scholar, and teacher. With Lewis Sperry Chafer and A. B. Winchester he cofounded Dallas Theological Seminary in Texas.

Tillich, Paul. *1886–1965*. Existential theologian who tried to make connections between theology and philosophy, religion and culture, Lutheranism and socialism, German and American thought. His *Systematic Theology* (1951–1964) attempted to offer theological answers to secular questions about reason, Being (i.e., God), and Jesus Christ.

Torrey, Reuben Archer. *1856–1928*. Congregational evangelist, teacher, and author.

Tozer, Aiden Wilson. *1897–1963*. Pastor with the Christian and Missionary Alliance Church in Toronto and Chicago. Prolific writer of books and editor of the *Alliance Weekly* he has been called a twentieth-century prophet.

Truett, George Washington. *1867–1944.* Southern Baptist preacher. One of the great preachers and evangelists of his day. Once president of the Southern Baptist Convention, for five years he was also president of the Baptist World Alliance.

Tyndale, William. *1494–1536.* Bible translator, Reformer, and martyr. His English NT was printed in 1525–1526.

Waldo (Valdez), Peter. *D. ca. 1217.* Founder of the Waldenses. He was a prosperous merchant of Lyons, France. After his conversion, he decided to dispose of his property, become a poor man, and preach to the common people. He became known as "the poor man of Lyons." He founded the Waldensian movement of people who went about preaching repentance.

Warner, Daniel Sidney. *1842–1925.* Founder of the Church of God (Anderson, Indiana).

Wesley, Charles. *1707–1788.* Brother of John Wesley and the hymnist of the English revival.

Wesley, John. *1703–1791.* Founder of Methodism. Forced out of the pulpits in the established Church of England, his founding of a separate denomination was inevitable. Out of his great revival work and the organizing of his converts into classes and societies, Wesley gradually developed the organization for the Methodist church.

Weymouth, Richard Francis. *1822–1902.* English Baptist philologist and NT scholar. He is remembered for "The New Testament in Modern Speech" translation.

White, Ellen Gould Harmon (Mrs. James White). *1827–1915.* Chief leader of the Seventh-day Adventists.

White, William. *1748–1836.* Patriarch of the Protestant Episcopal church.

Whitefield, George. *1714–1770.* English preacher and revivalist. An early associate of the Wesley brothers, he eventually parted company with them and started the Calvinistic Methodist Society.

Whyte, Alexander. *1836–1921.* Free Church of Scotland clergyman.

Williams, George. *1821–1905.* Congregationalist and founder of the Young Men's Christian Association.

Witherspoon, John. *1723–1794.* Presbyterian minister and signer of the Declaration of Independence.

Woolman, John. *1720–1772.* American Quaker preacher.

Wycliffe, John. *Ca. 1320–1384.* "The Morning Star of the Reformation." He wanted to provide England with a new translation of the Bible, acknowledging it as the only source of truth. He rejected the doctrine of infallibility of either pope or council, and held that papal decrees or pronouncements had authority only insofar as they were in harmony with the Scriptures. The clergy were not to rule, but to serve and help the people. He challenged transubstantiation, purgatory, and other Roman dogmas.

Xavier, Francis. *1506–1552.* Jesuit missionary.

Zinzendorf, Count Nicholas Ludwig von. *1700–1760.* Reorganizer of the Moravian or Bohemian Brethren.

Zwingli, Huldreich Ulrich. *1484–1531.* Swiss Reformer. He became chief pastor in the Great Minster Church in Zurich, where he expounded the Scriptures. He attacked the celibacy of the clergy, the worship of the image of Mary, the selling of indulgences, and other abuses of the church. His open break with Rome came when he rejected the Catholic coordination of Scripture and tradition and held the Bible as the only infallible authority.

Quotations and Allusions

"**D**on't make me your scapegoat," said a man who had no idea of the origin of his statement. Daily we fill our conversations with references to the Bible—and, like this man, we often do not know it.

Here are common expressions in our language, all with biblical roots.

Am I my brother's keeper? Cain answered God in this way after having killed his brother Abel. (See Gen. 4:9.) *The question refers to an unwillingness to assume responsibility for the welfare of others.*

Apple of the eye. An old English expression that referred to the pupil of the eye; the phrase is used in several English translations. God calls the psalmist the apple of his eye in Psalm 17:8. (See also Deut. 32:10; Prov. 7:2; Zech. 2:8.) *Apple of the eye refers to something cherished, precious, and protected.*

Baptism by fire. John the Baptist, in speaking of Jesus, said, "I indeed baptize you with water; but One mightier than I is coming, whose sandal strap I am not worthy to loose. He will baptize you with the Holy Spirit and fire." (See Luke 3:16.) *While John the Baptist probably meant fire in the sense of purifying, this phrase usually means facing a time of severe testing or pain. It is usually regarded as a life-changing experience. "He had his baptism of fire when he was a prisoner of war."*

Bread on the waters. From Ecclesiastes 11:1, "Cast your bread upon the waters, for you will find it after many days." *If we act generously toward others, we will be rewarded.*

Break bread. The actual phrase occurs only in Luke 24:35 where it refers to an ordinary meal, and in Acts 2:42 where it means the sacrament of the Lord's Supper. There are also several allusions to breaking of bread. *When we invite persons to break bread with us, we invite them to eat with us.*

Den of lions. Daniel was thrown into a den of lions so that they would kill him. (See Dan. 6.) *We use this phrase in reference to a naive person who faces sophisticated individuals or hostile situations.*

Do unto others as you would have them do unto you. Also known as the golden rule, it can read this way: "Whatever you want men to do to you, do also to them" (Matt. 7:12).

Eat, drink, and be merry, for tomorrow we may die. This quote alludes to Ecclesiastes 8:15 which reads, "So I commended enjoyment, because a man has nothing better under the sun than to eat, drink and be merry; for this will remain with him in his labor all the days of his life which God gives him under the sun." *As usually quoted, the phrase means we should enjoy life as much as possible now because we don't know what will happen in the future.*

Eye for an eye. When Moses gave the law he said that if men fight and hurt a pregnant woman and "if any harm follows, then you shall give life for life, eye for eye, tooth for tooth, hand for hand, foot for foot, burn for burn, wound for wound, stripe for stripe" (Exod. 21:23–24). These words stated the principle of justice in the Old Testament, meaning persons could not avenge themselves and exact more. For instance, if a man lost an eye he could not blind the other in both eyes. *This is usually a demand for revenge and exacting recompense.*

Eye of a needle. A figure of speech used by Jesus to illustrate the extreme difficulty in attaining salvation by those who put wealth first in life: "It is easier for a camel to go through the eye of a needle than for a rich man to enter the kingdom of God" (Matt. 19:24; Mark 10:25; Luke 18:25).

Fatted calf. (See Luke 15:23, 27.) In the parable of the prodigal son, this phrase referred to a calf especially fattened for a feast to celebrate the return of the wastrel son. *A fatted calf refers to a time of celebration.*

Fly in the ointment. This phrase comes from Ecclesiastes 10:1: "Dead flies putrefy the perfumer's ointment, and cause it to give off a foul odor." *Anything that hinders or prevents success is a fly in the ointment.*

Forbidden fruit. (See Gen. 3.) The fruit of the tree of knowledge of good and evil in the Garden of Eden that God commanded Adam and Eve not to eat. *Anything that is tempting but forbidden or dangerous (often associated with sexuality) is forbidden fruit to us.*

Get thee behind me, Satan. (See Matt. 16:23.) Jesus said these words to rebuke Peter, who did not want him to die. By trying to hold Jesus back from his divinely appointed mission, Peter was Satan, a tempter. *This is a rebuke for those who put any kind of temptation in our path.*

Go the second mile. Jesus' words were: "And whosoever compels you to go one mile, go with him two" (Matt. 5:41). In those days the Romans could compel a Jew to carry something for a mile. *To give more than expected or required, especially in an unpleasant task, is going the second mile.*

Golden calf. When Moses delayed coming down from the mountain with the Ten Commandments, the Israelites made an idol-image like a calf from gold jewelry and ornaments and worshiped it. (See Exod. 32.) *Any false god, anything worshiped or highly valued other than God, is a golden calf.*

Good Samaritan. Jesus told a parable about a Jew who was beaten, robbed, and left by the wayside. After others passed him by a Samaritan, an enemy of Jews, helped the man. (See Luke 10:25–37.) *Individuals who go out of their way to help others, especially strangers, are good Samaritans.*

Handwriting on the wall. When the proud Babylonian King Belshazzar was holding a feast, a hand mysteriously appeared and wrote words on the palace wall in a language no one understood. The king called for Daniel who interpreted the words that pronounced judgment upon Babylon (see Dan. 5). *Perceptive people foresee the doom that lurks ahead.*

Hide your light under a bushel. Jesus said, "You are the light of the world. A city that is set on a hill cannot be hidden. Nor do they light a lamp and put it under a basket, but on a lampstand, and it gives light to all who are in the house" (Matt. 5:14–15). *If we hide our light under a bushel, we hide our abilities.*

Jezebel. A wicked queen in ninth-century Israel who brought pagan worship to the nation. (See 1 Kings 16—21; Rev. 2:20.) *Jezebel has historically symbolized female wickedness, especially in connection with sexual matters. This label usu-*

ally refers to a woman who flaunts her charms or dresses inappropriately.

Job's comforters. In his misery, Job had a visit from three friends who offered him explanations for his misfortune. Everything they said was condemning, insisting that God sent Job's misfortune as punishment for secret sins. *Job's comforters are people who seemingly offer comfort or encouragement, but actually make us feel worse.*

Judas. This disciple of Jesus received thirty pieces of silver for betraying Jesus to the Romans. In the garden of Gethsemane, he kissed Jesus on the cheek so that the soldiers would know which man to arrest. *To call anyone a Judas is to call that person a traitor or betrayer. Sometimes we refer to the "Judas kiss" which has the same meaning but emphasizes that a close friend did the betraying.*

Judge not, that you be not judged. (See Matt. 7:1.) Jesus commanded his disciples not to judge, or condemn, because they would be just as harshly condemned. *Since we are all imperfect, none of us has the right to judge another harshly.*

Last shall be first. Jesus actually said, "But many who are first will be last, and the last first" (Matt. 19:30). *Those who prosper now through wicked means will, on the day of judgment, receive their recompense while those who suffer for living righteously will receive their reward.*

Leopard cannot change its spots. Jeremiah wrote the proverb this way: "Can the Ethiopian change his skin or the leopard its spots? Then may you also do good who are accustomed to do evil" (Jer. 13:23). *We cannot change our basic nature.*

Let him who is without sin cast the first stone. In an attempt to discredit Jesus, scribes and Pharisees brought a woman charged with adultery, saying that Moses commanded them to stone her and asking for his decision. They did this as a test. If Jesus forgave her, they could then ac-cuse him of disobeying the law. Jesus answered, "He who is without sin among you, let him throw a stone at her first" (John 8:7). The accusers, struck by their consciences, left. Jesus said to the woman, "Neither do I condemn you; go and sin no more" (v. 11). *None of us is sinless and, therefore, none of us is in the position to condemn others.*

Let the dead bury their dead. A would-be disciple wanted to follow Jesus but pleaded, "Lord, let me first go and bury my father" (Matt. 8:21). He was probably saying, "I will follow you someday when my father is dead and I'm free to go." Jesus replied, "Follow Me, and let the dead bury their own dead" (v. 22). *When people offer us frivolous excuses, we say, "Let the dead bury their own dead." Our words show that we give little credence to the excuse.*

Letter kills, but the spirit gives life. (See 2 Cor 3:6.) *Strict observance of laws or rules is less important than being true to the principles.*

Lion shall lie down with the wolf. This statement misquotes Isaiah 11:6: "The wolf also shall dwell with the lamb. The leopard shall lie down with the young goat, the calf and the young lion and the fatling together; and a little child shall lead them." Isaiah 65:25 reads, "The wolf and the lamb shall feed together, the lion shall eat straw like the ox, and dust shall be the serpent's food." *We use these words when we speak of natural enemies being at peace with each other.*

Love of money is the root of all evil. This is an incorrect quotation. When Paul wrote against those who make the gaining of wealth their primary aim in life, his words were: "For the love of money is a root of all kinds of evil, for which some have strayed from the faith in their greediness" (1 Tim. 6:10). Other versions say, "The root of all evil." *Evil and wrongdoing come from a yearning for wealth.*

Love your neighbor as yourself. Jesus summed up the law of Moses in two great commandments. First, we are to love God fully, and second, we are to love our neighbors as we love ourselves. (See Matt. 22:39; Lev. 19:18.) *This is a reminder to be kind and considerate of others. In recent years, the quotation has been used to remind us that God commands us to love ourselves. This then becomes the basis for a healthy sense of self-esteem. That is, we know God loves us and we are also commanded not only to love others but also ourselves.*

Man does not live by bread alone. When Satan tempted Jesus in the wilderness by telling him to turn stones into food, Jesus gave him this answer. (See Matt. 4:4.) *We have spiritual needs as well as physical and material ones.*

Manna from heaven. This expression does not appear in the Bible, but it alludes to God's miraculous provision of food for the Israelites during their years of wandering in the wilderness. *Manna from heaven refers to any unexpected good that comes our way, especially money.*

Meek shall inherit the earth. In the Sermon on the Mount, Jesus said, "Blessed are the meek, for they shall inherit the earth" (Matt. 5:5). *This statement is often used to console those who give up or ignore reward because they will receive it in God's eternal realm.*

More blessed to give than to receive. When Paul was giving his final farewell to the elders of Ephesus, he quotes the words of Jesus, not found in any of the four gospels: "It is more blessed to give than to receive" (Acts 20:35). *This is sometimes quoted as "It's better to. . . ."*

No man can serve two masters. Jesus said, "No one can serve two masters; for either he will hate the one and love the other, or else he will be loyal to the one and despise the other" (Matt. 6:24). The verse ends, "You cannot serve God and mammon." *We need a singular goal. Sometimes this quote is used as a rebuke that says we can't get the fullness from this world and still serve Jesus Christ.*

Nothing new under the sun. This quotation is adapted from Ecclesiastes 1:9, where the writer holds a pessimistic view of life and insists, "That which has been is what will be, that which is done is what will be done, and there is nothing new under the sun." *This is a cynical way of stating that nothing original can happen.*

Original sin. This is a theological term referring to the disobedience of Adam and Eve in the Garden of Eden. *The phrase often is used to refer to sexual sins.*

Patience of Job. In the NT, the book of James urges readers to be patient and says, "Indeed we count them blessed who endure. You have heard of the perseverance of Job [*patience* in some translations] and seen the end intended by the Lord—that the Lord is very compassionate and merciful" (James 5:11). Readers knew of Job who had suffered every kind of calamity except death, yet he still maintained his faith in God. *This is usually a description of someone who suffers or puts up with difficult and painful circumstances without complaining.*

Pearl of great price. Jesus told a parable about a trader who sold everything he owned to purchase an invaluable pearl, "who, when he had found one pearl of great price, went and sold all that he had and bought it" (Matt. 13:46). *This quote refers to giving ourselves to anything of immense value. Some use this to mean giving up everything for salvation.*

Pearls before swine. (See Matt. 7:6.) Adapted from the Sermon on the Mount where Jesus said, "Do not give what is holy to the dogs; nor cast your pearls before swine, lest they trample them under their feet, and turn and tear you in pieces." Jesus meant for the disciples to preach to those most likely to listen. *If we cast pearls before swine, we share or give things of value to those who have no appreciation for their worth.*

Physician, heal thyself. (Or *yourself* in modern translations). (See Luke 4:23.)

Jesus said he expected to hear this proverb from people in his hometown. He added, "Assuredly, I say to you, no prophet is accepted in his own country" (v. 24). (See *Prophet is not without honor.*) *We use this saying to tell individuals to look at their own shortcomings instead of judging others.*

Pride goes before a fall. This saying misquotes Proverbs 16:18, "Pride goes before destruction, and a haughty spirit before a fall." *When we feel smug or boastful we are setting ourselves up for big disappointments.*

Prophet is without honor in his own country. In Matthew's Gospel, when the people in the synagogue of his hometown of Nazareth rejected Jesus, he said, "A prophet is not without honor except in his own country and in his own house" (see Matt. 13:57). (See *Physician, heal thyself.*) *Those close to us do not appreciate us.*

Render to Caesar the things that are Caesar's and to God the things that are God's. (See Matt. 22:21.) Religious leaders plotted against Jesus and one of their questions was, "Is it lawful to pay taxes to Caesar or not?" Palestine was then under Roman rule and the term *Caesar* stood for Rome. *We have an obligation to give to the world whatever belongs to the world and give to God what belongs to God. Sometimes this statement is a way of saying that we give honor and respect to whoever deserves it.*

Salt of the earth. Jesus called his disciples *salt*, and the complete verse concludes with, "but if the salt loses its flavor, how shall it be seasoned? It is then good for nothing but to be thrown out and trampled underfoot by men" (Matt. 5:13). Jesus meant that true Christians add flavor (meaning) to life by the way they live. These words also contain a note of warning. *When we use this expression, we refer to someone who is solid and unflappable.*

Scapegoat. On the Day of Atonement, the high priest selected a goat and, laying his hands on the animal, confessed the sins of Israel. This act symbolized the transferring of the nation's guilt by placing it on the goat who was then killed. (See Lev. 16.) *An innocent person suffering for the wrongdoing of another is a scapegoat.*

Serve both God and mammon. *Mammon* was a Hebrew word that meant "material possessions" (see Matt. 6:24). (See *No man can serve two masters.*) *We cannot live with divided loyalties.*

Shibboleth. This Hebrew word was used by Jephthah and the men of Gilead at the Jordan River to capture the straggling Ephraimites they had not killed in battle. The Ephraimites could not pronounce *sh* and said *Sibboleth.* By their mispronunciation, they identified themselves as the men of Ephraim. *We use this saying derisively when we speak of another group's catchword or rallying cry.*

Soft answer turns away wrath. (See Prov. 15:1.) *Giving a gentle response to angry individuals will dissipate their venom.*

Spare the rod and spoil the child. The correct statement is "He who spares his rod hates his son, but he who loves him disciplines him promptly" (Prov. 13:24). *Parents who love their children discipline them.*

Strain at a gnat. Jesus, rebuking the religious leaders of his day, said, "Blind guides, who strain out a gnat and swallow a camel!" (Matt. 23:24). He referred to the the custom of straining wine to take out the impurities before it was served. *Some people exercise meticulous care over insignificant matters and ignore important items.*

Thirty pieces of silver. The money paid by the chief priests to Judas Iscariot for betraying Jesus. He later threw the money at the feet of the authorities who had paid him. (See *Judas.*) *This is sometimes called blood money—money (or position) received through betraying friends or a prin-*

ciple. This phrase can also refer to paying anyone to commit a deceptive or treacherous act.

Thorn in the flesh. Paul used this vague phrase to refer to an extreme difficulty he regularly encountered (see 2 Cor. 12:7). In context, Paul's experiences of visions and revelations came to him from God. (See 2 Cor. 12:1–6.) This difficulty came to prevent Paul from being "exalted above measure." He called the thorn a messenger of Satan, because it tried to prevent his work from going forward. Some scholars think Paul referred to a physical condition and have suggested a variety of diseases such as epilepsy, malaria, or bad eyesight. *Having a problem or burden that continues to trouble us is a thorn in the flesh. A woman with a congenital defect referred to it as her thorn in the flesh.*

Through a glass darkly. This saying refers to a mirror which, in the first century, poorly reflected the image. (See 1 Cor. 13:12.) *We don't understand things clearly at the present but we will eventually.*

Time to be born and a time to die. "To everything there is a season, A time for every purpose under heaven: A time to be born, and a time to die" (Eccles. 3:1–2). *There is a right moment for everything.*

Turn the other cheek. Adapted from Jesus' saying, "You have heard that it was said, 'An eye for an eye and a tooth for a tooth' But I tell you not to resist an evil person. But whosoever slaps you on your right cheek, turn the other to him also" (Matt. 5:38). (See *Eye for an eye.*) *We accept injury or insult without retaliating.*

Valley of the shadow of death. This phrase comes from Psalm 23:4, "Yea, though I walk through the valley of the shadow of death, I will fear no evil; For You are with me; Your rod and Your staff, they comfort me." *When our life is in peril, we can trust God to protect us or to give us peace. We often use this saying particularly in speaking of death itself.*

Vanity of vanities; all is vanity. The pessimistic tone of the book of Ecclesiastes begins, "'Vanity of vanities,' says the Preacher; 'Vanity of vanities, all is vanity.'" The writer scrutinizes life only to find it empty and meaningless. *Sometimes we use this phrase with a similar meaning of vanity in the sense of uselessness. More often, we use it in referring to an excessive concern with our appearance, as a way of saying that a person is vain or self-centered.*

Voice of one crying in the wilderness. Isaiah 40:3 reads, "The voice of one crying in the wilderness: 'Prepare the way of the LORD; make straight in the desert a highway for our God.'" Matthew quotes this verse (3:3) showing that John the Baptist's appearance fulfilled this prophecy because he heralded the coming of Jesus Christ. *When individuals take their stand and feel all alone or unsupported, they say they are like a single voice in the wilderness, that is, they are unheard or uncared about.*

Walking on water. This expression refers to Jesus walking from the shore of the Sea of Galilee to his disciples who were in a boat. The winds were raging and Jesus calmed them. (See Matt. 14:22–33.) *When individuals face particularly difficult tasks, they compare them to walking on water. Sometimes the phrase refers to the high regard some people have of others. "She thinks he's so wonderful that he can do anything, even walk on water."*

Wolf shall also dwell with the Lamb. (See *Lion shall lie down.*)

Sickness and Healing, Magic and Miracles

Sickness and Disease

Unquestionably the Hebrews knew less about science and the healing art than other ancient cultures such as the Egyptians, Babylonians, and Assyrians. From the Bible we find no evidence of medical practitioners. The heads of families or women probably performed the simple operation of circumcision. (See Gen. 17:10–14; 34:24; Exod. 4:25.)

The first medicines were probably introduced to the Israelites though the Egyptian people, especially the priests. Egyptians also embalmed their dead with spices and perfume—a custom that the Israelites soon came to accept.

In Bible times, medicines were made from minerals, animal substances, herbs, wines, fruits, and other parts of plants. Scripture often refers to the medicinal use of these substances.

For example, the "balm in Gilead" is mentioned as a healing substance (Jer. 8:22). The "balm" is thought to have been an aromatic excretion from an evergreen tree or a form of frankincense. Wine mixed with myrrh was known to relieve pain by dulling the senses. This remedy was offered to Jesus as he hung on the cross, but he refused to drink it (Mark 15:23). The Israelites anointed their sick with soothing lotions of olive oil and herbs. In the story of the good Samaritan, oil and wine were poured into the wounds of the beaten man (Luke 10:34). The early Christians continued this practice, anointing the sick as they prayed for them (James 5:14).

Matthew 23:23 mentions certain spices that were often used as antacids. Mandrakes were used to arouse sexual desire (Gen. 30:14). Other plants were used as remedies or stimulants.

In times of sickness, the Israelites tended to fall back on religious ritual and, ultimately, on God. (See Exod. 15:26; Pss. 103:3; 147:3; Jer. 17:14.) In one instance we find divine reproach for not turning to God during an illness. Asa went to the physicians instead of to God. (See 2 Chron. 16:12.)

By Jesus' time the Jews had become enlightened through their contacts with Egypt, Babylon, Greece, and Rome. They cultivated philosophy, law, and medicine. Throughout the NT (especially the Gospels and Acts), they name specific diseases such as palsy, bloody flux, and lunacy. Physicians were a profession as evidenced by Matthew 9:12 and other passages. Luke was the beloved physician (see Col. 4:14).

Sickness

Jesus healed the blind (Mark 10:51–52), the lame (Matt. 21:14), the deaf (Mark 7:33–35), and the maimed (Matt. 15:30). The Greek word translated as "maimed" referred to a person who was missing an arm or a leg. On one occasion, Jesus also restored a person's withered hand (Matt. 12:9–13)—an act of compassion that brought criticism from the Pharisees because he dared to heal on the Sabbath.

Another distinct disability in Bible times was impotence, or the inability of a male to father children. Sometimes a royal household servant was castrated as a precautionary measure, particularly if he worked with the members of the king's harem or other women of the palace. Such sterilized domestic servants were known as eunuchs (Acts 8:27–39). Sometimes impotence was caused by accident. Regardless of the cause, a person who was a eunuch (Lev. 21:20; *broken stones*, KJV; *crushed testicles*, RSV) was barred from serving as a priest under the Levitical law.

The law specifically stated that a person with an outward blemish or defect could not serve as a priest. This included "a man blind or lame, who has a marred face (*flat nose*, KJV), or any limb too long, a man who has a broken foot or broken hand, or is a hunchback (*crookbacked*, KJV), or a dwarf, or a man who has a defect in his eye" (Lev. 21:18–20).

The reasoning behind these strict regulations was that only those who were physically perfect were worthy of serving at the altar of the Lord.

Diseases

The Hebrews believed illness was caused by sin in the individual, which God had to punish (Gen. 12:17; Prov. 23:29–32), sin of a person's parents (2 Sam. 12:14–15), or seduction by Satan (Matt. 9:34; Luke 13:16).

However, several passages in the Bible show there is not always such a simple explanation for disease (for example, Job 34:19–20).

The Bible contains many general references to illness and disease without naming a specific malady. For example, the words *affliction* (Ps. 25:18) and *infirmity* (Jer. 10:19)

Ruins of the hospital used by the early Greek physician Hippocrates at Cos.

PHOTO BY HOWARD VOS

An elaborate sarcophagus, or coffin, at the city of Tyre, dating from the roman period.

PHOTO BY HOWARD VOS

often refer to an overwhelming sense of pain or sorrow that might have been caused by either illness or spiritual despair.

The words *pestilence* (Jer. 21:6) and *plague* (Num. 11:33) seem to refer to contagious diseases of epidemic proportions, which God sent occasionally as instruments of judgment. In the NKJV, the word *pestilence* is used of the mysterious disease that struck the livestock of the Egyptians (Exod. 9:3; *murrain*, KJV).

Other words in the Bible that indicate the presence or effects of illness or disease include *bruise* (Isa. 30:26), *sore* (Lev. 13:27), and *wound* (Job 34:6). A bruise occurs when the flesh beneath the skin is injured but the skin remains unbroken. Sores and wounds involve a puncture of the skin.

The following specific illnesses or diseases are mentioned or implied in the Bible. This list is keyed to the NKJV, with cross-references from five additional popular English versions: KJV, NASB, NEB, NIV, and RSV.

Ague.   (See *Fever*.)

Blains.   (See *Boils*.)

Blindness.   Three types of blindness are mentioned in the Bible: *sudden* blindness caused by flies and aggravated by dirt, dust, and glare; *gradual* blindness caused by old age; and *chronic* blindness.

Paul suffered temporary blindness on the road to Damascus (Acts 9:8). While Scripture often refers to the elderly as those whose eyes "grew dim" (see Gen. 27:1; 48:10; 1 Sam. 4:15), being blind usually refers to chronic blindness.

The Israelites had compassion for the blind. God placed a curse on those who made the blind wander out of their way (Deut. 27:18). Jesus ministered to many people who were blind. He said, "[God] has anointed Me to preach the gospel to the poor; He has sent Me to heal the brokenhearted, to proclaim liberty to the captives and recovery of sight to the blind" (Luke 4:18). Jesus healed a man born blind (John 9:1–41), a blind man whose healing was gradual (Mark 8:22–24), two blind men sitting by the wayside (Matt. 20:30–34), and a great number of others (Mark 10:46–52; Luke 7:21).

Blindness was often understood to be a punishment for evildoing. Examples are the men of Sodom (Gen. 19:11), the Syrian army (2 Kings 6:18), and Elymas at Paphos (Acts 13:6–11).

Blood, Flow of.   According to the Mosaic law, a woman suffering from menstrual disorders was considered ceremonially unclean (Lev. 15:25). One such woman who had suffered for 12 years (Luke 8:43–48) touched the hem of Jesus' garment and was healed immediately because of her great faith. The NASB refers to this condition as a *hemorrhage*.

Bloody flux.   (See *Dysentery*.)

Boils.   This term probably refers to *anthrax*, a disease transmitted to humans by cattle, sheep, goats, and horses. The disease is caused by a rod-shaped bacterium that forms spores. These spores, in turn, can infect humans, who develop a boil-like lesion with a pustule (blain). In the infectious stage, the blain is called a malignant pustule. God inflicted boils on the Egyptians when the Pharaoh refused to let the Hebrews go to the Promised Land (Exod. 9:9–10; *blains*, KJV). This was also one of the afflictions that God threatened to bring upon the Hebrew people because of their grumbling after the Exodus from Egypt (Deut. 28:27; *botch*, KJV).

Satan was permitted to afflict Job with boils from the top of his head to the tip of his toes (Job 2:7). King Hezekiah also was afflicted with boils (2 Kings 20:7), which Isaiah cured by applying a poultice of figs. A fresh fig poultice has a drawing effect. Before the advent of antibiotics, this type of treatment for boils was common. Other words for boils used by different translations of the Bible are *sores* and *scabs*.

Botch.   (See *Boils*.)

Bowels, Disease of. (See *Dysentery*.)

Cancer. This disease is mentioned only once in the Bible: "And their message will spread like cancer" (2 Tim. 2:17; *canker*, KJV; *gangrene*, NASB, NEB, NIV, RSV). The word refers to the circulatory deterioration known as gangrene, which spreads rapidly and eats up tissue.

Canker. (See *Cancer*.)

Consumption. Moses warned the rebellious Israelites, "The LORD will strike you with consumption, with fever, with inflammation, with severe burning fever" (Deut. 28:22; *wasting disease*, NIV). This disease is probably *tuberculosis*, a consumptive infection of the lungs.

Dropsy. This word describes an abnormal accumulation of serous fluid in the body's connective tissue or in a serous cavity. The accumulation causes swelling. Jesus met at least one victim of dropsy in a Pharisee's house. Asked by Jesus if he thought it lawful to heal on the Sabbath, the Pharisee declined to answer. Jesus then healed the sufferer (Luke 14:1–4).

Dumb, Dumbness. (See *Muteness*.)

Dumb spirit. (See *Mute spirit*.)

Dysentery. This disease rots the bowels, or the intestines, in its advanced stage (2 Chron. 21:15–19). The fibrine separates from the inner coating of the intestines and is expelled. The KJV refers to a severe form of dysentery as the "bloody flux." The father of a Christian named Publius lay sick with this disease (Acts 28:8). Paul prayed for him and the man was healed. Some scholars believe dysentery was also the strange malady afflicting King Hezekiah of Judah (2 Kings 20:1).

Eczema. A symptom of this disease was an inflammation of the skin, marked by redness, itching, and oozing lesions that become scaly, encrusted, or hardened (Lev. 21:20; 22:22; *scurvy*, KJV; *itching disease*, RSV).

Emerods. (See *Tumor*.)

Epilepsy. (See *Mute spirit*.)

Feet, Diseased. Excessive uric acid in the blood causes this kidney ailment and manifests itself through painful inflammation of joints. King Asa had a foot disease, apparently *gout* according to 2 Chronicles 16:12–13.

Fevers. The KJV uses the word *ague* to describe a burning fever. Moses warned the rebellious Israelites that "I will ever appoint over you terror, panic, consumption and the burning ague that shall consume the eyes" (Lev. 26:16, KJV).

When Jesus found Simon Peter's mother-in-law ill with this symptom, he rebuked the fever and she was able to rise from her bed and wait on the disciples (Luke 4:38–39). On another occasion, Jesus healed the feverish son of a government official (John 4:46–54). Many diseases in ancient Israel were characterized by high fevers, the most common of which were *malaria* and *typhoid*.

Gangrene. (See *Cancer; Feet, Disease of*.)

Hemorrhage. (See *Blood, Flow of*.)

Insanity. King Saul seems to have had symptoms of a *bipolar personality*, or *manic depressive* (see 1 Sam. 16:14–23). The Bible mentions others who may have suffered from mental or nervous disorders such as King Nebuchadnezzar (see Dan. 4:33–34). The words *mad* and *madness* are also used by various translations to refer to this malady.

Intestines, Disease of. (See *Dysentery*.)

Itch. This is a curse God threatened to send upon the Hebrew people if they departed from faith in him (Deut. 28:27). Itch is caused by a microscopic mite that burrows into the skin, causing extreme discomfort.

Itching disease. (See *Eczema*.)

Leprosy. Leprosy, or *Hansen's disease*, is one of the most dreaded diseases of the world. Leprosy is caused by a bacillus and is characterized by the formation of nodules that spread, causing loss of sensation and deformity. Now treated with sulfone drugs, leprosy is perhaps the least infectious of all known contagious diseases. It was often misdiagnosed in biblical times because people believed it was highly contagious and hereditary. Leviticus 13:1–17 condemns leprosy as a plague.

On the basis of a hair in a scab, a pimple, or a spot on the skin that had turned white, the priest would declare a person to be a leper and would quarantine him for seven days. If no change in the spot occurred by then, the quarantine would be extended another week. At that time, if the spot had started to fade, the "leper" would be pronounced cured and returned to his normal life. However, if the spot remained or had spread, the person was declared unclean and banished. The words *scurf* and *scall* are applied to these spots on the skin by various English translations (see Lev. 13:30).

Leprosy was common in the Near East. When Hebrews were healed of leprosy, they were to offer certain sacrifices and engage in rites of purification (Lev. 14:1–32). Jesus healed lepers on numerous occasions (Luke 5:12–13; 17:12–19).

Lunacy, Lunatic. (See *Mute spirit.*)

Mad, Madness. (See *Insanity.*)

Muteness. This is the temporary loss of speech, usually caused by a brain lesion but sometimes attributed to an emotional upset. Likely this happened to Ezekiel (Ezek. 33:22). When an angel told Zacharias that he would be the father of John the Baptist, the old man could not speak (Luke 1:22).

Mute spirit. The NKJV uses this phrase and it probably refers to *epilepsy.* This disorder was marked by erratic electrical discharges of the central nervous system and manifested by convulsive attacks. One

man brought his epileptic son to Jesus (see Mark 9:17–29; the KJV says the boy had a "dumb spirit"). Jesus healed him. Among the scores of people brought to Jesus for healing, many were epileptics (Matt. 4:24; *lunatics,* KJV).

Ancients believed that epilepsy was caused by the moon, and they referred to epileptics as being moonstruck. Psalm 121:6 might have this idea in mind when it says, "The sun shall not strike you by day, nor the moon by night."

Palsy. (See *Paralysis, Paralytic.*)

Paralysis, Paralytic. These words refer to total paralysis. The Gospels record an incident in which Jesus healed a paralyzed man at Capernaum (Mark 2:1–12). Acts declares that the apostles healed people with this disease (8:7; 9:33–34; *palsy,* KJV).

Scab, Scabs. (See *Boils.*)

Scall. (See *Leprosy.*)

Scurf. (See *Leprosy.*)

Scurvy. (See *Eczema.*)

Sore, Sores. (See *Boils.*)

Tumor. The specific nature of this disease is unknown, although some scholars believe the word refers to *hemorrhoids* (Deut. 28:27; 1 Sam. 6:11). Other versions prefer *ulcers* (RSV) or *emerods* (KJV).

Ulcer. (See *Tumor.*)

Wasting disease. (See *Consumption.*)

Worms. Isaiah warned that the rebellious people of Israel would be afflicted with worms (Isa. 51:8). He also predicted this fate for Babylon (see 14:11). This parasitic disease could be fatal because no medical remedies were available. Tapeworms and hookworms live as parasites in the human body and cause illness and disease.

The Bible says that an angel of the Lord struck Herod the Great so that worms ate him and he died (see Acts 12:23).

Healing Methods—Heathen and Holy

Ancient peoples sought healing from many sources. The Jewish nation tried many of the methods forbidden by God, taking up the customs of their healthen neighbors.

Here are various ways individuals in Bible times sought health and healing.

Child sacrifice. Passing a son or daughter through the fire refers to child sacrifice, and the fact that God outlawed it meant it must have been done in Bible times (Deut. 18:10). Second Kings 16:3 records that King Ahaz sacrificed his son in this way, possibly to appease a pagan god. His grandson, King Manasseh, sacrificed his sons two generations later (2 Kings 21:6; 2 Chron. 33:6).

Diet. Most of the laws about food consumption are included in the first five books of the OT. The restrictions involving meats were based on the simple fact that only animals with separated hooves who chewed the cud were suitable for eating (Lev. 11:3). This law excluded pigs, camels, rabbits, and mice.

Divination. (See *Soothsaying; Witchcraft.*)

Fortune telling. This term meant predicting the future through magic and enchantment. At Philippi, Paul healed a slave girl who earned a lot of money for her masters by fortune telling (Acts 16:16; *soothsaying*, KJV, RSV).

Hygiene. The law of Moses required that the body and clothes be washed after contact with a diseased or dead person. The regulations about contact with dead bodies specified a period of uncleanness lasting seven days.

Magic. The Hebrew word translated as *magic* appears only in connection with Egyptian and Babylonian magicians. The first cluster of verses relates to Joseph in Egypt (Gen. 41:8, 24); the second appears in connection with the plagues (Exod. 7:11–9:11); and the third deals with Daniel and the various government-supported magicians of Babylon (Dan. 1:20; 2:2, 10, 27; 4:7, 9; 5:11).

Magic comes from a Greek word that appears several times in the NT. Simon the sorcerer is one example (Acts 8:9–25) and Elymas the sorcerer another (Acts 13:6–8).

Mediums. Consulting mediums (Deut. 18:11) may be the same thing as practicing wizardry. It describes the witch at En Dor, whom Saul engaged to bring up the spirit of Samuel (1 Sam. 28:3, 9; *familiar spirits*, KJV).

Miracles. Historic events or natural phenomena that appear to violate natural laws are miracles, but to believers they also reveal God through the eyes of faith.

Necromancy. The phrase "calling up the dead" occurs only in Deuteronomy 18:11, although this is exactly what an OT witch did.

Occult practices. Occult practices were common among the pagan nations of the ancient world. But attempts to contact or control evil spirits were expressly forbidden to the Hebrew people. Deuteronomy 18:10–11 mentions specific occult practices that were forbidden by the law of Moses.

Omens, Interpreting. Behind the phrase "interpreting omens" (*enchantments*, KJV), lie four different Hebrew words. The most common of the four occurs in Genesis 30:27 where Laban says that he has learned from experience (that is, divination) that God was with Jacob. Other forms occur in Genesis 44:5 (Joseph's divining with his cup) and Leviticus 19:26 and Deuteronomy 18:10 (Baalam's activity).

Purification, Ritual. Temple priests had several medical functions. Leviticus describes seven kinds of ritual purification that had medical significance: post-childbirth (Lev. 12), leprosy (Lev. 13), sexually transmitted diseases (Lev. 15:12–15), male sexual function (Lev. 15:16–18), sexual intercourse (Lev. 15:18), menstruation (Lev. 15:19–30), and dead bodies (Lev. 21:1–3).

Sanitary rituals. Several rituals were observed among the Hebrew people to maintain sanitary conditions and to promote good health. One of these involved bodily discharge. Although not all bodily discharges were infectious, all were treated as potentially infectious.

Snake charming. (See *Omens, Interpreting*.)

Soothsaying. Soothsaying is a relatively rare word in the Bible describing some form of divination, the practitioner of which is also described by the KJV as "observer of times" (Deut. 18:10). Because the word sounds like a Hebrew word for "cloud," some scholars believe *soothsaying* refers to "cloud reading." This practice may have been similar to *tea leaf reading* or *astrology*.

Sorcery. Sorcery or witchcraft was forbidden in the law of Moses (Exod. 22:18; Deut. 18:10), although it was apparently practiced by the worst of the kings of Israel and Judah. (See 2 Kings 9:22; 2 Chron. 33:6; Nah. 3:4.) (See also *Spiritism*.)

Another NT word translated *"sorcery"* comes from the same Greek word as our English word, *pharmacy*.

Spells, Conjuring. Conjuring spells, also translated as *charm*, appears in Deuteuronomy 18:11, Psalm 58:5; Isaiah 47:9, 12. Sometimes the word is rendered as *enchantments*. A different Hebrew word, related to a word for *bind*, lies behind the translation of Isaiah 19:3 and may mean "casting a spell."

Spiritism. The word for "spiritist" (Deut. 18:11) always appears with "witch." The root of the word in Hebrew is the verb "to know." In modern English, *wizard* means "someone wise, inventive, clever, or skillful."

Washing, Ritual. The Bible records a few cases in which ailing persons performed a ritual washing in order to receive a cure.

When Naaman contracted leprosy, Elisha instructed him to submerge himself seven times in the Jordan River. Naaman did so and was healed (2 Kings 5:10).

Witchcraft. The practice of witchcraft (Deut. 18:10), or divination, was a means for extracting information or guidance from a god. The word describes the activity of Balaam the soothsayer or professional prophet, who was hired to curse Israel (Num. 22:7; 23:23; Josh. 13:22).

Miracles and Gifts————

Miracles in the Old Testament

Miracles in the OT are connected especially with the great events in Israel's history, such as the call of Abraham (Gen. 12:1–3), the birth of Moses (Exod. 1:1–2:22), the Exodus from Egypt (Exod. 12:1–14:31), the giving of the law (Exod. 19:1–20:26), and the entry into the Promised Land (Josh. 3:1–4:7).

These miracles are for salvation, but God also acts in history for judgment (Gen. 11:1–9).

• The plagues of the Exodus showed God's sovereign power in judgment and salvation (Exod. 7:3–5).

• In parting the water, God showed his love and protection for Israel as well as his judgment on Egypt for its failure to recognize God (Exod. 15:2, 4–10).

• During the wilderness journey, God demonstrated his love and protection in supplying the daily manna (Exod. 16:1–36).

• Elijah controlled the rain and successfully challenged the pagan priests of Baal (1 Kings 17:1; 18:1–40).

Through all of these events—and others—God revealed himself as Lord, as Savior of Israel, and as punisher of the nation's enemies.

Miracles in the New Testament

The NT miracles are essentially expressions of God's salvation and glory.

Why did Jesus perform miracles? Jesus answered this question himself. When in prison, John the Baptist sent some of his disciples to Jesus to see if he was the "Coming One" (Matt. 11:3). Jesus told them to inform John of what he had done: "The blind see, the lame walk; the lepers are cleansed and the deaf hear; the dead are raised up, and the poor have the gospel preached to them" (11:5). With these words, Jesus declared that his miracles were the fulfillment of the promises of the Messiah's kingdom as foretold by Isaiah (35:5–6; 61:1). Jesus' miracles were signs of the presence of the kingdom of God.

Jesus did not work miracles to prove his deity or messiahship. In fact, he refused to work miracles as proofs (Matt. 12:38–42; Luke 11:29–32). His death was the proof to Israel.

The Acts of the Apostles is a book of miracles. Again, these miracles are a continuation of the miracles of Jesus, made possible through the Holy Spirit. The miracles of the apostles were done in the name of Jesus and were manifestations of God's salvation (Acts

3:11). This thread of continuity is seen in Peter's miracles that paralleled those of Jesus. (See Luke 5:18–26; 7:22; 8:49–56; Acts 3:1–16; 9:32–35, 36–42.)

God began his church with a powerful display of miracles:
- At Pentecost, the Holy Spirit came on the people with power (Acts 2:1–13), leading to conversions (Acts 2:41).
- When Philip went to Samaria, the Spirit of God anointed him with power (Acts 8:4–40).
- When Peter met Cornelius, great power was in evidence (see Acts 10:1–48).
- Through Peter, judgment fell upon Ananias and Sapphira who acted in hypocrisy (Acts 4:32–5:11).
- The church's power became evident when they prayed (see Acts 4:23–31).
- Paul's transforming vision (Acts 16:6–10) was out of the ordinary.

Miraculous powers were also present in the apostles:
- Peter healed a lame man (Acts 3:1–6).
- Peter healed a paralytic (Acts 9:32–35).
- Peter raised the dead (Acts 9:36–42).
- The apostles performed mighty miracles (Acts 5:2–16).
- Peter was miraculously released from prison (Acts 12:1–11).
- Paul's conversion was a startling incident (Acts 9:1–19).
- The ability to work miracles was taken as a sign of apostleship by Paul (Rom. 15:18–19; 2 Cor. 12:12).

Spiritual Gifts in the New Testament

The lists of the gifts of the Spirit in the NT show that miracles were one of the means by which believers ministered to others—inside and outside the church (Rom. 12:6–8; 1 Cor. 12:8–10, 28–30; Eph. 4:11–12).

These gifts were given by the Holy Spirit to Christians for adding to and building up the church. These lists are scattered throughout the Bible and were probably never intended to be all-inclusive.

For example the spiritual gifts listed in 1 Corinthians 12:8–10 are

> Discerning of spirits
> Faith
> Healings (since the word is plural, some scholars have suggested that some were endowed with the ability to heal certain types of diseases)
> Interpretation of tongues
> Miracles
> Prophecy
> Speaking in tongues or other languages (Greek *glossalalia,* such as on the day of Pentecost in Acts 2:4)
> Wisdom
> Word of knowledge (implying specific and limited knowledge such as what Peter showed in Acts 5:1–9)

Different lists appear in Romans 12:3–8, Ephesians 4:7–12, and 1 Peter 4:10–11.

Paul indicated that these gifts are equally valid but not equally valuable—their value is determined by the need in the church. In explaining this matter to the Corinthians, who were endowed with gifts but engaged in much strife as well, he used the analogy of the human body. All members of the body, he said, have functions but some are more important than others. The service of Christians must be in proportion to the gifts they possess.

Sin
and Virtue

Sin

The Bible defines *sin* as "lawlessness" (1 John 3:4) and "transgression of God's will, either by omitting to do what God's law requires or by doing what it forbids." Transgression can occur in thoughts (1 John 3:15); words (Matt. 5:22); or actions and deeds (Rom. 1:32).

Here are some of the sins specifically stated in the Bible.

Abomination. This includes anything that offends the spiritual, religious, or moral sense and causes extreme disgust, hatred, or loathing. Among the items described as an abomination were the carved images of pagan gods (Deut. 7:25–26), the sacrifice to God of inferior, blemished animals (Deut. 17:1), and the practice of idolatry (Deut. 17:2–5).

Other abominations include sexual transgressions (Lev. 18) and the practice of magic and witchcraft (Deut. 18:9–12). Most of the Hebrew words translated *abomination* have the meaning of impure, filthy, and unclean—foul smelling and objectionable to a holy God.

Adultery. Adultery involves willful sexual intercourse with an individual other than one's spouse. Jesus expanded the meaning of adultery to include the cultivation of lust: "Whoever looks at a woman to lust for her has already committed adultery with her in his heart" (Matt. 5:28).

Ambition, Selfish. Paul condemned the spirit of strife and selfishness (2 Cor. 12:20; Gal. 5:20). This type of behavior is alien to the spirit of Christ and inappropriate for Christian believers.

Apostasy. An extremely strong word, *apostasy* means a falling away from the faith. The nation of Israel fell into repeated backslidings (Jer. 5:6). Jeremiah predicted the judgment of God upon such disloyalty: "Your wickedness will chasten you, and your apostasy will reprove you" (Jer. 2:19, RSV).

Backbiting. A graphic word, *backbiting* means to speak slanderously or spitefully about others when they are not present, i.e., behind their backs (Ps. 15:3; Rom. 1:30). Backbiting involves some element of deceit and cowardice.

Backsliding. This word means to revert to sin or wrongdoing; to lapse morally in the practice of religion. The term is found mainly in Jeremiah (2:19; 31:22; 49:4) and refers to the lapse of the nation of Israel into paganism and idolatry.

Bestiality. This word refers to sexual intercourse between a human being and an animal. According to the Mosaic law, both the beast and the guilty person were to be put to death for this abomination (Exod. 22:19; Lev. 18:23; Deut. 27:21).

Blasphemy. *Blasphemy* is the specific act of cursing, slandering, reviling, or showing contempt or lack of reverence for God. In the OT, blaspheming God was a crime punishable by death (Lev. 24:15–16).

Carnality. Anything sensual, worldly, nonspiritual, and relating to or given to the desires and appetites of the flesh or body is considered *carnal*. Paul contrasted spiritual people—that is, those under the control of the Holy Spirit—with the carnal—those under the control of the flesh (Rom. 8:5–7l; Cor. 3:1–4). The word *carnal* is usually reserved in the NT to describe immature Christians.

Covetousness. An intense desire to possess something (or someone) that belongs to another is referred to as *covetousness*. The Ten Commandments prohibit this attitude (Exod. 20:17; Deut. 5:21).

Curse. A curse is a prayer for injury, harm, or misfortune to befall others. Noah, for instance, pronounced a curse on Canaan (Gen. 9:25). Isaac pronounced a curse on anyone who cursed Jacob (Gen. 27:29). The soothsayer Balaam was hired by Balak, king of Moab, to pronounce a curse on the Israelites (Num. 22—24). Goliath, the Philistine giant of Gath, "cursed David by his gods" (1 Sam. 17:43).

Dishonesty. This word refers to deceit, usually for the sake of profit. To God, dishonesty is as despicable and morally destructive as sexual depravity (Ezek. 22:11–13). God struck Ananias and Sapphira dead for their deceit (Acts 5:1–11).

Disobedience. *Disobedience* refers to an unwillingness to comply with the guidance of authority, especially a neglect of God's will. The first and most crucial act of disobedience occurred when Adam and Eve ate of the forbidden fruit (see Gen. 3).

Dissension. *Dissension* is discord or strife that arises from a difference of opinion. The sin is in allowing this to continue and to do nothing to prevent its spread.

Dissipation. *Dissipation* refers to "indulgent or wasteful living, especially excessive drinking." Drinking much wine leads to dissipation (Eph. 5:18). Bishops should not be guilty of dissipation (Titus 1:6–7).

Drunkenness. *Drunkenness* is a drugged or deranged condition from drinking intoxicating beverages (1 Cor. 5:11; 6:10; Eph. 5:18). Drunkenness regularly appears in lists of vices in the NT (Luke 21:34; Rom. 13:13; Gal. 5:21).

Envy. Envy shows itself by feelings of resentment and jealousy toward others because of their possessions or good qualities. James linked envy with self-seeking (James 3:14, 16; *selfish ambition*, RSV).

Fornication. Sexual relationships *outside* the bonds of marriage is the technical distinction between fornication and adultery. Adultery involves married persons while fornication involves those who are unmarried. But the NT often uses the term in a general sense of any unchastity.

Gluttony. *Gluttony* is the sin of those who eat excessively. Yet gluttony is more than overeating. In its association with drunkenness it describes a life given to excess.

Gossip. *Gossip* describes the spreading of rumors or idle tales.

Hate *or* Hatred. *Hate* is defined as strong dislike, disregard, or even indifference toward someone or something. Both the emotions and the will are involved. Various degrees and types of hatred are described in the Bible. This makes it difficult to define hatred in simple, absolute terms. The people of God are to hate what God hates—sin (Deut. 12:31; Isa. 61:8; Heb. 1:9).

Holy Spirit, Sin against. The unpardonable sin is stated in the words of Jesus: "He who blasphemes [speaks evil] against the Holy Spirit never has forgiveness, but is subject to eternal condemnation" (Mark 3:29).

Homosexuality. Paul listed homosexuals (people attracted sexually to members of their own sex) among those who would not inherit the kingdom of God (1 Cor. 6:9) and declared that God's wrath stands against such behavior, whether practiced by men or women (Rom. 1:26–27). (See *Sodomy.*)

Hypocrisy. Hypocrites pretend to be what they are not. The NT meaning of hypocrisy (or hypocrite) reflects its use in Greek drama. In Greek theater, a hypocrite was one who wore a mask and played a part on the stage, imitating the speech, mannerisms, and conduct of the character portrayed.

Idolatry. *Idolatry* involves worshiping something created as opposed to worshiping the Creator. Scores of references to idolatry appear in the OT.

Immorality. *Immorality* is behavior contrary to established moral principles. It is a sexual sin, and it also describes Israel's worship of pagan gods (Ezek. 23:8, 17), an adulterous woman (Prov. 2:16), and sexual impurity (1 Cor. 5:1).

Incest. In the RSV *incest* refers to sexual relations with near kin, a sin expressly forbidden by the law of Moses (Lev. 20:12; *perversion*, NKJV). The word translated as *incest* by the RSV in this passage is a Hebrew word with the idea of a mixing of unnatural elements. The Hebrew people were called to a higher code of sexual ethics than was practiced by their Canaanite and Egyptian neighbors. Intercourse was forbidden with one's mother, stepmother, sister, granddaughter, stepsister, aunt, daughter-in-law, sister-in-law, or stepdaughter-granddaughter.

Iniquity. *Iniquity* means "unrighteousness" or "lawlessness." The Bible often uses this word to describe evil and wickedness. Iniquity refers to different types of evil, such as transgressions of spiritual law and crimes against God (2 Pet. 2:16; Rev. 18:5), moral or legal wrongs (1 Cor. 13:6), or depravity and sin in general (Gen. 15:16; Ps. 51:1, 5, 9).

Laziness. Condemned by biblical writers, laziness means "inactivity," "idleness," or "a refusal to work." "Because of laziness the building decays," wrote the author of Ecclesiastes, "and through idleness of hands the house leaks" (Eccles. 10:18).

Lewdness. *Lewdness* involves preoccupation with sex and sexual desire. It also refers to lust (Judg. 20:6; Hos. 2:10; 6:9; Rom. 13:13). The Hebrew word translated as *lewdness* means an "evil plan," "purpose," or "scheme." It can be a wicked thought, especially with reference to sexual unchastity.

Licentiousness. *Licentiousness* refers to undisciplined and unrestrained behavior, especially a flagrant disregard of sexual restraints (Mark 7:22; 2 Cor. 12:21; *lasciviousness*, KJV). The Greek word translated as *licentiousness* means "outrageous conduct," showing that licentious behavior is a disregard for what is right.

Lie. Any statement or act designed to deceive another person is a lie. The motivation for most lying is a desire to hurt others (Gen. 3:1–13; Rom. 3:13) or to protect oneself, usually out of fear or pride (Matt. 26:69–75; Acts 5:1–11).

Lust. *Lust* is a desire for what is forbidden, and means "obsessive sexual craving." Lust also refers to the desire for things that are contrary to the will of God (1 Cor. 10:6).

Murder. The unlawful killing of others constitutes murder, especially when done with premeditated malice. After the first sin in the Garden of Eden (Gen. 3:1–24), it was not long before the first murder occurred (Gen. 4:8) when Cain killed Abel, his brother.

Pride. The Greek word *huperephania*, which is translated *pride*, means "showing oneself above." It describes the attitude of those who have contempt for anyone, for those who see themselves as superior and others as inferior. James said that "God resists the proud" (cf. James 4:6).

Prostitution. This is the act or practice of promiscuous sexual relations, especially for money, and usually refers to women. Several words are used for a woman who engages in illicit sexual activity for pay, including *harlot, whore,* and *prostitute.*

Rape. This is the crime of forcing another person to submit to sexual intercourse. The word *rape* does not occur in many English translations of the Bible (KJV, RSV, NKJV). The NIV and the NEB, however, do use the word (Judg. 20:5; Zech. 14:2).

The Mosaic laws concerning rape and seduction are recorded in Exodus 22:16–17 and Deuteronomy 22:25–29.

Slander. Any evil, malicious talk intended to damage or destroy another person is slander (Pss. 31:13; 50:20; Ezek. 22:9). Slander is prohibited in the ninth commandment: "You shall not bear false witness against your neighbor" (Exod. 20:16; Deut. 5:20).

Sodomy. Sodomy refers to unnatural sexual intercourse, especially between two males. This English word is from Sodom, an ancient city in the land of Canaan noted for depraved activities.

The men of Sodom came to Lot's house, demanding that he allow them to have sexual relations with two people inside (Gen. 19:5). But Lot refused. The next day Lot escaped from Sodom, and God destroyed the city because of its great sin (Gen. 19). Sodomy was prohibited by the law of Moses (Deut. 23:17) and condemned by the apostle Paul (Rom. 1:27; 1 Cor. 6:9). (See *Homosexuality.*)

Suicide. To commit suicide is to murder oneself, to take one's own life. The word does not occur in the Bible. Neither are there any laws relating to it. But the Bible does give examples of suicide, including Saul and his armorbearer (1 Sam. 31:4–5), and Zimri, king of Israel, who "burned the king's house down upon himself with fire"

(1 Kings 16:18), when Tirzah was besieged. In the NT, Judas killed himself because of his shame and grief at betraying Jesus (Matt. 27:5).

Temptation. Temptation is not actually sin. It is an enticement or invitation to sin, with the implied promise of greater good to be derived from following the way of disobedience.

Transgression. This word refers to the violation of a law, command, or duty. The Hebrew word most often translated as *transgression* in the OT means "revolt" or "rebellion." The psalmist wrote, "Blessed is he whose transgression is forgiven, whose sin is covered" (Ps. 32:1). In the NT every occurrence of the word *transgression* (NKJV) is a translation of a Greek word that means "a deliberate breach of the law" (Rom. 4:15; 1 Tim. 2:14; Heb. 2:2).

Trespass. A trespass violates or cuts across a law. The Hebrew word translated as *trespass* means "a stepping aside from the (correct) path." (See Gen. 31:36; Exod. 22:9.) In the NT *trespass* is often a translation of a Greek word meaning "a falling aside" (Mark 11:25–26; Eph. 2:1, 5).

Unbelief. This means a lack of belief or faith in God and his provision. While unbelief does not hinder God's faithfulness (Rom. 3:3–4), it does affect the individual's capacity to receive the benefits of that faithfulness.

Vice. *Vice* is wicked or depraved conduct. Peter said that Christians are free from the law, but not free to do wrong. We should not use our Christian freedom "as a cloak for vice" (1 Pet. 2:16).

Winebibbers. This is the name for those who drink too much wine. The Bible warns against associating with such persons (Prov. 23:20).

Virtue

Biblical ethics refers not to human theories or opinions about what is right and wrong, but to what the Bible says about daily living. Questions of human conduct prevail throughout the Bible. God's revelation through the Bible narrates the story of human ethical failure, God's redeeming grace, and the ethical renewal of God's people.

While love is the summary of Christian ethics, the NT also contains specific ethical instructions. A basic pattern for this ethical teaching is the contrast between our life before faith in Christ and our new existence afterward. Christians are called to leave behind their old conduct and to put on the new (Eph. 4:22–24), to walk in newness of life (Rom. 6:4), and to exhibit the fruit of the Spirit (Gal. 5:22–23).

Following are the major Christian virtues mentioned in the Bible. These virtues also could be considered sanctification (holiness), fruit of the spirit, discipleship, or maturing.

Affliction. While affliction often means suffering as a result of God's judgment on sin (Isa. 53:4; Matt. 24:29; Rom. 2:9), as a Christian virtue there is a kind of suffering that brings about the purifying of believers (Rom. 5:3–5; 2 Thess. 1:4–7). (See *Chastening; Suffering.*)

Agape. (See *Love.*)

Bless, Blessing. As the act of declaring, or wishing, God's favor and goodness upon others, blessing is not only the good effect of words, but it also has the power to bring them to pass. In the Bible, important persons blessed those with less power or influence. The patriarchs pronounced benefits upon their children, often near their own deaths (Gen. 49:1–28). Even if spoken by mistake, once a blessing was given it could not be taken back (Gen. 27).

Brotherly love. (See *Love, Brotherly.*)

Chastisement. The word refers to infliction of punishment and is something done to us. In the Bible chastisement usually refers to punishment or discipline inflicted by God for the purpose of education, instruction, and training (Job 4:3; Ps. 6:7); corrective guidance (2 Tim. 2:25); or discipline, in the sense of corrective physical punishment (Prov. 22:15; Heb. 12:5–11; Rev. 3:19).

Confession. While confession can be a profession or statement of belief, it primarily means an admission of sin.

The Bible frequently urges confession of sin (see Ps. 32:5; James 5:16).

Consecration. This is the act of setting apart, or dedicating, something or someone for God's use. Believers are consecrated by Jesus Christ (John 17:17; 1 Pet. 2:9), and God urges them to consecrate themselves as well (Rom. 12:1; 2 Tim. 2:21).

Contrition. Contrition refers to an attitude that pleases God (Ps. 34:18; Ps. 51:17). Those with contrite spirits weep over wrongdoing and express genuine sorrow for their sin.

Correction. This word means "to reform," "to punish" or "to chasten" (see Prov. 3:11–12). It can mean "to reprove" (Prov. 13:18; 15:10), and "judgment" (Hab. 1:12). The NT declares that all Scripture is profitable for correction (2 Tim. 3:16).

Faithfulness. While faithfulness is one of God's attributes, it is a quality for us to cultivate. Faithfulness means dependability, loyalty, and stability. Paul lists faithfulness as a fruit of the Spirit (Gal. 5:22–23).

Forgiveness. The act of excusing or pardoning others in spite of their slights, shortcomings, and errors. We offer forgiveness because we have been forgiven (see Matt. 6:12 and Eph. 4:32).

Generosity. This virtue means being liberal in spirit, especially in contributing to the needy. True Christian giving is "a matter of generosity and not as a grudging obligation" (2 Cor. 9:5).

Godliness. This means piety or reverence toward God.

Goodness. This is the quality of being good and of praiseworthy character or moral excellence. It is also part of the fruits of the Spirit (see Gal. 5:22–23).

Humility. A freedom from arrogance grows out of the recognition that all we have and are comes from God. The Greek philosophers despised humility because it implied inadequacy, lack of dignity, and worthlessness. This is not the biblical meaning of humility. Jesus is the supreme example of humility (Matt. 11:29; Mark 10:45; John 13:4–17; Phil. 2:5–8).

Intercession. A true virtue is cultivating the habit of interceding—petitioning God or praying on behalf of others.

An early example of intercession occurs in Genesis 18, where Abraham speaks to God on behalf of Sodom. His plea was compassionate and came out of his concern for the well-being of others.

Longsuffering. Although translated as "longsuffering" in the KJV and NKJV, the word refers to patient endurance. This is part of the fruit of the Spirit (Gal. 5:22–23), and we are exhorted to cultivate this virtue in passages such as Eph. 4:2. (See *Patience.*)

Love. This word refers to attitude and action, not emotion. Someone defined Christian love as unconquerable benevolence. It means that no matter what others do to us, we seek only their highest good. The Greeks used four words for love (only the last two appear in the NT):

1. *Eros* refers to passion, sexual feelings.
2. *Storge* refers to affection, especially used of parents and children.
3. *Philia* refers to friendship, the warmth we feel toward those who are near to us.
4. *Agape* concerns the will even more than the emotions because love expresses itself through deliberate effort, which we can make only with God's help.

Love, Brotherly. This is the love *(agape)* of brothers—or sisters—for each other. Sometimes the NT uses the word *brother* to refer simply to another human being, whether a Christian or not (Matt. 25:40), or to people of our race (Rom. 9:3). Usually, however, it is used of believers in Christ.

Meekness. This means an attitude of humility toward God and gentleness toward others. Meekness grows out of a recognition that God is in control. Although weakness and meekness may seem similar, they are not. Weakness is negative, suggesting a lack of strength or courage. Meekness is personal conscious choice. Meekness refers to strength and courage under control, a strength that comes from God.

Paul pointed out that spiritual leaders of the church have great power in confronting sinners, but he cautioned them to restrain themselves in meekness (Gal. 4:1; 5:22–23).

Moderation. This word is better translated as "self-control," not given to sudden impulses or excesses (1 Tim. 2:9). Although the term rarely occurs in the Bible, the concept of moderation is common. The Pharisees were not moderate. Jesus described them as those "who strain out a gnat and swallow a camel" (Matt. 23:24).

Obedience. To obey is to carry out the will of another, especially God. In the Bible, obedience relates to hearing. Obedience is a positive, active response to what people hear. God summons individuals to active obedience to his revelation. Samuel said that God's pleasure was not in sacrifice but in obedience (1 Sam. 15:22).

Patience. This means longsuffering or forebearance under suffering and endurance in the face of adversity. Two Greek words are translated as patience:

1. *Makrothymia* (Heb. 6:12; James 5:10) expresses patience toward people.

2. *Hypmone* (Matt. 18:26, 29) meaning patience toward things or events. This is the quality that enables individuals to be "patient in tribulation" (Rom. 12:12).

Perseverance. This virtue means the steadfast effort to follow God's commands. The NT makes it clear that faith alone can save, but persevering in doing good works is the best indication that individuals' faith is genuine (James 2:14–26).

Restitution. Contrite Christians restore to the rightful owners anything that has been taken away, stolen, lost, or surrendered. Leviticus 6:1–7 gives the Mosaic law of restitution and establishes the procedure to be followed in restoring stolen property.

In the NT, the word *restitution* is not used, but the idea is expressed. Zacchaeus, a chief tax collector, said to Jesus, "If I have taken anything from anyone by false accusation, I restore fourfold" (Luke 19:8).

Sincerity. The word translated "sincerity" refers to purity of motive or freedom from hypocrisy. Paul compared sincerity to unleavened bread (1 Cor. 5:8), a biblical symbol of purity. The sincerity with which Christians conduct their lives testifies to their godliness (2 Cor. 1:12). (See *Godliness.*)

Suffering. While the Bible makes it clear that some suffering is the result of evil action or sin, all suffering does not fall into this category. Some suffering is not related to the past but is forward-looking, in that it serves to shape and refine God's children (1 Pet. 1:6–7; 5:10). Hebrews 5:8 declares that Jesus learned obedience by the things which he suffered and that he was perfected through suffering (see also Heb. 2:10). Suffering has the potential of demonstrating God's power (2 Cor. 12:7) and those who suffer can comfort others (2 Cor. 1:3–6).

Temperance. The meaning of temperate in English translations should not be restricted to the kind of self-control individuals exert by abstaining from alcoholic beverages. The temperance of which the Bible speaks is more inclusive. The word used, *egkrateia*, is the same word Paul used in 1 Corinthians 9:25 in speaking of athletes' disciplining of their bodies. *Egkrateia* indicates self-control that masters all sensual and sexual desires, and is the virtue of those who keep all their desires in control.

Thanksgiving. Praise thanks God for what he does for us. Ideally, thanksgiving springs from a grateful heart; but it is a virtue to cultivate, regardless of initial attitude (1 Thess. 5:18).

Spiritual Beings

God

The Bible never seeks to prove the existence of God; it simply affirms his existence by declaring, "In the beginning God . . ." (Gen. 1:1).

The greatest revelation of God comes through the Bible. Through the inspired written record, both the existence of God and the nature of God are revealed in and through Jesus Christ.

Attributes of God

God may be described in terms of attributes, that is, the inherent characteristics of his being.

Natural Attributes

The first group comprises the natural attributes of God.

God is spirit. God has no body, no physical or measurable form—God is invisible.

God is changeless. Progress and change may characterize some of his works, but God remains unchanged.

God is all powerful. God's power is unlimited. He can do anything that is not inconsistent with his nature, character, and purpose.

God is all knowing. God possesses all knowledge. Because God is everywhere at one and the same time, he knows everything simultaneously.

God is everywhere. God is not confined to any part of the universe but is present in all his power at every point in space and every moment in time (Ps. 139:7–12).

God is eternal. Eternity refers to God's relation to time. Past, present, and future are known equally to him.

Moral Attributes

The second group of attributes is called moral attributes. These refer to God's character, his essential nature.

God is holy. The word "holy" comes from a root word that means "to separate." "Holy" speaks of God as separated from or exalted above other things.

God is righteous. Righteousness as applied to God refers to his affirmation of what is right as opposed to what is wrong. The righteousness of God refers to his moral laws laid down to guide the conduct of humankind, as in the Ten Commandments.

Righteousness also refers to God's administration of justice. He brings punishment upon the disobedient. God's righteousness is redemptive.

God is love. Love is the essential, self-giving nature of God. God's love for humanity seeks to awaken a responsive love from all humankind toward God.

God is truth. All truth, whether natural, physical, or religious, is grounded in God.

God is wisdom. God's wisdom is revealed in his doing the best thing, in the best way, at the best time for the best purpose.

Names of God in the Old Testament

The titles or designations given to God throughout the Bible come about because of God's self-revelation.

Adonai. This name means "to judge," "to rule," and points to God as the almighty Ruler, to whom everything is subject. In early times it was the usual name for God.

Branch of Righteousness. Jeremiah 23:5–6 names the coming messianic figure, the "Branch of righteousness," who will descend from David and be raised up to reign as king to execute judgment and righteousness in the earth.

El. Another important root name for God in the OT is El. By itself it refers to a god in the most general sense. It was widely used in ancient Near Eastern cultures whose languages are similar to Hebrew and may refer either to the true God or to false gods.

The highest Canaanite god was El, whose son was Baal. In the Bible the word is often defined properly by a qualifier like "Yahweh": "I, the LORD [Yahweh] your God [Elohim], am a jealous God [El]" (Deut. 5:9).

Elohim. Derived from the same root as El, it points to God as the strong and mighty One, the object of awe.

Glory. God is described as Glory *(Shekinah)* (Exod.16:7; Ps.104:31; Isa.60:1).

King. This descendant of David will have several divine qualities. He will be a Branch of Righteousness, a King, and his name will be called "the Lord Our Righteousness" *(Yahweh Tsidkenu).*

Most High. This name for God appears frequently in the OT, particularly in the Psalms, Isaiah, and Daniel (Ps. 92:1; Isa. 14:14; Dan. 4:17). It emphasizes the might and power of God.

Servant. The name of Servant here identifies the divine person and his saving ministry on behalf of his people.

Shepherd. God is described in prophecy as the Shepherd who will feed his flock, gather the lambs in his arms, carry them in his bosom, and gently lead those with young.

Wisdom. This person also appears in Proverbs 8:1–36 as Wisdom, the speaker, who always says and does what is righteous, is equal to Yahweh and works with him in the creation of the universe.

Word of God. This term figures prominently in Scripture as another name of God. The Word is not as clearly a person in the OT as in the NT where Jesus Christ is identified as the personal Word of God (John 1:1, 14).

Yahweh, Jehovah. One of the most important names for God in the OT is *Yahweh* (or *Jehovah*), from the verb, "to be," meaning simply but profoundly, "I am who I am," and, "I will be who I will be," or, "I am the who always is and ever shall be."

The four-letter Hebrew word "Yhwh" was the name by which God revealed him-

God the Creator, from a painting by Michelangelo in the Sistine Chapel in Rome.

self to Moses in the burning bush (Exod. 3:14). Some English Bibles translate the word as "Yahweh," while others still use "Jehovah."

The following are other names in honor of God in the OT that stem from the basic name of Yahweh:

Yahweh Elohe Israel. The Hebrew name means "Lord-God-of-Israel," and it appears in Isaiah, Jeremiah, and the Psalms. Other names similar to this are *Netsah Israel*, "the Strength of Israel" (1 Sam. 15:29); and *Abir Yisrael*, "the Mighty One of Israel" (Isa. 1:24).

Yahweh-jireh. This name is translated as "the-Lord-will-provide," commemorating the provision of the ram in place of Isaac for Abraham's sacrifice (Gen. 22:14).

Yahweh-nissi. This name means "the-Lord-is-my-banner," in honor of God's defeat of the Amalekites (Exod. 17:15).

Yahweh-shalom. This phrase means "The-Lord-is-peace," the name Gideon gave the altar which he built in Ophrah (Judg. 6:24).

Yahweh-shammah. This phrase expresses the truth that "the-Lord-is-there," referring to the city which the prophet Ezekiel saw in his vision (Ezek. 48:35).

Yahweh-tsebaoth. This name, translated "the-Lord-of-hosts," was used in the days of David and the prophets, witnessing to God the Savior who is surrounded by his hosts of heavenly power (1 Sam. 1:3).

Names of God in the New Testament

Abba. *Abba* is an Aramaic word corresponding to our "Daddy" or "Papa." It occurs three times:

• In the garden of Gethsemane where Jesus prayed, "Abba, Father . . ." (Mark 14:36).

• Paul linked the Christians' cry of "Abba, Father" with the "Spirit of adoption" (Rom. 8:15).

• Paul writes, "Because you are sons, God has sent forth the Spirit of his Son into your hearts, crying out, 'Abba, Father!'" (Gal. 4:6).

Father. This name explains God's familial relationship to his people (Matt. 5:16; 28:19).

Highest. This name for God, which appears only in the gospel of Luke in the NKJV (Luke 1:32; 6:35), emphasizes the glory and majesty of God.

Descriptive Names of God

The more frequently used terms, such as Father, are ways to speak of God's personal nature. Other names may also be used that reflect God's nature and activity:

Creator	Ruler
Defender	Shepherd
Deliverer	Source
Protector	Sovereign
Provider	Sustainer

Metaphors used as names for God include:

God of Vision	Shelter
Light of world	Source of Life
Rock of Salvation	

Descriptive Names of Jesus

The incarnation of Jesus affirms his truly human nature. Jesus incorporates the humanity of both women and men. Scriptures ascribe to him qualities found in both genders: anger, patience, compassion, strength, grief, tenderness, love, understanding:

Brother	Great Physician	Redeemer
Example	Love incarnate	Rescuer
Friend	Messiah	Resurrected Christ
God incarnate	Our Savior	Son of Mary
Good Shepherd	Prophet	Teacher

Metaphors used as names for Jesus include:

Alpha and Omega	Lamb	Morning Star
Bread of Life	The Life	True Vine
Cornerstone	Lion of Judah	The Truth
The Door	Living Water	The Way

Descriptive Names of the Holy Spirit

Scripture refers to the Spirit in terms of personhood and activity. Names describe personal qualities and abilities:

Advocate	Giver of Life	Nourisher
Comforter	Helper	Nurturer
Convictor of sin	Illuminator	Sanctifier
Convincer	Keeper	Teacher
Counselor	Motivator	Transformer
Enabler	Mover	

Metaphors used as names for the Holy Spirit include:

Breath of God	Indwelling Spirit	Wisdom
Guarantee	Wind of God	

Facts About God

God is eternal	Deut. 33:27; Ps. 90:2	God is merciful	Ps. 103:8–17
God is faithful	Deut. 7:9; Ps. 89:1–2	God is omnipotent	Gen. 18:14; Rev. 19:6
God is good	Ps. 107:8	God is omnipresent	Ps. 139:7–12
God is gracious	Ps. 111:4; 1 Pet. 5:10	God is omniscient	Ps. 139:2–6; Isa. 40:13–14
God is holy	Lev. 19:2; 1 Pet. 1:15	God is one	Deut. 6:4–5; Isa. 44:6–8
God is immutable	Heb. 1:10–12; 13:8	God is righteous and just	Ps. 119:137
God is incomprehensible	Job 11:7–19; Rom. 11:33	God is self-existent	Exod. 3:13–14
		God is self-sufficient	Ps. 50:10–12
God is infinite	1 Kings 8:22–27; Jer. 23:24	God is sovereign	Isa. 46:9–11
		God is spirit	John 4:24
God is light	James 1:17; 1 John 1:5	God is trinity	Matt. 28:19; 2 Cor. 13:14
God is love	John 3:16; Rom. 5:8	God is true (truth)	John 17:3; Titus 1:1–2
		God is wise	Prov. 3:19; 1 Tim. 1:17

God the Son _____

The NT is the only substantial first-century source of information about the life of Jesus. He is hardly mentioned in Jewish or Roman literature of that time.

The first-century Jewish historian Flavius Josephus wrote a book on the history of Judaism, attempting to show the Romans that Judaism was really not far separated from the Greek and Roman way of life.

The four Gospels are our primary sources of information about Jesus Christ. They do not present a biography covering his life, but a picture of his person and work. From his birth to his thirtieth year hardly anything is said of him. Even the account of his ministry is not exhaustive. Much of what John knew and saw, for example, is left unrecorded (John 21:25).

What is recorded is sometimes compressed into a few verses. All the Gospels give considerably more coverage to the events of the last week of Christ's life than to anything else.

Because each writer wished to emphasize a somewhat different aspect of Jesus' person and work, the accounts vary in detail. It is evident that the original authors selected the facts that best suited their purposes, and they did not always observe a strictly chronological order. It is generally acknowledged that Luke comes nearest to following the actual sequence of events. The Gospels are interpretations more than chronicles, but there is no reason to doubt the complete truth of their accounts.

Prophecies Fulfilled by Jesus

Would be born of a woman	Gen. 3:15; Gal. 4:4
Would be from the line of Abraham	Gen. 12:3, 7; 17:7; Rom. 9:5; Gal. 3:16
Would be from the tribe of Judah	Gen. 49:10; Heb. 7:14; Rev. 5:5
Would be from the house of David	2 Sam. 7:12–13; Luke 1:31–33; Rom. 1:3
Would be born of a virgin	Isa. 7:14; Matt. 1:22–23
Would be given the throne of David	2 Sam. 7:11–12; Ps. 132:11; Isa. 9:6–7; 16:5; Jer. 23:5; Luke 1:31–32
Would be given an eternal throne	Dan. 2:44; 7:14, 27; Micah 4:7; Luke 1:33
Would be called Immanuel	Isa. 7:14; Matt. 1:23
Would have a forerunner	Isa. 40:3–5; Mal. 3:1; Matt. 3:1–3; Luke 1:76–78; 3:3–6

Prophecies Fulfilled by Jesus—*continued*

Would be born in Bethlehem	Mic. 5:2; Matt. 2:5–6; Luke 2:4–6
Would be worshiped by wise men and presented with gifts	Ps. 72:10; Isa. 60:3, 6, 9; Matt. 2:11
Would be in Egypt for a season	Num. 24:8; Hos. 11:1; Matt. 2:15
Would be the intended victim in a massacre of infants at his birthplace	Jer. 31:15; Matt. 2:17–18
Would be called a Nazarene ("branch")	Isa. 11:1; Matt. 2:23
Would be zealous for the Father	Pss. 69:9; 119:139; John 6:37–40
Would be filled with God's Spirit	Ps. 45:7; Isa. 11:2; 61:1–2; Luke 4:18–19
Would heal many	Isa. 53:4; Matt. 8:16–17
Would deal gently with the Gentiles	Isa. 9:1–2; 42:1–3; Matt. 4:13–16; 12:17–21
Would speak in parables	Isa. 6:9–10; Matt. 13:10–15
Would be rejected by his own	Ps. 69:8; Isa. 53:3; John 1:11; 7:5
Would make a triumphant entry into Jerusalem	Zech. 9:9; Matt. 21:4–5
Would be praised by little children	Ps. 8:2; Matt. 21:16
Would be the rejected cornerstone	Ps. 118:22–23; Matt. 21:42
Would not be believed in spite of his miracles	Isa. 53:1; John 12:37–38
Would be betrayed by a friend for 30 pieces of silver	Pss. 41:9; 55:12–14; Zech. 11:12–13; Matt. 26:14–16, 21–25
Would be a man of sorrows	Isa. 53:3; Matt. 26:37–38
Would be forsaken by his disciples	Zech. 13:7; Matt. 26:31, 56
Would be scourged and spat upon	Isa. 50:6; Matt. 26:67; 27:26
His betrayal money would be used to buy a potter's field	Jer. 32:6–9; Zech. 11:12–13; Matt. 27:9–10
Would be crucified between two thieves	Isa. 53:12; Matt. 27:38; Mark 15:27–28; Luke 22:37
Would be given vinegar to drink	Ps. 69:21; Matt. 27:34, 48; John 19:28–30
Would suffer the piercing of his hands and feet	Ps. 22:16; Zech. 12:10; Mark 15:25; John 19:34, 37; 20:25–27
Would have his garments parted and gambled for	Ps. 22:18; Luke 23:34; John 19:23–24
Would be surrounded and ridiculed by his enemies	Ps. 22:7–8; Matt. 27:39–44; Mark 15:29–32
Would be thirsty	Ps. 22:15; John 19:28
Would commend his spirit to the Father	Ps. 31:5; Luke 23:46
Would not have a bone broken	Exod. 12:46; Num. 9:12; Ps. 34:20; John 19:33–36
Would be stared at in death	Zech. 12:10; Matt. 27:36; John 19:37
Would be buried with the rich	Isa. 53:9; Matt. 27:57–60
Would be raised from the dead	Ps. 16:10; Matt. 28:2–7
Would ascend	Ps. 24:7–10; Mark 16:19; Luke 24:51
Would become a greater high priest than Aaron	Ps. 110:4; Heb. 5:4–6, 10; 7:11–28
Would be seated at God's right hand	Ps. 110:1; Matt. 22:44; Heb. 10:12–13
Would become a smiting scepter	Num. 24:17; Dan. 2:44–45; Rev. 19:15
Would rule the heathen	Ps. 2:8; Rev. 2:27

The Life of Jesus

Although each gospel was written to stand on its own merits, the four Gospels may be worked together into a harmonious, single account of Jesus' life. He lived in a Jewish society guided by OT precepts and basically under the influences of the Pharisaic interpretation of the Law.

About the year 6 B.C., toward the end of Herod's reign in Israel, the priest Zechariah was officiating in the temple in Jerusalem. He was burning incense at the altar during the evening prayer when an angel appeared to him, announcing the forthcoming birth of a son. This child would prepare the way for the Messiah; the spirit and power of Elijah would rest upon him (cf. Luke 3:3–6). His parents were to call him John.

Zechariah was a truly godly man but it was difficult for him to believe what he heard and consequently he was struck dumb until Elizabeth (his wife) gave birth. The child was born, circumcised and named according to the directions of God. Then Zechariah regained his voice and praised the Lord. This hymn of praise is called the Benedictus (Luke 1:5–25, 68–79).

Three months before the birth of John, the same angel (Gabriel) appeared to Mary. This young woman was betrothed to Joseph, a carpenter descended from King David (cf. Isa. 11:1). The angel told Mary she would conceive a child by the Holy Spirit, and that she should name the child Jesus.

Mary was amazed to learn that although she was a virgin, she would bear a child who was the Son of God and would be the Savior of his people (Luke 1:32–35; cf. Matt. 1:21). Yet she accepted this message with great meekness, glad to be living in God's will (Luke 1:38).

Gabriel also told her that her cousin Elizabeth was expecting a child, and Mary hastened to share their mutual joy. When these two godly women met, Elizabeth greeted Mary as the mother of her Lord (Luke 1:39–45). Mary also broke forth in a song of praise (*Magnificat*, vv. 1:46–56). She stayed three months with Elizabeth before returning home.

Joseph, Mary's betrothed husband, was utterly shocked at what appeared to be the fruit of terrible sin on Mary's part (Matt. 1:19–25). He decided to put her away quietly. Then an angel in a dream explained the situation to him and directed him to marry his intended wife as planned.

Jesus was born in Bethlehem to which the newlyweds had been summoned for registration at the command of the emperor, Augustus Caesar (Luke 2:1). Thus the prophecy of Micah 5:2 was fulfilled.

Early Years

We know of five events in the childhood of Jesus. First, in accordance with Jewish law, he was circumcised and named on the eighth day (Luke 2:21).

Second, Jesus was presented at the temple to seal the circumcision. He was also "redeemed" by the payment of the presented five shekels. For her purification, Mary gave a pair of turtledoves or pigeons, the offering of the poor (cf. Lev. 12:8; Luke 2:24).

Third, sometime later a group of wise men (perhaps Babylonian priests and astrologers) appeared in Jerusalem, inquiring about the birth of "the king of the Jews." They had seen his star in the sky (Matt. 2:2).

Fourth, after the departure of the wise men, God directed Joseph to flee to Egypt with his family (Matt. 2:13–15). Herod had ordered the execution of all infants aged two and younger who lived in and around Bethlehem.

Fifth, Jesus journeyed with his parents to Jerusalem when he was 12 years old (Luke

2:41–52). It was time for him to be inducted into the court of the men and this probably happened during Passover. He was formally presented to the religious leaders. Jesus returned later to the temple and continued discussions with the teachers or rabbis.

Scripture says that as a youth, Jesus "increased in wisdom and stature, and in favor with God and men" (Luke 2:52).

John the Baptist, Zechariah and Elizabeth's son and Jesus' cousin, was to prepare the way for the ministry of Jesus. He was known as the "Baptist" because he preached to his fellow Jews that they should repent and be baptized.

When Jesus was about 30, he went to John to be baptized. However, he repented of no sin, for he had none. He identified himself with sinners in order to be their sin-bearer. When Jesus came up from the water, the Holy Spirit visibly descended upon him in the form of a dove.

Jesus and John, and perhaps the onlookers as well, heard the voice of God declaring his approval of Jesus (Matt. 3:13–17; Mark 1:9–11; Luke 3:21–22; John 1:32–33).

The Holy Spirit at once led Jesus into the wilderness to face temptation by the devil (Matt. 4:1–11; Mark 1:12–13; Luke 4:1–13).

Early Judean Ministry

Only the gospel of John describes this period of Jesus' life. John first recounts the relationship between John the Baptist and Jesus. John the Baptist told delegates from the highest religious authorities that he was not the Messiah, although indicating that the Messiah was present (John 1:19–27). The next day as Jesus approached, he pointed to him as the Messiah (vv. 1:30–34) and said, "Behold the Lamb of God," implying that his own disciples should follow Jesus (vv. 1:35–37).

Jesus began to gather disciples to himself (John 1:38–51). As a result of John the Baptist's testimony, John and Andrew followed Jesus. Peter became a follower as a result of his brother's testimony. The fourth follower, Philip, immediately obeyed Jesus' summons. Philip brought Nathanael (Bartholomew) and when Jesus demonstrated that he knew Nathanael's inner thoughts, he also joined the band.

Jesus journeyed to Galilee. At a wedding feast in Cana, he turned water into wine. This act revealed to the disciples his authority over nature. After a brief ministry in Capernaum, Jesus and his followers went to Jerusalem for the Passover. There he publicly declared his authority over the worship of men by cleansing the temple. At this time Jesus hinted at his death and resurrection: "Destroy this temple, and in three days I will raise it up" (John 2:19).

One of the Jewish leaders, a Pharisee named Nicodemus, came to Jesus at night to talk about spiritual matters. Their well-known conversation focused on the necessity of being born again (literally "from above"; John 3:1ff.).

The next six months find Jesus ministering outside Jerusalem, but still in Judea where John the Baptist is also working.

Toward the end of this period, the Baptist was thrown into prison because he denounced Herod Antipas for taking the wife of his brother Philip (Matt. 14:3–5).

Perhaps John's imprisonment prompted Jesus to go to Galilee to minister.

Galilean Ministry

Jesus' first stop on his return to Galilee was at Cana. There he healed a nobleman's son. The fervency of the nobleman persuaded Jesus to fulfill his request (John 4:46–54). In Nazareth Jesus worshiped in the synagogue on the Sabbath. There he was asked to read (in Hebrew) and explain (perhaps in Aramaic) a portion of Scriptures.

Then Jesus went to Capernaum, which seems to have become his headquarters (cf.

Matt. 9:1). Here he officially called to travel with him the disciples Peter, Andrew, James, and John, who seem to have returned to their homes and occupations. Jesus taught in the synagogue each Sabbath and healed a demoniac there.

Back in Capernaum, Jesus demonstrated his authority to forgive sin by curing a paralytic and summoning Matthew, a tax collector, to become a follower (Luke 5:17–29). Matthew responded immediately.

During this period Jesus encountered increasing hostility from the high Jewish officials. While in Jerusalem for one of the annual feasts, he was attacked for healing a cripple on the Sabbath (John 5:1–16). This healing asserted Jesus' authority over the Sabbath, and the Jews at once understood this to be a claim for divine authority. Jesus said that he knew God's mind, that he would judge sin, and that he would raise people from the dead. His critics pointed out that only God can do such things.

Back in Galilee, the Sabbath controversy continued as Jesus defended his disciples for picking grain on the Sabbath. Ultimately he claimed divine lordship over the day. He healed a man with a withered hand on the Sabbath. From then on, the Jewish religious authorities began plotting to destroy him (Matt. 12:1–14; Mark 2:23–3:6; Luke 6:1–11).

Jesus singled out 12 of his disciples who were officially to carry on his ministry. The appointment of the 12 inaugurated a new period of Jesus' ministry, beginning with the Sermon on the Mount. Jesus delivered this same message (called the Sermon on the Plain) when he descended from the mountain with his newly appointed apostles (Luke 6:20–49; cf. Matt. 5:1–6:29).

We read of several interwoven incidents. Perhaps on the day he delivered the Sermon on the Mount, Jesus healed the centurion's servant. This Roman soldier was sympathetic toward the Jewish religion (Luke 7:5) and apparently embraced Jesus as the Messiah.

At Capernaum, about 11 kilometers (7 miles) from the site of the Sermon on the Mount, crowds continued to press upon Jesus. To escape this pressure, he set out for Nain (with many accompanying him). At the city's entrance Jesus restored a widow's son to life. This incident stirred the excitement of the crowd (Luke 7:11–15).

In one of the cities Jesus visited (perhaps Nain), he was anointed by an outcast woman. Jesus forgave her sins in the presence of his host, Simon the Pharisee. Simon was scandalized, but Jesus was happy to receive her love and repentance (Matt. 26:6–13; Mark 14:3–9; Luke 7:36–50).

This begins Jesus' second tour of the Galilean cities (Luke 8:1–4). The 12 disciples and certain devoted women (Mary Magdalene, Joanna wife of Herod's steward, Susanna, and others) accompanied him.

On this journey he cured a demoniac, and the Pharisees accused him of working with the devil (Matt. 12:22–37; Mark 3:22–30; Luke 11:14–26). He emphasized the blessedness of those who "hear the word of God and do it" (Luke 8:21). This same day he spoke many parables from a boat.

Jesus made a third tour of Galilee that included a number of miracles and a second rejection at Nazareth. Jesus yearned for more laborers to reap the spiritual harvest. He sent his disciples out by twos to call the cities of Israel to repentance, granting them power to heal and cast out demons. Their ministry extended his own (Matt. 10:5–42; Mark 6:7–13; Luke 9:1–6).

At this point, we read the report of John the Baptist's death. Herod Antipas had long hesitated before killing John because he feared the people. His wife Herodias plotted John's death using her daughter Salome to achieve her goal. Herod's guilty conscience led him to ask if Jesus was the resurrected John.

Grieving at John's death, beleaguered by crowds, and exhausted from work, Jesus gathered the 12 and crossed the Sea of Galilee. But the crowds got to the other side before them, and Jesus taught the masses all day. The session was climaxed when Jesus fed the entire multitude (5,000 men plus women and children) by dividing and multiplying five loaves and two fish. When the leftovers were gathered they filled twelve baskets (Matt. 14:13–21).

Immediately after the miracle Jesus put the 12 into the boat and sent them back across the sea, even though a storm was brewing. He retreated into the mountains to escape the enthusiastic crowd that wanted to make him king by force.

Three hours after midnight, the disciples were caught in a violent storm in the middle of the lake. They were frightened. But when disaster seemed certain, Jesus came walking toward them on the water (Matt. 14:24–33; Mark 6:47–52). After he calmed their fears, Peter asked Jesus to let him come and meet him on the waters. As Peter got out of the boat and started toward Jesus, he became fearful and began to sink. Jesus took his hand and led him back to the boat. The water was calmed immediately.

In Capernaum Jesus began to heal the sick who streamed to him from everywhere. Soon the crowd who had been fed arrived. Finding Jesus in a synagogue, they heard him explain that he was the true bread of life from heaven.

They were now faced with accepting the authority of this teaching, spelled out in terms of eating Jesus' flesh and drinking his blood. This offended many of them and they left (John 6:22–66). Jesus asked the 12 disciples if they were also going to leave. This elicited Peter's well-known confession, "Lord, to whom shall we go? . . . Also we have come to believe and know that You are the Christ, the Son of the living God" (v. 69).

In Bethsaida Jesus healed a blind man (Mark 8:22–26). Then he and his disciples journeyed north to the area of Caesarea Philippi, where Peter confessed him to be the Messiah, "the Christ, the Son of the living God."

Jesus replied that Peter's faith made him a rock, and that he would build his church upon this rock—that is, faith such as Peter's (Matt. 16:13–20; cf. Mark 8:27–9:1). At this point Jesus described his approaching suffering, death, and resurrection.

About a week later, Jesus took Peter, James, and John up a mountain and revealed to them his heavenly glory (the Transfiguration). He conversed before their eyes with Moses and Elijah (Matt. 17:1–13; Mark 9:2–13; cf. Luke 9:28–36).

Jesus again toured Galilee but this time secretly. He again told the 12 of his coming death and resurrection, and again they were unable to understand what he said.

After many months, Jesus went to Jerusalem to celebrate the Feast of Tabernacles. He had refused to go with his family, but later he made the trip privately. In Jerusalem the people's opinions about him were divided. Jesus publicly affirmed that he was sent from the Father and was the Savior of the world.

The religious leaders sent officers to arrest Jesus, but they were so impressed by him that they were unable to fulfill their task. Then these leaders attempted to discredit Jesus by getting him to violate the law. But they were not successful. They brought a woman before him taken in adultery, and he turned the incident completely against them (John 8:3–11).

Perean Ministry

About two months elapsed while Jesus went back to Galilee. Perhaps it was at this time that he sent 70 disciples to the cities of Israel to declare that the kingdom was near and that Jesus was the Messiah (Luke 10). Jesus attempted to pass through Samaria on his way to Jerusalem, but the people rejected him. He crossed the Jordan and traveled through Perea.

During this journey Jesus performed many miracles, such as healing an infirm woman and a dropsied man on the Sabbath (Luke 13:11–17; 14:1–6). The Sabbath miracles stirred yet more hostility among the Pharisees.

In Jerusalem at the annual Feast of Dedication, Jesus openly declared himself to be the Messiah. The Jews regarded this as blasphemy, and they again tried to seize him, but Jesus retreated across the Jordan to Beth-abara. The opposition of the religious authorities continued to grow.

The outcasts of society rallied to hear his teaching. Again Jesus taught primarily in parables. He privately explained the true meaning of his parables to the 12 and continued their special training. One day an urgent message arrived from the home of Mary and Martha: Lazarus, their brother, was gravely ill. By the time Jesus arrived in Bethany, Lazarus had died and been buried for four days. Jesus raised him from the dead. This miracle increased the determination of the Jewish leaders to get rid of him (John 11:1–48).

Jesus again retired from the crowds for a time. Then he turned toward Jerusalem and death (John 11:54–57). The way to Jerusalem was marked by miracle working, teaching, and confrontation with the Pharisees.

The Last Week

The last week before Jesus' crucifixion occupies a large portion of the gospel records. Jesus attended a feast in Jericho at the home of Simon the leper, where Mary anointed him with costly perfumes and wiped his feet with her hair. Some of the disciples protested this act because they felt it was a waste of money, but Jesus commended her. He pointed out that she was anointing him for his coming burial (Matt. 26:6–13; Mark 14:3–9).

On the next day (Sunday), Jesus rode into Jerusalem on a colt upon which his followers had spread their garments (John 12). The Passover pilgrims lined the road, waving palm branches and acclaiming Jesus as the Messiah.

On Tuesday the Jewish leaders demanded that Jesus explain the authority by which he acted as he did. Jesus replied by telling several parables. He successfully thwarted the Pharisees' traps to get him to contradict Moses and be discredited before the crowds. At one point Jesus pointedly denounced the scribes and Pharisees. This was followed by an expression of his concern and longing for the people to love him (Matt. 23).

Jesus spent Wednesday resting in Bethany. On Thursday evening he ate the Passover with his disciples (Matt. 26:17–30; Mark 14:12–25). He sent Peter and John to find the place where the meal would be eaten.

During the meal that evening, the disciples argued about which of them would be most important. Jesus arose and washed their feet, trying to teach them that they should serve one another (John 13:1–17). After the meal Jesus instituted the Lord's Supper, a rite to be observed until he returned. This symbolic meal consisted of eating bread (representing his body) and drinking wine (representing his blood).

Judas left the meal to finalize arrangements to betray Jesus. As he left, Jesus warned the others that they would lose their faith in him that night. But Peter assured Jesus of his loyalty. Jesus replied that he would deny him three times before the cock crowed at dawn.

Jesus and the 11 remaining disciples left the Upper Room and went to the garden of Gethsemane. While Jesus agonized in prayer, the disciples fell asleep. Three times he returned to find them sleeping. Finally he calmed his soul and was ready to face his death and all it would mean (Matt. 26:36–46; Mark 14:32–42). At this point Judas arrived with a company of armed men. He identified Jesus for the soldiers by kissing him (Matt. 26:47–56; Mark 14:43–52; Luke 22:47–53; John 18:1–14).

Jesus stood trial before both the religious and civil authorities. The religious trial was illegally convened during the night; but it confirmed its decision after daybreak. Even so, it was a mockery of justice (Matt. 26:59–68; Mark 14:55–65; Luke 22:65–71).

The civil trial occurred Friday morning before Pilate, who saw no threat or crime and sent Jesus to Herod, who mocked him and returned him to Pilate (Luke 23:6–16). The Roman official hoped to release Jesus by popular demand, but the crowd shouted for him to release Barabbas (a robber and murderer). They insisted that Pilate crucify Jesus.

Pilate proposed to scourge Jesus and release him to pacify the crowd, and he inflicted on him other mockeries and punishments. But again the crowd cried, "Crucify Him."

From Pilate's court, Jesus was taken outside the walls of Jerusalem to the hill of Golgotha, where he was crucified at about 9 A.M. on Friday (Matt. 27:32–56).

Jesus was buried before dark on Friday ("the first day," since the Jews reckoned days from dusk to dusk). His body remained in the tomb from dusk Friday to dusk Saturday ("the second day") and from dusk Saturday to dawn Sunday ("the third day"). On the morning of the third day the astonished guards felt the earth quake and saw an angel roll away the stone sealing the tomb. They fled from the scene.

At first light a group of women came to anoint Jesus' body with spices. They found the tomb empty. Running back to the city, they reported the news to Jesus' disciples. Peter and John raced to the tomb and found it just as they had said (Matt. 27:57–28:10 and parallels). Jesus had risen from the dead.

Jesus appeared to his followers on 10 recorded occasions after his resurrection. At one of these appearances, Jesus commissioned the 11 remaining apostles to go into all the world and make disciples, baptizing and teaching them. This is known as the Great Commission (Matt. 28:19–20).

As he appeared to his followers for the last time, Jesus ascended into heaven (Luke 24:49–53; Acts 1:6–11). He promised to return just as he was going—visibly and physically.

Christology

The Doctrine of Christ or Christology deals with the person and work of Jesus Christ.

His Person

Understanding Christ's person is no easy task, but there is general agreement on most aspects of the nature of Jesus Christ and his personality.

Of 12 titles of Jesus, five reflect something significant of his person and work (*Christ, Jesus, Lord, Son of God,* and *Son of Man*).

Alpha and Omega. The first and last letters of the Greek alphabet. This title is given to God the Father and God the Son (Rev. 1:8, 21:6). The risen Christ says, "I am the Alpha and the Omega, the Beginning and the End, the First and the Last" (Rev. 22:13). Calling Jesus Christ the Alpha and the Omega acknowledges that he is both the Creator and the Redeemer and the final judge of all things.

Beginning. A title that describes his existence before time began. The gospel of John declares that Jesus was present with the Father "in the beginning," and, therefore, the Creator of all things (John 1:2–3). Christ is called "the Beginning" (Col. 1:18), "the Beginning of the creation of God" (Rev. 3:14), and "the Beginning and the End" (Rev. 1:8; 21:6; 22:13).

Christ. The NT equivalent of *Messiah,* a Hebrew word meaning "anointed one" (cf. Acts 4:27; 10:38). This title emphasized that Jesus was divinely appointed to his mission, that he had an official relationship to God the Father—that is, he had a job to do and a role to discharge at the Father's appointing.

Desire of All Nations. A phrase interpreted by some translations of the Bible as a *prophecy of the Messiah* (Hag. 2:7, KJV, NKJV; *wealth of all nations*, NASB; *treasure of all nations*, NEB). Haggai envisioned a time when the choicest and costliest treasures of the Gentiles would be dedicated to the God of Israel.

Holy One of God. This title was given to Jesus by Peter (John 6:69, RSV) and remarkably, by a demon-possessed man (Mark 1:24). In their preaching, the apostles called Jesus "the Holy One and the Just" (Acts 3:14). This was a name belonging to him as the Messiah, indicating he was especially set apart for God.

This title also emphasized his positive goodness and complete dedication to the doing of his Father's will.

Jesus. The name *Jesus* (identical with *Joshua* and meaning "God is Savior") emphasizes his role as the Savior (Matt. 1:21).

Lord. A simple title for Jesus (somewhat like *Master*). It was a title of authority or ownership, and sometimes an indication of his equality with God (e.g. Matt. 7:22; Mark 12:36–37; Luke 2:11).

Only Begotten. A title used by John to designate Jesus' uniqueness (John 1:14, 18; 3:16, 18; 1 John 4:9). This title comes from combining two Greek words that mean "single kind." Therefore, it means "the only one of its kind" or "unique."

As the unique, sinless Son, Jesus accomplished our salvation through his death on the cross.

Son of God. A title applied to Jesus in an official or messianic sense (cf. Matt. 4:3, 6; 16:16; Luke 22:70; John 1:49). It emphasized that he was a person of the triune Godhead, supernaturally born as a human being.

Son of Man. The title used almost exclusively by Jesus himself (cf. Matt. 9:6; 10:23; 11:19). Some feel he used it because it most clearly distinguished his Messiahship from the erroneous ideas of his time.

Wisdom. Much that is said in the OT about the word of God is paralleled by what is said of the wisdom of God. The terms are interchangeable. "The Lord by wisdom founded the earth" (Prov. 3:19). In the NT Christ is portrayed as the personal Wisdom of God (1 Cor. 1:24, 30)—the one through whom all things were created (1 Cor. 8:6; Col. 1:16; Heb. 1:2).

Word. Jesus' perfect revelation of the Father is also expressed when he is described as the Word (*logos*) of God (John 1:1–18). The Word is the self-expression of God; that self-expression has personal status, existing eternally with God. The Word by which God created the world (Ps. 33:6) and by which he spoke through the prophets "became flesh" in the fullness of time (John 1:14), living among men and women as Jesus of Nazareth.

Christians believe that Jesus is both God and human—i.e., that he has two distinct natures united "inconfusedly, unchangeably, indivisibly, inseparably" in his one person (Chalcedonian Creed, A.D. 451).

The Bible reports that Jesus was worshiped at God's command (Heb. 1:6), while lesser spiritual beings decline to be worshiped (Rev. 22:8–9) because worship was to be rendered only to God. Only the divine Creator may be worshiped by his creatures. But Jesus Christ, God's Son, is cocreator with the Father (John 1:3; Col. 1:16; Heb. 1:2); therefore both must be worshiped.

Scripture declares that Jesus is the Savior of his people (Matt. 1:21), even though Yahweh (Jehovah) was the only Savior of his people (Isa. 43:11; Hos. 13:4). The Father himself has clearly called Jesus "God" (Heb. 1:8).

Scripture also teaches the true humanity of Jesus. The Jesus of the NT is no illusion or ghost but human in every sense. He called himself a man, as did others (e.g., John 8:40; Acts 2:22). He lived in his body (John 1:14; 1 Tim. 3:16; 1 John 4:2) and experienced human joys and sufferings (Luke 2:40, 52; Heb. 2:10, 18; 5:8). However, the Bible emphasizes that Jesus did not partake of the sin that characterizes all other human beings (cf. Luke 1:35; John 8:46; Heb. 4:15).

His Personality

Jesus Christ has two distinct natures but is a single person, not two persons under one skin. He is the eternal Logos (divine Word), the second person of the Trinity, yet he assumed human nature in such a way that there was no essential change in the divine nature. We can address Jesus Christ in prayer using titles that reflect both his human and divine natures, although his divine nature is the ultimate basis of our worship.

The incarnation manifested the triune (three-in-one) God by showing us the relationship between Father, Son and Spirit (cf. Matt. 3:16–17; John 14:15–26; Rom. 1:3–4; Gal. 4:4–5; 1 Pet. 1:1–12). Because Jesus is one person, and because the unity of his personal life embraces all his character and all his powers, Scripture speaks of him as being both divine and human. It ascribes divine acts and attributes to Jesus Christ the eternal Son of God (Acts 20:28).

His Position

As we seek to understand Jesus Christ, we need to examine his position before the law. He humbled himself before it, and, as a result, God exalted him over it. This is an interesting irony.

The Son laid aside his divine majesty and assumed human nature. He submitted himself to all the sufferings of his earthly life, including death itself. He did this to accomplish God's plan to redeem humanity from sin.

Jesus Christ was surrounded by sin. The devil repeatedly attacked him. His own people hated him and refused to believe he was the Savior. His enemies persecuted him. Finally, at the end of his earthly life, Jesus endured all the wrath of God against sin. No other person has suffered as intensely as Jesus did.

God the Father exalted Jesus by raising him from the dead, taking him away to heaven, and seating him at his own right hand. Jesus Christ will return from that place of honor to judge the living and the dead.

His Prophetic Office

The OT depicts prophets as persons who receive God's word (revelation) and pass it on to the people. In order to function as prophets, these individuals had to receive a clear word from God. They stood in God's stead before the people; God used their mouths to communicate what he wished to say.

The OT promised a great Prophet who would convey God's Word finally and decisively to his people (Deut. 18:15). Jesus was that Prophet (Acts 3:22–24). He acted prophetically even before he came to earth as a human being, for he spoke through the writers of the OT (1 Pet. 1:10–11).

His Priestly Office

While OT prophets represented God before the people, priests represented the people before God. So Christ represents his people before the Father (Heb. 3:1; 4:14).

Jesus presented himself as a priestly sacrifice. The OT sacrifices were *expiatory* (they put away sin, restoring worshipers to the blessings and privileges God intended for them) and *vicarious* (another life was offered for sin instead of the lives of worshipers).

Jesus Christ reconciles sinners to God. God expressed his love for humankind by sending Jesus to redeem them from their sins (John 3:16). In every event, God has attempted to bring his creatures back to him. When Jesus came into the world, there was no change in God himself, only a change in his relation to sinners.

Christ also intercedes for his people (Heb. 7:25). He entered the holy place of heaven by means of the perfect, all-sufficient sacrifice that he offered to the Father.

In the presence of God, Jesus Christ now answers the constant accusations of the devil against believers (Rom. 8:33–34).

Finally, Jesus Christ prays for believers. He pleads for the needs we do not mention in our prayers—things that we ignore, underestimate, or do not see.

His Kingly Office

As the second person of the Trinity, cocreator with the Father, Jesus Christ is the eternal king over all kings. As Savior, he is the king of a spiritual kingdom—that is, he rules in the hearts and lives of his people. By reason of his spiritual kingship, Jesus Christ is called the head of the church (Eph. 1:22).

Jesus Christ rules and governs all things on behalf of his church. He will not allow his purposes to be frustrated in the end. He received this universal kingship when God exalted him to his place of honor in heaven. He will deliver this kingdom to the Father when he accomplishes the final victory over evil (1 Cor. 15:24–28), i.e., when he destroys this world-order once for all and makes it new.

Seven Words from the Cross

While Jesus hung on the cross, he spoke seven different times.

Father, forgive them, for they do not know what they do. (Luke 23:34)
Jesus taught that we should forgive those who sin against us. How appropriate that his first words from the cross should be words of forgiveness.

Assuredly, I say to you, today you will be with Me in Paradise. (Luke 23:43)
As he hung on the cross, Jesus did not appear to be a king. Yet, what faith the repentant thief displayed when he pleaded, "Lord, remember me when You come into Your kingdom" (Luke 23:42). Jesus' reply was good news to the dying sinner.

Woman, behold your son! . . . Behold your mother! (John 19:26–27)
In spite of his own grief and pain, Jesus continued to think of others. His earthly father, Joseph, probably had died by this time. Jesus asked his beloved disciple, John, to take care of his mother and for Mary to be a mother to John.

Eli, Eli, lama sabachthani? . . . My God, My God, why have You forsaken Me? (Matt. 27:46; Mark 15:34)
These words came from Jesus' lips about 3 P.M., after he had hung on the cross for hours. Death was near; Jesus was feeling the pain and loneliness that sin causes. The sin in this case was our sin and not his. To express his anguish and grief, Jesus quoted the opening words of Psalm 22, using the same words that King David had used centuries earlier (Ps. 22:1).

I thirst! (John 19:28)
The OT had prophesied that Jesus would suffer for the sins of the world. In his death, that prophecy was being fulfilled. Jesus suffered spiritual torment as well as physical agony as he hung on the cross. His spirit thirsted to win the spiritual battle against evil while his body thirsted for water.

It is finished! (John 19:30)
The word translated "finished!" shows that Jesus' victory has been achieved. It carries the idea of perfection or fulfillment. God's plan of salvation has been accomplished through Jesus' sacrifice on the cross.

Father, into Your hands I commit My spirit. (Luke 23:46)
Jesus did not die a failure but a victorious Savior. He finished his work triumphantly and entrusted his spirit to God his Father.

God the Holy Spirit_____

The Holy Spirit is the third member of the Trinity who exercises the power of the Father and the Son in creation and redemption. Because the Holy Spirit is the power by whom believers come to Jesus Christ and see with new eyes of faith, the Holy Spirit is closer to us than we are to ourselves. Like the eyes of the body through which we see physical things, he is seldom consciously in focus or seen directly, because he is the one through whom all else is seen in a new light.

This may help to explain why the relationship of the Father and the Son is more visible in the Gospels—it is through the eyes of the Holy Spirit that the Father-Son relationship is viewed.

The Holy Spirit appears in the gospel of John as the power by whom Christians are brought to faith and helped to understand their lives with God. The Spirit brings a person to new birth: "That which is born of the flesh is flesh, and that which is born of the Spirit is spirit" (John 3:6), "It is the Spirit who gives life" (6:63).

The Holy Spirit is the *Paraclete,* or *Helper,* whom Jesus promised to the disciples after his ascension. The triune family of Father, Son, and Holy Spirit are unified in ministering to believers (John 14:16, 26). It is through the Helper that Father and Son abide with the disciples (15:26).

This unified ministry of the Trinity is also seen as the Spirit brings the world under conviction of sin, righteousness and judgment. He guides believers into all truth with what he hears from the Father (John 12:49–50); the Father witnesses to and glorifies the Son (8:16–18, 50, 54); the Father and Son honor the Holy Spirit by commissioning him to speak in their name (14:16, 26); the Holy Spirit honors the Father and Son by helping the community of believers.

During his ministry, Jesus refers to the Spirit of God (Matt. 12:28–29; Luke 11:20) as the power by whom he is casting out demons and invading the stronghold of Beelzebub and freeing those held captive. Accordingly, the Spirit works with the Father and Son in realizing the redeeming power of the kingdom of God. God's kingdom is not only the reign of the Son but also the reign of the Spirit, as all share in the reign of the Father.

The person and ministry of the Holy Spirit in the Gospels is confirmed by his work in the early church. The baptism with the Holy Spirit (Acts 1:5, 2:4ff.) is the pouring out of the Spirit's power in missions and evangelism (1:8).

This prophecy of Jesus (cf. Joel 2:28–32) begins on Pentecost (Acts 2:1–18). Many of those who hear of the finished work of God in Jesus' death and resurrection (vv. 2:32–38) repent of their sins. In this act of repentance, they receive the gift of the Holy Spirit, becoming witnesses of God's grace through the Holy Spirit.

Two special words in describing the person and work of the Holy Spirit are *helper* and *paraclete.*

Jesus used the term *helper* (John 14:16, 26; 15:26; 16:7). The Greek word has been translated into English in various versions of the Bible as "Comforter," "Advocate," and "Counselor," as well as "Helper." This Greek word is so filled with meaning that it is difficult to translate it with one English word. The basic meaning, however, is "helper."

The Holy Spirit is the one called to our side by Jesus to help us, to stand by us, to strengthen us, and to give assistance when needed. The Holy Spirit is the "other" Helper (John 14:16). Just as Jesus was the Great Helper while on earth, the Holy Spirit is now our Helper.

Paraclete is a transliteration of the Greek word *parakletos* which means "one who speaks in favor of," as an intercessor, advocate, or legal assistant.

The word appears only in the gospel of John. Jesus applied the term to the Holy Spirit, who would be an advocate on behalf of his followers after his ascension; the Spirit would plead their cause before God (John 14:16, 26; 15:26; 16:7).

Paul's teaching about the Holy Spirit harmonizes with the accounts of the Spirit's activity in the Gospels and Acts. According to Paul, it is by the Holy Spirit that believers confess that Jesus is Lord (1 Cor. 12:3). Through the same Spirit varieties of gifts are given to the body of Christ to ensure its richness and unity (vv. 4–27).

The Holy Spirit is the way to Jesus Christ the Son (Rom. 8:11) and to the Father (vv. 14–15). He is the person who bears witness to us that we are children of God (vv. 16–17). He "makes intercession for us with groanings which cannot be uttered" (vv. 26–27).

The Holy Spirit also reveals to Christians the deep things of God (1 Cor. 2:10–12) and the mystery of Christ (Eph. 3:3–5). The Holy Spirit acts with God and Christ as the pledge or guarantee by whom believers are sealed until the day of salvation (2 Cor. 1:21–22) and by whom they live (Rom. 15:13).

Against the lust and enmity of the flesh Paul contrasts the fruit of the Spirit: "Love, joy, peace, longsuffering, kindness, goodness, faithfulness, gentleness, self-control" (Gal. 5:22–23).

Since the Holy Spirit is the expressed power of the triune God, believers are not to grieve the Spirit (Eph. 4:30). Jesus made this clear in his dispute with the religious authorities who attributed his ministry to Satan rather than the Spirit and hence committed the unforgivable sin (Matt. 12:22–32).

Satan

Satan (literally, "adversary") is the great opposer or adversary of God and humanity. It is the personal name of the devil.

The Hebrew word from which Satan comes sometimes refers to human enemies (1 Sam. 29:4; Ps. 109:6). Once it refers to the angel of the Lord who opposed Balaam (Num. 22:22). But whenever this word is used as a proper name in the OT, it refers to the great superhuman enemy of God and humanity (1 Chron. 21:1; Job 1—2). This use of the word also occurs frequently in the NT.

History of Satan

Two OT passages—Isaiah 14:12–15 and Ezekiel 28:11–19—furnish a picture of Satan's original condition and the reasons for his loss of that position. These passages were addressed originally to the kings of Babylon and Tyre. In their long-range implications, many scholars believe, they refer to Satan himself. They tell of an exalted angelic being, one of God's creatures, who became proud and ambitious. He determined to take over the throne of God for himself. But God removed him from his position of great dignity and honor.

Building upon this foundation, Revelation provides glimpses of further stages in Satan's work of evil. In his fall from God's favor, Satan persuaded one-third of the angels to join his rebellion (12:3–4). Throughout the OT period he sought to destroy the messianic line. When the Messiah became a human being, Satan tried to eliminate him (vv. 4–5).

Characteristics

As a result of his original status and authority, Satan has great power and dignity. So great is his strength that Michael the archangel viewed him as a foe too powerful to oppose (Jude 9).

Satan's influence in worldly affairs is also revealed. His various titles reflect his control of the world system, such as "ruler of this world" (John 12:31), "god of this age" (2 Cor. 4:4), and "prince of the power of the air" (Eph. 2:2).

Satan exercises his evil power through demons (Matt. 12:24; 25:41; Rev. 12:7, 9). An outburst of demonic activity occurred when Jesus came to earth the first time because of the Savior's attack against Satan's kingdom (Matt. 12:28–29; Acts 10:38).

Satan also has high intelligence. Through it he deceived Adam and Eve and took over their rule of the world for himself (Gen. 1:26; 3:1–7). His cleverness enables him to carry out his deceptive work almost at will.

Yet Satan's attributes, impressive as they are, are not limitless. His power is subject to

God's restrictions (Luke 4:6; 2 Thess. 2:7–8). The reins of God on his activities are illustrated by Satan's request to God for permission to afflict Job (Job 1:7–12).

Satan is permitted to afflict God's people (Luke 13:16; 1 Thess. 2:18; Heb. 2:14), but he is never allowed to win an ultimate victory over them (John 14:30–31; 16:33).

Satan's nature is malicious. His efforts in opposing God, his people, and his truth are tireless (Job 1:7; 2:2; Matt. 13:28). He is always opposed to best interests of all individuals (1 Chron. 21:1; Zech. 3:1–2).

Methods

Of the various methods used by Satan in carrying out his evil work, none is more characteristic than temptation (Matt. 4:3 ff.; 1 Thess. 3:5). Satan leads people into sin by various means: by direct suggestion, as in the case of Judas Iscariot (John 13:2, 27); through his agents who disguise themselves as messengers of God (2 Thess. 2:9; 1 John 4:1); and through an individual's own weaknesses (1 Cor. 7:5).

Along with his work of tempting humankind, Satan also delights in deception (1 Tim. 3:6–7; 2 Tim. 2:26). His lying nature stands in bold contrast to the truth for which Christ stands (John 8:32, 44). The great falsehood he uses so frequently is that good can be attained by doing wrong. This lie is apparent in practically all his temptations (Gen. 3:4–5). As the great deceiver, Satan is an expert at falsifying truth (2 Cor. 11:13–15).

Defeat

Satan is destined to fail in his continuing rebellion against God. His final defeat is predicted in the NT (Luke 10:18; John 12:31; Rev. 12:9; 20:10). The death of Jesus on the cross is the basis for Satan's final defeat (Heb. 2:14–15; 1 Pet. 3:18, 22). This event was the grand climax to a sinless life during which Jesus triumphed over the enemy repeatedly (Matt. 4:1–11; Luke 4:1–13).

Personal victory depends on our will to offer resistance to Satan's temptations (Eph. 4:25–27; 1 Pet. 5:8–9). To help Christians win this battle against Satan, God has provided the power of the Holy Spirit, the continuing prayer of Jesus Christ in heaven for believers (Heb. 7:25), the leading of the Holy Spirit (Gal. 5:16), and various weapons for spiritual warfare (Eph. 6:13–18).

Reality

Some people have trouble accepting the existence of Satan. But his presence and activity are necessary to explain the problems of evil and suffering. The Bible makes it plain that Satan exists and that his main work is to oppose the rule of God in human affairs.

The devil is strong, but Christians are stronger through the Lord (Eph. 6:11). They have the protection needed to withstand his assaults. The devil tempts, but God provides a way of escape (1 Cor. 10:13); the devil tries to take advantage of people (2 Cor. 2:11), but he will flee if fought (James 4:7). The devil should not be feared, for Jesus is more powerful than this deceiving prince of the demons (1 John 4:4).

Beelzebub. Prince of demons. The religious leaders of Jesus' time were guilty of blasphemy against the Holy Spirit because they claimed the miracles of Jesus were actually conducted by the devil (see Matt. 9:34; 12:24). The KJV and some other versions incorrectly translate "demons" as "devil." There are many demons but only one devil.

Deceiver. Starting with Eve, the devil has tempted to deceive every living soul (see Rev. 20:10). Evil people operating under the power of the evil one will continue to deceive (2 Tim. 3:13).

Devil. Literally, "accuser." This is the main title for the fallen angelic being who is the supreme enemy of God and man. Satan is his name, and devil is what he is—the accuser or deceiver. The title "devil" appears 35 times in the NKJV. In every case it is preceded by the article "the," indicating a title rather than a name. The term comes from a Greek word that means "a false witness" or "malicious accuser."

Enemy. The devil is the worst enemy of humanity (see Matt. 13:25, 28, 39). This is one enemy Jesus does not want us to love. He is an enemy of Christ, the church, and the gospel. He is tireless in his efforts to uproot good and sow evil.

Lucifer. "Morning star." This is the Latin name for the planet Venus. The word "Lucifer" appears only once in the Bible (Isa. 14:12). Literally, the passage describes the overthrow of a tyrant, the king of Babylon. But many Bible scholars see in this passage a description of Satan, who rebelled against the throne of God and was "brought down to Sheol, to the lowest depths of the Pit" (Isa. 14:15). The same kind of interpretation is often given to Ezekiel 28:11–19.

Murderer. "He was a murderer from the beginning" are strong words from the lips of Jesus (John 8:44). The devil killed Abel and the prophets, and he wanted to kill Jesus before his time (v. 40).

Ruler of this world. Three times Jesus called the devil the "ruler of this world" (see John 12:31; 14:30; 16:11). The devil offered the world to Jesus if he would worship him, but the Lord refused with these words, "Get behind me, Satan" (Luke 4:5–8).

Wicked one *or* Evil one. A common term used in referring to Satan (see Matthew 6:13; 13:19, 38; 1 John 2:13). This phrase depicts the devil's fundamental nature. He is in direct opposition to everything God is and all he wishes to do. He is the source of all evil and wickedness. While the KJV reads, "Deliver us from evil," the NKJV more accurately reads, "Deliver us from the evil one." Humanity needs this deliverance, for the devil "walks about like a roaring lion, seeking whom he may devour" (1 Pet. 5:8).

Names for Satan

Accuser of God's people	Rev. 12:10	Liar	Gen. 3:4–5; John 8:44
Angel of light	2 Cor. 11:14–15	Lucifer, "light-bearer" or "shining one"	Isa. 14:12
Apollyon, "destroyer"	Rev. 9:11		
Beelzebub, "prince of demons"	Matt. 12:24	Murderer	John 8:44
Belial, "vileness" or "ruthlessness"	2 Cor. 6:15	Prince of the power of the air	Eph. 2:2
Deceiver	Rev. 20:10	Prince of this world	John 12:31
Devil, "slanderer"	occurs 35 times in the Bible	Roaring lion	1 Pet. 5:8
Dragon	Rev. 12:7	Ruler of darkness	Eph. 6:12
Enemy	Matt. 13:39	Satan, "adversary" (his most common name)	occurs 52 times in the Bible
God of this age	2 Cor. 4:4		
King of death	Heb. 2:14		
Leviathan, "one who dwells in the sea of humanity"	Isa. 27:1	Tempter	1 Thess. 3:5
		Wicked one	Matt. 13:38

Other Spiritual Beings

Angel. An angel is a member of an order of heavenly beings who are superior to humans in power and intelligence. By nature angels are spiritual beings (Heb. 1:14). They have superhuman power and knowledge (2 Sam. 14:17, 20; 2 Pet. 2:1). However, they are not all-powerful and all-knowing (Ps. 103:20; 2 Thess. 1:7).

Artistic portrayals of angels as winged beings are generally without basis in the Bible. Rarely is an angel so described. Angels are mentioned numerous times in more than half of the biblical books.

Angels, fallen. These heavenly beings or divine messengers created by God rebelled against him and were cast out of heaven. The lord or prince of these fallen angels is Satan (Rev. 12:7–9). Fallen angels, or messengers, continue to serve Satan; but their power is limited. Judgment awaits them in the future (Matt. 25:41; Rev. 12:9). Some believe that the fallen angels referred to in 2 Peter 2:4 and Jude 6 are possibly the beings referred to as "sons of God" in Gen. 6:1–4. There is no real distinction between fallen angels and demons.

Archangel. In the celestial hierarchy, a spiritual being next in rank above an angel. The word archangel occurs several times in the Bible. In the NT the voice of an archangel and the sounding of the trumpet of God will signal the coming of Jesus Christ for his people (1 Thess. 4:16).

Cherub, Cherubim. These creatures were usually portrayed with human or animal faces and with wings. They were considered angelic servants of God with the special task of guarding holy places and objects such as the ark of the covenant.

Demon. This is another name for a fallen angel who joined Satan in rebellion against God.

The origin of demons is not explicitly discussed in the Bible. But the NT speaks of the fall and later imprisonment of a group of angels (1 Pet. 3:19–20; 2 Pet. 2:4; Jude 6).

The group that participated in the fall apparently followed one of their own number, Satan. The fall occurred before God's creation of the world, leaving Satan and his angels free to contaminate the human race with wickedness (Gen. 3; Matt. 25:41; Rev. 12:9). Only part of the fallen angels took part in the wickedness at the time of the Flood (Gen. 6:1–4). These were the ones who were imprisoned. God left the rest free and they try to undermine the cause of righteousness in the world.

A symbolic view of the initial fall appears in Revelation 12:3–4 where the dragon (a symbol for Satan) "drew a third of the stars of heaven" (a symbol for angels) and "threw them to the earth." This shows that Satan has his own angels, presumably these demons (Matt. 25:41; Rev. 12:9).

Demons in the Old Testament.
Because the Jews believed God's power was unlimited, the OT contains little information about demons. The primitive status of the understanding of demons during this

Facts about angels

They were created by God	Gen. 2:1; Neh. 9:6; Eph. 3:9; Col. 1:16			68:17; Dan. 7:9–10; Matt. 26:53; Heb. 12:22; Rev. 5:11
They report directly to God	Job 1:6; 2:1		They possess intelligence	Dan. 9:21–22; 10:14; Rev. 19:10; 22:8–9
They were present at creation	Job 38:4, 7		They possess will	Isa. 14:1–15; Jude 6
They announced Jesus' birth to the shepherds	Luke 2:10–14		They rejoice	Job 38:7; Luke 2:13
They do not marry	Matt. 22:30			
They were created to live forever	Rev. 4:8		They display desire	1 Pet. 1:12
Their purpose is to glorify God	Rev. 4:8		They are stronger than human beings	Ps. 103:20; 2 Thess. 1:7; 2 Pet. 2:11
Angels help human beings	Heb. 1:14			
Fallen angels harm human beings	Mark 5:1–5		They are more intelligent than human beings	Dan. 9:21–22; 10:14
They are spirit beings	Ps. 104:4; Heb. 1:7, 14		They are not omnipresent	Dan. 10:12
They are invisible	Rom. 1:18–32; Col. 2:18		They are not omnipotent	Dan. 10:13; Jude 9
They are innumerable	Deut. 33:2; Ps.		They are not omniscient	Matt. 24:36

Names used for angels

Armies	Speaks of their military service	Josh. 5:14; 1 Sam. 17:45
Chariots	May refer to their swiftness	2 Kings 6:16–17; Ps. 68:17; Zech. 6:1–5
Holy Ones, Saints	Refers to their total separation to the will of God	Ps. 89:7; Dan. 8:13
Ministers	Signifies their religious virtues and spiritual service	Ps. 103:20–21; 104:4
Sons of God	Gen. 6:2, 4; Job 1:6; 2:1; 38:7	
Sons of the mighty	May refer to their awesome strength and power	Ps. 29:1; 89:6
Stars	May indicate both their number and their brightness	Job 38:7; Ps. 148:2–3; Rev. 12:3–4
Watchers	Speaks of their duties as supervisors and agents	Dan. 4:13, 17

time may be reflected in the way the OT relates the fallen angels to God. It was a "distressing (or evil) spirit from God" (1 Sam. 16:15–16, 23) that troubled King Saul. A "lying spirit" from the Lord is the one about whom Micaiah, the prophet of the Lord, spoke (1 Kings 22:21–23).

Pagan worship is also related to demon activity in the OT (Lev. 17:7; Ps. 106:37). Demons delight in making heathen idols the focus of their activities.

Demons in the New Testament. The NT accepts the OT teaching about demons and advances the doctrine significantly. Demons are designated in a number of different ways in the NT. Frequently they are called "unclean spirits" (Matt. 10:1; Mark 6:7). Another descriptive phrase for them is "wicked (or evil) spirits" (Luke 7:21; Acts 19:12–13).

In his writings Paul calls them "deceiving spirits" (1 Tim. 4:1). John refers to "the spirit of error" (1 John 4:6) and "spirits of demons" (Rev. 16:14). Luke describes one demon as a "spirit of divination" (Acts 16:16).

The only individual demon named in the NT (Satan himself is never referred to as a demon) is the one called *Abaddon* in Hebrew and Apollyon in Greek (Rev. 9:11). Some scholars believe this is another name for Satan or that this is an unfallen angel. But stronger evidence suggests he was a fallen angelic leader who is subject to the kingly authority of Satan.

Legion (Mark 5:9; Luke 8:30) is probably a collective name for a group of demons rather than the name of a single demon.

A prime purpose of Jesus' earthly ministry was to overcome the power of Satan. This included his conquest of the demonic realm (Matt. 12:25–29; Luke 11:17–22; John 12:31; 1 John 3:8). This explains the fierce conflict between Jesus and these evil spirits while he was on earth.

Yet Jesus' enemies accused him of being in alliance with Satan's kingdom, including his demons (Mark 3:22; John 8:48). This same accusation was made against his forerunner, John the Baptist (Matt. 11:18; Luke 7:33). Jesus' works of goodness and righteousness showed that these claims were not true (Matt. 12:25–29; Luke 11:17–22).

Following the resurrection of Jesus and his return to heaven, these demonic principalities and powers have continued their warfare against those who are his followers (Rom. 8:38–39; Eph. 6:12). Satan and his allies will finally be overthrown by God.

After Jesus returns, the devil and his angels will be defeated and thrown into the lake of fire and brimstone (Matt. 25:41; Rev. 20:10). This is a doom with which demons are quite familiar (Matt. 8:29). God will achieve the ultimate victory in this conflict, which has been going on since the beginning of time.

Demon possession. This is an affliction of persons in the NT who were possessed or controlled by demons (Matt. 4:24; 8:33).

The NT gives graphic descriptions of the effect of demons on people. Some of the diseases they caused included: muteness (Matt. 12:22; Mark 9:17, 25), deafness (Mark 9:25), blindness (Matt. 12:22), and bodily deformity (Luke 13:10–17).

Demons were not responsible for all physical ailments. The gospel writers frequently distinguished between sickness and demon possession (Matt. 4:24; Mark 1:32; Luke 6:17–18). Sometimes a problem caused by demons appears to have another cause in another situation (Matt. 12:22; 15:30).

Activities of fallen angels

Fallen angels cause blindness	Matt. 12:22	Fallen angels cause muteness	Matt. 9:32–33
Fallen angels cause deafness	Mark 9:25	Fallen angels cause personal injuries	Mark 9:18
Fallen angels cause disease	Matt. 10:1; Mark 1:23–26; 3:11; Luke 4:36; Acts 5:16; 8:7; Rev. 16:13	Fallen angels cause physical defects	Luke 13:11
		Fallen angels disseminate false doctrine	2 Thess. 2:2; 1 Tim. 4:1
Fallen angels cause epilepsy	Matt. 17:15–18	Fallen angels execute Satan's program	1 Tim. 4:1; Rev. 9; 16:12–14
Fallen angels cause insanity	Matt. 8:28; 17:15, 18; Mark 5:15; Luke 8:27–29	Fallen angels oppose God's purpose	Eph. 6:12

Facts about fallen angels.

Bottomless pit is under the control of an angel called *Abaddon* (Hebrew) and *Apollyon* (Greek)	Rev. 9:11	Fallen angels know who Jesus is	Luke 4:34
Eventually evil angels will be cast into the lake of fire forever	Matt. 25:41; 2 Pet. 2:4; Jude 6	Fallen angels possess great strength	Exod. 7:11–12; 8:7; Dan. 10:13; Mark 5:2–4; 9:17–26; Acts 19:16; 2 Cor. 10:4–5
Evil angels will be judged by Jesus Christ and the church	1 Cor. 6:3		
Fallen angels are evil and rule over the nations of the world	Dan. 10:13	Fallen angels speak	Matt. 8:29; Mark 3:11; 5:12; Luke 4:34, 41; 8:28; Acts 19:15
Fallen angels display disdain	Acts 19:15		
Fallen angels experience fear	Luke 8:28; James 2:19		
Fallen angels have names	Luke 8:30; Rev. 9:11	Wicked angel (demon) named Legion headed a large group of fallen spirits that possessed the maniac of Gadara	Mark 5:9
Fallen angels know of their future damnation	Matt. 8:29		

In NT times demons were also responsible for some mental problems (Matt. 8:28; Acts 19:13–16). The ranting and raving that they produced probably should be included with mental disorders (Mark 1:23–24; John 10:20). Uncontrolled fits were another form of demonic affliction (Luke 9:37–42; Mark 1:26). Sometimes a demon also caused a person to behave in an antisocial manner (Luke 8:27, 35).

Gabriel. An archangel. In the Bible, Gabriel appeared to Daniel to interpret his visions, to Zacharias to foretell the birth of John, and to Mary to announce that she would give birth to Jesus.

Host of heaven. They are heavenly beings created by God and associated with him in his rule over the world. God is a social being who brings other families into being and implants the divine image in them. The families of earth bear this image (Ps. 19:1–6; Rom. 1:19–20), as does the host of heaven (Isa. 45:12).

At the angel's announcement to the shepherds of the birth of Jesus, a multitude of the heavenly host praised God (Luke 2:13). They served as a great choir of created heavenly beings who glorified their Creator and participated in the background of the new age of salvation.

God is also called "the LORD of hosts" (Isa. 1:9; 10:23, RSV). The host of heaven consists of angelic beings and celestial bodies whom God has created and whose principal role is to serve and glorify him (1 Kings 22:19; Ps. 103:19–21; Isa. 40:26).

Living creatures. These are heavenly beings mentioned in the visions of Ezekiel and John.

In Ezekiel's vision (Ezek. 1:1–28) these creatures had four faces (man, lion, ox, and eagle) and four wings. The prophet also identified the four living creatures as cherubim (chapter 10).

These four heavenly beings are probably the same as the four living creatures mentioned by John in the NT (Rev. 4:6–9).

Michael. The name of the archangel who disputed with the devil about the body of Moses (Jude 9). In the OT, Michael is described as having power and authority

(Dan. 10:13) and is the guardian of Israel (Dan. 10:21).

He is mentioned by Daniel (Dan 10:13, 21) as the protector of God's people against the powers of Persia and Greece. His name appears in Jude and Revelation where he is called the archangel (Jude 9; Rev 12:7).

Queen of Heaven. This is the name of a fertility goddess to whom the Israelites, especially the women, offered sacrifice and worship in the days before the fall of the southern kingdom of Judah (Jer. 7:18; 44:17–19, 25). In the time of Jeremiah, many people in Jerusalem and other cities of Judah worshiped the queen of heaven. Their worship included burning incense and pouring out drink offerings to her (Jer. 44:17). This was obviously a form of idolatry, but it is not clear exactly which pagan god was worshiped.

The phrase "queen of heaven" may be a title for the goddess Ishtar (perhaps the same goddess as the biblical Ashtoreth). Or it may refer to the Canaanite goddess Anat. Cakes were also baked in honor of the "queen of heaven" (Jer. 7:18). These cakes may have been in the shape of stars, crescent moons, or the female figure. The worship of this goddess was one of the evils that brought God's judgment upon Judah (Jer. 7:20).

Rahab the Dragon. "Agitated." This was a mythological sea monster or dragon representing the evil forces of chaos that God subdued by his creative power. The name Rahab as it occurs in Job 9:13 (NIV), Job 26:12 (NIV), Ps. 87:4 and 89:10, Isa. 30:7 (NIV), and Isa. 51:9 has no connection with the personal name of Rahab, the harlot of Jericho (Josh. 2:1–21). The references to Rahab in the books of Job, Psalms, and Isaiah speak of an evil power overcome by God.

God's smiting of Rahab is described in Job 26:12 (NIV) to signify God's power over the chaos of primeval waters at the creation. The NKJV translates Rahab as "the storm."

Because the Rahab-dragon imagery was used in describing the deliverance from Egypt, the name Rahab also became a synonym for Egypt itself (Ps. 87:4; Isa. 30:7; *Rahab-Hem-Shebeth,* NKJV). In its widest sense, the dragon can represent any force that opposes God's will. It is a fitting symbol for Satan (Rev. 20:2).

Seraph, Seraphim. "Fiery, burning ones." These are angelic or heavenly beings associated with Isaiah's vision of God in the temple when he was called to his prophetic ministry (Isa. 6:1–7).

This is the only place in the Bible that mentions these mysterious creatures. Each seraph had six wings. They used two to fly, two to cover their feet, and two to cover their faces (Isa. 6:2). The seraphim flew about the throne on which God was seated, singing his praises as they called special attention to his glory and majesty.

These beings apparently also served as agents of purification for Isaiah as he began his prophetic ministry. One placed a hot coal against Isaiah's lips with the words, "Your iniquity is taken away, and your sin is purged" (Isa. 6:7).

Theological Words

Eschatology
(The Last Things)____

In the past twenty years, more and more Christians seem to be stressing the end of the time. Perhaps this may be the natural result of grappling with issues such as nuclear armament and the expanding number of nations around the globe now manufacturing their own nuclear bombs.

Aside from that, Christians from the time Jesus Christ ascended into heaven have awaited his return. And as they have waited they have raised questions about eschatology—the study of last things.

The Basics

Among Christians, certain events are clear and almost universally accepted: the visible and bodily return of Jesus Christ (called *rapture* by some); the judgment of all people in the world (Matt. 25:31–46); and the creation of the new heavens and the new earth where all the righteous will remain forever (Rev. 21—22).

Prior to the mid-nineteenth century, with some variations, the church as a whole saw the end of time in the following sequence: Jesus Christ would return to the earth; this return would usher in the end of the world and the judgment of all nations and individuals; and all will go to eternal bliss or damnation (Dan. 12:1).

With the rise of dispensationalism and popularized by the Scofield Reference Bible, a different theological position emerged. Generally speaking, dispensationalists see the end of the world in the following sequence:

1. The return of Jesus Christ—the rapture—when God's people will be snatched from the earth.
2. The great tribulation of seven years' duration will take place on this earth.
3. Jesus returns at the end of the seven years, and sets up his rule on earth for one thousand years—the millennium.
4. At the end of this period, Satan and his army rise up in a final but futile battle— the battle of Armageddon.
5. Jesus Christ and the angels of heaven cast Satan into the lake of fire.
6. Then follow the judgments—first, that of separating the righteous and the unrighteous (Matt. 24:31ff.), and second, the judgment of the great white throne (2 Cor. 5:10).

This second judgment of the great white throne is only for Christians and has to do with rewards. A preview of this judgment appears in 1 Cor. 3:5–16, where we are told that we build upon the foundation of Jesus Christ. Our work after that will be judged. Some will have their works utterly destroyed (i.e., as one theologian says, these people will make it into heaven by the skin of their teeth). Others will have varying degrees of reward.

Because of the differing viewpoints on the first three items above (the rapture, the great tribulation, and the millennium), more detailed explanations follow.

Prophecies Concerning the Last Days

Increase of wars and rumors of war	Joel 3:9–10; Matt. 24:6–7
Extreme materialism	2 Tim. 3:1–2; Rev. 3:14–19
Lawlessness	Ps. 78:8; Prov. 30:11–14; 2 Tim. 3:2–3
Population explosion	Gen. 6:1
Increase in speed and knowledge	Dan. 12:4
Departure from the Christian faith	2 Thess. 2:3; 1 Tim. 4:1, 3–4; 2 Tim. 3:5; 4:3–4; 2 Pet. 3:3–4
Intense demonic activity	Gen. 6:1–4; 1 Tim. 4:1–3
Unification of the world's religious, political, and economic systems	Rev. 13:4–8, 16–17; 17:1–18; 18:1–24
Universal drug usage (the word *sorceries* can refer to drugs)	Rev. 9:21
Abnormal sexual activity	Rom. 1:17–32; 2 Pet. 2:10, 14; 3:3; Jude 18
Widespread violence	Gen. 6:11, 13; Rev. 9:21
Rejection of God's Word	2 Tim. 4:3–4; 2 Pet. 3:3–4, 16
Rejection of God	Ps. 2:1–3
Blasphemy	2 Tim. 3:2; 2 Pet. 3:3; Jude 18
Self-seeking and pleasure-seeking	2 Tim. 3:2, 4
People minus a conscience	1 Tim. 4:2
Religious hucksters	2 Pet. 2:3
Devil worshipers	Rev. 9:20; 13:11–14
Rise of false prophets and Antichrists	Matt. 24:5, 11; 2 Pet. 2:1–2
False claims of peace	1 Thess. 5:1–3
Great political and religious upheavals in the Holy Land	Matt. 24:32–34

The Rapture

Derived from the Latin *apio,* the term *rapture* has two basic meanings. First, it means "to seize," such as the ecstasy of spirit mystics sometimes enjoy. The second meaning is "to snatch" or "a removal from one place to another by forcible means."

In eschatology the word is used only in this second sense—as a phase of the prophetic revelation dealing with the future coming of the Lord for his church.

Paul seeks to comfort believers at Thessalonica whose loved ones have recently died, with the assurance that at the return of Jesus Christ these shall be given first consideration. When they are raised, the living saints will be "caught up" (Greek *harpagesometha*) together with them in clouds to meet the Lord in the air, never more to be separated from him or from one another (1 Thess. 4:17). This will also be the time of the bodily transformation of believers (1 Cor. 15:51–52; Phil. 3:20–21).

The verbal form of *harpazo* occurs several times in the NT. For example, the Spirit caught up Philip near Gaza and brought him to Caesarea (Acts 8:39). Paul was caught up into paradise, where he experienced ineffable things (2 Cor. 12:2–4). There can be no doubt that Paul's language in 1 Thess. 4:17 requires a removal of the saints from earth at the time of the Lord's return.

Three views are held concerning the relation of this event to the tribulation period, which the prophetic Scriptures place immediately before the return of Christ.

Pre-Tribulationists

The most generally held view puts the Rapture before the Tribulation, holding that the tribulation is marked by the pouring out of the divine wrath upon a Christ-rejecting society, which is not intended for the church and is utterly unsuited to her, however much she may profit by the experience of tribulation in the general sense.

Advocates of this view believe that God has promised to exempt the church from this period of trouble and judgment that is coming upon the world. The Rapture is God's way of fulfilling his purpose.

The language of Paul requires a removal of believers from the earth scene. Pre-tribulationists argue that there would be little point in a translation into the air to be followed by an immediate return to the earth such as the post-tribulation view demands. In the interval between the Rapture and the public appearing of Christ before the world he will reward his people.

Mid-Tribulationists

They hold that it is improper to speak of the great Tribulation as coextensive with the seventieth week of Daniel 9:24, for both there and in the Revelation the period is conceived as divided. Only the latter half is to be marked by tribulation. It will be preceded by a period of peace and safety (1 Thess. 5:3). Since the saints will be spared the ordeal of tribulation, the Rapture will occur at this midway point. In substance, this view does not differ from the preceding, for both maintain the exemption of the church from the tribulation era.

Post-Tribulationists

They maintain that the church will remain on the earth during the predicted time of trouble and wrath, and will experience tribulation but not wrath. God's wrath comes upon humanity and troubles, testing, and tribulation upon God's people. Yet God will protect his own when his wrath is manifested.

For post-tribulationists, no interval will occur between the Rapture and the coming of the Lord with the resurrected saints to judge the world and set up the kingdom.

The differences among the three viewpoints occur because nowhere in the Bible is the Rapture treated in relation to the coming of Jesus Christ.

Post-tribulationists emphasize that their view is the more simple and natural solution. In 2 Thessalonians 1:6–10, where the effect of the coming upon both believers and unbelievers is sketched, there is no suggestion that the return has two phases.

Pre-tribulationists stress the difficulty involved in the exemption of the church from judgments that are represented as poured out on the earth as a whole, although this difficulty is lessened by the fact that the tribulation saints (Rev. 6:15) survive the ordeal.

They also argue that, just as the coming of the Lord in the OT was largely undifferentiated in its prophetic portrayal, but turned out to be a double coming, separated by the present age, so the future coming of Jesus Christ, although sometimes presented as a single event, may well be effected in two stages. One of these stages involves the saints only, and the other involves the unbelieving world as well.

The Nature of the Tribulation

Unbelievably bloody wars	Matt. 24:6–7; Rev. 6:2–4; 14:20
Drunkenness	Matt. 24:38; Luke 17:27
Illicit sex	Matt. 24:38; Luke 17:27; Rev. 9:21
Gross materialism	Luke 17:28; Rev. 18:12–14
Rise of false messiahs and prophets	Matt. 24:5, 11–24
Horrible persecution of believers	Matt. 24:10; Rev. 16:6; 17:6
People hiding in the caves of the rocks in fear of God	Isa. 2:19–21; Rev. 6:15–17
The pangs and sorrows of death similar to those of women in labor, to seize people	Isa. 13:8; Jer. 30:6
Terrible worldwide famines	Rev. 6:5–6, 8
Humans to be slaughtered by predatory wild beasts	Rev. 6:8
Disastrous earthquakes	Rev. 6:12; 11:13; 16:18
Fearful heavenly signs and disturbances	Luke 21:25; Rev. 6:12–13; 8:12
Universal tidal waves and ocean disasters	Luke 21:25; Rev. 8:8–9; 16:3
The stars, moon, and sun to be darkened	Isa. 13:10; Joel 2:10, 30–31; 3:15
The moon to be turned into blood	Joel 2:31; Rev. 6:12
The heavens to be rolled together like a scroll	Isa. 34:4; Rev. 6:14
Massive hailstones composed of fire and blood to fall upon the earth	Rev. 8:7; 16:21
Huge meteorites to fall upon the earth	Rev. 8:8–11
Stars to fall upon the earth	Rev. 6:13
Salt waters and fresh waters to become totally polluted	Rev. 8:8–11; 11:6; 16:3–4
Universal disaster of land ecology	Rev. 8:7
Events to steadily go from bad to worse	Amos 5:19
A time of thick darkness and utter depression	Joel 2:2
No period in history to compare to it	Jer. 30:7; Dan. 12:1; Matt. 24:21–22
A time of famine of the word of God	Amos 8:11–12
A time of absolutely no escape from God's fierce judgment	Amos 9:2–3
Worldwide drug usage	Rev. 9:21
Universal idolatry and devil worship	Rev. 9:20; 13:11–17
Murderous demonic invasions	Rev. 9:3–20
Subterranean eruptions	Rev. 9:1–2
Scorching solar heat	Rev. 16:8–9
Terrifying periods of total darkness	Rev. 16:10
Unchecked citywide fires	Rev. 18:8–9, 18
A plague of cancerous sores	Rev. 16:2
The total destruction of the earth's religious, political, and economic systems	Rev. 17—18
A universal dictatorial rule by the Antichrist	Rev. 13
An all-out, no-holds-barred attempt to destroy Israel	Rev. 12
Survivors of this period to be more rare than gold	Isa. 13:12
Human blood to be poured out like dust and their flesh like dung	Zeph. 1:17
The slain to remain unburied and the mountains to be covered with their blood	Isa. 34:3; 66:24

The Nature of Tribulation—*continued*

The earth to be removed out of its orbit	Isa. 13:13
The earth to be turned upside down	Isa. 24:1, 19
The earth to reel to and fro like a drunkard	Isa. 24:20
The most frightful physical plague in all history	Zech. 14:12
A 200-mile river of human blood to flow	Rev. 14:20
Scavenger birds to eat the rotted flesh of entire armies	Matt. 24:28; Rev. 19:17–19

Events Occurring with the Tribulation

Formal organization of the harlot church	1 Tim. 4:1–3; 2 Tim. 3:1–5; Rev. 17
Appearance of the Antichrist and his prophet	Rev. 13
Revival of the Roman Empire	Dan. 2:41; 7:7; Rev. 13:1; 17:12
The Antichrist's seven-year covenant with Israel	Isa. 28:18; Dan. 9:27
Pouring out of the first six seals	Matt. 24:4–8; Rev. 6
Mass return of the Jews to Palestine	Isa. 43:5–6; Ezek. 34:11–13; 36:24; 37:1–14
Conversion and call of the 144,000	Matt. 24:14; Rev. 7:1–4
Abomination of desolation	Dan. 9:27; 12:11; Matt. 24:15; 2 Thess. 2:4; Rev. 11:2
Ministry of the two witnesses	Rev. 11:3–13
Gog and Magog invade Palestine	Ezek. 38—39
Martyrdom of the two witnesses	Rev. 11:7
Martyrdom of the 144,000	Rev. 14:1–5
The casting out of Satan from heaven	Rev. 12:3–15
The destruction of the false church	Rev. 17:16
The full manifestation of Antichrist	Rev. 13:16–18
Worldwide persecution of Israel	Dan. 12:1; Zech. 11:16; Matt. 24:21; Rev. 12:13
Pouring out of the last seal judgment	Rev. 8—9; 11:15–19
The messages of three special angels	Rev. 14:6–12
The pouring out of the seven vials of judgment	Rev. 16
The sudden destruction of economic and political Babylon	Rev. 18
The battle of Armageddon	Ps. 2:1–5, 9; Isa. 34:1–6; 63:3–4, 6; Joel 3:2, 9–16; Zech. 12:2; 14:2–3, 12; Rev. 14:14–20; 16:16; 19:11–21

The Great Tribulation

This is a short but intense period of distress and suffering at the end of time. The exact phrase, the "great tribulation," is found only once in the Bible (Rev. 7:14). The great Tribulation is to be distinguished from the general tribulation believers face in the world (Matt. 13:21; John 16:33; Acts 14:22). It is also to be distinguished from God's specific wrath upon the unbelieving world at the end of the age (Mark 13:24; Rom. 2:5–10; 2 Thess. 1:6).

The great Tribulation fulfills Daniel's prophecies (Dan. 7—12). It will be a time of evil from false christs and false prophets (Mark 13:22) when natural disasters will occur throughout the world.

Names for the Coming World Calamity

The Day of the Lord	Isa. 2:12; 13:6, 9; Ezek. 13:5; 30:3; Joel 1:15; 2:1, 11, 31; 3:14; Amos 5:18, 20; Obad. 15; Zeph. 1:7, 14; Zech. 14:1; Mal. 4:5; Acts 2; 20; 1 Thess. 5:2; 2 Thess. 2:2; 2 Pet. 3:10
Indignation	Isa. 26:20; 34:2
The day of God's vengeance	Isa. 34:8; 63:1–6
The time of Jacob's trouble	Jer. 30:7
The wing of abominations	Dan. 9:27
The time of trouble such as never was	Dan. 12:1
The seventieth week	Dan. 9:24–27
The time of the end	Dan. 12:9
The great day of his wrath	Rev. 6:17
The hour of his judgment	Rev. 14:7
The end of this age	Matt. 13:40, 49
The great tribulation	Matt. 24:21

Reasons for the Great Tribulation

To harvest the crop that has been sown throughout the ages by God, Satan, and humankind	Matt. 13
To prove the falseness of the devil's claim	Isa. 14:12–15
To prepare a great martyred multitude for heaven	Rev. 7:9, 14
To prepare a great living multitude for the Millennium	Matt. 25:32–34
To punish the Gentiles	Rom. 1:18; 2 Thess. 2:11–12; Rev. 19:15
To purge Israel	Ezek. 20:23, 38; Zech. 13:8–9; Mal. 3:3
To prepare the earth itself for the Millennium	Rev. 16:20

The Millennium

This is the thousand-year period mentioned in connection with the description of Christ's coming to reign with his saints over the earth (Rev. 19:11–16; 20:1–9). Several OT passages refer to the Millennium (Isa. 11:4; Jer. 3:17; Zech. 14:9).

These and many other OT passages are often taken to refer only to the thousand-year period itself. However, it is difficult in these passages to see a clear dividing line between the earthly period of the Millennium and the eternal state of new heavens and earth. Therefore, it is best to let teaching about the Millennium be drawn specifically from the words in Revelation 20.

Dispensationalists teach that during that thousand-year period, Satan will be bound in the bottomless pit so he will not deceive the nations until his short period of release (Rev. 20:3, 7–8). The faithful martyrs who have died for the cause of Christ will be resurrected before the Millennium. They will rule with Christ on earth and will be priests of God and Christ (Rev. 5:10; 20:4). The unbelieving dead will wait for the second resurrection (Rev. 20:5). After the thousand years, Satan will be released to resume his work of deceit (Rev. 20:7–8).

The most important aspect of the Millennium is the reign of Christ. Peter taught that

Christ now rules from the right hand of God (Acts 2:33–36). That rule will last until his enemies are made his footstool (Ps. 110:1). Paul also understood Christ to be presently reigning in a period designed to bring all of God's enemies underfoot (1 Cor. 15:25–27). The impact of Christ's present rule over the earth from God's right hand must not be seen as unrelated to his future reign during the Millennium.

Again, three viewpoints on the thousand-year period:

Pre-Millennialism

The view held by dispensationalists. As discussed above, this interpretation teaches that this age will end in judgment at the return to Jesus Christ. However, the ultimate state will not occur then. Instead, Jesus Christ will restore the kingdom of Israel and reign for at least one thousand years.

The Millennium will be the last of the ordered ages of time. Eternity will dawn when the Millennium is complete (Isa. 65:17; 66:22; 2 Pet. 3:13; Rev. 21:1). The Millennium will be characterized by the binding of Satan and the severe limitation of sin. The perfect sinless state will take place after the Millenium.

Amillennialism or Nonmillennialism

Amillennialists hold that the Millennium refers to Christ's spiritual rule today from heaven. They point out that if we take the six references to the word *millennium* in Revelation 20 literally (see vv. 2–7), no other portion of the NT speaks about a literal reign upon earth of one thousand years. The rest of Revelation 20 is filled with symbols that cannot be taken literally (e.g., the bottomless pit and the great chain, v.1). Further, a literal interpretation would be contrary to the usual use of the word *thousand* in the NT. (See 2 Pet. 3:8.)

The reign of Christ on earth, amillennialists say, is taking place now and will continue until the return of Jesus Christ.

By taking a spiritualized interpretation of certain passages such as Revelation 20, amillenialists claim that Zion does not refer to Israel but to the Christian church—the new Zion of God. They make no distinction between the nation of Israel and the church and believe that the church is the true Israel of God.

Post-Millennialism

Held by relatively few, this position views Christ's spiritual rule as working through preaching and teaching to bring a gradual world improvement that leads up to Christ's return. This theory has been largely disproved by the progress of history.

Millenial Prophecies

The temple to be rebuilt	Isa. 2:2; Ezek. 40—48; Joel 3:18; Hag. 2:7–9; Zech. 6:12–13
Israel to be regathered	Isa. 43:5–6; Jer. 24:6; 29:14; 31:8–10; Ezek. 11:17; 36:24–25, 28; Amos 9:14–15; Zech. 8:6–8; Matt. 24:31
Israel to recognize Messiah	Isa. 8:17; 25:9; 26:8; Zech. 12:10–12; Rev. 1:7
Israel to be cleansed	Jer. 33:8; Zech. 13:1
Israel to be regenerated	Jer. 31:31–34; 32:39; Ezek. 11:19–20; 36:26
Israel to once again be related to God by marriage	Isa. 54; 62:2–5; Hos. 2:14–23
Israel to be exalted above the Gentiles	Isa. 14:1–2; 49:22–23; 60:14–17; 61:6–7

Israel to become God's witnesses	Isa. 44:8; 61:6; 66:21; Ezek. 3:17; Mic. 5:7; Zeph. 3:20; Zech. 8:3
Jesus to rule from Jerusalem with a rod of iron	Ps. 2:6–8, 11; Isa. 2:3; 11:4
David to aid in this rule as viceregent	Isa. 55:3–4; Jer. 30:9; Ezek. 34:23; 37:24; Hos. 3:5
All sickness to be removed	Isa. 33:24; Jer. 30:17; Ezek. 34:16
The original curse on creation to be removed (see Gen. 3:17–19)	Isa. 11:6–9; 35:9; 65:25; Joel 3:18; Amos 9:13–15
The wolf, lamb, calf, and lion to lie down together in peace	Isa. 11:6–7; 65:25
A little child to safely play with once poisonous serpents and spiders	Isa. 11:8
Physical death to be swallowed up in victory	Isa. 25:8
All tears to be dried	Isa. 25:8; 30:19
The deaf to hear, the blind to see, and the lame to walk	Isa. 29:18; 35:5–6; 61:1–2; Jer. 31:8
Knowledge about God to be increased	Isa. 41:19–20; 54:13; Hab. 2:14
No social, political, or religious oppression	Isa. 14:3–6; 49:8–9; Zech. 9:11–12
Full ministry of the Holy Spirit	Isa. 32:15; 59:21; Ezek. 36:27; 37:14; Joel 2:28–29
Jesus to be the Good Shepherd	Isa. 40:11; 49:10; 58:11; Ezek. 34:11–16
A time of universal singing	Isa. 35:6; 52:9; 54:1; 55:12; Jer. 33:11
A time of universal praying	Isa. 56:7; 65:24; Zech. 8:22
A unified language	Zeph. 3:9
The wilderness and deserts to bloom	Isa. 35:1–2
All nations to see God's glory	Isa. 60:1–3; Ezek. 39:21; Mic. 4:1–5; Hab. 2:14
Longevity of man to be restored	Isa. 65:20
Universal peace	Isa. 2:4; 32:18
Universal holiness	Zech. 14:20–21
Solar and lunar light to increase	Isa. 4:5; 30:26; 60:19–20; Zech. 2:5
Palestine to become greatly enlarged and changed	Isa. 26:15; Obad. 17—21
A river to flow east-west from the Mount of Olives into both the Mediterranean and Dead Seas	Ezek. 47:8–9, 12; Joel 3:18; Zech. 14:4, 8, 10
Jerusalem to become known as *Jehovah Tsidkenu* ("the Lord our righteousness") and *Jehovah Shammah* ("the Lord is there")	Jer. 33:16; Ezek. 48:35
Jerusalem to become the worship center of the world	Isa. 2:2–3; Mic. 4:1
Jerusalem's streets to be filled with happy boys and girls playing	Zech. 8:5
The city to occupy an elevated site	Zech. 14:10
The earthly city to be six miles in circumference	Ezek. 48:35
The heavenly, suspended city to be 1,500 by 1,500 by 1,500 miles	Rev. 21:10, 16

In conclusion, the time of the Second Coming is unknown along with all of the other issues of eschatology. Jesus stated that only the Father knew the time.

Eschatology and Prophecy

One-fourth of the Bible was prophetic when written, say conservative scholars. And yet, they cry, most of the thinking, knowledge, and understanding reduces prophecy to events immediately clustering around the second coming of Jesus Christ.

Properly understood, eschatology is a far broader subject.

Lewis Sperry Chafer wrote in his *Systematic Theology:*

> This, the last major division of systematic theology, is concerned with things to come and should not be limited to things which are future at some particular time in human history but should contemplate all that was future in character at the time its revelation was given.

General Prophecies

Prophecy	Stated	Fulfilled
The eating of the forbidden fruit to bring physical and spiritual death	Gen. 2:17	Gen. 3:7—5:5
The Flood to occur in 120 years	Gen. 6:3	Gen. 7:10
The Flood never to be repeated	Gen. 9:15	Testimony of history
Canaan to be a servant to his brothers	Gen. 9:25	Josh. 9:21–23, 27; Judg. 1:28
The people of Shem to be especially blessed by God	Gen. 9:26	John 4:22; Rom. 3:1–2; 9:4–5
The people of Japheth to share in Shem's blessing	Gen. 9:27	Rom. 9:30; 11:11–12, 25
The firstborn of all unprotected homes in Egypt to die in one night	Exod. 12:12–13	Exod. 12:29–30
The Red Sea to part	Exod. 14:13–18	Exod. 14:26–31
The Jordan River to part	Josh. 3:13	Josh. 3:14–17
Jericho to fall on the seventh day	Josh. 6:1–5	Josh. 6:20

Prophecies Concerning Births

Person	Stated	Fulfilled
Isaac	Gen. 15:4; 17:19, 21; 18:10, 14	Gen. 21:1–3
Jacob and Esau	Gen. 25:19–23	Gen. 25:24–26

Samson	Judg. 13:2–5	Judg. 13:24
Samuel	1 Sam. 1:17–18	1 Sam. 1:20
Shunammite woman's son	2 Kings 4:16	2 Kings 4:17
John the Baptist	Luke 1:13–17	Luke 1:57–64
Jesus	Luke 1:26–33	Luke 2:4–7

Prophecies Concerning Cities

City	Prophecy	Stated	Fulfilled
Tyre	The coastal city to be captured by Nebuchadnezzar	Ezek. 26:7	Testimony of history
	The island city to later be made flat	Ezek. 26:4, 14; 28:1–10	Testimony of history
	Both cities to become a place for the spreading of nets	Ezek. 26:14	Testimony of history
	Both to be devoured by fire and the debris thrown into the sea	Zech. 9:3–4	Testimony of history
	Neither to be rebuilt	Ezek. 26:24	Testimony of history
Jericho	To fall on the seventh day at the hands of Joshua	Josh. 6:1–5, 20	Josh. 6:20
Nineveh	The city to be totally destroyed	Nah. 1:3, 6	Testimony of history
	This destruction to be effected (in part) by the overflowing of the Tigris River	Nah. 1:8	Testimony of history
	The attackers of the city to wear red	Nah. 2:3	Testimony of history
Jerusalem	To become God's chosen place	Deut. 12:5–6, 11; 26:2; Josh. 9:27; 10:1; 1 Kings 8:29; 11:36; 15:4; 2 Kings 21:4, 7; 2 Chron. 7:12; Ps. 78:68	Testimony of history
	To be spared from invasion by Israel and Syria	Isa. 7:1–7	Testimony of history
	To be spared from invasion by the Assyrians	Isa. 37:33–35	Isa. 37:36–37
	To be destroyed by the Babylonians	Isa. 3:8; Jer. 11:9; 26:18; Mic. 3:12	2 Chron. 36:15–21
	The temple of Solomon to suffer destruction	1 Kings 9:7–9; Ps. 79:1; Jer. 7:11–14; 26:18; Ezek. 7:21–22; 24:21; Mic. 3:12	Lam. 7; 2 Chron. 36:19
	The temple vessels to be carried to Babylon and later returned to Jerusalem	Jer. 28:3	2 Kings 25:14–15; 2 Chron. 36:18; Ezra 1:7–11
	To be rebuilt by the Jews after spending 70 years in captivity	Isa. 44:28; Jer. 25:11–12; 29:10	Ezra 1:1–4
	To have its streets and walls rebuilt during a period of trouble	Dan. 9:25	Ezra 4—5; Neh. 2:6ff.
	The walls to be rebuilt 483 years prior to the crucifixion of Jesus	Dan. 9:26	Testimony of history
	To be destroyed by the Romans	Luke 19:41–44	Testimony of history

Prophecies Concerning Cities—*continued*

City	Prophecy	Stated	Fulfilled
	The temple of Herod also to be burned at this time	Matt. 24:1–2	Testimony of history
	To be trodden down by Gentiles until the Second Coming	Luke 21:24	Testimony of history
	To be occupied by the Antichrist during the Tribulation	Zech. 12:2; 14:2	Yet to be fulfilled
	To become the worship center of the world during the Millennium	Isa. 2:2–3; Mic. 4:1	Yet to be fulfilled

Old Testament Prophecies Concerning Individuals

Prophecy	Stated	Fulfilled
Joshua and Caleb to enter Canaan after a period of 40 years	Num. 14:24, 30	Josh. 3:7, 17; 14:6–12
Sisera to be defeated by a woman	Judg. 4:9	Judg. 4:21–22
Hophni and Phinehas to die on the same day	1 Sam. 2:34	1 Sam. 4:11
The priesthood to be removed from the line of Eli	1 Sam. 2:27–36; 3:11–14	1 Kings 2:26–27
Saul to become Israel's first king and save the country from the Philistines	1 Sam. 9:15–16	1 Sam. 11—14
Saul's kingdom not to continue	1 Sam. 13:14; 15:28; 24:20	2 Sam. 3:1; 5:1–3
Saul to die in battle on a certain day	1 Sam. 28:19	1 Sam. 31:1–6
Solomon, not David, to build the temple	1 Chron. 17:1–12	1 Kings 7:51
Jeroboam's dynasty to be destroyed	1 Kings 14:10–11	1 Kings 15:27–29
Ahab to win over the Syrians	1 Kings 20:28	1 Kings 20:29–30
Ahab to die in battle for killing Naboth	1 Kings 21:19; 22:17	1 Kings 22:37
The dogs would lick Ahab's blood from his chariot	1 Kings 21:19	1 Kings 22:38
Jezebel to be eaten by wild dogs	1 Kings 21:23; 2 Kings 9:10	2 Kings 9:30–35
Elisha to receive a double portion of Elijah's spirit	2 Kings 2:9–10	Testimony of history: he performed twice the miracles of Elijah
Naaman to recover from his leprosy	2 Kings 5:3, 8, 10	2 Kings 5:14
The starving citizens of Samaria to enjoy an abundance of food in 24 hours	2 Kings 7:1	2 Kings 7:16–17
An arrogant aide of the king to see this miracle at Samaria, but not eat of the food	2 Kings 7:2, 19	2 Kings 7:17, 20
A Syrian king (Ben-Hadad) not to recover from his sickness	2 Kings 8:10	2 Kings 8:15
Jehu to have four generations on the throne of Israel	2 Kings 10:30	2 Kings 15:12
Jehu's dynasty to then be destroyed	Hos. 1:4	2 Kings 15:8–12
Joash to defeat the Syrians three times	2 Kings 13:18–19	2 Kings 13:25
Jehoram to suffer with an intestinal disease because of his sin	2 Chron. 21:15	2 Chron. 21:18–19

Amaziah to die for his idolatry	2 Chron. 25:16	2 Chron. 25:20, 22, 27
Sennacherib not to invade Jerusalem	Isa. 37:33–35	Isa. 37:36–37
Sennacherib to fall by the sword in his own land	Isa. 37:7	Isa. 37:37–38
Hezekiah to be healed of a fatal disease	Isa. 38:5	Isa. 38:9
Jehoahaz never to return to Judah, but to die in his Egyptian captivity	Jer. 22:10–12	2 Kings 23:33–34
Josiah to burn the decayed bones of Jeroboam's pagan priests on the false altar Jeroboam had constructed	2 Kings 13:1–3	1 Kings 23:4–16
Jehoiachin to be captured by Nebuchadnezzar	Jer. 22:25	2 Kings 24:15
A false prophet named Hananiah to die within a year	Jer. 28:15–16	Jer. 28:17
Zedekiah to be captured by Nebuchadnezzar	Jer. 21:7	Jer. 52:8–9
Nebuchadnezzar to win over the Egyptians at Carchemish	Jer. 46	Testimony of history
Nebuchadnezzar to invade Egypt	Jer. 43:9–13; 46:26; Ezek. 29:19–20	Testimony of history
Nebuchadnezzar to be reduced to an animal for his pride	Dan. 4:19–27	Dan. 4:28–37
Belshazzar to have his kingdom taken from him	Dan. 5:5, 25–28	Dan. 5:30
Cyrus to allow the Jews to go back and rebuild Jerusalem	Isa. 44:28	Ezra 1:1–2
Alexander the Great to conquer Greece and establish a world empire	Dan. 2:32–39; 7:6; 8:5–8, 21; 11:3	Testimony of history
Alexander to defeat the Persians	Dan. 8:5–8	Testimony of history
Alexander to die suddenly and his kingdom to be divided into four parts	Dan. 8:8, 22; 11:4	Testimony of history
Antiochus I Epiphanes to persecute the Jews and profane their temple	Dan. 8:11–25	Testimony of history

New Testament Prophecies Concerning Individuals

Prophecy	Stated	Fulfilled
Zacharias to be mute until the birth of his son	Luke 1:20	Luke 1:57–64
John the Baptist to be Jesus' forerunner	Isa. 40:3–5; Mal. 3:1; Luke 1:76–77	Matt. 3:1–11; Luke 3:2–6
Simeon to live until he had seen the Messiah	Luke 2:25–26	Luke 2:28–32
Peter to deny Jesus	John 13:38	John 18:24–27
Peter to suffer martyrdom for Jesus	John 21:18–19; 2 Pet. 1:12–14	Testimony of history
Judas to give himself over to Satan	John 6:70	Luke 22:3; John 13:27
Judas to betray Jesus	John 6:71; 13:21	Matt. 26:47–50; Luke 22:47–48; John 18:2–5
Paul to suffer much for Jesus	Acts 9:16	2 Cor. 11:23–28; 12:7–10; Gal. 6:17; Phil. 1:29–30
Paul to be a minister to the Gentiles	Acts 9:15	Acts 13:46; 18:6; 22:21; 26:17;

New Testament Prophecies Concerning Individuals—*continued*

Prophecy	Stated	Fulfilled
		28:28; Rom. 11:13; Eph. 3:1; 1 Tim. 2:7; 2 Tim. 1:11
Paul to preach before kings	Acts 9:15	Acts 24—26
Paul to go to Rome	Acts 23:11	Acts 28:16

Prophecies Concerning Israel

Prophecy	Stated	Fulfilled
The people of Shem to be especially blessed of God	Gen. 9:26	Matt. 1:1ff.; John 4:22
A great nation to come from Abraham	Gen. 12:2	Num. 23:10
This nation to exist forever	Jer. 31:35–37	Testimony of history
Israel's kings to come from the tribe of Judah	Gen. 49:10	1 Sam. 16:1–2; 1 Chron. 28:4; Luke 1:26–27
Canaan to be given to Israel forever	Gen. 13:15	Josh. 21:43–45 (partial); Isa. 60:21; Ezek. 37:25 (future)
Israel to sojourn in another land for 400 years, there to serve and be afflicted	Gen. 15:13	Exod. 12:40
This oppressive nation (Egypt) to be judged by God	Gen. 15:14	Exod. 7:14—12:29
Israel to leave Egypt with great substance	Gen. 15:14	Exod. 12:35–36
Israel to return to Canaan from Egypt in the fourth generation	Gen. 15:16	Josh. 3:16–17
Israel to conquer Canaan gradually	Exod. 23:29–30	Judg. 1:19–36
Those (over 20) who sinned at Kadesh Barnea would not see the Promised Land, but would wander 40 years in the wilderness	Num. 14:32–34	Num. 26:63–65
Israel to set a king over themselves	Deut. 17:14–20	1 Sam. 10:24
Israel to suffer a tragic civil war after the death of Solomon	1 Kings 11:11, 31	1 Kings 12:16–17, 19–20
The northern kingdom to be carried away into Assyrian captivity	1 Kings 14:15–16; Hos. 1:5; 10:1, 6	2 Kings 17:6–7, 22–23
This would happen 65 years after the Isaiah and Ahaz meeting	Isa. 7:8	2 Kings 17:24
The southern kingdom to be carried away into Babylonian captivity	Jer. 13:19; 20:4–5; 21:10; Mic. 4:10	2 Kings 24—25
The temple to be destroyed	1 Kings 9:7; 2 Chron. 7:20–21; Jer. 7:14	2 Kings 25:9
The length of the Babylonian captivity would be 70 years	Jer. 25:11; 29:10	Dan. 9:2
Israel to then return to the land	Jer. 29:10	Ezra 1
The temple vessels once carried into Babylon to be brought back to the land	2 Kings 25:14–15; Jer. 28:3; Dan. 5:1–4	Ezra 1:7–11
Israel eventually to be scattered among the nations of the world	Lev. 26:33; Deut. 4:27–28; 28:25–68; Hos. 9:17	Testimony of history

Israel to "abide many days" without a king, an heir apparent, the Levitical offerings, the temple, or the Levitical priesthood	Hos. 3:4	Testimony of history
Israel also to be free from idolatry during this terrible time	Hos. 3:4	Testimony of history
Israel to become a byword among the nations	Deut. 28:37	Testimony of history
Israel to loan to many nations, but borrow from none	Deut. 28:12	Testimony of history
Israel to be hounded and persecuted	Deut. 28:65–67	Testimony of history
Israel nevertheless to retain her identity	Lev. 26:44; Jer. 46:28	Testimony of history
Israel to remain alone and aloof among the nations	Num. 23:9	Testimony of history
Israel to reject her Messiah	Isa. 53:1–9	Luke 23:13–25
Israel to return to Palestine in the latter days prior to the second coming of Jesus	Deut. 30:3; Ezek. 36:24; 37:1–14	Testimony of history

Prophecies Concerning Nations

Nation	Prophecy	Stated	Fulfilled
Egypt	To experience seven years of plenty and seven years of famine	Gen. 41:1–7, 17–24; 45:6, 11	Gen. 41:47–48, 53–57; 47:13, 20
	To host Israel for 400 years and afflict them	Gen. 15:13	Exod. 12:40; Acts 7:6
	To be judged for this by the 10 plagues	Gen. 15:14; Exod. 3:20; 6:1; 7:5	Exod. 7:14—12:29
	To pursue Israel but fail and perish	Exod. 14:3–4	Exod. 14:5–9, 23–28, 30–31
	To defeat Israel at Megiddo	Jer. 2:16–17, 19, 36–37	2 Kings 23:29–35
	To stumble and fall before Babylon at Carchemish	Jer. 46:5–6, 10–12	Testimony of history
	To be invaded by Nebuchadnezzar	Jer. 43:7–13; 46:13–26	Testimony of history
	To decline from its exalted position and become a base nation	Ezek. 29:1–2, 15	Testimony of history
	To suffer at the hand of the Antichrist during the Tribulation	Dan. 11:40–43; Joel 3:19	Yet to be fulfilled
	To be restored and blessed by God along with Assyria and Israel during the Millennium	Isa. 19:21–25	Yet to be fulfilled
Babylon	To expand under Nebuchadnezzar	Hab. 1:5–10	Testimony of history
	To defeat the Egyptians at Carchemish	Jer. 46	Testimony of history
	To defeat the Assyrians	Nah. 1—3	Testimony of history
	To be defeated by the Medes and Persians	Isa. 13:17; Jer. 51:11	Dan. 5
Three world powers	To follow Babylon	Dan. 2; 7	Testimony of history
Persia	To consist of an alliance between two peoples	Dan. 8:1–4, 20	Testimony of history
	To defeat the Babylonians	Dan. 2:39; 7:5	Dan. 5
	To be defeated by the Greeks	Dan. 8:5–8, 21–22	Testimony of history

Prophecies Concerning Nations—*continued*

Nation	Prophecy	Stated	Fulfilled
Greece	To be invaded by Persia	Dan. 11:2	Testimony of history
	Alexander the Great to conquer Greece and establish a world empire	Dan. 2:32–39; 7:6; 8:5–8, 21; 11:3	Testimony of history
	To defeat the Persians	Dan. 8:5–8	Testimony of history
	To be divided into four parts after Alexander's death	Dan. 8:8, 22; 11:4	Testimony of history
Rome	To defeat the Greeks	Dan. 2:40; 7:7; 11:18–19	Testimony of history
	To destroy Jerusalem	Matt. 23:37–39	Testimony of history
	To be revived during the Tribulation	Dan. 2:41; 7:7–8; Rev. 13:1; 17:12	Yet to be fulfilled
	To be destroyed by Jesus at the Second Coming	Dan. 2:34–35, 44; 7:9, 14, 27	Yet to be fulfilled
Unknown nation to the far north	To invade Israel during the Tribulation	Ezek. 28:7–11, 16	Yet to be fulfilled
	To be joined by various allies	Ezek. 38:4–7	Yet to be fulfilled
	To come down "to take plunder and to take booty"	Ezek. 38:12	Yet to be fulfilled
	To suffer a disastrous defeat at the hand of God, losing some 83 percent of its troops	Ezek. 39:2	Yet to be fulfilled

Theological Schools of Thought

The church—the people of God—has never been in full agreement as to doctrine. Within months of its beginning (see Acts 6), the first Christians were disputing over the distribution of food. Apparently the Greek-speaking widows felt they were not getting their rightful share. Seven deacons, chosen from the congregation for their faithfulness and level of spirituality, took on the job of food distribution and settled the first squabble.

In Acts 15, the leaders of the infant church met in Jerusalem to discuss serious theological differences about what demands to make on Gentile Christians. After a lengthy debate, they came to a resolution, and sent Paul and Barnabas and others through Asia Minor to tell the whole church (v. 22).

In Paul's letters (with the exception of Philippians), the apostle handles complex theological issues separating sincere Christians.

In the 2,000 years since the founding of God's church on the day of Pentecost, people have continued to disagree. Consequently, in this section, we present an overview of the more prominent schools of theological thought and discussion that have been and still are issues. Also included is a brief discussion of such classic issues as Arianism, Pelagianism, Calvinism, and Arminianism—major shifts of thought that still influence Christians today.

Arianism. The Arian controversy arose in the diocese of Alexandria, Egypt (ca. A.D. 320) and concerned primarily the person of Jesus Christ.

The dispute took its name from Arius, a presbyter in Alexandria, who taught that there is a difference between God the Father and Jesus Christ the Son.

Arius represented Christ as a created being, but the first and greatest, God's intermediary agent through whom all other things were created. Yet, because of the power and honor delegated to him, he was to be looked upon as God and was worthy of being worshiped.

Most Arians held that the Holy Spirit was the first and greatest of the creatures called into existence by the Son. This meant a God who had a beginning and who might therefore have an end.

This controversy continued longer and was more serious than any other that agitated the early church. Arianism had several repercussions. First, in denying the true deity of Jesus Christ while insisting on worshiping him, Arians opened the door to polytheism. Second and more significant for the church, they also attempted to destroy the basis for a belief in the Trinity.

Third, Arianism caused a number of disputes over the teachings of the church and set a precedent for civil authorities to interfere in church affairs.

Arminianism. A school of thinking founded by Jacob (or James) Hermann,

(Latin Arminius), (1560–1609), a Dutch theologian at the University of Leiden.

About 1588 Arminius started to reject the doctrine of predestination. In the plague of 1602, two of the Leiden theological professors died. The following year Arminius was appointed in the place of one of them.

His Calvinist orthodoxy was attacked but he defended himself and denied the doctrine of predestination while still insisting on the need of grace for salvation. After his death in 1609, his sympathizers carried matters considerably further than Arminius had done in his writings.

They produced the Remonstrance to the States-General, asking for a revision of the catechism and the Belgic Confession. In summary, they said:

1. God elects or reproves on the basis of foreseen faith or unbelief.
2. Jesus Christ died for all although only believers are saved.
3. The human race is so depraved that divine grace is necessary for faith or to accomplish any good deed. None can be saved without the help of God's grace.
4. All good works must be ascribed to grace, but this grace is not irresistible (Acts 7:51).
5. It is possible for believers to fall away from faith.

The Remonstrants were condemned at the Synod of Dort (1618–1619) and expelled by the Calvinists. The Remonstrant Brotherhood was formed in 1619 and still exists as a denomination.

In England, Arminianism was adopted by Anglican Archbishop Laud (1573–1645), influenced Puritan John Milton (1608–1674), and attracted John Wesley (1703–1791), so that Arminianism moved into all streams of English theology. Later, it spread in the American colonies. (See *Calvinism*.)

Calvinism. The theological doctrine of John Calvin (1509–1564), a Reformer in Geneva who was the son of a wealthy and influential notary.

Under his father's influence, Calvin studied law (1528–1531) at Orleans and Bourges. He also learned Greek in the process. Calvin turned from a legal career to pursue his deepening interest in Greek, Latin, and Hebrew. Nothing is known of his religious understanding until he was 25. In his writings he speaks of a sudden conversion.

Calvin's conversion involved an unreserved commitment to the study of the Bible as the source of authority for the church and the Christian life. He rejected the old order of the church under the papacy. He conceived of a new order—a reform that would follow a pattern based on Scripture. The rich resources of learning, his own brilliance, and his scholarly habits were priceless assets in forming and communicating his theological understanding.

The acronym TULIP has sometimes been used as a simple frame to incorporate the theology of Calvin with its emphasis upon the sovereignty of God:

T = Total depravity. All have inherited Adam's sin.
U = Unconditional election. Apart from human merit or divine foreknowledge, election is based on the sovereign will of God.
L = Limited atonement. The work on the cross is limited to those elected to salvation.
I = Irresistible grace. The elect will be saved apart from their own desire. No one desires salvation apart from the Holy Spirit at work in them.
P = Perseverance of the saints. The saved will continue and never be finally lost.

Charismatic. A term that has come to refer to those who believe in, seek, and use the charismatic gifts. They sometimes refer to their movement as the charismatic renewal—once again seeing the re-newing of spiritual gifts.

The Pentecostal movement gave birth to the charismatic renewal. Many charismatics today have no vital connection to the Pentecostal movement, but their movement has its historical roots in the holiness churches. Pentecostals separated from Methodism in the United States near the end of the nineteenth century.

The Assemblies of God—the largest of the Pentecostal churches—officially began in 1914, and since then many other Pentecostal churches and denominations have sprung up including the Church of God in Cleveland, Tennessee and the Foursquare Church.

In the mid-1950s a reemphasizing on these charismatic gifts emerged within the Pentecostal churches, partly in reaction against stringent legalism. The renewing movement had no marked effect on the more traditional historic denominations until the early 1960s, when it began to penetrate the mainline churches. Around 1967, it was felt in the Roman Catholic Church.

Sometimes called neo-Pentecostalism, the charismatic renewal has spread rapidly and now forms a strong current in Christianity.

It manifests itself principally in praying for the baptism in/of the Holy Spirit; the exercise of the gifts of the Spirit—such as prophecy, praying for healing, tongues (Greek *glossolalia*), teaching; experiential faith—an emphasis upon "feeling the faith" as well as believing it; and an ecumencity with other charismatics regardless of their denominational affiliation. (See *Pentecostalism.*)

Covenant theology. A term referring to the theology of the Reformed churches. The place which it gives to the covenants has its prototype in patristic theology as systematized by Augustine of Hippo.

Those who hold this viewpoint see the whole of Scripture as being covered by two covenants: (1) the covenant of works and (2) the covenant of grace.

In these covenants they identify four factors: the parties, the promise, the proviso (condition), and the penalty (for failure).

In the covenant of works, the parties were God and Adam, who represented the whole of humanity. The promise was life based on the provision of perfect obedience by Adam. The penalty for disobedience was death.

To save the human race from the penalty of Adam's disobedience, a second covenant came into operation which had been planned before the creation of the world—the covenant of grace.

This covenant is described as new, but it is the covenant under which believers lived in OT times before the law (see Rom. 4 and Gal. 3).

Salvation was shown to be of grace and not of merit, and the OT sacrifices prefigured the atoning death of Christ. Although the same covenant, it is called a better covenant because it is administered by Jesus Christ who is greater than Moses (Heb. 3:5–6).

There are two ways of examining the covenant of grace, both incorporating the fourfold requirements. First, from God's perspective. This is sometimes called the *covenant of redemption:* parties—God and Jesus Christ; promise—salvation for believers; proviso—Christ's perfect obedience, including suffering the penalty for human disobedience; and penalty—Jesus suffered death, the innocent for the guilty.

The second perspective is from the human side: parties—God and believers; promise—eternal life; proviso—faith in Jesus Christ as the only requirement; and penalty—Jesus paid the penalty in place of believers.

Dispensationalism, a later development in covenant theology, used its predecessor as the foundation of their theological stance. (See *Dispensationalism.*)

Dispensationalism. A theological position originating in the nineteenth century, which makes special reference to those periods of time under which the human race is answerable to God for their obedience—

or disobedience—according to the revelation from God they received.

The word "dispensation" occurs twice in the NKJV; "The dispensation of the fullness of the times" (Eph. 1:10) and "the dispensation of the grace of God" (3:2). The KJV uses the term four times (1 Cor. 9:17; Eph. 1:10; 3:2; Col. 1:25).

Dispensationalism considers its method a way of "rightly dividing the word of truth." Its theologians divide history into several dispensations, usually seven, all of which have been pointing toward the second coming of Christ, when salvation will be made complete.

The commonly identified dispensations are *innocence*, from Creation to the fall; *conscience*, the covenant with Adam, ending with the flood (see Gen. 9); *human government*, from Noah to Abraham; *promise*, from Abraham's call (Gen. 12:1–3) to Moses; *law*, from the giving of the law to Moses until the death of Jesus Christ; *grace*, from the death and resurrection of Christ to the second coming; and *kingdom*, the establishment of God's rule on earth and the thousand-year reign of Christ over the nations.

Docetism.   A theological term derived from the Greek verb *dokeo*, meaning "to seem." Docetism is the doctrine that Christ did not actually become flesh but only seemed to be a man. It was one of the first theological errors to appear in the history of the church.

As used today, the term applies to theologies that, by implication, undermine the full personhood of Jesus Christ. For example, those who believe that Jesus could not have sinned when tempted by Satan (Matt. 4:1ff.) because he was the Son of God, deny his human choices.

Ecumenism.   A word from the Greek that refers to attempts to reunite separated churches. In medieval times, there were attempts (e.g., Councils of Lyons, 1274, and Florence, 1438–1439) to bring together the Eastern and Western churches. In the early stages of the Protestant Reformation several attempts were made to unite the divided body.

Since then, sporadic attempts have been made to link Anglicans and Roman Catholics such as the negotiations between Archbishop Wake of Canterbury and French theologians in the early eighteenth century. The papal visit to Canterbury in 1982 sparked and renewed these ecumenical concerns.

Ecumenism, however, has been largely a phenomenon of the twentieth century and, until recently, flourished mostly within Protestantism. It is more of a spiritual mood or religious commitment than a precise theological position.

Ecumenists now say that many of the traditional reasons for division between Christians are no longer valid, being the products of historical circumstances that no longer exist. New needs and an appreciation of the deep doctrinal roots, shared by all Christians, have led to a sense of God's leading the churches not only toward closer institutional cooperation but the visible unity that expresses God's life and purpose. Oneness in Christ is the foundation on which all rests.

Concrete results of ecumenism are the establishment of the World Council of Churches in 1948; the closer move toward unity between Catholics and Protestants since Vatican II (1963); and the widespread union and reunion of churches, especially in the United States in the past thirty years, as in the merging of Methodists, Lutherans, Presbyterians, and United Church of Christ.

Evangelicalism.   That expression of the Christian faith which emphasizes the "good news" or the "glad tidings" that God has provided redemption for the human race and the need to spread the word. The term is derived from Greek *euangelion*, which means "evangel, gospel, good news."

Evangelicals affirm that salvation from sin is obtained through the grace of God, that it is not earned by good behavior or charitable works or given because of individual merit.

The term came into use during the Reformation to identify those Protestants who held to belief in salvation by grace through faith and to the final authority of Scripture. In this present century, evangelicalism refers to a "born-again Christianity."

Generally speaking, the meaning of the word has narrowed to mean those who stress at least four things: personal experience of a conversion to Jesus Christ, living a moral life, the Bible as God's infallible rule and guide for life, and a zeal for evangelism.

Evangelicalism in the late twentieth century expresses itself in various sub-communities:

Fundamentalist-evangelicals are characteristically militant and separatist, and view themselves as born-again Christians who hold unswervingly to the doctrine of biblical inerrancy and are loyal to the doctrinal propositions of the Bible

Old evangelicals are exponents of the life of personal piety and stress the conversion experience and promote either mass evangelism or individual witness, strict standards of personal morality and disciplined Bible study.

New evangelicals share the convictions of other evangelicals but also accent the rational defense of the faith and seek to relate them more aggressively to social issues.

Justice-and-peace evangelicals, or sometimes *young evangelicals,* are a vocal minority within conservative churches who call for a more radical stance against issues such as oppression, war, abortion, and acceptance of homosexuality.

Charismatic evangelicals stress the baptism of the Holy Spirit with an emphasis upon tongues (glossolalia) and a fervent life of prayer, praise and personal testimony.

Existentialism. This term represents a type of thinking rather than a unified school of thought. It emphasizes the place of personal commitment in an act of faith.

Existential faith believes with inward passion. It concerns itself with the relation between the self and the object of belief and choosing from within the center of moral freedom.

In the nineteenth century Soren Kierkegaard formulated the theology of existentialism. He was greatly disturbed by the dead orthodoxy in the church of Denmark. He found that Christians were substituting symbols of the faith for vital trust in Jesus Christ. They put their trust in externals such as baptism, confirmation, and doctrines. They recited the Apostles' Creed but took no account of the relation between what they recited and the state of their own lives.

Kierkegaard illustrated the peril of faith by Abraham's offering of Isaac. Cheap faith reads the account, sighs, and then turns back to daily affairs. Existential faith is troubled because it knows it must be personally responsible for what it believes.

The existentialist asks such questions as: *How can a holy God command a human sacrifice? How can a sinner love God so perfectly that his affection for his own son is transcended? How can the Christian's attitude of egocentric possessing survive at the expense of mutual, reciprocal, communal activity of being?*

Existential faith offers a corrective against a shallow and utopian optimism based on the idolatry of science or a belief in inevitable technological progress.

Feminist theology. A theological emphasis developed primarily in the United States, although conferences, publications, and teaching are spreading the movement to Britain, Western Europe, and Latin America. Most feminist theology has developed since 1968, although feminist criticism of biblical exegesis and Christian theology can be traced to earlier roots.

In 1667, Margaret Fell, influential early Quaker leader and wife of George Fox, founder of the Society of Friends, wrote a tract entitled "Women's Speaking Justified, Approved and Allowed of by the

Scriptures," and offering a biblical interpretation of women's equality in Christ and their consequent right to preach, teach, and minister in the church.

In nineteenth-century America, the Society of Friends was an important source for feminist leaders who typically argued the case for women's rights from a biblical basis. In 1837, Sarah Grimke, a Quaker abolitionist and feminist, campaigned for women's rights. On the basis of Genesis 1:27, Grimke asserted that women were equal with men in the original creation since both were created in the image of God.

Both women and men, she contended, were given dominion over nature, but men were not given dominion over women in the original creation. Patriarchalism was criticized as a sinful decline from the original place of woman in the divine plan. Grimke called on church and social leaders to reform their institutional structures to rectify this injustice. Nineteenth-century American feminists objected to use of the Bible as an instrument of male domination.

Modern feminist theology within the church focuses in two areas.

1. It criticizes the masculine bias in Christian theology that has excluded women from ordained ministry and higher theological education throughout much of the church's history.

Feminists argue that Christian theology has excluded and attempted to nullify women's experience. Classical theology reflects a negative bias against women in its anthropological teachings.

2. Feminists contend for the support of the full personhood of women and their inclusion in leadership roles in church and society.

Within the Judaeo-Christian tradition, feminists seek to uncover the fundamental meaning of concepts of God, Christ, human personhood, sin, and redemption and to reform the effects of male domination.

Fundamentalism. The term comes from the title of a series of booklets called *The Fundamentals,* published in the United States between 1910 and 1915. The movement arose to resist dangerous theological tendencies in what was then known as modernism, or liberalism.

In 1919, an organization called the World's Christian Fundamentals Association was formed. Its members stated their belief in nine points of doctrine:

1. The inspiration and inerrancy of the Bible.
2. The Trinity.
3. The virgin birth and deity of Jesus Christ.
4. God's creation of the world and the fall of the human race through sin.
5. The substitutionary atonement of Jesus Christ.
6. The bodily resurrection and ascension of Jesus Christ.
7. The regeneration of believers.
8. The personal and imminent return of Jesus Christ.
9. The resurrection and final assignment of all human beings either to eternal bliss or eternal woe.

Even today fundamentalism rests on the the foundation that the Bible is without error of any kind. This central tenet is supported by two others: the verbal inspiration of the Scriptures as originally written and the literal interpretation of the Bible.

Liberalism. Religious liberalism (often called modernism, and sometimes Neo-Protestantism) was a post-Enlightenment development in German theology that arose as a protest against the intense rationalism of the Enlightenment and against religious orthodoxy.

Positively, liberalism was an attempt to harmonize Christian theology with the variety of elements of the new learning. It is presumed to have begun with Friedrich Schleiermacher, ca. 1806.

Liberalism had a fourfold root:

1. Philosophically it was grounded in German idealism.
2. It accepts the authority of the new

critical studies of the Scriptures that contained implicitly or explicitly, a denial of the historic doctrines of revelation and inspiration.

3. It held that the developing sciences antiquated much of the Scriptures.

4. It sought a harmony of Christianity with the new learning.

It has consistently held for the right of free criticism of any and all theological claims. While the traditional, classical liberalism has lost its place of theological leadership, the seeds of its position are much in existence in theological circles today.

Pelagianism. The name given to the belief that human beings are able to achieve their salvation by their own powers. It was the teaching of Pelagius, a British lay theologian and exegete (his *Expositions on the Epistles of St. Paul* have come down to us), who at the end of the fourth century was influential among the Roman aristocracy, and later in North Africa and Palestine.

By means of free will, Pelagius argued, even atheists could become virtuous. Christians, however, had the added help of grace, which Pelagius understood in his own way as the example and motivation provided by Christ.

Original sin was no more than Adam's bad example, not an inherited defect which impaired the freedom of the will. Adult baptism served only to provide a psychological break with the past, not as the means of remitting inherited guilt.

The heresy was condemned by councils at Milevis and Carthage in 416 and 418, by Popes Innocent I and Zosimus and by the Emperor Honorius. After that, Pelagius' disciples Caelestius and Julian of Eclanum took the lead in defending and refining their master's doctrine.

Pentecostalism. A movement of Christian renewal patterned after the first Christian Pentecost when the Holy Spirit came upon the disciples in the upper room and transformed them into bold evangelists. It is characterized by the reappearance of the gift of glossolalia (speaking in tongues), healing and miracles.

In its more recent days it has come to be identified with the charismatic renewal, a movement that arose in midwestern America at the beginning of the twentieth century, although it had nineteenth-century antecedents in England and Armenia, as well as in American revivalism. The Welsh revival led by Evan Roberts in the early twentieth century also stimulated the American development.

The Pentecostal movement began at nondenominational Bethel Bible College in Topeka, Kansas in 1901, when Agnes Ozman, after being prayed with for the baptism in the Spirit, experienced a powerful renewal and began to praise God in an unknown tongue, later identified as Bohemian. As others shared this experience, especially in 1904 in Los Angeles, an enthusiastic movement took form.

Rejected by the Holiness, Baptist, and Methodist churches from which most of its early participants came, this movement engendered many new churches, commonly known as Pentecostal, Full Gospel or Foursquare. Today Pentecostalists embrace over twenty-two million adherents, making them the fifth largest Protestant group in the world.

From about 1960 on, Episcopalians, Lutherans, Methodists, Presbyterians, and members of other established Protestant churches, after receiving the Pentecostal experience, insisted on remaining in their denomination and are sometimes tagged as neo-Pentecostals.

Since 1967 some Roman Catholics have embraced Pentecostalism, while tending more and more to prefer the term charismatic renewal.

This renewal is based on belief in the Holy Spirit as a gift given by the glorified Lord Jesus to his disciples. Without limiting the working of the Spirit to the supernatural gifts listed in places such as 1 Corinthians 12 and 14, it holds to the reality and value of these charisms as manifestations of the Spirit's activity.

Until recent years Pentecostals regarded glossolalia as the sign of having received the Holy Spirit. Today, especially among neo-Pentecostalists, tongues are seen as one among many gifts of the Spirit, none of which is given to everyone. Even so, tongues is the most widespread of the gifts and has become a mark of the Pentecostal movement.

While the spiritual gifts have drawn attention to the charismatic renewal, they are not its chief strength. This lies the emphasis on inner peace and joy, a vivid awareness of the presence of the living God and his love, a strong sense of loving communion with other believers, and a new courage and power in witnessing to Christ. All of this, according to the Pentecostals, flows from the baptism in the Spirit.

Above all, Pentecostalism does not consider itself a doctrinal position, method, or strategy, but rather an experience—a personal experience of the inner working of the Holy Spirit.

Semi-pelagianism. A term applied to theories which imply that the first movement toward God is made by human efforts unaided by grace. The term seems to have come into use at the end of the sixteenth century in the controversy within the Roman Catholic Church over grace and free will.

In modern times the term is applied to writers of the fifth and sixth centuries, such as J. Cassian, Vincent of Lerins, and Faustus of Riez, who taught that individuals must take for themselves the first step toward salvation. None of these writers had any connection with Pelagius. Their teachings were condemned at the Second Council of Orange in 529; Pope Boniface II endorsed the verdict in 531.

Universalism. The doctrine of the ultimate well-being of every person. The doctrine has a pagan and a Christian form.

According to the former, all individuals will ultimately be happy because all are, by nature, the creatures and children of God.

The Christian universalist heresy, which has consistently been rejected by the tradition of the church—Eastern, Roman, and Protestant, teaches that although all the human creatures of God have fallen into sin and are lost, all will be saved through the universal redemption of Christ.

Christian universalism has manifested two distinct forms: restoration at death and restoration after future punishment.

The second position is the classical theory of Christian universalism taught from the time of Clement of Alexandria. This says that ultimately all people will be reconciled to God.

Probably the most celebrated adherent of this position was Origen (d. 254). He rejected the notion of endless punishment, teaching that the wicked, including the devil, after enduring the pains of hell for a season would come forth purified for heaven.

The universalist movement in America was divided by those who insisted on perfection of everyone at death without further purgatorial punishment. A declaration adopting the "orthodox" view of punishment before perfection was made in 1878, at Winchester, N.H. Since then, most universalists have opted for the first position—all will be reconciled to God at death.

The scriptural base of universalism hinges on three arguments:

1. The purpose of God: the restoration of all things to their original perfection (Acts 3:21)
2. The means of restoration: through Jesus Christ (Rom. 5:18; Heb. 2:9)
3. The nature of the restoration: union of every soul with God (1 Cor. 15:24–28)

Theological Words and Terms

"W ho is Jesus Christ?"

This may well have been the question that started early Christians in their quest to define what they believed. *Theology* comes from two Greek words (*Theos*, "God," and *logos*, "discourse," "word," or "study") and means "the study of God and religious doctrines." Without theology, we cannot talk about what we believe.

The roots of Christian theology lie deep in the civilizations of the ancient world, especially Israel, Rome and Greece. From the first days, Christians engaged in dialogue with non-Christians. This pushed them to define their views and to clarify their understandings. Who is Jesus Christ? Only a man like everybody else? God in a human form? Who is a Christian? What does it mean to believe? What is a heretic? The questions go on endlessly.

For centuries the sharpest minds in the church discussed and argued among themselves as well as with those outside the faith. Slowly Christians accepted certain views as orthodox (Greek *orthos*, "straight," and *doxa*, "opinion" or "understanding," and the term came to mean "correct thinking").

In arriving at these orthodox views, they had to find the words to explain what they meant. Sometimes theologians invented words such as *trinity* or took already-known words like *agape* ("love") and reframed them with new meanings.

Since the beginning of the church, theologians have continued to seek better ways to communicate the common faith of believers. In each generation different concerns emerge, and the church again strives to communicate the faith more clearly.

The following words are theological terms—many of them not found in the Bible—so integral a part of Christian thinking, most of us would have difficulty articulating what we believe without using them.

Abraham's bosom. In Jesus' parable (see Luke 16:22ff.), Lazarus is carried by the angels into Abraham's bosom. Most people see this as the poor man entering into the heavenly banquet, reclining at the table at Abraham's side (cf. John 13:23).

Rabbinic Judaism used the expression to mean "rest from the toil and neediness of earthly life in intimate fellowship with the father of the race, who is still alive and blessed in death."

Absolution. The word comes from the Latin, *absolve*, and means "to set free." It is used in theology to denote the forgiveness of sins, being specifically used by Roman Catholics of the remission given through or by the church.

Abstinence. The word refers to a refraining from external actions, such as drinking, eating, marriage, and participating in human society. In its wider meaning it includes the whole negative side of biblical spirituality and morality, but its usual sense involves abstinence from food or drink.

Accountability. This word does not appear in English versions of the Bible, but its cognates occur in several places (e.g., Luke 16:2; Rom. 1:20; 14:12).

The classic Scripture reference on the subject is Romans 14:12, "So then each of us shall give an account of himself to God." Obviously this text implies that there is a supreme moral Ruler of the universe to whom all creatures are ultimately responsible and accountable.

This same sentiment is expressed by the apostle in Romans 2:12 where he indicates that even those who knew not law are responsible. They will render an account to God since God has revealed himself to them in conscience.

Adam. The Hebrew word occurs about 560 times in the OT, nearly always meaning "man" or "humankind." However, in the opening chapters of the Bible it is used as the proper name of the first man, who was created by God in his image.

Admonition. Greek *nouthesia*. This word occurs three times in the NT (1 Cor. 10:11; Eph. 6:4; Titus 3:10) and denotes "a putting into the mind." Its verbal cognate, "to put in mind," appears four times (Rom. 15:14; Col. 3:16; 1 Thess. 5:12; 2 Thess. 3:15).

An admonition is supposed to put into another's mind God's expectation. It can and often has degenerated into the church's expectation, assumed to be God's as well.

Advent of Christ. Latin *adventus*. The word corresponds to the Greek *parousia*. The latter term, however, occurs only in referring to the second advent. But second-century Christian literature applied the word to both comings of Christ.

Advocate. The English word is used only in 1 John 2:1, a translation of the Greek *parakletos*, which occurs four other times in the NT (John 14:16, 26; 15:26; 16:7).

The word means "one who is called to the side of another," especially in a court of law and means simply "helper" or "intercessor." In 1 John 2:1 Jesus Christ is the advocate who intercedes for Christians. The efficacy of Christ's work as advocate rests on his propitiatory sacrifice (1 John 2:2).

Parakletos is a title given to the Holy Spirit in John's Gospel. Although the Latin translators used *advocatus* even here, the KJV translates it "comforter" in all four occurrences. This rendering goes back to Wycliffe, whose translation greatly influenced subsequent English versions.

Parakletos could easily be translated in John by "advocate" or a synonym, such as "counselor," "helper," or "intercessor."

Affections. This old English term referred to any bent, disposition or emotion, good or evil. The KJV used it to translate *splagchnon* ("bowels," "compassionate feeling") in 2 Corinthians 7:15; *phroneo* ("to mind," "think") in Colossians 3:2; and *pathos* ("feeling," "passion") in Colossians 3:5 and Romans 1:26.

Any states of pronounced feeling are affections, although generally we mean only those that incline the will to action. They are usually distinguished from passions as being less intense. Affections may be classified as natural or spiritual in accordance with their exciting cause.

Age. In the OT, the Hebrew word *olam* means "a long, indefinite period of time," whether past or future.

In the NT, the Greek word *aion* means "indefinite time."

In the past, *aion*, like *olam*, is used to mean "an indeterminate period of time." For example:

- The age of the prophets is "from the age," i.e., from long ago (Luke 1:70; Acts 3:21).
- God's revelation to Israel was "from the age" (Acts 15:18).
- "From the age" in John 9:32 means "from all past time."
- Jude 25 has a variant form, "before all the age," meaning before all time.

Used to indicate the future, *unto the age* occurs 27 times, and its meaning must be determined from the context. In Matthew 21:19, Mark 3:29, John 13:8, and 1 Corinthians 8:13, it means "never." In other contexts, the idea of a future eternity is apparent (e.g., John 6:51, 58; 11:26; 14:16; 2 Cor. 9:9; Heb. 5:6; 7:17, 21; 1 Pet. 1:25; 1 John 2).

The plural *ages* is used to strengthen the idea of endlessness:

Past. "Before the ages" (1 Cor. 2:7); "from the ages" (Eph. 3:9; Col. 1:26). In Ephesians 3:11 we have the "purpose of the ages," i.e., God's eternal purpose.

Future. "Unto the ages" (see e.g., Luke 1:33; Rom. 1:25; 11:36; 2 Cor. 11:31; Heb. 13:8). Jude 25 reads "unto all the ages."

The eternity of the future is strengthened by doubling the form:

Singular. "Unto the age of the age" (Heb. 1:8)

Plural. "Unto the ages of the ages" (Eph. 3:21)

This expression occurs 21 times, all in the writings of Paul or in Revelation, with the exception of Hebrews 13:21; 1 Peter 4:11; 5:11.

Sometimes *aion* refers not so much to a period of time but to that which fills the time period. The creation of the ages in Hebrews 1:2 refers to all that fills the ages—the world. In 11:3 *the ages* are further described by the phrase "that which is seen"—the visible world that fills the ages of time.

Since *aion* can bear spatial connotations, it can be used interchangeably with *kosmos* ("world"). Some examples are

- "The world to come" (Heb. 2:5)
- "The age to come" (Heb. 6:5)
- "Wisdom of this world" (1 Cor. 1:20; 3:19)
- "The wisdom of this age" (1 Cor. 2:6)
- Possibly the "cares of this world" in Mark 4:19 and Matthew 13:22 are synonymous with the care for "the things of the world" in 1 Corinthians 7:33. The assertion that God is the King of the ages (1 Tim. 1:17) means not only that he is Lord of time but of all that fills time.

The biblical concept of the "ages" stands in contrast to the Greek idea of time—eternity relationship, in which eternity is qualitatively different from time. Eternity is unending time. The future life has its setting in a redeemed earth (Rom. 8:21; 2 Pet. 3:13) with resurrection bodies.

Annunciation. Three people received an *annuntiatio* (Latin; *euaggelismos*, Greek) in the Gospels: Zechariah (Luke 1:13), Joseph (Matt. 1:20), and Mary (Luke 1:26ff.). The word usually refers to the annunication to Mary. Luke related the annunciation by Gabriel to Mary in her Nazareth home. Matthew wrote an account of the announcement of the birth and name of Jesus to Joseph in a dream.

Anointing. The practice of applying oil or perfumed oil upon persons or things. The references are most common to the anointing of kings and priests, using mainly olive oil. Directions are given for compounding it with perfumes for holy use (Exod. 30:22–25).

Athanasian theology. The beliefs or theology of Athanasius (293–373) who defended the orthodox view of the divinity of Christ. He opposed and defeated Arius at the Council of Nicea (325). Arius stated that Christ was created by, but not essentially different from the Father. (See *Creed.*)

Anthropomorphism. The term (not found in the Bible—derived from Greek *anthropos*, "human," and *morphe* "form") designates the view which conceives of God as having human form and characteristics.

Biblical expressions speak of God having feet (Gen. 3:8; Exod. 24:10), hands (Exod. 24:11; Josh. 4:24), mouth (Num. 12:8; Jer. 7:13), and heart (Hos. 11:8).

In a wider sense the term also includes human attributes, such as emotions (e.g., Gen. 2:2; 6:6; Exod. 20:5; Hos. 11:8).

Apostle. The biblical use of this word is confined to the NT, where it occurs 79 times.

English scholars transliterated the Greek *apostolos* (from *apostellein*, meaning "to send"). Several words for *send* occur in the NT, expressing the ideas of "releasing," "dispatching," and "dismissing." The verb emphasizes the elements of commission—authority of and responsibility to the sender.

This means that apostles are those sent on definite missions in which they act with full authority on behalf of the senders and are accountable to them.

Apostolic succession. This theory of ministry in the church did not arise before A.D. 170–200. The Gnostics claimed to possess a secret tradition handed down to them from the apostles. As a counterclaim the Roman Catholic church pointed to each bishop as a true successor to the apostle who had founded the papacy.

The bishop, as an authoritative teacher, preserved the apostolic tradition as the guardian of the apostolic Scriptures and the creed.

Ascension. The ascension refers to that act of the God-man by which he brought to an end his postresurrection appearances to his disciples. He finally departed from them and passed into the other world where he will remain until his second advent (Acts 3:21). Luke describes this event in Luke 24:51 and Acts 1:9.

According to John, Jesus spoke three times of his ascending into heaven (3:13; 6:62; 20:17). Paul speaks of Christ ascending far above all heavens in order to permeate the whole universe with his presence and power (Eph. 4:10).

Phrases that refer to this same event are "received up in glory" (1 Tim. 3:16), "gone into heaven" (1 Pet. 3:22), and "passed through the heavens" (Heb. 4:14).

Asceticism. Greek *askesis*, "exercise" or "training." Asceticism denotes the practice of self-discipline, particularly in relation to the body. This self-discipline normally takes the form of renunciation (e.g., fasting, celibacy), but has sometimes been given a more active form in such excesses as self-flagellation.

Asceticism can also refer to the surrender of possessions or withdrawal from various aspects of intellectual or cultural life for spiritual edification or service.

The consistent biblical emphasis upon a proper asceticism is impressive, yet there is no suggestion of anything evil in what ascetics leave (e.g., food, marriage, property, or ordinary relationships), no universal or permanent rule of asceticism, and no value in merely abstaining (rather, abstinence is undertaken with a view to something positive, such as repentance, hearing God's word or service).

Ash Wednesday. The first day of Lent, the traditional 40-day fast before Easter. The title derives from the discipline in the ancient Roman Church of sprinkling ashes on the heads of penitents and their being restored to communion at Easter. (See *Lent*.)

Assurance. The doctrine that those who belong to Jesus Christ may know without doubt that they are saved (Phil. 1:6; Col. 2:2; Heb. 6:11; 10:22).

Baptism. Greek *baptisma*. This transliteration denotes the action of washing, dipping or plunging into water. Since the earliest day of the church (Acts 2:41), this act has been used as the rite of Christian initiation.

Its origins go back to the OT purifications, but baptism as we know it begins with the baptism of John. Christ himself, both by precedent and precept (Matt. 3:13; 28:19), gives authority for its observance. On this basis it has been practiced by almost all Christians.

Three major positions exist among Christian groups.

1. Sacramental view. Baptism is a means by which God conveys grace. By undergoing this rite, those baptized receive remission of their sins, are regenerated (given a new nature), and are given a new or

strengthened faith. (Roman Catholics and Lutherans hold this position.)

Roman Catholics emphasize the rite itself—the power to convey grace is within the sacrament itself. Not the water but the sacrament as established by God and administered by the church, produces this change. Lutherans concentrate on the faith present in the person being baptized and stress the importance of the preaching of the Bible. Preaching awakens faith by entering the ears to strike the hearts and baptism enters the eyes to reach and move the hearts.

2. Covenantal view. Baptism is a sign and seal of the covenant—God's pledge to save the fallen race. Because of God's actions and promises, God forgives and regenerates. The benefits of the covenant are for all adults who receive baptism and for all infants who remain faithful to the vows made on their behalf in baptism. The covenant, rather than the sacrament or another's faith, is the means of salvation. Baptism is a vital part of this covenant relationship.

In the covenantal view, baptism serves the purpose that circumcision did in the OT. For the Jews, circumcision was the external and visible sign that they were within the covenant God established with Abraham. Converts to Judaism had to undergo this rite. Under the new covenant, baptism replaces circumcision.

Circumcision symbolizes a cutting away of sin and a change of heart (Deut. 10:16; Ezek. 44:7, 9). Similarly, baptism depicts a washing away of sin (Acts 2:38; Titus 3:5) and a spiritual renewal (Rom. 6:4; Col. 2:38; Titus 3:5). Colossians 2:11–12 links these two. (Presbyterians and the Reformed Churches hold this position.)

3. Symbolic view. This position stresses the symbolic nature by emphasizing that baptism does not cause an inward change or alter an individual's relationship to God. Baptism is a token—an outward indication—of the inner changes that have already occurred in believers. Baptism serves as a public identification of union with Jesus Christ and as a public testimony of the change that has taken place.

This position sees baptism not so much an initiation into the Christian life as into the Christian church. The church practices baptism and believers submit to it because Jesus commanded that it be done and gave us the example by being baptized himself. This makes baptism an act of obedience, commitment and proclamation. (Baptists and Pentecostals hold this view.)

The form of baptism has divided Christians into two major groups—those who insist upon the exclusive use of immersion and those who permit it but use other forms such as sprinkling or pouring.

Immersionists present four arguments.

1. Immersion is the only valid form since the Greek word for baptism predominantly means "to immerse" or "to dip"—implying that the candidates were plunged beneath the water.

2. Immersion was the form used in the early church. *The Didache*, a manual of Christian instruction written A.D. 110–120 stated that immersion should generally be used and that other forms should be used only when immersion was not possible.

3. The biblical descriptions of baptism imply immersion. John baptized in Aenon near Salim "because there was much water there" (John 3:23; see also Matt. 3:16; Acts 8:36).

4. Romans 6:4–6 identifies baptism with the believer's death (and burial) to sin and resurrection to new life, as well as the death and resurrection of Jesus Christ. Only immersion adequately depicts the meaning.

Those who argue against the exclusive use of immersion offer four arguments.

1. The Greek word for baptism is sometimes ambiguous in usage. Its most common meaning was to "dip," "plunge," or "immerse," but it also carried other meaning as well. The argument cannot be resolved purely on linguistic grounds.

2. By inference, immersion could not have been the exclusive method used in

NT times. Could John have been physically capable of immersing all those persons who came to him for baptism? On the day of Pentecost, could the disciples have immersed 3,000 people? Did the Philippian jailer leave his jail to be baptized? If not, how would he have been immersed? Was enough water for immersion brought to Cornelius' house? Did Paul leave the place where Ananias found him so that he could be immersed?

3. Immersion may not be the best form to show the meaning of baptism. The major significance of baptism is purification. The cleansing ceremonies of the OT were performed in a variety of ways—immersing, pouring, and sprinkling (Mark 7:4; Heb. 9:10).

4. Some people consider that the close association between baptism and the outpouring of the Holy Spirit, which came from above, requires the symbolism of pouring rather than immersion. (See *Baptism, believer's; Baptism, infant.*)

Baptism, believer's. Those who hold this view restrict baptism to individuals who actually exercise faith. This excludes infants who could not possibly have such faith. Candidates for baptism have already experienced the new birth by their faith in Jesus Christ and give evidence of this salvation in their lives.

Arguments for adult or believers' baptism include:

1. In every instance of NT baptism where the people are specifically identified, those baptized were adults.

2. In each of the preceding instances, those who were baptized expressed personal, conscious faith. This is especially true in Acts (see 2:37–41; 8:12; 10:47; 19:4–5; 28:8) as well as Matthew (see 3:2–6; 28:19).

3. In NT baptisms, repentance and faith come first, followed by baptism.

4. None of the instances that speak of households being baptized (e.g., Acts 16:34; 18:8) specifically state the inclusion of infants. Possibly all the people in the households could have been adults.

Baptism, infant. Groups that practice infant baptism (e.g., Episcopalians, Lutherans, Methodists, Presbyterians, and Roman Catholics) also baptize adults who come to faith in Jesus Christ.

Arguments in support of infant baptism include:

1. In NT times entire households were baptized as in Acts 16:15; 18:18. These households must have included children. This extends a practice begun with the apostles.

2. Jesus commanded the disciples to bring children to him, and when they did, he blessed them (Mark 10:13–16). Because of this example from Jesus, it seems consistent to baptize children.

3. Children participated in the OT covenant: "And I will establish My covenant between Me and you and your descendants after you in their generations, for an everlasting covenant, to be God to you and your descendants after you" (Gen. 17:7).

Children were present at the renewing of the OT covenant (Deut. 29:10–13; Josh. 8:35). God made promises to children as well as adults (Isa. 54:13; Jer. 31:17). Circumcision was administered to infants in the OT. Since baptism has now replaced circumcision, it is natural that it would be administered to children.

4. Historically, infant baptism has been practiced in the church from early times, certainly as early as the second century.

The dividing issue on infant baptism generally is that the covenant theologians (Presbyterians, Lutherans, and the various Reformed groups) insist that only the children of believing parents should be included. Roman Catholics tend to baptize children whose parents have not made such a commitment.

Barbarian. *Barbaros* is an onomatopoeic word that originated by imitating the unintelligible sounds of people who spoke a language foreign to Greek. It became a designation for those who spoke in such a tongue or possessed a foreign culture.

The word is used in four different places in the NT. Acts 28:2, 4 translates it as "natives" of Malta without derogatory overtones. Romans 1:14 mentions "barbarians" along with Greeks to indicate the universality of Paul's apostleship. 1 Corinthians 14:11 translates the word as "foreigner" or "language." Colossians 3:11 lists "barbarians" as a social distinction of NT times; division of people into classes like this is alien to the spirit of Christ.

Beelzebub. Some think the literal meaning is "dung-god," and he is called "lord of flies" (cf. 2 Kings 1:2ff.), referring to a god of the Philistines. In NT times the Jews used it as an epithet for the prince of demons (Matt. 12:24). Some of Jesus' contemporaries derogated our Lord by alleging that he was possessed by Beelzebub and did miracles through his power (Mark 3:22). Jesus exposed the baselessness of this charge.

Benediction. An act or pronouncement of blessing. The Aaronic benediction was given to Aaron and his sons as a part of their ministry in God's behalf toward the people and is epitomized as a putting of God's name upon them (Num. 6:22–27). The NT parallel is the apostolic benediction (2 Cor. 13:14), which reflects the progress of revelation by its emphasis on the Trinity.

In Roman Catholic theory the virtue of the benediction, regarded as quasiautomatic in its efficacy, increases with the rank of the one who pronounces it.

Binding and loosing. These are technical terms for the exercise of disciplinary authority bestowed by Jesus in conjunction with the keys of the kingdom, first to Peter in Matthew 16:19, then to all the disciples in 18:18.

Binding and loosing in Judaism also mean "to prohibit" and "to permit" (Num. 30:13).

Born again. The experience of a second birth by the Holy Spirit. (See *Salvation.*)

Blasphemy. To speak evil of someone. The Greek *blasphemeo* is usually translated "blaspheme," but also "defame," "rail

on," and "speak evil of." The law of blasphemy (Lev. 24:11–16) prescribed death for the person who cursed the name of the Lord or blasphemed (Hebrew *naqab*). It is not clear that this is a direct interpretation of the third commandment. Many think that commandment refers, principally at least, to nonfulfillment of oaths taken in God's name. Blasphemy is likely meant, not thoughtless utterance of the divine name as in modern swearing—evil though that may be—but a deliberate cursing of God that involves a denial of his deity and attributes.

Bread. The Greek words *lehem* (appearing more than 200 times) and *artos* (found about 100 times) mean either "bread" or other "food prepared from grain," such as wheat or barley.

Bull, papal. An apostolic letter bearing in its superscription the title of the pope in which the pope speaks to the church *ex cathedra* in matters pertaining to faith and morals and thus infallibly according to Roman Catholic doctrine. It is so named because of the leaden seal (Latin *bulla, seal*) by which papal documents were authenticated during the Middle Ages. The term was at first applied to all kinds of official documents emanating from the papal chancery, but a more precise definition has existed since the fifteenth century.

Call, Called, Calling. The developed biblical idea of God's summoning individuals to his service. They receive his power, symbolized by the laying on of hands.

Canon. The 66 books admitted to the Bible as authoritative: 39 in the OT and 27 in the NT.

Catechism. The form or guide used to instruct candidates for church membership. Catechism can also refer to a book that contains such instructional materials.

Catholic. A transliteration of the Greek *katholikos*, "throughout the whole," or "general." This word has been used in a variety of senses during the history of the church. In the earlier patristic period it meant universal.

When the term appears in the Apostles' Creed—"the holy catholic church" (ca. 450)—it retains the sense of universality and accents the unity of the church in spite of its wide diffusion. The Catholic Epistles of the NT were so designated by Origen, Eusebius, and others to indicate that they were intended for the whole church rather than a local congregation.

Celibacy. The state of being unmarried, required for Roman Catholic priests and the members of some orders.

Chastity. To suppress sexual desire or refrain from sexual relations in order to devote oneself to spiritual ends.

Chosen people. Name for the Hebrew people, whom God chose as his special instruments. As a holy people set apart to worship God, they were to make his name known throughout the earth (Deut. 7:6, 7; Ps. 105:43). In the NT Peter described Christians as members of a "chosen generation" (see 1 Pet. 2:9).

Christian. An adherent or follower of Jesus Christ. The word occurs three times in the NT (Acts 11:26; 26:28; 1 Pet. 4:16).

Church. A local assembly of believers that includes the redeemed of all ages who follow Jesus Christ as Savior and Lord.

In the four gospels, *church* occurs only in Matthew 16:18 and 18:17. This scarcity of usage in the books that report on the life and ministry of Jesus is because the church as the body of Christ did not begin until the day of Pentecost after the ascension of Jesus (Acts 1:1–4).

That the church began on the day of Pentecost rests on two understandings:

1. While still on earth, Jesus declared the church to be yet future.

2. The church was built on the death, resurrection, and ascension of Christ, and as such was not possible until Pentecost (Acts 1:1–4; Gal. 3:23–25).

The Greek word for church is *ekklesia* and occurs 115 times in the NT. In at least 92 instances the word refers to a local congregation. In the other references, the word refers to the church in general.

Clergy. The word is from the Greek *kleros*, "a lot," and may point to a method of choosing as in Acts 1:26 (cf. also Acts 1:17 where "part" is the translation of *kleros*).

In the NT the word is not used of a restricted class. It denotes either a lot or a heritage, and in 1 Peter 5:3 the plural is used of God's people as a whole. But by the time of Tertullian *kleros* was used of the class of ordained office-bearers in the church.

Collect. A brief prayer. In Episcopal/Anglican and Roman Catholic churches, this is a prayer read before the gospel and epistle readings.

Command, Commandment. A law, edict or statute. God's commandments are always directed toward the welfare of his people.

Commission, the great. Jesus' command to the disciples to preach the gospel on a worldwide basis.

Each of the gospels has its own statement of the commission, likely repeated in varying form by our Lord. Mark's account (16:15) emphasizes the obligation to go to every creature with the message. Luke's statement stresses the evangelization of the nations as the fulfillment of God's purpose set forth in the OT Scriptures.

In John, the words of Jesus impart dignity to this task. As the Father has sent him, so the Savior sends the apostles. The Spirit is the source of power for this mission, and "forgiveness of sins" points to the effectiveness of the gospel to the needs of sinful humanity (John 20:21–23).

The peculiarity of Acts 1:8 lies in its specification of the areas in which the witness is to be given. Galilee is omitted, perhaps on the assumption that the disciples, being Galileans, would not neglect their

Commands to Believers

Abstain from all appearances of evil	1 Thess. 5:22	Do not be deceived by evil companions	1 Cor. 15:33
Abstain from all fleshly lusts	1 Pet. 2:11	Do not be unequally yoked with unbelievers	2 Cor. 6:14–18
Avoid troublemakers	Rom. 16:17	Do not be drunk with wine	Eph. 5:18
Avoid profane and vain babblings	1 Tim. 6:20	Do not be weary in well-doing	Gal. 6:9
Avoid false science	1 Tim. 6:20	Do not be slothful	Heb. 6:12
Avoid foolish questions	Titus 3:9	Do not be influenced by strange doctrines	Heb. 13:9
Avoid arguments about the law	Titus 3:9	Beware of false prophets	Matt. 7:15; Phil. 3:2
Be reconciled to a brother	Matt. 5:24		
Be wise as serpents	Matt. 10:16	Beware of evil people	Matt. 10:17
Be harmless as doves	Matt. 10:16	Beware of covetousness	Luke 12:15
Be thankful	Col. 3:15	Beware of backsliding	2 Pet. 3:17
Be patient toward all	1 Thess. 5:14; 2 Tim. 2:24	Do not bid false teachers Godspeed	2 John 10–11
Be ready to give an answer for the hope that is in you	1 Pet. 3:15	Bring up children in the Lord	Eph. 6:4
Be transformed	Rom. 12:2	Cast your cares upon God	1 Pet. 5:7
Be patient in tribulation	Rom. 12:12	Have confidence in God	Heb. 10:35
Be children in avoiding malice	1 Cor. 14:20	Come out from among the world	2 Cor. 6:17
Be adult in understanding	1 Cor. 14:20	Count it joy when you are tempted	James 1:2
Be steadfast	1 Cor. 15:58	Treat others as you expect to be treated	Matt. 7:12
Be unmovable	1 Cor. 15:58		
Always abound in God's work	1 Cor. 15:58	Desire the milk of the word	1 Pet. 2:2
Be of one mind	Rom. 12:16	Do all to God's glory	1 Cor. 10:31; Col. 3:17, 23
Be separate from the unclean	2 Cor. 6:17		
Be angry and sin not	Eph. 4:26	Do all things without murmuring or disputing	Phil. 2:14
Be filled with the Spirit	Eph. 5:18	Earnestly contend for the faith	Jude 3
Be anxious for nothing	Phil. 4:6		
Be an example to other believers	1 Tim. 4:12	Give no place to Satan	Eph. 4:27
Be gentle to all	2 Tim. 2:24	Give thanks	Eph. 5:20; Phil. 4:6
Be ready to teach	2 Tim. 2:24		
Be content with what you have	Heb. 13:5	Give time to reading	1 Tim. 4:13
		Give no offense	1 Cor. 10:32
Be vigilant	1 Pet. 5:8	Give freely	2 Cor. 9:6–7
Do not pray like the hypocrites	Matt. 6:5	Give as God has prospered you	1 Cor. 16:2
Do not be afraid of people	Luke 12;4	Give willingly	2 Cor. 8:12
Do not be conformed to this world	Rom. 12:2	Give purposely	2 Cor. 9:7
Do not be children in understanding	1 Cor. 14:20	Do not grieve the Holy Spirit	Eph. 4:30
		Grow in grace	2 Pet. 3:18

Commands to Believers—*continued*

Have no fellowship with darkness	Eph. 5:11	Follow things that edify	Rom. 14:19
Have compassion	Jude 22	Walk in the Spirit	Gal. 5:15
Have a good conscience	1 Pet. 3:16	Do not provoke one another	Gal. 5:26
Hold forth the word of life	Phil. 2:16	Come boldly to the throne of grace	Heb. 4:16; 10:19–23
Hold fast sound words	2 Tim. 1:13	Do not forsake assembling together	Heb. 10:25
Honor fathers	Eph. 6:2		
Honor mothers	Matt. 19:19	Exhort one another	Heb. 10.25
Honor widows	1 Tim. 5:3	Lay aside every weight	Heb. 12:1
Honor rulers	1 Pet. 2:17	Run with patience the race before us	Heb. 12:1
Lay aside all envy	1 Pet. 2:1		
Lay aside all evil speaking	1 Pet. 2:1	Look to Jesus	Heb. 12:2
Do not lay up treasures on earth	Matt. 6:19	Offer the sacrifice of praise to God continually	Heb. 13:15
Let your light shine	Matt. 5:16	Do not judge one another	Rom. 14:1
Let everyone deny himself	Matt. 16:24	Do not cause others to stumble	Rom. 14:13
Let all share with the needy	Luke 3:11		
Let everyone obey civil laws	Rom. 13:1	Mark troublemakers	Rom. 16:17; Phil. 3:17
Let no man deceive himself	1 Cor. 3:18	Pray for your persecutors	Matt. 5:44; Luke 10:2
Let everyone examine himself at communion	1 Cor. 11:28	Pray for laborers	Matt. 9:38; Luke 10:2
Let God know your requests	Phil. 4:6	Present your body to God	Rom. 12:1
Let your speech be with grace	Col. 4:6	Put on the new man	Eph. 4:24; Col. 3:10
Do all things in decent order	1 Cor. 14:40	Put on the whole armor of God	Eph. 6:11,13
Let those who are taught support the teacher	Gal. 6:6	Do not quench the Spirit	1 Thess. 5:19
Let wives be subject to their husbands	Eph. 5:22; Col. 3:18	Consider yourself dead to sin	Rom. 6:11
Let husbands love their wives	Eph. 5:25	Redeem the time	Eph. 5:16
Let wives reverence their husbands	Eph. 5:33	Resist the devil	James 4:7; 1 Pet. 5:9
Let everyone be swift to hear, slow to speak, slow to wrath	James 1:19	Restore backsliders in meekness	Gal. 6:1
		Strengthen feeble knees	Heb. 12:12
Let the afflicted pray	James 5:13	Study to show yourself approved to God	2 Tim. 2:15
Let the adorning of women be more inward than outward	1 Pet. 3:3–4	Take no anxious thought of tomorrow	Matt. 6:34
Don't let the left hand know what the right hand is doing	Matt. 6:3	Take the Lord's Supper	1 Cor. 11:24–26
Do not let sin reign in the body	Rom. 6:12	Be careful not to despise little ones	Matt. 18:10
		Be aware of yourself and your doctrine	1 Tim. 4:16
Do not let the sun go down on your wrath	Eph. 4:26	Withdraw from disorderly people	2 Thess. 3:6, 14

own section. Each of the places mentioned has its own reason for emphasis. Jerusalem must not be avoided because of antipathy for those who there crucified the Lord. Such people advertise their need for the gospel. Judea is the probably home of the betrayer, but it must not suffer neglect on this account. Samaria conjures up feelings of animosity, but this must not deter the apostles from ministry there. Jesus himself had pointed the way (John 4). The uttermost part of the earth suggests the masses of paganism with their idolatry and immorality. These must be reached, and without the complaint that the Master confined his labors to the Jews.

In Matthew 28:19 the emphatic word is not "go" but "make disciples"—to make converts, as in Acts 14:21. The command is grounded in Jesus' universal authority (v. 18) and is implemented by his promise of unfailing presence and support (v. 20).

Communicant. A church member who participates in the sacrament of the Lord's Supper.

Communion. One of several words for the Lord's Supper (e.g., *Eucharist, Lord's Table*). Open Communion means any Christians may participate. Closed Communion is open only to those of a particular faith or belief. Occasionally *communion* is a synonym for *denomination*. (See *Lord's Table*.)

Communion of saints. The spiritual union of all Christians of all ages.

Confession of faith. A declaration of religious belief, an acknowledgment made publicly before witnesses (1 Tim. 6:12, 13). Occasionally the phrase is used to describe the creeds of the early church, but more particularly the formal statements made by the Protestant churches at the time of the Reformation and afterward.

The main Evangelical (Lutheran) confessions are the *Confession of Augsburg*, 1530, the work of Melanchthon, approved by Luther; *Articles of Smalkald*, 1573; *Formula*, 1577; and *Book of Concord*, 1580.

Reformed (Calvinist) confessions number nearly 30, of which the most important are: the *Helvetic Confession*, 1536 and 1566; the *Scottish Confession*, 1560; the *Heidelberg Catechism*, 1563; the *Canons of the Synod of Dort*, 1618; and the *Westminster Confession*, 1646, which was the work of the Westminster Assembly, a synod appointed by the Long Parliament in 1642 to revise the *Thirty-nine Articles* of the Church of England. This latter confession has been used by the Church of Scotland since 1647, and was approved by Parliament in 1648.

Confession of sins. The confession of sins is part of the confession or acknowledgment (Greek *homologia*) of the sovereignty of God. It is the admission of guilt when confronted with the revealed character and will of God. Confession is a test of repentance and belief in the gospel, as Mark 1:1–5 illustrates, and by God's grace is a condition of forgiveness (Ps. 32:5; 1 John 1:9) and of effectual prayer (1 Kings 8:33; Neh. 1:6; Ps. 66:18; Dan. 9:4; Luke 18:9–14).

The levitical law required confession (with restitution where possible) before remission of either individual or corporate trespasses (Lev. 5:5; Lev. 16:21; Num. 5:7).

Confirmation. The initiatory rite by which individuals become inducted into the church.

It is one of the seven sacraments of both the Roman Catholic and Eastern Orthodox Churches. The Roman Church teaches that it was instituted by Christ, through his disciples, for the church. Its early history is somewhat uncertain, and only gradually did it receive recognition as a sacrament. It was given a sacramental status by Peter Lombard in the twelfth century.

One of the two sacraments administered by a bishop in the Roman Catholic Church, its purpose is to make those who have been baptized in the faith strong soldiers of Jesus Christ. It is administered to children before they receive their first

Communion, generally at about the age of 12.

According to Roman Catholic theology, sanctifying grace is increased in the soul and a special sacramental grace consisting of the seven gifts of the Holy Spirit is conferred upon the recipient.

In the Lutheran Church confirmation is a rite rather than a sacrament, and the recipients offer it as a confirmation in their own hearts of those baptismal vows their parents assumed in their behalf. It is administered but once (at age 12–14) and admits the confirmands to the communion.

In the Protestant Episcopal Church it is a sacramental rite completing baptism.

Conversion. The act of conversion is represented by the Hebrew verb *sub* and the Greek *epistrepo*—both meaning "to turn" or "return" (either physically or spiritually).

Apostolic preaching insists (Acts 26:20) that people must turn from evil to God (Acts 14:15; 1 Thess. 1:9). Such an act translates them from Satan's power to God's kingdom (Acts 26:18). True conversion involves faith and repentance and results in the forgiveness of sins (Acts 3:19; 26:18).

Conviction. The process of being condemned by one's own conscience as a sinner. The concept of conviction is a major theme of Scripture, although the word is rarely used (e.g., Pss. 32; 51; Acts 2:37; Rom. 7:7–25). The agent of conviction is the Holy Spirit (John 16:7–11); and the means of conviction is either the word of God (Acts 2:37) or God's general revelation through nature and the consciousness of a sense of right and wrong (Rom. 1:18–20; 2:15).

Corban. This comes from the Hebrew word meaning "offering," and is used only once in the NT (Mark 7:11).

Jesus is referring to the despicable practice of children refusing to help needy parents on the pretense that money they might have used had already been dedicated as a gift to God. The scribal tradition of Jesus' day allowed this. Later scribal authorities modified it as they were able to see its clear misuse.

Cornerstone. In the NT the people of God are viewed as a spiritual temple in which Jesus Christ is the cornerstone.

Covenant. An agreement between people or groups that involves promises on the part of each to the other. The concept of covenant between God and his people is one of the most important theological truths of the Bible.

Covenants in the Bible.

1. The covenant with all repenting sinners to save them through Christ. This covenant is unconditional with no strings attached (see Titus 1:1–2; Heb. 13:20).

2. The covenant with Adam (Gen. 1:28; 2:15–16; 3:15–19). *Before the Fall*—that he could remain in Eden as long as he obeyed. This was conditional. *After the Fall*—that God would someday send a Savior. This was unconditional.

3. The covenant with Noah (Gen. 8:21–22) that the earth would not be destroyed by water again and that the seasons would continue until the end. This was unconditional.

4. The covenant with Abraham (Gen. 12:2–3, 7; 13:14–17; 15:5, 18; 17:8) that God would make Abraham the founder of a great nation and that God would someday give Palestine forever to Abraham's seed. This was unconditional.

5. The covenant with Moses and Israel (Exod. 19:3–8; Lev. 26; Deut. 28) that Israel could have the land at that time to enjoy if they obeyed and that Israel would forfeit all God's blessings if they disobeyed. This was conditional.

6. The covenant with David (2 Chron. 13:5; 2 Sam. 7:12–16; 23:5) that from David would come an everlasting throne, that from David would come an everlasting kingdom, and that from David would come an everlasting king. This was unconditional.

7. The covenant with the Church (Matt. 16:18; 26:28; Luke 22:20; Heb. 13:20–21) that Christ would build his Church with his own blood, that all the fury of hell would not destroy it, and that he would perfect all the members of his Church. This was unconditional.

8. The new covenant with Israel (Deut. 1:1–9; Isa. 42:6; 43:1–6; Jer. 31:31–34; Heb. 8:7–12) that God would eventually bring Israel back to himself, that God would forgive their iniquity and forget their sin, that God would use them to reach and teach Gentiles, and that God would establish them in Palestine forever. This was unconditional.

Creed. A brief, authoritative, formal statement of religious beliefs. The word *creed* comes from the Latin word *credo* meaning "I believe," the first word of both the Nicene Creed and the Apostles' Creeds.

Scholars believe that the first creed of the early church was simply, "Jesus Christ is Lord." As the church spread across the world, the need arose to formalize what the orthodox (true) church believed. In time this meant the emergence of the creeds, usually recited at baptisms and worship services.

The three earliest and most most historically significant of the church are:

1. The Nicene Creed adopted by the Council of Nicaea (A.D. 325) and revised by the Council of Constantinople (A.D. 381). The Council of Nicaea, convened by the Roman emperor Constantine the Great (ruled A.D. 306–337), rejected a heresy known as Arianism, which denied the divinity of Jesus. The Nicene Creed formally proclaimed the divinity and equality of Jesus Christ, the Son of God, in the Trinity.

Nicene Creed.

We believe in one God,
the only Son of God,
eternally begotten of the Father,
God from God, Light from Light,
true God from true God,

begotten, not made,
of one Being with the Father;
For us and for our salvation
he came down from heaven,
was incarnate of the Holy Spirit and
the Virgin Mary
and became truly human
For our sake he was crucified under
Pontius Pilate;
he suffered death and was buried.
On the third day he rose again
in accordance with the Scriptures;
he ascended into heaven
and is seated at the right hand of the
Father.
He will come again in glory
to judge the living and the dead,
and his kingdom will have no end.

We believe in the Holy Spirit, the Lord, the
giver of life,
who proceeds from the Father and the
Son,
who with the Father and the Son
is worshiped and glorified,
who has spoken through the prophets.
We believe in the one holy catholic and
apostolic church.
We acknowledge one baptism
for the forgiveness of sins.
We look for the resurrection of the dead,
and the life of the world to come.
Amen.

(From the *International Consultation on English Texts.*)

2. The Athanasian Creed, a Christian creed from the fourth century, relating especially to the doctrines of the Trinity and the bodily incarnation of Christ. This creed was originally ascribed to Athanasius (A.D. 293–373), but scholars now believe it to be the work of an unknown writer of a much later time.

Athanasian Creed.

1. Whosoever will be saved, before all things it is necessary that he hold the catholic [true Christian] faith.

2. Which faith except every one do keep whole and undefiled, without doubt he shall perish everlastingly.

3. But this is the catholic faith: That we worship one God in trinity, and trinity in unity.

4. Neither confounding the persons; nor dividing the substance.

5. For there is one person of the Father: another of the Son: another of the Holy Ghost.

6. But the Godhead of the Father, and of the Son, and of the Holy Ghost is all one: the glory equal, the majesty coeternal.

7. Such as the Father is, such is the Son, and such is the Holy Ghost.

8. The Father is uncreated: the Son is uncreated: the Holy Ghost is uncreated.

9. The Father is immeasurable: the Son is immeasurable: the Holy Ghost is immeasurable.

10. The Father is eternal: the Son eternal: the Holy Ghost eternal.

11. And yet there are not three eternals; but one eternal.

12. As also there are not three uncreated: nor three immeasurable: but one uncreated, and one immeasurable.

13. So likewise the Father is almighty: the Son is almighty: and the Holy Ghost is almighty.

14. And yet there are not three almighties: but one almighty.

15. So the Father is God: the Son is God: and the Holy Ghost is God.

16. And yet there are not three Gods; but one God.

17. The Father is Lord: the Son Lord: and the Holy Ghost Lord.

18. And yet not three Lords; but one Lord.

19. For like as we are compelled by the Christian verity to acknowledge every Person by himself to be God and Lord:

20. So are we forbidden by the catholic religion to say, there are three Gods, or three Lords.

21. The Father is made of none; neither created; nor begotten.

22. The Son is of the Father alone: not made; nor created; but begotten.

23. The Holy Ghost is of the Father and the Son: not made; neither created; nor begotten; but proceeding.

24. Thus there is one Father, not three Fathers: one Son, not three Sons: one Holy Ghost, not three Holy Ghosts.

25. And in this Trinity none is before or after another: none is greater or less than another.

26. But the whole three Persons are co-eternal together, and co-equal.

27. So that in all things, as aforesaid, the Unity in Trinity, and the Trinity in Unity is to be worshipped.

28. He therefore that will be saved, must thus think of the Trinity.

29. Furthermore, it is necessary to everlasting salvation, that we believe also rightly in the incarnation of the Lord Jesus Christ.

30. Now the right faith is, that we believe and confess, that our Lord Jesus Christ, the Son of God, is God and Man.

31. God, of the substance of the Father, begotten before the worlds: and Man, of the substance of His mother, born in the world.

32. Perfect God: perfect Man, of a reasonable soul and human flesh subsisting.

33. Equal to the Father as touching His Godhead: inferior to the Father as touching His Manhood.

34. And although He be God and Man; yet He is not two, but one Christ.

35. One, not by conversion of the Godhead into flesh; but by assumption of the Manhood into God.

36. One altogether, not by confusion of substance, but by unity of person.
37. For as the reasonable soul and flesh is one man; so God and Man is one Christ.
38. Who suffered for our salvation: descended into hades: rose again the third day from the dead.
39. He ascended into heaven: He sitteth on the right hand of God, the Father almighty:
40. From whence He shall come to judge the quick and the dead.
41. At whose coming all men must rise again with their bodies;
42. And shall give account for their own works.
43. And they that have done good shall go into life everlasting; but they that have done evil, into everlasting fire.
44. This is the catholic faith; which except a man believe truly and firmly, he cannot be saved.

3. The Apostles' Creed, the well-known creed that lies at that basis of most other religious statements of belief. Although it bears the name of the apostles, it did not originate with them, or at least not all of it. Not until the sixth century did the Apostles' Creed appear in its present form. Even so, this creed has held an important place through the centuries and is still recited in many churches around the world in each worship service.

The Apostles' Creed.
I believe in God, the Father Almighty,
　creator of heaven and earth.

I believe in Jesus Christ, his only Son, our Lord,
　who was conceived by the Holy Spirit,
　born of the Virgin Mary,
　suffered under Pontius Pilate,
　was crucified, died, and was buried;
　he descended to the dead.
　On the third day he rose again;
　he ascended into heaven,

is seated at the right hand of the Father,
　and will come again to judge the living and the dead.
I believe in the Holy Spirit,
　the holy catholic church,
　the communion of saints,
　the forgiveness of sins,
　the resurrection of the body
　and the life everlasting. Amen.
(From the *International Consultation on English Texts*.)

Day of Atonement. A full description of this ritual is given in Leviticus 16 (cf. 23:27–32; 25:9; Num. 29:7–11). It was held on the tenth of Tishri (October-November) and underlined by its elaborate symbolism the universal need for atonement. The people, the high priest and his house, and even the sanctuary shared in this need. Typically it points forward to Christ's atonement (Heb. 9).

Two main elements of the ritual are the sprinkling of blood at the mercy seat, not otherwise accessible, and the ceremony of the two male goats, one of which was sent into the wilderness as a scapegoat and the other to be slain. Together these two animals symbolized the expiation and removal of sin. (For a similar rite of removal, see Lev. 14:4–7, 49–51.)

Day of Christ. When Jesus Christ will return to claim faithful believers as his own (1 Cor. 1:8; 5:5; 2 Cor. 1:14; Philem. 1:10). A related concept, *Day of the Lord*, focuses on God's judgment against unbelievers. (See *Day of the Lord*.)

Day of the Lord. An event at the end of time when God's will and purpose for humanity and the created world will be fulfilled. Theologians don't agree on details. Some believe the Day of the Lord will be a lengthy period of time rather than a single day when God destroys heaven and earth in preparation for the eternal state of humanity. Others believe the Day of the Lord will be an instantaneous event when Christ will return to earth to claim faithful believers while consigning unbelievers to eternal damnation.

Amos 5:18–20 is probably the earliest occurrence of the phrase. He wrote that the day would be a time of darkness for any in rebellion against God, whether Jew or Gentile, a time of judgment (Isa. 13:6, 9; Jer. 46:10), as well as restoration (Isa. 14:1; Joel 2:28–32). (See *Judgment, Day of.*)

Death.　Under normal conditions, death is a universally lamented event in human experience. It is a phenomenon that cannot be regarded as wholly natural, but as a mystery calling for explanation. If human beings are truly the crown of the divine handiwork, why should they have a shorter existence than some forms of plant and animal life? If human beings are made in the image of the eternal God, they should not ever die. The answer Scripture provides is that human involvement in transgression of God's will and law has brought death as a penalty (Gen. 2:17). This does not mean that death, whether as to its timing or its manner, is directly related in each case to specific sin (Luke 13:1–4). It does mean that by reason of the very universality of sin, death is present as a necessary consequence (Rom. 5:12–14).

In the OT, death is set forth in various ways. It was sometimes described as a gathering to the fathers (2 Kings 22:20). More often it was stated as a going down into *sheol*, a cheerless abode where no work could be continued and where no communion was possible (Ps. 6:5; Eccles. 9:10).

Brighter expressions appeared with the expectation of continued fellowship with God (Ps. 73:24). An influence in this direction may well have been the inequalities in earthly existence—the suffering of the righteous and the prosperity of the wicked. Justice would be meted out in the life after death.

Because of the connection between sin and death, Christ's redemptive mission entailed his own death (Rom. 4:25; 1 Cor. 15:3; 1 Pet. 3:18). By submitting to death he triumphed over it, abolishing it and bringing life and immortality to light (2 Tim. 1:10). Believers in Christ, despite the im-

partation to them of spiritual life, are subject to physical death, for this is the last enemy to be overcome (1 Cor. 15:26). It will be banished at the return of Christ, when the Christian dead shall be raised incorruptible (1 Cor. 15:52; Phil. 3:20–21).

In view of the future bodily resurrection of the saints, death can be described as a sleep (1 Thess. 4:15).

The fear of death is overcome for Christians because they no longer have to cope with sin when they stand in the presence of God—sin that is the sting of death (1 Cor. 15:56). Christ has removed the sting by his atoning death. To depart this life is positive gain (Phil. 1:21). It brings a betterment of the condition of believers, even a sharing of the glorified presence of the Son of God (Phil. 1:23; 2 Cor. 5:8). Death has no power to effect separation from Christ (Rom. 8:38).

In the teaching of Paul, so intimate and effective is the union between Christ and their own lives that believers are regarded as having died to sin with Christ. For this reason Christians are under no obligation to serve sin any longer (Rom. 6:1–4; Col. 3:1–3). Death may also denote the moral failings of human nature (Rom. 7:24).

Unbelievers are dead because of their sins; they are unresponsive to God (Eph. 2:1; Col. 2:13). This strain of teaching occurs in John also (5:24) and Jude describes apostates as "twice dead" (Jude 12). The deadness of their natural state is matched by the deadness of their false teaching. When the wicked are finally punished, their doom of separation from God is called the *second death* (Rev. 21:8).

Death, Second.　The state of final condemnation and punishment to which unbelievers are consigned by God at the Last Judgment (Rev. 2:11; 21:8).

Deism.　Deism, as distinguished from theism, polytheism, and pantheism, designates no well-defined system or doctrine. The term denotes a certain movement of rationalistic thought that was manifested chiefly in England from the mid-seventeenth to the mid-eighteenth century.

The chief doctrines generally held by those who called themselves deists were

- The existence of a personal God, Creator and Ruler of the universe
- The obligation of divine worship
- The obligation of ethical conduct
- The necessity of repentance from sins
- Divine rewards and punishments, here, and in the life of the soul after death.

These points were stated by Lord Herbert of Cherbury (1583–1648), called "the father of Deism."

Demon. An evil spirit, or messenger and minister of the devil. In the NT demons afflicted people with mental, moral, and physical distempers. They entered into people and controlled them in demon possession (Mark 5:1–21), instigated "doctrines of demons" (1 Tim. 4:1), exercised power in the satanic world system (Eph. 6:12; cf. Dan. 10:13), energized idolatry, immorality and human wickedness (1 Cor. 10:20; Rev. 9:20–21), inspired false teachers (1 John 4:1–2), and in general assisted Satan's program of opposition to the will of God.

Depravity, Total. This theological term denotes the unmeritoriousness of humanity in the sight of God and is an inherent corruption of nature inherited from Adam.

Devil. The main title for the fallen angelic being who is the supreme enemy of God and humankind. Satan is his name, and devil is what he is—the accuser or deceiver. The term *devil* comes from a Greek word that means "false witness" or "malicious accuser."

Disciple. "Pupil" or "learner," an exact equivalent of the Greek, *mathetes.*

Disciples refers to
- Believers (Acts 11:26)
- Learners in the teachings of Jesus Christ
- Individuals committed to a sacrificial

life for Christ's sake (Luke 14:26, 27, 33)
- People who make disciples of others (Matt. 28:19)

Discipline. Discipline implies instruction and correction, training that improves, molds, strengthens, and perfects character. It is moral education by obedience through supervision and control. Usually the concept is translated *chastening, chastisement,* and *instruction.*

The discipline of believers by God our heavenly Father is illustrated by the correction made by the human father: "As a man chastens [*yasar*] his son, so the LORD your God chastens you" (Deut. 8:5; Pss. 6:1; 38:1). They are taught not to despise the chastening (*musar*) of the Almighty (Job 5:17; Prov. 3:11). The value of discipline by a human father is stressed in Proverbs 19:18.

Dispensation. Theological position that originated in the nineteenth century. Dispensationalists are those who set periods of time under which members of the human race are answerable to God for how they obeyed (or disobeyed) the divine revelations they received.

Dispensation occurs twice in the NKJV: "the dispensation of the fullness of the times" (Eph. 1:10) and "the dispensation of the grace of God" (Eph. 3:2). The KJV uses the term four times (1 Cor. 9:17; Eph. 1:10; 3:2; Col. 1:25).

They divide history into several dispensations, and they believe all history has been pointing toward the second coming of Christ, when salvation will be made complete.

They commonly identify seven dispensations:

1. Innocence: from creation to the Fall
2. Conscience: the covenant with Adam, ending with the Flood (Gen. 9)
3. Human government: from Noah to Abraham

4. Promise: from Abraham's call (Gen. 12:1) to Moses
5. Law: from the giving of the law to Moses until the death of Jesus Christ
6. Grace: from the death and resurrection of Christ to the Second Coming
7. Kingdom: the establishment of God's kingdom on earth and the 1,000-year reign of Christ over the nations

Dispersion. This is a technical term for Jews who were scattered abroad throughout the world beyond the borders of Palestine.

Doctrine. The teaching of Scripture on theological themes. Technically, *dogma* refers to an authoritative ecclesiastical affirmation, while *doctrine* refers to material used by councils and ecclesiastical hierarchies to formulate theological truth.

Dogma. Greek *dokein*, "think," "seem good." The word designates a doctrine authoritatively pronounced, especially in the Roman Catholic Church

Doxology. Greek *doxa*, "glory." The term refers to ascribing praise to the three persons of the Trinity.

Earth, New. The new physical universe that God will create at the end of time. After God created the heavens and the earth, humanity sinned and fell under God's curse (cf. Gen. 3). God promised to create a new heaven and new earth (Isa. 65:17; 66:22).

Easter. The annual festival of our Lord's resurrection. Sunday is also the weekly commemoration of that event. It is the oldest and greatest festival of the Christian church, having been observed from very early times. The importance of the feast comes from the centrality of the Resurrection in the church's faith and preaching.

The festival is preceded by the 40 days of Lent and extends for 40 days afterward. In the primitive church Easter was one of the special occasions for the baptism of catechumens and for the restoration of penitents to the Lord's Supper.

According to Bede, the name *Easter* is derived from Eastre, an Anglo-Saxon goddess whose festival was held in the spring. The original title given to the feast, in both the East and the West, was Pascha because of its association with the Jewish Passover.

Ecumenical councils. Although there have been many throughout the 2,000 years since the birth of the church, the first seven laid the foundation for all subsequent theological thinking.

The seven early church councils were

1. At Nicaea, 325
2. At Constantinople, 381
3. At Ephesus, 431
4. At Chalcedon, 451
5. At Constantinople, 553
6. At Constantinople, 680
7. At Nicaea, 787 (See *Creed.*)

Elect. An individual or group chosen by God for special favor and for the rendering of special service to him. In the OT the Hebrew people were designated as God's elect. The NT speaks of Jesus as God's chosen one (1 Pet. 2:4, 6) and of the church as God's new chosen people (Rom. 8:33; 2 John 1, 13).

Election. The gracious and free act of God in calling those who become part of his realm and special beneficiaries of love and blessings.

The Bible describes the concept of election in three ways:

1. Election refers to the selection of Israel and the church as a people for special service and privileges.

2. Election means the choice of a specific individual to some office or special service.

3. The election of individuals means they are children of God and heirs of eternal life.

Encyclical. A letter sent to local congregations, usually a communication from the pope. In recent years, this term has broadened to include the reports and actions of church conferences.

Epiphany. Greek *epiphaneia*, "manifestation." The feast of the Epiphany takes place on the twelfth day after Christmas (Jan. 6) and is of Eastern Orthodox origin. It is celebrated on the nativity of our Lord, his baptism in the Jordan, and the manifestation of his glory at Cana's wedding feast (John 2:11).

Epistle. Greek *epistole*, "letter." It is the regular word for a letter, and it is used often in Acts and the Pauline Epistles and twice in 2 Peter.

Eschatology. A theological term (from the Greek *eschatos*, "last," and *logos*, "study") that designates the study of what will happen at the end of history, particularly centering on the second coming of Christ. It is the study of last things.

Eternal life. New and redeemed existence in Jesus Christ granted by God as a gift to all believers. Eternal life refers to the quality of new existence in Christ as well as the unending character of this life.

Most references to eternal life in the NT are oriented to the future. The emphasis is upon the character of the life that will be enjoyed endlessly.

Jesus said that eternal life comes only to those who make a total commitment to him (Matt. 19:16–21; Luke 18:18–22). Paul's few references to eternal life usually have a future rather than a present orientation (Rom. 5:21; 6:22; Gal. 6:8).

John and 1 John emphasize eternal life as the present possession of Christians (John 3:36; 5:24; 1 John 5:13).

Eternal punishment. The Bible says that sin will be punished (e.g, Dan. 12:2; Matt. 10:15; John 5:28f.; Rom. 5:12ff.). Orthodox Christianity has always understood this to signify that eternal punishment is the lot of the finally impenitent.

In recent times, however, this has been disputed from two directions:

1. Some hold that eventually all will be saved. While this might, perhaps, be deduced from a few scriptural passages taken in isolation, it cannot be maintained that it accords with the general tenor of Bible teaching.

2. Others teach that human beings are no more than potentially immortal. Those who trust Jesus Christ enter into salvation (i.e., they attain immortal life). If they fail to do so, they simply die, and that is the end of them. Persons holding this view find support in passages that speak of death or destruction as the lot of the wicked.

Eternity. Infinite or unlimited time; time without beginning or end.

Ethics. The science of conduct. It is a systematic attempt to consider the purposeful actions of humanity, to determine their rightness or wrongness, their tendency to good or evil. The variety of terms in ethical usage testifies to the complexity of the problem of determining in the nature of morality. Such terms include *good, right, duty, ought, goodwill, virtue,* and *motive*.

Evangelical. *Eugangelion*, "evangel" or "good news." This was originally a technical term that came into use at the time of the reformation. *Evangelical* was used both to identify Protestants and to signify two important doctrines: (1) justification by faith and (2) the authority of the Scriptures.

Eventually the term *evangelical* narrowed and began to refer to whose who held to these cardinal doctrines and emphasized personal conversion and a rigorous moral life along with a zeal for spreading the Christian faith.

Today the important issues between evangelicals and others is in the area of biblical authority. Evangelicals insist that Scripture is the Word of God and infallible in its original form. With this comes the other doctrines of the evangelical faith:

- The Trinity
- The deity of Christ
- The personality of the Holy Spirit
- The substitutionary suffering and death of Jesus Christ as an atonement for his people
- Jesus' resurrection from the grave and ascension into heaven
- The second coming of Jesus Christ
- The resurrection and judgment of all people
- The belief in heaven and hell

Everlasting. That which lasts forever and is eternal. The Greek word translated as *everlasting* in the NT literally means "age-lasting," as contrasted with that which is brief or temporal.

Faith. A belief in or confident attitude toward God that involves commitment to his will for one's life.

Fall. The Fall refers to the disobedience and sin of Adam and Eve that caused them to lose the state of innocence in which they had been created. This event plunged them and all of humanity into a state of sin and corruption. The account of the Fall occurs in Genesis 3.

Fast, Fasting. The word means going without food or drink voluntarily, generally for religious purposes.

Fasting can take place in times of grief. A seven-day fast occurred when the bones of Saul and his sons were buried (1 Sam. 31:13). While the Jews were in exile they fasted on the fifth and seventh months, marking the date the siege of Jerusalem began and the date when Jerusalem fell to the Babylonians (Zech. 7:5).

Fasting was done by individuals in times of personal stress. David fasted upon hearing that Saul and Jonathan were dead (2 Sam. 1:12). Nehemiah fasted and prayed when he learned that Jerusalem had remained in ruins since its destruction (Neh. 1:4). The Persian king Darius fasted all night after placing Daniel in the lion's den (Dan. 6:18).

The Law of Moses required fasting only on one occasion—the annual Day of Atonement. This resulted in referring to the day as "the day of fasting" (Jer. 36:6) and "the fast" (Acts 27:9).

Several specific examples of fasts appear in the OT. Moses did not eat bread or drink water during the 40 days and 40 nights he spent on Mount Sinai receiving the law (Exod. 34:28). When the Benjamites defeated the other Israelites (Judg. 20:26), they fasted. Samuel gathered the people of Mizpah together during the war with the Philistines for a time of prayer and fasting (1 Sam. 7:6).

Jehoshaphat called for a fast when the Moabites and Ammonites opposed Israel (2 Chron. 20:3). After Jonah preached at Nineveh, by royal order the people fasted and put on sackcloth (Jon. 3:5).

In the NT, Anna "served God with fastings and prayers night and day" (Luke 2:37). John the Baptist taught his disciples to fast (Mark 2:18). Jesus fasted 40 days and 40 nights before his temptation (Matt. 4:2). Cornelius was fasting when he had a vision (Acts 10:30). The church in Antioch fasted (Acts 13:2–3) before sending Paul and Barnabas on their first missionary journey.

The Bible particularly links fasting with self-humiliation (or repentance as in Ps. 35:13). It is often mentioned with prayer (Matt. 17:21; Acts 13:3), especially of those pursuing Christian work or the seeking of God (cf. Acts 10:30).

The undertaking of a definite commission for God (Ezra 8:23; Acts 13:3) is an occasion for fasting. This is especially shown in the case of Jesus, whose baptism is followed at once by the 40 days of fasting in the wilderness (Matt. 4:2; cf. Paul's withdrawal to Arabia). In this connection, the fast was also a time of temptation and therefore of testing (Matt. 4:1–3ff.) to strengthen him in his future ministry.

Fasts

Moses' 40-day fast as he prayed concerning Israel's sin	Deut. 9:9, 18, 25–29; 10:10
David's fast as he lamented Saul's and Jonathan's deaths	2 Sam. 1:12
David's fast as he lamented Abner's death	2 Sam. 3:35
Daniel's fast as he lamented the vision God had given him	Dan. 10:3–14
Elijah's 40-day fast after he fled from Jezebel	1 Kings 19:7–18
Ahab's fast as he humbled himself before God	1 Kings 21:27–29
Darius's fast as he worried over Daniel's fate	Dan. 6:18–24
Daniel's fast as he read Jeremiah's prophecy and prayed for Judah's sins	Dan. 9:1–19
Daniel's fast as he prayed over a vision God had given him	Dan. 10:3–13
Esther's fast as she sorrowed over Haman's wicked plot to destroy her people	Esther 4:13–16
Ezra's fast as he wept over the sins of the returning remnant	Ezra 8:21
Nehemiah's fast as he wept over the broken-down walls of Jerusalem	Neh. 1:4—2:10
The Ninevites' fast after they heard the preaching of Jonah	Jon. 3
Anna's fast as she awaited the Messiah	Luke 2:37
Jesus' 40-day fast before the temptation	Matt. 4:1–11
John's disciples' fast	Matt. 9:14–15
The elders' fast in Antioch, prior to sending out Paul and Barnabas	Acts 13:1–5
Cornelius's fast as he sought out God's plan of salvation	Acts 10:30
Paul's three-day fast after his experience on the Damascus Road	Acts 9:9
Paul's 14-day fast while on a sinking ship	Acts 27:33–34

Feet-washing. Feet-washing ranked high among Eastern hospitality rites. Open sandals on hot, dusty, or muddy roads made feet-washing on arrival at the tent or house of a friend a necessity. A slave, or the guest himself, performed the act (Gen. 18:4; 19:2; 24:32; 43:24; Judg. 19:21). If the host wished to honor his guest and demonstrate affection and humility, he could personally perform the act (1 Sam. 25:41). Thus the failure of Simon (Luke 7:36–50) even to provide facilities for Christ to wash his own feet marks not only pride and lack of respect for him, but also discourtesy and unfriendliness.

Despite its place in rites of hospitality, feet-washing never became the ritual observance in the Jewish religion that hand-washing did. Only priests, in preparation for approach to God, observed such a rite (Exod. 30:18–21; 40:30–32).

The feet-washing in John 13:1–17 invested the hospitality rite with deeper meaning. The utensils were there, the servants were absent, but no disciple would humble himself to perform the act. Quarreling, arising from pride, had created tension (Luke 22:24). Christ's action, in addition to breaking their pride and antagonism, taught that the mark of greatness is service, that frequent spiritual cleansing is needed, and that service must be humbly received from Christ before it can be given to him.

The practice of washing the feet is observed regularly by some Protestant denominations as a sacrament and practiced on special occasions by others.

Foreknowledge. In theological language the word *foreknowledge* designates the prescience or foresight of God concerning the entire course of future events. The constant representation in Scripture is that God knows all things, actual or possible, past, present, and future. Whereas human knowledge is very limited and is derived from observation and from a process of reasoning, divine foreknowledge is unlimited and is intuitive, innate, and immediate.

Genuflection. The act of bending one knee in worship when entering the sanctuary or in approaching the altar as an act of reverence.

Glory. Beauty, power, or honor—a quality of God's character that emphasizes greatness and authority. The word is used in three senses in the Bible:

1. God's moral beauty and perfection of character.
2. God's moral beauty and perfection as a visible presence. While God's glory is not a substance, at times God does reveal his perfection to humanity in visible ways. Such a display of the presence of God is often seen as fire or dazzling light, but sometimes as an act of power.
3. Praise. At times God's glory may mean the honor and audible praise his creatures give to him.

Glossolalia. Speaking in tongues as a manifestation of the baptism with the Holy Spirit. This phenomenon is described in Acts 2 and occurred on the day of Pentecost. (See also Acts 19:1–6.)

Gnosticism. A system of false teachings that existed during the early centuries of Christianity. Its name came from the Greek word for knowledge, *gnosis*. Gnostics believed that special, esoteric knowledge was the way to salvation. Gnosticism was condemned as false and heretical by several writers of the NT.

This knowledge could be possessed only by the section of humanity that was "pneumatic," or spiritual. They alone were inevitably led back to the realm of light of the Supreme God.

There was a second class of humanity, those who were only "psychic" and could not get beyond faith. The prophets and other good Hebrews belonged to this class, but they must be eternally in a sphere much inferior to that occupied by those who had *gnosis*.

The third class represented the overwhelming mass of humankind. They were merely "hylic" (i.e., subject to matter), and their case was utterly hopeless because they were in endless bondage to Satan and their own lusts. Their end was to be completely destroyed.

One of the worst features of Gnosticism was elevating a limited number to a specially privileged class and consigning the vast majority of people to unredeemable destruction. This was totally contrary to the teachings of Christianity.

By the beginning of the third century nearly all the more intellectual Christian congregations in the Roman Empire were markedly affected by it. Its errors are clearly referred to in the NT (e.g., 1 John 2:22; 4:2–3, where reference is made to those who denied that Christ had come in the flesh). The system was eclectic, and its materials were drawn from many quarters such as the mythologies of Greece, Egypt, Persia, and India. Many of its leading ideas had existed before the Christian era, but its votaries felt that in the Christian religion were valuable elements that could be worked into their system.

Godhead. An Old English term that is a synonym for God, with an emphasis on that which makes the triune God essentially one (Rom. 1:20; Col. 2:9). Paul used the term to show the contrast between God's sinless nature and corrupt human character.

In Romans 1:20 Paul used *Godhead* to describe what mortals sought to see in nature as a result of God's creative handiwork—"His eternal power and Godhead," or Deity.

Gospel. The Greek word translated as *gospel* means a "reward for bringing good news" or simply "good news." This refers specifically to the good news of the death, burial, and resurrection of Jesus Christ as preached by the disciples. (See 1 Cor. 15:1–4.) The offer of the gospel is forgiveness and freedom from sin on the basis of faith in Jesus Christ. (See Eph. 2:8–9.)

Grace. God's kindness and graciousness toward humanity, shown without regard to the worth or merit of those who receive it and in spite of what they deserve. This denotes God's undeserved kindness toward us by which we receive a new birth (cf. John 3:3), become children of God by being adopted, and pray to God as our Father (Rom. 8:14–16). We become members of Christ's body (1 Cor. 12:27) and partakers of the divine nature (2 Pet. 1:4).

Heaven.

1. As used in a physical sense, heaven is the expanse over the earth (Gen. 1:8). The Tower of Babel reached upward to heaven (Gen. 11:4). God is the possessor of heaven (Gen. 14:19). Heaven is the location of the stars (Gen. 1:14; 26:4) as well as the source of dew (Gen. 27:28).
2. Heaven is the dwelling place of God (Gen. 28:17; Rev. 12:7–12). It is the source of the New Jerusalem (Rev. 21:2, 10).
3. Heaven is used as a substitute for the name of God (Luke 15:8–21; John 3:27). The kingdom of God and the kingdom of heaven are often spoken of interchangeably (Matt. 4:17; Mark 1:15).

Heavenly City. The city prepared and built by God for those who are faithful to him (Heb. 11:10, 16), and known as the heavenly Jerusalem (Heb. 12:22).

Heavens, New. When used with *new earth* the term refers to the perfected state of the created universe and the final dwelling place of the righteous. The phrase is found in Isaiah 66:22, 2 Peter 3:13, and in a modified form in Revelation 21:1.

Heilsgeschichte. A German theological term meaning "the history of salvation," which describes the Bible as essentially such a history. While the Bible says much about other matters, these are merely incidental to its single purpose of unfolding the story of redemption. This system traces in history and doctrine the development of the divine purpose in the salvation of the human race.

Hell. Place of eternal punishment for the unrighteous. The NKJV and KJV use this word to translate *sheol* (Hebrew) and *"hades"* (Greek) for the abode of the dead.

Hell as a place of punishment translates *Gehenna*, the Greek form of the Hebrew word that means the "vale of Hinnom"—a valley south of Jerusalem. In this valley the Canaanites worshiped Baal and the fire god Molech by sacrificing their children in fire that burned continuously. Ahaz and Manasseh, kings of Judah, were guilty of this terrible, idolatrous practice (2 Chron. 28:3; 33:6).

The word *Gehenna* occurs 12 times in the NT. Each time it is translated *hell*. With the exception of James 3:6, it is used only by Jesus (Matt. 5:22, 29–30; 10:28; 18:9; 23:15, 33; Mark 9:43, 45, 47; Luke 12:5). In Matthew 5:22; 18:9; and Mark 9:47, it is used with *fire* as *hell fire*.

In Mark 9:46, 48, hell is described as a place where "their worm does not die and the fire is not quenched." Jesus spoke of outer darkness and a furnace of fire, where there will be wailing, weeping, and gnashing of teeth (Matt. 8:12; 13:42, 50; 22:13; 24:51; 25:30; Luke 13:28). Obviously this picture is drawn from the valley of Gehenna.

Hope. The sense of expectation of good and something for which we wait. In the Bible, hope stands for the act of hoping (Rom. 4:18; 1 Cor. 9:10) and the thing hoped for (Col. 1:5; 1 Pet. 1:3).

Hope arises not from human desires or wishes but from God, who is himself the believers' hope: "My hope is in You" (Ps. 39:7). Genuine hope is not wishful thinking, but a firm assurance about things that are unseen and still in the future (Rom. 8:24–25; Heb. 11:1). Because of salvation in Christ and because God is the source of all our expectations, Paul refers to him as the God of hope (Rom. 15:13).

Immaculate Conception. Roman Catholic dogma (official teaching) that the Virgin Mary was preserved from all stain or original sin.

Immanence. The counterpart of transcendence. Theologically, the former connotes an indwelling of God within the world and its processes.

Pantheism discovers God in all things throughout the natural order and is a familiar form of the theology of immanence. Pantheism identifies God with the universe; it holds that God is not separate from the world but that he and his creation are one and the same.

The biblical viewpoint combines immanence and transcendence and says that God is immanent (i.e., everywhere present as in Ps. 139) and that the order of nature unmistakably reveals his handiwork, eternal power, and sovereignty (Ps. 19; Rom. 1:20). God is transcendent in being and majesty and is infinitely above all that is human and temporal. (See *Transcendence*.)

Immortality. Exemption from death; the state of living forever. In the Bible, the word *immortality* refers primarily to the spirit, but is also used of the resurrected or transformed body.

The Greeks had no concept of a bodily resurrection. Plato taught that spirit is everything and that the body (matter) is nothing. He believed the spirit lives on but the body returns to dust. In 1 Corinthians 15, Paul answered this concept and wrote of immortality and the resurrection in his sermon to the Greek philosophers on Mars Hill.

The biblical concept of immortality is rooted in humanity's being created in God's image and likeness (Gen. 1:26–27).

God is spirit. The reference in Genesis is not to bodily form but to spiritual nature. As the eternal, God is also immortal (1 Tim. 6:16). "And the LORD God formed man of the dust of the ground, and breathed into his nostrils the breath of life; and man became a living being" (Gen. 2:7). Only of a human being does the Bible say he "became a living being." God made members of the human race to live forever, physically and spiritually, and they would have, except for the entrance of sin.

Ancient Hebrews believed in the survival of the spirit, although they thought of the afterlife as a shadowy existence. The idea of a bodily resurrection gradually evolved (Job 19:26; Ps. 16:8–11; Dan. 12:2).

The tone of a hope of immortality pervades the entire OT, including the faith of Abraham, Isaac, and Jacob, because of God's promises (Heb. 11:13). Abraham's near-sacrifice of Isaac (Gen. 22) is interpreted in Hebrews 11:17–19 as an act that involved faith in a resurrection.

In Jesus' time the Sadducees denied a bodily resurrection, while the Pharisees believed in it.

In Jesus Christ we have God's full revelation about immortality of both body and spirit (John 11:23–26; Rom. 2:6–7; 2 Tim. 1:10). His bodily resurrection is proof of our immortality (1 Cor. 15:12–16).

The nature of the resurrection body is not clear. Some see it as like that of Jesus—a real body, but not subject to time, space, or density (Luke 24:31, 36–43; John 20:19–20, 26–29). But the matter should not be pressed too far. As our present bodies are fitted to conditions on earth, so will our resurrection bodies be suitable for conditions in heaven (1 Cor. 15:38–44).

Although death is an enemy (1 Cor. 15:26), Paul thought of death as necessary for believers to receive immortal, incorruptible bodies (1 Cor. 15:50–57).

In 1 Thessalonians 4:14–17 Paul taught that "the dead in Christ will rise first. Then we who are alive and remain shall be caught up together with them in the clouds to meet the Lord in the air. And thus we shall always be with the Lord."

Jesus spoke of "the resurrection of life" and "the resurrection of condemnation" (John 5:29). We can assume that both believers and unbelievers will receive resurrection bodies—but their eternal destiny will be different (Dan. 12:2).

Imputation. An accounting term used to ascribe the theological credit or debit to one another. Theologically this occurs in these ways:

1. Solidarity in sin means that the guilt and punishment of Adam are also ours.
2. The Atonement entails the laying of the cost of our sin to Christ's account.
3. *Justification* is the theological word for reckoning the righteousness of Christ and its benefits to believers.

Incarnation. The triune God, without in any way ceasing to be God, revealed himself to humanity for our salvation by coming among us as a human being. This person is Jesus, held to be the incarnate Son of God. Taken into God's eternity and glorified at the Resurrection, the Incarnate One remains forever the ultimate focus for God and human encounters. Jesus Christ as God incarnate mediates God to us but also in his perfect humanity represents us to God. (See *Kenosis*.)

Indulgence. In the Roman Catholic church, a remission of the temporal punishment due to sins, the guilt of which has already been remitted. This indulgence is granted only upon the showing of penance.

Inerrant. Without fault and totally truthful; a term applied to explain the infallibility of the Bible.

Infinity. A theological term implying that God is not bound by time and space (Col. 1:15; Heb. 1:3). God does experience everything that happens within the universe he has created.

Intermediate state. Realm or condition in which souls exist between the death of the body and the resurrection. That such a state is a reality is acknowledged by practically all branches of the Christian church. Differences of opinion regarding it have to do primarily with the nature of the state.

Differing positions say that

• Souls are in purgatory, whether or not the souls reform and repent.
• Souls are asleep—unaware of anything.
• Souls are conscious and have already entered into their reward.

The Bible has little to say about the intermediate state, and focuses attention on the return of Jesus and the new era that follows.

Generally, the church has affirmed the passages that teach a state of conscious existence for both the righteous and the wicked. For the righteous it is a time of rest and of blessedness and joy. And for the wicked it involves suffering. The parable of the rich man and Lazarus represents Lazarus as conscious and blessed in Abraham's bosom, while the rich man is in torment (Luke 16:19–31). While on the cross Christ promised the penitent thief, "Today you will be with Me in Paradise" (Luke 23:43). And John says: "'Blessed are the dead who die in the Lord from now on.' 'Yes,' says the Spirit, 'that they may rest from their labors, and their works follow them'" (Rev. 14:13). (See also 2 Cor. 5:8; Phil. 1:23; these verses imply that after the death of the body the saints live gloriously in the presence of God.)

Invocation. A religious act of calling upon God. The opening of many types of services is marked by a prayer of invocation in which God is called upon to bless and guide.

Jerusalem, New. The Holy City described in Revelation 21—22. It is God's perfect and eternal order of the future.

The New Jerusalem and the new Garden of Eden (symbols of righteousness, peace, and prosperity) are the dwelling place of God, Christ, and the church. John saw no temple in the New Jerusalem, "for the Lord God Almighty and the Lamb are its temple" (Rev. 21:22).

Revelation 14:8 draws a graphic contrast between the harlot city called Babylon the Great (see also 16:19; 17:1—18:24), the earthly and temporal city of humanity, and the New Jerusalem (Rev. 21:2—22:5), the heavenly and eternal city of God. Revelation 21:10 identifies the holy Jerusalem as the church, "the bride, the Lamb's wife" (Rev. 21:9).

Judgment Day. The act of judging on the last Judgment Day will occur when God gives both rewards and punishment. (See *Day of the Lord*.)

Kenosis. A theological term used in connection with the dual nature of Jesus as fully human and fully divine. It is taken from the Greek word *kenoo*, which means "to empty" (Phil. 2:7). The NASB translates this passage, "He emptied Himself," but the KJV and NKJV express it, "He made Himself of no reputation."

The Bible teaches that our Savior was both fully divine and completely human during his earthly life. But nowhere does Scripture explain exactly how Jesus' two natures coexisted. Theologians have struggled to explain this mystery. In the 1800s scholars formulated the kenosis theory that God's divine Son laid aside or "emptied himself" of divine attributes when he became human.

This theory of Jesus' incarnation has been rejected by many scholars because kenosis theology teaches that when the Son of God became a human being, he stopped being God. Or another way of stating it is that he was first God, then became a man, and after the Resurrection returned to being God.

Paul explained the emptying of Jesus in the next phrase: "Taking the form of a bondservant, and coming in the likeness of men" (Phil. 2:7). Opponents of kenosis say that Paul does not tell us that Jesus stopped being God or that he gave up any divine attributes. Although John 17:5 shows that Jesus' glory as God's eternal Son was veiled during his incarnation, they take the phrase "He emptied himself" figuratively as a reference to Christ's humility and willingness to partake "of flesh and blood" (Heb. 2:14). While not ceasing to be God's Son, Christ also became God's servant.

Kerygma. Transliteration of a Greek word that means "proclamation" or "preaching." It refers to the proclamation or preaching of the message of the gospel.

Kingdom of God *or* Kingdom of Heaven. God's rule of grace in the world, a future period foretold by OT prophets. The realm of God is the experience of blessedness like that of the Garden of Eden, where evil is fully overcome and those who live in this realm know only happiness, peace, and joy. This was the main expectation of the OT prophets about the future.

John the Baptist astonished his hearers when he announced that this expected and hoped-for kingdom was at hand—in the person of Jesus (Matt. 3:2). Jesus repeated this message (Matt. 4:17; Mark 1:15) and went further by announcing that the kingdom was already present in his ministry: "If I cast out demons by the Spirit of God, surely the kingdom of God has come upon you" (Matt. 12:28). Jesus was the full embodiment of the kingdom.

The entire ministry of Jesus is understood in relation to this important declaration of the presence of the kingdom. His ethical teachings cannot be understood apart from the announcement of the kingdom. The perfection to which they point makes no sense apart from the present experience of the kingdom. Participation in the new reality of the kingdom involves being followers of Jesus in a call to the highest righteousness (Matt. 5:20).

The acts and deeds of Jesus make sense only in the large context of proclaiming the kingdom. When John the Baptist asked if he was "the Coming One" (i.e., the Messiah), Jesus answered by recounting some of his deeds of healing (Matt. 11:5). The reference in these words to the expectation of a Messiah (especially of Isa. 29:18–19; 35:5–6; 61:1) could not have been missed by John. At the synagogue in Nazareth, Jesus read a passage from Isaiah 61 about the coming messianic age and then made the astonishing announcement, "Today this Scripture is fulfilled in your hearing" (Luke 4:21).

All that Jesus did is related to the dawning of the kingdom of God through his ministry. His healings were manifestations of the presence of the kingdom. In these deeds there was a direct confrontation between God and the forces of evil. Summarizing his ministry, Jesus declared, "I saw Satan fall like lightning from heaven" (Luke 10:18). Satan and evil are in retreat now that the kingdom has made its entrance into human history. This is an anticipation of the final age of perfection that will be realized at Christ's return.

Kiss of peace *or* Holy kiss. A religious greeting or ceremony, usually during the Eucharist (Lord's Supper).

Lent. The 40 days of fasting immediately preceding Easter, beginning on Ash Wednesday and concluding on Easter Eve. The 40 days do not include the six Sundays, which are feast days.

Likely in the early centuries the fast was one of forty hours, as part of the preparation of candidates for Easter baptism. Not until much later (ca. seventh century) did the 40-day period become universally recognized in honor of our Lord's fast in the wilderness (Matt. 4:2).

As a time of abstinence, almsgiving, and acts of devotion, Lent is intended to serve as preparation for the Easter festival. The name is derived from the Old English *lenckten* meaning "the spring."

Limbo. In Roman Catholic theology the term is based on the Latin *limbus*, from the Teutonic *hem* or *border*, and refers to the abode after death of souls excluded from heaven but not worthy of punishment in hell.

The limbo of infants is the permanent place of "natural happiness" for unbaptized children and the mentally incompetent dying "without grievous personal guilt."

Litany. A form of prayer made up of a series of petitions and offered by the worship leader with congregational responses.

Liturgy. While the word literally means the "work of the people" and applies to worship, usually it refers to a prescribed form of worship used in certain churches.

In ecclesiastical usage, the word is used (1) in a general sense with reference to any of the prescribed services and offices of the church's worship and (2) in a specific sense with reference to the rituals used at the celebration of the holy Communion, the eucharistic office being commonly referred to as the liturgy.

The earliest liturgical forms of this latter kind are in the Didache (ca. A.D. 100), which prescribes acts of thanksgiving for the cup and the bread, but also gives liberty to the "prophets" to use what words they like in setting apart the elements.

The account of the Lord's Supper given by Justin Martyr (mid-second century) also contains liturgical teaching, but indicates that a place was still found for extemporaneous prayers and thanksgivings. Probably by the beginning of the third century a set form of prayer was used for the consecration of the bread and wine, though the form varied from place to place.

Liturgies arising from the Reformation in the sixteenth century drew freely upon the ancient forms while introducing drastic and far-reaching changes. The principal schools of liturgical revision were those represented by Luther in Germany, Zwingli at Zurich, Bucer at Strasbourg, Calvin at Geneva, and Cranmer in England.

Logia. A term applied to collections of sayings credited to Jesus and used as source materials by the gospel writers in the writing of their gospels. The Greek word *logia* literally means "oracles," "divine responses," "utterances," or "sayings." Some scholars see many similarities between the gospel of Matthew and the gospel of Luke and believe an earlier source existed but is now lost, upon which both Matthew and Luke drew in writing their gospels. This speculative source they call the Logia.

When the apostle Paul spoke of "the words of the Lord Jesus" (Acts 20:35), he quoted a saying of Jesus not found in any of the four gospels. He may have been citing a quotation from the Logia: "It is more blessed to give than to receive." An example of this type of literature, containing quotations from Jesus not found in the canonical Gospels, is the gospel of Thomas, an early apocryphal gospel.

Logos. A Greek term used to refer to Christ, the Word of God (see John 1).

Lord. The usual Greek word for Lord, *kyrios,* is used in a wide variety of ways:
- Polite address to a superior
- Subjection to the master of a house
- Acknowledgment of the head of a family, or the supreme authority in a state
- Recognition of God (or Christ's) supremacy

In the first century there were "many lords" (1 Cor. 8:5), the title being used for each of the cult deities as well as for the Roman emperors. As applied to God in the OT, *Lord* denotes the active exercise of his power over the world as Creator and Ruler. *Lord* expresses not the metaphysical nature of deity, but his sovereign authority.

In the NT, *Lord* is applied to Jesus in three ways: as teacher, as rabbi, and as master by his disciples. At other times, he is spoken of as *my* or *our Lord* in the sense of the exalted Messiah reigning on his throne at the right hand of Yahweh (Jehovah).

Lord's Supper. Many of Jesus' actions and words at the Last Supper, such as breaking the bread, were part of the prescribed passover ritual. But when Jesus said, "This is My body" and "This is My blood" (Mark 14:22–24) while distributing the bread and the cup, he did something totally new. These words, intended for our blessing, have been the focus of sharp disagreement among Christians for centuries. In what sense are the bread and wine Christ's body and blood? What should the Lord's Supper mean to us? The answers to these questions are often grouped into four categories, although there are variations within these four broad views.

1. Transubstantiation.

This is the official position of the Roman Catholic church (especially before the Second Vatican Council of 1962–1965). This view holds that the bread and wine literally and actually become the body and blood of Christ when the words of institution are spoken by the priest. While the physical properties (taste, appearance, etc.) of the bread and wine do not change, the inner reality of these elements undergoes a spiritual change.

This view may help to foster a serious attitude toward the Eucharist, but it ignores the figurative nature of Jesus' language. Jesus could not have been holding his actual body and blood in his hands. He probably meant, "This bread represents My body" and "This wine represents My blood." Jesus often used figurative language (Luke 8:11, 21), just as a person does today when showing someone a photograph and saying, "This is my father."

2. Consubstantiation.

Martin Luther developed this view, and it is the official position of Lutherans today. Christ's body and blood are truly present "in, with, and under" the bread and wine. The elements do not literally change into Christ's body and blood. But in the same way that heat is present in a piece of hot iron, so Christ is present in the elements. Lutherans ascribe to Jesus' words the meaning, "This accompanies My body."

Consubstantiation encourages the recipients of the Eucharist to grasp that Jesus Christ is present at the Supper, but it misses the figurative use of Jesus' words.

3. Memorial (or Symbolic).

The memorial (or symbolic) understanding comes from the Swiss Reformer, Ulrich Zwingli, who denied the bodily presence of Christ while saying he is spiritually present in the faith of believers. For Zwingli, the Lord's Supper was mainly a symbol, a memorial of the death of Christ, and believers pledge their unity with one another and their loyalty to Christ. This is the viewpoint held by most Baptist and independent churches. This position tends to place more emphasis on what the Christian does and promises in the Supper than on what God does.

4. Spiritual (or Dynamic).

John Calvin took an intermediate position. Instead of the physical and local, he taught the spiritual presence of Christ in the Supper. In distinction from Zwingli, Calvin stressed the deeper significance of the sacrament, calling it a seal and pledge of what God does for believers rather than a pledge of their consecration to God. The virtues and effects of the sacrifice of Christ on the cross are present and actually conveyed to believers by the power of the Holy Spirit. This is the position of Presbyterians and Reformed churches.

Critics say that Calvin sometimes placed more emphasis on Jesus' glorified flesh and blood than the Scriptures teach. Yet this position helps to explain why the Eucharist is so important for Christians to observe, and why it is such a serious offense to misuse it. His view also corresponds well with those Scriptures that speak of God's nourishing and empowering work in his people (Eph. 3:14–21; Col. 2:6–10, 19).

Biblical References.

In 1 Corinthians 10:16, Paul rebuked the Corinthians for their involvement with idolatry. He called the cup "the communion of the blood of Christ" and the bread "the communion of the body of Christ." The Greek word for communion means

"fellowship," "participating and sharing." From the context it appears that Paul is saying that when Christians partake of the cup and bread, they are participating in the benefits of Christ's death (his blood) and resurrection life (his glorified body). The most important of these benefits are the assurance of sins forgiven through Christ's blood and the assurance of Christ's presence and power through his body.

The one body (the universal church) in 1 Cor. 10:17 connects with the body of Christ (v. 16) in the sense that the entire church of Christ is organically related to the living, glorified human body of Christ now in heaven. The one (loaf of) bread (v. 17), representing Jesus as the Bread of Life, is eaten by all believers at the Supper, symbolizing their unity and common participation in the one body of Christ (see John 6:35).

The great discourse of Jesus on the Bread of Life (John 6:25–68), while not intended to be a direct theological explanation of the Lord's Supper, helps to explain how receiving the sacrament can be one way in which Christians "feed" on the Lord (John 6:55–57). Other important ways are by prayer and the hearing of God's Word through the Scriptures.

In 1 Corinthians 11:17–34 Paul rebuked the Corinthians for their pride and greed during the meal that accompanied the Eucharist (vv. 17–22). Then (vv. 23–25) he described the institution of the Lord's Supper and emphasized the need for Christians to partake in a worthy manner. Many of them who had not been doing so were weak and sick, and many had even died as a result of God's judgment (vv. 27–34).

Why does Paul use such strong language when speaking of the abuse of the Lord's Supper? The Corinthians were not properly recognizing the Lord's body. Wealthy Corinthians shamed their poorer brothers and sisters by their selfish eating practices (vv. 21–22) and were not grasping the true nature of the church as Christ's body in which all distinctions of social class and race were blotted out (cf. Gal. 3:28).

Meaning for Today.

Three concepts can help us see the value of the Lord's Supper for today.

1. The Lord's Supper is a time of remembrance and focuses on the past. Jesus said, "Do this in remembrance of Me" (Luke 22:19; 1 Cor. 11:24–25). This is not so much our dwelling on the agonies of the Crucifixion as it is our remembering the marvelous life and ministry of our Savior. The sacrament is an occasion for expressing our deepest praise and appreciation for all Jesus Christ has done for us.

One step in the Jewish Passover meal was to proclaim the Hebrews' deliverance from Egyptian bondage (see Exod. 12:26–27). In the Supper, Christians proclaim deliverance from sin through the death of Christ, our Passover (cf. 1 Cor. 5:7; 11:26).

2. The Supper is a time of refreshing and communion. This focuses on the present. As we participate in the benefits of Jesus' death and resurrection life (Rom. 5:10; 1 Cor. 10:16), we are actually being nourished and empowered from the risen Christ through the Spirit.

John Wesley believed in this strengthening. On the average, he received Communion every four or five days throughout his long and fruitful ministerial career. It is not that God cannot empower us without the Lord's Supper, but that he instituted the Supper for us, even as he has designated prayer and the hearing of Scripture as means of communicating grace. While the Bible does not tell us how often to observe the Eucharist, Wesley's guideline—"as often as you can"—deserves our serious consideration.

3. The Supper is a time of recommitment and anticipation. This focuses on the future. We are to examine (literally, prove or test) ourselves and partake in a worthy manner (1 Cor. 11:28–29). In so doing, we renew our dedication to Christ and his people, in hopeful anticipation "till He comes" (1 Cor. 11:26). After Christ's return we shall partake with him—in his physical presence—in the kingdom (Matt. 26:29).

Manifestation. A term used several ways in the NT:

1. It indicates the eternal purpose of God, hidden from human gaze down the ages, but now revealed in Jesus Christ. Part of his saving work of redeeming fallen humanity is the revelation of the Father. In a general way this had been done through nature (Rom. 1:19–20), but in Jesus Christ revelation becomes personal (Heb. 1:1–2).
2. The appearances of the risen Christ to his own are called manifestations (John 21:1, NASB).
3. Jesus Christ continues to disclose himself through the life and service of his followers (2 Cor. 2:14; 4:10).
4. At the return of Christ, the glorified saints will be manifested together with him (1 John 3:2).
5. At the judgment seat of Christ the motivations of the redeemed will be made known (1 Cor. 4:5; 2 Cor. 5:10; cf. Mark 4:22).

Mansions. The translation of a Greek word in John 14:2 that means "rooms." Jesus promised many individual rooms, or dwelling places, within the one house. In heaven believers will experience the intimacy of dwelling with the Father and all other believers

Maranatha. "Our Lord, come!" or "Our Lord comes." An Aramaic expression written by Paul as he concluded his first letter to the Corinthians (1 Cor. 16:22, KJV).

Three interpretations are possible:
• Prayer for the Lord's return
• Confession of the Lord having come
• Assertion of the Lord's presence (as in the Lord's Supper)

Paul most certainly meant to use *maranatha* in the first sense. However, the word appears in the Didache at the end of a series of eucharistic prayers.

Martyr. A witness. Because the early Christians frequently suffered for their faith, the word *martyr* came to mean "those who suffered or died because of their witness to Jesus Christ." Paul calls Stephen a martyr (Acts 22:20). Revelation mentions "the martyrs of Jesus" (17:6).

Martyrs in the Bible include the following:

• Isaiah, traditionally said to have been sawed asunder by Manasseh (Heb. 11:37)

• Stephen, the church's first martyr, stoned by the Jews (Acts 7:59)

• James, the first of the 12 apostles to be martyred (Acts 12:1–2)

• Paul, believed to have been beheaded by Emperor Nero (2 Tim. 4:6)

• Peter, believed to have been crucified upside down by Nero (2 Pet. 1:14)

• Antipas, martyred in the city of Pergamos (Rev. 2:13)

• Two tribulational witnesses martyred by the Beast (Rev. 11:7)

Mass. The central worship service in the Roman Catholic church, which focuses on celebrating the holy Eucharist (the Lord's Supper).

Metempsychosis. This is the theory that souls are reincarnated many times, an essential part of Buddhism and Hinduism. It is also held by Theosophists, Anthroposophists, Rosicrucians, most occultists, and some spiritualists and philosophers. It is often coupled with the theory of *karma*, whereby the present allotment of good and evil is what has been merited in previous lives. Memories of earlier lives, sometimes induced under hypnosis, are open to doubt.

Although reincarnation was held by Gnostics and a few early Christians, the Bible lends no support. Hebrews 9:27 mentions "to die once." In John 9:2–3 Christ rejects the theory of sin in a previous life as an explanation of blindness. John the Baptist was not Elijah in person (Matt. 11:14; 17:10–12), but had "the spirit and power of Elijah" (Luke 1:17).

Millennium.

1. Premillennial or Dispensational Views.

In the theology of dispensationalists, this is the 1,000-year period mentioned in connection with the description of Christ's coming to reign with his saints over the earth (Rev. 19:11–16; 20:1–9). Several OT passages refer to the Millennium (Isa. 11:4; Jer. 3:17; Zech. 14:9).

These and many other OT passages are often taken to refer only to the 1,000-year period itself. However, it is difficult in these passages to see a clear dividing line between the earthly period of the Millennium and the eternal state of new heaven and new earth. Therefore, it is best to let teaching about the Millennium be drawn specifically from the words in Revelation 20.

During that 1,000-year period, dispensationalists teach Satan will be bound in the bottomless pit so he will not deceive the nations until his short period of release (Rev. 20:3, 7–8). The faithful martyrs who have died for the cause of Christ will be resurrected before the Millennium. They will rule as priests of God and Christ (Rev. 5:10; 20:4). The unbelieving dead will wait for the second resurrection (Rev. 20:5). After the 1,000 years, Satan will be released to resume his work of deceit (Rev. 20:7–8).

The most important aspect of the Millennium is the reign of Christ. Peter taught that Christ now rules from the right hand of God (Acts 2:33–36). That rule will last until his enemies are made his footstool (Ps. 110:1). Paul also understood Christ to be presently reigning in a period designed to bring all of God's enemies underfoot (1 Cor. 15:25–27).

2. Amillennial or Nonmillennial Position.

Persons who hold this position state that the Millennium refers to Christ's spiritual rule today from heaven. They point out that good exegesis forbids building a doctrine on the six references to the "thousand years" in Revelation 20 (see vv. 2–7)—a highly symbolic passage. Doctrines must be built on solid statements and can then be supported by figurative references. Revelation 20 is filled with symbols that cannot be taken literally (e.g., the bottomless pit and the great chain, v. 1). Further, it would be contrary to the usual use of "a thousand years" in the NT (see 2 Pet. 3:8). No other portion of the NT speaks about a literal reign upon earth of 1,000 years.

The reign of Christ is taking place now and will continue until his return.

3. Postmillennial Interpretation.

Although held by relatively few, this position views Christ's spiritual rule as working through preaching and teaching to bring gradual world improvement leading up to Christ's return.

Minister *or* Ministry. The consistent NT teaching is that the work of ministers is "for the equipping of the saints . . . for the edifying of the body of Christ" (Eph. 4:12). The minister is called of God to a position of responsibility rather than privilege, as the words for minister show (*diakonos*, "table waiter"; *hyperetes*, "under-rowers" in a large ship; *leitourgos*, "servant" usually of the state or a temple).

Two passages in the NT are of special importance. First, from 1 Corinthians 12:28 we gather that ministries in the early church were those of apostles, prophets, teachers, miracles, gifts of healings, helps, governments, diversities of tongues, and also interpretations. Second, from Ephesians 4 comes the addition of evangelists and pastors.

These works are the direct gift of God to the church. Both passages say this and are confirmed elsewhere in the case of some of the people mentioned. In Galatians 1:1 Paul insists that his apostolate was not of human origin. He entirely excludes the possibility of his receiving it by ordination.

This gives us a group of people directly inspired by the Holy Spirit to perform various functions within the church to build up the saints in the body of Christ.

Monasticism *or* Monachism. From the Greek *monos,* meaning "alone," this general term signifies the renunciation of life in the world for the ideal of unreserved devotion to God. It is not exclusive to Christianity, but is found in every religious system that has reached an advanced degree of ethical development. Monasticism is commonly extended beyond its strict implication of solitude to embrace the religious communities.

Christian monasticism originated in the latter half of the third century. Its rise came in three stages: (1) hermits (Paul of Thebes and Antony of Egypt were among the first); (2) lauras, or colonies of solitaries under one abbot, developed by Pachomiusa; and (3) monasteries.

Monasticism was introduced into the West in the fourth century and at first followed Eastern models. Benedict (ca. 525) founded Monte Cassino and formulated his famous Rule, which eventually became the monastic charter of the West for four centuries.

Monotheism. Worship of one supreme deity, an important characteristic of the worship system of the Hebrew people. One of the central teachings in the OT is Deuteronomy 6:4: "Hear, O Israel: The LORD our God, the LORD is one!" Against the idolatry of surrounding nations with their many gods (polytheism), God revealed this essential aspect of his nature to Israel.

Mystery. The NT use of *mystery* (Greek *musterion*) refers to God's plan that has previously been unrevealed. It is not a secret but something to proclaim (see 1 Cor. 4:1). Paul uses the word numerous times and means not only a previously hidden truth that is now presently divulged but one that contains a supernatural element that remains in spite of the revelation.

In the OT, *mystery* occurs only in the Aramaic sections of Daniel (Dan. 2:18, 27–30, 47; 4:9, NASB, RSV; *secret,* NKJV). Some of God's mysteries were revealed to Daniel and King Nebuchadnezzar.

Mysteries in the NT include:
- Translation of the church as the body of Christ at the end of this age (Eph. 3:1–11; 6:19; Col. 4:3)
- The church as the bride of Christ (Eph. 5:28–32)
- "Christ in [us], the hope of glory" (Col. 1:27)
- The mystery of iniquity (2 Thess. 2:7)
- The way by which humanity is restored to godliness (1 Tim. 3:16)

Mystery religions. Secret religions that flourished in Syria, Persia, Anatolia, Egypt, Greece, Rome, and other nations centuries before and after the time of Jesus Christ. The mystery religions were popular in the first century A.D. and provided strong religious competition for Christianity.

They were called mystery religions because their initiation and other rituals were kept secret. These religions included the cults of Eleusis, Dionysus, Isis and Osiris, Mithra, Cybele (the Magna Mater, or Great Mother), the Dea Syria, and many local deities, all of which promised purification and immortality.

By means of the secret rituals of these religions—which might involve ceremonial washings, blood-sprinkling, drunkenness, sacramental meals, passion plays, or even sexual relations with a priest or priestess—their followers became one with their god and believed that they participated in the life of that god.

Name. A label or designation that sets one person apart from another. In the Bible, personal (and place) names were formed from words that had their own meaning. People of the Bible were conscious of the meaning of names and believed in a vital connection between the name and the person it identified. A name represented the nature of the person.

The naming of a baby was important because in choosing a name, the parents could reflect the circumstances of the child's birth, their own feelings, their gratitude to God, their hopes and prayers for the child, and their commitment of the child to God.

Here are examples of names in the Bible:
- *Isaac* reflected the "laughter" of his mother at his birth (Gen. 21:6).
- *Esau* was named "hairy" because of his appearance.
- *Jacob* means "supplanter" because he grasped his brother Esau's heel (Gen. 25:25–26).
- *Moses* means "drawn out" as he was drawn out from the water (Exod. 2:10).

A popular custom of Bible times was to compose names by using the shortened forms of the divine name El or Ya (Je) as the beginning or ending syllable. Examples of this practice are the following:
- *Elisha* = means "God is salvation."
- *Daniel* = means "God is my judge."
- *Jehoiakim* = means "the Lord has established."
- *Isaiah* = means "the Lord is salvation."

Sometimes very specialized names, directly related to circumstances of the parents, were given to children. God told Isaiah to name one of his children Maher-Shalal-Hash-Baz, meaning "speed the spoil" or "hasten invasion of the nation of Judah" (Isa. 8:3–4). Hosea named a daughter Lo-Ruhamah, "no mercy," and a son Lo-Ammi, "not my people." Both names referred to God's displeasure with his people (Hos. 1:6–9).

The change of a name can also be of great importance in the Bible. Abram became Abraham in connection with his new calling to be "a father of many nations" (Gen. 17:5). Jacob became Israel ("God strives") because he "struggled with God and with men, and . . . prevailed" (Gen. 32:28; 35:10).

In the giving or taking of a new name, often a crucial turning point in the person's life has been reached. Simon became Peter because, as the first confessing apostle, he was the "rock" upon which the new community of the church would be built (Matt. 16:18). Saul became Paul, a Greek name for one destined to become the great apostle to the Gentiles.

The connection between a name and the reality it signified is nowhere more important than in the names referring to God. The personal name of God revealed to Moses in the burning bush—"I AM WHO I AM"—conveyed something of his character (Exod. 3:14). According to Exodus 34:5–6, when the Lord "proclaimed the name of the LORD," he added words that described his character. The name of the Lord was virtually synonymous with his presence: "For Your wondrous works declare that Your name is near" (Ps. 75:1).

To know the name of God is to know God himself (Ps. 91:14). To "take the name of the LORD your God in vain" (Exod. 20:7) is to act in any way that is inconsistent with the character of God.

NT writers emphasized the close relationship between names and what they mean. In Acts 4:12, Peter said, "For there is no other name under heaven given among men by which we must be saved." In this instance the name is interchangeable with the reality it represents.

Jesus taught his disciples to pray, "Hallowed be Your name" (Matt. 6:9). Christians were described by Paul as those who "name the name of Christ" (2 Tim. 2:19). A true understanding of the exalted Jesus is often connected with a statement about his name. Jesus "has by inheritance obtained a more excellent name" than the angels (Heb. 1:4). "God also has highly exalted Him and given Him the name which is above every name" (Phil. 2:9).

Natural theology. A quality in humans that enables them to know God as Creator if not as Redeemer, or at least to know of his existence and in some respects what he is like. This basic knowledge forms the starting point for a fuller understanding of God and the divine-human relationship.

The role allowed it in Christian theology has usually been preparatory to the theology of revelation.

Natural theology finds biblical support in Romans 1:18ff.; Acts 14:15–17; 17:22ff.; the "nature" psalms (e.g., 19 and 104); and the book of Job.

Nature, divine. The only biblical use of this phrase is in 2 Peter 1:4: "That through these you may be partakers of the divine nature." The reference is to our participation rather than to the divine nature as such.

Applied to God, the phrase obviously speaks of the intrinsic being of God in all of his perfections. As contrasted with human nature, the divine is self-existent, free, creative, eternal, omnipresent, omnipotent, constant, the sum of wisdom, righteousness, and love.

Referring to the Son, the divine nature refers to deity united with humanity. By his deity, Jesus Christ enjoys the fullness of being and attributes of the divine nature. In his incarnation he also assumed the essence and attributes of human nature, giving us one person with two natures or, as it is sometimes stated, two natures in one person.

New commandment. This phrase occurs first at John 13:34 where we would expect mention of the institution of the Lord's Supper. It occurs also in 1 John 2:8 as an echo of the original utterance.

Christians should love one another, even as Jesus loved them and laid down his life for them. John 15:13 is the substance of the new commandment.

New creation. A phrase that appears in 2 Corinthians 5:17 and Galatians 6:15. It suggests that the old is discarded and must be replaced by the new because the new is superior (cf. "the new covenant," Luke 22:20).

Paul's use of the phrase expresses the result of the conversion experience—which is not self-generated but accomplished by divine grace—a spiritual renewal. The need for a new creation is occasioned by the vitiating effect of sin upon the human race. Fallen human nature is such that only a new act of creation will render it fit for devotion and service to God. Both Pauline occurrences of the phrase are in contexts that stress the crucial significance of the death of Jesus in establishing the new order.

Two parallel expressions are "regeneration" (Matt. 19:28; Titus 3:5) and "born again" (John 3:3, 7; RSV reads "born anew," margin "born from above"). That Paul was not averse to using the metaphor of rebirth as well as new creation is demonstrated by 1 Corinthians 4:15, Galatians 4:19, and Philemon 10, all of which refer to birth and travail.

Oath. Scripture ascribes oaths to both God and humans. On God's part an oath is his solemn asseveration of the absolute truth of his divine word (Num. 23:19) so that his people can fully trust in his promises (Isa. 45:20–24). Since God cannot swear by anyone greater than himself (Heb. 6:13), as humans do (Heb. 6:16), he swears

- By himself (Heb. 6:13)
- By his holiness (Ps. 89:35)
- By his great name (Jer. 44:26)
- By his life (Ezek. 33:11)

God has confirmed with a most solemn oath the sure hope of human salvation through faith in Jesus, the Savior of sinners (Heb. 7:20–28). This anthropomorphic representation of God, swearing an oath on behalf of humanity's eternal welfare, must be regarded as a most loving condescension on his part and calls for our trust and faithful obedience.

Some oaths and vows in the Bible involve the following people: Jacob at Bethel (Gen. 28:20); the Nazirite (Num. 6:2–21); Jephthah, concerning the offering of a sacrifice (Judg. 11:30); Hannah, concerning a yet unborn child (1 Sam. 1:11); Absalom, used to deceive David (2 Sam. 15:7); Jezebel to kill Elijah (1 Kings 19:1–2); Jonah inside the fish (Jon. 2:9); Paul (Acts 18:18); four men and Paul (Acts 21:23–26); and certain Jews, to kill Paul (Acts 23:12).

Offices of Christ. Since the days of Eusebius, most theologians have looked upon the mediatorial work of Christ as that of prophet, priest, and king. All other christological offices such as advocate or intercessor fall under one of these three heads.

Three OT passages point prophetically in this direction, assigning to Jesus Christ this threefold office (Deut. 18:15; Ps. 110:4; Zech. 6:13). Jesus Christ's assumption of this threefold office is eternal, since he must reign forever (Isa. 9:6–7) and he is to be priest "forever according to the order of Melchizedek" (Heb. 6:20).

As prophet, Jesus Christ speaks the truth of God to humanity. This work includes both prediction and the telling forth of truth in general. Since he is the Truth, he is the infallible prophet. He was conscious of fulfilling this office (Mark 13:5–7). He has a divine commission in mediating as prophet (Isa. 61:1–3) demonstrated by his manner, message, and the results of his teaching.

There is a close connection between Jesus Christ's work as prophet and priest. In the prophetic role, he often spoke of what he would accomplish as priest, and as our priest he secures for believers what he proclaimed as prophet. The priest was one appointed to deal with God in behalf of people, and in this work Jesus Christ had two chief duties to perform. He had to bring a sacrifice and also to make intercession. Unlike other priests, he is both the offerer and the offering.

As king (Ps. 2:6; Isa. 9:6–7; 11:1–9), Christ rules for God. This office relates most directly to Israel, although its exercise affects the world. As Lord, Christ rules his church even now. His kingship is secured, and assuredly divine covenants were made with Abraham (Gen. 12 and 17) and with David (2 Sam. 7:8–17). His work as prophet is primarily in the past. His role as priest is past, present, and future while his work as king awaits (for the most part) future fulfillment.

Omnipotence. A theological term that refers to the all-encompassing power of God. The almighty God expects human beings to obey him, and he holds them responsible for their thoughts and actions. Nevertheless, he is the all-powerful Lord who has created all things and sustains them by the word of his power (Gen. 1:1–3; Heb. 1:3).

Omnipresence. A theological term that refers to the unlimited nature of God or his ability to be everywhere at all times. God is not like the manufactured idols of ancient cultures that were limited to one altar or temple area. God reveals himself in the Bible as the Lord who is everywhere. God is present as Lord in all creation (Ps. 139:7–12).

Omniscience. A theological term that refers to God's superior knowledge and wisdom, his power to know all things. God is the Lord who knows our thoughts from afar. He is acquainted with all our ways, knowing our words even before they are on our tongues (Ps. 139:1–6, 13–16). He needs to consult no one for knowledge or understanding (Isa. 40:13–14).

Ordination. This is a ceremony by which people are set apart, commissioned, and consecrated to an order or office. People are ordained to and established in ministries of service and leadership. It is also the process of commissioning a pastor or other officer of the church. This process is seldom mentioned in the NT. Some scholars doubt whether the solemn service we know today as ordination was practiced in the time of Jesus. However, while the technical sense of the term does not occur in the NT, several references do indicate an official commissioning ceremony.

The 12 apostles were chosen and sent by Jesus (Mark 3:13–19; Luke 6:12–16), but without any ordination service. There was no ordination service at the election of Matthias (Acts 1:26). The seven were commissioned by laying on of hands (Acts 6:6). Paul and Barnabas were commissioned by the Antioch church in the same manner (Acts 13:3). However, the laying on of hands was widespread in the ancient world and does not necessarily point to an ordination service.

The primary evidence of an ordination service comes from 1 Timothy 4:14, where Paul apparently speaks of an official ceremony. Timothy's special spiritual gift was given to him "by prophecy with the laying on of the hands of the eldership." From 2 Timothy 1:6 it would seem that Paul joined with them in this service.

The ordination of Christian leaders is an act of the church by which the responsibility of an office is passed on to an individual.

Orthodoxy. Belief in a doctrine or practice considered true and correct. The English equivalent of Greek *orthodoxia* (from *orthos*, "right," and *doxa*, "opinion"), meaning "right belief," as opposed to heresy or heterodoxy. The term is not biblical; no secular or Christian writer uses it before the second century.

Paradise. A place of exceptional blessedness, happiness, and delight, and a descriptive name for heaven.

Originally *paradise* was a Persian word meaning "a wooded park" or "an enclosed or walled orchard." Traditional Hebrew theology held that the dead descended to Sheol. After the emergence of belief in the afterlife, however, this view was drastically modified.

In the period between the OT and the NT, the Jews believed that, after the resurrection, the righteous would go to Paradise, a place much like the Garden of Eden before the Fall.

In the NKJV the word *paradise* occurs only three times: Luke 23:43; 2 Corinthians 12:4; Revelation 2:7.

To the repentant thief on the cross Jesus said, "Today you will be with Me in Paradise" (Luke 23:43). Various commentators have pointed out that when a Persian king wished to bestow upon one of his subjects a special honor, he made him a "companion of the garden." The subject was chosen to walk in the king's garden as a special friend and companion of the king. Jesus may well have promised the thief that he would be his companion in the garden of heaven.

Paradox. An assertion that is self-contradictory; two or more assertions that are mutually contradictory; or an assertion that contradicts commonly held positions or opinion.

Paradoxes may be either rhetorical or logical. A rhetorical paradox is a figure used to shed light on a topic by challenging the reason of another. The NT contains many effective examples of this use of the paradox (e.g., Matt. 5:39; 10:39; 2 Cor. 6:9–10).

Logical paradoxes arise from the attempt by the human mind to unify or to coordinate the multiple facets of experience. Because of the complexity of reality as well as the limitations of finite human reason, our best efforts to know reality bring us only to opposing truths. In such cases we may be nearer the truth when we accept both sides of a paradoxical issue rather than giving up one side in favor of the other.

Two differing interpretations of the logical paradox have emerged in the history of the church. One asserts actual paradoxes in which what is true also contradicts a right application of the laws of human thought. The other holds that paradoxical assertions are only apparent contradictions.

Often this difference resolves itself into a mere difference of psychological attitude. Those who take the first interpretation are willing to leave incoherent elements unresolved in thinking. Those who hold the second believe that all truth must fit with the laws of human thought such as the law of contradiction and, therefore, does not leave incoherencies.

Parousia. A transliteration of a Greek word that refers to the second coming, or the return, of the Lord Jesus Christ at the end of this age to set up his kingdom, judge his enemies, and reward the faithful.

The Greek word literally means "a being alongside," hence "appearance" or "presence." Christians are "looking for the blessed hope and glorious appearing of our great God and Savior Jesus Christ" (Titus 2:13).

Peace. A word with several different meanings in the OT and NT.

The OT meaning had to do with completeness, soundness, and well-being of the total person. This peace was considered God-given, obtained by following the Law (Ps. 119:165). Peace sometimes had physical meaning, suggesting security (Ps. 4:8), contentment (Isa. 26:3), prosperity (Ps. 122:6–7), and the absence of war (1 Sam. 7:14). The traditional Jewish greeting, *shalom*, was a wish for peace.

In the NT, peace often refers to the inner tranquillity and poise of Christians whose trust is in God through Christ. This understanding was originally expressed about the coming Messiah (Isa. 9:6–7).

The peace that Jesus Christ spoke of was a combination of hope, trust, and inner quietness brought about by a reconciliation with God. Such peace was proclaimed by the angels at Jesus' birth (Luke 2:14), and by Jesus himself in his Sermon on the Mount (Matt. 5:9) and during his ministry. He also promised this peace at the Lord's Supper, shortly before his death (John 14:27).

Paul wrote that such peace and spiritual blessedness was a direct result of faith in Christ (Rom. 5:1).

Pelagianism. A heresy named after Pelagius, a British monk of the fourth century. Pelagianism denied the doctrines of original sin and total depravity, and held that human beings are saved by their own free will and not by the sovereign grace of God.

Perdition. Destruction, ruin, or waste, especially through the eternal destruction brought upon the wicked by God (Heb. 10:39; 2 Pet. 3:7). Jesus contrasted the way that leads to life with the way that leads to destruction (Matt. 7:13).

Paul contrasted perdition with salvation (Phil. 1:28). The "desire to be rich" can lead some to "destruction and perdition" (1 Tim. 6:9). Peter speaks of "the day of judgment and perdition of ungodly men" (2 Pet. 3:7), a perishing far worse than those destroyed in the Flood.

The NT twice uses the phrase "the son of perdition": of Judas Iscariot (John 17:12) and of "the man of sin [or lawlessness]" whom some scholars identify with the Antichrist (2 Thess. 2:3).

The phrase portrays the progression of an evil character who produces ruin in others and is headed toward final judgment (Rev. 17:8, 11). Perdition in this passage refers to a place of eternal punishment, the final state of the damned.

Perfect *or* Perfection.   Without flaw or error, or a state of completion or fulfillment. God's perfection means that he is complete in himself, perfect in all the characteristics of his nature. He is the basis of and standard by which all other perfection is to be measured (Job 36:4; Pss. 18:30; 19:7; Matt. 5:48).

By contrast, human perfection is relative and dependent on God for its existence. As applied to an individual's moral state in this life, perfection may refer either to a relatively blameless life-style (Gen. 6:9; Job 1:1; James 3:2) or to maturity as a believer (Phil. 3:15; James 1:4). Because perfection in this life is never reached, people will continue to sin (Phil. 3:12–15; 1 John 1:8).

Some theologians consider that our perfection relates to our position or relationship that Paul describes as being "in Christ," and not our actual conduct.

Loving God perfectly and totally is the aim of all Christians while acknowledging that Christian perfection in this life is not possible. We aim at Christian perfection by striving to obey the great commandments of Jesus (Matt. 22:37–39)—to love God and our fellow human beings.

Perish.   The meaning of *perish* is explained primarily in three uses of the word.

1. Purely physical destruction in, or from, this world, without judgment or punishment. The word *abad* (Hebrew) used in this way applies mainly to animals and inanimate objects, but may refer to persons (2 Sam. 1:27; Job 4:11; so also Greek *apothnesko*, Matt. 8:32).

2. More frequently, the destruction, while purely physical, is regarded as the consequence or punishment for wrongdoing (Deut. 4:26).

3. The distinctive NT use is of a perishing of the soul as well as the body (Matt. 10:28; Luke 13:3). The antithesis to perishing is having eternal life.

Persecution.   Persecution (literally a pursuing) is the systematic attempt to suppress or exterminate Christianity by social pressure to the point of violence. Persecution of Christians began with the action of the Sanhedrin against Peter and John because of their proclamation of the resurrection of Jesus (Acts 4:1–3, 5ff.).

Another persecution took place after the stoning of Stephen. The Christians in Jerusalem were driven out of the city and scattered in every direction (Acts 8:1–4).

Organized persecution did not begin until the time of Nero, and was then probably only temporary and local. Scholars speak of several persecutions under the Roman Empire:

- Nero, A.D. 64
- Domitian, A.D. 95
- Trajan, A.D. 100
- Antoninus Pius, A.D. 161–180
- Septimius Severus, A.D. 197
- Maximinus, A.D. 235
- Decius, A.D. 249
- Diocletian, A.D. 303

Perseverance *or* Perseverance of the saints.   The continuous operation of the Holy Spirit in believers by which God's grace, once begun in them, continues forever (see John 10:28–29; Rom. 11:29; Phil. 1:6).

Polity.   A form or system of church government.

Pope.   Generally understood as referring to the bishop of Rome. In the early centuries of the church, *pope* was used as a form of address in several bishoprics, and is still applied to priests of the Eastern Orthodox church. It is a corruption of the classical name for father.

The pope is regarded by Roman Catholics as the head of the church on earth and called the Vicar of Christ. His prerogatives are said to be derived from Christ's appointment of the apostle Peter to this position, Peter's subsequent bishopric at Rome, and the transmission of his authority to his successors.

No early support for this understanding of Christ's words to Peter recorded in Matthew 16:18 exists, nor is there clear historical evidence that Peter was ever at Rome. But even if exegesis were to establish the first point, and recent archaeological research to confirm the early tradition that Peter was martyred at Rome under Nero, there is still no proof that he passed on his leadership to all subsequent occupants of the Roman see.

The controversy concerning the papacy is one of the oldest in church history. It led, in 1054, to the break of the Eastern churches from the Western and, in the sixteenth century, to the breakup of the Western church into the Protestant churches and present Roman Catholic church. While popes have generally been men of outstanding ability, contributing to the well-being of the whole church, a few have been men not worthy of the office. The doctrine of the infallibility of the pope has now been defined as an official dogma of the Roman Catholic church.

Prayers for the dead. No passage in either testament implies this practice. Of the single passage in the Apocrypha that appears to allude to it, the text, translation, and interpretation of 2 Maccabees 12:45 are all uncertain. Further, considerable evidence exists that orthodox Jews of the intertestamental period rejected prayers for the dead.

Preaching. Preaching is the proclamation of the good news by those who have been called by God. Preaching is the divinely ordained means for the transmission of the message to the world and serves also as a means of grace for the edification of the church of Christ.

Predestination. The teaching that declares the sovereignty of God over humanity in such a way that the freedom of the human will is also preserved.

Two major concepts are involved in the biblical meaning of predestination.

1. God, who is all-powerful in the universe, has foreknown and predestined the course of human history and the lives of individuals. If God were not in complete control of human events, he would not be sovereign and would not be God.

2. God's predestination of human events does not eliminate human choice. How God can maintain sovereignty and still allow human freedom seems to be reserved for his understanding alone. Great minds have struggled with this problem for centuries.

Two views of predestination are prominent among church groups today.

1. Calvinstic view: God offers irresistible grace to those he elects to save.

2. Arminian view: God's grace is the source of redemption, but it can be resisted through free choice.

Those who oppose the Calvinistic view say that this means God is unjust, deciding that some people will be saved and others lost. Calvinists reply that the human race, because of Adam's fall, sinned by free choice and no person deserves salvation.

Further, without divine intervention, no person wants salvation (Rom. 3:1–24). At the same time, Arminians would say that God's grace is universal and salvation is for "everyone who believes" (Rom. 1:16).

Simplistically stated, in Calvinism, God chooses believers; in Arminianism, believers choose God.

Although the word *predestination* does not appear in the Bible, Paul alludes to it in Ephesians 1:11: "We have obtained an inheritance, being predestined according to the purpose of Him who works all things according to the counsel of His will."

Christians do agree that creation is moving within the purpose of God of bringing the world into complete conformity to his will (Rom. 8:28). From the beginning of time, God predestined to save humankind by sending his Son to accomplish salvation. God "desires all men to be saved and to come to the knowledge of the truth" (1 Tim. 2:4).

Paul declared that he was a debtor to take the message of the gospel to other people (Rom. 1:14–15) so they might hear and obey. Paul clearly meant that no one is saved apart from the will of God and no one is lost apart from the will of God. But the will of God functions within an order that God himself has established.

Pre-existence of souls. Three major theories have been advanced concerning the origin of the soul.

1. Pre-existence: all souls, whether eternal or created by God in eternity past, exist in an abode or "treasury," from which they are called forth to inhabit people.

2. Creationism: each individual soul is a direct creation of God and is placed in the human body, either at birth or sometime prior to it.

3. Traducianism: the soul, as well as the body, is propagated by the parent.

The teaching of preexistence does not pretend to be a scriptural doctrine, for the Bible never speaks of creation of men prior to Adam and Eve. Nor is the present condition of the human race ascribed to any higher source than the sin of our first parents.

The idea of preexistence appears frequently in Talmudic literature, although it has been rejected by the majority of Jewish philosophers. According to Josephus it was held by the Essenes and may reflect the belief of the Jews at the time of Christ.

Among twentieth-century religionists, the Mormons are the chief exponents of this theory. They contend that the soul, being synonymous with the spirit, is with God in heaven until sent to indwell the baby. This is essentially a form of reincarnation, which has no scriptural foundation.

The Bible teaches that souls depart this life, either for eternal punishment or the presence of God (Heb. 9:27).

Prophet. A person (male or female) who spoke for God and who communicated the divine message to God's people.

Propitiation. The divine side of the work of Jesus on the cross. This is the atoning death of Jesus, through which he paid the penalty demanded by God because of human sin.

The term comes from old English, propitiate, "to appease." Propitiation expressed the idea that Jesus died on the cross to pay the price for human sin. Although Jesus was free of sin, he took all our sins upon himself and redeemed us from the penalty of death that our sins demanded. "He Himself is the propitiation for our sins, and not for ours only but also for the whole world" (1 John 2:2; expiation, RSV).

Providence. The continuous activity of God in his creation by which he preserves and governs. The doctrine of providence affirms God's absolute lordship over creation, confirms the dependence of all creation on the Creator, and denies the idea that the universe is governed by chance or fate.

Through his providence God controls: the universe (Ps. 103:19); the physical world (Matt. 5:45); the affairs of nations (Ps. 66:7); humans' birth and destiny (Gal. 1:15); human successes and failures (Luke 1:52); the protection of God's people (Ps. 4:8); insignificant things (Matt. 10:29–31); and apparent accidents (Prov. 16:33).

Divine government is the continued activity of God by which he directs all things to the ends he has chosen in his eternal plan. God is King of the universe and has given Jesus Christ all power and authority to reign (Matt. 28:18–20; Acts 2:36; Eph. 1:20–23).

God acts in accordance with the laws and principles he has established in the world. The laws of nature are human descriptions of how we perceive God at work in the world.

Punishment, everlasting. The final judgment of God upon the wicked. The classic example of eternal punishment in the OT is the destruction of Sodom and Gomorrah (Gen. 19:15–28).

When speaking about wicked angels who are being held in "everlasting chains," Jude likened these wrongdoers to the wicked men of Sodom and Gomorrah, who "are set forth as an example, suffering the vengeance of eternal fire" (Jude 6–7).

Paul wrote that those who do not know God "shall be punished with everlasting destruction from the presence of the Lord and from the glory of His power" (2 Thess. 1:9). This same idea was expressed by Jesus in the parable of the sheep and the goats (Matt. 25:31–46). After separating the two, Jesus blessed the sheep—those who have cared for the unfortunate and poor. Then he pronounced judgment upon the goats— those who did not have compassion: "Depart from Me, you cursed, into the everlasting fire" (v. 41).

The essential meaning of everlasting punishment involves banishment from the presence of God and Christ forever—a fate made vivid by the image of eternal fire (Rev. 19:20; 21:8).

Purgatory. A teaching of Roman Catholic and Greek Orthodox Churches. Purgatory is a place of temporal punishment in an intermediate realm in which all who die at peace with the church but are not perfect undergo penal and purifying suffering. Only believers who have attained a state of Christian perfection go immediately to heaven. All unbaptized adults and those who commit mortal sin after baptism go immediately to hell.

Protestantism rejects the doctrine, since this doctrine is not found in the Bible but in the Apocrypha (2 Macc. 12:39–45).

Quick, quicken. Old English word meaning "to make alive." (See Rom. 8:11; 1 Cor. 15:36.)

Reconciliation. The restoration of fellowship or relationship after an estrangement. The OT contains the idea of an atonement or covering for sin (Lev. 6:30; 16:20). In the NT the word means "to change thoroughly." (See 2 Cor. 5:18–19.)

By the death of Christ the world is changed in its relationship to God, who now accepts that event to bring us into right relationship.

The Bible teaches that God and humanity are alienated from each other because of God's holiness and human sinfulness. Although God loves sinners (Rom. 5:8), it is impossible for him not to judge sin (Heb. 10:27) and this judgment affects both parties.

The initiative in reconciliation was taken by God—while we were still sinners and enemies, Christ died for us (Rom. 5:8, 10; Col. 1:21). Reconciliation is God's own completed act that takes place before human actions such as confession, repentance, and restitution. God "has reconciled us to Himself through Jesus Christ" (2 Cor. 5:18).

Paul regarded the gospel as "the word of reconciliation" (2 Cor. 5:19). Knowing "the terror of the Lord," Paul pleaded, "Be reconciled to God" (5:20).

Redeemer. One who frees or delivers another from difficulty, danger, or bondage, usually by the payment of a ransom price. In the OT the redeemer could function in several ways. He could buy back property (even enslaved people) sold under duress (Lev. 25:23–32). He (usually as owner, not as a relative) often redeemed from the Lord dedicated property and firstborn livestock (Lev. 27:1–33; also Exod. 21:28–30). He could (as "an avenger of blood") take the life of one who had murdered his relative as a blood price (Num. 35:12–28).

Redemption. Deliverance by payment of a price. In the NT, redemption refers to salvation from sin, death, and the wrath of God by Christ's sacrifice. In the OT, redemption refers to redemption by a kinsman (Lev. 25:24, 51–52; Ruth 4:6; Jer.

32:7–8), rescue or deliverance (Num. 3:49), and ransom (Pss. 111:9; 130:7).

In the OT, redemption was applied to property, animals, persons, and the nation of Israel as a whole. In nearly every instance, freedom from obligation, bondage, or danger was secured by the payment of a price, a ransom, bribe, satisfaction, or a sum of money paid to obtain freedom, favor, or reconciliation. God alone, however, is able to redeem from the slavery of sin (Ps. 130:7–8).

Regeneration. The spiritual change brought about in a person's life by an act of God. In regeneration a person's sinful nature is changed, and he is enabled to respond to God in faith.

The word regeneration occurs only in the NT (Matt. 19:28; Titus 3:5), but the concept or idea is common throughout the Bible. The literal meaning of regeneration is "born again." The first birth, as Jesus said to Nicodemus (John 3:1–12) is "of the flesh" while the second birth is "of the Spirit." Being born of the Spirit is essential before a person can enter the kingdom of God. Every biblical command to undergo a radical change of character from self-centeredness to God-centeredness is, in effect, an appeal to be born again (Ps. 51:5–11; Jer. 31:33; Zech. 13:1).

Great religious experiences in the OT might well be regarded as new births, such as Jacob at the Jabbok (Gen. 32:22–32), Moses at the burning bush (Exod. 3:1–6), Josiah on hearing the reading of the law (2 Kings 22:8–13), and Isaiah in the temple (Isa. 6:1–8).

Regeneration involves an enlightening of the mind, a change of the will, and a renewed nature. It extends to the total human nature, changing persons' desires and restoring them to right relationships with God in Christ.

Remission. To be released or set free from sin (Acts 2:38; Heb. 9:22). Through the death of his Son, God has taken the initiative to break the grip of sin and set humanity free for a new way of life in God's Spirit.

Remnant. The part of a community or nation that remains after a dreadful judgment or devastating calamity, especially those who have escaped and remain to form the nucleus of a new community (Isa. 10:20–23). The survival of a righteous remnant rests solely on God's providential care for his chosen people and his faithfulness to keep his covenant promises.

The concept of the remnant has its roots in Deuteronomy 4:27–31; 28:62–68; 30:1–10. Moses warned the people of Israel that they would be scattered among the nations. But God also promised that he would bring the people back from captivity and establish them again in the land of their fathers. This concept was used by the prophets, who spoke of the Assyrian and Babylonian captivities. The concept was extended to apply also to the gathering of a righteous remnant at the time when the Messiah came to establish his kingdom.

In Amos and Isaiah the remnant consisted of those chosen by God who were rescued from the impending doom of the nation (Isa. 1:9; Amos 5:14–15). As such, they were labeled "the poor," those who suffer for God (Isa. 29:19; 41:17). At the same time, they serve God and stand before the nation as witnesses, calling the people to repent of their rebellion.

In the NT, Paul appropriated the teaching of Isaiah and other prophets and applied it to the church (Rom. 11:5). He showed that God's purpose is seen in the remnant of Israel who have joined the Gentiles to form the church, the new people of God.

Jesus' choice of twelve apostles built upon remnant themes. Symbolizing the twelve tribes, the apostles became the remnant who erected a new structure, the church, upon the foundation of Israel. In the church, both Jews and Gentiles find their true spiritual home when they believe in Christ.

Repentance. A turning away from sin, disobedience, or rebellion and a turning back to God (Matt. 9:13; Luke 5:32). In a more general sense, repentance means a change of mind (Gen. 6:6–7) or a feeling of remorse or regret for past conduct (Matt. 27:3). True repentance is a godly sorrow for sin, an act of turning around and going in the opposite direction. This type of repentance leads to a fundamental change in persons' relationship to God.

In the OT the classic case of repentance is King David after Nathan the prophet accused him of killing Uriah the Hittite and committing adultery with Uriah's wife, Bathsheba. David's prayer of repentance for this sin is Psalm 51.

In the NT John the Baptist's preaching was, "Repent, for the kingdom of heaven is at hand" (Matt. 3:2). To the multitudes he declared, "Bear fruits worthy of repentance" (Matt. 3:8; Luke 3:8). When Jesus began his ministry, he took up John's preaching of the message of repentance expanding the message to include the good news of salvation: "The time is fulfilled, and the kingdom of God is at hand. Repent, and believe in the gospel" (Mark 1:15).

In Jesus' preaching of the kingdom of God is seen the truth that repentance and faith are two sides of the same coin: by repentance, people turn away from sin; by faith, they turn toward God in accepting the Lord Jesus Christ.

Reprobate. Disapproved or rejected, translation of Hebrew *ma'as*. The word referred to things such as worthless offerings (Jer. 6:20) and the Greek *adokimos*, meaning "disqualified, morally corrupt, unfit for any good deed." The original meaning is not to stand the test and therefore to be disqualified. (See Rom. 1:28; 2 Cor. 13:5–7; 2 Tim. 3:8; Titus 1:6.)

In all these passages the condition of being reprobate is the result of perverse humanity that stubbornly refuses to obey God's will.

Respect of persons. Greek *prosopolepsia*, "receive the face"; Hebrew *nasa panim*, "to raise the face," or "to accept favorably those who should be rejected." In the OT the idea may be used in a good sense (see 1 Sam. 25:35; Mal. 1:8–9), but it frequently means "showing partiality," as in Leviticus 19:15, where a guilty person's poverty is no ground for being accepted favorably. In the NT the good sense disappears, and the word invariably means "to show partiality to a person because of external possessions, position, or privilege without regard to their true worth." God is no respecter of persons (Acts 10:34), neither accepting the Jews because of their privileges nor rejecting the Gentiles because of their lack of them.

Restoration of Israel.

Those who oppose the restoration of Israel argue:

1. OT prophecies often appealed to in support of national restoration (Isa. 11:11; Ezek. 37) were fulfilled in the return from the Babylonian captivity.
2. What was not fulfilled must be regarded as realized in the church of the NT, the new Israel.
3. Jesus told the Jews that the kingdom of God would be taken from them and given to a nation bringing forth its fruits (Matt. 21:43). This statement emphasizes that the restoration promises regarding Israel in the OT must have a conditional rather than an absolute character. Israel failed to meet the conditions.
4. In the unfolding of the divine purpose the NT church includes both Jews and Gentiles, the wall of partition between them being broken down by Jesus Christ. A return to special consideration for one nation would seem anachronistic once the church is a reality.
5. The return of the Jews to Palestine in considerable numbers in mod-

ern times, however interesting as a phenomenon of history, does not in itself guarantee a spiritual future in terms of national conversion.

Those who hold to the restoration of Israel argue:

1. OT prophecies relating to Israel's restoration as a people are too numerous, emphatic, and precise to be fulfilled by the return from captivity.
2. It is poor exegesis to assign to the church what was spoken about Israel. If the curses and judgments pronounced on Israel for disobedience belong to that people, then the future blessings ought to as well.
3. In the Annunciation the angel declared that the one to be born would rule over the house of Jacob for ever (Luke 1:33). It seems impossible to assign this reference to the church.
4. Jesus, despite his pronouncements of judgment on the nation of Israel for her sinful condition, and especially for her rejection of him, indicated blessing and glory for her in the future (Matt. 19:28; 23:39; Luke 21:24). In answering the query of the disciples about the restoration of the kingdom to Israel, he did not deny the fact, but only the present realization of the hope (Acts 1:6–7).
5. Paul's statement about divine wrath being visited on the Jews of his own time (1 Thess. 2:15–16) should not be taken as ruling out a glorious future for Israel because the restoration is stated so strongly in Romans 11:26–27.

Romans 11:26–27 has been the focal point of much discussion. If we understand Paul's statement that "all Israel will be saved" to refer to the totality of the elect, whether Jews or Gentiles—the new Israel—it overlooks the fact that from the beginning of this section (Rom. 9—11) Paul speaks of his kinsmen according to the flesh—Jews (9:3)—and contrasts Israel with Gentiles.

A second possibility is that "all Israel" means the sum total of Jewish believers in Christ. This viewpoint does not allow for the two stages in Paul's argument: (1) the existence of an election according to grace [Jews now in the church] and (2) the promise of a future conversion of Israel mentioned in 11:26–27.

The idea of remnant was in existence in Paul's day. He belonged to it himself. In Romans 11:26–27 God reasserted his pledge to the covenant nation. This position means that there will be a national turning of Israel to the Lord at his coming. The principal difficulty with this view is the absence of any teaching in the passage about the regathering of the people of Israel into their land and the institution of an earthly kingdom in which Israel fills the leading role.

Resurrection. Being raised from the dead. Resurrection has three primary meanings in the Bible:

1. Miraculous healings. These were individuals who were brought back to life in this present world such as the widow's son by Elijah (1 Kings 17:20–24).
2. Jesus' resurrection. This resurrection is linked with the overcoming of the powers of evil and death. Jesus' resurrection is the basis for the doctrine of general resurrection (1 Cor. 15:12–19).
3. General resurrection. The NT consistently teaches resurrection of believers based on the resurrection of Jesus as the first one risen from the dead (1 Cor. 15:12–58). This idea of resurrection is expressed in such images as a transformed body (Phil. 3:21), a new dwelling (2 Cor. 5:2), and new clothing (2 Cor. 5:4).

The NT also contrasts resurrection to life with resurrection to judgment (John 5:29; Acts 24:15).

Statements in the Bible about our resurrected bodies:

> It will be a recognizable body (1 Cor. 13:12).
> It will be a body like Christ's (1 John 3:2).
> It will be a body that will permit eating (Luke 24:41–43; John 21:12–13).
> It will be a body in which the spirit dominates (1 Cor. 15:44, 49).
> It will be a body unlimited by physical boundaries (Luke 24:31; John 20:19).
> It will be an eternal body (2 Cor. 5:1).
> It will be a glorious body (Rom. 8:18; 1 Cor. 15:43).

Revelation, natural. (See *Natural revelation.*)

Revelation, special. The term revelation means the disclosure of what was previously unknown. In Judeo-Christian theology, the term is used primarily of God's communication to humanity of divine truth—the manifestation of his will. Jesus Christ is the divine agent in all revelation.

This definition contrasts natural or general revelation (as in nature, history, and conscience) with special (sometimes called particular) revelation conveyed by wondrous acts and words. Special revelation is crowned by the incarnation of Jesus Christ, making the gospel of redemption not merely a series of abstract theses unrelated to specific historical events but the good news that God has acted in saving history (Heb. 1:2) for the salvation of lost humanity.

Reward, rewards. If all its related forms are included, reward occurs 101 times in most English translations. Four Greek words and several Hebrew words are rendered by this one word.

Its biblical usage is varied, including: a bribe (Ps. 15:5), a gift (1 Kings 13:7), punishment in this life for evil deeds (Matt. 6:5), and future punishment or retribution (Ps. 91:8).

Several times the word is used of evil done to people where good was expected (Gen. 44:4; Ps. 35:12).

Christ used rewards as an incentive for service. This has been a disturbing thought to some. This is more than materialism. Rewards are the result of human effort, but the Israelites, because of their covenant relationship, expected the fulfillment of divine promises as rewards. Christians may look for the completion of salvation as a reward for the fulfillment of the demands made upon them as disciples.

Paul teaches that all will appear before the judgment seat of Christ for the judgment of their works (Rom. 14:12; 2 Cor. 5:10). This kind of judgment is distinct from judgment for sins, because believers will not have to answer for them—they are forever gone (Rom. 5:1). Salvation is a gift (Eph. 2:8–9) but rewards are earned (1 Cor. 3:14). Both 1 Corinthians 3:9–15 and 9:16–27 discuss this idea at length. (See also 1 Cor. 9:25; Phil. 4:1; 1 Thess. 2:19; 2 Tim. 4:8; James 1:12; 1 Pet. 5:4; Rev. 2:10; 3:11.)

Righteousness. Holy and upright living, in accordance with God's standard. Righteousness comes from a word that means "straightness" and refers to a state that conforms to an authoritative standard. Righteousness is a moral concept. God's character is the definition and source of all righteousness (Gen. 18:25; Deut. 32:4; Rom. 9:14).

In the OT, righteousness defines human relationship with God (Ps. 50:6; Jer. 9:24) and with other people (Jer. 22:3). In the context of relationships, righteous action is that which promotes the peace and well-being of other human beings.

The sacrificial system in the OT and the cross of Jesus in the NT show human need for righteousness. Sin is disobedience to the terms that define human relationship with God and others. Since the Fall humanity is inherently unrighteous.

Sacrament. A formal religious act in which the actions and materials used are the channels by which God's grace is communicated, either actually or symbolically. The word *sacrament*, not used in most English versions of the Bible, comes from the Latin *sacramentum*, the word for a soldier's oath of allegiance. The word also came to have the idea of mystery associated with it. The Eastern Orthodox churches usually refer to the sacraments as "mysteries."

Roman Catholics and the Orthodox have seven sacraments:

1. The Eucharist (Lord's Supper)
2. Baptism
3. Confirmation
4. Penance (often called sacrament of reconciliation)
5. Matrimony
6. Holy orders
7. Of the sick (formerly extreme unction)

Roman Catholics and Orthodox hold that these sacraments are means of grace, or channels through which God imparts spiritual blessedness.

Some Protestant Christians prefer to use the word *ordinances* rather than sacraments. Virtually all Protestants consider baptism and the Lord's Supper the only true sacraments instituted by the Lord Jesus. These are the only two actions involving visible symbols (the water, and the bread and wine) that were clearly observed by Christ (Luke 22:14–20) and commanded by him (Matt. 28:19–20).

Saints. People who have been separated from the world and consecrated to the worship and service of God. Followers of the Lord are referred to by this term throughout the Bible, although its meaning is developed more fully in the NT. Consecration (setting apart) and purity are the basic meanings of the term. Believers are called *saints* in Romans 1:7 and *saints in Christ Jesus* in Philippians 1:1.

Salvation. The English word stands for several Hebrew and Greek words, the general idea being safety, deliverance, ease, soundness. In the OT the word *salvation* had many uses: "deliverance from danger" (Jer. 15:20); "deliverance of the weak from oppressors" (Ps. 35:9–10); "healing of sickness" (Isa. 38:20); "deliverance from blood-guilt and its consequences" (Ps. 51:14); "national deliverance from military threat" (Exod. 14:13); and "release from captivity" (Ps. 14:7).

Salvation finds its deepest meaning in the spiritual realm of life. The human need for salvation is one of the clearest teachings of the Bible.

The need for salvation goes back to the Fall, and life was marked by strife and difficulty. Increasingly, corruption and violence dominated this world (Gen. 6:11–13). When God destroyed the world with the Flood, he also performed the first act of salvation by saving Noah and his family. Eight people became the basis of another chance for humankind. The salvation of Noah and his family was viewed by the apostle Peter as a pattern of that full salvation we receive in Christ (1 Pet. 3:18–22).

The central OT experience of salvation is the Exodus (Exod. 12:40—14:31). Much of Israel's worship of God was a renewal of this mighty experience that brought the people from tyranny in Egypt to freedom in the Promised Land (Exod.13:3–16). The mighty saving power of God was demonstrated dramatically as the Israelites formed a holy nation of priestly servants of the Lord (Exod. 19:4–6). The Exodus became a pattern of salvation by which God's future deeds of redemption would be understood.

In the NT salvation comes through Christ and can be shown in three tenses:

• Past—when persons believe in Christ, they are saved (Acts 16:31).

• Present—they are also in the process of being saved from the power of sin (Rom. 8:13; Phil. 2:12).

• Future—they will be saved from the

presence of sin (Rom. 13:11; Titus 2:12–13).

God releases into lives today the power of Christ's resurrection (Rom. 6:4), and allows believers a foretaste of future life as his children (2 Cor. 1:22; Eph. 1:14). The experience of salvation will be complete when Christ returns (Heb. 9:28) and the kingdom of God is fully revealed (Matt. 13:41–43).

Sanctify, Sanctification. While the origin of the Hebrew root *qadas* is surrounded by obscurity, its fundamental meaning seems to be to set apart an object from ordinary usage for special or religious purposes, and in particular to set apart for God. In biblical Greek its equivalent is *hagiazein*, "to sanctify."

Savior. A person who rescues others from evil, danger, or destruction. The OT viewed God as the Savior: "There is no other God besides Me, a just God and a Savior" (Isa. 45:21). Because God is the source of salvation, he sent human deliverers to

Key Words in the Vocabulary of Salvation

Adoption	Wherein the believing sinner enjoys all the privileges and responsibilities of a child of God	Rom. 8:15–23; Gal. 4:4–5; Eph. 1:5
Election	Being chosen by God	2 Thess. 2:13; 1 Pet. 2:9
Faith	Turning to the Savior	Acts 20:21; Eph. 2:8–9; Heb. 11:6
Foreknowledge	Attribute of God that provided advance knowledge of all the facts concerning the elect	Acts 15:18; Rom. 8:29; 1 Pet. 1:2
Glorification	The ultimate, eternal, and absolute physical, mental, and spiritual perfection of believers	Rom. 8:18, 23, 30; 1 Cor. 15:43; Col. 3:4; 1 Pet. 5:1
Imputation	God adding Christ's righteousness to the believing sinner	Isa. 53:5, 11; Rom. 4:3–8; Phil. 3:7–8
Justification	God declaring a repentant sinner righteous	Rom. 5:1; 8:33
Predestination	God's eternal plan whereby all believing sinners are conformed to the image of Christ	Rom. 8:29–30; Eph. 1:9–12
Propitiation	Christ satisfying the holiness of God on the cross	Rom. 3:25; Eph. 2:13; Col. 1:20; 1 John 2:2; 4:10
Reconciliation	Bringing together two opposing parties	2 Cor. 5:18–20
Redemption	Salvation attained through the payment of a ransom	Luke 1:68; Gal. 3:13; Heb. 9:12
Regeneration	Receiving a new nature through the second birth	John 1:12–13; 3:3; 1 John 5:1
Remission	Putting away or carrying away our sins	Lev. 16:21–22; 13:12–13; Rom. 3:25; Eph. 4:32; Col. 2:13; Heb. 9:26
Repentance	Turning from sin	Matt. 9:13; Acts 17:30; 26:20
Sanctification	God setting us apart for growth and service	John 17:17; Eph. 5:26; 1 Thess. 4:3–4; 5:23
Substitution	Christ dying on the cross in our stead	John 10:11; 1 Pet. 3:18
Supplication (prayer)	Communicating with God	Luke 18:13; Acts 2:21; Rom. 10:13; Jude 20

rescue his people, Israel (Ps. 106:21; Isa. 43:3, 11).

This word also described the judges of Israel, those saviors or deliverers who rescued God's people from oppression by their enemies (Judg. 3:9, 15).

In the NT, the word for savior describes both God the Father (1 Tim. 1:1; Jude 25) and Jesus Christ the Son (Acts 5:31; Phil. 3:20). The apostles rejoiced that in Christ, God had become the "Savior of all men" (1 Tim. 4:10). He was the Savior of Gentiles as well as Jews.

Servant of the Lord. A theological concept from Isaiah that points forward to Jesus the Messiah. (See Isa. 42:1–4; 49:1–6; 50:4–9; 52:13—53:12.)

But even before Isaiah's time, the concept of God's servant was deeply rooted in the history of the nation of Israel. The term *servant* was frequently applied to those who performed some service, task, or mission for the Lord. The term was applied to Abraham (Gen. 26:24), Isaac (Gen. 24:14), Jacob (Gen. 32:10), and Moses (Deut. 34:5), as well as many of the prophets of the OT.

In the servant passages of his book, Isaiah used the phrase in a specialized or messianic sense. The Servant of the Lord not only would encounter and accept suffering in the course of his work, but he also would realize that his vicarious suffering would become the means by which he would give his life as a ransom for others.

The NT writers are unanimous: The Servant of the Lord is a messianic figure and Jesus is that Servant. The first of Isaiah's servant passages (Isa. 42:1–4) was quoted by Matthew as being fulfilled in Jesus (Matt. 12:18–21). Acts emphasized the suffering and hostility the Messiah underwent to accomplish redemption (Acts 3:13, 26; 4:27, 30).

In these passages Jesus is referred to as "His Servant Jesus" (Acts 3:13, 26) and "Your holy Servant Jesus" (Acts 4:27, 30). The violent treatment suffered by Jesus was precisely what the "Servant Songs" of Isaiah prophesied about God's Servant.

Jesus saw his role as that of a servant (Mark 10:45, in fulfillment of Isaiah 53:10–11). He taught his followers to view his mission, and theirs as well, in terms of servanthood. The Servant of the Lord, spoken of by Isaiah the prophet, is preeminently Jesus himself.

According to Isaiah, the Servant of the Lord would bring forth justice to the Gentiles (Isa. 42:1), establish justice in the earth (Isa. 42:4), bring Jacob (Israel) back to the Lord (Isa. 49:5), be "a light to the Gentiles" (Isa. 49:6), not hide his face from shame and spitting (Isa. 50:6), and be the sin-bearing servant, giving his life for the redemption of his people (Isa. 52:13—53:12).

Through Jesus the ancient mission given by God to Abraham—to be a blessing to all the families of the earth (Gen. 12:1–3)—is now entrusted to the church. The church's responsibility is to preach the gospel to all. To be a servant of God is to serve him continually (Dan. 6:20).

Seven Cardinal Virtues. As enunciated by the medieval church, they are

1. Faith
2. Hope
3. Love
4. Justice
5. Prudence
6. Temperance
7. Fortitude

They are "cardinal" in that all other Christian virtues hinge *(cardo)* on one or another of them.

Seven Deadly Sins. At an early stage in the life of the church, the influence of Greek thought (with its tendency to view sin as a necessary flaw in human nature) forced the church to determine the relative seriousness of various moral faults. This produced what is commonly referred to as the seven deadly sins—a concept that occupies an important place in the order and discipline of the Roman Catholic Church.

These seven deadly sins are

1. Pride
2. Covetousness
3. Lust
4. Envy
5. Gluttony
6. Anger
7. Sloth

Seventy Weeks. A term that Daniel used in his prophecy of the future (Dan. 9:24–27). In Daniel's vision, God revealed that the Babylonian captivity of his people would come to an end and they would be restored to glory as a nation within a period of 70 weeks of seven years each—or a total of 490 years.

Scholars interpret this 70 weeks prophecy in three different ways:

• Daniel is not a book of prophecy; he was writing about events that had already happened.

• The 490-year period climaxed with Jesus' death on the cross.

• The prophecy is yet to be fulfilled.

Shema. "Hear thou." The Jewish confession of faith that begins, "Hear, O Israel: The LORD our God, the LORD is one!" (Deut. 6:4). The complete *Shema* occurs three times: Numbers 15:37–41, Deuteronomy 6:4–9, and 11:13–21.

Sheol. Meaning unknown. In OT thought, the abode of the dead. Sheol is the Hebrew equivalent of the Greek *Hades*, which means "the unseen world."

Sheol was regarded as an underground region (Num. 16:30, 33; Amos 9:2), shadowy and gloomy, where disembodied souls had a conscious but inactive existence (2 Sam. 22:6; Eccles. 9:10). The Hebrews regarded Sheol as a place to which both the righteous and unrighteous went at death (Gen. 37:35; Ps. 9:17; Isa. 38:10).

God is present in Sheol (Ps. 139:8; *hell*, NKJV), suggesting that in death God's people remain under his care, and the wicked never escape his judgment.

Sin. Lawlessness (1 John 3:4) or transgression of God's will, by omitting to do what God requires or by doing what God forbids. The Bible makes it clear that all are sinners and there is none righteous except Jesus Christ (see Rom. 3).

Soul. Hebrew *nepesh*, Greek *psyche*. A term with two distinct meanings in the Bible:

1. That which makes a human or animal body live. This usage of soul refers to life in the physical body. *Nepesh* generally designates individuals or animals in their total essence.

The best examples of this usage are those passages in the NT in which the Greek word for *soul* is translated as *life*. "For whoever desires to save his life [soul] will lose it," Jesus declared, "but whoever loses his life [soul] for My sake and the gospel's will save it. For what will it profit a man if he gains the whole world, and loses his own soul?" (Mark 8:35–36).

This idea is also present in the OT. For example, the soul of a dying person departed at death (Gen. 35:18). The prophet Elijah brought a child back to life by stretching himself upon the child three times and praying that God would let the child's soul come back into him (1 Kings 17:19–23).

2. Soul also refers to the inner life of humanity, the seat of emotions and the center of human personality. The first use of soul in the OT expresses this meaning: "And the LORD God formed man of the dust of the ground, and breathed into his nostrils the breath of life; and man became a living being [soul]" (Gen. 2:7). This means more than being given physical life. The biblical writer declared that Adam became a "living soul"—a person, a human being, one distinct from all other animals.

Some passages describe the soul as the seat of emotions and desires for things such as food (Deut. 12:20–21), love (Song of Sol. 1:7), and God (Ps. 63:1).

In the NT, Jesus spoke of his soul as being "exceedingly sorrowful" (Matt. 26:38); Mary, the mother of Jesus, proclaimed that her soul "magnifies the Lord" (Luke 1:46);

and John prayed that Gaius would "prosper in all things and be in health, just as your soul prospers" (3 John 2).

Sovereignty of God. A theological term that refers to the unlimited power of God, who has sovereign control over the affairs of nature and history (Isa. 45:9–19: Rom. 8:18–39). God is working out his sovereign plan of redemption for the world, and the conclusion is certain.

Spirit. A word with three distinct meanings in the Bible:

1. The word is a general reference in the NT to the spirit of human beings (Matt. 5:3; Rom. 8:16; Heb. 4:12). Jesus made specific references to his spirit in a human sense (Mark 2:8; John 11:33), as did Paul (Acts 17:16; 2 Cor. 2:13). Paul sometimes referred to the spirits of those to whom he wrote (Gal. 6:18; 2 Tim. 4:22).

2. Spirit refers to good and evil spirits, meaning beings other than God and humans. An example of a good spirit is an angel (Ps. 104:4). The Bible contains many references to evil spirits (Mark 9:25; Acts 19:12–17; Rev. 18:2).

3. Spirit can mean the Spirit of God, the Holy Spirit. In the OT, the Spirit occasionally came upon people to give them power to do God's will or to enable them to serve God in a special way. For example, the Spirit of the Lord enabled Samson to kill a young lion with his bare hands (Judg. 14:5–6), gave Bezaleel wisdom and skill to build the tabernacle (Exod. 31:3), empowered judges to lead Israel to military victory (Judg. 3:10; 11:29), and enabled prophets to prophesy (Num. 24:2; Ezek. 11:5).

In the NT, the Holy Spirit was an even more active presence among the people of God. The Holy Spirit was the agent of fulfillment of OT prophecies (Acts 1:16; 2:16–21; 3:18; 28:25–27), continued to inspire Christian prophets and workers to do his will on earth (Acts 2:4; 19:6), came upon new Christians (Acts 10:44–48) to purify and sanctify them (2 Cor. 3:18; 2 Thess. 2:13), and guided the early Christian missionary work (Acts 10:19–20; 16:6–7).

This Holy Spirit is the Spirit of Jesus (2 Cor. 3:17). A person can relate to Jesus only by means of the Holy Spirit (Rom. 8:9; Gal. 4:6). John calls the Spirit the Helper (John 14:16–17).

Spiritual. Of the spirit or nonmaterial. The word *spiritual* refers to nonmaterial things, including a spiritual body (1 Cor. 15:44–46), things distinct from earthly goods (Rom. 15:27; 1 Cor. 9:11). But the most important use of the word is in reference to the Holy Spirit. The Spirit gave the law (Rom. 7:14) and supplied Israel with water and food (1 Cor. 10:3–4).

Theocracy. Direct government of the nation of Israel by God himself or his earthly representatives. Although theocracy is not a biblical word, the concept of God's rule on earth is thoroughly biblical.

In a theocracy human rulers interpret and carry out the divine ruler's will. In Israel's early days God ruled through men such as Moses, Aaron, and Joshua. Later, he ruled by using a group called the judges.

Deuteronomy 17:14–20 allowed for an Israelite monarchy under God and in cooperation with other ruling officials. Later, when Israel finally demanded a king, it was their attitude of being "like all the nations" rather than the request itself that God considered a rejection of his divine leadership (1 Sam. 8:5).

Samuel, the last judge and a great prophet, insisted that having an earthly king did not excuse Israel from obedience to God (1 Sam. 12:1–25). The human king was not an absolute monarch.

After the return from the Babylonian captivity (about 539 B.C.), the priest became an important agent of God's rule. Prophets such as Zechariah and Haggai mention the high priest as a ruler (Zech. 6:9–15). Apparently some Jews expected the Messiah to exercise priestly as well as kingly functions (Gen. 14:17–18; Ps. 110:4).

In the NT God's sovereign rule reestablished in Jesus Christ, the Prophet, Priest, and King appointed by God (Luke 24:19; Heb. 7:17; Rev. 19:16).

Theodicy. Greek *theos* and *dike,* "God" and "justice." Theodicy is the realm of theology or philosophy devoted to the vindication of God's goodness and justice despite the existence of evil.

The Bible makes no attempt to justify God. It is clear that he, as absolute sovereign, has willed the existence of both good and evil and that all this is for his own glory.

The sacrifice of Jesus does not give believers a solution, but it is a satisfying reply. There must have been some good reason for allowing evil, but this does not imply a defect in God or in his benevolence. If there had been any defect in God, he would not have sent his Son to save the world.

Theology. That which is thought and said about God. True theology is given by the Bible itself as the revelation of God in human terms.

Theophany. A visible manifestation of God. Usage restricts the term mainly to the theophanic manifestations during the OT period. These manifestations were direct messages (Exod. 19:9–25), messages in a dream (Gen. 20:3–7; 28:12–17), messages in a vision (Gen. 15:1–21; Isa. 6:1–13; Ezek. 1:1–3; 8:1–4), messages by an angel (Gen. 16:7–13; 18:1–33; 22:11–18; 32:24–30; Exod. 3:2–4:17; Josh. 5:13–15; Judg. 2:1–5; 6:11–24; 13:2–25), and messages in a dream by an angel (Gen. 31:11–13).

These theophanies appeared for specific purposes: to introduce momentous events (Exod. 3:1–12), to further reveal God's plan (Gen. 15:1–17; 28:12–17), to manifest the supernatural (Exod. 3:2f.; Josh. 5:13–15), and to support the wavering (Exod. 3:2–4:17; Judg. 6:11–24).

These appearances were only for God's people except where non-Israelites are specifically involved (Gen. 20:3–7; Num. 22:20–35).

The Angel of the Lord (better, *Angel of Yahweh*) frequently appears. We know this is God because:

• The Angel is identified as God (Gen. 16:7f., 13; 18:2, 10, 13; 22:10–12, 15–18; Exod. 3:2–6, 14, 18; Judg. 2:1, 5; 6:11, 14, 16).

• The Angel is recognized as God (Gen. 16:9–13; Judg. 6:22–24; 13:21–23).

• The Angel is described in divine terms (Exod. 3:5f., 14; Josh. 5:15).

• The Angel calls himself God (Gen. 31:11, 13; Exod. 3:2, 6, 14).

• The Angel receives worship (Josh. 5:14; Judg. 2:4f.).

• The Angel speaks with divine authority (Judg. 2:1–5).

The identification of the Angel of Yahweh with Jesus Christ is confirmed when he is

• Distinguished personally from God the Father (Gen. 21:17–20; 48:16; Exod. 23:20f.)

• Differentiated from angels in his acceptance of worship (Judg. 5:14f.; cf. Rev. 19:10; 22:8f.)

• Called by a messianic title (Judg. 13:18; cf. Isa. 9:6)

• Described as Redeemer (Gen. 48:15f.; Isa. 63:9)

• Predicted as the Angel (*messenger*) of the new covenant (Mal. 3:1; cf. also Exod. 14:19; 23:20 ff.; 32:34; 33:2, 14ff. with 1 Cor. 10:4)

• Equated with Christ's kingship (Josh. 5:13–15; cf. Rev. 19:11–16).

Theologically, the theophanies serve three purposes. They (1) corroborate the OT doctrine of the Trinity (Isa. 6:1–3, 8), (2) anticipate the NT doctrine of Christ's incarnation (John 1:14; 8:56), and (3) typify the biblical doctrine of God's eternal dwelling among the redeemed (cf. Exod. 25:8; 29:45f.; Rev. 21:3, 22; 22:3–5).

Transcendence. A nonbiblical term that refers to the relation of God to creation. God is wholly different or "wholly other" than his creation. He is also the holy one in the midst of his people (Hos. 11:9), independent and separate from his creatures.

Isaiah 6:1; 40:12–26 amplify this and show a remoteness, yet God is near in providence and grace (Ps. 139).

During the intertestamental period the remoteness of divine transcendence was overemphasized by refusing to use the divine name *Yahweh* (*Jehovah*). The incarnation and the coming of the Holy Spirit fulfills that OT revelation in the NT (Matt. 1:23; John 14:14–15, 23). In highest glory Christ is above his church, yet he is the head who is also one with it (Col. 1:18; 2:9–10; Heb. 4:14–15; Rev. 1:10–20). (See *Emanence*.)

Transform. To change radically in inner character, condition, or nature. In Romans 12:2 Paul exhorted, "Do not be conformed to this world, but be transformed by the renewing of your mind."

Followers of Christ are not to be conformed, inwardly or in appearance, to the values, ideals, and behavior of a fallen world. Believers continually renew their minds by the power of the Holy and become more like Christ (2 Cor. 3:18).

When he returns, Christ will "transform our lowly body that it may be conformed to His glorious body" (Phil. 3:21).

Tribulation, Great. A significant theological issue for dispensationalists. The exact phrase, the great tribulation, is found only once in the Bible (Rev. 7:14). It signifies a short but intense period of distress and suffering at the end of time.

According to this position, the Great Tribulation is different from the general tribulations believers face in the world (Matt. 13:21; John 16:33; Acts 14:22). It is also distinguished from God's specific wrath upon the unbelieving world at the end of the age (Mark 13:24; Rom. 2:5–10; 2 Thess. 1:6).

The Great Tribulation fulfills Daniel's prophecies (Dan. 7—12) and will be a time of evil from false christs and false prophets (Mark 13:22) when natural disasters will occur throughout the world.

Trinity. The coexistence of the Father, the Son, and the Holy Spirit in the unity of the divine nature.

The doctrine of the Trinity means that within the being and activity of the one God there are three distinct persons: Father, Son, and Holy Spirit. Although the word *trinity* does not appear in the Bible, the trinitarian concept appears in the Great Commission (Matt. 28:19) and in Paul's benediction (2 Cor. 13:14).

God revealed his oneness to the Israelites: "Hear, O Israel: The Lord our God, the Lord is one!" (Deut. 6:4). This was a significant religious truth because the surrounding nations worshiped many gods and had fallen into idolatry, worshiping the creation rather than the true Creator (Rom. 1:18–25). "But when the fullness of the time had come," Paul wrote (Gal. 4:4), "God sent forth His Son, born of a woman, born under the law." In the NT God revealed that he is not only one but a family of persons—an eternal, inexhaustible, and dynamic triune family of Father, Son, and Holy Spirit, who are one in will and purpose, love and righteousness. The unity of Father, Son, and Holy Spirit is portrayed by Jesus' teaching (John 14—16).

The Father serves the Son; the Son serves the Father; Father and Son defer to the Holy Spirit, who in turn, serves and defers to the Father and Son in a oneness that is eternally dynamic and inexhaustible.

Type. A figure, representation, or symbol of something to come, as an event in the OT foreshadows another in the NT. Types generally find their fulfillment in the person and ministry of Jesus, but they sometimes relate to God, the church, or some other reality.

Those using typology consider a wider range than those who tend to make practically everything in the OT point to a greater fulfillment in the NT and those who insist that the word *type* be explicitly mentioned in the NT before they recognize any OT type.

Between those extremes stand those

many scholars who feel that there are some OT correspondences to NT truths.

Although the word *type* is not specifically used, these scholars recognize such correspondences as:

• Melchizedek, the king-priest of Salem (Gen. 14:18–20; Ps. 110:4), typical of Christ (Heb. 6:20)

• The brazen serpent in the wilderness (Num. 21:4–9), typical of Jesus' own crucifixion (see John 3:14–15)

• The tabernacle, foreshadow of the person and work of Jesus Christ (Heb. 9—10)

The NKJV uses the word *type* in only one place: Paul mentions Adam as "a type of him [Jesus] who was to come" (Rom. 5:14; *pattern*, NIV).

Uncircumcision, uncircumcised. In the OT the uncircumcised are Israelites (Josh. 5:7) or Gentiles (Judg. 14:3; 15:18; 1 Sam. 17:26) who have not been circumcised. As circumcision represented obedience to God's covenant, uncircumcision represented rebellion and unbelief. The uncircumcised were excluded from the covenant, the Passover, the land, the sanctuary, and the Holy City.

Here is a summary of NT teaching on uncircumcision:

• All Gentiles are uncircumcised (Acts 11:3; Rom. 3:30; 1 Cor. 7:18; Gal. 2:7; Eph. 2:11).

• Uncircumcision is equated with the unregenerated state (Acts 7:51; Col. 2:13).

• Unbelieving Jews, although physically circumcised, are spiritually uncircumcised (Rom. 2:28f.; cf. Phil. 3:2ff.).

• Uncircumcised Gentiles who live righteously are counted spiritually circumcised. Jews, although physically circumcised, become uncircumcised by disobedience (Rom. 2:25–27).

• In Christ neither circumcision nor uncircumcision has any spiritual value (1 Cor. 7:19; Gal. 5:6; 6:15).

Victory. A religiously conditioned concept, rooted in the basic biblical principle that God is just and punishes sin and rewards righteousness (cf. Deut. 11:26–28).

Victory vindicates God's purposes and rewards righteous living on the part of God's people. In many passages righteousness equals victory. "Shall the prey be taken from the mighty, or the captives of the righteous [literally, *victor*] be delivered?" (Isa. 49:24; see also 41:2, 10; 54:17; Mal. 4:2).

In the OT victory refers to winning over foes and results in peace and security (Josh. 1:15; Jer. 23:6; Ps. 69:14). In the NT victory refers to spiritual forces and blessings.

Victory is over temptation and the powers of evil. The ultimate win will be Christ's victory over all physical and spiritual forces (Rev. 19:11–20:3).

The NT emphasizes the victory Christians have in their present daily life—over the enticements and assaults of the world. This happens when they appropriate by faith the power of Christ's victory on the cross (John 16:33; Rom. 8:37; Eph. 6:10; 1 John 5:4–5).

Vow. A voluntary obligation or promise made to God. People usually made vows on the condition of receiving special favors from God such as during sickness or other kinds of affliction.

They must then fulfill their vow when the calamity is over or the desire is granted (Gen. 28:20–22; Num. 21:2; 1 Sam. 1:11; 2 Sam. 15:8).

Three conditions of proper vows are a consciousness of dependence on God, a desire for something lawful and acceptable to God, and a yearning for spiritual self-edification.

Will of God. In the OT, the following Hebrew words express the concept of God's will: *hapes*, God's counsel or good pleasure (Isa. 44:28; 46:10; 48:10; 53:10); *rason*, God's goodwill and favor (Ezra 10:11; Pss. 40:9; 103:21; 143:10); and *esa*, God's counsel (i.e., planned by deliberation; Pss. 33:11; 73:24; Prov. 19:21; Is. 5:19; 46:10).

In the Aramaic of Daniel *seba* signifies God's will (Dan. 4:17, 25, 32; 5:21). The

NT uses three words: *bule*, God's eternal plan and purpose (Luke 7:30; Acts 2:23; 4:28; 20:27; Eph. 1:11); *thelema*, God's will (i.e., inclination; Acts 22:14; Rom. 12:2; Eph. 1:9; 5:17; Col. 1:9); and *eudokia*, God's good pleasure or delight (Luke 2:14; Eph. 1:5, 9; Phil. 2:13).

Although God's will is absolute and unconditioned by anything outside himself, it is not arbitrary, but in harmony with his holiness, righteousness, goodness and truth. God cannot do anything contrary to his essential nature. (See Num. 23:19; 1 Sam. 15:29; Heb. 6:18; 2 Tim. 2:13; James 1:13.)

God's will is inscrutable; humans cannot understand it any more than they can comprehend the being of God himself (Job 9:10; Rom. 11:33).

Witness, testimony. In legal terms, a witness (Greek *martys*) is a person who testifies (*martyreo*) to the truth. This is the testimony (*martyria*).

In Christian usage, the term means the testimony given by Christian witnesses to Christ and his saving power. In the early church, because such testimony often meant arrest and scourging, exile, or death, the Greek was transliterated to form the English word *martyr*, meaning "those who suffer or die rather than give up their faith."

World, worldliness. The Hebrew word *eres* means "earth contrasted with heaven" (Gen. 1:1) and is occasionally translated as "world." The more usual Hebrew word is *tebel*, signifying "the planet as habitable and fruitful" (Pss. 19:4; 90:2).

Three NT words (Greek) are translated as "world": *oikoumene*, "the populated world" (Luke 4:5); *aion*, usually translated as "age" (Heb. 1:2; 11:3); and *kosmos*, "order" or "system."

Kosmos, the usual word for "world," carries several meanings: "the material world" (Rom. 1:20); "the totality of heaven and earth" (Acts 17:24); "the sphere of intelligent life" (1 Cor. 4:9); "the place of human habitation" (1 Cor. 5:10); "humankind as a whole" (John 3:16); "hu-

mankind as alienated from God and under the sway of Satan" (1 John 5:19); and "the complex of ideas and ideals that govern those of the world in an ethical sense" (James 4:4; 1 John 2:15–17).

Among Greeks, *kosmos* was used for the universe, since it suitably expressed the order noted there. Hebrews thought in terms of the heavens (the abode of God) and the earth (the realm of human existence). God was the author of both, and the regularity of the movements of the heavenly bodies and the rhythm of the seasons bore witness to his creative power. NT writers largely followed the OT concept, using *kosmos* for the heavens and the earth combined (Acts 17:24).

Kosmos is readily applied in an evil sense. Frequently, particularly in John's writings, the world is presented as hostile to God.

The powers of spiritual evil with Satan as their head and organized with great efficiency (Eph. 6:12), dominate the life of unredeemed humanity. Satan rules a kingdom opposed to the kingdom of God (Luke 11:18).

Worldliness, although not a scriptural term, means "an affection for what is unlike God and contrary to his will" (James 4:4; 1 John 2:15–16).

Word, The. This theological phrase expresses the eternal being of Jesus Christ (John 1:1–14; 1 John 1:1; Rev. 19:13). The OT spoke of the word of God as the divine agent in the creation of the universe: "By the word of the Lord the heavens were made" (Ps. 33:6).

In the NT, it says "And the Word became flesh and dwelt among us" (John 1:14). Through the incarnation of Jesus Christ, God has come to dwell in our midst. Through the life and ministry of Jesus, a unique and final revelation of God has been given—one superior to the revelation given through the law and the prophets. In Christ, the Word of God, God's plan and purpose for humanity is revealed (2 Cor. 4:4; Heb. 1:1–3). (See *Logos*.)

War
and Warfare

K nowledge about arms and armor in the Middle East comes from archaeological discoveries, ancient engravings showing battle scenes, references and descriptions in the Bible, and other documents from the ancient world.

Arms and Armor

The forms and uses of weapons and armor changed from the beginning of the OT period until the end of the NT period. Certain weapons that were important in one period became outdated and fell from use in a later time. This occurred because nations competed with one another in developing more effective weapons. When one nation developed a shield that could not be penetrated effectively by the arrows of an enemy, then the enemy set out to develop a more powerful bow and better arrows.

In addition to their military application, arms and armor are spoken of figuratively in the Bible. For example, the Bible itself is often called a sword (Eph. 6:17), telling us that like a sword, it is able to slash to the very heart of people (Heb. 4:12). Jesus Christ is portrayed as bearing a sword in his mouth (Rev. 1:16; 19:15). The Psalms often refer to God as a shield because he protects his people (3:3; 28:7; 33:20).

The fullest development of armor imagery occurs in the epistle to the Ephesians in the NT. The apostle Paul compared the Christian's struggles with evil to a battle in which God provides believers with the armor and weapons needed to protect themselves against the enemy, Satan (see Eph. 6:10ff.).

The following offensive and defensive weapons and armor are mentioned in the Bible. This list is keyed to the NKJV, with cross-references from five additional popular translations—KJV, NASB, NEB, NIV, and RSV.

Arrow. (See *Bow*.)

Ax or Mace. *Battle-ax* (Jer. 51:20, NKJV, KJV, NEB) and *war club* (Jer. 51:20, NIV, NASB) were used by various translations of the Bible for the ancient ax, also known as the *mace*. Maces and axes are simple extensions of the club. A mace is a club with a metal head for greater efficiency in hand-to-hand combat. A mace was used frequently in the period before Abraham. With the development of helmets, the mace was less effective, although it continued to serve a symbolic function. For instance, the scepter, a symbol of authority used by ancient kings, probably had its origin in the war mace.

Axes remained important military weapons throughout the OT period. An ax also served as a domestic tool (1 Chron. 20:3). One major problem in making axes was the fastening of ax heads to handles. A fascinating miracle recorded in the OT concerns a poorly fastened ax head that flew off its handle into the Jordan River. The prophet Elisha recovered the ax head by causing it to float (2 Kings 6:5–7).

The ax was an important military weapon because of its ability to pierce armor. The OT describes the Egyptian (Jer. 46:22) and Babylonian armies (Ezek. 26:9) as attacking with axes. During Israel's early history, few axes existed in Palestine because the Philistines had a monopoly on metalwork (1 Sam. 13:19–23).

Battering ram. The battering ram was a war machine used to destroy a city's walls (Ezek. 26:9; *engine of war,* KJV). Although the battering ram was made in many shapes and sizes, a typical one featured a long, pointed pole that was driven with great force against a fortified city's massive stone walls. It took several men to operate the battering ram. Many models provided extensive protection for the crew, since the city's defenders usually fired upon them as they worked. The whole machine was mounted on wheels for easy movement.

Battle-ax. (See *Ax.*)

Battle bow. (See *Bow.*)

Belt. (See *Body armor.*)

Body armor. By about 3000 B.C., soldiers wore primitive body armor. The term *armor* describes anything from thick leather clothing to metal mail. General terms for body armor used in different translations of the Bible include *coat of mail* (Exod. 28:32, NKJV, NASB), *habergeon* (Exod. 28:32, KJV), and *brigandine* (Jer. 46:4, KJV).

Specific pieces of armor for the body mentioned in the Bible include breastplate (Neh. 4:16, NASB); belt, a wide piece of metal that protected a warrior's lower trunk and stomach (1 Sam. 18:4; *girdle,* RSV); and greaves, protective devices for the legs (1 Sam. 17:6, KJV).

Bow. Bows were the most characteristic weapons of warfare in the OT period, serving often as the decisive element in a battle. Simple bows were used in the prehistoric period, mostly for hunting.

Bows, composed of a piece of wood and string, were easy to make but did not have much power or range. The composite bow developed early in the history of the Middle East. The composite bow was a combination of wood and animal horn. This combination of materials provided the bow with the flexibility and strength needed for effective combat. But a composite bow was difficult to use, and only certain units within an army were specially trained to shoot the bow.

The bow was usually the first weapon fired in an open-field battle, because the archers of the hostile armies could send arrows from long distances. Chariot troops usually had bows. This combination of mobility and firepower made the army an effective war machine. When attacking a city, the archers would try to pick the defenders off the walls. Archers of the city would use their bows to keep the army from getting close enough to break down their defenses.

The destructive agent of a bow was the arrow, a long, slender shaft of wood with a tip of sharp stone or metal. The archer was also equipped with a quiver, a deep, narrow basket constructed especially for arrows.

Bows, arrows, and archers are mentioned often in the OT, beginning with the boy Ishmael (Gen. 21:20). Another term for bow used by some translations is *battle bow* (Zech. 9:10; NKJV, RSV, NIV).

Assyrian warriors in battle with an enemy force aboard a papyrus boat, in this carving from Sennacherib's palace at Nineveh.

PHOTO BY HOWARD VOS

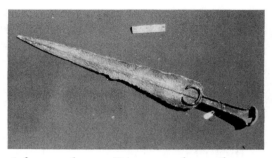

A bronze dagger. Daggers and swords were common weapons of Bible times.

PHOTO BY GUSTAV JEENINGA

Breastplate. (See *Body armor.*)

Brigandine. (See *Body armor.*)

Buckler. (See *Shield.*)

Chariot. The chariot rivaled the composite bow in its effectiveness as a weapon. Only wealthier nations could establish and maintain a chariot force.

Chariots were introduced in Mesopotamia (the land between the Tigris and Euphrates Rivers) about 2800 B.C. and served as mobile firing platforms. The chariot can bring great firepower quickly to the key point of the battle. Chariots came in many different forms, such as two-wheeled or four-wheeled, drawn by two to four horses. Some chariots would carry four warriors.

In combat a chariot usually carried two soldiers—a driver who controlled the reins and a warrior who needed both arms free to fire his bow. In some cases, depending on the nation and the period of history, a third person served as a shieldbearer to protect both the warrior and the driver. The warrior was usually equipped with a bow as well as a medium-range weapon, such as the javelin or spear.

The first chariots mentioned in the Bible belonged to Egypt. Joseph rode in a chariot behind the Pharaoh (Gen. 41:43). A later Pharaoh pursued Moses and the Israelites with his chariot (Exod. 14:6–9).

At first, the nation of Israel rejected chariots as tools of warfare (Josh. 11:4–9). Most of the country was not suitable for chariot warfare because of its high hills and deep ravines. Also, the spirit of conquest under Joshua was such that the use of a powerful weapon like the chariot might have led Israel to boast in their own power rather than God's. Solomon, however, developed a chariot corps in his army (1 Kings 4:26; 9:19).

Club. The most primitive weapon was the club, consisting in its early development of little more than a piece of wood especially shaped for hand-to-hand combat. In later years metal was added to these primitive weapons, and they evolved into a type of war club or mace. Another variation on the club was the *staff,* generally used by shepherds to care for their flocks but also mentioned in the Bible as a weapon of war (2 Sam. 23:21; 1 Chron. 11:23). Other words for club used by different translations of the Bible include *maul* (Prov. 25:18, KJV) and *cudgel* (Matt. 26:47, NEB).

Coat of mail. (See *Body armor.*)

Cudgel. (See *Club.*)

Dagger *or* Sword. Different translations of the Bible speak of the dagger and the sword as if these two weapons were basically the same. A sword was a piercing or cutting weapon so the warrior could stab or slash an enemy. Some swords were designed to pierce, others to slash. All swords had two parts, a handle (or hilt) and a blade. The blade was usually straight, but one unusual variation was the sickle sword. This weapon featured a curved blade with the sharp edge on the outside. The sword was the basic weapon of a Hebrew soldier. The biblical phrase that identified a man as a soldier was that he "drew the sword" (2 Kings 3:26).

Daggers were similar to swords in that they were composed of a hilt and a blade and were used to stab. Their advantage over swords was their ability to be hidden. Ehud, the judge, hid a dagger in his robes and stabbed the oppressor Eglon (Judg. 3:16–22).

Dart. (See *Javelin*.)

Engine of war. (See *Battering ram*.)

Girdle. (See *Body armor*.)

Greaves. (See *Body armor*.)

Handpike. (See *Javelin*.)

Handstaff. (See *Javelin*.)

Helmet. The helmet was a type of hat worn by warriors to protect their heads from physical blows in a military battle (1 Sam. 17:5; Jer. 46:4). Helmets came in various shapes and sizes and were made from many different materials, although metal was the most effective. Since the head is the most vulnerable part of the body, it was the first area covered by armor.

Javelin *or* Spear. In various translations of the Bible, these two terms are used interchangeably to refer to the same basic weapon—a long, slender shaft with a metal point. The only difference between them is that a spear was heavier and larger than a javelin. Therefore, a spear was used as a thrusting weapon as well as a throwing weapon.

Spears and javelins are mentioned often in the OT. At God's command, Joshua stretched out his spear toward Ai to show that the city would fall to the Israelites (Josh. 8:18–19). In a fit of jealousy, Saul tried to kill David with a spear (1 Sam. 18:10–11).

Other words for spear or javelin used in Bible translations include *dart* (2 Sam. 18:14, KJV, RSV); *handpike* (Ezek. 39:9, RSV); *handstaff* (Ezek. 39:9, KJV); *lance* or *lancet* (Judg. 5:8, NEB; 1 Kings 18:28, NKJV); and *throwing-stick* (Ezek. 39:9, NEB).

Lance *or* Lancet. (See *Javelin*.)

Mace. (See *Ax*.)

Maul. (See *Club*.)

Quiver. (See *Bow*.)

Shield. The shield was a hard object, generally made of metal, with which a warrior protected his body from the weapons of the enemy. In the biblical period, shields came in all sizes and shapes. Some shields were made of leather or wood. Another word for shield is *buckler* (1 Chron. 5:18, KJV).

Sling. Shepherds used and developed the sling to protect their livestock against wild animals. This was a simple weapon, generally composed of a small piece of leather or animal hide, and they used stones or pebbles as ammunition. While the sling is a simple weapon in terms of construction, it is difficult to fire with accuracy. Only trained soldiers used slings.

Next to archers, the slingmen were the most effective long-range warriors in OT times. The advantage of such a long-range weapon is illustrated by the most famous sling story of all—David's victory over Goliath. David had a decided advantage in the contest because Goliath was armed with a spear and a sword, both of which were short-range weapons.

Slingers were important elements in the Israelite army. The Benjamites had a unit of 700 left-handed slingers who could "sling a stone at a hair's breadth and not miss" (Judg. 20:16).

Spear. (See *Javelin*.)

Staff. (See *Club*.)

Sword. (See *Dagger*.)

Throwing-stick. (See *Javelin*.)

War club. (See *Club*.)

Military Men

General Commanders

Abner	Commander of King Saul's troops	1 Sam. 14:50
Amasa	Commander of Absalom's troops during the rebellion against David	2 Sam. 17:25
Claudius Lysias	Roman commander who sent Paul from Jerusalem to Felix, the Roman governor in Caesarea	Acts 23:12–33
Joab	Commander of King David's troops	1 Chron. 18:14–15
Joshua	Israel's first commander in chief	Exod. 17:8–10
Naaman	Leper and commander of the Syrian troops	2 Kings 5:1
Nebuzaradan	Commander of Nebuchadnezzar's troops	2 Kings 25:8
The Rabshakeh	Commander of the Assyrian troops when the angel struck them down	2 Kings 18:17—19:37
Sisera	Canaanite commander defeated by Barak and Deborah, and killed by Jael	Judg. 4

Regular Soldiers

Abishai	One of David's chief soldiers who personally killed 300 enemy soldiers in a battle	1 Chron. 11:20
Benaiah	One of David's captains	2 Sam. 8:18
Caleb	Loyal scout who, along with Joshua, gave a positive report about the land	Josh. 14:6–13; Num. 13:25—14:9
Irijah	Soldier of Judah who arrested Jeremiah, falsely accusing him of treason	Jer. 37:13
Ittai	Gittite who supported David during the rebellion by Absalom	2 Sam. 15:19–23
Potiphar	Egyptian soldier who employed Joseph as his servant and then imprisoned him on false charges	Gen. 39:1
Uriah	Hittite soldier whom David sent to his death in battle so he might marry his wife, Bathsheba	2 Sam. 11

Centurions

Centurion at Calvary	Recognized Jesus as the Son of God	Matt. 27:54
Centurion at Capernaum	Asked and received from Jesus healing for his dying servant	Luke 7:1–10
Cornelius	Led to Christ by Peter	Acts 10
Julius	Treated Paul kindly during his fateful ship voyage to Rome	Acts 27:1–44
Roman army commander	Rescued Paul from the Jews in Jerusalem	Acts 21:32; 22:25

Worship

Pagan Religions and Cultures

The Israelites of antiquity came into contact with Canaanites, Egyptians, Babylonians, and other people who worshiped false gods. God warned his people not to imitate their pagan neighbors, yet the Israelites disobeyed. They slipped into paganism again and again.

What did these pagan nations worship? And how did this worship pull the Israelites away from the true God?

By studying these pagan cultures we learn how the human race attempted to answer the ultimate questions of life before they found the light of God's truth. Also, we come to understand the world in which Israel lived—a world from which they were called to be radically different, both ethically and ideologically.

Common Features of Pagan Religions

Certain features were common to most of these pagan religions. They all partook of the same world view, which was centered on the locality and its prestige. The differences between Sumerian and Assyro-Babylonian religions or between Greek and Roman religions were marginal.

Many Gods

These religions were polytheistic, meaning that they acknowledged many gods and demons. Once admitted to the pantheon (a culture's collection of deities), a god could not be eliminated from it. He or she had gained divine tenure.

Each polytheistic culture inherited religious ideas from its predecessors or acquired

These scarabs, shapes in the image of sacred beetles, were used as charms by the ancient Egyptians in their superstitious form of religion. PHOTO BY GUSTAV JEENINGA

them in war. For example: *Nanna* (the moon god) or *Sin* (the fertility goddess and queen of heaven) to the Sumerians was *Ishtar* to the Babylonians.

The Romans simply took over the Greek gods and gave them Roman names. *Jupiter*, the Roman sky god, was the same as the Greek *Zeus; Minerva*, the Roman goddess of wisdom, was the same as the Greek *Athena; Neptune*, the Roman god of the sea, was the same as the Greek *Poseidon.*

The idea of the god was the same; the cultural wrapping was different. One ancient culture could absorb the religion of another without difficulty. Each culture claimed not only the gods of a previous civilization; it also laid claim to its myths and made them its own, with only minor changes.

The chief gods were often associated with some phenomenon in nature. *Utu / Shamash* is both the sun and the sun god; *Enki / Ea* is both the sea and the sea god. Pagan cultures made no distinction between an element of nature and a force behind that element. The ancients struggled against forces in nature they couldn't control, forces that could be either beneficent or malevolent.

Enough rain guaranteed a bumper crop at harvest, but too much rain would destroy that crop. Life was quite unpredictable, especially since the gods were thought to be capricious and whimsical, capable of either good or evil. Human beings and gods participated in the same kind of life; the gods had the same sort of problems and frustrations that human beings had. This concept is called *monism.*

When Psalm 19:1 says, "The heavens declare the glory of God, and the firmament shows His handiwork," it mocks the beliefs of the Egyptians and Babylonians. These pagan people could not imagine that the universe fulfilled an all-embracing divine plan.

The Egyptians also associated their gods with phenomena of nature: *Shu* (air), *Re / Horus* (sun), *Khonsu* (moon), and *Nut* (sky).

The same tendency appears in the Hittite worship: *Wurusemu* (sun goddess), *Taru* (storm), and *Telipinu* (vegetation).

Among the Canaanites: *El* was the high god in heaven; *Baal* was the storm god; *Yam* was the sea god; *Shemesh* the sun god; and *Yareah* was the moon god.

Because of this bewildering array of nature deities, pagans could never speak of a universe because they did not conceive of one central force that holds everything together. Pagans believed they lived in a multiverse.

Worship of Images or Icons

All these religions worshiped idols. Israel alone was officially aniconic (it had no images or pictorial representations of God). Images of Yahweh, such as Aaron's and Jeroboam's bull-calves (Exod. 32; 1 Kings 12:26–33) were forbidden by the second commandment.

Aniconic religion was not always the whole story. The Israelites worshiped pagan idols while they lived under Egypt's bondage (Josh. 24:14); and even though God banished their idols (Exod. 20:1–5), the Moabites lured them into idolatry again (Num. 25:1–2). Idolatry was the downfall of Israel's leaders in different periods of her history, and God finally allowed the nation to be defeated because "they sacrifice bulls" to pagan idols (Hos. 12:19).

Most pagan religions pictured their gods anthropomorphically (as human beings). In fact, only an expert can look at a picture of Babylonian gods and mortals and tell which is which. Egyptian artists usually represented their gods as men or women with animal heads. For example: *Horus* was a falcon-headed woman; *Anubis* was a jackal; and *Hathor* was a cow.

Hittite gods can be recognized by the drawing of a weapon they place on their shoulder, or by some other distinctive object such as a helmet with a pair of horns. The Greek gods also are pictured as humans, but without the harsh characteristics of the Semite deities.

Self-Salvation

What is the significance of portraying the gods like human beings? The Bible tells us that God made the human race in his image (see Gen. 1:27). Pagans, attempting to make gods in their own image, produced only amplified human beings to worship. The myths of the ancient world assumed that the gods had the same needs as humans, the same foibles and imperfections. If there was a difference between the pagan gods and people, it was only a difference of degree.

Sacrifice

Most pagan religions sacrificed animals to soothe their temperamental gods; some even sacrificed human beings. Because the heathen worshipers believed their gods had human desires, they also offered food and drink offerings to them (see Isa. 57:5–6; Jer. 7:18).

The Canaanites believed sacrifices had magical powers that brought the worshiper into sympathy and rhythm with the physical world. Because the gods were capricious, however, worshipers sometimes offered sacrifices to secure a victory over their enemies (see 2 Kings 3:26–27). Perhaps this is why the decadent kings of Israel and Judah indulged in pagan sacrifice (see 1 Kings 21:25–26; 2 Kings 16:13). They wanted magical aid in fighting their enemies, the Babylonians and Assyrians—preferably the aid of the same gods that had made their enemies victorious.

Painting depicting an Egyptian judgment scene. The dead man's heart is weighed on the scales in the afterlife, while the Egyptian god Thoth records their verdict.

PHOTO BY HOWARD VOS

Shown at right is an oven in Carthage, where infants were sacrificed as a worship ritual. This practice was strictly forbidden among the Hebrew people because of the high value which God placed on human life (Lev. 20:1–5; Jer. 32:35).   PHOTO BY HOWARD VOS

Jewish Religious Factions _____

By the time of Jesus, Judaism had become a sectarian religion. Jews holding different beliefs spent many hours arguing difficult questions of law, history, and politics. They debated such questions as:

Who is a true Jew?

What does God require of his people?

What is the destiny of Israel?

Their conflicting answers revealed sharp differences between the various Jewish sects of the time.

Old Testament Background

As we review the history of the OT, we find many factors that contributed to the hostility between the Jewish parties of Jesus' day.

Differences Among the Twelve Tribes

Many centuries had blurred the individual characteristics of Jacob's 12 sons (cf. Gen. 49). Nevertheless, the nation that grew out of the 12 brothers inevitably preserved some of their attributes. Sectarian divisions often followed family lines as descendants of the brothers continued their bitter rivalry.

People in Jesus' day were interested in tracing their lineage for at least four reasons:

1. To establish convenantal rights to position or property.
2. To identify themselves with the promised Messiah.
3. To identify themselves with well-known priests.
4. To establish their family roots.

Knowing one's family origin provided a certain amount of comfort and stability in the troubled times of the first century. No doubt this is why many Jews were careful to preserve a record of their family tree. They were proud to identify themselves with a Jewish tribe that had a long and noble heritage. Even Paul boasted of his family background in the tribe of Benjamin (2 Cor. 11:22; Phil. 3:5–6). Nation, tribe, breeding, and place of birth—these were the standards that first-century Jews used to evaluate themselves.

Jewish Sects in New Testament Times

When Jesus was born, the Jews of Palestine were divided into many sects of which there were three major factions: Pharisees, Sadducees, and Essenes.

Within each of these parties, small groups of Jews rallied around the teachings of a particular rabbi or his school of thought. In the three major parties of NT Judaism, the members in each group had a broad range of views.

Pharisees: Law Experts

During the time of John Hyrcanus, the Pharisees emerged from the old party of the Hasideans. The Pharisees were the master interpreters of the oral traditions of the rabbis. Most of them came from middle-class families of artisans and tradesmen (e.g., Paul was a tentmaker). They exerted a powerful influence over the peasant masses.

Josephus observed that when the Jewish people faced an important decision, they relied on the opinion of the Pharisees rather than that of the king or high priest (*Antiquities*, XII. x. 5). Because the people trusted them, the Pharisees were chosen for high government positions, including the Sanhedrin. Josephus estimates that only 6,000 Pharisees lived in Israel during the time of Jesus, so they needed popular support. Perhaps this is why they feared Jesus' ability to attract great crowds.

The Pharisees taught that righteous people would live again after death (Acts 23:8), while the wicked would be punished for eternity. Not many other Jewish groups accepted this view. Instead they espoused the Greek and Persian idea that death permanently separated the soul from the body.

Sadducees: Guardians of the Torah

After the Maccabeans drove the Syrians out of Palestine, the hellenistic Jews went into hiding. It was no longer safe for a Jewish scholar to endorse Greek ideas. Yet these Jewish intellectuals continued to apply Greek logic to the problems of the day, and they formed a new Jewish sect known as the Sadducees.

We are not sure what the name originally meant. Most scholars believe it is derived from the Hebrew word *saddig*, meaning "righteous" or that it comes from the priestly name "Zadok," since they were connected with the temple priesthood.

The Sadducees rejected the oral tradition of the rabbis and accepted only the written law of Moses, condemning any teaching that was not based on the written word. They saw too many Persian and Assyrian influences in the teachings of the Pharisees and felt they were traitors to the Jewish tradition. They rejected the Pharisaic belief in angels, demons, and resurrection after death (Matt. 22:23–32; Acts 23:8). Thus, they opposed Jesus when he agreed with the Pharisees.

The Sadducees adopted the beliefs of the Greek philosopher Epicurus, who held that the soul dies with the body. They taught that all individuals are the masters of their own fate.

Essenes: Righteous Radicals

The Essenes also emerged from the pious movement known as the Hasideans. Josephus reports that there were two groups of Essenes (*War*, II. 2). There may have been even more.

The name Essene comes from a Hebrew word that means "pious" or "holy." Although other Jews called them by this name, Essenes themselves probably rejected the label. They did not consider themselves to be especially holy or pious; but they did see themselves as the guardians of a body of mysterious truths that would govern the life of Israel when the Messiah appeared.

The Essenes planned to keep this information secret until the proper time. They probably identified themselves with the *maskilim* ("they that understand"), who, according to the prophet Daniel, would guide the Jews in their time of turmoil (Dan. 11:33; 12:9–10).

Most of the Essenes lived communally in remote desert areas. Some lived in a quarter of Jerusalem where there was even an Essenes' Gate. They practiced elaborate rites to purify themselves, physically and spiritually. Their writings (i.e., the Dead Sea Scrolls, which most scholars regard as Essene) show that they were careful to avoid being corrupted by the society around them, in the hope that God would honor their faithfulness. They called their leader the Teacher of Righteousness.

The Dead Sea Scrolls do not identify the people who lived in the Qumran community, where the scrolls were written, but the Roman historian Pliny said this area was the headquarters of the Essene sect.

In 1947 a Bedouin shepherd boy cast a stone into a cave at Khirbet Qumran (on the northwest coast of the Dead Sea) and heard the breaking of a clay jar. The boy entered the cave and found several jars containing ancient manuscripts. Scholars identified them as the book of Isaiah, a commentary on Habakkuk, and several documents that contained the teachings of the Qumran sect.

Eventually, 11 caves were located with ancient scrolls and fragments. The caves yielded fragments or copies of every book of the OT except Esther. Most of the manuscripts had been written in the time of the Maccabees. This discovery sparked archaeologists' interest in the ruins of Khirbet Qumran itself, where they found a large room for copying manuscripts.

Scholars still debate whether the people of Qumran were actually Essenes, since their writings disagree with known Essene teachings at several points. Some believe that Pharisees who fled from the rage of Janneus (88 B.C.) settled at Qumran (a commentary on the book of Nahum found at Qumran seems to refer to the life-style of the Pharisees). But if the people of Qumran were simply another splintered Essene group, that would account for their occasional departures from the mainstream of Essene teachings.

Among the other religious sects were such groups as Zealots, Herodians, and Samaritans.

Zealots

Pompey's invasion of Palestine in 63 B.C. destroyed the Jews' hopes of restoring their own government. Yet the Zealots stubbornly insisted that the Jews must repel the Roman invaders and tried to stir up rebellion among the Jews.

The best-known Zealot leader was Judas the Galilean (Acts 5:37). When Augustus decreed that "all the world should be registered" (Luke 2:2), Judas led an ill-fated revolt against the Romans. This was, according to Josephus, the beginning of the Jews' conflicts with the Roman Empire, which ended with the destruction of the temple in A.D. 70.

Judas and his followers resented any foreign control of their government. Their thinking probably inspired the questions that one Pharisee put to Jesus: "Is it lawful to pay taxes to Caesar, or not?" (Mark 12:14).

During Felix's term as procurator of Judea (A.D. 52–60), the Zealots formed a radical group known as the *Sicarii* ("dagger people"). The Sicarii circulated in crowds during festivals and killed Roman sympathizers with daggers they concealed in their clothing.

During the war with Rome (A.D. 66–70), the Sicarii escaped to the old Jewish fortress at Masada and made it their headquarters. Two years after the fall of Jerusalem, a Roman legion laid siege to Masada. Rather than die at the hands of the Gentiles, the Sicarii killed themselves and their families—960 people in all.

Herodians

Another Jewish sect known as the Herodians emerged during the Roman era. This was a political group that included Jews from various religious sects. They supported the dynasty of Herod the Great. They seemed to prefer Herod's oppressive home rule to the Romans' foreign supervision. The Herodians are mentioned three times in the NT (Matt. 22:16; Mark 3:6; 12:13) but none of these passages give us a clear picture of their beliefs.

Some scholars believe Herodians thought Herod was the Messiah, but there is no hard evidence to support this view.

Samaritans

The Samaritans were descendants of the Jews who remained in Palestine after the Assyrians defeated Israel in the eighth century B.C. They came from mixed marriages between Jews and Assyrian settlers who entered the Promised Land, so their very existence was a violation of God's law.

They worshiped God on Mount Gerizim, where they built their own temple and sacrificed animals. The Samaritans were despised by the Jews who returned from the Exile. They were called "the foolish people that dwell in Sichem [Shechem]" (Ecclesiasticus 50:25-26). In 128 B.C. John Hyrcanus destroyed the temple on Mount Gerizim. From this point on, Jews and Samaritans truly had no dealings with each other (cf. John 4:9).

In some ways, Jesus also stood aloof from the Samaritans. He told his disciples to stay away from the Gentiles and the cities of Samaria (Matt. 10:5-7). He brushed aside the Samaritan practice of worshiping only on Mount Gerizim (John 4:19-24). Yet Jesus was willing to visit one of their villages (Luke 9:52) and talk with the Samaritan woman. His parable of the good Samaritan suggests that in his view these despised people might be more faithful to the law than the Jews (10:25-37). When Jesus healed ten lepers, a Samaritan was the only man who returned to thank him (17:11-19). When Jesus commissioned his disciples and described their mission of preaching the gospel, he specifically included the land of Samaria (Acts 1:8).

Jesus' Response to the Factions

By the first century, the sects of Israel had changed the character of the Jewish faith. The narrow course that God originally had set before Israel had become a winding path through Oriental mysticism, Greek humanism, and ritualistic traditions.

Jesus spent much of his time responding to the misguided ideas of these groups. Jesus confronted these traditional sources of authority with a truer understanding of the law. He introduced Israel to the salvation and love of God. He countered the claims made by each group to righteousness, declaring all the sects and individuals to be sinners.

Jesus said that people's righteousness should exceed that of the Pharisees (Matt. 5:20). He warned his disciples to "beware of the leaven [the doctrine] of the Pharisees and the Sadducees" (16:6). He denounced the scribes and Pharisees for their hypocrisy and self-righteousness (23:1-36). He especially chided the Pharisees for their superficial methods of observing the Sabbath (Mark 2:23-3:6).

The NT never shows Jesus speaking directly to Essenes, but it is likely that their peculiar system of authority had displaced the authority of God and the coming Messiah, as the other Jewish sects had done. They needed to hear Jesus' message of truth, no less than the other Jews did.

Worship of Israel _____

T he people of Israel worshiped God, whom they called by the covenant name of *Yahweh* (some translations, *Jehovah*), in many ways and at many different places throughout the year. These worship rituals impacted upon their daily lives.

Moses told the people of Israel, "You are a holy people to the LORD your God; the LORD your God has chosen you to be a people for Himself, a special treasure above all the peoples on the face of the earth" (Deut. 7:6). God chose them not because of anything they had done or were, but because God loved them. (See Deut. 7:7.)

Before the Time of Moses

The first mention of a worship act occurs in Genesis 4:2–7: "Now Abel was a keeper of sheep, but Cain was a tiller of the ground. And in process of time it came to pass that Cain brought an offering of the fruit of the ground to the LORD. Abel also brought of the firstborn of his flock and of their fat."

The children of Adam and Eve recognized that God had given them "every herb" and "every beast" (Gen. 1:29–30), so they brought simple offerings to him. We do not know precisely where and how the offerings were made, but we are told that they brought two types of offering, and that Cain's was rejected while Abel's was accepted.

This is the first recorded instance of animal sacrifice. As time passed, the people learned that God honored and accepted their sacrificial offerings.

The patriarchs erected altars and made sacrifices wherever they settled (see Gen. 8:20; 12:7–8). They erected stone monuments as well. Jacob took the stone that he used as a pillow and "set it up as a pillar, and poured oil on top of it" (Gen. 28:18–22). He called it *Bethel* ("God's house").

The patriarchs also designated sacred trees (Gen. 12:6; 35:4; Deut. 11:30; Josh. 24:26) and sacred wells (Gen. 16:14). These objects reminded them of what God had done at particular times in their lives.

The patriarchs built simple earthen and stone altars for the slaughter of animal offerings. The Hebrew word usually translated as *altar (mizbeach)* literally means "a place of slaughter."

In the Time of Moses

Moses inaugurated a new period in Israel's worship practices—a period that extended far beyond his own lifetime. It began as Moses led the people of Israel out from Egypt (1446 B.C.). In this section, we focus on Moses' influence only until the time of the judges (which ended in 1043 B.C. with the naming of Saul as Israel's first king). During the time of the judges, God's people still worshiped in tents or tabernacles. But when David was king, plans were made for construction of a temple; our next section deals with that project.

The Worship Site

God sanctioned the use of earthen and stone altars (Exod. 20:24–26). In the days of Moses, God also sanctioned a new kind of worship site. When the great lawgiver climbed to the top of Mount Sinai, he received much more than the Ten Commandments. Among other things, he received a plan for an enclosed worship site with an altar housed in a cloth tent. It is difficult to construct a picture of this new site. Many artists have drawn their impressions, based upon the Bible's descriptions, but there is no complete agreement on the plan of the tabernacle.

We know that this worship site was different from the altars erected under the open sky. For one thing, it was much more elaborate. (See Exod. 27:1–3.) "You shall make an altar of acacia wood, five cubits long and five cubits wide—the altar shall be square— and its height shall be three cubits. You shall make its horns on its four corners; its horns shall be of one piece with it. And you shall overlay it with bronze. Also you shall make its pans to receive its ashes, and its shovels and its basins and its forks, and its firepans; you shall make all its utensils of bronze."

The Priesthood

After the giving of the Ten Commandments, an ordained priesthood came into being. According to God's command (Exod. 28:1), Moses consecrated his brother Aaron and Aaron's sons as priests. These men came from the tribe of Levi. From this point until intertestamental times, the official priesthood belonged to the Levites.

The high priest's most important function was to preside at the annual Day of Atonement. On that day, the high priest would enter the Holy of Holies of the tabernacle and sprinkle the mercy seat with the blood of sin offerings. By doing this, he atoned for his wrongs, those of his family, and those of all the people of Israel (Lev. 16:1–25). The high priest also sprinkled the blood from the sin offerings before the veil of the sanctuary and on the horns of the altar (Lev. 4:3–21).

As the spiritual head of Israel, the high priest had to attain a greater degree of ceremonial purity than did the ordinary priests. Leviticus 21:10–15 outlines the requirements for purity of the high priest. Any sin he might commit was a blight upon the entire people of Israel. He had to atone for such a sin with a specially prescribed offering (Lev. 4:3–12).

The high priest also offered the daily meal offering (Lev. 6:19–22) and participated in the general duties of the priesthood (Exod. 27:21).

Priests had many duties, such as presiding over all sacrifices and feasts, serving as medical advisors to the community (Lev. 13:15), administrating justice (Num. 5:11–13; Deut. 17:8–9; 21:5), blessing in the name of God (Num. 6:22–27), and blowing the trumpets that summoned the people to war or feast (Num. 10:1–10).

Levites served as priests from age 30 to 50 (Num. 4:39). After age 50, they were only allowed to assist their fellow priests.

The people's tithe provided food and clothing for the priests; a tenth of the tithe was given to the priests (Num. 18:21, 24–32). Since the tribe of Levi possessed no territory, 48 cities and surrounding pastures were given to them (Num. 35:1–8).

From the Monarchy to the Exile

Israel's worship patterns changed noticeably from the time of the monarchy (which began when Saul became king in 1043 B.C.) until the time of the exile (which began when the Babylonians seized Judah in 586 B.C.).

Before this time, the people of Israel worshiped God at many different places; but under the kings, their worship would be focused on a central place of sacrifice. Before, people could make offerings on the spur of the moment. Now they had to follow the procedures established by the law of Moses.

The Temple

Israel's first king, Saul, when faced with defeat at the hands of the Philistines, reverted to the old ways. He built an altar on the spot and asked for God's help. Samuel arrived later and reminded Saul that he could not worship just any place (1 Sam. 13:8–14).

Under the leadership of David, Israel became a strong and wealthy nation. David wanted to build a house of worship, but God said it was not for him to do but for Solomon (1 Chron. 22:6–19). Solomon built the temple—remarkably similar in many ways to the tabernacle. (See 1 Kings 6–7 and Exod. 25–28.)

In later days, Solomon's temple was desecrated in various ways by unfaithful Hebrew kings. (See 1 Kings 14:26; 2 Kings 12:4–15; 16:8; 18:15–16; 21:4; 23:1–12.)

Priest, Prophets, and Kings

A formal priesthood developed among the tribe of Levi in the time of Moses. However, under the monarchy there were examples of non-Levitical priests (2 Sam. 8:17; 1 Kings 4:5).

The king played an important role in Israel's worship. When he interacted with God, the whole nation was impacted (2 Sam. 21:1). The high priest anointed the king to signify that God had chosen him for his royal task. As the anointed representative of the people, the king had to make sacrifices (1 Kings 8). He gathered temple materials and ordered the construction. He had the power to affect everything Israel did concerning worship. Some of the later kings polluted temple activities with foreign rituals and idols.

Feasts

The primary festivals of this period were the Feast of Weeks, the Feast of Unleavened Bread (Passover), and the Feast of Booths.

Attendance was required, and the feasts were all held in Jerusalem. Previously, they were held wherever the ark of the covenant was located.

Foreign influences crept into Israel's worship and the prophets loudly denounced them. For example, Amos cried out against ritual lawbreaking (Amos 2:4), ritual prostitution (Amos 2:8), and worship not accompanied by repentance (Amos 4:4–6).

Even the temple itself came to show Canaanite, Phoenician, and Egyptian influences. Reform under King Josiah (639–608 B.C.) abolished local shrines and all sacrifice was done in Jerusalem once again. Josiah suppressed the local cults and rites of idolatry (2 Kings 23:4–26).

In the Time of Jesus

Jesus related to the temple in four distinct ways. First, as a pious Jew who was zealous for the Lord, Jesus showed respect for the temple. He referred to it as "the house of God"

(Matt. 12:4) and "My Father's house" (John 2:16). He taught that everything in it was holy because of the sanctifying presence of God (Matt. 23:17, 21).

Second, Jesus' zeal led him to purge the temple of the moneychangers (Mark 11:15–17; John 2:16) and to weep over it as he reflected on its coming destruction (Mark 13:1; Luke 19:41–44). Because Malachi 3:1–3 prophesied the cleansing of the temple as something the Lord would do, Jesus' act implied his deity and messiahship.

Third, because he was the Son of God incarnate, Jesus taught that he was greater than the temple (Matt. 12:6). Jesus' teaching that if the temple of his body was destroyed in three days he would raise it up (John 2:19) likewise affirms his superiority to the temple building.

Finally, Jesus taught that the church (Matt. 16:18) is the new eschatological temple (Matt. 18:19–20; John 14:23).

The first Christians were converted Jews. They continued to worship at the temple as Jesus had (Luke 24:52; Acts 2:46; 3:1; 5:12, 20–21, 42). As they began to understand the meaning and significance of Jesus' person, work, and teaching, they realized they were the new people of God, infused by God's Spirit. As such, they were part of a new, living temple. A new order had replaced the old.

Paul used the metaphor of the temple to express the unity of the new people of God that God is bringing about through the preaching of the gospel. The members of this new race are Jews and Gentiles who formerly were separated by the "middle wall of separation" and the "ordinances" that forbade them to mix (Eph. 2:14–15).

In a similar way, Peter used the word *house* to describe Christians as members of a new, spiritual temple (1 Pet. 2:4–10). Christ is the chief cornerstone (v. 6). He is "a stone of stumbling and a rock of offense" (v. 8), a "living stone, rejected . . . by men, but chosen by God and precious" (v. 4).

In addition to understanding the church as the new, spiritual temple of God on earth that replaced the temple in Jerusalem, the New Testament alludes to a heavenly temple in whose life the church participates. John (John 1:51; 14:2) and Paul (Gal. 4:26; Phil. 3:20) both allude to the heavenly temple, but the idea is most developed in Hebrews and Revelation.

Index